# THE ORIENTAL BIOGRAPHICAL DICTIONARY

# THE
# ORIENTAL
# BIOGRAPHICAL DICTIONARY

**THOMAS WILLIAM BEALE**
EDITED BY
**HENRY GEORGE KEENE**

GYAN

*Published by*

Gyan Publishing House
5, Ansari Road
Daryaganj, New Delhi-110002
Phone: 011-47034999, 9811692060
E-mail: books@gyanbooks.com

*Distribution Network*
gyanbooks.com
India, USA, Canada, UK, Australia, France



ISBN: 978-81-212-8720-3 (PB)
First Published, 1881

2nd Impression 2023

*Printed at:* Gyan Press, Delhi.



**THE ORIENTAL BIOGRAPHICAL DICTIONARY**
Author: Thomas William Beale

THE

# ORIENTAL BIOGRAPHICAL DICTIONARY.

BY THE LATE

THOMAS WILLIAM BEALE

(AUTHOR OF THE MIFTAH-UL-TAWARIKH.)

EDITED BY

THE ASIATIC SOCIETY OF BENGAL

UNDER THE SUPERINTENDENCE OF

HENRY GEORGE KEENE, M. R. A. S.

A FELLOW OF THE UNIVERSITY OF CALCUTTA; AUTHOR OF THE TURKS IN INDIA, ETC.

CALCUTTA:

PRINTED BY J. W. THOMAS, BAPTIST MISSION PRESS.

PUBLISHED BY THE

ASIATIC SOCIETY, 57 PARK STREET.

1881.

# PREFATORY NOTICE.

THE author of this Dictionary was formerly a Clerk in the office of the Board of Revenue, N. W. P. at a time when the Secretary was Henry Myers Elliot, afterwards well known as Sir H. M. Elliot, K. C. B. It is probable that, in preparing his extracts from the Mohamadan Histories of India, Elliot availed himself of the aid of Mr. Beale, of whose scholarship Prof. Dowson makes justly deserved mention in the eighth volume of his valuable edition of the work.* Mr. Beale died at a very advanced age in the summer of 1875, having before his death expressed a wish that I would see his MS. through the press, and reduce the transliteration into conformity with the system then recently adopted by the Government of India, and founded (as I need hardly observe) upon the system of Sir W. Jones.

Accordingly, on the 5th October of that year I laid the MS. before Sir John Strachey, the then Lieut.-Governor, in the name of the Archæological Society of Agra, of which he was a Vice-Patron, in a letter from which the following is an extract:—

"This is no ordinary book. I have used it as a work of reference, for years: and have lately had an opportunity of showing it to the eminent scholar Mr. E. B. Eastwick, C. B. who, I am authorised to say, concurs with me in thinking that the Dictionary will be of unique value to oriental students."

Sir J. Strachey took up the subject with that enlightened energy which always actuated him in dealing with the past history of the country over whose administration he then presided. The MS. and copyright were acquired at the expense of Government; and it was ultimately resolved—in view of the importance of the work and my own official occupations—that the editing should be entrusted to the Asiatic Society of Bengal.

The Society confided the labour of seeing the Dictionary though the press to their Philological Secretary, Principal Blochmann, of whose qualifications it would be presumptuous to say more than that they have an œcumenical reputation. That distinguished man (of whom it has been observed by Count v. Noer that he united the enthusiasm of an artist to the most patient accuracy of research†) undertook the task with his characteristic earnestness and ability. But unhappily for oriental scholarship Mr. Blochmann's lamented death occurred before he had completed the preparation of more than a few sheets; and the duty ultimately reverted to the local Archæological Society of Agra.

Being soon after transferred from Agra, and being besides prevented by my public duties from giving to the Dictionary the full attention which its importance required, I have availed to a great degree of the aid of my colleagues, Mr. Sáyad Mahmood, Prof. A. Thomson, and Lála Bahál Rai. I have also (in the latter sheets particularly) had valuable help from Dr. Hoernle, Philological Secretary of the Society. To these gentlemen, and to the Superintendent of the Baptist Mission Press the work is indebted for its handsome and practical appearance and character.

The substance is almost entirely Mr. Beale's; and I cannot close this notice more fitly than by giving the following extracts from the preface originally drafted by himself:—

"In preparing a work of this nature, intended to be used as a work of reference on matters connected with Oriental History, it is proper to state that the greatest care has been taken to ensure accuracy in the narrative, as also in the dates of births, deaths, and other events recorded.... Various MSS. have been collated whenever discrepancy was observed.... To remove all doubt, chronograms indicating the dates with a certainty not to be found by any other method and written when the events were fresh in the minds of men, have been inserted, when available."

* *The History of India, by its own Historians.* Trübner & Co. 1877.

† *Kaiser Akbar.* Leyden, 1880.

I may here add that it has been judged expedient to omit these chronograms, for the most part, in printing the book. In the chapter of Mr. Dowson's book already cited, will be found an account of this species of *memoria technica*. But it is chiefly interesting as machinery for producing a certain result; and when the result has been produced is not of much more use than the scaffolding of a building when the building is complete.

"The materials collected in this Biography are only from those works which were within the reach of the author, and therefore it is to be considered as a nucleus to which those who have access to other sources may add new materials.

"It may also be proper to add, that the difficulties and embarrassment which a writer of such a work is liable to meet with is so great, (I quote here the words of a learned gentleman) 'that though of a minor order, comprehends in itself such a number of annoyances that the writer of it, even if he had none other to make head against, might feel tempted to abandon his pen in despair when considering it.'

"'In the East' says he, 'there are but a few proper names of individuals. Abdullah, Alí, Hasan, Husain, Muhammad, for example, are common to thousands. To remedy the inconvenience that might be supposed to result from this tendency to homogenousness, the Orientals annex to the family-name of the chronicled person, 1, a Kunia, or surname taken from the name of his eldest son, as Abu Muhammad (father of Muhammad); Abú'l Hasan (father of Hasan); 2, the name of his father and often the name of his grandfather; 3, a name taken from his place of residence; 4, a name taken from his birthplace; 5, an honorary title, chiefly appended to the name of Kázís, Sheiks and Imáms, Monks and Doctors, as Baháuddín *(Splendour of Religion)*, Jaláluddín *(Glory of Religion)*, Tájuddín *(Crown of Religion)*; and in the order of this nomenclature, the last name is put first. Thus to designate aright the famous physician Abdul Latíf, we must call him Muwaffikuddín Abú Muhammad Abdul Latíf bin Yusaf Mousalí Baghdádí, *viz.*, The Protector of Religion, father of Muhammad, Abdul Latíf, son of Joseph, living at Mousal, born at Baghdád. Yet this is by no means an exaggerated specimen; several other surnames of the same kind are frequently added. The perpetual recurrence of such a multiplicity of names and titles must tend in many ways to confuse a literary historian; and the more naturally when he finds the same individual chronicled in one page under his honorary title only, as Jaláluddín, in another under his family-name, as Abdur Rahmán, in the third under his father's name as Ibn Arabsháh, somewhere else under the name of his sons, as Abú'l Abbás, and perhaps again, and where one would least look for it, under the name of his native province, Sháhristán. D'Herbelot has recorded no fewer than fourteen Persian writers, all of whom pass, under the common cognomen of Karamání, from their province Karamán. Here is perspicuity! But this is not all. The transcribers of the MSS. have frequently confounded the title Abú and Ibn, or else for abbreviation sake, have omitted them altogether and written down Abdullah, or Abdur Rahmán, him who was in fact the father or the son of Abdullah or Abdur Rahmán. Then there are a great many authors whom public celebrity has been accustomed to distinguish so exclusively by one only of their adjunctive titles, that even the native biographers find it impossible to trace either their family-names or their surnames. Lastly, many hundreds of books bear the same name, and the names of most books are conceived after such a many-worded and no-meaninged fashion, that de Sacy, Schlegel, Casiri and von Hammer, to mention but a few investigators out of many, have been foiled in the attempt to establish their signification.'

"To prevent such confusion and difficulties, the author has taken care to insert each individual under his different appellations, *viz.*, under his family-name, his surname, poetical name, under his title or under the name of the place of his birth, referring at the same time, if he is not to be found under one name, to look under the one referred to.

"In conclusion the author begs to add that most part of the materials collected in this volume were procured by the assistance of his son the late lamented Mr. J. W. Beale, 2nd Master of the Bareily College who was murdered by the insurgents on the 3rd June 1857 at that station, and since he is now no more, the author is obliged to drop his pen; but earnestly hopes that this work which is nearly the first of its kind in India, and the want of which has already been much felt, may prove useful to the Student, the Scholar, the Historian, and the general reader."

This notice may well terminate with a repetition of this hope: and with an appeal to scholars of larger leisure and opportunities for an indulgent treatment of a work produced by a man who had never been in Europe nor enjoyed the use of a complete Library. Mr. Beale had drawn up a list of more than thirty books in various languages which had furnished him with materials. In addition the editors have from time to time referred to the translation of the *Ain Akbari* and its invaluable notes by Mr. Blochmann, of which the 1st Volume (never, alas, continued) was published in Calcutta some years ago.

One word more as to the inexhaustible subject of transliteration. The English as is well known have three methods; the Haphazard (which indeed is no method at all), the Gilchristian, and the popularised Jonesian introduced by the Government of India under the inspiration of Mr. W. W. Hunter. None of these is quite satisfactory. The French adopt a system of their own, and so do the Germans. Mr. Beale had followed an orthography, compounded of the two first-named elements, which has been to some extent modified in printing these pages. For the convenience of Continental European scholars the names have also been printed in the Persian character; and it is hoped that no practical difficulty will be experienced by those who may have occasion to use the Dictionary.

H. G. KEENE.

MEERUT, *September*, 1881.

# A.



**A'azz-uddin,** ( اعزالدين ) Prince, second son of Sháh 'Alam Bahádur Sháh. He was born on the 17th Ẕí-Ḳa'da 1074 and appears to have died early.]

**A'azz-uddin,** ( اعزالدين ) son of Mu'izz-uddín Jahándár Sháh, emperor of Dilhí. He was blinded and imprisoned by Farrukh-siyar, in the end of 1124 H.]

**Aba Bakr** (Mirzá or Sulṭán), the son of Sháhrukh Mirzá the son of Amír Timur. He was murdered by order of his brother Mirzá Ulugh Beg, A. D. 1448 (852 A. H.)

**Aba Kaan** or **Abka Khan** or **Abaka Khan,** ابا قاآن or ابقا خان, a king of Persia of the tribe of Mughuls or Tartars, and descendant of Chingiz Khán, succeeded his father Hulákú Khán in February 1265, A. D. (Rabí'-uṣ-Ṣání 663 A. H.), and was crowned on Friday the 19th June following (3rd Ramaẓán.) He was a prince who added to the qualifications of courage and wisdom those of moderation, clemency, and justice. His ambassadors were introduced in 1274 to the ecclesiastical Synod at Lyons. He proved to be a formidable neighbour to the Christians who settled at Jerusalem. The intrigues of his court embittered the latter years of his reign; and his days were believed by many to have been shortened by poison given to him by his minister Khwája Shams-uddín Muhammad, which occasioned his death on Wednesday the 1st of April 1282 A. D., (20th Ẕil-ḥijja 680 A. H.) after a reign of 17 years and some months. He had married the daughter of Michael Palæologus, emperor of Constantinople, who had been betrothed to his father, but arrived at Marágha in Tabríz, the seat of his government, after the death of that prince. Abá-ḳá-án was succeeded by his brother Nekodár, who embraced Muhammadanism, and took the title of Ahmad Khán.

**'Abbas,** عباس, the son of 'Abdul-Muṭṭalib, and uncle of the prophet Muhammad. He at first opposed the ambitious views of his nephew, but when defeated in the battle of Badr, he was reconciled to him, warmly embraced his religion, and thanked heaven for the prosperity and the grace which he enjoyed as a Musalmán. He served the cause of Muhammad at the battle of Ḥunain by recalling his dismayed troops to the charge, and inciting them boldly to rally round their prophet, who was near expiring under the scimitars of the Ṣakafites. He died on the 21st February, 653 A. D., (17th Rajab, 32 A. H.); and 100 lunar years after, Abul-'Abbás, surnamed As-Saffáḥ, one of his descendants, laid the foundation of the 'Abbásí or Abbaside family of the Caliphs in Baghdád, which continued for 524 lunar years. The tomb of 'Abbás is in Madína.

**'Abbasa,** عباسه, a sister of Hárún-ur-Rashíd, the Khalífa of Baghdád, who bestowed her hand on Ja'far Barmakí, his minister, on condition that she abstained from the marriage rights. The promise was forgotten, and the husband's life was sacrificed by the tyrant, and 'Abbása was reduced to poverty. This circumstance took place in 803 A. D. (187 A. H.). There are still extant some Arabic verses which beautifully celebrate her love and her misfortunes. See Ja'far ul-Barmakí.

**'Abbas 'Ali,** عباس علی, a physician, and one of the Persian magi, who followed the doctrines of Zoroaster. He wrote A. D. 980, a book called 'Royal Work', at the request of the son of the reigning Khalífa of Baghdád, to whom it was dedicated. It was translated into Latin by Stephen of Antioch in 1127 A. D.

**'Abbas 'Ali** (Mírzá), whose poetical name is Betáb, is the son of Nawáb Sayádat 'Alí Khán, son of Ghulám Muhammad Khán, the son of Faiẓ-ullah Khán, Nawáb of Rámpúr.

**'Abbas bin-'Ali Shirwani,** عباس بن علی شروانی, author of a history, containing the narrative of Sher Sháh the Afghán, who drove Humáyún from Hindústán, A. D. 1539, and mounted the throne of Dilhí. This work was dedicated to the emperor Akbar, and is called Tuḥfa-i-Akbarsháhí. The first part of this work was translated into Urdú by Maẓhar 'Alí Khán in the time of Lord Cornwallis and is entitled 'Táríkh-i-Sher Sháhí.'

*Vide* Dowson, Elliot's History of India, IV, 301.]

**'Abbas Mirza,** a Persian prince, son of Fatḥ 'Alí Sháh, was born in 1783. He died in 1833. His death was a great loss to his country, although he could not prevent the encroachments of Russia. His eldest son, Muhammad Mirzá, mounted the throne in 1834, on the death of Fatḥ 'Alí, under the united protection of England and Russia.

**'Abbas Mirza,** عباس مرزا, whose title was Nawáb Iktidár-uddaula, was the author of a Maṣnawí in Urdú verse, containing a history of Christ. He was living in Lakhnau in 1849 A. D., and was then about eighty years of age.

**'Abbas (Shah) I,** عباس شاه, surnamed the Great, and seventh king of Persia of the Ṣafawí family, was born on Monday the 29th of January 1571 A. D. (1st Ramaẓán, 978 A. H.). He was proclaimed king of Persia, in his sixteenth year, by the chiefs of Khurásán, and took possession of the throne during the lifetime of his father, Sulṭán Sikandar Sháh, surnamed Muhammad Khudábanda, A. D. 1588, (996 A. H.). He was the first who made Iṣfahán the capital of Persia. He was brave and active, and enlarged the boundaries of his dominions. He took conjointly with the English forces, in 1622 A. D., the island of Ormus, which had been in the possession of the Portuguese for 122 years. He reigned 44 lunar years, was contemporary with Akbar and Jahángír, and died on Thursday, the 8th of January, 1629 A. D. (24th Jumáda I, 1038 A. H.). His grandson succeeded him and took the title of Sháh Ṣafí.

He was a bigoted Shí'a. In later histories he is generally called ماضی *mází; vide* Kín Translation, I, 445, 453.]

**'Abbas (Shah) II,** عباس شاه ثانی, great-grandson of Sháh 'Abbás I, succeeded his father Sháh Ṣafí to the throne of Persia in the month of May, 1642, A. D. (Ṣafar 1052, A. H.), when he was scarcely ten years old. Ḳandahár, which was lost by his father, was recovered by this prince before he was sixteen years of age. Sháh Jahán made many efforts to recover this city, but with no success. He reigned 25 lunar years, and was cut off by the *lues venerea* in his 34th year, on the 26th August 1666 A. D. (5th Rabí'-ul-awwal, 1077 A. H.) He was succeeded by his son Ṣafí Mirzá, who took the title of Sháh Sulaimán. According to Chardin, he died on the 25th September which corresponds with the 5th Rabí'-uṣ-Ṣání. *Vide* Orme's Historical Fragments of the Mogul Empire, p. 196.

**Abdal,** ( ابدال ) son of 'Alí Ráí, ruler of Little Tibet during the reign of Sháh Jahán. He was captured, and Ádam Khán was appointed governor of Little Tibet. *Vide* Dowson, Elliot's History of India, VII, 63.]

**Abdal Chak,** ( ابدال چک ) uncle of Yúsuf Khán Chak (last king of Kashmír, who succumbed to the emperor Akbar). *Vide* Ḿín Translation I, 478.]

**Abdali,** ابدالي, *vide* Ahmad Sháh Abdálí.

**Abdals,** the forty, hence called *Chihil-tanán*. After Muhammad's death, the Earth complained to God that she would henceforth be no longer honored by prophets walking on her surface. God promised that there should always be on earth forty (or, according to some, seventy-two) holy men, called *Abdáls,* for whose sake he would not destroy the earth. The chief of the Forty is called 'Ghauṣ.']

**Abdar Begam,** آبدار بیگم, one of the concubines of the Emperor Akbar.

**'Abdi,** عبدي, his proper name is not known. He is the author of the work called "Tarjama-i-Taḳmila," a translation of Yáfi'í's Legends of Ḳádiriya saints into Persian verse, completed in 1641 A. D., 1051 A. H., under Sháh Jahán.

**'Abdi of Tun,** عبدی, a poet who had a predilection for Maṣnawís, and is the author of the "Gauhar-i-Sháhwár," which is in the style of Nizámí's Makhzan-ul-Asrár. He came to celebrity in Khurásán in 1545 A. D., 950 H. *Vide* Khwája Zain-ul-'Ábidín 'Alí 'Abdí, who appears to be the same person.

**'Abdi,** عبدی, and **Nawedi,** نویدی, *vide* Khwája Zain-ul-'Ábidín 'Alí 'Abdí.

**Abdi,** ابدی, author of a heroic poem called Anwar-náma in praise of Nawáb Anwar-uddín Khán of the Karnátik, in which the exploits of Major Lawrence and the first contests between the English and French in India are recorded with tolerable accuracy. *Vide* Abjadí.

**'Abdul-'Ali (Maulana),** entitled "Baḥrul-'ulúm" (*i. e.* the Sea of Knowledge), the son of Mullá Niẓám-uddín Sihálí. He is the author of the 'Arkán Arba' Fiḳah' and several other works. He died A.D. 1811 (1226 A. H.).

**'Abdul-'Aziz,** عبد العزيز بن عمر, son of 'Umar (Omar) the second Khalífa after Muhammad. He did not succeed his father in the khiláfat. The Muhammadans consider him a great lawyer.

**'Abdul-'Aziz,** عبد العزيز, author of the Táríkh-i-Husainí, containing the Life of the famous Ṣadr-uddín Muhammad Husainí Gesú-Daráz, whose tomb is held in the highest veneration at Kulbarga in the Dakhin. This work was dedicated to Ahmad Sháh Bahmaní in 1445 A. D.

**'Abdul-'Aziz bin-Ahmad Dairini (Shaikh),** ديريني, an Arabian author who died 1294 A. D.

**'Abdul-'Aziz Khan,** *vide* 'Azíz.

**'Abdul-'Aziz (Maulana Shah),** son of Sháh Walí-ullah, a learned Musalmán of Dihlí. He is the author of a Persian commentary on the Ḳurán, entitled "Tafsír Fath-ul-'Azíz", and several other works. His death took place in June 1824 A. D. (7th Shawwál, 1239, A. H.)

**'Abdul-'Aziz** (Shaikh), شيخ عبد العزيز, of Dihlí, a learned man who died in the time of the emperor Akbar, A. D. 1567, 975 A. H. 'Abdul-Ḳádir of Badáon found the chronogram of his death in the following words—"Ḳuṭb-i-Ṭaríḳat-numá."

**'Abdul-'Aziz,** emperor of Turkey, son of Sulṭán Maḥmúd, succeeded his brother Sulṭán 'Abdul-Majíd on the 25th June 1861, 1277 A. H.

**'Abdul-'Aziz** (Shaikh), شيخ عبد العزيز. His poetical name was 'Izzat. He held a manṣab of 700 in the reign of Aurangzíb, and died in the year 1680 A. D., 1091 A. H. He is the author of a poem called Sáḳí-náma.

For a detailed biography *vide* the *Majma'-un-Nafáis.*]

**'Abdul-Baki,** عبدالباقی, author of the Maáṣir-i-Raḥímí, or Memoirs of 'Abdur-Raḥím Khán, Khán-Khánán, and of all the illustrious nobles, authors, and poets, who resided at the court of Akbar. He completed his work in 1616 A. D., 1025 A. H., and died about the year 1642 A. D., 1052 A. H., in the reign of Sháh Jahán.

For further notes *vide* Dowson, Elliot's History of India, VI, 237.]

**'Abdul Baki,** Mauláná. He was a *Ṣadr* in the beginning of Akbar's reign.]

**'Abdul-Basit,** (Mauláná), مولانا عبد الباسط, the son of Rustam 'Alí. He wrote a commentary on the Ḳurán which he left incomplete. He also wrote a work called 'Ajíb-ul-Bayán fí 'ulúm-il-Ḳurán. He died in 1808 A. D., 1223 A. H.

**'Abdul-Fattah,** عبد الفتاح, author of the Persian work called "Aurád-i-Ghauṣiya," on Sufism, and of one entitled "Jawáhir-ul-Káyinát."

**'Abdul-Ghaffar,** عبدالغفار, whose full title is Shaikh Najm-uddín 'Abdul-Ghaffár ush-Sháfi'í Ḳazwíní, is the author of the "Ḥáwí," "Fiḳah," "Lubáb," and "Sharḥ Lubáb." He died in the year 1265 A. D., 663 A. H.

**'Abdul-Ghafur,** of Láhor, عبد الغفور لاهوری, was an author and a pupil of 'Abdur-Raḥmán Jámí. He died in the year 1506 A. D., 912 A. H.

**'Abdul-Ghafur (Shah),** شاه عبد الغفور, commonly called Bábá Kapúr, a saint whose tomb is at Gwáliár. He was a native of Kálpí, and a disciple of Sháh Madár. He died in the year 1571 A. D., 979 A. H.

*Vide* Ḿín Translation, I, p. 539.]

**'Abdul-Ghafur,** Shaikh, of A'zampúr in Sambhal, a pupil of 'Abdul-Ḳuddús. He died in 995 H.]

**'Abdul-Ghani** (Mirzá), مرزا عبد الغنی, a native of Kashmír, wrote under the name of Ḳabúl. He died in the year 1726 A. D., 1139 A. H. ; *vide* Ḳabúl.

**'Abdul-Hakk** (Shaikh), شيخ عبد الحق دهلوی, of Dihlí, surnamed 'Muḥaddiṣ', son of Saif-uddín son of Sa'd-ullah Turk. He was a descendant of one of Amír Timur's followers, who had remained at Dihlí, after the return of the conqueror to his native land. He is the author of the "Táríkh-i-Haḳḳí," which is more frequently styled "Táríkh-i-'Abdul-Haḳḳ," compiled in the 42nd year of the emperor Akbar's reign, 1596 A. D., 1005 A. H. He went on a pilgrimage to Mecca and Madína, where he dwelt for a long time, and wrote works upon many subjects—Commentaries, Travels, Ṣúfí doctrines, religion, and history, and his different treatises amount altogether to more than one hundred. The best known are the "Madína Sakína," "Maṭla'-ul-Anwár," "Madárij-un-Nubuwwat," "Jazb-ul-ḳulúb", "Akhbár-ul-Akhyár" a book on the saints. He was born in the month of January 1551 A. D., Muḥarram 958 A. H. In the year 1637 A. D., although he was then ninety years old, he is said to have been in possession of his faculties. He died in the year 1642 A. D., 1052 A. H., aged ninety-four lunar years; lies buried on the bank of the Ḥauẓ Shamsí in Dihlí, and now holds a high rank among the saints of Hindústán. His son Shaikh Núr-ul-Haḳḳ is the author of the Zubdat-ut-Tawáríkh.

For further notes *vide* Dowson, Elliot's History of India, VI, 175, 483.]

**'Abdul-Hakim of Siyalkot,** عبدالحکیم, was a pupil of Mauláná Kamál-uddín of Kashmír. He wrote the Ḥáshiya, or marginal notes, on the Tafsír Baiẓáwí and a Ḥáshiya on the marginal notes of 'Abdul-Ghaffár. He died in the year 1656 A. D., 1066 A. H.

**'Abdul-Halim bin-Muhammad,** عبد الحلیم, surnamed *Kanalizáda*, an Arabian author, who died in the year 1589 A. D., 997 A. H.

**'Abdul-Hamid,** *vide* Ahmad IV, emperor of Turkey.

**'Abdul-Hamid of Lahor,** was the author of the Pádsháh-náma-i-Sháhjahání.

Regarding this history, *vide* Dowson, Elliot's History of India, VII, 3.]

**'Abdul-Hasan (Kazi),** author of an Arabic work on Jurisprudence called "Aḥkám-us-Sulṭání".

**'Abdul-Hay (Mir) Sadr,** میرعبد الحی صدر, a learned man who wrote a chronogram on the death of the emperor Humáyún, and one on the accession of Akbar in 1556 A. D., 963 A. H.

*Vide* Áín Translation I, 480.]

**'Abdul-Jalil (Mir or Sayyid)** عبد الجلیل بلگرامی میر, of Bilgrám in Audh. He was a great scholar and an elegant poet, and his poetical name was Wásiṭí. In 1699 A. D., 1111 A. H., he visited the camp of Aurangzíb at Bíjápúr; and being presented to that monarch by Mírzá 'Alí Beg, the royal intelligencer, obtained a manṣab and a jágír, with the joint offices of Bakhshí (Paymaster) and News-writer of Gujrát; from which place he was removed to Bhakar in Sindh, with similar appointments. Through some intrigues at court, he was recalled from Bhakar in the reign of Farrukh-siyar in 1714 A. D., 1126 A. H., but upon circumstances being explained, he was restored in the most honorable manner, and was at length permitted to officiate by deputy, whilst he himself remained at Dihlí until 1721 A. D., 1133 A. H., when he resigned in favor of his son Mír Sayyid Muhammad. He was the son of Sayyid Ahmad of Bilgrám, was born on the 2nd June 1661 A. D., 13th Shawwál 1071, and died on Monday the 28th December 1724 A. D., 23rd Rabí' I, 1137, aged 66 lunar years, and is buried at Bilgrám close to his father's tomb. He is the author of several works, one of which containing letters written in Persian is called "Ádáb-ul-Mursilín.

For a detailed biography, *vide* Ázád's *Sarw-i-Ázád*, and the *Tabṣirat-un-Náẓirín* by 'Abdul-Jalíl's son.]

**'Abdul-Kadir (Sultan),** was the descendant of a Marabaut family of the race of Háshim, who trace their pedigree to the Khalífas of the lineage of Fáṭima. His father died in 1834. His public career began at the time of the conquest of Algiers by the French. In 1847, he was defeated and surrendered himself, but was afterwards permitted to reside in Constantinople. He died in 1873.

**'Abdul-Kadir bin-Abil-Wafa al-Misri (Shaikh Muhiy-uddin)** الدین عبد القادر بن ابی الوفا مصری شیخ محی, author of the "Jawáhir-ul-Maziya fi Ṭabaḳát-il-Ḥanafiya, a biographical dictionary giving an account of the Ḥanafí lawyers, arranged in alphabetical order. He died in 1373 A. D., 775 A. H.

**'Abdul-Kadir Badaoni (Shaikh),** عبد القادر بداؤنی شیخ, was the son of Mulúk Sháh of Badáon̤ and pupil of Shaikh Mubárak of Nágor. He is the author of a work called "Muntakhab-ut-Tawáríkh". He was a very learned man, and was frequently employed by the emperor Akbar to make translations into Persian from the Arabic and Sanskrit, as in the case of "Mu'jam-ul-Buldán," "Jámi'-ur-Rashídí", and the "Rámáyan". He also composed a moral and religious work, entitled "Naját-ur-Rashíd," and translated two out of the eighteen Sections of the "Mahábhárat," and made an abridgment of the History of Kashmír in 1591 A. D., 999 A. H. The year of his death is not known, but he was living in 1596 A. D., 1004 A. H., in which year he completed the Muntakhab-ut-Tawáríkh. His poetical name was Ḳádirí.

He died at Badáon̤, in 1004. For a detailed biography *vide* Journal, Asiatic Society, Bengal, 1869, Pt. I, p. 118; and Dowson, V, 477.]

**'Abdul-Kadir Suhrawardi,** عبد القادر سہروردی, author of the work called "Ádáb-ul-Muríd."

**'Abdul-Kadir Bedil (Mirza),** میرزا عبد القادر بیدل a celebrated poet, better known by his poetical name of Bedil or Mirzá Bedil. He was a Tartar of the tribe of Birlás; in his youth he was employed by prince A'zam Sháh, son of Aurangzíb, but being one day ordered by the prince to write a panegyric in his praise, he resigned the service and never afterwards served any one. He is the author of several works, such as "Muḥíṭ A'zam"; "Chár 'Unṣur"; "Inshá-i-Bedil", also called Ruḳ'át-i-Bedil, and of a Díwán or book of Odes in Persian, containing 20,000 couplets. He died in the commencement of the reign of Muhammad Sháh, on the 24th November 1720 O. S., 4th Ṣafar, 1133 H. He is also the author of a work called "Nukát-i-Bedil," containing the memoirs of Shaikh Junaid, third in descent from the celebrated Shaikh Ṣafí, and grandfather of Sháh Ismá'íl Ṣafawí, king of Persia.

*Vide* Sprenger, Catalogue of Oudh MSS., p. 379.]

**'Abdul-Kadir Gilani or Jilani or Jili (Shaikh),** also called Pír-i-Dastgír and Ghauṣ-ul-A'zam Muḥiy-uddín, a saint, who is said to have performed a number of miracles during his lifetime. He was born in Gílán or Jílán in Persia, in the year 1078 A. D., 471 A. H., and was greatly revered for his learning, his piety, and the sanctity of his manners. He died on the 22nd February 1166 A. D., 17th Rabí' II, 561, aged 91 lunar years, and is buried at Baghdád, where he held the place of guardian of Abú-Ḥanífa's tomb. The order of Dervishes, called after him the Ḳádirís, acknowledge him as founder. His tomb is held in high veneration amongst the Muhammadans. He is said to have written many books on Mystical Theology, amongst which are the "Futúḥ-ul-Ghaib", "Malfúẓát-i-Ḳádirí" in Arabic, and a translation of the same in Persian, named "Malfúẓát-i-Jílání." Another work of his in Arabic on Jurisprudence is called Ghunyat-ut-Ṭálibín, and another work on Sufism is entitled Bahjat-ul-Asrár, and a book of Odes called Díwán-i-Ghauṣ-ul-A'zam. *Vide* Muhammad Ḳásim (Sayyid) and Abdáls.

Some say that he was born at Jíl, a village near Baghdád; hence he should be called Jílí.]

**'Abdul-Kadir (Maulana),** مولانا عبد القادر دهلوی, of Dihlí, the son of Maulawí Walí-ullah. He is the author of an Urdú commentary on the Ḳurán, entitled "Tafsír Múziḥ-ul-Ḳurán."

**'Abdul-Kadir Naini (Maulana),** عبد القادر نائینی, a poet who was a native of Náín near Iṣfahán, and contemporary with Shaikh Sa'di.

**'Abdul-Kadir,** a resident of Devi, a village in the district of Lakhnau. From the Jámi'-ut-Tawáríkh of Rashíd-uddín he translated that portion which is called the book of Pátanjal, into easy Persian, at the request of Major Herbert in May 1823. It is a collection of all the sciences, and one of the most valuable works of the sages of Hind. It contains an account of their various sects, and the history of their ancient kings, also the life of Sákyamuni.

**'Abdul-Kahir Jurjani (Shaikh),** عبد القاهر جرجانی son of 'Abdur-Raḥmán, was the author of the book called "Daláil-ul-I'jáz," and several other works. He died in 1081 A. D., 474 A. H.

**'Abdul-Karim,** عبد الکریم, surnamed Imám-uddín Abul-Ḳásim, author of the "Sharḥ Kabír" and "Sharḥ Ṣaghír".

**'Abdul-Karim bin-Muhammad al-Hamadani,** author of a Persian Commentary on the Sirájiya of Sajáwandí, entitled "Faráiẓ-ut-Tájí Sharḥ Faráiẓ-is-Sirájí".

**'Abdul-Karim Sindhi (Mulla),** عبد الکریم سندھی, a native of Sindh who served under Khwája Mahmúd Gáwán in the Dakhin, and was living about the year 1481 A. D., 886 A. H. He is the author of the history of Sultán Mahmúd Bahmaní, entitled "Táríkh-i-Mahmúd-Sháhí".

**'Abdul-Karim,** a native of Dihlí, who accompanied Nádir Sháh to Persia, and wrote a history of that conqueror about the year 1754 A. D., 1168 A. H., entitled "Bayán-i-Wáḳi'".

Regarding this work, *vide* Dowson, Elliot's History of India, VIII, 124.]

**'Abdul-Karim,** Mír, of Bukhárá, who died at Constantinople about 1246 H. (1830 A. D.) He is the author of a history of Afghánistán and Turkistán (1740 to 1818 A. D.), translated into French by C. Schefer, Paris, 1876.]

**'Abdul-Karim,** Munshi, who died about thirty years ago. He is the author of the *Táríkh-i-Ahmad*, a history of Ahmad Sháh Durrání and his successors. The Persian text was lithographed in 1266, and an Urdú translation under the title of *Wáḳi'át-i-Durrání* was issued at Kánhpúr in 1292 H. (1875 A. D.) 'Abdul-Karím also wrote a larger work, entitled *Muḥáraba-i-Kábul o Ḳandahár*, (1265 H.) which contains the heroic deeds of Akbar Khán, son of Dost Muhammad Khán, and is chiefly based on the Akbar-náma written in verse by Munshí Ḳásim Ján; and the *Táríkh-i-Panjáb tuḥfatan lil-aḥbáb*, (A. H. 1265) on the Sikh wars.]

**'Abdul-Kuddus Gangohi (Shaikh)** شیخ عبد القدوس گنگوھی, a native of Gangoh, near Dihlí, was a descendant of Abú-Ḥaníía of Kúfa, and a famous saint of India. He died on the 27th November, 1537 A. D., 23rd Jumáḍá II, 944 A. H., the chronogram of the year of his death being "Shaikh-i-ajall." His grandson Shaikh 'Abdun-Nabí held a high post in the reign of Akbar, but was subsequently imprisoned and murdered.

**'Abdullah,** عبد الله بن عبد المطلب, the father of Muhammad the Prophet, was a younger son of 'Abdul-Muṭṭalib the son of Háshim. He was remarkable for his beauty, and though a driver of camels, he is said to have possessed such merits, that his hand was solicited in marriage by the fairest and the most virtuous of the women of his tribe. He was so universally admired, that on the night of his nuptials one hundred young females expired in despair. His wife Ámina, though long barren, at last became the mother of Muhammad. 'Abdullah died during the lifetime of his father, eight days (some say eight years) after the birth of his son, and left his widow and infant son in very mean circumstances, his whole substance consisting of only five camels and one female Ethiopian slave. 'Abdul-Muṭṭalib, his father, was therefore obliged to take care of his grandson Muhammad, which he did and at his death enjoined his eldest son Abú-Ṭálib to provide for him for the future. 'Abdullah died about the year 571 A. D.

**'Abdullah bin-'Ali al-Halabi,** was one of the first writers on Shí'a jurisprudence, as he was amongst the earliest compilers of the traditions of that sect. It does not appear that any of his legal compositions are extant.

**'Abdullah,** عبد الله بن رواحة, son of Rawáḥa, was an Arabian poet who signalized himself in arms as well as poetry. He became an associate of Muhammad and was sent with the army, of which Zaid was the chief, against the Greeks, and was killed at Múta in Syria with Zaid and Ja'far the brother of 'Alí, in 629 A. D., 8 H.

**'Abdullah son of Zubair,** عبد الله بن زبیر, was the first Musalmán born at Madína amongst those who were called 'Muhájirín', that is to say, fugitives from Mecca. After the battle of Karbalá in 680 A. D., in which Husain the son of 'Alí was slain, the inhabitants of Mecca and Madína, perceiving that Yazíd did all that lay in his power to suppress the house of 'Alí, made an insurrection against Yazíd, the second khalífa of the house of Umayya, and proclaimed 'Abdullah khalífa in the city of Mecca. The Musalmáns of Syria also, after the death of Yazíd and Mu'áwiya the 2nd, acknowledged him for the space of 128 days, after which time Marwán the son of Ḥakam was proclaimed khalífa in the city of Damascus. 'Abdullah still remaining in the city of Mecca, was besieged there in 691 A. D., 72 A. H., by Ḥajjáj, general of the khalífa 'Abdul-Malik. The siege lasted 8 months and 17 days, after which 'Abdullah made a sally upon the enemy, destroyed a great number of them with his own hand, and was at length killed fighting valiantly in 692 A. D., 73 A. H. His head was cut off, and sent to the khalífa 'Abdul-Malik.

**'Abdullah,** عبد الله بن مسعود, son of Mas'úd, companion of Muhammad. He died in 652 A. D., 32 A. H.

**'Abdullah,** عبد الله بن عباس, son of 'Abbás the uncle of Muhammad, was distinguished as a teacher of the sacred book. Before he was ten years of age, he is said to have received inspiration from the angel Gabriel. He was born in 619 A. D., three years before the Hijra (622), and was considered the ablest interpreter of the Ḳurán then in existence. He was appointed governor of Baṣra by the khalífa 'Alí, and remained there for some time. He then returned to Ḥijáz, and died at Ṭáyif, a town lying 60 miles eastward of Mecca, in 687 A. D., 68 A. H., aged 70 years. His mother Umm-ul-Faẓl was the sister of Maimúna, one of the wives of Muhammad.

**'Abdullah,** عبد الله بن عمر, son of 'Umar the second khalífa after Muhammad, was one of the most learned Arabians amongst the contemporaries of Muhammad. He died in 692 A. D., 73 A. H. He is famous for his liberality.

**'Abdullah,** عبد الله بن یزید, son of Yazíd, was celebrated as a lawyer in the 7th century. He was the disciple of Abú-Huraira and Abú-'Abbás, companions of Muhammad, and lived till the hundredth year of the Hijra, or 718 A. D., 100 A. H.

**'Abdullah,** عبد الله بن علی, the son of 'Alí, son of 'Abdullah, son of 'Abbás, the uncle of Muhammad, was the uncle of the first two khalífas of the Abbasides, *viz.*, Abul-'Abbás al-Saffáḥ and Al-Manṣúr, under whom he served as general against the khalífa Marwán, and having vanquished that prince, proclaimed his nephew Al-Saffáḥ. He was guilty of horrible cruelties on the family of the Ommaides. When his eldest nephew died, his brother Al-Manṣúr took upon him the government, which displeased 'Abdullah so much, that he raised an army against him, but was defeated and afterwards perfidiously murdered in 754 A. D., 137 A. H.

**'Abdullah,** عبد الله بن راوند, the son of Ráwand, was the founder of an impious sect, who were called after him the Ráwandites, during the Khiláfat of Al-Manṣúr the Abbaside, about the year 776 A. D.

**'Abdullah,** عبدالله, the son of Shams-uddín, author of the marginal notes on the "Talwíḥ," entitled "Ḥáshiya bar Talwíḥ," a work on jurisprudence.

**'Abdullah,** عبد الله بن طاهر, the son of Ṭáhir, the general of Al-Mámún. He succeeded his brother Ṭalḥa in the government of Khurásán about the year 828 A. D., 213 A. H., reigned 17 years, and died in 844 A. D., 230 A. H. He was succeeded by his son Ṭáhir II.

**'Abdullah Abu-Muslim,** عبد الله ابومسلم, author of the Commentary on the Ḳurán, called "Ṣaḥíḥ Muslim." He was born in 817 A. D., 202 H., and died in the year 875 A. D., 261 H. He is called by some writers Abul-Husain Muslim bin-al-Ḥajjáj bin-Muslim al-Ḳushairí, and by others Muslim bin-Ḥajjáj Níshápúrí, which see.

**'Abdullah,** عبد الله بن طيب السرخسی, the son of Ṭayyib al-Sarakhsí, preceptor to the Khalífa Mu'taẓid Billah, by whom he was put to death A. D. 899, 286 A. H. He is the author of the "Baḥr-ul-Manṭiḳ," and Ísághújí (a commentary on the Isagoge of Porphyras).

**'Abdullah,** عبد الله بن عدی, the son of 'Adiy, author of the Kitáb Kámil. He died in 975 A. D., 365 A. H.

**'Abdullah,** author of a collection of Letters, entitled Inshá-i-'Abdullah.

**'Abdullah,** عبد الله بن مسلم بن قتيبة, the son of Muslim, the son of Ḳutaiba, was the author of the work called "Kitáb-ul-ma'árif," and several other works. He died in 889 A. D., 276 A. H.

**'Abdullah,** عبدالله, author of the Persian work on jurisprudence, called "Aḥkám us-Ṣalát."

**'Abdullah,** عبدالله کلبرگی, of Kulbarga, author of a work called "Fars-náma," writton in 1407, A. D.

**'Abdullah Ansari (Khwaja),** عبد الله انصاري, surnamed Shaikh Abú Ismá'íl, the son of Abú-Manṣúr, the son of Abú-Ayyúb. He was born at Hirát in May, 1006 A. D., Sha'bán, 396 A. H., and is the founder of the sect called Anṣárís in Hirát and Khurásán. He died on the 2nd July, 1088 A. D., 9th Rabí' I., 481 A. H., aged 84 lunar years, and is buried at Hirát in a place called Gázurgáh. 'Abdullah was struck with stones by the boys when he was doing penance, and expired.

**'Abdullah bin-'Ali bin-Abu-Shu'ba al-Halabi,** عبدالله بن على بن ابو شعبة الحلبی. One of the earliest writers both on the Ḥadíṣ and Law of the Imámiya sect. His grandfather, Abú-Shu'ba, is related to have collected traditions in the time of the Imáms Hasan and Husain. 'Abdullah wrote down these traditions, and presented his work, when completed, to the Imám Ja'far Ṣádiḳ, by whom it is said to have been verified and corrected.

**'Abdullah bin-'Ali,** author of the work called "Sírak ul-Hindí," which he paraphrased from the Persian into the Arabic, for it had been originally translated from Sanskrit into the Persian.

**'Abdullah Ahrar,** عبدالله احرار, author of the "Malfúẓát-i-Khwája 'Abdullah," containing the doctrines of the Naḳshbandís, and of the "Anís-us-Sálikín."

**'Abdullah,** عبدالله بن سلام, the son of Salám, author of the questions which Muhammad was asked on the subject of his prophecy. He is also the author of a work, called "'Aẓmat-ul-Manḳúl." Another work, called "Hazár Masáyil", is ascribed to him.

**'Abdullah,** عبد الله بن محمد, son of Muhammad, surnamed Ḳalánísí, an Arabian author. He died in 1121 A. D., 515 A. H.

**'Abdullah bin-Fazl-ullah,** of Shíráz, author of the "Tárikh-i-Waṣṣáf."

The first four volumes of this work, which may be looked upon as a continuation of the '*Jahán-kushá*', go as far as Sha'bán, 690, (March, 1300). Subsequently, the author added a fifth volume which relates the events down to the year 728 (1328 A. D.); *vide* Dowson, Elliot's History of India, III, 24.]

'ABDULLAH is also the name of the author of the *Táríkh-i-Dáúdí*, an Afghán History, written during the reign of Jahángír; *vide* Dowson, IV, 434.]

**'Abdullah,** عبدالله ابن اليافعی شافعی, the son of 'al-Yáfi'í Sháfi'í, author of the Arabic work called "Rauẓat-ur-Rayáḥín," containing a detailed account of the lives of Muhammad, the twelve Imáms, and of all the saints of Arabia, Persia, and Hindústán.

**'Abdullah Shattari** (Shaikh), عبد الله شطاری, a descendant of Shaikh Shiháb-uddín Suhrawardí. He came from Persia to India, and died in Málwá, A. D. 1406, 809 H., and is buried there.

Regarding the Shaṭṭárís *vide* Journal, Asiatic Society, Bengal, 1874, Pt. I, p. 216.]

**'Abdullah Hatifi,** *vide* Hátifí.

**'Abdullah Khan Uzbak,** عبد الله خان اُزبک, was a renowned officer in the time of Akbar. He was made governor of Mandú (Málwá) in 1562 A. D., and afterwards rebelled against the king, but was defeated and compelled to leave the country.

For further notes *vide Áín* Translation I, p. 320.]

**'Abdullah Khan,** عبد الله خان اُزبک, chief of the Uzbaks, was the son of Sikandar Khán, the son of Jání Beg Khán, a descendant of Júji Khán, son of Chingiz Khán. After the death of his father (during whose life he had several battles with him), he ascended the throne of Samarḳand and Bukhárá in 1582 A. D., 990 A. H., invaded Khurásán and took Hirát after a siege of nine months in 1585 A. D., 993 A. H. Its governor 'Alí Ḳulí Khán with several other chiefs were put to death, and the city was plundered. He was contemporary with Sháh 'Abbás of Persia and Akbar Sháh, and died after a reign of 15 years, aged 66, on the 12th February 1597 A. D., 5th Rajab 1005 A. H. The chronogram of the year of his death is "ḳiyámat ḳáyim shud." He was succeeded by his son 'Abdul-Múmin Khán.

**'Abdullah Khan Firuz-Jang,** عبد الله خان فيروزجنگ a descendant of Khwája 'Abdullah Aḥrár. He came to India in the latter end of the reign of the emperor Akbar, was raised to the rank of 6000 by the emperor Jahángír, and died in the time of Sháh Jahán, A. D. 1644, 17th Shawwál 1054, aged nearly 70 years.

**'Abdullah Khan** (Sayyid), سيد عبدالله خان, styled Ḳuṭbul-Mulk, was governor of Alláhábád from the time of Bahádur Sháh, emperor of Dihlí, and his younger brother Sayyid Husain 'Alí Khán, that of Bihár. These brothers sprung from a numerous and respected family of the descendants of the prophet, who were settled in the town of Bárha, and in consequence of this origin, they are best known in India by the name of Sádát, or Sayyids, of Bárha. Farrukh-siyar, who by the aid of these two brothers had ascended the throne of Dihlí, on his accession in January 1713 A. D., 1125 A. H., made the former his prime-minister, with the title of Ḳuṭb-ul-Mulk, and appointed the latter Amír-ul-Umará. Husain 'Alí Khán was assassinated by Mír Ḥaidar Khán at the instigation of the emperor Muhammad Sháh on the 18th September 1720 O. S., 27th Ẕil-ḳa'da 1132, and his brother 'Abdullah Khán, who made some resistance, was defeated and taken prisoner on the 4th November following, 14th Muḥarram 1133, and died in confinement after three years on the 19th September 1723 O. S., 30th Ẕil-ḥijja 1135. The remains of Husain 'Alí Khán were transferred to Ajmír for burial. His brother 'Abdullah was buried at Dihlí.

Regarding the Sayyids of Bárha, *vide* Áín Translation, I, p. 390; and for 'Abdullah Ḳuṭb-ul-Mulk, *vide* Dowson, VII, 447ff.]

**'Abdullah Kutb-Shah,** عبدالله قطب‌شاه, the sixth Sulṭán of the Ḳuṭb-Sháhí dynasty of Golkonda in Ḥaidarábád, Dakhin. He succeeded Muhammad Ḳuṭb Sháh, and reigned many years under the protection of the emperor Sháh Jahán, to whom he acknowledged himself tributary, and paid an annual sum; but in the year 1656 A. D., 1066 A. H., he displeased that monarch, and brought upon himself much trouble. The emperor had commanded him to permit his prime-minister Mír Muhammad Sa'íd and his son Muhammad Amín to repair with their effects to court. Ḳuṭb-Sháh disobeyed the mandate, and confining Muhammad Amín, then at Ḥaidarábád, seized part of his wealth. The prince Aurangzíb, then governor of the imperial territories in the Dakhin, enraged at this conduct, marched to Ḥaidarábád, which he took and plundered. 'Abdullah was obliged to purchase pardon by a contribution of a crore of Rupees, and the gift of his daughter in marriage to the son of his enemy, the prince Sulṭán Muhammad. From this time 'Abdullah, during the remainder of his life, was in fact a vassal of the empire. 'Abdullah Ḳuṭb-Sháh died in June 1674 A. D., Rabí' I 1085 H., and was succeeded by his son-in-law Abul-Hasan.

**'Abdullah Mansur,** عبد الله منصور, author of the Tarjama-i-Ṭabaḳát-i-Ṣúfiya, containing the lives of the most celebrated Ṣúfís and Shaikhs.

**'Abdullah Mirza,** عبد الله مرزا, was the son of Ibráhím Mirzá, the son of Sháhrukh Mirzá, and great-grandson of Amír Timur. Upon his father's death (about the year 1443 A. D.), he became possessed of the sovereignty of Fárs, or Persia; but four years after, he was dispossessed by one of his cousins-german, named Mirzá Abú-Sa'íd, and was obliged to fly to his uncle Mirzá Ulugh Beg, who then reigned in Transoxiana, and who gave him his daughter in marriage. Some time after, Ulugh Beg having been defeated in a battle against his son Mirzá 'Abdul-Laṭíf, and afterwards put to death by him in October 1449 A. D., Ramaẓán 853 A. H., and the latter not enjoying the success of his parricide above six months, 'Abdullah, as son-in-law to Ulugh Beg, took possession of his dominions: but Mirzá Abú-Sa'íd, his cousin-german, declared war against him, and defeated him in a pitched battle, in which he perished. This event took place in the year 1451 A. D., 855 A. H.

**'Abdullah** (Mauláná), مولانا عبد الله, son of Ilahdád. He is the author of Sharḥ Mízán-il-Manṭiḳ and several other works. He was a native of Dihlí, flourished in the reign of Sulṭán Sikandar, and died in 1516 A. D., 922 H.

**'Abdullah,** Mauláná of Sulṭánpúr, a learned bigoted Sunní at Akbar's Court. He had the title of 'Makhdúm-ul-Mulk.' He played a prominent part in the religious discussions which led Akbar to renounce Islám. He died, or was poisoned, in 990 H. *Vide* Áín Translation, p. 544, and p. vii (of Abul-Faẓl's Biography).]

**'Abdullah Tamimi,** عبد الله تميمى, author of the Arabic work called "Rauẓat-ul-Abrár," which contains the history of Muḥammad, and Memoirs of many of his companions.

**'Abdullah Tirmizi** (Mír), عبد الله ترمذي, waṣ an elegant poet and wrote an excellent Nasta'líḳ hand, for which he received from the emperor Jahángír the poetical name of Waṣfí, or praiseworthy, and the title of Mushkín-Ḳalam, that is to say, out of whose pen flowed musk. He is the author of several poems. His death happened in the year 1626 A. D., 1035 A. H. His tomb stands at a place in Ágra, called Naglá Jawáhir.

For the inscription on his tomb, and his son Muhammad Ṣáliḥ Kashfí, *vide* Proceedings, Asiatic Society Bengal, 1874, p. 162.]

**'Abdul-Latif,** عبد اللطيف, a celebrated physician, born at Baghdád A. D. 1261, 660 A. H. To the acquirement of medical knowledge he applied himself with diligence; and it was chiefly with this view that, in his 28th year, he left Baghdád in order to visit other countries. Having spent a year in Mauṣil, he removed to Damascus in Syria and thence to Egypt, where the people of the highest rank continued to vie with each other in cultivating his friendship. He afterwards travelled to Aleppo, and resided several years in Greece. Of 150 treatises which he composed on various subjects, only one, entitled "Historiæ Ægyti Compendium," has survived the ravages of time. He died suddenly at Baghdád in his 65th year.

**'Abdul-Latif,** عبد اللطيف, a great-grandson of Amír Timur. In October 1449 A. D., he defeated his father Mirzá Ulugh Beg in an action near Samarḳand, took him prisoner and put him to death. He did not long enjoy his success, for he had scarcely reigned six months, when he was murdered by his own soldiers on the 9th May 1450, 26th Rabí' I, 854 A. H. His head was separated from his body and sent to Hirát, where it was placed on the gate of the college built by his father.

**'Abdul-Latif,** عبداللطيف, a native of Ḳazwín, and author of the work entitled "Lubb-ut-Tawáríkh," a history of Persia, written in the middle of the 16th century.

**'Abdul-Latif (Mulla),** ملا عبد اللطيف, of Sulṭánpúr, was the tutor of the prince Aurangzíb. In the last years of his life he became blind, received from the emperor Sháh Jahán a few villages free of rent for his support, and died in the year 1632 A. D., 1042 A. H.

**'Abdul-Latif,** author of a collection of Letters called "Inshá-i-'Abdul-Laṭíf."

**'Abdul-Latif,** عبد اللطيف, author of the work called Laṭáif-i-Ma'nawí, a commentary on the difficult passages of the Maṣnawí of Mauláná Rúm, written in 1640 A.D. He also is the author of a Dictionary, called "Laṭáif-ul-Lughát."

Regarding the author *vide* Journal, Asiatic Society, for 1868, p. 32.]

**'Abdul-Maal,** عبدالمعال, author of a system of Geography, written in the Persian Language, and entitled "Masáḥat-ul-Arẓ," or the survey of the earth.

**'Abdul-Majid Khan,** عبد المجيد, the Turkish emperor of Constantinople, was born on the 23rd April, 1823, and succeeded his father Mahmúd II, on the 2nd July, 1839, A. D., 1277 A. H. He died on the 25th June, 1861, aged 39 years, and was succeeded by his brother 'Abdul-'Azíz.

**'Abdul-Majid Khan,** عبد المجيدخان, entitled Majd-ud-daula, a nobleman who was promoted by Ahmad Sháh of Dihlí to the rank of 3rd Bakhshígarí or paymastership, in 1748 A. D., 1161 A. H. He died in the year 1752 A. D., 1165 A. H.

**'Abdul-Majid (Shaikh),** شيخ عبد المجيد, a learned man who flourished in the time of Sháh Jahán, and wrote a history of that emperor entitled Sháh Jahán-náma.

This seems to be a mistake for 'Abdul-Ḥamíd.]

**'Abdul-Malik,** عبد الملک بن مروان, the son of Marwán I, was the 5th Khalífa of the house of Umayya (Ommaides). He succeeded his father at Damascus, on the 13th April, 685 A. D., 3rd Ramaẓán, 65 A. H., surpassed his predecessors in military exploits, and extended his power as far as Spain in the west, and India in the east. He was so generous as not to take a church from the Christians, which they had refused to grant him when he requested it. He was called Abul-Ẓubáb or "father of flies," because his breath was so offensive, that it killed the very flies that settled on his lips. He reigned upwards of 21 lunar years and died in October, 705 A. D., Shawwál, 86 A. H. He was succeeded by Walíd I, the eldest of his sixteen sons, who greatly extended the Moslem dominions.

**'Abdul-Malik,** عبد الملک بن صالح, the son of Ṣáliḥ, the son of 'Abdullah, the son of 'Abbás, was related in blood to the prophet Muhammad; was invested by Hárún-ur-Rashíd, the Khalífa of Baghdád, with the government of Egypt, in which he continued till about the year 794 A. D., 178 A. H., when Hárún, suspecting that he was engaged in some cabals, in order to obtain the empire, threw him into prison, where he remained till Hárún's death. His son released him, and invested him with the government of Syria, A. D. 809, 193 A. H.

**'Abdul-Malik,** عبد الملک ابن ظهر, the son of Ẓuhr, an eminent Arabian physician, commonly called by Europeans Avenzoar, a corruption of Ibn-Ẓuhr. His full name is Abú-Marwán 'Abdul-Malik ibn-Ẓuhr. He flourished about the end of the 11th or the beginning of the 12th century. He was of noble descent, and born at Sevilla, the capital of Andalusia, where he exercised his profession with great reputation. His grandfather and father were both physicians. It is said that he lived to the age of 135; that he began to practice at 40 or, as others say, at 20; and had the advantage of a longer experience than almost any one ever had, for he enjoyed perfect health to his last hour. He left a son, also known by the name of Ibn-Ẓuhr, who followed his father's profession, was in great favour with Al-Manṣúr, emperor of Morocco, and wrote several treatises on physic. Avenzoar wrote a book, entitled "Tayaṣṣur fi-l-mudáwát wat-tadbír", which is much esteemed. This work was translated into Hebrew in 1280 A. D., and thence into Latin by Paravicius, whose version has had several editions. The author added a supplement to it, under the title of Jámi', or Collection. He also wrote a treatise "Fil-adwiyat wal-aghziyat", *i. e.*, of medicines and food, wherein he treats of their qualities. Ibn-Ẓuhr was contemporary with Ibn-Rashíd (Averroes), who more than once gives him a very high and deserved encomium, calling him admirable, glorious, the treasure of all knowledge, and the most supreme in medicine from the time of Galen to his own.

**'Abdul-Malik,** عبد الملک, king of Fez and Morocco, was dethroned by his nephew Muhammad, but he afterwards defeated Sebastian king of Portugal, who had landed in Africa to support the usurper. The two African monarchs and Sebastian fell on the field, 1578 A. D. (986 A. H.)

**'Abdul-Malik** (Khwája), a native of Samarḳand who held the office of Shaikh-ul-Islám in that city in the reign of Amír Timur.

**'Abdul-Malik Samani I,** عبد الملک سامانی, a king of the house of Sámán, and son of Amír Núḥ I, whom he succeeded in 954 A. D. (343 A. H.). He reigned in Khurásán and Máwarán-nahr seven and a half years, and was killed by a fall from his horse while playing at ball in 961 A. D. (350 A. H.) He was succeeded by his brother Amír Manṣúr I.

**'Abdul-Malik Samani II,** عبد الملک سامانی, an Amír of the house of Sámán, was elevated to the throne of Khurásán, after his brother Amír Manṣúr II, in 998 A. D. (388 A. H.). He was the last Amír, or king, of the race of the Samanides. He reigned only a few months, and was defeated in battle against Sulṭán Mahmúd of Ghazní in 999 A. D., who took possession of his country. 'Abdul-Malik was shortly after murdered.

**'Abdul-Manaf,** عبد المناف, or 'Abd-Manáf, (*i. e.* slave of the idol Manáf) the great-great-grandfather of Muhammad, was the son of Ḳuṣayy, who aggrandized the tribe of the Ḳuraish by purchasing the keys of the Ka'ba from Abú-Ghassán, a weak and silly man, for a bottle of wine. Ḳuṣayy was succeeded by his second son 'Abdul-Manáf, to whom the prophetic light, which is said to have manifested itself in his face, gave the right of primogeniture. After his death, his son Háshim, the father of 'Abdul-Muṭṭalib, succeeded.

'Abd-Manáf is also the name of a son of the Prophet, who died in infancy.]

**'Abdul-Mannan (Mir),** میر عبد المنان, son of Mír Nu'mán Khán, son of Khwája 'Abdur-Raḥím Khán of Andiján. He served under the celebrated Niẓám-ul-Mulk Áṣaf-Jáh in the Dakhin for several years, was an excellent poet, and is known under the poetical name of 'Ibrat.

**'Abdul-Mumin,** عبد المومن, a man of obscure origin and son of a potter, who seized the crown of Morocco after destroying the royal family. He extended his dominions by the conquest of Tunis, Fez, and Tremezen. He meditated the invasion of Spain, when death stopped his career in 1156 A. D. His son Yúsuf who succeeded him, carried his ambitious views into effect.

**'Abdul-Mumin Khan,** عبد المومن خان, the son of 'Abdullah Khán, chief of the Uzbaks, was raised to the throne after the death of his father at Samarḳand in the year 1597 A. D., 1005 A. H. He took Mashhad and put the inhabitants to the sword. He was soon after assassinated by his own officers in 1598 A. D., 1006 A. H.; the chronogram of his death being contained in the words "Badbakht-i-sar-burída." After his death, Dín Muhammad Khán, the son of 'Abdullah Khán's sister, was placed on the throne; but he fell shortly after, in a battle fought at Hirát, against Sháh 'Abbás, king of Persia.

**'Abdul-Muttalib,** عبد المطلب, the grandfather of Muhammad, the son of Háshim of the tribe of Ḳuraish. He is said to have been extremely affable and easy of access, as well as just and generous. The well which God shewed Hagar the mother of Ishmael in the wilderness, is said to have been miraculously discovered to 'Abdul-Muṭṭalib, about five hundred years after it had been filled up by 'Amr, prince of the Jorhomites. The well is called Zamzam by the Arabs and is on the east side of the Ka'ba, covered with a small building and cupola. Its water is highly reverenced, being not only received with particular devotion by the pilgrims, but also sent in bottles as a great rarity to most parts of the Muhammadan dominions. 'Abdul-Muṭṭalib had ten sons, whose names are as follows: Abú-Ṭálib, the father of 'Alí; 'Abbás, the ancestor of the Abbasides who reigned at Baghdád; Ḥamza; Ḥáriṣ; Abú-Lahab; 'Abdullah the father of Muhammad; Al-Maḳawwam; Zubair; Zirár; Ḳuṣam. His younger son 'Abdullah, the father of Muhammad, dying eight days after the birth of his son, 'Abdul-Muṭṭalib was obliged to take care of his grandson Muhammad, which he not only did during his life, but at his death enjoined his eldest son Abú-Ṭálib to provide for him for the future. 'Abdul-Muṭṭalib died about the year 579 A. D., at which time Muhammad was about eight years old.

**'Abdul-Nabi (Shaikh),** شيخ عبد النبي, son of Shaikh Aḥmad, and grandson of Shaikh 'Abdul-Ḳuddús of Gangoh. He was the tutor of the emperor Akbar, and was honored with the dignity of Ṣadr-us-Ṣudúr. No Ṣadr during any former reign had so much favor. The king was for some time so intimate and unceremonious with him, that he would rise to adjust the Shaikh's slippers when he took his leave. At last, through the enmity of Mauláná 'Abdullah Makhdúm-ul-Mulk (*vide* p. 6) and others, he fell in the king's estimation, and began to be treated very differently. He was banished to Mecca, and after his return was murdered in the year 1583 A. D. (991 A. H.)

*Vide* Áín Translation I, 546, 538, and p. xiii (Abul-Fazl's Biography); also Proc. Asiatic Society, Bengal, January, 1876.]

**'Abdul-Nabi Khan,** served under Aurangzíb, and built the large Mosque at Mathurá; *vide* Proc. As. Socy. Bengal, 1873, p. 12.]

**'Abdul-Rahim bin-Ahmad Sur,** عبد الرحيم بن احمد سور, author of the Persian Dictionary 'Kashf-ul-Lughát. *Vide* Journal, As. Society, Bengal, for 1868, p. 9.]

**'Abdul-Rahim Khan,** عبد الرحيم خان خانان, Khán-Khánán, commonly called Khán Mírzá, was the son of Bairám Khán, the first prime-minister of the emperor Akbar. He was born on the 17th December 1556 A. D. (14th Ṣafar 964 H.) and was only four years old when his father was assassinated. When of age, he received the appointment of his father with the same title of Khánkhánán and the government of Gujrát in 1585 A. D. (993 H.) His daughter Jání Begam was married to prince Dányál in the year 1599 A. D. (1007 H.) He translated the "Wáḳi'át-i-Bábarí" (Memoirs of the emperor Bábar) from Turkí into Persian. After Akbar's death, he served under Jahángír for 21 years, and died a few months before that emperor, shortly after the suppression of Mahábat Khán's rebellion, in the year 1627 A. D. (1036 A. H.), aged 72 lunar years, and lies buried at Dihlí near the Dargáh of Shaikh Niẓám-uddín Auliyá, where his tomb is to be seen to this day. His poetical name was Raḥím.

For a detailed biography *vide* Áín Translation I, 334.]

**'Abdul-Rahim,** عبد الرحيم, one of the principal nobles who joined Prince Khusrau in his rebellion against his father Jahángír in 1606 A. D. He was taken prisoner with the prince and brought to the emperor at Láhor; by whose order he was sewn up in the raw hide of an ass, kept constantly moist with water, in which miserable condition he remained for twenty-four hours. He was afterwards pardoned; *vide* Áín Translation I, 455.

**'Abdul-Rahim Khan,** Khwája, خواجه عبد الرحيم خان, the son of Abul-Ḳásim. He was a native of Andiján in Farghána, came to India in the reign of the emperor Sháh Jahán, and served under Aurangzíb for several years. He died in 1692 A. D. (1103 A. H.)

**'Abdul-Rahman,** عبد الرحمن ابن ملجم, the son of Muljim, the murderer of 'Alí, son-in-law of Muhammad. He was killed by Hasan, son of 'Alí, in January 661 A. D. (Ramaẓán, 40 A. H.)

No Shí'a would now-a-days call his son 'Abd-urraḥmán, just as no Muhammadan would call his son Yazíd.]

**'Abdul-Rahman,** عبد الرحمن ابن ابوبكر, the son of Abú-Bakr, first Khalífa after Muhammad, and brother to 'Áyisha, the favorite wife of the prophet. He died in the same year that his sister died, *i. e.*, in 678 A. D., 58 A. H.

**'Abdul-Rahman,** عبد الرحمن بن محمد حنيف, son of Muhammad Ḥaníf son of 'Alí. He raised a formidable power against Ḥajjáj, the governor of Arabia, defeated him in several battles, and at last, rather than fall into his hands, threw himself from a house and died, 701 A. D., 82 A. H.

**'Abdul-Rahman,** a popular Afghán poet of Pesháwar. His verses are written with fiery energy, which has made them popular amongst a martial people, and yet with natural simplicity which is charming to the lover of poetry. Not far from the city is his grave, situated on the road to Hazárkhána, the poet's native village.

**'Abdul-Rahman,** عبد الرحمن, a Saracen general of the Khalífa Hishám, (called by some of our authors Abderames) who penetrated into Aquitain and Poitou, and was at last defeated and slain by Charles Martel near Poitiers, in 732 A. D., 114 A. H.

**'Abdul-Rahman Mustafa,** عبد الرحمن مصطفى, who in Watkin's Biographical Dictionary is called Babacauschi, was muftí of the city of Caffa, in Tauris. He wrote a book called 'The Friend of Princes'. He died in A. D. 1381, 783 A. H.

**'Abdul-Rahman,** عبد الرحمن, also called by old writers Abderames, a descendant of the Khalífas of the house of Umayya. He was invited to come to Spain, in 756 A. D., 139 A. H., by the Saracens who had revolted; and after he had conquered the whole kingdom, he assumed the title of king of Cordova. He was the founder of the Ommaides of Spain, who reigned above two hundred and fifty years, from the Atlantic to the Pyrenees. He died in 790 A. D., 174 A. H., after reigning 32 years.

**'Abdul-Rahman Ichi,** عبد الرحمن ايجي, or Íjí, the father of 'Ḳází 'Aẓd-uddín of Shíráz, a learned man and native of Ích, a town situated 40 farsakhs from Shíráz.

**'Abdul-Rahman,** عبد الرحمن, called by us Abderames, a petty prince in the kingdom of Morocco, who murdered 'Imád-uddín, his predecessor and nephew, and was himself after a long reign assassinated by a chieftain whose death he meditated, 1505 A. D., 911 A. H.

**'Abdul-Rahman,** the Sulṭán of Fez and Morocco, born 1778, was rightful heir to the throne when his father died; but was supplanted by his uncle, after whose death he ascended the throne in 1823. His eldest son Sídí Muhammad (born 1803) is heir to the throne.

**'Abdul-Rahman Khan,** عبد الرحمن خان, Nawáb of Jhajjar, who on account of his rebellion during the mutiny of the native troops in 1857 A. D, 1274 A. H., was found guilty and executed at Dihlí before the Koṭwálí on the 23rd December of the same year. He was a descendant of Najábat 'Alí Khán, to whom in 1806, when Sir G. Barlow was Governor-General of India, were granted the large territorial possessions held by the late Nawáb, yielding a yearly revenue of 12½ lacs, and consisting of Jhajjar, Badlí, Karaund with its fort, Nárnaul, &c. In addition to these, expressly for the purpose of keeping up 400 horsemen, the territory of Badwán and Dadrí was granted. Up to May 1857, he had always been looked upon as a staunch friend of the British Government; but when the rebellion burst forth, he forgot all his obligations to the British, and sided with the rebels.

**'Abdul-Rahman Khan,** عبد الرحمن خان, Ṣadr-us-Ṣudúr of Kánhpúr, a rebel and a staunch supporter of Náná Ṣáḥib, when that ruffian commenced his career. He was hanged at Kánhpúr, in June 1858, 1274 A. H.

**'Abdul-Rahman Sulami (Shaikh),** author of the "Ṭabaḳát Ṣúfiya", a work on Sufism. He died in 1021 A. D., 412 A. H. He is also called Abú-'Abdur-raḥmán.

**'Abdul-Rahman,** son of 'Abdul-'Azíz Naḳshbandí, the father-in-law of Sulaimán Shikoh, who married his daughter in A. H. 1062, the 25th year of Sháh Jahán.

**'Abdul-Rahman Chishti,** عبد الرحمن چشتي, author of the *Mir-át-i-Mas'údi*, which contains the legendary history of Sálár Mas'úd Ghází, buried at Bahráich in Audh. 'Abur-raḥmán died during the reign of Aurangzíb in 1094 H. For extract translations *vide* Dowson, Elliot's History of India, II, 513. An Urdú translation of the Mir-át-i-Mas'údí was lithographed at Kánhpur, 1287 H., under the title of 'Ghazá-náma-i-Mas'úd.']

**'Abdul-Rashid,** عبد الرشيد, was the son of Sulṭán Mas'úd of Ghazní. He began to reign, after deposing and confining his brother 'Alí in 1052 A. D., 443 H. He had reigned but one year, when Ṭughril, one of his nobles, assassinated him and mounted the throne of Ghazní. Ṭughril reigned only forty days, and was murdered on the Persian New Year's day in March 1053 A. D., 444 A. H., when Farrukh-zád, a brother of 'Abdur-Rashíd, succeeded him.

**'Abdul-Rashid** (Mír), مير عبد الرشيد, son of 'Abdul-Ghafúr-ul-Husainí. He lived in the time of the emperor Sháh Jahán, and wrote chronograms on his accession to the throne of Dihlí in 1628 A. D., 1037 A. H. He is the author of the Persian Dictionary called "Farhang-i-Rashídí", also of the "Muntakhab-ul-Lughát", a very useful Arabic Dictionary, with Persian explanations, dedicated to the emperor Sháh Jahán. Another work of his is called "Risála-i-Mu'arrabát."

The Farhang-i-Rashídí, which was written in 1064 (A. D. 1653), is the first critical dictionary of the Persian language, and has been printed by the Asiatic Society of Bengal; *vide* Journal, Asiatic Society, Bengal, 1868, p. 20.]

**'Abdul-Rashid Khan,** عبد الرشيد خان, son of Sulṭán Abú-Sa'íd Khán, king of Káshghar. He was the contemporary of Humáyún, the emperor of Dihlí. Mírzá Ḥaidar, author of the Táríkh-i-Rashídí, dedicated his work to him.

*Vide* Dowson, Elliot's History of India, V, 127; and A'ín Translation I, 460.]

**'Abdul-Razzak,** عبد الرزاق, a chief of the Sarbadáls of Sabzwár. He was at first employed by Sulṭán Abú-Sa'íd Khán as a Yasáwal, or mace-bearer, but after his death, when confusion took place, he possessed himself of Khurásán in 1336 A. D., 737 A. H., and was slain, after one year and two months, by his brother Wajíh-uddín Mas'úd in September 1337, Ṣafar 738 A. H. Mas'úd reigned seven years, and was deposed by his brother Shams-uddín, who after a reign of four years and nine months was slain at Sabzwár by Ḥaidar Ḳaṣṣáb. After him Amír Yahyá Ḳirátí made himself master of Khurásán, and gave the command of his troops to Ḥaidar Ḳaṣṣáb. In the month of December 1353 A. D., 754 A. H., Yahyá slew Tughán Timur, a descendant of the Mughul kings, in battle, and was himself slain by his nobles, after he had reigned four years and eight months. After him they raised Khwája Luṭf-ullah, the son of Khwája Mas'úd, to the masnad. He was slain after a short time by Hasan Dámghání, who reigned four years and four months, when Khwája 'Alí Muayyad slew him, and reigned eighteen years in Khurásán, after which he made over his country to Amír Timur who passed Khurásán in 1380 A. D., 782 A. H. 'Alí Muayyad was killed in a battle in the year 1386, 788 A. H., and with him terminated the power of the Sarbadáls.

**'Abdul-Razzak,** Kamál-uddín, son of Jalál-uddín Is-ḥáḳ, born at Hirát on the 12th Sha'bán, 816 (6th November, 1413). He is the author of the historical work entitled '*Maṭla'-us-sa'dain*. He died in 887 (A. D. 1482); *vide* below *sub* Kamál, and Dowson, IV, 90.]

**'Abdul-Razzak,** عبد الرزاق, the son of Mirzá Ulugh Beg, the emperor Bábar's uncle. He was killed by the command of that monarch, before his invasion of India, for raising disturbances at Kábul, about 1509 A. D., 915 A. H.

**'Abdul-Razzak (Mulla),** ملا عبد الرزاق, of Láhiján, author of the "Gauhar-i-Murád," a dissertation on the creation of the world and the pre-eminence then given by God to man, dedicated to Sháh 'Abbás II of Persia. He lived about the year 1660 A. D., 1072 H. His poetical name is Fayyáẓ.

**'Abdul-Salam,** عبد السلام بن محمد, son of Muhammad, a celebrated learned man, and author of the "Tafsír Kabír," a commentary on the Ḳurán. He died in the year 1095 A. D., 488 A. H.

**'Abdul-Salam,** قاضي عبد السلام بداوني, (Ḳázi) of Badáoṇ, son of 'Aṭá-ul-Ḥakk. He is the author of the commentary called "Tafsír Zád-ul-A'khirat" in Urdú, consisting of 200,000 verses, which he completed about the year 1828 A. D., 1244 H., as the name of the work shews.

**'Abdul-Salam,** عبد السلام, a famous philosopher and physician, who died at Damascus in 1443 A. D., 847 H.

**'Abdul-Salam,** ملا عبد السلام, (Mullá) of Láhor, a pupil of Amír Fatḥ-ullah Shírází. He died in the year 1628 A. D., 1037 A. H.

*Vide* A'ín Translation I, 545.]

**'Abdul-Salam,** ملا عبد السلام, (Mullá) of Dihlí, was the pupil of Mullá 'Abdus-Salám of Láhor. He wrote the Sharḥ, or marginal notes, on the commentaries called "Tahzíb", "Manár" &c., and is also the author of the work on Sufism in Arabic, called "Ḥall-ur-Rumúz."

**'Abdul-Samad,** عبد الصمد, uncle of the two first Khalífas of the house of 'Abbás, died at a great age during the khiláfat of Hárún-ur-Rashíd in the year 801 A. D., 185 A. H. It is said of him that he never lost a tooth, for both the upper and lower jaws were each of one single piece.

**'Abdul Samad,** Khwája, خواجه عبد الصمد, a noble of Akbar's court, also well-known as caligrapher. He was the father of Sharíf, Amír-ul-Umará under Jahángír (*vide* A'ín Translation, I, pp. 495, 517), and had the title of *Shírín-Ḳalam*, or sweet-pen.]

**'Abdul-Samad,** عبد الصمد, nephew of Shaikh Abul-Fazl, Secretary to the emperor Akbar. He is the compiler of the work called "Inshá-i-Abul-Fazl," which he collected and published in the year 1606 A. D., 1015 H.

**'Abdul-Samad Khan,** عبد الصمد خان, styled Nawáb Saif-uddaula Bahádur-Jang, was the son of Khwája 'Abdul-Karím, a descendant of Khwája 'Ubaid-ullah Aḥrár. The native country of his father was Samarḳand, but he was born at A'gra. In his childhood, he went with his father to Samarḳand, where he completed his studies. In the reign of Aurangzíb he returned to India, and was, at his first introduction to the emperor, raised to the rank of 600, and after a short time to that of 1500, with the title of Khán. In the reign of Jahándár Sháh, the rank of 7000 and the title of 'A'lí-Jang were conferred on him. He was made governor of Láhor in the time of Farrukh-siyar, and was sent with a great army against the Sikhs, whom he defeated and made prisoners with Bánda their chief. He was made governor of Multán by the emperor Muhammad Sháh with the title of Saif-uddaula, and his son Zakariyá Khán, Ṣúbadár of Láhor. He died in 1737 A. D., 1150 A. H., a year before the invasion of Nádir Sháh. *Vide* Khán-Daurán IV.

The Histories call him *Diler-jang*, not '*A'lí-jang*; *vide* also Dowson, VII, 456, 491, 511.]

**'Abdul-Samad Khan,** عبد الصمد خان, Faujdár of Sarhind, distinguished himself in the Maraṭha Wars, and was at last beheaded by Bháo in 1174 A. H. (A. D. 1760); *vide* Dowson, VIII, 278.]

**'Abdul-Shukur (Maulana),** مولانا عبد الشكور. His poetical name was Bazmí. He lived in the time of Sháh Jahán about the year 1634 A. D., 1044 A. H.; *vide* Bazmí.

**'Abdul Wahhab (Kazi),** قاضی عبد الوهاب, lived in the time of the emperor 'Álamgír, and died on the 26th November 1675 A. D., 18th Ramazán 1086 A. H. at Dihlí. He is the author of a Dastúr-ul-'Amal, which he dedicated to that monarch.

**'Abdul Wahhab (Mir),** میرعبد الوهاب, author of the "Tazkira-i-Be-nazír", which he wrote about the year 1758 A. D., 1172 A. H.

**'Abdul-Wahhab,** عبد الوهاب, author of the Manáḳib-i Maulawí Rúm, containing the memoirs of the celebrated Jalál-uddín Rúmí.

**'Abdul-Wahhab bin-Ahmad,** عبد الوهاب بن احمد, author of the Arabic work on theology, called "Anwár Aḥmadiya," written in 1548 A. D.

**'Abdul-Wahhab,** or Muhammad bin-'Abdul-Wahháb, founder of the sect of the Wahhábís, was born at Ḥuraimala in the province of Najd in Arabia about the year 1750 A. D.

**'Abdul-Wahid,** عبد الواحد, author of the Sab'a Sanábil, essays on the duties of Instructor and Student, written in the year 1561 A. D., 969 A. H.

**'Abdul-Wahid (Mir),** میرعبد الواحد, a native of Bilgrám, in Audh, whose poetical name was Sháhidí. He died in his native country on the 11th of December 1608 A. D., 3rd Ramazán 1017 A. H. His son's name was Mír 'Abdul-Jalíl, the father of Sayyid Uwais, whose son's name was Sayyid Barkat-ullah.

**'Abdul-Wahid (Mir),** میرعبد الواحد, of Bilgrám. He wrote under two assumed names, *viz.* Wáhid and Zauḳí, was an excellent poet in Persian and in Hindí, and is the author of a work in prose and verse, called "Shakaristán-i-Khayál," wherein he has mentioned the names of all kinds of sweetmeats. He was killed on the 13th October 1721 A. D., Friday, 2nd Muharram 1134 A. H., in an affray with the zamíndárs of Ráhún in the Panjáb, the settlement of which place was entrusted to his father Sayyid Muhammad Ashraf.

**'Abdul-Wahidi,** a Turkish poet, author of a Díwán comprising 30 Ḳaṣídas, 200 Ghazals, 29 Táríkhs, and 54 Rubá'ís.

**'Abdul-Wasi' of Hansi,** عبد الواسع هانسوی, author of a Persian grammar, called after his name "Risála-i-'Abdul-Wási'." He flourished in the last century, and is also the author of a Hindústání Dictionary, entitled "Gharáib-ul-Lughát".

For further notes *vide* Proceedings, Asiatic Society Bengal, for 1877, p. 121.]

**'Abdul-Wasi' Jabali,** عبد الواسع جبلي, a celebrated poet of Persia, who flourished about the year 1152 A. D., 547 A. H., in the time of Sulṭán Bahrám Sháh, son of Sulṭán Mas'úd, of Ghazní, and Sulṭán Sanjar Saljúḳí, in whose praise he wrote several beautiful panegyrics. He died in the year 1160 A. D., 555 A. H. 'Jabal' means a mountain, and as he was a native of Ghurjistán, a mountainous country, he chose "Jabalí" for his poetical title; *vide* Jabalí.

*Vide* Sprenger, Catalogue of Oudh MSS., p. 443.]

**Abengnefil,** (a corruption of an Arabian name, spelt so in Lemprière's Biographical Dictionary), was an Arabian physician of the 12th century, and author of a book, the translation of which entitled 'De virtutibus medicinarum et ciborum', was printed at Venice in 1581, folio.

**'Abhai Singh,** راجة ابهی سنگه, Rájá of Jodhpúr, who had acquired his power by the murder of his father Rájá Ajít Singh Ráṭhaurí in the beginning of the reign of Muhammad Sháh, emperor of Dihlí, about the year 1726 A. D., 1139 A. H. He served under the emperor, and having in a battle defeated Sarbaland Khán, the usurper of Gujrát, was appointed governor of that province in 1727 A. D., 1140 A. H.; but his younger brother Bakht Singh succeeded his father to the Ráj of Jodhpúr. Abhai Singh was poisoned in 1752 A. D., and after his death his son Bijai Singh succeeded him.

**'Abi Bakr,** author of the "Jawáhir-ul-Ganj," and of a another work on Sufism, called "Marṣád-ul-'Ibád."

**'Abi Bakr Muhammad,** ابی بکر محمد, author of an Arabic work in prose entitled "Ádáb-ul-Kitáb," written in 984 A. D., 374 A. H.

**'Abid-Khan,** عابد خان, a nobleman on whom Aurangzíb conferred the Ṣúbadárship of Multán.

**Abjadi,** ابجدی, the poetical name of Mír Muhammad Ismá'íl Khán, tutor of the Nawáb 'Umdat-ul-Umará of the Karnatik, who made him a present of 6,700 Rs. on the completion of the history, called "Anwar-náma," a maṣnawí, or epic, containing an account of the exploits of Nawáb Anwar Khán, the father of the patron of the author. It was completed in 1760 A. D. (1174 A. H.), and in 1774 the title of Malik-ush-shu'ará, or poet laureate, was conferred on the author. *Vide* Abdí.

**'Abka Khan,** ابقا خان, *vide* Abá Ḳáán.

**Abu-'Abbas,** ابوعباس, the first khalífa of Baghdád, of the race of 'Abbás. *Vide* Abul-'Abbás.

**Abu-'Abdullah,** ابو عبد الله. There are three Muhammadan saints of this name, whose lives are written by Abú-Ja'far. The first is surnamed Ḳuraishí, because he was of the family of the Ḳuraishites and a native of Mecca. The second bore the name of Iskandar, and the third that of Jauharí.

**Abu-'Abdullah Bukhari,** *vide* Muhammad Ismá'íl Bukhárí.

**Abu-'Abdullah,** ابوعبد الله, Muhammad Fázil, son of Sayyid Ahmad, the son of Sayyid Hasan of Ágra, author of the poem called "Mukhbir-ul-Wáṣilín", written in praise of Muhammad and his descendants, with the dates of their respective deaths in verse. The title of the book is a chronogram for 1106 A. H., in which year it was completed, corresponding with 1650 A. D. He flourished in the time of 'Álamgír and died in the year 1694 A. D. He is also called Maẓhar-ul-Ḥaḳḳ, which see.

**Abu-'Abdullah,** ابو عبد الله ابن مالک, commonly called Ibn-Málik, author of the "Sharḥ Saḥíḥ Bukhárí." He died at Damascus in 1273 A. D. (672 A. H.)

**Abu-'Abdullah,** ابو عبد الله, the surname of Sháfi'í, which see.

**Abu-'Abdullah,** ابوعبد الله بن احمد انصاری قرطبی, the son of Ahmad Anṣárí, an Andalusian author, who died A. D. 1272 (671 A. H.).

**Abu-'Abdullah,** ابوعبد الله حمیدی, Muhammad ul-Ḥamídí, son of Abú-Naṣr, author of the work called "Jam' baina-l-Ṣaḥíhain" and the history of Andalusia, called "Táríkh Undulus". The former comprehends the collections of al-Bukhárí and Muslim, and has a great reputation. He died in 1095 A. D. (488 A. H.).

**Abu-'Abdullah Maghribi,** ابوعبد الله مغربی, named Muhammad bin-Ismá'íl, tutor of Ibráhím Khawáṣ, Ibráhím

Shaibán of Kirmánsháh, and of Abú-Bakr of Bíkand, and pupil of Abul-Husain Zarrín of Hirát. Abú-'Abdullah died in the year 911 A. D. (299 A. H.), and was buried on Mount Sinai.

**Abu-'Abdullah Muhammad,** ابوعبد الله محمد, son of Sufyán, a native of Ḳairuwán in Africa. He is the author of the work called "Hádí." He died in 1024 A. D. (415 A. H.)

**Abu-'Abdullah Muhammad bin-'Ali ar-Rahibi,** ابوعبدالله محمد, author of a short treatise, entitled the "Bighyat-ul-Báḥiṣ" consisting of memorial verses, which give an epitome of the law of inheritance according to the doctrine of Zaid bin-Ṣábit.

**Abu-'Abdullah Muhammad Ha'kim Kabir,** ابو عبد الله محمد حاکم کبیر, author of the work called "Mustadrik". He died in 1014 A. D., 405 A. H.

**Abu-'Abdullah Muhammad bin-Muhammad al-Nu'mani,** surnamed Shaikh Mufíd and Ibn-Mu'allim, was a renowned Shí'a lawyer. Abú-Ja'far ut-Ṭúsí describes him in the Fihrist as the greatest orator and lawyer of his time, the most ancient Mujtahid, the most subtle reasoner, and the chief of all those who delivered Fatwas. Ibn-Kaṣír-ush-Shámí relates that, when he died, Ibn-Nakíb, who was one of the most learned of the Sunní doctors, adorned his house, told his followers to congratulate him, and declared that, since he had lived to see the death of Shaikh Mufíd, he should himself leave the world without regret. Shaikh Mufid is stated to have written 200 works, amongst which one, called the "Irshád", is well-known. He also wrote works on the law of inheritance. His death took place in A. D. 1022, 413 A. H., or as some say A. D. 1025, 416 A. H.

**Abu-'Abdullah Muhammad bin-'Umar al-Wakidi,** ابوعبد الله محمد بن عمر الواقدی, an author who wrote in Arabic the work, called "Ṭabaḳát Wáḳidí", containing the history of the conquest of Syria by the generals of 'Umar during the years 638-9 A. D. He is said by some to have died in the year 824 A. D., 219 A. H., but as he makes mention of Al-Mu'taṣim Billah, whose reign began in 833, he must have died about the year 834 and not 824 A. D., 209 A. H. *Vide* Wáḳidí.

**Abu-'Abdullah Muhammad bin-Husain al-Shaibani,** ابو عبد الله محمد بن حسین الشیبانی, commonly called Imám Muhammad, was born at Wásiṭ in 'Iráḳ-'Arab in A. D. 749, 132 A. H., and died at Rai, the capital of Khurásán in A. D. 802, 187 A. H. He was a fellow pupil of Abú-Yúsuf, under Abú-Ḥanífa, and on the death of the latter pursued his studies under the former. His chief works are six in number, of which five are considered of the highest authority, and are cited under the title of the "Ẓáhir-ur-Riwáyát; they are "Jámi'-ul-Kabír", "Jámi'-us-Ṣaghír", the "Mabsúṭ fí furú'-il-Ḥanafiya", the "Ziyádát fí furú'-il-Ḥanafiya", the "Siyar-ul-Kabír wal-Ṣaghír"; and the "Nawádir", the sixth and last of the known compositions of Imám Muhammad, which, though not so highly esteemed as the others, is still greatly respected as an authority.

**Abu-'Abdullah Salih,** *vide* Abú-'Alí, Wazír of Manṣúr I.

**Abu-'Abdul-Rahman Ahmad bin-'Ali bin-Shu'aib al-Nasai,** ابوعبد الرحمن احمد نسائی, author of the works called "Sunan Kubrạ" and "Sunan Ṣughrạ'." The first is a large work on the traditions; but as Nasáí himself acknowledged that many of the traditions which he had inserted, were of doubtful authority, he afterwards wrote an abridgement of his great work, omitting all those of questionable authenticity: and this abridgement which he entitled Al-Mujtabạ and is also called Sunan Ṣughrạ, takes its rank as one of the six books of the Sunna. Al-Nasáí was born at Nasá, a city in Khurásán, in 830 A. D., 303 A. H., and died at Makka in 915 A. D.

**Abu-'Abdul-Rahman Sulami,** *vide* 'Abdul-Raḥmán Sulamí.

**Abu-'Abdul-Rahman Yunas,** عبد الرحمن یونس, the son of Ḥabíb, an excellent grammarian who died in the year 798 A. D., 182 A. H.

**Abu-'Abdul-Wahid,** ابوعبد الواحد, an elegant Turkish poet who flourished in Constantinople, in the earlier part of the seventeenth century.

**Abu-Ahmad,** ابو احمد بن قاسم, the son of Ḳásim, was born in the city of Amasia in Natolia A. D. 1483, 888 A. H.; he publicly explained the book written by his father Aḥmad bin-'Abdullah ul-Kirmí on the fundamental points of Muhammadanism.

**Abu-'Ali,** ابوعلی, the wazír of Manṣúr I, the son of Núḥ, prince of the Samanian dynasty of Khurásán. In A. D. 963, 352 A. H., he translated the "Táríkh Ṭabarí" into the Persian language from the Arabic. It is a general history from the creation of the world, down to the 300th year of the Hijra. In the course of eight centuries the language of Abú-'Alí having become obsolete, Abú-'Abdullah Sáliḥ bin-Muhammad was persuaded by Núr-ullah Khán, prince of Túrán, to put it into modern Persian; *vide* Abu Ja'far at-Ṭabarí, and Ṭabarí.

**Abu-'Ali Ismail,** ابوعلی اسمعیل, an Arabian author who died in 967 A. D., 356 A. H.

**Abu-'Ali Kalandar,** ابوعلی قلندر, (Shaikh) commonly called Bú-'Alí Ḳalandar Shaikh Sharaf-uddín Pánipatí, a celebrated and highly respected Muhammadan saint, who is said to have performed numerous miracles during his life. He was born at 'Iráḳ in Persia, but came to India and fixed his residence at Pánipat, where he died, aged about 100 years, on the 30th August, 1324 A. D., 9th Ramaẓán 724 A. H. His tomb is held sacred and is visited by the Musalmans to this day.

*Vide* Proceedings, As. Society, Bengal, for 1870, p. 125, and for 1873, p. 97.]

**Abu-'Ali Ahmad bin-Muhammad,** the son of Ya'ḳúb bin-Maskawaihi Kházin of Rai, author of the Arabian work, entitled "Kitáb-ut-Ṭahárat", which was translated in Persian by Násir-uddín Ṭúsí, and named Akhláḳ-i-Náṣirí. He flourished about the 12th century.

**Abu-'Ali,** ابوعلی مهندس, surnamed Muhandis, 'the Geometrician', who excelled in that science. He flourished A. D. 1136, 530 A. H., in the time of Al-Ḥáfiẓ li-dín-illah, Khalífa of Egypt, and Al-Ráshid Billah, the son of Al-Mustarshid of Baghdád.

**Abu-'Ali Sina,** ابوعلی سینا, *vide* Abú-Síná.

**Abu-'Ali 'Umar,** ابوعلی عمر بن محمد, son of Muhammad, was the author of the commentary, called "Sharḥ Kabír" and "Sharḥ Ṣaghír." He died in the year 1247 A. D., 645 A. H.

**Abu-Ayyub,** ابو ایوب, a companion of Muhammad who had been with him in the battles of Badr and Uhud, and lost his life in the expedition of Constantinople (A. D. 668, 48 A. H.) in the reign of Mu'áwiya, the first Khalífa of the house of Umayya. His tomb is held in such veneration by the Muhammadans, that the Sultáns of the 'Usmán, or Ottoman, dynasty gird their swords on at it on their accession to the throne.

**Abu-Bakr,** or **Aba-Bakr,** ابوبکر or ابابکر, son of Míránsháh, was killed in battle A. H. 810, A. D. 1407.

**Abu-Bakr Ahmad bin-'Umar al-Khassaf,** ابوبکر احمد بن عمر الخصاف, author of several treatises, known by the name of "Ádáb-ul-Kází." Hájí Khalífa speaks very highly of this work. It contains 120 chapters, and has been commented upon by many learned jurists: the most esteemed commentary is that of 'Umar bin-'Abdul-'Azíz bin-Mája, commonly called Husám-ush-Shahíd, who was killed in 1141 A. D. Al-Khassáf died in 874 A. D., 261 A. H.

**Abu-Bakr Ahmad,** ابوبکر احمد, son of Husain Baihakí, *vide* Baihakí.

**Abu-Bakr Bakalani,** ابو بکر باقلانی, son of Tayyib. He was of the sect of Imám Málik, and author of the work called "Al-Tauhíd," and several other works. He died in 1012 A. D., 403 A. H. See Bákalání.

**Abu-Bakr Bikandi,** a pupil of Abú-'Abdullah Maghribí. He lived about the year 900 A. D.

**Abu-Bakr,** ابو بکر بن ابی شیبه, son of Abú-Shaiba, an Arabian author who died in the year 849 A. D., 235 A. H.

**Abu-Bakr Zangi,** ابو بکر بن سعد بن زنگی, son of Sa'd, son of Zangí, one of the Atábaks of Persia, who reigned at Shíráz for thirty-five years, and died in the year A. D. 1260, 658 A. H. The celebrated Shaikh Sa'dí of Shíráz dedicated his Gulistán to him in 1258 A. D.

**Abu-Bakr Kattani,** Shaikh Muhammed bin-'Alí Ja'far, a famous saint, who was born at Baghdád, and died in A. D. 934, A. H. 322.]

**Abu-Bakr bin-Mas'ud al-Kashani,** ابو بکر بن مسعود الکاشانی, author of the work on jurisprudence, entitled "Badái'." It is also called "Badái'-us-Sanái'." He died in A. D. 1191, 587 A. H.

**Abu-Bakr,** مولانا ابوبکر زین الدین, (Mauláná) surnamed Zain-uddín, a learned Musalmán, who died at Táíbád on Thursday the 28th of January 1389 A. D., 30th Muharram 791 H.

For further notes *vide* Áín Translation I, 366.]

**Abu-Bakr Muhammad al-Sarakhsi,** ابو بکر محمد السرخسی, whose title was Shams-ul-Aïmma; he composed, whilst in prison at Uzjand, a law book of great extent and authority, entitled the "Mabsút." He was also the author of the celebrated "Al-Muhít." He died in A. D. 1096, 490 A. H.

**Abu-Bakr Shadan,** شیخ ابوبکر شادان, (Shaikh) of Kazwín, a celebrated pious Musalmán who died at Kazwín in the year 1137 A. D., 531 A. H.

**Abu-Bakr Shashbani,** ابوبکر ششبانی, a valiant commander, born in a village called Shashbán in the province of Mázandarán. He was one of the greatest opponents of Amír Timur in his conquest of Asia.

**Abu-Bakr Shibli,** شیخ ابوبکر شبلی, (Shaikh) a celebrated doctor of divinity, born and brought up at Baghdád, but the native country of his parents was Khurásán. This Súfí followed the doctrines of the sect of Imám Málik, and had for his masters Junaid and other holy men of that epoch. He died at Baghdád on Friday, 31st July, 946 A. D., 27th Zil-hijja 334 A. H., aged 87 years.

**Abu-Bakr Siddik,** ابو بکر صدیق, the father of 'Áyisha, the wife of Muhammad the prophet, by whom he was so much respected that he received from him the surname of Siddík, which signifies in Arabic "a great speaker of truth," and at whose death, in June 632 A. D., he was elected successor in opposition to 'Alí, the son-in-law of the prophet. He supported with energy the new faith, and reduced several of the Arabian tribes who wished to abandon the new doctrines and return to the religion of their fathers. Afterwards, he turned his arms against foreign nations, and by the valour of his active general Khálid, he defeated an army of 200,000 men, whom the Greek emperor Heraclius had sent to ravage Syria. He did not enjoy his victories: a slow fever wasted his vigour, and he died the very day that Damascus was taken; but before he died he appointed for his successor 'Umar (Omar) the son of Khattáb. He had reigned two lunar years three months and nine days, and expired in his 63rd year on Friday the 23rd August, 634 A. D., 22nd Jumáda II, 13 A. H. He was buried close to the tomb of Muhammad in Madína.

**Abu-Bakr Tughluk,** ابوبکر تغلق, the son of prince Zafar Khán, and grandson of Fírúz Sháh Tughluk, was raised to the throne of Dihlí after the assassination of his cousin Ghiyás-uddín Tughluk, in February 1389 A. D., Safar 791 A. H. He reigned one year and six months, after which his uncle Prince Muhammad Tughluk, the son of Fírúz Sháh, who was at Nagarkot, (Kángra) proclaimed himself king, and proceeded with an army towards Dihlí. After some repulses he was victorious, entered Dihlí, and ascended the throne in the month of August 1390 A. D., Ramazán 792 A. H. Abú-Bakr who had fled towards Mewát, was taken prisoner on the 29th November of the same year, 20th Zil-hijja, and sent to the fort of Mírath, where he died some years after. *Vide* Dowson, IV, 20.

**Abu-Bakr Yahya,** ابوبکر یحیی, author of the "Bahjat-ul-Maháfil", or the Delight of Assemblies, containing various anecdotes recorded of Muhammad, the four Khalífas, and other illustrious persons, in Arabic.

**Abu-Darda,** ابودردا, a companion of Muhammad, who was governor of Syria in the time of the Khalífa 'Umar.

**Abu-Daud Sulaiman bin-al-Ash'as,** ابو داؤد سلیمان بن الاشعث, surnamed Al-Sijistání, author of a "Kitáb us-Sunan", which contains 4,800 traditions, selected from a collection made by him of 500,000. It is considered the fourth book of the Sunna. He was born in 817 A. D., 202 A. H., and died at Basra in 888 A. D., 275 A. H.

**Abu-Daud Sulaiman bin-'Ukba,** ابو داؤد سلیمان بن عقبة الظاهری, surnamed Az-Záhirí. He is the translator and commentator of Euclid in Arabic. He was also the founder of a Sunní sect, but had few followers, and was called Az-Záhirí, because he founded his system of jurisprudence on the exterior (*záhir*), or literal meaning of the Kurán and the traditions, rejecting the kiyás. He was born at Kúfa A. D. 817, 202 A. H., and died at Baghdád in 883 A. D., A. H. 270. Some authors say that he died in 275 A. H. (888 A. D.). He was a great partisan of Sháfi'í.

**Abu-Hafs al-Bukhari,** ابو حفص البخاری, a muftí of Bukhárá, and a very rigid Musalmán. He was surnamed Al-Kabír, the Great, to distinguish him from his son, who was surnamed Al-Saghír, the Little, or the Younger, and was also a learned teacher, but not so famous as his father.

**Abu-Hafs Haddad,** 'Amr, son of Salama, of Níshápúr, a saint, who died in 264 A. H.]

**Abu-Hafs 'Umar,** ابو حفص عمر بن احمد, son of Aḥmad, author of 330 works, among which are "Targhíb and Tafsír" and "Masnad". He died in 995 A. D., 385 A. H.

**Abu-Hafs 'Umar al-Ghaznawi,** ابو حفص عمر الغزنوی سراج الدین, surnamed Siráj-uddín, a follower of Abú-Ḥanífa, and author of the Arabic work called "Zubdat-ul-Aḥkám", which expounds the practical statutes of the different doctrines of the four Sunní sects. He died in 1371 A. D., 773 A. H.

**Abu-Ha'mid (Imam),** امام ابو حامد بن محمد غزالی, son of Muhammad, surnamed Ghazzálí. He is the author of the Arabic work on theology, called "Iḥyáu-'ulúm-id-dín" and of many other works. He died in 1111 A. D., 505 A. H. *Vide* Ghazzálí.

**Abu-Hamza bin-Nasr al-Ansari,** ابو حمزة بن نصر الانصاری, surnamed Aus bin-Málik, was one of the six authors most approved for Muhammadan traditions. He died at Basra, in the year 710 A. D., 91 A. H., aged 103 years, after having begot 100 children. He was the last that was styled Saḥába, that is to say, friends, companions, and contemporaries of Muhammad.

**Abu-Hanifa (Imam),** امام ابو حنيفه, surnamed Al-Nu'mán Kúfí, the son of Ṣábit, a celebrated lawyer among the Musalmáns, was born at Kúfa in the year 699 A. D., 80 A. H., and is said to have been a descendant of the Persian king Nausherwán the Just. Though he was imprisoned at Baghdád by the khalífa Al-Manṣúr for denying the doctrines of predestination, and died in his confinement, yet his learning, his virtues, and moderation found partizans in the East, and 335 years after his decease, Sultán Malik-sháh Saljúḳí erected a mausoleum in the city of Baghdád, where his remains were deposited. There were not wanting enthusiasts who declared that his name was mentioned in the Old Testament, and that his birth had been foretold as well as that of the prophet. He died in the year 767 A. D., 150 A. H., aged 70 lunar years. He was the founder of the first of the four chief sects of Sunnís, and the principal of the Mujtahid Imáms, who looked to the ḳiyás as the main authority upon which to base decisions. At the period of his birth, four, or as some authors say, six of the companions of the Prophet, were still living. *Vide* Ḥanífa (Imám).

**Abu-Hatim,** ابو حاتم, a celebrated Musalmán lawyer. *Vide* Ḥátim, surnamed Al-Asamm.

**Abu-Huraira,** ابو هريرة, that is "father of the kitten," so nicknamed by Muhammad, because of his fondness for a cat which he always carried about with him. He was so constantly called by this name, that his true name is not known, nor his pedigree. He was such a constant attendant upon Muhammad, that a great many traditions go under his name; so many, indeed, that the multitude of them make people suspect them. Nevertheless, others receive them without hesitation as of undoubted authority. He was Ḳázi of Mecca in the time of 'Uṣmán. He died in the year 679 A. D., 59 A. H.

**Abu-Husain Zarrin,** ابو حسين زرين, of Hirát, and master of Abú-'Abdullah Maghribí. He died at the age of 120.

**Abu-Ibrahim Ismail,** ابو ابراهيم اسمعيل بن يحيى المزني, son of Yaḥyá al-Mazaní, a distinguished disciple of Imám Sháfi'í, and author of the "Jámi' Ṣaghír" and other works. He died in the year 878 A. D., 264 A. H. He was the most celebrated amongst Sháfi'í's followers for his acquaintance with the legal system and juridical decisions of his preceptor, and for his knowledge of the traditions. Amongst other works, he wrote the "Mukhtaṣir," the "Manṣúr", the "Rasáil-ul-Mu'tabira" and the "Kitáb-ul-Waṣáiḳ." The Mukhtaṣir is the basis of all the treatises composed on the legal doctrines of Sháfi'í, who himself entitled Al-Mazaní "the champion" of his doctrine.

**Abu-Is-hak,** son of Alptigín, independent governor of Ghazní. Abú-Is-ḥáḳ handed over the reigns of the government to Subuktigín, who on Is-ḥáḳ's death in A. D. 977, A. H. 367, usurped the throne.]

**Abu-Is-hak,** ابو اسحق بن محمد, the son of Muhammad, an inhabitant of Syria, who wrote an excellent commentary to Mutanabbí. He died in 1049 A. D., 441 A. H.

**Abu-Is-hak Ahmad,** ابو اسحق احمد, or Abul-Is-háḳ Ibráhím bin-Ismá'íl, author of the "Ḳiṣaṣ-ul-Anbiyá" which contains an account of the creation of the world, and a history of all the prophets preceding Muhammad; also the history of Muhammad till the battle of Uḥud, A. D. 623. He died in 1036 A. D., 427 A. H.

**Abu-Is-hak al-Kaziruni,** ابو اسحق الكازرونی, a Muhammadan saint who, they say, lighted a lamp in the mosque of the college called "Takht Siráj," which continued burning for four hundred years till the time of Bin-Ḳásim.

**Abu-Is-hak Hallaj,** ابو اسحق حلاج اطعمه, generally called "Bus-ḥáḳ Aṭ'ima", a poet and cotton-thrasher, who never wrote a verse without mentioning in it the name of a dish; consequently they gave him the name of Aṭ'ima, *i. e.* meals. His poetical name is Bus-ḥáḳ. He lived in the time of Sikandar son of 'Umar Shaikh; *vide* Is-ḥáḳ.

**Abu-Is-hak Isfaraini,** ابو اسحق اسفراینی, son of Muhammad, author of the "Jámi'-ul-Jila," which refutes the doctrines of various sects. He died in 1027 A. D., 418 A. H.

**Abu-Is-hak Shami,** of Syria, a famous saint, who died on the 14th Rabí' II, 329, and lies buried at 'Akka.]

**Abu-Is-hak Shirazi,** ابو اسحق شیرازی, author of the "Ṭabaḳát ul-Fuḳahá," a collection of the lives of celebrated lawyers. He died A. D. 1083, 476 A. H.

**Abu-Is-hak,** شاہ شیخ ابو اسحق, (Sháh Shaikh). His father Amír Muhammad Sháh, a descendant of Khwája 'Abdullah Anṣárí, was governor of Shíráz in the reign of Sultán Abú-Sa'íd Khán, and was murdered during the reign of Arpá Khán in 1335 A. D., 736 A. H. His son Amír Mas'úd, who succeeded him was also slain shortly after, when his brother Abú-Is-háḳ took possession of Shíráz in 1336. He reigned 18 years; but when Amír Muhammad Muẓaffar besieged Shíráz in 1353 A. D., 754 A. H., Abú-Is-háḳ fled to Iṣfahán, where he was slain four years after, on Friday the 12th May 1357 A. D., 21st Jumáda I, 758 A. H.

**Abu-Ismail Muhammad,** ابو اسمعيل محمد, author of the history called "Táríkh Futúḥ-il-Shám" the conquest of Syria by the generals of 'Umar in forty-two battles, during the years 638 and 639 of the Christian Era, translated and abridged from the "Ṭabaḳát Wáḳidí."

**Abu-Ja'far,** ابو جعفر, *vide* Al-Manṣúr.

**Abu-Ja'far Ahmad bin-Muhammad Tahawi,** ابو جعفر احمد بن محمد طحاوی, an inhabitant of Ṭaḥá, a village in Egypt. He was a follower of the Ḥanafiya sect, and is the author of the commentary on the Ḳurán, called "Aḥkám-ul-Ḳurán," and other works, called "Ikhtiláf-ul-'ulamá", "Ma'ání-l-Aṣár", "Násikh and Mansúkh", all in Arabic. He died in the year 933 A. D., 321 A. H. He also wrote an abridgement of the Ḥanafí doctrines, called the "Mukhtaṣir ut-Ṭaḥáwí."

**Abu-Ja'far al-Haddad,** ابو جعفر الحداد, } Two great teachers of the spiritual life; **Abu-Ja'far al-Saffar,** ابو جعفر الصفار, } one was a locksmith, and the other a brazier.

The latter is called *Al-Haffár*, i. e., grave-digger, in Jámí's Nafhát-ul-Uns.]

**Abu-Ja'far al-Tabari,** ابو جعفر الطبری ابن جریر, son of Jarír, author of the Táríkh Tabarí, a very authentic history in Arabic, which he wrote in the year 912 A. D. This work was translated and continued by Abú-Muhammad of Tabríz in Persian. Tabarí was the founder of the seventh Sunní sect, which did not long survive the death of its author. He was born at Ámul in Tabaristán in 838 A. D., 224 A. H., and died at Baghdád in 922 A. D., 310 A. H. He is also the author of a commentary to the Kurán.

**Abu-Ja'far Muhammad bin-'Ali bin-Babwaihi al-Kumi,** ابو جعفر محمد بن علی بن بابویه الصدوق, surnamed As-Sadúk, one of the earliest of the many writers of commentaries on the Kurán among the Shí'as. He lived in the fourth century of the Hijra, and was a contemporary of Rukn-ud-daula Dailamí. He was one of the greatest of the collectors of the Shí'a traditions, and the most celebrated of all the Imámiya lawyers of Kum in Persia. This writer composed a large and a small Tafsír. There is considerable uncertainty as to the exact time when he lived. Shaikh Túsí says in the Fihrist that Abú-Ja'far died at Rai in 331 A. H., A. D. 942, but this appears to be erroneous. Shaikh Najáshí, who died in A. D. 1014, states that Abú-Ja'far visited Baghdád, whilst yet in the prime of life, in A. H. 355, A. D. 965, which might well have been the case, since Abul-Hasan 'Alí bin-Bábwaihi, the father of Abú-Ja'far, did not die until A. H. 329, A. D. 940. In addition to this, Núr-ullah relates, on the authority of the Shaikh ad-Dúryastí* that Abú-Ja'far lived in the time of Rukn-ud-daula Dailamí, and had repeated interviews with that prince, who, as is well-known, reigned from A. H. 338 to A. H. 366, A. D. 949—976. He is also the author of the "Man lá yahzarhu al-Fakíh," which is the fourth of the four authentic books on Shí'a tradition, called Kutub Arba'. He is said to have written in all 172 works, and to have been especially skilled in Ijtihád.

**Abu-Ja'far Muhammad bin-Hasan al-Tusi,** (Shaikh) who was one of the chief Mujtahids of the Imámiya or Shí'a sect, is the author of the work entitled "Fihristu-Kutub-ish-Shí'a wa Asmá-il-Musannifín." It is a bibliographical dictionary of Shí'a works, together with the names of the authors. The greater part of this author's works were publicly burnt in Baghdád in the tumult that arose between the Sunnís and Shí'as in 1056 A. D., 448—460 A. H. Abú-Ja'far died in 1067 A. D. He is also the author of a very extensive commentary on the Kurán, in twenty volumes, which is generally called the "Tafsír ut-Túsí," though it was entitled by its author the "Majma'-ul-Bayán li-'ulúm-il-Kurán." Among the Four Books on Shí'a Hadís, called Kutub Arba', the two first in order were composed by him entitled "Tahzíb-ul-Ahkám," and Istibsár. His chief works are the Mabsút and the Khiláf, which are held in great estimation, as are also the Niháya and the Muhít by the same author. The Risála-i-Ja'fariya is likewise a legal treatise by at-Túsí, which is frequently quoted.

**Abu-Jahl,** ابو جهل, the uncle of 'Umar ibn-ul-Khattáb. He was one of the most inveterate enemies of Muhammad and his religion. Though his son 'Ikrima became a convert to the tenets of Muhammad, yet his father was for ever shut out from paradise; and so violent is the resentment of the Musalmáns against this first enemy of their prophet, that they call the colocynth, in contempt, the melon of Abú-Jahl. Abú-Jahl was slain in the battle of Badr, which he fought against Muhammad, together with Al-Ás his brother, in the 70th year of his age, in the month of March 624 A. D., Ramazán 2, A. H.

**Abu-Lahab,** ابو لهب, the uncle of Muhammad, also called 'Abdul-'Uzza, was the son of 'Abdul-Muttalib and one of the bitterest enemies of Muhammad and his doctrines. He died of grief within a week after the defeat of Abú-Sufyán in the battle of Badr, which took place about the beginning of the year 624 A. D., 2 A. H. He was a man of wealth, of proud spirit and irritable temper. His son 'Utba was engaged, or according to some, married to, Muhammad's third daughter Rukayya, but when Muhammad appeared as a prophet, the contract was dissolved, and Rukayya married her lover 'Usmán. Abú-Lahab was also allied to the rival line of Kuraish, having married Umm-Jamíl, sister of Abú-Sufyán.

**Abul-'Abbas,** surnamed Al-Saffáh, which see.

**Abul-'Abbas bin-Muhammad,** ابو العباس بن محمد, author of the Arabic work "Ma'rifat-us-Sahába," and other books. He died in 1041 A. D., 432 A. H.

**Abul-'Abbas Ahmad bin-Muhammad,** commonly called Ibn-'Ukda, was one of the greatest masters of the science of traditions, and was renowned for his diligence in collecting them, and the long and frequent journeys which he undertook for the purpose of obtaining information on the subject. Al-Dárkutní, the Sunní traditionist, is reported to have said that Ibn-'Ukda knew 300,000 traditions of the Ahl-i-Bait and the Banú-Háshim. He died in A. D. 944, 333 A. H.

**Abul-'Abbas Fazl,** bin-Ahmad, of Isfaráín, was minister to Mahmúd of Ghazní.]

**Abul-'Aina,** ابو العیناء, a Musalmán lawyer celebrated for his wit. When Músa, son of the khalífa 'Abdul-Malik, put to death one of Abul-'Ainá's friends, and afterwards spread a report that he had escaped, Abul-'Ainá said in the words of the Lawgiver of the Hebrews, "Moses smote him and he died." The sentence was reported to the prince, and Abul-'Ainá was summoned to appear. Instead of dreading the threats of the tyrant, he boldly replied in the words of the following verse in Exodus, "Wilt thou kill me to-day as thou killedst the other man yesterday?" The ingenuity of the expression disarmed the anger of Músa, who loaded him with presents.

**Abu-Lais Nasir Samarkandi,** author of the work on jurisprudence in Arabic called "Fikh Abú-Lais," and the "Ghunyat-ul-Mubtadí."

**Abul-'Ala,** ابو العلا, entitled Malik-ush-Shu'ará, or royal poet, of Ganja, flourished in the time of Manúchihr, ruler of Shirwán. The poets Falakí and Khákání were his pupils, and to the latter he gave his daughter in marriage.

**Abul-'Ala Ahmad bin-'Abdullah al-Ma'arri,** المعری ابو العلا احمد بن عبد الله, a celebrated Arabian philosopher, free-thinker and poet, born at Ma'arra in Syria on Friday the 26th December 973 A. D., 1st Rabí' I, 363 A. H. Though he lost his sight in the 3rd year of his age by the small-pox, his poetry is animated and his descriptions are beautiful and striking. He died on Friday the 9th of May 1057 A. D., 1st Rabí' I, 449 A. H. He was the panegyrist of Al-káyim Billah, the khalífa of Baghdád, and has left a Díwán in Arabic. *Vide* Zeitschrift, D. M. G., xxix, p. 304.

**Abul-'Ala,** میر ابو العلا اکبرابادی, (Mír), of Akbarábád or Ágra, Mír Abul-Wafá Hasaní, was born in the year 1582 A. D., 990 A. H. His grandfather Mír 'Abd-us-Salám came to India from Samarkand, and went on a pilgrimage to Mecca, and died after some years. His father Mír Abul-Wafá died at Fathpúr Síkrí, from which place his remains were conveyed to Dihlí and buried close to the college situated near the Lál Darwáza. When Rája Mán Singh was appointed governor of Bengal, Mír Abul-

* Dúryast, a village near Rai, which is now called Darasht.

'Alá accompanied him, and was honored with the rank of 3,000, but he soon left him and proceeded to Ajmír, and thence to Ágra, where he passed the remainder of his life, and is said to have performed many miracles. He died on Friday the 21st, January 1651 A. D., 9th Ṣafar, 1061 A. H., aged 71 lunar years, and lies buried at Ágra, at a place near the karbalá, where every year on the anniversary of his death a great number of people assemble together and worship his tomb.

He was a Naḳshbandí and a descendant of Khwája Aḥrár.]

**Abul-Barakat Nishapuri,** ابو البرکات نیشاپوری, author of the work called "Dastúr-ul-Kitábat."

**Abul-Barakat 'Abdullah bin-Ahmad,** ابو البرکات عبد الله بن احمد, *vide* Nasafí.

**Abul-Barakat,** Shaikh, brother of Abul-Faẓl, born A. D. 1552; *vide* Áín Translation, p. xxxiii.]

**Abul-Farah,** of Wásiṭ, the ancestor of the Sayyid families of Bárha, Bilgrám, Khairábád, Fatḥpúr Hanswa, and other places. *Vide* Áín Translation I, 390.]

**Abul-Faraj,** ابو الفرج, (who in some of our Biographical Dictionaries is called Abulfaragius (George), was the son of Aaron, a Christian physician, born at Malatia in Armenia, near the source of the Euphrates in 1226 A. D. He followed his father's profession, but afterwards studied the Eastern languages and divinity, and was ordained bishop of Guba in his 20th year, from whence he was translated to Lacabena and Aleppo. He wrote a work on history, called "Mukhtaṣir-ud-Dawal," divided into dynasties, which is an epitome of universal history from the creation to his own time. The most excellent part of the work is that which relates to the Saracens, Mughuls, and the conquests of Chingiz Khán. Dr. Pococke, Professor of Hebrew and Arabic at Oxford, published this work in 1663, in the original Arabic, with a Latin version of it. Abul-Faraj died in 1286 A. D., 685 A. H.

**Abul-Faraj 'Ali,** ابو الفرج علی بن حسین, the son of Husain bin-Muhammad Ḳuraishí Iṣfahání, was born in the year 897 A. D., 284 A. H., and was brought up at Baghdád. He is the author of a famous work called Kitáb-ul-Aghání, or Book of Songs, an important biographical dictionary, notwithstanding its title, treating of grammar, history, and science, as well as of poetry. The basis is a collection of one hundred Arabian songs, which he presented to Saif-ud-daula, prince of the race of Ḥamdán, who ordered him a thousand dínárs. The minister of that prince, thinking this sum too small for the merit of the work, on which the author had laboured fifty years, doubled it. The author of this celebrated work died in 967 A. D., 356 A. H., having lost his reason previous to his death.

**Abul-Faraj al-Baghawi,** ابوالفرج البغوی, } two great
**Abul-Faraj al-Khalidi,** ابوالفرج الخالدي, } poets, who lived at the court of the Sulṭán Saif-ud-daula of the house of Ḥamdán, who was a protector of men of letters, on whom he bestowed large pensions.

**Abul-Faraj ibn-Jauzi,** ابوالفرج ابن جوزی, surnamed Shams-uddín, was the most learned man, the ablest traditionist, and the first preacher of his time. He compiled works on a variety of subjects, and was the tutor of the celebrated Shaikh Sa'dí of Shíráz. He died on the 16th June, 1201 A. D., 12th Ramaẓán, 597 A. H., and is buried at Baghdád. His father's name was 'Alí, and that of his grandfather Jauzí. One of his works is called "Talbís Iblís", "The Temptation of Satan."

**Abul-Faraj Runi,** ابو الفرج رونی, of Rún, said to be a place near Láhor. He is the author of a Díwán, and was the panegyrist of Sulṭán Ibráhím, (the grandson of Sulṭán Mahmúd of Ghazní) who reigned from 1059 to 1088 A. D., 451 to 481 A. H. Anwarí imitated his style; *vide* Sprenger Oudh MSS., p. 308. He is often wrongly called Abul-Faraḥ Ruwainí; *vide* Dowson iv, 205.]

**Abul-Faraj Sanjari,** ابو الفرج سنجری, a Persian poet who lived in the time of the great irruption of the Tartars under Chingiz Khán.

*Vide*, however, Sprenger, Oudh MSS., p. 308, from which it appears that Sanjarí is a mistake for Sijizí, *i. e.* of Sijistán.]

**Abul-Fath Lodi,** chief of Multán. Sulṭán Mahmúd of Ghazní took Multán in A. D. 1010, and carried away Abul-Fatḥ as prisoner to Ghazní.

**Abul-Fath Bilgrami,** ابو الفتح, (Ḳáẓí) commonly called Shaikh Kamál. It is mentioned in the work called "Sharáif-i-'Uṣmání, that he was born in the year 1511 A. D., 917 A. H., and that in the reign of the emperor Akbar he held the situation of Ḳáẓí of Bilgrám, and died in the year 1592 A. D., 1001 A. H. Mullá Fírúz 'Uṣmání found the chronogram of the year of his death in the letters of his name, *viz.:* Shaikh Kamál.

**Abul-Fath Busti,** ابوالفتح بستی, (Shaikh) a learned Musalmán of Bust, who lived in the time of Sulṭán Mahmúd of Ghazní, wrote excellent poetry on divinity, and died in July, 1039 A. D., Shawwál, 430 A. H. He is the author of a Díwán in Arabic.

**Abul-Fath,** author of a Persian work called "Chahár Bágh", or 'the four gardens', containing forms of letters on different subjects.

**Abul-Fath,** Muhammad bin-Abú-Bakr al-Marghínání al-Samarḳandí, author of the "Fuṣúl-ul-'Imádiya", which comprises forty sections containing decisions respecting mercantile matters, and being left incomplete at the author's death, which took place in A. D. 1253, 651 A. H., was finished by Jamál-uddín bin-'Imád-uddín.

**Abul-Fath Gilani,** ابو الفتح گیلانی, surnamed Masíḥ-uddín, the son of 'Abdur-Razzáḳ a nobleman of Gílán, was a physician in the service of the emperor Akbar. In the year 1589 A. D., he proceeded to Kashmír with that monarch, and during the emperor's progress from Kashmír to Kábul, he died at a place called Dhantúr, on the 20th June of the same year, 16th Sha'bán, 997 A. H., and was buried at Bábá Hasan Abdál. He had come to India with his two brothers Ḥakím Humám and Ḥakím Núr-uddín Ḳarárí about the year 1567 A. D., 974 A. H.

For further notes, *vide* Áín Translation I, 424.]

**Abul-Fath Muhammad al-Shahristani,** ابو الفتح محمد الشهرستانی, author of the Arabic work called "Kitáb ul-Milal wan-Niḥal," or the Book of Religions and Philosophical Sects. This book, which gives a full account of the various Sunní sects, was translated into Latin and published by Dr. Haarbrücker, in 1850 A. D., and into English by the Rev. Dr. Cureton. Shahristání died in A. D. 1153, 548 A. H.

**Abul-Fath Nasir bin-Abul-Makarim Mutarrizi,** ابوالفتح ناصر بن ابو المکارم مطرزی, author of the Arabic Dictionary called "Mughrib." He died in A. D. 1213, 610 A. H. in Khwárazm. He was a Mu'tazilite and invited people to that faith. He is also the author of the "Sharḥ Maḳámát Harírí, and of another work called "Kitáb Azharí." The inhabitants of Khwárazm used to call him the master of Zamakhsharí, and on his death the poets wrote more than seven hundred elegies in his praise.

**Abul-Fath Nasir bin-Muhammad,** ابوالفتح ناصر, author of the "Jámi'-ul-Ma'árif."

**Abul-Fath Rukn-uddin bin-Husam Nagori,** ابوالفتح رکن الدین, author of a work on jurisprudence, entitled the "Fatáwạ Ḥammádiya" which he composed and dedicated to his tutor, Ḥammád-uddín Ahmad, chief-ḳázi of Naharwála (Paṭan) in Gujrát. This work was lithographed in the original Arabic at Calcutta in A. D. 1825.

**Abul-Fath 'Usman,** ابوالفتح عثمان, surnamed Malik ul-'Azíz 'Imád-uddín, second king of Egypt of the Ayyúbite dynasty. He acted as viceroy of Egypt during the absence of his father, Sulṭán Ṣaláḥ-uddín Yúsuf ibn-Ayyúb, in Syria. On the demise of his father at Damascus in 1193 A. D., he took possession of the supreme power with the unanimous consent of the great military officers of the empire. He was born at Cairo on the 7th January 1172 A. D., 8th Jumádạ I, 567 A. H., reigned about five years, and died at Cairo on the 23rd November, 1198 A. D., 21st Muḥarram, 595 A. H.

**Abul-Fazl Baihaki,** ابوالفضل بیهقی, author of several works on history. *Vide* Baihaḳí.

**Abul-Fazl 'Abdul-Malik bin-Ibrahim al-Hamadani al-Mukaddasi,** ابوالفضل عبد الملک, author of the "Faráiẓ-ul-Muḳaddasí", a treatise on the law of inheritance according to the Sháfi'í doctrine. He died A. D. 1095, 489 A. H.

**Abul-Fazl Ja'far,** ابو الفضل جعفر, son of the khalífa Al-Muktafí, was a great astronomer; *vide* Al-Mutawakkil.

**Abul-Fazl Muhammad,** ابو الفضل محمد, author of the Arabic Dictionary called "Ṣuráḥ-ul-Lughát."

**Abul-Fazl** (Shaikh), شیخ ابوالفضل, Akbar's favorite Secretary and Wazír. His poetical name was 'Allámí. He was the second son of Shaikh Mubárak of Nágor, and brother of Shaikh Faiẓí. He was born in the year 1551 A. D., 958 A. H., and was introduced to the emperor in the 19th year of his reign. His writings testify him to be the most learned and elegant writer then in the East. He is celebrated as the author of the "Akbarnáma" and the "Áín-Akbarí", and for his letters, called "Maktúbát-i-'Allámí," which are considered in India models of public correspondence. The history of the Mughul emperors he carried on to the 47th year of Akbar's reign, in which year he was murdered. He was deputed with prince Sulṭán Murád in 1597 A. D., 1006 A. H., as Commander-in-Chief of the army of the Dakhin, and on his being recalled five years after, he was advancing towards Narwar with a small escort, when he fell into an ambuscade, laid for him by Birsingh Deo Bundelá, rájá of Uṛchá in Bundelkhand, at the instigation of Prince Salím (afterwards Jahángír) on suspicion of being the occasion of a misunderstanding between him and the emperor his father; and although Abul-Faẓl defended himself with great gallantry, he was cut off with most of his attendants, and his head was sent to the prince, who was then at Alláhábád. This event took place on Friday the 13th of August, 1602 A. D., 4th Rabí' I, 1011 A. H. Akbar was deeply afflicted by the intelligence of this event; he shed abundance of tears, and passed two days and two nights without food or sleep. Abul-Faẓl is also the author of the "'Ayár-Dánish" which is a translation of Pilpay's Fables in Persian.

For a detailed biography *vide* Áín Translation, I, pp. i to xxxvi.]

**Abul-Fazl Tahir bin-Muhammad Zahir-uddin Faryabi,** ابوالفضل محمد, a Persian poet; *vide* Ẓahír.

**Abul-Fida Ismail Hamawi,** ابو الفدا اسمعیل حموی, whose full name is Malik Muayyad Ismá'íl Abul-Fidá, son of Malik-ul-Afẓal, a learned and celebrated prince, who succeeded his brother Ahmad as king of Ḥamát in Syria in the year 1342 A. D., 743 A. H. When a private man, he published in Arabic an account of the regions beyond the Oxus called "Taḳwím-ul-Buldán," which was first edited by Grævius with a Latin translation, London 1650, and by Hudson, Oxford 1712. Abul-Fidá died in 1345, aged 72, at Ḥamát. The principal of Abul-Fidá's other works is his abridgment of Universal History down to his time, called "Táríkh Mukhtaṣir." He is very exact, and his style is elegant, on which account his works are very much esteemed.

**Abul-Faiz,** ابوالفیض. *Vide* Faiẓí.

**Abul-Faiz Muhammad bin-Husain bin-Ahmad,** surnamed Al-Kátib, or the Writer, is better known by the name of bin-Ahmad. He was a wazír of Sulṭán Rukn-ud-daula, of the Boyides. He was a great orator and a poet, and brought Arabian caligraphy to perfection. He died in 961 A. D., 360 A. H.

**Abul-Futuh Razi Makki,** ابوالفتوح رازی مکی, author of the Arabic work called "Risála" or "Kitáb Hasaniya", which has a great reputation amongst the Shí'as, particularly in Persia. It consists of an imaginary disputation between a Shí'a slave-girl and a learned Sunní lawyer, on the merits of their respective doctrines, in which, as a matter of course, the girl utterly discomfits her opponent. The argument is very ingenuously managed, and the treatise, taken altogether, furnishes a good and concise exposition of the tenets of the Shí'as, and the texts on which their belief is founded. This work was translated from Arabic into Persian by Ibráhím Astarábádí in 1551 A. D.

**Abul-Ghazi Bahadur,** ابو الغازی بهادر, Khán of the Tartars, was descended from the great Chingiz Khán. He came to the sovereignty of Khwárazm on the death of his brother; and after 20 years, during which he was respected at home and abroad, he resigned the sovereignty to his son Anúsha Muhammad, and retired to devote himself to literature. He wrote a valuable genealogical history of the Tartars, the only Tartar history known in Europe, but did not live to finish it. He died A. D. 1663, 1074 A. H., and on his death-bed charged his successor to complete his history, which he performed in two years after his father's death. This valuable work was translated into German by Count Strahlenberg, and a French translation appeared at Leyden in 1726.

**Abul-Ghazi Bahadur,** *vide* Sulṭán Husain Mirzá.

**Abul-Haras,** ابوالحرث المشهور به ذو الرمه بن عقبه, or Ḥaraṣ, commonly called Ẓul-Rama, son of 'Uḳba. He was an Arabian poet, and was contemporary with Farazdaḳ. He died in A. D. 735, 117 A. H.

**Abul-Hasan,** ابوالحسن, author of the "Siyar Núr Maulúd," a heroic poem on the wars of the prophet Muhammad.

**Abul-Hasan,** ابوالحسن, a poet who wrote a commentary on the Díwán of Anwarí, called Sharḥ-i-Díwán-i-Anwarí.

**Abul-Hasan 'Abdullah,** ابوالحسن عبدالله بن مقنع, (Imám), son of Muḳanna'. He translated Pilpay's Fables from the Pahlawí language into Arabic by order of Abú-Ja'far Manṣúr, the second khalífa of the house of 'Abbás, who reigned at Baghdád from 754 to 775 A. D. The book is called Kalíla Damna.

**Abul-Hasan 'Ali,** ابوالحسن علی, author of the works called "Sunan" and "'Ilal." He died A. D. 990, 380 A. H.

**Abul-Hasan 'Ali bin-al-Husain al-Kumi,** بابویه ابوالحسن بن حسین القمی, commonly called Bábwaihi, who is said to have died in A. D. 940, 329 A. H., was the author of several works of note, one of which is called "Kitáb-ush-Sharí'a." This writer is looked upon as a considerable authority, although his fame has been almost eclipsed by his more celebrated son, Abú-Ja'far Muhammad Ibn-Bábwaihi (p. 14). When these two writers are quoted together, they are called the two Ṣadúḳs. He is also the author of the Kitáb-ul-Mawáriṣ, a treatise on the law of inheritance.

**Abul-Hasan 'Ali,** ابوالحسن علی بن سلطان مسعود, the son of Sulṭán Mas'úd I, ascended the throne at Ghazní, on Friday, 29th December, 1049 A. D., 1st Sha'bán, 441 A. H., reigned little more than two years, and was deposed by his brother 'Abdur-Rashíd in 1052 A. D., 443 A. H.

**Abul-Hasan Ash'ari,** ابوالحسن اشعری ابن اسمعیل, son of Ismá'íl. He was a Mu'tazilite, but afterwards became a Sunní. He is the author of nearly 400 works. He died in the year 936 A. D., 324 A. H.

**Abul-Hasan Jurjani,** ابوالحسن جرجانی, a celebrated lawyer, a native of Jurján or Georgia. *Vide* Jurjání.

**Abul-Hasan Khan,** مرزا ابو الحسن خان, (Mirzá) Persian ambassador to the British Court in 1809 and 1819. He is the author of a work called "Ḥairat-náma," or book of wonders, which title was given by it by Fatḥ 'Alí Sháh, king of Persia. It contains a long account of the Khán's travels in India, Turkey, Russia, England, &c.

**Abul-Hasan Kutb-Shah,** ابوالحسن قطب شاه, whose original name was Táná Sháh, was the son-in-law of 'Abdullah Ḳutb-Sháh, after whose demise, about the year 1672 A. D., 1083 A. H., he succeeded to the throne of Golkonda in Ḥaidarábád, Dakhin. This place was conquered by 'Álamgír, after a siege of seven months, on the 22nd of September, 1687 A. D., 24th Ẓil-ḳa'da, 1098 A. H., and Abul-Hasan was taken prisoner and confined for life in the citadel of Daulatábád. Golkonda was then reduced to a province of the empire of Hindústán. Abul-Hasan died in confinement about the year 1700 A. D., 1112 A. H. He was the last Sulṭán of the Ḳuṭb-sháhí dynasty.

**Abul-Hasan Razin bin-Mu'awiya al-'Abdari,** ابو الحسن رضین بن معاویه العبدری, author of a collection of traditions bearing the same title as the one written by Baghawí, namely "Jámí' baina-l-Ṣaḥíḥain." It comprises the works of Al-Bukhárí and Muslim, the Muwaṭṭá of Málik ibn-Aus, the Jámí'-ut-Tirmizí, and the Sunans of Abú-Dáúd, and Al-Nasáí. He died in 1126 A. D., 520 A. H.

**Abul-Hasan,** شاه ابوالحسن, (Sháh) son of the famous Sháh Ṭáhir of Ahmadnagar in the Dakhin, and minister of 'Alí 'Ádil Sháh I, about the year 1572 A. D., 980 A. H.

**Abul-Hasan,** the son of I'timád-ud-daula, prime minister of the emperor Jahangír, had three daughters, *viz.*, Arjmand Bánú, also called Mumtáz-Maḥall, married to the emperor Sháh Jahán; Sulṭán Zamánia, the second daughter, was married to Sulṭán Parwíz; and the third Badr-uzza-mánia to Sháh 'Abdul-Laṭíf, the spiritual guide of the emperor 'Álamgír. *Vide* Áṣaf Khán.

**Abul-Hasan Turbati,** ابوالحسن تربتی, entitled Rukn-us-Salṭanat, an Amír who held the rank of 5,000 in the reign of the emperor Jahángír, and died in the sixth year of Sháh Jahán, A. D. 1632, 1042 A. H., aged 70 years.

**Abul-Hunain Ahmad bin-'Ali al-Najashi,** author of a biographical work entitled "Kitáb-ur-Rijál", comprising the lives of eminent Shí'as. Najáshí died in A. H. 405 (1014 A. D.).

**Abul-Husain bin-Abu-Ya'la al-Farra,** بن ابو یعلی ابوالحسین, (Ḳáẓí), author of the Ṭabaḳát-ul-Ḥanbaliya, which comprises the lives of the most famous lawyers of the sect of Ibn-Ḥanbal; it was commenced by our author, continued by Shaikh Zain-uddín 'Abdur-Raḥmân bin-Ahmad, commonly called Ibn-Rajab, and concluded by Yúsuf bin-Hasan al-Mukaddasí: these three writers died respectively in 1131, 1392, and 1466 A. D., 526, 795, and 871 Ḥ.

**Abul-Husain Kharkani,** ابوالحسین خرقانی, author of the "Sharḥ-i-Makhzan-ul-Asrár," and "Mir-át-ul-Muḥaḳḳiḳín," containing an explanation of the ceremonies used on the induction of a Ṣúfí, and the rules of the order. He died A. D. 986, 376 A. H.

**Abul-Husain 'Ali bin-'Umar al-Darkutni,** دارقطنی ابوالحسین علی بن عمر, a Sunní traditionist, whose collection of traditions, like those of Abú-Bakr Ahmad-bin-al-Husain al-Baihaḳí, are of the highest authority. He died in 995 A. D., 385 A. H.

**Abul-Husain Zarrin,** *vide* Abú-Husain Zarrín.

**Abul-Kasim al-Sahrawi,** ابوالقاسم الصحراوی called in Lemprière's English Biographical Dictionary "Alsaharavius", an Arabian physician who lived about the year 1085, 478 A. H., and is the author of the "Al-Taṣríf," a treatise in 32 books on medical practice.

**Abul-Kasim Namakin,** ابو القاسم نمکین, a Sayyid of Hirát, served with distinction under Akbar and Jahángír, and became a rich landowner in Bhakar in Sindh. He built the great mosque in Sukhar. His descendants served under Sháhjahán, 'Álamgír, and Farruk-siyar. *Vide* Áín Translation I, p. 470.]

**Abul-Kasim Nishapuri,** ابوالقاسم نیشاپوری, author of a Persian work on Ethics, called "Ganj-i-Ganj," and of another work, entitled "Ḥulyat-ul-Muttaḳín."

**Abul-Kasim 'Abdullah,** ابو القاسم عبدالله, son of Muhammad Baghawí, author of the book called Mu'jam, and several other works. He died in the year A. D. 929, 317 A. H.

**Abul-Kasim Isma'il bin-'Abbad,** ابوالقاسم اسمعیل, wazír of the Boyide prince Fakhr-ud-daula. One of the most splendid libraries ever collected by a private individual in the East was that of this nobleman. Ibn-Aṣír relates that four hundred camels were required to remove the books.

**Abul-Kasim Mirza,** son of Kámrán Mirzá, brother of the emperor Humáyún. In the year 1557 A. D., 964 A. H., he was confined in the fort of Gwáliár by the emperor Akbar, who, when going to punish Khán-Zamán, ordered him to be murdered.

**Abul-Kasim,** ابوالقاسم کاهی, Káhí, of Isfahán, though it is usually said that he was of Kábul. He died at Ágra. *Vide* Ḳásim-i-Káhí.

**Abul-Kasim,** ابوالقاسم الحلی, of Ḥilla, commonly called Shaikh Muayyad, author of the "Sharái'-ul-Islám", a treatise on lawful and forbidden things. This book is of great authority amongst the Muhammadans professing Shí'a doctrines. He is also called Shaikh Najm-uddín Abul-Ḳásim Ja'far bin-Muayyad. He died A. D. 1277, 676 A. H.

**Abul-Kasim** 'Ubaidullah bin-'Abdullah bin-Khurdádbih, died A. H., 300, A. D. 912. He is best known as IBN-KHURDÁDBIH. He wrote the "Kitáb-ul-Masálik wal-Mamálik," the 'Book of Roads and Kingdoms.' *Vide* Khurdádbih, and Dowson I, p. 12.]

**Abul-Khair,** مولانا ابوالخیر خوارزمی, Mauláná, of Khwárazm, a physician and poet whose poetical name was 'Áshiḳ. From his native country he went to Hirát in the latter part of the reign of Sulṭán Husain Mirzá, and was there till Muhammad Shaibání, commonly called Sháhí Beg Khán Uzbak, conquered that province, and took him to Máwarán-nahr, or Transoxiana, where he died in 1550 A. D., 957 A. H. The chronogram of the year of his death is "Faut-i-'Áshiḳ," the death of 'Áshiḳ.

**Abul-Ma'ali,** whose proper name is Muhammad Ṣadr-uddín, is claimed by the Turks as the first of their poets, though his labours were not confined to their language alone, for he wrote in Arabic also, and was in Persian the rival and opponent of Náṣir-uddín. He was contemporary with Jalál-uddín Rúmí and his son Walad, and died about the year 1270 A. D. He is not, however, according to Baron von Hammer, strictly considered to be a Turkish poet by his countrymen; but the mystic tone which he adopted from Persian literature, and which he was undoubtedly the first to impress upon the national mind, gives him an unquestionable right to the place assigned him. The names of his works, such as the "Seal of Perfection," and the "Key of Mysteries," indicate the peculiarity of his taste and genius; but amidst all the confusion of style and thought, some passages of great beauty and even simplicity are found in his works. He is lost, however, in the fame of his successor 'Áshiḳ.

**Abul-Ma'ali,** ابوالمعالی بن عبدالحمید, the son of 'Abdul-Majíd, the most eloquent of the Persians, who flourished in the time of Sulṭán Bahrám Sháh Ghaznawí, by whose order, in the year 1118 A. D., 512 A. H., he wrote in prose his "Kalíla Damna" (or Pilpay's Fables) from a copy which Rúdakí, the celebrated poet, had formerly used for poetry. This version continued in vogue till the time of Sulṭán Husain Mirzá, fourth in descent from 'Umar Shaikh, the second son of Amír Timur, when his prime-minister Amír Shaikh Ahmad Suhailí got Husain Wá'iẓ to modernize it, in A. D. 1505, 910 A. H., under the name of "Anwár Suhailí", or the Rays of Canopus. Abul-Fazl, the able prime minister of Akbar, compressed this work, and gave it the name of "'Ayár-Dánish," or the touch-stone of knowledge. He is called by Daulat Sháh, Ḥamíd-uddín Naṣr-ullah. *Vide* Naṣr-ullah, the son of 'Abdul-Ḥamíd.

**Abul-Ma'ali,** شاہ ابوالمعانی, (Sháh) a chief in the service of the emperor Akbar, who having revolted was compelled to seek safety in Kábul, where Mirzá Muhammad Ḥakím, the brother of Akbar, gave him his sister, named Mihr-un-Nisá Begam, in marriage, and raised him to the first office in that kingdom. The ungrateful refugee, however, had not been many months in office, before he aspired to the kingdom of Kábul, and in March 1564 A. D., Sha'bán, 971 A. H., basely assassinated Mirzá Muhammad Ḥakím's mother, his own mother-in-law, who was a woman of uncommon abilities, and might with truth be said to have ruled that kingdom. He then pretended to act as regent to the young prince, who was still in his minority, with a view to get rid of him as soon as he could conciliate the Umarás. In the meantime Mirzá Sulaimán, prince of Badakhshán, attacked him, and slew him in a battle on the 13th May, 1564 A. D., 1st Shawwál, 971 A. H., and took possession of that country, which he held for two years. Abul-Ma'álí was an elegant poet, and his poetical name was Shahbadí.

**Abul-Ma'ali,** شیخ ابو المعالی اللہ آبادی, (Shaikh) of Alláhábád, author of the work called "Tuḥfat-ul-Ḳádiriya," or the life of Shaikh 'Abdul-Ḳádir Gíláni. He resided in Láhor, and died there on the 6th April 1615, 16th Rabí' I, 1024.

**Abul-Mafakhir Razi,** ابو المفاخر رازی, a poet who flourished in the reign of Sulṭán Muhammad Saljúḳí.

**Abul-Mahasin,** ابوالمحاسن, author of the work called "Manhal-i-Ṣáfí."

**Abul-Makarim bin-'Abdullah.** There are three comments on the Niḳáya of 'Ubaidulla bin-Mas'úd, which are much esteemed: they were written respectively by Abul-Makárim in 1501 A. D., 907 A. H.; Abú-'Alí bin-Muhammad al-Birjindí in 1528 A. D., 935 A. H., and Shams-uddín Muhammad al-Khurásání in 1534 A. D., 941 A. H.

**Abul-Ma'shar,** ابوالمعشر, who is called by some older authors Albumassar and Albumazar, was a learned Arabian astronomer, who flourished in the ninth century in the reign of the khalífa Al-Mámún of Baghdád, and wrote a treatise on the revolutions of the years. His full name is Ja'far bin-Muhammad bin-'Umar Abul-Ma'shar. He is called the prince of the Arabian astrologers. He was born in Balkh. In his famous work, called "Ulúf" or "Kitáb-ul-Ulúf", which he wrote from a Sanskrit work on astronomy, he asserts that, when the world was created, the seven planets were together in the first point of the sign of Aries, and that it will end when the same planets shall meet again in the last point of Pisces in their exaltation or Dragon's head. He died in A. D. 885, 272 A. H. His works were printed in Latin at Venice in 1586, 8vo.

**Abul-Najib al-Bukhari,** ابو النجیب البخاری, poetically called also 'Am'aḳ, was a Persian poet who flourished in the fifth century of the Hijra at the court of the Sulṭán Ḳadr Khán, king or kháḳán of Turkistán, who made him president of the academy of poets which he had established. His poem of the loves of Yúsuf and Zalíkhá, which can be read in two different metres, is much admired. He was particularly famous for his elegies. He lived nearly 100 years. Daulat Sháh says, he lived in the time of Sulṭán Sanjar, who requested him to write an elegy on the death of his daughter Malik Khátún, which he did, although he was then blind on account of old age. He appears to have died some years before or after 1145 A. D., 540 A. H.

**Abul-Sa'adat Mubarak Ibn-Asir,** ابن اثیر الجزری ابوالسعادت مبارک, al-Jazarí, author of an Arabic Dictionary called "Al-Niháya fí gharíb-il-Ḥadíṣ." He died in 1209 A. D., 606 A. H.; *vide* Ibn-Aṣír.

**Abul-Wafa,** (Khwája), one of the great saints of Khwárazm, and author of several works on Sufism. He died 1432 A. D., 835 A. H.

**Abu-Maaz Muslim,** ابو معاذ مسلم, an Arabian grammarian, who died in 803 A. D., 187 A. H.

**Abu-Mansur,** surnamed al-Ḥákim bi-amr-illah, succeeded his father Al-'Azíz to the throne of Egypt in A. D. 990, 381 A. H., when only 11 years of age. In the latter part of his reign he fancied himself a god, and found no fewer than 16,000 persons who owned him as such. These were mostly the Darárians, a new sect sprung up about this time, who were so called from their chief, Muhammad Ibn-Ismá'íl, surnamed Darárí. He is supposed to have inspired the mad khalífa with this impious notion; and as Darárí set up for a second Moses, he did not scruple to assert that Abú-Manṣúr was the great creator of the universe. He was assassinated in the year 1020 A. D. His son Ṭáhir succeeded him.

**Abu-Mansur,** ابو منصور, author of the "Kitáb-ut-Tauḥíd," and several other works.

**Abu-Mansur 'Abdul-Kahir al-Baghdadi,** author of a treatise on the law of inheritance according to Sháfi'í. He died A. D. 1037, 429 A. H.

**Abu-Mas'ud,** surnamed Shaikh-ul-Islám, a native of Constantinople, and author of the valuable commentary on the Ḳurán, entitled "Irshád-ul-'aḳl," flourished in the reign of Sulṭán Salím Khán, emperor of Constantinople, and died in 1516 A. D., 922 H.

**Abu-Muhammad,** ابو محمد مکی, of Mecca, son of Abú-Ṭálib, author of a commentary on the Ḳurán, and several other works. He died in 1045 A. D., 437 A. H.

**Abu-Muhammad,** son of 'Abbás, the son of a sister of Abú-Ja'far bin-Muhammad bin-Jarír al-Ṭabarí. It is said that he had by heart 100,000 verses of different authors. He died in 993 A. D., 383 A. H., and was a contemporory of the author of the 'Ayyár.

**Abu-Muhammad Husain bin-Mas'ud Farra `al-Baghawi,** ابو محمد حسین فراء ابن مسعود البغوی, author of a collection of traditions, called the "Maṣábíḥ," in Arabic; also of the "Ma'álim-ut-Tanzíl" and "Sharḥ-us-Sunnat." He died in 1122 A. D., 516 A. H. He was a vendor of furs, consequently he was called Farrá. Baghawí also wrote a "Jámí' baina-l-Ṣaḥíḥain."

**Abu-Muhammad Hisham bin-al-Hakim al-Kindi al-Shaibani,** who lived in the time of the Khalífa Hárún-ur-Rashíd, and died in A. D. 795, 179 A. H., is famed as one of the first compilers of Shí'a traditions.

**Abu-Muhammad Nasihi,** ابو محمد ناصحی, was a man of eminent learning in the time of Sulṭán Mas'úd I of Ghazní. He wrote a book entitled "Mas'údí," in support of the doctrine of Abú-Ḥanífa, which he presented to the king. He flourished about the year 1035 A. D.

**Abu-Muhammad Rozbihan Bakali Shirazi,** ابو محمد روز بهان بقلی شیرازی, author of the "Ṣafwat-ul-Masháríb." He died in July 1209 A. D., Muḥarram, 606 A. H.; *vide* Rozbihán (Shaikh).

**Abu-Muhammad Shatibi,** ابو محمد شاطبی, a very learned Musalmán and author of the "Ḳasída Sháṭibiya." He died in 1194 A. D., 590 A. H. His proper name was Ḳásim; he was born at Sháṭibiya in Andalusia, from which he derived his title of Sháṭibí. He is also the author of several other works.

**Abu-Muhammad Tabrizi,** author of the Persian history, called "Táríkh-i-Ṭabarí". The original of this book was written in Arabic by Abú-Ja'far bin-Jarír Ṭabarí, in A. D. 912, 300 A. H., and was afterwards translated into Persian and continued by Abú-Muhammad, and dedicated to Abú-Ṣáliḥ bin-Núḥ, about the year 1118 A. D., 512 A. H.

**Abu-Musa, Ja'far al-Sufi,** whose poetical name is Jabar, was the founder of the Arabian school of chemistry, flourished towards the end of the 8th, or the commencement of the 9th century. According to the majority of authorities, he was born at Ṭús in Khurásán. He wrote an immense number of treatises on alchemy, also a work on astronomy. An edition of his works in Latin was published at Dantzic in 1662, and another in English by Russel in 1678.

**Abu-Musa al-Ash'ari,** ابو موسی الاشعری, one of the arbitrators between 'Alí and Mu'áwiya I, by whose decision 'Alí was deposed in the year 658 A. D., 37 A. H. Eight months after the battle of Ṣiffín between 'Alí and Mu'áwiya, the two arbitrators Abú-Músạ and 'Amr the son of 'Aṣ met at a place between Mecca and Kúfa, where a tribunal was erected. Abú-Músạ first ascending it, pronounced these words with a loud voice:—"I depose 'Alí and Mu'áwiya from the Khiláfat (or government) to which they pretend, after the same manner as I take this ring from my finger," and immediately came down. 'Amr then went up and said, "You have heard how Abú-Músạ has on his part deposed 'Alí; as for my part I depose him too, and I give the khiláfat to Mu'áwiya, and invest him with it after the same manner as I put this ring upon my finger; and this I do with so much the more justice, because he is 'Uṣmán's heir and avenger and the worthiest of all men to succeed him."

**Abu-Muslim,** a great general, to whom the Abbasides entirely owed their elevation to the khiláfat, for which he is commonly called Ṣáḥib-ud-Da'wat, or author of the vocation of the Abbasides. For his good conduct and bravery, he occupied the first posts in the service of the Ommaides. He was governor of Khurásán A. D. 746, when he proclaimed the Abbasides the lawful heirs of the khiláfat, and in 749 A. D. transferred the dignity of Khalífa from the family of Umayya to that of the Abbasides. This revolution occasioned the death of above 600,000 men; and when Abú-Ja'far Al-Manṣúr, the second Khalífa of the race of 'Abbás, was opposed on his accession by his uncle 'Abdullah, son of 'Alí, 'Abú-Muslim was despatched against him. This general having harassed him for five months together, at last brought him to a general action, and having entirely defeated him, forced him to fly to Baṣra. Notwithstanding all his services, however, Abú-Muslim was soon after, on Thursday the 13th February, 755 A. D., 24th Sha'bán 137 A. H., ungratefully and barbarously murdered by Al-Manṣúr, and his body was thrown into the Tigris. Abú-Muslim took his origin (as Iṣfahání, a Persian historian relates) from Ḥamza, who pretended to descend from Gaudarz, one of the ancient kings of Persia.

**Abu-Na'im,** ابو نعیم بن عبد الله, son of 'Abdullah, author of the works called "'Ulyá" and "Daláil-i-Nubuwwat." He died in the year 1012 A. D., 403 A. H.

**Abu-Nasr Farabi,** ابو نصر فارابی, *vide* Fárábí.

**Abu-Nasr,** author of a Persian work on Sufism, called "Anís-ul-Ṭálibín."

**Abu-Nasr Farahi,** ابو نصر فراهی, flourished about the year 1220 A. D. in the time of Bahrám Sháh, son of Táj-uddín, ruler of Sístán (also called Nímrúz), who began to reign in the year 1215 A. D. He is the author of a vocabulary in verse, called "Niṣáb-us-Ṣibyán".

His real name is Muhammad Badr-uddín, and he belongs to Faráh, a town in Sijistán; *vide* A'ín Translation I, 41*n*.]

**Abu-Nasr Isma'il bin-Hammad al-Jauhari,** ابونصر اسمعیل بن حماد الجوهری, is the author of the Dictionary called Ṣiḥáḥ-ul-Lughát. He was born at Fáráb, and died about the year 1003 A. D., 394 A. H.

**Abu-Nasr Khan,** نواب ابو نصر خان, (Nawáb) an amír of the reign of the emperor 'A'lamgír. The mosque of Jájnagar in Orísa was built by him in the year 1687 A. D., 1098 A. H.

**Abu-Nasr Maskati,** ابو نصر مسکطی, a native of Maskaṭ, and author of the book called "Maḳámát."

**Abu-Nasr Sabur,** (Shápúr) son of Ardsher. He built in the year 954 A. D. an edifice at Baghdád, dedicated to scientific and literary exercises, and collected a large quantity of books, designed for the use of Musalmáns; there were, it is said, upwards of 10,400 volumes of all kinds, including a hundred Ḳuráns, copied by the celebrated caligrapher Ibn-Muḳla.

**Abu-Nawas,** ابو نواس, al-Hasan bin-Hání, a celebrated Arabian poet, born in the city of Baṣra. His merit was acknowledged at the court of Hárún-ur-Rashíd. His principal works have been collected by several persons, on which account there is a great difference between the copies of his works. His proper name is Abú-'Alí. He died A. D. 810, 195 A. H.

**Abu-Raihan al-Biruni,** ابو ریحان البیرونی, or Abú-Raiḥán Muhammad bin-Ahmad al-Bírúní, was born about the year 971 A. D. in the town of Bírún, said to be situated in the province of Khwárazm. He was astronomer, geometrician, historian, scholar, and logician. Besides metaphysics and dialectics, he studied and appears to have drawn his chief lustre from attainments in the magical art. Of this, the following instance is related. One day Sulṭán Mahmúd ordered him to deposit with a third person a statement of the precise manner in which the monarch would quit the hall where he then was sitting. The paper being lodged, the king, instead of going out by one of the numerous doors, caused a breach to be made in the wall, by which he effected his exit;—but how was he amazed, when, on the paper being examined, there was found in it a minute specification of the precise spot through which he penetrated! Hereupon the prince with horror denounced this learned man as a sorcerer, and commanded him to be instantly thrown out of the window. The barbarous sentence was presently executed: but care had been taken to prepare beneath a soft cushion, into which the body of the sage sank without sustaining any injury. Abú-Raiḥán was then called before the monarch, and was required to say whether by his boasted art he had been able to foresee these events, and the treatment through which he had that day passed. The learned man immediately desired his tablets to be sent for, in which were found regularly predicted the whole of these singular transactions. He travelled into different countries, and to and from India for the space of 40 years. He wrote many works, and is said to have executed several translations from the Greek and epitomized the Almajest of Ptolemy. His works are said to have exceeded a camel load. The most valuable of all his works is the "Táríkh-ul-Hind." Another of his works is the Ḳánún Mas'údí, dedicated to Sulṭán Mas'úd of Ghazní, for which he received an elephant-load of silver coins. He lived in the time of Sulṭáns Mahmúd and Mas'úd Ghaznawí, and died in the year 1039 A. D., 430 A. H.

For further notes *vide* Dowson, Elliot's Histy. of India, II, 1.]

**Abu-Sa'id,** ابوسعید بن عبدالله, the son of 'Abdullah, an Arabian poet who flourished in the court of Ṣaláḥ-ud-dín, and was his prime minister. He died in the year 1201 A. D., 597 A. H.

**Abu-Sa'id,** ابو سعید بن کلیب شاشی, the son of Kulaib Sháshí, author of the book called "Masnad Kabír." He died in 946 A. D., 335 A. H.

**Abu-Sa'id 'Abdul-Malik bin-Kuraib,** ابوسعید عبدالملک بن قریب, commonly called Aṣma'í, celebrated for his grammatical knowledge and eloquence. He was born in the year 740 A. D., 122 A. H., and flourished in the time of Al-Manṣúr, khalífa of Baghdád (who reigned from 754 to 775 A. D.), and died at Baṣra during the reign of Hárún-ur-Rashíd, or, as some authors say, in A. H. 216 (A. D. 832).

**Abu-Sa'id 'Abdur-Rahman bin-Mamun al-Mutawalli,** author of the "Faráiẓ Mutawallí", a treatise on the law of inheritance according to Sháfi'í's doctrine. He died A. D. 1085, 478 A. H.

**Abu-Sa'id Baizawi,** ابو سعید بیضاوی, or Ḳáẓí Abú-Sa'íd 'Abdullah Baiẓáwí, author of the work called "Niẓám-ut-Tawáríkh," an epitome of Oriental History from Adam to the overthrow of the Khiláfat by the Tartars under Hulákú Khán A. D. 1258, 674 A. H., written about the year 1275. *Vide* Baiẓáwí.

**Abu-Sa'id Fazl-ullah,** ابو سعید فضل الله, son of Abul-Khair, a great Ṣúfí, of Mahna. His spiritual guide was Abul-Fazl Luḳmán of Sarakhs. He devoted himself to ascetic exercises and spent fourteen years in the wilderness. He is the author of the Quatrains, called Rubá'iyát-i-Abú-Sa'íd Abul-Khair. He died at the age of 44 in the year 1068 A. D., 440 A. H.

**Abu-Sa'id Khan Bahadur,** بوسعیدخان بهادر بن الجایتو, a Sulṭán of the family of Hulákú Khán, was the son of Oljáitú, commonly called Muhammad Khudá-banda, whom he succeeded to the throne of Persia in December 1316 A. D., Shawwál 716 A. H., when he was only twelve years of age. In his time Rashíd-ud-dín, the author of the Jámi'-ut-Tawáríkh, was put to death. This monarch may be termed the last of the dynasty of Hulákú Khán who enjoyed any power. The few princes of that sovereign's family who were raised to the throne after Abú-Sa'íd were mere pageants, whom the nobles of the court elevated or cast down as it suited the purposes of their ambition. Abú-Sa'íd reigned 19 lunar years, and died of fever on the 30th November 1335 A. D., 13th Rabí' II, 736 A. H. The following is a list of the princes of the family of Chingiz Khán, who were raised to nominal power after the death of Abú-Sa'íd Khán.

Arpá Khán (Mu'izz-uddín) was crowned in 1335, reigned five months, and was killed in battle in 1336 A. D.

Músa Khán was elevated in 1336, reigned two years, and was murdered in 1338 A. D.

Sákí, sister of Abú-Sa'íd Khán, was elevated to the throne in 1338. She was married to Jahán Timur who got the kingdom as her dowry, but was deposed the same year. After him

Sulaimán Khán was declared king; he left the kingdom and went to Diyár-bakr in 1344.

Nausherwán was elevated in 1334.

**Abu-Sa'id Mirza,** سلطان ابو سعید مرزا, (Sulṭán) the son of Sulṭán Muhammad Mirzá, son of Míránsháh, son of Amír Timur (Tamerlane). He was born in 1427 A. D. After the death of his father in 1441, he continued to live with Mirzá Ulugh Beg, son of Mirzá Sháhrukh at Samarḳand, and served in his army when he was at war with his son Mirzá 'Abdul-Laṭíf; but when that prince was murdered by his unnatural son in October 1449 A. D., Ramaẓán, 853 A. H., and he in his turn was slain after six or seven months by his own soldiers, and Samarḳand was taken possession of by Mirzá 'Abdullah, son of Mirzá Ibráhím and grandson of Mirzá Sháhrukh, Abú-Sa'íd with the assistance of Abú-Khair Uzbak having defeated and taken 'Abdullah prisoner in a battle, put him to death and ascended the throne of Samarḳand in 1451 A. D., 855 A. H. He also took possession of Khurásán after the death of Bábar Sulṭán, son of Báyasanghar Mirzá in 1457, 861 A. H., and greatly extended his dominions, but was at last taken prisoner in an ambuscade, and put to death on the 8th February, 1469 A. D., 25th Rajab, 873 A. H., after he had reigned 18 years. After his death, Sulṭán Husain Báiḳrá, surnamed Abul-Ghází, a descendant of Amír Timur, made himself master of the empire. Abú-Sa'íd at his death left eleven sons, *viz.*, Mirzá Sulṭán Ahmad, Mirzá Sulṭán Mahmúd, Mirzá Sulṭán Muhammad, Mirzá Sháhrukh, Mirzá Ulugh Beg, Mirzá 'Umar Shaikh, Mirzá Abá-Bakr, Mirzá Sulṭán Murád, Mirzá Sulṭán Khalíl, Mirzá Sulṭán Walíd, and Mirzá Sulṭán 'Umar; of whom four arrived to the dignity of kings, *viz.* Mirzá Ulugh Beg to the throne of Kábul; Mirzá Sulṭán Ahmad to the kingdom of Samarḳand; Mirzá 'Umar Shaikh to the united thrones of Andiján and Farghána; and Mirzá Sulṭán Mahmúd to those of Kunduz and Badakhshán. Abú-Sa'íd Mirzá, says Bábar Sháh, though brought up in the city, was illiterate and unrefined. *Vide* Genealogical Table attached to Á'ín Translation.]

**Abu-Sina Muhammad,** author of the Arabic work called "Daḳáiḳ-ul-Ḥaḳáiḳ," containing a collection of traditions.

**Abu-Sina,** ابو سینا, or Abú-'Alí Síná, whom we call Avicenna, was a famous Muhammadan physician and philosopher, who early applied himself to literature, botany, and mathematics. At the age of eighteen, he began to practise, and with such success that he became physician to the court of Baghdád. He was born in the city of Bukhárá in 983 A. D., 373 A. H., and died at Hamadán in July, 1037, 427 A. H., aged 54 lunar years, with the character of a learned man but too much addicted to wine and effeminating pleasures. His books on Medicine, &c., were in number 100, now nearly all lost. He is also called Ibn-Síná. The following are the titles of his works. Of the Utility and Advantages of Sciences, 20 books. Of Innocence and Criminality, 2 books. Of Health and

Remedies, 18 books. On the means of preserving Health, 3 books. Canons on Physic, 14 books. On Astronomical Observations, 1 book. On Mathematical Sciences. Of Theorems, or Mathematical and Theological Demonstrations, 1 book. On the Arabic language, 10 books. On the Last Judgment. On the Origin of the Soul, and the Resurrection of Bodies. Of the end we should propose to ourselves in Harangues and Philosophical Arguments. Demonstrations of the collateral lines in the sphere. Abridgment of Euclid. On Finity and Infinity. On Physics and Metaphysics. On Animals and Vegetables, &c., Encyclopædia, 20 volumes.

**Abu-Sufyan,** ابو سفيان بن حرب, the son of Ḥarb, the grandson of Umayya, and great-grandson of 'Abdul-Shams. He was an able and ambitious man, of great wealth and influence, and one of the most persevering and powerful opponents of Muhammad. He was the father of Mu'áwiya, the first khalífa of the house of Umayya, and one of the heads of the tribe of Ḳuraish, to which Muhammad also belonged. When Muhammad took up arms for the propagation of his faith, Abú-Sufyán was made generalissimo of his enemies against him: and after the battle of Badr, he stood very fair for the headship of that tribe. But he was at last convinced (as it seems, by a signal victory gained by Muhammad over his enemies), of the truth of the prophet's pretensions, and was converted in the 8th year of the Hijra, A. D. 629.

**Abu-Sulaiman Daud,** ابو سليمان داؤد, bin-Abul-Faẓl bin-Muhammad Fakhr Binákití, so called from having been born at Binákit, or Finákit, a town in Transoxiana, afterwards called Sháhrukhiya. He is the author of the "Táríkh-i-Binákití." Its correct name in full length is "Rauzatu úlí-l-albáb fí Tawáríkh-il-Akábir wal-Ansáb," *i. e.* the garden of the learned in the histories of great men and genealogies. It is chiefly an abridgment of the Jámi'-ur-Rashídí, and was compiled by the author only seven years after that work in A. D. 1317, 707 A. H., and is dedicated to Sulṭán Abú-Sa'íd, the ninth Mughul king of Persia. The author was a poet as well as an historian, and was appointed by Sulṭán Gházán Khán, poet laureate of his court. He died in or about the year 1330 A. D., 731 A. H.

*Vide* Dowson, Elliot's Histy. of India, III, 55.]

**Abu-Tahir,** ابو طاهر, of Tortosa in Spain, author of the "Dáráb-náma", an abridgement of Oriental Biography, containing the Lives of Ẓuḥák, of Darius, of Philip of Macedon, and of Alexander the Great: also Memoirs of Galen and other Greek Philosophers, &c.

**Abu-Tahir Khatuni,** ابو طاهر خاتونى, a poet who flourished in the 12th or 13th centuries of our era. He is the author of the History of the Saljúḳí kings, entitled "Táríkh-us-Saljúḳí," and of another work, called "Manáḳib-ush-Shu'ará."

**Abu-Talib,** ابو طالب, was the father of 'Alí and the uncle of Muhammad the prophet. He died 3 days before Khadíja, the first wife of Muhammad, in August, 619, A. D., aged 80 years.

**Abu-Talib Husaini,** author of the "Tuzuk-i-Timúrí." This work contains an account of the first forty-seven years of the life of Tamerlane, written by himself in Chaghtái Turkí, and translated into Persian by Abú-Ṭálib, who dedicated it to Sháh Jahán. It has been translated into English by Major Charles Stewart.

*Vide* Dowson, III, 389.]

**Abu-Talib Kalim,** ابو طالب كليم همدانى, whose poetical name was Kalím, was a great poet of Hamadán in Persia, and came to India, the first time in the reign of the emperor Jahángír, and returned home in 1619 A. D., 1028 A. H. After some years he again visited India in the time of Sháh Jahán, who employed him and conferred on him the title of "Malik-ush-Shu'ará", or Poet Laureate. He was twice weighed against gold and silver, and the amount was given to him as a reward for his poetical talents. He died at Láhor on the 19th November, 1651, 15th Ẕil-ḥijja 1061 A. H. He is the author of a poem, called "Ẓafar-náma-i-Sháh Jahán," or the conquests of Sháh Jahán, and of a Díwán in Persian.

**Abu-Talib Khan,** مرزا ابو طالب خان, (Mirzá) the son of Ḥájí Muhammad Beg Khán, by descent a Turk, was born at Lakhnau in the year A. D. 1752, 1165 A. H. He was appointed by Mukhtár-ud-daula, the prime minister of Nawáb Áṣaf-ud-daula of Lakhnau, in 1775 A. D., 'Amaldar of Iṭáwa and several other districts situated between the rivers Jamuná and Ganges. In this situation he continued for two years; and after the death of his patron, and the appointment of Ḥaidar Beg Khán to his office, he was superseded, and repaired to Lakhnau, and was allowed by the Nawáb 60,000 Rs. per annum for his support. After the expiration of one year, Colonel Alexander Hanny, having been appointed Collector of Gorakhpúr, requested the Nawáb to take him with him as an assistant, in which situation he continued for three years. He was afterwards employed by Mr. Middleton, the Resident of Lakhnau, in reducing the rebel rájá Balbhaddar Singh, whom, during two years, he frequently defeated and pursued. At length being surprised in his camp, the rájá in endeavouring to make his escape, was killed. Abú-Ṭálib, after this falling in distress for some years, embarked for Europe with Captain David Richardson, a Scotchman, and left Calcutta in February, 1799, Ramaẓán 1213 A. H. He visited England and other parts of Europe, and was well known in London under the title of the Persian Prince. During his travels he wrote a Journal in which he daily inserted every event, and committed to writing such reflections as occurred to him at the moment. On his return to Calcutta in 1803, 1218 A. H., having revised and abridged his notes, he published them under the title of "Maáṣir-ut-Ṭálibí fí Bilád-i-Ifranjí." This work was translated by Charles Stewart, and published in London in the year 1814. Abú-Ṭálib died about the year 1806 A. D., 1221 A. H. He is also the author of the "Khuláṣat-ul-Afkár."

*Vide* Dowson, VIII, 298.]

**Abu-Talib Mirza,** *vide* Sháista Khán.

**Abu-Talib,** شيخ ابو طالب, (Shaikh) the father of Shaikh Muhammad 'Alí Ḥazín. He died at Iṣfahán in 1715, 1127 A. H., and was interred in the cemetery, called Mazár Bábá Rukn-uddín, close to the tomb of the learned Mauláná Hasan, Shaikh-ul-Islám of Gílán.

**Abu-Tammam Habib ibn-Aus al-Tai,** ابو تمام حبيب ابن اوس الطائى, an Arabian poet. Having arrived in the city of Hamadán, he was received with great distinction by Abul-Wafá bin-Salama. When about to depart, a heavy fall of snow made the roads for a long time impassable. Abul-Wafá conducted the poet to his library, and placed it entirely at his disposal. Surrounded with these literary treasures, Abú-Tammám forgot his journey, read the precious volumes with avidity, and devoted his time to the composition of several works. The poetical collection, entitled "Khamsa", was the principal fruit of these researches, and attests the indefatigable attention with which the learned writer had ransacked this rich library. Amongst the other works that he wrote, one is called "Fuḥúl-ush-Shu'ará". He was born in A. D. 804, 188 A. H., at Jásim near Damascus, and died in A. D. 845, 231 A. H.

**Abu-Tayyib al-Mutanabbi,** ابو طيب المتنبى, *vide* Mutanabbí.

**Abu-Turab, Mir,** ميرابوتراب, a Salámí Sayyid of Shíráz, who served, with his son Mír Gadáí, in Gujrát, and then under Akbar. He died in 1005 H., and lies buried in Ahmadábád; *vide* Áín Translation I, p. 506.]

**Abu-'Ubaida,** ابوعبيده, a friend and associate of Muhammad, who had the command of the Moslem army in the time of Abú-Bakr, the first khalífa, but being defeated in a battle against the troops of the Greek emperor, he was deprived of the command, which was given to Khálid. 'Umar, on his accession to the khiláfat, replaced Abú-'Ubaida in the command of the army in Syria, being greatly displeased with the cruel and blood-thirsty disposition of Khálid. Abú-'Ubaida extended his conquests over Palestine and Syria, and drove the Greeks out of the whole country extending from the Mediterranean to the Euphrates. This conquest was completed in 639 A. D., 18 A. H., in which year Syria was visited by a dreadful plague, in which the Moslems lost 25,000 men, among whom were Abú-'Ubaida himself, Yazíd ibn Abú-Sufyán, and many other men of distinction.

**Abu-'Ubaida ibn-Mas'ud,** ابوعبيده ابن مسعود, a general in the time of the khalífa 'Umar. He was defeated and killed in battle by Farrukhzád, who commanded the army of Túrán-Dukht, queen of Persia, about the year 635 A. D.

**Abu-'Ubaida Kam bin-Salam,** author of a work on "Karáat."

**Abu-'Ubaida Ma'mar bin-Al-musanni,** ابوعبيده معمربن المثنى, a famous Arabian grammarian, born in Basra, who lived in the time of Hárún-ur-Rashíd, and died A. D. 824, 209 A. H., aged 99 lunar years.

**Abu-'Umar Minhaj al-Jurjani,** ابوعمر منهاج الجرجانى, author of the "Tabakát-i-Násirí", a celebrated history, written in 1252 A. D., 650 A. H., and dedicated to Sultán Násir-uddin Mahmúd of Dihlí. *Vide* Minháj-i-Siráj.

**Abu-Yahya bin-Sanjar,** ابويحيي ابن سنجر, author of a Díwán in Arabic. He died in 1234 A. D., 632 A. H.

**Abu-Yahya Ahmad bin-Daud al-Farazi al-Jurjani,** ابويحيى احمد بن داؤد, who was originally a Sunní, but became a convert to the Imámiya or Shí'a faith, is the author of a biographical work, entitled "Kitáb fí ma'rifat-ir-Rijál," containing the lives of eminent Shí'as.

**Abu-Ya'kub al-Warrak,** ابويعقوب الوراق, *vide* Muhammad bin-Is-hák an-Nadím.

**Abu-Yazid,** ابويزيد مكتبدار, Maktabdár, secretary of state in Egypt, who rebelled against Káim, the second khalífa of the race of the Fátimites. He was not punished for his rebellion till Ismá'íl al-Mansúr defeated him, and confined him in an iron cage where he ended his days.

**Abu-Yusuf,** امام ابويوسف, (Imám) bin-Habíb al-Kúfí, a celebrated Kází of Baghdád, and one of the first pupils of Abú-Hanífa, dignified with the title of Kází-l-Kuzát, or supreme judge, in the reigns of Hádí and Hárún-ur-Rashíd, khalífas of Baghdád. He supported the tenets of Abú-Hanífa, and maintained the dignity of his office by impartiality. When one day reproached for his ignorance of one of the causes brought before him, for the decision of which he received an ample allowance, he jocosely replied, that he received in proportion as he knew; but, said he, if I were paid for all I do not know, the riches of the khiláfat itself would not be sufficient to answer my demands. He was born 731 A. D., 113 A. H., and died on the 13th September 798, A. D., 27th Rajab, 182 A. H., at the age of 69 years, at Baghdád. The only work known to have been written by him, treats of the duties of a Magistrate, and is entitled "Ádáb-ul-Kází." The reputation of this work has been eclipsed by that of another, having a similar title, by al-Khassáf.

**Abu-Yusuf Ya'kub bin-Sulaiman Isfaraini,** ابويوسف يعقوب بن سليمان, author of the "Sharáit-ul-Khiláfat." He died in 1095 A. D., 488 A. H.

**Abn-Zakariya Yahya al-Nawawi,** *vide* Nawawí.

**Abu-Zarr,** ابوذر قرمطى, the father of the Karamatians in Arabia, who not only opposed the religion of Muhammad, but plundered and insulted the temple of Mecca and carried away the black stone which was believed to have fallen from heaven. He died 953 A. D., 342 A. H. *Vide* Karmat.

**Abu-Zarr Yakut Mausili,** ابوذرياقوت موصلى, a celebrated caligrapher.

**Abu-Zubaid,** ابوزبيد, an author who has written on the lion and all its names in the Arabic language.

**Abrakh Khan,** ابرخ خان, (the son of Kizilbásh Khán Afshár, governor of the fort of Ahmadnagar, who died there in the 22nd year of Sháh Jahán) was a nobleman of high rank in the time of 'Álamgír. A few years before his death, he was appointed governor of Barár, where he died on the 24th of July, 1685 A. D., 3rd Ramazán, 1096 A. H.

**Abru,** آبرو, *vide* Háfiz Ábrú.

**Abru,** آبرو, poetical name of Sháh Najm-uddín of Dihlí, *alias* Sháh Mubárak, who flourished in the reign of the emperor Muhammad Sháh. He died in 1161 H. *Vide* Sprenger, Oudh MSS., p. 196.]

**Abtin,** آبتين, the father of Farídún, seventh king of Persia of the first, or Peshdádian, dynasty. Ábtín pretended that he derived his origin from Jamshed, king of Persia of the same dynasty.

**Achanak Begam,** one of the concubines of the emperor Akbar. She had built a garden on the banks of the Jamuná at Ágra, called Achának Bágh. Some traces of it are yet to be seen.

**Achchhe,** اچهے, the poetical name of prince Baland-Akhtar, a brother of the emperor Muhammad Sháh of Dihlí. He was familiarly called Achchhe Sáhib, and therefore chose Achchhe for his 'takhallus.' He is the author of a beautiful poem, called "Náhíd-o-Ákhtar," *i. e.* Venus and the Star, containing 355 verses, which he completed in the year 1726 A. D., 1139 A. H.

**Adam,** the first man. The Muhammadans place Ádam's Paradise in heaven; hence after the fall Ádam and Hawwá (Eve) were hurled down to earth. As this event happened about 7,000 years before the Hijra, Ádam is often called haft-hazárí.]

**Adam Khan Gakkhar,** آدم خان گكهر, chief of the Gakkhars, who defied the power of the emperor Akbar. In 970, at the instigation of Kamál Khán Gakkhar, Ádam was attacked, and defeated and captured at Hilán, south of Chiliánwálá, near Dángalí, Ádam's stronghold. *Vide* Áín Translation, I, 457.]

**Adham,** ادهم, the poetical name of Mirzá Ibráhím, a Sayyid of the Safawí race. He came to India in the time of the emperor Sháh Jahán. He died, or was put to death in prison, in the year 1650 A. D., 1060 A. H. He is the author of a Díwán, and also of a Masnawí, called Rafík-us-Sálikín, and a Sákí-náma.

**Adham Artamani,** ادهم ارتمانی, author of a Díwán in Persian.

**Adham,** ادهم, *vide* Ibráhím-i-Adham.

**Adham Khan,** ادهم خان, the son of Máhum Anaga. He appears to be a royal bastard. His mother Máhum was one of Akbar's nurses *(anaga)*, who attended on Akbar 'from the cradle till after his accession.' She played a considerable part in bringing about Bairám's fall. Adham Khán (*i. e.* the Black Khán) was a commander of 5,000, and distinguished himself in keeping the rebellious Bhadauriya clan near Hatkánth, south-east of Ágra, in order. In 968 H., he defeated Báz Bahádur of Málwá. In the following year (A. D. 1562), he stabbed at court his enemy Atgah Khán, Akbar's foster-father, and was killed by the emperor's order. Máhum Anaga died forty days after from grief, and was buried with her son in Dihlí in a Mausoleum erected by Akbar. Adham's brother Bákí Khán, or Khán Bákí Khán, died in the 30th year of Akbar's reign, as Governor of Garha-Katanga (Central Provinces).]

**Adhan,** ادهن, Shaikh, a Chishtí saint, who died at Jaunpúr in 970 H.]

**Adib,** ادیب, the poetical name of Abú-Hasan 'Alí bin-Nasr, an excellent philosopher, who was a judge in Egypt, under the khiláfat of Ammár the Fátimite.

**Adib,** ادیب, surnamed Sábir, a poet who was contemporary with Asír-uddín Futúhí and Anwarí. *Vide* Shiháb-uddín Adíb Sábir.

**'Adil Khan,** عادل خان فاروقی, Fárúkí I, ruler of Khandesh, who is also called Mírán Ghaní, which see.

**'Adil Khan II, Faruki,** عادل خان فاروقی ثانی, entitled A'zam Humáyún, son of Hasan, and grandson of Nasír Khán Fárúkí by the daughter of Mahmúd Sháh of Gujrát. He succeeded to the throne of Khándesh after the death of Dáúd Khán Fárúkí in August, 1510 A. D., Jumáda I, 916 A. H., and removed from Tálner to Burhánpúr, which place he made the seat of his government, and died there after a reign of nine or ten years in 1520, 926 A. H., and was succeeded by Mírán Muhammad, his eldest son by the sister of Bahádur Sháh of Gujrát.

**'Adil Khan,** عادل خان, the eldest brother of Sultán Islám Sháh, king of Dihlí. He fled to Patna after his defeat in a battle against his brother, but he soon disappeared, and was never heard of afterwards.

**Adina Beg Khan,** آدینه بیگ خان, son of Channú, an Aráin by caste, was born at Sarakpúr near Láhor. He was brought up in a Mughul family, became a soldier, but devoted himself to accounts. He was governor of Sultánpúr when Nádir Sháh invaded India. Subsequently, he supported Abdálí Sháh Durrání. He died without heirs at Khánpúr near Hoshyárpúr, where a fine tomb was erected over his remains.]

**'Adli,** عدلی, the nickname of Muhammad 'Ádil Sháh, king of Dihlí. His name was Mubáriz Khán, son of Nizám Khán. He succeeded Islám Sháh in the very end of 960 H., defeated with the help of his general Hímú, in 962, Muhammad Sháh of Bengal at Chhapparghatta, east of Kálpí, and was at last, in 964, one year after Akbar's accession, defeated and killed in the battle of Súrajgarh, near Munger, by Bahádur Sháh, Sultán of Bengal. His nickname 'Adlí was often further corrupted to 'Andhlí', 'the blind woman.']

**'Adnan,** عدنان, one of the descendants of Ismá'íl the son of Abraham, with whom the genealogies of the Arabians, and also that of Muhammad, terminate. For reckoning up from 'Adnán to Ismá'íl, the descents are very uncertain, and the best historians confess that there is nothing certain beyond 'Adnán.

**Afi,** آفی, poetical name of Ahmad Yár Khan, author of a small poem in Persian called "Masnawí Gulzár-i-Khayál," containing the story of Sháhzáda and Gadá, written in 1848.

**'Afif,** *vide* Shams Siráj 'Afíf.

**Afrasyab,** افراسیاب, an ancient king of Túrán, the son of Pashang. He overcame Nauzar, king of Persia of the Peshdádian dynasty, and having killed him, ruled over Persia for twelve years. He was subsequently defeated in a battle against Kai-khusrau, king of Persia, of the 2nd or Kaiánian dynasty.

**Afrin,** آفرین, poetical name of Shaikh Kalandar Bakhsh of Saháranpúr, who is the author of a work, called Tuhfat-us-Sanái'.

**Afrin,** آفرین, the poetical name of Sháh Fakír-ullah of Láhor. He was a Gújar, embraced Muhammadanism, and is the author of a Díwán, and of an epic, called "Hír-wa-Ránjhá." Some say that he died in 1730, and others in 1741 A. D., 1143 or 1154 A. H.

**Afsah,** افصح, Sháh Fasíh, a pupil of Mirzá Bedil, died at Lakhnau in 1192 H., and left a Díwán.]

**Afsari,** افسری, the poetical name of a poet.

**Afshin,** افشین, the surname of Haidar ibn-Káús, a general of the khalífa al-Mu'tasim Billah of Baghdád. He was a Turk by origin, and had been brought up a slave at the khalífa's court, and having been employed in disciplining the Turkish militia, had acquired the reputation of a great captain. He was, however, executed about the year 840 A. D. by the khalífa, being accused of holding correspondence with the khalífa's enemies.

**Afsos,** افسوس, the poetical name of Mír 'Alí. He was first in the service of Nawáb Is-hák Khán, the uncle of Ásaf-ud-daula of Lakhnau, and subsequently of Mirzá Jawán-Bakht, and was finally recommended to Lord Wellesley and appointed a Munshí of the College of Fort William. He is the author of the Áráish-i-Mahfil in Urdú, and of the Gulistán, translated by him into the same language. He died in Calcutta in 1806 A. D., 1221 A. H.

**Aftab,** آفتاب, the poetical name of Sháh 'Álam, king of Dihlí, who died in the year A. D. 1806.

**Afzal,** the poetical name of Sháh Ghulám A'zam, which see.

**Afzal 'Ali Khan,** (Nawáb), *vide* below Afzal Khán (p. 24) whose original name was Shukr-ullah.

**Afzal,** the poetical name of Muhammad Afzal, which see.

**Afzali,** افضلی, the poetical name of Shaikh Muhammad Násir, son of Shaikh Khúb-ullah of Alláhábád. He died in 1750 A. D., 1163 A. H.

**Afzal Khan,** افضل خان, or Mír Muhammad Afzal. He flourished in the reign of the emperor Muhammad Sháh of Dihlí, and died in the year 1735 or 1738 A. D., 1148, 1151 A. H. His poetical name was Sábit, which see.

**Afzal Khan,** افضل خان, Shaikh 'Abd-urraḥmán, son of the celebrated Shaikh Abul-Fazl, minister and secretary to the emperor Akbar, was Jahángír's governor of Bihár in 1610 A. D., and died at A'gra in 1613.

*Vide* A'ín Translation, p. xxxv (Abul-Fazl's Biography), and Dowson, VI, 205.]

**Afzal Khan,** افضل خان, whose original name was Mullá Shukr-ullah, the son of 'Abdul-Ḥakk, came from Shíráz to the Dakhin, and was introduced by 'Abdur-Raḥím Khán, Khánkhánán, to the emperor Jahángír, who conferred on him the rank of an Amír. In the second year of Sháh Jahán, 1628 A. D., 1038 A. H., the office of Wizárat-i-kull having become vacant by the dismissal of Irádat Khán, the brother of A'saf Khán Ja'far Beg, he was honored with that appointment. In the eleventh year of the emperor, the mansab of 7,000 and 4,000 sawárs was conferred on him, but he died the next year at Láhor on the 7th January, 12th Ramazán, 1048 A. H., 1639 O. S., aged 70 years. His poetical name was 'Allámí. His tomb, called Chíní Rauza is in A'gra, on the left bank of the Jamuná.

**Afzal-ud-daula,** (Nawáb), Nizám of Ḥaidarábád, succeeded his father Nawáb Nasír-ud-daula in May 1857, 15th Zil-ka'da, 1285 A. H., and departed this life on the 26th of February 1869, aged 44 years, leaving an infant son who, according to the succession guarantee granted by Lord Canning, is now his successor.

**Afzal-uddin,** (Mír), Nawáb of Súrat. He died on the 7th August, 1840, at the age of 59 years, after enjoying his nominal nawábship about 21 years. His son-in-law, Mír Ja'far 'Alí, succeeded him.

**Agah Khan,** a eunuch of the emperor Sháh Jahán, who died on the 9th Rabí' I, 1067 A. H. His tomb is near the Mumtáz-Maḥall in Tájganj.

**Agah,** آگاه, the poetical name of Maulawí Muhammad Báḳir. His parents were of Bíjápúr, but he was born at Ellora in 1745 A. D., 1158 A. H., and died on the 3rd of March 1806 A. D., 14th Zil-ḥijja 1220 A. H. He is the author of a Díwán.

He was a Náita (pl. *Nawáit*, said to be a corruption of the Persian *nau-ámad*, a 'new arrival'), a name given to certain seafaring Arabs, settled in Western India.]

**Agha Ahmad 'Ali,** poetically styled Ahmad, son of A'ghá Shajá'at 'Alí, of Dháká, a Persian grammarian of note, who successfully defended, in his "Muayyid-i-Burhán," and the "Shamsher-i-Teztar," the author of the Burhán Ḳáṭi', a Persian Dictionary, against the famous Dihlí poet Ghálib. He also published the "Risála-i-Ishtiḳáḳ", the "Risála-i-Tarána", "Haft A'smán," a History of the Persian Masnawí, and edited several works for the Asiatic Society of Bengal. He was a Persian teacher in the Calcutta Madrasa, when he died (June 1873).]

**Agha Husain Khwansari,** آغا حسین خوانساری, *vide* Husain Khwánsárí.

**Agha Mir,** آغا میر, entitled Mu'tamad-ud-daula, minister of Ghází-uddín Ḥaidar, king of Audh. He was dismissed in 1826 A. D., 1242 A. H., and retired to Kánhpúr, where he died on Monday 7th May, 1832, 5th Zil-ḥijja, 1247.

**Agha Muhammad Khan,** آغا محمد خان, *vide* A'ḳá Muhammad Khán Ḳájár.

**Agha Mulla,** آغا ملا, surnamed 'Dawátdár', 'the inkstand-holder,' the ancestor of the three A'saf Kháns who served under Akbar and Jahángír. His genealogical table is given in A'ín Translation, I, 369.]

**Aghar Khan,** اغرخان, Pír Muhammad, who served during the reign of Aurangzíb against Prince Shujá', in A'sám, and in Kábul. He died in A. H. 1102. His son, Aghar Khán II, was still alive during the reign of Muhammad Sháh. The family traced their descent from Aghar, a descendant of Yáfiṣ (Japhet), son of Núḥ. Their villa Agharábád near Dihlí is often mentioned in the histories.]

**Ahi,** آهی, a poet who was a chief of one of the Chaghtái hordes, and had assumed originally the poetical name of "Nargisí," but changed it into "A'hí", because he found that another poet of his time had adopted it. He is the author of a Díwán which he dedicated to prince Gharíb Mirzá, the son of Sulṭán Husain Mirzá Báiḳrá. He died in the year 1520 A. D., 927 A. H.

**Ahl-i-Bait,** اهل بیت, 'the people of the house', a general name for the descendants of Muhammad, the Sayyids.]

**Ahl-i-Kitab,** اهل کتاب, 'the people of the book', a collective name for the Jews, Christians, and Muhammadans, who received a book, *i. e.*, revealed religion, from heaven.]

**Ahli Khurasani,** اهلی خراسانی, a poet who died at Tabríz in the year 1527 A. D., 934 A. H. He must not be confounded with Ahlí-i-Túrání, a Chaghtái nobleman of profligate character, who lived at the court of Sulṭán Husain Mirzá, and died in 1497 A. D., 902 A. H.

**Ahli Shirazi,** اهلی شیرازی (Mauláná) of Shíráz, an elegant poet in the service of Sháh Ismá'íl Safawí I. He is the author of several poems, amongst which are the "Siḥr-i-Ḥalál", "Sham' wa Parwána", "Risála-i-Naghz", Sáḳí-náma", and "Fawáid-ul-Fawáid." He died in the year 1535 A. D., 942 A. H., and is buried at Shíráz, close to the tomb of Ḥáfiẓ.

**Ahlia Bai,** the wife of Madhu Ráo Peshwá Sindia, built a place in the time of Sháh 'A'lam, called Bisnán Ghát, or a bathing-place for all men, on the banks of the river Jamuná. It extended from the trench of the fort to the house of Dárá Shikoh, and was in good preservation in the year 1830 A. D. On one of the corners a large gun of iron was lying, under the Hawelí of Dárá Shikoh, called Dhaul Dahaní.

**Ahlia Bai,** اهلیه بائی, the wife of Khánde Ráo, the son of Malhár Ráo Holkar I, of Indor, after whose death, in 1766 A. D., she had a jágír allotted to her yielding an annual revenue of 1,500,000 Rupees. Her husband Khánde Ráo was killed in battle at Díg against Súrajmal Jáṭ in 1754. Her son Malí Ráo, who had succeeded his grandfather Malhár Ráo in 1766, died nine months after. She was a woman of spirit and ability, and reserved in her own hands the right of nominating a successor, and elected Tokají to the ráj.

**Ahmad al-Makkari,** احمد, author of the History of the Muhammadan Dynasties in Spain. This work was translated by M. Pascual de Gayangos, an erudite Spaniard, London, 1810, in 4to., Vol. I. He was born in the 16th century, and died in Damascus in the year 1631 A. D., 1041 A. H. After having composed a very detailed biography of the celebrated and learned wazír of Granada, Muhammad Ibn-ul-Khaṭíb, he added to it, in the form of an introduction, a general history of the Arabs in Spain from the conquest to their final expulsion.

**Ahmad I,** احمد بن محمد, emperor of Turkey, son and successor of Muhammad III, whom he succeeded in January, 1604 A. D., Sha'bán, 1012 A. H. This prince was of a good constitution, strong and active; he would throw a horseman's mace, of nine or ten pounds weight, farther than any of his court. He was much given to sensual pleasures, and had 3000 concubines. He died on the 15th November, 1617 A. D., 15th Ẕil-ḳa'da, 1025 A. H., at the age of thirty, having reigned fourteen years. He was succeeded by his brother Muṣtafa I.

**Ahmad II,** احمد بن ابراهيم, son of Ibráhím, succeeded on the death of his brother Sulaimán II, in 1691 A. D., 1103 A. H., to the throne of Constantinople, and died in 1695, 1106 A. H. He was succeeded by Muṣtafa II, son of Muhammad IV.

**Ahmad III,** احمد بن محمد, son of Muhammad IV, was placed on the throne of Constantinople in 1703 A. D., 1115 A. H., by the heads of a faction which had deposed his brother Muṣtafa II. He granted a friendly asylum to Charles XII of Sweden, after the battle of Pultowa; and the kindness and the hospitality which marked the whole of his intercourse with that unfortunate monarch, are entitled to the highest encomium. He was preparing an expedition against Persia, when an insurrection hurled him from his throne, and exalted his nephew Mahmúd I from a prison to the sovereign power in 1730 A. D., 1142 A. H. He died of apoplexy in 1736, aged 74 years, 1148 A. H.

**Ahmad IV,** احمد بن احمد, (also called 'Abdul-Ḥamíd), son of Ahmad III, emperor of Turkey, succeeded his brother Muṣtafa III in 1774 A. D., 1188 A. H. He died after a reign of 15 years on the 7th April, 1789, Rajab 1203 A. H., and was succeeded by Salím III.

**Ahmad,** احمد, an Arabian author who is known as the writer of a book on the interpretation of dreams, a translation of which in Greek and Latin was published with that of Artemidorus on the same subject, at Paris, by Rigault A. D. 1603. He lived in the 4th century of the Hijra.

**Ahmad Abu-Tayyib al-Mutanabbi,** ابو طيب المتنبى احمد, a celebrated Arabian poet whom none excelled in poetry. He is the author of a Díwán. He died in the year 965 A. D., 354 A. H.; *vide* Mutanabbí.

**Ahmad al-Ghaffari,** احمد الغفاري; *vide* Ahmad bin-Muhammad al-Ghaffárí (p. 26).

**Ahmad 'Ali Hashimi,** شيخ احمد على هاشمى, (Shaikh), author of the Biographical Dictionary, called "Makhzan-ul-Gharáib", dedicated to Nawáb Ṣafdar-Jang of Faizábád, who died in 1754 A. D., 1167 A. H. His poetical name was Khádim.

**Ahmad 'Ali Khan,** Nawáb of Rámpúr; *vide* Faiz-ullah Khán.

**Ahmad 'Ali Khan,** نواب احمد على خان, Nawáb of Karnál. A remission of revenue to the extent of Rs. 5,000 per annum was granted to him in perpetuity by the British Government, and a khil'at of the value of Rs. 10,000 was conferred on him, in July 1858, for his distinguished loyalty and for the eminent services rendered by him during the rebellion of 1857. In 1806, the Pargana of Karnál consisted of a number of villages, yielding a revenue of Rs. 40,000 per annum. It was conferred by Lord Lake in jágír on three Mandal chiefs, named Muhammadí Khán, Ghairat 'Alí Khán, and Is-ḥáḳ Khán, for their lives, and after their death to descend to their heirs, subject to the payment of Rs. 15,000 per annum in perpetuity. Nawáb Ahmad 'Alí Khán is the lineal descendant of Muhammadí Khán, and holds 24 entire villages, besides a 3rd share in four others. These lands are assessed at Rs. 24,000, on which the Nawáb has hitherto paid a quit rent of Rs. 5,000, payment of which sum the Government has now remitted.

**Ahmad 'Ali Khan,** سيد احمد على خان, (Sayyid), Nawáb-Náẓim of Bengal, succeeded his brother 'Alí-Jáh. He died on the 30th October, 1824 A. D.

**Ahmad 'Ali Khan,** and Walídád Khán, the rebel Nawábs of Málágaṛh.

**Ahmad Ayaz,** Malik Khwája Jahán, served with distinction under Muhammad Sháh bin-Tughluḳ of Dihlí. On the death of the king at Tatta, in A. H. 752 (A. D. 1352), he tried to set up at Dihlí a son of the late king, but had to submit to Fírúz Sháh III, who allowed the nobles to execute him before he himself entered Dihlí.]

**Ahmad Bakhsh Khan,** (Nawáb), entitled Fakhr-ud-daula, was the jágírdár of Fírúzpúr and Lohárú in the district of Dihlí, after whose death his son Nawáb Shams-uddín Khán succeeded him. The latter was executed for murder in October, 1835.

**Ahmad Barani,** احمد برنى, author of a Persian work, called "Sifr-us-Siyar."

**Ahmad Beg Kabuli,** served in Kábul under Muhammad Ḥakím, Akbar's brother, and later under Akbar and Jahángír. He was for some time governor of Kashmír. He died about A. D. 1614.]

**Ahmad Beg Khan,** a son of (Muhammad Sharíf) Núr Jahán's brother. He served under Jahángír in Bengal, assisted Prince Sháhjahán during his rebellion, and was subsequently made by Sháhjahán governor of Tatta, Síwistán, and of Multán. He received as jágír Jáis and Ameṭhí in Audh, where he died.]

**Ahmad bin-'Abdullah al-Kirmi,** احمد بن عبدالله, author of a work on the fundamental points of Muhammadanism. *Vide* Abú-Ahmad, the son of Ḳásim.

**Ahmad bin-Abu-Bakr,** احمد بن ابى بكر, an Arabian author who wrote the "Mashra'-ul-Manáḳib", a minute account of the events of Muhammad's life, with memoirs of his successors and companions.

**Ahmad bin-Abu-Bakr bin-Nasir Mustafa al-Kazwini,** احمد بن ابوبكر, author of the "Táríkh-i-Guzída", which contains the history of the four ancient Persian Dynasties, *viz.* Peshdádians, Kaiánians, Ashkánians, and Sásánians, that is, from the year 890 B. C. to 636 A. D., and memoirs of the several dynasties who ruled over Persia, Tartary, &c., during the khiláfat, and to the year 1329 A. D. See also called Ḥamd-ullah Mustaufí.

**Ahmad bin-'Ali Razi, (Shaikh),** احمد بن على رازي شيخ, surnamed Jassás, a famous lawyer. He was born in the year 917 A. D., 305 A. H., and died in 980 A. D., 370 A. H., aged 65 lunar years.

**Ahmad bin-'Ali al-Khatib Kastalani,** احمد بن على الخطيب; *vide* Ḳasṭalání.

**Ahmad bin-Hasan Maimandi,** احمد بن حسن ميمندى, (Khwája) foster brother and fellow student of his sovereign Sulṭán Mahmúd of Ghazní. On the removal of Abul-'Abbás Fazl, two years after the succession of Mahmúd, Khwája Ahmad was appointed prime minister, which office he held uninterruptedly for a period of 18 years, when Altúntásh, the commander-in-chief, and a number of other Amírs, brought before the court of the king charges against him. He was in consequence disgraced and imprisoned for 13 years in one of the forts of India. He was released by Sultán Mas'úd, son and successor of Mahmúd, and reinstated in the responsible office of minister, which he held for some time. He died a natural death in the year 1033 A. D., 424 A. H.

**Ahmad bin-Idris,** احمد بن ادريس, a lawyer of the sect of Málik, was the author of many works, and died about the year 1285 A. D., 684 A. H.

**Ahmad bin-Israil,** احمد بن اسرائيل, a great astrologer who lived under the khiláfat of Wásik Billah of Baghdád.

**Ahmad bin-Kasir,** احمد بن كثير, also called Muhammad bin-Kaṣír and Kaṣír al-Farghání, is the same person whom we call Alfaraganius, a great astronomer, who lived during the reign of the Khalífa al-Mámún. *Vide* Farghání.

**Ahmad bin-Muhammad al-Ghaffari al-Kazwini,** احمد بن محمد الغفاري, a kází, and a descendant of 'Abdul-Ghaffár, the author of the "Ḥáwí". He is the author of the work called "Naskh-i-Jahán-ará" which he composed in the year 1563 A. D., 971 A. H., of which number the title forms the chronogram. It is also called "Táríkh-i-Mukhtaṣir," an abridged history of Asia, from Ádam down to Sháh Ṭahmásp of Persia, A. D. 1525. It also contains memoirs of the Muhammadan kings of Spain, from A. D. 755 to 1036. It was dedicated to Sháh Ṭahmásp. We are also indebted to him for the better known work, entitled "Nigáristán". We learn from the "Táríkh Badáoní" that, having resigned his employment in Persia, he went towards the close of his life on a pilgrimage to Mecca, and that landing in Díbal in Sindh, for the purpose of paying a visit to Hindústán, he died at that port in 1567 A. D., 975 A. H.

*Vide* Dowson, Elliot's Histy. of India, II, 504.]

**Ahmad bin-Muhammad al-Kastalani,** القسطلانى احمد بن محمد, an author who died in the year 1527 A. D., 933 A. H.; *vide* Ḳasṭaláni.

**Ahmad bin-Muhammad Kuduri,** بن محمد قدوري احمد, author of a work on jurisprudence, called "Ḳudúrí", and several other works. He died in 1046 A. D., 438 A. H.

**Ahmad bin-Muhammad bin-'Ali Bakr al-Hanafi,** author of the "Khazánat-ul-Fatáwa," a collection of decisions made towards the end of the eighth century of the Hijra, and comprising questions of rare occurrence.

**Ahmad bin-Tulun,** احمد بن طولون, the founder of the Túlúnide dynasty in Egypt; *vide* Ahmad Ibn-Ṭúlún.

**Ahmad bin-Yahya bin-Jabir al-Biladuri,** البلاذري or البلاذرى, surnamed also Abú-Ja'far and Abul-Hasan, was the instructor to one of the princes of the family of al-Mutawakkil, and died in A. H. 279, A. D. 892. His "Futúḥ-ul-Buldán" is one of the earliest Arabic chronicles. He also wrote a geographical work, entitled "Kitáb-ul-Buldán," the Book of Countries.]

**Ahmad bin-Yahya,** احمد بن يحيى, author of the marginal notes on the "Wiḳáya", a work on jurisprudence.

**Ahmad bin-Yusuf,** احمد بن يوسف, an historian and author of the "Akhbár-ud-dawal", written in 1599 A. D., 1008 A. H., which is said to be an abridgement of Janábí's "Táríkh-ul-Janábí", called also "Baḥr-uz-Zakhkhár".

**Ahmad Chap,** Malik, was Náib-Bárbak under Fírúz Sháh II (Khiljí) of Dihlí, whom he warned in vain against 'Alá-uddín. He was blinded by 'Alá-uddín after his accession.]

**Ahmad (Shaikh),** شيخ احمد غزنوي, of Ghazní, author of the work entitled "Maḳámát-i-Shaikh Ahmad," containing the Life of Ahmad Jám, Shaikh-ul-Islám of Níshápúr; with a minute account of the miracles performed by him. *Vide* Ahmad Jám.

**Ahmad (Shaikh),** شيخ احمد اميتهى, commonly called Mullá Jíwan, of Amethí, was the tutor of the emperor 'Álamgír, and author of the "Tafsír-i-Ahmadí." He died in 1718 A. D., 1130 A. H. *Vide* Mullá Jíwan.

**Ahmad, Shaikh,** second son of Shaikh Salím Chishtí of Fatḥpúr Síkrí. He served under Akbar, and died in 985 H.]

**Ahmadi,** احمدى, the poetical name of Mír Sayyid Luṭf-ullah, who died in 1633 A. D., 1043 A. H.

**Ahmadi,** احمدى, a Turkish poet, whose proper name was Khwája Ahmad Ja'farí, and of whom we have the following anecdote. The great Tartar conqueror Amír Timur (Tamerlane) being on his march through Anadoli, halted for a while at Amasia, where Ahmadí lived; and the poet took the opportunity of presenting him with an ode. This led to further intimacies, Timur being a patron of literary men; and one day when both were in the bath, the monarch amused himself by putting crochetty questions to Ahmadí, and laughing at his answers. "Suppose now," said he, pointing to the surrounding attendants, "you were required to value these beautiful boys, how much would you say each was worth?" Ahmadí answered with becoming gravity, estimating one at a camel-load of silver, another at six bushels of pearls, a third at forty gold wedges, and so made the circuit of the ring. "Very fair," said Timur, "and now tell me, What do you value Me at?" "Four and twenty aspers," replied the poet, "no more and no less." "What!" cried Timur, laughing, "why the shirt I have on is worth that." "Do you really think so?" asked Ahmadí, with the greatest apparent simplicity—"at that rate you must be worth nothing, for I included the shirt in the valuation!" Much to his credit, Timur, instead of being angry, applauded and rewarded the wit and boldness of the poet. Ahmadí was a contemporary of Shaikhí, and is the author of the "Kulliyát-i-Khwája Ahmad Ja'farí." He also composed a heroic poem on the actions of Tamerlane, and a Sikandar-náma in the Turkish language. He died in A. D. 1412.

**Ahmad Ghaffari,** *vide* Ahmad bin-Muhammad al-Ghaffárí.

**Ahmad Ghazzali,** *vide* Ghazzálí (Ahmad).

**Ahmad Ibn-'Arab-Shah,** *vide* 'Arab-Sháh.

**Ahmad Ibn-Hanbal,** *vide* Ḥanbal (Imám.)

**Ahmad Ibn-Tulun,** احمد ابن طولون, the founder of the Ṭúlúnide dynasty in Egypt, a Turkish slave, who being entrusted by al-Mu'tamid, the khalífa of Baghdád, with the government of that country and Syria in A. D. 879, set up for himself, and maintained his authority notwithstanding all attempts to depose him. He reduced Damascus, Ḥimṣ, Ḥamát, Ḳinnisrín, and ar-Raḳḳa, situated upon the eastern bank of the Euphrates. His mosque in Cairo may be seen to this day. He died in A. D. 884, 270 A. H., and was succeeded by his son Khumárwaih. Egypt continued to be governed by his successors for several years when it was again reduced in A. D. 905 by Muhammad, general of the khalífa of Baghdád al-Muktafí;

the last khalífa of Egypt having assassinated his predecessor, and thereby rendered himself very odious. In the year 933, Muhammad the son of Táj, or Tájíl, surnamed al-Ashhad, seized upon Syria and Egypt in the khiláfat of ar-Rází Billah, and his family retained the whole of it, except a small part which 'Ubaid-ulla al-Mahdí, the first of the Fáṭimite dynasty (the seat of whose empire was at Ḳairuwán near Tunis) had conquered in A. D. 910. His successor Abú-Tamím Ma'd, surnamed Mu'izz li-dín-illah, conquered the rest of Egypt about the year 970, by his general Ja'far, who built the city of al-Ḳáhira, commonly called Grand Cairo, whither his master soon removed his court. The Fáṭimite dynasty ended in A. D. 1176, when, upon the death of the last prince of this family, the kingdom was usurped by the famous Ṣaláḥ-uddín (Saladin).

*List of the Khalífas of Barbary.*

'Ubaid-ullah al-Mahdí, first of the Fáṭimite race.
Al-Ḳáim Mahdí, his son.
Ismá'íl, surnamed al-Manṣúr, son of al-Ḳáim.
Mu'izz li-dín-illah, son of al-Manṣúr, who conquered Egypt and became the first khalífa of the Fáṭimite dynasty in that country.

**Ahmad Ilkani,** احمد ایلکانی, also called Ahmad Jaláyir; *vide* Hasan Buzurg.

**Ahmad Jafari,** احمد جعفری, (Khwája) *vide* Ahmadí.

**Ahmad Jalal Bukhari,** (Sayyid) son of Sayyid Muhammad Bukharí.

**Ahmad Jalayir,** احمد جلایر, also called Ahmad Ílkání, a descendant of Hasan Buzurg, which see.

**Aḥmad Jam,** احمد جام, (Shaikh ul-Islám) entitled Abú-Naṣr and Zinda-Píl, a celebrated Muhammadan saint of Ṇíshápúr, born in the year 1049 A. D., 441 A. H. He passed 18 years of his life in devotion in wilds and mountains. He subsequently got married, and was blessed with 39 sons and 3 daughters. At the time of his death, besides the 3 daughters, 14 of his sons were living, all of whom became men of learning and authors of several works. Ahmad Jám himself was an author, and among the different works that he wrote, are the following: "Risála Samarḳandí", "Anís-ut-Ṭálibín", "Miftáḥ-un-Naját", "Baḥr-ul-Ḥaḳíkat", and "Siráj-us-Sáyirín". He died in the reign of Sulṭán Sanjar in February, 1142 A. D., Rajab 536 A. H.

**Aḥmad Jan** (Sulṭán) of Hirát. He died about the 6th of April 1863, 17th Shawwál 1279 A. H., and was succeeded by his son Shah Nawáz Khán.

**Aḥmad Kabir,** سید احمد کبیر, (Sayyid) a Musalmán saint, whose tomb is at Uchcha in Multán. He is the son of Sayyid Jalál, and the father of two other saints Sayyid Jaláluddín, surnamed Makhdúm Jaháníyán Jahán-gasht, and Rájú Ḳattál. Numerous miracles were wrought by these two brothers.

**Ahmad Khan,** (Sayyid) C. S. I., of 'Alígaṛh, a distinguished Muhammadan reformer. He wrote a book on the life and work of the Prophet, and founded the 'Alígaṛh College.

**Ahmad Khan,** احمد خان, surnamed Nekodár (or Nicholas) was raised to the throne of Persia after the death of his brother Abáḳá Khán, the son of Hulákú Khán, in April, 1282 A. D., Ẕil-ḥijja, 680 A. H., and was the first emperor of the race of Chingiz Khán who embraced the Muhammadan religion. He is said to have been baptized in his youth by the name of Nicholas, but policy, or conviction, led him to abandon the doctrine of Christ for that of Muhammad, when he assumed the name of Ahmad Khán. In the first year of his reign, Majd-ul-Mulk Yazdí, a nobleman of his court, being accused of sorcery, lost his life. He put his own brother to death, and was successful in obtaining possession of the person of his nephew, Arghún Khán: but that prince was not only rescued from his violence by the Mughul nobles, but by their aid was enabled to deprive him of his crown and life on the night of Thursday, 11th August 1284 A. D., 26th Jumáda I, 683 A. H., and become his successor.

**Ahmad Khan Bangash,** احمد خان بنگش, second son of Muhammad Khán Bangash, Nawáb of Farrukhábád. When the Wazír Ṣafdar-Jang, after the death of Ḳáim-Jang, the brother of Ahmad Khán, confiscated his estates in December 1749, A. D., 1163 A. H., he (Ahmad Khán) collected an army of Afgháns, defeated rájá Nawal Rái, the Wazír's deputy, who was slain in the action, and recovered the territories lately seized from his family. This circumstance took place on the 2nd August 1750, Friday, 10th Ramaẓán, 1163 A. H. After this, Ahmad Khán governed his country about 22 lunar years, and died in November 1771, Sha'bán, 1185 A. H., when he was succeeded by his son Diler Himmat Khán, who received the title of Muẓaffar-Jang from the emperor Sháh 'Alam, who was then on his way to Dihlí from Alláhábád.

**Ahmad Khan Mewati,** one of the petty rulers *(mulúk-i ṭawáif)* who had usurped the chief parts of the Dihlí empire, during the Sayyid dynasty (beginning of the 15th century). Ahmad Khán held Mewát, his frontier coming close up to Dihlí. He had to submit to Buhlúl Lodí.]

**Ahmad Khan Sur;** *vide* Sikandar Khán Súr.

**Ahmad Khattu,** شیخ احمد کهتو, (Shaikh) surname of Wajíh-uddín Ahmad Maghribí, who was the son of Malik Ikhtiyár-uddín, a nobleman at the court of Sulṭán Fíruz Sháh Tughluḳ of Dihlí, and related to him. After the death of his father, having squandered his wealth in pleasure and dissipation, he became a disciple of Shaikh Bábá Is-ḥáḳ Maghribí, and turned very pious and journeyed to Gujrát, where he acquired great fame. During his residence at that place, he obtained such celebrity, that Sulṭán Muẓaffar Gujrátí became his disciple. He died in that country in the reign of Sulṭán Muhammad of Gujrát, on Thursday, 6th of January 1446, 8th Shawwál 849 A. H., aged 111 years, and was buried at Sarkich, near Ahmadábád. Khaṭṭú is a place in Nágor, where Shaikh Ahmad was born.

**Ahmad bin-Khizrawaih,** احمد بن خضرویه, a celebrated Muhammadan saint, was the disciple of Khwája Ḥátim Aṣamm. He died in the year 854 A. D., 240 A. H., and is buried at Balkh.

**Ahmad Maghribi,** *vide* Ahmad Khaṭṭú (Shaikh).

**Ahmad Mirza,** سلطان احمد مرزا, (Sulṭán), son of Abú-Sa'íd Mirzá, after whose death, in 1469, he took possession of Samarḳand, and died about the year 1495 A. D.

**Ahmad (Mulla),** ملا احمد, the son of a ḳází of Tatta. His ancestors who resided in Sindh, were Fárúḳís of the Ḥanífa sect, but he was a Shí'a. He is the author of a work, called "Khuláṣat-ul-Ḥayát", the Essence of Life. He came from the Dakhin to the court of the emperor Akbar, in the year 1582 A. D., 990 A. H., and when that monarch ordered the "Táríkh-i-Alfí" to be compiled, several authors were employed in the compilation, but subsequently the chief labour devolved upon Mullá Ahmad. The compilation of the first two volumes up to the time of Chingiz Khán was just finished by him, when Mírzá Fúlád Birlás, during the month of January 1588, Ṣafar, 996 A. H., persuaded the Mullá, who was always openly reviling the first khalífas, to leave his own house at midnight on some pretence, and then murdered him in a street of Láhor. For this act Mírzá Fúlád was sentenced to death, was bound alive to the leg of an elephant in the city of Láhor, and dragged along till he died. The Mullá expired three or four days after the Mírzá. After the death of Mullá Ahmad, the remainder of the work was written by A'saf Khán Ja'far Beg, up to the year 997 A. H., or 1589 A. D. Mullá Ahmad was buried at Láhor, but being a Shí'a, who openly used to revile the first khalífas, the people of Láhor exhumated his remains and burnt them.

*Vide* A'ín Translation, I, 206.]

**Ahmad Nizam Shah Bahri,** احمد نظام‌شاه, the founder of the Niẓám-Sháhí dynasty of the Dakhin, was the son of Niẓám-ul-Mulk Baḥrí, prime minister to Sulṭán Mahmúd Sháh Bahmaní. He had conquered many places in the vicinity of his father's jágír, and was besieging the fort of Dundrájpúr about the year A. D. 1486, 891 A. H., when he received intelligence of the assassination of his father, and immediately returned and assumed the titles of the deceased, and was generally known by those of Ahmad Niẓám-ul-Mulk Baḥrí, to which the people of the Dakhin added the title of Sháh. As he had distinguished himself repeatedly as a general in the field, though the Sulṭán wished to remove him from power, none of his nobility would accept the task of reducing him. He, however, on the 3rd May 1490, 3rd Rajab 895 A. H., gained a victory over the army of the Sulṭán, and from that time he sat without opponent on the masnad of royalty, and by the advice of Yúsuf 'A'dil Sháh, who had already become independent, having discontinued to read the khuṭba in the name of the king, put in his own and spread a white umbrella over his head. He laid the foundation of the city of Ahmadnagar in A. D. 1495, 900 A. H., which was completed in two years, and became the first of the Niẓám-Sháhí kings of Ahmadnagar. He died in A. D. 1508, 914 A. H., and was succeeded by his son Burhán Niẓám Sháh I. The following is a list of the Niẓám-Sháhí kings of Ahmadnagar:—

Ahmad Niẓám Sháh I, A. D. 1490.
Burhán Niẓám Sháh, 1508.
Husain Niẓám Sháh I, 1553.
Murtaẓa Niẓám Sháh, 1565.
Mírán Husain Niẓám Sháh, 1587.
Ismá'íl Niẓám Sháh, 1589.
Burhán Niẓám Sháh II.
Ibráhím Niẓám Sháh, 1594.
Ahmad Niẓám Sháh II, son of Sháh Ṭáhir, 1594.
Bahádur Niẓám Sháh, 1595.
Murtaẓa Niẓám Sháh II, 1598.

The Niẓám Sháhí dominions fall under the control of Malik 'Ambar, 1607.

**Ahmad Pasha,** احمد پاشا, a general of Sulaimán I, emperor of Turkey, who when appointed governor of Egypt, revolted from his sovereign in 1524 A. D. He was soon after defeated by Ibráhím, the favorite of Sulaimán, and his head was sent to Constantinople.

**Ahmad Rumi,** احمد رومي, author of the Fáiḳ-ul-Ḥaḳáiḳ, a work written in imitation of the Maṣnawí of Jalál uddín Rúmí.

**Ahmad Samani,** امير احمد ساماني, (Amír) second king of the race of Sámán (Samanides), succeeded his father Amír Ismá'íl in the provinces of Khurásán, &c., in 907 A. D., 295 A. H. He was a cruel prince, and contended with his uncle, his brothers, and other relations for the extensive possessions of his father, more by intrigues at the court of Baghdád, than by arms. After a reign of seven years, he was murdered by some of his domestics on Thursday, 30th January, 914 A. D., 23rd Jumáda I, 301 A. H., and his son Amír Naṣr, then only eight years of age, was placed upon the throne of Khurásán and Bukhárá. Ahmad was buried in Bukhárá, and they gave him the title of Sulṭán Shahíd, *i. e.* the martyred king.

**Ahmad Sarhindi,** شيخ احمد سرهندی, (Shaikh) entitled Mujaddid-i-Alf-i-Ṣání, a dervish celebrated for his piety and learning, was the son of Shaikh 'Abdul-Wáḥid Fárúḳí, and was born at Sarhind in A. D. 1563, 971 A. H. He was a disciple of Khwája Báḳí, a celebrated saint of Dihlí, and is the author of several works. He died on Tuesday, 29th November 1624, the last Tuesday in the month of Ṣafar 1034 A. H., and is buried at Sarhind. He was called "Mujaddid-i-Alf-i-Ṣání", or the "Renewer of the second Millennium", because he adopted the general belief that every thousand years a man was born, who has a thorough knowledge of the Islám, and whose vocation it is to revive and strengthen it. He believed that he was the man of the second *(ṣání)* Millennium *(alf)*.

**Ahmad, Sayyid,** of Bárha, brother of Sayyid Mahmúd Bárha, served under Akbar in Gujrát. He was in charge of Akbar's hunting leopards. His son, Sayyid Jamáluddin, was killed by the explosion of a mine before Chítor.]

**Ahmad, Sayyid,** of Bukhárá, father of the renowned Shaikh Faríd-i-Bukhárí; *vide* below.]

**Ahmad Shah,** احمد شاه, entitled Mujáhid-ud-dín Muhammad Abun-Naṣr Ahmad Sháh Bahádur, was the son of Muhammad Sháh, emperor of Dihlí, whom he succeeded on the 15th April 1748, 27th Rabí' II, 1161 A. H. His mother's name was Udham Báí. He was born in the fort of Dihlí on Tuesday, 14th December 1725, 17th Rabí' II, 1138 A. H. and crowned in Pánípat on Monday 19th April 1748, 2nd Jumáda I, 1161 A. H. After a reign of 6 years 3 months and 8 days, he was deposed and imprisoned, and afterwards blinded, together with his mother, by his prime minister 'Imád-ul-Mulk Ghází-uddín Khán, on Sunday, 2nd June 1754, N. S. After this, he lived more than 21 years, and died on the 1st of January 1775, from bodily disease. He was buried in the front of the mosque of Ḳadam-Sharíf in Dihlí, in the mausoleum of Maryam-Makání. After his imprisonment, 'A'lamgír II, son of Jahándár Sháh, was raised to the throne.

*Vide* Proceedings, As. Socy. Bengal, for 1874, p. 208.]

**Ahmad Shah I,** احمد شاه, second king of Gujrát, was the son of Tátár Khán, and grandson of Muẓaffar Sháh, whom he succeeded as king of Gujrát. The author of the Muntakhab-ut-Tawáríkh states, that his grandfather placed him on the throne during his lifetime, in the year 813 H. or 1410 A. D., and that he survived that measure five months and sixteen days. In the same year, he laid the foundation of a new city on the banks of the Sábarmatí, which he called after his own name, Ahmadábád, and which afterwards became the capital of the kings of Gujrát. The date of the laying of the foundation of this city is contained in the words "Bá-khair", *i. e.* all well. He died after a reign of nearly 33 years, on the 4th July 1443 A. D., 4th Rabí' I, 847 H., and was succeeded by his son Muḥammad Sháh.

**Ahmad Shah II,** احمد شاہ ثاني, king of Gujrát. After the death of Mahmúd Sháh III, there being no relation on whom the succession might devolve, I'timád Khán, the prime minister, resolved rather than see the kingdom in absolute anarchy, to elevate a youth, whom he asserted to be the son of prince Ahmad Khán, formerly governor of Ahmadábád, and declared him the legal successor to the crown of Gujrát. He was forthwith placed on the throne on the 18th February 1554 A. D., 15th Rabí' I, 961 A. H. He reigned 7 years and some months, and was found murdered one morning at the foot of the palace wall. This event took place on Monday the 21st April 1561 A. D., 5th Sha'bán, 968 A. H. He was succeeded by Muzaffar Sháh III.

*Vide* Áín Translation, I, 335.]

**Ahmad Shah Abdali,** احمد شاہ ابدالي, commonly called Sháh Durrání, was the son of a chief of the Afghán tribe of Abdál, in the vicinity of the city of Hirát. He was taken prisoner in his infancy by Nádir Sháh, who gave him the post of a mace-bearer, and by degrees promoted him to a considerable command in the army. The morning after the assassination of Nádir Sháh, which took place in the night of the 12th May, 1747, O. S., he made an attack, supported by a corps of Uzbaks, upon the Persian troops, but was repulsed. He then left the army, and proceeding by rapid marches to Kandahár, not only obtained possession of that city, but took a large convoy of treasure which was coming from Kábul and Sindh to the Persian camp. By the aid of these means, he laid the foundation of a kingdom, which soon attained a strength that rendered it formidable to the surrounding nations. He not only subdued Kandahár and Kábul, but took Peshá-war and Láhor; and emboldened by this success, and the weakness of the empire, he resolved the conquest of the capital of Hindústán. In the beginning of the year 1748, 1161 A. H., he began his march from Láhor. Muhammad Sháh, the emperor of Dihlí, being at this time too indisposed to take the field, despatched his only son, prince Ahmad, against the enemy, under the command of the wazír Kamar-uddín Khán, Safdar Jang, governor of Audh, and several other chiefs, with a great army. For some days several skirmishes took place between the two armies near Sarhind. At length, on Friday 11th March, 1748, 22nd Rabí' I, 1161 A. H., Kamar-uddín Khán, the wazír, being killed as he was at his devotion in his tent by a cannon ball, a panic prevailed in the Mughul army; the battle, however, continued till a magazine of rockets taking fire in the enemy's camp, numbers of the troops were wounded by the explosion; and Sháh Abdálí, either disheartened by the loss, or satisfied by the plunder gained at Sarhind, thought it proper to retreat towards Kábul, which he did unmolested. In the year 1757 A. D., 1170 A. H., he again advanced as far as Dihlí and Ágra, and after having plundered and massacred the inhabitants of Mathurá, he returned to Kandahár. About the year 1758 A. D., 1172 A. H., the Maratha power had spread itself in almost every province of Hindústán, when Najíb-ud-daula, the Rohíla, Shujá'-ud-daula Nawáb of Audh, and not only the Musalmáns but Hindús also, joined in petition to Ahmad Sháh Abdálí, that he would march and assume the throne of Dihlí in which they promised to support him. The Abdálí enraged at the seizure of Láhor by the Marathas, rejoiced at the invitation, and advanced without delay across the Indus, and driving the Marathas before him, he did not stop till they reached the vicinity of Dihlí. He engaged the Marathas in several battles, and attained the highest renown among Muhammadans by the memorable defeat that he gave the hostile army on the plains of Pánípat. This famous action was fought in January, 1761. After this victory, Durrání Sháh returned to his own country, but before his departure, he acknowledged Sháh 'Álam, then in Bengal, as emperor of Hindústán, and commanded Shujá'-ud-daula and other chiefs to submit to his authority. He died after a reign of 26 years in 1772 A. D., 1182 A. H., aged 50 years, and was succeeded by his son Timur Sháh. His tomb, covered with a gilt cupola, stands near the king's palace, and is held sacred as an asylum.

**Ahmad Shah Wali Bahmani I,** احمد شاہ ولی بہمنی, (Sultán), was the second son of Sultán Dáúd Sháh of the Bahmaní race. He ascended the throne of the Dakhin on the 15th September, 1422 A. D., 5th Shawwál 825 A. H., ten days before the demise of his brother Sultán Fírúz Sháh, who had resigned the crown in his favor. He is the founder of the city and fort of Ahmadábád Bídar, the foundation of which he laid in the year 1432 A. D., 836 A. H. It is said that the Sultán, on his return from a war at Bídar, took to the amusement of hunting; and coming to a most beautiful spot, finely watered, resolved to build upon it a city, to be called after his name, Ahmadá-bád. A citadel of great extent and strength was erected on the very site of Bídar, the ancient capital of princes, who, according to the Hindú books, 5000 years back, possessed the whole extent of Mírhat, Karnatik, and Talingána. Rájá Bhím Sen was one of the most celebrated of this house, and the history of the loves of his daughter and Rájá Nal, king of Málwá, are famous through all Hindústán. Their story was translated from the Sanskrit by Shaikh Faizí, under the title of "Nal Daman", into Persian verse, at the command of the emperor Akbar Sháh. Ahmad Sháh reigned 12 lunar years and 10 months, and died on the 19th of February 1435 A. D., 18th Rajab, 838 A. H. He was buried at Ahmadábád Bídar, and was succeeded by his son Sultán 'Alá-uddín II.

**Ahmad Shah Bahmani, II** احمد شاہ بہمنی, (Sultán). On the death of his father Sultán Mahmúd Sháh II, in October 1518 A. D., Shawwál 924 A. H., Amír Baríd, his prime-minister, dreading that the surrounding powers would attack him should he assume open independence, placed prince Ahmad, son of the late king, upon the throne at Ahmadábád Bídar, leaving him the palace, with the use of the royal jewels and a daily allowance of money for his support. The sum not being equal to his expenses, the king broke up the crown, which was valued at 400,000 huns, or £ 160,000, and privately sold the jewels. He died two years after his accession to the throne, in the year 1521 A. D., 927 A. H. After his death Amír Baríd raised Sultán 'Alá-uddín III, one of the princes, on the throne. Two years after, he was imprisoned, and another son of Mahmúd Sháh, named Walí-ullah Sháh, was placed in his room. Three years after his accession, the minister conceiving a passion for his wife, he caused him to be poisoned, and espoused the queen. He then placed Kalím-ullah, the son of Ahmad Sháh II, on the throne. This prince enjoyed nothing but the name of sovereign, and was never allowed to leave the palace. He was afterwards treated with great rigour by Amír Baríd, whereupon he made his escape, first to his uncle Ismá'íl 'Ádil Sháh to Bíjápúr, and thence to Burhán Nizám Sháh of Ahmadnagar, where he resided till his death. With him ended the dynasty of the Bahmaní kings of the Dakhin. In fact before this event, the Dakhin was divided into five kingdoms—'Ádil-Sháhí or kings of Bíjápúr; Kutb-Sháhí, or kings of Golkonda; 'Imád-Sháhí, or kings of Barar; Nizám-Sháhí or kings of Ahmadnagar; and Baríd-Sháhí, kings of Ahmadábád Bídar.

**Ahmad Shah of Bengal,** احمد شاہ, succeeded his father Jalál-uddín to the throne of Bengal in 834 H. or 1430 A. D., reigned about 16 years, and died about the year 1446 A. D., 850 A. H. He was succeeded by Násir-uddín Mahmúd Sháh I, a descendant of Shams-uddín Ilyás Sháh.]

**Ahmad Shah,** or **Ahmad-ullah Shah,** احمد شاہ, commonly called "The Maulawí", a prominent character in the neighbourhood of Shahjáhánpúr and Muhammadí during the mutiny of 1857. He is said to have been the inspired Faķír who travelled through the upper provinces, a few years ago, on a miraculous mission. He made a pretty long stay at Ágra, astonishing the natives and puzzling the authorities. It seems probable that he was even then busy in sowing the seeds of rebellion. He held great power within the city of Lakhnau, in March, 1858, when the Commander-in-chief entered that city and commanded a stronghold in the very heart of the city. He was slain at Púsain, on the 15th June 1858, sixteen miles north-east of Sháhjahánpúr, and the rájá of that place sent the head and trunk to Mr. Gilbert Money, the Commissioner.

**Ahmad Shihab-uddin Talish,** احمد شهاب الدین تالش, *vide* Shiháb-uddín Ahmad Tálish.

**Ahmad Suhaili,** امیر احمد سهیلی, (Amír), seal-bearer to Sultán Husain Mirzá of Hirát, to whom several of the poets of his time dedicated their works. Husain Wáiẓ dedicated his "Anwár Suhailí" to him. *Vide* Suhailí.

**Ahmad-ullah Shah,** commonly called "The Maulawí"; see **Ahmad Shah.**

**Ahmad Yadgar,** احمد یادگار, author of the "Táríķ-i-Salátín-i-Afághina," a history of the Afghán kings of India from Buhlíd Lodí, composed by order of Dáúd Sháh, last king of Bengal. *Vide* Dowson, V, 1.]

**Ahmad Yar Khan,** احمد یار خان, whose poetical name is Yaktá, was of the tribe of the Turks called Birlás. His father Allah Yár Khán held at different periods the súbadárí of Láhor, Tatta, and Multán, and was afterwards appointed to the Faujdarí of Ghazní. Ahmad Yár Khán also held the Súbadárí of Tatta in the latter part of the reign of 'Álamgír. He was an excellent poet, and is the author of several poems. He died on the 21st September, 1734 A. D., O. S., 23rd Jumádạ I, 1147 A. H.

**Ahmad Yar Khan,** (Nawáb), of Barelí, the son of Nawáb Ẓul-fiķár-ud-daula Muhammad Ẓul-fiķár Khán Bahádur Diláwar-Jang of Barelí. He was alive in A. D. 1815, 1230 A. H.

**Ahmad Zarruk,** احمد زروق, surname of Abul-'Abbás Ahmad bin-Ahmad bin-Muhammad bin-'Ísá Barallusí, author of the commentary, called "Sharḥ Asmá'-il-Ḥusnạ." He died in 1493 A. D., 899 A. H.

**Ahsan,** احسن, poetical name of 'Ináyat Khán, the son of Nawáb Ẓafar Khán. He was governor of Kábul in the reign of 'Álamgír and is the author of a Díwán. *Vide* Áshná.

**Ahsan-ullah Khan,** حکیم احسن الله, (Hakím), so well known at Dihlí, died in September 1873 in that city.

**Ain-uddin (Shaikh),** شیخ عین الدین of Bíjápúr, author of the "Mulḥaķát", and Kitáb-ul-Anwár, containing a history of all the Muhammadan saints of India. He flourished in the time of Sulṭán 'Alí-uddín Hasan Bahmaní.

**'Ain-ul-Mulk,** حکیم عین الملک, Ḥakím, a native of Shíráz, and a well-educated and learned Musalmán, was an officer of rank in the time of the emperor Akbar. He was an elegant poet, and his poetical name was Wafá. He died in the 40th year of the emperor's reign in 1594 A. D., 1003 A. H.

For further notes, *vide* Áín Translation I, 481.]

**'Ain-ul-Mulk (Khwaja),** خواجه عین الملک, a distinguished nobleman of the court of Sulṭán Muhammad Sháh Tughluķ and his successor Sulṭán Fíruz Sháh, kings of Dihlí. He is the author of several works, one of which is called "Tarsíl 'Ain-ul-Mulkí." He also appears to be the author of another work called "Fatḥ-námá," containing an account of the conquests of Sulṭán 'Aláuddín who reigned from 1296 to 1316 A. D.

**'Aish,** عیش, the poetical name of Muhammad 'Askarí who lived in the reign of the emperor Sháh 'Álam.

**'Aishi,** عیشی, a poet, who is the author of a Masnawí called "Haft Akhtar", or the seven planets, which he wrote in 1675 A. D., 1086 A. H.

**Ajit Singh, Raja,** راجه اجیت سنگه, a Ráṭhaurí Rájpút, and hereditary zamíndár of Máṛwáṛ, or Jodhpúr, was the son of Rájá Jaswant Singh Ráṭhaurí. He was restored in 1711 A. D. to the throne of his ancestors, and gave his daughter in marriage to the emperor Farrukhsiyar in the year 1716 A. D. He was murdered one night, when fast asleep, at the instigation of his son Abhai Singh, who succeeded him. This took place in the beginning of the reign of the emperor Muhammad Sháh.

**Ajit Singh,** a Sikh chief and murderer of Mahárájá Sher Singh of Láhor. He also slew Dhaián Singh, another chief, and was himself seized by Hirá Singh, the son of Dhaián Singh, and put to death together with Lena Singh and others. This took place in September 1843.

**'Ajiz,** عاجز, the poetical name of 'Árif-uddín Khán, who lived about 1754 A. D., 1168 A. H.

**'Ajiz,** the poetical title of Lálá Gangá Bishn, father of Rámjas Munshí, which see.

**Ajaipal,** the rájá who founded Ajmír about 1183 A. D.

**Ajmal,** اجمل, (Sháh) or Sháh Muhammad Ajmal, a Pírzáda of Alláhábád, was a descendant of Sháh Khúb-ullah, and younger brother of Sháh Ghulám Ķuṭb-uddín, the son of Sháh Muhammad Fákhir, the respectability of whose family is well known at Alláhábád. He died in the year 1821 A. D., 1236 A. H.

**Ajmiri Khan,** an inhabitant of Ajmír. He walked with the emperor Akbar from Ágra to Ajmír, on which account he received the title of Ajmírí Khán from that emperor. He had built a garden on a spot of 28 bíghas of ground at Ágra. This place is now called Ajmírí Khán-ká Tíla.

**Aka Muhammad Khan Kajar,** آقا محمد خان قاجار, king of Persia, of the tribe of Ķájár, and son of Muhammad Hasan Khán Ķájár, ruler of Mázanderán. He was made an eunuch in his childhood by 'Ádil Sháh, the nephew and immediate successor of Nádir Sháh. After the death of 'Ádil Sháh, he obtained his release, and joined his father, who was afterwards slain by Karím Khán Zand, king of Persia. Ághá or Áķá Muhammad was obliged to surrender himself to him, and was a prisoner in the city of Shíráz. He had, for some time, been very strictly guarded, and was never allowed to go beyond the walls of the town, but afterwards he was permitted to go a-hunting. When the last illness of Karím Khán assumed a dangerous appearance, he contrived to leave that city on the usual pretext of hunting. When intelligence was brought to him that the founder of the Zand dynasty was no more, accompanied by a few attendants, he commenced his flight, and favored by the confusion of the moment, he reached his province of Mázandarán in safety, and proclaimed himself one of the competitors for the crown of Persia. Soon after the death of 'Alí Murád Khán, ruler of Persia, in 1785 A. D., he made himself master of Isfahán without a battle, but had for several years to contend with Lutf 'Alí Khán, the last prince of the Zand family, before he became sole master of Persia. Lutf 'Alí Khán was put to death by him in A. D. 1795, 14th Muharram, 1212 A. H. Áká Muhammad Khán was murdered on the 10th July, 1797, by two of his attendants, whom he had sentenced to death, in the 63rd year of his age. He had been a ruler of a great part of Persia for upwards of 20 years, but had only for a short period enjoyed the undisputed sovereignty of that country. He was succeeded by his nephew Fath 'Alí Sháh, who died in 1834, 1250 A. H. After him, his grandson Muhammad Sháh, the son of 'Abbás Mirzá, mounted the throne and died in 1847, when his son Násir-uddín Ahmad Sháh, the present king of Persia, succeeded him.

**Aka Razi,** آقارضی, a poet of Persia, who came to India, and after his return home, died in 1615 A. D., 1024 A. H.

**Aka Rihi,** of Níshápúr, an author.

**Akbarabadi Mahall,** اکبر ابادی محل, A'azz-un-Nisá Begam, was the name of one of the wives of the emperor Sháh Jahán. The large red stone mosque at Faizbázár in Dihlí was built by her in the year A. D. 1651, 1060 A. H., at a cost of 150,000 Rupees. She died on the 29th January, 1677 A. D., 4th Zil-hijja, 1087 A. H., in the reign of 'Álamgír. There is also a masjid inside the city of Ágra built by her, called Akbarábádí Masjid. She had a villa also built at Ágra.

**Akbar Ali Tashbihi,** اکبرعلي تشبيهي. He is mentioned in the Khulásat-ul-Ash'ár to have been the son of a washerman. He went to India, and turned fakír, but as he was an infidel, his ascetic exercises cannot have been of much use to his soul. He left a díwán of about 8000 verses, and a masnawí, called "Zarra wa Khurshed". He was alive in 1585 A. D., 993 A. H.

Regarding this poet *vide* Áín Translation, I, 596.]

**Akbar Khan,** the son of Dost Muhammad Khán, ruler of Kábul by his first wife. He shot Sir W. H. Macnaghten on the 26th December, 1841, when his father Dost Muhammad Khán was a State prisoner in India. When his father Dost Muhammad Khán came in possession of Kábul after the retreat of the English in 1842, he was appointed heir-apparent in preference to Muhammad Afzal Khán, his eldest son by his second wife. He died in 1848, when his full brother Ghulám Haidar Khán was nominated heir-apparent, after whose death, in 1858, Sher 'Alí his brother, the present Amír, was nominated.

**Akbar,** (Prince) the youngest son of the emperor 'Álamgír, was born on the 10th September, 1657, O. S., 11th Zil-hijja, 1067 A. H., raised the standard of rebellion against his father, and joined the Maratha chief Sambhují in June 1681. He afterwards quitted his court, and repaired to Persia, where he died in 1706, 1118 A. H., a few months before his father, and was buried at Mashhad in Khurásán. 'Álamgír, at one time, intended to make Akbar his successor, and this preference arose from Akbar being the son of a Muhammadan mother, the daughter of Sháh Nawáz Khán; whereas his brothers Sultáns Mu'azzam and A'zam were born of Rájpút princesses.

**Akbar Shah,** اکبر شاه, the Great, emperor of Hindústán, surnamed Abul-Fath Jalál-uddín Muhammad, was the eldest son of the emperor Humáyún, and was born in Amarkot in the province of Sindh on Sunday the 15th October, 1542 A. D., 5th Rajab, 949 A. H., at a time when his father, after being defeated by Sher Sháh, had taken refuge with Ráná Prashád. At the time of his father's death, Akbar was at Kálánúr, where he had been deputed by his father with a considerable force to expel the ex-king Sikandar Sháh Súr from the Siwálik mountains. When information reached the prince of this mournful event, Bairám Khán, and other officers who were present, raised him to the throne on Friday, 14th February, 1556, A D., 2nd Rabí' II, 963 A. H., Akbar being then only 13 years and 9 months old. He enlarged his dominions by the conquest of Gujrát, Bengal, Kashmír, and Sindh. Besides the forts of Atak, Ágra, and Alláhábád, many military works were erected by him. He also built and fortified the town of Fathpúr Síkrí, which was his principal residence, and which, though now deserted, is one of the most splendid remains of former grandeur of India. He died after a prosperous reign of 51 lunar years and 9 months on Wednesday, the 16th October, 1605, Old Style, 13th Jumáda II, 1014 A. H., aged 64 lunar years and 11 months. The words "Faut-i-Akbar Sháh," (the death of Akbar Sháh) are the chronogram of his death. He was buried in the village of Sikandra in the environs of Ágra, where a splendid mausoleum was built over his remains by his son Jahángír, which is still in a high state of preservation. He received after his death the title of "Arsh-'Ashyání," and was succeeded by his son Sultán Salím, who assumed the title of Jahángír. His mother's name was Hamída Bánú, commonly called Maryam-Makání. The history of this potentate has been written, with great elegance and precision by his wazír Abul-Fazl, in a work, entitled the "Akbar-náma." In order to keep his turbulent Umarás, Turks, and Afgháns, in check, Hindú chiefs were encouraged by Akbar, and entrusted with the highest powers, both military and civil, as was the case with Rájá Máldeo of Márwár, Bhagwán Dás of Amber, Mán Singh, his son, and Rájá Todar Mal. He also connected himself and his sons with them by marriage. Both Akbar and his successor, Jahángír, had amongst their wives several of Hindú origin. Towards the middle of his reign, Akbar became dissatisfied with the Muhammadan religion, and invited to his court teachers of the Christian, Hindú, and Parsí religions, and took an interest in their discussions. He adopted, however, neither, but attempted to found a new system of belief, called 'Dín-i-Iláhí', which acknowledged one God, and the king as his vicegerent.

**Akbar Shah II,** اکبر شاه ثانی, king of Dihlí, whose title in full is Abul-Nasr Mu'in-uddín Muhammad Akbar Sháh, was the son of the nominal emperor Sháh 'Álam; was born on Wednesday, 23rd April, 1760, New Style, 7th Ramazán, 1173 H., and succeeded his father at the age of 48, on the 19th of November, 1806 A. D., 7th Ramazán, 1221 H., as titular king of Dihlí. On his accession he made some weak attempts to increase his influence and power. These were properly resisted, but at the same time the pledge given by Lord Wellesley, to increase the allowance of the imperial family when the revenue of the country improved, was redeemed by an act of politic liberality. An augmentation of ten thousand rupees per mensem was appropriated for the support of his eldest son, whom he had declared heir-apparent. He sat on the throne of his ancestors nearly 32 lunar years; died on Friday, 28th September, 1837, 28th Jumáda II, 1253 A. H., aged about 80 lunar years, and was buried at Dihlí, close to the tomb of Bahádur Sháh. His son Bahádur Sháh II, the last king of Dihli, succeeded him. Akbar some time wrote poetry and used the word Shu'á' for his poetical name.

**Akhfash Ausat,** اخفش اوسط was called Akhfash, because he had small eyes. His proper name is Abul-Hasan Sa'íd. He was an author and died in the year 830 A. D. Some say he was born at Balkh and died in 376 A. H. There were three persons of this name, all of whom were authors. Akhfash Asghar, or the lesser, died in 845 A. D.

**Akhtar,** اختر, the poetical name of Kází Muhammad Sádik Khán, an excellent writer of prose and verse.

**Akhtar,** اختر, the poetical name of Wájid 'Alí Sháh, the last king of Audh, now of Garden Reach, Calcutta.

**'Akidat Khan,** عقیدت خان, title of Mír Mahmúd, brother of Asálat Khán Mashhadí. He came to India in the 14th year of 'A'lamgír, A. D. 1670, and was raised to the rank of 1,000 and 400 sawárs.

**'Akil,** عقیل, 'A'kíl the brother of 'Alí. There is a story of him that being displeased with his brother 'Alí the Khalífa, he went over to Mu'áwiya, who received him with great kindness and respect, but desired him to curse 'Alí; and as he would not admit of any refusal, 'Akíl thus addressed the congregation:—" O people! you know that 'Alí, the son of Abú-Tálib, is my brother: now Mu'áwiya has ordered me to curse him; therefore, may the curse of God be upon him." So that the curse would either apply to 'Alí or to Mu'áwiya.

**Akil Khan,** عاقل خان, 'A'kil Khán, nephew of Afzal Khán wazír, a nobleman of 3,000, who served under the emperor Sháh Jahán, and died A. D. 1649, 1059 A. H.

**Akil Khan, (Nawab),** نواب عاقل خان, the title of Mír 'Askarí. He was a native of Khawáf in Khurásán, and held the office of wizárat in the time of the emperor 'A'lamgír. He was an excellent poet; and as he had a great respect for Sháh Burhán-uddín, entitled Ráz-i-Iláhí, he chose the word Rázi for his poetical title. He is the author of several works, among which are a Masnawí and Díwán. He died A. D. 1695, 1108 A. H. *Vide* Rází.

**Akmal-uddin Muhammad bin-Mahmud,** (Shaikh) author of a commentary on the Hidáya, entitled "'Ináya" or "al-'Ináya". There are two commentaries on the Hidáya, commonly known by that name, but the one much-esteemed for its studious analysis and interpretation of the text, is by this author: it was published in Calcutta in 1837. This author died in 1384 A. D., 786 A. H.

**'Akrima,** or more correctly, **'Ikrima,** عکرمه, surname of Abú-'Abdullah, who was a freed slave of Ibn-'Abbás, and became afterwards his disciple. He was one of the greatest lawyers. He died in the year 725 A. D., 107 A. H.

**Aksir,** or more correctly, **Iksir (Mirza),** اکسیر اصفهانی مرزا, of Isfahán, author of a book of elegies. He served under Nawáb Nizám-ul-Mulk A'saf-Jáh and Safdar-Jang, and died in Bengal in 1756 N. S., 1169 A. H.

**Alahdad Sarhindi,** or more correctly, **Ilahdad,** poetically styled Faizí, a native of Sarhind, and author of a Persian Dictionary called "Madár ul-Afázil".

Regarding this dictionary and its author, *vide* Journal, As. Socy., Bengal, 1868, p. 10.]

**Al-Ahnaf,** الاحنف, uncle of Yazíd, the second khalífa of the house of Umayya. At the battle of Siffín he had fought on the side of 'Alí. Several sayings of this celebrated chief are recorded in the Biographical Dictionary of Ibn Khallikán. He outlived Mu'áwiya.

**Alahwirdi Khan,** الله وردی خان, or more correctly, **Ilahwirdi Khan,** a nobleman of the reign of the emperor Jahángír. He was raised to the rank of 5000 in the time of Sháh Jahán, and held several offices of importance. He was appointed governor of Patna, and espoused the cause of Sultán Shujá', brother of Aurangzíb, A. D. 1658, 1068 A. H., and after the defeat of Shujá', accompanied him to Bengal, where he was slain together with his son Saif-ullah by order of that prince in July 1659, Zil-ka'da, 1069 A. H.

The word *wirdi* or *wirdi* means "a rope", God being the *habl-i-matín*, the strong rope which the faithful seize so as not to perish.]

**Alahwirdi Khan,** الله وردی خان, or more correctly, **Ilahwirdi Khan,** title of Ja'far Khán, the son of Iláhwírdí Khán the first. He was raised to the rank of an amír by 'A'lamgír, with the title of Ilahwardí Khán 'A'lamgír-Sháhí. He was appointed Súbadár of Alláhábád, where he died A. D. 1669, 1079 A. H. He was an excellent poet and has left a díwán.

**Alahwirdi Khan** الله وردی خان مهابت جنگ, or more correctly, **Allahwirdi Khan,** styled Mahábat-Jang, the usurper of the government of Bengal, was originally named Mírzá Muhammad 'Alí. His father Mírzá Muhammad, a Turkmán, a officer in the service of the prince A'zam Sháh, on the death of his patron in 1707 A. D., falling into distress, moved from Dihlí to Katak, the capital of Orísá, in hopes of mending his fortune under Shujá'-uddín, the son-in-law of Nawáb Murshid Kulí Ja'far Khán, Súbadár of Bengal, who received him with kindness and after some time bestowed on his son the Faujdárí of Rájmahall, and procured for him from the emperor a mansab and the title of Allahwardí Khán, and afterwards that of Mahábat-Jang. After the death of Shujá'-uddín, and the accession of his son Sarfaráz Khán to the government of Bengal, Allahwírdí contrived to murder the latter in 1740 A. D., 1153 A. H., and usurped the government. He reigned sixteen years over the three provinces of Bengal, Bihár, and Orísá, and died on Saturday, the 10th April, 1756, N. S., 9th Rajab, 1169 A. H., aged 80 years. He was buried in Murshidábád near the tomb of his mother in the garden of Khush-Bágh, and was succeeded by his grand-nephew and grandson Mírzá Mahmúd, better known by his assumed name of Siráj-ud-daula. It does not appear that Allahwírdí ever remitted any part of the revenue to Dihlí.

**Alah Yar Khan,** شیخ الله یار خان, or more correctly, **Ilah Yar Khan,** (Shaikh), son of Shaikh 'Abdus-Subhán, was formerly employed by Nawáb Mubáriz-ul-Mulk Sarbaland Khán, governor of Gujrát, and in the reign of the emperor Farrukhsiyar was raised to the rank of 6,000, with the title of Rustam Zamán Khán. In the time of the emperor Muhammad Sháh, when Rájá Abhai Singh, the son of Rájá Ajít Singh Márwárí, was appointed governor of Gujrát in the room of Nawáb Sarbaland Khán, the latter made some opposition to his successor; a battle ensued, and Shaikh Iláh Yár, who was then with the nawáb, was killed in the action. This took place on the day of Dasahrá, 5th October, 1730, O. S., 8th Rabí' II, 1143 A. H.

**Alah Yar Khan,** الله یارخان ابن افتخار خان, or more correctly, **Ilah Yar Khan,** son of Iftikhár Khán Turkmán, a nobleman of the court of Sháh Jahán. He died in Bengal in A. D. 1650, 1060 A. H.

**Alah Yar Khan Mir-Tuzuk,** الله یار خان میر توزک, or more correctly, **Ilah Yar Khan,** a nobleman in the time of the emperor 'A'lamgír, who held the rank of 1,500, and died A. D. 1662, 1073 A. H.

**Al-Amin,** الامین, the 6th khalífa of the house of 'Abbás, succeeded his father Hárún-ur-Rashíd to the throne of Baghdád, in March, 809 A. D., 193 A. H. He was no sooner seated on the throne than he formed a design of excluding his brother al-Mámún from the succession. Accordingly, he deprived him of the furniture of the imperial palace of Khurásán; and in open violation of his father's will, who had bestowed on al-Mámún the perpetual government of Khurásán and of all the troops in that province, he ordered these forces to march directly to Baghdád. Upon the arrival of this order, al-Mámún expostulated with the general al-Fazl Ibn Rabí'a, who commanded his troops, and endeavoured to prevent his marching to Baghdád; but without effect, for he punctually obeyed the orders sent by the khalífa. Al-Fazl having ingratiated himself with the khalífa by his ready compliance with his orders, was chosen prime-minister, and governed with absolute sway, al-Amín abandoning himself entirely to drunkenness. Al-Fazl was a very able minister; but fearing al-Mámún's resentment, if ever he should ascend the throne, he gave al-Amín such advice as proved in the end the ruin of them both. He advised him to deprive al-Mámún of the right of succession that had been given him by his father, and transfer it to his own son Músa, though then but an infant. Agreeable to this pernicious advice, the khalífa sent for his brother al-Kásim from Mesopotamia, and recalled al-Mámún from Khurásán, pretending he had occasion for him as an assistant in his councils. By this ill-treatment al-Mámún was so much provoked, that he resolved to come to an open rupture with his brother. A war soon after broke out between them. Táhir ibn-Husain, the general of al-Mámún, laid siege to Baghdád, took it, and having seized al-Amín, cut off his head, and exposed it to public view in the streets of Baghdád. Afterwards he sent it to al-Mámún in Khurásán, together with the ring or seal of the khiláfat, the sceptre and the imperial robe. At the sight of these, al-Mámún fell down on his knees, and returned thanks to God for his success, making the courier who brought the insignia a present of a million of dirhams. The death of al-Amín took place on the 6th October, 813 A. D., 6th Safar, 198 A. H. He was then 30 years of age, and had reigned but four years and some months.

**Alamayo,** (Prince), the son of king Theodore of Abyssinia. After the fall of Magdala and the death of his father, 10th April, 1868, he was sent to England to be educated.

**'Alamgir I,** عالمگیر بادشاہ, emperor of Hindústán, surnamed Abul-Zafar Muhi-uddín Muhammad Aurangzíb, took the title of 'Álamgír on his accession to the throne. He was the third son of the emperor Sháh Jahán, born on Sunday, 10th October, 1619 O. S., 11th Zíl-ka'da, 1028 H. His mother's name was Arjmand Bánú, surnamed Mumtáz-Mahall. In his youth, he put on the appearance of religious sanctity, but in June, 1658, Ramzán, 1068 H., during his father's illness, he in conjunction with his brother Murád Bakhsh, seized Ágra, and made his father prisoner. Murád was soon after imprisoned by 'Álamgír, who marched to Dihlí, where he caused himself to be proclaimed emperor on the 21st July of the same year, 1st Zíl-ka'da, 1068 H., but was not crowned till the first anniversary of his accession, a circumstance which has introduced some confusion in the chronology of his reign. Soon after, he put Murád Bakhsh and his eldest brother the heir-apparent Dárá Shikoh to death. He greatly enlarged his dominions, and became so formidable, that all Eastern princes sent ambassadors to him. He was an able prince, but a bigoted Sunní, and attempted to force the Hindús to adopt that faith, destroying their temples, and levying the capitation tax *(jizya)* from every Hindú. The feudatory chiefs of Rájpútáná successfully resisted the impost. He died after a reign of 50 lunar years at Ahmadábád in the Dakhin, on Friday, the 21st of February, 1707 O. S., 28th Zíl-ka'da, 1118 H., aged 90 lunar years and 17 days, and was interred in the court of the mausoleum of Shaikh Zain-uddín, in Khuldábád, 8 *kos* from the city of Aurangábád. After his death, he received the title of "Hazrat Khuld-Makán", (*i. e.* He whose place is in paradise). He was married in the 19th year of his age to a daughter of Sháhnawáz Khán, the son of 'Ásaf Khán the prime minister of the emperor Jahángír, by whom he had 5 sons and 5 daughters. His eldest son, named Sultán Muhammad, died before his father; his second son was Muhammad Mu'azzam who succeeded him with the title of Sháh 'Álam Bahádur Sháh; the third A'zam Sháh was slain in battle fought against the latter; the fourth Muhammad Akbar, who revolted against his father, took refuge in Persia and died there; the fifth Kám Bakhsh who was also slain in battle. The names of his 4 daughters are,—Zeb-un-Nisá, Zínut-un-Nisá, Badr-un-Nisá, and Mihr-un-Nisá.

**'Alamgir II,** 'Azíz-uddín, was the son of the emperor Jahándár Sháh by Anúp Báí; was born in 1688 A. D., 1099 A. H., and raised to the throne in the fort of Dihlí by 'Imád-ul-Mulk Ghází-uddín Khán the wazír, on Sunday the 2nd June, 1754, N. S., 10th Sha'bán, 1167 A. H., after the deposition and imprisonment of Ahmad Sháh, the son of the emperor Muhammad Sháh. He was, after a nominal reign of 5 years and some months, assassinated by the same person who had placed him on the throne, on the 29th November, 1759, N. S., 8th Rabí' II, 1173 H., and was interred in the platform before the mausoleum of the emperor Humáyún. His son 'Álí Gauhar (afterwards Sháh 'Álam) being then in Bengal, Muhiy-ul-Sunnat, son of Kám Bakhsh, the son of the emperor Aurangzíb, was seated on the throne, with the title of Sháh Jahán, and insulted by the empty name of emperor for some months, after which on the 10th October 1760 N. S., 29th Safar, 1174 H., the Marathas having plundered Dihlí, prince Mírzá Jawán Bakht, the son of 'Álí Gauhar, was placed on the throne by the Maratha chief Bháo, as regent to his father, who was still in Bengal.

**Alap Arsalan,** *vide* Alp Arsalan.

**Alaptigin** or **Alptigin,** الپتگین, one of the chief nobles of Bukhárá, and governor of Khurásán during the reign of the house of Sámán. Having in 962 A. D. renounced his allegiance to that court, he retired, with his followers, to Ghazní, then an insignificant town, to escape the resentment of Amír Mansúr Sámání, whose elevation to the throne he had opposed, on the ground of his extreme youth. He established a petty principality, of which Ghazní became the capital. He died A. D. 976, 366 A. H., when his son Abú-Is-hák succeeded him; but that weak and dissipated prince survived his father but a short time; and the suffrage of all ranks gave the rule to Subiktagín, a chief in the service of Alaptigín in 977 A. D., 367 A. H.

**Al-Aswad,** الاسود, an impostor, *vide* Musailama.

**'Ala-ud-daula,** علاؤالدولہ, *vide* Alá-ud-daula.

**'Ala-ud-daula,** نواب علاؤالدولہ, (Prince), the son of Báisanghar Mirzá and grandson of Sháhrukh Mirzá, after whose death in A. D. 1447, he ascended the throne at Hirát, but was soon driven from it by his uncle Ulugh Beg. After the death of Ulugh Beg, A. D. 1449, he was imprisoned and blinded by his brother Sultán Bábar. He died in A. D. 1459, A. H. 863.

**'Ala-ud-daula,** نواب علاؤ الدولہ, a Nawáb of Bengal. *Vide* Sarfaráz Khán.

**'Ala-ud-daula, (Mir** or **Mirza),** میر علاؤ الدولہ, a poet whose poetical name was Káfí. He is the author of a biography of those poets who flourished in the reign of the emperor Akbar. The time of his death is not known, but he was living at the time of the conquest of Chítor by Akbar in 1567 A. D., 975 A. H. There is some mistake in his poetical name; he appears to be the same person who is mentioned under the poetical name of Kámí, which see.

**'Ala-ud-daula Samnani,** علاؤالدولہ سمنانی, one of the chief followers of the Súfí Junaid Baghdádí. In his youth he served Arghún Khán, the Tartar king of Persia, and his uncle Sharaf-uddín Samnání was a nobleman at the court. He died on Friday the 8th of March 1336 A. D., 23rd Rajab, 736 A. H., aged 77 lunar years, six years before Khwajá Kirmání.

**'Ala-uddin,** علاؤالدين, a Muhammadan prince of the Arsacides or Assassins, better known by the appellation of "The old man of the mountains". His residence was a castle between Damascus and Antioch, and was surrounded by a number of youths, whom he intoxicated with pleasures, and rendered subservient to his views, by promising still greater voluptuousness in the next world. As these were employed to stab his enemies, he was dreaded by the neighbouring princes. *Vide* Hasan Sabbáḥ.

**'Ala-uddin (Khwaja),** خواجه علاؤ الدين عطاملک, surnamed 'Atá Málik was the brother of Shams-uddín Muhammad Ṣáḥib, díwán, and is the author of a history called "Jahánkushá".

**'Ala-uddin 'Ali al-Kuraishi ibn-Nafis,** ابن نفيس علاؤالدين علي القريشي, author of the commentary termed "Mújiz-ul Ḳánún fil-Ṭibb", being an epitome of the canons of Avicenna. He died A. D. 1288.

**'Ala-uddin Atsiz,** علاؤ الدين التنز, the son of 'Alá-uddín Hasan Ghorí. He defeated Bahá-uddín Sám in 1210 A. D. and reigned four years in Ghor. He fell in battle against Táj-uddín Ildúz A. D. 1214, and was the last of the kings of Ghor, of the family of 'Alá-uddín Hasan.

**'Ala-uddin Hasan,** علاؤ الدين حسن غوري, prince of Ghór, entitled Jahán-sóz. His elder brother Ḳuṭb-uddín, prince of Ghór, was publicly executed by his brother-in-law Bahrám Sháh of Ghazní in 1119 A. D., 513 A. H. Saif-ud-daula brother of the deceased took possession of Ghazní in 1148 A. D., 543 A. H., but afterwards was defeated, taken prisoner and put to death by Bahrám Sháh in 1149 A. D., 544 A. H. When the mournful news of his brother's death reached 'Alá-uddín, he burnt with rage and being determined to take revenge, invaded Ghazní with a great army. He defeated Bahrám Sháh, who fled to Láhor, took possession of Ghazní in 1152 A. D., 574 A. H., and gave up the city to flames, slaughter, and devastation for several days, on which account he is known by the epithet of "Jahán-sóz," or the burner of the world. He carried his animosity so far as to destroy every monument of the Ghazní emperors with the exception of those of Sultán Mahmúd, Mas'úd, and Ibráhím; but he defaced all the inscriptions, even of their times, from every public edifice. 'Alá-uddín died in the year 1156 A. D., 549 A. H., after a reign of 6 years, and was succeeded by his son Malik Saif-uddín or Saif-ud-daula who in little more than a year fell in battle with the Ghiza Turkmáns. He was succeeded by his eldest cousin Ghiyáṣ-uddín Muhammad Ghorí.

The following is a list of the kings of Ghór:

1. 'Alá-uddín Hasan Ghorí.
2. Malik Saif-uddín, son of do.
3. Ghiyáṣ-uddín Muhammad Ghorí, son of Bahá-uddín Sám, the younger brother of 'Alá-uddín.
4. Shiháb-uddín, brother of Ghiyáṣ-uddín.
5. Ghiyáṣ-uddín Mahmúd, son of Ghiyáṣ-uddín.
6. Bahá-uddín Sám, son of Ghiyáṣ-uddín Mahmúd.
7. Atsiz, son of Jahán-sóz and last of the kings of Ghór of this branch.

**'Ala-uddin (I),** علاؤ الدين حسن کانگوه بهمني, Hasan Kángoh Bahmaní, the first Bahmaní king of the Dakhin. He was a native of Dihlí, and in the service of a Brahmanical astrologer named Kángoh, or Gángoh, enjoying high favor with the prince Muhammad Tughluḳ, afterwards king of Dihlí. This Brahman assured Hasan that he perceived from his horoscope that he would rise to great distinction, and be eminently favored of the Almighty; and made him promise that if he ever should attain regal power, he would use the name of Kángoh and employ him as his minister of finance, a request with which Hasan readily complied. The governor of Daulatábád and others having revolted took possession of the place, and selected Hasan (who had then the title of Ẓafar Khán and a jágír in the Dakhin) to be their king. On Friday, the 3rd August, 1347 A. D., 24th Rabí' II, 748 A. H., they crowned him and raised him on the throne, with the title of 'Alá-uddín Hasan Kángoh Bahmaní at Kulbarga, which place became the royal residence and capital of the first Muhammadan king of the Dakhin, and was named Ahsanábád. Towards the end of the reign of Muhammad Tughluḳ of Dihlí, he subdued every part of the Dakhin previously subject to the throne of Dihlí. The death of 'Alá-uddín Hasan happened 10 years, 10 months and 7 days after his accession to the throne, about the 10th of February 1358 A. D., 1st Rabí' I, 759 A. H. He was succeeded by his son Muhammad Sháh I Bahmaní. The following is a list of the kings of the Bahmaní dynasty of Kulbarga or Ahsanábád with the years of their accessions:

| | | |
|---|---|---|
| 'Alá-uddín Hasan I, .......... | 748 H., | 1347 A. D. |
| Muhammad Sháh I, .......... | 759 H., | 1358 A. D. |
| Mujáhid Sháh, .............. | 776 H., | 1375 A. D. |
| Dáúd Sháh,.................. | 780 H., | 1378 A. D. |
| Mahmúd Sháh, .............. | 780 H., | 1378 A. D. |
| Ghiyáṣ-uddín,................ | 799 H., | 1397 A. D. |
| Shams-uddín, ................ | 799 H., | 1397 A. D. |
| Fírúz Sháh Roz-afzún, ........ | 800 H., | 1397 A. D. |
| Ahmad Sháh Walí, .......... | 825 H., | 1422 A. D. |
| 'Alá-uddín Ahmad II, ........ | 838 H., | 1435 A. D. |

Humáyún the cruel.
Niẓám Sháh.
Muhammad Sháh II.
Mahmúd II.
Ahmad Sháh II.
'Alá-uddín III.
Walí-ullah.
Kalím-ullah, with whom the Bahmaní dynasty terminates, and is succeeded by Amír Baríd at Ahmadábád Bídar.

**'Ala-uddin II,** سلطان علاؤ الدين ثاني, (Sulṭán) son of Sulṭán Ahmad Sháh Walí Bahmaní, ascended the throne at Ahmadábád Bídar in the Dakhin, in the month of February 1435 A. D., 838 A. H., and died after a reign of 23 years, 9 months and 20 days in the year 1457 A. D., 862 A. H. He was succeeded by son Humáyún, a cruel prince.

**'Ala-uddin Khilji,** سلطان علاؤالدين خلجي سکندرثاني, (Sulṭán) styled Sikandar-i-Ṣání, 'the second Alexander' was the nephew and son-in-law of Sulṭán Jalál-uddín Fírúz Sháh Khiljí, whom he murdered at Kaṛa-Mánikpúr in the province of Alláhábád on the 29th July, 1296 A. D., 17th Ramaẓán, 695 A. H., and marching thence with his army ascended the throne of Dihlí in the month of October the same year, Ẓil-ḥijja, 695 A. H., after having defeated and removed Rukn-uddín Ibráhím, the son of Fírúz Sháh. He was the first Musalmán king who made an attempt to conquer the Dakhin. He took the fort of Chítor in August, 1303 A. D., 3rd Muḥarram, 703 H. It is said that the empire never flourished so much as in his reign. Palaces, mosques, universities, baths, mausolea, forts and all kinds of public and private buildings, seemed to rise as if by magic. Among the poets of his reign, we may record the names of Amír Khusrau, Khwája Hasan, Ṣadr-uddín 'Alí, Fakhr-uddín Khawáṣ, Ḥamíd-uddín Rájá, Mauláná 'Arif, 'Abdul-Ḥakím and Shiháb-uddín Ṣadr-Nishín. In poetry Amír Khusrau and Khwája Hasan had the first rank. In philosophy and physic, Mauláná Badr-uddín Dámishḳí. In divinity, Mauláná Shitábí. In astrology, Shaikh Niẓám-uddín Auliyá acquired much fame. 'Alá-uddín died, according to Firishta, on the 6th Shawwál, 716 A. H. (or 19th December, 1316 A. D.) after having reigned more than 20 years. He was buried in the tomb which he had constructed in his life-time near the Manihár Masjid in Old Dihlí. Amír Khusrau in that part of his Díwán, called "Baḳiya-i-Naḳiya" says that he died on the 6th Shawwál, 715 H., *i. e.* about the 30th December 1315 A. D. After his death, Malik Náib Káfúr, one of the eunuchs of the king, placed his youngest son Sulṭán Shiháb-uddín 'Umar, who was then only seven years old, on the throne. After a short time, however, the eunuch Káfúr was slain, and Shiháb-uddín was set aside, and his elder brother Mubárak Khán under the title of Mubárik Sháh ascended the throne on the 1st April, 1316 A. D., 7th Muḥarram, 716 H. but according to Firishta in 1317. It was the boast of 'Alá-uddín, that he had destroyed one thousand temples in Banáras alone. He is best known now by the beautiful gateway to the Kutb Mosque and the unfinished tower by which he hoped to rival the Kutb Minár.

**'Ala-uddin 'Imad Shah,** علاءالدين عماد شاه, succeeded to the government of Barár in the Dakhin after the death of his father Fatḥ-ullah 'Imád Sháh about the year 1513 A. D., and following the example of other chiefs of the house of Bahmaní, declared himself king of Barár, and established his royal residence at Gawal. He contracted an alliance by marriage with the sister of Ismá'íl 'Adil Sháh, named Khadíja, in 1528 A. D., 935 A. H., and died some time about the year 1532 A. D., 939 A. H. He was succeeded by his son Daryá 'Imád Sháh.

**'Ala-uddin Kaikubad,** علاؤالدين كيقباد, (Sulṭán) a prince of the Saljúkian dynasty. When Sulṭán Malik-Sháh conquered Rúm or Anatolia in Asiatic Turkey, he conferred on Sulaimán the son of Kutlumish that kingdom, whose descendants reigned there till the time of Abáḳá Khán, the Tartar king of Persia. 'Alá-uddín Kaikubád was a descendant of Sulaimán Sháh and died about the year 1239 A. D., 637 A. H.; *vide* Sulaimán bin-Kutlumish.

**'Ala-uddin Majzub,** شاه علاؤ الدين مجذوب, (Sháh) a Muhammadan saint of Agra, commonly called Sháh 'Alá-wal Baláwal, son of Sayyid Sulaimán. He died in the beginning of the reign of Islám Sháh, son of Sher Sháh in the year 1546 A. D., 953 A. H. His tomb is in Agra at a place called Náí-kí Manḍí, where crowds of Musalmáns assemble every year to worship it. The adjacent mosque has sunk into the ground to the spring of the arches.

**'Ala-uddin Mas'ud,** علاؤ الدين مسعود, Sulṭán of Dihlí, was the son of Sulṭán Rukn-uddín Fírúz, and grandson of Shams-uddín Iltitmish, was raised to the throne of Dihlí after the murder of Bahrám Sháh in May, 1242 A. D., Ẕil-ḳa'da, 639 A. H. He died on the 10th June, 1246 A. D., 23rd Muḥarram, 644 H., after a reign of four years, and was succeeded by his brother (or uncle) Sulṭán Náṣir-uddín Mahmúd.

**'Ala-uddin Muhammad al-Samarkandi,** قندي محمد علاؤ الدين السمر, (Shaikh) author of a compendium of Al-Kudúrí's Mukhtaṣir, which he entitled the "Tuḥfat-ul-Fukahá." This work was commented upon by his pupil Abú-Bakr bin-Mas'úd al-Káshání, who died in 1191 A. D., 587 A. H. This comment is entitled al-Badái' as-Ṣanái'.

**'Ala-uddin Ali Shah,** علاؤالدين على شاه, king of Western Bengal. He usurped the government of that country after defeating Fakhr-uddín Mubárak Sháh and was assassinated about 746 A. H. by the instigation of Khwája Ilyás, who succeeded him under the title of Shams-uddín Ilyás Sháh.]

**'Ala-uddin Husain Shah,** علاؤالدين حسين شاه, king of Bengal. He was the son of Sayyid Ashraf, and after defeating Muẓaffar Sháh at Gaur in 899 A. H., ascended the throne of Bengal. He reigned with justice for a considerably longer period than any of his predecessors until the year 1521 A. D., 927 A. H. when he died a natural death, after a reign of 28 years. His son Nuṣrat Sháh succeeded him.

**'Ala-uddin (Sultan),** سلطان علاؤالدين سلجوقى, a king of the race of Saljúḳ, who reigned in Iconium, and died in the year 1301 A. D., 700 A. H.

**'Ala-uddin (Sultan),** سلطان علاؤالدين پادشاه دهلى, the last king of Dihlí of the Sayyid dynasty, succeeded his father Sulṭán Muhammad Sháh to the throne in January 1446 A. D., Shawwál, 849 A. H. Bahlól Lodí in 1451, 855 A. H., at the instigation of Ḥamíd Khán wazír, took possession of Dihlí during the absence of the king who was then at Badáoṇ. 'Alá-uddín continued to reside at Badáoṇ unmolested till his death, which happened in the year 1478 A. D., 883 A. H. His reign at Dihlí being about six years, and his government of Badáoṇ 28 years.

**'Ala-uddin (Sayyid),** of Oudh, whose poetical name was Wáṣilí, is the author of a Tarjí'band, commonly called "Mámuḳímán," with which word it commences. He was a native of Khurásán, came to India about the year 1300 A. D., became a disciple of Niẓám-uddín Auliyá and fixed his residence in Oudh.

**'Ala-uddin Takash,** علاؤالدين تكش, a Sulṭán of Khwárizm, *vide* Takash.

**'Ala-ul-mulk Kotwal,** ملک علاؤالملک کوتوال, (Malik). He served under Sulṭán 'Alá-uddin Khiljí, king of Dihlí, and was the uncle of Ẓiyá-uddín Barni, the author of the "Táríkh Fíruz-Sháhí." He was then very old and so fat that he was not able to attend the court more than once a month. He was living in A. D. 1300, 699 A. H.

**'Al-AzizBillah Abu-al-Mansur Tarar,** ابوالمنصورطرار العزيز بالله, son of Mu'izz-ud-dín-allah, second khalífa of Egypt of the Fáṭimite dynasty, succeeded his father in A. D. 976, and committed the management of affairs entirely to the care of Jauhar or Ja'far, his father's long-experienced general and prime-minister. This famous warrior after several battles with Al-Aftakín, the amír of Damascus and the Karmatians, died in 990 A. D., 381 A. H. 'Al-Aziz died in his way to Syria in the 21st year of his reign and 42nd of his age and was succeeded by his son Abul-Manṣúr.

**Al-Baghawi,** البغوى, *vide* Abul-Faraj-al-Baghawí and Abú-Muhammad Farráí ibn-Mas'úd al-Baghawí.

**Al-Batani,** البطنى, commonly called by European writers Albategnius, was an Arabian astronomer who wrote a treatise on the knowledge and the obliquity of the Zodiac of the stars. He died in 929. He greatly reformed astronomy, comparing his own observations with those of Ptolemy. This book was printed at Nüremberg, in 1537, 4to., and at Bologna in 1545. He died A. D. 929.

**Al-Biruni,** ابروني, an Arabian author whose original work, entitled "Táríkh Hind", was compiled in India in about A. D. 1030-33. See Abú-Raiḥán.

**Al-Bukhari,** البخارى, who received this name from Bukhárá, the place of his birth or his chief residence, was a famous lawyer by name of Muhammad Ismá'íl. His collection of traditions on the Muhammadan religion, commonly called Ṣaḥíḥ-ul-Bukhárí, is of the greatest authority of all that have ever been made; he called it "Al-Ṣaḥíḥ," *i. e.* genuine, because he separated the spurious ones from those that were authentic. He says, he has selected 7,275 of the most authentic traditions out of 10,000, all of which he looked upon to be true, having rejected 200,000 as false. He died at Bukhára in the year 870 A. D., 256 A. H. *Vide* Muhammad Ismá'íl Bukhárí.

**Al-Dawani,** *vide* Dawání.

**'Ali,** علی ابن ابی طالب, son of Abú-Ṭálib, was the cousin and son-in-law of Muhammad. He was born 23 years before the Hijrí, *i. e.*, in the year 599 A. D., at the very temple itself. His mother's name was Fáṭima, daughter of Asad the son of Háshim. After the death of Muhammad, he was opposed in his attempts to succeed the prophet by 'Uṣmán and 'Umar, and retired into Arabia where his mild and enlarged interpretation of the Ḳurán, increased the number of his proselytes. After the death of 'Uṣmán, the 3rd khalífa, he was acknowledged khalífa by the Egyptians and Arabians in July, 655 A. D., but in less than 5 years after, he was compelled to resign that title, and Mu'áwiya was proclaimed khalífa at Damascus. 'Alí was subsequently wounded by 'Abdur-Rahmán ibn-Muljim in a mosque at Kúfa, whilst engaged in his evening prayers, on Friday, the 22nd January, 661, A. D., 17th Ramaẓán, 40 A. H., and died four days after. 'Alí after the decease of his beloved Fáṭima, the daughter of the prophet, claimed the privilege of polygamy, and had 18 sons and 18 daughters. The most renowned of them are the two sons of Fáṭima, *viz.*, Hasan and Husain, as also Muhammad Ḥaníf, by another wife. Among the many surnames, or honorable titles bestowed upon 'Alí, are the following—Wasí' which signifies "legatee and heir;" Murtaẓa, "beloved by God;" Asad-ullah-ul-Ghálib, "the victorious lion of God;" Ḥaidar, a "lion;" Sháh Mardán, "king of men;" Sher Khudá, "the lion of God." His memory is still held in the highest veneration by the Muhammadans, who say that he was the first that embraced their religion. They say, moreover, that Muhammad, talking of him, said, "'Alí is for me and I am for him; he stands to me in the same rank as Aaron did to Moses; I am the town in which all knowledge is shut up, and he is the gate of it." However, these great eulogies did not hinder his name, and that of all his family, from being cursed, and their persons from being excommunicated through all the mosques of the empire of the khalífas of the house of Umayya, from Mu'áwiya down to the time of 'Umar ibn-'Abdul-'Azíz, who suppressed the solemn malediction. There were besides several khalífas of the house of 'Abbás, who expressed a great aversion to 'Alí and all his posterity; such as Mu'taẓid and Mutawakkil. On the other hand, the Fátimite khalífas of Egypt caused his name to be added to that of Muhammad in the call to prayer, *(azán)* which is chaunted from the turrets of the mosques. He is the first of the twelve Imáms, eleven of whom were his descendants. Their names are as follows:

1. 'Alí, the son of Abú-Ṭalib.
2. Imám Hasan, eldest son of 'Alí.
3. " Husain, second son of 'Alí.
4. " Zain-ul-'Ábidín, son of Husain.
5. " Muhammad Báḳir, son of Zain-ul-'Ábidín.
6. " Ja'far Sádiḳ, son of Muhammad Báḳir.
7. " Músa Káẓim, son of Ja'far Sádiḳ.
8. " Alí Músa Raza, son of Músa Káẓim.
9. " Muhammad Taḳí, son of Músa Razá.
10. " 'Alí Naḳí, son of Muhammad Taḳí.
11. " Hasan 'Askarí, son of 'Alí Naḳí.
12. " Mahdí, son of Hasan 'Askarí.

As to the place of Alí's burial, authors differ; but the most probable opinion is, that he was buried in that place which is now called Najaf Ashraf in Kúfa, and this is visited by the Muhammadans as his tomb.

The followers of 'Alí are called Shí'as, which signifies sectaries or adherents in general, a term first used about the fourth century of the Hijra.

'Alí is reputed the author of several works in Arabic, particularly a collection of one hundred sentences (paraphrased in Persian by Rashíd-uddín Waṭwáṭ), and a Díwán of didactic poems, often read in Madrasahs.

In mentioning Alí's name, the Shí'a use the phrase "'alaihi as-salám," which is used after the names of prophets; the Sunnís say, "karrama alláhu wajhahu," 'may God honor his face.'

**'Ali,** علی بن احمد بن ابوبکر کوفی, son of Ahmad bin-Abú-Bakr Kúfí, a resident of Uch and author of the history of Sindh in Arabic called "Tuḥfat-ul-Kirám". This work was translated into Persian and called "Chách Náma", a translation of which was made in English by Lieutenant Postans and published in the Journal of the Asiatic Society in 1838.

**'Ali,** علی بن احمد المشهور بواحدی, son of Ahmad, commonly called Wáḥidí, was an Arabian author who wrote three Commentaries, *viz.*: "Wasít," "Zakír", and "Basiṭ", and also "Kitáb Nuzúl". He died in 1075 A. D., 468 A. H.

**'Ali,** علی بن حمزه, son of Ḥamzá, author of the "Táríkh Iṣfahání".

**'Ali,** علی بن حسین واعظ, son of Husain Wáiẓ Káshifí, the famous writer of the *Anwár-i-Sohaili*, author of the work called "Laṭáif-uz-Ẓaráif", containing the anecdotes of Muhammad, of the twelve Imáms, of the ancient kings of Persia, and of various other persons. He is also the author of another work entitled "Rushḥát", containing the Memoirs of the Ṣúfí Shaikhs of the Nakshbandí order. 'Alí died in 1532 A. D., 939 A. H. He is also called 'Alí Waez. *Vide* Ṣafí-uddín Muhammad.

**'Ali,** علي بن محمد قوسنجي, son of Muhammad Ḳúsanjí, an astronomer, and author of the "Sharḥ-ul-Jadíd", the new commentary. He died A. D. 1474, 879 A. H.

**'Ali,** علي بن عثمان, son of 'Uṣmán Gilání, author of the "Kashf-ul-Maḥjúb", containing a minute description of the twelve orders of Ṣúfís, &c., written in 1499 A. D., 905 A. H. He is also called Pír 'Alí Hajwírí.

**'Ali,** علی ملقب به ابوالحسن, surnamed Abul-Hasan, *vide* Abul-Hasan 'Alí.

**'Ali,** علی تخلص ملا ناصرعلی, the poetical name of Mullá Náṣir 'Alí, which see.

**'Ali,** علی, the poetical name of a poet who converted the Ghazals of Ḥáfiz into Mukhammas.

**'Ali 'Adil Shah I,** علی عادل شاه بیجاپوری, of Bíjápúr, surnamed Abul-Muẓaffar, succeeded to the throne of that kingdom after the death of his father Ibráhím 'Ádil Sháh I, in 1558 A. D., 965 A. H. He reigned about 22 lunar years, and, as he had no son, he appointed in the year 1579 A. D. his nephew, Ibráhím, son of his brother Ṭahmásp, his successor; and the following year on the night of Thursday the 10th of April, 1580, 23rd Ṣafar, 988 A. H., he was assassinated by a young eunuch. He was buried in the city of Bíjápúr, where his tomb or mausoleum is called by the people, "Rauẓa 'Alí."
*Vide* Áín Translation, I, 466.]

**'Ali 'Adil Shah II,** علی عادل شاه ثاني بیجاپوری, of Bíjápúr, succeeded his father Muhammad 'Adil Sháh in his childhood in November, 1656 A. D., Muharram, 1067 H., and was unable to remedy the disorders which had occurred in his kingdom, by the rebellion of the celebrated Marhatta chief Sewájí, who had possessed himself of all the strongholds in the Kokan country, and erected several new forts. Under pretence of making his submissions to the Sulṭán, he begged an interview with the Bíjápúr general, Afzal Khán, whom he treacherously stabbed in an embrace. Rustam Khán was afterwards sent against him, and defeated. 'Alí 'Adil Sháh died in the year 1672 A. D., 1083 A. H. after a turbulent reign of 11 or 12 years. He was succeeded by his son Sikandar 'Adil Sháh.

**'Ali Ahmad,** شيخ علي احمد**,** (Shaikh) the son of Shaikh Husain Nakshí, a learned man and engraver who died suddenly on hearing a verse of the poet Khwája Hasan of Dihlí repeated in the presence of the emperor Jahángír on the 13th of April, 1609 O. S., 18th Muharram, 1018 H.

**'Ali Akbar,** علي اكبر**,** the eldest son of Imám Husain, killed in battle together with his father on the 10th October, 680 A. D.

**'Ali Akbar,** علي اكبر**,** author of the work called "Majma'-ul-Auliá", containing a detailed account of all the Muhammadan saints, dedicated to the emperor Sháh Jahán who was a great admirer of saints, A. D. 1628, 1038 A. H.

**'Ali Akbar,** على اكبر الہ ابادی**,** of Allahábád, author of the "Fasúl Akbarí", and "Usúl Akbarí", and several other works.

**'Ali Asghar,** علي اصغر**,** proper name of Imám Zain-ul-'Abidín, which see.

**'Ali Asghar,** على اصغر قنوجی**,** of Kanauj, author of a commentary on the Kurán called "Sawákib-ut-Tanzíl". He died in the year 1727 A. D., 1140 A. H.

**'Ali Bae,** علي بای**,** (whose name is spelt in our English Biographical Dictionaries Alí Bey) was a native of Natolia, son of a Greek priest. In his 13th year he was carried away by some robbers as he was hunting, and sold to Ibrahím, a lieutenant of the Janissaries, at Grand Cairo, who treated him with kindness. 'Alí distinguished himself against the Arabs, but when his patron was basely assassinated in 1758, by Ibrahím the Circassian, he avenged his death, and slew the murderer with his own hand. This violent measure raised him enemies, and his flight to Jerusalem and to Ptolemais or Acre with difficulty saved him from the resentment of the Ottoman Porte, that had demanded his head. Time, however, paved the way to his elevation. Those who had espoused the cause of the Circassian were sacrificed to the public safety; and 'Alí recalled by the public voice, governed the country with benevolence and equity. In a battle fought against a rebellious Mamlúk to whom he had entrusted part of his army, 'Alí saw some of his troops desert, and unwilling to survive a defeat, he defended himself with the fury of a lion, till he was cut down by a sabre and carried to the conqueror's tent, where eight days after he expired of his wounds, April 21st, 1773, in his 45th year, and left behind him a character unrivalled for excellence, for courage, and magnanimity.

**'Ali Bae,** علي بائي**,** the titles by which he was known in the Muhammadan countries, were, al Amír, al-Hakím, al-Fakíh, al-Sharíf, al-Háj 'Alí Báe ibn Usmán Báe al-Abbás, Khádim Baitulláh al-Harám, *i. e.* the prince, the learned, doctor of the law, of the blood of Muhammad, pilgrim, 'Alí Báe, son of Usmán Báe, of the race of the Abbasidesí, servant of the house of God. He was master of the Arabic language, and had carefully studied the mathematical and natural branches of science and knowledge. It was in 1802 that he visited England. In June 1803 he sailed from Spain to Morocco, and travelled through Tripoli, Cyprus, Egypt, Arabia, Syria, and Turkey, and wrote a history of his travels, which was translated into English and published in London in the year 1816, entitled "The Travels of 'Alí Báe." In his visit to the isle of Cyprus he surveyed some curious remains of antiquity that have been usually overlooked. Having been admitted in his character of a Muhammadan prince to sweep the interior of the Ka'ba at Mecca, the most sacred office that a Musalmán can perform, and to visit it repeatedly, he has given, from personal inspection a more minute and exact account of the temple of Mecca than other travellers could lay before the public. His notice of the venerated mountain beyond Mecca, the last and principal object of the pilgrimage to that city, and his description of the interior of the Temple of Jerusalem, which no Christian is permitted to enter, is said to contain much new information.

**'Ali Bahadur,** نواب على بہادر**,** Nawáb of Banda, eldest son of Shamsher Bahádur I, and grandson of the Marhatta chief Bájí Ráo Peshwá I. He received the investiture of Bundelkhand from Náná Farnawís, the Púna minister, about the year 1790 A. D. and accompanied by his brother Ghání Bahádur, and supported by a powerful army, invaded Bundelkhand, but was opposed by Nána Arjun, (the guardian of Bakhat Singh a descendant of Rájá Chatursál) who falling in the contest, and Rájá Bakhat Singh being taken prisoner, Alí Bahádur acquired the whole of that part of the ráj of Banda which belonged to Bakhat Singh and all the ráj of Panna. He reigned about 11 or 12 years, and as at the time of his death, which happened in 1801 or 1802 A. D., his eldest son Shamsher Bahádur II was absent at Púna, his youngest son Zulfikár Alí was proclaimed (in violation of the title of his eldest brother) as his successor by his uncle Ghání Bahádur and his Díwán Himmat Bahádur Gosháin. Ghání Bahádur, however, was soon after expelled by Shamsher Bahádur who took possession of the ráj.

**'Ali Bahadur Khan,** على بہادر خان**,** the last Nawáb of Banda and son of Zulfikár Alí Khán Bahádur. He is the author of a díwan and a masnawí called "Mehr-úllah." He was removed for alleged complicity in the rebellion of 1857.

**'Ali Barid I,** على بريد**,** succeeded his father Amír Baríd to the throne of Ahmadábád Bídar in the Dakhan in the year 1542 A. D. and was the first of this family who assumed royalty. He died after a reign of more than 20 years in 1562 A. D., 970 A. H. and was succeeded by his son Ibráhím Baríd.

**'Ali Barid II,** succeeded his father Kasim Baríd II in the government of Ahmadábád Bídar in 1572 A. D. and was deposed in 1609 by his relative Amír Baríd II, who succeeded him, and was the last of this dynasty.

**'Ali Beg,** على بيگ a Pole, born of Christian parents. When young he was made prisoner by the Tartars and sold to the Turks, who educated him in the Muhammadan faith. He rose in the Turkish court, and was appointed interpreter to the Grand Signior, and translated the Bible and the English Catechism into the Turkish language. His great work is on the liturgy of the Turks, their pilgrimages to Mecca, and other religious ceremonies, translated into Latin by Dr. Smith. He died 1675 A. D.

**'Ali Beg, (Mirza),** مرزا على بيگ**,** a native of Badakhshán who held a high rank in the service of the emperor Akbar; and was honored with the office of 4,000 in the reign of Jahángír. He accompanied the emperor one day to visit the shrine of the celebrated saint, Shaikh Maín-uddín Chishtí at Ajmír, and happening to see the tomb of Sháhbáz Khán Kambú, he embraced it, and crying out with a loud voice, that, "he, when living, was one of his oldest and best friends," gave up the ghost. This happened on the 11th of March, 1616 O. S., 2nd Rabí I, 1025 A. H.

**'Ali bin al-Husain al-Masa'udi al-Hudaili,** مسعودی على بن الحسين**,** the far-famed author of the Marúj-uz-Zahab, and who has been, with some justice, termed the Herodotus of the East, was also a writer on the Shia' traditions. He died in 957 A. D., 346 A. H.

**'Ali Boya** or **Ali ibn Boya,** علي بويه, entitled Imád-ud-daula, the first of a race of kings of Fars and 'Irák. The flatterers of this family, which is called Dílamí or Diálima (from the name of their native village, Dílam) and Bóya or Buyites (from that of one of their ancestors named Bóya), trace their descent to the ancient kings of Persia: but the first of this race that history notices, was a fisherman of Dílam whose name was Bóya. His eldest son, 'Alí Boya, was employed by a governor of his native country named Murawij, and was in the command of the chief part of his army, with which he encountered and defeated Yákút, the governor of Isfahán, and by the immense plunder that he obtained from that victory, he became at once a leader of reputation and of power. He pursued Yákút into Fars, defeated him again, and took possession of the whole of that province as well as those of Kirmán, Khúzistán and 'Irák in 933 A. D., 321 A. H. This chief was afterwards tempted, by the weak and distracted state of the Khiláfat or Caliphate, to a still higher enterprize: accompanied by his two brothers, Hasan and Ahmad, he marched to Baghdád. The Khalíf al-Rází Billáh fled, but was soon induced to return: and his first act was to heap honors on those who had taken possession of his capital. 'Alí Bóya, on agreeing to pay annually 600,000 dinars of gold, was appointed viceroy of Fars and 'Irák, with the rank of Amír-ul-Umrá, and the title of 'Imád-ud-daula. His younger brother Ahmad, received the title of Maizz-ud-daula, and was nominated wazír to the khalif. Hasan, who was his second brother, received the title of Rukn-ud-daula, and acted, during the life of Alí Bóya, under that chief. Alí Bóya fixed his residence at Shiráz, and died on Sunday the 11th November, 949 A. D., 16th Jamad I, 338 H., much regretted by his soldiers and subjects. He was succeeded by his brother Rukn-ud-daula.

Sultáns of the race of Boya who reigned 108 lunar years in Persia:

'Imád-ud-daula 'Alí Bóya; Maizz-ud-daula Ahmad; Rukn-ud-daula Hasan, sons of Bóya.

Azd-ud-daula; Mouyyad-ud-daula; Fakhr-ud-daula Abúl Hasan, sons of Rukn-ud-daula.

Majd-ud-daula, son of Fakhr-ud-daula.

Izz-ud-daula Bakhtyár, son of Maizz-ud-daula.

**'Ali Durdazd,** مولانا علی رد دزداسترابادي, (Mouláná) of Astarábád. A poet who was cotemporary with Katibí Tarshízí who died in A. D. 1435, 840 A. H. He is the author of a díwán. He was living in A. D. 1436, in which year his wife died, on which account he wrote a beautiful elegy.

**'Ali Ghulam Astarabadi,** علي غلام استرآبادی, a poet who served under the kings of Dakhin and was living in 1565 A. D., 972 A. H., in which year Rámráj the rájá of Bíjánagar was defeated and slain in a battle against the Muhammadan princes of Dakhin, of which event he wrote a chronogram.

**'Ali Hamdani,** علي همداني, *vide* Sayyid 'Alí Hamdání.

**'Ali Hamza,** علي حمزه, author of the "Jawáhir-ul-Asrár", a commentary on the abstruse meaning of the verses of the Kurán &c., being an abridgment of the "Miftáh-ul-Asrár", written in 1436 A. D. 'Alí Hamza's poetical name is 'Azurí, which see.

**'Ali Hazin,** علي حزين (Shaikh Muhammad) *vide* Hazín.

**'Ali ibn Isa,** علي ابن عيسى, general of the khalíf al-Amín, killed in battle against Táhir ibn Husain, the general of the khalíf al-Mámún in the year 811 A. D., 195 A. H., and his head sent as a present to the khalíf.

**'Ali ibn ul-Rijal,** علي ابن الرجال, author of the Arabic work on astronomy called "Albára' ahkám Najúm."

**'Ali Ibrahim Khan,** علي ابراهيم خان, a native judge of Banaras who is the author of 28 mans and several other works and a tazkira or biography of Urdú poets which he wrote about the year 1782 A. D., 1196 H. His poetical name is Khalíl.

**'Ali Jah,** علي جاه, the eldest son of the Nizám of Haidarábád. He rebelled against his father in June 1795 A. D. was defeated and made prisoner, and died shortly after.

**'Ali Kusanji,** علي قسنجي, (Mullá) *vide* Mullá 'Alí Kúsanjí.

**'Ali Kusanji,** علي قوسنجي, (Mulla) author of the "Sharah Tajríd", and Háshia Kashsháf. He died in 1405 A. D., 808 A. H.

**'Ali Kuli Beg of Khurasan,** علي قلي بيگ, author of a tazkira or biography of poets.

**'Ali Kuli Khan,** علي قلي خان, (Nawab) *vide* Ganna Begam.

**'Ali Lala,** (Shaikh Razí-uddín) a native of Ghazní. His father Sayyid Lálá was the uncle of Shaikh Sanáí the poet. He was a disciple of Najm-uddín Kubrá and his title Shaikh ul-Shaiukh. He died A. D. 1244, 642 A. H., aged 76 lunar years.

**'Ali Mahaemi,** علي مهايمي, a native of Mahaem in the Dakhín, was the son of Shaikh Ahmad, and is the author of the commentary on the Kurán entitled "Tafsír Rahmání." He died A. D., 1431, 835 A. H.

**'Ali Mardan Khan,** علي مردان خان, Amír-ul-Umra, was a native of Persia and governor of Kandahár on the part of the king of Persia, but finding himself exposed to much danger from the tyranny of his sovereign Sháh Safí, he gave up the place to the emperor Sháh Jahán, and himself took refuge at Dihlí in the year 1637 A. D., 1047 A. H. He was received with great honour, was created Amír-ul-Umrá, and was at different times, made governor of Kashmír and Kábul, and employed in various wars and other duties. He excited universal admiration at the court by the skill and judgment of his public works, of which the canal which bears his name at Dihlí still affords a proof, and the taste and elegance he displayed on all occasions of show and festivity. He died on his way to Kashmír, where he was going for change of air, on the 16th of April, 1657 A. D., O. S., 12th Rajab, 1067 A. H., and was buried at Lahor in the mausoleum of his mother. He left three sons, *viz.*, Ibráhím Khán, Isma'íl Beg and Is-hák Beg, of whom the two last were slain in the battle which took place between Dára Shikóh and 'Alamgír at Dhaulpúr on the 29th May, 1658, O. S., 7th Ramazan, 1068 H. He is believed to have introduced the bulbous Tartar dome into Indian architecture.

**'Ali Musi Raza,** علي موسي رضا, the eighth Imám of the race of Alí, and the son of Músí Kázim the seventh Imám. His mother's name was Umm Sayyid; he was born in the year 764 or 769 A. D., 147 A. H. and died on Friday the 12th of August 818 A. D., 9th Safar, 203 H. His wife's name was Umm Habíl the daughter of the Khalíf al-Mámún. His sepulchre is at Tús in Khurásán. That town is now commonly called Mash-had, that is, the place of martyrdom of the Imám. To the enclosure wherein his tomb is raised, the Persians give the name of "Rauzat Rizawí," or the garden of Razá, and esteem it the most sacred spot in all Persia. The chief ornament and support of Mash-had is this tomb, to which many thousands of pious pilgrims annually resort, and which had been once greatly enriched by the bounty of sovereigns. Nasír-ulláh Mirzá the son of Nádir Sháh carried away the golden railing that surrounded the tomb, and Nádir Mirzá son of Sháh-rukh Mirzá and grandson of Nádir Sháh, took down the great golden ball which ornamented the top of the dome over the grave, and which was said to weigh 60 maunds or 420 pounds. The carpets fringed with gold, the golden lamps, and everything valuable were plundered by these necessitous and rapacious princes. Alí Músí Razá was poisoned by the khalíf al-Mámún, consequently is called a martyr.

**'Ali Muhammad Khan,** علي محمد خان, founder of the Rohila government. It is mentioned in Forster's Travels, that in the year 1720 A. D. Basharát Khán and Dáúd Khán, of the tribe of Rohilas, accompanied by a small number of their adventurous countrymen came into Hindústan in quest of military service. They were first entertained by Madan Sháh, a Hindú chief of Seraulí, (a small town in the north-west quarter of Rohilkhand) who by robbery and predatory excursions maintained a large party of banditti. In the plunder of an adjacent village, Dáúd Khán captured a youth of the Ját sect, whom he adopted and brought up in the Muhammadan faith, by the name of 'Alí Muhammad, and distinguished this boy by pre-eminent marks of paternal affection. Some years after, the Rohilas quarrelling with Madan Sháh, retired from his country, and associating themselves with Chánd Khán the chief of Barelí, they jointly entered into the service of Azmat Khán, the governor of Moradábád. After the death of Dáúd Khán, who was slain by the mountaineers in one of his excursions, the Rohila party in a short space of time seized on the districts of Madan Sháh and 'Alí Muhammad Khán was declared chief of the party. From the negligence of government and the weak state of the empire of Dihlí in the reign of Muhammad Sháh, he possessed himself of the district of Katir (now called from the residence of the Rohilas, Rohilkhand) and assumed independence of the royal authority. He was besieged in March, 1745 A. D., Safar 1158 A. H., in a fortress called Bankar and 'Aoulá and taken prisoner, but was released after some time, and a jágír conferred on him. The emperor Muhammad Sháh died in April 1748, A. D. 1161 A. H. and 'Alí Muhammad Khán some time after him in the same year at 'Aoulá, which he had ornamented with numerous public and private edifices. He left four sons, *viz.*, Sa'd-ulláh Khán, Abdulláh Khán, Faiz-ulláh Khán and Dúnde Khán. Sa'd-ulláh Khán succeeded to his father's possession being then twelve years old. *Vide* Sa'd-ullah Khán.

**'Ali (Mulla),** ملا علي, Muhaddis or the traditionist whose poetical name was "Tárí", died in the year 1573 A. D., 981 A. H., and Mullá 'Alam wrote the chronogram of his death.

**'Ali Murad Khan,** علي مراد خان, a king of Persia of the Zand family. He succeeded to the throne after the death of Sádiḳ Khán in March, 1781 A. D., and assumed the title of wakíl. He reigned over Persia five years and was independent of the government two years prior to this period. Persia during this time, enjoyed a certain degree of peace. He continued to confine his rival 'Aká Muhammad Khán to the province of Mázindarán. He died in 1785 A. D.

**'Ali Murad,** (Mír) present chief of Khairpúr (1869).

**'Ali Naki,** امام علي نقي, (Imám) was the tenth Imám of the race of 'Alí, and the son of Imám Muhammad Taḳí who was the ninth Imám. He was born in the year 828 A. D., 213 A. H., and died on the 17th of June, 869 A. D. 3rd Rajab, 255 A. H. His tomb is in Sarmanráe (which is also called Sámira) in Baghdád, where his son Muhammad Askarí was also buried afterwards.

**'Ali Naki Khan,** نواب علي نقي خان, (Nawáb) the father-in-law and prime minister of Wájid 'Alí Sháh, the last king of Lakhnau. He died at Lukhnau of cholera about the 1st December, 1871, 17th Ramẓán, 1278 A. H.

**'Ali Naki,** علي نقي Díwán of Prince Murad Bakhsh, son of Shalyahí, whom he slew with his own hand.

**'Ali Nawedi,** علي نويدى, a poet and pupil of Sháh Ṭáhir Andjání, came to India, where he was patronized by Abúl Fatha Husain Nizám Sháh I. For some time he was in disgrace with his patron and changed his Takhallus or poetical name from Nawedí to Ná-umaidí (or hopeless). He died in 1567 A. D., 975 A. H., at Ahmadnagar in the Dakhan.

**'Ali Quli Beg,** *vide* Sháh Afghán Khán.

**'Ali Shahab Tarshizi,** علي شهاب ترشيزى, a poet who was a native of Tarshish. He flourished in the reign of Sháh-rukh Mirzá, and found a patron in his son Muhammad Jogí, in whose praise he wrote several panegyrics. He was co-temporary with the poet Azurí, who died A. D. 1462, 866 A. H.

**'Alisher,** امير عليشير, (Amír) surnamed Nizám-uddín, was the prime minister of the Sulṭán Husain Mirzá ruler of Khurásán. He sprang from an illustrious family of the Jaghtaí or Chaghtaí tribe. His father Gajkína Bahádur, held one of the principal offices of government during the reign of Sulṭán Abúl Ḳásim Bábar Bahádur, a descendant of Amír Taimúr. His grandfather, by his mother's side, was one of the principal Amírs of Sulṭán Báiḳara Mirzá, the grandfather of Sulṭán Husain Mirzá. Alísher attached himself originally to Sulṭán Abúl Ḳásim Bábar Mirzá, who was greatly attached to him, and called him his son. After his death he retired to Mash-had and continued his studies there; which place he subsequently quitted for Samarḳand, on account of the disturbances which broke out in Khurásán, and applied himself diligently to the acquirement of knowledge in the college of Khwája Fazl-ulláh. When Sulṭán Husain Mirzá became uncontrolled ruler of Khurásán, he requested Sulṭán Ahmad Mirzá, at that time ruler of the countries beyond the Oxus, to send 'Alísher to him. On his arrival, he was received with the greatest distinction, and raised to the highest posts of honor. 'Alísher's palace was open to all men of learning: and notwithstanding that the reins of government were placed in his hands, in the midst of the weightiest affairs, he neglected no opportunity of improving both himself and others in the pursuit of knowledge. He was not only honored by his own Sulṭán and his officers, but foreign princes also esteemed and respected him. After being employed in the capacity of díwán and prime minister for some time, love of study induced him to resign, and bidding a final adieu to public life, he passed the remainder of his days in composing Turkish and Persian works, of which Sám Mirzá recounts the names of no less than twenty-one. Daulat Sháh the biographer, Mírkhúnd and his son Khúndamír, the historians, dedicated their works to him, and amongst other men of genius who were cherished by his liberality may be mentioned the celebrated poet Jámí. His collection of Odes in the Chaghtaí or pure Turkish dialect, which he wrote under the poetical name of Nawáí, amounts to 10,000 couplets, and his parody of Nizámí's five poems, containing nearly 30,000 couplets, is universally admired by the cultivators of Turkish poetry, in which he is considered to be without a rival. In the Persian language also he wrote a collection of Odes, under the poetical name of Fání or Fanáí, consisting of 6,000 distiches. 'Alísher was born in the year 1440 A. D., 844 A. H., and died on Sunday the 6th of December, 1500 A. D., 15th Jamad I, 906 A. H., five years before his royal friend and master Sulṭán Husain Mirzá. Khúndamír has recorded the year of his death in an affectionate chronogram: "His highness the Amír, the asylum of divine guidance, in whom all the marks of mercy were conspicuous, has quitted the thorny brake of the world, and fled to the rose-garden of pity. Since the 'light of mercy' has descended on his soul, those words represent the year of his departure." One of his works is called "Majális-ul-Nafáes."

**'Ali Tabar,** شهزاده علي طبار, (Prince) was the son of prince 'Azim Sháh, and grandson of the emperor 'Alamgír. He died in the year 1734 A. D., 1147 A. H.

**'Ali Waez,** علي واعظ, the son of the famous Husain Wáez Káshifí of Hirát. *Vide* 'Alí son of Husain Wáez.

**'Ali Wardi Khan,** علی وردی خان, also called Alahwardí Khán, which see.

**'Ali Yezdi,** علي يزدي, *vide* Sharaf-uddín 'Alí Yezdí.

**Alexander the Great,** *vide* Sikandar Zul-karnyn.

**Al-Farghani,** الفرغاني, surname of Ahmad ibn Kathír or Kasír, an Arabian astronomer of the ninth century, author of an introduction to astronomy. *Vide* Farghání.

**Al-Faryabi,** الفاريابي, *vide* Fáryábí.

**Al-Ghazzali,** الغزالي, *vide* Ghazzálí.

**'Alha** and **Udal,** آلہا و اودل, princes of Mahóba. There is a heroic ballad sung or recited by the Hindú sepoys in a kind of monotonous, but not unmusical sort of chaunt, accompanied by a sotto voce beat of the dhól, which rise to a constrepito in the pause between the verses. Whoever has resided in a military cantonment must have frequently observed the sepoys, when disengaged from military duty, collected in small knots, listening to one of the party reciting some poem or tale to a deeply interested audience. The subject of this lay is the prowess of 'Alhá', the rájá of Mahóba, a town in Bundelkhand, of which extensive ruins remain. The hero is described as the terror of the Muhammadans; his triumphs over whom are attributed not only to his own valour, but the favor of the goddess Kálí, whom he had propitiated by the offering of his life. There are many songs, it is said, of this prince, and his brother Udal, a warrior of equal estimation; but they are preserved only traditionally by the Powárs, and their amateur students. The verses are in Bhakha.

**Al-Hadi,** الهادي, the fourth khalíf of the house of 'Abbás succeeded his father al-Mahdí on the 4th of August, 785 A. D., 23rd Muharram, 169 H., to the throne of Baghdád. He reigned one year and one month, and having formed a design to deprive his younger brother Hárún-al-Rashíd of his right of succession and even to assassinate him, was poisoned by his prime minister about the month of September 786 A. D., Rabí I, 170 A. H. On his death his brother the celebrated Hárún-al-Rashíd ascended the throne.

**Al-Hakm,** also called ibn Abdúl Hakm, an Arabian author who (according to the chronological arrangement of the Arab authorities by Howard Vyse and Dr. Sprenger, in the former's second volume of 'The Pyramids of Gizeh') lived about 1450 A. D., or six hundred years after the death of the khalíf al-Mamún of Baghdad, but by a manuscript note recorded by a gentleman of the British Museum, (1868) it appears that al-Hakm was nearly contemporary with that prince who flourished between 813 and 842 A. D. Al-Hakm writes that the Great Pyramid in Egypt was built by a certain antediluvian king Saurid, and filled by him chiefly with celestial spheres and figures of the stars; together with the perfumes used in their worship; and that khalífa al-Mamún found the body of a man deposited, with jewels, arms, and golden writing, in the coffer, when he broke into the king's chamber of the Great Pyramid. But neither Abú Múshar Jáfar bin Muhammad Balkhi, who wrote in about 890 A. D. nor ibn Khurdalbeh, in 920 A. D. have one word about al-Mamún, or any opening of the pyramid. But when we descend to Masaúdi, in 967 A. D. he, after an astonishing amount of romancing on what took place at the building of the pyramids 300 years before the Flood,—mentions that, not al-Mamún, but his father, khalífa Harún-al-Rashíd, attempted to break into the Great Pyramid; and after penetrating 20 cubits, found a vessel containing 1000 coins of the finest gold, each just one ounce in weight, and making up a sum which exactly repaid the cost of his operations; at which, it is added, he greatly wondered. About the year 1170 A. D. or 340 years after al-Mamún's age, that prince is mentioned by Abú Abd-ullah Muhammad bin Abdur Rahím Alkaisi, who states that he was informed that those who went into the upper parts of the Great Pyramid in the time of al-Mamún, came to a small passage, containing the image of a man in green stone, and within that a human body with golden armour &c. &c.

**Al-Hasan,** الحسن, an Arabian who wrote on optics, about the year 1100 A. D.

**Alif bin Nur Kashani,** الف بن نورکاشني, author of another "Matla'-ul-Anwár", besides the one of the same name written by Mullá Husain Wáez. This is a complete history of Muhammad, his descendants, with Memoirs of the khalífs.

**Aljaitu,** الجايتو, a Tartar king of Persia, who assumed the title of Muhammad Khudá Bandá on his accession to the throne, which see.

**Al-Kadir Billah,** القادر بالله, the twenty-fifth khalíf of the Abbaside family, was the son of Is-ḥáḳ the son of Muḳtadir Billah. He ascended the throne of Baghdád after the dethronement of al-Taya' in 991 A. D., 381 A. H. He was a contemporary of Sulṭán Mahmúd of Ghazní; reigned 41 lunar years and 3 months, and died in 1031 A. D., 422 A. H. He was succeeded by al-Káem-bi-amr-illáh.

**Al-Kadiri** or **Kadiri,** القادري, a sect of Muhammadans. These are a branch of the Muetazillís, and differ in their opinions from the orthodox Musalmáns, in that they deny God's decree, and assert free will; affirming that the contrary opinion makes God the author of evil.

**Al-Kaim Billah** or **Al-Kaim-bi-amr-illah,** القايم بالله, surnamed Abú Ja'far Abdulláh, the 26th khalíf of the house of 'Abbás. He succeeded his father Kádir Billah to the throne of Baghdád in 1031 A. D., 422 A. H., reigned 44 lunar years and 8 months, and died in 1075 A. D., 467 A. H., which was soon after Sulṭán Maliksháh the Saljúḳí had ascended the throne of Persia, and as that monarch was the real master of the empire, the nomination of a successor was deferred till he was consulted. He deputed a son of his prime minister Nizám-ul-Mulk to Baghdád with orders to raise al-Muḳtadí the grandson of al-Káim to the (nominal) rank of the commander of the faithful.

**Al-Kaim,** القايم second khalíf of the Fátimite race of Barbary; he succeeded his father Obeid-ullah al-Mahdí A. D. 924, 312 A. H. During his reign we read of nothing remarkable, except the revolt of Yezíd ibn Kondat, a man of mean extraction. Al-Káem reigned nearly 12 years and died in A. D. 945, 334 A. H. His son Ismaíl al-Mansúr succeeded him.

**Al-Kahir Billah,** القاهر بالله, the nineteenth khalíf of the race of the Abbasides, and the third son of al-Mo'tazid Billáh, succeeded his brother al-Muḳtadir to the crown of Baghdád in October, 932 A. D., Shawwál, 320 A. H. He had reigned only one year five months and twenty-one days, when his wazír ibn Maḳla deprived him of his sight with a hot iron on Wednesday the 23rd April, 934 A. D.,

6th Jamad I, 322 A. H. and raised al-Rází Billah the son of Muḳtadir to the throne. It is said that al-Ḳáhir, after this, as long as he lived, was obliged to beg for charity in the mosque of Baghdád, calling out to the people that assembled there, "Have pity and give charity to one, who had once been your khalífa."

**'Al-Kama,** علقمه, son of Ḳys was one of the pupils of Abd-ullah bin Masaúd, and an eminent man. He died in 681 A. D., 61 A. H.

**Al-Khassaf,** الخصّاف, *vide* Abú-Bakr Ahmad bin-'Umar al-Khaṣṣáf.

**'Allama Dawani,** *vide* Dawání.

**'Allama Hilli,** شيخ علامه حلي, (Shaikh) the great Shia lawyer, whose full name is Shaikh al-'Alláma Jamál-uddín Hasan bin Yúsuf al-Mutakhir Hillí, was the author of the "Khulásat-ul-Aḳwál" a biography of eminent Shias. His chief works on the subject of traditions, are the Istiksá al-Ya'tbár, the Masábíh al-Anwár and the Durar-wa al-Marján. He died in 1326 A. D., 726 A. H. *Vide* Jamál-uddín Hasan bin Yúsaf.

**'Allami,** *vide* Afzal Khán.

**'Allami,** علامي, the poetical name of Shaikh Abúl Fazl the favorite wazír and secretary of the emperor Akbar.

**'Allami Shirazi,** علامي شيرازي, or the philosopher of Shíráz, a very learned man, so generally called that his proper name is almost forgotten. He is the author of a celebrated collection of tracts on pure and mixed mathematics, entitled Durrat-ut-Táj.

**Al-Mahdi,** المهدي, the third khalíf of the race of Abbás, succeeded his father Abú Ja'far al-Mansúr to the throne of Baghdád, and was inaugurated on Sunday the 8th of October, 775 A. D., 6th Ẓil-ḥijja, 158 A. H. From the accession of al-Mahdí to the year 781 A. D., 164 A. H., the most remarkable event was the rebellion of al-Maḳna (or al-Maḳanna) which see. All this time war had been carried on with the Greeks, but without any remarkable success on either side. But after the suppression of the rebellion of al-Maḳna, the khalíf ordered his son Harún-al-Rashíd to penetrate into the Greek territories with an army of 95,000 men. Harún, then, having entered the dominions of the empress Iráne, defeated one of her commanders that advanced against him; after which he laid waste several of the imperial provinces with fire and sword, and even threatened the city of Constantinople itself. By this the empress was so terrified, that she purchased a peace with the khalíf by paying him an annual tribute of 70,000 pieces of gold, which for the present at least, delivered her from the depredations of these barbarians. After the signing of the treaty, Harún returned home laden with spoils and glory. This year (*i. e.* the 164th year of the Hijrí or 781 A. D.) according to some of the oriental historians, the sun one day a little after his rising, totally lost his light in a moment without being eclipsed, when neither any fog nor any cloud of dust appeared to obscure him. This frightful darkness continued till noon, to the great astonishment of the people settled in the countries where it happened. Al-Mahdí was poisoned, though undesignedly, by one of his concubines, named Hasana. She had designed to destroy one of her rivals whom she imagined to have too great an ascendancy over the khalíf, by giving her a poisoned pear. This the latter, not suspecting anything, gave to the khalíf; who had no sooner eaten it than he felt himself in exquisite torture, and soon after expired. This event took place on the eve of Thursday the 4th of August, 785 A. D., 23rd Muhurram, 169 H. in a village called Ar Rád in the dependencies of Másabadán. He was succeeded by his eldest son al-Hádí.

**Al-Mahdi,** المهدي, a khalíf of Barbary, *vide* Obeid-ullah al-Mahdí and Muhammad al-Mahdí.

**Al-Makna, or al-Makanna,** المقنع, a famous impostor of Khurásán who lived in the reign of al-Mahdí the khalífa of Baghdád. His true name was Hákam ibn Hásham, and had been an under secretary to Abú Muslim governor of that province. He afterwards turned soldier, and passed thence into Máwarunnahr, where he gave himself out as a prophet. The name of al-Maḳna, as also that of al-Burḳaí, that is, the veiled, he received from his custom of covering his face with a veil or girdle mask, to conceal his deformity; he having lost an eye in the wars, and being otherwise of a despicable appearance, and a stutterer; though his followers pretended he did this for the same reason that Moses did, *viz.*, lest the splendor of his countenance should dazzle the eyes of his beholders. In some places he made a great many proselytes, deluding the people with a number of juggling tricks which they swallowed as miracles, and particularly by causing the appearance of a moon to rise out of a well for many nights together; whence he was also called in the Persian tongue, Sázinda Máh, or the Moon-maker. This wretch, not content with being reckoned a prophet, arrogated to himself divine honors; pretending that the Deity resided in his person. He had first, he said, assumed the body of Adam, then that of Noah and subsequently of many other wise and great men. The last human form he pretended to have adopted was that of Abú Muslim a prince of Khurásán, from whom it proceeded to him. At last this impostor raised an open rebellion against the khalíf, and made himself master of several fortified places in Khurásán, so that al-Mahdí was obliged to send one of his generals with an army against him about the year 780 A. D., 163 H. Upon the approach of the khalífa's troops, al-Maḳna retired into one of his strong fortresses which he had well provided for a siege. But being closely besieged by the khalífa's forces, and seeing no possibility of escaping, he gave poison in wine to his whole family and all that were with him in the castle; when they were dead, he burnt their bodies, together with all their furniture, provisions, and cattle; and lastly he threw himself into the flames. He had promised his followers, that his soul should transmigrate into the form of an old man riding on a greyish coloured beast, and that after so many years he would return and give them the earth for their possession; which ridiculous expectation kept the sect in being for several years. English readers will remember the use made of this story by the author of Lalla Rookh.

**Al-Mamun,** المامون, surnamed 'Abdulláh, was the seventh khalíf of the race of the Abbasides, and the second son of Hárún-al-Rashíd. He was proclaimed khalíf at Baghdád on the 6th October, 813 A. D., 6th Safar, 198 A. H., the day on which his brother al-Amín was assassinated. He conferred the government of Khurásán upon Ṭáhir ibn Husain his general, and his descendants with almost absolute and unlimited power. This happened in the year 820 A. D., 205 A. H., from which time we may date the dismemberment of that province from the empire of the khalífs. During the reign of this khalíf nothing remarkable happened; only the African Moslems invaded the island of Sicily, where they made themselves master of several places. Al-Mámún conquered part of Crete, had the best Greek writers translated into Arabic, and made a collection of the best authors. He also calculated a set of astronomical tables and founded an academy at Baghdád. In Khurásán he made Tús, at that time the capital of the kingdom, his place of residence. Under his patronage Khurásán became the resort of learned men; and the city of Tús, the great rival of Baghdád. He died of a surfeit on the 18th of August, 833 A. D., 17th Rajab 218 A. H., after a reign of 20 years and some months in Asia Minor, aged 48 years, and was buried at Tarsus a city on the frontiers of Asia Minor. His wife named Búrán, daughter of Hasan ibn Sahl his prime minister, outlived him 50 years, and died on Tuesday the 22nd September, 884 A. D., 27th Rabí I., 271 A. H , aged 80 years. Al-Mámún was succeeded by his brother al-Mo'tasim Billah.

**Al-Mansur,** المنصور, 2nd khalíf of Barbary of the Fatimite race, *vide* Ismáíl, surnamed al-Mansúr.

**Al-Mansur,** المنصور, whose former name was Abú Ja'far, was called al-Mansúr, the victorious, by his overcoming his enemies. He was the second khalíf of the noble house of Baní Abbás or Abbasides, and succeeded to the throne of Baghdád after the death of his brother Abúl Abbás surnamed al-Saffáh, in 754 A. D., 136 A. H. He was opposed by his uncle, 'Abdulláh son of Alí, who caused himself to be proclaimed khalíf at Damascus, but was defeated by al-Mansúr's general, Abú Muslim. He laid the foundation of the city of Baghdád on the banks of the Tigris in 762 A. D. and finished it four years after. He was a prince of extraordinary talent and taste, and an ardent lover of science and literature. He got the Pahlawí copy of Pilpay's Fables translated into Arabic. In the year 775 A. D., 158 A. H., the khalíf set out from Baghdád in order to perform the pilgrimage to Mecca; but being taken ill on the road, he expired at Bír Maimún, whence his body was carried to Mecca; where, after 100 graves had been dug, that his sepulchre might be concealed, he was interred, having lived, according to some 63, according to others 68 years, and reigned 22 lunar years. He is said to have been extremely covetous, and to have left in his treasury 600,000,000 dirhams, and 24,000,000 dínars. He is reported to have paid his cook by assigning him the heads and legs of the animals dressed in his kitchen, and to have obliged him to procure at his own expence all the fuel and vessels he had occasion for. He was succeeded by his son al-Mahdí. A Christian physician, named Bactishua, was very eminent at the court of al-Mansúr, who understanding that he had an old infirm woman for his wife, sent him three beautiful Greek girls and 3,000 dínars as a present. Bactishua sent back the girls and told the khalíf that his religion prohibited his having more than one wife at a time; which pleased the khalíf so much, that he loaded him with presents, and permitted him, at his earnest request, to return to his own country of Khurásán.

**Al-Mo'tamid Billah,** المعتمد بالله, the fifteenth khalíf of the house of Abbás, was the son of al-Mutwakkil Billah. He was raised to the throne of Baghdád by the Turks after the murder of al-Muhtadí in 870 A. D., 256 A. H. This year the prince of the Zanjiáns, Alí or al-Habíb, made incursions to the very gates of Baghdád, doing prodigious mischief wherever he passed. In the year 874 A. D., Ya'kúb-bin-Lys having taken Khurásán from the descendants of Táhir, attacked and defeated Muhammad ibn Wásil (who had killed the khalíf's governor of Fars, and afterwards made himself master of that province) seizing on his palace, where he found a sum of money amounting to 40,000,000 dirhams. In the year 879 A. D., 265 A. H., Ahmad ibn Túlan rebelled against the khalíf and set up for himself in Egypt. There were now four independent powers in the Moslem dominions, besides the house of Umyya in Spain; *viz.* The African Moslems, or Aghlabites, who had for a long time acted independently; Ahmad ibn Túlan in Syria and Egypt; Ya'kúb ibn al-Lys in Khurásán, and al-Habíb in Arabia and I'rák. In the year 883 A. D., 270 A. H., al-Habíb was defeated and slain by al-Muwafik the khalíf's brother and coadjutor, who ordered his head to be cut off, and carried through a great part of that region which he had so long disturbed. In the year 891 A. D., 278 A. H. the Karmatians first made their appearance in the Moslem empire, and gave almost continual disturbance to the khalífs and their subjects. Al-Mo'tamid reigned 22 lunar years 11 months and some days, and died in the year 892 A. D., 279 A. H. He was succeeded by his nephew al-Mo'tazid Billah the son of al-Muwafiḳ.

**Al-Mo'tasim Billah,** المعتصم بالله, was the fourth son of Harún-al-Rashíd, and the eighth khalíf of the house of Abbás. He succeeded to the throne by virtue of his brother al-Mamún's express nomination of him to the exclusion of his own son al-'Abbas, and his other brother al-Ḳásim, who had been appointed by Harún-al-Rashíd. In the beginning of his reign 833 A. D., 218 A. H., he was obliged to employ the whole forces of his empire against one Bábak, who had been for a considerable time in rebellion in Persia and Persian Iráḳ, and had taken upon himself the title of a prophet. He was, however, defeated and slain. In the year 838 A. D., 223 A. H., the Greek emperor Theophilus invaded the khalíf's territories, where he behaved with the greatest cruelty, and by destroying Sozopetra the place of al-Mo'tasim's nativity, notwithstanding his earnest entreaties to the contrary, occasioned the terrible distinction of Amorium. He is said to have been so robust, that he once carried a burden of 1,000 pounds weight several paces. As the people of Baghdád disturbed him with frequent revolts and commotions, he took the resolution to abandon that city, and build another for his own residence. The new city he built was first called Sámira, and afterwards Sarmanrí, (for that which gives pleasure at first sight) and stood in the Arabian 'Iráḳ. He was attached to the opinion of the Matazalites who maintain the creation of the Ḳurán; and both he and his predecessor cruelly persecuted those who believed it to be eternal. Al-Mo'tasim died on Thursday the 5th January, 842 A. D., 18th Rabí I., 227 H. He reigned 8 years 8 months and 8 days, was born in the 8th month (Shaban) of the year, was the 8th khalíf of the house of Abbás, ascended the throne in the 218th year of the Hijrí, died on the 18th of Rabí I., lived 48 years, fought 8 battles, built 8 palaces, begat 8 sons and 8 daughters, had 8,000 slaves, and had 8,000,000 dínars, and 80,000 dirhams in his treasury at his death, whence the oriental historians gave him the name of al-Musamman, or the Octonary. He was the first khalíf that added to his name the title of *Billah*, equivalent to the *Dei Gratia* of Christian sovereigns. He was succeeded by his son al-Wáthiḳ or Wásiḳ Billáh.

**Al-Mo'tazid Billah,** المعتضد بالله, the son of al-Muwafiḳ, the son of al-Mutwakkil Billáh, was the sixteenth khalíf of the race of Abbas. He came to the throne of Baghdád after the death of his uncle al-Mo'tamid Billáh in 892 A. D., 279 A. H. In the first year of his reign, he demanded in marriage the daughter of Khamarawia, Sultán or khalíf of Egypt, the son of Ahmad ibn Túlan; which was agreed to by him with the utmost joy, and their nuptials were solemnized with great pomp in the year 895 A. D., 282 A. H. He carried on a war with the Karmatians, but very unsuccessfully, his forces being defeated with great slaughter, and his general al-Abbás taken prisoner. The khalíf some time after his marriage granted to Hárún, son of. Khamarawia, the perpetual prefecture of Awásam and Kinnisrin, which he annexed to that of Egypt and Syria, upon condition that he paid him an annual tribute of 45,000 dínars. He reigned 9 years 8 months and 25 days, and died in 902 A. D., 289 A. H. His son al-Muktafí Billáh succeeded him.

**Al-Mughira,** المغيرة, the son of Sayyid and governor of Kúfa in the time of Mu'áwia the first khalíf of the house of Umyya. He was an active man, and of very good parts; he had lost one of his eyes at the battle of Yersnouk, though some say that it was with looking at an eclipse. By the followers of Alí he was accounted to be of the wrong party, and one of the chief of them. For thus they reckon, there are five elders on Alí's side; Muhammad, Alí, Fátima, Hasan and Husain; and to these are opposed, Abú Bakr, 'Umar, Muáwia, Amrú and al-

Mughíra. He died in the year 670 A. D., 50 A. H., at Kúfa. A great plague had been raging in the city, which made him retire from it; but returning upon its violence abating, he nevertheless caught it, and died of it.

**Al-Muhtadi,** المهتدي, the fourteenth khalíf of the Abbasides, was the son of one of al-Wáthiḳ's concubines named Kurb, who is supposed by some to have been a Christian. Al-Muhtadí was raised to the throne of Baghdád after the dethronement of al-Muttai'z Billáh in 869 A. D., 255 A. H. The beginning of his reign is remarkable for the irruption of the Zanjians, a people of Nubia, Ethiopia and the country of Caffres, into Arabia, where they penetrated into the neighbourhood of Basra and Kúfa. The chief of this gang of robbers, was 'Alí ibn Muhammad ibn Abdúl Rahmán, also called al-Habíb, who falsely gave himself out to be of the family of Alí ibn Abú Taleb. This made such an impression upon the Shías in those parts, that they flocked to him in great numbers; which enabled him to seize upon the cities of Basra and Ramla, and even to pass the Tigris at the head of a formidable army. In the year 870 A. D., 256 A. H., al-Muhtadí was barbarously murdered by the Turks who had raised him to the throne. He reigned only eleven months and was succeeded by al-Mó'tamid.

**Al-Mukhtar,** المختار, a celebrated Muhammadan chief who had beaten all the generals of the khalífs Yezíd, Marwán, and Abdúl Málik, and had made himself sole master of Babylonian I'ráḳ, whereof Kúfa was the capital. He persecuted all those he could lay his hands on, who were not of Husain's party; he never pardoned any one of those who had declared themselves enemies to the family of the prophet, nor those who, as he believed, had dipped their hands in Husain's blood or that of his relations. He sent an army against Ubeid-ullah the son of Zayád, who was sent by the khalíf Abdúl Málik towards Kúfa with leave to plunder it for three days, and slew him in battle in August, 686 A. D., Muharram, 67 A. H. al-Mukhtár was killed at Kúfa in a battle fought with Misaa'b the brother of Abdulláh the son of Zuber, governor of Basra, in the month of April, 687 A. D., Ramzan 67 A. H., in the 67th year of his age. It is said that he killed nearly 50,000 men.

**Al-Muktadi Billah,** المقتدي بالله, surnamedAbúl Ḳásim Abd-ulláh, the son of Muhammad, and grandson of al-Ḳáem Billáh, was raised to the throne of Baghdád after the death of his grandfather in 1075 A. D., 467 A. H., by orders of Sulṭán Malikshàh Saljúkí who was then the real master of the empire. He was the 27th khalíf of the race of Abbas, reigned 19 lunar years and 5 months and died in 1094 A. D., 487 A. H. His death induced Barkayáraḳ the Saljúkí, the reigning Sulṭán of Persia, whose brother Mahmúd had died about the same period, to go to Baghdád, where he confirmed al-Mustazhir the son of the late khalíf as his successor, and was himself hailed by the new lord of the faithful, as Sulṭán of the empire.

**Al-Muktadir Billah,** المقتدربالله, the eighteenth khalíf of the house of Abbás, was the son of al-Mó'tazid Billáh. He succeeded his brother al-Muktafí to the throne of Baghdád in 908 A. D., 295 A. H. He reigned 24 lunar years 2 months and 7 days, and was murdered by a eunuch on the 29th October, 932 A. D., 25th Shawwal, 320 H. He was succeeded by his brother al-Ḳáhir Billáh.

**Al-Muktafi Billah,** المكتفي بالله, was the seventeenth khalíf of the house of Abbás who reigned in Baghdád. He succeeded his father al-Mó'tazid Billáh in 902 A. D., 289 A. H., and proved a warlike and successful prince. He gained several advantages over the Karmatians, but was not able to reduce them. The Turks, however, having invaded the province of Máwarunnahr, were defeated with great slaughter; after which al-Muktafí carried on a successful war against the Greeks, from whom he took Seleucia. After this he invaded Syria and Egypt, which provinces he recovered from the house of Ahmad ibn Túlan in 905 A. D., 292 A. H.; he then renewed the war with success against the Greeks and Karmatians. Al-Muktafí died in 908 A. D., 295 A. H., after a reign of about six years and a half. He was the last of the khalífs who made any figure by their warlike exploits. His successors al-Muḳtadir, al-Ḳáhir and al-Rází, were so distressed by the Karmatians and numberless usurpers who were every day starting up, that by the 325th year of the Hijrí 937 A. D., they had nothing left but the city of Baghdád.

**Al-Muktafi Bi-amr-illah,** المقتفي بامرالله, the son of al-Mustazahr was the 31st khalíf of the house of Abbás. He succeeded his nephew al-Ráshid in A. D. 1136, 530 A. H., reigned about 24 lunar years and died in 1160 A. D., 555 A. H., leaving his kingdom to his son al-Mustanjad.

**Al-Mustaa'li Billah,** المستعلي بالله, the sixth Fatimite khalíf succeeded his father al-Mustanasar Billáh in the government of Egypt and Syria. During his reign, the power of that dynasty was impaired, and its authority weakened, their political influence having ceased in most of the Syrian cities, and the provinces of that country having fallen into the possessions of the Turkmans on one hand, and the Franks on the other. This people (the Crusaders) entered Syria and encamped before Antioch in the month of October, 1097 A. D., Zil-ḳada 490 A. H.; they obtained possession of it on the 20th June, 1098, 16th Rajab, 491 A. H.; the following year they took Maaratun Nomán, and in the month of July, 1099, Sha'ban, 492 A. H., they became masters of Jerusalem, after a siege of more than 40 days. This city was taken on a Friday morning; during the ensuing week, a great multitude of Moslems perished, and upwards of 70,000 were slain in the Masjid al-Aḳsá (or mosque of Umar) —— al-Musta-a'lí was born at Cairo on the 24th August, 1076, 20th Muharram, 469 A. H., proclaimed khalíf on Thursday the 28th of December, 1094, 18th Ẓil-ḥijja 487 A. H., and died in Egypt on the 10th December, 1101 A. D., 16th Safar, 495 A. H. His son Amar bi Ahkám-ulláh Abú Alí Mansúr succeeded him.

**Al-Mustaa'sim Billah,** المستعصم بالله, surnamed Abú Ahmad Abdulláh, was the thirty-seventh and last khalíf of the race of Abbás. He succeeded his father al-Mustanasar to the throne of Baghdád in 1142 A. D., 640 A. H. In his time Halakú Khán Tartar, emperor of the Mughals and grandson of the great conqueror Changiz Khán, besieged Baghdád for two months, and having taken that place, seized al-Mustaa'sim and his four sons whom he put to a most cruel death with 800,000 of its inhabitants. Halákú Khán was very desirous of seizing upon Baghdád, and of adding the whole kingdom of Mesopotamia to his already vast and numerous conquests; but, partly on account of his own scruples, and partly from fear of offending the prejudices of his Sunní followers, who were all of the same faith with the khalíf, he refrained for a time from entering the sacred dominion of one who was considered as the head of their holy religion, and the true representative of their beloved prophet. But the glorious days of the house of Baní Abbás had already been numbered, the effeminate Mustaa'sim had personal vices enough to lead to and excuse the final extinction of his race! Ibn al-Ḳama, his prime minister (who hated him more than any other of his oppressed subjects) from within, and Nasír-uddín Túsí, the preceptor of the Mughal prince (who owed him an old grudge) from without, urged the conqueror to the gates of Baghdád. Nasir-uddín had a few years before been at Baghdád, seeking shelter from persecution, when he was introduced to Mustaa'sim, the latter asked him to what country he belonged? "Tús, please your holiness", answered Nasír-uddín. "Art thou of the asses, or of the oxen of Tús?" said the khalíf (meaning the two principal branches of the Shia faith—Akhbarís and Usúlís). Mortified as the illustrious refugee was at this inhospitable insult, he still submissively answered, "Of the oxen of Tús, please your highness." "Where, then, are thy horns", said the insolent buffoon. "I have them not with me", replied Nasír-uddín, "but, if your holiness permit, I will go and fetch them." "Make haste, hence, then, thou deformed animal", said the khalíf, "and never again appear in my presence in so imperfect a state!" Nasír-uddín kept his promise well, for, at the moment when Baghdád was on the point of being surrendered, and the khalíf driven to the last extremity, he sent him a message to the effect that the ox of Tús was at the gate with *his horns*, and inquiring, when it would please his holiness to receive him? Nasír-uddín had in the city another old offender, whom he was anxious also to chastise. This was ibn Hájib, also one of the khalíf's ministers, and a person of great reputation for his learning; but being an Arabian Sunní, and a very bigoted one too, he had behaved still more cruelly than his master to the distressed Persian Shia when he sought protection at Baghdád. Ibn Hájib having been seized with depression of spirits, the physicians had recommended him (and the priests had granted him dispensation) to take, occasionally, a little wine. This happened when Nasír-uddín was at Baghdád. One day, ibn Hájib feeling himself particularly melancholy, and having, in consequence, taken a larger dose than usual, he became unusually merry, and requested Nasír-uddín to accompany him on the Tigris. Having reached the middle of the stream, he stopped the boat, and produced the several volumes of Nasír-uddín's works, which the learned refugee had presented to the khalíf—some of them in the original manuscript, and not yet transcribed, and in the presence of their anxious author, he threw them all, one after another, into the river, with such spiteful force, that the water was splashed about in every direction; when turning himself, on each occasion, to his mortified guest, he exclaimed with a sarcastic smile of triumph, "How wonderfully it bubbles!" When the turn of Nasír-uddín came, he, too, gave full vent to his revenge. He ordered ibn Hájib to be cased up to his neck, in an ox's hide, just taken off the animal, and, having filled the skin with air, he laid it for a few hours in the sun, till it became quite dry, and sounded like a drum. Then the victor advanced close to his half exhausted enemy, gave him a kick of triumph, and, as he rolled on the ground, exclaimed, "How wonderfully it rattles!" This melancholy event took place on Sunday the 10th of February, 1258 A. D., 4th Safar, 656 A. H., from which time Baghdád was added to the other conquered provinces of this proud emperor. Al-Mustaa'sim reigned 15 lunar years and 7 months.

**Al-Musta'in Billah,** المستعين بالله, the son of Muhammad, the son of al-Mo'tasim Billáh was the twelfth khalíf of the race of Abbás. He ascended the throne of Baghdád in 862 A. D., 248 A. H., after the death of his cousin or brother al-Mustanasar Billáh, but was forced to abdicate the throne in 866 A. D., 252 A. H., by his brother al-Mó'tiz Billáh, who afterwards caused him to be privately murdered.

**Al-Mustakfi Billah,** المستكفى بالله, was the 22nd khalíf of the Abbaside family, and the son of al-Muktafí the son of al-Mó'tazid Billáh. He succeeded his uncle al-Muttaķí in 945 A. D., 333 A. H, reigned in Baghdád one year and four months, and was deposed by his wazír in 946 A. D., 334 A. H. After him al-Mutía' Billáh was raised to the throne.

**Al-Mustansir Billah,** المستنصر بالله, the son of Táhir, was the fifth khalíf of Egypt of the Fátimite race. He succeeded his father A. D. 1036, and with the assistance of a Turk named Basásirí, conquered Baghdád and imprisoned al-Káem Billáh about the year 1054 A. D., and for a year and half was acknowledged the only legitimate chief of all the Musalmáns. Basásirí was defeated and killed by Tughral Beg A. D. 1059, 487 A. H. *Vide* Basásirí. Al-Mustanasar died in 1094, having reigned 60 years; and was succeeded by his son al-Mustaa'lí Billáh Abúl Ķásim.

**Al-Mustansir Billah I,** المستنصر بالله, the eleventh khalíf of the race of Abbás, ascended the throne of Baghdád after the murder of his father al-Mutwakkil in December 861 A. D., Shawwal, 247 A. H., and had reigned only six months, when he was cut off by the hand of death in 862 A. D., 248 A. H. He was succeeded by his cousin al-Musta'ín Billáh.

**Al-Mustansir Billah II,** المستنصر بالله, surnamed Abú Ja'far al-Mansúr, ascended the throne of Baghdád after the death of his father al-Táhir, in 1226 A. D., 623 A. H. He was the 36th khalíf of the house of Abbás, reigned about 17 years, and died in 1242 A. D., 640 A. H., leaving his kingdom to his son al-Mustaa'sim Billáh the last of the khalífs.

**Al-Mustanjid Billah,** المستنجد بالله, the thirty-second khalíf of the race of Abbás, succeeded to the throne of Baghdád after the death of his father al-Muktafí, in 1160 A. D., 555 A. H., reigned 11 lunar years and died in 1171 A. D., 566 A. H., when his son al-Mustazí succeeded him.

**Al-Mustarshid Billah,** المسترشد بالله, the twenty-ninth khalíf of the Abbaside family, succeeded his father al-Mustazahr to the throne of Baghdád in 1118 A. D., 512 A. H. It is related by ibn Khallikán that when Sultán Masaúd the son of Muhammad the son of Maliksháh Saljúkí was encamped outside of the town of Marágha in Azurbeján, al-Mustarashid was then with him, and on Thursday the 28th or according to ibn Mustaufí, the 14th or 28th Zil'ķada 529 A. H. (corresponding with the 24th August or 7th September, 1135 A. D.) a band of assassins broke into the khalíf's tent and murdered him. Al-Mustarashid reigned 17 lunar years and some months, and was succeeded by his son al-Ráshid Billáh.

**Al-Mustazhir Billah,** المستظهر بالله, the son of al-Muktadí, was the twenty-eighth khalíf of the dynasty of Abbás. He was placed on the throne of Baghdád after the death of his father in 1094 A. D., 487 A. H., by Barkyaraķ Saljúkí, the Sultán of Persia. He reigned 25 lunar years and some months, and at his death which happened in the year 1118 A. D., 512 A. H., he was succeeded by his son al-Mustarashid.

**Al-Mustazi Bi-amr-illah,** المستضي بامر الله, the thirty-third khalíf of the Abbaside family, succeeded his father al-Mustanjad to the throne of Baghdád in 1171 A. D., 566 A. H. He reigned about seven years and died in 1179 A. D., 575 A. H., when his son al-Násir Billáh succeeded him.

**Al-Mutaa'zz Billah,** المتعز بالله, the son of al-Mutwakkil, was the thirteenth khalíf of the race of Abbás. He deposed his brother al-Mustaín in 866 A. D., 252 A. H., and having caused him to be murdered privately, ascended the throne of Baghdád. He did not, however, long enjoy the dignity of which he had so iniquitously possessed himself, being deposed by the Turkish Militia (who now began to set up and depose khalífs as they pleased) in the year 869 A. D., 255 A. H. After his deposition, he was sent under an escort from Sarr Manrae to Baghdád, where he died of thirst and hunger, after a reign of three years and about seven months. The fate of this khalíf was peculiarly hard: the Turkish towns had mutinied for their pay; and al-Mutaazz not having money to satisfy their demands, applied to his mother named Kabíha for 50,000 dínars. This she refused, telling him that she had no money at all, although it afterwards appeared that she was possessed of immense treasure. After his deposition, however, she was obliged to discover them, and even deposit them in the hands of the new khalíf al-Muhtadí. They consisted of 1,000,000 dínars, a bushel of emeralds, and another of pearls, and three pounds and three quarters of rubies of the colour of fire.

**Al-Mutia' Billah,** المطيع بالله, the twenty-third khalíf of the race of Abbás was the son of al-Muḳtadir Billáh. He ascended the throne of Baghdád after al-Mustakfí in 946 A. D., 334 A. H., reigned 29 lunar years and 4 months and died in 974 A. D., 363 A. H. His son al-Taya' succeeded him.

**Al-Muttaki Billah,** المتقى بالله, the son of al-Muḳtadir was the twenty-first khalíf of the dynasty of Abbás. He succeeded his brother al-Rází Billáh to the throne of Baghdád in 941 A. D., 329 A. H., reigned 3 years 11 months and 15 days and died in 945 A. D., 333 A. H. He was succeeded by his nephew, al-Mustaḳfí the son of al-Muktafi.

**Al-Mutwakkil, 'Al-allah,** المتوكل على الله. This was the name and title assumed by Abúl Fazl Ja'far on his accession to the throne of Baghdád. He was the tenth khalíf of the house of Abbás, and the son of al-Mó'tasim Billáh. He succeeded his brother al-Wáthik or Wásiḳ in the year 847 A. D., 232 A. H., and began his reign with an act of the greatest cruelty. The late khalíf's wazír having treated al-Mutwakkil ill in his brother's lifetime, and opposed his election to the khiláfat, was on that account now sent to prison, and afterwards thrown into an iron furnace lined with spikes or nails heated red hot, where he was miserably burnt to death. During this reign nothing remarkable happened, except wars with the Greeks, which were carried on with various success. He was very intolerant, especially of the Jews and Christians, on whom he heaped many indignities. He did not stop there. In his imbecility and ferocity he forbade the pilgrimage to Karbala, and caused the sacred repository of the ashes of Husain and the other martyrs interred there to be razed. He reigned 14 years 9 months and 9 days, and was assassinated and cut into seven pieces on the 24th December, 861 A. D., 17th Shawwal, 247 A. H., at the instance of his son al-Mustanasar who succeeded him.

**Al-Muwaffik Billah,** الموفق بالله, the son of al-Mutwakkil Billáh, the khalíf of Baghdád and brother and coadjutor of the khalíf al-Ma'tamid, to whom he was of much service in his battles against his enemies. He died of the elephantiasis or leprosy in the year 891 A. D., 278 A. H., and while in his last illness, could not help observing, that of 100,000 men whom he commanded, there was not one so miserable as himself. His son Mó'tazid, after the death of his brother al-Mó'tamid in 892 A. D., succeeded to the throne of Baghdád.

**Al-Muwyyid (Isma'il),** المويد اسمعيل, whose name is spelt in Lempriere's Universal Biographical Dictionary, "Alombuadad", and in Watkin's Biographical Dictionary "Almuvadad", was an Arabian historian, who gave a chronological account of the Saracen affairs in Sicily from 842 to 904 A. D. This MS. is in the library of the Escurial, in Spain, and a Latin version of it is inserted in Muratoris' Rerum Italicarum Scriptores.

**Al-Muzani,** المزنى, *vide* Abú Ibráhím Ismaíl.

**Al-Nasir Billah,** الناصر بالله, or al-Nasir-uddin allah, the son of al-Mustazí succeeded his father to the throne of Baghdád in 1179 A. D. He professed the Shía' faith, and after a long reign of 46 lunar years and 11 months, died in the year 1225 A. D. He was the 34th khalíf of the house of Abbás, and was succeeded by his son al-Táhir Billáh.



**Alp Arsalan,** الپ ارسلان, (which means in the Turkish language "the valiant lion") was a king of Persia of the Saljúkian dynasty, and the son of Dáúd Beg Saljúkí. He succeeded his uncle Tughral Beg in 1063 A. D., 455 A. H., married the sister of the khalíf Ḳáem Billáh, and his name, after that of the khalíf, was pronounced in the public prayers of the Muhammadans. He was a warlike prince; and, having spoiled the Church of St. Basil in Cæsarea, defeated Romanus Diogenes, emperor of the Greeks in 1068 A. D., 460 A. H., who was seized and carried to the conqueror. Alp Arsalan demanded of his captive, at the first conference, what he would have done if fortune had reversed their lot. "I would have given thee many a stripe", was the imprudent and virulent answer. The Sulṭán only smiled and asked Romanus what he expected would be done to him. "If thou art cruel", said the emperor, "put me to death. If vain-glorious load me with chains, and drag me in triumph to thy capital. If generous, grant me my liberty." Alp Arsalan was neither cruel nor vain-glorious, he nobly released his prisoner, and gave all his officers who were captives dresses of honor, and sent them away. Alp Arsalan after a reign of more than nine years was stabbed about the 15th of December, 1072 A. D., 30th Rabí I, 465 A. H., by a desperate Khwárizmian, whom he had taken prisoner and sentenced to death. He was buried at Marv in Khurásán, and the following is the translation of the inscription engraved on his tomb: "All ye who have seen the glory of Alp Arsalan exalted to the heavens, come to Marv, and you will behold it buried in the dust." He was succeeded by his son Malikshâh.

**Alp Arsalan,** who is by some called Apal Arsalan, was the son of Atsiz, a Sulṭán of Khwárizm, whom he succeeded in A. D. 1166, 551—557 A. H. and died in 1162 A. D.

**Alptakin or Alpṫagin,** الپتكين, *vide* Alaptakín.

**Al-Rashid or Harun al-Rashid,** هارون الرشيد, the celebrated hero of the Arabian Nights, was the fifth khalíf of the race of Abbás and son of al-Mahdí, he succeeded his eldest brother al-Hádí to the throne of Baghdád in 786 A. D., 170 A. H. This was one of the best and wisest princes that ever sat on the throne of Baghdád. He was also extremely fortunate in all his undertakings, though he did not much extend his dominions by conquest. In his time the Moslem empire may be said to have been in its most flourishing state, though, by the independency of the Moslems in Spain, who had formerly set up a khalíf of the house of Umyya, his territories were not quite so extensive as those of some of his predecessors. He, possessed the provinces of Syria, Palestine, Arabia, Persia, Armenia, Natolia, Media or Azurbeján, Babylonia, Assyria, Sindh, Sijistan, Khurásán, Tabristán, Jurján, Zábulistán, Mawarunnahr, or great Bukhária, Egypt, Libya, Mauritania &c., so that his empire was by far the most powerful of any in the world, and extended farther than the Roman empire ever had done.

In the beginning of the year 802 A. D., 186 A. H., he divided the government of his extensive dominions among his three sons in the following manner: To al-Amín the eldest, he assigned the provinces of Syria, Irák, the three Arabias, Mesopotamia, Assyria, Media, Palestine, Egypt, and all the part of Africa extending from the confines of Egypt and Ethiopia to the Straits of Gibraltar, with the dignity of khalíf; to al-Mámún the second, he assigned Persia, Kirmán, the Indies, Khurásán, Tabristán, Kábulistán and Zabulistán, together with the vast province of Máwarunnahr, and to his third son al-Ḳásim, he gave Armenia, Natolia, Jurján, Georgia, Circassia, and all the Moslem territories bordering upon the Euxine sea. As to the order of succession, al-Amín was to ascend the throne immediately after his father's decease; after him, al-Mámún; and then al-Ḳásim, whom he had surnamed al-Mó'tasim.

The most considerable exploits performed by this khalíf were against the Greeks, who by their perfidy provoked him to make war upon them, and whom he always overcame. In the year 803 A. D., 187 A. H., the khalíf received a letter from the Greek emperor Nicephorus, commanding him to return all the money he had extorted from the Empress Iráne, or expect soon to see an imperial army in the heart of his territories. This insolent letter so exasperated Hárún, that he immediately assembled his forces and advanced to Heraclea, laying the country, through which he passed, waste with fire and sword. For some time also he kept that city straitly besieged; which so terrified the Greek emperor that he submitted to pay an annual tribute.

In the year 804 A. D., 188 A. H., war was renewed with the Greeks, and Nicephorus with a great army attacked the khalíf's forces with the utmost fury. He was, however, defeated with the loss of 40,000 men, and received three wounds in the action; after which the Moslems committed terrible ravages in his territories, and returned home laden with spoils. The next year Harún invaded Phrygia; defeated an imperial army sent to oppose him, and having ravaged the country, returned without any considerable loss. In the year 806, 190 A. H., the khalíf marched into the imperial territories with an army of 135,000 men, besides a great number of volunteers and others who were not enrolled among his troops. He first took the city of Heraclea, from which he is said to have carried 16,000 prisoners; after which he made himself master of several other places, and, in the conclusion of the expedition, he made a descent on the island of Cyprus, which he plundered in a terrible manner. This success so intimidated Nicephorus, that he immediately sent the tribute due to Hárún, the withholding of which had been the cause of the war; and concluded a peace upon the khalíf's own terms. Charlemagne respected his character, and Hárún in token of his friendship presented to the European prince a clock, the mechanism and construction of which were regarded among the prodigies of the age. Hárún reigned 23 years and died in Khurásán on the eve of Saturday the 24th March, 809 A. D., 3rd Jamad II, 193 A. H., and was buried at Tús which is now called Mashhad. He was succeeded by his eldest son al-Amín.

**Al-Rashid Billah,** الراشد باالله, the thirtieth khalíf of the Abbasides succeeded his father al-Mustarashad in August or September, 1135 A. D., Zil'kad, 529 A. H., and died in the year 1136 A. D., 530 A. H. He was succeeded by al-Muktafí the son of al-Mustazahir.

**Al-Razi,** see Rází.

**Al-Razi Billah,** الراضى باالله, the son of al-Muktadir and the twentieth khalíf of the house of Abbás, was the last who deserved the title of the Commander of the Faithful. He was raised to the throne of Baghdád, after the dethronement of his uncle al-Káhir Billáh by the wazír ibn Makla in April 934 A. D., Jamad I, 322 A. H. In the year 936, the khalíf finding himself distressed on all sides by usurpers, and having a wazír of no capacity, instituted a new office superior to that of wazír, which he entitled Amír-ul-Umra. This great officer, Imád-ud-daula Alí Bóya, was trusted with the management of the finances in a much more absolute and unlimited manner than any of the khalíf's wazírs ever had been. Nay he officiated for the khalíf in the great mosque at Baghdád, and had his name mentioned in the public prayers throughout the kingdom. In short the khalíf was so much under the power of this officer, that he could not apply a single dínar to his own use without the leave of the Amír-ul-Umra. In the year 937 A. D. the Moslem empire so great and powerful, was shared among the following usurpers:

The cities of Wasat, Basra, Kúfa with the rest of the Arabian Irák, were considered as the property of the Amír-ul-Umrá, though they had been in the beginning of the year seized upon by a rebel called al-Baridi, who could not be driven out of them.

The country of Fars, Faristan, or Persia properly so called, was possessed by Imad-ud-daula Alí ibn Boya, who resided in the city of Shíráz.

Part of the tract denominated al-Jabal, together with Persian Irák, which is the mountainous part of Persia, and the country of the ancient Parthians, obeyed Rukn-ud-daula, the brother of Imad-ud-daula, who resided at Isfahán. The other part of the country was possessed by *Washmakin* the Dílamite.

Dayár Rabia, Dayár Bikr, Dayár *Modar*, and the city of Mousal, acknowledged for their sovereign a race of princes called Hamdanites.

Egypt and Syria no longer obeyed the khalífs, but Muhammad ibn Táj who had formerly been appointed governor of those provinces.

Africa and Spain had long been independent.

Cicily and Crete were governed by princes of their own.

The provinces of Khurásán and Málvarunnahr were under the dominions of al-Nasr ibn Ahmad, of the dynasty of the Samánians.

The provinces of Tabristán, Jurjan or Georgia, and Mázindarán, had kings of the first dynasty of the Dílamites.

The province of Kirmán was occupied by Abú Alí Muhammad ibn Eylia al-Sámání, who had made himself master of it a short time before. And

Lastly, the provinces of Yemama and Bahryn, including the district of Hajr, were in the possession of Abú Táhir the Karmatian.

Thus the khalífs were deprived of all their dominions, and reduced to the rank of sovereign pontiffs; in which light, though they continued for some time to be regarded by the neighbouring princes, yet their power never arrived to any height. In this low state the khalífs continued till the extinction of the Khiláfat by Halákú Khán the Tartar in the year 1258 A. D., 656 A. H.

Al-Rází Billáh reigned 7 years 2 months and 11 days and died in 941 A. D., 329 A. H. He was succeeded by his brother al-Muttakí.

**Al-Saharawi,** الصحراوي, *vide* Abúl Kásim.

**Al-Saffah,** السفاح, surname of Abúl Abbás, the son of Muhammad, the son of Alí, the son of 'Abdulláh, the son of Abbás the uncle of the prophet. He was proclaimed khalífa by the inhabitants of Kúfa on Friday the 29th of November, 749 A. D., 13th Rabí II, 132 A. H., upon which a battle took place between him and Marwán II the last khalífa of the house of Umyya or Ommaides, in which the latter was slain, 5th of August, 750 A. D., 26th Zil-hijja, 132 A. H. Al-Saffáh after this victory investing himself with sovereign power, laid the foundation of the dynasty of the Abbasides, which continued to be transmitted to his family from father to son for 524 lunar years, during a succession of 37 khalífs, till they were dispossessed by Halákú Khán the Tartar king of Persia in 1258 A. D., 656 A. H. By the elevation of the house of Abbás to the dignity of khiláfat, began that glorious period during which Arabic and Persian literature reached its highest perfection. With some few exceptions these khalífas were the noblest race of kings that ever adorned the throne of sovereignty. Abúl Abbás died, after a reign of more than four years, of the small-pox, on Sunday the 9th of June, 754 A. D., 13th Zil-hijja 136 A. H., and was succeeded by his brother Abú Ja'far Almansúr.

*List of the khalífas of the race of Abbás who reigned at Baghdád.*

1. Al-Saffáh or Abúl 'Abbás al-Saffáh.
2. Al-Mansúr.
3. Al-Mahdí son of al-Mansúr.
4. Al-Hádí, son of Mahdí.
5. Al-Rashíd or Hárún al-Rashíd son of Mahdí.
6. Al-Amín, son of Hárún.
7. Al-Mamún, son of Hárún.

Ibrahím son of Mahdí, competitor.

8. Al-Mo'tasim Billáh, son of Hárún.
9. Al-Wáthiḳ or Wásiḳ, son of Mo'tasim.
10. Al-Mutwakkil.
11. Al-Mustanasir Billáh.
12. Al-Mustaín Billáh.
13. Al-Mo'tiz Billáh.
14. Al-Muhtadí Billáh.
15. Al-Mo'tamid.
16. Al-Motazid Billáh.
17. Al-Muktafí Billáh.
18. Al-Muḳtadir Billáh.
19. Al-Kahir Billáh.
20. Al-Rází Billáh.
21. Al-Muttakí Billáh.
22. Al-Mustakfí Billáh.
23. Al-Mutía Billáh.
24. Al-Táyá Billáh.
25. Al-Ḳádir Billáh.
26. Al-Ḳáem be-amr-ulláh.
27. Al-Muḳtadí Billáh.
28. Al-Mustazahir Billáh.
29. Al-Mustarashid Billáh.
30. Al-Rahhid Billáh.
31. Al-Muktafí bi-amr-ulláh.
32. Al-Mustanjad Billáh.
33. Al-Mustazí bi-amr-ulláh.
34. Al-Násir Billáh.
35. Al-Táhir bi-amr-ulláh.
36. Al-Mustanasar Billáh II.
37. Al-Mo'tasim Billáh, the last khalíf.

**Al-Tahir bi-amr-illah Muhammad,** بامرالله محمد الطاهر, succeeded his father al-Násir Billáh to the throne of Baghdád in 1225 A. D., 622 A. H. He was the thirty-fifth khalíf of the house of Abbás, reigned 9 months and 11 days and died in 1226 A. D., 623 A. H. His son al-Mustanasar II succeeded him.

**Al-Taya' (or al-Tayi') Billah,** الطايع بالله, the son of al-Mutía' Billáh was the twenty-fourth khalíf of Baghdád. He succeeded his father in 974 A. D. reigned 17 years and 4 months, and was deposed by Bahá-ud-daula in 991 A. D., when Kádir Billáh the son of Is-ḥáḳ the son of Muḳtadir was raised to the throne.

**Altimsh,** التمش, *vide* Shams-uddín Altimsh.

**Al-Walid,** الوليد, *vide* Walíd.

**Al-Wathik or al-Wasik Billah,** الواثق, the ninth khalíf of the family of the Abbasides succeeded his father al-Mó'tasim Billáh on the 5th January, 842 A. D., 18th Rabí I, 227 A. H., to the throne of Baghdád. The following year, he invaded and conquered Sicily. Nothing remarkable happened during the rest of his reign. He reigned 5 lunar years 7 months and 3 days, and died in 847 A. D., 232 A. H. He was succeeded by his brother al-Mutwakkil.

**'Alwi,** علوى, poetical name of Shaikh Wají-uddín, which see.

**'Alwi,** علوى, poetical name of Mír Táhir 'Alwí who died at Kashmír previous to the year 1723 A. D., 1136 A. H. He is the author of a díwan and a Masnawí, the latter contains the story of the blacksmith and the cotton cleanser, called Ḳissae Haddád wa Halláj.

**'Alwi Khan (Hakim),** علوى خان, a physician, who was invited from Persia by the emperor Muhammad Sháh and died at Dehlí in 1748 A. D., 1161 A. H. His title was Mo'tmid-ul-Malúk Sayyid 'Alwí Khán Hakím. He is the author of a medical work called "Jáma'-ul-Jawa'-ma'."

**'Amad,** عماد, 'Amád Sháh, 'Amád-uddín &c. *vide* Imád, Imád Sháh &c.

**'Ama-'ak or Uma-'ak Bukhari,** عمعق, *vide* Abúl Najíb-al-Bukhárí.

**Amanat,** امانت, poetical name of Sayyid Ághá Hasan son of Ághá Razwí, author of a Díwán.

**Amanat 'Ali,** امانت‌علي, (Maulwí) author of a small work entitled "Bahár Ajam", containing 121 letters written by him to different persons, in pure Persian.

**Amanat Khan Mirak,** امانت خان ميرک, title of Mír Ma'ín-uddín Ahmad Khán Khwáfí, a native of Khwáf in Khurásán. He was a nobleman of high rank in the time of the emperor 'Alamgír, and died in the year 1684 A. D., 1095 A. H., at Aurangábád. He is the author of the work called "Shariat ul-Islám."

**Amanat Khan,** امانت خان, title of Mír Husain, son of Amánat Khán Khwáfí. He was honored with the title of his father about the year 1688 A. D., 1100 A. H., by the emperor 'Alamgír, and raised to the rank of a nobleman. He held different offices under that emperor and died at Surat A. D. 1699, 1111 A. H.

**Amanat Khan,** امانت خان, a celebrated Nastálíḳ writer, who in the eleventh year of the reign of the emperor Sháh Jahán wrote the inscriptions on the Táj at Ágra.

**Amani,** ميرامانى, (Mír) of Kábul died in 981 A. H. or 1573 A. D.

**Amani,** امانى, poetical name of Mirzá Amán-ulláh the eldest son of Mahabat Khán. He flourished in the time of the emperor Sháh Jahán, and died in the year 1637 A. D., 1047 A. H. He is the author of a díwán. *Vide* Khán Zamán Bahádur and Mahábat Khán.

**Aman-ullah,** حافظ امان الله, (Háfiz) of Benares was an author and Ḳází of Lakhnau in the time of the emperor 'Alamgír. He died in 1721 A. D., 1133 A. H.

**Aman-ullah Husaini,** امان الله حسيني, author of an Insha which goes by his name, "Insháe Amán-ulláh Husainí."

**Ahmad Shah Abdali,** احمد شاه ابدالي, on his seventh invasion of Hindustan arrived at the Satlaj in 1764, A. D. Amar Singh waited on him, but was ordered to shave his head and beard before entering the royal presence. By a nazarana or present of a lac of Rupees, he purchased permission to appear bearded and unshorn, and received investiture with the title of Maha Raja Rájagán Mahindar Bakashr, which title is now borne by the head of the Patiala family.

**Amar Singh,** امرسنگه rájá of Patiala, was the son of Sardal Singh who survived his father Rájá Ala Singh two or three years. Ahmad Amar Singh *vide* Rana Amar Singh.

**Amar Singh Rana,** son of Rama Pallal Singh of Chittore, died in 1028 A. H.

**Amar Singh,** امرسنگه, son of Gaj Singh, a rajpút chief of the tribe of Ráṭhor. He killed Salábat Khán Mír Bakhshí in the 17th year of Sháh Jahán in the presence of the emperor, on Thursday evening the 25th of July, 1644 O. S., 30th Jamadi I, 1054 H., and was by the order of the emperor pursued and cut to pieces after a gallant defence near one of the gates of the fort of Agra, which is to this day called Amar Singh Darwáza or Amar Singh Gate. An account of this prince's early history will be found in Tod's *Rájasthán.*

**Amar Singh,** امرسنگه, of Benares whose poetical name was Khushgó, held a government appointment in the Koel district. He compiled a short history of Akbar's palace and of the Táj of Agra and put the Bahár Dánish into verse and called it Tarjuma Bahár Dánish. This book is to be distinguished from the Izhár Dánish, an Urdú Translation of Bahár Dánish by Mullazáda at Palnar.

**Amar Singh,** (Rana) son of Rana Purtab Singh *vide* Rana Sankar.

**Ambaji Inglia,** a rája of Gwaliar who was living in 1803.

**Amin,** امين, the sixth khalíf of the house of Abbás. *Vide* al-Amín.

**Amin,** امين, poetical name of Sháh Amín-uddín of Azímábád who flourished about the year 1715 A. D., 1127 H., and left a diwán of Ghazals &c.

**Amina Begum,** امينه بيگم, *vide* Ghasítí Begum.

**Amin Ahmad** or **Amin Muhammad Razi,** امين احمد رازي the author of the Biographical Dictionary called "Haft Aklím." (The seven climates.) This book, which he finished in the time of the emperor Akbar in 1594 A. D., 1002 A. H., contains a short description of the seven climates of the Temperate Zone, and the Topography of their principal cities; with memoirs of the illustrious persons and eminent poets which each has produced.

**Amin-uddin Khan,** Nawab of Loharí, one of the eldest and most worthy of the chiefs of Dehlí. He died on the 31st of December, 1869 A. D., aged 70 years. His eldest son Mirzá 'Ala-uddín Khán succeeded to his estates at Saharú, on the 11th of January 1870.

**Amini,** اميني, poetical name of Amír Sulṭán Ibrahím, a contemporary of Khwája 'Asafí who died in 1520 A. D. 926 A. H. Amíní wrote a chronogram on that occasion.

**Amin-uddin,** مير امين الدين, (Mír) a poet and a great jester, was contemporary with the poets Moulana Alí Káhi and Khwája Alí Shaháb.

**Amin-uddin,** امير يمين الدين, (Amír) *vide* Yemín-uddín (Amír) and Tughrái.

**Amin-ud-daula Abul Jin,** امين الدولة ابوالجن, surnamed the Samaritan, was a physician and had been wazír to Málik Sálah Isma'íl. He was strangled at Cairo in 1250 A. D., 648 A. H., and there were found in his house, amongst other precious articles, about 10,000 volumes of valuable works, copied by the most celebrated calligraphers.

**Amin-ud-daula Khan,** امين الدوله خان, a rebel, was blown from the mouth of a gun on the 3rd August, 1857, at Agra.

**Amir bi Ahkam Allah,** امربا حكام الله, surnamed Abú Alí Mansúr seventh khalíf of the Fatimite dynasty of Egypt, succeeded his father al-Mustaa'lí Billáh in December 1101. From this time to the reign of 'Azid li-dín Allah, during which period five khalífs ascended the throne of Egypt, the history of that country affords little else than an account of the intestine broils and contests between the wazírs or prime ministers, who were now become so powerful, that they had in a great measure stripped the khalífs of their civil power, and left them nothing but a shadow of spiritual dignity. These contests at last gave occasion to a revolution, by which the race of Fatimite khalífs were totally extinguished. *Vide* 'Azid li-dín Allah.

**Amir,** امير, poetical name of Amír-ud-daulá Nasír Jang commonly called Mirza Menḍhú, son of Nawab Shuja-ud-daulá and brother to Nawab Asaf-ud-daulá.

**Amiran Shah,** اميران شاه, *vide* Mírán Sháh.

**Amira Singh Tappa,** اميره سنگه تپه, a chief of Nipál. He was the highest in rank and character of all the military chiefs of Naipál. In 1814 during his campaign against Sir David Ochterlony in the Kamáon hills, he evinced equal valour and patriotism.

**Amir Barid, I,** امير بريد, the son of Ḳásim Baríd whom he succeeded in the government of Ahmadábád Bídar in 1504 A. D., 910 A. H. During his rule the king Sulṭán Mahmúd Sháh Bahmaní died in 1517, A. D. 923 A. H., when Amír Baríd placed Sulṭán 'Alá-uddín III, on the throne, and after his death Sulṭán Kalím Ullah, who being treated with great rigour by the Amír, fled from Bídar to Ahmadnagar, where he died shortly after. With Kalím Ulláh ended the dynasty of the Bahmaní kings of Dakhan. Amír Baríd reigned over the territories of Ahmadabád Bídar with full power more than 25 years, and died at Daulatábád in 1542 A. D., 949 A. H. He was buried at Ahmadábád Bídar, and succeeded by his son Alí Baríd.

**Amir Barid, II,** اميربريد ثاني, succeeded to the government of Ahmadábád Biwar after deposing his relative Alí Baríd Sháh II in 1609 A. D., and was the last of the Baríd Shahí dynasty.

**Amiri,** اميري, the poetical name of Mauláná Sulṭán Muhammad, a distinguished man who lived in the time of Sháh Tahmasp Safwí I. He praised this sovereign in his poems, and is the translator of Amír Alí Sher's Tazkira, called "Majális-ul-Nafáes", from Turki into Persian. He is also the author of the "Bostán ul-Khayál."

**Amir Khan,** اميرخان, title of Mír Abúl Wafá, the eldest son of Mír Ḳásim Khán Namkín, was a nobleman in the time of the emperors Jahangír and Sháh Jahán. At the time of his death he was governor of Ṭhaṭṭa, where he died A. D. 1647, 1057 A. H., aged more than 100 years. His former name was Mír Khán, but having made a present of one lac of rupees to Sháh Jahán, he was honored with the title of Amír Khán.

**Amir Khan,** اميرخان ميرميران, surnamed Mír Mírán, the son of Khalíl-ulláh Khán Yezdí, was a nobleman of high rank in the time of the emperors Sháh Jahán and 'Alamgír, and a great favorite of the latter. He died at Kábul on the 28th April, 1698 A. D., 27th Shawwal 1109 H., and the emperor conferred the title of Amír Khán on his son.

**Amir Khan,** نواب اميرخان, (Nawáb) entitled U'mdat-ul-Mulk, was the son of the principal favorite of the emperor 'Alamgír, of the same name, and a descendant of the celebrated Sháh Na'mat-ulláh Walí. He was himself a favorite of the emperor Muhammad Sháh; was appointed governor of Allahabad in 1739 A. D., 1152 A. H., and recalled to court in 1743 A. D., 1156 A. H. He was naturally free of speech, and the emperor, fond of his repartee, had allowed him more license in conversation than was consistent with respect to his own dignity, when he was on business with the emperor, which by degrees disgusted Muhammad Sháh and made him wish his removal from office. He was consequently, with the consent of the emperor, stabbed with a dagger by a person who had been discharged from his service, and fell down dead on the spot. This circumstance took place on Friday the 26th December, 1746, 23rd Ẕil-ḥijja, 1159 H. He was buried after four days in the sepulchre of Khalíl-ulláh Khán his grandfather, which is close to the Saráe of Rúh-ulláh Khán at Dehlí. His poetical name was Anjám. He composed chiefly logographs, and has left Persian and Rekhta Poems.

**Amir Khan,** امیر خان, the famous chief of the Pindarís and ancestor to the present Nawab of Tonk. He was originally in the service of Jaswant Ráo Holkar, who becoming insane in 1806 and incapable of the administration of his own affairs, this Muhammadan chief endeavoured to establish an ascendancy at his court, but soon left it with the army he commanded to pursue the separate object of his own ambition, and became the chief of the Pindarís. Treaty was ratified with him by the British Government on the 19th December, 1817. He had on various pretexts avoided the ratification of the engagements which his agent had concluded with the resident of Dehlí, but the movement of troops to his vicinity, and their occupation of positions which left him only the option between engaging in an unequal conflict and signing this treaty, induced him to adopt the safer course. He was confirmed in the possession of all the territories he held from the Holkar family, but compelled to surrender his large trains of artillery to the English Government, and to disband that great body of plunderers which had been for more than two years the scourge of Málwa and Rájputána. Amír Khán died A. D. 1834, 1250 A. H.

**Amir Khan,** امیر خان, whose proper name was Mír Khán, but was changed by the emperor 'Alamgír by adding an alif to it into Amír Khán. On a spot of seven bíghas of ground, he had built his house close to the place called Guzar Tijara including the mahalla of Chhípitolá. In the first year of the emperor 'Alamgír he was appointed governor of the fort of Sháhjahanabad, and in the 11th year of the reign of the emperor he was appointed Súbadár of Kábul.

**Amir Khan Sindhi,** امیرخان سندهي, title of Mír Abdul Karím, son of Amír Khán the son of Mír Abul Kásim Namkín. He was employed in various offices during the reign of 'Alamgír, Bahádur Sháh and Farrukh-siyar, and died some time before the accession of Muhammad Sháh to the throne of Dehlí.

**Amir Khoand,** امیر خواند, *vide* Mír Khúnd or Khawind Sháh.

**Amir Khusro,** امیرخسرو, *vide* Khusro (Amír).

**Amir Mahmud,** فخرالدین امیرمحمود, a native of Fareomud, surnamed Fakhr-uddín and commonly called Ibn-Yemín, was the son of Amír Yemín-uddín entitled Málik-ul Fuzlá, *i. e.*, the prince of the learned. Amír Mahmúd was an excellent poet and died on Saturday the 29th of January, 1368 A. D., Jumáda II, 769 A. H., in Persia. He is mentioned in Dr. Sprenger's Catalogue, p. 67, to have died in 749 Hijrí corresponding with 1348 A. D., and in the Tazkira Daulat Shahí it is mentioned, that he died in 745 A. H., 1344 A. D. He has left a Díwán.

**Amir Mirza,** نواب امیرمیرزا, (Nawáb) was the son of George Hopkins Walters, a pensioned European Officer, who with his family, consisting of a wife, two daughters and one son, had established himself in Lakhnau as a merchant, many years ago. After his death his family through the intrigues of one Bakhsh Alí Khán, embraced the Muhammadan religion, and the younger daughter not long after was consigned to the Seraglio of king Nasír-uddín Hydar and became one of the queens of that monarch, under the title of Wilayetí Mahal, or the King's European consort. The elder daughter also received the name and title of Ashraf-un-nisa Begam. She remained unmarried all her life. The brother Joseph Walters received the name of Amír Mirzá. He was brought up as a Musalmán of the Shí'a sect, and always took a pride in showing himself as an orthodox follower of the Crescent. After Wilayetí Mahal's death, her elder sister Ashraf-un-nisa Begam succeeded to her estate, consisting of Government Securities valued at 1,14,00,000 rupees besides jewellery, moveable and immoveable property of considerable value. In 1832 Ashraf-un-nisa died, and was succeeded by Amír Mirzá her brother, who, squandered almost the whole property by his reckless prodigality. Amír Mirzá died on the 10th of January, 1870, in his 66th year.

**Amir Mo'izzi,** امیر معزي, a celebrated poet of Samarkand who served under Sultán Malik Sháh and Sultán Sanjar Saljúkí, and was honored with the title of Málik-ush-Shua'rá, or the Royal Poet. He was accidentally killed by an arrow shot by the latter prince. His Díwán contains 15,000 verses. His death happened in the year 1147 A. D., 542 A. H. His proper name was Amír Alí.

**Amir Shahi,** امیر شاهي سبزداري, of Sabzwár, a poet who flourished in the time of Sháhrukh Mirzá about the year 1436 A. D. *Vide* Sháhí (Amír).

**Amir Taimur,** امیرتیمور صاحبقران, styled Sáhib Kirán, because he reigned more than 30 years. He is also called Timarlang (Tamerlane) from some defect in his feet; was born at Kush in ancient Sogdania on Tuesday the 9th April, 1336, A. D. 27th Sha'bán, 736 A. H. Some say he was the son of a shepherd, and others, that he was descended in a right line from Kájulí Bahádur, son of Túmana Khán, of the same lineage with Changez Khán the celebrated conqueror of Persia. His father's name was Amír Turágháí and mother's Takína Khátún; however, his obscurity was soon forgotten in the glory of his exploits. Distinguished by his courage and unbounded ambition, he gained a number of faithful adherents, and seized the city of Balkh, the capital of Khurásán, and having put to death Amír Husain the ruler of that place, whose sister he had married, he ascended the throne on Wednesday the 10th of April, 1370 A. D., 12th Ramzán, 771 A. H. He then subdued Kandahár, Persia, and Baghdád, and seconded by an enthusiastic army, he penetrated to India, took Dehlí on Tuesday the 17th December, 1398 A. D., 7th Rabí' II, 801 A. H., with its immense treasures, and returned to punish Baghdád that shook off his yoke. The offending city was given up to pillage, and 80,000 of her inhabitants put to the sword. Now master of the fairer part of Asia, he interfered, at the request of the Greek emperor, in the affairs of Báiazíd (Bajazet) emperor of the Turks, and commanded him to abandon the siege of Constantinople. The message roused the indignation of Báiazíd; he marched against the new enemy, and was defeated by him in Phrygia, after a battle of 3 days, on Friday the 21st of July, 1402 A. D., 19th Zil-hijja, 804 A. H. Baiazíd fell into the hands of the emperor, and was carried about in mockery in an iron cage. To these conquests Taimúr added Egypt and the treasures of Cairo, and then fixed the seat of his empire at Samarkand, where he received the homage of Manuel Palæologus, emperor of Constantinople, and of Henry III, King of Castile, by their ambassadors. Taimúr was preparing fresh victories by the invasion of China, when death stopped his career on Wednesday the 18th of February, 1405 A. D., 17th Sha'bán, 807 A. H., in the 36th year of his reign, aged 71 years, and was buried at Samarkand. He was the first who founded the dynasty of the Mughul emperors of Dehlí. After his death he received the title of "Firdaus Makání," *i. e.*, "May paradise be his place of residence." He had four sons, *viz.*, Jahángír Mirzá, Umar Shaikh Mirzá, Mírán Sháh and Sháhrukh Mirzá. Tamerlane on his death-bed named his grandson Pír Muhammad son of Jahángír Mirzá, the universal heir of all his dominions; but the contempt with which his will was treated after his death, was equal to the veneration which had been paid to his authority during his life. The Sultán Khalíl, another of his grandsons, immediately took possession of the capital of Samarkand, and proclaimed himself emperor. Pír Muhammad did not live long enough to assert his rights, but was assassinated six months after the death of his grandfather. After his death, Sháhrukh Mirzá the youngest of the two surviving sons of Tamerlane, succeeded to the inheritance assigned for Pír Muhammad.

*List of the kings of Samarkand of the race of Amír Taimúr.*

Khalíl Sulṭán, the son of Mírán Sháh.
Sháhrukh Mirzá, son of Amír Taimúr.
Ala-ud-daula Mirzá.
Ulugh Beg Mirzá, son of Sháhrukh.
Mirzá Babar who subsequently conquered Dehlí and became the first emperor of the Mughuls in India.
Mirzá Abdul-Latíf.
Mirzá Sháh Muhammad.
Mirzá Ibrahím.
Sulṭán Abú Sayyid.
Mirzá Yádgár Muhammad.

**Amir Yemin-uddin,** اميريمين الدين, entitled Málik-ul-Fuzlá, *i. e.*, the prince of the learned, was a Turk and an excellent poet. He flourished in the time of Sulṭán Muhammad Khudá Banda, and died in 1324 A. D., 724 A. H., *vide* Tughardí.

**Amili,** آملي, a poet who is the author of a Díwán. This person appears to be the same with Shaikh Baha-uddín 'Amilí.

**Amina,** آمنه, the wife of 'Abdullah, and mother of Muhammad the prophet of the Musalmáns. She was the daughter of Wahab the son of 'Abdul Manáf. She is represented as the most beautiful, prudent and virtuous lady of her tribe, and consequently the most worthy of such an extraordinary person as 'Abdullah. She died six years after the birth of her son Muhammad, about the year 577 A. D.

**Amjad 'Ali Shah,** امجد علي شاه, was the son of Muhammad Alí Sháh whom he succeeded on the throne of Lakhnau as king of Oudh with the title of Suriá Jáh, on the 17th of May, 1842, 5th Rabí' II, 1258 A. H., and died on the 16th March, 1847 A. D., 26th Safar, 1263 A. H. He was succeeded by his son Wájid Alí Sháh, in whose time Oudh was annexed to the British Goverment on the 7th of February, 1856 A. D.

**'Ammar ibn Hissan,** عمّار ابن حسان, was Alí's general of the horse, and was killed in battle fought by Alí against Mu'áwia the first khalíf of the house of Umaia, in the month of July, 657 A. D., Safar, 37 A. H. He was then about 90 years of age, and had been in three several engagements with Muhammad himself. He was one of the murderers of Usmán the 3rd khalíf after Muhammad.

**Amra-al Kais,** امراء القيس, the son of Hajar, one of the most illustrious poets the Arabians had before Muhammadanism. He is one of the seven poets whose poems have, for their excellency, been hung in the temple of Mecca. These poems were called "Muallakat," (suspended), and as they were written in letters of gold, they were also called "Muzahhibát." The names of these seven celebrated poets, are Amra-al-Kais, Tarafa, Zuhír, Labíd, Antár, Amrú and Hárath.

Amra-al-Kais is the same person who is commonly called Majnún, the lover of Laila, and Labíd was his friend and master. *Vide* Lover of Majnun and Laila translated into English.

**Amrit Rao,** امرت راو, a Mahrattá chief who had been placed on the masnad of Púná by Holkar in 1803 A. D., but deposed by the British and a pension of 700,000 rupees was assigned for his support annually. He was the son of Raghunáth Ráo commonly called Raghoba. For some time he resided at Banaras and then in Bundelkhand; and died at the former station in 1824, A. D.

**Amru bin Mua'wia,** عمرو بن معاويه, an ancient Arabian poet whose collection of poems are to be found in the Royal Library at Paris, No. 1120.

**'Amru ibn Al-'As,** عمرو ابن العاص, a celebrated Muhammadan, at first the enemy and afterwards the friend of Muhammad, of whom, it is reported by tradition, that Muhammad said, "There is no truer Musalman, nor one more steadfast in the faith than 'Amrú." He served in the wars of Syria, where he behaved with singular courage and resolution. Afterwards Umar the khalíf sent him into Egypt, which he reduced in 641 A. D., 20 A. H., and became lieutenant of the conquered country. Usmán continued him in that post four years, and then removed him; whereupon he retired to Palestine, where he lived privately till Usmán's death. Upon this event, he went over to Mu'áwia upon his invitation; and took a great part in the dispute between 'Alí and Mu'áwia. The latter restored him to the lieutenancy of Egypt, and continued him in it till his death, which happened in 663 A. D., 43 A. H. Before he turned Muhammadan, he was one of the three poets who were famous for writing lampoons upon Muhammad, in which style of composition 'Amrú particularly excelled. There are some fine proverbs of his remaining, and also some good verses. He was the son of a courtezan of Mecca, who seems to have numbered some of the noblest of the land among her lovers. When she gave birth to this child, the infant was declared to have most resemblance to 'As, the oldest of her admirers, whence, in addition to his name of Amrú, he received the designation of Ibn-al-'As.

**'Amru,** عمرو بن سعيد, the son of Sa'íd was a cousin of the khalíf 'Abdul-Malik. In the year 688 A. D., 69 A. H., the khalíf left Damascus to go against Misaa'b the son of Zuber, and appointed Amrú to take care of Damascus, who seized upon it for himself, which obliged 'Abdul-Malik to return. After three or four days the khalíf sent for him and killed him with his own hand.

**'Amru bin Lais,** عمرو بن ليث, brother of Ya'kúb ibn Lais, whom he succeeded in the government of Khurásán, &c., in 878 A. D., 265 A. H., and ruled over those countries for 23 years. He was at last seized by Amír Isma'íl Sámání in 900 A. D., 288 A. H., and sent to Baghdád where he was confined for some time; his execution was the last act of the Khalíf Al-Mo'tazid, who gave orders for it a few months before his own death in 901 A. D., 289 A. H. He was blind of one eye. With Amrú fell the fortunes of his family. His grandson Táhir, struggled for power in his native province: but after a reign of six years, during which he conquered Fárs, his authority was subverted by one of his own officers, by whom he was seized and sent prisoner to Baghdád. The only other prince of the family of Baní Lais that attained any eminence, was a chief of the name of Khaláf, who established himself in Sístán and maintained his power over that province till the time of Sulṭán Mahmúd of Ghazní, by whom he was defeated and made prisoner.

**Amurath,** names of several emperors of Turkey written so by English writers, being a corruption of Murád, which see.

**Anandpal,** انندپال, son of Jaipál I, rájá of Láhor whom he succeeded about the year 1001 A. D., and became tributary to Sulṭán Mahmúd of Ghazní. He died about the year 1013, and was succeeded in the government by his son Jaipál II.

**Anarkali,** انار كلي a famous lady, who lived in the time of the emperor Jahángír. Her mausoleum is at a place called Anárkalí in Láhor, which is now used as a church. Different stories are told concerning the name Anárkalí by which the mausoleum as well as the bazár in its vicinity is known. According to some, it was the name of a princess in Jahángír's time, while others say, that Anárkalí was a beautiful handmaid with whom Jahángír fell in love, and who, on Sháh Jahán becoming aware of it, was buried alive. These stories may or may not be true, but this much is at least certain, that the woman, after whose name the building is called, lived in the time of the emperor Jahángír or Sháh Jahán, that Jahángír or some other prince was madly in love with her, and that her death took place under such mournful circumstances, as broke the heart of the fond lover, and led him in the height of his passion and love for the princess who was no more, to compose the following couplet, and have it engraved on her tombstone: "Oh could I see again the face of my angel, for ever would I repeat thanks to the Almighty."

**Anand Rao, Gaikwar,** انند راو گیکوار, a Marhattá chief of Baróda, with whom the English Government, had in 1812 concluded a subsidiary alliance. Before the treaty he was a nominal dependant of the Peshwa.

**Anas,** آنس, a poet of Arabia.

**'Andalib,** عندليب, *vide* Khwája Násir.

**Anis,** انس, poetical name of Mohan Lál, which see.

**Anisi Shamlu,** انیسی شاملو, a poet named Yúl Kulí Beg. He was an intimate friend and constant companion of prince Ibráhím Mirzá, a grandson of Sháh Isma'íl Safwí, consequently took the takhallas of Anísí. When 'Abdullah Khán Uzbak took Hirát he made a proclamation in his army, that the life of Anísí be spared, and treated him with great respect. He came to India and received a salary of 50,000 rupees, and a jagír. He died at Barhánpúr in 1605 A. D., 1014 A. H., and has left a Díwán and a Masnawí called Mahmúd Aiáz.

**Ang** or **Ungh Khan,** a king of the Trit Tartars who resided at Karakoram, and to whom the celebrated Jangez Khán was at one time a tributary. He is also called Prester John by the Syrian Missionaries. Jangez Khán having thrown off his allegiance, a war ensued, which ended in the death of Ang Khán in 1202 A. D.

**Anjam,** انجام, the poetical name of Nawáb Umdat-ul-Mulk Amír Khán, *vide* Amír Khán.

**Anup Bai,** انوپ بائي, the wife of the emperor Jahándár Sháh, and mother of Alamgír II, king of Dehlí.

**Anushtakin,** انوشتکین, the cup-bearer of Sultán Sanjar, and father of Sultán Kutb-uddín Muhammad of Khwárizm.

**Ans bin Malik,** آنس بن مالک, *vide* Abu Hamza bin Nasr-al-Ansárí.

**'Ansuri,** عنصري, a poet of the court of Sultán Mahmúd *Vide* Unsarí.

**Antar,** انتار one of the seven Arabian poets, whose poems were hung up in the temple of Mecca in golden letters and from that circumstance were called Mua'llakát (suspended), or Muzahhibát (golden). The first volume of the history of Antár, called "the Life and Adventures of Antár," was translated into English and published in December 1818, in England. *Vide* Amra-al-Kais.

**Anwari,** انوري, a famous Persian poet surnamed Ashad-uddín. He formerly took for his poetical name, "Kháfwarí," but he changed it afterwards to "Anwarí." From the superiority of his poetical talents, he was called the king of the poets of Khurásán. He was a native of Abiward in Khurásán, was the favorite of Sultán Sanjar Saljúkí, and the rival of the poet Rashídí surnamed Watwát, who espoused the cause of Atsiz the Sultán of Khwárizm. Whilst the two princes were engaged in war, the two poets assailed one another by rhymes sent on the point of arrows. He is also said to have been the greatest astronomer of his age. It so happened in the year 581 or 582 A. H., September, 1186 A. D., that there was a conjunction of all the planets in the sign of Libra; Anwarí predicted a storm which would eradicate trees and destroy every building. When the fatal day arrived, it was perfectly calm, and there was the whole year so little wind, that the people were unable to winnow their corn. He was therefore accused for his predictions as an astrologer, and was obliged to fly to Balkh where he died in the reign of Sultán Aláuddín Takash in 1200 A. D., 596 A. H. His death is mentioned in the Khulásat-ul-Asha'ár to have taken place in 587 A. H. and others have written 592 A. H. Anwarí, when very young, was sitting at the gate of his college called Mansúria in Tús, when a man richly dressed rode by him on a fine horse, with a numerous train of attendants; upon his asking who it was, he was told, that it was a poet belonging to the court. When Anwarí reflected on the honor conferred on poetry, for which art he had a very early bent, he applied himself to it more ardently than ever, and having finished a poem, presented it to the Sultán, who approved the work and invited him to his palace, and raised him even to the first honors of the State. He found many other poets at court, among whom were Salmán, Zahír and Rashídí, all men of wit and genius. Anwarí has left us a collection of highly esteemed poems, on various subjects called Díwán Anwarí. Verses from his poems are quoted by Sa'dí in his Gulistán.

**Anwari Khan,** انوري خان, a corruption of Abú Raihán, which see.

**Anwar-uddin Khan,** انور الدين خان, nawáb of the Karnatic, a soldier of fortune, who had attained power by treacherous connivance to the murder of the legitimate heir, a child whose guardian he had been appointed by Nizám-ul-Mulk. He at first served under one of the emperors of Dehlí, and was appointed governor of Korá Jahánábád. Ill success, or perhaps ill conduct, preventing him from being able to pay the usual revenues of his government to the throne, he quitted it privately, and went to Ahmadábád, where Ghází-uddín Khán the father of Nizám-ul-Mulk, gave him a post of considerable trust and profit in the city of Súrat. After the death of Ghazí-uddín, his son who had succeeded in the Súbadarí of the southern provinces, appointed him Nawáb of Yalore or Vellore and Rájmandrum, countries which he governed from 1725 to 1741 A. D., and in 1744 he was appointed governor of the Karnatic. He was killed in battle fought against Muzaffar Jang the grandson of Nizám-ul-Mulk, on the 23rd of July 1749 O. S., 1162 A. H., who took possession of the Karnatic. Anwar-uddín was then 107 years old. His eldest son was made prisoner and his second son Muhammad Alí fled to Trichinopoly. A heroic poem called "Anwar Náma," in praise of this Nawáb was written by Abdí, in which the exploits of Major Lawrence, and the first contests between the English and French in India, are recorded with tolerable accuracy. (*Vide* Sa'ádat-ullah Khán.) His son Muhammad Alí was confirmed by Nawáb Nasir Jang in the government of the Karnatic in 1750, A. D.

**Aohad Sabzwari,** خواجة اوحد سبزواري, (Khwája) poetical name of Khwája Fakhr-uddín, a physician, astronomer and poet of Sabzwár. He died A. D. 1463, 868 A. H., aged 81 lunar years, and left a Díwán in Persian containing Ghazals, Kasídas, &c.

**Aohadi,** اوحدي, the poetical name of Shaikh Aohad-uddín of Isfahán or Maragha, a celebrated Persian poet who put into verse the "Jám-i-Jam," a book full of Muhammadan spirituality, which he wrote in imitation of the Hadíka of Sanáí; he also wrote a Díwán containing verses. He was liberally rewarded by Arghún Khán, the king of the

Tartars. He was a pupil of Aohad-uddín Kirmání; died in 1337 A. D., 738 A. H., and was buried at Marágha in Tabreiz.

**Aohad-uddin Isfahani,** اوحدالدين اسفهاني, (Shaikh) a Persian poet, *vide* Aohadí.

**Aohad-uddin Kirmani,** اوحدالدين كرماني, (Shaikh) author of the "Misbah-ul-Arwáh." He flourished in the reign of Al-Mustanasar Billáh, khalíf of Baghdád, and died in the year 1298 A. D., 697 A. H. His poetical name is Hámid. He was a cotemporary of Shaikh Sa'dí of Shíráz.

**Aohad-uddin,** اوحدالدين, the surname of the celebrated Anwarí, which see.

**Aoji,** اوجي, a poet who died in 1640 A. D., 1050 A. H.

**Aurang,** اورنگ, name of a lover whose mistress was Gulchehra.

**Aurangabadi Begam,** اورنگاباوي بيگم, one of the wives of the emperor Aurangzeb 'Alamgír.

**Aurangzeb,** اورنگزيب, the son of Sháh Jahán emperor of Dehlí. On his accession to the throne, he took the title of 'Alamgír, agreeably to the custom of the Eastern princes, who always assume a new one on that occasion. *Vide* 'Alamgír.

**Apa Sahib,** آپا صاحب, a nephew of Rághójí Bhonsla II, and cousin to Parsarám Bhonsla, commonly called Bálá Sáhib, raja of Nágpúr or Beṛáṛ. The latter succeeded his father in March 1816, but being an idiot and unfit to rule, 'Apá Sáhib assumed the chief authority under the title of Regent, and had the sole conduct of the public affairs. Although he was in a great degree indebted for his elevation to the English Government, he early evinced a disposition as inconsistent with the gratitude which he owed to that State, as with the obligations of good faith. It was also discovered that he had secretly murdered his predecessor Bálá Sáhib (Parsarám) in order to obtain that elevation which he had so disgraced. He was consequently seized in the beginning of the year 1818, and brought to the Residency, where he continued in confinement till directed to be sent under a strong escort to the Company's territories. When arrived at Raichora, a village within one march from Jabalpúr, he contrived by bribing some of his guards, to make his escape. It is believed that, after having for a short period found a refuge in Asírgurh, he fled to the Panjáb where he remained a miserable dependant on the charity of Rája Ranjít Singh. After the dethronement of 'Apá Sáhib, the grandson of Raghojí Bhonsla was raised to the masnad of Nágpúr. *Vide* Partáp Singh Naráyan.

**Apa Sahib,** آپا صاحب, also called Shalyi, third brother of Partáp Singh Naráyan, rája of Satára. After the dethronement of his brother in 1839, he was placed on the masnad of Satára by the British Government, and died on the 5th April, 1848. Before his death he expressed a wish that he might adopt as a son, a boy by name Balwant Ráo Bhonsla, it was, however, determined to annex Satára.

**'Arabshah,** عربشاه, author of a history of Amír Taimúr (Tamerlane) called "Ajáeb-ul-Makdúr," and of a treatise on the unity of God. He was a native of Damascus, where he died in 1450 A. D., 854 A. H. He is also called Ibn 'Arabsháh, and Ahmad Ibn Arabsháh.

**Aram Bano Begam,** آرام بانو بيگم, a daughter of the emperor Akbar, who died in the 40th year of her age in 1624 A. D., 1033 A. H., during the reign of Jahángír her brother, and is buried in the mausoleum of Akbar at Sikandra in Ágra. Her tomb is of white marble. Her mother's name was Bíbí Daulat Shad, and her sister's name Shakr-un-nisa Begam.

**Aram Shah,** آرام شاه, (Sulṭán) king of Dehlí, succeeded his father Sulṭán Kutb-uddín Aibak in 1210 A. D., 607 A. H., and had scarcely reigned one year when he was deposed by Altimsh, (the adopted son and son-in-law of Kutb-uddín) who assumed the title of Shams-uddín Altimsh.

**Araru,** آرارو, a zamíndár of Koṛá in the province of Allahábád, was of the tribe of Khíchaṛ, who taking advantage of the weakness of the empire, slew Nawáb Ján Nisár Khán (brother to the wazír's wife), chakladár of that district in 1731 A. D., 1144 A. H., upon which 'Azim-ulláh Khán the son of the deceased was sent with an army to chastise him, but the zamíndár took refuge in his woods, and for a long while eluded his pursuer, who, tired out, returned to Dehlí, leaving his army under the command of Khwárizm Beg Khán. Aṛáṛú, emboldened by the Nawáb's retreat, attacked and slew the deputy; upon which the wazír Kamar-uddín Khán applied for assistance to Burhán-ul-Mulk Sa'ádat Khán Súbadár of Oudh, for the reduction of the rebel. Sa'ádat Khán marched against Aṛáṛú in 1735 A. D., 1148 A. H., killed him in a battle and sent his head to the emperor Muhammad Sháh. The skin of his body was flayed off, and sent stuffed with straw to the wazír.

**Ardai Viraf,** اردي وراف, a priest of the Magian religion, who lived in the time of Ardisher Bábagán king of Persia, and is the author of the "Ardai Viráf Nama" which he wrote in the Zend, or the original Persian language. See Nousherwán Kirmání.

**Ardisher Babakan,** اردشير بابكان, or Bábagán, the son of Bábak, was, we are told a descendant of Sásán the son of Bahman and grandson of Isfandiár. He was the first king of the Sásánian dynasty. His father Bábak, who was an inferior officer in the public service, after putting to death the governor appointed by Ardawán (Artabanes) made himself master of the province Fars. The old man survived but a short time. His son Ardisher, after settling the affairs of Fars, not only made himself master of Isfáhán, but of almost all Irák before Ardawán, who was the reigning prince, took the field against him, about the year 223 A. D. The armies met in the plains of Hurmuz, where a desperate battle ensued, in which Ardawán lost his crown and his life; and the son of Bábak was hailed in the field with the proud title of Sháhan Sháh, or King of kings. He was contemporary with Alexander Severus the Roman emperor. Ardisher (whom the Roman historians call Artaxerxes) having reigned 14 years as absolute sovereign of Persia, resigned the government into the hands of his son, Sháhpúr, called by the Romans, Sapor or Sapores, in the year 238 A. D.

*The following is a list of the kings of Persia of the Sásánian race.*

| | | | |
|---|---|---|---|
| 1. | Ardisher. | 16. | Hurmuz or Hurmuzd III. |
| 2. | Sháhpúr I. | 17. | Fíróz. |
| 3. | Hurmuzd I. | 18. | Balas or Palash. |
| 4. | Bahrám I. | 19. | Kubád. |
| 5. | Bahrám II. | 20. | Jámásp. |
| 6. | Bahrám III. | 21. | Naushterwán (Kasra). |
| 7. | Narsí. | 22. | Hurmuzd. |
| 8. | Hurmuzd II. | 23. | Khusro Parwez. |
| 9. | Sháhpúr II. | 24. | Sheròya. |
| 10. | Ardisher II. | 25. | Ardisher III. |
| 11. | Sháhpúr III. | 26. | Shahriár. |
| 12. | Bahrám IV. | 27. | Túrán or Púrán Dukht. |
| 13. | Yezdijard I. | 28. | Azarmí Dukht. |
| 14. | Bahrám Gór. | 29. | Farrukhzád Bakhtiár. |
| 15. | Yezdijard II. | 30. | Yezdijard III. |

**Ardisher,** اردشير, (or Artaxerxes) II succeeded his father Sháhpúr II in the year 380 A. D., and sat on the throne of Persia only four years, during which period no event of consequence occurred. He was deposed in 384 A. D., by his brother Sháhpúr III, who succeeded him.

**Ardisher,** اردشير, (or Artaxerxes) III, a king of Persia, of the Sásánian race, who reigned about the year 629 A. D., at Sheroyá.

**Ardisher Darazdast,** اردشير درازدست, an ancient king of Persia, the Artaxerxes Longimanus of the Greeks, surnamed Bahman, was the son of Isfandiár. He succeeded his grandfather, Gashtasp, as king of Persia in 464 B. C. He is celebrated for the wisdom he displayed in the internal regulation of his empire. In the commencement of the reign of this monarch, the celebrated Rustam was slain by the treachery of his brother. This prince is named Ahasuerus in Scripture, and is the same who married Esther, and during the whole of his reign shewed the greatest kindness to the Jewish nation. The long reign of this monarch includes that of two or more of his immediate successors, who are not noticed by Persian writers. According to them, he ruled Persia 112 years, and was succeeded by his daughter Queen Humái.

**Arghun Khan,** ارغون خان, the son of Abáká Khán and grandson of Halákú Khán, was raised to the throne of Persia after the murder of his uncle Ahmad Khán, surnamed Nekódár, in August, 1284 A. D., Jamad I, 683 A. H. His reign was marked by few events of consequence. He recalled the celebrated Shams-ud-dín Muhammad Sáhib Díwán his father's wazír, who, disgusted with court, had retired to Isfahán: but this able minister was hardly re-established in his office, before his enemies persuaded the prince that he had actually poisoned his father; and the aged wazír was in the same year made over to the public executioner. Amír Búká, the rival of Shams-ud-dín, rose, upon his fall, to such power that he was tempted to make a grasp at the crown: but he was unsuccessful, and lost his life in the attempt. Arghún Khán died on Saturday the 10th of March, 1291 A. D., 5th Rabí' I, 690 A. H., after a reign of 6 years and 9 months, and was succeeded by his brother Kaijaptú or Kaikhatú.

**Arghun Shah Jani Kurbani,** ارغون شاه جاني قرباني امير, (Amír) who reigned in Naishapúr and Tús about the year 1337 A. D., and was defeated by the Sarbadals of Sabzwár.

**'Arif,** عارف, the poetical name of the son of Ghulám Husain Khán. He was an excellent Urdú poet of Dehlí, and died in 1852 A. D., 1268 A. H.

**'Arifi,** عارفي (Mauláná) a Persian poet who flourished in the time of the wazír khwája Muhammad bin Is-hák, and wrote a work in his name called "Dah Náma." He lived in the 9th century of the Hijrí era.

**'Arifi,** عارفي, (Mauláná) son of Mubárik Maskhara, was a learned Musalmán, and was living in 1580 A. D., 988 A. H., when he wrote a chronogram on the death of Kásim Káhí who died in that year, during the reign of the emperor Akbar.

**Arjumand Bano Begam,** ارجمند بانو بيگم, entitled Mumtáz Mahál (now corrupted into Táj Mahál, and Táj Bíbí) was the favorite wife of the emperor Sháh Jahán, and daughter of 'Asaf Khán, wazír, the brother of the celebrated Núr Jahán Begam. She was born in the year 1592 A. D., 1000 A. H., and married to the prince Mirzá Khurram (afterwards Sháh Jahán) in 1612 A. D., 1021 A. H., by whom she had several children. She died in child-bed a few hours after the birth of her last daughter, named Dahar Ará, on the 7th of July, 1631 O. S., 17th Zil-hijja 1040 A. H., at Burhánpúr in the Dakhan, and was at first buried there in a garden called Zainábád, and afterwards her remains were removed to Agra, where a most splendid mausoleum was built over her tomb, all of white marble decorated with mosaics, which for the richness of the material, the chasteness of the design, and the effect at once brilliant and solemn, is not surpassed by any other edifice either in Europe or Asia. It was completed in 1645 A. D., 1055 A. H, and is now called the "Táj," or "Táj Mahál," which is said to have cost the enormous sum of £750,000. The chronogram of her death contains in the word "Gham," or Grief. She was also called Kudsia Begam.



**Arjun Singh,** ارجن سنگه, was one of the three sons of Rája Mánsingh. *Vide* Ain Translation, I, 485.

**Arpa Khan,** اريا خان, one of the princes of the Tartar family, was crowned king of Persia after the death of Abú Saíd Khán Bahádur, in November, 1335 A. D., 736 A. H. He reigned five months and was killed in battle against Músí Khán in 1336 A. D., who succeeded him. *Vide* Abú Saíd Khán Bahádur.

**Arsalan Khan,** ارسلان خان, title of Arsalán Kulí, the son of Alahwardí Khán I, was a nobleman in the service of the emperor Alamgír, and was living about the year 1696 A. D., 1108 A. H.

**Arsalan Shah,** ارسلان شاه, the son of Sultán Masa'úd III of Ghazní. He murdered his brother Sherzád in 1115 A. D., 509 A. H., and having ascended the throne, he imprisoned all his other brothers excepting Bahrám Sháh, who fled to Khurásán and sought assistance of Sultán Sanjar his uncle. Sanjar in the year 1118 A. D., 512 A. H., marched to Ghazní and in a battle defeated Arsalán Sháh, who made his escape to Láhor but was soon after taken prisoner and put to death, when Bahrám Sháh ascended the throne.

**Arsalan Shah,** ارسلان شاه, a king of Khwarizm and son of Atsiz. *Vide* Alp' Arsalán.

**Arsalan Shah Saljuki,** ارسلان شاه سلجوقي, the son of Tughral II, and grandson of Sultán Muhammad, brother to Sultán Sanjar. Arsalán Sháh died in January, 1176 A. D., 571 A. H. His son Tughral III who succeeded him, was the last Sultán of the family of the Saljúkides who reigned in Persia.

**'Arsh-Ashaiani,** عرش آشياني the title given to the emperor Akbar I, after his death.

**'Arshi,** عرشي, whose proper name was Mír Muhammad Momin, was a brother of Mír Sálah Kashifí the son of Mír Abdulláh Mushkín Kalam Husainí, who was a celebrated calligrapher under Jahángír. Arshí is the author of a poem called "Sháhid-Arshí," composed in the year 1659 A. D., 1070 A. H., also of another work entitled "Mehr wa Wafá," and of a Díwán.

**Artaxerxes,** *vide* Ardisher.

**Arzami Dukht,** ارزمي دخت, a queen of the Persians, whose general named Mehrán being killed in a battle against the Saracens, she was deposed by the people, who placed Yezdijard III upon the throne in her stead, a young man of the royal family. But this did not much mend the matter, the government of the new king of theirs, being even more inauspicious than that of the queen; for in her reign the confines of the empire were only invaded, but in his, all was entirely lost, and the whole kingdom and country of the Persians fell into the hands of the Musalmáns. The accession of Yezdijard is placed by Sir John Malcolm in 632 A. D., 11 A. H., but Major Price fixes it in 635 A. D., 14 A. H. *Vide* Túrán-dukht.

**Arzani Begam,** ارزاني بيگم, was the daughter of Shahriar who was married, in the 16th year of Jahángír's reign, to Mihr-un-nisá the daughter of Nur Jahán. *Vide* Ain Translation, I, 331.

**Arzu,** آرزو, the poetical name of Siráj-ud-dín Alí Khán, which see.

**Asa Ahir,** آسا اهير, a shepherd chief, who built the fortress of Asírgarh in the Dakhan in the 14th century; he had some 2000 retainers. The hill had long before been encircled by a wall to protect the cattle, and it was to employ the poor that Ásá constructed instead of the fortifications which still remain beyond all comparison, the strongest native built fortress in India. Ásá was put to death by Malik Nasír, the Muhammadan chief of Khandais, who possessed himself of the stronghold by treachery, and completed the fortifications. Two centuries later Asírgarh and all Nimar were conquered by Akbar and incorporated with the Mughal empires. It was taken by the British in 1817.

**Asad,** اسد, the poetical name of Mirzá Asad-ulláh Khán usually called Mirzá Noushâh. His ancestors were of Samarḳand, but he was born at Agra; but was brought up and lived at Dehlí where he rose to great fame as a poet and writer of the Persian language, whilst his compositions in Urdu were not less admired. He won the favour of Bahádur Sháh, the last king of Dehlí, who conferred upon him the title of Nawáb and appointed him royal preceptor in the art of poetry. He is the author of a Persian Inshá, a Masnawí in praise of 'Alí, and a Díwán in Persian and another in Urdu. Both have been printed. He was in 1852 A. D., sixty years of age, living at Dehlí, and was engaged in compiling a history of the Mughal emperors of India. His poetical name is Ghálib, which see. He died in the year 1869, 1285 A. H.

**Asadi Tusi,** اسدي طوسي, a native of Túsin the province of Khurásán, and one of the most celebrated Persian poets at the court of Sulṭán Mahmúd of Ghazní, whom the Sulṭán often intreated to undertake the Sháh Náma, but he excused himself on account of his age. His best work is supposed to be lost. He was the master of Firdausí, who afterwards composed the Sháh Náma. It is said that Firdausí on his departure from Ghazní requested him to finish the Sháh Náma which was yet incomplete, and that Asadí composed that part of the poem between the Arabian conquest of eastern Persia under the khalíf 'Umar, to the end, consisting of 4,000 couplets. The year of Asadí's death is unknown, but it appears from the above circumstance, that he was living in 1010 A. D., 401 A. H., in which year Firdausí departed from Ghazní. The most celebrated of the other works of Asadí now extant, is his dispute between Day and Night, a translation of which in English verse is to be found in the "Rose Garden of Persia," by Louisa Stuart Costello, published, London, 1845.

**Asad Khan,** نواب اسد خان, (Nawab) entitled Asáf-ud-daula and Jumlat-ul-Mulk, was descended from an illustrious family of Turkmans. His father who fled from the oppressions of Sháh Abbas of Persia into Hindústan, was raised to high rank by the emperor Jahángír with the title of Zulfiḳár Khán, and married to the daughter of a new relation to his empress Núr Jahán. His son Asad Khán (whose former name was Ibrahím) was very early noticed by Sháh Jahán, who married him to a daughter of his wazír 'Asaf Khán, and promoted him to the office of second Bakhshí, which he held till the 15th year of 'Alamgír (1671 A. D.) when he was raised to the rank of 4,000, and a few years afterwards to the office of wazír and highest order of nobility, seven thousand. In the reign of Bahádur Sháh he was appointed Wakíl Mutlaḳ (an office superior to wazír), and his son Isma'íl made Mír Bakhshí or chief paymaster with the title of Amír-ul-'Umra Zulfikár Khán; but on the accession of Farrukhsiar, he was disgraced, his estates seized, and his son put to death. Since that period, he lived upon a scanty pension in a sort of confinement, but much respected by all ranks. He died in the year 1717 A. D., 1129 A. H., aged 90 lunar years, and was buried with great funeral pomp at the expense of the emperor, in a mausoleum, erected by his father for the family.

**Asad-ullah al-Ghalib,** اسد الله الغالب, the conquering lion of God, an epithet of Alí the son-in-law of Muhammad.

**Asad-ullah Asad Yar Khan,** اسد الله اسديار خان, (Nawáb), he lived in the time of the emperor Muhammad Sháh, and died in 1745 A. D., 1158 A. H. His poetical name was Insán, which see.

**Asad-ullah Khan,** ميرزا اسد الله خان, (Mirzá) *vide* Asad, and Ghálib.

**Asaf,** آصف, a native of Kumm in Persia, who came to India in the reign of the emperor Sháh Jahán, and is the author of a Díwan.

**Asafi,** خواجه آصفي, (Khwája) son of Khwája Na'mat-ulláh, was an elegant poet. Ásafí is his poetical name, which he took on account of his father having served in the capacity of wazír to Sulṭán Abú Sa'íd Mirzá; for, they say, that Ásaf or Asaph of the Scriptures, was wazír to king Solomon. He was one of the contemporaries and companions of Jámí, and took instructions from him in the art of poetry. He died about the month of August, 1520, A. D., 16th Shaban 926 A. H., aged more than 70, and was buried at Hirát; but according to the work called Khulásat-ul-Asha'ár, he died in 920 A. H. He is the author of a Díwán or book of Odes called Díwán Ásafí, and a Masnawí in the measure of "Makhzan-ul-Asrár."

**Asaf Jah,** آصف جاه, the title of the celebrated Nizám-ul-Mulk of Haidarábád.

**Asaf Khan I,** آصف خان, surnamed Abdul Majíd, was a nobleman in the time of the emperor Akbar, who in 1565 A. D., 973 A. H., distinguished himself by the conquest of Garrakóṭa, a principality on the Narbada, bordering on Bundelkhand. It was governed by a queen or Rání named Durgáwatí, who opposed the Muhammadan general in an unsuccessful action, and when seeing her army routed and herself severely wounded, she avoided falling into the hands of the enemy by stabbing herself with a dagger. Her treasures, which were of great value, fell into the hands of Ásaf Khán; he secreted a great part, and the detection of this embezzlement was the immediate cause of his revolt. He was, however, subsequently pardoned, and after the conquest of Chittour, that country was given to 'Asaf Khán in jágír.

**Asaf Khan II,** آصف خان title of Khraj-Ghayas-ud-dín Alí Qaiwaní, the son of Áqá Mulland uncle to Ásaf Khán Jáfar Beg. He held the Bakhshígarí in the time of the emperor Akbar, and after the conquest of Gujrat in 1573 A. D., 981 A. H. in which he distinguished himself, the title of Abbás Khán was conferred on him. He died at Gujrat in 1581 A. D., 989 A. H., and after his death his nephew Mirzá Jáfar Beg was buried with the title of Ásaf Khán.

**Asaf Khan III,** آصف خان جعفربيگ, commonly called Mirzá Ja'far Beg, was the son of Mirzá Badí-uz-Zamán, and grandson of Aḳá Mullá Ḳazwíní. He was born at Ḳazwín, and came to India in his youth 1577 A. D., 985 A. H. At the recommendation of his uncle Mirzá Ghaiás-ud-dín, who was a nobleman at the court of the emperor Akbar, and bore then the title of A'saf Khán, was received with honor, and after the death of his uncle the office of Bakhshígarí was conferred on him with the title of A'saf Khán, 1581 A. D., 989 A. H. He was an excellent poet, and was one of the many that were employed by the emperor in compiling the "Táríkh Alfí," and after the assassination of Mullá Ahmad in 1588 A. D., 996 A. H. the remainder of the work was written by him up to the year 997 A. H. He is also called Asaf Khán Mirzá Ja'far Bakhshí Begí, and is the author of a poem called "Shírín wa Khusro." The office of chief Díwán was conferred on him by the emperor in 1598 A. D., 1007 A. H., and in the reign of Jahángír, he was raised to the high post of wazárat. He died in the year 1612 A. D., 1021 A. H. In his poetical compositions he used the name of Ja'far. One of his sons who also bore the name of Ja'far became an excellent poet and died in the time of 'Alamgír, A. D. 1682, 1094 A. H.

**Asaf Khan IV,** آصف خان, the title of 'Abúl Hasan, who had several other titles conferred on him at different times, such as Ya'tḳád Khán, Yemín-ud-daula, &c., was the son of the celebrated wazír Ya'tmád-ud-daula, and brother to Núr Jahán Begam. After his father's death in 1621 A. D., 1030 A. H., he was appointed wazír by the emperor Jahángír. His daughter Arjumand Báno Begam also called Mumtáz Mahal, was married to the prince Sháh Jahán. 'Asaf Khán died at Láhór in the 15th year of Sháh Jahán on the 10th November, 1641 O. S., 17th Sha'ban, 1051 A. H., aged 72 lunar years, and was buried there on the banks of the Ráwí opposite to the city of Láhór. Besides Mumtáz Mahal, he had four sons: *viz.*, Sháista Khán; Mirzá Masíh who was drowned in a drunken frolic in the river Behaṭ in Kashmír; Mirzá Husain, of moderate abilities, and little note; and Sháhnawáz Khán who rose to much reputation and distinction.

**Asaf-ud-daula,** آصف الدوله, a title of Asad Khán, which see.

**Asaf-ud-daula,** نواب اصف الدوله, (Nawáb) the eldest son of Nawáb Shujáa'-ud-daula of Audh, after whose death in January 1775, A. D., Ẕil-ḳada 1188 A. H., he succeeded to his dominions, and made Lakhnau the seat of his government, which formerly was at Faizábád. He died, after a reign of 23 lunar years and seven months, on Friday the 21st of September, 1797 A. D., 28th Rabí I, 1212 A. H., and was buried in the Imám Báṛa at Lakhnau of which he was the founder. His eldest adopted son, Wazír Alí Khán, agreeably to his request, was placed on the masnad, but was after four months deposed by Sir John Shore, then Governor of Calcutta, and Sa'ádat Alí Khán, the brother of the deceased, raised to the masnad. Asaf-ud-daula is the author of a Díwán in Urdú and Persian.

**Asalat Khan,** اصالت خان, title of Mír Abdul Hádí son of Mír Mírán Yezdí, was a nobleman in the service of the emperor Sháh Jahán. He died in the year A. D. 1647, 1057 A. H.

**Asalat Khan,** اصالت خان, title of Mirzá Muhammad son of Mirzá Badía' of Mashhad. He came to India in the 19th year of Sháh Jahán 1645, A. D., 1055 A. H., and was raised to the rank of 5,000 by the emperor 'Alamgír, in whose time he died 1666, A. D., 1076 A. H.

**Asam** or **Atham,** اثم, poetical name of Hafíz-ulláh, which see.

**Asar,** اثر, poetical name of Akhúnd Sháfa'í or Shafía'áí of Shíráz who died at Lár in the year 1701 A. D., 1113 A. H., and left a Díwán containing 10,000 verses.

**Asar,** اثر, poetical name of Nawáb Husain Alí Khán, son of Amír-ud-daula Haidar Beg Khán. He is the author of a Díwán.

**'Asi,** عاصي, the poetical name of Ghulám Sarwar, author of the Ḳáf Náma, which consists of Ghazals, all the verses of which end in Ḳáf, hence the name; another peculiarity is that the first letter of every verse of the first Ghazal is Alif, of the second Be, of the third Te, &c., a ghazal for every letter of the alphabet.

**Asir,** اسير, poetical name of Sayyid Gúlzar Alí, the son of Nazír, a poet of A'gra. He is the author of an Urdú Díwán, and is still living in A'gra, (1878).

**Asir,** اسير, commonly called Mirzá Jalál Asír, a celebrated poet of Persia and a relation of Sháh Abbás the great. He flourished about the year 1600 A. D., never came to India, and is the author of a Díwán in Persian. He died in 1630 A. D., 1040 A. H.

**Asir-ud-din Akhsikati,** اسير الدين اخسيكتي a native of Akhsíkat a city in the province of Farghána, was an excellent poet and contemporary with Khákání. He died in A. D., 1211, 608 A. H. He spent the greatest part of his life at the courts of the Atábaks, and stood in high favor with Arsalán Sháh, the son of Tughral, Eldiguz and Ḳizil Arsalán.

**Asir-ud-din Aomani** or **Aamani,** اسير الدين اوماني, a poet of Hamdán, who was a pupil of Nasír-ud-dín Túsí. He is the author of a Díwán in Persian and Arabic.

**Asir-ud-din ibn-Umar al-Abhari,** اسير الدين ابن عمر الابهري, author of the "Kashf," "Zubda," and "Hidáya," which is also called Hidáyet-ul-Hikmat, the Guide to Philosophy. He died in 1344 A. D., 745 A. H.

**Asghar,** اصغرحسين خان, Husain Khán (Nawáb) of Furrukhábád in 1874 went to Bombay intending to proceed to Mecca on a pilgrimage.

**'Ashrati,** عشرتي, *vide* Ishratí.

**Asha'ri,** اشعري, the surname of one of the most celebrated doctors among the Musalmáns, named Abúl Hasan Alí bin-Isma'íl. He died in 936 or 941 A. D., 324 or 329 A. H.

**'Ashik,** عاشق, poetical name of Mahdí Alí Khán, grandson of Nawáb Alí Mardán Khán. He is the author of 3 Díwáns in Urdú, two in Persian, a book called Hamla Haidari and several works.

**'Ashik,** عاشق, poetical name of Shaikh Núr-ud-dín Muhammad, the author of the Masnawí called "Aish wa Tarab," Enjoyment and Merriment, composed in 1668 A. D., 1079 A. H.

**'Ashik Pasha,** عاشق پاشا, a Turkish poet, who was born at Hirshari, in the reign of Sulṭán Orkhan the successor of Othman, and died at no very advanced age, in the reign of Murád I. He was, says Von Hormuz, one of the richest Shaikhs of his time, but lived nevertheless the life of a simple darvesh, from conscientious motives. His Díwán or great work, in imitation of Jalal-ud-dín Rúmí's is a collection of mystical poetry exceeding ten thousand distichs, and divided into ten books, each book into ten parts.

**'Ashik,** عاشق, poetical name of Mauláná Abúl Khair of Khwárizm, which see.

**Ashk** اشک, poetical name of Muhammad Khalíl-ullah Khán, which see.

**Ashna,** آشنا, poetical name of Mirzá Muhammad Táhir who had the title of Ináit Khán. He was a son of Nawáb Zafar Khán Ihsán, and died in 1666 A. D., 1077 A. H. His complete work is called "Kulliát 'Ashná," in which Kasídas are to be found in praise of Sháh Jahán and Dárá Shikóh.

**Ashna,** آشنا, the poetical name of Ghaiás-ud-dín who died in A. D. 1662, 1073 A. H.

**Ashob,** آشوب, the poetical name of Muhammad Bakhsh, a poet who flourished in Audh during the reign of Ásaf-ud-daula and his father Shujáa'-ud-daulá. He is the author of a Díwán.

**Ashraf,** اشرف, or Darwesh Ashraf. He flourished under Báisanghar's son, and has left a Díwán.

**Ashraf Ali Khan Koka,** اشرف علي خان کوکه, *vide* Fighán.

**Ashraf,** اشرف, poetical name of Mirzá Muhammad Sa'íd of Mázandarán, son of Mullá Muhammad Ḳána'. He came to India and was appointed to instruct Zebun Nisá Begam, the daughter of the emperor 'Alamgír. He died at Múngair. He is the author of a Díwán and several Masnawís.

**Ashraf,** اشرف, the poetical name of Muhammad Hasan, son of Sháh Muhammad Zamán of Allahábád. He was probably alive in 1852 A. D., and is the author of a Masnawí called "Ma'dan Faiz."

**Ashraf Khan,** اشرف خان, title of Mirzá Muhammad Ashraf the son of Islám Khán Mashhadí. In the reign of Sháh Jahán, he held the rank of 1500, and the title of Ya'tmád Khán. In the time of 'Alamgír he was raised to the rank of 3000 with the title of Ashraf Khán, and died five days after the conquest of Bíjápúr on the 17th September, 1686 A. D., 9th Ẕil-ḳada, 1097 A. H.

**Ashraf Khan,** اشرف خان, whose proper name was Muhammad Asghar, was a Sayyad of Mashhad, and held the office of Mír Munshí in the time of the emperor Akbar. He wrote a beautiful hand, and was an excellent poet. He composed a chronogram on the death of Muhammad Yúsaf in 1562 A. D., 970 A. H., another on the completion of the mosque of Shaikh Salím Chishtí at Fathapúr Sikrí in 1571 A. D., 979 A. H., and one on the conquest of Súrat by Akbar on the 1st of January, 1573, A. D., 25th Sha'bán, 980 A. H. He accompanied Munaim Khán Khánkhánán to Bengal and died at Lakhnautí in the year 1575 A. D., 983 A. H. At the time of his death he held the rank of 2,000.

**Ashraf,** اشرف, a chief of the Afgháns of the tribe of Ghilzaí, who was elected on the 22nd of April 1725 O. S., by the Afgháns as successor of his cousin or uncle Mahmúd, another chief of the same tribe, who had usurped the throne of Persia in the time of sSultán Husain Safwí whom he kept in confinement. A hraf on his accession múrdered the latter, and sent his corpse to be interred in Ḳumm. He was defeated by Nádir Ḳulí (afterwards Nádir Sháh) in 1729 A. D., 1142 A. H., who placed Sháh Tahmásp II, son of Sulṭán Husain on the throne. Ashraf was afterwards seized and murdered by a Billoch chief between Kirmán and Ḳandahár in January, 1730 A. D., 1143 A. H., and his head sent to Sháh Tahma sp.

**'Ashrat,** عشرت, *vide* Ishrat.

**'Ashrati,** عشرتي, name of a poet, *vide* Ishratí.

**'Asif Khan,** *vide* Ásaf Khán.

**'Asimi,** عاصمي, an Arabian poet who lived in the time of Khwája Nizám-ul-Mulk, and wrote beautiful panegyrics in his praise.

**'Asjudi,** عسجدي, a powerful poet at the court of Sulṭán Mahmúd of Ghazní, was a native of Marv, and one of the scholars of 'Unsarí. He evinced in his works much genius; but they are scarce, and the greatest part of them are lost.

**Askaran,** راجه اسکرن, (Rájá) brother of Rájá Bihárí Mal Kachhwáha. He served under the emperor Akbar for several years, and died some time after the year 1588 A. D., 996 A. H. After his death, his son Ráj Singh was raised to high rank and honors.

**'Askari,** امام عسکري, (Imám) *vide* Hasan Askarí.

**'Askari,** مرزا عسکري, (Mirzá) third son of the emperor Bábar Sháh. On the accession of his eldest brother Humáyún to the throne of Dihlí, the district of Sarkár Sambhal was conferred on him as jágír. He was subsequently kept in confinement for some time on account of his rebellious conduct by Humáyún on his return from Persia. He afterwards obtained permission to go on a pilgrimage to Mecca, but died on his way across the deserts of Arabia in the year 1554 A. D., 961 A. H. He left one daughter who was married to Yúsaf Khán, an inhabitant of Mashhad.

**Asmai,** اصمعي, surname of Abú Saíd Abdul Malik bin Ḳureb, which see.

**'Asmat,** عصمت, or Ismat, poetical name of Khwája Asmat-ullah of Bukhára. He was descended from a noble family of Bukhára tracing his ancestry to Ja'far, the son of Abú Tálib the father of Alí. He was successful in all kinds of poetical composition; and flourished in the time of prince Mirzá Khalíl, the grandson of Amír Taimúr, whom he instructed in the art of poetry. He died in the year 1426 A. D., 829 A. H., and has left a Díwán consisting of 20,000 verses.

**'Asmat-ullah,** عصمت الله, *vide* Asmat.

**'Asmat-ullah,** ملا عصمت الله, (Mullá) of Sahāranpúr, was the author of the work called "Shurah Khulásat ul-Hisáb." He died in 1626 A. D., 1035 A. H.

**Asoka,** اسوکه, the son of Bindusára, and grandson of Chandragupta rájá of Pataliputra in Magadha. He reigned for about 40 years, until the year 223 B. C. His reign is most important. Numerous inscriptions made by his order have been discovered in various parts of India.

**'Assar,** عسار, (oil-presser) the poetical name of Shams-ud-dín Muhammad. He was a native of Tabrez, and author of a romantic poem called "Mehr wa Mushtarí," the Sun and Jupiter, which he completed on the 20th February, 1377 A. D., 10th Shawwál, 778 A. H., and died in the year 1382 A. D., 783 A. H.

**Aswad,** اسود, or Al-Aswad, *vide* Musailima.

**'Ata,** عطا, the poetical name of Shaikh Atá-ulláh a pupil of Mirzá Bedil. He died at Dihlí in 1723 A. D., 1135 A. H.

**Atabak,** اتابک, or Atabig. This is a Turkish title, formed from the word Atá, father or tutor, and Beg, lord; and signifies a governor or tutor of a lord or prince. From the time of the decline of the dynasty of Saljúk to the conquest of Persia by Halákú Khán (which occupies a period of more than a century,) that country was distracted by the contests of a number of petty princes, or governors, called Atábaks; who taking advantage of the weakness of the last monarchs of the race of Saljúk, established their authority over some of the finest provinces of the empire. One of the most distinguished of these Atábegs, was Eldiguz, a Turkish slave, whose descendants reigned over 'Azurbeján. The Atábegs of Fars were descended from Salghur, a Turkish general. *Vide* Eldiguz and Salghur, also 'Imad-ud-dín Zangí. There were four dynasties of these Atábaks.

**Atabak Abu Bakr,** ابو بکر اتابک, the son of Atábak Muhammad, the son of Eldiguz, succeeded his uncle Ḳizal Arsalán as prime minister to Tughral III Saljúkí, in 1191 A. D., 587 A. H. He appears to have contented himself with the principality of 'Azurbeján, and fixed his residence at Tabrez. His long reign was only disturbed by one war with his brother Ḳutlaḳ, in which he was victorious. Ḳutlaḳ fled into Khwarizm and encouraged Ala-ud-dín Takash to advance against Tughral III whom he defeated and slew in 1194 A. D., 590 A. H. Abú Bakr died in 1210 A. D., 607 A. H., and was succeeded by his brother Atábak Muzaffar.

**Atabak Abu Bakr bin-Sa'd bin-Zangi,** اتابک ابو بکر بن سعد بن زنگي, *vide* Sunḳar.

**Atabak 'Ala-ud-daula,** اتابک علاء الدولہ, the son of Atábak Sám, one of the Atábaks of Isfahan of the race of the Dílamites. He died in 1227 A. D., 624 A. H., aged 84 years.

**Atabak Eldiguz,** اتابك يلدگز, *vide* Eldiguz.

**Atabak Muhammad,** اتابک محمد, was the eldest son of Eldiguz, whom he succeeded as prime minister in 1172 A. D., 568 A. H. When Tughral III a prince of the Saljúkian dynasty (who was a child of seven years of age) was placed on the throne in 1176 A. D., Muhammad, who was his uncle, became the actual ruler of Persia. This chief after enjoying power 13 years died in March, 1186 A. D., Ẕil-hijja 581 A. H., in which year the conjunction of all the planets took place. He was succeeded by his brother, Ḳizal Arsalán.

**Atabak Muzaffar,** اتابك مظفر, the son of Atábak Muhammad. He succeeded his brother Abú Bakr in 1210 A. D., 607 A. H., and not only inherited Azurbeján, but a considerable part of 'Iraḳ. He enjoyed this power 15 years; after which 'Azurbeján was invaded and conquered by Sulṭán Jalál-ud-dín the monarch of Khwárizm A. D. 1225, 622 A. H. Muzaffar shut himself up in the fort of Alanjaḳ, where he died; and with him perished the power of the family of Eldiguz.

**Atabak Muzaffar-ud-din Zangi,** اتابک مظفر زنگي, a prince of Shíraz, and brother of Sunḳar, which see.

**Atabak Sa'd bin-Zangi,** *vide* Sunḳar.

**'Ata Husain Khan,** عطا حسين خان, whose poetical name was Tahsín, is the author of the "Nautarz Murassa'," an Urdú translation of the "Chahár Darwesh." He flourished in the time of Nawáb 'Asaf-ud-daula of Lakhnau, about the year 1776 A. D., 1189 A. H. As a specimen of the Urdú language the Nautarz Murassa' was rendered objectionable for students, by his retaining too much of the phraseology and idiom of the Persian and Arabic. On this account a simple version was executed by Mír Amman of Dihlí in 1802 A. D., 1217 A. H., which is styled the "Bágh-o-Bahár," *vide* Tahsín.

**Atal,** اٹل, a name assumed by Mír Abdul Jalíl of Dehlí in his poetical compositions, who gave out that he was by inspiration the pupil of Ja'far Zaṭallí, and wrote poetry in Persian and Arabic.

**'Ata Malik,** عطا ملك *vide* Atá-ud-dín surnamed 'Atá Malik.

**Atash,** آتش, poetical name of Khwája Haidar Alí of Lakhnau, who is the author of two Díwáns or books of Odes consisting of Persian and Urdú verses. He died in 1847 A. D., 1263 A. H.

**'Ata-ullah,** عطا الله, surname of several Musalmán authors, but particularly of Táj-ud-dín Muhammad bin-Ahmad bin-Atá-ulláh, who is the author of a book entitled "Hakam-ul-Atia" which treats on Musalmán law, and is to be found in the Royal Library at Paris, No. 672. There is one Atá-ulláh who is the author of a dictionary called "Firdaus-ul-Lughát."

**'Ata-ullah,** عطا الله, bin-Muhammad-al-Husainí Naishápúrí, author of the "Rauzat-ul-Ahbáb," containing the history of Muhammad, of his companions, and of the twelve Imáms. This book was written at Hirat and dedicated to Amír 'Alísher in 1494 A. D., 899 A. H. He is also called Amír Jamál-ud-dín Atá-ulláh. He also wrote another work on the art of writing poetry, entitled "Kitáb Takmíl-us-Sanaa't" dedicated to the same Amír in which he calls himself 'Atá-ulláh bin-Muhammad-al-Husainí Naishápúrí. He was wazír to Sulṭán Husain Mirzá of Hirat, and died in the beginning of the year 917 A. H.

**At-har** or **Athar Khan,** اطهر خان, the son of Amír Nizám-ud-dín Razwí; he was a native of Bukhára, and came to India in the time of the emperor 'Alamgír, where he collected his poems into a Díwán.

**Ashir-ud-din,** اشير الدين, pronounced by the Indians Asír-ud-dín, which see.

**Atma',** اطمعه, poet whose proper name is Abú Is-háḳ Halláj, which see.

**Atsiz,** اتسز, one of the Sulṭáns of Khwárizm called Atsiz ibn-Auk by Ibn Khallikán. Tutush or Turtush son of Alp Arsalán, who was lord of the countries to the east of Syria, caused him to be arrested, and having put him to death on the 21st of October 1078, A. D., 11th Rabí II, 471 A. H., took possession of his kingdom.

**Atsiz,** اتسز, a Sulṭán of Khwárizm called by ibn-Khallikán, Atsiz the son of Ḳutb-ud-dín Muhammad the son of Anushtakín. He was cotemporary with Sulṭán Sanjar Saljúkí, with whom he had several battles. He died in 1166 A. D., 6th Jamad II, 551 A. H., and was succeeded to the throne by his son Alp Arsalán who is also called Apa Arsalán. He died in 1162 A. D., 19th Rajab, 557 A. H.

**Atsiz,** اتسز, son of Ala-ud-dín Hasan Jahán Sóz, king of Ghór. He reigned after Bahá-ud-dín Sám, and was killed in a battle against Táj-ud-dín Eldúz prince of Ghazní some time about the year 1211 A. D., 608 A. H. He was the last of the kings of Ghór of this branch.

**'Attar,** عطار, poetical name of Faríd-ud-dín Attár, which see.

**Aurangzeb,** اورنگزيب, a name of the emperor 'Alamgír, which see.

**Avank Khan,** اونک خان, or Ung Khán, a prince of the tribe of Karit or Kirit, a tribe of Mughals or Oriental Tartars, who made profession of the Christian religion.

He was surnamed Málik Yúhanná or king John. From the name of this prince we have made John the Priest, who was stripped of his dominions by Changez Khán in 1202 A. D., 599 A. H. They have since applied the name of John the Priest or Prestre John, to the king of Ethiopia, because he was a Christian. Avank Khán is by some authors called Avant Khán. He was a very powerful sovereign, and the greatest part of Tartary was tributary to him; but he was defeated and put to death by Changeiz Khán.

**Aven Rosch,** *vide* Ibn Rashíd.

**Avenzur,** *vide* Abdul Malik bin-Zohr.

**Averroes,** *vide* Ibn Rashíd.

**Avicenna,** *vide* Abú Sína.

**Aweis Karani, اویس قرني,** (Khwája) an upright Musalmán of the Súfí sect, who had given up the world, used to say to those that sought him, "Do you seek God? If you do, why do you come to me? And if you do not seek God, what business can I have with you?" He was an inhabitant of Yeman and of the tribe of Ḳáran. He was slain in a battle fought by Alí against Mu'áwia I. in 657 A. D., 17th Shawwal, 37 A. H. This man had never seen Muhammad, and yet the Musalmáns say, that when he heard that Muhammad had lost a tooth in battle, and not knowing which, he broke all his teeth.

**Aweis Jalayer, سلطان اویس جلایر,** (Sulṭán) succeeded his father Amír Hasan Buzurg as king of Baghdád in July 1356, A. D., Rajab 757 A. H., and after a reign of nearly nineteen lunar years died on Tuesday the 10th October, 1374 A. D., 2nd Jamad I, 776 A. H. He was succeeded by his son Sulṭán Husain Jaláyer.

**Aweis Mirza, اویس مرزا,** a prince nearly related to Baiḳara Bahádur, was nephew to Abúl Ghází Sulṭán Husain Bahádur. He was murdered by Sulṭán Abú Sáíd Mirzá between the years 1451 and 1457 A. D.

**'Ayani, عیاني,** whose proper name was Abú Is-háḳ Ibráhím, probably flourished previous to the 8th century of the Hijrat. He is the author of a Masnawí called "Anbia Náma," a history of the prophets who preceded Muhammad.

**Ayaz, ایاز,** a slave of Sulṭán Mahmúd of Ghazní, who being a great favourite of his master, was envied by the courtiers; they therefore informed the Sulṭán that they frequently observed Ayáz go privately into the Jewel office; whence they presumed he had purloined many valuable effects. The next time when the slave had entered the treasury, the Sulṭán followed by a private door, and unobserved, saw Ayáz draw from a large chest a suit of old dirty garments with which having clothed himself, he prostrated himself on the ground and returned thanks to the Almighty for all the benefits conferred on him. The Sultán, being astonished, went to him, and demanded an explanation of his conduct. He replied, "Most gracious Sire, when I first became your Majesty's servant, this was my dress, and till that period, humble had been my lot. Now that, by the grace of God and your majesty's favor, I am elevated above all the nobles of the land, and am intrusted with the treasures of the world, I am fearful that my heart should be puffed up with vanity; I therefore daily practice this humiliation to remind me of my former insignificance." The Sulṭán being much pleased, added to his rank, and severely reprimanded his slanderers.

**'Ayaz (Kazi), قاضي عیاض,** son of Músa, and author of the "Sharah Sahíh Muslim," Masháriḳ-ul-Anwár, and several other works. He died in 1149 A. D., 544 A. H.

**'Ayesha, عایشه,** daughter of Abú Bakr, and one of the most beloved wives of Muhammad, though she bore him no child. She was his third wife, and the only one that was a maid, being then only of seven years of age. On which account (some say) her father, whose original name was Abd-ulláh, was named Abú Bakr, that is to say, the father of the virgin. An Arabian author, cited by Maracci, says, that Abú Bakr was very averse to the giving him his daughter so young, but that Muhammad pretended a divine command for it; whereupon he sent her to him with a basket of dates, and when the girl was alone with him, he stretched out his hand, and rudely took hold of her clothes; upon which she looked fiercely at him, and said, "People call you the faithful man, but your behaviour to me shews you are a perfidious one." But this story is most probably one of those calumnies against Muhammad, which were invented and found favour during the Middle Ages. After the death of her husband, she opposed the succession of Alí, and had several bloody battles with him; although violent, her character was respected, and when taken prisoner by Alí, she was dismissed without injury. She was called prophetess and mother of the faithful. She died aged 67 in the year 678 A. D., 58 A. H. Her brother Abdur Rahmán, one of the four who stood out against Yezid's inauguration, died the same year. There is a tradition that 'Ayesha was murdered by the direction of Mu'áwia I, and the following particulars are recorded. 'Ayesha having resolutely and insultingly refused to engage her allegiance to Yezíd, Mu'áwia invited her to an entertainment, where he had prepared a very deep well or pit in that part of the chamber reserved for her reception, and had the mouth of it deceptively covered over with leaves and straw. A chair was then placed upon the fatal spot, and 'Ayesha, on being conducted to her seat, instantly sank into eternal night, and the mouth of the pit was immediately covered with stones and mortar. There is, however, no trustworthy authority in support of this story.

**'Ayn-uddin (Shaikh), شیخ عین الدین,** of Bíjápúr, author of the "Mulhiḳat," and Kitáb-ul-Anwár containing a history of all the Muhammadan saints of India. He flourished in the time of Sulṭán Ala-uddín Hasan Bahmaní.

**'Ayn-ul-Mulk (Hakim), حکیم عین الملک,** a native of Shíráz, and a well educated and learned Musalmán, was an officer of rank in the time of the emperor Akbar. He was an elegant poet, and his poetical name was Wafá. He died in the 40th year of the emperor in 1594 A. D., 1003 A. H.

**'Ayn-ul-Mulk (Khwaja), خواجه عین الملک,** a distinguished nobleman in the court of Sulṭán Muhammad Sháh Tughlaḳ and his successor Sulṭán Fíroz Sháh Bárbak, kings of Dehlí. He is the author of several works, one of which is called "Tarsíl 'Ayn-ul-Mulkí." He also appears to be the author of another work called "Fatha Náma," containing an account of the conquests of Sulṭán 'Alá-uddín Sikandar Sání, who reigned from 1296 to 1316 A. D.

**'Aysh, عیش,** poetical name of Muhammad 'Askarí who lived in the reign of the emperor Sháh 'Alam.

**'Ayshi, عیشي,** a poet who is the author of a Masnawí called "Haft Akhtar," or the seven planets, which he wrote in 1675 A. D., 1086 A. H.

**Azad, آزاد,** the poetical name of Mír Ghulám Alí of Bilgarám. His father Sayyad Núh who died in 1752 A. D., 1165 A. H., was the son of the celebrated Mír Abdúl Jalíl Bilgarámí. He was an excellent poet and is the author of several works in Persian, among which are

"Kasáed 'Uzzá", "Sab-hat-ul-Mirján," "Khazána 'Amira," and "Tazkira Sarv 'Azád." He died in the year 1786 A. D., 1200 A. H.

**Azad,** آزاد, the poetical name of Captain Alexander Hiderley, in the service of the Rájá of Alwar. He was a good poet and has left a small Díwán in Urdú. His father's name is Mr. James Hiderley and his brother's Thomas Hiderley. He died on the 7th of July 1861, Zilhij 1277 A. H., at Alwar, aged 32 years.

**Azad Khan,** آزاد خان, governor of Kashmír of the Afghán tribe, succeeded his father Hájí Karím Dád, a domestic officer of Ahmad Sháh Abdálí, and who was at the death of that prince advanced to the government of Kashmír by Taimúr Sháh, as a reward for quelling the rebellion of Amír Khán the former governor. Azád Khán was only 18 years of age (in 1783) when he was governor of Kashmír, but his acts of ferocity exceeded common belief.

**'Azaeri,** عضايری, *vide* Uzáerí.

**Azal,** ازل, poetical name of Mirzá Muhammad Amín who died in 1728 A. D., 1141 A. H.

**'Azd-uddin (Kazi),** قاضي عضد الدين, of Shíráz, author of several works, one of which is called the "Muwákif 'Azdia," a celebrated work in Arabic on Jurisprudence. He flourished in the time of Sháh Abú Is-hák governor of Shíráz, to whom he dedicated the above work. He died A. D. 1355, 756 A. H.

**'Azd-ud-daula,** عضد الدوله, a Sultán of the Boyites, succeeded his father Rukn-ud-daula in September, 976 A. D., Muharram, 366 A. H., to the government of Fars and 'Irák, as well as in the office of wazír or Amír-ul-Umrá to the khalíf Al-Táya Billáh of Baghdád, in the room of his cousin Izz-ud-daula the son of Maizz-ud-daula, whom he killed in battle in 978 A. D., 367 A. H. He built the mausoleum of 'Alí at Najaf Ashraf, embellished Baghdád and other places by magnificent public buildings, and died on Monday the 27th of March, 983 A. D., 8th Shawwal, 372 A. H., aged 47 lunar years. At his death the reigning khalíf read the prayers at the funeral of this good and great man. His name is still fondly cherished in a country, over which he endeavoured during the reign of his father and his own, being a space of 34 years, to diffuse prosperity and joy. His power and possessions became from the moment of his death, a subject of contest between his brothers and nephews.

**'Azim,** عظیم, the son of Mullá Kaidí, and a nephew of Mullá Nazírí, was a Persian poet of Naishápúr. He flourished about the year 1663 A. D., 1074 A. H., and is the author of a Díwán, and a Masnawí called "Fauz Azím," *vide* Azím Naishápúrí.

**'Azim Jah (Nawab),** نواب عظیم جاه, Siráj-ul-Umrá the son of Azím-ud-daula, Nawáb of the Karnatic, was installed by the British Government as Nawáb on the 3rd February, 1820. He died on the 12th November, 1825, aged 34 years.

**'Azim Jah,** عظیم جاه, Nawáb of Arkat, died 14th January, 1874, aged 74. He was the second son of Azim Jáh, one of the Nawábs of the Karnatic, and the uncle of the late Nawáb Ghulám Muhammad Ghaus Khán. He received a pension of 2500 rupees from the Government.

**'Azim-ud-daula (Nawab),** نواب عظیم الدوله, of the Karnatic, was the son of Nawáb Amír-ul-Umrá, the brother of Umdat-ul-Umrá. On the death of Umdat-ul-Umrá, the English resolved to take the functions of government into their own hands, 'Alí Husain the next heir refused to comply, consequently Ayím-ud-daula the nephew of the deceased was placed on the masnad by the British Government on the 31st of August, 1801. He died on the 2nd August, 1819, A. D. His son 'Azím Jáh was installed as Nawáb of the Karnatic on the 3rd February, 1820, A. D. In 1698, he allowed the Company to purchase the zamíndarship of Sutánuti, Calcutta and Govindpúr.

**'Azim-ul-Umra,** عظیم الامرا, minister of the Nizám of Hydarábád. He succeeded Rukn-ud-daula about the year 1794 A. D.

**'Azim-ullah Khan,** عظیم الله خان, says Mr. Sheppard in his Narrative of the Mutiny, was a charity boy, having been picked up, together with his mother, during the famine of 1837-38, when they were both in a dying state from starvation. The mother being a staunch heathen, she would not consent to her son being christened. He was adopted in the Kanpúr Free School under Mr. Patan, School Master. After 10 years, he was raised to be a teacher. After some years he attached himself to the Nawáb, who sent him to England for the purpose of making a last appeal. Failing in his endeavours, he returned to India breathing revenge in his heart.

**'Azimush Shan,** عظیم الشان, second son of the emperor Bahádur Sháh of Dehlí. He was appointed by his grandfather, the emperor 'Alamgír, governor of Bengal; he made Patna the seat of his government and named it Azímábád. On the news of his grandfather's death, leaving his own son Farrukhsiar (afterwards emperor) to superintend the affairs of that country, he came to Agra, and was present in the battle which took place between his father and his uncle 'Azim Sháh in June 1707, A. D., 1119 A. H. He was slain in the battle which ensued after his father's death between Jahándár Sháh and his other brothers in the month of February 1712, O. S., Muharram 1124, A. H. His second son Muhammad Karím was taken prisoner after the battle, and murdered by order of Jahándár Sháh who ascended the throne.

**'Aziz,** عزيز, whose proper name was Abdúl Azíz Khán, was a native of Dakhan. He is the author of a Díwán, also of a prose composition called "Gulshán Rang."

**'Aziz Koka (Mirza),** میرزا عزیز کوکه, the foster-brother of the emperor Akbar, *vide* 'Azim Khán, the son of Khán 'Azim commonly called Anka Khán.

**'Aziz-ullah Zahidi,** عزیز الله زاهدی, author of a Masnawí which he composed in the year 1407 A. D., 810 A. H. He is commonly called Azíz.

**'Azid le din-allah-bin-Yusaf-bin-Hafiz,** عاضد لدين الله بن يوسف بن حافظ, the eleventh and last khalíf of Egypt of the Fatimite dynasty, succeeded his father Fáez-bi-nasr-alláh Ísá bin-Záfir in the year 1158 A. D., 553 A. H. But the state of affairs in Egypt was now tottering to its fall. The descendants of 'Alí from the death of Al-Musta'alí Billáh A. D. 1101, had become puppets in the hands of their wazír or Amír-ul-Jayúsh (generalissimo), who wielded all the regal authority of the state: two Amírs, Dargam and Sháwar, had contested in arms this high dignity; and the latter, defeated and expelled from Egypt, sought refuge and aid from Núr-uddín styled Málik-ul-'Adil Núr-uddín Mahmúd, the celebrated ruler of Syria. The sovereign of Damascus eagerly embraced the opportunity of obtaining a footing in Egypt, and in 1163 A. D., 558 A. H., despatched a force under Asad-ud-dín Shirakoh (the brother of Aiyúb) and his nephew Sálah-uddín to reinstate Sháwar; whose rival called in the Christians of Palestine to his support: but ere Amauri (the brother and successor of Baldwin III) could enter Egypt, Dargam had been overpowered and slain by Shirakoh, who replaced Sháwar in his former power. But Sháwar, faithless alike to friend and foe, now entered into arrangements with the Franks in order to elude the fulfilment of his engagements with Núr-uddín; and Shirakoh, after maintaining himself for some time in Belbes against the joint forces of Jerusalem and Egypt, was compelled to enter into a convention with Amauri and evacuate the country. But he was soon recalled by Sháwar to deliver him from the vengeance of his new allies to whom he had proved as perfidious as to those of his own faith; Cairo was closely besieged by the Franks, and the Fatimite khalíf 'Azid le-dín-allah sent the hair of his women, the extreme symbol of Oriental distress, to implore the succour of Núr-uddín (1168 A. D.). Shirákoh again entered Egypt with an army, forced Amauri to retreat, and after beheading the double traitor Sháwar, installed himself in the twofold office of wazír to the Fátimite khalíf, and lieutenant of Egypt in the name of Núr-uddín; but dying the same year, was succeeded in his dignities by his famous nephew Sálah-uddín, who after the death of Núr-uddín in May, 1173 A. D., Shawwal, 569 A. H., became the sole master of Egypt and Syria. The khalíf 'Azid died in 1171 A. D., 567 A. H., and the name of the Abbaside khalíf Mustazí was substituted in the public prayers till the death of Núr-uddín.

**'Azim,** اعظم, poetical name of Siráj-ud-daula Muhammad Ghaus Khán, Nawáb of the Karnatic.

**'Azim,** اعظم, poetical name of Sayyad 'Azim 'Alí of Allahábád, author of a Díwán in Urdú, composed in 1855 A. D.

**'Azim Ali (Mir),** میر اعظم علي, of Ágra, author of a Sikandar Náma in Urdú verse, translated from the one in Persian, in 1844 A. D.

**'Azim Humayun,** اعظم همايون, *vide* Adil Khán Fárúkí II.

**'Azim Humayun Shirwani,** اعظم هماون شرواني, a nobleman of the court of Sultán Sikandar Sháh Lódí. He was imprisoned by Sultán Ibráhím and died in prison.

**'Azim Khan,** اعظم خان, or Khán 'Azim, an officer of state in the time of Humáyún and Akbar, emperor of Dehlí. He was commonly called Anka Khán, surnamed Shams-uddín Muhammad, was the father of Mirzá Azíz Kóka who also afterwards held the title of 'Azim Khán. He was a native of Ghazní, and formerly served under Prince Kámrán Mirzá. It is said that he saved the life of Humáyún, or had been of some service to him after his defeat by Sher Sháh at Kanauj; for which service he was handsomely rewarded by that emperor after his having recovered the kingdom. He accompanied the emperor to Persia, and as his wife Jíjí Begam became the wet-nurse of Akbar, the emperor's son, he was consequently called Anka Khán. He was the first person that was honored with the rank of "Haft Hazárí," or Seven Thousand, by Akbar. The office of Wakíl Mutlak, which was taken away from Máham Anka, was also conferred on him; on which account, Adham Khán Kokaltásh, the son of Máham Anka, took offence, and assassinated Khán 'Azim on Monday the 18th of May, 1562 A. D., 12th Ramzan, 969 A. H., in a room adjoining to that occupied by the emperor. Adham Khán was immediately bound hand and foot, by order of the emperor, and thrown down headlong from a window of the court at Ágra, where this circumstance had taken place, and crushed to death. The remains of Khán 'Azim were sent to Dehlí, and buried in the vicinity of the Dargáh of Nizám-uddín Auliá, where a mausoleum was erected over his grave by his son Mirzá Azíz Kóka which is still to be seen at Dehlí. Máham Anka died with grief one month after the death of his son Adham Khán. The tomb of Adham Khán, who is also buried at Dehlí, is called Bhúl Bhulián.

**'Azim Khan,** اعظم خان, the inhabitants of the town of Azimgaṛh, which is near Jaunpúr, say that the fortress and town of Azimgaṛh was founded by a person who belonged to the family of the Rájás of that place, and who was forced by the emperor Jahángír to become a Muhammadan and received the title of Azim Khán.

**'Azim Khan,** اعظم خان, commonly called Mirzá Azíz Kóka or Kokaltásh, was the son of 'Azim Khán or Khán 'Azim. He was called Kóká or Kokaltásh on account of his being foster-brother and playmate of Akbar; for his mother whose name was Jíjí Begam, was Akbar's wet-nurse. He was one of the best generals of the emperor, who, in the 16th year of his reign conferred on him the title of 'Azim Khán. He held the government of Gujrát for several years together, and being absent from the presence from a long period, was summoned to court by Akbar in 1592 A. D., 1001 A. H., but as that chief had always entertained the wish to proceed on a pilgrimage to Mecca, and his friends representing to him that the king was displeased with him, and merely sought an opportunity to imprison him, he placed his family and treasure on board a vessel, and on the 13th of March, 1594 O. S., 1st Rajab, 1002 A. H., set sail for Hejáz without leave or notice. In a short time, however, he found his situation irksome in that country, and returned to India, where he made his submission, and was restored at once to his former place in the emperor's favor and confidence. He died at Ahmadábád Gujrát in the 19th year of the reign of Jahángír 1624 A. D., 1033 A. H. His remains were transported to Dehlí and buried close to his father's mausoleum, where a splendid monument was erected over his tomb all of marble. It consists of 64 pillars, and is called by the people "Chaunsa'th Khambh."

**'Azim Khan,** اعظم خان, title of Mír Muhammad Bákir, the brother of 'Asaf Khán Jáfar Beg. In the second year of the reign of the emperor Jahángír 1606 A. D. 1015 A. H., he was honored with the mansab of 1000 and title of Irádat Khán. In the first year of Sháh Jahán, 1628 A. D., 1037 A. H., the rank of 2000 was conferred on him with the office of Wizárat Kull; in the third year of his reign he received the title of 'Azim Khán. He was appointed at different times governor of Bengal, Allahábád, Gujrát and latterly of Jaunpúr, where he died in 1649 A. D., 1059 A. H., aged 76 lunar years, and was buried there. After his death the title of 'Azim Khán was conferred on his eldest son, who was slain in the battle which took place between Dárá Shikoh and his brother Alamgír in 1658 A. D., 1068 A. H., at Ágra. His second son Mír Khalíl was honored with the title of Khán Zamán. During the government of this viceroy in Bonga 1634 A. D., the English obtained permission to trade with their ships in Bengal by the emperor Sháh Jahán, but were restricted to the port of Pipley where they established their factory.

**'Azim Khan Koka,** اعظم خان كوكه, the title of Muzaffar Husain commonly known by the appellation of Fidáí Khán, a title conferred on him by the emperor Sháh Jahán. His elder brother held the title of Khán Jahán Bahádúr Kokaltásh, and were both foster-brothers to the emperor Alamgír. Fidáí Khán was honored with the title of 'Azím Khán by Alamgír about the year 1676 A. D., 1086 A. H., and appointed governor of Bengal in 1676 A. D., 1087 A. H., which situation he held for a whole year and died on his way to Behar on the 21st April, 1678 O. S., 9th Rabí I, 1089 A. H.

**'Azim Khan,** اعظم خان, ex-amír and a brother of Sher Alí Khán, Amír of Kabul, died at Sháh Rúd on the 6th of October, 1869.

**'Azim Naishapuri,** اعظم نيشاپوری, author of a Díwán found in the Library of Típú Sultán.

**'Azam Shah,** اعظم شاہ, the third son of the emperor Alamgír, was born on the 11th July, 1653 O. S., 25th Shábán, 1063 A. H. After his father's death (his eldest brother Bahádur Sháh being then at Kábul) he was crowned in the garden of Shálimar at Ahmadábád in the Dakhan on the 4th March, 1707 O. S., 10th Zil-hijja 1118 A. H., but was soon after slain, together with his two sons Bedár Bakht and Wálájáh, in a battle fought against his eldest brother at Jajowan between Agra and Dholpur. This circumstance took place on Sunday the 8th of June, 1707 O. S., 18th Rabí' I, 1119 A. H., three lunar months and eighteen days after his father's death. His mother's name was Báno Begam, the daughter of Sháhnawáz Khán. He was buried in the mausoleum of Humáyún at Dehlí. His two youngest sons who survived him were 'Alí Tabār and Bedar Dil.

**'Azmat-ullah,** عظمت الله, (or Uzmat-ulláh) Sháh, author of the "Mazhar-ul-Asrár," being a long dissertation on the nature of the divinity, the soul, and other abstruse subjects on Súfiism.

**'Azra,** عذرا, name of the celebrated mistress of Wámiķ.

**Azraki,** حکیم ازرقي, commonly called Hakím Arzaķí, or Azraķí, was a physician and a poet. He was a native of Mars, and flourished in the reign of Tughral III, Saljúkí, king of Persia, in whose name he wrote several books. Arzaķí died in 1189 A. D., 585 A. H. His Díwán contains nearly 2,000 verses. He is also said to be the author of a work called "Kitáb Sindbád." His proper name is Abú'l Mahásin Abú Bakr Zain-ud-dín, son of Isma'íl Warráķ. He introduced himself into the society and confidence of the Saljúkí prince Tughán Sháh I, the seat of whose government was Naishapúr, by the composition of a most obscene book which he called "Alfia Shalfia," illustrated with pictures. This book appears to be a version of the Kók Sháshtar. He is called Azraķí in the Journal of the Asiatic Society of Bengal for 1844, Vol. XIII, Part II, p. 520, and stated to be the author of a history of Mecca, of which ancient work several MSS. are in Europe, especially one at Cambridge which has been left there by Dr. Burckhardt, who in the preface to his Travels in Arabia, professes to have largely made use of it.

**Azur,** آذر, the poetical name of Lutf 'Alí Beg, author of the Tazkira called "'Ataishkada Azur." He was engaged in the compilation of this work in 1765 A. D., 1179 A. H., and was alive in 1782 A. D., 1196 A. H. He never came to India.

**Azuri Razi,** آذری رازی, a native of Rei in Persia, was a celebrated poet who lived at the court of Sultán Mahmúd of Ghazní. On one occasion he received a present of 14,000 dirhams from the Sultán for a short panegyric.

**Azuri (Shaikh),** شیخ آذری, Isfaráení, whose original name was Jalál-uddín Hamza, was a pious Musalmán and an excellent poet. He came to Dakhan from Persia in the reign of Sultán Ahmad Sháh Walí Bahmaní, 1432 A. D., 835 A. H., and returned again to Khurásán, his native country, where he died in the year 1462 A. D., 866 A. H., aged 82 lunar years. He is the author of several works, among which are "Jawáhir-ul-Asrár," "Tughráe Humáyún," and "Samrát Fruits," which consists of four books, *viz.* "Almakrí Táma," "'Ajáeb-ud-dunia, "'Ajáeb-ul-'Ala," and "Sa'í-us-Safá." He also left a Díwán of 30,000 verses. He adopted the poetical name of 'Azurí, because he was born in the Persian month of Azur. His tomb is at Isfaráen, and was at the time of Daulat Sháh so sacred, that convicts found an asylum there from the hands of justice. He is also the author of another poetical work called "Bahman Náma." *Vide* Alí Hamza.

**'Azz-uddin Abdul Aziz,** عز الدین عبد العزیز, *vide* 'Azz-uddín.

# B.

**Baba,** بابا, a Turkish impostor, who announced himself in 1260 A. D., as the messenger of God; and collected a number of adherents, at whose head he laid waste Natolia. He was at last overpowered and his sect dispersed; *vide* Babak.

**Baba Afzal Kashi,** بابا افضل کاشی, an author.

**Baba Fighani,** بابا فغاني, a poet of Persia who served under Sultán Ya'kúb the son of Uzzan Hasan, and died in the year 1519 A. D., 925 A. H., at Khurasán. He has left a Díwán containing 6,000 verses.

**Baba Kaighusiz,** باباکیغوسز (Father without Anxiety) a dervish who flourished in the reign of Murád III, and was author of the 'Abdullah-Náma.

**Baba Lal Guru,** بابا لال گورو, a Hindú of the tribe of Khattrís, who was a Hindí poet and flourished in the time of Jahángír. He was an inhabitant of Málwa.

**Baba 'Isa,** باباعیسی or 'Ísa Langotesband. His tomb is in Tatta in Sindh. The inscription gives the year 1514 A. D., 920 A. H.

**Babak,** بابک, the father of Ardsher Bábakán, which see.

**Babak,** بابک, an impostor, who first appeared in 816 A. D., 201 A. H., when he began to take upon him the title of a prophet. What his particular doctrine was, is now unknown; but his religion is said to have differed from all others then known in Asia. He gained a great number of proselytes in 'Azarbáiján and Persian 'Iráķ, where he soon grew powerful enough to wage war with the khalíf Al-Atámún, whose troops he often beat, so that he was become extremely formidable in the beginning of the khalífa Al-Mu'ta'sim's reign. The general sent by the khalíf to reduce him, was Haidar-ibn-Káús, surnamed Afshín, a Turk by birth. By him Bábak was defeated with prodigious slaughter, no fewer than 60,000 men being killed in the first engagement. The next year 835 A. D., 220 A. H., he received a still greater overthrow, losing 100,000 men either killed or taken prisoners. By this defeat he was obliged to retire into the Gordian mountains, where he fortified himself in such a manner, that Afshín found it impossible to reduce him till the year 837 A. D., 222 A. H., when he was forced to surrender to Afshín, upon that general's promising him pardon. But Afshín no sooner had him in his power, than he first caused his hands and feet, and afterwards his head to be cut off. Bábak had supported himself against the power of the khalífs for upwards of 20 years, during which time he had cruelly massacred 250,000 people, it being his custom to spare neither man, woman, nor child of the Muhammadans or their allies.

**Baba Ratan,** ابورضا بابا رتن, surnamed Abú Razá, a pious Musalmán, who is said, by Daulat Sháh, to be one of the disciples of Jesus Christ, and that he lived to an advanced age of 1400 years, and died about the beginning of the 13th century of the Christian era.

**Babar Shah,** ظهیر الدین محمد بابر شاہ, surnamed Zahír-ud-dín Muhammad, the ancestor of the Mughal emperors of Dehlí, was the sixth in descent from Amír Taimúr (Tamerlane). His father 'Umar Shaikh Mirzá, was the son of Abú Sa'íd Mirzá, the son of Muhammad Mirzá, the son of Míránsháh, the son of Amír Taimúr. His mother's name was Kutlagh Nigár, Khánam, daughter of Yúnas Khán, king of Mughálistán and sister to Mahmúd Khán, a descendant of the famous Changez or Jenghiz Khán. He was born on the 15th February 1483, 6th Muharram. 888 A. H., and succeeded his father in the government of Farghána, the capital of which is Andján, in June 1494, Ramaẓán, 899 A. H. During eleven years he fought several battles with the Tartar and Uzbak princes, but was at last obliged to leave his country and fly towards Kábul, which place he conquered, without opposition, together with Kandahár and Badakhshán. He reigned for 22 years over those countries before his conquest of India. He then proceeded to Hindústán, slew Ibrahím Husain Lodí, the Paṭhán king of Dehlí, in a battle at Pánipat on Friday the 20th of April 1526, A. D., 7th Rajab, 932 A. H., and became the founder of the Mughal dynasty of India which ended in 1857. Babar wrote his own life in the Turkish language, called "Túzak Bábarí" with such elegance and truth, that the performance is universally admired. It was translated in the reign of his grandson Akbar, by Abdúl Rahím Khán, Khánkhánán into Persian, and recently into English from the Jaghatai Turkí, by J. Leyden, Esq., and Wm. Erskine, Esq. This monarch ascended the throne in his 12th year and reigned 38 years, *viz :* at Andján 11 years, at Kábul 22, and nearly 5 years in India, and died in Agra on Monday the 26th of December, 1530 A. D., 6th Jamád I, 937 A. H. He was at first buried in a garden on the left bank of the Jamna, then called the Núr Afshán, and now Rámbágh, from which place his remains were transported after six months to Kábul, where a splendid mausoleum was built on his tomb by his great-great-grandson, the emperor Sháh Jahán in 1646 A. D. His tomb on a hill near the city, surrounded by large beds of flowers, commands a noble prospect. The chronogram of the year of his death was found to consist in the words "Bahisht-rozíbád," or "May heaven be his lot." After his death, he received the title of "Firdaus-Makání. He was succeeded on the throne of Dehlí by his eldest son, the emperor Humáyún. His other three sons were Mirzá Kámrán, Mirzá 'Askarí, and Mirzá Handál. Firishtá says, that Bábar, who was much addicted to women and wine, on occasions when he was inclined to make merry, used to fill a reservoir in a garden in the neighbourhood of Kábul, with some wine, over which was inscribed a verse to this purpose—

Give me but wine and blooming maids,
All other joys I freely spurn :
Enjoy them, Bábar, while you may—
For youth once past, will ne'er return.

**Babar (Sultan),** سلطان بابر, surnamed Abúl Ḳásim, was the son of Mirzá Baisanghar and grandson of Sháhrukh Mirzá. After the death of Mirzá Ulagh Beg and his son 'Abdúl Latíf, he succeeded in January 1452, A. D., Ẕil-ḥija 855 A. H., in murdering his own brother Sulṭán Muhammad and establishing himself in the government of Khurásán and the neighbouring countries. A few months before his death, the comet of 1456 A. D., 860 A. H., made its appearance and alarmed the inhabitants of Khurásán. He died at Mashhad on Tuesday the 22nd of March 1457, 25th Rabí II, 861 A. H. After his death Khurásán was taken possession of by Mirzá Abú Sa'íd, the grandfather of the emperor Bábar Sháh of Dehlí.

**Baba Soudai,** *vide* Soudáí (Bábá). باباسودائي

**Babawia,** بابويه, or Bin Bábawia, father of Ibn Bábawia, *vide* Abú'l Hasan Alí Bin-al-Husian at Kumarí.

**Badakhshi,** بدخشي, a Persian poet who was a native of the province of Badakhshán. He flourished in the reign of the khalíf Al-Muktafí, about the year 905 A. D., 294 A. H. His Díwán or collection of poems is written upon the fortunes of the great men of the court; and he says that the varied scene in human affairs ought not to create surprise as we see that life is measured by an hour-glass, and that an hour is always above and the other below in alternate succession.

**Badakhshi (Maulana),** مولانا بدخشي سمرقندی, of Samarḳand, flourished in the reign of Ulagh Beg Mirzá, the son of Sháhrukh Mirzá, and is the author of a Díwán.

**Badan Singh Jat,** بدن سنکه جاٹ, the son of Chúráman Ját, a rájá of Bhartpúr and the founder of the fort at Ḍíg. He was living at the time of Nádir Sháh's invasion of India in 1739 A. D., 1152 A. H. After his death his son Súrajmal Jáṭ succeeded him, *vide* Chúráman Ját.

**Badaoni,** بداؤني Abdúl Kadír of Badaon.

**Badi-uddin,** بديع الدين *vide* Sháh Madár.

**Badi-uddin (Shaikh),** شيخ بديع الدين, of Saháranpúr, was a disciple of Shaikh Ahmad Sarhindí. He died in the year 1632 A. D., 1042 A. H., and lies buried in the yard of the masjid erected by him at Saháranpúr.

**Badi'-uzzaman Mirza,** مرزا بديع الزمان, was the eldest son of Sulṭán Husain Mirzá, after whose death in 1506 A. D., 912 A. H., he reigned conjointly with his younger brother, Muzaffar Husain Mirzá, over Khurásán. He was subsequently compelled by the victorious Uzbaks, and the usurpation of his brother, to take refuge in 'Iráḳ ; and in the year 1514 A. D., 920 A. H., went to the court of the Ottoman Sulṭán, Salím I, where, after a few months' residence, he died of the plague. He was the last of the race of Taimúr who reigned in Persia. In a work called "Ship of the Time," a Persian Anthology, there are to be found some verses of the royal poet's composition. The following is a translation of a few lines :

Since not for me thy cheek of roses shines,
My bosom like the fading tulip pines ;
Who in his burning heart conceals its flame,
And mine, in absence, perishes the same.
Pour wine—and let me as I drink suppose.
I see the colours of that blushing rose ;
Pour wine—and let it borrow every hue
Born in the tulip's petals wet with dew ;
Till I believe thou may'st e'en yet be mine—
And let me never wake, nor that sweet dream resign.

**Badr,** بدر, poetical title of Gangá Parshád, a Hindú.

**Badr Chachi,** بدر چاچي, surnamed Fakhr-uz-zamán, a celebrated poet of Chách (the ancient name of Táshkand) who flourished in the reign of Sulṭán Muhammad Tughlaḳ Sháh, king of Dehlí, and died some time after the year 1344 A. D., 745 A. H.

**Badr Muhammad,** بدر محمد دهلوی of Dehlí, author of the Persian Dictionary called "Adáb-ul-Fuzalá," dedicated to Ḳadr Khán bin Diláwar Khán, written in 1419 A. D., 822 A. H.

**Badr Shirwani (Maulana),** مولانا بدر شيرواني, a Musalmán scholar and poet who was contemporary with Kátibí who died in 1435 A. D.

**Badr (Pir),** *vide* Pír Badar.

**Badr-uddin Aintabi,** بدرالدين اينتبي, an historian who relates that the Ḳází Ibn-al-Maghúlí who died in 1231 A. D., 628 A. H., bequeathed a part of his vast collection of books to the library of the college founded in Cairo by Málik 'Ashraf Borsabaí.

**Badr-uddin (Balbaki),** بدرالدين بعلبكي, a Syriac physician, who wrote a book called "Musarrah-al-Nafs." He lived in the 7th century of the Hijrah.

**Badr-uddin, Isma'il-al-Tabrizi,** اسمعيل التبريزي بدرالدين, an Arabian author, surnamed Bázil.

**Badr-uddin Jajurmi,** بدرالدين جاجرمي, an author who died in 1287 A. D., 686 A. H., in which year also died Majd-uddín Hamkar. He was a cotemporary of Shams-uddín Muhammad Sáhib Díwán, and of Sa'dí.

**Badr-uddin Lulu,** بدرالدين لولو, ruler of Mausal who was living in the reign of Halákú Khán the Tartar in 1258 A. D., and was in his 90th year.

**Badr-uddin Mahmud,** بدر الدين محمود, known by the name of Ibn-al-Ḳází Simáwana, is the author of the Jáma'-al-Fusúlain," a collection of decisions on mercantile matters. He died 1420 A. D., 823 A. H.

**Badr-uddin Mahmud Bin Ahmad-al-'Aini,** بدرالدين محمود بن احمد العيني, author of a commentary on the "Kanz-ul-Daḳáeḳ," called "Ramz-ul-Haḳáeḳ." He died in 1451 A. D., 855 A. H. He is also the author of a collection of decisions entitled the "Masáel-al-Badria."

**Badr-uddin Muhammad Bin Abdur Rahman-al-Dairi,** بدرالدين محمد بن عبدالرحمان الديري, author of a commentary on the "Kanz-ul-Daḳáeḳ," entitled "Matlab-ul-Fáeḳ," which is much esteemed in India.

**Badr-uddin Shashi Shirwani,** بدرالدين شاشي شيرواني, died in 754 or 854 A. H.

**Badr-uddin Sufi,** بدرالدين صوفي, author of the "Bahr-ul-Hayát," "the sea of life," containing many good rules for moral conduct.

**Badr-uddin,** بدر الدين, of Sarhind, author of a Persian work called Hazrát-ul-Ḳuds containing the miracles performed by Ahmad Sarhindí.

**Badshah Bano Begam,** بادشاه بانو بيگم, one of the wives of the emperor Jahángír. She died in 1620 A. D., 1029 A. H.

**Baghdad Khatun,** بغداد خاتون, a daughter of Amír Chobán or Jovian who governed the empire of the Tartars in the reign of Sultán Abú Sa'íd, the son of Aljáitú. Her father refusing to give her in marriage to that prince, because she had been betrothed to Shaika Hasan Jaláiar, was the occasion of the Amír's disgrace and death. Hasan who had married her, afterwards repudiated her, and gave her into the hands of Abú Sa'íd. The prince publicly married her, and for some time was entirely governed by her; but being at last disturbed, and dying a short time after in 1335 A. D., 736 A. H., she was suspected to have poisoned him, and Báidú Khán, the successor of Abú Sa'íd, put her to death.

**Badr-un-nisa Begam,** بدر النسا بيگم, the daughter of 'Álamgir died in March 1670 A. D., Ẕi-Ḳa'da 1080 A. H.

**Badshah Begam,** بادشاه بيگم, wife of the emperor Jahángír, died in the year 1029 A. H.

**Baghuri,** بغوي, or Baghshúrí, surname of Muhammad bin Is-háḳ, an Arabian author who wrote on moral subjects, died in the year 1280 A. D., 679 A. H.

**Baghwi,** بغوي, *vide* Abú Muhammad Farái-ibn-Masa'úd al-Baghwí.

**Bahadur Ali Husaini (Mir),** مير بهادر علي حسيني, chief Munshi of the college of Fort William, author of the Akhláḳ Hindí, or Indian Ethics, translated from a Persian version, also of the "Nasir Benazír," a prose translation of the enchanting Fairy Tale entitled "Sehr-ul-Bayán" commonly called "Mír Hasan's Masnawí." This latter work was written by the request of Dr. Gilchrist in 1802 A. D., 1217 A. H., and published at Calcutta in 1803.

**Bahadur Khan Faruki,** بهادر خان فاروقي, succeeded his father Rájá Ali Khán in the government of Khándesh in 1596 A. D., 1005 A. H. When the emperor Akbar a few years afterwards arrived at Mánḍo, with the avowed intention of invading the Dakhan, Bahádur Khán instead of adopting the policy of his father in relying on the honor of Akbar, and going with an army to co-operate with him, shut himself up in the fort of Asír, and commenced preparations to withstand a siege. When Akbar heard of these proceedings, he sent orders to the Khán-khánán 'Abdur Rahím Khán, and the prince Dániál Mirzá to continue the siege of Ahmadnagar, while he himself marched to the south and occupied Burhánpúr, leaving one of his generals to beseige Asír. The blockade of this fortress continued for a length of time, till it surrendered, and Bahádur Khán, the last of the Fárúḳí dynasty humbled himself before the throne of Akbar in the year 1599 A. D., 1008 A. H., while the impregnable fortress of Asír with ten years' provisions and countless treasures fell into the hands of the conqueror.

**Bahadur Khan Rohila,** بهادرخان روهيله, son of Dariá Khán, was an amír of high rank in the reign of the emperor Sháh Jahán. He accompanied prince Aurangzib to Ḳandahár, and died there during the siege, on the 19th of July 1649 A. D., 19th Rajab, 1059 A. H.

**Bahadur Nizam Shah,** بهادر نظام شاه, the last of the Nizám Sháhí kings of Ahmadnagar in the Dakhan. On the death of his father Ibráhím Nizám Sháh, which took place in August 1595 A. D., Ẕil-hijja 1003 A. H., several factions arose in Ahmadnagar, each setting up a nominal sovereign. Mián Manjú, who possessed the city, and acknowledged the title of Bahádur Nizám Sháh, then an infant, being besieged by his competitors, invited Sulṭán Murád, son of the emperor Akbar, then governor of Gujrát, to his assistance, for which he offered to become tributary to the Mughal power. Sulṭán Murád embraced the proposal, and arrived before Ahmadnagar with a considerable army. Mián Manjú by this time, having overcome his rivals, repented of his offers, and prepared to oppose the prince. Having committed the city to the charge of Nasír Khán his deputy, and the care of Chánd Bíbí, great aunt to Sulṭán Bahádur, he departed to raise levies, and implore the assistance of Kutb Sháh of Gólkanḍa and 'Adil Sháh of Bijápúr. Sulṭán Murád beseiged Ahmadnagar, on the 16th of December 1595 O. S., 23rd Rabí II, 1004 A. H., which was gallantly defended. Breaches were made, but were immediately repaired by the heroic conduct of Chánd Bíbí, who covering herself with a veil, headed the troops. At length in the month of March 1596, Rajab, 1004 A. H., supplies growing scarce in the camp, and the allies of Bíjápúr and Gólkanḍa approaching, Sulṭán Murád thought proper to accept of some offers of tribute from Chánd Bíbí, and raise the seige. Some money was paid, and the districts in Berar belonging to the Nizám Sháhí government were ceded to the Mughals. In the year 1600 A. D., beginning of 1009 A. H., Ahmadnagar was taken by the Mughals, and Bahádur Sháh with all the children of both sexes of the royal family were taken prisoners and sent to perpetual confinement in the fortress of Gwáliar.

**Bahadur Singh Kuchwaha,** بهادر سنگه کچواها, brother to Sakat Singh, died of hard-drinking in the year 1621 A. D., 1030 A. H.

**Bahadur Shah,** بهادر شاه افغان, an Afghán, succeeded his father Mahmúd Khán as governor of Bengal in the time of Salím Sháh, and became independent and reigned five years. He was deposed in 1549 A. D., 956 A. H. and succeeded by another of the nobles of Salím Sháh named Sulaimán Ḳiráni.

**Bahadur Shah,** بهادر شاه بن مظفر شاه گجراتي, the second son of Muzaffar Sháh II, of Gujrát. At the time of his father's death, he was absent at Jaunpúr, but when Mahmúd Sháh his younger brother ascended the throne of Gujrát, after the murder of his eldest brother Sikandar Sháh, Bahádur returned from thence, and having deprived Mahmúd of his kingdom, ascended the throne on the 20th of August 1526, A. D., 15th Ẕi-Ḳa'da 932 A. H. He conquered Málwá on the 26th February 1531, 9th Shabán, 937 A. H., and the king of that place, Sulṭán Mahmúd II, who was taken prisoner and sent to Champanir, was put to death on the road. In the year 1536 A. D., 942 A. H. Málwá was taken by the emperor Humáyún, and Bahádur being defeated was obliged to fly towards Cambay, where, on his arrival, he heard that a fleet, in which there were between 4 or 5,000 Europeans, had arrived off the island of Diu. He immediately repaired thither with a reinforcement of troops, and on his arrival there, he ordered his barge and went to visit the admiral, with the intention of killing him; but perceiving that he was betrayed, he arose, and was attacked on all sides by the Portuguese, when a soldier struck him over the head with a sword and threw him into the water, where he was drowned. This event took place on the 14th of February 1537, 3rd Ramaẕán, 943 A. H., and has been commemorated in two Persian chronograms, comprising the numerals which form the date of the year when it occurred. Their meaning is this: "The Europeans were the slayers of Bahádur," and "The king of the land became a martyr at Sea." Bahádur Sháh was 20 years of age when he ascended the throne, reigned 11 lunar years, and was slain at the age of 31. After his death his nephew Mírán Muhammad Sháh was raised to the throne of Gujrát.

**Bahadur Shah I,** قطب‌الدين شاه عالم بهادر شاه, surnamed Kutb-uddín Sháh 'Alam, formerly called prince Mua'zzim, was the second son of the emperor 'Alamgír I, born at Burhánpúr in the Dakhan on the 4th October 1643 O. S., 30th Rajab, 1053 A. H. At the time of his father's death, which took place at Ahmadábád, on the 21st February 1707 O. S., 28th Ẕi-Ḳa'da 1118 A. H., he being then at Kábul, his younger brother, prince 'Azim, was proclaimed sovereign of all India in perfect disregard of the late emperor's will. Prince Mua'zzim, with better reason, assumed the crown at Kábul with the title of Bahádur Sháh; and both brothers prepared to assert their pretensions by force of arms. They assembled very large armies, and met at length at Dhaulpúr not far to the south of Ágra. A bloody battle ensued on Sunday the 8th June 1707, O. S., 18th Rabí' I, 1119 A. H., in which prince 'Azim and his two grown-up sons Bedár Bakht and Wálájáh, were killed. Bahádur Sháh reigned nearly five lunar years and died at Láhor on Monday the 18th of February 1712, O. S., 21st Muḥarram, 1124 A. H., in the 71st lunar year of his age. He was buried in the environs of Dehlí, near the tomb of Khwája Kutb-uddín, where he had built during his life a mosque entirely of white marble named Motí Masjid. His tomb is also built of the same stone. He received the title of "Khuld Manzil," *i. e.*, "May his mansion be in paradise," after his death. He left four sons, *viz.*, Ma'iz-uddín Jahándár Sháh, Azím-ush-Shán, Rafí-ush-Shán, and Jahán Sháh, among whom a battle ensued, wherein the three latter brothers were killed, and Jahándár Sháh ascended the throne.

**Bahadur Shah II,** ابوالمظفر سراج الدين محمد بهادر شاه, the present and last king of Dehlí whose title in full is Abú'l Muzaffar Siráj-uddín Muhammad Bahádur Sháh, a lineal descendant from Amír Taimúr; is the son of Akbar Sháh II, on whose death he succeeded him on the 28th September 1837, 28th Jumáda II, 1253 A. H. He was born on Tuesday the 24th of October 1775, 28th Shabán, 1189 A. H.; and Abú'l Muzaffar is the chronogram of his birth. His mother's name was Lál Bái. A stipend or pension of one lakh of rupees monthly was allowed him by the British Government. He is an excellent Persian scholar and an elegant Urdú poet, and Zafar is his poetical name. His Díwán or Book of Odes was printed some years ago at Dehlí. He is supposed to be the principal instigator of the mutiny of the native troops throughout India in 1857, and is now deposed and tried, but his life has been guaranteed. In October 1858 he was sent down to Calcutta, from which place he embarked on board H. M. Ship "Megara" on Saturday the 4th December 1858, for Rangoon, accompanied by two of his wives, a son and a grandson, and thus ended the royal race of Taimúr in India. His sons Mirzá Mughal and Mirzá Khwaja Sulṭán, and a grandson named Mirzá 'Abú Bakr, who were known to have taken a prominent part in the atrocities attending the insurrection, were captured on the 22nd September 1857 at the tomb of Humayún, and shot on the spot. During the mutiny in 1857, Bahádur Sháh had struck a new coin with the following inscription:—

بزرزد سكۀ نصرت طرازی,
سراج الدين بهادر شاه غازی.

**Bahadur Singh (Rao),** *vide* Ráo Bahádur Singh.

**Bahai,** بهائي, *vide* Bahá-uddín 'Amilí.

**Bahar,** بهار, poetical name of Ṭek Chand, which see.

**Baha-uddin,** بهاء الدين, a learned Arabian, known as a favorite of Sulṭán Sálah-uddín (Saladdin) and the historian of that prince's life. He flourished about the year 1190 A. D., 586 A. H. An edition of his work appeared at Leyden in 1755.

**Bahar Bano,** بهار بانو, Daulat-un-Nisa, and Begam Sulṭán, daughters of the emperor Jahángír. All of them died in their childhood.

**Bahar Bano,** بهار بابو, daughter of the emperor Jahángír, married to Prince Tahmuras, the son of Prince Dániál in their childhood.

**Bahar Bano Begam,** بهار بانو بيگم, another daughter of Jahángír, was married to Tahmúr a son of prince Dániál.

**Baha-uddin,** بهاء الدين بن شمس‌الدين, the son of Shams-uddín, the son of Fakkhr-uddín. His father was the first king of the second branch of the Sulṭáns of Ghór. Baha-uddín was the second king, and is said to have reigned 14 years. Imám Fakhr-uddín Rází who flourished in his time and died in 1210 A. D., 606 A. H., dedicated the work called "Risála Haiyat," or book of geometry to him. After the death of Baha-uddín, his son Jalál-uddín succeeded him. He was slain by Sulṭán Muhammad of Khwárizm, and appears to have been the last of this branch.

**Bahadur Singh,** بهادر سنگه, the only surviving son of Rájá Mán Singh Kachwaha.

**Baha-uddin,** بهاء الدين حاكم اصفهان, governor of Isfahán, and author of the "Muntakhab-ul-Akhbár," an abridged history of the patriarchs and prophets, also of Muhammad and his descendants, with a good description of the cities of Mecca and Madina. He flourished about the year 1271 A. D., 670 A. H.

**Baha-uddin 'Amili (Shaikh),** شيخ بهاالدين عاملي, a native of 'Amul in Persia, and son of Shaikh Husain. His poetical name is Bahái. He is the author of several works, one of which is a Masnawí or poem called "Nán-wa-Halwá," Bread and Pudding. He flourished in the time of Sháh 'Abbás the Great, king of Persia; died at Isfahán on Tuesday the 21st of August 1621, O. S., 12th

Shawwál, 1030 A. H., and was buried, agreeably to his request, at Mashhad. Imád-uddaula Abú Tálib, the prime minister of Sháh 'Abbás, found the chronogram of the year of his death in the words "Shaikh Bahá-uddín Wáe." Besides the above-mentioned Masnawí and many Arabic works, he has left a Díwán and a Kashkól, or Adversaria.

**Baha-uddin Muhammad,** شيخ بها الدين محمد جليل, Jalal or Jalíl (Shaikh) of 'Amil. This person is mentioned by H. M. Elliot, Esq., in his "Historians of India," and appears to be the same with the preceding. He was a Persian mathematician, says he, and lived in the reign of Sháh 'Abbás the Great. He was celebrated among his countrymen for a supposed peculiar power which he possessed over the magi and writers of talismans, and was one of the most pious devotees of his time. His works on various subjects are much read in Persia, particularly one entitled "Kashkól," or the Beggar's Wallet, being an universal miscellany of literature. The "Já'ma' ul-Abbasí," a concise and comprehensive treatise on Shia law in twenty books, is generally considered as the work of Bahá-uddín Muhammad 'Amilí, but that lawyer only lived to complete the first five books, dedicating his work to Sháh 'Abbás. The remaining fifteen books were subsequently added by Nizám Ibn-Husain-al-Sáwaí.

**Baha-uddin Nakshband (Khwaja),** الدين نقشبند خواجه بها, a famous learned Musalmán who died on Monday the 1st of March 1389 A. D., 2nd Rabí' I, 791 A. H., and was buried at Bukhára.

**Baha-uddin Nakshband (Shaikh,)** بها الدين نقشبند شيخ, a celebrated saint and the founder of an Order of Súfís, distinguished by the title of Nakshbandí. He is the author of the "Haiát Náma," an esteemed moral poem. He died at Harafa in Persia 1453 A. D., 857 A. H. He appears also to be the author of a work on Súfiism called "Dalíl-ul-'Ashiḳín."

**Baha-uddin Sam,** بها الدين سام, son of Ghayás-uddín Mahmúd, king of Ghór and Ghazní. He succeeded his father in 1210 A. D., 607 A. H., at the age of fourteen years, but was after three months defeated by Alá-uddín Atsiz, son of Jahán Sóz, who reigned four years in Ghór and Ghazní, and fell in battle against Taj-uddín Elduz in 1214 A. D. Bahá-uddín Sám was, after his defeat, taken captive by the governor of Hirát, and sent to Khwárizm Sháh, who at the time of the invasion of Chingiz Khán, threw him along with his brother into a river where both were drowned.

**Baha-uddin Shirazi,** بها الدين شيرازي, a celebrated Ḳází of Shiráz, who died in the year 1380 A. D., 782 A. H.

**Baha-uddin Wald (Maulana),** مولانا بها الدين ولد, a native of Balkh and the father of the celebrated Jalál-uddín Maulawí Rúmí. He flourished and enjoyed distinguished honors in the time of Sulṭán Muhammad, surnamed Ḳutb-uddín of Khwárizm. He was an enthusiastic follower of the doctrine of the Súfís, and became so celebrated as a preacher and expounder, that people flocked from all parts of Persia to hear him discourse. In the latter part of his life, he left his native country and went and dwelt at Ḳonia (Iconium) in Asiatic Turkey, where he died about the year 1230 or 1233 A. D., 628 or 631 A. H., and his son succeeded him as the head of the sect.

**Baha-uddin Zikaria (Shaikh),** شيخ بها الدين زكريا, a Muhammadan saint of Multán, was the son of Ḳutb-uddín Muhammad, the son of Kamál-uddín Ḳureshí. He was born at Kótkaroṛ in Multán in 1170 A. D., 565 A. H. After his studies he journeyed to Baghdád and became a disciple of Shaikh Shaháb-uddín Suharwardí. He afterwards returned to Multán where he became intimate with Faríd-uddín Shakarganj. He died at Multán on the 7th November, 1266 A. D., 7th Ṣafar, 665 A. H., aged 100 lunar years, and is still considered one of the most revered saints of India. He left enormous wealth to his heirs. His son Shaikh Sadr-uddín died at Multán in 1309 A. D., 709 A. H.

**Baha-uddin,** بها الدين, (Badí'-uddín or Bogo-neddín) a Muhammadan saint whose tomb is in the neighbourhood of Bukhára, called Mazári Bogo-neddín. During the invasion of the Russians at that place, it is said, that a book, written in verse in the Persian language, was found in the tomb of this saint. It is said in this book that in the 82nd year of the Hijrah (1865 A. D.,) the Christians will rush upon Tashkand like a river. In the 84th year (1867 A. D.,) they will occupy Samarkand, and sweep it away like a prickly thorn. In the 88th year (1871 A. D.,) the Christians will take Bokhára, and convert it into a level like the steppe. In the year 90th but one (1872) the Khwárizmians will run out of their own accord to meet them like children.

**Bahishti,** بهشتى, poetical name of Sheikh Ramzán, the son of 'Abdul Muhsin, an author who died 1571 A. D., 979 A. H.

**Bahjat,** بهجت, or Behjat, author of a Díwán which contains chiefly Ghazals, and at the end a very silly Ḳaseada in praise of the Europeans. He was living in Lakhnau in 1797 A. D., 1212 A. H.

**Bahlol,** بهلول, who lived during the reign of the khalíf Hárún-al-Rashíd, was one of those people who pass amongst the Musalmáns either for saints or madmen. Although surnamed Al-Majnún, or the Fool, he was possessed of a great deal of wit.

**Bahloli,** بهلولي, a poet whose Díwán was found in the Library of Típú Sulṭán.

**Bahlol Lodi (Sultan),** سلطان بهلول لودي, a king of Dehlí of the tribe of Afgháns called Lódí. His father Málik Kálá was the son of Ibrahím Khán or Málik Bahrám governor of Multán. In the year 1450 A. D., 854 A. H., Bahlól, during the absence at Badáon of Sulṭán Alá-uddín, son of Muhammad Sháh, took possession of Dehlí. He, however, gave place to the name of the Sulṭán for some time in the khutba; but when that prince promised to cede to him the empire, upon condition that he would permit him to live quietly in the possession of Badáon, Sulṭán Bahlól immediately threw the name of 'Alá-uddín out of the khutba and caused himself to be crowned on the 18th of January, 1452 A. D., 25th Ẕil-ḥijja, 855 A. H. Bahlól reigned 38 lunar years, seven months and seven days, and died on the 1st of July, 1489 A. D., 2nd Sha'bán, 894 A. H. He is buried at Dehlí near the tomb of Nasír-uddín Mahmúd, surnamed Chirágh Dehlí, a Musalmán saint, and was succeeded by his son Nizám Khán, who assumed the title of Sikandar Sháh.

*The following is a list of the kings of Dehlí of the tribe of Lódí Afgháns.*

Bahlól Lódí.
Sikandar Sháh, son of Bahlól.
Ibrahím Husain, son of Sikandar who was the last of this race, and was defeated by Bábar Sháh.

**Bahman,** بهمن, an ancient king of Persia, better known in history by his title of Ardisher Darázdast, which see.

**Bahman Yar Khan,** بهمن يار خان, son of Sháista Khán and grandson of Ásaf Khán, a nobleman of the court of the emperor 'Alamgír.

**Bahu Begam,** بهو بيگم, the mother of Nawáb Ásf-uddaula of Lakhnau. She died on the 28th December 1815.

**Bahram I,** بهرام, (Varanes of the Greeks), the fourth king of the Sasánian race, was the son of Hurmuz (Hormisdas) whom he succeeded to the Persian throne in the year 273 A. D. He was a mild and munificent prince, and much beloved by his subjects. The most remarkable act of his reign was, the execution of the celebrated Máni (Mani) the founder of the sect of the Manichœans. *Vide* Máni. Bahrám reigned only three years and three months, after which he left the crown to his son Bahrám II, about the year 276 A. D.

**Bahram II,** بهرام, (some authors term him the fourth of that name), was the son of Bahrám I, whom he succeeded to the crown of Persia in 276 A. D. He reigned 17 years, and after his demise, was succeeded by his son Bahrám III, about the year 293 A. D.

**Bahram III,** بهرام, succeeded his father Bahrâm II to the Persian throne about the year 293 A. D., reigned only four months, and was succeeded by his brother, Narsí, or Narses.

**Bahram IV,** بهرام, the twelfth king of Persia of the Sasanian race, succeeded his brother Sháhpúr (Sapores) about the year 390 A. D., and is distinguished from other princes of the same name, by his title of Kirmansháh, which he received from having, during the reign of his brother, filled the station of ruler of the province of Kirmán: and he has perpetuated it by founding the city of Kirmánsháh. He reigned, according to some accounts, eleven years: and to others fifteen. He was killed by an arrow when endeavouring to quell a tumult in his army, and was succeeded by Yezdijard I, who is called Isdigerdes by the Greek authors.

**Bahram V,** بهرام, (or Varanes V,) the fourteenth king of Persia of the Sasanian dynasty, who is known, in Persian history, by the name of Bahrám Gór. He was the son of Yezdijard I, whom he succeeded to the throne of Persia in 420 A. D. The word Gór signifies a wild ass: an animal to the chase of which this monarch was devoted; and it was in pursuit of one of these that he lost his life; having suddenly come upon a deep pool, into which his horse plunged, and neither the animal nor his royal rider were ever seen again. The first rhythmical composition in the Persian language is recorded to have been the production of Bahrám and his mistress Dilárám. Bahrám visited India, was contemporary with Theodosius the emperor of Constantinople, and ruled Persia eighteen years. He died in 438 A. D., and was succeeded by his son Yezdijard II.

**Bahram,** بهرام, an author who wrote the History of the Parsís of Bombay in 1599 A. D., entitled Ḳissai Sanján.

**Bahram Chobin,** بهرام چوبين, or Jovián, a general of Hurmuz III, king of Persia, whom he deposed; he reigned eight months about the year 590 A. D. *Vide* Hurmuz III.

**Bahram Mirza,** بهرام مرزا, son of Sháh Samá'íl Ṣafawí. He was a good poet and died in the prime of youth in 1550 A. D., 957 A. H.

**Bahram Saqqa,** بهرام سقه, a poet, was of Turkish extraction and belonged to the Bayát tribe. It is said that the prophet Khizr appeared to him, and a divine light filled him. He renounced the world and became a water-carrier. *Vide* Ain Translation, Vol. I, p. 581.

**Bahram Sarkhasi,** بهرام سرخسي, a Prosodian of Sarakhs, a town between Naishápúr and Marv.

**Bahram Shah,** بهرام شاه, son of Sulṭán Masa'úd III, ascended the throne of Ghazní by the assistance of Sulṭán Sanjar his uncle, after his brother Arsalán Sháh, who was put to death in 1118 A. D., 512 A. H. Bahrám Sháh after a prosperous reign of 35 lunar years was defeated in 1152 A. D., 547 A. H., by 'Alá-uddín Hasan Ghórí, and fled to Láhor where he died the same year, and his son Khusro Sháh succeeded him in the government of Láhor. The poets Shaikh Sa'náí and Abú'l Majd-bin-'Adam-al-Ghaznawí flourished in the time of Bahrám Sháh.

**Bahram Shah,** بهرام شاه, surnamed Ma'iz-uddín, was the son of Sultán Rukn-uddín Fíróz. He was raised to the throne of Dehlí after the murder of Sulṭána Razia the queen, on Monday the 21st of April, 1240 A. D. He reigned little more than two years, and was slain by the instigation of Mahzab-uddin wazír, about the 15th of May, 1242 A. D., when Sulṭán 'Alá-uddín Masa'úd, another son of Sulṭán Altimsh, was raised to the throne. Firishta says that Bahrám was the son of Altimsh and brother of Sulṭána Razia.

**Bahramand Khan,** بهرمند خان, son of Mirzá Bahrám, and one of the emperor 'Alamgír's oldest nobility and his friend. After the death of Rúh-ulláh Khán, he was raised to the post of Mír Bakhshí or chief paymaster by the emperor in 1692 A. D., 1103 A. H., and died in the Dakhan on the 17th October, 1702 O. S., 5th Jumáḍa II, 1114 A. H. He was buried at his own request in a small tomb at Bahádurguṛh. He was succeeded in his office by Zulfiḳáṛ Khán Nasrat Jang, who notwithstanding this appointment continued in the command of the army against the Marhattas in the Dakhan.

**Bahr-ul Hifz,** بحرالحفظ, (or the Sea of Memory,) is the title of Abú Usmán-bin-'Amrú who wrote a book on the manners and qualities of princes. He died 869 A. D., 255 A. H.

**Baidu Khan,** بايدو خان, the son of Turagháí and grandson of Halákú Ḳhán, succeeded Kaikhatú or Kaijaptú Khán in January, 1295 A. D., Ṣafar, 694 A. H., and enjoyed the crown of Persia only seven months: he was dethroned and slain by his nephew, Gházán Khán, the son of Arghún Khán; who was compelled to attack his uncle and sovereign to preserve himself from destruction. This event took place in October the same year, Ẓil-ḥijja 694 A. H. In English Histories he is called Batu. In 1235, at the head of half a million of Keptchak Mongols, he conquered the east of Russia, destroying Riazan, Moscow, Vlandimir and other towns.

**Baikara Mirza (Sultan),** سلطان بايقرا مرزا, the son of Umar Shaikh Mirzá, the second son of Amír Taimúr. Báiḳara succeeded his brother as governor of Persia in 1394 A. D., 796 A. H. His eldest brother, Pír Muhammad Jahángír was slain in 1405 A. D., 808 A. H. Báiḳara Mirzá was slain by his uncle Sháhrukh Mirzá in 1416 A. D., 819 A. H., he left a son named Mansúr, who became the father of Sulṭán Husain Mirzá, surnamed Abú'l Ghází Bahádur.

**Baihaki,** بيهقي, surnamed Abú'l Fazl, and whose proper name is Abú Bakr Ahmad, was the son of Husain Baihaḳí. He is the author of the works in Arabic called "Sunan Kubra and Sughra," and of one entitled "Sha'b-ul-Imán." He died in the year 1066 A. D., 458 A. H. His collection of Traditions is also of the highest authority.

**Baiju,** بيجو, one of the most celebrated songsters of India, besides Náek, Gopál, and Fansin.

**Bairam Khan,** بيرام خان, styled Khán Khánán, or Lord of lords, was one of the most distinguished officers of the Mughal court. He was a Turkmán and descended from a line of ancestors who served for many generations in the family of Taimúr. Bairám accompanied the emperor Humáyún from Persia to India, and on the accession of his son Akbar, he was honored with the title of Khán Khánán and the office of prime minister; and had the whole civil and military powers vested in his hands. When Akbar in 1558 A. D., 965 A. H., thought he was capable of acting for himself, he dismissed Bairám Khán from the wizárat. Bairám at first had recourse to rebellion, but being unsuccessful, was compelled to throw himself on the clemency of his sovereign, who not only pardoned him, but assigned to him a pension of 50,000 rupees annually for his support. Bairám soon after took leave of the emperor with the design of making a pilgrimage to Mecca, and had proceeded to Gujrát in order to embark for Mecca, but was slain by one Mubárik Khán Lohání, whose father Bairám Khán had slain in battle with his own hand during the reign of the emperor Humáyún. This event took place on Friday the 31st of January, 1561 A. D., 14th Jumáda I, 968 A. H. He was at first buried near the tomb of Shaikh Hisám at Gujrát, but afterwards his remains were transported to Mashhad and buried there. He is the author of a Díwán.

**Bairam,** بيرام, sometimes erroneously written by us for Bahrám.

**Bairam Beg,** بيرام بيگ, was father of Muním Khán. The latter was a grandee in Humáyún's Court. *Vide* Ain Translation, Vol. I, p. 317.

**Baizawi,** قاضي بيضاوى, (Kazi) the surname of Nasir-uddín Abú'l Khair Abd-ulláh-ibn-Umar al-Baizáwí. He was a native of Baizá, a village of Shíráz, on which account he is styled Baizáwí. He held the office of Kází or Judge of the city of Shíráz for a considerable time, and died at Tabriz or Tauris in the year 1286 A. D., 685 A. H., or as others say in 1292 A. D., 691 A. H. He is the author of the well-known Commentary on the Ḳurán called "Tafsír Baizáwí," which is also called "Anwár-ul-Tanzíl," and "Asrár-ul-Táwíl". Some say that he is also the author of a history entitled "Nizámut Tawáríkh," but the author of this work is said by others to be Abú Sa'íd Baizáwí, which see.

**Baisanghar (Mirza),** مرزا بايسنغر, son of Mirzá Sháhrukh, the son of Amír Taimúr. He was a learned and noble prince, a great protector of letters and learned men. He himself wrote six different hands, composed verses in the Persian and Turkish languages, and constantly had in his employment forty copyists for transcribing MSS. He was born in the year 1399 A. D., 802 A. H., and died before his father in 1434 A. D., 837 A. H., at Hirát, aged 35 lunar years.

**Baisanghar (Mirza),** مرزا بايسنغر, son of Sulṭán Husain Mirzá of Hirát. He was killed by Khusro Sháh, king of Ḳundaz.

**Bajazet,** name of several Turkish emperors spelt so in English, being a corruption of Báyezíd, which see.

**Baji Bai,** باجي بائي, also called Bíja Báí, which see.

**Baji Rao I,** باجي راؤ پيشوا, (Peshwá,) the son of Bálájí Ráo Bishwanáth Peshwá, whom he succeeded in October 1720, A. D. He was the ablest of all the Bráhmaṇ dynasty, and of all the Marhaṭṭa nation, except Sewájí. He died on the 28th April 1740, O. S., 12th Ṣafar 1153, A. H., and left three sons: *viz.*: Bálájí Ráo who succeeded him as Peshwá: Rághunáth Ráo commonly called Rághoba, who was at one time much connected with the English, and was the father of the last Peshwá Bájí Ráo II; and Shamsher Bahádur to whom (though an illegitimate son by a Muhammadan woman, and brought up in his mother's religion), he left all his possessions and pretensions in Bundelkhand.

**Baji Rao II,** باجي راوپيشوا, the last Peshwa, was the eldest son of Rághoba or Rághunáth Ráo of infamous memory. He succeeded Mádho Ráo, the infant Peshwá, who died suddenly in October 1795, A. D. During the reign of Mádho Ráo, he and his brother Chimnájí were confined in the fort of Juneir, near Púna, and after his death Chimnájí was furtively invested, but he was soon after deposed and Bájí Ráo was publicly proclaimed Peshwá by Daulat Ráo Scindhia on the 4th December, 1796 A. D. In May, 1818 a proclamation was issued by Government deposing him; and the Rájá of Sitára, Partáp Singh Náráyan released from confinement, had a part of the Púna territories assigned for his support, and was vested with the reality of that power of which his ancestors, in latter times, had enjoyed only the name. Bájí Ráo was compelled to surrender himself to the English, and was pensioned on the 3rd June, 1818. The pension allowed him by Government was 800,000 rupees per annum. He died at Biṭhúr near Cawnpúr in December, 1852 A. D., and was succeeded by his adopted son Dhondú Pant, commonly called Náná Sáhib, who became a rebel in the disturbances of 1857.

**Bakai (Mulla),** ملا بقائي, a poet who lived in the time of the emperor Bábar Sháh. He is the author of a poem or Masnawí which he dedicated to the emperor.

**Bakai,** بقائي, surname of Ibrahím-bin-'Umar, a learned Musalmán who is the author of several treatises on ancient philosophers, on divination by numbers, a commentary on the Ḳurán, &c. He died in the year 1480 A. D., 885 A. H.

**Bakalani,** باقلاني, the author of a work called "Ai'jáz-ul-Ḳurán," or of the difficult things in the Ḳurán. See Ábú Bakr Báḳalání.

**Baki Muhammad Khan Koka,** محمد خان كوكه باقي, eldest brother of Adham Khán, the son of Máham Anka, was an officer of 3000 in the time of the emperor Akbar. He died at Garh Kaṭka, where he had a jagír, in 1585 A. D., 993 A. H.

**Baki Khan,** باقي خان, a nobleman of the court of the emperor Sháh Jahán, by whom he was appointed governor of the fort of Ágra. In the 24th year of the reign of the emperor he was raised to the rank of 1500. In the 49th year of the emperor's reign, he still held the governorship of the fort of Ágra, and was raised to the rank of 2000 the following year. He had built in the front of the gate called Hathiapol, which is situated towards the Chauk and the Jama Misjid, a fine bungalow which was still standing about the year 1830 A. D.

**Bakhat Singh,** بخت سنگه, or Bakht Singh Ráṭhor, son of Ajít Singh and brother of Abhai Singh, rájá of Jodhpúr. He was poisoned in 1752 A. D.

**Bakhshi 'Ali Khan,** بخشي علي خان, whose poetical name was Hashmat, flourished in the time of Nawáb Salábat Jang of Haidarábád about the year 1751 A. D., 1164 A. H.

**Bakhshi Bano Begam,** بخشي بانو بيگم, a sister of the emperor Akbar the Great.

**Bakshu,** بخشو, a singer, lived at the Court of Rájá Bikramájit Mansur; but when his patron lost his throne, he went to Rájáh Kirát of Kálinjar. Not long afterwards he accepted a call to Gujrát, where he remained at the Court of Sulṭán Bahádur 1526 to 1536 A. D. *Vide* Ain Translation, Vol. I, p. 611.

**Bakhtari,** بختري, one of the most celebrated Arabian poets, who died in the year 823 A. D. According to some writers, he was born in 821 A. D., 208 A. H., flourished in the time of the khalíf Al-Musta'ín Billáh, and died in his 63rd year at Baghdád. He is also called Bin-Bakhtarí.

**Bakhtawar Khan,** بختاور خان, an amír who served under the emperor Alamgír. The Saráe of Bakhtáwar-nagar near Dehlí was constructed by him in 1671 A. D., 1082 A. H. He is the author of the work called "Mirat-ul-'Alam," a history of the first part of the reign of 'Alamgír. He died in 1684 A. D., 1095 A. H., *vide* Názir Bakhtaiár Khán.

**Bakhtaiar Beg Gurdi Shah Mansur,** گرد ساه بختیار بیگ, Turkman, was an Amír and governed (1001) Siwistan. *Vide* Ain Translation, Vol. I, p. 474.

**Bakhtaiar Khilji,** بختیار خلجي *vide* Muhammad Bakhtaiár Khiljí.

**Bakili,** بقلي, surname of Abú'l Fazl Muhammad-bin-Ḳásim al-Khwárizmí, who from his learning has the title of Zain-uddín and Zain-ul-Masháekh, or the ornament of the doctors. He wrote a book on the prayers of the Musalmáns, on the glory and excellence of the Arabs, called "Salát-ul-Baḳilí." He died in 1167 A. D., 562 A. H., but according to Hájí Khalfa in 1170 A. D., 566 A. H. There was another Baḳilí, also a Muhammadan doctor, who died in 982 A. H.

**Bakir,** باقر, the poetical name of Muhammad Báḳir Alí Khán who flourished in the time of the emperor Muhammad Sháh and wrote a Masnawí or poem called "Ramúz-ut-Táhirín", composed in 1726 A. D., 1139 A. H., also another work entitled "Gulshani Asrár," which he wrote in 1732 A. D., 1145 A. H. He is also the author of a Díwán, and another poem called "Mirat-ul-Jamál.

**Bakir Ali Khan,** باقر علي خان, *vide* Báḳir.

**Bakir (Imam),** امام باقر, *vide* Muhammad Báḳir (Imám).

**Bakir Kashi,** باقر کاشي, whose poetical name is Khirad, was a contemporary of Zahúrí who flourished about the year 1600 A. D., and is the author of a Díwán.

**Bakir Khan,** باقرخان, a nobleman in the service of the emperor Sháh Jahán. In the latter part of his life, he was appointed governor of Allahábád, where he died in 1637 A. D., 1047 A. H., in which year died also Khán Zamán Bahádur in Daulatábád.

**Bakir Khan,** باقرخان نجم ثاني, surnamed Najm Sání, an amír of the reign of Sháh Jahán. He was a very liberal man; fond of literature; and was himself a poet. He died in 1640 A. D., 1050 A. H., but, according to the work "Másir-ul-Umrá," in 1637 A. D., 1047 A. H. He is the author of a Díwán or Book of Odes.

**Baktash Kuli,** بکتاش قلي, a Musalmán writer of the Persian sect, who wrote a book, called "Bostán-al-Khayál" or the Garden of Thoughts. Watkin's Biographical Dictionary. See also Amírí, who also wrote a book of that name.

**Bakhtishu,** بختیشوع, name of a Christian physician in the service of Harún-al-Rashíd.

**Balaji Rao Bishwa Nath Peshwa,** بالاجي راؤ بشوناتهہ پیشوا, the founder of the Bráhman dynasty of Peshwá, was the hereditary accountant of a village in the Kokan. He afterwards entered into the service of a chief of the Jádo family, whence he was transferred to that of the rájá Sáhú, son of Sambhájí, chief of the Marhattas. His merits were at length rewarded with the office of Peshwá, at that time second in the State. He died in October 1720, and was succeeded by his son Bájí Ráo Peshwá I.

*List of Hereditary Peshwás of Púna.*

Bálájí Ráo Bishwanath Peshwá.
Bájí Ráo Peshwá I, son of Bálájí.
Bálájí Ráo, son of Bájí Ráo.
Mádho Ráo Bilál, son of Bálájí, succeeded under the regency of his uncle Rághunáth Ráo.
Náráyan Ráo Peshwá, brother of Mádho Ráo.
Rághunáth Ráo, son of Bájí Ráo Peshwá I.
Mádho Ráo II, posthumous son of Náráyan Ráo.
Bájí Ráo II, son of Rághunáth Ráo, proclaimed himself, and was taken by Scindhia.
Chimnájí, furtively invested at Púna, 26th May, 1796.
Bájí Ráo II, publicly proclaimed, 4th December, 1796.
Surrendered to, and pensioned by the English, 3rd June, 1818, and Partáp Singh Náráyan the rájá of Sitára released from confinement.

**Balaji Rao,** بالاجي راو, also called Bálá Ráo Panḍit Pradhán, was the son of Bájí Ráo Peshwá I, and succeeded his father in April, 1740 A. D. He was at Púna when the battle between the Marhattas and Ahmad Sháh Abdálí took place in January, 1761 A. D., but died some time after in the same year, leaving three sons, *viz.:* Biswás Ráo who was killed in the battle of Pánípat, Mádho Ráo, and Náráyan Ráo.

**Baland Akhtar,** بلند اختر, a brother of the emperor Muhammad Sháh. *Vide* Achchhe.

**Balash,** بالاش, *vide* Pálásh or Pálás.

**Balban,** بلبن, a king of Dehlí, *vide* Ghayás-uddín Balban.

**Balbhaddar Singh,** بلبهدر سنگهہ, a rájá lineally descended from the ancient Hindú monarchs of Audh, who having 100,000 Rájpúts at his command, considered himself as equal to the Nawáb Wazír of Lakhnau, whose authority he disclaimed. To reduce this rájá, an army was sent, about the year 1780 A. D., composed partly of the Nawáb's troops, and partly of the Company's sepoys; but owing to the intrigues of Haidar Beg Khán, the minister of the Nawáb Wazír Asaf-uddaula, and the native collectors who extorted large sums from the zamíndárs, this measure failed of success. During two years he was frequently defeated and pursued; and at length being surprised in his camp, he was killed in endeavouring to make his escape.

**Baldeo Singh,** بلدیو سنگهہ, the Jáṭ rájá of Bhartpúr, was the second son of Ranjít Singh. He succeeded to the ráj after the death of his eldest brother Randhír Singh.

**Baligh,** بلیغ, author of the "Daláel Zahira," "Talauwan Ḳudrat," and Makálima. He was a native of India and was living in 1772 A. D., 1186 A. H.

**Balin,** erroneously written by some for Balban, which see.

**Balkini,** بلقیني, *vide* Bilḳainí.

**Balwan Singh,** بلوان سنگهہ, (who was always called by the natives of A'gra as the Kashí-wala rájá) was the son of the celebrated Chait Singh, rájá of Banaras. Balwan Singh was born at Gwaliar, and after his father's death, he and his family lived in the city of A'gra for many years on a monthly pension of 2000 rupees. He lost his only son Kúwar Chakarbatí Singh on the 17th of December, 1871, and after a few days, on the 26th of the same month, he resigned his unusually prolonged life. The only surviving members of this family are the widow of Chakarbatí Singh and his children, a boy aged 9 and a girl aged 11 years. Balwan Singh is the author of a Díwán in Urdú.

**Balwant Singh,** بلونت سنگهہ, a rájá or zamíndár of Banaras. He was the father or brother of the famous Chait Singh who rebelled against the British, and was arrested and deposed by Mr. Hastings in 1781. Balwant Singh succeeded his father Mansa Ram in 1740, A. D., reigned 30 years, died in 1770, and was succeeded by Rájá Chait Singh.

**Balti,** بالتي, (*vide* Jodh Baí), the daughter of rájá Udaia Singh Ráthor, commonly called Motha rájá, she was married to the emperor Jahangír and became the mother of Sháh Jahan. She died in 1619 A. D., 1028 A. H.

**Balwant Singh,** بلونت سنگه, rájá of Bhartpúr, succeeded his father Baldeo Singh in August 1824; was displaced by one of his cousins, named Durjan Sál, in March 1825, but reinstated by the British Government on the 19th of January 1826. Bhartpúr was stormed and taken by the Bengal troops under Lord Combermere, on the 18th January. The British lost during the siege 45 officers killed and wounded, and 1500 men; the enemy lost some thousands, and the usurper Durjan Sál was seized and sent to Allahábád. His father Baldeo Singh was the second brother of Randhír Singh, the eldest of the four sons of Ranjít Singh, the son of Kehrí Singh, the brother of Ratan Singh, the brother of Jawáhir Singh, the son of Súrajmal, the son of Chúráman Ját, the founder of the principality. Balwant Singh died aged 34 years on the 16th of March 1853, and was succeeded by his infant son Jaswant Singh.

**Banana,** بنانه, an Arabian poet whose full name is Abú Bakr-bin-Muhammad bin-Banána. There has been another Bin-Banána, *viz.*, Abú Nasr-ibn-ul-'Azíz-bin Banána, who was a poet also, and died at Baghdád in 1009 A. D., 400 A. H.

**Banda,** بنده, *vide* Razí (Mauláná).

**Banda,** بنده, a gurú or chief of the Sikhs, and successor of Gurú Gobind. This man obtained great power, and committed great depredations in the province of Láhor, in the reign of Bahádur Sháh I, and while the emperor was in Dakhan against his brother Kám Bakhsh, Banda collected his followers, to revenge the death of his predecessor's sons who were taken prisoners, and had been put to death some time ago. He committed the greatest cruelties on the Musalmáns, in every advantage shewing no quarter to age or sex, and even ripping up women with child. The emperor found it necessary to march in person against him, and he was besieged in the fortress of Lohguṛh, which was taken, but Banda found means to escape, and raise new insurrections. In the reign of the emperor Farrukhsír, 'Abdus Samad Khán governor of Kashmír was sent against the rebels with a great army. After many severe engagements, he forced Banda to take refuge in a fortress, which was blockaded so effectually, as to cut off every supply. The garrison was reduced to the necessity of eating cows, horses, asses, and other animals forbidden by their laws; when at length, having no provision of any sort left, and being reduced to the extremity of famine and disease, they begged for quarter. 'Abdus Samad Khán, having planted a standard on the plain, commanded them to come out and lay their arms under it, which they did. He then divided the meaner sort among his chiefs, who cut off their heads; and threw their bodies into a river near the fortress. Banda and other captives were sent to Dehlí, through which he was carried in an iron cage upon an elephant, dressed in a robe of gold brocade. The Sikhs bore the insults of the populace with the greatest firmness, and steadily refused the emperor's offers of life if they would embrace the Muhammadan faith. They were put to death, a hundred each day, on the ensuing seven days. On the eighth day Banda and his son, were put to death without the city. A dagger was put into his hands, and he was commanded to kill his infant son; but refusing, the child was slain by the executioner, his heart torn out, and forced into the father's mouth. Banda was then put to death by the tearing of his flesh with red hot pincers and other tortures, which he bore with the greatest constancy. This event took place in the year 1715 A. D., 1127 A. H.

**Bano Begam,** بانو بيگم, the daughter of Sháhnawáz Khán, the son of the Wazír Asaf Khán, wife of the emperor Alamgír, and mother of 'Azim Sháh.

**Barahman,** برهمن, poetical title of a Bráhman whose name was Chandar Bhán, which see.

**Barbak,** باربك, the son of Bahlol Lodí, king of Dehlí. *Vide* Husain Sháh Sharḳí.

**Barbak Shah,** باربک شاه, Púrbí, the son of Násir Sháh, whom he succeeded to the throne of Bengal in 1458 A. D. He reigned for a period of 17 years and died in 1474 A. D., 879 A. H.

**Barbarassa (Aruch),** بار بارسّه, a famous pirate. Being called in to assist Salím, prince of Algiers, against the Spaniards, he murdered that monarch, and took possession of his throne. He afterwards laid siege to Tunis, which he took, and caused himself to be proclaimed sovereign. He was besieged by the Marquis of Gomarez and reduced to the greatest distress. He escaped by a subterraneous passage, but was overtaken with a small number of Turks, the whole of whom died sword in hand in 1518, A. D.

**Barbarassa,** بار بارسه, the famous Corsair. Sulaimán, emperor of the Turks, gave him the title of Khair-uddín, and made him afterwards Páshá of the sea. He succeeded his brother Aruch, who conquered the kingdom of Algiers, after having killed Salím the Arabian king. He took Tunis, 1533 A. D., 940 A. H., after having driven out the Venetians, but Andre Doria retook it again, 1536 A. D., 943 A. H. After this, he ravaged several parts of Italy, and reduced Yemin, in Arabia Felix, to the Turkish government. Khair-uddín died at Constantinople in 1546 A. D., 953 A. H., aged 80.

**Barbud,** باربد, a famous Persian musician, master of music to Khusro Parwez king of Persia. He composed an air called Aorangí, and invented a musical instrument (a sort of lyre) which bears his name: *viz.*, Bárbud or Bárbut.

**Barizi,** بارزي, the son of 'Abdul Rahím, an Arabian author who wrote a commentary on the work called "Asrar-ul Tanzíl." He died in 1337 A. D., 738 A. H. This author appears to be the same with Báziri, which see.

**Bark,** برق, poetical name of Muhammad Razá.

**Barkali,** بركلي, the name of two Muhammadan doctors; the one died in 1553 A. D., 960 A. H., and the other in 1573 A. D., 982 A. H. They are sometimes called Bingilí, which see.

**Barkat-ullah (Sayyad),** سيد بركت الله, styled "Sáhib-ul-Barkát," was the son of Sayyad Aweis, the son of Mír 'Abdul Jalíl, the son of Mír 'Abdul Wáhid Sháhidí of Bilgarám. His poetical name was 'Ishḳí, and as his grandfather's tomb was in Máhaṛa in the district of Agra, he went and lived in that village till the day of his death which happened on the 25th of July, 1729 A. D., 10th Muḥarram, 1142 A. H.

**Barkayarak (Sultan),** سلطان بركيارق, the eldest son of Sultán Maliksháh Saljúḳí, whom he succeeded in 1092 A. D., 485 A. H. His usual residence was Baghdád. His brother, Muhammad ruled over Azur-beján; while Sanjar, his third brother, established a kingdom in Khurásán and Transoxiana, from whence he extended his conquests over the fallen princes of Ghazní. Barkayárak reigned twelve years and died in December, 1104 A. D.

498 A. H. His brother Sulṭán Muhammad succeeded him.

**Barmak,** برمک, the name of a noble family, originally from Balkh in Khurásán, and highly celebrated all over the East for their generosity, magnificence, and distinguished patronage of men of genius. One of the most illustrious was governor to the khalíf Harún-al-Rashíd, and his son Ja'far, afterwards minister to that prince; but having incurred his displeasure, he with several of the heads of the family was put to death. *Vide* Ja'far-al-Barmakí.

**Baroda,** برودا, rájá of. *Vide* Pelají.

**Basasiri,** بساسيري, (a glutton) was the nickname, and afterwards the surname of Arsalán, who from a slave became Commander-in-Chief of the armies of Bahá-ud-daula, the wazír of the khalíf of Baghdád. Having quarrelled with him he fled to Egypt and put himself under the protection of Al-Mustanasir Billáh, the fifth khalíf of Egypt of the Fatimite dynasty. After some time he came to Baghdád. He took Ḳáem, the 26th khalíf of the Abbasides, prisoner in Baghdád, deposed him, and caused Mustanasir, to be acknowledged the only and legitimate chief of all the Musalmáns. He maintained Mustanasir in the khiláfat for one year and a half, after which Tughral Beg, Sultán of the Saljúḳides, put Ḳáem on the throne of Baghdád again, defeated and killed Basásírí 1059 A. D., 451 A. H., and sent his head to Ḳáem, who caused it to be carried on a pike through the streets of Baghdád.

**Bashir-ibn-ul-Lais,** بشير ابن الليث, or Laith, the brother of the arch-rebel Rafa-ibn-ul-Lais, who had revolted against Harún-al-Rashíd the khalíf of Baghdád in the year 806 A. D., 190 A. H., at Samarḳand, and assembled a considerable force to support him in his defection; notwithstanding all Harún's care, the rebels made in 807 A. D., 191 A. H., great progress in the conquest of Khurásán. According to Abúl Faraj, in the year 809 A. D., 193 A. H., Bashír was brought in chains to Hárún, who was then at the point of death. At the sight of him the khalíf declared, that if he could speak only two words he would say kill him; and immediately ordered him to be cut to pieces in his presence.

**Basiti,** باسطي, poetical name of a person who is the author of the biography of poets called "Tazkira Básití.

**Basus,** باسوس, an Arabian woman, from whom originated a war, called Harb-i-Basús, which has since become a proverb to express, "Great events from little causes." Two Arabian tribes fought about 40 years, because a camel belonging to this woman broke a hen's egg; the owner of the egg wounded the camel with an arrow, and the two tribes were instantly in arms.

**Batalmiyusi,** بطلميو سى, an Arabian author, who died in 1030 A. D., 421 A. H. He wrote a treatise on the qualities requisite in a secretary and good writer, and another on genealogies.

**Batu Khan,** باتوخان, the son of Jújí Khán, and grandson of Changez Khán. He ruled at Ḳipchak and was cotemporary with Pope Innocent IV.

**Bauwab,** بوّاب, (or Bouwáb) surname of Abú'l Hasan 'Alí Kála, who is better known under the name of ibn-Bouwáb. It is he who improved the form of the Arabic Alphabet after Ibn-Maḳla. He died in 1022 A. D., 413 A. H., or as some say in 1032 A. D., 423 A. H. After him Yá'kúb, surnamed Mustaa'simí, reduced it to its present form.

**Baian,** بيان, the poetical name of Khwája Ahsan-uddín or Ahsan-ullah Khán of Agra, who was living at Dehlí in 1760 A. D., 1174 A. H.

**Baiazid I (Sultan),** سلطان بايزيد, whom we call Bajazet, surnamed Ilderim, or Lightning, succeeded his father Murád I (Amurath) in 1389 A. D., 791 A. H., as Sulṭán of the Turks. He caused his elder brother Ya'kúb, his rival for the throne, to be strangled, an act of barbarity which since his time has become a custom at the Turkish court. He conquered Bulgaria, Macedonia, and Thessaly; and after he had made the emperor of Constantinople tributary to his power, he marched to attack Tamerlane in the east. He was, however, totally defeated near Angoria on Friday the 21st July, 1402 A. D., 19th Ẕil-ḥijja, 804 A. H., and taken prisoner; and when the proud conqueror asked him what he would have done with him if he had obtained the victory, Báiazíd answered that he would have confined him in an iron cage. "Such then shall be thy fate," rejoined Tamerlane, and ordered him to be carried about with his camp in an iron cage. Báiazíd died on the 8th of March, 1403 A. D., 13th Sha'bán, 805 A. H., at Antioch in Pisidia during his confinement in Taimúr's camp. His son Músa, who was with his father at the time of his death, brought his remains to Brusa and buried there. During his (Músa's) absence in the camp, his brother Sulaimán had ascended the throne.

**Baiazid II,** سلطان بايزيد, (Sulṭán) emperor of Turkey succeeded his father Muhammad II. to the throne of Constantinople in May, 1481 A. D., Rabí' I, 886 A. H. He extended the boundaries of his kingdom; and obliged the Venetians to sue for peace. His reign was distracted by intestine discord, and he fell by the perfidy of his son Salím I, who caused him to be poisoned in 1512 A. D., 918 A. H., in the 60th year of his age and 31st of his reign. He was a man of uncommon talents, and did much for the improvement of his empire, and the promotion of the sciences.

**Baiazid Ansari,** بايزيد انصاري, the Afghán Apostle, called Pír Róshan, founder of the Súfí sect called "Róshania," or "the enlightened." He had established amid the mountains of Afghánistán a temporal power upon the authority of his spiritual character, which enabled him and his successors to disturb the tranquillity of the Empire of Dehlí, when, under the celebrated Akbar, it had reached the very zenith of its power.

**Baiazid Bustami (Khwaja),** خواجه بايزيد بسطامي the famous ascetic of Bustám, whose original name was Taifúrí; he is therefore sometimes called Báiazíd Taifúrí-al-Bustámí. His father's name was 'Isa-ibn-Ádam-ibn-'Isa-ibn-'Alí. His grandfather was a Gabr or magian, but became a convert to Islámism. These two brothers Ádam and 'Alí, were like himself, devout ascetics, but in an inferior degree. He was born in the year 777 A. D., 160 A. H., lived to a great age, and died between the years 845 or 848 A. D., 231 or 234 A. H., but according to Ibn-Khalikán his death took place in 875 or 878 A. D., 261 or 264 A H. He is said to have been a cotemporary of Ahmad Khizroya who died 240 A. H.

**Baiazid Khan,** بايزيد خان, faujdár of Sarhind, who was commanded by the emperor Farrukh-siyar to punish the Sikhs, who had risen in rebellion; he took the field, but was assassinated in his tent when alone at evening prayers, by a Sikh commissioned for that purpose by Banda their chief, and the murderer escaped unhurt. This circumstance took place about the year 1714 A. D., 1126 A. H.

**Baiazid (Sultan),** سلطان بايزيد. There is a cenotaph at Chaṭigáon, called the Rauza of Sulṭán Báiazíd. It is related that he was born at Bustám in Khurásán, of which country he was king; but abandoning regal pomp and cares for the tranquillity of the ascetic life, he came with twelve attending disciples to Chaṭigáon. Their arrival was promptly opposed by the king of the fairies and the attendant genii, who desired them forthwith to depart. Sultán Báiazíd, with feigned humility, entreated to be allowed to remain that night and to occupy only as much ground as could be illumed by a single lamp, called in Bengáli, chatí or chat; on obtaining their consent, he kindled from his urine a lamp of such radiance, that its light extended to Tík Naof, a distance of 120 miles, and scorched the terrified genii, who fled from its flame in dismay. In commemoration of this event, the place was named Chatigram, in common parlance, Chatgáon, signifying the village of the lamp. This insult and breach of confidence, led to implacable war on the part of the genii, whom Sultán Báiazíd, in various conflicts, drove from the field; and in his strenuous exertions dropped a ring where the cenotaph now stands—his Karanphúl, or ear-ring, fell in the river, which thence was named the "Karanphúlí;" and a sankh, or shell, dropped from his hand, into the other stream, from which it derived the name of Sankhautí. Sultán Baiazíd then become a Gorchela (*i. e.*, did penance in the tomb) for 12 years: after endowing it with lands to keep it in repair and defray the expenses of pilgrims and the twelve disciples,—he proceeded to Makanpúr, and was succeeded by his disciple Sháh—who in the hope of an eternal reward, performed the penance of standing for 12 years on one leg, after which he also proceeded to Makanpúr; leaving the cenotaph under the charge of Sháh Pír, an attending disciple of Báiazíd. This place was therefore in after ages held in great repute, and visited by numerous pilgrims from distant parts. It is situated on a hill, ascended by a flight of steps, inclosed by a wall about 30 feet square and 15 high, with mitred battlements, and a pillar rising two feet above them at each angle, similar to the buildings of the time of Akbar. The tomb, about 12 feet by 9, is in the centre of the area, with some shells and corals deposited at its head.

**Baiazid Taifuri-al-Bustami,** بایزید طیفوری البسطامي, *vide* Baiazíd Bustámí.

**Baz Bahadur,** باز بهادر, whose original name was Málik Báiazíd, succeeded his father Shujáa' Khán to the government of Málwa in 1554 A. D., 962 A. H., and having taken possession of many towns in Málwa which were previously almost independent, he ascended the throne under the title of Sultán Báz Bahádur. His attachment to Rúpmaní, a celebrated courtezan of that age, became so notorious, that the loves of Báz Bahádur and Rúpmaní have been handed down to posterity in song. He reigned about 17 years, after which the kingdom of Málwa was taken, and included among the provinces of the empire of Dehlí, by the emperor Akbar in the year 1570 A. D., 978 A. H. Báz Bahádur afterwards joined Akbar at Dehlí and received a commission as an officer of 2000 cavalry. Báz Bahádur and Rúpmaní both are buried in the centre of the tank at Ujjain.

**Bazil,** باذل, *vide* Rafí Khán Bázil.

**Bazil,** باذل, the poetical name of Badr-uddín Ismaíl-al-Tabrizí, an Arabian author.

**Baziri,** بازری, author of a poem entitled "Koukab-al-Darriat" or the Brilliant Star, in praise of Muhammad, who cured him, as he said, of the palsy in a dream. Every line of the poem ends with an M, the initial of the prophet's name, and it is so highly valued, that many of the Muhammadans learn it by-heart, on account of its maxims. Lempriere's Universal Dictionary under Bausirri. Bárizí and Bázirí appears to be the same person.

**Baz Khan,** باز خان, an amír in the service of the emperor Bahádur Sháh. He was killed in the battle against Azim Sháh on the 8th June, 1707 O. S., 18th Rabí' I, 1118 A. H., at Dhaulpúr.

**Bazmi,** بزمي, author of the Padmáwat in Persian verse. He was a native of Karkh and resided for some time at Shíráz. He came to Gujrát during the reign of the emperor Jahángír, and composed the abovementioned poem in 1619 A. D., 1028 A. H. He was living at Dehlí in the time of Sháh Jahán, about the year 1634. His proper name is 'Abdul Shakúr.

**Bazzaz,** بزاز, the author of the "Adáb-al-Mufridát" or a treatise on the particular conditions and properties of traditions, and some other works on the Muhammadan theology.

**Bebadal Khan,** بی بدل خان, a poet of Persia who came to India in the reign of the emperor Jahángír, and flourished in the time of Sháh Jahán, who conferred on him the title of Bebadal Khán. Under his superintendence the Peacock throne was constructed. Bebadal Khán appears to be the former title of Abú Tálib Kalím.

**Bedar,** بیدار, the poetical name of Sanáth Singh, a Hindú, who was living in 1753 A. D., 1166 A. H.

**Bedar,** بیدار, an author whose proper name was Imám Bakhsh, a native of Ambála. He is the author of the work called "Táríkh Sa'ádat," being an account of the progress of the dynasty which ruled over Audh from Shujáa'-uddaula to Sa'ádat 'Alí Khán, to whose name the title is an illusion. It was composed in 1812 A. D., 1227 A. H. He is also the author of several Masnawís, one of which contains the praises of Nawáb Sa'ádat 'Alí Khán, called "Gulshán-i-Sa'ádat." He was living in the time of Nasír-uddín Haidar, king of Audh.

**Bedar Bakht,** بیدار بخت, (Prince), son of 'Azim Sháh. He was killed in the battle fought by his father against the emperor Bahádur Sháh on the 8th June, 1707 O. S., 1119 A. H.

**Bedar Bakht,** بیدار بخت, son of Ahmad Sháh, king of Dehlí. He was elevated to the throne of Dehlí on the 1st September, 1788 A. D., 27th Zi-Ka'da 1202 A. H., when Ghulám Kadir imprisoned Sháh Alam. Bedar Bakht continued to reign until the approach of the Marhattas towards Dehlí, when he fled upon the 12th October, 1788, but was subsequently apprehended and murdered by the orders of Sháh Álam.

**Bedil (Mirza),** مرزا بیدل, the poetical name of Saídaí Gilaní, which see.

**Begam Sultan,** بیگم سلطان, a lady of rank, whose tomb is to be seen to this day, outside of the gate of Ya'tmád-uddaula's mausoleum in Agra. From the inscription that is on her tomb, it appears that she died in the time of the emperor Humayún in 1538 A. D., 945 A. H., and that she was the daughter of Shaikh Kamál.

**Begana,** بیگانه, the poetical name of Abú'l Hasan.

**Bekasi (Maulana),** مولانا بیکسي, a poet who lived in the time of the emperor Akbar.

**Bekasi (Maulana),** مولانا بیکسی, a poet of Shíráz who was cotemporary with Ghizalí, who died in the year 1111 A. D., 505 A. H.

**Bekhabar,** بیخبر, the poetical name of Mír 'Azmat-ullah, son of Lutf-ullah of Bilgarám. He died in 1729 A. D., 1142 A. H., at Dehlí. He is the author of the work called "Safínae Bekhabar."

**Bekhud,** بیخود, poetical name of Mulla Jámí Láhaurí Namdár Khání, which see.

**Bekhud,** بيخود, poetical name of Sayyad Hadí 'Alí, son of Sayyad Násir 'Alí Sehr, and author of a Díwán.

**Betab,** بيتاب, whose proper name is Abbas 'Alí Khán, which see.

**Bengal,** Sultáns and Governors of, *vide* Muhammad Bakhtaiár Khiljí, and Khán Jahán.

**Berar,** راجه برار, rájá of, *vide* Rághójí Bhósla.

**Bhagwan Das (raja),** راجه بهگوانداس, called by Abú'l Fazl Bhagwant Dás, was the son of Rájá Bihára Mal Kachhwáha of Ambhar or Amer, now Jaipúr. His daughter was married to the prince Mirzá Salím (afterwards Jahángír) in the year 1585 A. D., 993 A. H., by whom he had a daughter named Sultán-un-nisá Begam, and then a son who now was Sultán Khusro. Bhagwán Dás died five days after the death of Rájá Todar Mal, *i. e.*, on the 15th November, 1589 A. D., 19th Muharram 998 A. H., at Láhor. After his death, the emperor Akbar, who was then at Kábul, conferred the title of Rájá on his son Mán Singh with the rank of 5000.

**Bhagwant Singh,** بهگونت سنگه, ráná of Dhaulpúr (1857). He died on the 14th February, 1873.

**Bhanbu Khan,** بهنبوخان, the son of Zabitá Khán, which see.

**Bhau,** بهاؤ, a Marhatta chief. *Vide* Sadásheo Bháú.

**Bhau Singh,** بهاو سنگه, also called Mirzá Rájá, was the second son of Rájá Mán Singh, the son of Rájá Bhagwán Dás Kachhwáha. He succeeded to the ráj after his father's death in 1614 A. D., 1023 A. H., was raised to the rank of 5000 by the emperor Jahángír, and died of drinking 1621 A. D., 1030 A. H. Two of his wives and eight concubines burnt themselves on his funeral pyre. Among Jahángír's courtiers the rájás of Ambúr were the most addicted to drinking. His eldest brother Jagat Singh, and Maka Singh his nephew, had likewise paid with their lives for their drunken habits, but their fate was no lesson for Rájá Bháú.

**Bhara Mal (Raja),** بهارا مل, *vide* Bihárí Mal.

**Bhartpur,** راجه بهرت پور rájá of, *vide* Chúráman Ját.

**Bhaskar Acharya,** بهسكر اچاريا, a most celebrated astronomer of the Hindús, who was born at Bídae, a city in the Dakhan, in the year of Saliváhana, 1036, corresponding with the year 1114 A. D., 508 A. H. He was the author of several treatises, of which the Líláwatí and the Bíjá Ganita, relating to arithmetic, geometry and algebra, and the Siromaní, an astronomical treatise, are accounted the most valuable authorities in those sciences which India possesses. The Siromaní is delivered in two sections, the Góla-Adhyáya, or the Lecture on the Globe, and the Ganita Adhyáya, or the Lecture on Numbers, as applied to astronomy. The Líláwatí was translated into Persian by Faizí in the reign of Akbar, and an English translation has also been lately made by Dr. Taylor and published at Bombay. Bhaskar died at an advanced age, being upwards of 70 years. Líláwati was the name of his only daughter who died unmarried.

**Bhim Singh,** بهيم سنگه, ráná of Udaipúr, was living in 1750 A. D.

**Bhim Singh Rathour,** بهيم سنگه راتّهور. He usurped the throne of Jodhpúr in 1793 A. D., on his grandfather's death by defeat of Zálim Singh, and died in 1803. He was succeeded by Mán Singh.

**Bhim,** راجه بهيم, rájá of Gujrát, in whose time Sultán Mahmúd Ghaznawí took the famous temple of Somnáth in 1027 A. D.

**Bhoj (Raja),** راجه بهوج, *vide* Rájá Bhój.

**Bhori Rani,** بهوري راني, the last of the wives of Maharájá Ranjít Singh, she died childless at Láhor on the 5th of April, 1872. Her adopted son Kúwar Bhúp Singh distributed large sums of money before and after her death as alms to the poor. The funeral was very grand. Her remains were burnt near the *samádh* of the late Maharájá, and the ashes were sent to be thrown into the Ganges at Hardwár. She drew a pension of 800 rupees per mensem from our Government and held jágírs of upwards of 60,000 rupees per annum.

**Bhuchchu,** بهچو, *vide* Zarra.

**Bhuya,** ميان بهو يه, a nobleman of the court of Sultán Sikandar Lodí, who built the masjid Math in Dehlí, but was afterwards assassinated by that prince without any crime, only because people used to assemble at his place.

**Bibi Bai,** بي‌بي بائي, the sister of Muhammad Sháh 'Adil king of Dehlí, married to Salím Sháh Súr by whom she had a son named Fíróz. After the death of Salím Sháh, when Fíróz, then an infant, was being murdered by his uncle Muhammad Sháh, she defended her son for some time in her arms, presenting her body to the dagger, but her cruel brother tore the young prince from her embrace, and in her presence severed his head from his body. This event took place in May, 1554 A. D.

**Bibi Daulat Shad Begam,** بي‌بي دولت شاد بيگم, one of the wives of the emperor Akbar and the mother of Shakrunnisa Begam, who survived her father, and died in the time of Jahángír.

**Bibi Marwarid,** بی‌بی مرواريد, wife of the late Amír Afzal Khán, died in September, 1874 A. D.

**Bibi Zinda Abadi,** بي‌بي زنده ابدی, commonly called Bíbí Jind Wadí by the people of Uchcha, was one of the descendants of Sayyad Jalál. She is buried at Uchcha in Multán. The dome in which she rests is erected of burnt bricks and cemented by mortar. The whole of the edifice is ornamented by various hues, and *lapis lazuli* of the celebrated mines of Badakhshán. The size of this grand building may be estimated at 50 feet high, and the circumference 25.

**Bihari Lal,** بهاري لعل, a celebrated Hindí poet, called by Gilchrist the Thomson of the Hindús, and much admired among them; he appears to have flourished about the beginning of the 16th century. Being informed that his prince Jaisáh of Jaipúr was so infatuated with the beauty of a very young girl he had married, as to neglect entirely the affairs of his country; for he never came abroad, having shut himself up to contemplate the fascinating charms of his beauteous, though immature bride; Bihárí boldly ventured to admonish him by bribing a slave girl to convey a couplet, which he had composed, under his pillow; the translation of which is thus given by Gilchrist, "When the flower blooms, what will be the situation of the *tree*, that is now captivated with a *bud*, in which there is neither fragrance, sweets, or colour." This had not only the desired effect of rousing the prince from his lethargy, but excited in his breast a generous regard for the man, whose advice came so seasonably and elegantly disguised. Bihárí received, ever after, a pension from court, with a present of more than one thousand pounds, for a work he published under the name of "Satsaí," from its consisting of seven hundred couplets.

**Bihari Mal,** بهاری مل, also called Bharamal and Púranmal, a rájá of Ambhar or Ameir, now Jaipúr, was a rájpút of the tribe of Kachhwáha. He paid homage to Bábar about the year 1527 A. D., and was on friendly terms with the emperor Akbar, and had at an early period given his daughter in marriage to him, of whom was born the emperor Jahángír. Both he and his son Rájá Bhagwán Dás were admitted at the same time to a high rank in the imperial army by the emperor. Bhagwán Dás gave his daughter in marriage to Jahángír in 1585 A. D., who was married next year (1586) to the daughter of Rájá Udai Singh, son of Rao Maldeo Rathor.

**Bija Bai,** بيجا بائى, or Bájí Báí, the wife of Maháraja Daulat Ráo Scindhia of Gwaliár. After the death of her husband who died without issue, she elected Jhanko Ráo Scindhia as his successor on the 18th June, 1827. She was expelled by him in 1833, and went over to Jhansí where she had a large estate. She died at Gwáliar about the middle of the year 1863.

**Bijaipal,** بجي پال, a famous or fabulous rájá of Bayána, regarding whose power, riches, and extent of dominion, many curious tales are still current among the Bhartpúr Játs who assert their (spurious) descent from him. In the "Bijaipál Rasa," a metrical romance or ballad (written in the Birj Bhákha) the Hindú scholar will find a full and particular account of this great Hindú monarch, who is fabled to have conquered rájá Jumeswar, the father of Pirthí Ráj, the celebrated chauhán king of Dehlí, and to have ruled despotically over the whole of India. The Karaulí rájá too boasts his descent from Bijaipál, and if any faith can be placed in a "Bansáolí or genealogical tree," he has a fair claim to the benefits, real or imaginary, resulting therefrom.

**Bijai Singh,** بجي سنگه, son of rájá Abhai Singh, the son of Mahárájá Ajít Singh, Ráthor of Jódhpúr, succeeded to the ráj in 1752 A. D., 1167 A. H. He became infatuated with fondness for a young concubine; his chiefs rebelled, his family were in hostility with each other, and he left at his death the throne itself in dispute. Rájá Mán Singh at length succeeded, in 1804, to the honors and the feuds of Bijai Singh.

**Bijai Singh,** بجي سنگه, son of Rájá Bhagwán Dás. *Vide* Rámji.

**Bikrami,** بكرامي, the poetical name of Mír 'Abdur Rahmán Wizárat Khán, brother of Kásim Khán, the grandfather of Samsam-uddaula Sháhnawáz Khán. He was promoted in the reign of the emperor 'Alamgír to the Díwání of Málwa and Bíjápúr. He was an excellent poet, and has left a Díwán composed in a most beautiful style.

**Bikramajit,** بكرماجيت, or more properly Vikramáditya, a celebrated sovereign of Málwa and Gujrát, whose capital was Ujain. His era called the Sambat is still used in the north of India. Bikramájít died or ascended the throne in the Kálí Jug, year 3044, according to Wilford, whose essays in the 9th and 10th volumes of the Asiatic Researches, contain the fullest information on the history of the three supposed princes of this name, and of their common rival Saliváhana. The first Sambat year, therefore, concurs with the year 3045 of the Kalí Jug year, or 57 years before the birth of Christ. This prince was a great patron of learned men; nine of whom at his court are called the nine gems, and are said to have been Dhanwantari, Kshapanaka, Amera Siñha, Sanku, Vetálabhatta, Ghatakarpara, Kálidása, Virahamihira, and Varáruchi.

**Bikramajit (Rajah),** راجه بكرماجت, *Vide* Rae Patr Dás. A Khatre.

**Bilal,** بلال, the name of the crier, who used to announce to the people when Muhammad prayed. He was an African, and a freed slave of Muhammad. He died in the time of Umar the second Khalíf after Muhammad, in the year 641 A. D., 20 A. H.

**Bilal Kunwar,** بلال كنور, the wife of the emperor 'Alamgír II, and mother of Sháh 'Alam, king of Dehlí. Her title was Zínat Mahal.

**Bilkaini,** بلقيني, whose proper name was Abú Hafs, is the author of the works called "Mahásin-ul-Istiláh," "Sharah Bukhárí," and "Tarandí." He died in 1402 A. D., 805 A. H. See Siráj-uddín son of Núr-uddín, and Abú Hafs-al-Bukharí.

**Binai,** بنائى, (Mauláná), his father was a respectable architect at Hirát, the birthplace of the poet, and his takhallus or poetical name, is derived from Biná or Banna, a builder. He is the author of a work called "Bahrám-wa-Bahróz," a story which he dedicated to Sultán Ya'kúb the son of Uzzan Hasan. His conceit had roused the jealousy of Amír Alísher, Bináí tried to conciliate his favour by writing a Kasída in his praise, but received no reward, he therefore substituted the name of Sultán Ahmad Mirzá for that of Alísher, saying that he would not give away his daughters without dowry. Alísher was so enraged at this, that he obtained a death-warrant against him. Bináí fled to Máwarunnahr. He was killed in the massacre of Sháh Isma'íl in 1512 A. D., 918 A. H. He has also left a Díwán consisting of 6,000 verses.

**Bin Ahmad,** بن احمد, *vide* Abú'l Faiz Muhammad.

**Binakiti,** بناكتي, *vide* Abú Sulaimán Dáúd.

**Binayek Rao (raja),** راجه بنايك راو, the son of Amrit Ráo, a Marhatta chief. He died in July 1853, aged 50 years.

**Bin Banana,** بن بنانه, surname of Abú Nasr-ibn-ul-'Azíz bin-'Amrú, an Arabian poet who died at Baghdád in 1009 A. D., 400 A. H.

**Bindraban,** بندرابن, a Hindú author who flourished in the reign of the emperor 'Alamgír, and wrote a work called "Lubb-ut-Tawáríkh," a summary history of Hindústán.

**Birbal,** بيربل, or Bírbar, was a Bráhman of the tribe of Bhát. His proper name was Mahes Dás. He was a man of very lively conversation, on which account he became one of the greatest personal favorites of the emperor Akbar, who conferred on him the title of rájá and the rank of 5000. He was also an excellent Hindí poet, and was honored with the title of Kabráe or the royal poet. He was slain together with Mulla Sherí and other officers of note, in a battle fought against the Yúsafzaí Afgháns of Sawád and Bijor (places between Kábul and Hindústán) in February 1586 A. D., Rabí' I, 994 A. H. Akbar was for a long time inconsolable for the death of Bírbal, and as the rájá's body was never found, a report gained currency that he was still alive among the prisoners, and it was so much encouraged by Akbar, that a long time afterwards an impostor appeared in his name; and as this second Bírbal died before he reached the court, Akbar again wore mourning as for his friend. Many of Bírbal's witty sayings are still current in India.

**Bir Singh,** راجه بيرسنگه, a rájá of the Bundelá tribe of Rájpúts. He was the founder of this family, and from him the family of the Urcha chief is descended. The greater part of his dominions was wrested from him by Rájá Chatar Sál, who was the last sole possessor of the Bundelkhand province. At that period its capital was Kalanger, but the residence of the rájá was Panná, celebrated for its diamond mines.

**Birgili**, برگلي, surname of Mullá Muhammad-bin-Pír 'Alí, a celebrated Arabian author, who wrote the "Sharah Arba'ín," and died 1573 A. D., 981 A. H. He is by some called Barkalí.

**Birjis Kadar**, برجيس قدر, whose original name was Ramzán 'Alí, is the son of Wájid 'Alí, the ex-king of Lakhnau. His mother's name is Ma'shúk Begam. At the outbreak, he was created king with the unanimous consent of the rebel soldiery in 1857 at the instance of Barkat Ahmad, Risaladár, late 15th Regiment Irregular Cavalry, who subsequently fell in battle. Birjís Ḳadar was then 10 years of age. Before his accession, his uncle Sulaimán Sẖikoh was much persuaded by the rebels to accept the crown, but refused. Birjís Ḳádar was driven out of India and is now with his mother at Katmandú in Nepal.

**Bisati Samarkandi**, بساطي سمرقندي, a poet of Samarḳand who flourished in the time of Sulṭán Khalíl-ullah, grandson of Amír Taimúr. He was formerly a weaver of carpets, and had assumed for his poetical title "Hasírí," but he changed it afterwards to Bisátí. He was cotemporary with 'Asmat-ullah Bukharí.

**Bishr Hafi**, بشرحافي, (*i. e.*, Bishr the barefoot) a Muhammadan doctor who was born at Marv, and brought up at Baghdád, where he died on Wednesday the 10th of November 840 A. D., 10th Muḥarram, 226 A. H. Different dates are given of his death; but it is certain that he died several years before Ahmad Hanbal, and the one given here appears to be very correct.

**Bishun Singh (Kachwaha)**, بشن سنگه, rájá of Ambhar or Ameir, was the son of Rám Singh and the father of Mirzá Rájá Jaisingh Sewáí. He died about the year 1693 A. D., 1105 A. H.

**Bismil**, بسمل, the poetical name of Mirzá Muhammad Sha'fí of Naishápúr, uncle of Nawáb Safdar Jang.

**Bismil**, بسمل, the poetical name of Amír Hasan Khán of Calcutta, who was living in 1845 A. D., 1261 A. H.

**Biswas Rao**, بسواس راو, the eldest son of Bálá Ráo Peshwá, the Marhatta chief. He was killed in the battle against Ahmad Sháh Abdálí on the 14th January, 1761 N. S., together with Sadásheo Bháú and other Marhatta chiefs.

**Bithal Das Gaur**, بيهتل داس گور, son of Gopál Dás, rájá of Sheopúr. On a spot of 10 bhigas towards Tájganj on the banks of the river Jamna he had built his house and a garden. In the town of Shaligahan he was raised to 3000, and appointed Kiladár of the fort of Ágra. He was afterwards raised to the rank of 5000, and in the year 1062 A. H. went home and died there.

**Bo 'Ali Kalandar**, بوعلي قلندر, *vide* Abú 'Alí Ḳalandar.

**Boya**, بويه, *vide* 'Alí Bóya.

**Bughra Khan**, بغرا خان, surname of Náṣir-uddín Mahmúd, the second son of Sulṭán Ghayáṣ-uddín Balban, king of Dehlí. He was made governor of Lakhnauṭí in Bengal by his father, at whose death in 1286 A. D., he being then in that province, his son Kaiḳubád was raised to the throne of Dehlí. *Vide* Náṣir-uddín Mahmúd.

**Bukhari**, بخاري, *vide* Al-Bukhárí.

**Bulbul**, بلبل, *vide* Mirzá Muhammad surnamed Bulbul.

**Burandak**, برندق, the poetical name of Maulána Bahá-uddín. He was a native of Samarḳand, and a sprightly satirical poet; much dreaded by his contemporaries, on account of his wit and caustic humour. He was the especial panegyrist of Sulṭán Báiḳara Mirzá, the son of Umar Shaikh and grandson of Amír Taimúr. When Prince Báiḳara ascended the throne in 1394 A. D., he ordered that the sum of five hundred ducats (in Turkí bish yúz altún) should be paid to Burandaḳ. By a mistake of the Secretary, he received only two hundred; and therefore addressed the following lines to the Sulṭán:—

"The Sháh, the terror of his foes,
Who well the sound of flatt'ry knows,
The conqueror of the world, the lord
Of nations vanquish'd by his sword,
Gave, while he prais'd my verse, to me
Five hundred ducats as a fee.
Great was the Sulṭán's gen'rous mood,
Great is his servant's gratitude,
And great the sum; but strange to say,
Three hundred melted by the way!
Perhaps the words in Turkish tongue
Convenient meaning may contrive;
Or else my greedy ear was wrong,
That turn'd two hundred into five."

The Sulṭán was extremely entertained at the readiness of the poet; and sending for him, assured him that the words "*bish yúz altún*" signified in Turkish a *thousand* ducats, which he ordered to be immediately paid. Dublin University Magazine for 1840. The year of Burandaḳ's death is unknown. He was cotemporary with Khwája 'Asmat-ullah Bukhárí who died in 1426 A. D., 829 A. H.

**Burhan**, برهان, a poet of Mázindarán, came to Dehlí and died there shortly after Nádir Sháh had pillaged that city. He is the author of a Díwán.

**Burhan**, برهان, the poetical name of Muhammad Hasan, the author of the Persian Dictionary called Burhán Ḳáta, *vide* Muhammad Hasan.

**Burhan 'Imad Shah**, برهان عماد شاه, one of the princes of the 'Imád Sháhí dynasty. He succeeded his father Daria 'Imád Sháh in the government of Beraṛ, when but a child. His minister Taufal Khán, became regent; and before the prince was of an age to assume the reins of his empire, Taufal Khán, assisted by the ruler of Khándesh and by the Nizám Sháhí court, usurped the government. He eventually confined his sovereign in irons in the fort of Parnála, and assumed the title of king. In the year 1568 A. D., 980 A. H., Nizám Sháh marched against Taufal Khán, under the pretence of releasing the imprisoned prince from his confinement. He took the fort of Gáwal by capitulation, defeated Taufal Khán and made him prisoner with his son; but instead of placing the captive monarch on the throne of Beṛár, sent him with the usurper and his son to be confined in one of the Nizám Sháhí forts, where they were all subsequently strangled by the king's order. Thus the family of 'Imád Sháh and that of the usurper Taufal Khán became extinct.

**Burhan Nakid**, برهان ناقد, a poet who is the author of the poem entitled "Dil Áshób," dedicated to the emperor Sháh Jahán.

**Burhan Nizam Shah I**, برهان نظام شاه, ascended the throne of Ahmadnagar in the Dakhan after the death of his father Ahmad Nizám Sháh in 1508 A. D., 914 A. H., in the seventh year of his age. He reigned 47 lunar years and died at the age of 54 in 1554 A. D., 961 A. H., and was buried in the same tomb with his father.

**Burhan Nizam Shah II,** برهان نظام شاه, brother of Murtazá Nizám I, ascended the throne of Ahmadnagar in the Dakhan on the 15th May, 1591 O. S., 1st Sha'bán, 999 A. H., after deposing and confining his own son Isma'íl Nizám Sháh, who had been placed on the throne during his absence at the court of the emperor Akbar. He was advanced in years; but notwithstanding his age, gave himself up to pleasures unbecoming his dignity. His reign was marked by an unsuccessful war with the king of Bíjápúr, and a disgraceful defeat from the Portuguese, who had seized the sea coasts of his dominions. He died after a reign of 4 years and 16 days, on the 18th of April, 1595 A. D., 18th Sha'bán, 1003 A. H., in the 40th year of the reign of Akbar, and was succeeded by his son Ibráhím Nizám Sháh. Maulána Zahúrí dedicated his Sákináma to Burhán Nizám Sháh, containing nearly 4,000 verses.

**Burhan-uddin Abu Is-hak-al-Fazari,** برهان الدين ابو اسحق, commonly called Ibn-Firkáh, author of the "Faráez-al-Fazárí" a treatise on the law of Inheritance according to Sháfa'í's doctrine. He died in 1328 A. D., 729 A. H.

**Burhan-uddin Bin Mazah-al-Bukhari** برهان الدين author of the "Zukhírat-ul-Fatáwa," sometimes called Zakhírat-ul-Burhania", and of the "Muheet-al-Burhání."

**Burhan-uddin Ali Bin Abu Bakr-al-Marghinani (Shaikh),** شيخ برهان الدين علي, author of the "Hidáya Sharah Badáya, or the Lawyer's Guide," a very celebrated book of Muhammadan Jurisprudence, which during the period that Mr. Hastings governed the British dominions in India, was by his orders most ably translated by Charles Hamilton, Esq., and published in London, in the year 1791 A. D. Burhán-uddín was born at Marghínán, in Transoxania in 1135 A. D., 529 A. H., and died in 1197 A. D., 593 A. H. The Hidáya which is a commentary on the Badaya-al-Mubtada, is the most celebrated law treatise according to the doctrines of Abú Hanífa, and his disciples Abú Yúsaf and the Imám Muhammad. A Persian version of the Hidáya was made by Maulwí Ghulám Yehiá Khán and others and published at Calcutta in 1807. He also wrote a work on Inheritance entitled the "Faráez-ul-Usmání," which has been illustrated by several comments.

**Burhan-uddin Gharib (Shah or Shaikh),** شاه برهان الدين غريب, a celebrated Musalmán saint much venerated in the Dakhan. He died in 1331 A. D., 731 A. H., and his tomb is at Burhánpúr in Daulatábád, and is resorted to in a pilgrimage by the Muhammadans. He was a disciple of Shaikh Nizám-uddín Aulia who died in 1325 A. D., 725 A. H.

**Burhan-uddin Haidar Bin Muhammad-al-Hirwi,** برهان الدين بن محمد author of a commentary on the Sirájia of Sajáwandí. He died in 1426 A. D., 830 A. H.

**Burhan-uddin Ibrahim Bin Ali Bin Farhun,** برهان الدين ابراهيم بن علي بن فرحون, chief biographer of the Málikí lawyers, and author of the "Díbáj-ul-Muzahhib." He died in 1396 A. D., 799 A. H.

**Burhan-uddin (Kazi),** قاضي برهان الدين, Lord of the city of Sivas in Cappadocia or Caramenia who died in 1395 A. D., 798 A. H. After his death Báyezíd I, Sultán of the Turks, took possession of his States.

**Burhan-uddin Mahmud Bin Ahmad,** برهان الدين محمود بن احمد, author of a "Muhít," which, though known in India, is not so greatly esteemed as the Muhít as-Sarakhsí. The work of Burhán-uddín is commonly known as the Muhít-al-Burhání.

**Burhan-uddin Muhammad Bakir (Mir),** قاضي مير برهان الدين محمد باقر, Kází of Káshán. He wrote a Díwán containing about 5000 verses. He was living about the year 1585 A. D., 993 A. H.

**Burhan-uddin (Shaikh),** شيخ برهان الدين, or Sayyad *vide* Kutb 'Alam.

**Burhan-uddin (Sayyad),** سيد برهان الدين, surnamed Muhakkik. He died in the year 1247 A. D., 645 A. H., and was buried at Cæsarea.

**Burhan-ul-Mulk Sa'adat Khan,** برهان الملك سعادت خان, *vide* Sa'ádat Khán, and Mirzá Nasír.

**Burzui,** برزوي, a Persian physician who lived under Naushirwán the Just. He was sent by that prince to India to procure a copy of the book called the Wisdom of all Ages; which he afterwards translated into Persian. That which now exists is greatly altered from the original version.

**Bus-hak,** بوسحاق the abbreviated poetical name of Abú Is-hák Atma', which see.

**Buzarjimehr,** بزرجمهر, the celebrated minister of Naushirwán the Just, king of Persia. He is said to have imported from India the game of Chess and the Fables of Pilpay. Such has been the fame of his wisdom and virtues, that the Christians claim him as a believer in the gospel; and the Muhammadans revere him as a premature Musalmán. He lived to a great age, and died in the time of Hurmuz III, son and successor of Naushirwán the Just, between the years 580 and 590 A. D.

**Buzarjmehr Kummi,** بزرجمهر قمي, a celebrated Persian Prosodian of Kumn, who lived before the time of Saifí, the author of the Urúz Saifí.

**Buzurg Khanam,** بزرگ خانم, the daughter of Saif Khán, by Malika Báno Begam, the daughter of Asaf Khán Wazír, and wife of Zafar Khán, a nobleman of the reign of the emperor 'Alamgír. She died before her husband in the month of May, 1659 A. D., Shawwál 1069 A. H.

**Buzurg Umaid Khan,** بزرگ اميد خان, son of Sháista Khán, an officer of rank in the time of the emperor Alamgír. At the time of his death, which took place in 1694 A. D., 1105 A. H., he was governor of Behár.

**Buzurg Umaid,** بزرگ اميد or Kaia Buzurg Umaid, one of the Ismaílís, who succeeded Hasan Sabbáh, the Old Man of the Mountains, in June, 1124 A. D., Rabí' II, 518 A. H., and reigned 24 years. After his death his son Kaia Muhammad succeeded him and reigned 25 years.

---

# C.

**Caragossa,** *vide* Kara Ghuz.

**Chaghtai Khan,** چغتاء خان, or Káán, the most pious and accomplished of all the sons of Changez Khán; and although he succeeded, by the will of his father, to the kingdoms of Transoxania, Balkh, Badakhshán, and Káshghar in 1227 A. D., 624 A. H., he governed these countries by deputies, and remained himself with his eldest brother, Okta Káán, by whom he was regarded with the reverence which a pupil gives to his master. He died seven months before his brother in the month of June, 1241 A. D., Zi-Ka'da, 638 A. H. Karáchár Nawián, who was the fifth ancestor of Amír Taimúr, was one of his Amírs, and, at length, captain general of all his forces. The dynasty that founded the so-called "Moghul Empire" of India was named after Chaghtai.

**Chaghta Sultan,** چغتا سلطان, a handsome young man of the tribe of the Mughals and favorite of the emperor Bábar Sháh. He died at Kábul in 1546 A. D., 953 A. H.

**Chait Singh,** چیت سنگھ, son of Balwant Singh, a rájá or zamíndár of Banáras. He succeeded his father in 1770 A. D. In August 1781 demands were made upon him, by the Governor-General, for additional tribute to be paid to the Company, as the sovereign power now requiring assistance in its exigency. The rájá declined, pleading willingness, but inability. He was seized by Mr. Hastings' order, at Banáras; a revolt took place in his behalf on the 20th August; nearly two companies of sepoys and their officers were destroyed,—and the rájá escaped in the confusion. The Governor-General immediately assumed control of the province; and troops were called in to oppose the rájá, who now headed the numbers flocking to his support. He was defeated at Latífpúr—and lastly, his stronghold of Bijaigurh was seized, and his family plundered by a force under Major Popham. The rájá had fled, on his reverses at Latífpúr, to Bundelkhand. His government was declared vacant, and the zamíndarí bestowed on the next heir, a nephew of the rájá, a minor. After these transactions at Banáras, the Governor-General proceeded to Audh, to obtain an adjustment of the heavy debts due to the Company by the Wazír 'Asaf-ud-daula. The territories of the Begams, (one, the mother of Shuja'-ud-daula, the late Nawáb—the other, the mother of the Wazír) were seized, on a charge of aiding the insurrection of Chait Singh. The rájá found an asylum in Gwáliar for 29 years, and died there on the 29th March, 1810 A. D. The lands were transferred to a collateral branch of the family, the present representative of which is named Rájá Udat Narain. See Balwant Singh. His estates, with title of Rájá, were presented to his nephew Babú Muhíp Narain, grandson of Rájá Balwant Singh.

**Chand,** چاند, or Chánd, called also Trikala, from his supposed prophetic spirit, was a celebrated Hindú poet or bard. He flourished towards the close of the twelfth century of the Christian era. He may be called the poet laureate of Prithiráj, the Chauhán emperor of Dehlí who, in his last battle with Shaháb-uddín Ghórí, was taken prisoner, and conveyed to Ghazní, where his bard, Chánd, followed him. Both perished by their own hands, after causing the death of their implacable foe, Shaháb-uddín. Like the Greek bard, Homer, countries and cities have contended for the honor of having been the place of birth of this the most popular poet of the Hindús. Dehlí, Kanauj, Mahóba, and the Panjáb, assert their respective claims, but his own testimony is decisive, whence it appears that he was a native of Láhor. In his 'Prithiráj Chauhán Rása," when enumerating some of the heroes, friends and partizans of his hero, he says, "Niddar was born in Kanauj, Siluk and Jait, the father and son, at Abú; in Mundava the Parihár, and in Kurrik Kángra the Haolí Ráo, in Nágor, Balbhaddar, and Chánd, the bard, at Láhor."

**Chand Saudagar,** چاند سوداگر, a Bangali merchant.

**Chand,** چاند, *vide* Teik Chand.

**Chanda Kunwar,** چندا اکنور, the wife of Mahárájá Kharag Singh of Láhor.

**Chanda,** چندا ماہ لقا, also called Máh-liká, a dancing girl, or queen of Haidarábád, was a poetess of much taste and merit. She is the author of a Díwán which was revised by Sher Muhammad Khán Imán. In the year 1799 A. D., in the midst of a dance, in which she bore the chief part, she presented a British officer with a copy of her poems, accompanied with the following complimentary observations, in the form of the usual gazal:—

> Since my heart drank from the cup of a fascinating eye,
> I wonder beside myself, like one whom wine bewilders.
> Thy searching glances leave nothing unseated;
> Thy face, bright as flame, consumes my heart.
> Thou soughtest a *Nazar:* I offer thee my head;
> Albeit thy heart is not unveiled to me.
> My eyes fixed on thy lineaments—emotion agitates my soul,
> Fresh excitement beats impatient in my heart.
> All that Chandá asks is, that, in either world,
> Thou wouldst preserve the ashes of her heart by thy side.

Garcin de Tassy informs us that there is a copy of her Díwán in the East India House Library, which she herself presented to Captain Malcolm on the 1st of October, 1799 A. D.

**Chanda Sahib,** چندا صاحب, surname of Husain Dost Khán, a relation of Dóst 'Alí Khán, Nawáb of Arcot, whose daughter he had married. He had made his way to the highest offices of the government by the services of his sword, and was esteemed the ablest soldier that had of late years appeared in the Carnatic. He inveigled the queen of Trichinopoly, and got possession of the city in 1736 A. D. He was taken prisoner by the Marhattas on the 26th March, 1741 A. D., and imprisoned in the fort of Sitára, but was released by the aid of Mons. Dupleix in 1748, and appointed Nawáb of the Carnatic by Muzaffar Jang. He was put to death in 1752 A. D., 1st Sha'bán, 1165 A. H. by the Marhattas, and his head sent to Muhammad 'Alí Khán who was made Nawáb of Arcot by the English, who treated it with ignominy.

**Chandar Bhan,** چندربہان برہمن, a Bráhmaṇ of Paṭiála, well-versed in the Persian language, was employed as a Munshí in the service of the prince Dárá Shikóh, the eldest son of the emperor Sháh Jahán. He is the author of several Persian works, *viz.:* "Guldasta," "Tuhfat-ul-Anwár," "Tuhfat-ul-Fus-há," "Majma'-ul-Fukrá," one entitled "Chár Chaman," another called "Manshát Bráhmaṇ" being a collection of his own letters written to different persons, and also of a Díwán in which he uses the title of Bráhmaṇ for his poetical name. After the tragical death of his employer, he retired to Banáras where he died in the year 1662 A. D., 1073 A H. He had also built a house at Ágra, of which no traces now remain.

**Chand Bibi (Sultana),** چاند بی بی, was the daughter of Husain Nizám Sháh I of Ahmadnagar in the Dakhan, sister to Murtaza Nizám Sháh, and wife of 'Alí 'Adil Sháh I, of Bíjápúr. After the death of her husband in 1580 A. D., 988 A. H., she had been queen and dowager-regent of the neighbouring kingdom of Bíjápúr during the minority of her nephew Ibráhím 'Adil Sháh II, and was one of the most able politicians of her day. The Mughals under prince Murád, the son of Akbar, proceeded in November, 1595 A. D., Rabí' II, 1004 A. H., and besieged Ahmadnagar for some months, while Chánd Sultána defended the place with masculine resolution. At the same time there being a scarcity of provisions in the Mughal camp, the prince and Khán-Khánán thought it advisable to enter into a treaty with the besieged. It was stipulated by Chánd Bíbí that the prince should keep possession of Berar, and that Ahmadnagar and its dependencies, should remain with her in the name of Bahádur, the grandson of Burhán Sháh. She was put to death by the Dakhanís in the year 1599 A. D., 1008 A. H.

**Chandu Lal,** راى چندولال, a Hindú, who was appointed Díwán to the Nizám of Haidarábád in 1808 A. D. His poetical name is Shádán. He died in the year 1863 A. D.

**Chandragupta,** چندرگپت, (called by the Greeks Sandracottus). He seized the kingdom of Magadha, after the massacre of the survivors of the Naida dynasty, whose capital was the celebrated city Patáliputra, called by the Greeks Palibothra.

**Changez Khan,** چنگيز خان, also called by us Gengis, Jengis, and Zingis, surnamed Tamújin, was the son of Yesukí, a Khán or chief of the tribe of Mughals. He was born in 1154 A. D., 549 A. H., and at the age of 13 he began to reign, but the conspiracies of his subjects obliged him to fly for safety to Avant Khán, a Tartar prince, whom he supported on his throne, and whose daughter he married. These ties were not binding. Avant Khán joined against Changez, who took signal vengeance on his enemies, and after almost unexampled vicissitudes, he obtained, at the age of 49, a complete victory over all those who had endeavoured to effect his ruin, and received from the Kháns of Tartary the title of Kháḳán in 1206 A. D., 602 A. H., and was declared emperor of Tartary. His capital was Ḳaráḳurm. In the space of 22 years he conquered Corea, Cathay, part of China, and the noblest provinces of Asia, and became as renowned a conqueror as Alexander the Great. He died on Sunday the 29th August, 1227 A. D., Ramaẓán 624 A. H., aged 75 lunar years, leaving his dominions (which extended 1800 leagues from east to west, and 1000 from north to south) properly divided to his four sons, Jújí, Oḳtái, Chaghtái and Túlí Khán.

*List of the Mughal emperors of Tartary.*

Changez Khán, ........................ 1206
Túlí Khán, his son, ...................... 1227
Oḳtái, brother of Túlí, .................... 1241
Turkína Khátún, his wife, regent for 4 years.
Kayúk Khán, son of Oḳtái, ................. 1246
Ogúlgan-mish, his wife, regent on his death,.. 1248
Mangú Khán, son of Túlí Khán, ........1251, died 1259

After the death of Mangú, the empire of the Mughals was divided into different branches, in China, Persia, in Ḳapcháḳ, &c.

Ḳablái Khán, the brother of Mangú Khán, succeeded in China, and founded the Yuen dynasty, ............................ 1260
Chaghtái Khán, son of Changez Khán, founded the Chaghtái branch in Transoxiana, .... 1240
Jújí, son of Changez Khán, founded the Ḳapcháḳ dynasty, ......................... 1226

*Vide*, Halákú Khán.

**Chatrapati Appa Saheb,** چتراپتي اپا صاحب, rájá of Sitae, who died in, or a year before, 1874 A. D., whose adopted son was Rájá Rám.

**Char Bagh,** چار باغ, name of a garden constructed by the emperor Bábar on the bank of the Jamna, which it is said was also called Hasht Bahisht; it bore all sorts of fruits; no traces of this famous garden are left now.

**Chatur Sal,** چتر سال, Chhattar Sál, or, according to the author of the "Másir-ul-Umrá," Satar Sál, was the son of Chait Singh, chief of the Bundelas or inhabitants of Bundelkhanḍ, of which province he was rájá. To secure the independence of his posterity against the encroaching power of the Marhaṭṭas, he entered into a close alliance with the Peshwá Bájí Ráo I about the year 1733 A. D., 1146 A. H., and at his demise, he bequeathed him a third of his dominions, under an express stipulation, that his posterity should be protected by the Peshwá and his heirs. Chatur Sál died 1735 A. D., leaving two sons, Hirde Sáh and Jagat Ráj. The division of the dominions of Bundelkhanḍ, bequeathed to the Peshwá, comprised the Maháls of Kálpí, Sirounj, Kúnch, Garra Koṭa and Hirdainagar. Gangadhar Bála was nominated by the Peshwá as his náib to superintend the collections. Afterwards the principal leaders in Bundelkhanḍ having fallen in battles, and the ruin of the country having been completed by the subsequent conquest of the ráj of Panna by Náná Arjún, the grandson of Bakhat Singh, a descendant of Chatur Sál, it hence became the object of Náná Farnawís, the Púna minister, notwithstanding the stipulations by which the former Peshwá obtained from Chatur Sál one-third of his dominions, to annex the whole of Bundelkhanḍ to the Marhaṭṭa States. For this purpose he gave the investiture of it to 'Alí Bahádur, son of Shamsher Bahádur, an illegitimate son of the Peshwá Bájí Ráo, whose descendants now are called the Nawábs of Banda. *Vide* Muhammad Khán Bangash.

**Chatur Mahal,** چتر محل, one of the Begams of the ex-king of Audh. One Ḳurbán 'Alí, who had held a subordinate position, and was latterly a Sharistadár under the British Government, suddenly became a rich man by marrying her. He formed the acquaintance of this young and beautiful woman, and they resolved to be married. But the Begam did not wish the union with a man so inferior to herself to take place where she was known, and so obtained the permission of the Chief Commissioner to leave Audh on the pretence of making a pilgrimage to Mecca. Once clear of Lakhnau, she was joined by Kurbán 'Alí, and made for his home at Bijnaur in Bundelkhanḍ.

**Chin Kalich Khan,** چين قليچ خان, *vide* Kulich Khán.

**Chin Kalich Khan,** چين قليچ خان, former name of Nizám-ul-Mulk Asaf Jáh.

**Chimnaji 'Apa,** چمناجي آپا, the younger son of the Marhaṭṭa chief Raghunáth Ráo, (Raghóba) was furtively raised to the masnad at Púna some time after the death of Mádho Ráo II, the son of Naráyan Ráo, on the 26th May, 1796 A. D.; but was deposed afterwards, and succeeded by his elder brother Bájí Ráo II, who was publicly proclaimed on the 4th December following.

**Churaman,** چورامن, an enterprising Jáṭ who having enriched himself by plundering the baggage of the emperor 'Alamgír's army on his last march to the Dakhan, built the fortress of Bhartpúr, fourteen kós from Ágra, with part of the spoil, and became the chief of that tribe. The present rájás of Bhartpúr are his descendants. He was killed by the royal army in the battle which took place between the emperor Muhammad Sháh and Ḳutb-ul-Mulk Sayyad 'Abd-ulláh Khán in November, 1720 A. D., Muḥarram, 1133 A. H. His son Badan Singh succeeded him.

*The following is a list of the Rájás of Bhartpúr.*

Chúráman Jáṭ.
Badan Singh, the son of Chúráman.
Súrajmal Jáṭ, the son of Badan Singh.
Jawáhir Singh, the son of Súrajmal.
Ráo Ratan Singh, brother of Jawáhir Singh.
Kehrí Singh, the son of Ratan Singh.
Nawal Singh, the brother of Ratan Singh.
Ranjít Singh, the nephew of Nawal Singh and son of Kehrí Singh.
Randhír Singh, the son of Ranjít Singh.
Baldeo Singh, the brother of Randhír Singh.
Balwant Singh, the son of Baldeo Singh.
Jaswant Singh, the son of Balwant Singh and present rájá of Bhartpúr.

**Chosroes I,** of Persia, *vide* Naushirwán the Just.

**Chosroes II,** *vide* Khusro Parviz.

# D.

**Dabir-ud-daula Amin-ul-Mulk (Nawab),** نواب دبير الدوله امين الملک, title of Khwája Faríd-uddín Ahmad Khán Bahádur Muslah Jang, the maternal grandfather of Sayyid Ahmad Khán, Munsif of Dehlí. Whilst the British were in Bengal, and the Wakíl of the king of Persia was killed in Bombay in an affray, it became urgent for the British Government to send a Wakíl on deputation to Persia. Dabír-ud-daula was selected for this high office. On his return, after fully completing the trust, he was appointed a full Political Agent at Ava. After this, in latter times, he held the office of Prime Minister to Akbár Sháh II.

**Dai,** داعی, whose full name is Nizám-uddín Muhammad Dáí', was a disciple of Sháh Na'mat-ulláh Walí, and is the author of a Díwán which he completed in the year 1460 A. D., 865 A. H.

**Daghistani,** داغستاني, a poet of Dághistán in Persia, who is the author of a Persian work called "Rayáz-ush-Shu'ará," *vide* Wálih.

**Dahan,** داهان, whose proper name is Abú Muhammad Sa'íd, son of Mubárik, better known as Ibn Dáhán-al-Baghdádí, was an eminent Arabic grammarian, and an excellent poet. He died in 1173 A. D., 569 A. H.

**Dailamites,** the, a dynasty.

**Dakiki,** دقيقي, a famous poet at the court of Amír Núh II, son of Amír Mansúr Sámání, by whose request he had commenced to write the Sháh Náma, but before he could finish a thousand verses of the story of Gashtasp, he was slain by one of his slaves. The year of his death is not known, but this event appears to have taken place during the reign of his royal master, who reigned in Khurásán twenty years, and died in 997 A. D., 387 A. H. His proper name, according to the Aitáshkada, was Mansúr bin-Ahmad.

**Dalpat Sah,** دلپت ساه, the husband of Rani Durgáwátí, which see.

**Dalpat,** دلپت, rájá of Bhojpúr near Buxar, was defeated and imprisoned, and when he was at length set at liberty by Akbar, on payment of an enormous sum, he again rebelled under Jahángír, till Bhojpúr was sacked, and his successor Rájá Partáb was executed by Shah Jahán, whilst the Rání was forced to marry a Muhammadan courtier.

**Dalip Singh (Maharaja),** مهاراجه دليپ سنگه, the youngest son of Mahárájá Ranjít Singh, ruler of the Panjáb. He was only ten years of age when he was raised to the masnad at Láhor after the death of his nephew, Rájá Sher Singh, in September, 1843. In his time the Panjáb was annexed to the British Government, 1846 A. D. "On the 19th of March," (1849) says Marshman, "the young Mahárájá took his seat for the last time on the throne of Ranjít Singh, and in the presence of Sir Henry Lawrence, the Resident, and Mr. Elliot, the Foreign Secretary, and the nobles of his court, heard Lord Dalhousie's proclamation read in English, Persian, and Hindí, and then affixed the initials of his name in English characters to the documents which transferred the kingdom of the five rivers to the Company, and secured him an annuity of five lakhs of rupees a year. Dalíp Singh was baptized on the 8th March, 1835 A. D., and went to England where he is still living.

**Damad,** داماد, poetical name of Muhammad Bákir, which see.

**Damaji,** داماجي, the first Gaekwár of Baroda. His successor was Pelájí.

**Damishki,** دمشقی, an illustrious Persian poet, named Muhammad Damishkí, who flourished in the time of Fazl, the son of Ahia or Yahia, the Barmecide or Barmakí.

**Danial Mirza (Sultan),** سلطان دانيال مرزا, the third son of the emperor Akbar. He was born at Ajmír on Wednesday the 10th September, 1572 A. D., and received the name of Dániál on account of his having been born in the house of a celebrated Darwesh named Shaikh Dániál. His mother was a daughter of Rájá Bihárí Mal Kachhwáha. After the death of his brother, prince Sultán Murád, he was sent to the Dakhan by his father, accompanied by a well appointed army, with orders to occupy all the Nizám Sháhí territories. Ahmadnagar was taken in the beginning of the year 1009 A. H. or 1600 A. D., Sultán Dániál died on the 8th April, 1605 A. D., 1st Zil-hijja, 1013 A. H., in the city of Burhánpúr, aged 33 years and some months, owing to excess in drinking. His death and the circumstances connected with it, so much affected the king his father who was in a declining state of health, that he became every day worse, and died six months after. From the chronogram it appears that the prince Dániál died in the year 1012 A. H., or 1604 A. D., a year and six months before his father.

**Danish,** دانش, poetical name of Mír Rází who died in 1665 A. D., 1076 A. H.

**Danishmand Khan,** دانشمند خان, whose proper name was Muhammad Shafí' or Mullá Shafí', was a Persian merchant who came to Súrat about the year 1646 A. D., 1056 A. H., from which place he was sent for by the emperor Sháh Jahán. He was soon after raised to the mansab of 3000 and paymastership of the army, with the title of Dánishmand Khán. In the reign of 'Alamgír he was honored with the mansab of 4000, and after some time to that of 5000, and appointed governor of Sháh Jahánábád, where he died in the month of July, 1670 A. D., 10th Rabí' I, 1081 A. H. He used to speak much about the Christian religion. Bernier, the French Traveller, who accompanied 'Alamgír to Kashmír in 1664, has mentioned him in his Travels.

**Danishmand Khan,** دانشمند خان, whose original name was Mirzá Muhammad, and poetical, Alí, was a native of Shíráz. In the year 1693 A. D., he was honored with the title of Na'mat Khán, and the superintendence of the royal kitchen by the emperor 'Alamgír. After the death of that monarch, the title of Nawáb Dánishmand Khán Alí was conferred on him by Bahádur Sháh, by whose order he had commenced writing a Sháhnáma or history of the reign of that emperor, but died soon after in the year 1708 A. D., 1120 A. H. *Vide* Na'mat Khán Alí.

**Dara** or **Darab I,** دارا داراب, the eighth king of the second or Kaiánian dynasty of the kings of Persia, was the son of Queen Humai, whom he succeeded on the Persian throne. His reign was distinguished by several wars; particularly one against Philip of Macedon. He reigned twelve years, and was succeeded by his son **Dárá** or **Dáráb** II.

**Dara** or **Darab II,** دارا داراب, is the celebrated Darius Codomanus of the Greeks. He succeeded his father **Dárá** I, as king of Persia, and was slain in battle against Alexander the Great in the year 331 B. C. He was the last and ninth king of the 2nd or Kaiánian dynasty of the kings of Persia.

**Dara Bakht (Mirza),** مرزا دارا بخت, son of Bahádúr Sháh, the ex-king of Dehlí. His poetical title is Dárá, and he is the author of a Díwán.

**Darab Beg (Mirza),** مرزا داراب بیگ, *vide* Jóyá.

**Darab Khan,** داراب خان, commonly called Mirzá Dáráb, was the second son of Abdul Rahím Khán, Khán Khánán. After the death of his eldest brother Sháhnawáz Khán in 1618 A. D., 1027 A. H., he was honored with the rank of 5000 by the emperor Jahángír and appointed governor of Beŗár and Ahmadnagar in the Dakhan. He was also governor of Bengal for some time, and on his return to the Dakhan, the emperor, being displeased with him on some account, ordered Mahábat Khán to strike off his head, which he did, and sent it to the king. This circumstance took place 1625 A. D., 1034 A. H.

**Darab Khan,** داراب خان, son of Mukhtár Khán Sabzwárí, a nobleman in the service of the emperor 'Alamgír. He died on the 24th June, 1679 A. D., 25th Jumáḍa I, 1090 A. H.

**Dara Shikoh,** دارا شکوه, the eldest and favorite son of the emperor Sháh Jahán, was born on the 20th March, 1615 O. S., 29th Ṣafar, 1024 A. H. His mother, Mumtáz Mahal, was the daughter of 'Asaf Khán, wazír, the brother of Núr Jahán Begam. In the 20th year of his age, *i. e.*, in the year 1633 A. D., 1043 A. H., he was married to the princess Nádira, the daughter of his uncle Sulṭán Parwez, by whom he had two sons, *viz.*, Sulaimán Shikóh and Sipehr Shikóh. In 1658 A. D., during the illness of his father, several battles took place between him and his brother Aurangzib 'Alamgír for the throne, in which Dárá being defeated, was at last obliged to fly towards Sindh, where he was captured by the chief of that country and brought to the presence of Aurangzib, loaded with chains, on a sorry elephant without housings; was exposed through all the principal places and then led off to a prison in old Dehlí, where after a few days, in the night of the 29th of August, 1659 O. S., 21st Ẓil-ḥijja 1069 A. H., he was murdered by the order of Aurangzib; his body exhibited next morning to the populace on an elephant, and his head cut off and carried to the emperor, who ordered it to be placed on a platter, and to be wiped and washed in his presence. When he had satisfied himself that it was the real head of Dárá, he began to weep, and with many expressions of sorrow, directed it with its corpse to be interred in the tomb of the emperor Humáyún. Sipehr Shikóh, his son, who was also taken captive and brought with his father, was sent away in confinement to Gwáliar. Sulaimán Shikóh, his eldest son, who, after the defeat of his father had taken refuge in Srínagar for some time, was subsequently, in 1670 A. D., 1071 A. H., given up by the rájá of that place to the officers of Aurangzib and conveyed to Dehlí. He was then sent to Gwáliar, where he and his brother Sipehr Shikóh both died within a short space. Dárá Shikóh is the author of the work called "Safínat-ul-Aulia," an abridgment of the Life of Muhammad, with a circumstantial detail of his wives, children, and companions, &c., also of a work entitled "Majma'-ul-Bahrain," (*i. e.*, the uniting of both seas,) in which he endeavours to reconcile the Bráhmaṇ religion with the Muhammadan; citing passages from the Ḳurán to prove the several points. In 1656 he likewise, with the same intent, caused a Persian translation to be made by the Bráhmaṇs of Banáras, of the Apnikhat, a work in the Sanskrit language, of which the title signifies "the word that is not to be said;" meaning the secret that is not to be revealed. This book he named "Sarr-i-Asrár," or Secret of Secrets; but his enemies took advantage of it, to traduce him in the esteem of his father's Muhammadan soldiers, and to stigmatize him with the epithets of Káfir and Ráfizí (unbeliever and blasphemer), and finally effected his ruin; for Aurangzib his brother made a pretence of that, and consequently had all his bigoted Muhammadans to join him. Monsieur Anquctil du Perron has given a translation of this work, in two large volumes in quarto, on which a very good critique may be found in the Second Number of the "Edinburgh Review." There is also a copy of the Persian version of this work in the British Museum, with a MS. translation, made by N. B. Halhed, Esq. He is also the author of the three following works, "Hasnát-ul-'Arifín," "Risála Haḳ Náma" and "Sakínat-ul-Aulia." His poetical name was Ḳádirí. Catrou says that Dárá died a Christian.

**Dard (Mir),** میر درد, is the poetical name of Khwája Muhammad Mír of Dehlí, a son of Khwája Násir who was one of the greatest Shaikhs of the age. Dard was the greatest poet of his time. He was formerly in the army, but he gave up that profession on the advice of his father and led the life of a devotee. When during the fall of Dehlí every body fled from the city, Dard remained in poverty contented with his lot. He was a Súfí and a good singer. A crowd of musicians used to assemble at his house on the 22nd of every month. Some biographers say that he was a disciple of Sháh Gulshan, meaning Shaikh Sa'd-ulláh. Besides a Díwán in Persian and one in Rekhta, he has written a treatise on Súfiism called "Risála Wáridát." He died on Thursday the 3rd of January, 1785 A. D., 24th Ṣafar, 1199 A. H.

*List of his Works.*

| | |
|---|---|
| A'lí Nála-wa-Dard. | Ilm-ul-Kitáb. |
| A'lí Sard. | Díwán in Persian. |
| Dard Dil. | Díwán in Urdú. |

**Dardmand,** دردمند, poetical name of Muhammad Taḳíh of Dehlí, who was a pupil of Mirzá Ján Jánán Mazhar, and the author of a Sáḳínáma and of a Díwán. He died at Murshidábád in the year 1762 A. D., 1176 A. H.

**Daria Imad Shah,** دریا عماد شاه, the son of 'Alá-uddín 'Imád Sháh whom he succeeded on the throne of Beŗáŗ in the Dakhan about the year 1532 A. D., 939 A. H. In 1543 A. D., 950 A. H., he gave his sister Rabia' Sulṭána in marriage to Ibráhím 'Adil Sháh, and the nuptials were celebrated with royal magnificence. In 1558 A. D., 966 A. H., he gave his daughter in marriage to Husain Nizám Sháh and reigned in great tranquillity with all the other kings of the Dakhan until his death, when he was succeeded by his son Burhán 'Imád Sháh.

**Ḍaria Khan Rohila,** دریا خان روهیله, a nobleman in the service of prince Sháh Jahán, who on his accession to the throne, raised him to the rank of 5000. He afterwards joined the rebel Khán Jahán Lodí. In a battle which took place between him and Rájá Bikarmájít Bundela, son of Rájá Chhajjar Singh, he was killed, together with one of his sons and 400 Afgháns 1630 A. D., 1040 A. H. His head was sent to the emperor.

**Darikutni,** دارقطنی, *vide* Abú'l Husain 'Alí-bin-'Umr.

**Darimi,** دارمی, the son of 'Abdul Rahmán of Samarkand, is the author of the work called "Musnad Dárimí." He died in the year 869 A. D., 255 A. H. He is also called by some authors Abú Muhammad 'Abd-ulláh-al-Dárimí.

**Darki,** درکی قمی, of Kumm in Persia, was a contemporary of Sháh 'Abbás. He died in the Dakhan and left a Persian Díwán.

**Dasht Baiazi,** دشت بیاضی, *vide* Walí of Dasht Bayáz.

**Dastam Khan,** دستم خان, son of Rustam Khán Turkistání, was an Amír of 3000 in the service of the emperor Akbar. He died in 1580 A. D., 988 A. H. of his wounds which he had received in battle against the three nephews of Rájá Bihárí Mal, who had rebelled against the emperor and were also killed.

**Data Ram Brahman,** داتا رام بامن, a poet who wrote beautiful Persian verses.

**Dattaji Sindhia,** دتاجي سيندهيه, son of Ránájí and brother of Jaiápá Sindhia, a Marhaṭṭa chief who had a cavalry of 80,000 horse under him, and was slain in battle against Ahmad Sháh Abdálí in the month of January, 1760 A. D., Jumáda II, 1173 A. H., a year before the death of Bháú, the famous Marhaṭṭa chief. *Vide* Ránájí Sindhia.

**Daud Bidari (Mulla),** داؤد بيدري, a native of Bídar in the Dakhan. When twelve years of age, he held the office of page and seal-bearer to Sulṭán Muhammad Sháh Bahmaní I, king of Dakhan about the year 1368 A. D., 770 A. H. He is the author of the "Tahfat-us-Salátín Bahmaní."

**Daud Khan Faruki,** داؤد خان فاروقي, succeeded his brother Mírán Ghaní to the throne of Khándesh in September, 1503 A. D., 1st Jumáda I, 916 A. H., reigned seven years and died on Wednesday the 6th of August, 1510 A. D. He was succeeded by 'Adil Khán Farúkí II.

**Daud Khan Kureshi,** داؤد خان قريشي, son of Bhíkan Khán, was an officer of 5000 in the reign of the emperor 'Alamgír. In the year 1670 A. D., 1081 A. H., he was appointed governor of Allahábád.

**Daud Khan Panni,** داؤد خان پني, son of Khizir Khán Panní, a Paṭhán officer, renowned throughout India for his reckless courage, and his memory still survives in the tales and proverbs of the Dakhan. He served several years under 'Alamgír, and when Bahádur Sháh, on his departure from the Dakhan, gave the viceroyalty of that kingdom to the Amír-al-Umra, Zulfikár Khán, as that chief could not be spared from court, he left the administration of the government to Dáúd Khán, who was to act as his lieutenant. In the reign of Farrukh-siyar when the Amír-ul-Umra Husain 'Alí Khán marched towards Dakhan, Dáúd Khán received secret orders from the emperor to oppose and cut him off. Accordingly when the Amír-ul-Umrá arrived at Burhánpúr, Dáúd Khán, who regarded himself as the hero of his age, prepared to receive him. The engagement was very bloody on both sides; a matchlock ball struck Dáúd Khán, and he fell down dead on the seat of his elephant. This event took place in the year 1715 A. D., 1127 A. H.

**Daud Kaisari (Shaikh),** شيخ داؤد قيصري, author of another commentary called "Sharah Hadís-ul-Arba'ín," besides the one written by Birgilí. He died 1350 A. D., 751 A. H.

**Daud Shah Bahmani (Sultan),** داؤد شاه بهمني سلطان, the son of Sulṭán 'Alá-uddín Hasan, ascended the throne of Dakhan, after assassinating his nephew Mujáhid Sháh on the 14th of April, 1378 A. D., 21st Muḥarram, 780 A. H. He reigned one month and five days, and was murdered on the 19th May the same year in the mosque at Kulbarga where he went to say his prayers. He was succeeded by his brother Mahmúd Sháh I.

**Daud Shah,** داؤد شاه گجراتي, a king of Gujrát, who was placed on the throne after the death of his nephew Kutb Sháh in 1439 A. D., and was deposed after seven days, when Mahmúd Sháh, another nephew of his, a youth of only 14 years of age, was raised to the throne.

**Daud Shah,** داؤد شاه, the youngest son of Sulaimán Kiráni succeeded to the kingdom of Bengal after the death of his eldest brother Báiazíd in the year 1573 A. D., 981 A. H. This prince was much addicted to sensual excesses; and the propensity was rendered more degrading by his inclination to associate with persons of low origin and mean connections, by whom he was induced to attack the frontiers of the kingdom of Dehlí. He had several skirmishes with Munaim Khán, Khán Khánán, governor of Jaunpúr, who was subsequently joined by his master, the emperor Akbar, when an obstinate battle took place on the 30th of July, 1575 A. D., 21st Rabí' II, 983 A. H., in which Dáúd Sháh was defeated and obliged to retire to a fort on the borders of Kaṭak. After this a peace was concluded, by which Dáúd Sháh was invested with the government of Orisa and Kaṭak, and the other provinces of Bengal were occupied by Munaim Khán in the name of the emperor. The year of this event is commemorated in a Persian Hemistich. After the death of Munaim Khán which took place the same year at Lakhnautí, Dáúd Khán re-took the provinces of Bengal, but was soon attacked by Khán Jahán Turkmán, who was appointed governor, when after a severe engagement Dáúd Khán was taken prisoner, and suffered death as a rebel. From that period, the kingdom of Bengal was subdued, and fell under the subjection of the emperor Akbar. Thus ended the rule of the Púrbí or independent eastern kings of Bengal.

**Daud Tai,** داؤد طاي, a Musalmán doctor who was master of several sciences. He had served Abú Haníſa for 20 years, and was one of the disciples of Habíb Ráí. He was contemporary with Fazail Aiáz, Ibráhím Adham and Ma'rúf Karkhí, and died in the reign of the khalíf Al-Mahdí, the son of Al-Mansúr, about the year 781 or 782 A. D., 164 or 165 A. H.

**Daud Khan,** داؤد خان, a general of Aurangzíb.

**Dawal Devi,** داول ديوى, or Dewal Deví, *vide* Kaulá Deví.

**Dawani,** دواني, the philosopher, whose proper name is Jalál-uddín Muhammad Asa'd Aldawání, the son of Sa'd-uddín Asa'd Dawání. He flourished in the reign of Sulṭán Abú Sa'íd and died, according to Hájí Khalfa, in the year 908 A. H., (corresponding with 1502 A. D.). He is the author of the "Sharah Haiákal," "Akhlák Jalálí," "Isbát Wájib," (on the existence of God) "Risála Zaura," (on Súfíism), "Háshia Shamsia," and "Anwár Sháfia." He also wrote the "Sharah 'Akáed," and marginal notes on "Sharah Tajríd." The Akhlak Jalálí is a translation from the Arabic, the original of which appeared in the 10th century under the name of "Kitáb-ut-Tahárat," by an Arabian author, minister of the imperial house of Bóyá. Two centuries after, it was translated into Persian by Abú Nasr, and named "Akhlák Násirí," or the morals of Násir, being enriched with some important additions taken from Abú Sína. In the 15th century, it assumed a still further improved form, under the present designation, the Akhlák Jalálí or morals of Jalál. This book which is the most esteemed ethical work of middle Asia, was translated into English by W. F. Thompson, Esq. of the Bengal Civil Service, London, 1839.

**Dawar Bakhsh (Sultan),** سلطان داور بخش, surnamed Mirzá Bulákí, was the son of Sulṭán Khusro. When his grandfather, the emperor Jahángír, died on his way from Kashmír to Láhor in October, 1627 O. S., Ṣafar 1037 A. H., 'Asaf Khán, wazír, who was all along determined to support Sháh Jahán, the son of the late emperor, immediately sent off a messenger to summon him from the Dakhan. In the meantime, to sanction his own measures by the appearance of legal authority, he released prince Dáwar Bakhsh from prison, and proclaimed him king. Núr Jahán Begam, endeavouring to support the cause of Sháhriár, her son-in-law, was placed under temporary restraint by her brother, the wazír, who then continued his march to Láhor. Shahriár who was already in that city, forming a coalition with two, the sons of his uncle, the late prince Dániál, marched out to oppose 'Asaf Khán. The battle ended in his defeat; he was given up by his adherents, and afterwards put to death together with Dáwar Bakhsh and the two sons of Dániál, by orders from Sháh Jahán who ascended the throne. Elphinstone in his History of India, says that Dáwar Bakhsh found means to escape to Persia, where he was afterwards seen by the Holstein ambassadors.

**Daya Mal,** دیا مل, *vide* Imtiyáz.

**Daya Nath,** دیا ناتهه *vide* Wafá.

**Dayanat Khan,** دیانت خان, title of Muhammad Husain, an amír of 2500, who served under the emperor Sháh Jahán, and died at Ahmadnagar in the Dakhan 1630 A. D., 1040 A. H.

**Daya Ram,** دیا رام, Paṭṭha, a hero, renowned in the west of Hindústán for extraordinary strength of body, extraordinary courage, and extraordinary achievements. He was a Gwála by caste, and flourished in the reign of the Emperor Farrukh-siyar. The wonderful feats of this man are sung or recited accompanied by the beat of a *ḍhól* throughout Hindústán. A full and affecting account of this hero is given in the "Bengal Annual" published at Calcutta in 1833, p. 169.

**Daya Ram,** دیا رام, a chief of Hátras, tributary to the Honorable Company, who, about the year 1814 A. D., confiding in the extraordinary strength of his fort, shewed a spirit of contumacy and disobedience. A train of Artillery was brought against this place from Cawnpúr, and a few hours of its tremendous fire breached the boasted fortification.

**Dilami** دلامی and Sámání were two dynasties which divided between them the kingdom of Persia towards the beginning of the 10th century. They both rose to power through the favor of the Khalífs of Baghdád, but they speedily threw off the yoke. The Dílámí divided into two branches, exercised sovereign authority in Kirmán, Iráḳ, Fáris, Khuzistán, and Laristán, always acknowledging their nominal dependence on the Khalífí, and during the whole period of their rule, one of the southern branch of this family was vested with the dignity of Amír-ul-Umra, or vizír, and managed the affairs of the khalifate. Several of the Dílámí were able and wise rulers, but Mahmúd of Ghazní put an end to the rule of the northern branch in 1029 A. D., and the Saljúḳs subjugated the southern one in 1056 A. D., by the capture of Baghdád, their last stronghold. Their more powerful rivals, the Sámání, had obtained from the Khalíf the government of Transoxiana in 874 A. D.; and to this, Isma'íl, the most celebrated prince of the family, speedily added Khwárizm, Balkh, Khurásán, Sístán, and many portions of northern Turkistán. Rebellions of provincial governors distracted the Samanida monarchy towards the end of the 10th century; and in 999 A. D. their dominions north of Persia were taken possession of by the Khán of Káshghar, the Persian provinces being added by Mahmúd of Ghazní to his dominions. See Sámání.

**Din Muhammad Khan,** دین محمد خان, the son of Iání Beg Sulṭán, and 'Abd-ulláh Khán Uzbak's sister, was raised to the throne of Samarḳand after the death of 'Abdul Mómin Khán, the son of 'Abd-ulláh Khán, in 1598 A. D., 1006 A. H. He was wounded in a battle fought against Sháh 'Abbás the Great, king of Persia, and died shortly after.

**Diwana,** دیوانه, poetical name of Muhammad Ján, who died in the year 1737 A. D., 1150 A. H.

**Diwana,** دیوانه, poetical name of Ráe Sarabsukh, a relation of rájá Mahá Naráyan. He wrote two Persian Díwáns of more than 10,000 verses; most poets of Lákhnau were his pupils. He died in 1791 A. D., 1206 A. H.

**Diwana,** دیوانه, poetical name of Mirzá Muhammad 'Alí Khán of Banáras, who was employed in the office of Mr. Colebrooke at Jahanábád.

**Diwanji Begam,** دیوانجی بیگم, she was the mother of Arjumand Bano Begam Mumtaz Mahal, and the wife of 'Asaf Khán, Wazír. On a spot of fifty bighas of land on the bank of the river Jamna, close to the Rauza of Tájganj, is to be seen her Rauza bust of white marble.

**Deo Narain Singh,** دیونراین سنگهه, (K. C. S. I., Sir, Rájá) of Banáras, died suddenly on the 28th August, 1870.

**Dewal Devi,** دیول دیوی, *vide* Kaulá Deví.

**Dhara,** دهارا, the son of Rájá Todarmal. He was killed in a battle fought against Mirzá Jání Beg, ruler of Thatta, in November, 1591 A. D., Muḥarram 1000 A. H.

**Dhola Rao,** دهولا راو, the ancestor of the Kachhwaha Rájás of Ambír or Jaipúr, he lived about the year 967 A. D.

**Dhundia Wagh,** دهوندیه واگهه, the free-booter, who had for several years with a formidable band, pillaged and laid waste the frontiers of Mysore. This robber assumed the lofty title of king of the two worlds, and aimed, doubtless, at carving out for himself some independent principality, after the example of Hydar 'Alí, in whose service he originally commenced his adventurous career. Subsequently he incurred the displeasure of Típú Sulṭán, who chained him like a wild beast to the walls of his dungeons in Serangapatam, from which "durance vile" he had been liberated by the English soldiers after the taking of Serangapatam. He now threatened Mysore with 5,000 cavalry. The Government of Madras instructed Colonel Wellesley to pursue him wherever he could be found and to hang him on the first tree. His subjugation and subsequent death (in 1800) with the extirpation of his formidable band of free-booters, relieved the English Government from an enemy, who, though by no means equal to Hydar and Típú, might eventually have afforded considerable annoyance.

**Dil,** دل, poetical name of Zorawar Khán of Sirkar Kol. He is the author of a Díwán and a few Masnawís.

**Dilawar Khan,** دلاورخان, founder of the dynasty of the Muhammadan kings of Málwa. The Hindú histories of the kingdom of Málwa go back as far as the reign of Rájá Bikarmájít, whose accession to that kingdom has given rise to an era which commences 57 years before Christ. After him reigned Rájá Bhój and many others who are all mentioned among the rájás of Hindústán. During the reign of Ghayás-uddín Balban king of Dehlí in the year 1310 A. D., 710 A. H., the Muhammadans first invaded and conquered the provinces of Málwa; after which it acknowledged allegiance to that crown until the reign of Muhammad Sháh Tughlaḳ II, 1387 A. D., 789 A. H. At this period Diláwar Khán, a descendant on his mother's side from Sulṭán Shaháb-uddín Ghórí, was appointed governor of Málwa, previously to the accession of Muhammad Tughlaḳ, and he subsequently established his independence. In the year 1398 A. D., 801 A. H., Mahmúd Sháh, king of Dehlí, being driven from his throne by Amír Taimúr (Tamerlane,) made his escape to Gujrát, and then to Málwa, where he remained three years, after which, in 1401 A. D., 804 A. H., he, at the instance of the Dehlí nobles, quitted Málwa, in order to resume the reins of his own government. Diláwar Khán shortly afterwards assumed royalty and divided his kingdom into estates among his officers whom he ennobled. Diláwar Khán on assuming independence, took up his residence in Dhár, which place he considered as the seat of his government, but he frequently visited the city of Mándo, remaining there sometimes for months together. He only survived his assumption of the royal titles a few years; for in the year 1405 A. D., 808 A. H., he died suddenly, and his son Alp Khán ascended the throne under the title of Sultán Hóshang Sháh. Including Diláwar Khán eleven princes reigned in Málwa till the time of the emperor Humáyún, whose son Akbar eventually subdued and attached it to the Dehlí government. Their names are as follow:

1. Diláwar Khán Ghórí.
2. Hóshang Sháh, son of Diláwar.
3. Sultán Muhammad Sháh.
4. Sultán Mahmúd I, Khiljí, styled the Great, son of Malik Mughís.
5. Ghayas-uddín Khiljí.
6. Nasir-uddín.
7. Mahmúd II.
8. Bahádur Sháh, king of Gujrát.
9. Kadar Sháh.
10. Shujáa' Khán, and
11. Báz Bahádur, son of Shujáa' Khán.

**Dilawar Khan,** دلاورخان, a nobleman of the reign of the emperor Sháh Jahán, was the son of Bahádur Khán Rohila. He died at Kábul in the year 1658 A. D., 1068 A. H.

**Dildar Aga,** دلدار آغا, one of the wives of the emperor Babar, and mother of Mirzá Handál.

**Diler Himmat Khan,** دلیر همت خان, original name of Nawáb Muzaffar Jang of Farrukhábád, which see.

**Diler Khan,** دلیرخان, a Dáúdzaí Afghán, whose proper name was Jalál Khán. He was the younger brother of Bahádur Khán Rohila, and one of the best and bravest generals of the emperor 'Alamgír. He held the rank of 5000, and died in the year 1683 A. D., 1094 A. H., in the Dakhan.

**Diler Khan,** دلیرخان, title of 'Abdul Raúf, the son of 'Abdul Karím, formerly in the service of the king of Bíjápúr. After the conquest of that country, he joined 'Alamgír and received the title of Diler Khán and the mansab of 7000. He died in the reign of Bahádur Sháh in the Dakhan, where he held a jágír.

**Dilras Bano Begam,** دلرس بانو بیگم, daughter of Shahnawáz Khán Safwí, the son of Mirzá Rustam Kandharí, and wife of the emperor 'Alamgír. She had another sister who was married to Murád Bakhsh, brother of 'Alamgír.

**Dilshad Khatun,** دلشاد خاتون, daughter of Amír Damishk, the son of Amír Juban or Jovian, and wife of Sultán Abú Sa'íd Khán. Amír Hasan Buzurg, who after the death of the Sultán in 1335 A. D., took possession of Baghdád, married her, but the reins of government were in her hands.

**Dilsoz,** دلسوز, poetical title of Khairátí Khán, a poet who lived about the year 1800.

**Dost 'Ali,** دوست علی, Nawáb of Arkat and a relative of Murtaza Khán. Under him the atrocious seizure of Trichinopoly was perpetrated by Chanda Sahib. He was succeeded by his son Safdar 'Alí, who, after overcoming the effects of poison prepared for him by Murtaza Khán, fell by the poniard of a Pathán assassin, hired for the work by the same person. A storm was raised which he had not the courage to encounter; and disguising himself in female attire, he escaped from Arkat to his own fort of Vellore.

**Dost Muhammad Khan,** دوست محمد خان, ruler of Kábul and Kandahár, was one of the brothers of Fatha Khán, the celebrated wazír of Mahmúd, ruler of Hírat and chief of the Barakzaí clan. He was the most powerful chief in Afghánistan, and had for some years previous to the restoration of Sháh Shujáa'-ul-Mulk by the British in 1838, ruled that country. On the death of this prince, Dost Muhammad again assumed the reins of government.

On the base and cruel murder of Fatha Khán by Mahmúd at the instigation of Prince Kámrán, his brothers revolted from their allegiance under the guidance of 'Azím Khán, the governor of Kashmír, and drove Mahmúd and his son Kámrán from Kábul. Azím Khán in the first instance offered the vacant throne to Sháh Shujáa', but offended by some personal slight, withdrew his support, and placed in his room, Aiyúb, a brother of Sháh Shujáa', who was content to take the trappings with the power of royalty. On Azím Khán's death, his brothers dissatisfied with their position conspired against his son, Habíb-ulláh Khán, and seizing his person, by threats of blowing him from a gun, induced his mother to deliver up the residue of Azím Khán's immense wealth. Aiyúb's son was killed in these disputes, and he himself, alarmed by these scenes of violence, fled to Láhor. Dost Muhammad Khán, the most talented of the brothers, then took possession of the throne and became *de facto* king of Kábul. Sher Dil Khán, accompanied by four brothers, carried off about half a million sterling of Azím Khán's money, and seated himself in Kandahár, as an independent chieftain. He and one of his brothers died some years ago; and Kandahár was until lately ruled by Kohan Dil Khán, assisted by his two surviving brothers Rahím Dil and Mír Dil. In the year 1839 the British army entered Kábul and placed Sháh Shujáa'-ul-Mulk on the throne on the 8th May, and Dost Muhammad Khán surrendered to the British Envoy and Minister in Kábul on the 4th November, after having defeated the 2nd Bengal Cavalry by a desperate charge. He was subsequently sent down to Calcutta, where he arrived, accompanied by one of his sons, on the 23rd May, 1841. He was set free in November 1842 and returned to Kábul, where he reigned as before till his death, which took place on the 9th June, 1863 A. D., 21st Zil-hijja 1279 A. H., and his youngest son Amír Sher Alí succeeded him.

**Doulat Khan Lodi,** دولت خان لودی, who, according to Firishta, was an Afghán by birth, originally a private Secretary, who after passing through various offices was raised by Sultán Mahmúd Tughlak, and attained the title of 'Azíz Mumálik. After the death of Mahmúd, the nobles raised him to the throne of Dehlí in April, 1413 A. D., Muharram, 816 A. H. In March 1414, 15th Rabí I, 817 A. H., Khizir Khán, governor of Multán, invaded Dehlí, and after a siege of four months obliged Doulat Khán on the 4th June 1414, Jamáda I, 817 A. H., to surrender. He was instantly confined in the fort of Fírózábád, where he died after two months.

**Doulat Khan Lodi,** دولت خان لودی, who invited Bábar Sháh to India, was a descendant of the race of that name who heretofore reigned at Dehlí. He was a poet and a man of learning. He died a short time l efore Bábar conquered Dehlí, *i. e.*, in the year 1526 A. D. 932, A. H.

**Doulat Khan Lodi Shahu Khail,** دولت خان لودی ساهو خیل, was the father of the rebel Khán Jahán Lodí. He served under Mirzá 'Azíz Kóka, 'Abdul Rahím Khán Khán Khánán, and prince Dáníál for several years and was raised to the rank of 2000. He died in the Dakhán 1600 A. D., 1009 A. H.

**Doulat Rao Sindhia (Maharaja),** دولت راوسیندهیه مهاراجه, of Gwáliar, a Marhattá chief, was the grand-nephew and adopted son of Madhojí Sindhia, whom he succeeded to the ráj of Gwaliar in March, 1794 A. D., 1208 A. H. His violence, rapacity and lawless ambition, were the main causes of the war in 1802 with the confederate Marhatta chieftains. Hostilities having broken out with the British, Sir Arthur Wellesley (afterwards Duke of Wellington) defeated Doulat Ráo at Assaye in 1803, while Lord Lake drove the Marhattas from the whole of the Doab. He married Bají Bái, reigned 33 years, and died on the 21st March, 1827, 21st Sh'aban 1242 A. H. He was succeeded by Jhanko Ráo Sindhia.

**Doulat Shah,** دولت شاه, son of Bakht Sháh of Samarḳand, and author of the Biography of Poets called "Tazkira Doulat Sháhí." He flourished in the reign of Sulṭán Husain Mirzá of Hirát, surnamed Abúl Ghazí Bahádur, and dedicated the work to his prime minister, the celebrated Amír Nizám-uddín 'Alísher. This work was written in 1486 A. D., 891 A. H., and contains the Lives or Memoirs of ten Arabian, and one hundred and thirty-four Persian poets, with various quotations from their works, and anecdotes of the princes at whose court they resided. It also gives an account of six poets then residing in Hirát; two of whom were principal ministers of the Sulṭán; *viz.*, 'Alísher, and Amír Shaikh Ahmad Suhelí. *Vide* Fáezí Kirmaní. He died in 1495 A. D.

**Dundey Khan,** دوندے خان روهيله, a Rohila chief, and son of 'Alí Muhammad Khán, the founder of the Rohila Government. In the partition of lands which were assigned to the chiefs, in the time of Háfiz Rahmat Khán, Dúndey Khán obtained the districts of Bisaulí, Murádábád, Chándpúr and Sambhal in Rohilkhanḍ. He died previous to the Rohila war which took place in 1774 A. D., leaving three sons, the eldest of whom Muhib-ullah Khán, succeeded to the largest portion of his territories.

**Dunyapat Singh (raja),** راجه دنياپت سنگه. His father died in 1790 A. D., at which time he was only seven years of age. He inherited from his grandfather Rúp Ráe the Chaklas of Kóṛá, Fathapúr and Kaṛa, but was dispossessed by the Nawáb Wazír, and a Nánkar allowance of 24,000 rupees granted to the rájá on his exclusion. This was subsequently reduced to 7,500 rupees. The original grant amounted to 52,000 per annum, payable from 14 mahâls, but in 1770 A. D., the Nawáb Najaf Khán acquiring unlimited dominion over these provinces, dispossessed his father of eleven of the villages, by which his income was reduced to 20,000 rupees. In 1787 his father was dispossessed of the remaining three villages by Zain-ul-'Abidín Khán, the 'Amil,but as the rájá was about to proceed to hostilities, the 'Amil agreed to allow him 10,000 Rs. for the first year, and 20,000 thereafter, but failed in the fulfilment of his promise. In 1792 A. D., Zain-ul-'Abidín died, and was succeeded by his son Báḳar 'Alí Khán, and from that period up to 1802, the rájá Duniápat Singh was allowed 8,000 rupees per annum, which was confirmed by Government in 1805 in perpetuity.

**Dupleix,** a French officer, governor of Pondicherry. In 1750 A. D., he was elevated to the rank of a Haft Hazárí, or Commander of seven thousand horse, and permitted to bear an ensign, assigned to persons of the highest note in the empire, by Muzaffar Jang, viceroy of the Dakhan, after his victory over his brother Násir Jang who fell in battle.

**Durduzd,** دردزد, *vide* 'Alí Durduzd of Astrabad.

**Durgawati (Rani),** راني درگاوتي, daughter of Rana Sarika. *Vide* Silhaddí.

**Durgawati (Rani),** راني درگاوتي, the daughter of the rájá of Mahóba, who was much celebrated for her singular beauty. Overtures had been made for an union with Dalpat Sáh, rájá of Singalgurh (which is situated on the brow of a hill that commands a pass on the road about half way between Garha and Sangar;) but the proposal was rejected on the ground of a previous engagement, and some inferiority of caste on the part of the Garha family, who was of the race of the Chandeil ráj-púts. Dalpat Sáh was a man of uncommonly fine appearance, and this added to the celebrity of his father's name and extent of his dominions, made Durgáwatí as desirous as himself for the union, but he was by her given to understand, that she must be relinquished or taken by force, since the difference of caste would of itself be otherwise an insurmountable obstacle. He marched with all his troops he could assemble, met those of her father and his rival,—gained a victory and brought off Durgáwatí as the prize to the fort of Singalgurh. Dalpat Sáh died four years after their marriage, leaving a son named Bír Naráyan about three years of age, and his widow as regent during his minority. Asaf Khán, the imperial viceroy at Kaṛa Mánikpúr on the Ganges in the province of Allahábád, invited by the prospect of appropriating so fine a country and so much wealth as she was reputed to possess, invaded her dominions in the year 1564 A. D., at the head of 6,000 cavalry and 12,000 well disciplined infantry, with a train of artillery. He was met by the queen at the head of her troops, and an action took place in which she was defeated. She received a wound from an arrow in the eye; and her only son, then about 18 years of age, was severely wounded and taken to the rear. At this moment she received another arrow in the neck; and seeing her troops give way and the enemy closing around her, she snatched a dagger from the driver of her elephant, and plunged it in her own bosom. Her son was taken off the field, and was, unperceived by the enemy, conveyed back to the palace at Chúrágarh, to which Asaf Khán returned immediately after his victory and laid siege. The young prince was killed in the siege; and the women set fire to the place under the apprehension of suffering dishonor if they fell alive into the hands of the enemy. Two females are said to have escaped, the sister of the queen, and a young princess who had been betrothed to the young prince Bír Naráyan; and these two are said to have been sent to the emperor Akbar. In this district of Jabbalpúr, the marble rocks and the palace called Madan Mahal is worth seeing. There is some doggrel rhyme about this palace which is not generally known, though of some interest. This building stands on a single granite boulder, and was constructed by the Gond princess Raní Durgawatí, at the time of the Muhammadan invasion of Central India. Years after the cession of the country to the British, a wag of a Panḍit wrote on the entrance door of the palace the following lines:

Madan Mahal ké chhain mé,<br>
Do tángón ké bích,<br>
Gaṛá nau lakh rupí,<br>
Aur soné ká do íṇt.

Translation—

In the shade of Madan Mahal<br>
Between two boulders<br>
There are buried nine lakhs of rupees<br>
And two bricks of gold.

It did not take long for the news of the appearance of this writing on the door to spread abroad, and the very person to fall a dupe to the Pandit's trick was Captain Wheatley, at that time a Political Assistant at Jabalpúr. He mustered some peons and laborers, and having proceeded to the spot, commenced digging for the treasure on the part of Government. The native lady, in whose possession was the village lands on which the palace stood, came rushing down to the Agent to the Governor-General and represented that she was being plundered of her treasure by Captain Wheatley. "Paglí," replied Sir Wm. Sleeman, "he is as mad as you are; the Pandit would not have divulged the secret were it of much value." Many years have since elapsed, and many others not possessed of Sir William's wisdom have fallen dupes to the Pandit's poetical trick; and, but for the very durable nature of the martas, there have been enough of excavations made in and about the building to raze it to the ground.

# E.

**Egypt,** kings of, *vide* Moizz-li-dín-alláh Abí Tamím Ma'd.

**Ekkoji,** يكوجي, the founder of the Tanjore family was the son of Shahjí Bhosla, and brother of Seiwájí, but from another consort. The principality of Tanjore was one of the oldest in the Marhaṭṭa confederacy, of which province Ekkojí obtained possession in 1678 A. D.

# F.

**Faek,** فايق, or Fáyeḳ, poetical name of Moulwí Muhammad Fáeḳ, author of the work called "Makhzan-ul-Fawaed."

**Faez,** فايض, or Fáyez, poetical name of Shaikh Muhammad Fáez, a pupil of Muhammad Sa'íd Ayáz. He is the author of a short Díwán, and was probably living in 1724 A. D., 1136 A. H.

**Faezi Kirmani,** فايضى كرماني, a poet who rendered the Tazkira of Doulat Sháh in Persian verses in the time of the emperor Akbar, and altered the division of the original, making ten periods instead of seven. *Vide* Lutf-ullah Muhammad Muhaddis.

**Faghfur,** فغفور, the general name of the kings of China.

**Faghfur Yezdi,** حكيم فغفوريزدي, (Hakím) a physician and poet of Persia, born at Yezd. He is the author of a Díwán or Book of Odes, and has written several panegyrics in praise of the kings of Persia. He came to India in 1603 A. D., 1012 A. H., and was employed by prince Parwez, and died at Allahábád about the year 1619 A. D., 1028 A. H.

**Fahmi Kirmani,** مولانا صدرالدين محمد فهمی کرمانی, (Moulana Sadr-uddín Muhammad), a poet who is the author of a Masnawí called "Súrat-wa-Ma'aní," and also of some Ḳasídas, Ghazals, Satires, &c. He died in the year 1584 A. D., 993 A. H., in the fort of Tabrez, during the time it was besieged by the Turks.

**Faiz,** فيض, the distinguished mystical philosopher and theologist, Mullá Muhsin of Káshán, commonly called Akhúnd Faiz. He flourished under Sháh 'Abbás II of Persia, who treated him with great respect. He has written a great number of books, of which "Kitáb 'Asafí" and "Kitáb Safí are two Commentaries on the Ḳurán. He died at Káshán under, or after Sháh Sulaimán of Persia, and his tomb is a place of pilgrimage.

**Faiz,** فيض, poetical title of Mír Faiz 'Alí, an Urdú poet of Dehlí. His father Mír Muhammad Taḳí was also an elegant poet, and had assumed the title of Mír for his poetical name. Both Faiz 'Alí and his father were living at Dehlí in the year 1785 A. D., 1196 A. H.

**Faiz,** فيض, a pupil of Mirzá Ḳatíl, and author of a poetical work containing amorous songs in Persian, called "Díwán Faiz." He was living in the time of Muhammad 'Alí Sháh, king of Lákhnau, about the year 1840 A. D., 1256 A. H.

**Faiz,** فيض, poetical title of Faiz-ul-Hasan of Sahâranpúr, author of the "Rauzat-ul-Faiz," a poem composed in 1847 A. D., 1263 A. H.

**Faizi (Shaikh),** شيخ فيضي, whose proper name was Abú'l Faiz, was the son of Shaikh Mubárik of Nágor, and eldest brother of Shaikh Abú'l Fazl, prime-minister and secretary to the emperor Akbar Sháh. He was born on the 16th September 1547, A. D., 1st Shában, 954 A. H., and was first presented to Akbar in the 12th year of his reign, and introduced his brother Abú'l Fazl six years later.. After the death of the poet laureate Ghizálí of Mashhad, about the year 1572 A. D., or some years after, or, according to the "Másir-ul-Umrá," in the 33rd year of the emperor, Faizí was honored with the title of "Malik-ush-Shua'rá" or king of poets. In history, philosophy, in medicine, in letter writing, and in composition, he was without a rival. His earlier compositions in verse, bear his titular name of Faizí, which he subsequently dignified into Faiyází, but he survived to enjoy his last title only one or two months, and then met his death. Being desirous of rivalling the Khamsa or the five poems of Nizámí, he wrote in imitation of them his "Markaz Adwár," "Sulaiman and Bilkais," "Nal Daman," "Haft Kiskwár," and "Akbar Nama." The story of Nal Daman is an episode of the Mahábhárat, which he translated into Persian verse at the command of the emperor Akbar. He was the first Musalmán that applied himself to a diligent study of Hindú literature and science. Besides Sanskrit works in poetry and philosophy, he made a version of the "Bíja Ganitá," and "Lílawatí," of Bhaskar Achárýá, the best Hebrew works on Algebra and Arithmetic. He was likewise author of a great deal of original poetry, and of other works in Persian. He composed an elaborate Commentary upon the Ḳurán, making use of only those 13 out of the 28 letters of the Alphabet which have no dots, and which he named "Sawáta'-ul-Ilhám"; a copy of this extraordinary monument of wasted labour (says Mr. Elliot) is to be seen in the Library of the East India House. There is also another book of the same description which he wrote and called "Mawarid-ul-Kalam." Faizí suffered from asthma and died at Ágrah on Saturday the 4th of October, 1595 O. S., 10th Ṣafar, 1004 A. H., aged 49 lunar years and some months; and, as many supposed him to have been a deist, several abusive chronograms were written on the occasion, of which the following is one—"The Shaikh was an infidel." There is also an Insha or collection of Letters which goes after his name. His mother died in January, 1590 A. D., 998 A. H., and his father in August, 1593 A. D., Ẕeḳa'd, 1001 A. H. He was a profound scholar, well versed in Arabic literature, the art of poetry and medicine. He was also one of the most voluminous writers that India has produced and is said to have composed 101 books. Faizí had been likewise employed as teacher to the princes; he also acted as ambassador. Thus in 1000 A. H., he was in the Dakhin, from whence he wrote the letter to the historian Budáoni, who had been in temporary disgrace at Court. Vide *Ain Translation* I, 490.

**Faizi,** فيضي, of Ṣarhind, *vide* Alahdad.

**Faiz-ullah Anju (Mir),** ميرفيض الله انجو, a Ḳází who presided on the seat of justice in the reign of Sulṭán Mahmúd Bahmaní, king of Dakhan, who reigned from 1378 to 1397 A. D., 780 to 799 A. H. He was a good poet, and a contemporary of the celebrated Khwája Háfiz. Once presenting the Sulṭán with an ode of his own composition, he was rewarded with a thousand pieces of gold, and permitted to retire, covered with honors, to his own country.

**Faiz-ullah Khan,** فيض الله خان, chief of the Rohelas and Jagírdar of Rámpúr, was the son of 'Alí Muhammad Khán Rohela. After the battle of Kutra in 1774 A. D., he retired to the Kamaon hills. By the treaty under Colonel Champion, he had a territory allotted to him of the annual value of 14 lakhs of rupees. He chose the city of Rámpúr as the place of his residence, and after an uninterrupted and prosperous administration of 20 years, he died in September, 1794 A. D., Safar 1209 A. H., and was succeeded by his eldest son Muhammad 'Alí Khán. This prince, in the course of a few days, in 1794 was imprisoned and assassinated by his younger brother Ghulám Muhammad, who forcibly took possession of the government. The English, having espoused the cause of Ahmad Alí, the infant son of the murdered prince, defeated and took Ghulám Muhammad prisoner at Bithoura. He was conveyed to Calcutta, where, under pretence of going on a pilgrimage to Mecca, he embarked on board a ship, probably landed at one of the ports in Típú Sultán's dominions, and thence made his way to the court of Kábul in 1797 A. D., 1212 A. H., where, united with the agents of Típú in clamours against the English, he urged Zamán Sháh, the son of Taimúr Sháh, to invade Hindustán, promising that, on his approach to Dehlí, he should be joined by the whole tribe of Rohelas. The Nawáb Ahmad Alí Khán died about the year 1839 A. D., 1255 A. H. After the death of Ahmad Alí Khán, Muhammad Saíd Khán ascended the Masnad in 1840; after him Muhammad Yusuf Alí Khán succeeded in 1855, who was living in 1872.

**Fakhri,** فخری, son of Moulana Sultán Muhammad Amírí of Hirát. He is the author of the "Jawáhir-ul-'Ajáeb," Gems of Curiosities, being a biography of poetesses. He informs us that with the intention to perform the pilgrimage to Mecca, he came during the reign of Sháh Tahmásp Husainí to Sindh, the ruler of that country was then I'sa Turkhán (who died about the year 1566 A. D., 974 A. H.). Iláhí the poet calls the above-mentioned work "Tazkirat-ul-Nisá." He is also the author of the "Tahfat-ul-Habíb," a collection of Ghazals from the best authors.

**Fakhri,** فخری, a poet who wrote a Díwán of 10,000 verses in which he imitated most of the ancient masters, but as he had not much education, he was not acknowledged by other poets. He dug a grave for himself outside the Isfahán Gate and made himself a tomb-stone, and visited his grave every Friday. He was living in 1585 A. D., 993 A. H.

**Fakir (Mir Shams-uddin),** میر شمس الدین فقیر, of Dehlí, who had also the poetical name of Maftún. From Dehlí he went to Lákhnau in 1765 A. D., 1179 A. H., and is said to have been drowned about the year 1767. He is the author of a Díwán and also of a Masnawí called "Taswír Muhabbat," containing the story of Rám Chánd, the son of a betel-vender, composed in 1743 A. D., 1156 A. H., and of several other poems.

**Fakir,** فقیر, poetical name of Mír Nawázish 'Alí of Bilgaram. He died in the year 1754 A. D., 1167 A. H.

**Fakhr-uddin,** فخرالدین, one of the princes of the Druses, who, early in the 17th century, conceived the idea of rendering himself independent of the Porte. He was betrayed, carried a prisoner to Constantinople, where he was strangled by order of Sultán Murád IV. in 1631 A. D., 1041 A. H.

**Fakhr-uddin Abu Muhammad-bin-Ali az-Zailai,** فخر الدین ابو محمد بن علي زيلعی, author of a Commentary on the Kanz-ul-Dakáek, entitled "Ta'ba'ín-ul-Hakáek" which is in great repute in India, on account of its upholding the doctrines of the Hanafí sect against those of the followers of Sháfa'í. He died in 1342 A. D., 743 A. H.

**Fakhr-uddin Bahman, (Malik),** فخرالدین بهمن ملک, third Sultán of the dynasty of Kart or Kard, was the son of Málik Shams-uddín Kart II, whom he succeeded to the throne of Hirát, Balkh and Ghazní in September, 1305 A. D., 705 A. H. He was contemporary with Sultán Aljaitú, surnamed Muhammad Khudá Banda, king of Persia, who sent an army against him which he defeated. He died about the beginning of the year 1307 A. D., 706 A. H., and was succeeded by his brother Málik Ghayás-uddín Kart I, who died in 1329 A. D.

**Fakhr-uddin Iraki (Shaikh),** شیخ فخرالدین عراقي, was the son of Shaikh Shaháb-uddín's daughter, and disciple of Shaikh Bahá-uddín Zikaria of Multán, whose daughter he married. He died on the 23rd November, 1289 A. D., 8th Zil-ká'da 688 A. H., and lies buried at Damascus. He was a native of Irák, and assumed the poetical name of Irákí in his poetry. Doulat Sháh says that 'Irákí died during the reign of Muhammad Khuda Banda in the year 1307 A. D., 709 A. H. *Vide* Irákí.

**Fakhr-uddin Ismat-ullah Bukhari,** فخرالدین عصمت الله بخاری. He died in 1426 A. D., 829 A. H., *vide* Asmat.

**Fakhr-uddin Junan (Malik),** ملک فخرالدین جونان, eldest son of Sultán Ghayás-uddín Tughlak Sháh I. On the accession of his father to the throne of Dehlí, he was declared heir-apparent, with the title of Ulagh Khán, and all the royal ensigns conferred upon him. The names of his other brothers were Bahrám Khán, Zafar Khán, Mahmúd Khán and Nasrat Khán. After the death of his father in 1325 A. D., 725 A. H., he succeeded him with the title of Muhammad Sháh Tughlak I.

**Fakhr-uddin Kha'lidi (Maulana),** مولانا فخرالدین خالدي, who was commonly called "Bihishtí," is the author of a work called "Sharah-Faráez." He was the master of Mouláná Mo'ín-uddín Jawíní.

**Fakhr-uddin Mahmud Amir,** امیر فخرالدین محمود, son of Amír Yemín-uddín Muhammad Mustúfí. He is generally known by his Takhallus or poetical name, Ibn Yemín, *i. e.*, the son of Yemín-uddín. According to Dr. Sprenger's Catalogue, he died in 1344 A. D., 745 A. H., and left panegyrics on the Sarabdál princes and some ghazals, but it is particularly his Kita's which are celebrated. *Vide* Amír Mahmúd.

**Fakhr-uddin Malik,** ملک فخر الدین, *vide* Málik Fakhr-uddín, king of Bengal.

**Fakhr-uddin Mirza,** مرزا فخر الدین, the eldest son of Bahádur Sháh II, ex-king of Dehlí. He died before the rebellion, on 10th July, 1856.

**Fakhr-uddin (Moulana),** مولانا فخرالدین, son of Nizám-ul-Hak, was styled Saiyad-ush-Shúa'rá, or chief of the poets. He is the author of several works, among which are the following "Nizám-ul-'Akáed," "Risála Marjia" and "Fakhr-ul-Hasn." He died in the year 1785 A. D., 1199 A. H., aged 73 years, and lies buried close to the gate of the Dargáh of Kutb-uddín Bakhtyár Kákí in old Dehlí. His tomb is of white marble and has an inscription mentioning his name and the year of his demise. His grandson Ghulám Nasír-uddín, surnamed Kálí Sáhib, was a very pious and learned Musalmán; he too was a good poet and died in the year 1852 A. D., 1268 A. H.

**Fakhr-uddin Muhammad Razi (Imam),** رازي امام فخرالدين محمد, was a doctor of the Sháfa'í sect. He surpassed all his contemporaries in scholastic theology, metaphysics and philosophy. He is the author of several instructive works, among which is one called "Hadáyek-ul-Anwar," a book on different subjects which he dedicated to Sultán 'Alá-uddín Takash, ruler of Khwárizm; and another called "Risála Haiyat," or Geometry, dedicated to Sultán Bahá-uddín Ghorí. He was born at Rei on the 26th January, 1150 A. D., 25th Ramazán, 544 A. H., and died at Hirát on Monday the 29th of March, 1210 A. D., 1 Shawwal, 606 A. H., aged 62 lunar years. His father's name was Ziyá-uddín-bin-Umar. The title of Rází attached to his name is because he was born at Rei in Tabristan. He is the father of Khwája Nasír-uddín Túsí.

**Fakhr-uddin Sultan,** فخرالدين سلطان, also called Fakhra, was the king of Sonárgáon in Bengal, which adjoins the district of Pandúa. He was put to death by Shams-uddín king of Lakhnautí about the year 1356 A. D., 757 A. H., who took possession of his country.

**Fakhr-ud-daula,** فخرالدولة, title of Abú'l Hasan 'Alí, a Sultán of the race of Bóya, was the son of Sultán Rukn-ud-daula. He was born in 952 A. D., 341 A. H., and succeeded his brother Mowaiyad-ud-daula to the throne of Persia in January, 984 A. D., Sha'bán, 373 A. H. He was a cruel prince, reigned 14 years, and died in August, 997 A. D., Sha'bán, 387 A. H. He was succeeded by his son Majd-ud-daula.

**Fakhr-ud-daula,** فخرالدولة, a nobleman who was governor of Patna in the reign of Muhammad Sháh emperor of Dehlí; he held that situation till the year 1735 A. D., 1148 A. H., when it was taken away from him and conferred upon Shujaa'-uddín Náwab of Bengal, in addition to that government, and of the province of Urissá.

**Fakhr-ul-Islam,** فخرالاسلام برودى, of Baród, the son of 'Alí. He is the author of the works called "Usúl-ud-dín" and "Usúl Fikha," and several other works. He died in 1089 A. D., 482 A. H.

**Fakhr-ullah Asad Jurjani,** فخرالله اسعد جرجاني. He flourished under the Saljúk princes, and is the author of the love adventures of Wais and king Rámín, originally in the Pahlawí language, called "Wais-wa-Ramín."

**Fakhr-un-nissa Begam,** فخرالنسا بيگم, the wife of Nawáb Shujá'at Khán. She is the founder of the mosque called "Fakhr-ul-Masájid," situated in the Kashmírí Bázár at Dehlí, which she erected in memory of her late husband in the year 1728 A. D., 1141 A. H.

**Falaki,** فلكي, takhallus of a Persian poet whose proper name was Abú'l Nizám Muhammad Jalal-uddín Shirwání. He is also commonly styled Shams-ush-Shuá'rá, the sun of the poets, and Málik-ul-Fuzla, king of the learned. His poems are preferred to those of Khákání, and Zakír. Hamd-ulláh Mustaufí calls him the master of Khákání, but Shaikh 'Azurí makes mention in his Jawáhir-ul-Asrár that Khákání and Falakí both were the pupils of Abú'l 'Alá of Ganja. There has been also another Falakí surnamed Abú'l Fazl, who was an author. Falakí died in 1181 A. D., 577 A. H. His patron was Manochehr Shirwání.

**Fanai,** فنائي, poetical name of Shams-uddín Muhammad-bin-Hamza. He was an author and died in the year 1430 A. D., 834 A. H.

**Fani,** فاني, (perishable) the poetical name of Muhsin Fání, which see.

**Fani,** فاني, the Takhullus of Khwája Muhammad Mo'ín-uddín-bin-Muhammad-bin-Mahmúd Dihdár Fání. He came to India and stood in high favor with Abdul Rahím Khán the Khán Khánán. He died in 1607 A. D., 1016 A. H., and left several works on Súfyism, as "Sharah Khutba," "Háshia Rashahát," "Háshia Nafhát," "Háshia bar-Gulshan Ráz," and "Albayán." He is also the author of a Díwán in Persian, and a Masnawí or poem called "Haft Dilbar," *i. e.*, the seven sweethearts, dedicated to the emperor Akbar.

**Farabi,** ابو نصر فارابي, commonly called so, because he was a native of Fáráb, a town in Turkey. His proper name is Abú Nasr. He was one of the greatest Musalmán philosophers, remarkable for his generosity and greatness of talents, whom we call Alfarabius. He was murdered by robbers in Syria in 954 A. D., 343 A. H., thirty years before the birth of Abú Sína. Imád-uddín Mahmúd and Ahmad-bin-Muhammad were two authors who were also called Fárábí.

**Faraburz,** فرابرز, the son of Kaikáús, (Darius the Mede) king of Persia.

**Faraghi (Mir),** مير فراغي, the brother of Hakím Fath-ulláh Shírází. He was living in 1563 A. D., 971 A. H., in which year the fort of Ranthanbúr was conquered by the emperor Akbar, on which occasion he wrote a chronogram.

**Farai,** فراء, whose proper name was Abú Zikaria Yehia, was an excellent Arabic grammarian who died in the year 822 A. D., 207 A. H.

**Faramurz,** فرامرز, son of Rustam, the Hercules of the Persians. He was assassinated by the order of Bahman, also called Ardisher Darazdast, king of Persia. There has also been one Muhammad bin-Farámurz, styled Shadíd, who was an author.

**Faraskuri,** فرسقوري, surname of Muhammad bin-Muhammad-al-Hanífa, Imám of the mosque named Gouride, at Grand Cairo, who flourished about the year 1556 A. D., 964 A. H., and was an author.

**Fard,** فرد, poetical name of Abú'l Hasan, the son of Sháh Na'mat-ulláh. He died in the year 1848 A. D., 1265 A. H., and left a Díwán.

**Farghani,** فرغاني, commonly called so because he was a native of Farghána, but his full name is Ahmad or Muhammad-ibn-Kasír-al-Farghání, a famous Arabian astronomer whom we know under the name of Alfragan or Alfraganius. He flourished in the time of the khalíf Al-Mámún, about the year 833 A. D., 218 A. H., and is the author of an introduction to Astronomy, which was printed by Golius, at Amsterdam, in 1669, with notes.

**Farhad,** فرهاد, the lover of the celebrated Shírín, the wife of Khusro Parwez, king of Persia. The whole of the sculpture at Bístún in Persia is ascribed to the chisel of Farhád. He was promised, we are told in Persian Romance, that if he cut through the rock, and brought a stream that flowed on the other side of the hill to the valley, the lovely Shírín (with whom he had fallen distractedly in love) should be his reward; he was on the point of completing his labour, when Khusro Parwez fearing to lose his mistress, sent an old woman to inform Farhád, that the fair object of his desire was dead. He was at work on one of the highest parts of the rock when he heard the mournful intelligence. He immediately cast himself headlong, and was dashed in pieces. *Vide* Shírín.

**Farhat,** فرحت, poetical name of Shaikh Farhat-ulláh, son of Shaikh Asad-ulláh. He wrote a Díwán in Urdú and died in the year 1777 A. D., 1191 A. H., at Murshidábád.

**Farhat Kashmiri,** فرحت کشمیری, a poet who was living in 1724 A. D., 1136 A. H.

**Farid Bukhari (Shaikh),** شیخ فرید بخاری, commander of the Agra city guards when Akbar died. Great honors were conferred on him by the emperor Jahángír. on account of his services. He received the title of Murtaza Khán, and managed the affairs of the empire till he was rendered unfit for business, by a stroke of the palsy, which opened the way for the promotion of Ya'timad-uddaula the father of the empress Núr Jahán. He died 1616 A. D., 1025 A. H.

**Farid Katib,** فرید کاتب, *vide* Faríd-uddín Kátib.

**Farid** or **Farid-uddin Ahwal,** فرید الدین احول, (the squinting) a poet of Persia who was a native of Asfaráen in Khurásán and co-temporary with Imámí Hirwí. Khwája Nizám-uddín Abú Bakr the Wazír of Azd-uddín Sa'd was his patron. He died at Isfahán and left a Díwán containing 5,000 verses.

**Farid** or **Farid-uddin (Shaikh),** فریدالدین شکر گنج فرید شیخ, a celebrated Muhammadan saint, who is styled "Shakar Ganj," on account of his having, it is said, miraculously transmuted dust or salt into sugar. His father's name was Shaikh Jalál-uddín Sulaimán, a descendant of Farrukh Sháh of Kábul. He was a disciple of Khwája Kutb-uddín Bakhtyár Kákí, and was contemporary with Shaikh Sa'd-uddín Hamwia, Saif-uddín Mákharzí, and Bahá-uddín Zikaria, all of whom died successively a short time after one another. He was born in 1173 A. D., 569 A. H., died on Saturday the 17th October, 1265 A. D., 5th Muharram, 664 A. H., aged 95 lunar years, and is buried at Ajúdhan, a place commonly called Patan or Pák Patan in Multán. The anniversary of his death is celebrated every year on the 5th of Muharram, when a great crowd of Muhammadans assemble together to pray at his tomb.

**Farid-uddin,** فریدالدین کاتب, commonly called Faríd Kátib, was a pupil of Anwarí, a good poet and secretary to Sùltán Sanjar. When that prince was defeated by the monarch of Kara Khatái in 1140 A. D., 535 A. H., and fled with a few followers to Khurásán, Faríd consoled him by composing an ode upon the occasion, in which he says, "that every thing must change, but that the condition of God alone was not liable to change."

**Farid-uddin Attar (Shaikh),** شیخ فریدالدین عطار, surnamed Muhammad Ibráhím, was a dealer in perfumes, from which he took his poetical name "'Attar." He afterwards retired from the world, became a disciple of Shaikh Majd-uddín Baghdádí, and lived to a great age, namely, that of 114 lunar years. He was born at Shádyákh, a village in Naishápúr in the reign of Sultán Sanjar in November, 1119 A. D., Sha'ban, 513 A. H., and, when at the siege of Naishápúr, the son-in-law of Changez Khán, the Tartar, was killed, a general massacre of the inhabitants of that place was made by the Mughals, among the number that were slain, Faríd-uddín was one. This circumstance took place on the 26th April, 1230 A. D., 10th Jamad II, 627 A. H. He is the author of 40 poems and several prose works, amongst the latter "Tazkirat-ul-Aulia."

*The following are his poems.*

| | |
|---|---|
| Asrár Náma. | Iláhí Náma. |
| Ashtur Náma. | Khayát Náma. |
| Ausat Náma. | Kanz-ul-Hakaek. |
| Besar Náma. | Lisán-ul-Ghaib. |
| Bulbul Náma. | Mansúr Náma. |
| Gul-wa-Khusro or Hurmuz. | Miftáh-ul-Fatúh. |
| Haidar Náma. | Mazhar-ul-'Ajáeb. |
| Haft Wádí. | Pand Náma. |
| Hakáek-ul-Jawáhir. | Musíbat Náma. |
| Halláj Náma. | Wald Náma. |
| Jawáhir-ul-zát. | Wasiat Náma. |
| Khusro Náma. | Mantik-ul-Tair. |
| Kanzan Makhfia. | Mukhtár Náma. |
| Kunt Kauz Makháfia. | Sipáh Náma. |

Besides the above, he is also the author of a Díwán containing 40,000 verses.

**Faridun,** فریدون, an ancient king of Persia, the son of Abtín, an immediate descendant of Tahmurs, king of Persia. He had escaped, it is said in a miraculous manner, from Zohák, when that prince had seized and murdered his father. At the age of 16 he joined Káwa or Gáwa, a blacksmith, who had collected a large body of his countrymen: these fought with enthusiasm under the standard of the blacksmith's apron, which was afterwards converted into the royal standard of Persia, called the Durafsh Káwání. Zohák, after numerous defeats, was made prisoner, and put to a slow and painful death. Faridún, who was a very just and virtuous king, had three sons, *viz.:* Salm, Túr, and Erij. among whom he divided his kingdom; but the two elder, displeased that Persia, the fairest of lands and the seat of royalty, should have been given to Erij their junior, combined to effect his ruin, and at last slew him, and sent his head to Faridún. The old man fainted at the sight, and when he recovered, he called upon Heaven to punish the base perpetrators of so unnatural and cruel a deed. The daughter of Erij was married to the nephew of Faridún, and their young son Manúchehr proved the image of his grandfather. When he attained manhood, the old king made every preparation to enable him to revenge the blood of Erij. A war commenced; and in the first battle Salm and Túr were both slain. Fareidún soon afterwards died, and was succeeded by Manúchehr. Persian authors assure us that Fareidún reigned 500 years.

**Faridun,** فریدون, a Turk who wrote a Commentary in the Turkish language on the Ghazals of Hafiz.

**Farigh,** فارغ, author of the poem called "Masnawí Fárigh," which he composed in 1592 A. D., 1000 A. H., in which year, he says, Sháh 'Abbás conquered Gílán, and to whom it was dedicated.

**Faris Ecchidiak,** فارس, (from Chambers' Encyclopædia) an Arab poet and litterateur, born about the year 1796 A. D. In religion he was a Syrian Christian. He is the author of several works. When in London, he published his revised text of the New Testament in Arabic. His Díwán in Arabic is highly spoken of by those who have seen it. He was living in 1860.

**Fariz,** فارض, or Ibn Fáriz, surname of Abú Hafs Sharaf-uddín Umar bin-al-Asa'dí, bin-al-Murshid, bin-Ahmad al-Asa'dí, a very illustrious Arabian poet. He was born at Cairo 1181 A. D., 577 A. H., and died there in the year 1234 A. D., 632 A. H.

**Farkhari,** فرخاري, a poet who was in the service of Amír Kaikáús, and is the author of the story of "Wámiḳ-wa-Uzra," in verse.

**Farkhunda Ali Khan (Mir),** مير فرخنده على خان, Nizám of Dakhan. He succeeded his father Sikandar Jáh in the government of Haidarabád in 1829 A. D. *Vide* Afzal-uddaula.

**Faroghi Kashmiri,** فروغي كشميرى, a poet who died in 1666 A. D., 1077 A. H.

**Faroghi (Maulana),** مولانا فروغي, of Ḳazwín in Isfahán; he was a dealer in perfumes, but an excellent poet, and lived in the time of 'Abbás the Great.

**Farrukhi,** فرخي, or Farkhí, a poet who flourished in the time of Sulṭán Mahmúd of Ghazní, was a pupil of Unsarí the poet, and a descendant of the royal race of the kings of Sístán. He is the author of a work called "Tarjumán ul-Balághat" and of a Díwán in Persian. He wrote several panegyrics in praise of Abú'l Muzaffar, the son of Amír Nasr and grandson of Násir-uddín, ruler of Balkh.

**Farrukh Fa'l,** فرخ فال, a son of the emperor Humáyún by Máh Chúchak Begam, born at Kábul in 1555 A. D., 962 A. H.

**Farrukh-siyar (Muhammad),** محمد فرخ سير, emperor of Dehlí, born on the 18th July, 1687, O. S., 18th Ramazán, 1098 A. H., was the son of Azím-ush-Shán, the second son of Bahádur Sháh I, and great-grandson of the emperor Alamgír. His father was killed in the battle fought against Jahándár Sháh his uncle and predecessor. One of Jahándár Sháh's first acts on his accession to the throne had been to put all the princes of the blood within his reach, to death: among those whom he could not get into his power, was Farrukh-siyar, who was in Bengal at the time of his grandfather Bahádur Sháh's death. But when the information of his father's death reached him, he threw himself on the compassion and fidelity of Saiyad Husain Alí Khán, the governor of Behár, who warmly espoused his cause, and prevailed on his brother, Saiyad Abdullah Khán, governor of Allahábád, to adopt the same course. By the aid of these noblemen, Farrukh-siyar assembled an army at Allahábád, marched towards Agra, defeated Jahándár Sháh, took him prisoner, and having murdered him, he ascended the throne in the fort of Dehlí on Friday the 9th of January, 1713, O. S., 23rd Ẕil-ḥijja, 1124 A. H. The former Amír-ul-Umrá Zulfiḳár Khán and many other nobles and dependants of the late emperor were put to death by the bow-string and other punishments. Rájá Subhchand, Díwán to the late Amír-ul-Umrá, had his tongue cut out: Azíz-uddín, son of Jahándár Sháh, 'Alí Tabár, the son of 'Azim Sháh, and Humáyún Bakht, younger brother to Farrukh-siyar were deprived of their sight by a red hot iron drawn over their eyes. On Farrukh-siyar's accession, Abdulláh Khán, the eldest brother, was made Wazír with the title of Ḳutb-ul-Mulk, and Husain Alí Khán raised to the rank of Amír-ul-Umrá (Commander-in-Chief) which was the second in the State. His nuptials with the daughter of Rájá Ajít Singh of Márwár, were celebrated with unprecedented splendour in the year 1716 A. D., 1128 A. H. Farrukh-siyar had not long enjoyed the throne, when a jealousy arose between him and the Wazír Ḳutb-ul-Mulk. And on the emperor's trying to form schemes for the recovery of his independence, he was deposed, blinded and imprisoned by the two brothers. This event took place on the 18th February, 1719, O. S., 8th Rabí' II, 1131 A. H., and not long after he was murdered on the 16th May, A. D., 9th Rajab, 1131 A. H., following, and buried in the court of the mausoleum of the emperor Humáyún at Dehlí. He reigned 6 years 3 months and 15 days. After his deposal the Saiyads set up a prince of the blood to whom they gave the title of Rafí-ud-Darját. It was from Farrukh-siyar that the East India Company obtained their Farmán of free trade, with leave to purchase thirty-seven districts in Bengal, besides various privileges, but little attention was however paid to it by the Súbas, till the English acquired force to give it weight.

**Farrukhzad,** فرخزاد, a prince of Persia of the Sásánian race. *Vide* Túran Dukht.

**Farrukhzad,** فرخزاد, son of Sulṭán Masa'úd I, of Ghazni, began to reign after the death of his brother Sulṭán Abdul Rashíd in March 1053, A. D., 444 A. H. He reigned 6 years and died in the latter part of the year 1058 A. D., when his brother Sulṭán Ibrahím succeeded him.

**Farsi,** فرسي يا فارسي or Farasí, surname of Abú'l Fawáris Ibrahím, a Persian author.

**Farsi,** فرسي, poetical name of Sharíf Khán Amír-ul-Umrá, which see.

**Faryabi,** *vide* Zahír-uddín Fáryábí.

**Faryad,** فرياد, the poetical name of Lálá Sáhib Ráe, a Káyeth of Lákhnau. He originally had assumed Ḳurbán for his poetical name, but latterly changed it to Faryád. He was living in 1782 A. D., 1196 A. H.

**Farzada Kuli,** فرزدا قلي, author of a Catalogue of books in the Arabic, Persian, and Hindí languages, amounting, on a rough estimate, to upwards of 2,000 volumes. From its mentioning the Díwán of Sauda, it appears that it was written within the last fifty or sixty years. It also mentions the "Mustafá Náma," in the metre of the Sháh Náma, embracing the history of Persia from Muhammad to Tahmasp Sháh Safwí, amounting to 104,000 couplets; also of a Persian translation of the Muḳámát of Harízí. Journal of the Royal Asiatic Society, No. 11.

**Farzadak,** فرزدق, the son of Ghálib, called the master of Arabian poets, was an author, and had the whole Ḳurán by heart. He died in 728 A. D., 110 A. H., aged upwards of 70 years. He flourished in the reign of Abdul Málik, the son of Marwan I, who imprisoned him because he wrote a panegyric in praise of Imám 'Alí Zain-ul-'Abidín, son of Imám Husain, but was released, after the death of the khalíf, by his son Walíd. His Díwán in Arabic is much esteemed in Hujáz and Iráḳ.

**Fasihi Ansari,** فصيحي انصاري هروي of Hirat, a Persian poet, who flourished about the year 1595 A. D., 1004 A. H. He never came to India. He died in 1636 A. D., 1046 A. H.

**Fasih-uddin Muhammad Nizami Maulana,** مولانا فصيح الدين محمد نظامي, author of the "Sharah Jughmíní."

**Fassi,** فسي, surname of Faḳíh-uddín Muhammad-ibn-Ahmad 'Alí-al-Husainí; he was a native of Fass (Fez) on which account he was called Fassí. He was an author and Ḳází of the city of Mecca, and died 1429 A. D., 833 A. H.

**Fatha Ali Husaini,** فتح علي حسيني, author of the biography called "Tazkirat-ush-Shua'ráe Hindí." It contains the Memoirs of 108 Hindí and Dakhaní authors, with numerous extracts from their works.

**Fatha 'Ali Shah,** فتح علي شاه, king of Persia, was an Afghán of the tribe of Káchár. He succeeded his uncle 'Aká Muhammad Khán to the throne of Persia in 1797 A. D., 1212 A. H. He had received an excellent education, and possessed some literary accomplishments; was a tolerable poet, and fond of the society of the learned, whom he generously patronized. He reigned nearly 40 years and died in the year 1834 A. D., 1250 A. H. After him Muhammad Sháh, the son of 'Abbás Mirzá, and grandson of Fatha 'Alí Sháh, mounted the throne and died in 1847 A. D., when his son Nasír-uddín Ahmad Sháh, the present king, succeeded him. It was to the court of Fatha 'Alí Sháh that Sir John Malcolm in 1800 led the magnificent embassy which Lord Wellesly had despatched from Calcutta, with the view of trumping Bonaparte's cards in the East, and of playing off a Persian ally on our Indian frontiers against an Afghán ill-wisher, the ambitious Zamán Sháh.

**Fatha Haidar,** فتح حيدر, the eldest son of Tippú Sulṭán.

**Fatha-puri Mahal,** فتح پوری محل, or Begam, one of the wives of the emperor Sháh Jahán. She was the founder of the Fathapúrí Masjid in Dehlí.

**Fathi,** فتحي, a poet of Ardastán, who died in 1635 A. D., 1045 A. H.

**Fatha Khan,** فتح خان, the son of Sulṭán Fíroz Sháh Bárbak, king of Dehli, and brother of Zafar Khán. *Vide* Fíroz Sháh Bárbak.

**Fatha Khan,** فتح خان, Nawáb of Bháwalpúr.

**Fatha Khan,** فتح خان, brother of Dost Muhammad Khán, ruler of Kábul. The celebrated Wazír of Mahmúd, ruler of Hirat, and chief of the Barakzaí clan, whose family drove away the descendants of Ahmad Sháh Abdálí from Kábul.

**Fatha Khan,** فتح خان, the son of Malik 'Ambar, the Abyssinian chief of Ahmadnagar in the Dakhan, who had the Nizám Sháhí dominions under his control for some years. After his father's death in 1626 A. D., 1035 A. H., he succeeded to his authority; but Murtaza Nizám Sháh II, being weary of his control, took him prisoner by treachery, and confined him in the fort of Khybar. Having made his escape, he rebelled, but was again taken, and confined in Daulatábád. He was released in time, and appointed generalissimo by the influence of his sister, mother to Nizám Sháh. He shortly, to prevent another removal from office, confined the Sultán under pretence of insanity, and put to death twenty-five of the principal nobility in one day, writing to the emperor Sháh Jahán, that he had thus acted, to prevent them from rebelling against him. The emperor in reply commended his attachment, and ordered him to put the captive prince to death, which he did about the year 1628 A. D., 1038 A. H., and placed his son Husain, an infant of ten years, on the throne. Fatha Khán, by offering a present of eight lacs of rupees, and agreeing to pay tribute, was allowed to keep what territory yet remained to the Nizám Sháhí sovereignty. In the year 1634 A. D., 1044 A. H., Fatha Khán was forced to surrender; and the fall of this place put a final period to the Nizám Shahí dynasty, which had swayed the sceptre for 150 years. Husain Nizám Sháh was confined for life in the fortress of Gwáliar, but Fatha Khán was received into favour, and was allowed to retire to Láhor on a pension of two lacs of rupees, which he enjoyed till his death.

**Fatha Naek,** فتح نایک, the father of Haidar 'Alí Khán, the usurper of Mysore and Seringapatam. He died in 1738 A. D., and was buried at Kolár, a capital of seven parganas, about 35 miles east of Bangalore.

**Fatha Shah,** فتح شاه پوربي Púrbí, succeeded Yúsaf Sháh to the throne of Bengál in 1482 A. D., 887 A. H., and after a reign of about eight years was murdered in 1491 A. D., 896 A. H., by the eunuch Sulṭán Sháhzáda, who succeeded him.

**Fatha-ullah Imad Shah,** فتح الله عماد شاه, originally in the service of Sulṭán Mahmúd Sháh II, Bahmaní, king of Dakhan, was made governor of Berar. He became independent about the year 1484 A. D., and died about the year 1513. His son 'Alá-uddín 'Imád Sháh succeeded him. *Vide* 'Imad-ul-Mulk.

**Fatha-ullah, Mustaufi,** فتح الله مستوفي, surnamed Fakhr-uddín, was a good poet and served under Khwája Rashíd-uddín, Fazl-ulláh and his son Ghayás-uddin Muhammad, as secretary. He is the brother of Khwája Hamd-ullah Mustaufí, who died in 1349 A. D.

**Fatha-ullah Shirazi Amir,** امير فتح الله شيرازی, one of the most learned men of his time. He came from Shíráz to Dakhan and passed a few years in the service of Sulṭán Alí Adil Sháh of Bíjapúr. After the death of that king, he left Dakhan and came to Dehlí in the year 1582 A. D., 990 A. H., and had an honorable office assigned to him by the emperor Akbar, near his person, with the title of Azd-ud-daula. He died on Wednesday, the 3rd Shawwál 997 Hijri, the 24th Amardád Mah Iláhí, in the 34th year of Akbar's reign, corresponding with the 6th of August, 1589 O. S., at Sirínagar the capital of Kashmir, where he had proceeded with his royal master. The king was much grieved at his loss; and Sheikh Faizí wrote an appropriate epitaph on the occasion. Fifteen days after his death died also the Hakím Abú'l Fatha Gilání, the brother of Hakím Hamám, who was then with the king proceeding to Kábul. Sarfí Sáwají wrote the chronogram of their death.

**Fatima,** فاطمة, the daughter of Muhammad and his wife Khudija. She was born at Mecca five years before her father gave himself out for a prophet, *i. e.*, about the year 606 A. D., and died about six months after him in the city of Medina on the night of Monday, the 23rd of November, 632 A. D., 3rd Ramazán, 11 A. H. She was married to Alí, Muhammad's cousin-german, and became the mother of the Imams Hasan and Husain. She passes for a very holy woman amongst the Musalmáns, and is also called by them Batúl, Táhira, Mathara, and Zahra.

**Fatima bint Asad,** فاطمة بنت اسد, the daughter of Asad, the son of Háshim. She was the wife of Abú Tálib and mother of 'Alí.

**Fatima Sultan,** فاطمة سلطان, one of the wives of Umar Sheikh Mirzá, and mother of the prince Pír Muhammad Jahángír.

**Fatimites,** or kings of Barbary and Egypt of the Fatimite dynasty, *vide* Muizz-li-dín-allah, and Obeid-ullah Almahdí.

**Fattahi Naishapuri Moulana,** مولانا فتاحي نيشاپوری, an author, who died 1448 A. D., 852 A. H., *vide* Yahia (Mulla).

**Fawad Muhammad Pasha,** فواد محمد پاشا, a Turkish statesman and litterateur of Constantinople, son of Izzat Mulla, and nephew of Laila Khatún, a Turkish poetess. He is the author of several works. He was living in 1870 A. D., and has been loaded with distinctions by European sovereigns.

**Fayyaz,** فياض, *vide* 'Abdul-Razzaḳ of Láhiján.

**Fayyazi,** فيضي, *vide* Faizí (Shaikh).

**Fazal Khan,** فضل خان, governor or kiladar of the fort of Agra, was turned out by Súrajmal Ját, who took possession of the fort and plundered every thing he could lay his hands upon.

**Fazil,** فاضل, a poet who flourished about the year 489 A. D.

**Fazl Ali Khan,** فضل علي خان, a poet who flourished in the time of the emperor Muhammad Sháh of Dehlí, and was living in 1739 A. D., 1152 A. H.

**Fazl Ali Khan,** فضل علي خان, whose entire title was "Nawáb Ya'timad-ud-doula Zayá-ul-Mulk Saiyad Fazl 'Alí Khán Bahádur Sohráb Jang," was the prime minister of the king of Audh Ghází-ud-dín Haidar, and was living in 1829 A. D.

**Fazl Barmaki,** فضل برمكي, brother of 'Jafar-al-Barmaki, the minister of Hárún-al-Rashíd Khalífa of Baghdád. *Vide* Jafar-al-Barmakí.

**Fazli,** فضلي, a poet and author of the Loves of "Sháh-wa-Máh" a poem containing 12,260 Persian verses which he completed in the year 1641 A. D.

**Fazl Hak,** فضل حق, the son of Fazl Imám. He also wrote prose and poetry as well as his father. His Ķasídas are much esteemed. At the outbreak of 1857, he joined the rebel Nawáb of Banda and others, and was at last killed at Narod in an attack made by General Napier on the 17th December, 1858 A. D., 1274 A. H. The "Dehlí Gazette" of May 17th, 1859 mentions, that sentence of transportation was passed on the rebels Loní Sangh, Ex-rájá of Mitaulí, and the Maulwí Fazl Haķ,

**Fazl Imam,** فضل امام, an inhabitant of Khairábád, who wrote prose and poetry, and died in the year 1828 A. D., 1244 A. H.

**Fazl Rasul Moulvi,** مولوى فضل رسول بداوني, of Badáon, son of Maulví Abdul Majíd, and author of the works called "Bawáriķ," and "Tashíh-ul-Masáel." He was living in 1854 A. D., 1271 A. H.

**Fazl-ullah,** فضل الله, surnamed Khwája Rashíd-uddín, a native of Ķazwín or Hamdan and a Persian historian who wrote at the desire of his master the Sulţán of Persia a history of the Mughals, finished in 1294 A. D., to which he afterwards added a supplement. He was beheaded in July 1318, A. D. His name is spelt in some of our Biographical Dictionaries, Fadl-allah. From the work of Rashíd-uddín, called Jáma'-ut-Tawáríkh, and from other materials, Abú'l Ghází, king of Khwárizm, composed in the Mughal language, his Genealogical History. *Vide* Rashid-uddín.

**Fazl-ullah Moulana,** مولانا فضل الله, Physician to Amír Taimúr, and the most celebrated and skilful practitioner of the age in which he lived.

**Fazl-ullah Khan Nawab,** فضل الله خان, an Amír of the court of the emperor Babar, who built a mosque in Dehlí in the year 1529 A. D., 936 A. H., which is still standing.

**Fazuli Baghdadi,** فضولي بغدادى, an author who was a native of Baghdád, and died in the year 1562 A. D., 970 A. H., and left us a Díwán in the Persian and Turkish language.

**Fidai Khan,** فدائي خان, former title of 'Azim Khán Kóka, which see.

**Fidai Mirza,** مرزا فدائي, name of a poet.

**Fidwi,** فدوي, of Láhor, the poetical name of a person, who was cotemporary with Mirzá Rafí-us-Saudá. He is the author of a poem in Urdú entitled "Yúsaf-wa-Zaleikhá," (the Loves of Joseph and Potiphar's wife). Mír Fatha Alí Shaidá has satirized him in his story of the "Búm and Baķķál."

**Fidwi,** فدوي, author of a Persian Díwán. He flourished, or was living in the year 1649 A. D., 1059 A. H.

**Fighan,** فغان, the poetical title of Ashraf 'Alí Khán, the son of Mirzá 'Ali Khán, and the Kóka or foster-brother of the emperor Ahmad Sháh of Dehlí. He is the author of a Díwán in the Urdú language, containing about 2,000 verses. He died at Patna in 1772 A. D., 1186 A. H., and was buried there.

**Fighani,** فغاني, *vide* Bábá Fighání.

**Fikrat,** فكرت, poetical title of Mirzá Ghaiás-uddin.

**Fikri,** فكري, poetical title of Sa'íd Muhammad of Hirát. He was a weaver and is therefore called Jámabáf. He came to India in 1561 A. D., 969 A. H., and gained through his great talents for making epigrams, the favor of the emperor Akbar. He composed only Rubạ'ís, and died in 1565 A. D., 973 A. H.

**Firaki,** فراقي, poetical title of an author named Abú'l Barkát, who died in the year 1507 A. D., 913 A. H.

**Firdausi** or **Firdausi Tusi,** فردوسي يا فردوسي طوسي, the poetical title of Abú'l Kásim Hasan-bin-Sharaf Sháh, a famous Persian poet, styled by us the Homer of Persia, whose epic poem, called Sháhnáma, written by order of Sultán Mahmúd of Ghazní, is much celebrated. It contains the annals of the ancient kings of Persia, from the reign of the first king, Kaiamurs, to the death of Yezdijard III, the last monarch of the Sásánian race, who was deprived of his kingdom 641 A. D., by the invasion of the Arabs during the Khiláfat of 'Umar, the second Khalif after Muhammad. It is the labour of 30 years, and consists of 60,000 verses, each of which is a distich. The following circumstances respecting the origin of the poem and the life of the poet, are chiefly derived from the preface to the copy of the Sháhnáma, which was collated 1426 A. D., 829 A. H., by order of Báisanghur Mirzá the grandson of Amír Taimúr. It appears from that preface, that Yezdijard, the last king of the Sásánian race, took considerable pains in collecting all the chronicles, histories, and traditions connected with Persia and the sovereigns of that country, from the time of 'Kaiomurs to the accession of the Khusros, which by his direction were digested and brought into one view, and formed the book known by the name of "Siar-ul-Maluk," or the Bástán Náma. When the followers of Muhammad overturned the Persian monarchy, this work was found in the plundered library of Yazdijard. In the tenth century one of the kings of the Sásánian dynasty, directed Daķíķí the poet to verify that extensive work, but the poet only lived to finish a thousand distichs, having been assassinated by his own slave. Nothing further was done till the reign of Sulţán Mahmúd, when a romantic accident furnished the Sulţán with a copy of the Bástán Náma, the existence of which was till then unknown to him. From this work, he selected seven stories which he delivered to seven poets to be composed in verse, that he might be able to ascertain the merits of each competitor. The poet Unsarí gained the palm, and he was accordingly engaged to arrange the whole in verse. Firdausí was at this time at Tus, his native city, where he cultivated his poetical talents with assiduity and success. He had heard of the attempt of Daķíķí, and of the determination of the reigning king Mahmúd, to patronize an undertaking which promised to add lustre to the age in which he lived. Having fortunately succeeded in procuring a copy of the Bástán Náma, he pursued his studies with unremitting zeal, and soon produced that part of the poem in which the battles of Zuháḳ and Fareidún are described. The performance was universally read and admired, and it was not long before his fame reached the ears of the Sulṭán, who immediately invited him to his court. It is related that when Firdausí, on the invitation of the Sulṭán, reached the capital of Ghazní, he happened to pass a public garden where the three royal poets, Unsarí, Asjadí and Farrukhí were enjoying themselves. The poets observed him approach and at once agreed that if the stranger chanced to have any taste for poetry, which they intended to put to test, he should be admitted to their friendship, and in order to decide as to his merits they settled among themselves to repeat each in his turn a hemistich, and leave to Firdausi to complete the fourth, but at the same time satisfied in their own minds, that there was no other word in the Persian language that would rhyme with the three, which they had taken care to pre-occupy. Firdausí joining them and hearing the proposal, promised to exert his powers. They then commenced each with an extemporaneous hemistich:

Unsarí...... The light of the moon to thy splendour is weak,

Asjadí...... The rose is eclipsed by the bloom of thy cheek;

Farrukhí.... Thy eye-lashes dart through the folds of the Joshan,

Firdausí .... Like the javelin of Geo in the battle with Pushan.

The poets were astonished at the readiness of the stranger, and ashamed at being totally ignorant of the story of Geo and Pushan, which Firdausí related as described in the Bástán Náma. They immediately treated him with the greatest kindness and respect, and afterwards introduced him to Mahmúd, as a poet capable of undertaking the Sháhnáma. Mahmúd considered himself never so much honored as when Firdausí set his foot at Ghazní; he was never more proud, than that Firdausí was by his command, composing, in his faultless verse, a history of the monarchs of Persia, his predecessors. No reward then appeared to him too great to offer, to induce the poet to undertake the task, no promises too splendid to excite him. "Write, unequalled one," cried he, "and for every thousand couplets a thousand pieces of gold shall be thine." Firdausí obeyed, but resolved to accept no reward till he had completed the work he had undertaken, and for thirty years he studied and laboured that his poem might be worthy of eternal fame. In this he succeeded, and presented an elegant copy of his book to Mahmúd, but the patience of the Sulṭán was exhausted, his enthusiasm was gone, his liberality had faded away, and when the 60,000 couplets of the Sháhnáma was ended, there was a pause, which brought to the poet disappointment and to the monarch such everlasting disgrace as has obliterated all his triumphs. Mahmúd received the book, coldly applauded his diligence and dismissed him. Many months elapsed, and Firdausí heard no more of his work: he then took occasion to remind the king of it by the following epigram:

'Tis said our monarch's liberal mind,
Is like the ocean unconfined,
Happy are they who prove it so,
'Tis not for me that truth to know.
I've plunged within its waves, 'tis true,
But not a single pearl could view.

Shamed, picqued, and offended at this freedom, the Sulṭán ordered 60,000 pieces of silver dirhams to be sent to the author, instead of the gold which he had promised. Firdausí was in the bath at the time the money arrived, and his rage and amazement exceeded all bounds when he found himself thus insulted. He immediately distributed the paltry sum amongst the attendants of the bath and the slave who brought it. The excited poet then relieved his mind by a satire full of stinging invective, and caused it to be transmitted to the favorite Wazír who had instigated the Sulṭán against him; it was carefully sealed up, with directions that it should be read to Mahmúd on some occasion when his mind was perturbed with affairs of State, as it was a poem likely to afford him entertainment. Firdausí having thus prepared his vengeance, quitted the court and was safely arrived in Mázandarán where news reached him that his lines had fully answered the purpose he had intended they should do. Mahmúd had heard and trembled, and too late discovered that he had ruined his own reputation for ever. After his satire had been read by Mahmúd, the poet feared to remain too long in one place: he sought shelter in the court of the Khalíf of Baghdád, in whose honor he added a 1000 couplets to the Sháhnáma, and who rewarded him with 60,000 gold dinars which had been withheld by Mahmúd. Mahmúd pretended to have discovered that his Wazír had deceived him in attributing impiety to Firdausí, and he at once sacrificed that favorite, dismissing him with disgrace. Thinking, by a tardy act of liberality, to repair his former meanness, Mahmúd dispatched to Firdausí the 60,000 pieces he had promised, a robe of State, and many apologies and expressions of friendship; but the poet was dead, having expired in his native town full of years and honours, surrounded by his friends and kindred. Firdausí died at Tús (now called Mashhad) his native country in 1020 A. D., 411 A. H., aged 89 years; but Hají Khalfa says, he died in 1025 A. D., 416 A. H. Besides the Sháhnáma, he is the author of other poems called "Abiát Firdausí."

**Firdausi-al-Thauil,** فردوسي التهيهل, a Turkish historian, and author of the Turkish work called "Sháhnáma" which comprises the history of all the ancient kings of the East. Bayazíd or Bajazet II, to whom the book was dedicated, ordered the author to reduce it from its original bulk of 300 volumes to 80. Firdausí, however, felt so mortified at this proposal, that he preferred leaving the country altogether, and emigrated to Khurásán, in Persia. Firdausí flourished in 1500 A. D.

**Firishta,** فرشته, whose proper name is Muhammad Ḳásim, and who is the author of the history called "Táríkh Firishta," was born at Astrabád on the borders of the Caspian Sea, about the year 1570 or 1550 A. D., 978 or 958 A. H. His father, a learned man, by name Ghulám 'Alí Hindú Sháh, left his native country when our author was very young and travelled into India. He eventually reached Ahmadnagar in the Dakhan during the reign of Murtazá Nizám Sháh I, and was appointed by the Sulṭán to instruct his son Mírán Husain, in the Persian language, but he soon died after his selection, and Firishta was left an orphan in early youth. After the death of Murtazá Nizám Sháh in 1589 A. D., 996 A. H., he proceeded to Bijápúr, and was presented by Diláwar Khán, minister to Ibráhím 'Adil Sháh II, by whose request he wrote the history which goes by his name, in the year 1023 Hijrí (1614 A. D.) The year of his death is altogether unknown. Briggs supposes that it occurred in 1612 A. D., 1021 A. H., making him only 41 years of age. M. J. Mohl supposes him to have revised his work up to at least 1623 A. D., 1033 A. H., making his age not less than 73, as he supposes him to have been born in 1550 A. D. Firishta styles his work, "Gulshan-i-Ibráhímí," and "Nauras Náma." Its former name is derived from the king to whom it was dedicated; and hence it is frequently quoted under the name of "Táríkh Ibráhímí." The latter name was given to it in commemoration of the new capital, Nauras, which his patron Ibráhím 'Adil Sháh, commenced building in the year 1599 A. D. The first and second books, giving an account of the Dehlí emperors down to Akbar, were translated into English by Colonel Dow in 1768. The history of the Dakhan by Captain Jonathan Scott. But the translation of the entire work by General Briggs in four volumes 8vo., 1829, has (according to Elliot) thrown others into the shade, and is by far the most valuable store-house of facts connected with Muhammadan dynasties of India.—[*v.* Dowson's *Elliot*, VI, 207.]

**Firoz,** فيروز, a celebrated Súfí of Agra, author of a Persian work on Theology called "'Aḳáed Súfia," written in 1626 A. D., 1036 A. H.

**Firoz I,** فيروز, (the Peroses of the Greeks), a king of Persia of the Sásánian race, was the eldest son of Yezdijard II. He succeeded his younger brother Hurmuz, whom he dethroned and put to death in 458 A. D. He lost his life in a battle against the king of Transoxiana, after a reign of 26 years, in 484 A. D. Balás or Palas or Balasus, his son, succeeded him; and after his death his brother Ḳubád mounted the throne.

**Firozabadi,** فيروز ابادى, surname of Majd-uddín Muhammad-bin-'Yaḳúb bin-Muhammad, a learned Persian, so called from his birth-place Fírozábád, a village in Shíráz. The stupendous work called Ḳámús or "Ḳámús-ul-Lughát," renowned as the most perfect Arabic Dictionary, was written by him. Those who are acquainted with the peculiarities of the Arabic language cannot open this work without feeling amazed at the literary wonders wrought by this learned man. He died 1414 A. D., 817 A. H. *Vide* Majd-uddín Muhammad-bin-'Yaḳúb.

**Firozabadi,** فيروز ابادي, a learned Musalmán, author of "Al Tanbidh," or Tanbiz, or general information on the Muhammadan law in the 11th century. Lempriere's Universal Dictionary. Majd-uddín Muhammad-bin-'Ya'ḳúb, author of the Ḳámús, is also called Fírozábádí.

**Firoz Mulla,** ملا فيروز بن كاؤس, son of Káús, chief priest of the Pársí Kadímís of Bombay, author of the "George Náma," a history of India from its discovery by the Portuguese to the conquest of Púna by the English in 1817 A. D., 1233 A. H.

**Firoz Jang Khan,** فيروز جنگ خان, the inscription on the gate of the old fort of Patna, dated in the Hijra year 1042, attributes its erection to Fíroz Jang Khan.

**Firoz Khan Khwaja Sara** فيروزخان خواجه سراء, who held the rank of 300 in the time of Shahjahan.

**Firoz Shah,** فيروز شاه, the son of Salím Sháh, was raised to the throne of Dehlí at Gwáliar after the death of his father when he was only about 12 years old. He had scarcely reigned three months (or only 3 days) when his mother's brother Mubárík Khán murdered him on the 2nd May, 1554, A. D., 29th Jumáda I. 961 A. H., and ascended the throne with the title of Muhammad Sháh 'Adil. See Bíbí Báí.

**Firoz Shah Bahmani Sultan,** سلطان فيروز شاه بهمني, king of the Dakhan, was the son of Sulṭán Dáúd Sháh. After having deposed and confined Sulṭán Shams-uddín, he ascended the throne on the 15th November, 1397 A. D., 800 A. H., with the title of Sulṭán Fíróz Sháh Róz Afzún. He excelled his predecessors in power and magnificence, and in his reign the house of Bahmaní attained its greatest splendour. On ascending the throne, he appointed his brother Ahmad Khán, Amír-ul-Umrá, with the title of Khánkhánán, and raised Mír Faizullah Anjú, his preceptor, to the office of Wazír-us-Saltanat, with the title of Malik Náeb. He reigned 25 years, 7 months and 15 days, and died on the 25th of September, 1422 A. D., 15th Shawwal, 825 A. H., ten days after his resigning his crown in favour of his brother Ahmad Khán, who ascended the throne with the title of Sulṭán Ahmad Sháh Walí Bahmaní.

**Firoz Shah Khilji Sultan,** سلطان فيروز شاه خلجي, surnamed Jalál-uddín, son of Ḳáem Khán, ascended the throne of Dehlí after the murder of Sulṭán Muiz-uddín Kaiḳubád in 1282 A. D., 688 A. H. He reigned about 8 years, after which he was obliged to go down to Kaṛá Mánikpúr in the province of Allahábád to punish his nephew and son-in-law 'Alá-uddín, the governor of that place, who had rebelled against him. 'Alá-uddín hearing of the king's departure from Dehlí, crossed the Ganges and encamped near Mánikpúr upon the opposite bank. When the king reached the landing place, 'Alá-uddín appeared upon the bank with his attendants, whom he ordered to halt. He advanced alone, met his uncle and fell prostrate at his feet. The king taking him by the hand, was leading him to the royal barge, when 'Alá-uddin made a signal to his guards, and one of his officers struck his head off. 'Alá-uddín caused it to be fixed on the point of a spear and carried through the camp and city. This circumstance took place on the 19th of July 1296, A. D., 17th Ramaẕán, 695 A. H., and 'Alá-uddín ascended the throne of Dehlí with the title of Sikandar Sání. Firóz Sháh was the first Sulṭán of the second branch of the Turk of Afghan dynasty, called Khiljí.

*List of Kings of the Khiljí dynasty.*

1. Fíróz Shah Khiljí.
2. 'Ala-uddin Khiljí.
3. Shahab-uddín Umar.
4. Mubarik Sháh Khiljí, the last of this dynasty, was murdered in 1321 A. D., by Málik Khusro, a favorite slave, who ascended the throne, but was soon after slain by Ghaias-uddín Tughlaḳ Sháh, the first of the 3rd branch of Afghan.

**Firoz Shah Purbi,** فيروز شاه پوربي, a king of Bengal, whose former name was Málik Andíl, an Abyssinian chief, who after killing the eunuch Sulṭán Sháhzáda, was elevated to the throne of Bengal in 1491 A. D., 896 A. H., with the title of Fíróz Sháh. He repaired the city of Gour, commonly called Lakhnauṭí, where he gave universal satisfaction to all classes of his subjects. He died in 1494 A. D., 899 A. H.

**Firoz Shah Tughlak Sultan,** سلطان فيروز شاه تغلق, called Fíróz Sháh Bárbak, was the son of Sipahsálár Rajab, the brother of Sulṭán Ghaiás-uddín Tughlaḳ, and cousin to Sulṭán Muhammad Tughlaḳ, whom he succeeded to the throne of Dehlí on the 20th March, 1351, A. D., 21st Muharram, 752 A H., at Ṭhaṭṭa. He was a just and learned prince. His soldiers and his subjects were equally happy under his administration, nor did any one dare to exercise oppression in his time. He was himself the author of the work called "Fatúhát Fíróz Sháhí," *i. e.*, the conquests of Fíróz Sháh. In August, 1387 A. D., he abdicated the throne and resigned the reins of government to his son Násir-uddin Muhammad, but the prince giving himself up entirely to pleasure, was soon after expelled and obliged to fly with a small retinue to the mountains of Sirmour, and Fíróz Sháh again resumed his full authority. He constructed numerous buildings and canals, as also the fort of Fírózábád at old Dehlí, and after a reign of 38 lunar years and eight months, died on the 21st of September, 1388, A. D., 18th Ramaẕán, 790 A. H., aged upwards of 80 years. The words "Wafát Fíróz," (the death of Fíróz) comprise the numerical letters of the year of his demise. He was buried on the banks of the Hauz Khás, built by him in old Dehlí, and was succeeded by his grandson Ghaiás-uddín (the son of Fatha Khán) who was slain after five months. After him another grandson of the late king, named Sulṭán Abú Bakr, the son of Zafar Khán, was raised to the throne. He had reigned one year and six months, when his uncle Násir-uddín Muhammad Sháh, the son of Fíróz Sháh deposed him and ascended the throne of Dehlí in August 1390.

**Firoz Shah,** فیروز شاہ, one of the sons of the ex-king Bahádur Sháh II, king of Dehlí, and one of the chief rebels in the outbreak of 1857. He took a prominent part in the rebellion of 1857, and the British Government offered a reward of 10,000 rupees for his apprehension. It was reported in 1864 that he made his appearance in the Serony Jungles. Some Arabs, who have recently arrived at Haidarábád, state that he is now (1866) in Arabia, and supports himself by begging among the rich merchants.

**Fitrat,** فطرت, the poetical name of Mír Móiz-uddín Muhammad Múswí Khán, a mansabdár in the time of 'Alamgír employed as Díwán of Súba Behár. He was a Sayyad and lineal descendant of 'Alí Músí Razá. He subsequently chose for his poetical name, Múswí. He was born in Persia in 1640 A. D., 1050 A. H., and came to India, where he was much esteemed for his talents as a poet and a critic. He is the author of a Tazkira or biography called "Gulshan-i-Fitrat," also of a Díwán. He died in 1690 A. D., 1100 A. H. *Vide* Múswí.

**Fouji,** فوجي, poetical name of Mirzá Muhammad Muḳím; he was born at Shíráz, but came to India in the time of Sháh Jahán, and was attached to the service of his son Sháh Shujá'a in Bengal. After a long residence in India he returned to his father-land, but died in a short time after his arrival there. He was living in 1649 A. D., 1059 A. H., and has left a Díwán in Persian verse. As he was employed in the army he derived his poetical title from "Fouj," *i. e.*, army.

**Foulad Khan (Shidi),** فولاد خان شيدى, an Abyssinian who was a Kotwal in the time of the emperor Muhammad Sháh, about the year 1737 A. D., 1150 A. H., and on whom a satire was written by the poet Sauda. He had built a fine garden in Ágrah, of which no traces are to be seen now.

**Fourak,** فورق, surname of Abú Bakr Muhammad, bin-Hasan, bin-Fouraḳ, commonly called ibn-Fouraḳ, was a great Metaphysician and Schoolman, for which reason he is styled Mutkallim. He was born at Isfahán, and died in the city of Naishápúr, in Khurásán, 1015 A. D., 406 A. H.

**Furati,** فراتي, *vide* Mulla Furátí.

**Furkati,** فرقتي, whose proper name was Abú Turáb, was a poet. He died in the year 1617 A. D., 1026 A. H.

**Fursat,** فرصت, poetical title of Muhammad Beg, a poet, who was in the service of Sháh 'Abbás II, and died under Sháh Sulaimán, kings of Persia. He has left a Díwán of Ghazals.

**Fursi,** فرسي, poetical title of Husain Alí Sháh, author of the "Nisbat Náma Shahraiárí," a history of the Ḳutbsháhí dynasty of Golkanḍa in 18,600 verses, from its commencement to Muhammad Ḳulí Ḳutbsháh, who died in 1612 A. D., 1021 A. H.

**Fuzail Ayaz,** فضيل عياض, a pious Musalmán whose native country was either Kúfa, Khurásán or Samarkand. He received instructions from Imám Ja'far Sádíḳ, and was the master of Bishr Hafí and Sarí Saḳtí. He suddenly fell down and died at the time of prayers at Mecca in January, 803 A. D. Muḥarram 187 A. H.

---

# G.

**Gaj Singh Rathor,** گج سنگه راتهور كچهواهه, a rájá of Már wár or Jodpúr of the tribe of Raṭhor rájpúts, was the son of Súraj Singh and the father of Jaswant Singh. He reigned about 18 years and died in the year 1630 A. D. in Gujrát. The building called Kálá Mahál at Pípal Manḍí in Ágrah, was constructed by him. His son Amar Singh killed Salabut Khán. Sulṭán Parwez married Gaj Singh's sister in 1624 A. D., and Sulaiman Shíkoh, the son of Sulṭán Parwez, married the daughter of Gaj Singh in the year 1065 A. H.

**Gakkhar,** گکهر, a tribe whose residence is amongst the mountains that lie between Bhat and Sindh. *Vide* Kamál Khán Gikhar.

**Ganga Bai,** گنگا بائي, Ráni of Jhánsí and widow of Rájá Gangádhar Ráo. At the outbreak of 1857, she joined the rebels, and was the cause of the massacre at Jhánsí. She was killed in the battle of Gwáliar on the 17th of June, 1858. She fell with her horse, and was cut down by a Hussar; she still endeavoured to get over, when a bullet struck her in the breast; and she fell to rise no more. The natives hastily burnt her dead body to save it from apprehended desecration by the Firingís on the night of the 17th and 18th.

**Ganna Begam,** گنا بيگم, *vide* Gunna Begam.

**Gajpati,** گج پتي, a rájá of Jagdespúr in south Bihár, who, and his brother Bairí Sál, during the reign of the emperor Akbar, defied the Mughal armies for several years, though the unequal combat led to their destruction.

**Garshasp,** گرشاسپ, an ancient king of Persia, *vide* Karshásp.

**Gashtasp,** گشتاسپ, was, according to Persian history, the son of Lohrásp, and the fifth king of the Kaianian dynasty of Persia. In his time flourished Zardasht or Zoroaster, who converted the Persians to the worship of fire. Gashtásp, they say, reigned 60 years, and was succeeded by Bahman his grandson, whose father Isfandaiár was a great warrior and was killed by Rustam some time before.

**Gilan Shah,** *vide* Kabús.

**Gesu Daraz,** گيسو دراز, *vide* Muhammad Geisu Daráz.

**George Thomas,** جارج طامس. The district of Hurriana was once the field of the exploits of this famous adventurer. The Jats are a stalwart and brave race, and showed what they could do under his leadership, but when left to themselves they are so divided by factions, that Hurriana has always fallen an easy prey to every adventurer who has taken it into his head to subdue it. Thus it was overrun by the Marhaṭṭas, under Messrs. Louis and Perron, by the Rohillas under Amír Khán, and another leader, and finally by the British. George Thomas came out to India as a common seaman, and having deserted his ship, first took service with Madho Rao Scindhia about the year 1770 A. D. The famous Begam of Sirdhana was then in the zenith of her power, and he left Scindhia to serve her, and shortly after, having collected a body of men, he left her, and marched down to Hurriana, and in no time carved out a kingdom for himself. He made the city of Hansi his capital and built a strong fort in it. He built another fort about 20 miles to the south of the town of Rohtak, and called it after his own Christian name Georgegaṛh, or as the natives call Jahájgaṛh. After a few years the Marhaṭṭas under Mons. Louis invaded his territories. He hastened to give them battle, and throwing himself into the small fort of Jahájgaṛh, he fought them for three days, though his force was infinitely smaller than theirs. His cavalry, which was composed principally of that rascally tribe the Raughars, having gone over to the enemy, and his Lieutenant, an Englishman, of the name of Hopkinson, being killed, his troops at length gave way, and he fled on a favourite Arab horse, to Hansi, a distance of about 60 miles. We are not aware how long he lingered in the neighbourhood after his defeat, but he died at Banáras on his way to his native country, Ireland. His great-granddaughter is the wife of a writer on a humble salary at present (1867) in one of the Government Offices in Ágrah. There is a "Life of George Thomas" written by a friend of his in the Dehli Institute Library.

**Ghaeb,** غايب, a poet who died in 1750 A. D., 1163 A. H.

**Ghafil,** غافل اكبر ابادي, a poet of Ágrah.

**Ghairat Khan,** غيرت خان, title of Khwája Kángár, the nephew of 'Abdullah Khán, Fíroz Jang and son of Sardár Khán. In the year 1631 A. D., he brought the head of Khán Jahán Jodí to Sháh Jahán, and was raised to the rank of 2000 with the title of Ghairat Khán. He died in 1640 A. D., 1050 A. H., at Ṭhaṭṭa of which place he was governor. He is the author of the "Jahángír Náma."

**Ghalib,** غالب, the poetical title assumed by Muhammad Sa'd, author of a Díwán which he completed in the year 1690 A. D., 1101 A. H.

**Ghalib,** غالب, the poetical name of Mír Fakhr-uddín, author of a book of Ḳasídás which he finished in the 6th year of Muhammad Sháh the emperor of Dehlí, 1734 A. D., 1136 A. H.

**Ghalib,** غالب, poetical title of Sheikh Asad-ulláh, son of the sister of Sheikh Muhammad Afzal of Allahábád. He died in 1750 A. D., 1163 A. H.

**Ghalib,** غالب, poetical name of Mirzá Asád-ullah Khán, author of a Díwán, and a history of the Mughal emperors of India. He was the son of 'Alí Bakhsh Khán, the brother of Nawáb Ahmad Bakhsh Khán of Fírozpúr and Lohárí. He died at Dehlí in the month of February or March, 1869 A. D., 1285 A. H.

**Ghani,** غني, the poetical name of Mirzá Muhammad Táhir. He is commonly called Ghaní Kashmírí on account of his being a native of Kashmír. He was a pupil of Sheikh Muhsin-Fání, whom he excelled in his learning and became an elegant poet. He wrote a book of Odes called "Díwán Ghaní," and died at Kashmír two years before his master 1668 A. D., 1079 A. H. It is said that the emperor 'Alamgír wrote to Saif Khán the governor of Kashmír to send Ghaní to his presence. Ghaní refused to go, telling him at the same time to inform the emperor that Ghaní had become insane and was not worthy to be sent to his presence. Saif Khán said, that he could not call a wise man like him mad; upon which Ghaní immediately got mad, tore his clothes, and died after three days. He was a young man at the time of his death, having enjoyed a brilliant reputation for poetical excellence for about eighteen years. He sometimes uses Táhir for his poetical name.

**Ghani Bahadur,** غني بهادر, son of Shamsher Bahádur I, and younger brother of 'Alí Bahádur, the Nawáb of Banda. *Vide* 'Alí Bahádur.

**Ghanimat,** غنيمت, poetical name of Muhammad Akram, author of a short Díwán and a Masnawí containing an account of the Loves of Azíz and Sháhid, called "Nairang Ishḳ," composed in the reign of Alamgír.

**Gharib,** غريب, poetical name of Sheikh Nasír-uddin of Dehlí. He is the author of a Díwán in Persian.

**Gharib,** غريب, poetical name of Sayyad Karím-ullah of Bilgrám.

**Ghasiti Begam,** گهسيتي بيگم و آمنه بيگم, the wife of Shahámat Jang, and Amina Begam the mother of Nawáb Siráj-uddaula, were daughters of Nawáb Mahabat Jang of Bengal; they were drowned in the river, close to Jahángírnagar, by order of Míran the son of Nawáb Ja'far 'Alí Khán, in June, 1760 A. D.

**Ghayas Halwai,** غياث حلواى, of Shíráz, was blind and died by a fall from the terrace of a house in the time of Sháh Safí. He is the author of a Díwán.

**Ghayas-uddin,** غياث الدين, author of a Persian Dictionary called "Ghayás-ul-Lughát," *vide* Muhammad Ghayás-uddín.

**Ghayas-uddin Bahmani,** سلطان غياث الدين بهمني (Sulṭán) the eldest son of Sulṭán Mahmúd Sháh I. He ascended the throne of the Dakhan in his seventeenth year, after the death of his father in April, 1397 A. D. He had reigned only one month and twenty days, when Lalchín, one of the Turkish slaves, not being appointed prime minister to which office he had aspired, put out his eyes with the point of his dagger, and having sent him in confinement to the fortress of Ságar, placed Shams-uddín, the late king's brother on the throne. This circumstance took place on the 14th of June, 1397 A. D., 17th Ramaẓán, 799 A. H.

**Ghayas-uddin Balban,** سلطان غياث الدين بلبن, (Sulṭán) king of Dehlí. In his youth he was sold as a slave to Sulṭán Altimsh, who raised him by degrees to the rank of a noble, and gave him his daughter in marriage. On the accession of his son Násir-uddín Mahmúd to the throne of Dehlí, Ghayás-uddín was appointed his wazír. After the king's deposal or death in February, 1266 A. D., 664 A. H., he ascended the throne and reigned 20 years. He died in 1286 A. D., 685 A. H., aged 80 years, and was succeeded by his grandson Móiz-uddín Kaiḳubád, the son of Násir-uddín Baghrá Khán, governor of Bengal, who was then absent in that province.

**Ghayas-uddin Kart I (Malik),** ملک غياث الدين كرت, fourth king of the race of Kart or Kard. He succeeded his brother Málik Fakhr-uddín Kart in 1307 A. D., 706 A. H., reigned more than 21 years over Hirát, Balkh, and Ghazní, and died in the year 1329 A. D., 729 A. H. He was succeeded by his son Málik Shams-uddín Kart.

**Ghayas-uddin Kart II (Malik),** غياث الدين كرت ملک, the eighth and last king of the dynasty of Kart or Kard. He succeeded his father or grandfather Móiz-uddín Husain Kart in 1370 A. D., 771 A. H., and reigned 12 years over Hirát, Ghor, Sarakhsh and Naishápúr, and conquered Tús and Jám. He was a great tyrant, and had several battles with the Sarbadáls of Sabzwár and the chiefs of Jání Ḳurbání. In the year 1381 A. D., 783 A. H., Amír Taimúr (Tamerlane) conquered Hirát, when Ghayás-uddín together with his son and brother were taken prisoners and put to death. This dynasty lasted one hundred and nineteen lunar years and two months.

**Ghayas-uddin Khilji (Sultan),** غياث الدين خلجي سلطان, succeeded his father Sulṭán Mahmúd Khiljí on the throne of Gujrát in May, 1469 A. D., Ẕi-Ḳa'da, 873 A. H. When he had reigned 33 years and arrived at an advanced age, his two sons anxiously looked for his death as an event which would secure to one of them the throne of Málwa; a jealousy arose between the two brothers who conspired against each other, till Násir-uddín, the eldest, having put his brother, Shujá'at Khan to death on the 22nd of October, 1500 A. D., 24th Rabí' II, 906 A. H., assumed the reins of government. A few days after, his father was found dead in the seraglio; and it was supposed that poison had been administered to him by his son.

**Ghayas-uddin Mahmud,** غياث الدين محمود, the son of Ghayás-uddín Muhammad Ghorí, succeeded his uncle Shaháb-uddín in the kingdom of Ghór and Ghazní in 1205 A. D., 602 A. H. He reigned about four years, and was assassinated by the people of Mahmúd Alí Sháh on Saturday night, the 31st of July, 1210 A. D., 7th Ṣafar, 607 A. H. He was at first buried at Fíróz Kóh, but was afterwards transported to Hirát and buried there. He was succeeded by his son Bahá-uddín Sám, who was after three months defeated by 'Alá-uddín Atsiz (son of Alá-uddín Hasan surnamed Jahán Sóz) who reigned in Ghór and Ghazní for four years, and fell in battle against Málik Násir-uddín Husain Amír Shikár in the year 1214 A. D., 611 A. H. After his death Alá-uddín Muhammad son of Abú Alí, cousin of Málik Ghayás-uddín Muhammad was raised to the throne by Táj-uddín Eldúz.

**Ghayas-uddin Muhammad, (Sultan),** سلطان غياث الدين محمد, the son of Málik Sháh of the Saljúk dynasty. In the time of his eldest brother Barkayárak the empire was divided, Barkayárak retaining Persia; Ghayás-uddín Muhammad, Syria and Azurbeján; and Sultán Sanjar, Khurásán and Mawarunnahr. He reigned about the year 1095 A. D. *Vide* Muhammad (Sulṭán).

**Ghayas-uddin Muhammad Ghori,** غياث الدين محمد غوري, king of Ghór and Ghazní, was the son of Bahá-uddín Sám, the youngest brother of Alá-uddín Hasan Ghórí. He succeeded to the throne of Ghór and Ghazní after the death of his cousin Málik Saif-uddín the son of the latter, about the year 1157 A. D., and conferred the government of Ghazní on his brother Shaháb-uddín surnamed Mo'iz-uddín Muhammad; this illustrious general subdued Khurásán and a great part of India in the name of his brother Ghayás-uddín, who annexed those countries to his own dominions. Ghayás-uddín died on Wednesday, the 12th of March, 1203 A. D., 27th Jumádạ I, 599 A. H., and was succeeded by his brother Shaháb-uddín.

**Ghayas-uddin Mahmud Ghori,** فياث الدين محمود غوري, the son of Ghayás-uddín Muhammad Ghorí, and nephew of Shaháb-uddín Muhammad Ghorí, whom he succeeded to the throne of Ghor and Ghazní in 1206 A. D. Mahmúd being naturally indolent, remained satisfied with the throne of Ghor, and proclaimed Taj-uddín Eldúz, king of Ghazní. He died in 1210 A. D.

**Ghayas-uddin Purbi,** غياث الدين پوربى, succeeded his father Sikandar Púrbí on the throne of Bengal in 1367 A. D., 775 A. H., reigned for a period of seven years, and died in 1373. He was succeeded by his son Sulṭán-us-Salátín.

**Ghayas-uddin Tughlak Shah I (Sultan),** سلطان غياث الدين تغلق, king of Dehlí. His father Tughlaḳ was a slave of Sulṭán Ghayás-uddín Balban. He ascended the throne of Ḍehlí after murdering Khusro Sháh on the 26th August, 1321 A. D., 1st Shabán, 721 A. H., reigned three years and some months, and was crushed to death by the fall of a temporary wooden building which his son had raised for his entertainment on his return from Lakhnautí in February, 1325 A. D., Rabí' I, 725 A. H. His son Muhammad Tughlaḳ succeeded him. The celebrated poet Amír Khusro of Dehlí, who lived to the end of this king's reign and received a pension of 1000 tangas monthly, wrote the history of this prince under the title of "Tughlaḳ Náma." Ghayás-uddín was the first king of the 3rd branch of the Afghán dynasty which is called Tughlaḳ Sháhi. The following is a list of the Sulṭáns of this branch :—

| | |
|---|---|
| Ghayás-uddín Tughlaḳ I. | Mahmúd Sháh Tughlaḳ last |
| Muhammad Shah Tughlaḳ I. | of this family expelled by |
| Fíroz Shah Tughlaḳ. | Amír Taimúr. |
| Ghayás-uddín Tughlaḳ II. | (Nasrat Khán). |
| Abú Bakr Sháh. | (Ikbal Khán). |
| Muhammad Sháh Tughlaḳ II. | Mahmúd Sháh restored. |
| Ala-uddín Sikandar Sháh. | |

**Ghayas-uddin Tughlak II, (Sultan),** سلطان غياث الدين تغلق, was the son of prince Fatha Khán and grandson of Fíroz Sháh Tughlaḳ. He ascended the throne in place of Fíroz Sháh in Dehlí on the death of his grandfather in 1388 A. D., 790 A. H., but giving loose to his youthful passions, and neglecting the affairs of the State, the chiefs together with the household troops revolted, and put him to death on the 19th February, 1389 A. D., 21st Ṣafar, 791 A. H., after he had reigned six months. He was succeeded by his cousin Abú Bakr Tughlaḳ the son of prince Zafar Khán, the third son of Fíroz Sháh.

**Ghazali,** غزالي, *vide* Ghazzálí.

**Ghazanfar Khan,** غضفرخان, son of Alawardí Khán I and brother of Alawardí Khán II, a nobleman of the reign of Sháh Jahán and 'Alamgír. He was three times at different periods appointed governor of Saharanpúr and afterwards of Ṭhaṭṭa in Sindh, where he died on the 1st May, 1666 A. D., 17th Ẕi-Ḳa'da, 1077 A. H. His remains were brought to Dehlí and buried there.

**Ghazan Khan,** غازان خان, seventh king of Persia of the Tartar tribe and fourth in descent from Halákú Khán, was the son of Arghún Khán. He succeeded to the crown of Persia after the dethronement of Báidú Khán his uncle in October, 1295 A. D., Ẕil-ḥijja, 694 A. H. He was the first emperor of the race of Changez Khán who embraced the religion of Muhammad, and with him near one hundred thousand of his followers followed their leader into the pale of Islám. He was the first of this race of kings who threw off all allegiance to the Kháḳán of Tartary, by directing that the name of that monarch (whom he now deemed to be an infidel) should not, in future be struck on the coins of Persia. After embracing Muhammadanism, he took the title of Sulṭán Mahmúd. He reigned nearly nine years and died on Sunday, the 17th of May, 1304 A. D., 11th Shawwál, 703 A. H., at Ḳazwín; he was interred in a superb mosque which he had constructed near Tauris or Tabrez. He was succeeded by his brother Aljaitú, who took the title of Muhammad Khudá Banda.

**Ghazi,** غازي, the poetical title of a person who served as Kúrbegí under the prince Sulṭán Muhammad Muázzim the son of the emperor 'Alamgír.

**Ghazi,** غازي, or Al-Ghází, the son of Ortak, the first of the Turkmán Ortakite princes who seized Jerusalem and reigned in Mardin and Miafarkin in Syria. The following princes are his descendants :

| | A. D. | A. H. |
|---|---|---|
| Husám-uddín Taimúrtásh son of Alghází, began to reign, ........ | 1122 | 516 |
| Najm-uddín Abú'l Muzaffar Albí or Alpí, son of Taimúrtásh, ........ | 1152 | 547 |
| Ḳutb-uddín Alghází, son of Albí, ........ | 1176 | 572 |
| Husám-uddín Yúlak Arsalan, the son of Ḳutb-uddín, ........ | 1184 | 580 |
| Málik Almansúr Násir-uddín Ortak Arsalan, son of Ḳutb-uddín, ........ | 1201 | 597 |
| Málik-us-Saíd Najm-uddín Ghází, son of Násir-uddín Ortak, ........ | 1239 | 637 |
| Málik-ul-Mazaffar Ḳará Arsalán, son of Najm-uddín, ........ | 1255 | 653 |
| Shams-uddín Daúd, ........ | 1291 | 691 |
| Málik-al-Mansúr Najm-uddín Ghází, .... | 1293 | 693 |
| Albí Málik-ul-Adil 'Imád-uddín 'Alí, .... | 1312 | 712 |
| Málik-us-Sálah Shams-uddín Sálah, the last prince of this race, ........ | 1312 | 712 |

**Ghazi-uddin Haidar,** غازی الدین حیدر, the eldest of the ten sons of Nawáb Sa'ádat 'Alí Khán of Audh. On his father's death, which took place on the 11th July, 1814 A. D., 22nd Rajab, 1229 A. H., he succeeded to his dominions as Nawáb Wazír, and five years after, assumed, with the concurrence of the British Government, the regal dignity. His coronation took place on Saturday, the 9th October, 1819 A. D., 18th Zil-hijja, 1234 A H., at Lakhnau, when he took the title of Abú'l Muzaffar Maiz-uddín Sháh Zaman Ghazí-uddín Haidar Pádsháh. On ascending the first step of the throne, the minister delivered to him a radical crown, studded with diamonds and jewels of great value. He then put it on his head and was congratulated on the occasion by the Resident who saluted him as king of Audh. Jewels and pearls to the value of 30,000 rupees were then scattered over the heads of the spectators, many were picked up by our fair ladies. Ghazí-uddín Haidar died after a reign of more than 13 years, on the 19th of October, 1827 A. D., 27th Rabi' I, 1243 A. H., aged 58 lunar years, and was succeeded by his son Sulaimán Jáh Nasír-uddín Haidar.

**Ghazi-uddin Khan I,** غازي الدين خان فيروز جنگ, styled Fíróz Jang, whose original name was Mír Shaháb-uddín, was the son of Kulich Khán Sadr-us-Sudúr, and was raised to the rank of an Amír with the title of Fíróz Jang, after his father's death, by the emperor 'Alamgír in 1687 A. D., 1098 A. H. His son was the famous Nizám-ul-Mulk 'Asaf Jáh whose descendants are known to Europeans as Nizáms of the Dakhan. In the reign of Bahádur Sháh he was appointed governor of Gujrát, and died at Ahmadábád in 1710 A. D., 1122 A. H. His remains were transported to Dehlí, and interred in the yard of the college built by him outside the Ajmírí Gate.

**Ghazi-uddin Khan II,** غازي الدين خان امير الامرا, Amír-ul-Umrá, also styled Fíróz Jang, was the eldest son of the celebrated Nizám-ul-Mulk 'Asaf Jáh. He was elevated to the rank of Amír-ul-Umrá after the death of Khán Daurán, and departure of Nádir Sháh to Persia, in 1739 A. D., 1152 A. H., by the emperor Muhammad Sháh. Some years after the death of his father, when his brother Násir Jang, who had succeeded him, died in the Dakhan, he proceeded from Dehlí to regain his possessions in that country, but died on his way at Aorangábád on the 16th of October, 1752 A. D., 7th Zil-hijja, 1165 A. H. New Style. His remains were brought to Dehlí and buried there. After his death the office of Amír-ul-Umrá was conferred on his son Shaháb-uddín with the title of 'Imád-ul-Mulk Ghází-uddín Khán.

**Ghazi-uddin Khan III,** امير الامرا غازي الدين خان, Amír-ul-Umrá, styled 'Imád-ul-Mulk, was the son of Ghází-uddín Khán Fíróz Jang, the son of Nizám-ul-Mulk 'Asaf Jáh. His original name was Shaháb-uddín, but after the death of his father in 1752 A. D., 1165 A. H., he was, by the recommendation of Nawáb Safdar Jang, wazír, appointed Amír-ul-Umrá, by the emperor Ahmad Sháh of Dehlí with the title of 'Imád-ul-Mulk Ghází-uddín Khán. This is that Ghází-uddín Khán, who afterwards became wazír, imprisoned and blinded his master the emperor Ahmad Sháh, and assassinated 'Alamgír II. His wife was the celebrated Gunna Begam, who died in the year 1775 A. D., 1189 A. H. The year of Ghází-uddín Khán's death is unknown, but according to the biography of the poet called Gulzár Ibráhím, he was living in 1780 A. D., 1194 A. H., in straitened circumstances. His poetical name was Nizám. According to the work called Másir-ul-Umrá, he went to the Dakhan 1773 A. D., 1187 A. H., and received a jágír in Málwa; subsequently he proceeded to Súrat and passed a few years with the English, and thence on a pilgrimage to Mecca. He composed Persian and Reikhta poetry and left Arabic and Turkish Ghazals and a thick Persian Díwán and a Masnawí in which the miracles of Mauláná Fakhr-uddín are related. Some say he died at Kalpí.

**Ghaznawi,** غزنوی, *vide* Muhammad Khán (Mír).

**Ghazzal,** غزال, (a seller of thread) title of Wásil-bin-'Atá, a celebrated Musalmán doctor who was thus surnamed.

**Ghazni,** غزني, kings of, *vide* Subaktagín.

**Ghazzali,** امام احمد غزالي, or Ghazálí (Imam Ahmad), younger brother of Imám Muhammad Ghazzálí. He was a doctor of the sect of Sháfa'í, and died at Kazwín in the year 1123 A. D., 517 A. H., but according to Ibn Khallikán in 520 A. H., corresponding with 1126 A. D.

**Ghazzali,** امام محمد غزالي, or Ghazálí (Imam Muhammad) who is also entitled Hujjat-ul-Islám, is the surname of Abú Hámid Muhammad Zain-uddín-al-Túsí, one of the greatest and most celebrated Musalmán doctors, and author of a treatise on the different classes of science which concern religion, called, "Kímiáe Sa'ádat," and many other works such as the Yákút-ut-Tawíb, also called "Tafsír Jawáhir-ul-Kurán," "Akáed Ghazzálí," "Ahia-ul-'Ulúm," and "Tuhfat-ul-Filasafa." He was born in the year 1058 A. D., 450 A. H., in a village called Ghazzála or Ghazála in Tús, whence he and his brother Ahmad, derived their names of Ghazzálí. He died on the 18th December, 1111 A. D., 4th Jumáda II, 505 A. H., aged 55 lunar years. Some authors say that his name should be spelt Ghazálí and not Ghazzálí, but the following verses from the Mukhbir-ul-Wásilín, confirms the latter.

احمد انكس كه ماه غزالي است
در دو عالم بدرجهٔ عالي است

He is said to have written ninety-nine works, mostly in Arabic, a few in Persian.

**Ghizali (Moulana),** مولانا غزالي, of Tús or Mashhad, the royal poet. He mentions in one of his Kasídas named Rauzat-us-Safá, that he was born in the year 1524 A. D., 930 A. H. He first came from Mashhad his native country to the Dakhan, where being disappointed in his prospects, he went over to Jaunpúr, and was employed for some years by Khán Zamán 'Alí Kulí Khán, governor of that province, during which time he wrote a poem called "Naksh Badí'a," for which he received from his patron a piece of gold for each couplet. After the death of Khán Zamán, who was slain in battle against the emperor Akbar in 1568 A. D., 975 A. H., he fell into the hands of that monarch, who took him into his service, and conferred on him the title of Málik-ush-Shua'rá, or the King of poets. He was the first poet that was honoured with this title in India. He accompanied his royal master to the conquest of Gujrát, and died there of venereal disease, on Friday the 5th of December, 1572 A. D., 27th Rajab, 980 A. H. He is buried at Ahmadabád, Gujrát, at a place called Sarkíj. He is also the author of a Díwán, and three Masnawís or poems, containing from 40 to 50,000 verses; their titles are: "Kitáb Asrár," "Rishahát-ul-Haiát," and "Mirat-ul-Káenát."

**Ghous Muhammad Khan,** غوث محمد خان, whose title is Mohtashim-uddaula, is the present Nawáb of Jáwara.

**Ghous-ul-'Alam,** غوث العالم, a famous Súfí, *vide* Muhammad Ghous of Gwáliar.

**Ghous-ul-'Azim,** غوث الاعظم, a title of the Muhammadan saint 'Abdul Kádir Gilání.

**Ghouwasi,** غواصي يزدي, of Yezd, a poet, whose proper name is Izzuddín. He is said to have composed 100,000 verses. This fertile poet, in a work which he wrote in 1543 A. D., 950 A. H., says: "The poetry which I have written amounts to 1,950 books." He made 500 verses a day, and it would appear that he put the "Rauzat-ush-Shohada," the history of Tabarí, the legends of the prophets, Kaleila-wa-Damna, and the Medical work called "Zakhíra Khwárizm Sháhí," and many other works into verse. He died in 1553 A. D., 960 A. H., at an age of more than one hundred years.

**Ghulam 'Ali, Mir,** ميرغلام علي آزاد, a poet whose poetical title is 'Azád, which see.

**Ghulam 'Ali Khan,** غلام علي خان, author of the "Lama'át-ut-Táhirín," a panegyric on the actions of Muhammad, and a number of mystical poems, dedicated to the emperor 'Alamgír.

**Ghulam 'Ali,** غلام علي, author of the work called "Sháh 'Alam Náma," a history of the reign of the Emperor Sháh 'Alam, who died in 1806 A. D., 1221 A. H.

**Ghulam Husain Khan, Nawab Sayyad,** طباطبائي نواب سيد غلام حسين خان, surnamed Tiba Tibáí, son of Hidáet 'Alí Khán, Bahádur Asad Jang, author of a Persian work called "Siar-ul-Mutákhirín," written in the year 1780 A. D., 1194 A. H., and translated soon after into English by a French Renegade, called Mustáfá. It was again translated into English by F. C. Balfour, Esq., LL. D. He is also author of a Poem entitled "Basharát-ul-Imámat."

**Ghulam Husain Khan,** غلام حسين خان, author of the Persian History of Bengal called "Rayaz-ussalatín" which he wrote about the year 1780 A. D. at the request of Mr. George Udney of Málwa. He was a learned and respectable character, once of greater consequence, and afterwards a member of the native court of judicature under the most worthy Nawáb 'Alí Ibrahím Khán.

**Ghulam Imam Shahid, Maulana,** غلام امام شهيد مولانا, a poet who is the author of a Persian Díwán, and of a celebrated Ḳasída comprising the dispute between Love and Beauty. His poetical title is Shahed and he is living still, 1879 A. D.

**Ghulam Kadir Khan,** غلام قادرخان, son of Zábita Khán, and grandson of Najíb-uddaula, the Rohila chief. This is that traitor who after extorting as much money as he could from his royal master, the emperor Sháh 'Alam of Dehlí, ordered his Rohilas to pluck out his eyes from their sockets and placed Beídar Bakht, son of Ahmad Sháh, and grandson of Muhammad Sháh on the throne. This mournful event happened on the 10th of August, 1788 A. D., 7th Ẕi-Ḳa'da, 1202 A. H. After this, the traitor endeavoured to make his retreat to his own territory Ghousgaṛh, but was pursued by the Marhaṭṭas who took him prisoner, cut off his ears, nose, arms, and legs, and in this mutilated state he was sent to Dehlí; but died on the road in the month of December the same year, Rabí I, 1203 A. H. His tomb is in Aul, Parganna Furrah, Zila Ágrah.

**Ghulam Kutb-uddin Shah,** قطب الدين الله ابادي شاه غلام of Allahábád, whose poetical name is Musíbat, was the son of Sháh Muhammad Fákhir. He was an elegant poet eminently learned and accomplished, and is the author of a work called "Nán Ḳalia," (Cakes and Steaks) which he wrote in answer to a work entitled "Nán Halwá" (Cakes and Pudding). He was born on the 29th August, 1725 O. S., 1st Maḥarram, 1138 A. H., went on a pilgrimage to Mecca, and died there in the year 1773-4 A. D., 1187-8 A. H.

**Ghulam Muhammad,** غلام محمد, (Prince,) son or grandson of Tippú Sulṭán, was installed as a Knight Commander of the Star of India on the 27th February, 1871 A. D. Seventy-two years ago he was a prisoner in the hands of the English, and since then a recipient of the highest honors. He died in Calcutta on the night of the 11th August, 1872, aged 78 years.

**Ghulam Muhammad Khan,** غلام محمد خان, present nawáb of the Karnatic, whose title is Amír-ul-Hind Wálá Jáh Umdat-ul-Umrá Mumtáz-ul-Mumálik.

**Ghulam Muhammad Khan, Nawab,** محمد خان نواب غلام, *vide* Faiz-ulláh Khán.

**Ghulam Ahia,** غلام يحيى, author of an Arabic work on Logic, which goes after his name. Its marginal Notes written by another author are called "Shams-uz-Zuhá."

**Ghunchachae Ummaid,** غنچهٔ اميد, (*i. e.,* a small bud of hope), was one of the wives of Umar Shaikh Mirzá, the son of Sulṭán Abú Sa'íd Mirzá, and mother of Násir Mirzá, and Mahd Báno Begam. She was a native of Andjan.

**Girami,** گرامي, the poetical name of a poet whose Díwán was found in the Library of Típú Sulṭán.

**Girdhar Das,** گردهر داس, of Dehlí, author of the history of Rám, entitled "Rámáyan," translated from the Sanskrit in 1722 A. D. This is a very celebrated Hindí poem, containing the exploits of the famous demigod Rám, who reigned over India for many years. His capital was at Audh, and his conquests extended to Ceylon, where the chain of rocks which nearly unite that island to the continent, is still called Rám's Bridge. Besides this, there are two other Rámáyans, one translated by Tulshí Dás in the Bhákhá dialect, and another by Khushtar in Urdú.

**Girdhar Singh,** گردهر سنگه, or Girdhar Bahádur, a Rájpút chief who was governor of Málwa in the reign of the emperor Muhammad Sháh, and fell in battle against the Peshwá Bájí Rao's officers in 1729 A. D. His nephew, Dayá Rám, who succeeded him, and had opposed a gallant resistance for some time, was defeated by Chimnájí the Peshwá's brother, and lost his life in battle about the year 1732 A. D.

**Gobind Guru,** گرو گوبند, a chief of the Sikhs, *vide* Gurú Gobind.

**Gopal** or **Nayek Gopal,** نايك گوپال, a celebrated singer of India, who was a native of the Dakhan, and flourished during the reign of Sulṭán 'Alá-uddín Sikandar Sání. He was a contemporary of Amír Khusro who died in 1325 A. D. It is related that when Gopál visited the court of Dehlí, he sung that species of composition called "Gít," the beauty of which style, enunciated by the powerful and harmonious voice of so able a performer, could not meet with competition:—At this the monarch caused Amír Khusro to remain hid under his throne, whence he could hear the musician unknown to him. The latter endeavoured to remember the style, and on a subsequent day, sung "Qoul" and "Tarána" in imitation of it, which surprised Gopál, and, fraudulently deprived him of a portion of his due honor.

**Goshyar,** گوشيار, an astronomer whose proper name is Abú'l Hasan.

**Gouhar Shad Begam,** گوهر شاد بیگم, the wife of Mirzá Sháhrukh, the son of Amír Taimúr. She was slain by Sulṭán Abú Sa'íd Mirzá for creating disturbances, in 1457 A. D., 861 A. H., at Hirát, where she lies buried on the left bank of a stream called Anjír. The grave is shaded by a very high gilt dome. She is said to have been the most incomparable lady in the world. Some erroneously say that she was the daughter of Amír Taimúr, and the sister of Sháhrukh Mirzá, and that she never married, but devoted herself to the perusal of the Ḳurán, *vide* Mohan Lal's Journal.

**Goya,** گویا, poetical name of Hisam-uddaula Nawáb Faḳír Muhammad Khán of Lakhnau. He is the author of a Díwán.

**Goya,** گویا, the poetical name of Mirzá Kámrán, a brother of Jóyá, which see.

**Goya,** گویا, poetical name of Shaikh Haiát-ulláh of Furrukhábád.

**Gujar,** گوجر, grandson or son of the daughter of the Peshwá Rághójí Bhosla's daughter. He was raised to the masnad of Nágpúr after the dethronement of 'Apá Sáhib in 1818 A. D.

**Gulab Singh,** گلاب سنگھ, of Jammú (Mahárájá) the independent ruler of Kashmír and the hills, which were made over to him by the British "for a consideration," after the battle with the Sikhs in 1846. He died 2nd August, 1857 A. D , about three months after the outbreak of the native troops. He was succeeded by his son Ranbír Singh.

**Gulbadan Begam,** گلبدن بیگم, a daughter of the emperor Bábar Sháh, sister to Humayún and aunt to Akbar Sháh. She was married to Khizir Khán, a descendant of the kings of Káshghar. Khizir Khán was made governor of Lahor in 1555 A. D., 963 A. H., and afterwards of Behár, where he died about the year 1559 A. D., 966 A. H.

**Gulbarg Begam,** گلبرگ بیگم, daughter of the emperor Babar Sháh, she is also called Gulrang Begam, and Gulrukh Begam, which see.

**Gulchehra Begam,** گلچهره بیگم, a daughter of the emperor Bábar Sháh and youngest sister of Humáyún, by whom she was given in marriage to Abbás Sulṭán, an Uzbak prince, at Kábul in 1548 A. D.

**Gul Muhammad Khan,** گل محمد خان ناطق, a poet of Dehlí who died in the year of the Christian era 1848 A. D., 1264 A. H. His poetical name was Nátik, which see.

**Gulrukh Begam,** گلرخ بیگم, a daughter of the emperor Bábar, who was married to Mirzá Núr-uddín Muhammad, a person of respectable family, by whom she had a daughter named Salíma Sulṭána Begam, who was married in the beginning of the reign of the emperor Akbar, to Berám Khán, Khánkhánán, after whose death in 1561 A. D., 968 A. H., the emperor married her himself. Gulrukh Begam is called in the Másir-ul-Umrá, Gulbarg Begam, and by some Gulrang Begam.

**Gulrukh Begam,** گلرخ بیگم, a daughter of Kámrán Mirzá, the brother of the emperor Humáyún, and first cousin to Akbar. She was married to Ibrahím Husain Mirzá, the son of Muhammad Sulṭán Mirzá a descendant of Amír Taimúr. Ibrahím Husain, who together with his other brothers had created great disturbances in the country, was taken prisoner in 1573 A. D., 981 A. H., and shortly after put to death and his head sent to Akbar, who ordered it to be placed over one of the gates of Ágrah. Gulrukh Begam survived him for several years and was living at Ágrah in 1614 A. D., 1023 A. H.

**Gulshan,** گلشن, the poetical name of Shaikh Sa'd-ulláh, a mystical poet, who resided for some years at Dehlí, and left nearly 100,000 verses of Ghazals. He was a disciple of Sháh 'Abdúl Ahad Sarhindí, and made with him a pilgrimage to Mecca. He died in 1728 A. D., or 1141 A. H.

**Gulshani,** گلشنی, the poetical title of Shaikh Sa'd-ulláh, which see.

**Gunna** or **Ganna Begam,** گنا بیگم, a princess, celebrated for her personal accomplishments, as well as for the vivacity of her wit, and the fire of her poetical genius. Several of her lyric compositions, in the Hindustání language are still sung and admired, one of which is to be seen in the first volume of the Asiatic Researches, p. 55. She was the daughter of Nawáb 'Alí Ḳulí Khán commonly called Chhangá or Shash Angushtí (from having six fingers on each hand), a mansabdár of 5000 horse. Ganná Begam was betrothed to Shujá'-uddaula, the son of Nawáb Safdar Jang, but afterwards married to 'Imád-ul-Mulk Ghází-uddín Khán, wazír, and this rivalship is said to have in part laid the foundation of the mortal enmity which afterwards subsisted between that wazír and Safdar Jang. Adjoining to the village of Núrábád near Dhoulpúr, two miles from Cholá Saráe, is a pretty large garden, the work of the emperor Alamgír, built in the year 1688 A. D., 1160 A. H., over the gate of which is an inscription bearing the chronogram of the year of its erection, *viz.*, "Dida Bágh Jámál." Within this garden is the monument of Ganná Begam. Her shrine bears the following inscription, "Ah gham Gunná Begam," which is the chronogram of the year of her death, *viz.*, 1775 A. D., 1189 A. H. The poets, Sóz, Souda, and Minnat corrected her verses.

**Guru Gobind,** گرو گوبند, the son of Tegh Bahádur, a famous chief of the Sikhs. After the death of his father who was executed by order of the emperor 'Alamgír in the year 1673 A. D., having collected his followers, he gave them arms and horses, which till his time they had never used, and began to commit depredations, but he was soon obliged to fly, and two of his sons being taken prisoners, were put to death. Being desirous of returning to his home, he prevailed on some Afgháns to conduct him, disguised as one of their devotees, through the army stationed at Sarhind; and for the remainder of his life kept himself retired, having lost his faculties in grief for his sons. He ordered his disciples to wear blue, and leave their beards and the hair of their heads unshaved, which they do to this day. He was succeeded by Banda, one of his followers.

---

# H.

**Habib Ajmi, Khwaja,** خواجه حبیب عجمی, he was called 'Ajmí or the Persian, on account of his not being able to read the Ḳurán, or that he could not pronounce the words of it distinctly. He was a pious Musalmán and disciple of Khwája Hasan Basrí. He died on the 28th August, 738 A. D., 7th Ramazán, 120 A. H.

**Habib-ullah,** حبیب الله, author of an Arabic work on philosophy called "Bahr-ul-Mantiḳ," or the Sea of Logic.

**Habib-ullah, Shaikh,** شيخ حبيب الله, a celebrated poet of Ágrah.

**Habib-ullah, Shah** or **Mir,** شاہ حبيب الله, a descendant of Sháh Ni'mat-ulláh Walí, and an amír in the service of the Bahmaní kings of the Dakhan. He was imprisoned, and afterwards put to death in June, 1460 A. D., Sha'bán 864 A. H., by Sulṭán Humáyún Sháh II, Bahmaní, a tyrant, who at the same time cast his brother Hasan Khán, who had rebelled against him, before a voracious tiger, that soon tore the wretched prince to pieces.

**Habshi** or **Habashi,** حبشي, a poet who having lost an eye in a scuffle, was asked by Ibráhím Páshá, "Where is thine other eye?" and making answer, "It grew tired of stopping at home in the socket, and flew out to see the world;" was imprisoned ten years for his wit in the tower of Hero and Leander, where he daily gave vent to his feelings in such verses as the following:—

I will groan, till every stone in this cold prison-tower shall weep,
I will cry, till earth and sky, and each dark rolling hour shall weep,
I will make, that hearts shall break, and even the dewless flower shall weep,
Yea, for me, the wronged Habshí, both Musalmán and Gabr shall weep!

**Hadi,** هادي, a khalíf of Baghdád, *vide* Al-Hádí.

**Hadi,** هادي, poetical name of Mír Muhammad Jawád 'Alí Khán, who died in the year 1800 A. D., 1215 A. H., and left a Díwán in Urdú.

**Hafi,** حافي, which means barefoot, is the surname of Zain-uddín Muhammad, an author, who led an austere life, and who always walking barefoot, was thus surnamed.

**Hafiz-uddin Ahmad, Moulwi,** حفيظ الدين احمد مولوي, author of the "Khirad Afróz," an Urdú translation of the "Ayár Danish," or Pilpay's Fables, which he translated for the use of the College of Fort William in 1803 A. D., 1218 A. H.

**Hafiz-uddin Nasafi-bin-Ahmad,** نسفي بن احمد حفيظ الدين, author of the Commentaries called "Madárik-ut-Tanzíl" and "Hakáek-ut-Tanáwíl," in Arabic. He died in the year 1310 A. D., 710 A. H., *vide* Nasafí or Al-Nasafa.

**Hafiz-ullah, Shaikh,** شيخ حفيظ الله, a relation of Siráj-uddín 'Alí Khán Arzú. His poetical name was Asam. He died in the 21st year of the emperor Muhammad Sháh of Dehlí, 1767 A. D., 1181 A. H.

**Hafiz Abru,** حافظ آبرو, surnamed Núr-uddín-bin-Lutf-ulláh, author of the history called "Táríkh Háfiz Abrú." He was born in the city of Hirat, but passed his infancy in Hamdán, where he received his education. He was fortunate enough to secure the esteem of Amír Taimúr, who sought every occasion to do him service. After the death of that tyrant, he attended the court of his son Sháhrukh Mirzá, and received from the young prince Mirzá Báisanghar every demonstration of kindness and regard. To him he dedicated his works under the name of "Zubdat-ut-Tawáríkh Báisangham," which contains a complete history of the world, and an account of the institutions and religions of different people down to 1425 A. D., 829 A. H. He died five years afterwards in the city of Zanján, about the year 1430 A. D., 834 A. H.

**Hafiz Adam,** حافظ آدم, a Musalmán devotee and disciple of Shaikh Ahmad Sarhindí, who about the year 1673 A. D., in conjunction with the Sikh Gurú Tegh Bahádur, having collected his followers, levied contributions with the greatest oppression from the inhabitants of his neighbourhood and pretended to royalty. He was banished from the kingdom across the Indus by order of the emperor 'Alamgír.

**Hafiz Halwai,** حافظ حلواى, a confectioner and poet of Hirat who flourished in the reign of Sháhrukh Mirzá, the son of Amír Taimúr about the year 1430 A. D., 834 A. H.

**Hafiz, Khwaja,** خواجه حافظ, whose proper name is Shams-uddín Muhammad, was the most elegant lyric poet of Persia. He was born at Shíráz in the reign of the Muzaffarians, and was living at the time when Amír Taimúr (Tamerlane) defeated Sháh Mansúr the last Sulṭán of that dynasty. The language of Hafiz has been styled among the Musalmáns, "Lisán-ul-Ghaib," the language of mystery. From his frequent celebration of love and wine in his odes he has not improperly been denominated, by some Orientalists, the Anacreon of Persia. He died in 1389 A. D., 971 A. H. at Shíráz, where his tomb is yet to be seen at a place called Musalla, and is visited as a sacred spot by pilgrims of all ages. After his death a collection of 569 of his odes was made by Sayyad Ḳásim Anwár, entitled "Díwán Hafiz." A few of his poems may be understood in a literal sense; but in general they are figurative, and allude to the Súfí doctrines; most of them have been at different times translated into some of the European languages. At the head of the English translators, stand Sir W. Jones, Messrs. Richardson and Carlyle. There have been two other Persian poets of the name of Háfiz, one of them surnamed Halwáí, that is to say, the confectioner, who lived in the reign of Sulṭán Sháhrukh, the son of Tamerlane, and the other was named Aján Rúmí. Many zealous admirers of Háfiz insist, that by wine he invariably means *devotion;* and they have gone so far as to compose a dictionary of words in the *language*, as they call it, of the Súfís: in that vocabulary, *sleep* is explained by *meditation* on the divine perfections, and *perfume* by *hope* of the divine favor; *gales* are *illapses* of grace; *kisses* and *embraces*, the raptures of piety; *idolators, infidels*, and *libertines*, are men of the purest religion, and their *idol* is the Creator himself; the *tavern* is a retired oratory, and its *keeper*, a sage instructor; *beauty* denotes the perfection of the Supreme Being; *tresses* are the expansion of his glory; *lips* the hidden mysteries of his essence; *down* on the cheek, the world of spirits, who encircle his throne; and a *black mole*, the point of indivisible unity; lastly, *wantonness, mirth*, and *inebriety*, mean religious ardour and abstraction from all terrestrial thoughts.

**Hafiz Muhammad,** author of the "Hawí Saghír."

**Hafiz Rahmat Khan,** حافظ رحمت خان, a celebrated Rohila chief. He joined his countrymen during the administration of 'Ali Muhammad Khán, who advanced him to an important station, and Pílíbhít and Bareily were given to him and Muradábád to another chief named Dúnde Khán. Having attained his office, by military ability and genius, he at length wholly superseded the authority of Sa'd-ulláh Khán, the son of 'Alí Muhammad Khán, and was advanced to the supreme administration of affairs. He failed in his engagement to pay forty lacs of rupees to Nawáb Shujá-uddaula of Audh for the protection of his country from the ravages of the Marhaṭṭas, was killed in a battle fought by the nawáb by the assistance of the English on the 23rd April, 1774 A. D., 10th Safar, 1188 A. H. His Life is translated by Mr. Elliott.

**Hafiz Rakhna,** حافظ رخنه, is the name of the person who planted a large garden at Sarhind in the reign of the Emperor Akbar and called it "Bágh Noulakh." He died in 1592 A. D., 1000 A. H., and a beautiful chronogram was written on the occasion.

**Hafs,** حفص, *vide* Abú Hafs-ul-Bukhárí.

**Hafsa,** حفصه, a daughter of the Khalíf Umar, and wife of Muhammad, in whose hands Abú Bakr, the successor of the prophet, deposited the original Ḳurán. She outlived her husband 33 years and died in 665 A. D., 45 A. H.

**Haibat Jang,** هيبت جنگ, title of Zain-uddín Ahmad, the youngest son of Hájí Ahmad, and nephew and son-in-law of Alahwardí Khán Mahábat Jang, governor of Bengal. He was the father of Nawáb Siráj-uddaula, who succeeded Mahábat Jang in the government of Bengal in 1756 A. D.

**Haibat Khan,** هيبت خان. He is the author of the "Taríkh Khán Jahán Lodí," "Makhzan-i-Afghání," containing the history of Khán Jahán Lodí and of the Afghans. Khán Jahán was a general of great reputation during the reign of the emperor Jahángir, but rebelling against Sháh Jahán, was killed in an engagement with the royal troops 1631 A. D., 1087 A. H. The above work was written in 1676 A. D. There is also an abridgement of this work, by the same author, called "Majmua' Afghání."

**Haidar,** حيدر, a title of 'Alí, the son-in-law of Muhammad.

**Haidar,** حيدر كليچه يا حيدر كلوچ, also called Haidar Kulúj or Haidar Kulícha, because he was by profession a baker. He was a native of Hírát, and is the author of a Díwán in Persian and one in Urdú.

**Haidar,** حيدر, or Mír Haidar Sháh of the Dakhan, a gallant soldier in the service of Nawáb Sarfaráz Khán governor of Bengal. He put the Díwán of Walí of the Dakhan into Mukhammas and interspersed that of Háfiz with verses of his own. He died at Húglí in the reign of the emperor Ahmad Sháh, a year or two before or after 1750 A. D., 1164 A. H., aged 100 years. Gracin-de-Tassy thinks that he is the author of a Masnawí entitled "Kissae Chandar Badon and Máhyár."

**Haidar Ali Moulwi,** مولوي حيدر علي فيض ابادي, of Faizábád, author of the "Muntahí-ul-Kalám," and several other works. He was living in Dehlí 1854 A. D., 1270 A. H.

**Haidar Mir,** حيدر مير, *vide* Haidar Mirzá.

**Haidar Mirza,** حيدر مرزا, who is also called Mír Haidar and Mirzá Haidar Doghlát, was the son of Muhammad Husain, and his wife was the aunt of Babar Sháh. He was formerly in the service of Kámrán Mirzá, brother of the emperor Humáyún, but being disgusted with his conduct abandoned his standard about the year 1539 A. D., 946 A. H., and joined the emperor, to whom he was afterwards of great service. In 1540 A. D., 947 A. H., he was deputed by the emperor to conquer Kashmír, which he took in a short time; but as that emperor was soon after expelled from India by Sher Sháh, Haidar became the king of that country. In the year 1548 A. D., 955 A. H., he invaded Little Thibet, and not only succeeded in conquering that country, but subsequently added Great Thibet, Rajora and Pogla to his dominions. He reigned nearly ten years and was killed by an arrow in a night-attack made upon his camp in 1551 A. D., 958 A. H.

**Haidar Khan, Mir,** مير حيدر خان, the grandson of Mír Haidar who was the author of the "Taríkh Rashídí." This person, on plea of presenting a petition, killed Husain 'Alí Khán Amír-ul-Umrá, at the instigation of the emperor Muhammad Sháh, on the 18th September, 1720 O. S., 27th Ẕi-Ḳa'da 1132 A. H., and was himself cut to pieces.

**Haidar Malik,** حيدر ملک, entitled Raís-ul-Mulk Chughtáí, author of the most authentic history of Kashmír, down to his own time. He was a nobleman in the service of the emperor Jahángír, and was living about the year 1619 A. D., 1028 A. H., in which year he accompanied that emperor to Kashmír.

**Haidar Muammai, Mir,** مير حيدر معماي, surnamed Rafísgí Káshí, a punster who flourished in the time of Sháh Ismaíl II, king of Persia, and wrote a chronogram at his death, which took place in 1577 A. D., 985 A. H. He was distinguished by his skill in making chronograms and enigmas. He came to India in the time of Akbar, and was drowned when returning by sea to Persia. He was in charge of copies of Faizí's works for distribution in Persia, and they were also lost. *Vide* Mír Haidar.

**Haidar Razi,** حيدر رازي, a Persian historian who wrote in the 17th century of the Christian Era.

**Haidar, Sheikh or Sultan,** سلطان حيدر, father of Sháh Ismaíl I, Safwí. He was the son of Sulṭán or Shaikh Junaid, the son of Shaikh Ibrahím, the son of Shaikh or Khwája Alí, the son of the celebrated Shaikh Sadar-uddín Músa, the son of Shaikh Safí or Safí-uddín Ardibelí, who was the 21st in a direct line from Músí Kázim, the seventh Imám. He was killed in a battle against Ya'kúb Beg the son of Uzzan Husan, at Shirwán in the month of July, 1488 A. D., Sha'ban, 893 A. H.

**Hairan,** حيران, poetical name of Mír Haidar 'Alí. He was killed in zillah Bihár, but had the assassin put to death before he expired.

**Hairani, Moulana,** مولانا حيراني همداني, of Hamdán. He is the author of several Masnawís or poems, *viz.*, "Bahrám-wa-Nahíd." Dispute between Heaven and Earth, entitled "Manazira Arz-wa-Samá;" Dispute between the Candle and the Moth, called "Manázira Shama'-wa-Parwana;" and Dispute between the Roasting Spit and the Fowl, named "Manázira Síkh-wa-Murgh." He died in 1497-8 A. D., 903 A. H.

**Hairat,** قيام الدين حيرت, poetical name of Ḳayám-uddín, the author of the biography called "Tazkira Maḳálát-ush-Shua'rá," which he completed in 1760 A. D., 1174 A. H.

**Hairat,** حيرت, poetical title of Pandit Ajuddhia Parshad, a native of Kashmír, who resided at Lakhnau. He is the author of a small Díwan and a few Masnawís. He died 1234 A. H., in the 35th year of his age.

**Hairati,** حيرتي, a poet of Marv. In reward of a Ḳasída which he composed in praise of Sháh Tahmásp I, Safwí, he obtained the title of Malik-ush-Shua'rá or king of poets. Besides the work called "Bahjat-ul-Mubáhij," he is the author of a Masnawí to which he gave the title of Gulzár. All his verses amount to about 40,000. He was murdered at Káshán 1554 A. D., 962 A. H.

**Hairati,** حيرتي, was the greatest poet of his time. He had studied at Isfahán, and was alive when Taḳí Káshání wrote his Tazkira, 1585 A. D. Though he received a liberal allowance from the Persian government, owing to his extravagance, it was quite insufficient for his support, and in 1581 A. D., 989 A. H., he came to India being attracted by the prodigality of the Kutb-Sháhí kings of Golkanḍa.

**Hajar,** حجر, a very great man among the followers of 'Alí, and remarkable for his singular abstinence, piety and strictness of life, his constant purifications according to Muhammadan law, and exactness in observing the hours of devotion. He was put to death in 666 A. D., by order of Mu'áwia I for speaking reproachfully of him, affronting his brother Zayád governor of Kúfa, and affirming that the government did not, of right, belong to any but the family of 'Alí.

**Hajari,** *vide* Hijrí.

**Haji Begam,** حاجي بيگم, wife of the emperor Humáyún. *Vide* Hamída Báno Begam.

**Haji Khalfa,** حاجي خلفه, a celebrated author commonly called Mustaufí Hájí Khalfa. He is the author of the work called "Fazlaka," also of the Biographical Dictionary called "Kashf-uz-Zunún," and the work called "Taķwím-ut-Tawáríkh Rúmí." The latter is a Chronological Table of remarkable events from the Creation of the world to 1648 A. D., 1058 A. H., translated from the Turkish, during the reign of Sultán Muhammad IV of Constantinople. The "Kashf-uz-Zunún" was printed for the Oriental Translation Fund in 1835-50, together with a Latin translation by Professor Fluegel. It appears that Hájí Khalfa formerly bore the title of "Kátib Chilpí," (which see,) and if this is correct, he died in 1657 A. D., 1067 A. H.

In Chamber's Encyclopædia the month and year of his death is September, 1658 A. D., and that he is also said to be the author of the Taríkh Kabír "the Great History," which is a history of the world from the creation of Adam to 1655 A. D., containing notices of 150 dynasties, principally Asiatic; also a history of the Ottoman empire from 1591 to 1658 A. D., and a history of the maritime wars of the Turks, which has been translated into English.

**Haji Muhammad Beg Khan,** حاجي محمد بيگ خان, the father of the celebrated Mirzá Abú Tálib Khán, author of the "Masír Tálibí." He was by descent a Turk, but born at 'Abbásábád in Isfahán. Whilst a young man, dreading the tyranny of Nádir Sháh, he fled from Persia, and on his arrival in India, was admitted into the friendship of the Nawáb Abú'l Mansúr Khán Safdar Jang. Upon the death of Rájá Nawul Ráe, Deputy Governor of Audh in 1750 A. D., 1163 A. H., Muhammad Ķulí Khán, the nephew of the Nawáb, was appointed to that important office, and he (Hájí) was nominated one of his assistants. On the death of Safdar Jang in 1753 A. D., 1167 A. H., his son Shujá-uddaula became jealous of his cousin Muhammad Ķulí Khán, arrested him and put him to death. Hájí fled with a few of his faithful servants to Bengal, where he passed a number of years, and died at Murshidábád in April, 1769 A. D., Ẕil-ḥijja, 1182 A. H.

**Haji Muhammad Jan,** حاجي محمد جان مشهدي, of Mashhad. His poetical name is Ķudsí. He flourished in the reign of the emperor Sháh Jahán, who conferred on him the title of "Malik-ush-Shua'ra," or the Royal poet. He is the author of a poem containing the conquests of the emperor, which he named "Zafarnáma." He died in the year 1645 A. D., 1055 A. H., and after him the title of the royal poet was conferred on Abú Tálib Kalím. He is also the author of a Díwán, and an Insha.

**Haji Muhammad Kandahari,** حاجي محمد قندهاري. He is the author of a history which goes by his name, *viz.*, "Taríkh Hájí Muhammad Ķandahárí."

**Haji Muhammad Kashmiri Moulana,** كشميري مولانا حاجي محمد. One of his forefathers who was a native of Hamdán, came to Kashmír with Mír Said 'Alí Hamdání. Hájí was born in that province, but came to Dehlí in his youth where he received his education. He was an excellent poet, flourished in the time of Akbar, and died on Thursday the 22nd of September, 1597 A. D., 19th Şafar, 1006 A. H., O. S. He was a religious man, and had many disciples, one of whom, named Mouláná Hasan, wrote the chronogram of his death.

**Haji Muhammad Khan Sistani,** خان سيستاني حاجي محمد. He was at first in the service of Bairám-Khán, Khánkhánán, after whose dismissal he was honored with the rank of 3000 by the emperor Akbar. He accompanied Munaim Khán, Khánkhánán to Bengal and died at Gour in 1575 A. D., 983 A. H.

**Hajjaj-bin-Yusaf-al-Sakafi** or **Thakafi,** الثقفي حجاج بن يوسف, one of the most valiant Arabian captains, who was made governor of Arabia and Arabian Iráķ by Abdulmalik the fifth Khalíf of the Ommaides, after he had defeated and killed Abdulláh-bin-Zubeir, who had taken the title of Khalífa at Mecca. In the year 693 A. D., 74 A. H., he pulled down the temple of Mecca, which Abdulláh had repaired, placing the black stone on the outside of it again and restoring it to the very form it had before Muhammad's time. He was a great tyrant; it is said of him, that in his lifetime, he had put to death a hundred and twenty thousand persons, and when he died had 50,000 in his prisons. He died in the reign of the Khalíf Walíd I, in the year 714 A. D., 95 A. H., aged 54 years.

**Hakikat,** حقيقت, poetical title of Saiyad Husain Sháh, son of Saiyad Arab Sháh. He accompanied Col. Kydd to Chinápatan in Madras as head Munshí and died there. He is the author of an Urdú Díwán and seven other works, some of which are named "Tahfat-ul-'Ajam," "Khazínat-ul-Amsál," "Sanamkada Chín" and "Hasht Gulgusht." *Vide* Husain Sháh.

**Hakim I,** حكيم, the poetical title of a person who was a native of Mashhad, and was living about the year 1688 A. D., 1100 A. H. He was an Arabic and Persian scholar, and is the author of a Díwán and a Masnawí.

**Hakim II,** حكيم, the poetical name of Sháh Abdul Hakím of Láhor. He is the author of a work called "Mardum Dída," compiled at Aurangábád in 1761 A. D., 1175 A. H. It contains an account of those poets with whom the author was acquainted.

**Hakim-Ain-ul-Mulk,** حكيم عين الملك, of Shiráz. He was a learned man and a clever writer. He traced his origin, on his mother's side, to the renowned logician Muhaķķiķ-i-Dawaní. The Historian Badaoni was a friend of his. Akbar also liked him very much. Hakím was a poet and wrote under the Lakhalus of Dawani. He died at Handiah on the 27th Ẕil-ḥijja 1003 A. H. *Vide* Ain, I. 481.

**Hakim Ali,** حكيم علي گيلاني, of Gilán, came to India in indigent circumstances, but was fortunate enough to become in course of time a personal attendant and friend of Akbar. In the 39th year of Akbar's reign, he constructed the wonderful reservoir which is so often mentioned by Mughal Historians. In the 40th year Alí was a commander of 700 and had the title of Jalinus Uzzamani the 'Galinus of the Age.' By Jahángír he was made a commander of 2000. He died on the 5th Muḥarram, 1018 A. H. *Vide* Ain, I. 466.

**Hakim Muhammad,** محمد حكيم. He was half-brother to the emperor Akbar, being born of a different mother. *Vide* Muhammad Hakím.

**Hakim Nur-uddin Shirazi,** حكيم نور الدين شيرازي, who appears to have been either grandson or sister's son of

Abú'l Fazl, asserts in his preface to the "Haját Dara Shikohí," that he commenced his work in the 14th year of the reign of Sháh Jahán 1642 A. D., 1052 A. H., the above name of the book gives the year of the Hijra, and brought it to a conclusion in 1056 A. H.

**Hakim-ul-Mumalik,** حكيم الممالك, title of Mír Muhammad Mahdí, a physician who held the rank of 4000 in the reign of the emperor 'Alamgír.

**Hakiri,** حقيري, poetical name of Mouláná Shaháb-uddín Mua'mmáí.

**Halaki,** هلاكي همداني, of Hamdán, a Persian poet, though illiterate, wrote a panegyric on the accession of Sháh Isma'íl Safwí II, to the throne of Persia, in the year 1576 A. D., 984 A. H., for which he received a handsome present from the king, while other poets who wrote on the same occasion, received nothing.

**Halaku Kaan** or **Khan,** هلاكو قاآن, also called Elkhán, was the son of Túlí Khán, and the fourth successor and grandson of Changez Khán the Tartar. In the reign of his brother Mangú Káán, king of Tartary, he was detached, in May, 1253 A. D., Rabí' I, 651 A. H., attended by one hundred and fifty thousand horse to subdue Persia, which he soon conquered, after which he extirpated the power of the Isma'ílís, the descendants of Hasan Sabbáh, the founder of the sect, and destroyed their strongholds in November, 1256 A. D., Ẕil-ḳada, 654 A. H. He next intended to march direct to Constantinople, but was persuaded by Nasír-uddín Túsí (whom he had made his prime minister) to turn his arms against Baghdád. He marched against that capital, and after a siege of some months, took it in February, 1258 A. D., 4th Ṣafar, 656 A. H. The Khalífa Mustaa'sim Billáh and his son were seized, and with 800,000 of its inhabitants were put to death. After these successes Halákú was desirous of returning to Tartary to take possession of the government of his native country, which had become vacant by the death of his brother, Mangú Káán: but the great defeat which the general whom he had left in Syria suffered from Saif-uddín Fíróz, the prince of the Mamlúks of Egypt, compelled him to abandon his design: and after he had restored his affairs in Syria, he fixed his residence at Marágha, in Azurbejan, where he died on Sunday the 8th February 1265 A. D., 19th Rabí' II, 663 A. H., after a reign of twelve years from his first coming to Persia, and eight years from the death of his brother. During his auspicious reign, the literature of Persia resumed its former flourishing state. The venerable Persian Bard Sa'dí of Shíráz was living in his time. Halákú was succeeded by his son Abákáán in the kingdom of Persia.

*List of Mughal-Tartar or Ilkhání dynasty of Persia.*

Halákú Khán, the son of Túlí Khán, succeeded his brother Mangú Káán in the kingdom of Persia.
Abá Káán, the son of Halákú.
Níkodár or Ahmad Khán, brother of Abáká.
Arghún Khán, son of Abáká.
Kaikhatú Khán, son of Abáká.
Baidú, grandson of Halákú.
Ghazán Khán, son of Arghún Khán.
Aljaitú, the son of Arghún Khán.
Abú Saíd Bahadur Khán, the son of Aljaptú, after whose death the dynasty became dependent.

**Halati,** حالتى, poetical title of Kásim Beg, who was born and brought up in Teherán, and spent the greater part of his life at Ḳazwín. He flourished in the reign of Sháh Tahmásp Safwí, and wrote the chronogram of the accession of Sháh Ismaíl II, in 1576 A. D., 984 A. H. He is the author of a Díwán in Persian.

**Halima,** حليمه, the name of Muhammad's nurse, who, it is said, had formerly no milk in her breasts, but immediately obtained some when she presented them to the new born prophet to suck.

**Hallaj,** حلاج. This word, which properly signifies the person that prepares cotton before it is manufactured, was the surname of Abú Mughís Husain-bin-Mansúr. *Vide* Mansúr Halláj.

**Hamd-ullah Mustoufi-bin-Abu Bakr-al-Kazwini, Khwaja,** حمد الله مستوفي بن ابو بكر القزويني خواجه, also called Hamíd-uddín Mustoufí, a native of Ḳazwín, and author of the "Táríkh Guzída," or "Selected History," which he composed in 1329 A. D., 730 A. H., and dedicated to the minister Ghayás-uddín, the son of Rashíd-uddín, author of the "Jáma'-ut-Tawáríkh," to both of whom Hamd-ulláh had been Secretary. The "Táríkh Guzída" ranks among the best general histories of the East. Eleven years after the completion of this history, the author composed his celebrated work on Geography and Natural History, entitled "Nuzhat-ul-Ḳulúb," "The delight of hearts," which is in high repute with Oriental Scholars, and which has obtained for him from D'Herbelot, the title of "le Geographe Persan." Hamd-ulláh died 1349 A. D., 750 A. H. He was the brother of Fakhr-uddín Fath-ulláh Mustoufí. See also Ahmad-bin-Abú Bakr.

**Hamid,** حميد, a poet, who is the author of a poem called "Ismat Náma," containing the loves of Sátin and Mína, composed in the year 1607 A. D., 1016 A. H., during the reign of Jahángír.

**Hamida Bano,** حميده بانو, the daughter of Malika Bano, the sister of Mumtáz Mahal, was married to Khalíl-ulláh Khán, who died in 1662 A. D.

**Hamida Bano Begam,** حميده بانو بيگم, styled (after her death) Mariam Makání, and commonly called Hájí Begam, was a great-granddaughter of Sheikh Ahmad Jám. She was married in 1541 A. D., 948 A. H., to the emperor Humayún, and became the mother of the emperor Akbar. She is the founder of the Saráe called Arab Sará, situated near the mausoleum of her husband at old Dehlí. She had gone on a pilgrimage to Mecca, and on her return, brought with her 300 Arabs, for whom she built this place in 1560 A. D., 968 A. H. She died at Ágrah on Monday, the 29th of August, 1603 A. D., 17th Shahrewar, 1012 A. H., aged about 78 years, and was buried in the mausoleum of Humáyún at Dehlí.

**Hamid-uddin Kazi,** قاضي حميدالدين دهلوي, of Dehli, was the author of the "Sharah Hidáet-ul-Fiḳah," and several other works. He died in 1363 A. D., 764 A. H.

**Hamid-uddin Mustoufi, Khwaja,** خواجه حميد الدين مستوفي. *Vide* Hamd-ulláh Mustoufí.

**Hamid-uddin Nagori, Kazi,** قاضي حميد الدين ناگوري, a native of Nágor who held the appointment of Ḳází, and died on the 11th July, 1296 A. D., 11th Ramazán, 695 A. H., and is buried at Dehlí close to the tomb of Khwája Kutb-uddín Bakhtiár, commonly called Kutb Sháh. He is the author of the book called "Tawála-ush-Shamús," containing religious contemplations and speculative opinions on the essence and nature of the divinity &c., &c. The year of his death is taken from an inscription over his tomb.

**Hamid-uddin Umar, Kazi,** قاضي حميد الدين عمر, flourished in the time of Sulṭán Sanjar, the Saljúkí king of Persia, was a contemporary of the poet Anwarí, and is the author of a Commentary on the Ḳurán called "Muḳámát."

**Hamid Ali, Mirza,** مرزا حامد علي, or more properly Prince Mirzá Hámid 'Alí, son of Wájid 'Alí Sháh, the last king of Lakhnau. He accompanied his grandmother the Dowager Queen of Lakhnau to England to claim his right, in 1856. *Vide* Jawád Alí.

**Hamid,** حامد, or Abdúl Hámid Yahia, a celebrated calligrapher, who reformed the Arabian characters in the reign of the Khalíf Muáwia II, of the house of Umaiya. He died in 749 A. D., 132 A. H.

**Hamid-uddin Ali-al-Bukhari,** حميد الدين علي البخاري, author of a short Commentary on the Hidáya, entitled the "Fawáed." He died in 1268 A. D., 667 A. H.

**Hamid Kirmani,** حامد كرماني, poetical name of Sheikh Aohad-uddín Kurmání.

**Hamid-ullah Khan,** حميد الله خان, author of the Aḥádís-ul-Khawánín, also called "Táríkh-i-Ḥamíd," which contains a history of Cháṭgawn (Chittagong). Printed at Calcutta in 1871.

**Hammad,** حماد, the son of Abú Hanífa, who was a learned man, and died in the year 792 A. D., 176 A. H.

**Hamza, Amir,** امير حمزة, the son of Abdul Muttalib, and uncle of Muhammad, who gave him the title of Asad-ulláh, or the lion of God, because of his courage and valour, and put into his hands the first standard he ordered to be made, which was called "Ráet-ul-Islám," the standard of the faith. Hamza, who was also called Abú 'Umar, was killed in the battle of Ohad which Muhammad fought with the Ḳureshites, of whom Abú Sufián was the chief. After the battle, Hinda, the wife of Abú Sufián, pulled out Hamza's liver out of his body and chewed and swallowed somo of it. This battle took place in the month of March, 625 A. D., Shawál, 3 A. H.

**Hamza Bano Begam,** حمزة بانو بيگم, daughter of Sháh Jahán by Kandaharí Begam, daughter of Muzaffar Husain Mirzá of the royal race of Sháh Isma'íl Safwí. She was born in the year 1019 A. H.

**Hamza Mirza,** حمزة مرزا, the eldest son of Sulṭán Muhammad Khuda Banda, and the grandson of Sháh Tahmásp I of the Safwí family of Persia. His father, on account of a natural weakness in his eyes, which rendered him almost blind, had at first entrusted the charge of the empire to his wazír, Mirzá Sulaimán; when that nobleman was slain, he created his own son, Hamza Mirzá, regent of the empire. This prince, by his valour, extricated his weak father from all the difficulties with which he was surrounded. But this gleam of good fortune soon vanished. This gallant prince was stabbed by a barber, in his own private apartments on the 24th of November, 1586 A. D., 22nd Ẕil-ḥijja 994 A. H.

**Hanbal, Imam,** امام حنبل, or Ahmad Ibn Hanbal, the son of Muhammad-ibn-Hanbal, was the fourth Imám or founder of one of the four orthodox sects of the Sunnís called Hanbalites. This sect made a great noise in Baghdád in the reign of the Khalíf Al-Muḳtadir in 929 A. D., 317 A. H., Merouzí chief of the sect, had asserted that God had placed Muhammad on his throne, which assertion he founded upon the passage of the Ḳurán: "Thy Lord shall soon give thee a considerable place or station." All the other sects of the Musalmáns regard the explication of the Hanbalites as a shocking impiety. They maintain that this '*considerable place or station*,' was the post or quality of a mediator, which they affirm to belong to their prophet. This dispute passed from the schools to the public assemblies. At length they came from words to blows which cost the lives of several thousands. In the year 935 A. D., 323 A. H., the Hanbalites became so insolent, that they marched in arms on the city of Baghdád, and plundered the shops on pretence that wine was drunk in them. Ahmad was a traditionist of the first class, and composed a collection of authenticated traditions called "Masnad" more copious than those any other person had till then been able to form: it is said that he knew by-heart one million of those traditions. He was born in the year 780 A. D., 164 A. H., and died on the 31st July, 855 A. D., 12th Rabí' I, 241 A. H., in the reign of the Khalíf Al-Mutwakkil, and was buried at Baghdád. It was estimated that the number of men present at his funeral was 800,000, and women 60,000; and it is said that 20,000 Christians, Jews and Magians became Moslems on the day of his death. In the year 835 A. D., Ramaẓán, 220 A. H., some time in the month of September, he was required by the Khalíf Al-Motasim Billáh to declare that the Ḳurán was created, but would not, and although beaten and imprisoned, persisted in his refusal. The eternity of the Ḳurán, considered as the word of God, is the orthodox Moslem doctrine.

**Handal Mirza,** هندال مرزا, son of the emperor Bábar Sháh, and brother of Humáyún, was born in the year 1518 A. D., 924 A. H. He lost his life in a night attack made by his brother Kámrán Mirzá on the emperor Humáyún near Khaibar in the province of Kábul, on the 19th of November, 1551 A. D., 21st Ẕi-Ḳa'da, 958 A. H. He is buried at Kábul close to the tomb of the emperor Bábar Sháh. Humáyún, out of affection to the memory of Handál Mirzá, in the same year, gave the daughter of that prince, Razia Sulṭána, to his son Akbar in marriage.

**Hani,** حني, surname of Muhammad-bin-'Alí, a poet who died in the year 1333 A. D., 733 A. H.

**Hanifa Imam,** امام حنيفة, also called Abú Hanífa and Imám 'Azim, was one of the four Jurisconsults of Mecca; *viz.*, Imám Hanifa, Imám Hanbál, Imám Sháfa'í and Imám Málik, from whom are derived the various Codes of Muhammadan Jurisprudence. He was one of the most celebrated doctors of the Musalmáns, and chief of the sect of Hanífites; and though his sect is the principal of the four which they now indifferently follow, he was ill-used during his lifetime, and died in the prison at Baghdád 767 A. D., 150 A. H. His principal works are, the "Musnad," *i. e.*, the foundation or support, wherein he established all the points of the Musalmán faith: a Treatise entitled "Filkalám," or Scholastic Divinity; and a Catechism called "Mua'llim-ul-Islám" *i. e.*, the Instructor.

His principal work is entitled the "Fiḳh-ul-Akbar," it treats of the Ilm-ul-Kalám, and has been commented upon by various writers, many of whom are mentioned by Hájí Khalfa. *Vide* Abú Hanífa. Some say that the Musnad was written by Imám Hanbál. By the Shias he is as much detested and censured, as by their antagonists he is admired and exalted. For allowing his disciples to drink *nabíz*, which is a wine made of dates, he is accused by the Persians of departing from the clear injunction of the Prophet against all intoxicating beverages.

**Harindar Narain Bhup, Maharaja,** مهاراجه هرندر نراين بهوپ, the rája of Kúch Behár, who died at Benáres on the 30th May, 1839, aged 70 years. He was of the Rajbansí caste, and a follower of Siva, but his style of living was very unlike that of a Hindú. He used to marry without any regard to caste, and entered into the connubial relation with any woman he took a fancy to. He did not even spare married women. The number of his wives or ránís was no less than 1200!

**Hari Rao Holkar,** هري راو هلكر, rájá of Indor, was the cousin and successor of Malhár Ráo III, the adopted son and successor of Jaswant Ráo Holkar. He died on the 24th of October, 1843 A. D.

**Hariri,** حريري, whose full name is Abú Muhammad Kasim-bin-'Alí-bin-'Usmán-al-Harírí-al-Basrí, was a native of Basra. He was one of the ablest writers of his time, and is the author of the "Mukámát Harírí," a work consisting of 50 Oratorical, Poetical, Moral, Ecomiastic, and Satirical discourses, supposed to have been spoken or read in public assemblies; but which were composed by the author at the desire of Anúsherwán-ibn-Khálid, wazír to Sultán Muhammad Saljúkí. He died at Basra in the year 1122 A. D., 516 A. H. Poets, historians, grammarians and lexicographers look upon the Mukámát as the highest authority, and next to the Kurán, as far at least as language is concerned. His book has been translated either entirely or partially into nearly every Eastern and European tongue.

**Harkaran,** هركرن, the son of Mathura Dás, a Kambóh of Multán, was a Munshí in the service of Nawáb Ya'tbár Khán, and is the author of a collection of letters called "Insháe Harkaran," or the Forms of Harkaran, translated into English by Dr. Francis Balfour, M. D. The second edition of this work was printed in England in 1804.

**Harun-al-Rashid,** هارون الرشيد. *Vide* Al-Rashíd.

**Hasan,** حسن بن سهيل, son of Suhail or Sahl, was governor of Chaldea about the year 830 A. D., under the Khalíf Al-Mámún, who married Túrán Dukht his daughter. Some attribute to this Hasan the translation of the Persian book entitled "Jáwedán Khirad" into Arabic.

**Hasan,** حسن, poetical name of Muhammad Hasan who flourished in the reign of the emperor Sháh 'Alam of Dehlí.

**Hasan Abdal,** حسن عبدال, or Baba Hasan Abdál, a famous saint who was a Sayyad at Sabzwár in Khurásán. He came to India with Mirzá Shahrukh, son of Anser Taimúr, and died at Kandahár where his tomb is resorted to by pilgrims. Jahángír says in the Túzak that the place Hurasadak is 75 kos from Kashmir.

**Hasan 'Ali,** حسن علي, the poet laureate in the service of Típú Sultán of Mysore. He is the author of a book called "Bhogbal," or the "Kok Shástar." It is a curious but obscene satire on women, said to be a translation or paraphrase from the Sanskrit in Hindí verse. There is another translation of the same book in Persian prose called "Lazzat un-Nisa," by Ziyá-uddín Nakhshabí.

**Hasan Askari, Imam,** حسن عسكري, or Abú'l Hasan 'Alí-al-'Askarí, was the eleventh Imám of the race of 'Alí, and the eldest son of Imám 'Alí Nakí who was the tenth. He was born at Madína in the year 846 A. D., 232 A. H., and died on the 6th November 874 A. D., 22nd Muharram, 261 A. H., aged 28 years. He is buried at Sarmanráe in Baghdád close to the tomb of his father.

**Hasan Basri, Khwaja,** خواجه حسن بصري, a native of Basra and a very pious Musalmán, who is said to have possessed all the branches of science, and was noted for self-mortification, fear of God and devotion. He is the author of a Díwán or book of Odes in Arabic. He was born in 642 A. D., 21 A. H., and died on the 11th October, 728 A. D., 1st Rajab, 110 A. H., aged 89 lunar years, and was buried at Basra.

**Hasan Beg, (Khani, Badakhshi),** بيگ خاني بدخشي حسن, Shaikh Umari was a good soldier. He was made a commander of 2500 for his services in Bangash, and was put towards the end of Akbar's reign, in charge of Kabul, receiving Fort Rohtas in the Panjáb as jagir. Hasan Beg, after making a useless attempt to incriminate others, was put into a cow-hide and in this state he was tied to donkeys and carried through the bazar. He died after a few hours from suffocation. *Vide* Ain, I. 454.

**Hasan-bin-Muhammad Khaki-al-Shirazi,** حسن بن محمد خاكي الشيرازي, who came to India in the time of the emperor Akbar and obtained different offices under the government. He is the author of a history also called "Muntakhib-ut-Tawáríkh," besides the one written by Abdul Kádir Badáoní. He commenced the work before the close of Akbar's reign, and completed it in the fifth year of the emperor Jahángír, *i. e.*, 1610 A. D., 1019 A. H., in which year, he tells us, he was appointed Díwán of Patna.

**Hasan-bin-Muhammad Sharif,** حسن بن محمد شريف, author of the "Anís-ul-'Ushshák," the lover's companion, containing an explanation of all the metaphors and phrases used by the poets; with numerous quotations from those held in the greatest estimation. *Vide* Khadim.

**Hasan-bin-Sabah,** حسن بن صباح, *vide* Hasan Sabbah.

**Hasan Buzurg,** حسن بزرگ, also called Sheikh Hasan, Amír Hasan Ílkání, and Amír Hasan Navián, Kayúkái, the son of Amír Ílkán Jaláyer. He was an immediate descendant of Sultán Arghún Khán, king of Persia, (whose sister was his mother,) and one of the principal chiefs of the Mughals in the reign of Sultán Abú Sa'íd. He married Baghdád Khátún, daughter of Amír Chobán or Jovián, but the prince being deeply enamoured of her charms, Amír Hasan, after the death of her father, was forced to resign his consort to him in 1327 A. D., 728 A. H. A few years after the death of Abú Sa'íd, Amír Hasan married his widow Dilshád Khátún, went to Baghdád, seized that city, and became the founder of a petty dynasty of princes. His life was passed in contests to establish his authority over the territories of Baghdád, and he died before this object of his ambition was accomplished, in July 1356 A. D., Rajab, 757 A. H. His son Sultán Owes Jaláyer was more fortunate: he not only succeeded in completing the conquest his father had commenced, but carried his arms into Azurbeján and Khurásán. Sultán Owes died in October 1374 A. D., 776 A. H., and left his government to his second son Sultán Husain Jaláyer. This excellent prince, who is also alike celebrated for his benevolence and love of justice, lost his life in an action in 1382 A. D., 784 A. H., with his brother Ahmad, surnamed Ílkání, a cruel and unjust ruler, whose enormities compelled his subjects to invite Amír Taimúr (Tamerlane) to their relief in 1393 A. D., and almost the whole of the future life of Ahmad passed in an ineffectual struggle with that conqueror. He fled to Egypt for safety, and when, after the death of Taimúr, he returned to recover his dominions, he was taken and put to death by Kara Yúsaf, a Turkman chief in 1410 A. D., 813 A. H.

**Hasan Imam,** امام حسن, the eldest son of 'Alí, the son of Abú Tálib, and Fátima, the daughter of Muhammad; was born on the 1st March 625 A. D., 15th Ramazán, 3 A. H. After the death of his father in January 661 A. D., Ramazán, 40 A. H., he succeeded him as second Imám, and was proclaimed Khalíf by the Arabians, but perceiving the people divided and himself ill-used, he after six months resigned the Khiláfat to Mu'áwia, who assigned to him about 150,000 pounds a year, besides large presents. After this Hasan and his brother Husain retired and lived privately at Madína, where after a few years he died of poison, administered to him by one of his wives, whom Yazíd, the son of Mu'áwia suborned to commit that wickedness, on the promise of marrying her afterwards. But instead of a new husband, she was forced to be contented with a good sum of money which Mu'áwia gave her for her pains; for Yazíd was not so mad as to trust himself to her embraces. This mournful event took place on the night of the 17th March, 669 or 670 A. D., 7th Safar, 49 A. H. He was buried in Madína at a place called Baķía. Hasan is said to have been in person very like his grandfather Muhammad, who, when he was born, spit in his mouth and named him Hasan. He had twenty children, fifteen sons and five daughters. Though his wives were remarkably fond of him, yet he was apt very frequently to divorce them and marry new ones.

**Hasan Kashi, Moulana,** مولانا حسن كاشي, a poet who was a native of Káshán. He is the author of many Ķasídas and Ghazals. The year of his death is not known, but he appears to have flourished about the 8th century of the Hijrí era.

**Hasan Khwaja,** خواجه حسن, *vide* Hasan Sanjarí.

**Hasan Khwaja,** خواجه حسن, a darwesh, the son of Khwajá Ibrahím. He is the author of a Díwán of Ghazals, in the last verses of each he has mentioned the name of his beloved.

**Hasan Kochak, Sheikh,** شيخ حسن كوچک, a grandson of Amír Choubán or Jovián. He was one of the chiefs, who, during the period of trouble and confusion which took place after the death of Sulṭán Abú Sa'íd, king of Persia, in 1335 A. D., rose to eminence. He fought several battles with Amír Hasan Buzurg, and met his death accidentally by the hands of his quarrelsome wife, in December 1343 A. D., Rajab, 744 A. H.

**Hasan Maimandi,** حسن ميمندى. It is recorded by some that he was one of the ministers of Sulṭán Mahmúd of Ghazní. This statement is altogether incorrect and unfounded, says Mr. Elliot, as it is not mentioned by any great historian. But his son who is commonly called Ahmad-bin-Hasan Maimandí was a minister of that monarch. Hasan Maimandí was, during the lifetime of Sulṭán Násir-uddín Subaktagín, employed as Díwán or Collector of Revenues at Ķasba Bust; but Násir-uddín was led by the secret machinations of his enemies to entertain an unfavourable opinion of him, till he was at last, in consequence of his having been convicted of extortion and fraud to a large amount, hanged by order of that Sulṭán; so that the general notion which prevails that he was the wazír of Sulṭán Mahmúd, is erroneous.

**Hasan, Mir,** ميرحسن, a Hindústání poet of Lakhnau, and author of the novel called "Masnawí Mír Hasan," containing the loves of Badr-i-Munír and Benazír in Urdú verse, which he completed and dedicated to Nawáb 'Asaf-uddaula in the year 1785 A. D., 1199 A. H. It is also called "Sahr-ul-Bayán." His ancestors were of Hirát, but he was born at Dehlí and went early in life to Lakhnau, where he was supported by Nawáb Safdar Jang and his son Mirzá Nawázish Alí Khán. He is also the author of a Díwán of about 8000 verses, and of a Tazkira of Urdú poets. He died in 1790 A. D., 1204 A. H. His father's name was Mír Ghulám Husain Záhik.

**Hasan Mirza,** مرزا حسن, son of Mulla Abdur Razzáķ of Lahiján. He has left some noble compositions, such as, "The True Light on the articles of Faith." "The Beauty of good Men in their Works." A pious treatise, and some others. He died in the beginning of the 18th century.

**Hasan, Moulana,** مولانا حسن, a learned Musalmán who lived in the time of the emperor Jahángír and wrote a chronogram on the sudden death of Sheikh 'Alí Ahmad, son of Sheikh Husain Naķshí, in the year 1609 A. D., 1018 A. H.

**Hasan Mutkallim, Moulana,** مولانا حسن متكلم, a poet and pupil of Mouláná Muzaffar of Hirát. He flourished in the reign of Malik Ghayás-uddín Kart II, in whose name he composed a book on the art of poetry.

**Hasan Rafi,** حسن رفيع, a Persian poet.

**Hasan Sabba** حسن صباح, the founder of the dynasty of the Isma'ilís in Persia. He was styled Sheikh-ul-Jabal, an Arabic title, which signifies "the chief of the mountains." The name by which this ruler and his descendants are indiscriminately known in European history, is, "The Old Man of the Mountain." His followers or descendants were also called Hasaní, and the English word "assassin," is supposed to have been formed from a corruption of this term. Hasan Sabbáh was at first a macebearer to Sulṭán Alp Arsalán; but in consequence of a quarrel with Nizám-ul-Mulk, the minister of that prince, he retired to Rai, his native country: and from thence, to Syria, where he entered into the service of a chief of the family of Isma'íl the son of Ja'far Sádiķ, and adopted the tenets of that sect. The first object of Hasan was to possess himself of a stronghold; and he succeeded in gaining by stratagem the mountain fort of Alahmút, situated between Ķazwín and Gílán. The fort was built by Hasan-bin-Zaid in the year 860 A. D., 246 A. H., and Hasan Sabbáh took it in 1089 A. D., 482 A. H. From this fortress he commenced depredations on the surrounding country, and added several other hill forts to the one he had already seized. That of Ródbár, which is also near Ķazwín, was next to Alahmút in consequence. Malik Sháh Saljúķí, the reigning Sulṭán, had sent a force to reduce him, but without any success. In the month of October, 1092 A. D., Ramazán, 485 A. H., Nizám-ul-Mulk, who was then following the royal camp from Isfahán to Baghdád, was stabbed by one of the followers of Hasan Sabbáh who was his personal enemy. Hasan Sabbáh died in 1124 A. D., 26th Rabí' II, 518 A. H. Rukn-uddín, who was the last of this family, and who is better known under the name of Ķáhir Sháh or Khúr Sháh, after a weak and ineffectual struggle fell before Halákú. That conqueror not only made him prisoner, but took and dismantled all his strongholds. This event took place in the month of November, 1256 A. D., Ẓi-Ķada' 654 A. H. It was his father Alá-uddín Muhammad who forced Nasír-uddín Túsí to remain with him for some years, till he was released by Halákú Khán. *Vide* Ismaíl and Ismaílís. The successor of Hasan was Buzurg Umed.

**Hasan Salimi,** حسن سليمي, *vide* Salímí.

**Hasan Sanjari, Khwaja,** خواجه حسن سنجرى, also called Khwája Hasan Dehlawí, a celebrated Persian poet of Dehlí, who was a contemporary of the famous Amír Khusro, and had become at the age of 50 years a disciple of Sheikh Nizám-uddín Aulia. He died, according to the author of the "Mirat-ul-Khayál," in the Dakhan in the year 1307 A. D., 707 A. H., and is buried at Daulatábád. He is the author of several works, amongst which is a Díwán, and one called "Fawáed-ul-Fawád," a collection of letters written by Nizám-uddín Aulia to his disciples. Tálib says he died in 1337 A. D., 738 A. H. His father's name was Aláí Sanjarí.

**Hasan, Shaikh,** شيخ حسن, the son of Shaikh Nazar-ulláh. He is the author of a work called "Sarat Istakam." He died in Mírat in the year 1078 A. H.

**Hasan Khan Shamlu,** حسن خان شاملو, governor of Hirát under Sháh Abbás II, and his son Sháh Sulaiman. He died in 1697 A. D., 1109 A. H., and is the author of a Díwán.

**Hasan, Sayyad,** سيد حسن غزنوي, of Ghazní, a poet who flourished in the reign of Sultán Bahrám Sháh the Ghaznavida, and is the author of a Díwán. He is also called Sayyad Hasan-al-Husainí. He died in the way while returning from Mecca, in the year 1170 A. D., 565 A. H.

**Hasham,** هشام بن عبد الملك, the son of Abdúl Malik, and the tenth Khalíf of the house of Umaiya or Ummaides, succeeded his brother Yazíd II in 724 A. D., 105 A. H. He conquered the Khákán of Turkistán, and made war against Leo III, the Isaurian. He was always attended by 600 camels to carry his splendid wardrobe. He died after a reign of 19 years 7 months and 11 days in the year 743 A. D., 125 A. H., and was succeeded by Walíd II, son of Yezíd II. In his time lived the celebrated Majnún, the lover of Lailí.

**Hashim,** هاشم, a poet who flourished at Burhánpúr in the Dakhan in the reign of the emperor Jahángír and was a disciple of Shaikh Ahmad Fárúkí, commonly called Shaikh Ahmad Sarhindí. He is the author of a Díwán and several other books, and was alive in 1646 A. D., 1056 A. H.

**Hashim,** هاشم, the son of Abdúl Manáf, was the father of Abdúl Muttalib, who was the father of Abdulláh and grandfather of Muhammad the prophet of the Musalmáns. He succeeded his father as president of the Ka'ba, and raised the glory of his people to the highest pitch; insomuch that the neighbouring great men and heads of tribes made their court to him. Nay, so great veneration is the memory of Hashim held in by the Arabs, that from him the family of Muhammad among them are called Háshimites. He died at Ghaza in Syria, and was succeeded by his son Abdúl Muttalib, who became president of the Ka'ba.

**Hashimi Kirmani,** هاشمي كرماني, author of a poem or Masnawí called "Mazhar-ul-Ásár." He died in 1541 A. D., 948 A. H.

**Hashmat,** حشمت, the poetical name of Mír Muhtashim Alí Khán, whose ancestors were of Badakhshán, but he was born in Dehlí. He died about the year 1748 A. D., 1161 A. H., and left a Díwán of 7000 verses.

**Hashmat,** حشمت, the poetical name of Bakhshí Alí Khán, which see.

**Hasrat,** حسرت, the poetical name of Sayyad Muhammad, who died in the reign of the emperor Muhammad Sháh.

**Hasrat,** حسرت, poetical name of Mír Muhammad Hayát of Patna who had the title of Haibat Kulí Khán. He was for some time attached to the service of Nawáb Shaukat Jang at Purania, and for some time to that of Siráj-uddaula of Murshidábád. He died in 1800 A. D., 1215 A. H., and left a Díwán of 2000 verses.

**Hasrat,** حسرت, poetical appellation of Mirzá Ja'far 'Alí, an Urdú poet who flourished in the latter part of the 18th century, and gave instructions in the art of poetry to Nawáb Muhabbat Khán at Lakhnau.

**Hasrati,** حسرتي, *vide* Shefta.

**Hatifi, Moulana,** مولانا هاتفي, the poetical name of Abdulláh, the son of Mouláná Abdur Rahmán Jámí's sister. He was born in Jám a city of Hirát, and died there in the year 1521 A. D., 927 A. H., and was buried in the village of Kharjard. He was a good poet, and author of several works. Having finished his studies, under the patronage and instruction of his uncle, Hátifí, with his permission, secluded himself from the world. When Sháh Isma'íl Safwí fought the Uzbak Tartars in Khurásán, and slew Sháhíbeg Khán their chief in 1508 A. D., 914 A. H., he prevailed on our poet to quit his cell, and come to court. Solely ambitious of rivalling the Khamsa or five poems of Nizámí, he wrote in imitation of them his "Lailí and Majnún," "Khusro and Shírín," "Haft Manzar," the "Taimúr Námá," which is also called "Zafarnáma," and in imitation of the Sikandar Náma, he undertook a heroic poem in praise of his patron, called "Fatúhát Shahí," which he did not live to finish. Among the numerous Persian poems on the story of Lailí and Majnún, that of Hátifí seems universally esteemed the simplest and most pathetic.

**Hatim,** حاتم طائي, commonly called Hátim Táí, a famous Arabian Chief of the tribe of Táí, celebrated for his liberality, wisdom and valour. He flourished before the birth of Muhammad, and his sepulchre may still be seen at a little village, called Anwarz in Arabia. There is an account of his adventures in the Romance entitled "Hátim Táí" in Persian, which has also been translated into Urdú. An English translation of this Romance was made by Duncan Forbes, A. M., from the Persian.

**Hatim,** حاتم اصم, surnamed Al-Asamm, that is to say, the deaf, was a great Musalmán doctor, much-esteemed for his piety and doctrine. He was a disciple of Shakík Balkhí and master of Ahmad Khizroya. He died 851 A. D., 237 A. H., in the reign of Mutwakkil the Khalíf of Baghdád, and was buried at Balkh in Khurásán his native country.

**Hatim Kashi, Maulana,** مولانا حاتم كاشي, a poet of Káshán in Persia, who flourished in the reign of Sháh Abbas the Great.

**Hatim,** حاتم, or Sháh Hátim, poetical name of Shaikh Zahír-uddín, a poet who was a contemporary of Walí. He was born at Dehlí in 1699 A. D., 1111 A. H., and was a soldier by profession. He gave the first impulse to Urdú poetry in Dehlí. In 1720 A. D., 1132 A. H., the Díwán of Walí was brought to Dehlí and verses of it were on every body's lips; this induced him and three friends of his, Nájí, Mazmún, and 'Abrú to apply themselves to Rekhta poetry. Up to the time of Hátim, it would appear, that Indian poets wrote in Persian. He is the author of two Díwáns in Urdú, one in imitation of Walí, and the other in imitation of Sauda and Mír Takí.

**Hatim Ali Beg, Mirza,** مرزا حاتم علي بيگ, *vide* Mehr.

**Hawas,** هوس, poetical title of Nawáb Mirzá Takí, son of Nawáb Mirzá Alí Khán. He is the author of the story of Lailí and Majnún in Urdú, and of a Díwán in which every Ghazal contains the name of Lailí and Majnún.

**Haya,** حيا, poetical title of Shio Rámdás, a Hindú, and brother of Rájá Dayá Mal Imtiyáz. He was a pupil of Mirzá Abdúl Kádir Bedil, and is the author of a Díwán of about 5000 verses.

**Hayat-ullah Ahrari,** حيات الله اراري, author of the work called "Hahata Alarfin," which contains the life of Abrsala. He died in 1061 A. H., and his tomb is in Ágrah.

**Hayati Mulla,** ملاحیاتي, of Gílán, a poet.

**Hazin,** مولانا شیخ محمد علي حزین, the poetical name of Moulána Shaikh Muhammad 'Alí, a Persian of distinction, eminently learned, and accomplished. He fled into Hindústán from his native country to avoid the persecution of Nádir Sháh in 1733 A. D., 1146 A. H. He was a voluminous author both in prose and verse. He wrote his Memoirs in 1741, eight years after his settlement for life in India, and it contains a variety of personal and historical anecdotes, excellent observations on men and manners, besides an interesting account of his travels, and remarks on many modern literary productions. A translation of this work, entitled, "The Life of Shaikh Muhammad Alí Hazín," was made by T. C. Balfour, Esquire, and published in 1830. His father's name was Shaikh Abú Tálib of Gílán, a descendant of Shaikh Táj-uddín Ibráhím, commonly called Shaikh Záhid Gíláni, who was the spiritual guide of Shaikh Safí-uddín Ardibelí. He was born at Isfahán on the 7th January, 1692 O. S., 27th Rabí' II, 1103 A. H., was in Dehlí at the time of Nádir Sháh's invasion, and died in 1766 A. D., 1180 A. H., aged 77 lunar years, at Benaras (where he had built his own tomb some time before his death) equally admired and esteemed by the Musalmán, Hindú and English inhabitants of that place. He is the author of several works in Persian and Arabic.

**Hazik, Hakim,** حکیم حاذوق, son of Hakím Humám, the brother of Abú'l Fatha Gíláni. He was a noble of the reign of the emperor Sháh Jahán, a physician and a poet, and is the author of a Díwán in Persian. He died 1658 A. D., 1068 A. H.

**Hessing, Colonel John William,** of Holland. He came to India and was at first employed by the Nawáb Nizám Alí Khán of the Dakhan in the year 1763 A. D., 1177 A. H., and afterwards by Mádho Ráo Scindhia in 1784, after whose death in 1794, he continued in the service of his nephew Daulat Ráo Scindhia, by whom he was appointed a Colonel in 1795, with the command of the fortress and city of Ágrah. He died on the 21st of July 1803, and was buried in the Roman Catholic Burial-ground at Ágrah, where a splendid mausoleum of red stone was built by his children, with an English inscription on his tomb which is of white marble.

**Hidaet,** هیدایت, poetical name of Hidaet Khán, the uncle of Nisár-ulláh Khán Firák. He died in the year 1215 A. H., and left a Díwán.

**Hidaet-ullah,** هیدایت الله, author of a work on arts and sciences called "Hidáet-ul-Ramal," written in 1601 A. D.

**Hidaet-ullah Khan,** هیدایت الله خان, great-grandson of Khán 'Azim Mirzá Koka. He is the author of a History called "Taríkh Hidaet–ulláh Khán" written in the year 1659 A. H.

**Himu,** هیمو, a banian or Indian shopkeeper of the caste of Dhúsar, whom Salím Sháh, king of Dehlí, had made superintendent of the markets. In the reign of Muhammad Sháh 'Adil, he was appointed his wazír, and intrusted with the whole administration of affairs. This person in the beginning of the reign of the emperor Akbar laid siege to Ágrah, and having reduced it proceeded to Dehlí which also surrendered, and Tardí Beg, governor of that place, who fled to Sarhind, was seized by Bairám Khán, the minister of Akbar, and beheaded for abandoning Dehlí, where he might have defended himself. Hímú was afterwards defeated and made prisoner in a battle fought at Panípat on Thursday the 5th of November, 1556 A. D., 2nd Muharram, 964 A. H., and brought into the presence of the king by Bairám Khán, who begged him to kill the infidel with his own hand. Akbar (who was then in his fifteenth year) in order to fulfil the wish of his minister, drew his sword and touched the head of the captive, while Bairám Khán, drawing his own sabre, at a single blow severed the head of Hímú from his body.

**Hijri,** هجري, the poetical title of a poet who was a native of Konbán but lived in Bengal. He is the author of a Díwán in which there is a Ḳasída of a most wonderful composition. If you read the first letter of every Misra', you have a Ḳita' in praise of Nawáb Sayyad Muhammad Riza Khán Muzaffar Jang. Some letters in the Ḳasída are written in red, if you read them by themselves, you have a Ghazal, and certain letters in the Ghazal form a Ruba'í, and certain letters in the Ruba'í form a Misra'. He was living in 1766 A. D., 1180 A. H.

**Hilal Kazwini,** هلال قزویني, an author who died in 1527 A. D., 934 A. H.

**Hilali,** هلالي استرابادي, of Astarábád, was a Tartar of the tribe of Jughtai or Chughtai, and author of a Díwán consisting of amorous odes. In his youth he travelled to Khurásán, and resided in Hirát, where the illustrious Amír 'Alísheir conferred on him many favours. He was a Sunní by religion, and was, by the contrivance of his enemies, who were Shías, put to death by order of one of the Uzbak chiefs in the year 1530 A. D., 936 A. H., but according to a book called Tuhfa Sháhí, in 1533 A. D., 939 A. H. He is the author of the following works, *viz.* "Sháh-wa-Darwesh," "Lailí-wa-Majnún," "Sifát-ul-'Ashiḳím," and a Díwán.

**Hilm,** حلم, poetical name of Prince Mirzá Saíd-uddín, commonly called Mirzá Faiyáz-uddín, son of Mirzá Rayáz-uddín *alias* Mirzá Muhammad Ján, son of Mirzá Khurram Bakht, son of Mirzá Jahandar Sháh, son of Sháh Alam, king of Dehlí. He is the author of a Díwán.

**Himmat Bahadur Gushain,** همت بهادرگشاین, Díwán of Ghaní Bahádur, Nawáb of Banda, and one of the Peshwa's (Bájí Rao II) principal officers in Bundelkhand. He joined the British troops under the command of Lieut.-Col. Powell in September, 1803, and gave battle to Shamsher Bahádur, Nawáb of Banda, who was defeated and compelled to retreat with loss. Himmat Bahádur was a powerful commander of a large body of horse, and of a numerous party of Gusháíns or Nagas, a peculiar class of armed beggars and religious devotees of whom he was not only the military leader, but also the spiritual guide. He died in 1814 and his family is provided for by the British Government.

**Himmat Khan,** همت خان, was the son of Khán Jahán Sháesta Khán, the son of the wazír Asaf Khán. He built his house on the banks of the river Jamna in a year with many other buildings such as gardens, reservoirs, baths, &c., &c., of which nothing remain now. But a bath, a reservoir, a Baolí, &c. &c., are still to be seen. His proper name was Sayyad Muzaffar. Sháh Jahán conferred on him the name of Himmat Khán. In the 19th year of Alamgír he was appointed governor of Allahábád. In the 24th year of Alamgír, the appointment of Bakhí-gani was conferred on him; and in the 30th year of Alamgír, he was again appointed governor of Allahábád.

**Hinda,** هنده, the daughter of Utba and wife of Abú Sufián. *Vide* Hamzá (Amír).

**Hindal Mirza,** هندال مرزا, *vide* Handal Mirzá.

**Hindu Rao,** هندو راو, the brother of Bíjá Báí, the wife of Maharájá Daulat Ráo Sindhia. His Kothí or Rekka House on a hillock is well-known at Dehlí. He died in 1855 A. D.

**Hira Singh,** هرا سينگ, a Sikh Chief and minister of Mahárájá Dalíp Singh of Láhor. He was murdered with many others about the beginning of January, 1845.

**Hirpaldeo,** هرپالديو, the son-in-law of Rámdeo, Rájá of Deogír, who by the assistance of the other rájás of the Dakhan, had recovered his country from the Musalmáns, but Mubárik Sháh, the son of Alá-uddín Khiljí, in the second year of his reign, 1318 A. D., 718 A. H., marched towards the Dakhan, took Hirpáldeo prisoner, flayed him alive, and hung his body at the gate of Deogír which is now called Daulatabád.

**Hisam-bin-Jamil,** حسام بن جميل, surname of Abú Sahl-al-Baghdádí, who passed for one of the best traditionists of Musalmánism. He died in 722 A. D., 104 A. H.

**Hissan,** حسان بن ثابت, the son of Sábit was a poet and companion of Muhammad. He is the author of a Díwán in Arabic. When Muhammad overcame his enemies at the battle of Khandaḳ, Hissán wrote a few verses on that occasion; the prophet was so much delighted, that he gave him Shírín the sister of Mária Ḳabtí, for wife.

**Hissan-al-Hind,** حسان الهند, that is, the Hissán of India, a title which Mír Gulám 'Alí Azád assumed.

**Holkar,** *vide* Mulhár Ráo I.

**Hormisdas,** *vide* Hurmuz.

**Hoshang,** هوشنگ, second king of the first or Pishdádian dynasty of Persia, was the son of Sayámak, and grandson of Kyómurs whom he succeeded. He reigned 40 years and was succeeded by his son Tahmurs, commonly called Deoband, or the Magician binder, a title he derived from the success with which he warred against the enemies of his family.

**Hoshang Shah,** هوشنگ شاه, (formerly called Alp Khán) was the first Muhammadan king of Málwa, and the son of Diláwar Khán Ghorí who was governor of that place from the time of Muhammad Sháh, son of Fíroz Sháh Tughlaḳ, king of Dehlí. After his father's death, which happened about the year 1405 A. D., 808 A. H., taking advantage of the times, he became entirely independent and assumed the title of Sulṭán Hoshang Sháh. He reigned 30 lunar years, and died on the 17th July, 1434 A. D., 9th Ẕil-ḥijja, 837 A. H. He was buried in a stone vault, and a splendid mausoleum of white marble was built over it which is still to be seen at Manḍo. The date of his death is to be found in the three last words of a distich translated thus by General Briggs.

When death had sealed the glorious Hoshang's fate,
And he prepared to tread on Lethe's shore,
I asked a poet to record the date,
Who briefly said, "Sháh Hoshang is no more."

He was succeeded by his son Sulṭán Muhammad Sháh, who was poisoned after a reign of one year and nine months by Mahmúd Khán (the son of his Wazír), who took the title of Mahmúd Sháh and ascended the throne of Málwa on Tuesday the 15th of May, 1436 A. D., 29th Shawwál, 839 A. H.

*List of the kings of Málwa, whose capitals were Dhár, Mando or Shádiábád.*

Diláwar Khán Ghorí, governor.
Hoshang Sháh Ghorí.
Muhammad Sháh Ghorí (also called Ghazní Khán).
Mahmúd Sháh Khiljí.
Sulṭán Ghayás-uddín Khiljí.
Sulṭán Násir-uddín Khiljí.
Sulṭán Mahmúd II, the last of the Khiljís.

In his time Málwa was incorporated with the kingdom of Gujrat by Bahádur Sháh.

**Hoshdar Khan,** هوشدارخان, a title of Hidáet-ulláh Khán, the son of Irádat Khán Wázah. He was honoured with this title by the emperor Farrukh-siyar, and after his father's death with that of Irádat Khán and the Faujdárí of Dúhipereya in the province of Málwa. In the sixth year of Muhammad Sháh, 1724 A. D., 1136 A. H., he attended Nizám-ul-Mulk 'Asaf Jáh to the Dakhan, and after the victory over Mubáriz Khán, was appointed Díwán of the Dakhan with the rank of 4000. He was afterwards appointed governor of Kulburga in the Dakhan and died in the year 1744 A. D., 1157 A. H. He had many sons, most of whom died in his lifetime. His eldest surviving son, Háfez Khán, succeeded him in the government of Kulbarga which he held at the time. Sháhnawáz Khán wrote the "Másir-ul-Umra," or Biography of Nobility.

**Hoshmand Begam,** هوشمند بيگم, daughter of Sulṭán Khusro, married to Prince Hushang, the son of prince Dánial in the year 1035 A. H.

**Hujjat,** حجت, poetical name of Násir Khusro, which see.

**Hujjat-ul-Islam,** حجت الاسلام, a title of Muhammad Ghazzálí, a celebrated doctor of the Musalmán law, *vide* Ghazzálí.

**Huma,** هما, poetical name of Sayyad Imtiyáz Khán, a son of Mo'tmid Khán, and a brother of Sayyad Ahmad, whose takhallus was Zamír. Ḥe is the author of a Díwán.

**Humai, Queen,** هماى, was the daughter of Bahman, who is also called Ardisher Darázdast (Artaxerxes Longimanus of the Greeks). She succeeded her father as queen of Persia, in the fourth century before Christ. She built the city called Simrah, which the author of the "Labb Tawaríkh" says, bore also the name of Simirem, and is the same which is at this day called Jarbadakan. The Persian authors state, that when she ascended the throne, she was pregnant by her own father. Shame led her to conceal this circumstance: and the child, of which she was delivered, was given over to a nurse to be put to death. The life of the child, however, was miraculously preserved; and the unnatural mother first recognised her son, when his fortune and valour had advanced him to the rank of a victorious general in her army. Humái immediately resigned the crown to him, and retired to a private life after she had reigned 32 years. Her son reigned about 12 years, and is called by the Persians Dárá or Dáráb I.

**Humam, Hakim,** حكيم همام, brother of Hakím Abú'l Fatha Gíláni, a well educated and learned man in the service of the emperor Akbar. He was sent by that monarch on an embassy, in company with Sayyad Sadr Jahán, to Abdulláh Khán Uzbak, ruler of Khurásán, about the year 1589 A. D., 997 A. H. He died in 1595 A. D., 1004 A. H., and left two sons, Hakím Sádiḳ and Hakím Khúshhál.

**Humam,** همام, poetical name of Kamál-uddín Muhammad bin-Abdul-Wahháb, styled by Arabsháh, "One of the most illustrious doctors of the member of the Sádát," that is to say, of the race of Alí. He lived in the time of Amír Taimúr (Tamerlane) and died in 1457 A. D., 861 A. H. He is author of a Commentary on the Hidáya. His proper name is Kamál-uddín Muhammad-al-Siwásí, which see.

**Humam Tabrezi, Khwaja,** همام تبريزي, a celebrated Persian poet of Tauris or Tabrez, and author of a collection of Rubáís or quatrain verses called "Rubáyát Mír Humám." He was a cotemporary and rival wit of Shaikh Sa'dí. Meeting one day in a bath, Humám, observing Sa'dí to be very bold, presented to him a bason with the bottom upwards; asked him, "Why do the heads of the people of Shíraz resemble this?" Sa'dí, having turned the bason with the empty side upwards, replied, "First tell me, why do the heads of the people of Tabrez resemble this?" Many other anecdotes are related of them. Humám died in the reign of Aljaitú, emperor of the Mughals, in the year 1313 A. D., 713 A. H., and was buried at Tabrez. He is also called Khwája Humám-uddín Tabrezí.

**Humam-uddin Tabrezi,** همام الدين تبريزي, *vide* Humám Tabrezí.

**Humayun,** نصير الدين محمد همايون, emperor of Hindústán, surnamed Nasír-uddín Muhammad, was the eldest son of the emperor Bábar Sháh, was born at Kábul on the night of Tuesday the 7th of March, 1508 A. D., 4th Zi-Ḳa'da, 913 A. H., and his mother's name was Máham Begam. He succeeded his father on the throne at Ágrah on the 26th December, 1530 A. D., 6th Jumáda I, 937 A. H., and conferred the government of Kábul, Ḳandahár, Ghazní, and the Panjáb on his brother Mirzá Kámirán, to Mirzá Askarí he gave the government of Sarkár Sambhal, to Mirzá Handál, Sarkar Alwar, and the government of Badakhshán to Mirzá Sulaimán, the son of Khán Mirzá, the son of Sulṭán Muhammad, the son of Sulṭán Abú Saíd. Humáyún was defeated the first time by Sher Khán (afterwards Sher Sháh) in a battle fought on the banks of the Chaunsá in Behár on the 26th June, 1539 A. D., 9th Safar, 946 A. H., and the second time at Ḳannoj on the 17th of May, 1540 A. D., 10th Muharram, 967 A. H. The capital no longer afforded him a place of refuge; even his brothers became his enemies, and would not grant him shelter in their provinces. He fled from one place to another, subject at times to the greatest hardships; and was at last obliged to quit the kingdom and seek an asylum in Persia, where he arrived in July, 1544 A. D., 951 A. H., and was hospitably and honorably entertained for some time by Sháh Tahmásp of Persia, who assisted him with troops. During the absence of Humayún, which extended to a period of fifteen years, five kings ascended the throne of Dehlí, *viz.* Sher Sháh, his son Salím Sháh, Muhammad Sháh Ádilí, Ibráhím Khán, and Sikandar Sháh. Humáyún having overcome his brothers at Kábul and Ḳandahár, commenced his march from the former city in the month of January, 1555 A. D., Safar, 962 A. H., towards India. He took the Panjáb, and advancing towards Dehlí, defeated Sikandar Sháh on the 22nd of June, 1555 A. D., 2nd Shabán, 962 A. H., in a battle fought at Sarhind. Sikandar, after his defeat, fled to the mountains of Sewálik, and Humáyún having reached Dehlí in triumph, became a second time emperor of Hindústán. Bairám Khán, to whose valour and talent the king was principally indebted for his restoration, was rewarded with the first offices in the state with the title of Khán Khánán. The year of this victory was found by Bairám Khán to be contained in the words, "The sword of Humáyún." Seven months after this victory, on the 21st January, 1556 A. D., as Humáyún was coming down at the time of evening prayers from the terrace of the Library at Dehlí, he fell headlong over the steps, and died on the 25th January, 1556 A. D., 11th Rabí' I, 963 A. H. The words "Alas! my sovereign fell from the terrace," contain the year of his demise. He was buried at Gílokharí, a distance of four kos from the city of Sháhjáhánábád on the banks of the river Jumna; and a splendid monument was erected over his remains some years after, by his son Akbar, who succeeded him. Humáyún died at the age of 49, after a reign of 25 years, including the fifteen years of his banishment from his capital. The foundation of his mausoleum was laid in 1565 A. D., 973 A. H., was superintended by Hájí Begam mother of Akbar, and was finished in 16 years at a cost of 15 lakhs of rupees. Farrukh-siyar, 'Alamgír II, Dára Shikóh and other princes are also buried in this mausoleum. Hamáyún, after his death, received the title of Jannat 'Ashiání.

**Humayun, Amir,** امير همايون, of Isfaráen, a poet who went early in life to Tabrez, and was supported by Ḳází 'I's'a and Sulṭán Yá'ḳúb, who called him Khusro Sání, that is, the second Khusro and Khusro Kóchak. After the death of his patron, he went to Káshán and died there in 1496 A. D., 902 A. H. He is the author of a Díwán.

**Humayun Shah, Bahmani, Sultan,** شاه بهمني سلطان همايون, surnamed Zálim, or the Cruel, was the eleventh king of the Bahmaní dynasty. He succeeded his father Sulṭán 'Alá-uddín II Bahmaní in the year 1458 A. D., 862 A. H., and causing his brother Hasan Khán's eyes to be put out, ascended the throne of the Dakhan. According to the will of his father, he conferred the office of Wakíl-us-Saltanat on Khwája Mahmúd Gáwán, with the title of Malik-ut-Tajjár and the government of Bíjápúr. He was an unjust prince and a great tyrant, on which account he was surnamed "the Cruel." He reigned 3 years 6 months and 6 days, and was murdered with one stroke of a heavy club on the 1st of September, 1461 A. D., 28th Zi-Ḳa'da, 865 A. H., during a fit of intoxication by his own servants who were wearied out with his inhuman cruelties. He was succeeded by his son Sulṭán Nizám Sháh, then only eight years of age.

**Hunain,** حنين, surname of Abú Zaid 'Abdur Rahmán Hunain, son of Is-hák, son of Hunain, was a celebrated Christian physician who translated many books out of the Greek into Syriac and Arabic.

**Hurmuz** or **Hurmuzd I,** هرمز يا هرمزد, the third king of Persia, of the Sasanian race, was the son of Sháhpúr I, whom he succeeded in 272 A. D. He is the Hormisdas of the Greek authors, and is said to have resembled, both in person and character, his grandfather Ardisher. The mother of this monarch was the daughter of Máhrukh a petty prince, whom Ardisher had put to death, and whose family he had persecuted, because an astrologer had predicted that a descendant of Máhrukh should attain the throne of Persia. This lady had fled to the tents of a shepherd where she was seen by Sháhpúr when hunting. This prince became enamoured, and married her privately. His father Ardisher, going one day unexpectedly to his son's house saw young Hurmuz. He was greatly pleased with the appearance of the child and made enquiries, which compelled Sháhpúr to confess all that had happened. The joy of the old king was excessive. "The prediction of the astrologers," he exclaimed, "which gave me such alarm, is, thank God, confirmed, and a descendant of Máhrukh shall succeed to my crown." Hurmuz was a virtuous prince, but reigned only one year and ten days. He died about the year 273 A. D., and was succeeded by his son Bahrám I.

**Hurmuz** or **Hurmuzd II,** هرمزد ثاني, the eighth king of Persia of the Sásánian race. He succeeded his father Narsí about the year 303 A. D., ruled Persia seven years and five months and died 310 A. D. No events of any consequence occurred during the reign of this prince. At his death he left no son: and the kingdom was on the point of being thrown into confusion, when it was declared that one of the ladies in the harem was pregnant, and that there were certain indications of the embryo being a male. When the child was brought forth, it was named Sháhpúr: and every care was taken to give the young sovereign an education suited to his high duties.

**Hurmuz** or **Hurmuzd III,** هرمزد ثالث, the second son of Yezdigard II, succeeded his father, of whom he was always the favourite, 456 A. D. His elder brother Fíroz, though at first compelled to fly across the Oxus, soon returned to assert his right at the head of a large army, which aided by a general defection of the Persians, who deserted his weak brother, obtained an easy victory, and the unfortunate Hurmuz was, after a short reign of little more than one year, dethroned and put to death 457 A. D.

**Hurmuz** or **Hurmuzd IV**, هرمزد رابع, (the Hormisdas III of the Greeks) was declared successor to his father the great Chosroes, surnamed Nausherwán the Just, and ascended the throne of Persia 579 A. D. His subjects revolted against him at the instigation of Bahrám Chobín or Varanes his general, whom he had offended by sending him a female dress because he had been defeated by the Romans. They confined Hurmuz and put out his eyes to disqualify him from ascending the throne, and soon after put him to death 590 A. D. His son Khusro Purvez having collected a force to oppose Bahrám, who with the intention of taking the government into his own hands was advancing towards Madáin, was defeated; and with great difficulty effected his escape to the territories of the Romans, from whose emperor, Maurice, he met with the most friendly and hospitable reception. Bahrám Chobín took possession of the vacant government: but his rule was short: for within eight months from the period of his taking possession of Madáin, he was defeated by an army of Romans and Persians commanded by Khusro, and fled to Tartary.

**Husain**, حسين, poetical name of Muzaffar Husain, an author who is also called Shahíd or Martyr. He is the author of the work called "Rayáz-us-Sálikím."

**Husain Ali Khan Bahadur**, حسين علي خان بهادر, second son of Alahwardí Khán, a nobleman of high rank who served under the emperor 'Alamgír, and died on the 3rd of October, 1686 A. D., 25th Ẕi-Ḳa'da 1097 A. H., a day after the fort of Bíjápúr was taken.

**Husain Ali Khan, Sayyad**, سيد حسين علي خان, Amír-ul-Umrá. *Vide* Abdulláh Khán (Sayyad).

**Husain-bin-Alim**, حسين بن عليم, author of the "Nuzhat-ul-Arwáh," containing interesting anecdotes of the most celebrated Súfís, *vide* Husain-bin-Hasan-al-Hasaní.

**Husain-bin-Muhammad, as-Sama'ani**, السمعاني حسين بن محمد, author of the "Khazánat-al-Muftiín" which contains a large quantity of decisions, and is a book of some authority in India. It was completed in 1339. A. D., 740 A. H.

**Husain-bin-Hasan-al-Husaini**, بن حسن الحسيني حسين, a native of Ghór and author of several works, *viz.* "Kanz-ul-Ramúz," "Sí Nama," "Nuzhat-ul-Arwáh," "Zád-ul-Musáfarín," "Tarab-ul-Majális," "Rúh-ul-Arwáh," "Sirát-ul-Mustaḳím," and of a Díwán in Arabic and Persian. He died, says Jámí, in the year 1317 A. D., 717 A. H., and is buried at Hírát. Firishta calls him Amír Husainí Sádát, and says, that he with his father Sayyad Najm-uddín came to India as merchants and became the disciples of Shaikh Bahá-uddín Zikaria at Multan, and died at Hírát on 1st December, 1318 A. D., 6th Shawwál, 718 A. H.

**Husain Dost Sambhali, Mir**, حسين دوست سنبهلي مير, son of Abú Tálib of Sambhal. He is the author of a biography of poets called "Tazkira Husainí," which appears to have been compiled a few years after the death of Muhammad Sháh the emperor of Dehlí who died in 1748 A. D., 1161 A. H.

**Husaini**, حسيني, author of the "Asmáe Husainí" and "Maktúbát Husainí."

**Husain Ghaznawi**, حسين غزنوي, author of the story of Padmáwat in Persian poetry called "Ḳissae Padmáwat."

**Husain Hallaj, Shaikh**, شيخ حسين حلاّج, the son of Mansúr Halláj. Many fables have been invented to account for the imprudence of this wise teacher. One of these states, that he observed his sister go out every evening: he followed her; having seen her communicate with the Húries, and receive from these celestial nymphs a cup of nectar, he insisted on drinking one or two drops that remained of this celestial liquor. His sister told him he could not contain it, and that it would cause his death. He persisted; from the moment that he swallowed it, he kept exclaiming An-ul-Haḳ! that is, "I am the truth!" till he was put to death. *Vide* Mansúr Halláj.

**Husain, Imam**, امام حسين, the second son of 'Alí, the son-in-law of Muhammad. He was born at Medina in January, 626 A. D., Shabán, 4 A. H., and was the third Imám of the race of 'Alí. Having refused to acknowledge Yazíd the son of Mu'áwia, for the lawful Khalíf, he was obliged to leave Medina, and to fly to Mecca, but was overtaken on his way and killed by order of Ubaidulláh-ibn-Zayád, one of Yazíd's captains, on the 10th October, 680 A. D., 10th Muḥarram, 61 A. H. When his head was brought to Ubaidulláh at Kúfa, he struck it over the mouth with a stick, and treated it with great contempt. He then sent it along with his family who were made captives, to Damascus where Yazíd then reigned. The day on which he was killed, is still a great day amongst the Musalmáns. He is buried at a place called Karbala in Babylonian Irák or Chaldea near Kúfa. Some pretend to show that Husain's head was buried near the river of Karbala; others say, that there are no traces of it remaining. However, the first Sulṭán of the race of Boyaides built on that spot a sumptuous monument, which is visited to this very day with great devotion by the Musalmáns. It is called "Gunbaz Faiz," or the dome of grace.

**Husain-ibn-Muin-uddin Maibadi**, الدين ميبدي حسين ابن معين, author of a work on religion, entitled "Fawátah."

**Husain Jalayer, Sultan**, سلطان حسين جلاير, grandson of Amír Hasan Buzurg, succeeded his father Sulṭán Awes Jaláyer, to the throne of Baghdád in October, 1374 A. D., 776 A. H., and lost his life in an action with his brother Sulṭán Ahmad in 1382 A. D., 784 A. H. *Vide* Hasan Buzurg.

**Husain Kashi**, حسين كاشي, an author, who died in 1544 A. D., 951 A. H.

**Husain, Kashmiri**, حسين كشميري, author of the Persian work, entitled, "Hidáyat-ul-'Amí," the Guide to the Blind, containing essays on various religious subjects, Súfí doctrines, &c.

**Husain Khonsari**, حسين خوانساري, was one of the celebrated philosophers of Persia, surnamed from his birth-place Khonsár, a town between Teheran and Kashan. He flourished in the latter part of the 17th century.

**Husain Langa I**, حسين لنگا, third king of Multán, succeeded his father Ḳutb-uddín Mahmúd Langa in 1469 A. D., 874 A. H. He entered into a treaty of alliance with Sikandar Lodí, king of Dehlí, and died about the year 1498 A. D., 904 A. H., or according to some, on Sunday the 28th August, 1502 A. D., 26th Ṣafar, 908 A. H., after a reign of 30 or 34 years. He was succeeded by his grandson Mahmúd Khán Langa. Firishta says, that the "Tawáríkh Bahádur Sháhí," which contains the history of this prince, is full of errors, and the author of the "Mirat-Sikandarí" declares it to be absolutely unintelligible.

**Husain Langa II**, حسين لنگا, fifth and last king of Multán, was, after the death of his father Mahmúd Khán Langa in 1524, raised to the throne, although a minor. He was only a pageant in the hands of his sister's husband, Shujáa'-ul-Mulk, who assumed the office of protector. Sháh Husain Arghún, king of Ṭhaṭṭa, under the orders of the emperor Bábar Sháh, soon after besieged the place which was at length, in the year 1526 A. D. 932 A. H., carried by escalade, after a siege of fifteen months. Husain Arghún having nominated one Lashkar

Khán his deputy, returned to Ṭhaṭṭa. When Bábar Sháh, during his illness, abdicated the throne in favor of his son Humáyún, the latter prince gave the Panjáb in jágír to Mirzá Kámrán his brother, who on his arrival at Láhor, sent for Lashkar Khán and made over the district of Kábul to him, in lieu of that of Multán, since which time the kingdom of Multán has continued a province of the empire of Dehlí.

**Husain Marwi,** حسين مروي, *vide* Khwája Husain Marwí.

**Husain Mirza,** حسين مرزا, *vide* Sulṭán Husain Mirzá.

**Husain Mashhadi,** حسين مشهدي, a Persian poet.

**Husain Moin-uddin,** حسين معين الدين, author of the "Fawátah Sabạ" on Theology.

**Husain Maibazi, Muin-uddin,** الدين حسين ميبذي معين, author of the "Sajanjal-ul-Arwáh," or Mirror of Spirits, a selection from the Persian and Turkí poets. He flourished in the tenth century of the Hijra.

**Husain Muammai, Mir,** مير حسين معماى, a celebrated punster who died in the year 1498 A. D., 904 A. H.

**Husain Nakshi, Mulla,** ملا حسين نقشي, a learned Musalmán of Dehlí who was a good poet and an excellent engraver in the time of the emperor Akbar. He died on the 16th of July, 1581 A. D., 14th Jumáda II, 989 A. H.

**Husain Nizam Shah I,** حسين نظام شاه, ascended the throne of Ahmadnagar in the Dakhan in the 30th year of his age, after the death of his father Burhán Nizám Sháh I in the year 1554 A. D., 961 A. H. In 1565 A. D., 972 A. H., an alliance was formed between him and the three Sultáns, *viz.*, 'Alí 'Adil Sháh of Bíjápúr, Ibráhím Ḳutb Sháh of Gólkanḍa and Amír Baríd of Ahmadabád Bídar, against Rámráj, rájá of Bíjanagar, who was defeated and slain. Husain Nizám Sháh died eleven days after his return from this expedition, on Wednesday the 6th of June, 1565 A. D., 7th Ẓi-Ḳa'da, 972 A. H., and his son Murtazá Nizám Sháh succeeded him. The death of Nizám Sháh has been commemorated in the following chronogram: "The sun of the Dakhan has become obscured."

**Husain Nizam Shah II,** حسين نظام شاه ثاني, a nominal prince of the Nizám Sháhí dynasty. *Vide* Fatha Khán, the son of Málik 'Ambar.

**Husain Sabzwari,** حسين سبزواري, a native of Sabzwár, and author of the works entitled "Latáef Wazáef," and "Ráhat-ul-Arwáh," books on Súfyism, containing the best means of obtaining salvation, and rules for moral conduct.

**Husain Sadat, Mir,** مير حسين سادات, *vide* Husain bin-Hasan-al-Husainí.

**Husain Shah Lohani, Pir,** حسين شاه لوهاني پير a Muhammadan saint whose tomb is in Múnghír, where both Hindús and Muhammadans make offerings especially on their marriages and other special occasions.

**Husain Shah Sharki, Sultan,** حسين شاه شرقي سلطان, ascended the throne of Jaunpúr after his brother Muhammad Sháh, who was slain in battle about the year 1452 A. D., 856 A. H. He fought several battles with Bahlól Lodí, the king of Dehlí, and was at last defeated, and so closely pursued that he left his horse and escaped on foot. The army of Dehlí advanced without any other check to Jaunpúr which fell to the arms of Bahlól, while Husain Sháh, abandoning his capital, was obliged to content himself with a small tract of country yielding only a revenue of five lakhs of rupees. Bahlól having delivered over Jaunpúr and its kingdom to his own son Bárbak, enjoined him not to deprive Husain Sháh of the small tract to which he was confined, terming it his family estate. This event took place about the year 1476 A. D., 881 A. H., and the subversion of the Sharkí dynasty may be dated from that year. The reign of Husain Sháh lasted for a period of 19 lunar years. Some years after the death of Bahlól Lodí (which happened in 1489 A. D., 894 A. H.) Husain Sháh incited the prince Bárbak to rise up against his brother Sikandar Lodí, king of Dehlí, and wrest the government out of his hands; but Bárbak was defeated in the first action and retired to Jaunpúr, to which place he was pursued by the king. Jaunpúr fell shortly after, and was added to the kingdom of Dehlí. Husain Sháh was now induced to seek refuge with 'Aláuddín Púrbí, king of Bengal, by whom he was treated with the respect due to his station till his death which took place in 1499 A. D., 905 A. H. With him the royal line of Jaunpúr was extinguished.

**Husain Shah,** حسين شاه of Bengal; *vide* 'Alá-uddín Husain Sháh.

**Husain Shah, Sayyad,** سيد حسين شاه, author of the story of Bahram Gór, entitled "Hasht Gulgasht," which he made into prose from the "Hasht Bahisht" of Amír Khusro in the year 1800 A. D., 1215 A. H., on the requisition of M. Charles Perron, who served under Daulat Ráo Scindhia, *vide* Hak-ík-at.

**Husain Waez, Maulana,** مولانا حسين واعظ surnamed Káshifí, was a man of consequence in the time of Sulṭán Husain Mirzá, surnamed Abú'l Ghází Bahádur of Khurásán, and held the office of sacred herald in the city of Hirát till the Hijrí year 910, on the last day of which he expired, *i. e.*, on the 3rd June, 1505 A. D., 30th Ẓil-ḥijja, 910 A. H. He is the author of a commentary on the Ḳurán, commonly called "Tafsír Husainí," which he entitled "Mawáhib 'Uliát," also of one entitled "Jawáhir-ut-Tafásír." Besides these, he wrote several other works, amongst which are the "Rouzat-ush-Shuhadá," an excellent history of Muhammad with a minute detail of the battle of Karbala, dedicated to Sulṭán Husain Mirzá in 1501 A. D., an abridgment of which is called "Dah Majlis." The "Akhlák Muhsiní," a very valuable system of Ethics, treating upon worship, prayer, patience, hope, chastity, &c., dedicated to the same Sulṭán 1494 A. D., 900 A. H., the title of which gives the year of its completion. The "Anwár Suhelí," (Emanations of the star Canopus) being a translation of Pilpay's Fables in Persian, dedicated to Amír Shaikh Ahmad Suhelí, seal-bearer to the Sulṭán. He calls himself in this book Maulána Husain-bin-'Alí-al-Waez surnamed Káshifí. He also made an abridgment of Moulwí Rúmí's Masnawí which he called "Lubb-i-Labáb." He is also the author of the works called "Makhzan-ul-Inshá," "Sabạ" Káshifia (on astrology), "Asrár Ḳásimí," "Matla-'ul-Anwár," and of a collection of Anecdotes called "Latáef-ut-Tawáef." This author is by some writers called Kamál-uddín Husain-al-Wáez-al-Káshifí-us-Subzwárí.

**Husain-uddin Husain-bin-Ali,** حسين بن علي حسين الدين, who is said to have been a pupil of Burhán-uddín 'Alí, was the first who wrote a commentary on the Hidáya, entitled the Niháya.

**Huzuri, Mir,** مير حضوري, son of Amír Sayyid 'Alí Muhtasib. He lived in the time of Sháh Isma'íl Safwí, and wrote a chronogram on his accession to the throne of Persia in the year 1576 A. D., 984 A. H. He is the author of a Díwán.

# I.

**Ibn-Abi Tai,** ابن ابی طی, author of the work called Kitáb "Ar Rauzatain."

**Ibn-Abu Usaibia, Muwaffik-uddin Abu'l Abbas Ahmad,** موفق الدین ابوالعباس احمد ابن ابوعسیبیا, author of the Arabic work called "'Ayún-al-Anbá-fi-Tabkát-ul-Atibbá," *i. e.*, Fountains of Information respecting the classes of Physicians. This book was translated by the author into Arabic from the Sanskrit at the commencement of the 13th century of our era. In the 12th chapter of this work, he gives an account of all the Physicians who were from India. Of one, whom he calls Kanka-al-Hindí, he says, He was skilful as a philosopher amongst the ancient philosophers of India, and one of the greatest of men. He investigated the art of physic, the power of medicines, the nature of compound substances, and the properties of simple substances. He was the most learned of all men in the form of the universe, the composition of the heavenly bodies, and the motions of the planets. An extract from the above work is given in the "Journal of the Royal Asiatic Society, No. 11," by the Rev. W. Cureton; with remarks by Professor H. H. Wilson. Ibn-Abú Usaibia died in 1269 A. D., 668 A. H.

**Ibn-Arabi,** ابن عربی, surname of Shaikh Muhí-uddín Abú'Abdulláh-bin-Muhammad-bin-'Alí-al-Táí-al-Hatimí-al-Andalusí, a celebrated doctor of Damascus to whom, the Muhammadans pretend, was dictated or inspired, or sent from heaven, by their prophet in the year 1229 A. D., a book of mystical divinity, called "Fasús-ul-Hakam." It contains 27 Hukams or Instructions; each of which is attributed to one of the ancient patriarchs or prophets, excepting the last, which belongs to Muhammad, and is entitled "Hakam Fardiyát Muhammadiat." The Musalmán doctors are very much divided as to the merit of this work; for some praise it, and others absolutely reject it, as being full of superstition and falsehood. He is also the author of several other works, one of which is called "Fatúhát Makkia." He died in 1240 A. D., 638 A. H. There appears to be another Ibn-'Arabí who died in Sarmanrae in Baghdád in the year 1040 A. D., or 431 A. H., and who was also an author of several works.

**Ibn-Arabshah,** ابن عربشاه, surname of Ahmad-bin-Muhammad, a native of Damascus, who besides a collection of Tales, wrote several other works in a very polished style, the most celebrated of which is a history of the Life of Amír Taimúr (Tamerlane) entitled "'Ajáeb-ul-Makdúr." He died at Damascus in the year 1450 A. D., 854 A. H. *Vide* Arab Sháh.

**Ibn-Amin,** ابن امین, *vide* Ibn-Yamín or Amír Mahmúd.

**Ibn-Asir,** ابن اثیر, al-Shaibání Majd-uddín, also called Jazarí, a most celebrated Arabian author of whom we have several works. He is the author of the Arabian work on Jurisprudence entitled "Jáma'-ul-Usúl," a work having great authority. Another of his works is called "Kamil-ut-Tawaríkh." He is by some authors called Abú'l Sa'ádat. Mubárik-bin-Asír-al-Jazarí, commonly called Ibn-Asír. He died 1209 A. D., 606 A. H. *Vide* Jazarí.

**Ibn-Askar,** ابن عسکر, an author who wrote the history of Damascus.

**Ibn-Babawia,** ابن بابویه, *vide* Abú Ja'far Muhammad bin-'Alí-bin-Bábawia.

**Ibn-Batuta,** ابن بتوته, the Arab traveller whom Muhammad Tughlak made Judge of Dehlí, was the author of the work called "Travels of Ibn-Batúta," which has been translated from Arabic by the Rev. S. Lee, B. D. London, 1829. Ibn-Batúta performed his pilgrimage to Mecca in 1332 A. D., 732 A. H. His work contains few facts concerning Arabia. His whole account of Mecca is "May God ennoble it."

**Ibn-Bauwab,** ابن بواب, *vide* Bauwáb.

**Ibn-Dahan,** ابن دهانه, *vide* Dáhán.

**Ibn-Darastuya,** ابن درستویه, commonly called so, but his proper name is Abú Muhammad 'Abdulláh, the son of Ja'far, a very learned Musalmán who died 958 A. D., 347 A. H., at Baghdád.

**Ibn-Dured,** ابن درید, author of a dictionary and of a work entitled "Gharíb-ul-Kurán" which is also called "Jamhira." He died at Baghdád in 933 A. D., 321 A. H.

**Ibn-Fakhr-uddin Anju,** ابن فخرالدین انجو, author of the "Farhang Jahángírí," *vide* Jamal-uddín Husain Anjú.

**Ibn-Farat,** ابن فرات, author of the Geographical Memoirs of Egypt.

**Ibn-Farghani,** ابن فرغانی, Shaikh Abú Bakr Wasiti, a saint, who died about 320 A. H.

**Ibn-Fourak,** ابن فورق, *vide* Fourak.

**Ibn-Ghayas,** ابن غیاث, *vide* Kamál-uddín Muhammad (Khwája).

**Ibn-Hajar, Shahab-uddin,** شهاب الدین ابن حجر, son of 'Alí 'Uskaláni, an Arabian author who wrote more than a hundred books, among which are "Lisán-ul-Mízán," and Asába. He died in 1449 A. D., 853 A. H., *vide* Shaháb-uddin Abú'l Fazl-al-'Uskalání.

**Ibn-Hajar Yehsami** or **Yehthami,** ابن حجر یهسمی, son of Badr-uddín, author of the work called "Sawáik Muhrika," and several other books. He died in 1566 A. D., 974 A. H.

**Ibn-Hajib,** ابن حاجب, an Arabian author of several works. He died at Alexandria in the year 1248 A. D., 646 A. H. He is the author of the two commentaries called "Káfia and Shafia."

**Ibn-Hanbal,** ابن حنبل, whose proper name is Abú 'Abdulláh Ahmad-ash-Shaibání-al-Marwazí, but generally known by the name of Ibn-Hanbal, was the founder of the fourth Sunní sect. This learned doctor, who was a pupil of Sháfa'i, strenuously upheld the opinion that the Kurán was uncreated, and that it had existed from all eternity. Since, however, it happened unfortunately that the Khalífa Al-Mustansir maintained tho contrary doctrine, Ibn-Hanbal was greatly persecuted for his persistent opposition to that monarch's favorite belief. *Vide* Hanbal.

**Ibn-Hanbali,** ابن حنبلی, surname of Muhammad-bin-Ibráhím Hanbalí, author of the "Uddat-ul-Hásib-wa-Umdat-ul-Masáhib," a book of Arithmetic. He died 1563 A. D., 971 A. H., and is the author of several other works.

**Ibn-Hasham,** ابن هشام, the author of the Sírat-ul-Rasúl or Biography of the Prophet. His native place was Old Cairo, where he died in 828 A. D., 213 A. H. An abridgment of his work was made at Damascus in 1307 A. D., 707 A. H., by one Ahmad Ibn-Ibráhím.

**Ibn-Hasham,** ابن هشام بن یوسف, son of Yúsaf, author of several Arabic works, among which are "Touzíh," "Sharah Alfia," &c. &c. He died 1361 A. D., 762 A. H.

**Ibn-Hibban,** ابن حبان, whose proper name was Asir-uddín Muhammad, the son of Yúsaf. Was the author of several works. He died at Damascus in the year 1344 A. D., 745 A. H.

**Ibn-Hilal,** ابن هلال, also called 'Aláí, is the author of a work, entitled "Minháj-ul-Tálibín," which is also called "Táríkh 'Aláí," and is dedicated to Sháh Shujáa' Kirmání.

**Ibn-Houbal,** ابن هوبل, a celebrated physician and author, who died in the year 1213 A. D.

**Ibn-Houkal,** ابن هوكل, an Arabian, and author of the work, entitled "Ashkál-ul-Bilád," containing maps and geographical description of several countries, which he wrote in the year 977 A. D., 367 A. H.

**Ibn-Humam,** ابن همام, author of a Commentary on the Hidáya, entitled "Fath-ul-Kadír," which is also called "Sharah Hidáya." He died in the year 1457 A. D., 861 A. H. He is also called Humám, which see.

**Ibn-Husam,** ابن حسام, of Khawáf, surname of Shams-uddín Muhammad, author of an heroic poem in praise of 'Alí, containing the principal events of his life; his disputes, wars, &c., entitled "Khâwar Náma." He died 1470 A. D., 875 A. H.

**Ibn-Ibad,** ابن عباد, surname of Abú'l Kasim Ismáí'l, Káfí, who was wazír and first minister of state to the Sultáns Muwaiyad-uddaula and Fakhr-uddaula of the race of Bóya. He died 995 A. D., 385 A. H., and is said to have left a library consisting of 112,000 volumes, and to have passed for the most generous and most liberal man of his time. He was also styled Káfí-ul-Kafát.

**Ibn-Imad,** ابن عماد, a poet of Khurásán who flourished in the latter end of the 14th century of the Christian Era. He resided in Shíráz, and is author of a Díwán or a love-story, called "Dah Náma", in Persian.

**Ibn-Jinni,** ابن جنّی, whose proper name was Abú'l Fatha 'Usmán, a learned Musalmán, but blind of one eye. He died at Baghdád 1002 A. D., 392 A. H.

**Ibn-Jouzi,** ابن جوزی, *vide* Abú'l Farah-ibn-Jouzí.

**Ibn-Kamal Pasha,** ابن كمال پاشا, surname of Muftí Shams-uddín Ahmad-bin-Sulaimán, author of the "Sharah Hadís-al-'Arbaín." He died 1533 A. D., 940 A. H.

**Ibn-Kattaa,** علي بن جعفر صقلي المشهوربه ابن قطاع, surname of 'Ali-bin-Ja'far Sikillí, an Arabian author, who died 1121 A. D., 515 A. H.

**Ibn-Khaldun,** ابن خلدون, the African philosopher. His name and titles are in Arabic: "Walí-uddín Abú Zaid 'Abdurrahman-bin-Muhammad-al-Hazramí-al-Ishbílí," but he is better known by the single patronymic name of Ibn-Khaldún. His father surnamed Khaldún was a native of Amazirg or Berber (in Africa), but his wife, descending from a family of the Arabian province Hazramát, made her son adopt the surname of Al-Hazramí. He was born in Tunis in the year 1332 A. D., and passed his youth in Egypt. He then served a short time under Taimúr, as chief justice at Damascus. He returned to Egypt where he became Supreme Judge, and died in the year 1406 A. D. His principal and most remarkable work is the History of the Arabs, the Persians, and the Barbers. The whole composition is commonly called Taríkh-ibn-Khaldún.

**Ibn-Khallikan,** ابن خليكان, whose full name is Shams-uddín Abú'l Abbás Ahmad-ibn-Muhammad-ibn-Abu Bakr-ibn-Khallikán, drew his descent from a family of Balkh. This very eminent scholar and follower of Sháfa'í doctrines, was born at Arbela, but resided at Damascus, where he had filled the place of chief Kází till the year 1281 A. D., 680 A. H., when he was dismissed, and from that time till the day of his death he never went out of doors. He was a man of the greatest reputation for learning, versed in various sciences, and highly accomplished; he was a scholar, a poet, a compiler, and an historian. By his talents and writings, he merited the honorable title of "the most learned man," and the ablest historian. His celebrated Biographical work, called the Wafiát-ul-Aiyán or deaths of eminent men, is the acme of perfection. This work was translated from the Arabic by Baron MacGucklin De Slane, Member of the Council of the Asiatic Society of Paris, &c., and published in 1842 A. D. This translation is a most valuable work to those who wish to gain a knowledge of the legal literature of the Muhammadans, as he has added to the text numerous learned notes, replete with curious and interesting information relating to the Muhammadan law and lawyers. Ibn-Khallikán was born on Thursday the 22nd of September, 1211 A. D., 11th Rabí' II, 608 A. H., and died on Thursday the 31st of October, 1282 A. D., 26th Rajab, 681 A. H., aged 73 lunar years, in the Najíbia College at Damascus and was interred at Mount Kásiyún.

**Ibn-Khurdadbih,** ابن خردادبه, an historian, who died about the year 912 A. D. *Vide* Khurdáziba.

**Ibn-Kutaiba,** ابن قتيبة, surname of Shaikh al-Imám Abú Muhammad Abdullah-bin-Muslim Dínwarí, author of the "Ayún-ul-Akhbár," and many other works. He died 889 A. D., 267 A. H.

**Ibn-Maja,** ابن ماجه, whose proper name is Abú Abdullah Muhammad-bin-Yezíd-bin-Mája-al-Kazwíní, was the author of a collection of traditions, and of a commentary on the Kurán. The first, which is entitled "Kitab-us-Sunan," is the sixth book of the Sunna, and is commonly called "Sunan Ibn-Mája." Ibn-Mája was born in the year 824 A. D., 209 A. H., and died in 886 A. D., 273 A. H.

**Ibn-Makla,** ابن مقله, wazír of the khalíf al-Káhir Billáh of Baghdád, whom, with the consent of other Umras, he deposed and having deprived him of sight, raised Al-Rází Billáh to the throne. Not long after, his hands and tongue were cut off by the order of Rází, because he had written a letter to the Khalíf's enemy without his knowledge, from which he died in the year 939 A. D., 327 A. H. Ibn-Makla is the inventor of the present Arabic character which was afterwards improved by Ibn-Bauwáb.

**Ibn-Marduya,** ابن مردويه, commonly called so, but his proper name is Abú Bakr. He is the author of the work "Mustakharij Bíkhárí" and of a commentary and history. He died 410 A. H.

**Ibn-Malik,** ابن مالک, *vide* Abú Abdulláh-ibn-Málik.

**Ibn-Muallim,** ابن معلم, *vide* Shaikh Mufíd.

**Ibn-Rajab,** *vide* Zain-uddín-bin-Ahmad.

**Ibn-Rashid,** ابن رشيد, surname of Abú'l Walíd Muhammad-bin-Ahmad, whom the Europeans call Averroes and Aven Rosch, was one of the most subtile philosophers that ever appeared among the Arabians. He was born at Corduba in Spain, where his father held the office of high priest and chief judge, under the emperor of Morocco. His knowledge of law, divinity, mathematics, and astrology was very extensive, and to this was added the theory rather than the practice of medicine. On the death of his father, he was appointed to succeed him. Falling under the suspicion of heresy, he was deprived of his posts, and thrown into prison, from whence he was at last delivered and reinstated in his office of judge. He wrote a treatise on the art of physic, an Epitome of Ptolemy's Almagest, a treatise on astrology, and many amorous verses; but when he grew old, he threw the three last into the fire. As to religion, his opinions were, that Christianity is absurd; Judaism, the religion of children; and Muhammadanism, the religion of swine. The best edition of his works is that of Venice, published in 1608. He is said to have died in 595 A. H., corresponding with 1199 A. D., but Lamprière in his Universal Biography says, that he died at Morocco in 1206 A. D.

**Ibn-Sabbagh-al-Shafai,** ابن صباغ الشافعي, surname of Abú Nasr 'Abdúl Sáíd-bin-Muhammad, author of the "Uddat-ul-'Alim Wát Taríḳ-ul-Sálim." He died 1084 A. D., 477 A. H.

**Ibn-Sad,** ابن سعد, author of the Tabaḳát.

**Ibn-Sina,** ابن سينا, *vide* Abú Sína.

**Ibn-Shahab-uz-Zohri,** ابن شهاب الظهري, an Arabian author who flourished during the Khiláfat of 'Umar-ibn-'Abdul 'Azíz.

**Ibn-Siraj,** ابن سراج, whose proper name is Abú Bakr Muhammad, was an Arabian author, and died in 928 A. D. 316 A. H.

**Ibn-Ukba,** ابن عقبة, surname of Jamal-uddín Ahmad, author of the "Umdat-ut-Tálib." He died 1424 A. D., 828 A. H.

**Ibn-Ukda,** ابن عقدة, *vide* Abú'l 'Abbás Ahmad-bin-Muhammad.

**Ibn-ul-Arabi,** ابن العربي, *vide* Ibn-Arabí.

**Ibn-ul-Hajar,** ابن الحجر, *vide* Ibn-Hajar.

**Ibn-ul-Jazari-bin-Muhammad,** ابن الجزري, an Arabian author who died in the year 1430 A. D., 833 A. H.

**Ibn-ul-Khashab,** ابن الخشاب, whose proper name is Abú Muhammad 'Abdullah, was an excellent penman. He died at Baghdád in 1172 A. D., 567 A. H.

**Ibn-ul-Rumi,** ابن الرومي, a famous Arabian poet who was co-temporary with Avicenna. He is the author of a Díwán in Arabic.

**Ibn-ul-Warda,** ابن الوردا, author of an Arabic history called "Mukhtásir Jáma-ut-Tawáríkh," a valuable general history from 1097 to 1543 A. D.

**Ibn-us-Saleh,** ابن الصالح, whose proper name is Abú 'Amrú 'Usmán-bin-'Abdur Rahmán-ash-Shahrzúrí, author of a collection of decisions according to the doctrine of Sháfa'í, entitled "Fatáwá Ibn-us-Saleh." He died in 1244 A. D., 642 A. H.

**Ibn-Yemin,** ابن يمين, a celebrated poet, whose proper name was Amír Mahmúd, which see.

**Ibn-Yunas,** ابن يونس, astronomer to the Khalíf of Egypt, who observed three eclipses with such care, that by means of them, we are enabled to determine the quantity of the moon's acceleration since that time. He lived about a century or more after Al-Batání.

**Ibn-Zohr,** ابن ظهر, *vide* Abdul Malik Ibn-Zohr.

**Ibn-Zuryk,** ابن ظريک, Tanúkí, an author.

**Ibrahim,** ابراهيم the patriarch Abraham.

**Ibrahim,** ابراهيم, an emperor of the Moors of Africa in the 12th century, who was dethroned by his subjects, and his crown usurped by 'Abdul Múmin.

**Ibrahim, Sultan,** سلطان ابراهيم, emperor of the Turks, was the son of Ahmad (Achmat). He succeeded his brother Murád IV (Amarath) in February, 1640 A. D., 1049 A. H., and spent a great part of his reign in the war of Crete against the Venetians, but without any great success. He was assassinated for his debaucheries and repeated cruelties in 1649 A. D., 1059 A. H. His son Muhammad IV, succeeded him.

**Ibrahim,** ابراهيم, the son of Alashtar, killed in 690 A. D., 71 A. H., in a battle fought between the khalíf 'Abdul Malik and Misaa'b the brother of 'Abdullah, the son of Zubair whose faithful friend he was.

**Ibrahim,** ابراهيم, the son of Ibráhím Mahrán, a very famous doctor of the sect of Sháfa'í, and author of several works.

**Ibrahim Adham,** ابراهيم ادهم, a king of Balkh, who retired from the world, became a Dervish and died between the years 875 and 880, aged 110 years. It is said that he saw in a dream, a man on the top of a house looking for something. He asked him, what he was looking for? The man replied, that he had lost his camel. What a fool you must be, said the king, to be looking for your camel on the roof of a house. The man rejoined, And what a fool you must be to look for God in the cares and troubles of a crown! Ibráhím from that day abdicated his throne, and became a wandering Dervish.

**Ibrahim 'Adil Shah I,** ابراهيم عادل شاه, Sulṭán of Bíjápúr, surnamed Abú'l Nasr, son of Ismaíl 'Adil Sháh, succeeded his brother Mallú Adil Sháh, on the throne of Bíjápúr in the Dakhan in 1535 A. D., 941 A. H. He married the daughter of 'Ala-uddín 'Imád Sháh, named Rabia Sulṭána in 1543 A. D., 950 A. H., reigned 24 lunar years and some months, and died in 1558 A. D., 965 A. H. He was buried at Kúkí near the tombs of his father and grandfather, and was succeeded by his son 'Alí 'Adil Sháh.

**Ibrahim 'Adil Shah II,** ابراهيم عادل شاه, of Bíjápúr, surnamed Abú'l Muzaffar, was the son of Tahmásp the brother of 'Alí 'Adil Sháh, whom he succeeded in April, 1580 A. D., Safar, 988 A. H., being then only in his ninth year. The management of public affairs was given to Kamál Khán Dakhaní, and Chánd Bíbí Sulṭána, widow of the late king, was entrusted with the care of the education of the minor monarch. For some time Kamal Khán behaved with due moderation in his office; but at length was guilty of some violence towards Chánd Sulṭána, who turned her thoughts to effect his destruction. She secretly sent a message to Hájí Kishwar Khán, an officer of high rank, who caused him to be murdered. After this event Kishwar Khán, by the support and patronage of Chánd Bíbí, grasped the authority of the State, and ruled with uncontrolled sway, till he was assassinated. Akhlás Khán next assumed the regency; but after some time he was seized by Diláwar Khán, who put out his eyes, and became regent of the empire. He was expelled by the king in 1590 A. D., and his eyes put out and himself confined in 1592 A. D. Ibráhím 'Adil Sháh died after a reign of more than 38 lunar years in 1626 A. D., 1036 A. H., and was succeeded by his son Muhammad 'Adil Sháh. The first building of any importance we meet at Bíjápúr, is the Ibráhím Rauza, the tomb of Ibráhím 'Adil Sháh II. On a high-raised platform of stone, separated by a square, in the midst of which is a houz or fountain, stand the rouza and mosque opposite each other, and corresponding in size and contour. The tomb is most elaborately ornamented, the walls being covered with inscriptions from the Ḳurán in raised stone Arabic letters, which formerly were gilt, on a blue ground, though now the colouring has worn away. The mosque also is a beautiful building.

**Ibrahim Ali Khan,** ابراهيم علي خان, the new chief of Maleir Kotla is a minor of about 15 years of age (1872), and is receiving his education in the Wards' School at Umballa.

**Ibrahim Ali Khan,** ابراهيم علي خان, nawáb of Tonk, grandson of the famous Pindara chief Amír Khán. His father Muhammad 'Ali Khán was deposed by the British Government on account of the Lowa massacre in 1867. He was installed as nawáb of Tonk on the 19th January, 1871 by the British Government.

**Ibrahim Astarabadi,** ابراهيم استرابادي, an author who translated the Risala or "Ḳitáb Hasania" of Abú'l Fatúh Rází Makkí from the Arabic into Persian in 1551 A. D., 958 A. H.

**Ibrahim Barid Shah,** ابراهيم بريد شاه, succeeded his father 'Alí Baríd in the government of Ahmadábád Bídar about the year 1562 A. D., 970 A. H. He reigned seven years and died about the year 1569 A. D., 977 A. H. His brother Ḳasim Baríd II, succeeded him.

**Ibrahim Bayu, Malik,** ملک ابراهيم بيو. In the province of Behar there is a hillock called Pír Pahárí, on the top of which there is a tomb with Persian inscriptions in verse, intimating that Málik Ibráhím Bayú died in the reign of Sulṭán Fíroz Sháh on a Sunday in the month of Ẓil-ḥijja 753 A. H., which corresponds with January, 1353 A. D., but who he was we are not informed.

**Ibrahim-bin-Aghlab,** ابراهيم بن اغلب, an Arabian captain who was appointed governor of Egypt and Africa by the Khalíf Hárún-al-Rashíd in 800 A. D., 184 A. H. The descendants of this governor who settled in Africa, bore the name of Aghlabia or Aghlabites, and formed a dynasty of princes who reigned there till the year 908 A. D., 296 A. H., when they were driven out by the Fatimites.

**Ibrahim-bin-Ali,** ابراهيم بن علي, author of the work called "Majma'-ul-Ansáb," or the Genealogy of the different dynasties of Persia, till 1233 A. D., 630 A. H.

**Ibrahim-bin-Hariri,** ابراهيم بن حريری, author of the "Táríkh Ibráhímí," an abridged history of India, from the earliest times, to the conquest of that country by the emperor Bábar Sháh, who defeated Sultán Ibráhím Hussain Lodí, king of Dehlí, and became the founder of the Mughal dynasty. It was dedicated to Bábar Sháh in 1528 A. D., 934 A. H.

**Ibrahim-bin-Muhammad-al-Halabi, Shaikh,** شيخ ابراهيم بن محمد الحلبي, author of a Persian work on Theology called "Aḳáed Sunnia," and of the "Multaḳá-al-Abhár." This work, which is an universal code of Muhammadan law, contains the opinions of the four chief Mujtahid Imáms, and illustrates them by those of the principal jurisconsults of the school of Abú Hanífa. He died 1549 A. D., 956 A. H., *vide* Imám 'Alam-bin-'Ata.

**Ibrahim-bin-Nayal,** ابراهيم بن نيال, brother of Tughral Beg's mother, a chief who defeated Tughán Sháh I, a prince of the Saljúḳian family, in battle, took him prisoner and blinded him. Ibráhím was murdered after some time in 952 A. D., 451 A. H., by Tughral Beg, the uncle of Tughán Sháh.

**Ibrahim-bin-Saleh,** ابراهيم بن صالح, cousin of Hárún-al-Rashíd. A curious story is given of him in the Journal of the Royal Asiatic Society, No. 11, that when he died, Mauka-al-Hindí the philosopher restored him to life, and that Ibráhím lived long after this circumstance, and married the princess 'Alí 'Abbasa, daughter of Al-Mahdí, and obtained the government of Egypt and Palestine, and died in Egypt.

**Ibrahim-bin-Walid II,** ابراهيم بن وليد ثاني, a Khalíf of the race of Umaiya, succeeded his brother Yazíd III, in 744 A. D., 126 A. H., and had reigned but seventy days, when he was deposed, and slain by Mu'áwia II, who ascended the throne in Syria.

**Ibrahim Husain, Khwaja,** خواجه ابراهيم حسين, a celebrated caligrapher in the service of the emperor 'Akbar, who wrote a beautiful Nastalíḳ hand. He died in the year 1593 A. D., 1001 A. H., and 'Abdul Ḳádir Badáoní found the chronogram of his death to be contained in his very name with the exception of the first letter in Ibráhím, *viz.*, Alif.

**Ibrahim Husain Lodi, Sultan,** ابراهيم حسين لودي سلطان, ascended the throne of Agra, after the death of his father Sikandar Sháh Lodí in February, 1510 A. D., Ẓi-ḳa'da 915 A. H. He reigned 16 years, and was defeated and slain in a battle fought at Pánípat with the emperor Bábar Sháh on Friday the 20th April, 1526 A. D., 7th Rajab, 932 A. H., an event which transferred the empire of Dehlí and Agrah to the family of Amír Taimúr. From this battle we may date the fall of the Paṭhán empire, though that race afterwards made many efforts, and recovered it for a few years in the time of the emperor Humáyún.

**Ibrahim Husain Mirza,** ابراهيم حسين ميرزا, a son-in-law of the emperor Humáyún, and the second son of Muhammad Sulṭán Mirzá, who had four other sons besides him, *viz.*, 1st, Muhammad Husain Mirzá, 2nd, Ibráhím Husain Mirzá, 3rd, Masa'úd Husain Mirzá, 4th, Ulagh Mirzá, who died in 1567 A. D., 975 A. H., and 5th, Sháh Mirzá. They were styled, "The Mirzás," and were, on account of their ill-conduct, confined in the Fort of Sambhal by order of the emperor Akbar. When that monarch marched in the year 1567 A. D., 975 A. H. for the purpose of subduing Málwá, they made their escape and sought an asylum with Chingiz Khán, a nobleman at Baroach. They took Champaneir and Súrat and also Baroach in 1569 A. D., 977 A. H., and created a great disturbance in the surrounding countries. Ibráhím Husain was taken prisoner in 1573 A. D., 981 A. H., and shortly after put to death by Makhsús Khán, governor of Multán, and his head sent to the emperor; who ordered it to be placed over one of the gates of Agrah, (*vide* Gulrakh Begam) and caused his brother Masa'úd Husain Mirzá to be confined in the fort of Gwáliar where he soon after died.

**Ibrahim-ibn-Aghlab,** ابراهيم ابن اغلب, a king of Barbary. This country was reduced by the Saracens in the Khiláfat of 'Umar, and continued subject to the Khalíf of Arabia and Baghdád till the reign of Hárún-al-Rashíd, who having appointed Ibráhím-ibn-Aghlab governor of the western parts of his empire, that prefect took the opportunity, first of assuming greater powers to himself than had been granted by the Khalíf, and then erecting a principality altogether independent of the Khalífs. The race of Aghlab continued to enjoy their new principality peaceably till the year 910 A. D., 298 A. H., during which time they made several descents on the island of Sicily, and conquered a part of it. About this time, however, one Obeidulláh surnamed 'Al-Mahdí, rebelled against the house of Aghlab, and assumed the title of Khalíf of Ḳairwán.

**Ibrahim, Imam,** امام ابراهیم. This Ibráhím who bears the title of Imám, or chief of the religion of Muhammad, is not of the number of the twelve Imáms of the posterity of 'Ali. He was a son of Muhammad, the son of 'Alí, the son of 'Abdullah, the son of 'Abbás the uncle of the prophet, and eldest brother of the two first Khalífs of the house of 'Abbás; but was himself never acknowledged for a Khalíf. He was put to death by order of Marwán II, surnamed Himár, last Khalíf of the house of Umayya, in the month of October, 749 A. D., Ṣafar, 132 A. H.

**Ibrahim Khan,** ابراهیم خان, the son of the celebrated Amír-ul-Umrá 'Ali Mardán Khán. He was honoured with the rank of 5000 in the second year of the emperor 'Alamgír 1659, A. D., and appointed governor, at different periods, of Kashmír, Lahor, Bihár, Bengal and other places, and died in the reign of Bahádur Sháh.

**Ibrahim Khan Fatha Jang,** ابراهیم خان فتح جنگ, was a relation of the celebrated Núr Jahán Begam, whose mother's sister he had married. When Ḳasim Khán the grandson of Shaikh Salím Chishtí was recalled to court from the government of Bihár in the twelfth year of the emperor Jahángír 1616 A. D., 1025 A. H., Ibráhím Khán was appointed governor of that province with the rank of 4000. He was killed at Dacca 1623 A. D., 1032 A. H., in battle against prince Khurram (afterwards Sháh Jahán) who had rebelled against his father Jahángír. His wife Rúh Parwaz Khánam lived to a great age, and died in the reign of the emperor 'Alamgír.

**Ibrahim Khan Sur,** ابراهیم خان سور, son of Ghází Khán, governor of Bayána, was the brother-in-law of Muhammad Sháh 'Adilí, whose sister he had married. He raised a considerable army and took possession of Dehlí and Ágrah on the 28th February, 1555 A. D., 6th Jumạda' I, 962 A. H. He had no sooner ascended the throne, than another competitor arose in the province of the Panjáb, in the person of Ahmad Khán, a nephew of the late Sheir Sháh. He defeated Ibráhím Khán in a battle, and the latter retreated to Sambhal, while Ahmad Khán took possession of Ágrah and Dehlí, and assumed the title of Sikandar Sháh in May the same year. Ibráhím Khán was killed by Sulaimán, King of Bengal, in Orissa in a battle fought in 1567 A. D., 975 A. H., and is buried there. Amongst the incidents of the year 1555 A. D., 962 A. H., was the explosion in the fort of Ágrah, when enormous stones and columns were sent flying several *kós* to the other side of the Jamna, and many people were destroyed. As the whole Fort was called Bádalgaṛh, the date was found in the words, "The fire of Bádalgaṛh."

**Ibrahim Khawas,** ابراهیم خواص, a pupil of Abú 'Abdullah Maghrabí who died 911 A. D. He was called Khawás, which means a basket-maker.

**Ibrahim Kutb Shah,** ابراهیم قطب شاه, was the son of Ḳulí Ḳutb Sháh I, sovereign of Golkanḍa. On the death of his brother Jamsheid Ḳutb Sháh, the nobles of the court elevated his son Subhán Ḳulí, a child of seven years of age, to the throne; but as he was unable to wield the sceptre, Ibráhím was sent for from Bíjánagar, where he then resided, and was crowned on Monday the 28th of July, 1550 A. D., 12th Rajab, 957 A. H. In the year 1565 A. D., 972 A. H., he, in conjunction with the other Muhammadan monarchs of the Dakhan, marched against Ramráj, the rájá of Bíjánagar, who was defeated and slain, and his territories occupied by the conquerors. In 1571 A. D., 979 A. H., the fort of Rájmandrí was taken from the Hindús by Rafa't Khán, the general of Ibráhím; the following chronogram commemorates the date of its occurrence: "The temple of the infidels has fallen into our hands." Ibráhím Ḳutb Sháh, after a prosperous reign of 32 years, died suddenly on Thursday the 5th of June, 1581 A. D., 21st Rabí' II, 989 A. H., in the 51st year of his age, and was succeeded by his son Muhammad Kutb Sháh.

**Ibrahim Mirza,** ابراهیم مرزا, the son of Bahram Mirzá and grandson of Sháh Ismaí'l Safwí. His poetical name was Jáhí. He was murdered by order of his grandfather.

**Ibrahim Mirza, Sultan,** سلطان ابراهیم مرزا, was the son of Sháhrukh Mirzá and grandson of Amír Taimúr. He was governor of Fars during the life of his father, and died a few years before him in 1435 A. D., 839 A. H. After his death, his son 'Abdullah Mirzá succeeded him, and was killed in battle against Mirzá Abú Sa'íd his cousin-german in 1451 A. D., 855 A. H.

**Ibrahim Mirza,** ابراهیم مرزا, his poetical name was Ádam, which see.

**Ibrahim Mirza,** مرزا ابراهیم, the son of Mirzá Sulaimán of Badakhshán, was born in the year 1534 A. D., 941 A. H. When his father with the intention of conquering Balkh went to that country, prince Ibráhím accompanied him, and was taken prisoner in battle and put to death by order of Pír Muhammad Khán, ruler of Balkh in the month of September, 1560 A. D., Ẓil-ḥijja, 967 A. H.

**Ibrahim Nayal,** ابراهیم نیال, *vide* Ibráhím-bin-Nayál.

**Ibrahim Nizam Shah,** ابراهیم نظام شاه, succeeded his father Burhán Nizám Sháh II, in the kingdom of Ahmadnagar Dakhan in the month of April, 1595 A. D., Sha'bán, 1003 A. H., and was slain in action against the troops of Ibráhím 'Adil Sháh II, of Bíjápúr, after a reign of only four months in the month of August, 1595 A. D., Ẓil-ḥijja, 1003 A. H. Mían Manjú, his Wazír, raised to the throne one Ahmad a boy, said to be of the Nizám Sháhí family.

**Ibrahim Pasha,** ابراهیم پاشاه, an adopted son of Muhammad 'Ali Pasha of Egypt, was born in 1789 A. D., and gave the first proofs of his gallantry and generalship in 1819 A. D., in quelling the insurrection of the Wahabís. He afterwards made several conquests. In 1848 A.D. when Muhammad 'Ali had sunk into absolute dotage, Ibráhím went to Constantinople, and was installed by the Porte as Viceroy of Egypt; but on the 9th November, 1848, he died at Cairo.

**Ibrahim Shah Sharki, Sultan,** سلطان ابراهیم شاه شرقي, ascended the throne of Jaunpúr, after the death of his brother Mubárik Sháh in 1402 A. D., 804 A. H. He was famous during his reign for the encouragement he afforded to literature; and we find that in those times of anarchy and confusion which prevailed in Hindústán, Jaunpúr became the seat of learning; as appears (says Firishta) from several works now extant, dedicated to Ibráhím Sháh. He died in 1440 A. D., 844 A. H., after a long reign of upwards of 40 years. He was beloved in life, and he was regretted by all his subjects. His eldest son Mahmúd Sháh Sharḳí succeeded him.

**Ibrahim Shah Pir,** ابراهیم شاه پیر, a Muhammadan saint whose tomb is in the district of Kach thirty miles above Lakpat. *Vide* Transactions Royal Asiatic Society, Vol. III, p. 558.

**Ibrahim Shaikh,** شیخ ابراهیم, the son of Shaikh Músa, the brother of Shaikh Salím Chishtí. He served Akbar for several years in the military line, and when that emperor was proceeding to Kábul after the death of his brother, Muhammad Hakím, Shaikh Ibráhím accompanied him as for as Thánesar, where he fell sick through excess of drinking and died on the 16th Mehr, in the 30th year of Akbar's reign, corresponding with September, 1585 A. D., Shawwál, 993 A. H. According to the work "Másir-ul-Umrá," he was left behind by the emperor and ordered to take charge of the fortress of Ágrah, where he died 1591 A. D., 999 A. H.

**Ibrahim, Shaikh, ibn-Mufrij-us-Souri,** شیخ ابراهیم ابن مفرج الصوری, author of the history of Alexander the Great and of Khizir in Arabic, called "Kitáb Tarikh al-Iskandar Zulkarnain-al-Rúmí-wa-Wazírat-al-Khizr." This is one of those substructures of truth upon which Eastern nations have erected a large and romantic edifice of fable, much in the same manner as the tales of chivalry of the Middle Ages, which though fictitious, were partly attributed to real characters, as in the romances of the Knights of the Round Table and the Peers of Charlemagne.

**Ibrahim Shirwani, Shaikh,** شیخ ابراهیم شروانی, ruler of Shirwán, who reigned about the beginning of the ninth century of the Hijra. Mauláná Kátibí flourished in his time and died in 1435 A. D.

**Ibrahim Shaibani,** ابراهیم شیبانی, of Kirman Sháh, a pupil of Abú 'Abdulláh Maghrabí. He lived about the year 900 A. D.

**Ibrahim, Sultan,** سلطان ابراهیم, the son of Sultán Masa'úd I of Ghazní, succeeded his brother Farrukhzád in 1059 A. D., 450 A. H. He was a pious, liberal and just prince. In the first year of his reign he concluded a treaty of peace with Sultán Sanjar the Saljúkide, at the same time his son Masa'úd espoused the daughter of Malikshah, sister to Sultán Sanjar, and a channel of friendship and intercourse was opened between the two nations. He afterwards came to India and took several forts and obtained the title of conqueror by the extent of his victories. Sultán Ibráhím had 36 sons and 40 daughters by a variety of women, the latter of whom he gave in marriage to learned and religious men. He died after a reign of more than forty years in 1098 A. D., 492 A. H., aged 76 lunar years, and was succeeded by his son Sultán Masa'úd II or III. According to the work called "Taríkh Guzída" he reigned 30 years and died in the year 1088 A. D., 481 A. H.

**'Ibrat,** عبرت, the poetical name of Ahmad 'Alí Khán, cousin of Nawáb Sa'ádat Khán Zulfikar Jang.

**'Ibrat,** عبرت, the poetical title of Mír Zaya-uddín, a poet, who wrote the first part of the story of Padmáwat in Urdú verse, and died; consequently the second part was written by Ghulám 'Alí 'Ishrat, and finished in the year 1796 A. D., 1211 A. H., the chronogram of which he found to contain the words "Tasnif Dosha'ir."

**'Ibrat,** عبرت, the poetical name of 'Abdul Mannán, which see.

**'Ibrat,** عبرت, the poetical name of Ahmad, a musician of Dehlí, who, from the instructions that he received from Mirzá 'Abdul Kádir Bedil, became an excellent poet. He at first had assumed "Maftún" for his poetical name, but afterwards changed it for "Ibrat." He was a contemporary of Násir 'Alí the poet, and was living about the year 1688 A. D., 1100 A. H.

**'Ibrat,** عبرت, the poetical title of Mír Ziazá-uddín, author of the first portion of the story of Padmáwat in Urdú verse. He died about the year 1795. A. D. *Vide* Padmáwat.

**Idris** or **Adris-bin-Hisam-uddin, Mulla,** ملا ادریس بن حسام الدین, author of the history called "Taríkh Hasht Bahisht," or the Eighth Paradise, containing the Memoirs of the most illustrious characters of the Muhammadan religion, who flourished from 1451 to 1506 A. D.

**'Idrisi,** ادریسی, (Abú 'Abdullah Muhammad-ibn-'Abdullah Idrís), also called Sharíf-al-Idrísí-al-Sikilí, author of a system of Arabian geography, composed in 1153 A. D. He is said to be one of the most eminent Arabic geographers and descendant of the royal family of the Idrísites. He was born at Ceuta or Sibtá (Civitas) in the year 1090 A. D. The title of the above work is "Nuzhat-al-Mushtak," and it has been translated into Latin by several authors.

**Iftikhar Khan,** افتخار خان, title of Sultán Husain, the eldest son of Mír 'Abdúl Hádí, entitled Asálat Khán Mír Bakhshí, who died at Balkh in the 20th year of the emperor Sháh Jahán 1647 A. D., 1057 A. H. In the first year of 'Alamgír, Sultán Husain was honored with the title of Iftikhár Khán. Some time before his death he was appointed Faujdár of Jounpúr, where he died in 1681 A. D., 1092 A. H.

**Iffat Bano,** عفت بانو, daughter of the emperor Jahángír. Her mother was the daughter of Saíd Khán of Kashghar. She died at the age of 3 years.

**Ihsan,** احسان, the poetical name of Mirzá Ihsánulláh, commonly known by the title of Nawáb Zafar Khán, who at one time was governor of Kábul when the poet Muhammad 'Alí Sáeb of Persia came to see him there. He died in 1662 A. D., 1073 A. H., and is the author of a Díwán in Persian.

**Ihsan,** احسان, the poetical name of 'Abdur Rahmán Khán of Dehlí, who wrote excellent poetry in Urdú, and died some time after the year 1844 A. D., 1260 A. H.

**Ihsan,** احسان, the poetical title of a Hindú named Chunní Lál, who was living at Ágrah in 1760 A. D., 1174 A. H.

**Ihtisham Khan,** احتشام خان, title of Shaikh Faríd of Fathapúr Síkrí, the son of Kutb-uddín Shaikh Khúban. He served under the emperors, Jahángír, Sháh Jahán and 'Alamgír; and was raised to the rank of 3000. He died in 1664 A. D., 1075 A. H.

**Ijad,** ایجاد, the poetical name of Mír Muhammad Ihsán, who died in the year 1721 A. D., 1133 A. H.

**Ika Pandit,** اقا پندت, a Marhatta who, in the time of Sháh Alam and Madho Ráo Scindhia, held the appointment of the Súbadarship of the fort of Ágrah.

**Ikbal Khan,** اقبال خان, was the son of Zafar Khán, the son of Fíroz Sháh Tughlak. He defeated Nasrat Khán and ascended the throne of Dehlí about the beginning of the year 1400 A. D., 802 A. H., and was slain in a battle against Khizr Khán, the governor of Multán, in November, 1405 A. D., 19th Jumáda I, 808 A. H. After his death Sultán Mahmúd Sháh, who was defeated by Amír Taimúr and had fled to Gujrát and then to Kanauj, returned on the invitation of Daulat Khán Lodí who commanded at Dehlí, and took possession of the empire.

**Ikbal-uddaula Muhsin Ali Khan,** محسن علی خان اقبال الدوله, the son of Shams-uddaula Ahmad 'Alí Khán, the son of Nawáb Sa'ádat 'Alí Khán of Lakhnau. He sailed for England to claim the throne of Audh in January, 1838, A. D., and after trying in vain to obtain the recognition of his claim in England, determined upon passing the remainder of his days in a life of sanctity in Turkish Arabia. He is the author of the work called "Iḳbal Firang."

**Ikhlas Khan Husain Beg,** اخلاص خان حسین بیگ, a nobleman of the reign of the emperor Sháh Jahán who died in the year 1639 A. D., 1049 A. H.

**Ikhlas Khan Ikhlas Keish,** اخلاص خان اخلاص کیش, was a Hindú of the tribe of Khattrí of Láhor. He was well-versed in Persian, and served under the emperor 'Alamgír, who conferred on him the above title. In the time of Farrukh-siyar he was raised to the rank of 7,000. He wrote the history of that emperor and called it "Bádsháh Nama." See Kishun Chand.

**Ikram Khan,** اکرام خان, the son of Islám Khán and Ládlí Begam, the sister of Abú'l Fazl, the prime minister of the emperor Akbar. *Vide* Islám Khán.

**Ikram Khan,** اکرام خان, title of Sayyad Hasan, an amír, who served under the emperor 'Alamgír, and died in 1661 A. D., 1072 A. H.

**Ikram Ali,** اکرام علی, author of the Urdú "Akhwán-us-Safá," which he translated from the Persian in the year 1810 A. D., 1225 A. H.

**Ikram-uddaula,** اکرام الدوله, the brother of 'Alí Nakí Khán, the prime minister of Wajid 'Alí Sháh, king of Lakhnau, died August 1869, A. D.

**'Ikrima,** عکرمه, son of Abú Jahl.

**'Ikrima,** عکرمه, *vide* Akrima.

**Iksir, Mirza,** اکثیر مرزا, *vide* Aksír.

**Ilah Wirdi Khan,** الله وردي خان, } *vide* Alah Wirdi Khán.
**Ilah Yar Khan,** الله یار خان, }

**Ilahi,** الهي, an author who, according to the work called "Khulásat-ul-Asha'ár," died in 1538 A. D., 945 A. H.

**Ilahi, Mir,** میر الهی, name and poetical title of a person who was a descendant of the Sayyads of Rashídábád in Humdán. He came to India in the latter part of the reign of Jahángír, and served under his son Sháh Jahán. He is the author of a biography called "Khazína Ganj Iláhí," and of a Díwán containing amorous songs. The author of the "Mirat Jahán" says, he died in 1648 A. D., 1057 A. H., but from the chronogram which Ghaní Kashmírí wrote at his death, it appears that he died in 1654 A. D., corresponding with 1064 A. H.

**Ilahi, Shaikh,** شیخ الهی, a philosopher of Bayána, who in the time of Salím Sháh, king of Dehlí, made a great stir, by introducing a new system of religion. He called himself Imám Mahdí, who, according to the Shía's, is still living and is to conquer the world. Having raised a great disturbance in the empire, he was in the year 1547 A. D., 954 A. H., scourged to death by order of that emperor.

**Ildiguz, Atabak,** اتابک یلدگز, was a Turkish slave, sold to Sulṭán Masa'úd, one of the Saljúkí princes. He is said to have so completely established himself in the favor of his royal master, that he advanced him to the highest stations in the kingdom: and the able manner in which Ildiguz executed every duty that was assigned to him, led at last, not only to his being charged with the education of one of the young princes, which gave him the title of Atábak or Atábeg, but to his marriage with the widow of Tughral II (the brother of Masa'úd, and nephew of Sulṭán Sanjar), and within a short period he became the most powerful noble of the Persian empire. He died at Hamdán in 1172 A. D., 568 A. H., in the reign of Arsalán Sháh, and left his power and station to his eldest son Atábak Muhammad.

*List of the Atábaks of the race of Ildiguz.*

| | | A. D. |
|---|---|---|
| Atábak Ildiguz, ........................ | died | 1172 |
| " Muhammad, son of Ildiguz, ........ | " | 1186 |
| " Kizal Arsalán, son of Ildiguz, ...... | slain | 1191 |
| " Ábú Bakr, son of Muhammad, .... | died | 1210 |
| " Muzaffar, son of Muhammad, he was defeated by Sulṭán Jalal-uddín of Khwarizm, and died some time after. He was the race of Ildiguz who reigned in 'Azurbejan. | | 1125 |

**Ilham,** الهام, *vide* Malúl.

**Ilmas 'Ali Khan,** الماس علي خان, the celebrated rich and powerful eunuch of the Court of Nawáb Asif-uddaula. He died in 1808 A. D.

**Iltitmish,** التمش, *vide* Altamish.

**'Imad-al-Katib** or **Imad-uddin-al-Katib,** عماد الکاتب یا عماد الدین الکاتب, that is, 'Imád the Secretary, was the surname of Muhammad, the son of 'Abdulláh, the son of Samad, also called Isfahání. He was a celebrated author, and has written in Arabic the history of Sáláh-uddín (Saladin) the Sulṭán of Egypt and Syria, in seven volumes, entitled "Barḳ-ush-Shámí," the Lightning of Syria. He died 1201 A. D., 597 A. H.

**'Imadi,** عمادی, surname of Jamál-uddín-bin-Imad-uddín Hanafí, author of the Arabic work called "Fusúl-ul-'Imádí."

**'Imad Fakih Kirmani, Khwaja,** عماد فقیه کرماني خواجه, a Muhammadan doctor who lived in the time of Sháh Shujáa' of Shíráz. His death is mentioned in the "Jawáhir-ul-Asha'ár" to have happened in 1391 A. D., 793 A. H., but according to the poets Iláhí and Daulat Sháh he died in the year 1371 A. D., 773 A. H., which appears to be correct. Ilahí also mentions to have seen 12,000 verses of his composition, and that he is the author of the works called "Muhabbat Náma," and "Mehnat Nama," adding that he wrote in all a "Panj Ganj," that is to say, five Masnawís or Poems. It is mentioned in the "Habíb-us-Siar," that Khwája 'Imád had a cat that would stand up to prayers with him, and do what he did. This was believed by Sháh Shujáa' to be a miracle of the Khwája; but Khwája Háfiz who was his cotemporary, and would not take it for a miracle, but a deceit of the doctor, wrote a ghazal on that occasion; the following is the translation of a couplet from the same: "O thou charming bird, where art thou going, stand still, and be not proud (or think thyself to be safe) because the cat of the saint says prayers." Imád Khwája was buried at Kirman, the place of his nativity.

**'Imad Khwaja,** خواجه عماد, *vide* Imád Faḳíh.

**'Imad Shah,** عماد شاه, *vide* Imádul Mulk, commonly called Fatha-ulláh.

**'Imad-uddin Katib,** عمادالدین کاتب, *vide* 'Imád-al-Kátib.

**'Imad-uddin,** عمادالدین, surname of Ḳara Arsalán-bin-Dáúd-bin-Sukmán-bin-Artaḳ. Núr-uddín Mahmúd was his son, to whom Sálah-uddín (Saladín) the Sulṭán of Egypt gave the city of 'Amid or Ḳara Amid, 1183 A. D., 579 A. H.

**'Imad-uddin,** عماد الدين, author of a poem called the "Guldasta" or the Nosegay, which he composed in 1664 A. D., 1075 A. H. He was a native of India.

**'Imad-uddin,** عماد الدين, author of the history of the Saljúkides.

**'Imad-uddin Zangi,** عماد الدين زنگي, the son of Afsa-ḳar, was one of the Atábaks or ruling ministers under the latter princes of the Saljúkian race. He was the first of that branch that had the government of Mousal. He received the governorship of that province in 1127 A. D., 521 A. H., from Sulṭán Muhammad, the son of Sultán Malikshāh Saljúkí, reigned 19 years, and was murdered by one of his slaves in 1145 A. D., 540 A. H.

*The following is a list of the princes of this race.*

| | A. D. |
|---|---|
| 'Imád-uddín Zangí, .................... began | 1127 |
| Saif-uddín Ghazí-bin-Zangí who defeated the French at Damascus, .................. began | 1145 |
| Ḳutb-uddín Maudúd, son of Zangí, .... 569 A. H. | 1149 |
| Núr-uddín Mahmúd, son of Zangí, he reigned at Aleppo and formed another branch, died 569 A. H., .................................... | |
| Malik Sálah, son of Núr-uddín, succeeded his father and reigned at Aleppo and died 1174, .... | |
| Al-Muizz Saif-uddín Ghazí-bin-Maudúd, .. began | 1170 |
| Azz-uddín Masa'úd-bin-Maudúd, ............... | 1180 |
| Núr-uddín Arsalan Sháh-bin-Masaúd, .......... | 1193 |
| Malik-ul-Káhir Azz-uddín Masa'úd-bin-Núr-uddín, | 1210 |
| Núr-uddín Arsalán Sháh-bin-Ḳáhir, ............ | 1218 |
| Násir-uddín Mahmúd-bin-Ḳáhir, .............. | 1219 |
| Al-Malik-al-Rahím Badr-uddín Lúlú, .......... | 1222 |
| Al-Malik-us-Sálah Isma'íl-bin-Lúlú, ........... | 1259 |

*Halab or Aleppo branch.*

| | |
|---|---|
| 'Imád-uddín Zangí, .......................... | 1127 |
| Núr-uddín Mahmúd-bin-Zangí, ................ | 1145 |
| Al-Malik-us-Sálah Isma'íl-bin-Núr-uddín, ........ | 1174 |
| 'Imád-uddín Zangí-bin-Ḳutb-uddín-bin-Maudúd, delivered Aleppo to Sálah-uddín (died 1197 A. D. | 1181 |

His son Muhammad reigned at Singara.

**'Imad-uddaula,** عماد الدوله علي بويه, surnamed 'Alí Bóya, was the son of Bóya, a fisherman who rose to the command of the armies of the Sulṭán of Dílam and obtained possession of Persia, &c., which he divided with his two brothers. He fixed his residence at Shíráz 933 A. D., 321 A. H., and died in the year 949 A. D., 338 A. H. *Vide* 'Alí Bóya.

**'Imadul Mulk,** عماد الملك, commonly called Fathulláh 'Imád Sháh, founder of the 'Imád Sháhí dynasty in the Dakhan, was descended from the Kanarese infidels of Bíjanagar. Having been taken prisoner in the wars with that country when a boy, he was admitted among the bodyguards of Khán Jahán, commander-in-chief and governor of Beṛáṛ. In the reign of Muhammad Sháh Bahmaní, through the influence of Khwája Mahmúd Gáwán, he received the title of 'Imád-ul-Mulk, and was subsequently raised to the office of commander of the forces in Beṛáṛ. After the murder of his patron Khwája Mahmúd Gáwán in 1481 A. D., 886 A. H., he retired to his government of Beṛáṛ. On the accession of Sulṭán Mahmúd Bahmaní, he was honored with the office of wizárat, which he held for some time, but being soon after disgusted with the court, he left it and declared his independence in the year 1485 A. D., 890 A. H. Elichpúr was his capital. He died about the year 1513 A. D., 919 A. H., and was succeeded by his eldest son 'Alá-uddín 'Imád Sháh.

*List of the kings of the 'Imád Sháhí dynasty of Beṛár.*

Fath-ulláh 'Imád Sháh.
'Alá-uddín 'Imád Sháh, son of Fath-ulláh.
Daria 'Imád Sháh, son of 'Alá-uddín.
Burhán 'Imád Sháh.
Tufal Khán, prime minister of Burhan 'Imád Sháh, who usurped the throne, but was opposed from Ahmadnagar, and the family of 'Imád Sháh and Tufal extinguished in 1568 A. D.

**'Imad-ul-Mulk,** عماد الملك, title of that Ghází-uddín Khán who murdered his master 'Alamgír II, emperor of Dehlí. *Vide* Ghazí-uddín Khán III.

**'Imad Zangi,** عماد زنگی, *vide* 'Imád-uddín Zangí.

**Imam,** امام, a high priest or head or chief in religious matters, whether he be the head of all Muhammadans, as the Khalífa or the priest of a mosque, or the leader in the prayers of a congregation; but this sacred title is given by the Shías only to the immediate descendants of 'Alí, the son-in-law of the prophet, which are twelve, 'Alí being the first. The last of these, Imám Mahdí, is supposed by them to be concealed (not dead), and the title which belongs to him, cannot, they conceive, be given to another: but among the Sunnís it is a dogma, that there must be always a visible Imám or "father of the church." The title is given by them to the four learned doctors who are the founders of their faith, *viz.*: Imáms Hanífa, Málik, Sháfa'í, and Hanbal. Of these four sects, the Hanbalite and Málikite may be considered as the most rigid, the Sháfa'ite as the most conformable to the spirit of Islámism, and the Hanífite as the wildest and most philosophical of them all. Two other Imáms, Abú Dáúd-uz-Záhirí, and Sufián-us-Saurí were also chiefs of the orthodox sects, but their opinions had not many followers, and after some time were totally abandoned. Ibn-Jarír-ut-Tabarí, whose reputation as an historian is so familiar to Europeans, founded also a particular sect, which disappeared soon after his death. The following are the names of the twelve Imáms of the race of 'Alí.

Imám 'Alí, the son-in-law of the prophet.
" Hasan.
" Husain.
" Zain-ul 'Abidín.
" Báḳir or Muhammad Báḳir.
" Jafar Sádiḳ.
" Músí Kázim.
" 'Alí Músí Raza.
" Taḳí or Muhammad Taḳí.
" 'Alí Naḳí.
" Hasan Askarí.
" Mahdí.

**Imam 'Alam-bin-'Ala-al-Hanafi,** عالم بن علا الحنفي امام, author of a large collection of Fatwas in several volumes, entitled "Fatáwá Tátárkhánia," taken from the "Muhít-al-Burhání," the "Zakhírat," the "Khánia" and "Zahíria." Afterwards, however, a selection was made from these decisions by the Imám Ibráhím-bin-Muhammad-al-Halabí, and an epitome was thus formed, which is in one volume, and still retains the title of "Tátárkhánia."

**Imam Bakhsh, Shaikh,** شيخ امام بخش, *vide* Sahábí.

**Imam Bakhsh, Shaikh,** شيخ امام بخش, *vide* Násikh.

**Imam Bakhsh, Moulvi,** مولوي امام بخش, *vide* Sahbáí.

**Imam 'Azim,** title of Abú Hanífa.

**Imami Hirwi, Moulana,** مولانا امامي هروي, he is called Hirwí, because he was a native of Hirát. He was an excellent poet and co-temporary with the celebrated

Shaikh Sa'dí of Shíráz, whom, in the opinion of some writers, he surpassed in the Kasída. He died about the year 1281 A. D., 680 A. H., and has left a Díwán.

**Imam Malik,** امام مالك ابن آنس, son of Anas, one of the four Imáms or Jurisconsults of Mecca. He died on the 28th of June, 795 A. D., 7th Rabí' II, 179 A. H., in the time of the Khalíf Hárún-al-Rashíd. *Vide* Málik-ibn-Anas.

**Imam Muhammad,** مفتي امام محمد, a Muftí in the reign of Hárún-al-Rashíd the Khalífa. He died at Baghdád in 802 A. D., 186 A. H., and is said to have written 999 works. He was a pupil of Imám Abú Yúsaf, who committed his notes to him, and he (Muhammad) made great use of them in the composition of his works. *Vide* Abú 'Abdulláh Muhammad-bin-Husain.

**Imam-uddin Amir Katib-bin-Amir Umar,** امام الدين اميركاتب بن اميرعمر, author of a Commentary on the Hidáya entitled "Kifáya" which he finished in 1346 A. D., 747 A. H. He had previously written another explanatory gloss of the same work, and entitled it the "Gháyat ul-Bayán."

**Imdad Ali,** امداد على, the rebel Deputy Collector, who was hanged at Banda together with the rebel Tahsíldár of Pailání Muhammad Muhsin on the 24th of April, 1858.

**Imrit Rao,** امرت راو, *vide* Amrit Ráo.

**Imtihani,** امتحانى, poetical name of Imám-uddín Beg.

**Imtiyaz,** امتياز, the poetical name of rájá Dayá Mal, whose father was Díwán of Asad Khán the Wazír of 'Alamgír, and he of Ghazí-uddín Khán, styled 'Imád-ul-Mulk.

**Imtiyaz Khan, Sayyad,** سيد امتياز خان خالص, whose poetical name is Khális, was a native of Isfahán or Mashhad. He came to India in the time of the emperor 'Alamgír, was appointed governor of Gujrát for some time, and was slain by Khudá Yár Khán in 1710 A. D., 1122 A. H., in Sindh. It is said that Kásim Alí Khán, the Nawáb of Bengal, was his grandson. He is the author of a Díwán.

**Ina'amullah Khan,** انعام الله خان, *vide* Yekín.

**Inayet Khan,** عنايت خان آشنا, whose poetical title is 'Ashná or Ahsan, and proper name Muhammad Táhir, was the son of Zafar Khán. He was an excellent poet, and is the author of the work called "Sháh Jahán Nama," a history of the emperor Sháh Jahán. Besides the abovementioned work, he is the author of a Díwán and a Masnawi. He died in 1666 A. D., 1077 A. H.

**'Inayet-ullah, Shaikh,** شيخ عنايت الله دهلوي, of Dehlí, author of the work called "Bahár Dánish," a collection of amusing tales, principally satires on women. Several of these tales were published by Colonel Dow, under the title of "The Tales of 'Ináyet-ulláh," and the whole work was translated in the year 1799 A. D., by Jonathan Scott, Esq., in three volumes, octavo.

**'Inayet-ullah Khan,** عنايت الله خان, the son of Shukulláh Khán, a descendant of Sayyad Jamál of Naishápúr. His mother Háfiz Mariam was tutor of the princess Zeibun Nisá Begam, the daughter of the emperor 'Alamgír; by her influence her son 'Ináyet-ulláh Khán was raised by degrees to the rank of 2500. In the reign of Farrukhsiyar the rank of 4000 was conferred on him, and in that of Muhammad Sháh, of 7000. He is the author of the work called "Ahkám 'Alamgírí," and compiler of the "Kalmát Taiyabát." He died 1726 A. D., 1139 A. H.

**Indarman Bundela, Raja,** راجة اندرمن بنديله, the brother of Rájá Suján Singh. He died in the Dakhan about the year 1675 A. D., and his zamíndárí of Urcha and the title of rájá were conferred upon his son Jaswant Singh by the emperor 'Alamgír.

**Insaf,** انصاف, the poetical name of Muhammad Ibráhím. His father was a native of Khurásán, but he was born in India. He was a cotemporary of Sarkhush the poet, was living about the year 1688 A. D., 1100 A. H., and died young.

**Insan,** انسان, the poetical title of Nawáb Asad-ulláh Asad Yár Khán. He held the mansab of Haft Hazárí in the reign of Muhammad Sháh, and died in April, 1745 A. D., Rabí' I, 1158 A. H. His remains were brought to Agrah and buried there in the cemetery of his ancestors.

**Insha** or **Insha Allah Khan,** انشا يا انشاالله خان, a poet and son of Máshá Alláh Khán. He is the author of four Díwáns of different kinds.

**Intikhabi,** انتخابى, a poet who was a native of Khurásán, but was brought up in India. He is the author of a Díwán.

**Intizam-uddaula Khan Khankhanan,** خان خانان انتظام الدوله, the second son of Nawáb Kamar-uddín Khán Wazír. He was appointed to the rank of second Bakhshí on the accession of Ahmad Sháh to the throne of Dehlí in 1748 A. D., 1161 A. H., and was honored with the appointment of Wazír in 1753 A. D., 1165 A. H., after the dismissal of Nawáb Safdar Jang from the office. He was murdered by 'Imád-ul-Mulk Ghází-uddín Khán on the 26th November, 1759 A. D., 5th Rabí' II, 1173 A. H., three days before the assassination of the emperor 'Alamgír II.

**Iradat Khan,** ارادت خان, the title of Mír Isháḳ or Isháḳ Khán, the son of Nawáb 'Azim Khán who held a high rank in the reign of the emperor Jahángír. Irádat Khán held various offices under Sháh Jahán, and in the first year of 'Alamgír's reign he was appointed governor of Audh, but died after two months in October, 1658 A. D., Zil-hijja 1068 A. H.

**Iradat Khan,** ارادت خان واضح, the title of Mirzá Mubarik-ulláh, whose poetical name was Wázah. His father Is-hák Khán (who afterwards held the title of Kifáyet Khán) was the son of Nawáb 'Azim Khán. Both his grandfather and father were noblemen of high rank. The former was Mír Bakhshí to the emperor Jahángír, and was afterwards appointed Faujdár of Jaunpúr, where he died in 1649 A. D., 1059 A. H., the latter held various offices of importance under Sháh Jahán and 'Alamgír, and died soon after his appointment to the government of Audh in 1658 A. D., 1068 A. H. His title was also Irádat Khán which was conferred on his son after his death. In the 33rd year of 'Alamgír our present poet was appointed Faujdár of Jágná, and at other periods, of Aurngábad and Mándo in Málwa. In the reign of Sháh 'Alam Bahádúr Sháh, he was governor of the Doáb, and the intimate friend of Mua'zzim Khán, Wazír. In the latter part of his days, he led a retired life, became a Kalandár, and died in 1716 A. D., 1128 A. H. His abilities as a poet were great, and he left a volume of poems behind him. He is the author of the "Kalmát 'Aliát," (Sublime discourses,) "Mína Bázár" and of a history of Aurangzeb's Successors, which latter was translated into English by Jonathan Scott, Esq., in 1786 A. D. After his death, which happened in the time of Farrukh-siyar, his son Mír Hidáet-ulláh received the title of Hoshdár Khán, held the rank of 4000, and died at Aurangábád 1744 A. D., 1157 A. H.

**'Iraki,** عراقی, whose proper name is Fakhr-uddín Ibráhím-bin-Shahryár, was a native of Hamdan in 'Irák, and a pupil and grandson by the mother's side of the great Shaikh Shaháb-uddín Suharwardí, author of a host of mystical works highly esteemed by the Súfís. 'Irakí offended his parent and master, in consequence of some love attachment, and went to India, where he remained some time, regretting his native country, and uttering his complaints in moving verse. He lived in company with the Shaikh Bahá-uddín Zikaria of Multán, whom he accompanied on his journey and became his disciple. 'Irákí, after a long sojourn in India, proposed returning to his own master, Shaháb-uddín; but the latter had died, and our poet continued his wanderings to Syria, where he expired after a long life of eighty-two years on the 23rd November, 1289 A. D., 8th Zi-Ka'da, 688 A. H., and was buried at Sálahí in Damascus close to the tomb of Shaikh Muhí-uddín Ibn-ul-'Arabí. His son Shaikh Kabír-uddín is also buried there. 'Irákí is the author of a work called "Lama'át," *vide* Fakhr-uddín 'Irákí.

**'Irfan,** عرفان, poetical name Muhammad Rizá, the son of Muhammad Ján Irfán, author of the "Kár Náma," containing the exploits of 'Alí Mardán Khán, the Amír-ul-Umrá of the emperor Sháh Jahán.

**Irtiza 'Ali Khan Bahadur,** ارتضا علی خان بہادر, author of the "Faráez Irtizia," a concise treatise in Persian on the law of Inheritance, which appears to be the principal authority of that law in the Dakhin. It was printed in Madras, but without a date.

**'Isam-uddin Ibrahim-bin-Muhammad Isfaraeni,** عصام الدین ابراهیم بن محمد اسفرینی, an Arabian author, who died 1536 A. D., 943 A. H., and is the author of the marginal notes in Arabic called "Háshia Isám-uddín."

**'Isa-ibn-Musa,** عیسی ابن موسی, the cousin-german of the Khalíf Abú Ja'far Mansúr, after whose death in 775 A. D., 158 A. H., he entertained thoughts of setting up for himself at Kúfa where he then resided; and in order to facilitate the execution of his scheme, fortified himself in that city. But al-Mahdí, the son of Mansúr, being apprised of his defection, sent a detachment of 1000 horse to bring him to Baghdád; which being done, al-Mahdí not only prevailed upon him to own allegiance to him, but also to give up his right to the succession (he being the next apparent heir to the crown) for 10,000 according to some, and according to others 10,000,000 dinars.

**'Isa Sawaji,** عیسی ساوجی, a poet of Sáwa who was a Kází. He died in 896 A. D., 291 A. H.

**'Isi Turkhan, Mirza,** مرزا عیسی ترخان, was a Turkmán and commander-in-chief of Sháh Beg Arghún, king of Sindh's army, after whose death he took possession of Thatta of which he was then governor, and assumed the title of king. He reigned 13 years and died in 1567 A. D., 975 A. H., when he was succeeded by his eldest son Mirzá Muhammad Bákí Turkhán, who, during his rule always maintained a friendly intercourse with the emperor Akbar of Dehlí, frequently sending presents, and acknowledging fealty to that monarch. He died after a reign of 18 years in 1585 A. D., 993 A. H., and was succeeded by his grandson Mirzá Jání Beg.

**Isdigertes,** ایزدجرد, *vide* Yezdijard.

**Isfahani,** اصفهانی, author of the "Dánish Náma," a system of natural philosophy.

**Isfan** or **Stephen,** اسفان, is the name and takhallus of a Christian, born at Dehlí. His father was a European. He was alive in 1800 A. D., 1215 A. H.

**Isfandiyar,** اسفندیار, the son of Kishtásp or Gashtásp (Hystaspus) the fifth king of the Kayánián dynasty of Persia, was a great warrior, and appears to be the Xerxes of the Greeks. He was killed by Rustam before his father's death.

**Is-hak,** اسحاق, the poetical title of Jamál-uddín, a cotton-thrasher of Shíráz. He was an elegant poet, and has left us a Díwán called "Aksír-ul-Ishtihá," the Elixir of Hunger, full of amorous songs and parodies on the odes of Khwája Háfiz, each verse of which contains either the name of a sweetmeat or a dish. He lived in the time of prince Sultán Sikandar, the son of Umar Shaikh, who much esteemed him. His proper name is Abú Is-hák, which he uses in poetry by abbreviating it into Bus-hák, *vide* Abú Is-hák.

**Is-hak-bin-'Ali,** اسحاق بن علی, author of a Díwán in Arabic, and of a work called "Zuhr-ul-'Adáb." He died in 1022 A. D., 413 A. H.

**Is-hak-bin-Husain** or **Hunain,** اسحاق بن حسین, یا حنین an Arabian author who translated the Almagastí of Ptolemy from the Greek into Arabic under the title of "Tahrír-al-Majastí." This book is to be found in the French King's Library, No. 887. Shírází has written a commentary on this work, and entitled it "Hall Mushkilát-al-Majastí."

**Is-hak Khan,** اسحاق خان, styled Mó'tamin-uddaula, whose original name was Mirzá Ghulám 'Alí, was a nobleman of high rank, and a great favourite of the emperor Muhammad Sháh of Dehlí. He was a good poet, and used for his poetical name Is-hák. He died in the 22nd year of the emperor 1740 A. D., 1153 A. H., and after his death, his daughter was married to Shujá-uddaula, the son of Nawáb Safdar Jang, and the nuptials were celebrated with uncommon splendour, 1746 A. D., 1159 A. H.

**Is-hak, Maulana,** مولانا اسحاق, a learned Musalmán who was born at Uchcha in Multán. In his youth he dedicated himself under the guidance of his uncle Sayyad Sadr-uddín Rájú Kattál, whose sister was his mother. He died in 1456 A. D., 860 A. H., and was buried in the compound of his own house at Saháranpúr.

**Is-hak Mousali,** اسحاق موصلی, a celebrated Arabian author, born at Mousal. It is related in the Kitáb Alaghání, that when he was on a journey, he carried with him eighteen coffers full of books, though he declared, that if he had not been anxious to make his luggage as light as possible, he would have brought double the quantity.

**'Ishk,** عشق, poetical title of Sháh Rukn-uddín who flourished in the reign of the emperor Sháh 'Alam.

**'Ishki,** عشقی, the title of a poet who flourished in the reign of the emperor Muhammad Sháh, and is the author of a Díwán. He died in 1729 A. D., 1142 A. H.

**'Ishki,** عشقی, poetical title of Shaikh Muhammad Wajíh, son of Ghulám Husain Mujrim of Patna. He was for ten years under the English government Tahsildár of Kharwar; was living in 1809 A. D., 1224 A. H., and is the author of a Díwán.

**'Ishrat,** عشرت, poetical name of Mirzá 'Alí Rizá, who collected his poems into a Díwán under Muhammad Sháh in 1747 A. D., 1160 A. H., and died shortly after.

**'Ishrat,** عشرت, author of the last part of the story of Padmawat in Urdú verse, which was completed by him 1796 A. D. *Vide* Padmáwat and Ibrat.

**'Ishrati,** عشرتي, poetical name of a poet who is the author of a small Díwán. His name is Aka 'Alí of Isfahán, he came to India, and on his return died at Mashad.

**Ishtiyak,** اشتیاق, poetical name assumed by Sháh Walí Ulláh of Sarhind, who was the grandson of Shaikh Ahmad Sarhindí. He was a distinguished Theologian and Súfí. He died in 1748 A. D., 1161 A. H., and left several works. Sháh 'Abdul 'Azíz of Dehlí, the most celebrated Indian Theologian in modern time, was one of his sons.

**Ishuri** or **Ishwari Singh,** ایسري سنگه, the son of Rájá Jai Singh Sawáí, whom he succeeded to the ráj of Jaipúr in 1743 A. D. He died in 1760 A. D., and was succeeded by his son Mádho Singh.

**Ishuri Parshad Narain Singh Bahadur** ایشري پرشاد نراین سنگه بهادر, rájá of Benaras (1869).

**Iskandar,** اسكندر, Alexander the Great. *Vide* Sikandar Zulkarnain.

**Iskandar Manishi,** اسکندر منشي, whom Stewart in his "Catalogue of Tippú Sulṭán's Library," calls Sikandar Hamnashíní, is the author of the "Táríkh 'Alam 'Aráe 'Abbásí," a history of the Persian kings of the Safwí dynasty, from Sháh Isma'íl I to Sháh 'Abbás the Great, to whom it was dedicated in 1616 A. D., 1025 A. H.

**Islam Khan,** اسلام خان, title of Mír Zayá-uddín Husain Badakhshí, whose poetical name was Wálá. He served under the emperor 'Alamgír, and was raised to the rank of 5000 with the title of Islám Khán. He died in the year 1663 A. D., 1074 A. H., at A'grah, and the chronogram of his death was written by Ghaní Kashmírí. He was the father of Nawábs Himmat Khán, Saif Khán and 'Abdur Rahím Khán.

**Islam Khan,** اسلام خان, the son of Safí Khán and grandson of Islám Khán Mashhadí, was Súbadár of Lahór in the time of the emperor Farrukh-siyar, and was raised to the rank of 7000 in the reign of Muhammad Sháh.

**Islam Khan Mashhadi, Nawab,** اسلام خان مشهدي نواب, (he is by some called Islám Khán Rúmí, but that is a mistake). He was a native of Mashhad, and his original name was Mír 'Abdus Salám. In the time of Jahángír he held the mansab of 5000, and the Súbadárí of Bengal; and in the time of Sháh Jahán was raised to the rank of 6000 with the title of Motam-uddaula and held the appointment of second Bakhshigárí and governorship of the Dakhin. He afterwards was again appointed governor of Bengal. In the 13th year of Sháh Jahán he was raised to the rank of Wizárat with the title of Jumdat-ul-Mulk. Shortly after he was raised to the rank of 7000, and the Súbadárí of the Dakhin. He was wazír to Sháh Jahán and held the manṣab of 7000, with the title of Islám Khán. He was some time before his death appointed governor of the Dakhin where he died in the 21st year of the emperor, on the 2nd of November, 1647 A. D., 14th Shawwál, 1057 A. H., and was buried at Aurangábád.

**Islam Khan Rumi,** اسلام خان رومي, title of Husain Páshá, son of 'Alí Páshá. He was governor of Basra, but being deprived of that situation by his uncle Muhammad, he left that country and came to India in 1689 A. D., 1080 A. H., where he was received by the emperor 'Alamgír with the greatest respect, and honored with the rank of 5000 and title of Islám Khán. He was killed in the battle of Bíjápúr in the Dakhin on the 13th of June, 1676 A. D., 11th Rabí' II, 1087 A. H. He had built his house at A'grah on a piece of ground consisting of four bígas and seven cottas, and a garden on a spot of three bígas and nine cottas, on the banks of the river Jamna near the Ghát called Tajára close to the fort of A'grah.

**Islam Khan, Shaikh,** شیخ اسلام خان, styled Nawáb Ya'tzád-uddaula, was a grandson of Shaikh Salím Chishtí, and son-in-law of Shaikh Mubárik, the father of the celebrated 'Abú'l Fazl, whose sister, named Láḍlí Begam, he had married. He was appointed governor of Bengal by the emperor Jahángír in 1608 A. D., 1017 A. H. Nawáb Ikrám Khán was his son, and Ḳásim Khán his brother. The latter succeeded him in the government of Bengal in 1613 A. D., 1022 A. H., in which year Islám Khán had died. His remains were transported to Fathapúr Síkrí where he was buried.

**Islam Shah,** اسلام شاه, *vide* Salím Sháh.

**Isma'il,** اسمعیل, or Ishmael, the son of the paṭriarch Abraham.

**Isma'il,** اسمعیل بن امام جعفر صادق, the eldest son of Imám Ja'far Sádiḳ, from whom the sect of Isma'ílís or Isma'ílias take their name. They maintain, that Isma'íl, who was the eldest son, but died during his father's life, should have succeeded to the dignity of Imám, and not Músí Kázim, who was his younger brother, and became the seventh Imám. Hasan Sabbah was of this sect. *Vide* Isma'ílís.

**Isma'il I, Safwi, Shah,** شاه اسمعیل صفوی, the son of Sulṭán Haidar, was the first monarch of the Safwian dynasty of kings who reigned in Persia. He traced his descent from Músí Kázim the seventh Imám, who was descended in a direct line from 'Alí, the son-in-law of Muhammad. Almost all his ancestors were regarded as holy men, and some of them as saints. The first of this family who acquired any considerable reputation was Shaikh Safí-uddín, who had settled at Ardibel, and from whom this dynasty takes its name of Safwía or Safwí. His son Sadr-uddín Músa, as well as his immediate descendants, Khwája Alí, Shaikh Ibráhím, Sulṭán Junaid, and Haidar, acquired the greatest reputation for sanctity. Cotemporary monarchs, we are informed, visited the cell of Sadr-uddín. The great Taimúr (Tamerlane), when he went to see this holy man, demanded to know what favour he should confer upon him. "Release those prisoners you have brought from Turkey," was the noble and pious request of the saint. The conqueror complied; and the grateful tribes, when they gained their liberty, declared themselves the devoted disciples of him to whom they owed it. Their children preserved sacred the obligation of their fathers; and the descendants of the captives of Taimúr became the supporters of the family of Safí, and enabled the son of a devotee to ascend one of the most splendid thrones in the world. Khwája 'Alí, after visiting Mecca, went on a pilgrimage to Jerusalem, and died at that city. His grandson Junaid, sat on the masnad as a spiritual guide after the death of his father Shaikh Ibráhím; and so great a crowd of disciples attended this holy man, that Jahán Sháh, the chief of the tribe of the Black Sheep, who at that time ruled Azurbeján, became alarmed at their numbers, and banished him from Ardibel. Junaid went to Dayárbikar, whose ruler, the celebrated Uzzan Hasan, received him kindly, and gave his sister in marriage to Junaid. He afterwards went with his disciples to Shirwán, where he was slain in a conflict with the troops of the king of that province in 1456 A. D., 860 A. H. His son Sulṭán Haidar succeeded him, and his uncle, Uzzan Hasan who had now by his overthrow of Jahán Sháh and Sulṭán Abú Saíd, become sovereign of all Persia, gave him his daughter in marriage. The name of this princess according to Muhammadan authors, was 'Alam Shoa', but we are informed by a cotemporary European writer, that she was called Martha, and was the daughter of Uzzan Hasan by the Christian lady Despina, who was a daughter of Calo Joannes, king of Trebizond. Sulṭán Haidar also lost his life from the wound of an arrow which he received in a battle with the troops of Shirwán Sháh and Ya'ḳúb Beg in July, 1488 A. D., Shabán, 893 A. H. Sulṭán Haidar had three sons by this princess; Sulṭán 'Alí, Ibráhím Mirzá and Sháh Isma'íl. When Isma'íl attained the age of fourteen (his elder brothers having died some years before), he put himself at the head of his adherents, and marched against the great enemy of his family the ruler of Shirwán, called Shirwán Sháh, whom he defeated 1500 A. D., 906 A. H., and soon after; by another victory gained over Alwand Beg, the son of Ya'ḳúb Beg, a prince of the dynasty of the White Sheep, he became the master of the province of Azurbeján, and established his residence at the city of Tabrez; and in less than four years became the acknowledged sovereign of the kingdom of Persia. He was born on the 17th July, 1487 A. D., 25th Rajab, 892 A. H., died after a reign of 24 lunar years on Monday the 23rd of May, 1524 A. D., 19th Rajab, 930 A. H., aged 38 years, and was buried at Ardibel. Muhammadan historians fix the commencement of his reign from the year 1500 A. D. He left four sons; Tahmasp, who succeeded his father, Sam Mirzá, Bahrám, and Ikhlás Mirzá, and five daughters. He composed a Turkish Díwán in which he uses the Takhallus of Khitabí.

*The following is a list of the Safwí kings of Persia.*

1. Sháh Isma'íl Safwí, 1st son of Sulṭán Haidar.
2. Sháh Tahmasp Safwí I, son of Isma'íl Safwí.
3. Sháh Isma'íl II.
4. Muhammad Khudá Banda.
5. Hamza, son of Khudá Banda.
6. Sháh Isma'íl III, son of Khudá Banda.
7. Sháh 'Abbás I, son of Khudá Banda.
8. Sháh Safí, the son of Safí Mirzá, the son of 'Abbás.
9. Sháh 'Abbás II, son of Sháh Ṣafí.
10. Sháh Sulaimán, son of 'Abbás II.
11. Sháh Husain, son of Sulaimán.
12. Sháh Tahmasp II, last of the Safwí dynasty.
    Mahmúd, an Afghán.
    Ashraf, an Afghán.
13. Sháh 'Abbás III, *vide* Nádir Sháh.
    Nádir Sháh.

**Isma'il II, Safwi, Shah,** شاه اسمعيل صفوى ثاني, second son of Sháh Tahmasp I, Safwí, whom he succeeded on the throne of Persia in May, 1576 A. D., Ṣafar, 984 A. H., by the aid of his sister Parí Khánam, who sent for him from the fort of Ḳahḳah where he was confined by his father for the last 18 years. The short reign of this unworthy prince was marked by debauchery and crime. Immediately on his accession, he directed the massacre of all the princes of the blood-royal that were at Ḳazwín, except 'Alí Mirzá whose life was spared: but even he was deprived of sight. His eldest brother Muhammad Mirzá, who had a natural weakness in his eyes, which rendered him almost blind, and was during his father's life, employed as governor of Khurásán, was then at Shíráz. Orders were sent to murder him and his son 'Abbás, but before they could be executed, Isma'íl was found dead one morning in a confectioner's house, supposed to have been poisoned by his sister. His death happened at Ḳazwín on Sunday the 24th November, 1577 A. D., 13th Ramaẓán, 985 A. H., after a short reign of one year and six months. He was succeeded by his eldest brother, Muhammad Mirzá who, on his accession to the throne, took the title of Muhammad Khudá Banda.

**Isma'il,** اسمعيل, surnamed al-Mansúr, third or fourth Khalíf of Barbary of the race of the Fátimites, succeeded his father al-Káem 945 A. D., 334 A. H., and having defeated and slain Yezíd-ibn-Kondat who had rebelled against his father, caused his body to be flayed, and his skin stuffed and exposed to public view. Al-Mansúr died after a reign of seven years and sixteen days in 952 A. D., 30th Shawwál 341 A. H., and was succeeded by his son Abú Tamím Ma'd surnamed Mo'izz-uddín-alláh.

**Isma'il 'Adil Shah, Sultan,** اسمعيل عادل شاه, of Bíjápúr, surnamed Abú'l Fatha, succeeded his father Yúsaf 'Adil Sháh on the throne of Bíjápúr in the Dakhin in 1510 A. D., 915 A. H., and died after a glorious reign of 25 lunar years on Wednesday the 27th of August, 1534 A. D., 16th Ṣafar, 941 A. H., and was buried at Kúkí near the tomb of his father. He was succeeded by his son Mallú 'Adil Sháh.

**Isma'il-bin-Hasan,** اسمعيل بن حسن, author of the work called "Zakhíra Khwárizm Sháh." He flourished in the reign of Alá-uddín Takash, Sulṭán of Khwárizm who died in 1200 A. D., 596 A. H., and was a cotemporary of Khaḳání the poet.

**Isma'il, Sayyad-bin-Husain Jurjani,** اسمعيل سيد بن حسين جرجاني, author of two medical works in Persian, called "Aghráz-ut-Tibb," and "Khiff-i-'Aláí," which he dedicated to Alp Arsalán, Sulṭán of Khwárizm.

**Isma'ili,** اسمعيلي or **Isma'ilia,** اسمعيليه, a family of chiefs, who had through the means of superstition, established an influence over the minds of their followers, that enabled them to strike awe into the bosoms of the most powerful sovereigns, and to fill a kingdom with horror and dismay for a period of nearly two centuries. Their ruler, who may be justly termed the chief of the assassins resided on a lofty mountain, called Alahmút, and fate was in his hands; for there was no shape which his followers could not assume, no danger that they could not brave, to fulfil his mandates. These were the Isma'ílís or assassins, well-known by the Crusaders, as subjects of the Old Man of the mountain. They were completely extirpated by Halákú, the Tartar king of Persia, in the year 1256 A. D. *Vide* Isma'íl and Hasan Sabbáh.

**Isma'il Hakki, Shaikh,** شيخ اسمعيل حقي, author of a commentary on the Ḳurán called "Rúh-ul-Bayán," and of the "Hadís-ul-Arba'ín."

**Isma'il Mirza,** اسمعيل ميرزا, of Isfahán, an author.

**Isma'il Nizam Shah,** اسمعيل نظام شاه. His father, prince Burhán Sháh, having been defeated in an attempt to dethrone his brother Murta'zá Nizám Sháh, had fled for protection to the court of the emperor Akbar. On his departure he left behind him two sons, named Ibráhím and Isma'íl, who were kept confined in the fortress of Láhágurh. On the death of Míran Husain Sháh, the younger being raised to the throne of Ahmadnagar by Jamál Khán in the month of March, 1589 A. D., Jumádạ I. 997 A. H., took the title of Isma'íl Nizám Sháh. His father Burhán Sháh having received assistance from the emperor Akbar, marched against his son, but was defeated. However in a short time after this, he renewed his attempts, and being joined by a great majority of the chiefs and people, attacked Jamál Khán the king's minister, who was killed in the action on the 27th April, 1591 O. S., 13th Rajab, 999 A. H. Isma'íl, who had reigned little more than two years, was taken prisoner and confined by his father, who ascended the throne of Ahmadnagar with the title of Burhán Nizám Sháh II.

**Isma'il Pasha,** اسمعيل پاشا, the present Khaddev or king of Egypt, son and successor of Muhammad 'Alí Pasha, who died in August, 1849 A. D.

**Isma'il Samani, Amir,** امير اسمعيل ساماني, the first King or Amír of the race of Sámán, called Sámání, traced his descent from Bahrám Chobín, the warrior who contended for the crown of Persia with Khusro Parvez. Sámán, the great-grandfather of Isma'íl, is termed, by European writers, a keeper of herds, and a robber: but this merely designates the occupation of a Tartar chief. His father Nasr Ahmad, the son of Asad, the son of Sámán, was appointed governor of Máwarun Nahr by the Khalíf Mo'tamid in the year 875 A. D., 261 A. H. On his death his son Isma'íl succeeded him. Ismaíl, after his conquest over Amrú-bin-Lais, whom he seized and sent to Baghdád, in 900 A. D., became independent. The power of the dynasty of the Sámánís extended over Khurásán, Seistán, Balkh and the countries of Trans-Oxania, including the cities of Bukhárá and Samarkand. This justly celebrated prince died after a reign of twenty years in 907 A. D., Safar 295 A. H., aged 60 years, and was succeeded by his son Amír Ahmad Sámání.

The names of the kings of this family who were called Amírs, and who continued to reign for a period of 128 lunar years, are as follow:—

1. Amír Isma'íl Sámání.
2. „ Ahmad Sámání.
3. „ Nasr-bin-Ahmad.
4. „ Núh I, son of Nasr.
5. „ Abdul Málik.
6. Amír Mansúr I.
7. „ Núh II.
8. „ Mansúr II.
9. „ 'Abdul Málik II, the last of this race.

**'Ismat,** عصمت, *vide* Asmat.

**'Istarushi,** عسترشي, *vide* Muhammad-bin-Mahmúd.

**Istaghana,** استغنا, poetical title of 'Abdul Rasúl.

**'Itabi,** عتابي, a poet, who died in the year 1614 A. D., 1023 A. H.

**Itkad Khan,** اعتقاد خان, the brother of 'Asaf Khán, Wazír, and son of Ya'tmád-uddaula. He was appointed governor of Kashmír by the emperor Sháh Jahán, which situation he held for several years. He died at Ágrah in 1650 A. D., 1060 A. H.

**Itkad Khan,** اعتقاد خان, the title of Mirzá Bahman Yár, the son of 'Asaf Khán and grandson of Ya'tmád-uddaula. He was raised to the rank of 4000 in the 25th year of Sháh Jahán 1651 A. D., 1061 A. H., with the title of Ya'tkád Khán, which his father held for some time as well as his uncle the brother of 'Asaf Khán. In the 5th year of 'Alamgír 1662 A. D., 1072 A. H., the rank of 5000 was conferred on him. In 1667 A. D., 1077 A. H., he proceeded to Dacca in Bengal, to visit his brother Sháista Khán who was then governor of that province, and died there in the year 1671 A. D., 1082 A. H.

**Itkad Khan,** اعتقاد خان, former title of Zulfikár Khán Nasrat Jang.

**Itmad Khan Khwaja Sara,** اعتماد خان خواجه سرا, an eunuch and officer in the service of the emperor Akbar. He was stabbed by his servant Maksúd 'Alí in 1578 A. D., 986 A. H., and was buried at a place called Itmádpúr, twelve miles from Ágrah, which he had founded in his lifetime.

**Itmad Khan,** اعتماد خان, title of Shaikh 'Abdúl Kawí, an Amír of the reign of the emperor 'Alamgír. He was murdered by a Kalandar in 1666 A. D., 1077 A. H.

**Itmad-uddaula,** اعتماد الدوله, title of Khwája Ayás or Ghayás the father of the celebrated Núr Jahán Begam, the favourite wife of the emperor Jahángír. He was a Tartar and came from Persia to India in the reign of the emperor Akbar. In the time of Jahángír, he was raised to the high rank of Wazír, with the title of Itmád-uddaula, and his two sons to the first rank of 'Umra with the titles of 'Asaf Khán and Itkád Khán. He died near Kót Kángrá where he had accompanied Jahángír on his way to Kashmír in February, 1621 O. S., Rabí' I, 1030 A. H. His remains were transported to Ágrah, and buried on the left bank of the Jamná, where a splendid mausoleum was built over his relics by his daughter Núr Jahán. It was completed in 1628 A. D., and is still in a high state of preservation. It is said, but it seems not to be true, that she intended to raise a monument of silver to his memory, but was reminded by her architect, that one of less covetable material stood a fairer chance of duration. After his death, his son 'Abú'l Hasan was appointed Wazír with the title of 'Asaf Khán. No private family ever made such alliances with royal blood, as this Tartar; for, his own daughter, his son's daughter and the daughter of his grandson, were married to three successive emperors of Hindústán; and another daughter of his grandson, to prince Murád Bakhsh, who disputed the throne with 'Alamgír, and for some days thought himself in possession of it. The place where he is buried, was a garden built by Itmád-uddaula during his lifetime. There are two tombs of yellow stone under the Rauza, one of which is of Itmád-uddaula and the other is said to be his wife's. It has a very large gate towards the east, built of red stone. It has two minars on both sides in the same number as there are two on the side of the Jamna towards the west. There is on the chabútra towards the Jamna a fish made of stone; if the water runs in and rises as far as its mouth, the whole of Allahábád will be inundated.

**'Itmad-uddaula,** عتماد الدوله, title of Muhammad Amír Khán, the prime minister of the emperor Muhammad Sháh. *Vide* Muhammad Amír Khán.

**Itmad-uddaula,** اعتماد الدوله, son of Muhammad Amín Khán, Wazír. *Vide* Kamar-uddín Khán.

**Itsam-uddin, Shaikh,** شيخ اعتصام الدين, author of the "Shagarf Nama-i-Wiláet," being the travels of the author in Great Britain and France, some time before or after the year 1766 A. D., 1180 A. H. This work has been translated into English.

**Ihia-bin-'Abdul Latif-al-Husaini of Kazwin, Amir,** اميريحيى بن عبد اللطيف الحسيني, author of the "Lubbut Tawáríkh," which he composed in 1541 A. D., 948 A. H. Hájí Khalfa gives his name as Isma'íl-bin-'Abdul Latíf, and in the Másir-ul-Umra, he is called Mír Ihia Husainí Saifí. He was patronized by Sháh Tahmásp Safwí, but his enemies, envious of his good fortune, endeavoured to poison his patron's mind against him, and at last prevailed so far as to induce the king to order him together with his son Mír Abdul Latíf, to be imprisoned, the latter, however, made his escape, but Mír Iahia died in prison after one year and nine months' imprisonment in 1555 A. D., 962 A. H., aged 77 years. His second son Alá-uddaula known by the poetical name of Kámí, is the author of the work called "Nafáis-ul-Másir." His eldest brother Mír 'Abdul Latíf who had fled to Gílán, came afterwards to Hindústán with his family some time after Akbar had ascended the throne. By him he was received with great kindness and consideration, and was appointed his preceptor. He is said by some authors to have died at Síkrí in 1563 A. D., 971 A. H., but the author of the "Másir-ul-'Umra" writes that his death took place in 1573 A. D., 981 A. H., and that Kásim Arsalán found the chronogram of his death to be "fakharályas." His eldest son Ghayás-uddín 'Alí was also endowed with an excellent disposition, and served Akbar for a long period. In the 26th year of Akbar's reign, 1581 A. D., he was honored with the title of Nakíb Khán, by which he is now best known. In the time of Jahángír he attained still further honors, and died at Ajmir in 1614 A. D., 1023

A. H. He was buried there in a marble tomb within the area of Mo'ín-uddín Chishtí's mausoleum, where his wife also lies buried by his side. Nakíb Khán was one of the compilers of the first portion of the "Táríkh Alfí," and the translator of the "Mahábhárat," though this honour is usually ascribed to Faizi. He left a son named Mír 'Abdul Laṭíf who was a person of great worth and ability and attained high honours, but died insane.

**Iyar Muhammad Khan, Mir,** میریار محمد خان, the son of Mír Murád 'Alí, former ruler of the Haidarábád portion of Sindh. He is a brother of Muhammad Khán, who being dispossessed and kept for some time a prisoner on the annexation of Sindh under Sir Charles Napier, was allowed to return, and now resides at Haidarábád as a private gentleman upon a pension from Government.

**Izid Bakhsh, Mirza,** میرزا ایزد بخش. His poetical name was Rasá; he was the grandson of 'Asaf Khán Ja'far Beg who was Wazír to Jahángír. Izid Bakhsh was at first employed by the prince 'Azim Sháh, and then by his father the emperor 'Alamgír in the capacity of Munshí. On the accession of Farrukh-siyar, he was disgraced by that emperor on account of his casting some reflections on his father Azím-ush-Shán at the time of the battle which took place between 'Azim Sháh and his brother Bahádur Sháh. By the order of the emperor, the hairs of his mustaches were plucked out one by one, and afterwards he was cruelly murdered. This event took place about the beginning of the year 1713 A. D., 1125 A. H. His tomb is still to be seen in the compound of the Ágrah College.

**'Izzat,** عزت, poetical name of (Shaikh) 'Abdul 'Azíz, which see.

**'Izzat,** عزت, poetical name of Sangham Lál, which see.

**'Izzat,** عزت, poetical title of Jaikishun, which see.

**'Izzat,** عزت, poetical appellation of Shaikh Wajíh-uddín.

**'Izzat-uddaula Mirza Muhsin,** عزت الدوله مرزا محسن, brother of Nawáb Safdar Jang. He was sent to Persia on an embassy to Nádir Sháh after his invasion of Hindústán, by the emperor Muhammad Sháh. *Vide* Najaf Khán and Muhammad Ḳulí Khán.

**'Izz-uddin Abdul Aziz-bin-Abdus-Salam Damishki, Shaikh,** عزالدین عبدالعزیز بن عبدالسلام دمشقي شيخ, author of the "Shajrat-ul-Ma'árif." He died in the year 1261 A. D., 660 A. H.

**'Izz-uddin Husain,** عزالدین حسین. He was created by Sulṭán Ibráhím of Ghazní, Amír Hájib, in which station he conducted himself so well, that the king gave him a princess of the house of Ghazní in marriage. He rose daily in favour and estimation, till Sulṭán Masa'úd the son of Ibráhím, put him in possession of the principality of Ghór. By the princess of Ghazní, he had seven sons entitled the seven stars. One of them, Fakhr-uddín Masa'úd, became king of Bámyán. The second was Kutb-uddín Muhammad, who married his cousin, a princess of Ghazní, the daughter of Sulṭán Bahrám Sháh. The third was 'Alá-uddín Hasan, prince of Ghór, who destroyed Ghazní. Izz-uddín during his lifetime paid tribute to the Saljúḳs as well as to the Ghaznavides.

**'Izz-uddin Khalid Khani,** عزالدین خالد خاني, author of the work called "Daláel Fíróz Sháhí," which he translated into Persian by order of Fíróz Sháh, from a Hindí book which treated on philosophy, astrology and divination.

**'Izz-uddaula Bakhtyar,** عزالدوله بختيار, the son of Mu'izz-uddaula-ibn-Bóya. He succeeded to the kingdom of 'Irák the same day on which his father died, *viz.*, Monday the 1st of April, 967 A. D., 17th Rabí' II, 356 A. H. The Khalíf al-Táya Billáh in the year 974 A. D. gave him his daughter in marriage, on whom a dowry of one hundred thousand dínárs was settled by her husband. He was a noble prince, and possessed such bodily strength that he would seize an enormous bull by the horns and throw him to the ground. A contest which arose between him and his cousin 'Azd-uddaula relative to their respective possessions, caused a breach between them which led to a war, and on Wednesday the 29th May, 978 A. D., they met and fought a battle, in which Izz-uddaula was slain, aged 36 years. His head was placed on a tray and presented to 'Azd-uddaula, who on seeing it, covered his eyes with his handkerchief and wept.

---

# J.

**Jabali,** جبالي, the son of Ayham, last king of the tribe of Ghassán, who were Christian Arabs. He became a Muhammadan, and afterwards attempted to assassinate Umar, the second Khalíf after Muhammad. He died 673 A. D., 53 A. H.

**Jabali,** جبالي, surname of Abú 'Alí Muhammad-bin-'Abdul Wahák, who was the master of the celebrated Abú'l Hasan al-Asha'rí, chief of the sect of the Asharians, and one of the four Imáms of Musalmanism.

**Jabali,** جبلي, poetical name of 'Abdul Wáṣa, who was born in the mountains of Ghurjistán, hence his takhallus which means mountaineer. He found a patron in Bahrám Sháh of Ghazní, and served Sulṭán Sanjar Saljúkí fourteen years. He died in 1160 A. D., 555 A. H., and left a Díwán of Kasídas. *Vide* 'Abdul Wáṣa.

**Jabar,** جبر, poetical name of Abú Músa Ja'far-al-Ṣafí, which see.

**Jabila Ram Nagar,** جیله رام نگر, a Hindú chief who was governor of Allahábád, and died there in the commencement of the reign of Muhammad Sháh in 1720 A. D., 1132 A. H. His nephew Girdhar was appointed governor of Audh after his death, and in 1724 A. D., 1136 A. H., the government of Málwá was conferred on him, and the Súbadárí of Audh was given to Burhán-ul-Mulk Sa'ádat Khán. Rájá Girdhar died at Málwá during the invasion of Bájí Ráo Marhaṭṭa, the general of Rájá Sáhú, about the year 1729 A. D., 1142 A. H., and was succeeded by Dayá Bahádur his relation, who continued gallantly to resist the enemy, and fell in battle about the year 1730 A. D., 1143 A. H., when Muhammad Khán Bangash was appointed governor of that province.

**Jabir,** جابر بن عبدالله, the son of 'Abdullah, was a companion of Muhammad and a traditionist. He was present in nineteen battles which Muhammad fought, and died in the year 692 A. D., 73 A. H., aged 94 years.

**Ja'far,** جعفر, poetical title of 'Asaf Khán, commonly called Mirzá Ja'far Beg.

**Ja'far,** جعفر, a soldier by profession. He is the author of a Maṣnawí, which he dedicated to the emperor Sháh Jahán.

**Ja'far-al-Barmaki,** جعفر البرمكي بن يحيى, son of Ahia or Yahia and grandson of Khálid, the son of Barmak who was originally a fire-worshipper. He succeeded his father Ja'far as wazír to the Khalíf Hárún-al-Rashíd; his grandfather having been wazír to Abú'l 'Abbás Saffáh, who was the first of all the Khalífs who had a wazír. This wazír Ja'far, was a great favourite of Hárún-al-Rashíd, who gave him 'Abbása, his sister, in marriage, under the condition to have no carnal connection with her, but he transgressed the command, for which the Khalíf ordered his head to be struck off. He also threw his brother al-Fazl and his father Ahia into prison, and there left them to die. Ja'far was only 28 years old when he was executed, having been in the favour of Hárún-al-Rashíd for the space of seventeen years. Ja'far was beheaded on Sunday the 29th of January, 803 A. D., 1st Safar 187 A. H., his body was gibbetted on one side of the bridge of Baghdád, and the head stuck up on the other.

**Ja'far Ali Khan,** جعفر علي خان, commonly called Mír Ja'far, whom the English placed on the masnad as Nawáb of Bengal, Behar and Orissa, after the defeat and death of Nawáb Siráj-uddaula, in June, 1757 A. D., Shawwál 1170 A. H. He was, however, deposed in 1760 A. D., 1174 A. H., on account of his neglect in the affairs of his government, and was obliged to retire on an ample pension, when his son-in-law, Mír Ḳásim 'Alí Khán was raised to the masnad. This man after his elevation, intending to drive out the English from Calcutta, was defeated in a battle fought at Udwa Nala on the 2nd of August, 1763 A. D., 22nd Muḥarram, 1177 A. H., and expelled, and Mír Ja'far was again placed on the masnad by the English. He died on Tuesday the 5th February, 1765 A. D., 14th Shabán, 1178 A. H., and his son Mír Phúlwárí, who assumed the title of Najm-uddaula, was elevated to the masnad. Ja'far Alí's cemetry is at Murshidábád, where his Begam and his son Míran are also buried.

*List of the Nawábs of Murshidábád.*

| | |
|---|---|
| Ja'far 'Alí Khán, ......... | died 5th February, 1765. |
| Najm-uddaula, son of Ja'far Alí Khán, ................ | died 3rd May, 1766. |
| Saif-uddaula, 2nd son of Ja'far 'Alí Khán, ............... | died 10th March, 1770. |
| Mubarik-uddaula, 3rd son of Ja'far 'Alí Khán, ........ | died September, 1793. |
| Nazir-ul-Mulk, son of Mubarik-uddaula, ............... | died April, 1810. |
| Zain-uddín 'Alí Khán. | |
| Sayyad Ahmad 'Alí Khán, .. | died 30th October, 1824. |
| Humáyún Jáh. | |
| Mansúr 'Alí Khán Nasrat Jang, present Nawáb (1858). | |

**Ja'far Barmaki,** جعفر برمكي, see Ja'far-al-Barmakí.

**Ja'far-bin-Abu Ja'far-al-Mansur,** جعفربن ابوجعفر المنصور, the Khalíf of Baghdád. His daughter Zubeda was married to Hárún-al-Rashíd. He died in the year 802 A. D., 186 A. H.

**Ja'far-bin-Abu Talib,** جعفر بن ابو طالب, was the brother of 'Alí the son-in-law of the prophet. He was killed in a battle fought at Muta in Syria against the Roman army in 629 A. D., 8 A. H.

**Ja'far-bin-Muhammad Husaini,** جعفربن محمد حسيني, author of the "Muntakhib-ut-Tawáríkh," a very judicious abridgment of Oriental history from Ádam down to Sháhrukh Mirzá, son of Amír Taimúr. This work was dedicated to Báisanghar Bahádur, third son of Sháhrukh, in 1417 A. D., 820 A. H. Many authors have compiled works under this title, one of which was written by Shaikh 'Abdul Ḳádir Badáoní.

**Ja'far-bin-Tufail,** جعفر بن طفيل, an Arabian philosopher in the 12th century, author of a romance, called the "history of Hai-ibn-Yokdhan," in which he asserts that by the light of nature, a man may acquire a knowledge of things, and of God. *Vide* Lempriere's Universal Dictionary, under Jaaphar.

**Ja'far Khan,** جعفرخان, entitled "Umdat-ul-Mulk," was the son of Sádiḳ Khán Mír Bakhshí, and sister's son and son-in-law of Yemín-uddaula 'Asaf Khán, wazír. He held the rank of 5000 under the emperor Sháh Jahán, was appointed prime minister by 'Alamgír about the year 1662 A. D., 1073 A. H., and died in the 13th year of that emperor, 1670 A. D., 1081 A. H., at Dehlí. After his death the office of wizárat was conferred upon, Asad Khán with the title of Asad-uddaula. It seems that after the death of Ja'far Khán his remains were transferred to Ágrah, where his tomb is to be seen still standing on the right bank of the Jamna.

**Ja'far Khan,** جعفرخان, whose original name was Murshid Ḳulí Khán, was appointed governor of Bengal by the emperor 'Alamgír in 1704 A. D., 1116 A. H. He founded the capital of Murshidábád and named it after his original title. He was the son of a Bráhmaṇ converted to Muhammadanism by Ḥájí Shafia' Isfahání. He died in the reign of the emperor Muhammad Sháh about the year 1726 A. D., 1138 A. H., and was succeeded by his son-in-law Shujá-uddín (also called Shujá-uddaula). The following is a list of his successors :—

| | A. D. |
|---|---|
| Murshid Ḳulí Ja'far Khán, .................. | 1704 |
| Shujá-uddín, son of Ja'far Khán, ............ | 1726 |
| 'Alá-uddaula Sarfaráz Khán, ................. | 1739 |
| Alahwardí Khán Mahábat Jang, ................ | 1740 |
| Siráj-uddaula, grandson of ditto, ............ | 1756 |
| Ja'far 'Alí Khán (dethroned in 1760), ......... | 1757 |
| Ḳásim 'Alí Khán, son-in-law of ditto, ........ | 1760 |
| Ja'far 'Alí Khán, restored in ............... | 1763 |
| Najm-uddaula, son of ditto, ................. | 1764 |
| Saif-uddaula, brother of Najm-uddaula, ....... | 1766 |
| Mubarik-uddaula, ........................... | 1769 |
| Názim-ul-Mulk Wazír-uddaula, (died April 28th, 1810, .................................. | 1796 |
| Sayyad Zain-uddín 'Alí Khán, son of ditto, ...... | 1810 |
| Sayyad Ahmad 'Alí Khán. | |
| Humáyún Jáh. | |
| Mansúr 'Alí Khán, Nasrat Jang. | |

**Ja'far Khan,** جعفرخان بن صادق خان, son of Sádiḳ Khán, king of Persia. He was recognised by the principal noblemen in Fars, after the death of 'Alí Murád Khán in 1785, and the people were forward in acknowledging his authority, but unable to resist his enemy 'Aḳá Muhammad Khán, who now ventured to embrace a more extensive field for the exertion of his talents, and commenced his march against Isfahán. Ja'far Khán was treacherously murdered in 1788; his head was severed from his body, and cast before the citadel, the sport of children, and the outcasts of the city.

**Ja'far Khan,** جعفرخان, a nobleman who in the first year of the emperor Bahádur Sháh was appointed governor of Kashmír in the room of Nawázish Khán 1707 A. D., 1119 A. H. He proved to be a bad governor and a mob set fire to his residence. He died in Kashmír of drink and excess 1709 A. D., 1121 A. H., and according to the record of his death, must be faring badly at present.

**Ja'far Nasiri,** جعفر نصیری, an author who completed the work called "Lataef Khayál," in 1742 A. D., 1155 A. H., which was commenced by Mirzá Muhammad Sálah.

**Ja'far Sadik,** جعفر صادق, or Ja'far the Just. He was the eldest son of Muhammad Bákir, the grandson of Imám Husain. He is reckoned the sixth Imám; was born at Madina about the year 702 A. D., 83 A. H., and died in the same city under the khiláfat of Abú Ja'far Al-Mansúr, in 765 A. D., 148 A. H. He was very famous for his doctrine amongst the Musalmáns, was invited to court by Al-Mansúr, that he might profit by his counsel: Ja'far returned for answer, "Whoever has a view duly to this world, will not give you sincere advice, and he who regards the next, will not keep your company." He was buried in the cemetry of Al-Bakía at Madina. The same tomb contains the bodies of his father, Imám Bákir, his grandfather 'Alí Zain-ul 'Abidín, and his grandfather's uncle, Hasan, son of 'Alí. His mother's name was Umm Farwáh, daughter of Kásim, the son of Muhammad, the son of Abú Bakr Sadík, the first Khalíf after Muhammad. He is said to be the author of a book of fate called "Fál Náma."

**Ja'far Zatalli, Mir,** میر جعفر زٹلی, a Sayyad of Nárnoul, cotemporary with Mirzá Bedil. He served under prince 'Azim Sháh, the son of the emperor 'Alamgír, who was slain in battle in 1707 A. D., 1019 A. H. Ja'far was the most celebrated humoristic poet of Hindústán; his compositions are a mixture of Persian and Urdú. He is the author of a Sháhnáma in Rekhta. He was put to death in 1713 A. D., 1225 A. H., by order of the emperor Farrukh-siyar, on account of a satirical verse he had written on the accession of that emperor to the throne of Dehlí.

**Jagat Goshaini,** جگت گوشاینی *vide* Jodh Báí.

**Jagat Narayan,** جگت ناراین, a Hindú poet who wrote some kasídas in praise of Nawáb 'Asaf-uddaula of Lakhnau, who died in 1797 A. D., 1212 A. H.

**Jagannath, Raja,** راجا جگناتهه the son of Bhara Mal. He held the rank of 5000 in the time of the emperor Jahángír, about the year 1605 A. D., 1014 A. H.

**Jagat Singh,** جگت سنگه, the son of Makund Singh Hara, lived in the time of the emperor 'Alamgír 1659 A. D.

**Jagat Singh,** جگت سنگه, rájá of Jaipúr or Jainagar, was the son of rájá Partáp Singh, the son of Madho Singh, the son of Ishurí Singh, the son of the celebrated rájá Jai Singh Sawáí, who lived in the time of the emperor Muhammad Sháh. Jagat Singh succeeded his father in 1803 A. D., and is said to have been an effeminate prince. Though he died without issue, he was succeeded by rájá Jai Singh, a posthumous son, believed supposititious.

**Jagnath Kalanwat,** جگناتهه کلاوت, a musician who was employed by Sháh Jahán, who conferred on him the title of Mahá Kabráj.

**Jaghtai,** جغتای *vide* Chaghtaí Khán.

**Jagnath,** جگناتهه, brother of Rájá Bhagwán Dás. He distinguished himself in the war with Rájá Partáp Singh. He slew the renowned champion Rám Dás, son of Jagmah.

**Jahan Ara Begam,** جهان آرا بیگم, daughter of the emperor Sháh Jahán, by Mumtaz Mahal, daughter of 'Asaf Khán, wazír; was born on Wednesday the 23rd of March, 1614 A. D., 21st Safar, 1023 A. H. One of the most beautiful examples of female modesty to be found in the annals of woman is recorded of this princess, celebrated in song and history as the heroic, the witty, the generous, the elegant, the accomplished, and the beautiful Jahán Ára Begam. One night, (26th March, 1644 A. D., 27th Muharram, 1054 A. H.) as she was returning from her father's apartments to the harem, in one of the passages which connect the latter building with the body of the palace, her flowing drapery was unhappily ignited by the flame of a lamp. Her whole dress, which was of the finest muslin, was instantly in flames, and of course her life was in imminent peril; but, knowing that she was then within hearing of many young nobles of the court, she would not raise an alarm, lest they should run to her assistance, and behold her unveiled, or lay their hands upon her in order to extinguish the flames. Heroically enduring all the agonies which fire could inflict, she withheld her cries, and rushed forward until she reached the women's apartments, and there sunk upon the floor, almost lifeless. For a long period, no hopes were entertained of her recovery, but she was ultimately restored to health by an English physician named Dr. Boughton who was then at Súrat, and had been sent for by the emperor her father then in the Dakhin, although her beauty was cruelly impaired. The emperor, in reward for Dr. Boughton's services, besides other favours, granted him, at his disinterested request, a patent for his countrymen to trade free of customs throughout his dominions. The large Masjid of red stone adjoining the fort of Ágrah near the Tripolia (now demolished) was built by her in the year 1648 A. D., 1058 A. H., at a cost of five lacs of rupees. She died in the reign of her brother the emperor 'Alamgír on the 5th September, 1680 A. D., 3rd Ramazán, 1092 A. H., and lies buried in the yard of the mausoleum of Nizám-uddín Aulia at Dehlí. The name of Jahán Ára will ever adorn the pages of history as a bright example of filial attachment and heroic self-devotion to the dictates of duty, more especially when we view it in contrast with the behaviour of her sister Roshan Ára, who, by aiding the ambitious designs of Aurangzíb, enabled him to dethrone Sháh Jahán. The amiable and accomplished Jahán Ára not only supported her aged father in his adversity, but voluntarily resigned her liberty and resided with him during his imprisonment in the fort of Ágrah. Her tomb is of white marble, open at the top, and at the head is a tablet with a Persian inscription inlaid in black marble letters, to the following effect: "Let no one scatter over my grave anything but verdure, for such best becomes the sepulchre of one who had a humble mind." On the margin is written, "The perishable fakír Jahán Ára Begam, daughter of Sháh Jahán, and the disciple of the saints of Chishtí, died in the year of the Hijra, 1092 A. H."

**Jahan Bano Begam,** جهان بانو بیگم, the daughter of Prince Murád, the son of the emperor Akbar. She was married to Prince Parwez, the son of Jahángír, by whom she had Nadira Begam, who was married to Dara Sheko, the eldest son of Sháh Jahán.

**Jahandar Shah,** جهاندار شاه, surnamed Muhammad Mui'zz-uddín, was the eldest son of the emperor Bahádur Sháh, and grandson of 'Alamgír. He was born in the Dakhin on Wednesday the 8th April, 1663 A. D., 10th Ramazán, 1073 A. H. The death of his father, which took place in February, 1712 A. D., Muharram, 1124 A. H., was followed by the usual struggle among his sons for the crown. The incapacity of Jahándár Sháh the eldest, had given a great ascendancy to the second whose name was Azím-ush-Shán. He was supported by most of the nobility and of the army, but his other brothers joined their interests, and were kept together by the persuasions and false promises of Zulfikár Khán the Amír-ul-'Umrá. Their concord was of short duration, and lasted only until the defeat and death of Azím-ush-Shán; after which a bloody battle ensued between the three surviving brothers, two of whom, *viz.*, Jahán Sháh with his son Farkhunda Akhtar, and Rafí-ush-Shán, being killed, Mui'zz-uddín by the intrigues and support of the Amír-ul-'Umrá, remained undisputed master of the throne, and was crowned at Láhór on Thursday the 10th of April, 1712 A. D., 14th Rabí' I, 1124 A. H., with the title of Jahándár Sháh. He was in himself a weak man, effeminately careful of his person, fond of ease, indolent, and totally ignorant of the art of government. He made the vast empire of Hindústán an offering to the foolish whims of a public courtezan, named Lál Kúnwar, which tortured the minds of worthy subjects loyal to his family. He reigned only nine months, was defeated in a battle fought near Ágrah, and afterwards taken prisoner and murdered in the month of January, 1713 A. D., Ẕil-ḥijja, 1124 A. H., by order of his nephew Farrukh-siyar (the son of the late Azím-ush-Shán), who became emperor. His corpse was exposed to public view, and then interred in the platform before the mausoleum of the emperor Humáyún at Dehlí. His mother's name was Nizám Bái.

**Jahandar Shah, Prince,** شهزاده جهاندار شاه, the eldest son of the emperor Sháh 'Alam. In April, 1784 A. D., on account of the unsettled affairs of his father, he made his escape from Dehlí and repaired to Lákhnau, where Mr. Hastings had arrived to regulate the concerns between the wazír, Asaf-uddaula, and the Company. He accompanied Mr. Hastings to Benaras, which place he chose for his residence. He had an allowance of five lacs of rupees per annum from the Nawáb wazír at the earnest request of Mr. Hastings. He died in Benaras on the 1st of April, 1788 A. D., 25th Shabán 1202 A. H., after an illness of little more than twenty-four hours; aged about 35 years, and was buried with every honour due to his rank near the tomb of a venerated Muhammadan in Benaras. The English Resident and principal people of the city attended his funeral. He left behind him three sons, whom, with the rest of his family, he recommended to the care of the English, under whom they still enjoy a comfortable asylum and allowance at Benaras. Garçin-de-Tassy informs us, that there is a work of his in the India House, which has the title of "Bayáz Ináyet Murshidzada." He is also called Mirzá Jawán Bakht, and his poetical title is Jahándár. The narrative written by this prince, was translated by Mr. Scott, and published in the appendix to Mr. Hastings' Review of the state of Bengal.

**Jahangir,** نورالدين محمد جهانگير, (emperor) surnamed Núr-uddín Muhammad, was the eldest son of the emperor Akbar the Great; was born in the village of Síkrí on Wednesday the 31st of August, 1569 A. D., 17th Rabí' I, 977 A. H., and was named Mirzá Salím on account of his coming into the world, as supposed, by the prayers of Shaikh Salím Chishtí, a venerable Shaikh and dervish who resided in the village of Síkrí, now called Fathapúr Síkrí, in the province of Ágrah. His mother, who received the title of Mariam Zamman, was the daughter of Rájá Bihárí Mal Kachhwáhá. After the death of his father, which took place on the 16th of October, 1605 A. D., he succeeded him by the title of Núr-uddín Muhammad Jahángír. He reigned 22 lunar years, 8 months and 15 days from the day of his father's demise; and died in camp on Sunday the 28th of October, 1627, A. D., 28th Safar, 1037 A. H., on his way to Láhór from Kashmír, aged 59 lunar years, 11 months and 12 days; and was interred in the suburbs of Láhór in the garden of his favourite wife Núr Jahán Begam. He was succeeded by his son Mirzá Khurram, who took the title of Sháh Jahán. His favourite Sulṭána Núr Jahán, who survived him 18 years, is also buried in the same mausoleum. Jahángír, after his death, received the title of "Jannat Makání." It was to this prince that Sir Thomas Roe was sent as ambassador by King James I. Sir Thomas has given a good description of the grandeur of the court of Hindústán; but very little notice is taken of this embassy in the chronicles of the East. In 1612, Jahángír permitted the Company to establish factories at Súrat, Ahmadábád, and Cambay. Jahángír wrote his own Memoir in Persian, called, "Túzak Jahángírí" which has been translated by Major David Price, London, 1829, 184 pages 4to. It is also called Jahángír Náma.

**Jahangir Kuli Khan, Kabuli,** جهانگيرقلي‌خان کابلي, an amír of the rank of 5000, who was appointed governor of Bengal by the emperor Jahángír in 1607 A. D., 1016 A. H., and died there in 1608 A. D., 1017 A. H.

**Jahangir,** جهانگير, a cousin and husband of Sikandar Begam of Bhopal. His uncle was one of the Paṭhán or Afghán soldiers of fortune, who under Aurangzíb carved out principalities, and on that emperor's death, declared himself independent at Bhopal; and on his death his wife was declared Regent by the army, and his daughter Sikandar Begam, heir. She married Jahángír who died in the year 1845 A. D.

**Jahangir Kuli Khan,** جهانگير قلي خان, son of Khán 'Azim Mirzá 'Azíz Kóka, served under the emperors Akbar and Jahángír, and died in the fifth year of Sháh Jahán 1631 A. D., 1041 A. H.

**Jahangir Mirza,** جهانگير مرزا, the eldest son of Amír Taimúr. He died before his father 1574 A. D., 776 A. H. His son's name was Pír Muhammad, which see.

**Jahangir, Mirza,** مرزا جهانگير, the eldest son of Akbar Sháh II, king of Dehlí. He was, in consequence of having fired a pistol at Mr. Seton the Resident at Dehlí, sent as a State prisoner to Allahábád, where he resided in the garden of Sulṭán Khusro for several years, and died there in 1821 A. D., 1236 A. H., aged 31 years; a salute of 31 guns was fired from the ramparts of the fort of Allahábád at the time of his burial. He was at first interred in the same garden, and subsequently his remains were transferred to Dehlí, and buried in the court-yard of the mausoleum of Nizám-uddín Aulia.

**Jahanian Jahan Gasht, Makhdum,** جهانيان جهانگشت مخدوم, *vide* Shaikh Jalál.

**Jahan Khatun,** جهان خاتون, a famous lady, who after the death of her first husband, got married to Khwája Amín-uddín, minister of Sháh Abú Is-háḳ, ruler of Shíráz. She is said to have been a very beautiful woman, and a good poet.

**Jahan Shah Turkman,** جهان شاه ترکمان, son of Ḳará Yúsaf Turkmán, was the brother of Sikandar Turkmán, after whose death in 1437 A. D., 841 A. H., the government of Azurbeján was conferred on him by Sháhrukh Mirzá, the son of Amír Taimúr. He held it till the death of that prince in 1447 A. D., 850 A. H., after which he conquered most part of Persia, and carried his arms as far as Dayárbikar, and fell in a battle which he fought against Hasan Beg, commonly called Uzzan Hasan, the ruler of that province, on the 10th of November, 1467 A. D., 12th Rabí' II, 872 A. H., aged 70 years. He reigned more than 30 lunar years, and as he was slain in battle against Hasan Beg, the chronogram of the year of his death was found to contain the words "Slain by Hasan Beg."

**Jahan Shah,** شهزاده جهان شاه, (prince) the third son of the emperor Bahádur Sháh. He was slain in the battle which took place at Láhor after the death of his father between his brothers in March, 1712 A. D. His mangled body with that of his brother Rafí-ush-Shán and his son, was conveyed to Dehlí and interred without ceremony and pomp in the mausoleum of the emperor Humáyún, the general receptacle of the murdered princes of the imperial family.

**Jahan Soz,** جهان سوز, a title of Sulṭán 'Alá-uddín Hasan Ghorí.

**Jahi,** جاهي, the poetical name of Ibráhím Mirzá (Sulṭán) which see.

**Jahiz** or **Aljahiz,** جاحظ يا الجاحظ, the surname of Abú 'Usmán 'Umar bin-Mahbúb Kana'ána, a man of great learning, but of a very eccentric tendency of mind. He wrote a book on the Commerce of the Arabians early in the third century of the Hijra, entitled "Kitáb-al-Nazrat fil Tajárat," which is frequently quoted by Nawerí. Jáhiz died 868 A. D., 255 A. H., at the age of 96 years.

**Jaiapa,** جياپا سيندهيا, Sindhia, succeeded his father Ránoji Sindhia, the founder of the Sindhia family, in 1750 A. D., 1163 A. H. and was murdered in his tent in 1759 A. D., 1172 A. H. He was succeeded by his brother Mádhojí Sindhia.

**Jaichand,** جيچند راتّهور, the last Ráṭhór monarch of Kanauj. He ruled the country from Buxar to Kanauj and reigned about the Sambat year 1400 A. D., 1343 A. H. His favourite residence was near the city of Jounpúr which he had built in 1359 A. D., 1416 Sambat. The present city of Jounpúr was built by Fíróz Sháh in the year 1370 A. D., 772 A. H., in the name of his uncle Fakhr-uddín Muhammad Júnán, the date of which is found in the words "Shahr Jounpúr." According to Colonel Tod, Jaichand reigned about the 12th century of the Christian era, and one of his grandsons named Seojí, with a few retainers, planted the Ráṭhór standard in Máṛwár in the year 1212 A. D.

**Jai Chand,** جي چند, a rájá of Nagarkot or Kángra, who lived in the time of the emperor Akbar.

**Jaikishun,** جي كشن, a Kashmírí Bráhman whose poetical name was 'Izzat, was the agent of Nawáb Is-hák Khán.

**Jaimal,** جيمل, a rájá, famous in history as "the bravest of the brave." In 1568 A. D. Udai Singh, the son of Rana Sanka or Sanga, and the founder of the capital Udaipúr in Chittór, came under the displeasure of the emperor Akbar. The recreant chief fled and left the defence of his capital (Chittór) to Rájá Jaimal, who was killed by Akbar himself in 1568 A. D.

**Jaipal I,** جيپال اول, son of Hitpál, rájá of Láhor of the Bráhman tribe, who reigned over the country extending in length from Sarhind to Lamghan, and in breadth from the kingdom of Kashmír to Multán. He was once defeated by Subaktagín, the Sulṭán of Ghazní, with great slaughter, and again on Monday the 27th November, 1001 A. D. by his son Sulṭán Mahmúd, when Jaipál with fifteen of his principal chiefs, being his sons and brethren, were taken prisoners, and 5000 of his troops were slain on the field of battle. He was afterwards released by Mahmúd, but in compliance with a custom which prevailed among the Hindús, that whatever rájá was twice overpowered by strangers, became disqualified to reign, he ordered a funeral pile to be prepared, and having set fire to it with his own hands, perished therein. He was succeeded by his son Anandpál.

**Jaipal II,** راجه جيپال ثاني, rájá of Láhor, son of Anandpál whom he succeeded in 1013 A. D. He was routed in a great battle by Sulṭán Mahmúd in 1022 A. D. on the banks of the river Raví, the result was the permanent occupation of Láhor by a Muhammadan governor, and the appointment of a Viceroy of Láhor by Mahmúd. This was the foundation of the Muhammadan empire in India.

**Jai Singh I,** راجه جي سنگه اول, (rájá) of the tribe of Kachhwáhá, commonly called Mirzá Rájá, was the son of rájá Máhá Singh, the son of Partáp Singh, the son of rájá Mán Singh. He served under the emperor Sháh Jahán, and was made governor over the conquered provinces of the Dakhin about the year 1664 A. D. by the emperor 'Alamgír. He was recalled to court in 1666 A. D., but died on the road, soon after his arrival at Burhánpúr, 28th Muḥarram 1078 A. H. According to Orme's Historical Fragments of the Mughul Empire, Jai Singh died at Burhánpúr soon after the pretended revolt of Sulṭán Muazzim the son of the emperor, and seems to have been poisoned by the procurement of 'Alamgír. There never was a prince among the rájpúts equal to him in accomplishments. He was completely learned in Hindí, and understood the Turkish, Persian, and Arabic languages. He left two sons, Rám Singh his eldest, and Kírat Singh. The former was honoured after his father's death with the title of rájá, and put in possession of his father's territories. Jai Singh had built several fine edifices at Ágrah of which no sign remains now, but the name and place on which the buildings stood is still called Jaisinghpúra.

**Jai Singh II, Sawai,** جي سنگه سوائي ثاني, a rájá of the tribe of Kachhwáhá rájpúts, was the son of Bishun Singh, the son of Kishun Singh, the son of Rám Singh, the son of Mirzá Rájá Jai Singh. He is commonly called Mirzá Rájá Jai Singh Sawáí. He was the zamíndár or rájá of a considerable territory in the province of Ajmír named Amer, but since the prince's founding a new city called Jaipúr, the rájáship has also taken that name. Bishun Singh, the father of Jai Singh and Bijai Singh, died about the year 1693 A. D., Sambat 1750, and after his death the title of rájá was bestowed on Jai Singh by the emperor 'Alamgír with the rank of 1500, and subsequently with that of 2000. After the death of that emperor, he espoused the cause of 'Azim Sháh, the son of 'Alamgír, whilst his brother Bijai Singh aided Bahádur Sháh, who on his accession to the throne conferred the rank of 3000 on the latter. Bijai Singh quarrelled with his brother for the ráj; and the emperor, not willing to displease either, confiscated their estate, and appointed Sayyad Husain Alí Khán of Bárha, as Faujdár of that place. When the emperor marched to the Dakhin to punish his brother Kámbakhsh, 1708 A. D., 1120 A. H., Jai Singh, with the aid of rájá Ajít Singh Ráṭhór, engaged the Faujdár in battle and having killed him took possession of the province. In the reign of Farrukh-siyar he was honoured with the title of Dhíráj Rájá Jai Singh, and in the time of Muhammad Sháh, with that of Sawái. In the year 1732 A. D., 1145 A. H., he was appointed governor of Málwá. His love of science makes him one of the most remarkable persons of his nation. He built five observatories for astronomical studies, namely, at Dehlí, Banaras, Mathrá, Ujain and Jaipúr, and published a work on astronomy called "Zíj Muhammad Sháhí." He also erected a Karavánsarae and market in every province of Hindústán for the convenience of travellers at his own expence. After his death, which took place in September, 1743 A. D., 9th Shabán, 1156 A. H., three of his wives with many concubines burned themselves on his funeral pile. He was succeeded by his son Ishurí

Singh, after whose death in 1760 A. D., Madho Singh his son succeeded him.

*List of Kachhwáhá Rájás of Amer or Jaipúr.*

| | |
|---|---|
| Bhara Mal. | Jai Singh Sawáí. |
| Bhagwán Dás. | Ishurí Singh. |
| Mán Singh. | Madho Singh. |
| Bháo Singh. | Pirthí Singh. |
| Mahá Singh. | Partáb Singh. |
| Jai Singh Mirzá Rájá. | Jagat Singh. |
| Rám Singh. | Jai Singh. |
| Bishnu Singh. | |

**Jai Singh III,** جي سنگه ثالث, (rájá) of the tribe of Kachhwáhá rájpúts and rájá of Jaipúr, was a posthumous son of Rájá Jagat Singh who died in 1818 A. D. Jai Singh was murdered by his kámdár, whose name was Jhota Rám, in the Sambat year 1891, or in January, 1834 A. D., and his infant son Rám Singh succeeded him.

**Jai Singh,** جي سنگه, or Rána Jai Singh of Udaipúr, a descendant of Rána Sanka who lived in the time of the emperor Akbar, succeeded his father Rána Ráj Singh, 1680 A. D., 1091 A. H.

**Jai Singh,** جي سنگه, (rájá) who held the súbahdárship of Ágrah in the time of the emperor Muhammad Sháh. He built the Sháharpanah round the city of Ágrah. It had several gates, but only three recently were remaining, *viz.*, (1) Ajmirí Darwazá, (2) Kara at Chhanga Mudí's bridge, (3) Kans Darwazá at Gokalpúra. After the mutiny of 1857, the British for some reason or other, pulled down the Ajmirí Darwazá.

**Jalal Asir,** جلال اسير, *vide* Asír.

**Jalal 'Uzd, Sayyad,** سيد جلال عضد, a poet who flourished in the reign of Muhammad Muzaffar, ruler of Fars and his descendants. He is the author of a Díwán.

**Jalal Bukhari,** سيد جلال بخاري, or Sayyad Jalál Bukhárí. He came to India from Bukhárá and became a disciple of Shaikh Bahá-uddín Zikariá of Multán. He resided at Uchcha in Multán and died there. He had three sons, Sayyad Ahmad Kabír, Sayyad Bahá-uddín and Sayyad Muhammad. Sayyad Ahmad Kabír, who succeeded his father as spiritual guide, had two sons, Makhdúm Jahanian, also called Shaikh Jalál, and Shaikh Sadar-uddín, commonly called Rájú Ḳattál.

*N. B.*—There is some confusion between this man and Shaikh Jalál. *Vide* Shaikh Jalál.

**Jalal Bukhari, Sayyad,** سيد جلال بخارى, a descendant of Sayyad Ahmad Kabír, and son of Sayyad Muhammad Bukhárí. He was born in the year 1594 A. D., 5th Jumádạ II, 1003 A. H., and was highly respected by the emperor Sháh Jahán, who conferred on him the office of Sadárat of all India with the manṣab of 6000. He sometimes amused himself in writing poetry, and had adopted the word Razá for his poetical title. He died on the 25th of May, 1647 O. S., 1st Jumádạ I, 1057 A. H., and is buried at Tájganj in Ágrah. His grandfather Sayyad Ahmad Kabír lies buried at a place in Dehlí called Bijai Mandil. Jalál Bukhárí left three sons, *viz.*, Sayyad Ja'far, Sayyad Alí styled Razwí Khán, and Sayyad Músa, on whom high titles were conferred by Sháhjahán, but his eldest son Ja'far obtained the place of his father.

**Jalal, (Hakim),** حكيم جلال شرواني, a physician and poet, who was a native of Shírwán. He flourished in the reign of Muhammad Muzaffar and his son Sháh Shujáa', rulers of Shíráz, both of whom reigned from 1353 to 1384 A. D. He is the author of a poem entitled "Gul-wa-Nauroz," which he wrote in 1334 A. D., 734 A. H. He is also called Jalál-uddín Tabíb.

**Jalali or Jalal,** جلالي يا جلال, commonly called Sayyad-i-'Alám Jalál or Jalálí, was a native of Ahmadabád, and his father and spiritual guide was Mír Ṣayyad Jalál bin-Hasan. He is the author of a Díwán.

**Jalal, Shaikh,** شيخ جلال, *vide* Shaikh Jalál, commonly called Makhdúm Jahánián. He was the son of Sayyad Ahmad Kabír, and grandson of Sayyad Jalál Bukhárí the first.

**Jalal, Shaikh,** شيخ جلال تهانيسرى, of Thanesar, *vide* Shaikh Jalál of Thanesar.

**Jalali,** جلالي, poetical name of Badr-uddín.

**Jalal-uddin Ahmad Afzal-bin-Muwaiyad,** جلال الدين احمد افضل بن مويد, an author.

**Jalal-uddin Aldawani,** جلال الدين الدواني, author of several works. *Vide* Dawání.

**Jalal-uddin Farahani,** جلال الدين فرهاني, a poet.

**Jalal-uddin Firoz Khilji,** جلال الدين فيروز خلجي, *vide* Fíróz Sháh Khiljí.

**Jalal-uddin Mahalli,** جلال الدين محلي, see Jalál-uddín Sayútí. He is sometimes called Jalál-uddín Muhammad bin-Ahmad-al-Mahlí.

**Jalal-uddin Malikshah,** جلال الدين ملكشاه, *vide* Malikshάh.

**Jalal-uddin Khan,** جلال الدين خان, the brother of Mahmúd Khán, nawáb of Bijnór, a rebel of 1857. *Vide* Sa'd-ulláh Khán.

**Jalal-uddin Muhammad-bin-Asa'd Aldawani,** جلال الدين محمد بن اسعد الدواني, *vide* Dawání.

**Jalal-uddin Muhammad Akbar,** جلال الدين محمد اكبر, *vide* Akbar.

**Jalal-uddin Purbi,** جلال الدين پوربي, king of Bengál, whose original name was Jítmal, ascended the throne of Bengál on the death of his father Rájá Kans in 1392 A. D., 794 A. H. He became a convert to the Muhammadan faith and received the name of Jalál-uddín. He ruled with such justice, that he became entitled to the appellation of the Nausherwán of the age. He reigned 17 years and died in 1410 A. D., 812 A. H., when his son Ahmad succeeded him.

**Jalal-uddin Rumi, Maulana,** مولانا جلال الدين رومي, commonly called Mauláná or Maulwí Rúmí, was the son of Bahá-uddín Wald Balkhí. He is not less esteemed as a poet than as a metaphysician, and is the author of the astonishing work entitled the "Maṣnawí Maulwí Rúmí." He founded an order of Derwishes or Súfís in the city of Conia (Iconium) in Asiatic Turkey. He was born at Balkh on the 30th of September, 1207 A. D., 6th Rabí' I 604 A. H., and died in the time of Abká Khán on the 17th of December, 1273 A. D., 5th Jumádạ II, 672 A. H. He was buried in a monastery at Conia, and his tomb was visited for many centuries by his devout countrymen who considered his works as the effect of inspiration, and only inferior to the Ḳurán. His Díwán contains 30,000 verses, and his Maṣnawi more than 47,000. In his Díwán, instead of his own title, he has inserted the name of Shams Tabrezí his master.

**Jalal-uddin Sayuti,** جلال الدين سيوطي, son of 'Abdur Rahmán bin-Abí Bakr, an Egyptian author of some merit, who died in 1505 A. D., 911 A. H. He is said to be the author of 400 works, amongst which are the commentary on the "Durr-al-Munshúr," and the last half of the "Tafsír Jalálain," the author of the other half was Jalál-uddín Mahalí who died in 1450 A. D., 854 A. H. Another work of Sayútí is called "Lubb-ul-Lubáb." It is a dictionary of patronymic names, and of others under which the Arabic authors are much more frequently quoted than under their proper names. The confusion under which the Arabs labour to identify men known under different names, has induced them to prepare dictionaries for obviating this difficulty. Sámání (or Samnání) in the sixth century of the Hijra published one, entitled, "Fil Ansáb," in which he does not only explain the sense and origin of these names, but also mentions with regard to every word the true names of the authors who have had them. This work was abbreviated in the succeeding century by Ibn-ul-Asír, and this extract shortened by Sayútí. There is another work of Sayútí called "Kashfus-Salsala-un-Wasfuz Zalzala," containing an account of all the earthquakes which took place from the year 713 A. D., 94 A. H., to his time. He wrote this work on the occasion of an earthquake in Egypt, with a view of shewing to his countrymen, that earthquakes are ordained by God to punish men for their sins. This work was translated from the Arabic by A. Sprenger, Esq., M. D. *Vide* Journal, Asiatic Society, Vol. XVII, Part II, p. 741. Sayútí is also the author of the "Jáma'-ul-Jawáma," containing a collection of Traditions of which he afterwards made an abridgement and called it Jáma'-us-Saghír."

**Jalal-uddin, Sultan,** سلطان جلال الدين, the son of Sulṭán Muhammad, surnamed Kutb-uddín, Sulṭán of Khwárizm. *Vide* Muhammad (Sulṭán).

**Jalayer,** جلاير, the name given to a race of kings of Baghdád, the first of whom was Hasan Buzurg, commonly called Hasan Jaláyer.

**Jalinus,** جالينوس, prince of the Greek physicians after Hippocrates, whom we call Galen.

**Jam Afra,** جام افرا, *vide* Násir-uddín Ḳabbácha.

**Jama Baf,** جاما باف, *vide* Mír Sayyad Jáma Báf.

**Jamal,** جمال, the name assumed by Abú'l Fazl Muhammad, the son of 'Umar, the son of Khálid. He is the author of the "Saráh," a dictionary of Arabic words explained in Persian by him, being a translation of a very celebrated Arabic dictionary, entitled the "Saháh."

**Jamali Khalifa,** جمالي خليفه, surname of Is-háḳ Karamání, another author of the commentary called "Sharah Hadís-ul-Arba'ín." He died 1526 A. D., 933 A. H.

**Jamali, Shaikh,** شيخ جمالي, *vide* Shaikh Jamálí.

**Jamal Fakih, Khwaja,** خواجه جمال فقيه, a poet.

**Jamal Kili, Shaikh,** شيخ جمال كيلي, an inhabitant of Ḳazwín in Isfahán. He lived in the time of Sulṭán 'Alá-uddín the Ismá'ílí, ruler of the fort of Alahmút, who highly respected him. It is said that he secretly followed the tenets of the Ismá'ílís, but the people thought otherwise. He died on Monday the 29th September, 1253 A. D., 4th Shawwál, 651 A. H.

**Jamal Khan,** جمال خان, a commander of 5000 horse in the reign of Sháh Jahán. It is related that the emperor had ordered that all the ladies at court should provide precious stones, and bring them to a market-place that he had erected, and there shew their wares publicly to all the noblemen at court, who were ordered to buy them at whatever prices the ladies put upon them; and that the king himself was to be a buyer, to put the greater honour on the new erected market. The ladies obeyed, and took their booths, as they thought fit. On the market day, the king and the noblemen came to market, and bought the jewels and other trifles the ladies had to dispose of. The king coming to the booth of a very pretty lady, asked her what she had to sell. She told him she had one large fine rough diamond still to dispose of. He desired to see it, and he found it to be a piece of fine transparent sugar-candy of a tolerable diamond figure. He demanded to know what price she set on it, and she told him with a pleasant air, that it was worth a lakh of rupees, or £12,500 sterling. He ordered the money to be paid, and, falling into discourse with her, found her wit was as exquisite as her beauty, and ordered her to sup with him that night in his palace. She accordingly went and stayed with him three nights and days, and then went back to her husband, whose name was Jamál Khán. The husband received her very coldly, and told her that he would continue civil to her, but would never live with her again but in the same manner as if she was his sister. Upon which she went to the palace, fell at the emperor's feet, and told him what her husband had said. The king in a rage gave orders to carry her husband to the elephant garden, and there put him to death by an elephant. The poor man was soon apprehended, and as they dragged him from his house, he begged to have leave to speak to the king. A friend of his ordered the messengers of death to stop awhile, till he had acquainted the king with the request, which was accordingly done, and he was ordered to be carried into the court of the palace, that the king might hear what he had to say; and being carried thither, the king demanded what he would have. He answered, that what he had said to his wife was the greatest honour which he was capable of doing his king, because, after he had honoured his wife with his embraces, he thought himself unworthy ever after to cohabit with her. The king, after pausing a little, ordered him to be unbound, and brought to his own room, where, as soon as he came, the king embraced him, and ordered a royal suit to be put upon him, and gave him command of five thousand horse more, but took his wife into his own harem.—*Asiatic Journal*, Vol. XXX, p. 215.

**Jamal-uddin Ahmad, Shaikh,** جمال الدين احمد شيخ, a celebrated Muhammadan saint of Hansí, and grandfather of Shaikh Kutb-uddín Manawwar.

**Jamal-uddin Ataullah, Amir,** جمال الدين عطا الله امير, nephew of Sayyad Asíl-uddín 'Abdullah. He is the author of the work called "Rauzat-ul-Ahbáb," *vide* Atáulláh bin-Muhammad al-Husainí Nishápúrí.

**Jamal-uddin-bin-'Abdul Razzak,** جمال الدين بن عبدالرزاق, a celebrated poet of Isfahán, and author of a Díwán. He is the father of Kamál-uddín Ismá'íl and Mu'ín-uddín 'Abdul Karím, both of whom were also poets. Jamál-uddín died in 1192 A. D., 588 A. H.

**Jamal-uddin Hasan bin-Yusaf bin-al-Matahhir al-Hilli,** جمال الدين حسن بن يوسف, entitled Shaikh al-'Allàma, is called the chief of the lawyers of Hilla. He is the author of the "Khulasat-ul-Aḳwál."

His legal works are very numerous, and frequently referred to as authorities of undisputed merit. The most famous of these are, the "Talkhís-ul-Marám," the "Ghâet-ul-Ahkám" and the "Tahrír-ul-Ahkám," which last is a justly celebrated work. The "Mukhtalif-ush-Shiạ" is also a well-known composition of this great lawyer; and his "Irshád-al-Azhan" is constantly quoted as an authority, under the name of the "Irshád-i-'Allâma." *Vide* Allâma al-Hilli.

**Jamal-uddin Husain Anju,** جمال الدين حسين انجو, son of Fakhr-uddín Kashmírí, author of the Persian Dictionary called "Farhang Jahángírí," which he dedicated to the emperor Jahángír in 1605 A. D., 1014 A. H. The author of the "Másir-ul-'Umra" calls him Mír Jamál-uddín Anjú, and says that he is a descendant of the Sayyads of Shíráz, and came to the Dakhin and thence to Ágrah 1585 A. D., 993 A. H. in the time of Akbar who raised him by degrees to the rank of 3000. In the reign of Jahángír, the rank of 4000 was conferred on him with the title of 'Azd-uddaula.

**Jamal-uddin-ibn-Malik,** جمال الدين ابن مالک, author of an Arabic work on philosophy, called "Alfia."

**Jamal-uddin Kashi,** جمال الدن كاشي, author of the history called "Zubdat-ut-Tawáríkh." A work of the same title is mentioned under Shaikh Núr-ul-Haḳ of Dehlí.

**Jamal-uddin Muhammad Abdul Razzak,** جمال الدين محمد عبدالرزاق, *vide* Jamál-uddín bin-'Abdul Razzák.

**Jami,** نور الدين عبدالرحمان جامي, the poetical name of Núr-uddín 'Abdur Rahmán, a celebrated Persian poet, the son of Mauláná Muhammad or Ahmad Isfaháni; was born on the 7th November, 1414 A. D., 23rd Shabán, 817 A. H., at a village in Hirát called Jám, from which he derived his poetical name "Jámí." He was remarkably polite, of a very gentle disposition, and endued with such extensive learning, that it was supposed there was not throughout the empire of Persia, so complete a master of the language as himself. Even princes, who were themselves men of erudition and exalted talents, have lavished upon him the most unbounded praises and the highest honours. He was very intimate with Sulṭán Abú Sa'íd Mirzá of Hirát, who continued the friend of Jámí so long as he lived. After his death, our poet enjoyed the same favours from his son and successor Sulṭán Husain Mirzá. He was a cotemporary of the esteemed Biographer, Daulat Sháh, who recorded his fame in the Lives of the Persian poets, called "Tazkira Daulat Sháhí." Jámí was the author of more than 44 works. His poem on the Loves of Joseph and Zalikha is one of the finest compositions in the language; it contains about 4000 couplets. He is also the author of the book called "Nafahát-ul-Ins," a very celebrated abridgement of the Lives of the Súfí Shaikhs, translated from the Arabic "Tabkát-us-Súfía," and dedicated to the celebrated wazír 'Alísher in 1476 A. D., 881 A. H. It may be here observed, that the celebrated poets, as Háfiz, Sádí, Jámí, &c. &c., were professed Súfís. The following are the works, commonly known, composed by Jámí:—

| These together are called Haft Aurang. | | |
|---|---|---|
| | 1. Silsilat-uz-Zahab, dedicated to Bayazíd II. | Sikandar-náma. |
| | 2. Salámán-wa-Absál. | Nafahát-ul-Ins. |
| | 3. Tuhfat-ul-Ahrár. | Baháristán. |
| | 4. Sabhat-ul-Abrár. | Fatúh-ul-Haramain. |
| | 5. Yúsaf-wa-Zalikha. | Khurshed-wa-Máh. |
| | 6. Lailí-wa-Majnún. | Lawaeh Jámí. |
| | 7. Khirad-náma. | Shawáhid-ul-Nabúat. |

Jámí died at the advanced age of 81 lunar years, on Friday the 9th of November, 1492 A. D., 18th Muḥarram, 898 A. H., mourned by the whole city of Hirát: his funeral expenses were defrayed by Sulṭán Husain, and a magnificent train of the most illustrious nobles accompanied his body to the tomb. 'Alísher, his friend laid the first stone of a monument which he caused to be raised to his memory, and his fame became immortal in the minds of his countrymen. He is also the author of a Tafsír or commentary of some note.

**Jami Lahouri, Mulla,** ملا جامي, *vide* Mulla Jámí.

**Jamila,** جميله, the poetical name of a Persian poet.

**Jamil-ibn-Mi'mar,** جميل ابن معمار, a celebrated Arabian poet who lived in the time of the khalíf 'Abdulmálik, and died in the year 701 A. D., 82 A. H. He was cotemporary with two other famous poets named 'Umar the son of 'Abdullah, and Kathír Azza. Jamíl was the lover of Shanba, one of those pairs of lovers, whose constancy and fidelity the orientals praise in their histories and poems.

**Jamshed,** جمشيد, (also called Jam) was one of the ancient kings of Persia, and the fourth of the First or Pishdádian dynasty. He is celebrated as the founder of Persepolis, which is to this day called Istakhr and Takht Jamshed. He introduced the solar year and ordered the first day of it, when the sun entered Aries, to be celebrated by a splendid festival. His country was invaded by Zuhák, a Syrian king, and the unfortunate Jamshed was obliged to fly before the conqueror. He was pursued by the agents of Zuhák, through Sístán, India, and China, and was at last seized and carried before his cruel enemy like a common malefactor, who ordered him to be placed between two boards and sawn asunder with the bone of a fish. We are told by Firdausí that his reign lasted 700 years. He is supposed to have flourished 800 years before the Christian era. His goblet, called Jám Jamshed and Jám Jam, was wondrous. A hundred marvellous tales are told of his celebrated cup, which used to dazzle all who looked on it, and has often been employed by the poets to furnish a simile for a bright eye.

**Jamshed,** جمشيد, this title is sometimes given by the Musalmáns to king Solomon the son of David, and they say that his magic ring and throne possessed extraordinary powers, and his control was absolute over genii and men.

**Jamshed Kutb Shah,** جمشيد قطب شاه, son of Ḳulí Ḳutb Sháh I, ascended the throne of Gólkonḍa in the Dakhin after the death of his father in September, 1543 A. D., Jumáḍa II, 950 A. H. He reigned seven years and some months, and was succeeded by his brother Ibráhím Ḳutb Sháh in 1550 A. D., 957 A. H.

**Janabi,** جنابي, the surname of Abú Muhammad Mustafa bin-Sayyad Hasan-al-Husainí, a celebrated historian and author of a work called "Táríkh-al-Janábí," of which the correct name is supposed to be "Bahr-uz-Zakhkhár," the Swelling of the Sea; it comprises a general history from the beginning of the world to 1589 A. D., 997 A. H. It was originally written in Arabic, and translated by the author into Turkish. Janábí died in 1591 A. D., 999 A. H.

**Jani,** جاني. There have been three authors of this name. The first Abú 'Abdullah Muhammad ibn-Málik Atáí, a native of Damascus. The second Basar Jání; and the third Mansúr bin-'Umar-al-Adib, a native of Isfahán, who died 1025 A. D.

**Jani,** جاني, the poetical name of Mirzá Ján, the father of Mirzá Ján Jánán.

**Jani Begam,** جاني بيگم, daughter of 'Abdul Rahím Khán, Khán-Khánán, who was married to prince Dániál, the son of the emperor Akbar in 1599 A. D., 1007 A. H.

**Jani Beg Sultan,** جاني بيگ سلطان, son of 'Abdullah Khán Uzbak's sister. His son, Dín Muhammad Khán, was raised to the throne of Samarkand after the death of 'Abdul Momin Khán, the son of 'Abdullah Khán Uzbak.

**Jani Beg Turkhan, Mirza,** مرزا جاني بيگ ترخان, ruler of Thatta, succeeded his grandfather Mirzá Muhammad Bákí, in the government of Thatta, the remaining province of Sindh, in 1584 A. D., 993 A. H. Akbar Sháh who before the death of Muhammad Bákí had gone to Láhor, and had remained there for some years, expected a personal visit from Jání Beg; but being disappointed he proceeded to take measures for the subjugation of that country. He therefore in the year 1591 A. D., 999 A. H. directed his commander-in-chief 'Abdul Rahím Khán, the son of Bairám Khán to proceed and occupy the place in his name. The first action took place on the 3rd November, 1591 A. D., 26th Muharram 1000 A. H. when the Sindhís were totally defeated. Notwithstanding, daily skirmishes took place between the two armies; at last Mirzá Jání Beg offered to acknowledge fealty to the emperor and to proceed to the presence. Shortly after, 'Abdul Rahím Khán celebrated the nuptials of his son Mirzá Írich with the daughter of Jání Beg, and after the rainy season of the year 1592 A. D., 1001 A. H. accompanied Mirzá Jání Beg to the presence of Akbar who created the latter a noble of the realm; and from that date the whole kingdom of Sindh reverted to the sovereignty of the empire of Dehlí. Mirzá Jání Beg died at Burhánpúr in 1599 A. D., 1008 A. H., and the government of Thatta was conferred on his son Mirzá Ghází.

**Jan Fishan Khan Bahadur,** جان فشان خان بهادر نواب, nawáb, of Sardhána. He, for his conspicuous loyalty during the mutiny of 1857, was ordered by Government to be rewarded with a pension of 1000 rupees a month in perpetuity to his male heirs, and a perpetuity in confiscated villages of 10,000 rupees per annum to be conferred upon him with remission of one half of revenue for his life, and a quarter for two generations.

**Jangez Khan,** جنگيز خان, *vide* Changez Khán.

**Jan Janan, Mirza,** مرزا جان جانان, son of Mirzá Ján, a learned Musalmán and a good poet, distinguished no less for the grace and spirit of his compositions than for the independent spirituality and anti-idolatrous nature of his sentiments. His poetical name was Mazhar; was born at Agrah about the year 1698 A. D., 1110 A. H., but resided at Dehlí. In the month of Muharram or 3rd January, 1781 A. D., 7th Muharram, 1195 A. H. having expressed his contempt for a superstitious ceremony—the commemoration of the death of Husain—he was shot on the terrace of his own house, by a vindictive partizan of that martyr, and died on the 6th of that month, 10th Muharram, 1195 A. H. He is the author of a Díwán.

**Jan Muhammad, Munshi,** منشي جان محمد, author of an Inshá or collection of letters which goes by his name.

**Jannat Ashyani,** جنت آشاني, the title given to the Emperor Humáyún after his death.



**Jannati,** جنتي, a poetical name.

**Jan Nisar Khan,** جان نثار خان, title of Kamál-uddín Husain, an Amír of 3000 under the emperor Sháh Jahán. At the time of his death he was governor of Sístan, and died there 1639 A. D., 1049 A. H.

**Jan Nisar Khan, Nawab,** نواب جان نثار خان, was the brother-in-law to the wazír Kamar-uddín Khán who had married his sister. He was appointed Chakladár of the districts of Korá Jahánábád in the province of Allahábád, and was assassinated by Arárú named Bhagwant Singh, a zamíndár of that place in 1731 A. D., 1144 A. H.

**Jan Nisar Khan, Sayyad,** سيد جان نثار خان, son-in-law of the wazír Kamar-uddín Khán, was put to death, together with several others by Nádir Sháh, on account of the resistance shewn by them in endeavouring to protect their family in the general massacre. This event took place in March, 1739 A. D., Zil-hijja 1151 A. H.

**Janoji Bhosla,** جانوجي بهوسله, the second rájá of Berar, succeeded his father Rághójí Bhósla in 1749 A. D., and died in 1772 A. D. He was succeeded by his younger brother Madhóji Bhósla. *Vide* Rághójí Bhósla the first rájá of Berar.

**Janubi,** جنوبي بدخشان, of Badakhshán, a poet and punster who flourished about the year 1521 A. D., 927 A. H.

**Januni,** جنوني, *vide* Junúní.

**Jan,** جان صاحب, or Ján Sahib, poetical name of Mír Yar 'Alí, who is the author of a Díwán.

**Jansipar Khan Turkman,** جان‌سپار خان تركمان, an Amír of 4000 in the reign of the emperor Jahángír. He was appointed governor of Allahábád in the first year of Sháh Jahán 1628 A. D., 1037 A. H., and died there the same year.

**Jansipar Khan,** جان‌سپار خان, second son of Mukhtár Khán Sabzwárí, an amír of the reign of the emperor 'Alamgír. At the time of his death he held the súbadárí of Haidarábád, and died there in 1701 A. D., 1113 A. H.

**Jarbardi,** جاربردي, surname of Fakhr-uddín Ahmad bin-Hasan, an author who wrote the "Sharah Sháfia," and the marginal notes on the "Kashsháf." He died 1345 A. D., 746 A. H.

**Jarir,** جرير, *vide* Jurír which is the correct pronunciation.

**Jarjis,** جرجيس, George, and in particular St. George the martyr, very well-known in the East, and even by the Muhammadans, who put him amongst the number of the prophets, and confound him with Elias.

**Jarj Tamas,** جارج طامس, *vide* George Thomas.

**Jarraz,** جراز, the surname of Ahmad bin-Ibráhím-al-Tabíb-al-Afríkí, who is often cited under the name of Ibn-Jarráz. He was a physician and an author, and a native of Africa. He died 1009 A. D., 400 A. H.

**Jarullah Zamakhshari,** جارالله زمخشري, surname of Mahmúd bin-'Umar-al-Zamakhsharí, the Ma'tzalite of

Zamakhshar, a village in Khwarizm. He is the author of an excellent commentary on the Ḳurán called "Kashsháf," which he wrote in the name of one of the princes of Mecca. He obtained the surname of Járulláh (or neighbour of God) on account of his residing for a long period at Mecca. He was born in 1074 A. D., 467 A. H., and died in the place of his nativity in the year 1142 or 1144 A. D., 537 or 539 A. H. He is also the author of many other works, such as—

Kitáb Fasl-dar-Nahr.
Asás-ul-Balághat-dar-Loghat.
Rabí-ul-Abrár.
Fasús-ul-Akhbar-wal-Faráez-dar-Ilm Faráez.
Raus-ul-Masáel-dur-Fiḳa.
Sharah Abiát Sebúya.
Mustaḳazí-dur-Amsál 'Arab.
Himam-ul-Arbia.
Sawáer-ul-Islám.
Shakáek-ul-Na'mán-wal-Kistás-dar-urúz.
Mu'ajjam-ul-Hadúd.
Manháj-dar-Usúl.
Muḳaddima-al-Adab.
Díwán-ul-Tamsíl.
Díwán-ul-Rasáel.
Díwán-ush-Shua'rá.

**Jassas,** جصاص, surname of Shaikh Ahmad bin-'Alí Rází, which see.

**Jaswant Rae,** جسونت رای, a Hindú who was a poet and the author of a Díwán. His Díwán was found in the Library of Típú Sulṭán.

**Jaswant Rao Holkar,** جسونت راو هلکر, the son of Takojí Holkar, and brother of Káshí Ráo, whom he succeeded on the masnad of Indor about the year 1802. He made a rapid incursion into the Doab and committed some ravages, but was defeated and pursued by Lord Lake to the Sikh country as far as the Bias in 1803, and all his territories occupied by a British force. The whole was restored to him at the peace. He became insane in 1806, and Tulshí Bái, his wife was acknowledged regent. He died on 20th October, 1811, and was succeeded by Malhár Ráo III, his son, by a woman of low birth. Tulshí Bái, however, continued to act as regent. On the 20th December, 1816, a company of armed men seized Tulshí Bái, conveyed her forcibly to the neighbouring river of Sípra, and cutting off her head on the bank, threw the lifeless trunk into the water.

**Jaswant Singh Bundela,** جسونت سنگھ بندیله, son of Rájá Indarman. He held a suitable rank in the army in the reign of the emperor 'Alamgír, and died about the year 1687 A. D., 1099 A. H. After his death the zamíndárí of Urcha was conferred on Bhagwant Singh his son, an infant of four years, with the title of Rájá, but he dying about the year 1693 A. D., 1105 A. H., there remained no one of the family of Rájás Shuján Singh or of his brother Indarman, to succeed him; upon which the Rání Amar Kúnwar, grandmother to the deceased prince, placed on the ráj Udaut Singh, who was descended from Madhukar Sáh, father to Rájá Bír Singh Deo, which was approved by the emperor, who conferred on him the title of rájá, and a suitable manṣab.

**Jaswant Singh, Maharaja,** مهاراجه جسونت سنگه, the celebrated rájá of Jodhpúr or Máṛwár, of the tribe of Ráṭhor Rájpúts, who acted so capital a part in the competitions of 'Alamgír and his brother Dárá Shikóh whose cause he espoused, and was guilty of great impropriety. He was the son of Rájá Gaj Singh and a descendant of Ráo Máldeo. Jaswant Singh, subsequently, became one of the best generals of 'Alamgír, and held the rank of 7000 for several years. He died near Kábul about the 11th December, 1678 A. D., 6th Ẕil-ḳada 1089 A. H. He had built a fine house at Ágrah on the banks of the Jamna, the surrounding walls of which are still standing, and his followers brought his infant children and his women who did not burn with him, towards their native country. Orders were sent by the emperor 'Alamgír to conduct them to court, where on their arrival, he insisted on the children being made Musalmáns. Upon this the rájpút attendants, determined to die rather than submit to this order, fled with their charge towards the rájá's territories, and being pursued by the emperor's troops, fought valiantly, and were mostly cut to pieces, but the women and infants arrived safe at Jodhpúr; they were, however, compelled to take refuge in the hills and the woods, and on the death of 'Alamgír in 1707 A. D., regained their former possession. Ajít Singh, his son, was restored to the throne of his ancestors in the year 1711 A. D., by the emperor Farrukh-siyar who married his daughter. Ajít Singh was murdered by his son Abhai Singh in 1724 A. D.

**Jaswant Singh,** جسونت سنگھ, rájá of Jodhpúr Máṛwár, succeeded to the gaddí after the death of his father Takhat Singh in February, 1873 A. D., 1289 A. H.

**Jaswant Singh,** جسونت سنگھ, son of Balwant Singh Mahárájá of Bhartpúr. He was born on the 28th February, 1851, and succeeded his father on the 16th of March, 1853 when he was but two years old.

**Jaswant Singh, Kunwar,** کنور جسونت سنگھ, *vide* Parwána.

**Jat,** جاٹ, a tribe of Hindú labourers who made no figure in the Mughul empire, as a nation, till the reign of 'Alamgír, in whose expedition to the Dakhin, they were first heard of as a gang of banditti, under an intrepid fellow called Chúráman. They were then so daring as to harrass the rear of the imperial army. After the death of that monarch they took advantage of the growing imbecility of the empire, and fortifying themselves, spread their depredations to the gates of Ágrah. Mukham Singh, who after the death of Chúráman commanded the Jáṭs, took upon himself the title of rájá, but their power increased under Badan Singh and Súrajmal, which last was dignified with titles from the emperor. *Vide* Chúráman Jáṭ.

**Jawad 'Ali, Mirza,** جواد علي مرزا, or more properly Prince Mirzá Muhammad Jawád 'Alí Sikandar Hashmat Bahádur, son of Amjád 'Alí Sháh, and brother of Wájid 'Alí Sháh the ex-king of Lakhnau. He accompanied his mother, the dowager Queen of Lakhnau, after the annexation of that country to the British possessions in 1856, to England, and died there after the death of his mother, on the 25th February, 1858, aged 30 lunar years. The body of the prince was transferred from London to Paris, to be buried on French soil beside that of the Queen his mother. An immense crowd had assembled to witness the procession, attended by Prince Mirzá Hamid 'Alí, the nephew of the deceased.

**Jawahir Singh,** جواهر سنگھ, *vide* Jouhar.

**Jawahir Singh,** جواهر سنگھ, the Jáṭ rájá of Ḍíg and Bhartpúr, was the son of Súrajmal Jáṭ. He succeeded to the ráj after his father's death in December, 1763 A. D., 1177 A. H., was secretly murdered in 1768, and was succeeded by his brother Ráo Ratan Singh, who did not escape suspicion of having been accessory to his brother's murder. Ratan Singh reigned ten months and thirteen days and was stabbed by a faḳír named Rúpánand, who pretended to transmute copper into gold. *Vide* Ratan Singh.

**Jawahir Singh,** جواهر سنگه, a Sikh chief who became the minister of Mahárájá Dalíp Singh after the death of Hírá Singh, and was murdered by the troops at Láhor on the 21st September, 1845. Rájá Lál Singh succeeded him.

**Jawahir Singh, Maharaja,** مهاراجه جواهر سنگه, son of Dhyan Singh and nephew of Mahárájá Guláb Singh, ruler of Káshmír.

**Jawan,** جوان, the poetical appellation of Mirzá Ḳázim 'Alí, a Hindústání lyric poet, attached to the college of Fort William. He is the author of an Urdú Díwán and also of a Bárah Másá which he composed in 1802 A. D., 1217 A. H. He was alive in 1812.

**Jawan Bakht, Mirza,** جوان بخت مرزا, the youngest son of Bahádur Sháh, the ex-king of Dehlí, who accompanied his father to Rangoon in 1858, and now resides under surveillance at that place. Government has sanctioned the grant of a separate pension and an allowance of 250 rupees to his wife Zamaní Begam in 1873 A. D.

**Jawed Khan,** جاوید خان, an eunuch and a great favourite of the emperor Ahmad Sháh and his mother, who raised him to the rank of an amír with the title of Nawáb Bahádur. Nawáb Safdar Jang, who was much disgusted at the influence he had over the emperor, invited him to an entertainment, and murdered him during the banquet. This event took place on the 28th of August, 1752 O. S., 28th Shawwál 1165 A. H.

**Jaweni,** جوینی, whose proper name was Abú'l Ma'álí 'Abdulmalik bin-'Abdullah, was a doctor and a very celebrated metaphysician, who bore the title of "Imám-ul-Haramain." He flourished in the reign of Málik Sháh the Saljúkide, and professed the doctrine of Shúfa'í at Naishapúr, where the famous Ghazzálí was his disciple. He is the author of several works, amongst which are the two following: "Táríkh Jahán Kusháe," and "Aḳídat-ul-Nizámiat." He died in 1085 A. D., 478 A. H.

**Jaweria,** جویره, one of the wives of Muhammad whom he married in the sixth year of the Hijra 627 A. D. She is said to be a woman of great beauty, and was brought among the captives. She died about the year 670 A. D., 56 A. H.

**Jawini,** جویني, *vide* Moín-uddín Jawíní.

**Jayesi,** جایسي, *vide* Málik Muhammad Jáyesí.

**Jazari,** جزري, surname of those who were born at a city called Jazarat-ul-'Umar, situated on the Tigris, to the northward of Nineveh and Mausal. One of the most illustrious amongst the men of letters this city has produced, was Ibn-Asír ul-Shaibaní Majd-uddín, who died 1209 A. D., 606 A. H., and of whom we have several works. *Vide* Ibn-Asír.

**Jenghis Khan,** جنگیز خان, *vide* Changez Khán.

**Jent Parkas, Lala,** جینت پرکاس, author of a poem called "Dastúr Ishḳ," containing the story of Sassí and Panún in Persian verse. It appears that his correct name is Jót Parkásh.

**Jhankoji Sendhia,** جهنکوجي سیندهیه, son of Jíápa or Jyápá Sendhia, was killed in the last battle which took place between Ahmad Sháh Abdálí and the Marhaṭṭas on the 14th of January, 1761 N. S., at Panípat.

**Jhanko Rao Sendhia,** جهنکو راو سیندهیه, also called Mukkí Ráo, on the death of Daulat Ráo Sendhia was elected by his widow Bájí Bái as rájá of Gwáliar, and was put on the masnad on the 18th June, 1827; but being then only nine years of age, Bájí Bái acted as regent. He assumed the reins of government in 1833, reigned 15 years and some months, and died on the 4th of February, 1843, aged 24 years. He was succeeded by his adopted son Jíájí Sendhia the present rájá of Gwáliar, with whom Bíjá Bái appears to have resided until the time of the mutiny.

**Jiaji Rao Sendhia,** جیاجي راو سیندهیه, the present rájá of Gwáliar, whose name in full is, Mahárájá 'Alí Jáh Jíájí Ráo Sendhia, was the adopted son of Jhanko Ráo Sendhia, on whose death he succeeded to the government on the 4th February, 1843. His installation took place on the 20th of January, 1844 when Lord Ellenborough visited the fort.

**Jiapa Sendhia,** جیاپا سیندهیه, *vide* Jyapa Sendhia.

**Jiji Begam,** جیجي بیگم, the wet-nurse of the emperor Akbar, and the mother of Mirzá 'Azíz Kóka, who was raised to a high rank by the emperor with the title of Khán 'Azim. She died in the year 1599 A. D., 1008 A. H. The king carried her coffin on his shoulders and shaved his beard and mustachoes.

**Jiwan, Mulla,** جیون ملا, *vide* Mulla Jíwan.

**Jodha Rao,** جودها راو, rájá of Máṛwár, and a descendant of Seojí, the grandson of the celebrated Jaichánd, the last Ráṭhór monarch of Kanauj. He in the year 1432 A. D. founded the modern capital of Jódhpúr, to which he transferred the seat of government from Mandór.

**Jodh Bai,** جوده بائي, (whose maiden name appears to be Jagat Goshaini and also Bálmatí), was the daughter of Rájá Udai Singh of Jodhpúr or Máṛwár, the son of Rájá Maldeo. She was called Jodh Báí, because she was a princess of Jódhpúr. She was married to Mirzá Salím (afterwards Jahángír) in 1585 A. D., 994 A. H., and became the mother of the emperor Sháh Jahán who was born in 1592 A. D., 1000 A. H. at Láhor. She died at Ágrah in 1619 A. D., 1028 A. H., and was buried in Sohágpúra built by her where her palace and tomb are still to be seen in a ruinous state.

**Jogi, Sultan,** جوگي سلطان, *vide* Muhammad Jogí.

**Josh,** جوش, poetical title of Ahmad Hasan Khán, who is familiarly called Achchhe Sáhib. He was living in Lakhnau in 1853 A. D., 1269 A. H., and is the author of an Urdú Díwán. He is the son of Nawáb Muḳím Khán, the son of Nawáb Muhabbat Khán, the son of Háfiz Rahmat Khán.

**Joshish,** جوشش, poetical title of Muhammad Hasan or Muhammad Róshan of Patna, who flourished in the time of the emperor Sháh 'Alam.

**Jot Parkash, Lala,** جوت پرکاش لالا a Hindú Káyeth and an author. This appears to be the correct for Jeint Parkásh, which see.

**Jouhar,** جوهر, the poetical appellation of Jawáhir Singh, a Hindú, who was the pupil of the poet Mulla Nátiḳ of Naishápúr. He is the author of a Díwán in Persian and Urdú, and was living in 1851 A. D., 1267 A. H.

**Jouhar,** جوهر, the poetical name of Munshí Sewa Rám of Sháhjahánpúr, who flourished in the time of Akbar Sháh II, and is the author of several works in Persian, such as "Jouhar-ul-Talím," "Jouhar-ul-Tarkíb," &c., the last-named work he wrote in 1820 A. D., 1235 A. H.

**Jouhari Farabi,** جوهری فارابی, surname of Abú Nasr Ismá'íl bin-Hammád. Although he was a Turk, yet he made such progress in the Arabic language, which he studied in Mesopotamia and Egypt, that he was styled "Imám-ul-Lughát," or master of the language. He is the author of a very large Arabic Dictionary entitled "Sahah-ul-Lughát," the purity of the tongue. He is often called after this work, "Sáhib-us-Sahah" or the author of the Saháh. He is commonly called Fárábí or Fárábí-al-Turkí, because he was a native of Fáráb in Turkistán. He died 1002 A. D., 393 A. H. Some authors say that his death took place in 992 A. D., 382 A. H.

**Jouhari Zargar,** جوهري زرگر, a poet who flourished in the time of Sulaimán Sháh and Arsalán Sháh of the house of Saljúḳ. He is the author of a poem containing the story of "Amír Ahmad and Mahastí."

**Jounpur,** جونپور, kings of, *vide* Khwája Jahán.

**Jouzi,** جوزي, *vide* Abú'l Faraj ibn-Jauzí.

**Joya,** جويا, poetical appellation of Mirzá Daráb Beg, a poet whose native country was Káshmír. He died in 1706 A. D., 1118 A. H., and is the author of a Díwán. The poetical name of his brother Mirzá Kámrán, was Góyá.

**Juban Choban** or **Jovian, Amir,** امير جوبان, the tutor and general of the armies of Sulṭán Abú Sa'íd Khán, son of Aljáitú, king of Persia. He was put to death by Málik Ghayás-uddín Kart in November, 1327 A. D., Muḥarram, 728 A. H., by order of the Sulṭán, because he refused to give him his daughter, Baghdád Khátún, in marriage. *Vide* Baghdád Khátún.

**Juber,** جبير, a companion of Muhammad.

**Judat,** جودت, a poetical appellation.

**Jughtai,** جغتاي, *vide* Chaghtai.

**Jugal Kishor,** جگل كشور, an inhabitant of Dehlí whose poetical name was Sarwat. He was wakíl to the Názim of Bengal for several years.

**Juji Khan,** جوجي خان, was the eldest son of Chingiz Khán the Tartar, from whom he had received for his share the wide regions of Ḳapcháḳ; but this prince died a few months before his father in 1226 A. D., and left his territories to his son Batú Khán, who conquered Russia and Bulgaria, and ravaged the countries of Poland, Moravia, and Dalmatia, and had marched into Hungary in order to attack Constantinople, when death ended his victorious career.

**Juna Shah,** جونا شاه, a brother of Muhammad Tughlaḳ Sháh, king of Dehlí, who built the city of Jounpúr which goes after his name.

**Junaid Baghdadi, Shaikh,** شيخ جنيد بغدادي, a celebrated ascetic whose father was a glass-blower of Nahâwand. He was born and brought up at Baghdád, and became one of the best disciples of Shâfa'í, but followed the system of Súfián Sourí. He made thirty pilgrimages to Mecca, alone and on foot. He died at Baghdád in the year 911 A. D., 298 A. H., and was buried near the tomb of his master and maternal uncle, Sarí Saḳtí.

**Junaid, Shaikh** or **Sultan,** سلطان جنيد, third in descent from the celebrated Shaikh Safí-uddín Ardibelí, and grandfather of Sháh Ismá'íl I of Persia, founder of the Safwí dynasty which was extirpated by Nádir Sháh. He was a Súfí or mystic philosopher, but being expelled from Azurbeján by the Turkmán ruler Jahán Sháh, established himself in Dayarbikar. In the latter period of his life, he went to Shirwán with his disciples, and was killed in 1456 A. D., 860 A. H., in a conflict with the troops of Amír Khalíl-ulláh, ruler of that province. *Vide* Ismá'íl I Safwí. The book called Nukkát Bedil, written by Mirzá Bedil, contains his Memoirs.

**Jununi,** جنوني, author of a poem called "Lataef Shouḳ," a collection of entertaining and witty tales which he composed in the year 1689 A. D., 1100 A. H., and dedicated to the emperor 'Alamgír, but many were rather obscene.

**Jununi, Maulana,** مولانا جنوني, a sprightly satirical poet of Hirát who flourished in the time of Amír Ghayás-uddín Sulṭán Husain, son of Fíroz Sháh about the 9th century of the Hijrí era.

**Jurat,** جرات, poetical title of Kalandar Bakhsh, a son of Yehia Amán and pupil of Hasrat. He was first supported by Nawáb Muhabbat Khán, but in 1800 A. D., 1215 A. H., he was in the service of prince Sulaimán Shikóh at Lakhnau. Though in the prime of life, he became blind, but became a good musician and an excellent player on the guitar. It appears that Jurat and his family had the family name of Yehia Mán, because they said that they were descended from Yehia Ráe Mán who resided in a street at Dehlí which is close to the Chándní Chouk, and is still called the Ráe Mán street. It is also stated that this Ráe Mán was executed by Nádir Sháh. Jurat died in the year 1810 A. D., 1225 A. H. He is the author of an Urdú Díwán and two Maṣnawis.

**Jurir,** جرير, or Abú Hazrá Jarír ibn-Atiya, was one of the greatest and most celebrated poets. He flourished in the reign of the Khalíf 'Abdulmalik of the house of Umayya, and received from him a handsome salary. He was once rewarded by the prince for a single panegyrical ode, with 100 camels, 18 slaves and a silver jug. Abú'l Faraj ibn-ul-Jauzí places the death of Jurír in the year 111 Hijrí or 729 A. D., 111 A. H., aged 80 years.

**Jurir-ibn-'Abdullah,** جرير ابن عبدالله, a general of the army in the time of 'Umar, the second Khalífa after Muhammad.

**Jurir-ibn-ul-Tabari,** جريرابن الطبري, or Jurír-ut-Tabarí, a celebrated Arabian historian, author of the "Táríkh Tabarí." He died in the year 922 A. D., 310 A. H. His son Muhammad, who was also an author, died in 942 A. D., 330 A. H. *Vide* Abú Ja'far-at-Tabarí.

**Jurjani,** جرجاني, which see.

**Jurjani,** جرجاني, a native of Jurján or Georgia. Al-Sayyad-ush-Sharíf Abú'l Hasan (or Husain) 'Alí, was thus surnamed because he was born in that country. He was one of the most celebrated Musalmán doctors; was born in 1339 A. D., 740 A. H., and died at Shíráz 1413 A. D., 816 A. H. There have been several other authors of this surname, as Al-Sharíf-al-Husainí, a son of the first, who was a famous physician and lived in the time of Atsiz, Sulṭán of the Khwárizmiáns. Also Abú'l Wafa, a mathematician, Abú Bakr bin-'Abdul Káhir, a grammarian, and Muhammad Jirjání, a valiant captain of the Sulṭán of Khwárizm, and governor of the city of Hirát who was killed in defending that place against Túlí Khán, son of Changez Khán.

# K.

**Kaan,** *vide* Khán.

**Ka'b,** كعب ابن زهير, or Kaa'b ibn-Zahír of Mecca, was an Arabian poet, and author of the "Ḳasáed Bánat Sa'ád," a poem in Arabic held in the highest estimation, containing a panegyric on Muhammad. A translation of part of it may be found in Sir William Jones's Second Volume of the Asiatic Researches. The author was a Jewish Rabbi, contemporary and opponent of Muhammad, and had written some satirical verses upon him; but afterwards being desirous of a reconciliation with the prophet, he wrote the above poem, which had the desired effect. Some authors say that he died in the first year of the Hijra, that is, 622 A. D., 1 A. H. But, according to Ockley's History of the Saracens, "Kaa'b came in the ninth year of the Hijra, and made his peace with Muhammad, with a poem in his praise." By this it appears that he was living in 631 A. D. He is said to have assisted Muhammad greatly in the compilation of the Ḳurán. *Wilkin's Biographical Dictionary under Coab.*

**Ka'b-al-'Ahbar,** كعب العهبر, a famous traditionist of the tribe of Hamyar, who embraced Islámism in the reign of 'Umar, and died in 652 A. D., 32 A. H., during the reign of 'Usmán.

**Kabir,** كبير, a celebrated Hindí poet, by trade a Musalmán weaver, who, according to the Akbar-náma, was cotemporary with Sikandar Sháh Lódí, king of Dehlí. Kabír was a Súfí or Deist of the most exalted sentiments and of benevolence unbounded. His poems which are still universally esteemed, inculcate the purest morality, good will and hospitality towards all men; and breathe so fine a spirit of toleration, that both Hindús and Musalmáns contend for the honour of his having been born of their religion. From the disinterested, yet alluring, doctrines his poems contain, a sect has sprung up in Hindústán, under the name of Kabír Panthí, who are so universally esteemed for veracity, and other virtues, among both Hindús and Musalmáns, that they may be with propriety considered the Quakers of this country. The time of Kabír's death seems involved in equal obscurity with the manner of his decease and burial. They relate that he lived a long time at Kásí (Benáras) and Gayá, and sojourned also at Jagarnáth, where he gave great offence to the Bráhmaṇs, by his conduct and tolerant doctrine. When stricken in years, he departed this life among a concourse of his disciples both Musalmáns and Hindús. He is buried at Ratanpúr, where his tomb is said to be seen to this day.

**Kabir, Shaikh,** شيخ كبير, surnamed Bala Pír, was the son of Shaikh Ḳásim Ḳádirí, whose tomb is at Chunár. Shaikh Kabír died at Ḳanauj on Monday, the 4th of November, 1644 A. D., 12th Ramaẓán, 1054 A. H., where a splendid Mausoleum was built on his tomb by one of his sons named Shaikh Mahdí who died in 1677 A. D., 1088 A. H., and is also buried there.

**Kabir-uddin,** كبير الدين بن تاج الدين عراقي, son of Táj-uddín 'Iráḳi, lived in the time of Sulṭán Alá-uddín king of Dehlí, and wrote a book on his conquests.

**Ḳablai Kaan,** قبلاء قاآن, or Khán, or more properly Ḳawaila Káán, Grand Khán of the Mongols and Emperor of China, was the son or brother of Mangú Khán emperor of Tartary, and great-grandson of Chingiz Khán. He succeeded his brother about the year 1259 A. D., 655 A. H., and founded the Yueen dynasty in China. Being ordered by his brother Mangú, then Khakan of the Mongols, to subjugate Corea and China, he entered China with an immense army in 1260 A. D., drove out the Tartars of the Kin dynasty and took possession of North China. In 1279 he completed the ruin of the Song dynasty by invading and subduing Southern China so that his dominion now extended from the Frozen Ocean to the Straits of Malacca and from Corea to Asia Minor—an extent of territory, the like of which had never before, and has never since, been governed by any one monarch. The rule of the Mughuls, hitherto severe and barbarous, changed its character in the reign of this prince, who adopted entirely the manners of the Chinese, and who is regarded, even by that people, as one of the best and most illustrious of their emperors. He died in 1294 A. D., 693 A. H.

**Ḳabul,** قبول, the poetical appellation of Mirzá 'Abdul Ghání Beg of Kashmír, who was a Súfí and a pupil of Jóyá, the brother of Góyá. He died in 1726 A. D., 1139 A. H.

**Ḳabus,** قابوس, a prince of the house of Shamgír, or Dashmagír, whose capital was Rei, and afterwards Jurján in Khurásán. Shamgír was succeeded by his son Bístún, of whom nothing particular is related. But the next of this family, Ḳábús, whose title was "Shama'-ul-Mulk," or the candle of the kingdom, is celebrated for his extraordinary wisdom and learning. He was, by the instigation of his son Manúchchr, slain by his own mutinous officers 1012 A. D., 403 A. H., whose excesses he had probably desired to restrain. He was succeeded by his son Manúchchr, who submitted to the power of Sulṭán Maḥmúd of Ghazní: but that monarch not only continued him in his family possessions, but gave him his daughter in marriage. He died 1070 A. D., 463 A. H., and was succeeded in the government of Jurján by his son Gílán Sháh. Ḳábús is the author of several works, one of which is called "Kamál-ul-Balághat."

**Kabuli Mahal,** كابلي محل, a wife of Sháhzahan.

**Kachhwaha,** the title of the Rájás of Amber or Jaipúr. *Vide* Bhará Mal.

**Ḳadard,** قادرد, the son of Ja'far Beg Dáúd, and brother of Alp Arsalán of the race of Saljúk. He was installed by Tughral Beg his uncle in 1041 A. D., 433 A. H., and became the first Sulṭán of the Saljúk dynasty of Kirmán where he reigned 32 years and died of poison in 1072 A. D., 465 A. H., by order of Malik Sháh.

*The following is a list of the Sulṭáns of Kirmán of the race of Saljúk.*

| | A. D. | A. H. |
|---|---|---|
| Ḳádard, the son of Ja'far Beg Dáúd, began | 1041 | 433 |
| Sulṭán Sháh, the son of Ḳadard, .......... | 1072 | 465 |
| Túrán Sháh, brother of Sulṭán Sháh, ...... | 1074 | 467 |
| Írán Sháh, son of Túrán Sháh, a tyrant who was slain in 1100, ............... | 1096 | 489 |
| Arsalán Sháh, son of Kirmán Sháh, reigned 42 years, ......................... | 1100 | 494 |
| Mughís-uddín Muhammad, son of Arsalán, | 1141 | 536 |
| Tughral Sháh, son of Muhammad, ........ | 1156 | 551 |
| Bahrám, Arsalán, and Túrán Sháh, sons of Tughral, dispute succession,........... | 1169 | 565 |
| Muhammad Sháh, son of Bahrám Sháh who after the death of his father and two uncles ascended the throne of Kirmán, was dispossessed by Malik Dínár, a Turk of the tribe of Ghuz in 1187 A. D., 583 A. H. Thus ended the Saljúk dynasty of Kirmán of the race of Ḳádard. | | |

**Ḳadar Khan,** قادرخان. *Vide* Ḳadr Khán.

**Ḳadir,** قادر, the poetical title of Shaikh 'Abdul Ḳádir Badáoní. *Vide* 'Abdul Ḳádir.

**Ḳadir,** قادر, the poetical appellation of Wazír Khán, an inhabitant of Ágrah, who was in great favour with 'Alamgír and his two successors. He died in 1724 A. D., 1136 A. H., and is the author of a Díwán.

**Ḳadir,** قادر, the poetical name of Shaikh 'Abdul Ḳádir, who was employed as Munshí by Prince Muhammad Akbar, son of 'Alamgír. He is the author of a Díwán.

**Ḳadir Billah,** قادر بالله. *Vide* Al-Ḳádir Billah.

**Ḳadir** or **Ḳadiri,** قادر یا قادري, the poetical name of 'Abdul Ḳádir of Badáon.

**Ḳadiri,** قادري, the poetical title of Prince Dárá Shikóh, the eldest son of the emperor Sháh Jahán.

**Ḳadir Shah,** قادر شاه, of Málwá. After the occupation of Málwá by the emperor Humáyún, that monarch had left his own officers in the government of that kingdom, but shortly after his return to Ágrah, Mallú Khán, one of the officers of the late Khiljí government, retook all the country lying between the Narbada and the town of Bhilsa, after a struggle of twelve months against the Dehlí officers; whom having eventually subdued, he caused himself to be crowned in Manḍo, under the title of Ḳádir Sháh of Málwá. He reigned till the year 1542 A. D., 949 A. H., when Sher Sháh took Málwá, and conferred the government to Shujaa' Khán his minister and relative.

**Ḳadr Khan,** قدر خان, king of Khutan, who was a contemporary of Sulṭán Mahmúd of Ghazní. He was living between the years 1005 and 1024 A. D. It is related of him that he was very fond of music, and that four bags were constantly placed round his sofa, and as he listened to the song, he cast handfuls of gold and silver to the poets.

**Ḳael,** قایل, poetical name of 'Abdullah, a Persian poet.

**Ḳaeli** or **Ḳabili,** قایلي, of Sabzwár, is the author of a biography or Tazkira of poets. He died in 1548 A. D., 955 A. H.

**Ḳaem-bi-amr-ullah,** قایم بامرالله, was the son of Mahdí, the first Khalíf of the Fatimites in Africa. He rebuilt the city of Massilah in Africa in the year 927 A. D., 315 A. H., and called it Muhammadia.

**Ḳaem Billah,** قایم بالله, Khalífa of Baghdád, *vide* Al-Ḳáem Billah.

**Ḳaem Jang** or **Ḳayum Jang,** قایم جنگ, the son of Muhammad Khán Bangash, nawáb of Farrukhábád, whom he succeeded in June, 1743 O. S., Jumáda I, 1156 A. H. He made war by the instigation of the wazír, nawáb Safdar Jang, with the Rohelas of Kaṭer now called Rohilkhanḍ, after the death of their chief, 'Alí Muhammad Khán, but was defeated and slain on the 10th November, 1749 O. S., 10th Ẕil-ḥijja, 1162 A. H., and his estates confiscated by the wazír. The principal servants of the deceased were sent prisoners to Allahábád; but his mother was allowed to keep the city of Farrukhábád and twelve small districts for the support of the family, as they had been conferred on it in perpetuity by the emperor Farrukh-siyar. The conquered country was committed to the care of the wazír's deputy, Rájá Nawáb Ráe, who was soon after slain in battle against Ahmad Khán the brother of Ḳáem Jang, who took possession of the country.

**Ḳaem,** قایم, poetical appellation of Ḳáem Khán who held the post of Captain in the service of Wazír Muhammad Khán, Nawáb of Tónk, the son of Amír Khán. He is the author of an Urdú Díwán, which he completed and published in 1853 A. D., 1270 A. H.

**Kafi,** کافي, surname of Taḳí-uddín 'Alí bin-'Alí, an Arabian author who died in the year 1355 A. D., 756 A. H. His name is spelt in some of our Biographical Dictionaries, Cafi.

**Kafi** or **Kami,** کافي, poetical name of Mirzá 'Alá-uddaula who flourished in the reign of the emperor Akbar. *Vide* Alá-uddaula (Mirzá), and Kámí.

**Kafi,** کافي, whose proper name was Kifáyet 'Alí, was a poet of Muradábád, and author of the "Bahár Khuld," which is a translation of the "Shimáel."

**Kafi-ul-Kafat,** کافي الکفات, *vide* Ibn-'Ibád.

**Kafur, Malik,** ملک کافور, a favourite eunuch of Sulṭán 'Alá-uddín Khiljí, king of Dehlí, who was raised to the high rank of wizárat. After the king's death, the first step which the traitor took, was to send a person to Gwáliár, to put out the eyes of Khizir Khán and Shádí Khán the two sons of the deceased Sulṭán. His orders were inhumanly executed. He then placed Shaháb-uddín the king's youngest son (a boy of seven years of age) on the throne, and began his administration; but was assassinated thirty-five days after the king's death, in January, 1317 A. D., 716 A. H., and Mubárik the third son of the king was raised to the throne.

**Kahaj Tabrezi, Shaikh,** شیخ کہج تبریزي, a learned Musalmán who held the office of Shaikh-ul-Islám at Tabrez during the reign of Sulṭán Aweis and Sulṭán Husain of Baghdád. He is the author of a Díwán.

**Kahi,** کاهي, *vide* Ḳásim Káhí.

**Ḳahir Billah,** قاهر بالله, *vide* Al-Káhir Billah, Khalífa of Baghdád.

**Ḳahkari,** قہقري, *vide* Najm-uddín Abú'l Hasan. In some of our Biographical Dictionaries his name is spelt Cahcari.

**Kaikaus,** کیکاوس, second king of the Kayanian dynasty of Persia, was the son of Kaiḳubád. He was vain and proud: and appears to have been in continual distress from the unfortunate result of schemes that his ambition led him to form, but which he wanted ability to execute. His life is connected with a thousand fables, which though improper in this place, form excellent materials for Firdausí, who has given, in his history of this period, the extraordinary and affecting tale of the combat between Rustam and his unknown son, Suhráb, who is killed by his father. This part of the Sháh-náma has been beautifully translated in English verse by J. Atkinson, Esq., Assistant Surgeon on the Bengal Establishment, and member of the Asiatic Society in 1814. Kaikáús when grown old, resigned his crown in favour of his grandson Kaikhusro, the son of Siáwakhsh.

**Kaikaus, Amir,** امیر کیکاوس, grandson of Ḳábús, prince of Jurján, and one of the noblemen who lived at the court of Sultán Maudúd, the grandson of Sultán Mahmúd of Ghazní. He is the author of the work called "Ḳábús-náma."

**Kaikhusro,** كيخسرو, the third king of the Kayanian dynasty of Persia and the grandson of Kaikáús. He ascended the throne in the lifetime of his father who resigned the crown in his favour. He had several battles with Afrásiáb the king of Túrán, who was at last defeated, taken prisoner, and slain. Soon after these events Kaikhusro resolved to devote the remainder of his life to religious retirement: he delivered over Kábul, Zábulistán and Nímróz to Rustam, as hereditary possessions; and resigned his throne to Luhrásp the son-in-law of Kaikáús and his own son by adoption and affection. After these arrangements, he went accompanied by some nobles to a spring which he had fixed upon as the place of his repose. Here he disappeared, and all those that went with him were destroyed on their return by a violent tempest. He lived 90 years and reigned 60.

**Kaikhusro,** كيخسرو, the son of Sultán Muhammad Khán, governor of Multán, who was the eldest son of Sultán Ghayás-uddín Balban, king of Dehlí. After his father's death in 1285 A. D., he was made governor of Multán by his grandfather, and after his decease in 1286 A. D., was murdered at Rohṭak by Malik Nizám-uddín, wazír of Kaiḳubád who ascended the throne as king of Dehlí.

**Kaikubad,** كيقباد, the founder of the second or Kayanian dynasty of the kings of Persia, was a lineal descendant of Manúchchr, according to some accounts he was his great-grandson. This prince had retired to the mountain of Alburz, from which place he was brought by Rustam the son of Zál and proclaimed king of Persia. He committed the administration of government into the hands of Zál, whose son Rustam, was appointed to lead the Persians against the dreaded Afrásiáb who had again passed the Oxus and invaded Persia. In this battle, Rustam overcame Afrásiáb, and afterwards a peace was concluded, by which it was agreed that the Oxus should remain as it had been heretofore, the boundary between the two kingdoms. Kaiḳubád lived some time after this in peace: he is said to have reigned 120 years. He left four sons: Kaikáús, Arish, Rúm and Armen. To the former he bequeathed his throne, and enjoined all the others to obey him.

*List of kings of the second or Kayanian dynasty.*

1. Kaiḳubád.
2. Kaikáús.
3. Kaikhusro (Cyrus the Great).
4. Luhrásp.
5. Gushtásp (Hystaspes of Grecian History).
6. Isfandiar (Aspanda or Astyages of ditto).
7. Bahman or Ardisher Darázdast (Artaxerxes Longimanus).
8. Humai, daughter and wife of Bahman.
9. Dáráb or Dárá, son of Bahman.
10. Dárá, son of Dáráb (Darius overcome by Alexander the Great).

**Kaikubad,** كيقباد, surnamed Mu'izz-uddín, the grandson of Sultán Ghayás-uddín Balban, whom he succeeded in 1286 A. D., 685 A. H., on the throne of Dehlí in the absence of his father Násir-uddín Baghrá Khán who was then in Bengal. In the year 1287 A. D., 686 A. H., his father having heard the state of affairs at Dehlí, marched from Bengal to visit and advise his son. They met on the banks of the Ghágra at Behár, and the whole scene was so affecting, that almost all the court shed tears. On this occasion the celebrated poet Amír Khusro wrote the poem called the "Kirán-us-Sadain," or the conjunction of the two planets. Kaiḳubád was assassinated through the instigation of Fíróz Malik Khiljí in 1288 A. D., who ascended the throne by the title of Jalál-uddín Fíróz Sháh Khiljí, and became the first Sulṭán of the 2nd branch of the Turk dynasty called Khiljí.

**Kaiomurs,** كيومرس, the first monarch of Persia according to all Muhammadan writers. This king is stated to have reclaimed his subjects from a state of the most savage barbarity. They say he was the grandson of Noah, and the founder of the first dynasty of Persian kings called Pishdádian. His son Siámak was killed in one of the battles with the barbarians or Devs; and when that monarch carried Hoshang, the infant son of Siámak, to share in the revenge he meant to take upon his enemies, his army was joined by all the lions, tigers and panthers in his dominions, and the Devs were routed and torn to pieces by the auxiliaries, who had left their native forest to aid the just king. After this victory, Kaiomurs retired to his capital Balkh. He reigned 30 years, and was succeeded by his grandson Hoshang.

*The following is a list of kings of the first or Pishdádian dynasty.*

1. Kaiomurs.
2. Hoshang.
3. Tuhmurs, surnamed Deoband.
4. Jamshed reigned at Persipolis.
5. Zuhák, surnamed Alwaní.
6. Faridún, restored by Kawa.
7. Manúchchr.
8. Naudar or Nauzar.
9. Afrásiáb, king of Turkistán.
10. Záb, brother of Naudar.
11. Garshásp.

**Ḳaisar,** قيصر, a poet of the tribe of Shámlú, who is commonly called Ḳaisar Shámlú.

**Ḳaisar,** قيصر, poetical name of Prince Khurshaid Ḳadr the son of Mirzá Asmán Ḳadr, the son of Mirzá Khurram Bakht, the son of Prince Mirzá Jahándár Sháh, the son of Sháh 'Alam, king of Dehlí.

**Ḳaisari Kirmani,** قيصرى كرماني, a poet of Kirmania.

**Kaiuk Khan,** كيوک خان, *vide* Kayúk.

**Kakafi,** كاكفي, *vide* Ahmad bin-Idrís. He is mentioned in some of our Biographical Dictionaries under the name of Cakafí.

**Kakafi,** كاكفي, *vide* Ahmad bin-Idrís.

**Ḳalandar,** قلندر, author of the work called "Sirát-ul-Mustaḳím," which he composed in 1405 A. D., 808 A. H., and dedicated to Abú'l Muzaffar Husain Sháh bin-Mahmúd Sháh bin-Ibráhím Sháh of Jaunpúr.

**Ḳalanisi,** قلانيسي, surname of 'Abdullah bin-Muhammad, an Arabian author, who died in 1121 A. D., 515 A. H.

**Kalb Ali Khan,** كلب علي خان, Nawáb of Rámpúr in 1869-70.

**Kalb Husain Khan, Mirza,** مرزا كلب حسين خان, Deputy Collector of Etáwah, the son Ahtarám-uddaula Dabír-ul-Mulk Kalb 'Alí Khán Bahádur. He is the author of four Díwáns and a biography called "Shaukat Nádirí." He was living in 1864 A. D., 1281 A. H.

**Kalhana,** كلهانه, a Bráhman and author of a history of Kashmír called "Rájátarangini." There are four chronicles of the history of Kashmír written in Sanskrit verse; the first by Kalhaná, bringing the history of Kashmír to about 1148 after Christ; the second, a continuation of the former, by Jaúarájá, to 1412 A. D.; the third, a continuation of the second by Srivara, a pupil of Jaúarájá, to 1477 A. D.; and the fourth, by Prajyábhaṭṭa, from that date to the conquest of the valley by the emperor Akbar. The author of the work, the Paṇḍit Kalhaná, of whom we merely know that he was the son of Champaka, and lived about 1150 A. D., under the reign of Siñha Deva of Kashmír—reports that before entering on his task, he had studied eleven historical works written previously to his time, and also a history of Kashmír by the sage Níla, which seems to be the oldest of all. Kalhaná begins his work, with the mythological history of the country, the first king named by him is Gonarda, who, according to his chronology, would have reigned in the year 2448 B. C., and the last mentioned by him is Siñha Deva, about 1150 after Christ.

**Kali Das,** كالي داس, a celebrated Hindú poet who lived towards the commencement of the Christian era. He was one of the nine splendid gems that adorned the court of Rájá Bikarmájít (Vikrámaditya). Some say that he flourished in the time of Rájá Bhój. He wrote the "Nalodia" for the purpose of exhibiting his unbounded skill in alliteration. In four books, containing on the average fifty-four stanzas each, he has given such illustrations of their subject as can never be surpassed. This work has been published in Europe, with a Latin translation by a continental scholar, Ferdinandus Benary. No reason can be imagined, why Kálí Dás should again write the history of Nala and Damayanti, after it had been so elegantly written in flowing verse by Vyása Deva, except that he intended in this simple story to shew forth his ingenuity in alliteration. He is also the author of the poem called "Kumára Sambhava," and of another called "Mahá Náṭak."

**Kali Sahib,** كالي صاحب, surname of Ghulám Nasír-uddín, the son of Mauláná Kutb-uddín, the son of Mauláná Fakhr-uddín. Although he was the Murshid or spiritual guide of the king of Dehlí, he preferred the habit of a Derwish. He died in 1852 A. D., 1268 A. H.

**Kalim,** كليم, the poetical name of Abú Tálib Kalím, which see.

**Kalim-ullah,** كليم الله, a title of Moses the prophet.

**Kalim-ullah,** كليم الله, the last king of the Bahmaní dynasty of Kulbarga or Ahmadábád Bídar in the Dakhin. He was expelled in 1527 A. D., by Amír Baríd his wazír, who mounted the throne and took possession of that kingdom.

**Kalim-ullah,** كليم الله, author of a work called "Kashkol Tasauwaf," an exposition of the mystical phrases of the Súfís.

**Kamal,** كمال, a poet of Isfahán.

**Kamal,** كمال, poetical title of Mír Kamál 'Alí of Gaya Mánpúr. He wrote Persian and Rekhta verses, and is the author of a large work called "Kamál-ul-Hikmat," on philosophy, and one called "Chahárdah Darúd," *i. e.*, the fourteen blessings containing an account of the Imáms. He died in 1800 A. D., 1215 A. H., and the chronogram of the Hijrí year of his death is contained in the word Dareghá.

**Kamal Ghayas, Maulana,** مولانا كمال غياث شيرازي, of Shíráz, a poet and physician who flourished in the time of Ibráhím Sulṭán.

**Kamal Ḳazi,** قاضي كمال, *vide* Abúl-Fath Bilgrámí.

**Kamal Khan, Gikhar,** كمال خان گكهر, prince of the Gikhars, was the son of Sulṭán Sárang, the son of Malik Kalán II, the son of Malik Kalán I, the son of Malik Khar, who was the founder of the principality of the Gikhars. Their country lies among the mountains between Bhaṭ and Sindh, which formerly belonged to the government of Kashmír. Malik Kalán II had several battles with Sher Sháh, but was at last taken prisoner and put to death by that monarch, and his son or grandson Kamál Khán imprisoned in the fortress of Gwáliár. He was, however, after some years released by Salím Sháh the son of Sher Sháh, but during his confinement, his uncle Sulṭán Ádam had taken possession of the country. In the first year of the reign of Akbar he was introduced to that monarch and was employed in his service. He by degrees rose to the rank of 5000, and was afterwards put in possession of his dominions by that emperor, and Sulṭán Ádam his uncle taken prisoner and made over to Kamál Khán who put him in confinement where he died. Kamál Khán who became tributary to Akbar, died in 1562 A. D., 970 A. H.

**Kamal Khujandi,** كمال خجندي, *vide* Kamál-uddín Khujandí.

**Kamal-uddin 'Abdul Razzak, Shaikh,** شيخ كمال الدين عبدالرزاق, is the author of several works, among which are the following "Tafsír Táwílát," "Kitáb Istiláhát Súfía," "Sharah Fasús-ul-Ḥikam," "Sharh Manázib-ul-Sábirín," &c. He was a contemporary of Shaikh Rukn-uddín 'Alá-uddaula. [He died in 1482 A. D.] 887 A. H. *Vide* 'Abdul Razzáḳ.

**Kamal-uddin Isma'il,** كمال الدين اسمعيل, son of Jamál-uddín Muhammad 'Abdul Razzáḳ of Isfahán, a celebrated poet of Persia, styled, Malik-ush-Shu'ará, that is to say, king of the poets, and is the author of a Díwán. In the year 1237 A. D., 2nd Jumáda I, 635 A. H., on the 21st of December, when Oḳtái Khán, the son of Changez Khán, invaded Isfahán, and massacred the inhabitants of that city, he also fell a martyr. It is said that he was tortured to death by the Mughuls who expected to find hidden property in his house.

**Kamal-uddin Khujandi, Shaikh,** شيخ كمال الدين خجندي, was a great Shaikh and lyric poet, and a cotemporary of Háfiz, who, though they never saw each other, much esteemed him, considering him and Salmán Sáwají as amongst the first poets of their time. He is commonly called Kamál Khujandí, born at Khujand, a town situated in one of the most beautiful and fertile districts of Persia. After having made the pilgrimage to Mecca, he settled at Tabrez, a place which he found extremely agreeable during the reign of the princes of the family of Jaláyer. The principal personages of Tabrez became his pupils, and he led a life of literary ease and enjoyment; but when Tuḳtamish Khán surprised Tabrez, Shaikh Kamál was made prisoner, and was carried to Serai in Kapják by order of Mangú Khán the grandson of Changez Khán, where he remained four years, after which he was permitted to return to Tabrez, near which city the Sulṭán Awes Jaláyer built him a house. Kamál did not sing the praise of princes in Ḳasída, nor did he write Maṣnawis, but only Ghazals, and fragments. He died in the year 1390 A. D., 792 A. H., and was buried at Tabrez. A MS. of the Díwán of Kamál, which had been the property of a Sulṭán, is possessed by the Imperial Library at Vienna, and is a great treasure as a specimen of splendid writing, and, also, for the superbly executed miniatures which adorn it, illustrating the poems. These pictures are not more than a square inch in size: there are two on each side of the concluding verse; and though so small, represent, with the greatest correctness, either allegorically or simply, the meaning of the poet.—*Dublin University Magazine for* 1840.

**Kamal-uddin Masa'ud, Maulana,** مولانا كمال الدين مسعود شرواني, of Shírwán, a celebrated logician and author of the marginal notes on the "Sharah Hikmat Áín."

**Kamal-uddin Muhammad bin-'Abdul Muna'im Jujari, Shaikh,** شيخ كمال الدين محمد بن عبد المنعم جوجاري, an author who died in 1484 A. D., 889 A. H.

**Kamal-uddin Muhammad-al-Siwasi,** كمال الدين محمد السواسي, commonly called Humám and Ibn-Humám, author of a commentary on the Hidáya entitled "Fath-ul-Ḳádir lil 'Ajiz-al-Faḳír." It is the most comprehensive of all the comments on the Hidáya, and includes a collection of decisions which render it extremely useful. He died in 1457 A. D., 861 A. H. *Vide* Humám and Ibn-Humám.

**Kamal-uddin Muhammad, Khwaja,** كمال الدين محمد خواجه, ibn-Ghayás-uddín Shírází, was a physician and a poet, and flourished in the time of Sulṭán Ibráhím Mirzá. For his poetical title he used Ibn-Ghayás.

**Kamal-uddin Musa bin-Yunas bin-Malik,** كمال الدين موسى بن يونس بن ملك, name of an Imám, who was one of the most celebrated Musalmán doctors.

**Kamal-uddin, Shah,** كمال الدين شاه, *vide* Lutf-ulláh.

**Ḳamar-uddin, Mir,** قمرالدين مير, whose poetical title is Minnat, which see.

**Ḳamar-uddin Khan, wazir,** قمر الدين خان وزير, whose original name was Mír Muhammad Fázil, was the son of Ya'tmád-uddaula Muhammad Amín Khán, wazír, and was himself appointed to that office with the title of Ya'tmád-uddaula Nawáb Ḳamar-uddín Khán Bahádur Nasrat Jang, by the emperor Muhammad Sháh, after the resignation of Nizám-ul-Mulk Asaf Jáh, in 1724 A. D., 1137 A. H. He was sent under Prince Ahmad on the first invasion of Ahmad Sháh Abdálí to oppose him, but was killed by a cannon ball, while at prayers in his tent during the battle of Sarhind on the 11th March, 1748 O. S., 11th Rabí' I, 1161 A. H.

**Kam Bakhsh,** شهزاده كامبخش, (prince) youngest son of the emperor 'Alamgír, a vain and violent young man, who had received from his father the kingdom of the Dakhin, but as he refused to acknowledge the sovereignty of the emperor Bahádur Sháh, his eldest brother, and struck coin in his own name, that monarch after attempting in vain to win him over by concessions, marched against him with a powerful army to the Dakhin, and defeated him in a battle near Haidarábád, where Kám Bakhsh died of his wounds on the same day in the month of February or March, 1708 A. D., Ẕil-ḥijja, 1119 A. H. His mother's name was Udaipúrí Muhal, and he was born on the 25th February, 1667 A. D., 10th Ramaẕán 1077 A. H.

**Ḳambari,** قنبري نيشاپوري, or Ḳanbarí, a poet of Naishápúr, flourished in the time of Sulṭán Bábar who died 1457 A. D., 861 A. H.

**Kami,** كامي, whose proper name is Mirzá Alá-uddaula Ḳazwíní, was the son of Mír Yahya bin-'Abdul Laṭíf, and is the author of the work called "Nafáis-ul-Másir," a Biographical Dictionary of Persian poets. It contains notices of about 350 poets in alphabetical order. Most of them flourished in India during the reign of Akbar to whom the book is dedicated. It was finished in 1571 A. D., 979 A. H., but there occur much later dates in it. He is supposed by some to have died in 1563 A. D., 971 A. H., and by others in 1573 A. D., 981 A. H., but the latter date appears to be correct. The discrepancy arises from the chronogram of his death, in which the number of the last word is considered by some to be 60 and by others 70, a difference of ten years. *Vide* Yahya bin-'Abdul Laṭíf.

**Kamil,** كامل, author of a poetical work, entitled "Chirágh-náma." It consists of Ghazals all of which rhyme in Chirágh (lamp) and the first letter of every verse of the first Ghazal is ا or A, of the second ب or B, and so on.

**Kamran Mirza,** كامران مرزا, second son of the emperor Bábar Sháh, and brother to the emperor Humáyún who, after his accession to the throne in 1530 A. D., 937 A. H., conferred on him the government of Kábul, Ḳandahár, Ghazní and the Panjáb. He was deprived of his sight by Humáyún when at Kábul in the year 1553 A. D., 960 A. H., on account of his repeated offences, and continually raising disturbances in the government. The operation was performed by piercing his eyes repeatedly with a lancet. Kámrán bore the torture without a groan until lemon-juice and salt were squeezed into his eyes, when he called out "O Lord my God! whatever sins I have committed I have been amply punished in this world, have compassion on me in the next." Kámrán eventually obtained permission to proceed to Mecca, where he resided three years and died a natural death in 1556 A. D., 964 A. H. He left three daughters and one son named Abú'l Ḳásim Mirzá, who was imprisoned in the fort of Gwáliar, and put to death by order of the emperor Akbar his cousin in the year 1565 A. D., 973 A. H.

**Kamran Shah,** شاه كامران, the present ruler of Hirát, is the son of Mahmúd Sháh, the son of Timur Sháh, the son of Ahmad Sháh Abdálí. On the death of his father Mahmúd Sháh, in (1829 A. D.) he succeeded him on the throne of Hirát.

**Ḳandahari Begam,** قندهاري بيگم, the first wife of the emperor Sháh Jahán. She was the daughter of Muzaffar Husain Mirzá Safwí, of the royal house of Persia, who was the son of Sulṭán Husain Mirzá, the son of Bahrám Mirzá, the son of Sháh Ismá'íl I of Persia. When Akbar Sháh, in the third year of his reign, made over Ḳandahár to Sháh 'Abbás, king of Persia, the latter conferred the government of that province on his nephew Sulṭán Husain Mirzá, after whose death his son Muzaffar Husain succeeded him. His three brothers came to India in the 38th year of Akbar (1592 A. D.), and Muzaffar Husain followed them afterwards, was received by the emperor with the greatest kindness, and honoured with the rank of 5000, and the jágír of Sambhal. His sister Ḳandahárí Begam, was married in September, 1610 A. D., Rajab, 1019 A. H. to Prince Khurram (afterwards Sháh Jahán) the son of the emperor Jahángír, and received the title of Ḳandahárí Begam, because she was born at Ḳandahár. The year of her death is unknown. She lies buried at Ágrah, in the centre of a garden called Ḳandahárí Bágh. The building on her tomb, which is in the vault, is converted into a dwelling place; it is a beautiful edifice, and now belongs to the Rájá of Bhartpúr.

**Kaus,** *vide* Kaikáús.

**Ḳaplan Beg,** قپلان بيگ, of the Ḳushchí family, was born in India and served under Khán-Khánán in the Dakhin with great distinction, and was in high favour with Jahángír. He is the author of a Díwán and a Maṣnawi, the latter is called "Máh Dost," which celebrates the love of Rustam and Rúdába.

**Kapurthala Rajah.** *Vide* Nihal Singh.

**Ḳara Arsalan,** قرا ارسلان, (which signifies in Turkish, a black lion,) was surnamed 'Imád-uddín, the son of Dáúd, the son of Sukmán bin-Artaḳ. Núr-uddín Mahmúd was his son, to whom Sálah-uddín (Saladin) gave the city of 'Amid or Ḳara 'Amid in Mesopotamia 1183 A. D., 597 A. H. His name is to be found in some of our Biographical Dictionaries under Cara Arslan.

**Ḳarachar Nawian,** قراچار نویان, name of the wazír and son-in-law of Changez Khán.

**Ḳara Ghuz,** قراغز, a Beglarbeg of Natolia whom our historians call Caragossa. He was impaled near Ḳara Hisár by Sháh Ḳulí in the reign of Báyazíd II, emperor of the Turks.

**Ḳara Khan,** قرا خان, *vide* Sadr-uddín bin-Ya'kúb.

**Ḳarak Shah,** قرک شاه, *vide* Sháh Ḳaṛak.

**Karam,** کرم, author of the "Harbae Haidarí," a history of Alí and his son Husain in verse, composed in 1723 A. D., 1135 A. H.

**Ḳara Muhammad Turkman,** قرا محمد ترکمان. The Turkmáns of Asia Minor were divided into two great tribes, the Ḳara Koinlú, and Aḳa Koinlú, *i. e.*, the tribes of "black and white sheep," from their carrying the figures of these animals in their respective standards. Ḳara Muhammad, the founder of the first dynasty, left his small territories, of which the capital was Van, in Armenia, to his son, Ḳara Yúsuf, who though possessed of considerable power, was compelled to fly before the sword of Timur. When that conqueror died, he returned from Egypt, and was victorious in an action with Sulṭán Ahmad Jaláyer I'lkání, the ruler of Baghdád, whom he made prisoner and put to death in 1410 A. D., 813 A. H. After this success he collected an army of 100,000 men, and was preparing to attack Sulṭán Sháhrukh the son of Amír Timur, when he was suddenly taken ill and died near Tabrez in 1411 A. D., 814 A. H. He was succeeded by his son Sikandar Turkmán, who was defeated by Sháhrukh in 1421 A. D., 824 A. H. Sikandar after this had several battles with Sháhrukh, but was at last slain by his son Ḳubád 1437 A. D., 841 A. H., when Sháhrukh added Rei to his own possessions, and gave Tabrez to Jahán Sháh the brother of Sikandar. Jahán Sháh, after a long reign of 30 lunar years, fell in one of the first actions he fought with Uzzan Hasan, chief of the Turkmáns of the white sheep, in November, 1467 A. D., Rabí' II, 872 A. H.

**Ḳarari,** قراري, a Persian poet, *vide* Abul Fath Gílání.

**Ḳara Yusuf,** قرا یوسف, *vide* Ḳara Muhammad.

**Karim,** کریم, poetical name of Mír Muhammad Kázim the son of Fikr. He flourished in the time of Kutbsháh of the Dakhin, and is the author of a Díwán.

**Karim Khan,** کریم خان, the murderer of Mr. W. Fraser, Commissioner of Dehlí. See Shams-uddín Khán (nawáb).

**Karim Khan,** کریم خان, a Pinḍarí chief, who surrendered himself to the British Government on the 15th February, 1818, and received for his support the Tálúḳa of Burhiápár in the Gorakhpúr district, which was held by his descendants up to the mutiny in 1857.

**Karim Khan Zand,** کریم خان زند. The history of Persia, from the death of Nádir Sháh till the elevation of 'Aḳá Muhammad, though it occupies nearly half a century, presents no one striking feature, except the life of Karím Khán, a chief of the tribe of Zand. He collected an army chiefly composed of the different tribes of Zand and Mafí, defeated the Afgháns in several engagements, finally drove them out of the country, and secured to himself the kingdom of Fárs, or the southern division of Persia, while Khurásán partially remained in possession of the descendants of Nádir Sháh; and the countries bordering on the Caspian Sea were retained by Muhammad Hasan Khán Ḳáchár, ruler of Mázindarán the great-grandfather of 'Aḳá Muhammad Sháh Ḳáchár. Karím Khán, after subduing his enemies, enjoyed independent power for twenty-six years; and during the last twenty, *viz.*, from 1759 to 1779, he had been, without a competitor, the acknowledged ruler of Persia. His capital was Shíráz. He died at an advanced period of life on the 2nd March, 1779 A. D., 13th Ṣafar, 1193 A. H., being nearly 80 years of age. After his death Zakí Khán assumed the reins of government, and was assassinated two months after. Sádiḳ Khán, brother of Karím Khán took possession of Shíráz after the death of Zakí Khán, and was put to death on the 14th of March, 1781 A. D., 18th Rabí' I, 1195 A. H., by 'Alí Murád Khán, who now became the sovereign of Persia, and died on the 11th January, 1785 A. D., 28th Ṣafar, 1199 A. H. After his death Lutf 'Alí Khán reigned for some years at Shíráz. He was defeated in 1794 and slain afterwards by 'Aḳá Muhammad Khán Ḳáchár, who took possession of Persia.

**Ḳarmat,** قرمط, or Ḳarmaṭa, a famous impostor, named Abú Zar, who in the year 891 A. D. became the head of a sect called Ḳarmaṭí or Karamatians, which overturned all the principles of Muhammadanism. He came from Khózistán to the villages near Kúfa, and there pretended great sanctity and strictness of life, and that God had enjoined him to pray fifty times a day; pretending also to invite people to the obedience of a certain Imám of the family of Muhammad; and this way of life he continued till he had made a very great party, out of whom he chose twelve apostles to govern the rest, and to propagate his doctrines. Afterwards his courage failing him, he retired to Syria, and was never heard of any more. This sect began in the Khiláfat of Al-Mo'tamid: they multiplied greatly in Arabian Iráḳ or Chaldea, and maintained perpetual wars against the Khalíf. In the year 931 A. D., they beseiged and took the city of Mecca, filled the well Zamzam with dead bodies, defiled and plundered the temple and carried away the black stone; but they brought it again in 950 A. D., and fastened it to the seventh pillar of the portico, giving out, that they had both taken it away, and brought it back again, by express order from heaven. This sect was dissipated by degrees, and at last became quite extinct. *Vide* Abú-Zarr Ḳarmaṭí.

**Ḳarmati,** قرمطي, or Karamatian, a follower of Ḳarmaṭ, which see.

**Karshasp,** کرشاسپ, or Garshásp, the son of Zú, and the last king of the first or Pishdádian dynasty of Persia. *Vide* Zú.

**Kart,** کرت, kings of the dynasty of,—*Vide* Shams-uddín Kart I.

**Kashi, Mulla,** ملا کاشي, surname of Kamál-uddín Abú'l Ghanam 'Abdul Razzáḳ bin-Jamál-uddín, a celebrated doctor, placed amongst the Musalmán saints, was author of several works. He died young about the year 1320 A. D., 720 A. H.

**Kashi Rao Holkar,** كاشي راو هلكر, the eldest of the four sons of Takójí Holkar, after whose death in 1797 A. D. disputes arose between Káshí Ráo and his brother Mulhár Ráo, and both repaired to the court of the Peshwá at Púna; where, on their arrival, Daulat Ráo Sindhia, with a view of usurping the possessions of the family, espoused the cause of Káshí Ráo, and made a sudden and unexpected attack in the month of September on Mulhár Ráo, whom he slew with most of his adherents. After this Sindhia pretended to govern the possessions of the Holkar family in the name of Káshí Ráo, whom he kept in a state of dependence and appropriated the revenue to his own use. A long contest ensued between Daulat Ráo and Jaswant Ráo Holkar, the brother of Káshí Ráo, and continued till the year 1802, when Jaswant Ráo appears to have taken possession of Indor the territory of his father.

**Kashfi,** كشفي, the poetical name of Sháh Muhammad Salámat-ulláh. He is the author of a Díwán in Persian which was printed and published before his death in 1279 A. H.

**Kashfi,** كشفي, takhullus of Mír Muhammad Sálah, who flourished in the reign of the emperor Jahángír, and is the author of a Tarjíhband called "Majmúa' Ráz," which he composed in 1621 A. D., 1030 A. H., containing 270 verses. He died in the year 1650 A. D., 1060 A. H., at Ágrah and lies buried there.

**Kashifi,** كاشيفي, the poetical name of Mauláná Husain bin-Alí, also known by that of Wâez or the preacher. He wrote a full commentary on the Ḳurán in the Persian language. He was a preacher at the royal town of Hirát in Khurásán. He died in 1505 A. D., 910 A. H. *Vide* Husain Wáez.

**Kashmir,** kings of,—*vide* Sháh Mír.

**Ḳasim,** قاسم اكبر ابادي, of Ágrah, author of the "Zafarnáma Akbarí," or book of the victory of Akbar Khán, the son of Dost Muhammad Khán, which he completed in 1844 A. D., 1260 A. H. It is a poem and contains an account of the late wars in Kábul by the British.

**Ḳasim,** قاسم, the poetical name of Hakím Mír Ḳudrat-ulláh who is the author of a Tazkira or Biography of poets.

**Ḳasim Ali Khan, Mir,** ميرقاسم عليخان, commonly called Mír Ḳásim, was the son-in-law of Mír Ja'far 'Alí Khán the Nawáb of Bengal. The English, deceived by his elegance of manners, and convinced of his skill in the finances of Bengal, raised him to the maṣnad in the room of his father-in-law in 1760 A. D., 1174 A. H. He, in the latter years of his government, retired to Munger, and actuated by a keen resentment against the English, for their extensive encroachments on his authority, and the commerce of his country, formed the plan of throwing off their yoke, and annihilating their influence in Bengal; but was deposed and defeated, in a battle fought on the Odwa Nála on the 2nd August, 1763 A. D., 22nd Muḥarram, 1177 A. H., and the deposed Nawáb Ja'far 'Alí Khán was again placed on the maṣnad. Ḳásim 'Alí, incensed to madness at these reverses, fled to Patna from Munger, and there cruelly ordered the massacre of the English in his power: there were 50 gentlemen, Messrs. Ellis, Hay, Lushington, and others, and 100 of lower rank. On the 5th October, they were brought out in parties, and barbarously cut to pieces, or shot under the direction of a German, named Samrú or Sombre. Munger fell to the English early in October. Patna was stormed on the 6th November, and the Ex-Nawáb Ḳásim 'Alí fled to the wazír of Audh, with his treasures, and the remnant of his army. On the 23rd of October, 1764 A. D., Major Carnac fought the celebrated battle of Buxar, completely routing the wazír Shuja-uddaula's army. The following day the Mughul emperor Sháh 'Alam threw himself on the protection of the British, and joined their camp with the imperial standard of Hindústán. The British army advanced to overrun Audh. The wazír refused to deliver up Ḳásim 'Alí, though he had seized and plundered him. Ḳásim 'Alí made his escape at first into the Rohela country, with a few friends and some jewels, which he had saved from the fangs of his late ally, the wazír, and found a comfortable asylum in that country; but his intrigues rendered him disagreeable to the chief under whose protection he resided, he was obliged to leave it, and took shelter with the Ráná of Gohad. After some years' residence in his country, he proceeded to Jódhpúr, and from thence came to try his fortune in the service of the emperor Sháh 'Alam about the year 1774 A. D., 1188 A. H., but was disappointed, and died shortly after in 1777 A. D., 1191 A. H., at Kotwal an obscure village near Dehlí, unpitied even by his own family. With Ḳásim 'Alí ended, virtually, the powers of the Súbadárs of Bengal.

**Ḳasim Ali Khan, Nawab,** نواب قاسم عليخان, uncle to the nawáb of Rámpúr. He was living in Bareli in 1869, and his daughter was murdered on the 22nd December of that year.

**Ḳasim Anwar, Sayyad,** سيد قاسم انوار, surnamed Ma'ín-uddín Alí, a great mystical poet, called from his knowledge and writings, the "diver into the sea of truth," the "falcon of the transcendant plains," the "profound knower of the world of spirits," the "key of the treasury of secrecy," &c. He was born at Tabrez; and was a member of a considerable family of the tribe of Sayyad, descended from the same stock as the Prophet. In his youth he dedicated himself, under the guidance of Shaikh Sadr-uddín Músá Ardibelí, to the contemplative life and deep study of the Súfís. He then journeyed to Gílán, where he soon acquired great fame; and subsequently went into Khurásán. During his residence at Hirát, he obtained such celebrity, and was surrounded by so many princes and learned men, his followers, that Mirzá Sháhrukh (the son of Amír Timur), moved by jealousy of the Sayyad, and attentive to the danger of the increase of the Súfí creed, commanded him to retire from the capital. In order to mitigate the harshness of this command, Báisanghar, the son of Sháhrukh, a learned and noble prince, took upon himself to make it known to the Sayyad, which he did in the most humane manner, inquiring of him, in the course of conversation, why he did not follow the counsel contained in his own verse. The Sayyad inquired in which verse, and Báisanghar immediately quoted the following:—

"Ḳásim cease at once thy lay;
Rise and take thy onward way;
Other lands have waited long,
Worthy thy immortal song:
Give the bird of paradise
What the vulture cannot prize;
Honey let thy friends receive,
To thy foes the carrion leave."

The Sayyad thanked him, and immediately set out for Balkh and Samarḳand, where he remained for a time. He afterwards, however, returned to Hirát, where as before, he was constantly followed by great and powerful men. His death occurred in the village of Kharjard in Jám near Hirát, where a garden had been bought for him by his disciples, in which he greatly delighted. This event took place in the year 1431 A. D., 835 A. H., and his tomb was erected in the very garden which he so much enjoyed. Amír Alísher afterwards piously endowed it. A book of Odes is the only work he has left behind, in which he uses "Ḳásim" for his poetical name.

**Ḳasim Arsalan,** قاسم ارسلان مشهدي, of Mashhad, a poet who was a descendant of Arsalán Jázib, a general of Sulṭán Mahmúd of Ghazní. He flourished in the time of the emperor Akbar, and was in great favour with that monarch. He died in 1587 A. D., 995 A. H., and has left a Díwán.

**Ḳasim Barid Shah I,** قاسم برید شاه, was the founder of the Baríd Sháhí dynasty in the Dakhin. He was a Turkish or Georgian slave, became by degrees the wazír of Mahmúd Sháh II, king of the Dakhin, and assumed such power as to take upon himself the entire government of the kingdom. He treated the king as a mere pageant, and about the year 1492 A. D., 898 A. H., by the advice of 'Adil Sháh, Nizám Sháh and 'Imád Sháh, became entirely independent, and leaving to the king only the town and fort of Ahmadábád Bídar, read the public prayers and coined money in his own name. After having ruled his estate for a period of twelve years, during the lifetime of his sovereign, he died in the year 1504 A. D., 910 A. H., and his son Amír Baríd succeeded him in office, and assuming still greater power, deprived Mahmúd Sháh of what little power had been left him by his father. Seven persons of this family have reigned since their establishment in the capital of Ahmadábád Bídar; their names are as follow:

| | | A. D. |
|---|---|---|
| Ḳásim Baríd I., ........................ | Began | 1492 |
| Amír Baríd,............................. | „ | 1504 |
| Alí Baríd; first who assumed royalty, .... | „ | 1542 |
| Ibráhím Baríd Sháh,.................... | „ | 1562 |
| Ḳásim Baríd Sháh II, ................... | „ | 1569 |
| Alí Baríd Sháh II,....................... | „ | 1572 |
| Amír Baríd Sháh II, ..................... | „ | 1609 |

**Ḳasim Barid Shah II,** قاسم برید شاه, succeeded his brother Ibráhím Baríd Sháh to the government of Ahmadábád Bídar in 1569 A. D., 977 A. H., and died after a reign of three years in 1572 A. D. He was succeeded by his son Mirzá 'Alí Baríd II, who was deposed after a reign of 27 years by his relative Amír Baríd II who ascended the throne in 1609 A. D., and was the last of this dynasty.

**Ḳasim Beg Halati,** قاسم بیگ حالتي, *vide* Hálatí.

**Ḳasim Diwana,** قاسم دیوانه, a poet who was probably alive in 1724 A. D., 1136 A. H., and is the author of a Díwán.

**Ḳasim Ḳadiri, Shaikh,** شیخ قاسم قادري, also called Sháh Ḳásim Sulaimání, a Musalmán saint whose tomb is at Chunár. His son Shaikh Ḳabír commonly called Bálá Pír is buried at Ḳanauj where he died in the year 1644 A. D., 1054 A. H. The shrine of Sháh Ḳásim Sulaimání at Chunár is the only notable Muhammadan endowment in the Mirzápúr District supported from the income of rent-free lands and a Ma'ásh Rozína pension.

**Ḳasim Kahi, Maulana,** مولانا قاسم کاهي, a Sayyad, whose proper name was Najm-uddín and surname Abú'l Ḳásim. He was a pupil of 'Abdul Rahmán Jámí; he accompanied Mirzá Kámrán, the brother of the emperor Humáyún, on a pilgrimage to Mecca from Hirát, and after the death of that prince in 1557 A. D., 964 A. H., he came to India in the reign of the emperor Akbar. For a long period he remained with Bahádur Khán the brother of 'Alí Ḳulí Khán at Benáras, and after his demise he came to Ágrah, where he passed the remainder of his life, and died there on the 17th of April, 1580 A. D., 2nd Rabí' II, 988 A. H., aged 110 lunar years. He was buried at Ágrah at a place called Madár Darwáza. Mauláná Ḳásim Arsalán another poet and Shaikh Faizí wrote the chronograms of his death. 'Abdul Ḳádir Badáoní calls him an atheist and a disgusting cynic.

**Ḳasim Khan,** قاسم خان, Súbadár of Kábul in the reign of the emperor Akbar Sháh. He was murdered by one Muhammad Zamán, who gave out that he was the son of Sháhrukh Mirzá. He had held possession of Badakshán for some years, but after his defeat by 'Abdullah Khán Uzbak, he came to Kábul and was confined by Ḳásim Khán whom he murdered about the year 1600 A. D., and was consequently put to death by Muhammad Háshim the son of Ḳásim Khán.

**Ḳasim Khan Jawini, Nawab,** قاسم خان جویني نواب, was a nobleman of the court of the emperors Jahángír, and Sháh Jahán, and held the rank of 5,000. He was a native of Sabzwár and was married to Manija Begam, the sister of Núr Jahán, consequently he was sometimes in jest called by the officers of the court "Ḳásim Khán Manija." He is the author of a Díwán, and his poetical name is Ḳásim. He succeeded Fidáí Khán in the government of Bengal in the first year of Sháh Jahán 1628 A. D., 1037 A. H. He slew about 10,000 Portuguese (men and women) and drove the rest from Huglí, of which place he took possession and died three days after, 1631 A. D., 1041 A. H. He had built a very grand house at Ágrah on 20 bighas of land and on 10 bighas of land the garden was built, of which no traces now remain.

**Ḳasim Khan, Shaikh,** شیخ قاسم خان فتحپورے, of Fathapúr Síkrí, entitled Muhtashim Khán, brother of Islám Khán. He was a noble of the rank of 4,000, in the reign of the emperor Jahángír who appointed him governor of Bengal after the death of his brother in 1613 A. D., 1022 A. H. He invaded Asám, and his troops were mostly killed in a night-attack by the Asámís, on which account he was recalled to court and died some time after.

**Ḳasim Shah,** قاسم شاه, *vide* Sháh Ḳásim.

**Ḳasim Shirazi,** قاسم شیرازي, a native of Shíráz, and author of the "Timur-náma," a very beautiful poem on the conquest of Amír Timur.

**Ḳasim Sulaimani,** قاسم سلیماني, *vide* Ḳásim Ḳádirí.

**Ḳasim Tibbi,** قاسم طبیبي, author of an Inshá.

**Ḳasimi,** قاسمي, his proper name is Mauláná Majd-uddín, a poet of Khwáf in Khurásán. He is the author of the work "Rauzat-ul-Khuld" which he wrote in imitation of the Gulistán of Sa'dí.

**Ḳasimi,** قاسمي توني, (Dervish) of Tún in Persia, who went about like a derwish and wrote poetry. He lived in the 9th century of the Hijra.

**Kasir,** کثیرعزا, or Kathír Azzá, one of the celebrated Arabian poets of the court of the Khalíf 'Abdul Malik. *Vide* Jamíl.

**Ḳassab,** قصاب, the poetical name of an author.

**Ḳastalani,** قسطلاني, the surname of Ahmad bin-Alí al-Khatíb. He is so called because he was born at Ḳastalá. He is the author of several works among which is the history called "Mawáhib Ladina," or "Mawáhib-ud-Dunní," an accurate history of the first forty years of Muhammad, being the period previous to his assuming the prophetic character. He died in the year 1517 A. D., 923 A. H. Besides him there were other authors of this surname, *viz.*, Ahmad bin-Muhammad al-Ḳastalání, who died 1527 A. D., 933 A. H., Ahmad bin-Ibráhím bin-Yahya-al-Yazdí-al-Ḳastalání, and Mulla Maslah-uddín Mustafá

Ḳastalání who died 1495 A. D., 901 A. H. They were all born at Ḳastalá, a city in Persia.

**Kathir,** كثير, *vide* Kasír.

**Katib Chilpi,** كاتب چلپي, of Constantinople, author of several works, among which is one called "Kashf-uz-Zanún," and another "Tuhfat-ul-Kabár," this latter work was translated by James Mitchell, Esq. It contains a detailed account of the maritime wars of the Turks in the Mediterranean and Black Seas, and on the Danube. He died in the year of the Christian era 1657 A. D., 1067 A. H. Kátib Chilpí appears to be a Turkish title of Hájí Khalfa, which see.

**Katibi,** كاتبي ترشيزي, poetical name of Mauláná Shams-uddín Muhammad bin-'Abdullah-al-Naishápúrí and Tarshízí. He wrote a very beautiful hand, on which account he assumed the title of "Kátibí." He came to Hirát in the reign of Báisanghar Mirzá, and afterwards became one of the best poets of the court of the prince Sulṭán Mirzá Ibráhím of Shírwán, in whose praise he once wrote a panegyric, and received from that prince a present of 10,000 dínars. We have several of his works in the Persian language. In the latter period of his life he fixed his residence at Astrabád, and died there in 1435 A. D., 839 A. H. His works which contain five poems are called "Majma'-ul-Bahryn," the story of Násir and Mansúr, which can be read in two different metres; "Dah Báb," "Husnwa Ishḳ" and "Bahrám and Gulandám."

**Ḳatil, Mirza,** ميرزا قتيل, the poetical name of Mirzá Muhammad Hasan. He was a native of Dehlí, and a Hindú of the tribe of Khattrí, but became a convert to Muhammadanism. He was an excellent Urdú and Persian poet, and died at Lakhnau in the time of Ghází-uddín Haidar, then nawáb of that country 1817 A. D., 1232 A. H. He is the author of several works, amongst which are:

Nuskha Shajrat-ul-Amání, dedicated to Mír Amán 'Alí.
Nahr-ul-Fasáhat, a Persian grammar.
Chahár Sharbat, and a Díwán.

**Ḳatran,** قطرن, *vide* Ḳitrán.

**Ḳawami Matarzi,** قوامي مطرزي, a great poet who was a native of Mutaráz, a city in Persia, and is an author. He was a brother of Shaikh Nizámí Ganjwí.

**Ḳawami Maulana Muzaffar,** مولانا مظفر قوامي, a celebrated poet.

**Ḳawam-uddin Hasan, Haji,** حاجي قوام الدين حسن, wazír to Sháh Shaikh Abú Is-háḳ, ruler of Shíráz. He was a man of great liberality, and one of the patrons of the celebrated Persian poet Khwája Háfiz, who has praised him in many of his odes. He died during the seige of Shíráz by Mubáriz-uddín Muhammad Zafar, on Friday the 12th of April, 1353 A. D., 6th Rabí' I, 754 A. H.

**Kawam-uddin, Khwaja,** خواجة قوام الدين, surnamed Sáhib Ayár, was the wazír and favourite companion of Sháh Shujáa', the son of Mubáriz-uddín Muhammad Zafar, commonly called Muzaffar Sháh, who took Shíráz in 1353 A. D. He was put to the rack and beheaded by Sháh Shujáa' in August, 1363 A. D., Zi-Ḳa'da, 764 A. H.

**Ḳawela Ḳaan,** قويلا قاآن *vide* Kiblai Ḳáán.

**Kayomurs,** كيومرث, *vide* Kaiomurs.

**Kayuk Ḳaan,** كيوك قاآن, or Kayúk Khán, was the son of Oḳtái Ḳáán, the son of Changez Khán. He succeeded his father in January, 1242 A. D., 639 A. H., to the kingdom of Tartary, and his uncle Jughtai or Chughtai Ḳáán to the kingdom of Transoxania, Badakhshán and Káshghar. He reigned one year, and died about the beginning of 1243 A. D., 640 A. H., when Mangú Ḳáán, the eldest son of Túlí Khán, the son of Changez Khán, succeeded him and reigned nine years.

**Ḳaza,** قضا, poetical name of Muhammad Hafíz-ulláh Khán.

**Ḳazi Khan,** قاضي خان, he is commonly called by this name, but his full name is Imám Fakhr-uddín Hasan bin-Mansúr-al-'Uzjandí-al-Farghání. He died in 1195 A. D., 592 A. H. He is the author of a work entitled "Fatáwa Ḳází Khán," a collection of decisions which is held in the highest estimation in India. Yúsuf bin-Junaid, generally known by the name of Akhí Chalabí-at-Túkátí, epitomised this work and compressed it into one volume.

**Ḳazib-ul-Ban,** قضيب البان, surname of Shaikh Muhín-uddín 'Abdul Ḳádir bin-Sayyad Muhammad, an Arabian author who died in 1630 A. D., 1040 A. H.

**Kazim, Hakim,** حكيم كاظم, a physician who had the title of Háziḳ-ul-Mulk and was the son of the Mujtahid Haidar Alí Tushtarí Najafí. He is the author of the work called "Farah-náma Fáṭima," which he composed in 1737 A. D., 1150 A. H.

**Kazim, Hakim,** حكيم كاظم, *vide* Sáhib.

**Kazim Ali Khan,** حكيم كاظم علي خان. He had built a garden at Ágrah on the banks of the Jamna opposite to Rám Bágh. Some traces of this garden still remain called Hakím ka Bágh. It was built in the year 1551 A. D.

**Kazim Zarbaya,** كاظم زربايه, a Persian poet who died at Isfahán in the year 1541 A. D., 948 A. H.

**Ḳazwini,** قزويني, author of the "'Ajáeb-ul-Makhlúkát," *vide* Zikaria bin-Muhammad bin-Mahmúd.

**Kerat Singh,** كيرت سنگه, second son of Mirzá Rájá Jaisingh. He served under the emperor 'Alamgír, and after his father's death was honoured with the rank of 3000. He was living in the Dakhin 1673 A. D., 1084 A. H.

**Kesari Singh,** كيسري سنگه, rájá of Jaipúr who lived in the time of Muhammad Sháh, emperor of Dehlí.

**Kesho Das Rathor, Raja,** راجة كيشو داس راتهور, who gave his daughter in marriage to the emperor Jahángír, by whom he had Bahar Bano Begam.

**Khadija,** خديجه, Muhammad's wife. Although this is the correct pronunciation of the name, yet, see under Khudyja.

**Khadim,** خادم, the poetical name of Nazar Beg, a poet. He was a pupil of Muhammad Azfal Sábit, and died some time before the year 1760 A. D., 1174 A. H.

**Khadim,** خادم, the takhallus or poetical appellation of Shaikh Ahmad 'Alí of Sandíla and son of Muhammad Hájí. He is the author of several works, among which is one called "Anís-ul-'Ushsháḳ," an Anthology. He flourished about the year 1752 A. D., 1165 A. H. See Hasan bin-Muhammad Sharíf.

**Khaef Kashmiri, Maulana,** خايف كشميري مولانا, a poet.

**Khafi,** خافي, poetical title of Mír Abúl Hasan Khán, author of a poem called "Chahár Dervish."

**Khafi Khan,** خافي خان, whose original name is Muhammad Háshim, was the author of the work called "Táríkh Kháfí Khán," which is also called "Muntakhib-ul-Lubáb," an excellent history of Hindústán, commencing with the invasion of the emperor Bábar Sháh, 1519 A. D., 925 A. H., and continued to the accession of Muhammad Sháh; comprehending the whole of the reign of the emperor 'Alamgír, also those of Bahádur Sháh, Jahándár Sháh, Farrukh-siyar, and Rafí-ud-darját; all of which, except the first ten years of 'Alamgír's reign, Colonel Dow was obliged to pass over, for want of documents. There are few works in the Persian language (says Stewart) so worthy of being translated. The author was a person of good family, who resided at Dehlí during the latter part of the reign of 'Alamgír, where he compiled his history; but in consequence of the well-known prohibition of that monarch, he was obliged to conceal his intentions, and for some other causes did not publish it till the 14th year of the emperor Muhammad Sháh, 1732 A. D., 1145 A. H. The work was well received, and the author was honoured with the title of Kháfí Khán, or the Clandestine Lord.

**Khaiyam,** خيام, *vide* 'Umar Khaiyám.

**Khaju,** خاجو, *vide* Khwájú.

**Khakan,** خاقان, the title of Changez Khán and his descendants. It means an emperor in the Turkish dialect.

**Khakani,** خاقاني, a celebrated Persian poet surnamed Afzal-uddín Ibráhím bin-'Alí Shírwání. He was a native of Shírwán, and the pupil of Falakí the poet. He flourished in the reign of Kháḳán Manúchchr, prince of Shírwán, who conferred on him the title of Kháḳání. He is the author of the book called "Tuhfat-ul-Iráḳín," a poetical description of the two provinces of 'Iráḳ 'Ajam and 'Iráḳ 'Arab, composed by him while travelling through them on a pilgrimage to Mecca. He is considered the most learned of the lyric poets of Persia, and was called "Sulṭán-ush-Shu'ará" or king of poets. He is also the author of a Díwán, according to Daulat Sháh, and the book called "Haft Aḳlím," he died at Tabrez in the year 1186 A. D., 582 A. H., and is buried at Surkháb, where, close to his tomb, Zahír-uddín Faryábí and Sháh Ghafúr Naishápúrí are also interred. The chronogram of the year of his death given in the work "Mukhbir-ul-Wasilín," shews that he died in 1199 A. D., 595 A. H.

**Khaki,** خاكي, author of the "Munáḳib-ul-'Arifín." This book contains the memoirs of three very celebrated Súfí Shaikhs, *viz.*, Khwája Bahá-uddín, Burhán-uddín, and Jalál-uddín. The former of these was reputed a great saint, and was the founder of an Order of Súfís, distinguished by the title of Naḳshbandí. He died at Haráfa in Persia, 1453 A. D., 857 A. H. The two others were authors of commentaries on the Ḳurán, and were held in much veneration. The above-mentioned book was dedicated to Bahá-uddín.

**Khaki Shirazi,** خاكي شيرازي, author of a Persian Díwán.

**Khaksar,** خاكسار, poetical name of Shukr-ulláh Khán, who died in 1696 A. D., 1108 A. H., and has left a Díwán.

**Ḳhaldun,** خالدون, *vide* Khálidún.

**Khalif** or **Khalifas,** خليفه, of the house of Muhammad, see Abú Bakr Siddíḳ.

**Khalif** or **Khalifas,** خليفه اميه, of the race of Umayya who reigned at Damascus, *vide* Mu'áwia I.

**Khalif** or **Khalifas,** خليفه عباسي, of the house of 'Abbás called 'Abbásí or 'Abbásides, who reigned at Baghdád, *vide* Al-Saffáh.

**Khalif** or **Khalifa,** خليفه, this Arabic word, which signifies vicar or successor, of which we have formed that of Khalíf or Caliph, is the name of a sovereign dignity amongst the Musalmáns, which comprehends an absolute power, and an independent authority over all that regards religion and political government. Not only the first four immediate successors of Muhammad, but the rulers of the house of Umayya, written by us Ommaides, who reigned in Damascus, and the 'Abbásides who reigned in Baghdád, were also called Khalífas. There were in all 56 Khalífas, 4 of whom were of the house of the prophet, 15 of the house of Umayya, and 37 of the house of 'Abbás.

**Khalid ibn-Barmak,** خالدبن برمک, was the first of the Barmakides, who acted as wazír to Abú'l 'Abbás Saffáh. He was the grandfather of Ja'far, wazír to Hárún-al-Rashíd. He died in the year 780 or 782 A. D., 163 or 165 A. H.

**Khalid ibn-Walid,** خالد ابن وليد, who became a proselyte to Muhammadanism in 630 A. D., and afterwards so terrible to the Greeks; was called from his courage, the Sword of God. In spreading the doctrines of the Ḳurán, and the dominion of the prophet, he committed atrocious cruelties, and was at last cut off by the plague in 639 A. D., but according to Ockley's History of the Saracens, Abú Ubeda died that year, and Khálid survived him about three years, and then died.

**Khalid ibn-Yezid ibn-Mua'wia,** خالد ابن يزيد, he is reported to have been the most learned of the tribe of Ḳuresh in all the different branches of knowledge, and skilled in the art of alchymy. He died in 704 A. D., 85 A. H.

**Khalidi,** خالدي, surname of Abú'l Faraj, one of the first poets of the court of the Sulṭán Saif-uddaula Hamdání. He was a native of Kháldia or Chaldea, consequently he is called Khálidí.

**Khalidun,** خالدون, or 'Abdul Rahmán bin-Muhammad bin-Khálidún, surnamed Alhazramí, was an author and Ḳází of the city of Aleppo when Amír Timur took it, who carried him away to Samarḳand as a slave, where he died 1405 A. D., 808 A. H.

**Khalil bin-Ahmad,** خليل بن احمد بصري, of Basra, a very learned man who is said to be the first that wrote on the art of writing poetry. He wrote several works and died about the year 175 A. H.

**Khalil ibn-Is-hak,** خليل ابن اسحاق, author of a Mukhtasir which goes after his name. This is a work professedly treating of the law according to the Málikí doctrines, and has been translated into French by M. Perron and published in the year 1849.

**Khalil,** خليل, the poetical title of Alí Ibráhím Khán, which see.

**Khalil,** خليل, the poetical appellation of Mirzá Muhammad Ibráhím, whose title was Asálat Khán. He served under the emperor 'Alamgír, and was living in Patna in 1690 A. D., 1102 A. H. He was a native of Khurásán, but brought up in India.

**Khalil Khan,** خليل خان, a manṣabdár of 5000 of the court of Sháh Jahán but of a very bad temper. It was he who instigated 'Alamgír to confine his father Sháh Jahán. He had built a fine house at Ágrah on the banks of the Jamna, of which some traces are still to be seen.

**Khalil, Maulanà,** مولانا خليل, a poet of Persia, who flourished in the time of Sháh Tahmásp Safwí, and was living about the year 1539 A. D., 946 A. H.

**Khalil Sultan,** سلطان خليل, son of Shaikh Ibráhím Shírwání, ruler of Shírwán. He reigned about the beginning of the 15th century of the Christian era.

**Khalil, Sultan,** سلطان خليل, also called Mirzá Khalíl and Khalíl-ulláh, was the son of Míránsháh, and grandson of Amír Timur at whose death, he being present with the army at Samarḳand, took possession of that country. This prince, who was a person of excellent temper, and had many good qualities, might have preserved the power he had acquired, had not his violent love for Shád-ul-Mulk, a celebrated courtezan, whom he had secretly married, diverted him from the cares of government. He had scarcely reigned four years, when he was seized by the chiefs who had raised him to the throne, and sent a prisoner to the country of Káshghar in 1408 A. D., 811 A. H., where instead of endeavouring to effect his release and recover his power, he spent the whole of his time in writing verses to his beloved mistress, who had been exposed, by the reverse of his fortune, to the most cruel indignities. He was at last released by Mirzá Sháhrukh his uncle, who had taken possession of his kingdom, and who not only gave him the government of Rei, Kum and Hamdán, but restored his beautiful mistress to his arms. After this he lived two years and a half and died 6th November, 1411 A. D., 18th Rajab, 814 A. H., aged 28 years, and Shád-ul-Mulk, on the occurrence of this event, acted a part which has given fame to her memory—she struck a poniard to her breast: and the lovers were buried in one tomb in the city of Rei.

**Khalil-ullah,** خليل الله, the Friend of God, a title of Abraham the patriarch.

**Khalil-ullah Hirwi, Mir,** مير خليل الله هروي, a descendant of Shaikh Na'mat-ulláh Walí.

**Khalil-ullah Khan,** خليل الله خان, entitled Umdát-ul-Mulk, brother of Asálat Khán Mír Bakhshí, served under the emperor Sháh Jahán, was appointed governor of Dehlí about the year 1653 A. D., 1063 A. H., and was raised to the rank of 6000 in the first year of 'Alamgír 1658 A. D., 1068 A. H. He died on the 11th February, 1662 A. D., 2nd Rajab, 1072 A. H.

**Khalil-ullah Mirza,** خليل الله مرزا, *vide* Khalíl Sulṭán.

**Khaliṣ,** خالص, the poetical name of Imtiyáz Khán of Isfahán, which see.

**Khallikan,** خليكان, *vide* Ibn-Khallikán.

**Khamosh,** خاموش, poetical name of Ráe Sáhib Rám of Dehlí. He was for some time Tahsíldár under Mr. J. Duncan in Benaras. He has left a large Díwán.

**Khan,** خان. This word which appears to be a corruption of Ḳáán, is a Turkish title and means powerful lord. The most powerful kings of Turkistán, of Great Tartary and of the Khatáyans have borne this title. Changez, the great conqueror, had no other, and it makes even part of his name, for he is called by the Orientals, Changez Khán. It means the same as Khákán or Ḳáán.

**Khan,** خان, the poetical name of Mirzá Sharíf.

**Khanam Sultan,** خانم سلطان, a daughter of the emperor Akbar, married to Muzaffar Husain Mirzá, the son of Ibráhím Husain Mirzá in 1593 A. D.

**Khanam Sultan,** خانم سلطان, a daughter of the emperor Akbar, married to Muzaffar Husain Mirzá, the son of Ibráhím Husain Mirzá by Gulrukh Begam.

**Khan 'Alam,** خان عالم, title of Mirzá Barkhurdár, son of Mirzá 'Abdul Rahmán Dauldí, a nobleman who served under the emperor Sháh Jahán and was raised to the rank of 5000; and in the reign of 'Alamgír he was honoured with the dignity of 6000. In the latter part of his life, he was pensioned by the emperor and received one lac of rupees annually. He had a house and garden in Ágrah on the banks of the river Jamna built of red stone touching the northern Burj of the Rauza of Tájganj in a spot consisting of 50 bighas. In the latter part of his life he was raised to 6000 by Sháh Jahán and appointed governor of Bihár.

**Khan 'Alam,** خان عالم, title of Ikhlás Khán, the son of Khán Zamán Shaikh Nizám. He served under the emperor 'Alamgír and was raised to the rank of 5000 in 1689 A. D., 1100 A. H., with the title of Khán 'Alam. In 1696 A. D. the rank of 6000 was conferred on him. After the death of that emperor he espoused the cause of 'Azim Sháh against his brother Bahádur Sháh, and fell in battle 1707 A. D., 1119 A. H. After his death his son was honoured with the same title.

**Khan 'Azim,** خان عظم, *vide* 'Azím Khán.

**Khan Bahadur,** خان بهادر, son of Rájá Mittra Jít of Patna. He is the compiler of the work called "Jáma' Bahádur Khání," an epitome of European Sciences in the Persian language, including treatises on astronomy, optics, and mathematics, and copious tables of logarithms for natural numbers, sines, tangents, &c., also of a small octavo volume of Perspective called "'Ilm-ul-Manázarat," in the Persian language, which he presented to the Asiatic Society in 1835 A. D., 1251 A. H.

**Khanazad Begam,** خانهزاد بيگم, the sister of the emperor Bábar was five years older than him. Another daughter of 'Umar Shaikh was Mehr Báno, eight years younger than Bábar. Another daughter was Yadgar Sultán Begam, whose mother's name is Aghá Sultán Ghunchichí; the fourth daughter was named Ruqia Sulṭán Begam, whose mother's name was Makhdúma Sulṭán Begam who was also called Qará Qúr Begam—the last two daughters were born after the death of their father.

**Khanazad Khan,** خانهزاد خان, *vide* Khán Zamán Bahádur and Rúh-ulláh Khán.

**Khanazad Khan,** خانهزاد خان, son of Sarbuland Khán, was governor of Peshâwar in 1723 A. D., 1135 A. H. When the government of Allahábád was conferred on his father by the emperor Muhammad Sháh in 1732 A. D., 1145 A. H., he was deputed to act for him as governor of that province.

**Khan Bahadur Khan,** خان بهادر خان, the son of Jalál-uddín Khán, the son of Háfiz Rahmat Khán. *Vide* Masrúf.

**Khande Rao Gaekwar,** کھاندي راو گه‌قوار, rájá of Baroda. He died in 1870 A. D., and was succeeded by his brother Malhár Ráo the present (1875) Rájá of Baroda.

**Khande Rao Holkar,** کھاندي راو هلکر, the only son of Malhár Ráo Holkar I. He was killed in a battle at Díg against Súraj Mal Ját in 1754 A. D. many years previous to his father's death, and left an only son Malí Ráo, who succeeded his grandfather and died nine months after. *Vide* Malhár Ráo I, and Ahlia Báí.

**Khan Douran I,** خان دوران اول, whose proper name is Sháh Beg Khán Kábulí, was an Amír in the time of the emperor Akbar. He received the title of Khán Dourán from Jahángír in the year 1607 A. D., 1016 A. H., and was appointed governor of Kábul. He died in Láhor in the year 1620 A. D., 1029 A. H., aged 90 years.

**Khan Douran Khan II,** خان دوران خان نصرت جنگ ثاني, Nasrat Jang, title of Khwája Sábir, son of Khwája Hisárí Nakshbandí. He was an officer of state in the service of the emperor Sháh Jahán and held the rank of 7000. He was stabbed one night whilst asleep by a young Kashmírian Bráhman whom he had converted to Muhammadanism, and died after a few days on the 12th of July, 1645 A. D., 27th Jumáda I, 1055 A. H., at Láhor. His remains were transported to Gwáliár and buried there in the cemetery of his ancestors.

**Khan Douran III,** خان دوران نصرت خان سيوم, Nasrat Khán, son of Khán Dourán Nasrat Jang. He held the rank of 5000 in the reign of the emperor 'Alamgír. In the latter part of his life he was appointed governor of Orissa, which post he held for several years and died there 1667 A. D., 1077 A. H.

**Khan Douran IV,** خان دوران چهارم, an amír of the reign of the emperor Farrukh-siyar, who soon after the accession of Muhammad Sháh and the assassination of Sayyid Husain Alí Khán, and imprisonment of his brother Kutb ul-Mulk, was appointed Amír-ul-'Umrá with the title of Samsám-uddaula in 1721 A. D., 1133 A. H. He was dangerously wounded in battle against Nádir Sháh and died the third day following, the 16th of February, 1739 A. D., 17th Zi-Ka'da, 1151 A. H. His original name was Khwája Muhammad 'Asim. He is also called Abdus Samad Khán Bahádur Jang.

**Khan Jahan,** خان جهان, title of Husain Kulí Beg, an amír of 5000 in the reign of the emperor Akbar. He was appointed governor of Bengal after the death of Munai'm Khán, about the year 1576 A. D., 984 A. H. He defeated, took prisoner, and slew Dáúd Khán, the ex-king of Bengal who had again rebelled against the emperor, and sent his head to Agrah, the same year. Khán Jahán died at Tánda in 1578 A. D., 986 A. H., and was succeeded by Muzaffar Khán.

*Governors of Bengal.*

| | A. D. | | A. D. |
|---|---|---|---|
| Khán Jahán, ...... | 1576 | Mukarram Khán, .. | 1626 |
| Muzaffar Khán, .... | 1579 | Fidaí Khán, ...... | 1621 |
| Rájá Todar Mal, .. | 1580 | Kasim Khán Jobun, | 1628 |
| Khán 'Azim, ...... | 1582 | 'Azim Khán, ...... | 1632 |
| Sháhbáz Khán, .... | 1584 | Sultán Shuja', .... | 1639 |
| Rájá Mán Singh, .. | 1589 | Mír Jumla, ........ | 1660 |
| Kutb-uddín, ...... | 1606 | Shaista Khán, .... | 1664 |
| Jahángír Kulí, .... | 1607 | Fidaí Khán, ...... | 1677 |
| Islám Khán, ...... | 1608 | Sultán Muhammad 'Azim, ........ | 1678 |
| Kasim Khán, ...... | 1613 | Shaista Khán, .... | 1680 |
| Ibráhím Khán, .... | 1618 | Ibráhím Khán, .... | 1689 |
| Sháh Jahán, ...... | 1622 | 'Azím-us-Shán, .... | 1697 |
| Khánázád Khán, .. | 1625 | | |

**Khan Jahan Barha,** خان جهان بارها, title of Sayyid Muzaffar Khán of Bárhá, an officer of the rank of 6000 who died in the time of the emperor Sháh Jahán at Láhor, 1645 A. D., 1055 A. H.

**Khan Jahan Kokaltash,** خان جهان کوکلتاس, whose proper name was Mír Malik Husain, the son of Mír Abú'l Ma'álí Khwáfí. He was a nobleman of true dignity, and being the foster-brother of the emperor 'Alamgír, thought himself superior to all the other 'Umrá. He was appointed governor of the Dakhin in 1670 A. D., 1081 A. H., and promoted by that monarch about the year 1674 A. D. from the rank of 700 to that of 7000 horse, and the title of Khán Jahán Bahádur Kokaltásh Zafar Jang. His former title was Bahádur Khán. He died on the 24th November, 1697 A. D., 19th Jumáda I, 1109 A. H. He seems to be the author of the "Tárikh Asám," or the invasion of Asám.

**Khan Jahan Kokaltash Khan Zafar Jang,** خان جهان کوکلتاس خان ظفرجنگ, a title of Alí Murád, a foster-brother of Jahándár Sháh. In the time of Bahádur Sháh, he was honoured with the title of Kokaltásh Khán, and when Jahándár Sháh ascended the throne, the rank of 9000 was conferred on him with the title of Khán Jahán Zafar Jang, and the office of Mír Bakhshígarí. But he did not long enjoy this high station, for he soon after fell in the battle which took place between his master and Farrukh-siyar 1713 A. D., 1125 A. H.

**Khan Jahan Lodi,** خان جهان لودی, an Afghán probably of low birth, but with all the pride and unruliness of his nation in India. He is by some said to be a descendant of Sultán Bahlól Lódí, and by others of Daulat Khán Lodí Sháhú Khail. He had held great military charges, was raised to the rank of 5000 in the reign of the emperor Jahángír, and commanded in the Dakhin under prince Parwez at the time of that prince's death. On the accession of Sháh Jahán, he entered into a close intimacy with his late enemies, and seemed to be aiming at independence. He was at last killed together with his son in an engagement with the royal troops on the 28th January, 1631 A. D., 1st Rajab, 1040 A. H., and their heads sent as a most acceptable present to Sháh Jahán. An affecting account of his death may be found in the 3rd Volume of Dow's History. The "Táríkh Khán Jahán Lódí" which is also called "Makhzan Afghání," contains the memoirs of this chief, written by Haibat Khán in 1676 A. D.

**Khan Jahan Makbul, Malik,** خان جهان مقبول ملک, entitled Kawám-ul-Mulk, was the prime-minister of Sultán Fíróz Sháh Bárbak who ascended the throne of Dehlí in 1351 A. D. He was originally a Hindú by name Kattú. On his conversion to Muhammadanism in his youth, Sultán Muhammad, the predecessor of Fíróz Sháh, changed his name to Makbúl, and appointed him to the government of Multán. He afterwards became Náib Wazír under the wazírship of Khwája Jahán, whom he at first supported in his attempt to place a son of Sultán Muhammad on the throne, but went over to Sultán Fíróz, on his approach to Dehlí, and was appointed by him wazír of the kingdom. According to the historian Shams Siráj Afíf, he died in the year 1374 A. D., 776 A. H., but by others in 772 A. H. After his death his son Jahán Sháh was honoured with his place and title of Khán Jahán by the king, who placed as much confidence in him as he had done in his father. He filled the office of prime-minister for twenty years.

**KhanKhanan,** خانخانان, this word is a title of honour and means Lord of Lords. Bairám Khán and his son 'Abdur Rahím Khán, both ministers to the emperor Akbar, and several others were honoured with this title.

**Khan Mirza,** خان مرزا, ruler of Badakhshán, was the son of Sultán Mahmúd Mirzá, the son of Sultán Abú Saíd Mirzá, a descendant of Amír Taimúr. He died in 1521 A. D., 927 A. H., leaving behind a son of seven years of age named Mirzá Sulaimán. Khán Mirzá was a cousin of the emperor Bábar, who on Mirzá's death appointed his own son Humáyún to that government.

**Khan Mirza,** خان مرزا, surname of 'Abdur Rahím Khán, KhánKhánán in the time of the emperor Akbar.

**Khan Zaman,** خان زمان, title of 'Alí Ḳulí Khán, who and his brother Bahádur Khán were the sons of Haidar Sultán Uzbak who was an officer of state in the service of the emperor Humáyún. In the reign of Akbar Sháh, these two brothers for their good services were raised to higher ranks and honoured with the jágír of Jaunpúr and the lower provinces; they at last became rebellious, which induced the emperor to march against them with a large force; a battle ensued wherein both brothers were slain. This event took place on Monday the 9th of June, 1567 A. D., 1st Ẕil-ḥijja, 974 A. H., at a place six kos west of Allahábád, which on account of this victory, was named Fathapúr. The date of this transaction is commemorated in the words "Fatha Akbar Mubárik," *i. e.*, May this great victory be prosperous.

**Khan Zaman,** خان زمان, title of Mír Khalíl, second son of 'Azim Khán the brother of 'Asaf Khán Ja'far Beg, and son-in-law of Yemín-uddaula 'Asaf Khán. He served under the emperor Sháh Jahán for several years, and in the reign of 'Alamgír was raised to the rank of 5000. At the time of his death he was governor of Málwá, where he died 1684 A. D., 1095 A. H.

**Khan Zaman Bahadur,** خان زمان بهادر, whose former title was Khánazád Khán and proper name Mirzá Amánullah, was the eldest son of Mahábat Khán surnamed Zamána Beg. He was an officer of state in the time of the emperor Jahángír, and was appointed governor of Bengal 1625 A. D., 1033 A. H. In the first year of Sháh Jahán, the rank of 5000 was conferred on him with the title of Khán Zamán Bahádur. He was a good poet, and is the author of a work called "Majmúa" containing the history of all the Muhammadan kings who reigned in different parts of the world before his time, and of a Díwán. He died in Daulatábád in 1637 A. D., 1047 A. H., in which year Báḳir Khán died also. His poetical name was Amáni.

**Khan Zaman Fatha Jang,** خان زمان فتح جنگ, was the title of Shaikh Nizám Haidarábádí. He at first served under Abú'l Hasan ruler of Haidarábád for several years, and then left him and was employed by the emperor 'Alamgír. In the year 1689 A. D., 1100 A. H., he took prisoner Sambha the Marhaṭṭa chief together with his wife and children; on which account he was raised to the rank of 7000 with the above title. He died 1696 A. D., 1108 A. H.

**Khair-uddin Muhammad, Maulvi,** مولوی خیر الدین محمد, author of the history of Jaunpúr.

**Khairun Nisa Khatun,** خیر النسا خاتون, a poetess, who was the daughter of the Ḳází of Samarḳand, and lived at Khurásán.

**Kharag Singh, Maharaja,** مهاراجه کهرگ سنگه, the ruler of Láhor and the Panjáb, was the eldest son of Mahárájá Ranjít Singh whom he succeeded on the 27th of June, 1839 A. D., 1255 A. H. He reigned one year and four months, and died on the 5th of November, 1840 A. D., 1256 A. H., aged 46 years. He was succeeded by his son Rájá Nau Nihál Singh, who, after having performed the customary rites at his father's funeral was returning home, and as he passed the Láhor gate, a part of the building gave way and fell over him from which he died. This event took place on the 17th of November the same year. After his death his mother Rání Chánd Kúnwar managed the affairs of her country for two months, when her second son Rájá Sher Singh deprived her of that power, and became the sole manager of the government. He reigned about two years and eight months, and was murdered together with his son Rájá Partáb Singh by Sardár Ajít Singh on the 13th of September, 1843 A. D. Rájá Dalíp Singh, the youngest son of Mahárájá Ranjít Singh, who was only ten years of age, was then raised to the maṣnad.



**Khasha,** خاشع, the poetical title of a person who is the author of a Díwán which he completed in 1681 A. D., 1092 A. H.

**Khassaf** or **Al-Khassaf,** خصاف, *vide* Abú Bakr Aḥmad bin-'Umar-al-Khassáf.

**Khatib,** خطیب, surname of Shams-uddín Muhammad bin-Ibráhím-al-Málikí, commonly called Khatíb-al-Wazírí, an author who died in the year 1486 A. D., 891 A. H.

**Khatun Jannat,** خاتون جنت, *i. e.*, the lady of paradise, a title of Fátima, the daughter of Muhammad, and wife of 'Alí.

**Khatun Turkan,** خاتون ترکان, this name or title means the "Turkish lady," and was always given to princesses of Turkish descent. The wife of Sultán Malikshâh Saljúkí bore the same title. She was the mother of Mahmúd, a boy of four years of age, whom she raised to the throne after the death of her husband in 1092 A. D., 485 A. H., but he died soon after, and Barkayáraḳ his eldest brother mounted the throne. The wife of Sulṭán Sanjar was also called Khátún Turkán. She died in 1156 A. D.

**Khattabi,** خطابي, surname of Abú Sulaimán Hamíd bin-Muhammad, an author who died in 998 A. D., 388 A. H.

**Khawari,** خاوري, poetical title of Mír 'Abú'l Fatha.

**Khawas Khan,** خواص خان, an amír in the service of Salím Sháh justly renowned for personal courage, strict honour, great abilities in war, and extensive generosity, was long driven about from place to place, on account of his fighting against the king in favour of his brother 'Adil Sháh. He at last took protection with Táj Khán, governor of Sambhal, who to ingratiate himself with Salím Sháh basely assassinated him about the year 1551 A. D., 958 A. H. His body was carried to Dehlí and there interred. His tomb is frequented by the devout to this day, they numbering him among their saints.

**Khawas Khan,** خواص خان, an amír in the service of the emperor Jahángír. He had a jágír in Kanauj, and died there in the year 1521 A. D., 1024 A. H.

**Khawind Shah** or **Khawand Shah,** امیر خاوند شاه, also called Mír Kháwand, and Amír Khán, and Sháh, a celebrated Persian historian, known amongst us by the name of Mirkhond as he calls himself in the preface of the life of Muhammad, but his true name at length is Muhammad bin-Kháwand Sháh bin-Mahmúd. He is the author of the work called "Rauzat-us-Ṣafá," the Garden of Purity. He was born towards the close of the year 1433 A. D., or the beginning of 1434 A. D., 836 or 837 A. H. His father's name was Sayyad Burhán-uddín Kháwand Sháh, a native of Mávarunnahr, after whose death he found means to be introduced to the excellent Amír 'Alísher, prime-minister to Sulṭán Husain Mirzá of Hirát, from whom he experienced every mark of kindness and encouragement, and to whom he dedicated the above work. He died at Balkh after a lingering illness on the 23rd of June, 1498 A. D., 2nd Ẕi-Ḳa'da, 903 A. H., aged 66 years. There is no other Oriental work (says Sir H. M. Elliot) that stands higher in public estimation than the Rauzat-us-Ṣafá. This work is written in seven books, the author had just completed the 6th book when he died, and his son Khonda Mír wrote the 7th book, and finished it in 1523 A. D., 929 A. H.

**Khayal,** خيال, the poetical title of Mír Muhammad Taḳí, author of a work called "Bóstán Khayál," the Garden of Imagination. He flourished about the year 1756 A. D., 1170 A. H.

**Khayali,** خيالي بخاري, of Bukhárá, a pupil of Khwája 'Ismat-ullah, and though he spent the greater part of his life in his native country, he was two years at Hirát in the service of Mirzá Ulugh Beg, during whose reign he died and left a Díwán.

**Khazini,** خازني, an astronomer whose proper name is 'Abdul Rahmán.

**Khink Sawar,** خنک سوار, *vide* Sayyad Husain Khink Sawár.

**Khirad,** خرد, the poetical name of Báḳir Káshí, which see.

**Khitabi,** خطابی, the poetical title of Sháh Ismá'íl Ṣafawí I.

**Khizir Khan,** خضرخان, king of Dehlí. Firishta says that both the authors of the "Tabkát Mahmúd Sháhí," and of the "Tawáríkh Mubárik," style him a Sayyad or a descendant of the prophet. His father Malik Sulaimán was governor of Multán, and he succeeded him in that office. He defeated Daulat Khán Lodí in a battle, and having taken him prisoner, ascended the throne of Dehlí on the 4th of June, 1414 A. D., 15th Rabí' I, 817 A. H. He died after a reign of seven lunar years two months and two days on the 4th June, 1421 A. D., 17th Jumáda I, 824 A. H., and was succeeded by his son Mubárik Sháh. Khizir Khán did not assume the title of emperor, but pretended to hold the empire for Sháhrukh Mirzá, the son of Amír Taimúr, in whose name he struck coins.

*The following is a list of the kings of the 4th or Sádát Dynasty of Dehlí.*

| | | A. D. | A. H. |
|---|---|---|---|
| Khizir Khán, a Sayyad, ............ | began | 1414 | 817 |
| Mubárik Sháh, son of Khizir Khán,.. | " | 1421 | 824 |
| Muhammad Sháh, the son of Faríd, the son of Khizir, .................. | " | 1434 | 837 |
| 'Alá-uddín, son of Muhammad Sháh, the last of the Sayyads who abdicated in favour of Bahlol Lódí,...... | " | 1446 | 849 |

**Khizir Khan,** خضرخان, the son of Sulṭán 'Alá-uddín Khiljí. This prince fell in love with Dewal Deví, the daughter of Ráe Karan, rájá of Gujrát, and married her. The history of their loves is written in a poem, entitled, "Ishḳia," by Amír Khusro. *Vide* Kaula Deví.

**Khizir Khan, Khwaja,** خواجه خضرخان, a descendant of the kings of Káshghar. He served under the emperor Humáyún who gave him his sister, named Gulbadan, in marriage, and appointed him governor of Láhor and afterwards of Behár, where he died about the year 1559 A. D., 966 A. H.

**Khizir, Khwaja,** خواجه خضر, name of a prophet who, the Orientals say, is still living, and sometimes appears to travellers who have lost their way. He is said to have accompanied Alexander the Great to the dark regions of Zulmát, where he was told he would find the Water of Life.

**Khojam,** خوجم, the poetical name of Khwája Sulṭán, the author of a poem in Urdú containing the story of Shamshád Sháh, dedicated to Sa'ádat 'Alí Khán, the Nawáb of Lakhnau.

**Khondamir,** خوندامير, the son of the celebrated Amír Khawand Sháh (Mirkhond). His full name is Ghayásuddín Muhammad bin-Hamíd-uddín Khond Amír. He is the author of the history called "Khulásat-ul-Akhbár," which is considered to be an abridgment of the "Rauzat-us-Ṣafá;" this book he wrote in 1498 A. D., 904 A. H., and dedicated it to Amír 'Alísher his patron. He was born, says Sir H. M. Elliot, at Hirát about the year 1475 A. D., 880 A. H., for he states in the preface to the "Habíb-us-Siar," that when he commenced it in the year 1521 A. D., 927 A. H., he had advanced through seven or eight stages beyond the fortieth year of his life. It was after the name of his patron Karím-uddín Habíb-ullah, a native of Ardibel, that he entitled his work "Habíb-us-Siar." Besides the abovementioned works, he composed the "Másir-ul-Malúk," the "Akhbár-ul-Akhiár," the "Dastúr-ul-Wazra," the "Mukárim-ul-Akhláḳ," and the "Muntakhib Táríkh Waṣṣáf." There are two other works ascribed to him, called "Gharáeb-ul-Asrár," and "Jawáhir-ul-Akhbár". He was compelled to leave Hirát on account of the disturbed state of the country in 1527 A. D., 933 A. H., and afterwards took a journey to Hindústán in company with Mauláná Shaháb-uddín the punster, and Mirzá Ibráhím Ḳánúní, esteemed the most literary men of the age. On Saturday the 19th of September, 1528 A. D., 4th Muḥarram, 935 A. H., they reached the metropolis of Ágrah, and were introduced to the emperor Bábar Sháh. They were loaded with presents and directed to remain in future about his person. Khondamír accompanied the emperor on his expedition to Bengal, and upon his death attached himself to his son Humáyún, in whose name he wrote the "Ḳanún Humáyúní," which is quoted by Abú'l Fazl in the Akbar-náma. He afterwards accompanied that monarch to Gujrát, and died in camp during the emperor's march from Khandesh to Mandú in pursuit of Bahádur Sháh Gujrátí. This event took place in 1535 A. D., 942 A. H., some time after the death of his friend Mauláná Shaháb-uddín, who died the same year. At his own request his body was conveyed to Dehlí, and was buried by the side of Nizám-uddín Aulia and Amír Khusro. The last and 7th book of the "Rauzat-us-Ṣafá" was written by him.

**Khub,** خوب, the poetical appellation of Kamál-uddín Shístání, the author of a mystical maṣnawi in the Gujrátí dialect, composed in 1578 A. D., 986 A. H. He also wrote a Persian translation and commentary on it in 1582 A. D., 990 A. H.

**Khub-ullah, Shaikh,** شيخ خوب الله, of Allahábád, surnamed Shaikh Muhammad Yahia, was the nephew and son-in-law of Shaikh Afzal of that place, whom he succeeded on the masnad of Irshád, that is to say, as a spiritual guide. He died at Allahábád on Monday the 1st of November, 1731 A. D., 1144 A. H., and his son Shaikh Muhammad Násir, whose poetical name was Fazlí, succeeded him. Khúb-ullah is the author of several works.

**Khuda Banda,** خدا بنده, *vide* Muhammad Khudá Banda.

**Khuda Banda Khan,** خدا بنده خان, son of Amír-ul-

'Umrá Sháistá Khán. In the lifetime of his father he held the Faujdárí of Bahráich with the rank of 1000, and after his father's death, in 1694 A. D., he was recalled to the presence, and was married to the daughter of Jumlat-ul-Mulk Asad Khán. In the year 1700 A. D., 1112 A. H. he was appointed governor of Bídar in the Dakhin by the emperor 'Alamgír, and subsequently of Karnatic Bíjápúr. After the death of Rúh-ullah Khán II, in 1703 A. D., he was honoured with the post of grand steward of the household with the rank of 2,500 horse. At the time of 'Alamgír's death, he held the rank of 3000. He espoused the cause of 'Azim Sháh against his brother Bahádur Sháh, and died of his wounds a few days after the battle in June, 1707 A. D., 1119 A. H.

**Khudyja,** خديجه, or Khadíja, the first wife of Muhammad. She was a widow and dealt in merchandise. She had employed Muhammad for some time to drive her camels, and afterwards married him. Muhammad had several children by her, but all of them died young, excepting three daughters, one of whom was Fátima, who was married to 'Alí. After her marriage with Muhammad she lived 22 years, and died at Mecca three years before the commencement of the Hijrí era, and three days after the death of Abú Ṭálib the father of 'Alí, and uncle of Muhammad, in August, 619 A. D., aged 62 lunar years. Mr. Burckhardt informs us that the tomb of Khudyja is still remaining, and is regularly visited by pilgrims. It is enclosed by a square wall, and presents no objects of curiosity except the tombstone, which has a fine inscription in Kufic characters, containing a passage from the Ḳurán, from the chapter entitled, "Súrat-ul-Kursí".

**Khurdadbih,** خردادبه, or Ibn-Khurdáziba, surname of Abú'l Ḳasim 'Ubaid-ullah bin-Aḥmad (or 'Abdullah) Ibn-Khurdáziba. This author has been the object of considerable controversies among the orientalists of Europe. Khurdáziba (the grandfather of our author) was a magian, and was converted to Islám by the Barmakides. Abú'l Ḳasim (our author) was consequently appointed over the post and intelligence department in the provinces belonging to the Jabal, (mountain); subsequently he came to the court of the Khalifa Mo'tamid, and became one of his privy counsellors. He is the author of several works, among which are—1, "Kitáb Adab-us-Samá," (from which Masa'údí gives a very interesting extract in his life of Mo'tamid); 2, "Kitáb Jamhúr Ansáb-ul-Fars" containing the most celebrated Genealogies of the Persians; 3, "Kitáb-al-Masálik-wal-Mumálik," a geographical work on the roads and kingdoms; 4, "Kitáb-al-Sharáb," on drink; 5, "Kitáb-ul-Lahwwal-Maláhí," on playing and amusements; 6, "Kitáb-al-Anwá," on the stars, and 7, "Kitáb-ul-Nudamá-wal-Julasá" on courtiers and companions. The Geography of Ibn-Khurdáziba, says Sir H. M. Elliot, is the only work which we possess of this author, and of this there is only one copy in Europe. The MS. in question is ancient, bearing the date of 1232 A. D., 630 A. H., but it wants in most instances the diacritical points. It is preserved in the Bodleian Library at Oxford, No. 993. Ibn-Khurdáziba died about the year 912 A. D., 300 A. H.

**Khurram Bakht, Mirza,** مرزا خرم بخت, the son of Mirzá Jahándár Sháh, the son of Sháh 'Alam, king of Dehlí.

**Khurram Begam,** خرم بيگم, the wife of Mirzá Sulaimán Badakhshí.

**Khurram, Mirza,** مرزا خرم, original name of the emperor Sháh Jahán before he came to the throne. Khurram was built by him before he came to the throne.

**Khurshed Mirza, Nawab,** نواب خورشيد مرزا, son-in-law to the late Nawáb Said-'uddaula, eldest son of Nawáb Mumtáz-uddaula, Bahádur, of Lakhnau. He died on the 19th of January, 1875 A. D. He had a Wasiḳa of 1200 Rs. per annum, which it is stated, will be continued to his widow, a young woman of 20.

**Khursindi,** خرسندي, a poet of Bukhárá, and author of the "Kanz-ul-Gharáeb," a commentary in verse on the "Mukhtasir" of Aḥmad Mansúrí, which can be read in different metres.

**Khushdil,** خوشدل, poetical name of Maulví Mustafa 'Alí Khán.

**Khushgo,** خوشگو, poetical title of 'Amar Singh of Benaras, which see.

**Khushgo,** خوشگو, poetical name of Bindrában, a Bania, who was a native of Benaras. He is the author of a Tazkira called "Safínae Khushgo;" the title is a chronogram, and consequently contains the date when he completed it, *i. e.*, in 1734 A. D., 1147 A. H. He was a pupil of 'Arzú, who by Khushgo's request in 1742 A. D., 1155 A. H., made some glosses and added a preface to it. *Vide* also Amar Singh of Benaras.

**Khushi,** خوشي, poetical title of a poet.

**Khushtar,** خوشتر, the poetical name of a poet who was the son of Mirzá Muhammad Afzal Sarkhush.

**Khushtar,** خوشتر, poetical name of Munshí Jagannáth, a Káyeth of Lakhnau, and author of the Rámáyan in Urdú verse translated from the Bhákhá of Tulshí Dás, in the year 1852 A. D., 1268 A. H. *Vide* Tulshí Dás and Girdhar Dás.

**Khushwakt Rae,** خوشوقت راي, he was for many years the agent and intelligencer of the British Government at Amritsar after the treaty with Mahárájá Ranjit Singh, which was concluded in the year 1809 A. D.

**Khusro, Amir,** امير خسرو, one of the most celebrated poets of Hindústán who served under several emperors of Dehlí, and wrote 99 poetical works. His father Amír Maḥmúd Saif-uddín, a Turk of the tribe of Láchín, came from Balkh to India and fixed his residence at Patiála where Khusro was born in the year 1253 A. D., 651 A. H. Khusro died six months after the death of Niẓám-uddín Aulia, who was his spiritual guide, and was buried close to his tomb at Ghayáspúr in old Dehlí. His death happened in September, 1325 A. D., Ramaẓán, 725 A. H. Khusro unfortunately lived at a period, says Sir H. M. Elliot, when vice was triumphant throughout Hindústán. He, however, had the happiness, during the last few years of his life, to see a just prince, Ghayás-uddín Tughlaḳ, on the throne, whose virtues he has commemorated in his history, called "Tughlaḳ-náma," and whom he survived but a few months. The following beautiful poems are particularly admired by his countrymen; and in fact they rival those of the most esteemed poets of Persia.

1. Tuhfat-ul-Saghír.
2. Shatt-ul-Hayát.
3. Ghurrat-ul-Kamál.
4. Baḳia Naḳia.
5. Hasht Bahisht.
6. Sikandar-náma.
7. Risala Nasr.

Besides these there are several other poems, *viz.*, "Nuḥ Sipehr," or the nine spheres, a beautiful mystical poem; the "Ḳirán-us-Sa'dyn" or the auspicious conjunction, a poem in praise of Sulṭán Mu'izz-uddín Kaiḳubád, king of Dehlí, and his father Násir-uddín Baghra Khán, king of

Bengal, who came to visit him. The "Maḳála" containing memoirs of the first four Khalífas, *viz.*, Abú Bakr, 'Umar, Usmán and 'Alí, with a treatise on the Súfi tenets, written in 1324 A. D., the "Ishḳia," a collection of poems on love subjects; the "Matla'-ul-Anwar," on the Súfí doctrines, and his Díwán which is held in great estimation in India, containing poems chiefly on mystical theology and divine love: many of them have been set to music, and are chanted by the devotees or Súfís; frequently producing extravagant ecstasies, termed by them *wajd*, or spiritual delirium. The Khamsa or the five celebrated books of Amír Khusro, which contains about 18,000 verses, are the following:

1. Hasht Bahisht.
2. Sikandar-náma.
3. Panj Ganj.
4. Lailí-wa-Majnún.
5. Shírín-wa-Khusro.

Khusro is said to have written 99 books, some of which, besides the abovementioned, are the following:

1. Aijáz Khusrowí.
2. Aína Sikandarí.
3. Khizir Khání.
4. Insháe Amír Khusro.
5. Jawáhir-ul-Bahr.

**Khusro Malik,** خسرو ملك, son of Khusro Sháh, was the last Sulṭán of the race of Ghaznavides. He ascended the throne at Láhor after the death of his father in 1160 A. D., 555 A. H., was defeated in 1184 A. D., 580 A. H., by Sháháb-uddín Ghorí, then governor of Ghazní, who took him prisoner and sent him to his brother Ghayás-uddín to Fíróz Kóh, where he died after some years.

**Khusro Malik,** خسرو ملك, the brother-in-law of Sulṭán Muhammad Sháh I, Tughlaḳ, whose sister named Khudáwandzáda he had married. He had once formed the project of taking the life of Sulṭán Fíróz Sháh the successor of Muhammad Sháh, by concealing a number of persons in the rooms adjacent to where the king sat, but was saved by Dáwar Malik, the son of Khusro Malik, who made a sign to him that danger was to be apprehended, upon which the king left the room and took refuge on the top of the house.

**Khusro Parwez,** خسرو پرویز, the son of Hurmuz III (or IV), king of Persia of the Sassanian race. He, by the assistance of the Roman emperor Maurice, after defeating Bahrám Chobín, his father's general, who had taken possession of the kingdom, ascended the throne of Persia 591 A. D. The moment he was firmly established on the throne, he fulfilled in the most faithful manner the engagements he had entered into with his ally; and publicly adopted the emperor Maurice as his father; but when that emperor was slain in 603 A. D., he instantly declared war, on the grounds of avenging his father and benefactor. His generals invaded the Roman territories; Dara, Edessa, and other strong places on the frontier, were soon subdued; Syria was completely pillaged, Palestine overrun, Jerusalem taken, and the true cross, which had been enclosed in a golden case, and buried deep in the earth, was discovered, and borne in triumph to Persia. His reign of more than 30 years, was marked by a success never surpassed by the most renowned of his ancestors. Persia was, however, invaded by Heraclius the Roman emperor, who defeated the troops of Khusro wherever he encountered them, and marched, in one direction, as far as the Caspian, in another to Isfahán; destroying in his progress all his splendid palaces, plundering his hoarded treasures, and dispersing, in every direction, the countless slaves of his pleasure. The subjects of Khusro had lost all regard for a monarch whom they deemed the sole cause of the desolation of his country: a conspiracy was formed against him: he was seized by his eldest son Sheroya or Siroes; his 18 sons were massacred before his face, and he was cast into a dungeon, and soon afterwards died or was put to death in 628 A. D., 7 A. H., after he had reigned 38 years. The glory of the house of Chosroes (Nausherwán) ended with the life of Khusro: his unnatural son enjoyed only eight months the fruit of his crime.

The Muhammadan authors say, that Khusro had received an epistle from Muhammad, inviting him to acknowledge Muhammad as the apostle of God. He rejected the invitation, and tore the epistle. "It is thus," exclaimed the Arabian prophet, "that God will tear the kingdom, and reject the supplications of Khusro." The historians of Muhammad, says Gibbon, date this embassy in the seventh year of the Hijrí which commenced 11th May, 628 A. D. Their chronology is erroneous since Khusro died in the month of February of the same year. Gibbon, Vol. VIII, p. 205.

**Khusro Shah,** خسرو شاه, a descendant of the ancient kings of Badakhshán, whom Bábar Sháh defeated about the year 1505, and took possession of his country and made it over to his cousin Khán Mirzá.

**Khusro Shah,** خسرو شاه, surnamed Nizám-uddín, was the son of Bahrám Sháh of Ghazní. He succeeded his father at Láhor in 1152 A. D., 547 A. H., and died there after a reign of seven years in 1160 A. D., 555 A. H. He was succeeded by his son Khusro Malik.

**Khusro Shah,** خسرو شاه, called also Malik Khusro, a favourite slave and wazír of Sulṭán Mubárik Sháh Khiljí, king of Dehlí, whom he murdered on the 4th April, 1321 A. D., 5th Rabí' I, 721 A. H., and ascended the throne by the title of Násir-uddín Khusro Sháh. He was soon after assassinated on the 26th August, 1321 A. D., 30th Rajab, 721 A. H., by Ghází Beg Tughlaḳ, who, the next day, mounted the throne and assumed the title of Ghayás-uddín Tughlaḳ Sháh I.

**Khusro, Sultan,** سلطان خسرو, the eldest son of the emperor Jahángír; was born in the month of August, 1587 A. D., Ramaẓán, 995 A. H., at Láhor. His mother was the sister of Rájá Mán Singh, the son of Rájá Bhagwán Dás, and after the birth of Khusro she got the title of Sháh Begam. He died in the Dakhin on the 16th of January, 1622 A. D., 13th Rabí' I, 1031 A. H., aged 36 lunar years, and his remains appear to have been transported to Allahábád, where he lies buried in a garden surrounded by pukka walls, called the garden of Sulṭán Khusro, and where his mother Sháh Begam is also buried. The dome over his tomb has an inscription of several Persian verses, and contains the chronogram of the year of his death in the words "Faiz Láeḳ." It is related in the work called "Maáṣir Ḳutb Sháhí" that Khusro was strangled by a man named Razá by the order of Sháh Jahán his younger brother.

**Khuzai,** خذاعی, a celebrated author, descendant from a tribe of Arabs called Khuzáạ. *Vide* Abú 'Abdullah Muhammad bin-Husain-al-Khuzáí.

**Khuzaima,** خزیمه, a companion of Muhammad.

**Khwaja Baki Billah,** خواجه باقي بالله, a Muhammadan saint. *Vide* Muhammad Baḳí (Khwája).

**Khwaja Hasan,** خواجه حسن, *vide* Hasan Sanjarí.

**Khwaja Hasan Basri,** خواجه حسن بسري, *vide* Hasan Basrí.

**Khwaja Hasan Sadr Nizami,** خواجه حسن سدر نظامي, author of the work entitled "Táj-ul-Maáṣir" which he dedicated to Sulṭán Ḳutb-uddín Eybak, king of Dehlí about the year 1208 A. D., 605 A. H.

**Khwaja Hashim Kashmin,** خواجه هاشم کشمین, author of a Persian work, entitled, "Zubdat-ul-Muḳámat," containing the (pretended) miracles of Aḥmad Sarhindí, a Muhammadan saint, and others.

**Khwaja Husain Marwi,** خواجه حسین مروی, a native of Marv in Persia, was an excellent poet. He flourished in the time of the emperor Akbar, and wrote chronograms at the birth of Sulṭán Sháh Murád, second son of the emperor, who was born in the year 1570 A. D., 978 A. H. He put the "Singhasan Battísí" into Persian verse, but did not complete it. He is the author of a Díwán.

**Khwaja Husain Sanai,** خواجه حسین سنائی مشهدی, of Mashhad. He and his father were protéges of Sulṭán Ibráhím Mirzá. He flourished about the beginning of the 11th century of the Hijra, left Ḳaṣídas and a Maṣnawi called "Sadde Sikandar."

**Khwaja Husain Sanai,** خواجه حسین ثنائی, a Persian poet, and son of Ghayás-uddín Muhammad. He came to India in the time of Akbar, died in 1588 A. D., 996 A. H., and left a thick Díwán.

**Khwaja Ibrahim Husain,** خواجه ابراهیم حسین, *vide* Ibráhím Husain (Khwája).

**Khwaja 'Imad,** خواجه عماد, *vide* 'Imád Faḳíh.

**Khwaja Imami,** خواجه امامي, author of a story in Persian, entitled, "Máli Dohafta." He was a cotemporary of Mirzá Ḳatíl.

**Khwaja Jahan,** خواجه جهان, original name of Malik Sarwar, founder of the race of the kings of the East, or Sharḳí dynasty of Jaunpúr. The different rulers who have governed in the provinces of Jaunpúr and Antarbed (territories south of Dehlí lying between the rivers Jamna and Ganges) are styled by historians the Sharḳí kings. It appears from the Tawáríkh Mubárik Sháhí, that Sultán Muhammad Sháh, son of Fíróz Sháh Tughlaḳ, king of Dehlí, created one of his eunuchs, named Malik Sarwar, his prime-minister, and honoured him with the title of Khwája Jahán; that upon the death of Muhammad Sháh, and on the accession of his son Sulṭán Mahmúd Sháh Tughlaḳ, a boy of ten years of age, in 1394 A. D., 796 A. H., he was appointed governor of the Eastern provinces of the empire, *viz.*, Ḳanauj, Audh, Kaṛa and Jaunpúr, the latter of which he made the seat of his government. The reign of Mahmúd Sháh was interrupted by serious internal commotions; and Khwâja Jahán taking advantage of these circumstances, and perceiving the weakness of the government arising out of the king's minority, assumed the title of Malik-ush-Sharḳ (King of the East), founded an independent kingdom at Jaunpúr, and died in the year 1400 A. D., 802 A. H., after a short reign of six years. He was succeeded by his adopted son Malik Wásil or Ḳaranfal, who assumed the title of Mubárik Sháh Sharḳí, and died in 1402 A. D., 804 A. H. After his death his brother Ibráhím Sháh Sharḳí succeeded him, and died about the year 1441 A. D., 845 A. H., after a reign of more than forty years. He was succeeded by Sulṭán Mahmúd Sháh Sharḳí, who died in 1452 A. D., 856 A. H., and left the kingdom to his son Muhammad Sháh, who was killed in battle about the year 1458 A. D., 861 or 862 A. H., when Husain Sháh, his brother, succeeded him. He had several battles with Bahlól Lodí, king of Dehlí, and was at last obliged to seek refuge in the court of Sulṭán 'Alá-uddín, king of Bengal, where he died in 1499 A. D., 905 A. H.

**Khwaja Jahan,** خواجه جهان, an Amír of 5000, who died in the time of Jahángír, in the year 1619 A. D., 1029 A. H., at Láhor.

**Khwaja Jahan,** خواجه جهان, *vide* Mahmúd Gáwán.

**Khwaja Kamgar,** خواجه کامگار, *vide* Ghairat Khán.

**Khwaja Kirmani,** خواجه کرمانی, an excellent Persian poet of Kirmánia, surnamed Malik-ul-Fuzlá, or king of the learned. He assumed for his poetical title Khwája and Khwájú; was cotemporary with Sa'dí of Shíráz and a disciple of Shaikh 'Alá-uddín Samnání whom he outlived, and died some years after 1345 A. D., 746 A. H., for he completed his "Gauhar-náma" in that year. He has written about 20,000 verses, and one of his poetical compositions is called "Humáe Humáyún." Mír or Amír Kirmání, and Ahmad Kirmání, were also two Persian poets. *Vide* Kirmání.

**Khwaja Mansur Ḳarabuka,** خواجه منصور قرابوقه طوسی, a poet of Tús who flourished in the reign of Sháhrukh Mirzá, and was employed by the Prince 'Alá-ud-daula. He died 1450 A. D., 854 A. H.

**Khwaja Mansur Shirazi,** خواجه منصور شیرازی, also called Sháh Mansúr, an excellent accountant who served under the emperor Akbar in the capacity of Díwán, and afterwards as his wazír for four years. He was falsely accused of embezzlement by Rájá Toḍarmal, Bírbal and others on account of his being too strict with them, and was imprisoned and afterwards impaled on the 27th February, 1581 A. D., 23rd Muḥarram, 989 A. H., on a supposition that he had been carrying on a correspondence with Mirzá Muhammad Hakím (half brother of Akbar), who had at that time invested Láhor.

**Khwaja Masa'ud,** خواجه مسعود, of Bak, *vide* Masa'úd (Khwája).

**Khwaja Masa'ud,** خواجه مسعود, a poet who died in the year 1131 A. D., 525 A. H., and left three thick Díwáns, one in the Persian, one in the Arabic, and one in the Hindústání language of that day. He is the earliest Musalmán poet who wrote in Hindústání of whom we have any account.

**Khwaja Masa'ud,** خواجه مسعود, a poet of an illustrious family of Kun, and one of the most celebrated writers of Maṣnawís in the last cycle of the Persian poets. He chose the admired subject of Yúsuf and Zalekha for one of his poems. He was called to Hirát, in the time of the Sulṭán Husain Mirzá, to celebrate the events of his reign in verse, and appears to have devoted himself to the task in rather a laborious manner, for he wrote 12,000 lines of a poem on the subject dictated; and would, no doubt, have added as many more, had not death put an end to his enthusiasm. He was the author of many admired poems; among others, "A Dispute between the Sun and the Moon," and "Between the Pen and the Sword." He flourished about the year 1480 A. D., 885 A. H.

**Khwaja Mua'zzam,** خواجه معظم, a man of a very mischievous character, was the brother of Hamída Báno Begam, and husband of Bíbí Fátima, the emperor Akbar Sháh's aunt. He was banished the kingdom several times for improper behaviour, but he soon returned; and when in the year 1564 A. D., 973 A. H., he killed his wife, he was thrown into prison, where, by the command of the emperor, he was murdered in 1565 A. D.

**Khwaja Muhammad Asim,** خواجه محمد اثم, *vide* Khán Dauran.

**Khwaja Muhammad Baki,** خواجه محمد باقي, *vide* Muhammad Baḳí (Khwája).

**Khwaja Muhammad Mukim,** خواجه محمد مقيم, *vide* Nizám-uddín Aḥmad.

**Khwaja Nasir,** خواجه نصير, author of the works called "Bustán-ul-Kirám," and "Aosáf-ul-Ashráf."

**Khwaja Nasir,** خواجه ناصر, a poet who was a cotemporary of Salmán Sáwají.

**Khwaja Nasir,** خواجه ناصر, whose poetical name is 'Andalíb, was the father of Mír Dard the poet.

**Khwaja Nizam-ul-Mulk,** خواجه نظام الملك, minister of Sulṭán Alp Arsalán. *Vide* Niẓám-ul-Mulk.

**Khwaja Parsa,** خواجه پارسا, surname of Muhammad bin-Muhammad Háfiz Bukhárí, author of the book called "Fazl ul-Kitáb fil Muházarát," containing the memoirs of all the celebrated Súfí Shaikhs of the Naḳshbandí Order; and of several other books. He flourished in the reign of Sháhrukh Mirzá, and died 1419 A. D., 822 A. H.

**Khwaja Rustam Khozyani,** خواجه رستم خزياني, *vide* Rustam (Khwája).

**Khwaja Sadr Nizami,** خواجه صدر نظامي, author of the book called "Táj-ul-Másir." He is also called Khwája Hasan Sadr Niẓámí.

**Khwaja Shakir Nasir-uddin 'Abdullah,** خواجه شاكر ناصرالدين عبدالله, one of the greatest saints of Turkistán.

**Khwaja Wafa,** خواجه وفا, Khwája Sara of Sháh Jahán.

**Khwaja Zain-ul 'Abidin 'Ali 'Abdi Beg Nawedi,** خواجه زين العابدين علي عبدى بيگ نويدي, of Shíráz, was for many years Mustaufí or Secretary. He was particularly distinguished in the Masnawí, and composed two Khamsas in imitation of Niẓámí. He is also the author of several other works, one of which is called "Jám Jamshed," and has left three Díwáns, the first is called "Ghurrae Ghurra," in this he uses his poetical name of Nawedí, in the second of 'Abdí. He died at Ardibel in 1580 A. D., 988 A. H. See 'Abdí of Tún and 'Alí Nawedí.

**Khwaja Zikaria,** خواجه زكريا, son of Khwája Muhammad Ahia, a nobleman of the time of the emperor Jahángír.

**Khwaju Kirmani,** خواجو كرماني, *vide* Khwája Kirmání.

**Khwansari** or **Khonsari,** خوانساري, poetical name of Mír Abúl Fatha.

**Khwansari,** خوانسارى, *vide* Husain Khónsárí.

**Khwarizm,** خوارزم, kings of, *vide* Ḳuṭb-uddín Muhammad, son of Anúshtakím.

**Kirmani,** كرماني, a native of Kirmánia. This is the surname of several authors, and amongst others of Ya'kúb bin-Idrís, who died in the year 1430 A. D., 833 A. H., *vide* Khwája Kirmání.

**Kisai, Hakim,** حكيم كسائي, a celebrated poet and physician of Marv in Persia, who was born on Wednesday the 23rd of March, 953 A. D., 27th Shawwál, 341 A. H. The year of his death is not known. There was another Kisáí whose proper name was Abúl Hasan, who was one of the seven eloquent readers of the Ḳurán, and died 796 A. D., 180 A. H.

**Kishna Raja,** كشنا راجه, of Mysore, was placed on the masnad on the 30th June, 1799 A. D., *vide* Krishná Rájá.

**Kishtasp,** كشتاسپ, also called Gashtásp, the son of Luhrásp, fifth king of Persia, of the Kayanian dynasty. He was the first who embraced the religion of the Magi, and built several temples for the worship of fire. *Vide* Gashtásp.

**Kishun Chand,** كشن چند, whose poetical appellation was Ikhlás, was the son of Achal Dás Khattrí of Dehlí, whose house was the resort of the learned. Kishun Chand, after his father's death, applied himself to poetry and became the author of a Tazkira or biography, entitled "Hamesha Bahár," *i. e.*, Eternal Spring, which he compiled in the year 1723 A. D., 1136 A. H. It contains, in alphabetical order, an account of about 200 poets who flourished in India from the time of Jahángír to the accession of Muhammad Sháh. See Ikhlás Khán Ikhlás Kesh.

**Kishun Singh, Kachwaha,** كشن سنگه, Rájá of Kishungaṛh, and eldest brother of Rájá Súraj Singh Ráthor, who served under the emperor Jahángír to whom his sister was married. Kishun Singh was slain by his brother Súraj Singh 1615 A. D., 1024 A. H., in the 10th year of the emperor Jahángír, who was married to his sister by whom he had Sháh Jahán.

**Ḳitran,** قطران بن منصور اجلي, or Ḳutrán bin-Mansúr Ajlí, a celebrated poet of Tabrez, was contemporary with the poet Rashíd Watwát. He is the author of a poem called "Ḳaus-náma," which he dedicated to Amír Ahmad or Muhammad bin-Amír Ḳammáj, ruler of Balkh, who was cotemporary with Sulṭán Sanjar.

**Ḳizal Arsalan,** قزل ارسلان, (which means the red lion), was the second son of Atábak Eldiguz. He succeeded his brother Atábak Muhammad in the office of prime-minister to his nephew Sulṭán Tughral III, 1186 A. D., 582 A. H., and in combination with Násir, the reigning khalíf of Baghdád, seized and imprisoned Tughral, and resolved to usurp the name as well as the power of a monarch. But the day before that fixed for his coronation, he fell by the blow of an assassin 1191 A. D., 587 A. H., and was succeeded by his nephew Atábak Abú Bakr, the son of Atábak Muhammad.

**Kizal Bashi,** قزل باشي. This is a Turkish word and means, red-headed.

**Ḳizal Bash Khan,** قزل باش خان, an amír of 4000, who served under the emperor Sháh Jahán, and died in the year 1648 A. D., 1058 A. H.

**Ḳizal Bash Khan,** قزل باش خان همدانے, of Hamdán, whose proper name was Muhammad Razá, came to India in the reign of the emperor Bahádur Sháh, and was honoured with the title of Ḳizalbásh Khán. He subsequently served under Mubáriz Khán, governor of Haidarábád, and after his death under Nizám-ul-Mulk 'Asaf Jáh, and died at Dehlí in the year 1746 A. D., 1159 A. H. He was a good musician and knew the Indian and Persian systems of musical compositions. His poetical name is Umaid.

**Kochak,** کوچک, poetical name of Prince Mirzá Wajíh-uddín who died in the East, though his remains were brought to Dehlí and buried close to the Dargah of Sultán-ul-Masháekh which is about 6 or 8 miles distant from Dehlí.

**Koukab,** کوکب, poetical name of Munshí Mahdí in the service of Nádir Sháh, author of "Durr-i-Nádira," "Táríkh Nádirí" and a poem entitled "Nádir-náma."

**Koukab,** کوکب, poetical name of a poet who died in the year 1840 A. D., 1256 A. H.

**Koula Devi** or **Kawaldah,** کولا دیوی, the beautiful wife of Ráe Karan, rájá of Gujrát, which place was taken by Sultán 'Alá-uddín Khiljí in the year 1297 A. D., 697 A. H., and among the captives was Koula Deví whom the king married. Her daughter Dewal Deví also was taken captive in the year 1306 A. D., 706 A. H. A few days after her arrival, her beauty inflamed the heart of the king's son, Khizir Khán, to whom she was eventually given in marriage. The history of the loves of this illustrious pair is written in an elegant poem called "Ishkia," composed by Amír Khusro of Dehlí. Mubárik Sháh, in the second year of his reign, put to death his brother Khizir Khán who was imprisoned at Gwáliar, and took Dewal Deví to be his wife.

**Koura Mal, Choudhari,** چودهري کورامل, author of the story of Kámrúp, a poem in Persian verse. He died on the 16th of May, 1848 A. D.

**Kousari Bukhari,** کوثری بخاری, an author who died in the year 1475 A. D., 880 A. H.

**Kousi,** قوسي, poetical name of Majd-uddín 'Alí, an author.

**Krishn,** کرشن, a god of the Hindús, was in the world in the time of the Kauras and Pandús, or the 7th century after the commencement of the Kálíjug, according to this shlók, "When something more than 650 years of the Kálíjug were expired, then were the Kauras and Pandús, in whose time the Great War took place."

**Krishna Raj Odawar,** کرشنا راج اوداور, the lineal descendant of the ancient family of Mysore, whose power Haidar 'Alí Khán had usurped in the year 1761 A. D. But after the defeat and death of Típú Sultán, and the departure of his sons from Seringapatam to Vellore, Mysore was divided between the Nizám and the English. The English took the southern portion, and the city of Seringapatam, by which accession their territory reached from sea to sea. The Nizám took an equal portion on the north-east. Some districts on the north-west, equal in value to more than half of each of their own portions, were offered by the allies to the Marhattas, which they refused to take, and they were divided between the Nizám and the English. The remainder was given to Krishná Rájá, then a child of three years of age, who was raised to the throne of his ancestors, on the 30th June, 1799 A. D., and Purania, a Bráhman of great ability and reputation, who had been the chief financial minister of Típú, was appointed Díwán to the young prince by the British Government. He was afterwards created Knight Grand Commander of the Most Exalted Order of the Star of India. He died on Friday the 27th of March, 1868 A. D., aged 72 years. His adopted son Chamrajaindra Odáwar, has been recognized and proclaimed as Mahárájá of Mysore. The young Mahárájá now being a minor, the government and administration of the territories of Mysore will, during his minority, be conducted under the direction of the Commissioner.

**Kuar Singh,** کنور سنگه, or Kúnwar Singh of Jagdíspúr, a rebel of 1857, was killed in battle in May or June, 1858.

**Kubad,** قباد, (Cavades of the Greeks), was the son of Fíróz I, king of Persia of the Sassanian race, and the successor of his brother Palásh. We are told that when his brother Palásh came to the throne, Kubád, who had aspired to it, fled towards the territories of the Khákán, or king of Transoxania; and as he passed Naishápúr, he spent one night with a beautiful young lady of that city, who, when he returned four years afterwards accompanied by a large army, presented him with a fine boy, the fruit of their casual amour. He was delighted with the appearance of the child; and as he was contemplating him, he received accounts that his brother Palásh was no more, and that the crown of Persia awaited his acceptance. This intelligence reaching him at such a moment, made him conclude, that fortune already smiled on his son, whom he, from that day, treated with the greatest favour, and gave the infant prince the name of Nausherwán. Kubád succeeded his brother in 488 A. D., and carried on a successful war against the Roman emperor Anastasius: and died, after a long reign of 43 years, 531 A. D. His son Nausherwán succeeded him.

**Kubadi,** قبادي, surname of Shís bin-Ibráhím, an Arabian author, who died in the year 1202 A. D., 599 A. H.

**Kublai Khan,** کبلاي خان, (*vide* Yule's Marco Polo) more properly Khublai, overthrew the Kin dynasty in 1260 A.D., and conquered the whole of China 19 years later; died at Pekin 1296 A. D.

**Kudrat,** قدرت, the poetical name of Sháh Kudrat-ullah of Dehlí, a Persian and Urdú lyric poet, and author of the work called "Nataej ul-Afkár" and a Díwán. He was living at Murshidábád in 1782 A. D., 1191 A. H. He was one of the most fertile Persian poets; his Díwán consists of 20,000 verses. He died in 1791 A. D., 1205 A. H., at Murshidábád.

**Kudrat,** قدرت, the poetical name of Shaikh Kudrat-ullah of Bhopal.

**Kudrat-ullah, Shaikh,** شيخ قدرت الله, Superintendent of Stamps at Bhopal, and author of several works in Persian and Urdú which were published by him in the year 1863 A. D., 1280 A. H., at Bhopal.

*List of Books composed by him.*

*Poetry.*

| | |
|---|---|
| Of Ghazals called, ............ | Díwán Kudrat. |
| Of Panegyrics or Kasídas, .. | Agwán Kudrat. |
| Poems, ...................... | Gulzár Kudrat. |
| Ditto, ...................... | Izhár Kudrat. |
| Malcom's History, ........ | Májrí Kudrat. |
| Mutiny of 1857, ............ | Tamásháe Kudrat. |
| Promiscuous pieces, ........ | Kímiyáe Kudrat. |

*Prose.*

| | |
|---|---|
| On Miracles, ............... | Ajáebát Kudrat. |
| On Medicine, ............... | Mujarribat Kudrat. |
| Letters, ..................... | Rukkát Kudrat. |
| Stories, ..................... | Hikáyát Kudrat. |

**Ḳudsi,** قدسي, *vide* Hájí Muhammad Ján Kudsí.

**Ḳudsi Ansari,** قدسي انصاري, of Isfahán, whose proper name is Shaikh 'Abdul Karím, was a celebrated learned and pious Musalmán of Isfahán. He died on the 3rd of February, 1615 A. D., 14th Muharram, 1024 A. H.

**Ḳudsia Begam,** قدسيه بيگم, daughter of 'Asaf Khán wazír, the son of the celebrated Yatmád-uddaula, wife of the emperor Sháh Jahán, niece to the empress Núr Jahán Begam, and mother of the emperor 'Alamgír, *vide* Arjumand Bano Begam and Mumtáz Mahal.

**Ḳuduri,** قدوري, surname of Abúl Husain Ahmad bin-Muhammad, a celebrated Musalmán doctor of Baghdád, of the Hanífa sect, who died 1036 A. D., 428 A. H. He is the author of the "Mukhtasir-ul-Ḳudúrí," which is one of the most esteemed of the works which follow the doctrines of Abú Hanífa, and is of high authority in India. It is a general treatise on law, and contains upwards of 12,000 cases. A well-known commentary on the Mukhtasir ul-Ḳudúrí is entitled "Al-Joharat ul-Naiyarat" and is sometimes called "Al-Joharat ul-Munírat."

**Ḳulich Khan,** قليچ خان, title of 'Abid Khán, who came to India in the reign of Sháh Jahán, was raised to the rank of 4000. He died by a cannon ball at the siege of Golkanḍa on the 8th of February, 1686 A. D., 24th Rabí' I, 1097 A. H. He is the father of Ghází-uddín Khán Fíróz Jang I, and grandfather of the celebrated Niẓám ul-Mulk 'Asaf Jáh of Haidarábád.

**Ḳulich Khan,** قليچ خان, of Andján, of the tribe of Jání Kurbání, was an amír of 4000, who served under the emperors Akbar and Jahángír from the year 1572 to 1611 A. D., 980 to 1020 A. H. His poetical name was Ulfatí.

**Ḳulich Khan Turani,** قليچ خان توراني, an amír who served under the emperors Jahángír and Sháh Jahán; was raised by the latter to the rank of 5000, and appointed governor of Kábul and Kandahár. He died 1654 A. D., 1064 A. H.

**Ḳuli Ḳutb Shah I, Sultan,** سلطان قلي قطب شاه اول. This prince was the founder of the sovereignty of Golkanḍa. His father Ḳuṭb ul-Mulk was originally a Turkish adventurer who came to try his fortune in the Dakhin and embraced the service of Muhammad Sháh Bahmaní. By degrees he was promoted to high rank; and in the reign of Mahmúd Sháh obtained the title of Ḳuṭb ul-Mulk and the Tarafdárí or government of Telingána. In 1493 A. D., 899 A. H., he received orders to besiege the fortress of Jámkonda, and as he was reconnoitring, was killed by an arrow from the walls. After his death, his office and titles were conferred by the king on his son Sulṭán Ḳulí with the territory of Golkanḍa, part of Telingána, in jágír. On the decline of the Bahmaní authority, when 'Adil Sháh and others assumed royalty, he also in the year 1512 A. D., 918 A. H., styled himself Sulṭán of Telingána under the title of Ḳulí Ḳuṭb Sháh. He was a chief of great abilities and ruled the country for a period of 50 years; 18 of which he governed Telingána in the name of Mahmúd Sháh, and reigned as king 32 lunar years; at the end of which he was assassinated by a Turkish slave supposed to have been bribed by his son and successor, Jámshed Ḳuṭb Sháh. His death happened on Sunday the 2nd September, 1543 A. D., 2nd Jumáḍa II, 950 A. H. The kings of the Ḳuṭb Sháhí dynasty who reigned at Golkanḍa, are as follows:—

1. Ḳulí Ḳuṭb Sháh.
2. Jámshed Ḳuṭb Sháh.
3. Ibráhím Ḳuṭb Sháh.
4. Muhammad Ḳulí Ḳuṭb Sháh.
5. Muhammad Ḳuṭb Sháh.
6. 'Abdullah Ḳuṭb Sháh.
7. Abú'l Hasan.

**Ḳuli Ḳutb Shah II, Sultan,** سلطان قلي قطب شاه, who is also called Muhammad Ḳulí Ḳuṭb Sháh, was the son of Ibráhím Ḳuṭb Sháh, upon whose death in June, 1581 A. D., Rabí' II, 989 A. H., he ascended the throne of Golkanḍa in his twelfth year. In the beginning of his reign he was engaged in war with 'Adil Sháh of Bíjápúr, with whom he concluded peace in the year 1587 A. D., giving him his sister in marriage. The air of Golkanḍa not agreeing with his constitution, he founded a city at about eight miles distance, which he called Bhágnagar, after his mistress Bhágmatí a celebrated courtezan; but being afterwards ashamed of his amour, he changed it to Haidarábád. Sháh 'Abbás, emperor of Persia, courted his alliance, by asking his daughter in marriage for one of his sons; and Ḳuṭb Sháh, esteeming connection with so august a monarch as an honour, complied with the request. He was much esteemed for his abilities, was an encourager of literature, and is the author of the work called "Kulliát Ḳuṭb Sháh," a very copious volume, containing Hindí, Dakhaní, and Persian Poems, on a variety of subjects. He was the fourth Sulṭán of the Ḳuṭb Sháhí dynasty and reigned 31 years. He died on Saturday the 11th of January, 1612 A. D., 17th Ẓi-Ḳa'da, 1020 A. H., and having no son, was succeeded by his brother Muhammad Ḳuṭb Sháh.

**Kulini,** قليني, *vide* Muhammad bin-Ya'ḳub.

**Kummi,** قمي, *vide* Malik Kummí.

**Ḳumri,** قمري, poetical name of Siráj-uddín.

**Ḳutb 'Alam,** قطب عالم, a celebrated Muhammadan saint, whose original name is Shaikh or Sayyid Burhán-uddín, but he is commonly known by the former; he was the grandson of Makhdúm Jahánián Sayyid Jalál Bukhárí. He chose Gujrát for his place of residence, and died there on the 9th of December, 1453 A. D., 8th Ẓil-hijja, 857 A. H. His tomb is at Batúh, six miles from the city of Ahmadábád in Gujrát. There is a slab kept at the door of his mausoleum, which some say is stone, others think it to be wood or iron. His son named Sháh 'Alam was also a pious Musalmán and is likewise buried at Gujrát.

**Ḳutb 'Alam,** قطب عالم, another Musalmán saint whose proper name is Shaikh Núr-uddín Ahmad. He was born at Láhor, and died in the year 1444 A. D., at Pinḍúa in Behar, where he is buried. Shaikh Hisám-uddín, whose tomb is at Kaṛa Mánikpúr, and who is also considered a saint, was one of his disciples.

**Ḳutb Shah,** قطب شاه, a title of the kings of Golkanḍa. *Vide* Muhammad Ḳuṭb Sháh and Ḳulí Ḳuṭb Sháh.

**Ḳutb Shah,** قطب شاه, a king of Gujrát, *vide* Kuṭb-uddín (Sulṭán).

**Ḳutb Shah,** قطب شاه, a celebrated Muhammadan saint of Dehlí, *vide* Kuṭb-uddín Bakhtiár.

**Ḳutb-uddin 'Abdul Karim ibn-'Abdul Nur,** قطب الدين عبدالكريم بن عبدالنور, is the author of the work called "Sharah Saḥíḥ Bukhárí," and of a history of Egypt entitled "Táríkh Misr." He died in the year 1333 A. D., 733 A. H.

**Ḳutb-uddin 'Allama, Maulana,** قطب الدين علامه مولانا, a learned Muhammadan poet who was cotemporary with the celebrated Shaikh Sa'dí of Shíráz, and is the author of several works, among which are the "Tuhfa Sháhí," "Sharah Kulliát Ḳánún," and "Sharah Miftáh ul-'Ulúm." He died at Tabrez on Sunday the 7th February, 1311 A. D., 17th Ramaẓán, 710 A. H.

**Ḳutb-uddin Bakhtiar Kaki, Khwaja,** خواجه قطب الدين بختيار كاكي, a celebrated Muhammadan saint of Dehlí, commonly called Ḳuṭb-Sháh, and sometimes called Ushí from his native country Ush near Andján in Persia. He died at old Dehlí on the 27th of November, 1235 A. D., 14th Rabí' I, 633 A. H. His tomb is still conspicuous in that district, and is visited by devotees. He is the author of a Díwán. Shaikh Faríd-uddín Shakar Ganj was one of his disciples.

**Ḳutb-uddin Eybak,** قطب الدين ايبک, king of Dehlí, originally a slave of Shiháb-uddín Muhammad Ghórí, prince of Ghór and Ghazní, who raised him to the rank of a chief in his army, and in the year 1192 A. D., 588 A. H., after his victory over Pithaura the Rájá of Ajmer, he left him as his deputy in India. The same year Ḳuṭb-uddín conquered Mirath and Dehlí and extended his conquest as far as Bengal. After the death of Shiháb-uddín in 1206 A. D., 602 A. H., his nephew Ghayás-uddín Mahmúd who succeeded him, sent Ḳutb-uddin all the insignia of royalty, a canopy, a crown and a throne, and conferred on him the title of Sulṭán. On the 27th June the same year, 18th Ẓi-Ḳa'da, 602 A. H., Ḳuṭb-uddín having invested himself with sovereign power ascended the throne, and made his residence the capital of Dehlí. His reign properly speaking, lasted only four years, though he enjoyed all the state and dignities of a king for upwards of twenty years. He died at Láhor by a fall from his horse in 1210 A. D., 607 A. H., and was succeeded by his adopted son Sulṭán 'Arám Sháh. The Jáma' Masjid in old Dehlí, which is famous under the name of "Ḳúwat ul-Islám," and stands close to the Ḳuṭb Minár, was formerly a Hindú temple, Ḳuṭb-uddín first converted it into a masjid, and afterwards Shams-uddín Altimsh and 'Ala-uddín Khiljí made some additions to it. The following is a list of the Sulṭáns of the Slave (or Turk) dynasty of Ghór who reigned at Dehlí.

| | | | A. D. | A. H. |
|---|---|---|---|---|
| 1. | Ḳuṭb-uddín Eybak of the first Turk dynasty, .............. | began | 1206 | 602 |
| 2. | 'Arám Sháh, son of Ḳuṭb-uddín, .. | „ | 1210 | 607 |
| 3. | Shams-uddín Altimsh, .......... | „ | 1210 | 607 |
| 4. | Rukn-uddín Fíróz, son of Altimsh, | „ | 1236 | 633 |
| 5. | Sulṭána Razia, daughter of Altimsh, ...................... | „ | 1236 | 634 |
| 6. | Bahrám Sháh, son of Altimsh,.... | „ | 1240 | 637 |
| 7. | 'Ala-uddín Masa'úd, son of Fíróz, | „ | 1242 | 639 |
| 8. | Náṣir-uddín Mahmúd, son of Altimsh, .................... | „ | 1246 | 644 |
| 9. | Ghayás-uddín Balban (a slave of Altimsh), ................ | „ | 1266 | 664 |
| 10. | Kaiḳubád, grandson of Altimsh (last of the 1st branch), ...... | „ | 1286 | 685 |
| 11. | Jalál-uddín Fíróz Sháh Khiljí, first Sulṭán of the 2nd branch of the Turk dynasty called Khiljí, which see, .................. | „ | 1288 | 688 |

**Kutb-uddin Khan,** قطب الدين خان, brother of Shams-uddín Auka, entitled 'Azím Khán. He was an amír of 5000 in the reign of the emperor Akbar; was made governor of Bahroch, and was treacherously slain by Sulṭán Muzaffar king of Gujrát in 1583 A. D.

**Ḳutb-uddin,** قطب الدين, a grandson of Shaikh Salím Chishtí.

**Ḳutb-uddin Khan Kokaltash,** قطب الدين خان كوكلتاش, whose original name was Shaikh Khúban, was the son of Shaikh Salím Chishtí's sister, and foster-brother of the emperor Jahángír who raised him to the rank of 5000. He was made governor of Bengal in 1606 A. D., 1015 A. H., and was killed at Bardwán by Sher Afgán Khán, the former husband of Núr Jahán Begam in 1607 A. D., 1016 A. H. His remains were transported to Fathapúr Síkrí and buried there.

**Ḳutb-uddin Mahmud bin-Muhammad Shirazi,** قطب الدين محمود بن محمد شيرازي, author of the "Ghurrat-ut-Táj," (splendour of the crown) and several other works. He died 1310 A. D., 710 A. H.

**Kutb-uddin Mahmud Langa,** قطب الدين محمود لنگا, second king of Multán of the tribe of Langa, who having secured the person of Shaikh Yúsuf his predecessor and son-in-law, sent him to Dehlí and ascended the throne of Multán in the reign of Sulṭán Bahlól Lodí. He reigned for a period of sixteen years and died much lamented in 1469 A. D., 874 A. H. He was succeeded by his son Husain Langa.

**Kutb-uddin Muhammad,** قطب الدين محمد, the son of Anúshtakín, the cup-bearer of Sulṭán Sanjar Saljúḳí. He was installed by the Sulṭán about the year 1140 A. D., and became the first king of Khwárizm of the race called Khwárizm Sháhí. The following is a list of the kings of this race.

1. Ḳuṭb-uddín Muhammad.
2. Atsiz, the son of Ḳuṭb-uddin Muhammad.
3. Alp Arsalán, the son of Atsiz.
4. Sulṭán Sháh, the son of Alp Arsalán.
5. 'Ala-uddín Takash Khán, his brother.
6. Sulṭán Muhammad, son of Takash. He was defeated by Changez Khán in 1218 A. D.
7. Jalál-uddín, the son of Sulṭán Muhammad, and last king of this race, slain 1230 A. D.

**Ḳutb-uddin Muhammad Ghori,** قطب الدين محمد غوري, was the son of 'Izz-uddín Ghórí. He married the daughter of Sulṭán Bahrám Sháh, king of Ghazní, and having founded the city of Fírózkoh in Ghór, made it his capital, and assumed all the dignities of a sovereign. At length he was induced to attack Ghazní. Sulṭán Bahrám obtaining intimation of his intentions contrived to get him into his power, and eventually put him to death. This is the origin of the feuds between the houses of Ghór and Ghazní. Saif-uddín Súrí, prince of Ghór, brother of the deceased, raised an army to revenge his death, with which he marched direct to Ghazní, which was evacuated by Bahrám, who fled to India. After some time Saif-uddín was betrayed into the hands of Sulṭán Bahrám by the inhabitants of Ghazní. The unhappy prince had his forehead blackened, and was seated astride on a bullock with his face towards the tail. In this manner he was led round the whole city; after which, being put to torture, his head was cut off and sent to his uncle Sulṭán Sanjar Saljúḳí, while his wazír Sayyad Majd-uddín was impaled.

**Ḳutb-uddin Munouwar, Shaikh,** قطب الدين شيخ منور, a Muhammadan saint of Hánsí, who was a grandson of Shaikh Jamál-uddín Aḥmad. He lived in the time of Sulṭán Fíróz Sháh Bárbak, king of Dehlí. He was a contemporary of the celebrated saint Shaikh Naṣir-uddin

Chiragh Dehlí; both of whom were disciples of Shaikh Nizám-uddín Aulia; and both of whom died the same year. Náṣir-uddín died on the 16th September, 1356 A. D., 18th Ramazán, 757 A. H., and Kutb-uddín on the 22nd November, 1356 A. D., 26th Zi-Ka'da, 757 A. H. The former lies buried at Dehlí and the latter at Hánsí.

**Kutb-uddin, Sultan,** سلطان قطب الدين, also called Kutb Sháh, was the son of Muhammad Sháh, king of Gujrát. After the death of his father in February, 1451 A. D., Muharram, 855 A. H., he ascended the throne of Gujrát, reigned more than eight years, and died on the 25th of May, 1459 A. D., 23rd Rajab, 863 A. H. He was buried in the vault of his father Muhammad Sháh, and was succeeded by his uncle Dáúd Sháh who reigned only a few days and was deposed.

**Kutbul-Mulk,** قطب الملك, the father of Kulí Kutb Sháh I, which see.

**Kutbul-Mulk,** قطب الملک, the title of 'Abdullah Khán (Sayyid) which see.

**Kutlamish,** قتلمش, a descendant of Saljúk, was taken prisoner by Maliksháh Saljúkí. *Vide* Sulaimán bin-Kutlamish.

**Kutlagh Nigar Khanam,** قتلغ نگار خانم, daughter of Yúnas Khán king of Mughalistán, and sister to Mahmúd Khán, a descendant of the famous Changez Khán. She was married to 'Umar Shaikh Mirzá, and became the mother of Bábar Sháh, king of Dehlí. She died at Kábul on the 4th of June, 1505 A. D., 1st Muharram, 911 A. H.

**Kutlak Khan,** قتلق خان, the title of Atábak 'Abú Bakr bin-Sa'd bin-Zangí.

**Kutran,** قطران, *vide* Kitrán.

**Kutrib,** قطرب, an author who was a cotemporary of Seboya the poet, and received this title from him, but his original name is Muhammad. He is the author of several works. He died 821 A. D., 206 A. H.

**Kutyba,** قتيبة, the son of Mushní ibn-Amar, was governor of Khurásán in the reign of khalíf 'Abdulmalik. He was slain in the time of Sulaimán, son of 'Abdulmalik in September, 715 A. D., Zil-hijja, 96 A. H.

**Kya Muhammad,** کیا محمد, *vide* Buzurg Umaid.

**Kyjaptu,** کیجپتو, second son of Sultán Abka Khán, the son of Halálú Khán, the Tartar king of Persia. He was raised to the throne by the voice of the majority of the Amírs on the death of his brother Arghún Khán in March, 1291 A. D., Rabí' I, 690 A. H. The resentment of a personal injury led Báidú Khán, a grandson of Halákú Khán, to rebel against him, and the unfortunate monarch was, after a short struggle, made prisoner, and put to death in January, 1295 A. D., Safar, 694 A. H. Báidú Khán succeeded him.

---

# L.

**Labid,** لبيد, whose full name is Abú A'kíl Labíd bin-Rabiat, was one of the most distinguished Arabian poets, and one of the seven whose verses constituted the Mua'l-lakát, a series of prizes suspended in the Ka'ba. He was still an idolater when Muhammad commenced publishing his laws. One of his poems commenced with this verse: "All praise is vain which does not refer to God: and all good which proceeds not from Him is but a shadow;" no other poet could be found to compete with it. At length the chapter of the Kurán, entitled *Barát*, was attached to a gate in the same temple, and Labíd was so overcome by the verses at the commencement, as to declare that they could only be produced by the inspiration of God, and he immediately embraced Islámism. When Muhammad was apprised of the conversion of Labíd, the finest genius of his time, he was exceedingly delighted, and requested him to answer the invectives and satires of Amra-alkys and other infidel poets who wrote against the new religion and its followers. The following sentence is also attributed to him, which is the finest which ever fell from the lips of an Arab :—"All is vain which is not of God." Labíd is said to have lived to the age of 140 years, and died at the city of Kúfa in 141 of the Hijra (758 A. D.) (There is some mistake in the year of his death.)—*Ockley's History of the Saracens.* Labíd is supposed to be the friend and tutor of Amra-alkys, commonly called Kaisand Majnún, the lover of Lylu.

**Lachhmi Narayan,** لچهمي نارايں, of Benares. He is the author of a biography or Tazkira called "Gul-e-Ra'ná."

**Lachhmi Ram,** لچهمي رام, a Hindú who was a poet and had adopted the word "Surúr" (happiness) for his poetical appellation.

**Lachhmi Bai,** لچهمي بائي, the wife of Malhár Ráo, rájá of Baroda, who married her under suspicious circumstances; a child was born in 1874 and it has been recognised as legitimate.

**Laddardeo,** لدرديو, a rájá of Telangana who became tributary to Sultán 'Ala-uddín Sikandar Sání in the year 1310 A. D., 710 A. H.

**Ladli Begam,** لاڈلي بيگم, was the daughter of Shaikh Mubárik of Nágór, and sister to Abú'l Fazl the minister of the emperor Akbar. She was married to Nawáb Islám Khán who had been governor of Bengal about the year 1608 A. D., 1017 A. H. She died at Ágrah, and is supposed to have been buried there in the cemetery of her father, which is now called (1844) Rauza Ladlí.

**Laila,** or **Laili,** ليلى, the name of the mistress of the celebrated Majnún, whose original name was Kais. These two lovers are very famous throughout the East. Lailí was the daughter of a neighbouring Chief. She was equally accomplished with her lover: and nothing seemed likely to disturb the happiness which their permitted attachment promised, till the avarice of her father destroyed at once all their hopes. Lailí was commanded to think of Kais no more, as she was destined to be the bride of one more rich and powerful; and in spite of the grief and remonstrances of the unfortunate pair, they were separated. Kais became insane from disappointment, and his name was therefore changed to Majnún, (the distracted). Death at length put a period to his miseries, and his faithful mistress soon followed him, leaving her cruel parent to his late and vain remorse, and the memory of these victims of avarice to eternal honour and regret. *Vide* Majnún.

**Lais,** or **Laith,** ليث, is the proper name of a brazier, who by his valour raised himself to the highest posts in the dominions of Darham, who then reigned in Sajistán. He left three sons, Ya'kúb, A'mrú, and 'Alí, of whom the first, called Ya'ḳúb bin-Lais, was founder of the dynasty of the Safarides.

**Lal Chand,** لال چند, whose poetical name was Uns, is the author of a Persian Díwán. He died in the year 1852 A. D., 1268 A. H.

**Lal Khan,** لال خان, a celebrated songster of India who died in the fourth year of the emperor Jahángír's reign, 1609 A. D., 1018 A. H.

**Lal Kunwar,** لال كنور, the favourite mistress of Jahándár Sháh, emperor of Dehlí. This woman had been a public dancer, and her family were of the same discreditable class: yet they were exalted to high stations by the emperor, to the exclusion of the nobles, whom they were also allowed on several occasions to insult with impunity.

**Laludin,** لالودين, the younger Nawáb of Najíbábád who turned a rebel in 1857, and was hanged in April 1858.

**Lal Singh (Raja),** لال سنگه راجا, a Sikh Chief and paramour of Rání Chánd Kúnwar. After the death of Rájá Jawáhir Singh, the office of prime-minister remained vacant for some time and was disposed of by lot to Lál Singh in November 1845. Lál Singh lived at Ágrah as a state prisoner for several years before the outbreak.

**Lama'i,** لامعی, (also called Láma'í Bukhárí because he was a native of Bukhára), his proper name is Mahmúd bin-'Usmán, and he is the author of the works called "Sharaf-ul-Insán," "Ibrat-náma," and "Shama'wa-Parwána," in the Turkish language. He died 1533 A. D., 940 A. H. He was a pupil of Sozní.

**Laek,** or **Layek,** لايق, the poetical name of the author of the poem called "Dastúr Himmat," containing the story of Kámrúp in Persian verses which he dedicated to Himmat Khán Bahádur his patron. He completed this work in 1685 A. D., 1096 A. H., and found the chronogram of that year to be contained in Himmat Khán.

**Largeiran Gun,** لرگيرن گون, *vide* Ahlía Báí.

**Lashkar Khan,** لشكرخان, a nobleman of the court of the emperor Jahángír.

**Lashkar Khan,** لشكرخان, a nobleman of the court of Jahángír and Sháh Jahán who held the manṣab of 5000. He had built his house near Naíkí Mandí on a spot of ground of 20 bígas which had a large gate.

**Latif-unnisa Begam,** لطيف النسا بيگم, a widow of the late Nawáb Shams ul-'Umra and Wikár ul-'Umra's mother, died at Hydarábád Dakhin on the 24th August, 1864 at the good old age of 74 lunar years. She survived her husband only sixteen months, and thirteen days. She was buried with great pomp in the sepulchre of her husband.

**Lilawati,** ليلاوتي, *vide* Bhaskar Ácháryá.

**Lisani (Maulana),** مولانا لساني, poetical name of Wajíh-uddin 'Abdullah Shírází, a son of Mír Muhammad Mushkfarósh. He died at Tabrez according to Khushgo in 1583 A. D., 991 A. H., and left a Díwán containing 4000 verses.

**Lodi,** لودي, a tribe of Paṭháns or Afgháns in India. *Vide* Khán Jahán Lodí.

**Lonkaran,** لنكرن, *vide* Ráe Lonkaran.

**Luhrasp,** لهراسپ, the son-in-law of Kaikáús, and successor of Kaikhusro, king of Persia. He was the fourth king of the Kayanian dynasty; and obliged both the rulers of Tartary and of China to do him homage. In his time Bakht un-Nasar (Nebuchadnezzar) the governor of 'Irák, took Jerusalem, and carried away into bondage such of its inhabitants as were not put to the sword. Luhrásp is stated to have reigned 120 years, and was succeeded by his son Kishtásp or Gashtásp, who is believed to be Darius Hystaspes of the Greeks.

**Luhrasp,** لهراسپ, original name of Mahábat Khán, the second son of the celebrated Mahábat Khán Jahángírí. He had been governor of Kábul for several years in the time of the emperor 'Alamgír, but was recalled to the presence about the year 1670 A. D., and shortly after ordered to command the army of the Dakhin in the room of Mahárája Jaswant Singh who was recalled to court. *Vide* Mahábat Khán Luhrásp.

**Lukman Hakim,** لقمان حكيم. He flourished about a thousand years before the Christian era, and is said to have been cotemporary with David the king of Israel. He is the greatest of the Oriental moralists, and held in the highest esteem by the Orientals for his wisdom and virtues; even Muhammad speaks of him in the 31st chapter of the Ḳurán which is called "Súra Luḳmán," with profound reverence. Luḳmán's wisdom, like Solomon's, is supposed to have been of divine origin. One day as he was in his room, working at his trade (he was a carpenter) several angels invisibly entered and saluted him. Luḳmán, hearing voices, looked around him, but not seeing any one, made no reply. The angels then said: We are messengers from God, thy Creator and ours, who hath sent us to thee to inform thee, that He designs to make thee a monarch and His vicegerent on earth. Luḳmán answered: If it be the absolute will of God that I shall become a monarch, that will must be accomplished; and I trust that He will grant me grace to execute His commands faithfully; but if the liberty of choice be given me, I should prefer abiding in my present condition; the only favour that I ask from God being, that He would preserve me from offending Him, for were I to offend Him, all the dignities of the earth would be but a burden to me. This reply was so agreeable to God that He at once bestowed on Luḳmán the gifts of Knowledge and Wisdom to a degree hitherto unparalleled. The Maxims of Luḳmán are ten thousand in number; and "any one of these," says an Arabian commentator, "is of much greater value than the whole world." His wisdom and the striking morality of his fables, are so like those of Æsop that he is considered by some as the same personage.

**Lutf,** لطف, the poetical name of Mír Amman, a Hindústání lyric poet, and one of the learned natives formerly attached to the College of Fort William. He is the author of the "Bágh-o-Bahár," a simple version of the "Nautarz Murassa" in Urdú, completed in 1802 A. D., 1217 A. H.

**Lutf 'Ali Khan,** لطف علي خان, the eldest son of Ja'far Khán, king of Persia, whom he succeeded in the year 1788 A. D.; had several battles with the troops of Aḳa Muhammad Khán Kachár, by whom he was defeated, taken prisoner, and afterwards murdered in 1795 A. D. He was the last prince of the Zand family.

**Lutfullah,** لطف الله, a Muhammadan gentleman, who was born in the ancient city of Dháránagar, in Málwá, on Thursday the 4th of November, 1802 A. D., 7th Rajab, 1217 A. H. His father Maulví Muhammad Akram, was a Muhammadan of the sacred order, a descendant of Sháh

Kamál-uddín, who was a great saint of his time in the province of Málwá, being the spiritual guide as well as general preceptor of Sultán Mahmúd Khiljí, during a period of 30 years. After his death, the Sultán built a magnificent mausoleum at the western gate of the city, and endowed therein a shrine to the memory of the holy man; opposite to it he caused to be raised another edifice, surmounted by a superb dome, which was intended as a resting-place for his own mortal remains, and there they still repose. Lutfullah proceeded to England as secretary to Mír Ja'far 'Alí the son-in-law of Mír Afzal-uddín, Nawáb of Súrat in March 1844, and after his return from England he wrote his adventures in 1854, entitled the "Autobiography of Lutfullah" in English, and dedicated it to Colonel W. S. Sykes, F. R. S., London, and published in June 1857.

**Lutfullah Khan,** لطف الله خان, son of Sa'dullah Khán, wazír of the emperor Sháh Jahán. After his father's death in 1656 A. D., 1066 A. H., though he was then only eleven years of age, the mansab of 700 and 100 sawárs were conferred on him. In the reign of the emperor 'Alamgír, he was raised to a higher rank, and died at the time when that emperor was engaged in conquering the fort of Gandána in the Dakhin. This event took place on the 28th December, 1702 A. D., 18th Shabán, 1114 A. H.

**Lutfullah Maulana,** مولانا لطف الله, a native of Naishápúr in Persia. He was an excellent poet and flourished in the time of Amír Timur. The poet Shaikh Azurí has mentioned him in his work called "Jawáhir ul-Asrár." He is the author of the "Táríkh Sháhrukh," which is an abridgment of the history of Amír Timur, with memoirs of the first nine years of the reign of his son and successor Sháhrukh Mirzá to whom he dedicated the work 1413 A. D., 816 A. H., and died the same year.

**Lutfullah Muhammad Muhaddis bin-Ahmad,** لطف الله محمد محدث بن احمد, author of the work called "'Asmán Sakhun," a rhymed abridgment of the "Tazkira Daulat Sháhí." We are informed in the preface that Fáezí Kirmání rendered the Tazkira of Daulat Sháh in Persian verses in the reign of Akbar and altered the division of the original, making ten periods instead of seven; Lutfullah, who was a contemporary of Aurangzíb 'Alamgír, remodelled this version and added two periods more to make the number correspond with the signs of the Zodiac; and in allusion to it, he gave it the above title. It consists of 250 verses; every verse contains the name of a poet.

**Lutf-unnisa Begam,** لطف النسا بیگم, the wife of Siráj-uddaula, nawáb of Bengal. She was murdered in the time of Nawáb Ja'far 'Alí Khán with several other women of the house of the late Nawáb in June 1760.

# M.

**Madaeni,** مدايني, a celebrated historian who was a native of Madáen in Persia.

**Madan Pal, Maharaja,** مدنپال مهاراجه, G. C. S. I., of Karaulí, died of cholera on the 17th August, 1869. This event has deprived Rájpútána of one of the best native rulers. The Mahárája having died without a son, the Government of India has recognised Lachhman Pál, the son of his younger brother Bishan Pál as successor to the Ráj of Karaulí. This young man had not long been at Karaulí, when he became the subject of an ailment from which he died in a few days. His death certainly wears a somewhat suspicious appearance.

**Madari Mal,** مداري مل, a Hindú and author of the work "Badáya ul-Fanún," containing forms of letters on different subjects, in Persian.

**Madar Shah,** مدار شاه, a celebrated Muhammadan saint whose tomb is at Makanpúr in Kanauj. *Vide* Sháh Madár.

**Madhogarh,** مادهوگر, a fort built by Mádhójí Sindhia in Agrah with stones, brick and sand.

**Madhoji Bhosla,** مادهوجي بهوسله, the third rájá of Berar of the Bhosla family, was the son of Raghojí Bhosla I. He succeeded his eldest brother Ránójí or Jánojí Bhosla in 1772 A. D., and died at an advanced age on the 29th May, 1788 A. D. He was succeeded by his son Rághojí Bhosla II, the fourth rájá of Berar or Nágpúr.

**Madho Ram,** مادهو رام, a learned Hindú who is the author of a book of Letters which goes after his name, called "Insháe Mádhó Rám," containing forms of letters on different subjects in Persian.

**Madho Rao I, Bilal Peshwa,** مادهوراو اول بلال پيشوا, second son of Bálájí Ráo Peshwá whom he succeeded as nominal Peshwá in 1761 A. D., under the regency of his uncle Raghunáth Ráo. He died in November, 1770 A. D., and was succeeded by his brother Náráyan Ráo.

**Madho Rao II, Peshwa,** مادهوراوثاني پيشوا, of the Marhattas, also called Sewájí Mádhó Ráo, was the posthumous son of Náráyan Ráo Peshwá, who was murdered in August, 1772 A. D., by his paternal uncle Raghunáth Ráo also called Rághóbá, who usurped the masnad. A few months after this event Náráyan Ráo's widow was delivered of a son, who was named Sewájí Mádhó Ráo, and was raised to the masnad, on which he continued until his death which took place on the 27th October 1795 A. D., by a fall from the terrace of his palace. He was succeeded by Chimnájí 'Apá, the younger son of the Marhatta chief Raghunáth Ráo.

**Madho Rao,** مادهوراو, or Mádhójí Sindhia, rájá of Gwáliár, was the son of Ránójí Sindhia. He succeeded his brother Jíápá Sindhia in 1759 A. D. to the management of his patrimonial inheritance, of which Ujjain was the capital; and by a train of successful operations was enabled to appropriate to himself a considerable part of the province of Málwá, belonging to the government of Púna, as well as to extend his domains over a great part of Hindústán; and to obtain possession of the person and nominal authority of the emperor Sháh 'Alam, of whom he was ostensible minister. He died on the 12th February 1794 A. D., without male issue, and was succeeded by his grand-nephew and adopted son Daulat Ráo Sindhia. He had built a small fort close to a place called Gazar Tijára in Agrah, and named it Mádhógarh, the ruins of which were still to be seen about the year 1830 A. D.

**Madho Singh Kachhwaha,** مادهو سنگه کچهواهه, the son of Rájá Bhagwán Dás and brother-in-law of Jahángír.

**Madho Singh Kachhwaha,** مادهو سنگه کچهواهه,

succeeded Ishurí Singh his father to the government of Jaipúr in the year 1760 A. D. He died in 1778 A. D. and was succeeded by his son Pirthí Singh, a minor, who was soon after deposed, and his brother Partáp Singh ascended the gaddí the same year, and died in 1803 A. D.

**Mael,** مایل, the poetical name of Mirzá Ḳuṭb-uddín, a nobleman of the reign of the emperor 'Alamgír. He was an excellent poet, but latterly became distracted and died eight days after Mullá Náṣir 'Alí, in the month of March 1697 A. D., Ramaẓán, 1108 A. H. His brother Mirzá Niẓám-uddín surnamed Tála was also an elegant poet.

**Maftun,** مفتون, poetical name of Momin 'Alí a poet.

**Maftun,** مفتون, the poetical title of Ghulám Mustafa, a brother of Razí-uddín Sarúrí who was usually called Ghulám Murtazá. He is the author of a Díwán. He died at the age of 30, about the year 1755 A. D., 1168 A. H.

**Maghmum,** مغموم, poetical name of Rámjas, a Hindú of Lakhnau, and author of an Urdú Díwán. He was employed by Mumtáz-uddaula, Mr. Johnson, and was living in 1785 A. D., 1199 A. H.

**Maghrabi Shaikh,** شیخ مغربي, poetical appellation of Muhammad Shírín. He was a friend of Kamál Khujandí, and like him a profound Súfí. He died at Tabrez 1416 A. D., 819 A. H., and is buried at Surkháb. Having been given to the most disgusting vices during his lifetime, he is considered as a saint. He is the author of a Díwán called "Ḳasáed Maghrabí," and several other works.

**Mahabat Jang,** مهابت جنگ, *vide* 'Alí Wardí Khán.

**Mahabat Khan,** مهابت خان, whose proper name was Zamána Beg, was the son of Ghór Beg, a native of Kábul. He had attained the rank of a commander of 500 under Akbar, and was raised to the highest dignities and employments by the emperor Jahángír. He enjoyed a high place in the opinion of the people, and was considered as the most eminent of all the emperor's subjects. In the month of February, 1626 A. D., Jumáda II, 1035 A. H., he seized the emperor's person, (because he (the emperor) never consulted him, but followed the advice of his wife Núr Jahán in all affairs), and carried him to his own tents where he remained a state prisoner for some time, but was soon released after a severe battle, by his wife Núr Jahán. In the second year of the emperor Sháh Jahán, the government of Dehlí was conferred on him. He died in the Dakhin in 1634 A. D., 1044 A. H., and his corpse was conveyed to Dehlí and buried there. After his death his eldest son Mirzá Amán-ullah received the title of Khán Zamán, and his second son Luhrásp was honoured with the same title of Mahábat Khán.

Mahábat Khán had his house built on the bank of the river Jamna on a plot of land of 50 bigas in Ágrah, though little of it now remains, there are some parts of its ruins still to be seen.

**Mahabat Khan,** مهابت خان, whose original name is Luhrásp, was the second son of the celebrated Mahábat Khán of the reign of Jahángír after whose death in 1634 A. D., 1044 A. H., he received this title. He was twice made governor of Kábul, and had the command of the army in the Dakhin. He died in 1674 A. D., 1085 A. H., in the reign of 'Alamgír on his way from Kábul to the presence. *Vide* Luhrásp.

**Mah Afrid,** ماه آفرید, daughter of Fíróz the son of Yezdijard, the last monarch of the Sasánian dynasty of Persian kings, and mother of Yezíd III, twelfth khalíf of the house of Umayya.

**Maham Anka,** ماهم انکه, mother of 'Azím Khán. *Vide* 'Azím Khán.

**Maham Begam,** ماهم بیگم, a granddaughter of Shaikh Ahmad Jám. She was married to the emperor Bábar Sháh, and became the mother of Humáyún. She was living about the year 1561 A. D., 969 A. H., as appears from an inscription on the gate of an old Madrasa (or college) and masjid constructed by her in that year near the fort of old Dehlí called Dín Panáh. The numerical words of the inscription from which the year of the buildings is known, are "Khair Manazil" or the Mansions of Bliss. She must have been then more than 70 years of age.

**Maha Singh,** مها سنگه, the grandson of Rájá Mán Singh Kachhwáhá of Ameir (now Jaipúr), and son of Partáp Singh. He served under the emperor Jahángír, and died in 1617 A. D. He was the father of Mirzá Rájá Jai Singh. *Vide* Mán Singh.

**Maha Singh,** مها سنگه, a Sikh Rájá of Láhor, who was the father of Mahárájá Ranjít Singh. He extended his rule and died in 1792 A. D., when his wife became regent with Lakhpat Singh minister.

**Mah Bano,** ماه بانو, sister of Khán 'Azím Kóka. She was married to 'Abdul Rahím Khán, KhánKhánán, son of Bairám Khán about the year 1572 A. D., 980 A. H., and died 1597 A. D., 1005 A. H.

**Mahbub 'Ali Khan,** محبوب علي خان, His Highness Ásaf Jah Muzaffar ul-Mulk Niẓám-uddaula Nawáb Mír Mahbúb 'Alí Khán Bahádur Fatha Jang is the Niẓám of Haidarábád Dakhin.

**Mah Chuchak Begam,** ماه چوچک بیگم, one of the wives of the emperor Humáyún, and mother of the prince Farrukh Fál, surnamed Muhammad Hakím.

**Mahdi,** مهدي, the first khalíf of the Fátimites in Africa. His son who succeeded him was named Káem-bi-amr-ullah.

**Mahdi,** مهدي, the third khalíf of the house of 'Abbás, *vide* Al-Mahdí.

**Mahdi 'Ali Khan,** مهدي علي خان, the grandson of Ghulám Husain Khán, the historian. He resided in Behar in 1801 A. D.

**Mahdi 'Ali Khan, Hakim,** حکیم مهدي علي خان, prime-minister of Náṣir-uddín Haidar, king of Audh. The Iron Suspension Bridge over the Kálínadí at Khodáganj near Fathagarh which was seven years in progress was built at his expence for Rs 70,000, and finished in July, 1836 A. D. He was dismissed from his post in 1832 A. D., which was again restored to him on the accession of Muhammad 'Alí Sháh in 1837 A. D. After this he lived only a few months and died in December, 1837 A. D.

**Mahdi, Imam,** امام مهدي, surnamed Abú'l Ḳásim Muhammad, the last of the twelve Imáms who are held in the highest veneration by the Muhammadans. The first of these was 'Alí, and the last Mahdí, the son of Hasan 'Askarí who was the eleventh Imám. He was born at Sarmanrai in Baghdád on Friday the 29th of July, 860 A. D., 15th Sha'bán, 255 A. H., and when he was about four or five years of age, his father died. The Shí'as or Shí'ites say, that he, at the age of 10, entered into a cistern at his father's house, whilst his mother was looking on, and that he never came out again. This occurred in 879 A. D., 265 A. H. They believe him to be still alive, and concealed in some secret place, and that he will appear again with Elias the prophet, on the second coming of Jesus Christ for the conversion of infidels to the Muhammadan religion.

**Mahdi Khan, Mirza,** مرزا مهدی خان, styled Munshí ul-Mumálik, was the confidential Secretary to Nádir Sháh, and is the author of the "Táríkh Nádirí" which is also called "Nádir-náma," or the history of Nádir Sháh, and "Táríkh Jahán Kushá." This work was translated into French by Sir William Jones.

**Mahdi, Mirza,** مرزا مهدی, author of the work called "Majmúa Mirzá Mahdí," a chronological table of the remarkable events of the house of Timur, commencing 1423 A. D., with Abú Sa'íd Mirzá, (third in descent from Timur, and grandfather of the emperor Bábar Sháh) who reigned over Khurásán and Transoxania; and terminating with the emperor Bahádur Sháh 1708 A. D.

**Mahfuz,** محفوظ, author of the "Story of Sháh Bedár Bakht," which is also called "Rashk-i-Chaman," in Urdú verse dedicated to Ghází-uddín Haidar, king of Audh in 1823 A. D., 1238 A. H.

**Mahip Narayan,** مهیپ نارایں, rájá of Benares. A pottah was granted him by the English on the 14th September, 1781 A. D.

**Mahir,** ماهر, the poetical name of Mirzá Muhammad 'Alí, a native of Agrah. His father was a Hindú in the service of Mirzá Ja'far Mua'mmáí or the punster, who having no children, converted the boy to the Muhammadan religion, adopted him as his own son, and gave him a good education. After the death of Mirzá Ja'far he attached himself to Dánishmand Khán and remained with him till his death, when he retired from the world and died in 1678 A. D., 1089 A. H. He was an excellent poet, and is the author of several works, one of which is called "Gul-i-Aurang" which he wrote in praise of the emperor "Aurangzeb 'Alamgír on his accession to the throne.

**Mahjur,** مهجور, *vide* Muhammad Bakhsh.

**Mahmud,** محمود ملقب به برهان الشریعت, surnamed Burhán-ush-Shariat, who lived in the seventh century of the Hijra, is the author of the work on jurisprudence called "Wikáya" which he wrote as an introduction to the study of the Hidáya. This work has been comparatively eclipsed by its commentary, the Sharh al-Wikáya by 'Ubaid-ullah bin-Masa'úd; this author's work combines the original text with a copious gloss explanatory and illustrative. Both the Wikáya and the Sharh al-Wikáya are used for elementary instruction in the Muhammadan Colleges. Other commentaries on the Wikáya exist, but they are of no great note.

**Mahmud,** محمود, an Afghán chief of Kandahár of the tribe of Ghilzaí, was the son of Mír Wais, after whose death in 1715 A. D. he succeeded him. He besieged Isfahán in 1722 A. D., and compelled Sultán Husain Safwí, king of Persia, to surrender and resign his crown to him. The king went forth with all his principal courtiers in deep mourning, surrendered himself to Mahmúd, and with his own hands placed the diadem on the head of the conqueror. The event took place on the 11th October of the same year, 11th Muhurram, 1135 A. H. After two years' possession of the sovereign power, he gave orders for the death of the Safwián princes, who were his prisoners, and thirty-nine of them, some grown up, others in their childhood, were barbarously slaughtered. It is said that he became deranged the same night, and not only tore his own flesh, but ate it. Every person that approached him, he overwhelmed with abuse, and in this condition died in 1725 A. D. But before his death the Afgháns, being threatened by an attack of the Persian prince, Tahmásp Mirzá, the son of Sultán Husain, who had fled from Isfahán, elected Ashraf, the cousin of Mahmúd, to be their ruler, who in April, 1725 A. D., 12th Sha'bán, 1137 A. H. murdered Mahmúd, and became the king of Persia.

**Mahmud,** محمود, the son of Sultán Muhammad Saljúkí. He held the government of Irák and Azurbeján for several years as deputy to his uncle Sultán Saryar who gave him his two daughters in marriage named Sítí Khátún and Máh Malik. He died in 1131 A. D., 525 A. H.

**Mahmud,** محمود بن عبد الله قان فیروزی, son of 'Abdullah Kán Fírózí, is the author of the History entitled "Maásir Kutb Shahí," and also of another work of the same description called "Táríkh Jáma ul-Hind." He served Kulí Kutb Sháh II for 30 years, and was living at the time of that monarch's death, which happened in 1612 A. D., 1020 A. H.

**Mahmud,** محمود شبشوی, of Shustar, (Shabishtarí) author of a religious book called Hak-ul-Yekín which is held in great estimation among the Persians.

**Mahmud I, Sultan,** سلطان محمود اول, emperor of Constantinople, was the son of Mustafa II and nephew of Ahmad III, whom he succeeded in 1730 A. D., 1142 A. H. His Janisárís expected from him the recovery of the conquered provinces, but he lost Georgia and Armenia, which were conquered by Nádir Sháh. Mahmúd died in 1754 A. D, 1168 A. H., and was succeeded by his brother 'Usmán II.

**Mahmud II, Sultan,** سلطان محمود ثاني, emperor of Constantinople, was the son of Sultán 'Abdul Hamíd, commonly called Ahmad IV, the son of Mustafa III. He was born on the 20th July, 1785 A. D., and ascended the throne after the deposition of his uncle Salím III and Mustafa IV, on the 28th of July, 1808 A. D. He was of the eighteenth generation from 'Usmán I who founded the dynasty, and the thirtieth sovereign of that family. He died on the 30th June, 1839 A. D., 1255 A. H., and was succeeded by his son 'Abdul Majíd. The reign of Mahmúd has been full of important events. The Greeks, in 1821 A. D. threw off the Ottoman yoke, and after a sanguinary contest have been declared independent; and in 1828 A. D., a war with Russia took place, in which the armies of Mahmúd were uniformly defeated, and the Russians were only prevented from advancing to Constantinople by large concessions on the part of the Turks, and the mediation of the European powers.

**Mahmud bin-Faraj,** محمود بن فرج, a famous impostor who gave himself out for Moses risen from the dead: but was flogged to death by the order of the khalíf Mutwakkil.

**Mahmud Boria, Pahlawan,** پهلوان محمود بوریا, a Muhammadan saint of Persia who followed the occupation of a boatman, and is the author of the work called "Kitáb Kanz."

**Mahmud Gawan, Khwaja,** خواجه محمود گاوان, styled Malik-ut-Tajjár Khwája Jahán, was the wazír of

Nizám Sháh Bahmaní, king of the Dakhin. In the reign of Muhammad II, the duties of Wakíl-us-Sulṭánat were conferred on him. His enemies lost no opportunity of poisoning the king's mind, and at last they brought this great man to destruction by contriving an infamous forgery, upon which the king without investigating the matter, ordered him to be put to death in the 78th year of his age. This event took place on the 5th of April, 1481 A. D., 5th Ṣafar, 886 A. H. Mahmúd had great learning and much judgment in composition of prose and verse. A little before his death, he had written a poem in praise of Muhammad Sháh. He is the author of the "Rauzat ul-Inshá," and some poems. Mauláná 'Abdul Rahmán Jámí corresponded with him, and some of his letters are to be seen in his works.

**Mahmud ibn-Masa'ud,** محمود ابن مسعود, author of a work called "Zínat-uz-Zamán."

**Mahmud Khan Langa,** محمود خان لنگا, the fourth king of Multán, son of prince Fíróz, succeeded his grandfather Husain Langa on the throne in August, 1502 A. D., Safar, 908 A. H. He reigned 23 years. In 1524 A. D., 931 A. H. some time before his death the emperor Bábar Sháh having conquered the country of the Panjáb proceeded to Dehlí, from whence he wrote an order to Husain Arghún, governor of Ṭhaṭta informing him that he intrusted him henceforward with the directions of affairs in Multán. That chieftain in consequence, crossed the Indus and marched with a large army to Multán; but before his arrival the king died and was succeeded by his son Husain Langa II.

**Mahmud Khan,** محمود خان, nawáb of Bijnor and a rebel of 1857. He was the great-grandson of Zabita Khán the son of Najíb-uddaula Amír ul-Umrá. *Vide* Sa'd-ulláh Khán.

**Mahmud Khwarizmi, Maulana,** مولانا محمود خوارزمي, a poet of Khwárizm.

**Mahmud, Mulla,** ملا محمود, of Jaunpúr, the son of Muhammad Fárúḳí, was the author of the work called "Shams Bázigha," and of the "Hawáshí Faríd fí Sharah ul-Fawáed," which he wrote in 1632 A. D., 1042 A. H., and died in 1652 A. D., 1062 A. H.

**Mahmud Parsa, Khwaja,** خواجه محمود پارسا, a poet who flourished in the time of Prince 'Alá-uddaula, and Sulṭán Abú Sa'íd Mirzá, and died 1477 A. D., 822 A. H.

**Mahmud Sa'id, Erchi,** محمود سعيد, author of the "Tuhfat-ul-Majális;" he was a contemporary of Shaikh Aḥmad Khaṭṭú whom he mentions therein.

**Mahmud Shah,** محمود شاه, one of the sons of Timur Sháh, the son of Aḥmad Sháh 'Abdálí, who being driven from Kábul by Dost Muhammad Khán, took possession of Hirát which country he ruled for some years, and after his death in 1829 A. D., his son prince Kámrán succeeded him.

**Mahmud Shah I, Bahmani,** محمود شاه بهمني اول, the fifth Sulṭán of the race of Bahmaní kings of the Dakhin, was the youngest son of Sulṭán 'Alá-uddín Hasan. He was raised to the throne at Kulbarga after the assassination of his brother Dáud Sháh in May, 1378 A. D., Muḥarram, 780 A. H., reigned 19 lunar years 9 months and 24 days, and died of a putrid fever on the 20th April, 1397 A. D., 21st Rajab, 799 A. H. He was succeeded by his son Sulṭán Ghayás-uddín Mahmúd, was a patron of literature, had a taste for poetry, and wrote elegant verses himself. In his reign the poets of Arabia and Persia resorted to the Dakhin and were benefitted by his liberality. Mír Faiz-ulláh Anjú, who presided in the seat of justice, once presented him with an ode, was rewarded with a thousand pieces of gold, and permitted to retire, covered with honours, to his own country. In his time the celebrated poet of Shíráz, Khwája Háfiz, determined to visit the Dakhin; but was prevented by a train of accidents.

**Mahmud Shah II, Bahmani,** محمود شاه بهمني ثاني, the fourteenth Sulṭán of the race of Bahmaní kings of the Dakhin, succeeded his father Muhammad Sháh II on the throne at Ahmadábád Bedar in March, 1482 A. D., Safar, 887 A. H., in the twelfth year of his age. He reigned 37 lunar years, and died on the 18th December, 1517 A. D., 4th Ẕil-ḥijja, 923 A. H. The reign of this prince though a long one, passed in troubles and civil wars, and the royal authority fell from the house of Bahmaní. On his death the governors in their respective provinces threw off the small portion of allegiance which they latterly paid to the late king, and proclaimed their independence. He was succeeded by his son Sulṭán Aḥmad Sháh II.

**Mahmud Shah I,** محمود شاه بيقره اول, surnamed Baiḳara the son of Muhammad Sháh and brother of Ḳuṭb-uddín or Ḳuṭb Sháh, was raised to the throne of Gujrát after the deposition of Dáúd Sháh his uncle in June, 1459 A. D., Sha'bán, 863 A. H. He caused the city of Ahmadábád to be surrounded by a wall and bastions in 1487 A. D., 892 A. H.; and on its completion had the sentence من دخله كان امنا in commemoration of the date of that event, inscribed on one face of the fortification, the meaning of which is, "Whosoever is within is safe." He made two expeditions to the Dakhin, reigned 55 lunar years, and died on the 23rd of November, 1511 A. D., 2nd Ramaẓán, 917 A. H., in the 70th year of his age. He was buried in Sarkíj or Sarkích near Ahmadábád in the mausoleum of Shaikh Aḥmad Khaṭṭú. He was succeeded by his son Muzaffar Sháh II.

**Mahmud Shah II,** محمود شاه ثاني, whose former name was Náṣir Khán, was the third son of Muzaffar Sháh II. He was raised to the throne of Gujrát after the murder of his eldest brother Sikandar Sháh in May, 1526 A. D, Sha'bán, 932 A. H. He reigned about three months, after which his brother Bahádur Sháh returning from Jaunpúr, deprived him of his kingdom and mounted the throne on the 20th August the same year, 15th Ẕi-Ḳa'da, 932 A. H. Mahmúd Sháh died in 1527 A. D., 933 A. H.

**Mahmud Shah III,** محمود شاه ثالث, was the son of Laṭíf Khán the brother of Bahádur Sháh. He was raised to the throne of Gujrát after the death of Mírán Muhammad Sháh in April, 1537 A. D., Ẕi-Ḳa'da, 943 A. H. In his reign, about the year 1540 A. D., 947 A. H., the fort of Súrat (Surat) on the shore of the sea, was completed by Khudáwanda Khán, before which time the Portuguese were in the habit of attacking the Muhammadans along that coast. Mahmúd Sháh reigned about 18 years, and was slain on the 16th of February, 1554 A. D., 13th Rabí' I, 961 A. H., while he was asleep, by one Daulat, at the instigation of Burhán, private chaplain to the king, who hoped by that means to ascend the throne of Gujrát. The same year died also Salím Sháh king of Dehlí, and Nizám Sháh Bahrí the Sulṭán of Ahmadnagar in the Dakhin. The words "Zawál Khusroán," *i. e.*, Destruction of Kings, commemorate the date of this event. Mahmúd Sháh was buried in the vault of Sulṭán Mahmúd Baiḳara, close to the mausoleum of Shaikh Aḥmad Khaṭṭu, and was succeeded by Aḥmad Sháh II.

**Mahmud Shah I, Khilji,** محمود شاه خلجي اول, was the son of Khán Jahán Khiljí styled Malik Mughís and 'Azím Humáyún the prime-minister of Hoshang Sháh, after whose death Mahmúd in conjunction with his father, having succeeded in poisoning his sovereign Muhammad Sháh the son of Hoshang Sháh, ascended the throne of Málwá on Tuesday the 15th of May, 1436 A. D., 29th Shawwál, 839 A H. He reigned 34 lunar years, and died on the 27th of May, 1469 A. D., 19th Zi-Ḳa'da 873 A. H., aged 68 years. The numerals of the two Persian words جنت نشيني give the year of his death. He was succeeded by his son Ghayás-uddín Khiljí who reigned 33 years and left his kingdom to his son Sulṭán Náṣir-uddín. He reigned 11 years and 4 months and was succeeded by his son Sulṭán Mahmúd II, who was defeated and slain by Sulṭán Bahádur Sháh of Gujrát in 1531 A. D., 937 A. H., and Málwá incorporated with the kingdom of Gujrát.

**Mahmud Shah II,** محمود شاه ثاني, the third son of Sulṭán Náṣir-uddín, after whose death he ascended the throne of Málwá on the 3rd May, 1511 A. D., 3rd Safar 917 A. H. Málwá was taken by Bahádur Sháh king of Gujrát on the 26th February, 1531 A. D., 9th Shabán 937 A. H., and Mahmúd Sháh taken prisoner with his seven sons and ordered into confinement. He was sent to the fort of Champaner, but died or was murdered on his way to that place, and the kingdom of Málwá became incorporated with that of Gujrát. After the death of Bahádur Sháh, one Ḳádir Khán and after him Shujáạ Khán ruled over Málwá for some years, and after the demise of the latter his son Báz Bahádur reigned till the year 1570 A. D., 978 A. H., when that kingdom was entirely subdued by the emperor Akbar.

**Mahmud Shah Purbi,** محمود شاه پوربي, succeeded his father Fíróz Sháh to the throne of Bengál in 1494 A. D., 899 A. H. He reigned about one year and was murdered by Siddí Badr who succeeded him and assumed the title of Muzaffar Sháh in 1495 A. D., 900 A. H.

**Mahmud Shah Sharki, Sultan,** محمود شاه شرقي, ascended the throne of Jaunpúr after the death of his father Sulṭán Ibráhím Sháh Sharḳí in 1440 A. D., 844 A. H. He reigned about 17 years and died in 1457 A. D., 862 A. H., when his eldest son Bhíkhan Khán succeeded him, and assumed the title of Muhammad Sháh Sharḳí.

**Mahmud Shah Tughlak, Sultan,** محمود شاه تغلق سلطان, surnamed Náṣir-uddín, was the son of Muhammad Sháh, the son of Fíróz Sháh Tughlaḳ. He was raised to the throne of Dehlí after the death of his brother Humáyún Sháh in April, 1394 A. D., Jumádạ II, 796 A. H., at the age of ten years. His minority and the dissensions of the nobles encouraged many of the surrounding chiefs to revolt and become independent. In his time Amír Timur invaded India, and defeated Mahmúd Sháh in a battle fought (according to Firishta on the 15th of January, 1399 A. D., 7th Jumádạ I, 801 A. H..) and according to Sharaf-uddín Yezdí, on Tuesday the 7th of Rabí' II, 801 A. H., corresponding with the 17th December, 1398 A. D., when Mahmúd fled to Gujrát, and Timur the next day took possession of Dehlí:

On the eighth of Rabí'-us-Sání, with the sun
In Capricorn, Timur died Dehlí won.

Timur soon after his conquest of Dehlí returned to Persia with an immense treasure from India. After the departure of that conqueror, Nasrat Khán, son of Fatha Khán, the son of Fíróz Sháh took possession of Dehlí, and ascended the throne with the title of Nasrat Sháh. He was succeeded in 1400 A. D., by Iḳbál Khán, after whose death Mahmúd Sháh, who was then at Ḳanauj, returned, and ascended the throne of Dehlí the second time in December, 1405 A. D., 22nd Jumádạ II, 808 A. H. But the governors of provinces no longer acknowledged allegiance to the throne, having established their independence during the civil war. Mahmúd Sháh died on the 4th of March, 1413 A. D., 29th Ẕi-Ḳa'da 815 A. H., and was succeeded by Daulat Khán Lodí. With Sulṭán Mahmúd the empire of Dehlí fell from the race of the Turks who were adopted slaves of Sulṭán Shaháb-uddín Ghórí.

**Mahmud, Sultan,** سلطان محمود غزنوي, the celebrated king of Ghazní, was the eldest son of Sulṭán Náṣir-uddín Subaktagín. His father at his death, 997 A. D., 387 A. H., unmindful of the superior right of Mahmúd (who was then employed in the government of Khurásán,) bequeathed his kingdom to Isma'íl, a younger son. Isma'íl attempted to confirm himself in the power to which he was raised, but on the approach of Mahmúd, after a vain attempt at resistance, he was compelled to throw himself upon the clemency of his offended brother. Mahmúd reigned more than 33 lunar years, during which time he made twelve expeditions into India; took Láhór, Dehlí, Kanauj and other parts of Hindústán; many hundred temples of the Hindús he levelled with the ground; many thousand idols he demolished, and broke to pieces the famous idol of Sómnáth, the fragments of which he distributed to Ghazní, Mecca and Medina. He was born on the 15th December, 967 A. D., 9th Muḥarram 357 A. H., and died on Thursday the 23rd of Rabí' II, 421 A. H., which year and date is inscribed on his tomb at Ghazní, corresponding with the 30th April, 1030 A. D. On a tombstone of white marble lies the mace of Mahmúd of such a weight that few men can wield it. He was succeeded by his son Muhammad, who reigned only five months, and was deposed and deprived of sight by his brother Masa'úd who ascended the throne.

**Mahmud, Sultan,** محمود سلطان, the son of Muhammad (Sulṭán), the son of Malik Sháh, which see.

**Mahmud, Sultan,** سلطان محمود غوری, of Ghór. *Vide* Ghayás-uddín Mahmúd Ghórí.

**Mahmud Tabrezi,** محمود تبريزی, author of the "Miftáh ul-Ya'jáz," or the Key to Miracles, describing the happiness of those who have obtained the light of Súfíism and other mysteries. Written in 1482 A. D., 887 A. H.

**Mahmud Tistari, Shaikh,** شيخ محمود تستري, a native of Tistar a town in Persia, and author of the poem called "Gulshan-e-Ráz," which he wrote in 1317 A. D., 717 A. H. He died in the year 1320 A. D., 720 A. H., and was buried at Tistar his native country.

**Mahtab Bagh,** مهتاب باغ, name of a place or garden, which Sháh Jahán had commenced building on the other side of the Jamna opposite to the Rauza of Tájganj and similar to it where he intended he should be buried after his death, but 'Alamgír his son took away all the materials for the construction of some other buildings after his father's death; some of its ruins are still to be seen.

**Maili,** ميلي هروی, poetical appellation of Mirzá Muhammad Ḳulí of Hirát who came to India in 1571 A. D., 979 A. H., and is the author of a Díwán.

**Majahid Shah Bahmani,** مجاهد شاه بهمني, *vide* Mujáhid Sháh.

**Maimuna,** ميمونة, the daughter of Hárith or Háris, was one of the wives of Muhammad, who married her in the eighth year of the Hijrí, *i. e.*, in 629 A. D. This was doubtless another marriage of policy, for Maimúna was 51 years of age, and a widow, but the connexion gained him two powerful proselytes. One was Khálid, the son of Walíd, a nephew of the widow, who by his prowess obtained the appellation of "The Sword of God." The other was Khálid's friend, 'Amrú the son of 'As; the same who assailed Muhammad with poetry and satire at the commencement of his prophetic career. Maimúna was the last spouse of the prophet, and, old as she was at her marriage, survived nearly all his other wives. She died many years after him in a pavilion at Sarif, under the same tree in the shade of which her nuptial tent had been pitched, and was there interred. This event took place about the year 671 A. D., 51 A. H.

**Maisana,** ميسنة, the Bedouin bride of the khalíf Mu'áwia I, and the mother of Yezíd, was a daughter of the tribe of Kalab; a tribe remarkable for the purity of dialect spoken in it. She was married to Mu'áwia whilst very young; but this exalted situation by no means suited the disposition of Maisana, and amidst all the pomp and splendour of Damascus, she languished for the simple pleasures of her native desert. She was an excellent poetess, and had pleased Mu'áwia's fancy to that degree with some of her verses, that he made her go back into the desert amongst her own relations, and take her son Yezíd along with her, that he also might be brought up a poet. This part of his education succeeded, for he was reckoned to excel in that way, though his chief talent consisted in making himself a drunken wretch. Maisana did not revisit Damascus till after the death of Mu'áwia, when Yezíd ascended the throne.

**Majd Hamkar Farsi,** مجد همكر فارسي, also called Majd-uddín Haibat-ulláh, *vide* Majd-uddín Hamkar.

**Majd, Maulana,** مولانا مجد, author of the work called "Rauzat ul-Khuld."

**Majd-uddaula,** مجد الدولة, a Sultán of the race of Boya called Boyaites, was the son of Fakhr-uddaula, the brother of 'Azd-uddaula, Sultán of Fars and Irák. He had for a short time governed Khurásán and assumed a regal state, but was taken prisoner in Rei, by the victorious Sultán Mahmúd of Ghazní in 1029 A. D., 420 A. H. He had been raised by the death of his father in August, 997 A. D., Sha'bán 387 A. H. when very young, to the government of the city and the surrounding country. During the minority of this prince, all the power was in the hands of his mother. Mahmúd commanded one of his officers to inform the lady, that she must submit to his authority, or prepare for war. "Had such a message been sent," replied the heroine, "in the life of my deceas ed lord, it must have occasioned great embarrassment. That is not the case now. I know Sultán Mahmúd; and from his character, am assured he will never undertake an expedition without calculating all the chances. If he attack and conquer a weak woman, where is the glory of such an achievement? If he be repulsed, the latest ages will hear of the shame of such a defeat!" Mahmúd, either swayed by the above reasons, or others of more weight, did not prosecute his designs upon Rei, till Majd-uddaula was of age, and had assumed the reins of government. He then advanced an army; by the leader of which the prince was deluded to an interview, and seized: his treasures and dominions passed into the hands of Mahmúd; who sent him, and his family prisoners to Ghazní.

**Majd-uddaula,** مجد الدولة, title of 'Abdul Majíd Khán, which see.

**Majd-uddin Ahmad ibn-Muhammad Sajawandi,** مجد الدين احمد ابن محمد سجاوندی, author of a commentary or Tafsír called "'Aín ul-Ma'ání." There is another work of the same title on Súfíism written by Shaháb-uddín Burhánpúrí.

**Majd-uddin Baghdadi,** مجد الدين بغدادی, a pupil and disciple of Shaikh Najm-uddín Kubrá. He is stated to have been a very religious and upright man, and was employed as a physician to Sultán Muhammad surnamed Kutb-uddín king of Khwárizm. It is said that he privately got married to the mother of the Sultán, who no sooner heard of it, than he ordered Majd-uddín to be thrown into a lake where he died. This circumstance took place 1219 A. D., 616 A. H., and a short time after, the Sultán was defeated and his country pillaged by Changez Khán.

**Majd-uddin Bilkani,** مجد الدين بيلقاني, an author.

**Majd-uddin Hamkar Farsi,** مجد الدين همكر فارسي, also called Majd-uddín Haibat-ulláh and Majd Hamkar, *i. e.*, Majd the weaver. His poetical title is Majd and Rihí. He was a native of Shíráz and derived his descent from Anúsherwán. He was in high favour with the Atábak Sa'd Abú Bakr bin-Zangí and a cotemporary of Sa'dí. Under Abákáán, the Tartar king of Persia, he was made governor of Shíráz where he died upwards of 90 years of age in 1287 A. D., 686 A. H., and left a Díwán in Persian. In his time, people used to call him the king of poets.

**Majd-uddin Isma'il, Shaikh,** شيخ مجد الدين اسمعيل, was Kází of Shíráz in the reign of Sháh Shaikh 'Abú Is-hák Khwája Háfiz who praises him in one of his odes, and has found the year of his demise to be contained in the words "Rahmat Hak" *i. e.*, the mercy of God. He died on Wednesday the 29th of July, 1355 A. D., 18th Rajab, 756 A. H.

**Majd-uddin Khalil,** مجد الدين خليل, a poet who was a contemporary of Khákání and wrote poetry in his praise.

**Majd-uddin Muhammad bin-Ya'kub bin-Muhammad,** مجد الدين بن محمد بن يعقوب بن محمد, commonly called Fírózábádí, is the author of the much-esteemed and very copious Lexicon in Arabic called the "Kámús," or "Bahr ul-Muhít," The Ocean, dedicated to bin-Abbás, prince of Arabia Felix. He died 1414 A. D., 817 A. H., *vide* Fírózábádí.

**Majd ul-Mulk,** مجد الملك, a nobleman of the court of Sultán Abká Khán. He was put to death at the instigation of Shams-uddín Muhammad commonly called Sáhib Díwán, on suspicion of sorcery, in the reign of Sultán Ahmad Khán, in August, 1282 A. D., 20th Jumáda I, 681 A. H., and not long after Shams-uddín had to undergo the same fate.

**Majir,** مجير, *vide* Mujír.

**Ma'jiz,** معجز, *vide* Nizám Khán Ma'jiz.

**Ma'jizi,** معجزی, a poet who was a cotemporary of Rukn-uddín Kabáí, and master of the poet Badr-uddín Jájurmí.

**Majju Khan, Nawab,** مجو خان نواب, a chief of the rebels who caused himself to be proclaimed Nawáb of Murádábád, and instigated the people to murder and plunder Europeans, was captured with his son in the latter part of April, 1858 A. D.

**Majlisi,** مجلسي, *vide* Muhammad Bákir Majlisí.

**Majnun,** مجنون, this name was given to a person whose proper name was Ḳais, after he had fallen in love with Lailá or Lailí. The meaning of the word is a madman; also a man who is transported by love either divine or profane. *Vide* Lailí. Majnún lived in the time of the khalíf Hashám of the house of Umayya, about the year 721 A. D., 103 A. H.

**Majnun,** مجنون, the poetical title of two poets, one of Dehlí and the other of Lakhnau.

**Majruh,** مجروح, takhallus of Munshí Kishun Chand, a Kashmírian, who was living in 1782 A. D., 1196 A. H., at Lakhnau.

**Majzub,** مجذوب, Mirzá Muhammad Majzúb of Tabrez. He is the author of several Masnawís and also of a Díwán which he completed in 1653 A. D., 1063 A. H.

**Majzub,** مجذوب, poetical name of Mirzá Ghulám Haidar Beg, an adopted son of the celebrated poet of India, Souda; was living at Lakhnau in 1800 A. D., 1215 A. H., and had written two Díwáns in Urdú.

**Majzub,** مجذوب, poetical title of Najábat 'Alí Sháh an Urdú poet who died in the year 1819 A. D., 1234 A. H.

**Makanna',** مقنع, *vide* al-Makna' or Makanna.

**Makbul,** مقبول, named Makbúl Ahmad. He is the author of the "Núr-náma," and "Káf-náma," also of a Masnawí in Urdú called "Dard Ulfat." He was living at Lakhnau in 1853 A. D., 1270 A. H.

**Makhdum Jahanian Jahangasht,** مخدوم جهانيان جهان‌گشت, *vide* Shaikh Jalál.

**Makhdum Sharki,** مخدوم شرقي, author of the "Kitáb un-Nawáfiz."

**Makhfi,** مخفي, the poetical title of the princess Zeb un-Nisá Begam, daughter of the emperor 'Alamgír. She is the author of a Díwán and of a Tafsír or Commentary on the Kurán. Makhfí was also the takhallus of Núr Jahán Begam. *Vide* Zeb-Un-Nisá Begam.

**Makin,** مكين, poetical name of Mirzá Muhammad Fákhir a native of Dehlí, who came to Lakhnau in 1759 A. D., 1173 A. H. He is the author of a Díwán. He died in the year 1806 A. D., 1221 A. H.

**Makna',** مقنع, *vide* al-Makna' or Mukanna.

**Makrizi,** مقريزى, author of the work entitled "Kitáb us-Sulúh." He lived about the year 1229 A. D., 626 A. H.

**Makrizi,** مقريزي, whose proper name is Takí-uddín Ahmad was an eminent Arabic historian and geographer, born in 1366 A. D., in Makríz near Balbec. He early devoted himself to the study of history, astrology &c., at Cairo, where also he afterwards held the offices of inspector of weights and Imám of different mosques. Some of his works have been translated into French and Latin. He died in 1442 A. D., aged 82 years.

**Maktabi,** مكتبي, a school-master of Shíráz, who is the author of a poem called "Lailí wa-Majnún," composed in 1490 A. D., 895 A. H.

**Maktub Khan,** مكتوب خان, superintendent of the library of the emperor Sháh Jahán.

**Makunda Bramhchari,** مكندہ برمہچاري, a famous Bráhman ascetic. The Hindús insist that the emperor Akbar was a Hindú in a former generation. The proximity of the time in which this famous emperor lived, has forced them, however, to account for this in the following manner:—"There was a holy Bráhman of the above name, who wished very much to become emperor of India, and the only practicable way for him was to die first, and be born again. For this purpose he made a desperate *Tapassia*, wishing to remember then every thing he knew in his present generation. This could not be fully granted; but he was indulged with writing upon a brass plate a few things which he wished more particularly to remember; then he was directed to bury the plate, and promised that he should remember the place in the next generation. Makunda, went to Allahábád, buried the plate and then buried himself. Nine months after he was born in the character of Akbar, who, as soon as he ascended the throne, went to Allahábád, and easily found the spot where the brass plate was buried." (*Mill's British India*, Vol. II, page 152.) The translation of the inscription on the brass plate, is as follows: "In the Sambat year 1598 on the 12th day of the 2nd fortnight of the month of Mágh, I Makunda Bramhchárí, whose food was nothing but milk, sacrificed myself at Parág (Allahábád) the grand place of worship, with the design that I should become the ruler of the whole world." The above date corresponds with the 27th of January, 1542 A. D., and Akbar was born on Sunday the 15th of October the same year, being three or four days less than nine lunar months after the above circumstance.

**Maldeo Rao,** مالديو راو, a rájá of Márwár of the Ráthor tribe of rájpúts, and a descendant of Jodhá Ráo who founded Jódhpúr. He acquired a pre-eminence in Rájpútána in 1532 A. D., and is styled by Firishta, "the most potent prince in Hindústán." Powerful as he was, however, he was compelled to succumb to the emperor Akbar, and to pay reluctant homage at the court of the Mughal. After his death his son Udai Singh succeeded him.

**Malhar Rao Gaekowar,** ملهار راو گايكهوار, Rájá of Baroda succeeded to the ráj after the death of his brother Khánde Ráo on the 29th November, 1870, aged 42. His father was called Mahárájá Kharide Ráo Gaekowar, Sona Khaskhail Shamsher Bahádur, G. C. S. I. He is fifth in descent from Piláji, the second Gaekowar and sixth from Damají the first Gaekowar. When Sir Seymour Fitzgerald sent a peremptory message directing his brother Khánde Ráo to replace his minion (Díwán) by some man of character, the Gaekowar fell into so violent a rage, that the conflict of passion deprived him of life. At that time Malhár Ráo the present ruler was a prisoner. He had been confined for years on suspicion of having attempted his brother's life, and from his captivity at Padra he was called to a throne by the British Government. Colonel Phayre narrowly escaped lately being poisoned by him.

**Malhar Rao Holkar I,** ملهار راو هلكر. The Holkar family are of the Dhúngar or Shepherd tribe. The derivation of the name Holkar or more properly Halkar, is from Hal a village, and Kar an inhabitant. Malhár Ráo who was the first prince of this family, was an officer in the service of the first Peshwá Bájí Ráo, and was one of the earliest Marhatta adventurers in the expeditions to the northward; he killed Girdhar Bahádur Súbadár of Málwá in 1726 or 1729 A. D. The time when he obtained any local authority was in 1728 A. D., the district of Indor was assigned to him by the Peshwa in jágír about the year 1733. He was present at the battle of Panipat 14th January 1761, died in 1768 A. D., and was succeeded by his wife Ahlia Baí, who resigned the military power to Tokají Holkar. The original family being thus extinct, Ahlia Bái, Khánde Ráo's widow, elected Takóji Holkar the nephew of Malhár Ráo to the principality. He had four sons, Káshí Ráo and Malhár Ráo by his wife, and Jaswant Ráo and Etojí by his mistress.

*The Holkar Family.*

1. Malhár Ráo Holkar I.
2. Mallhí Ráo, grandson of ditto, succeeded under regency of Ahlia Bái, his mother, and died in 1767 A. D.
3. Takojí Holkar.
4. Káshí Ráo.
5. Jaswant Ráo.
6. Malhár Ráo II.
7. Harí Ráo Holkar.

**Malhar Rao Holkar,** ملهار راو هلکر, a son of Takojí Holkar, rájá of Indor, killed in battle against Daulat Ráo Sindhia in September, 1797 A. D. *Vide* Káshí Ráo.

**Malhar Rao Holkar II,** ملهار راو هلکر, the adopted or illegitimate son and successor of Jaswant Ráo Holkar the son of Takojí Holkar. He succeeded his father as rájá of Indor in 1811 A. D. After the battle of Mahadpúr, a peace was concluded by Government with Malhár Ráo on the 6th January, 1818 A. D. He died in 1834 and was succeeded by Martand Ráo his adopted son who was soon after dispossessed by Harí Ráo Holkar, and after him succeeded by Khánde Ráo who dying without issue, the East India Company assumed the right of nominating Mulkerjí Ráo.

**Malika Bano Begam,** ملكه بانو بیگم, the eldest daughter of 'Asaf Khán, wazír, and sister of Mumtáz Mahal. She was married to Saif Khán surnamed Mírzá Safí, son of Amánat Khán; he was an amír of 5000, and died in Bengal 1639 A. D., 1049 A. H. Malika Báno died in 1640 A. D., 1050 A. H., during the reign of Sháh Jahán.

**Malika Jahan,** ملكه جهان, a princess of Dehlí married to Husain Sháh Sharkí, king of Jaunpúr.

**Malika Jahan,** ملكه جهان, a wife of the emperor Jahángír and daughter of Rawal Bhím of Jísalmír whose brother's name was Rawal Kalyán.

**Malika Zamana,** ملكه زمانه, the daughter of the emperor Farrukh-siyar, married to Muhammad Sháh, emperor of Dehlí in 1722 A. D., 1135 A. H. The year of her death is not known, but she lies buried in a small tomb out of the Kábul gate of Dehlí.

**Malik Alashtar,** ملك الاشتر, a Saracen chief who served under 'Abú 'Ubaida and subsequently under 'Alí. He was poisoned on his way to Egypt by order of Muáwia I, in 658 A. D., 38 A. H.

**Malik Ambar Habshi,** ملك عنبر حبشي, an Abyssinian, who rose from the condition of a slave to great influence and command in the Dakhin. When Ahmadnagar was taken by prince Dánìál in 1600 A. D., 1009 A. H., Malik Ambar and Rájú Minnán a Dakhin chief, divided the remaining territories between them, leaving to a nominal Sultán, Murtazá Nizám Sháh II whom they had placed on the throne on the capture of Bahádur Nizám Sháh, only the fortress of Ousa with a few villages for his support. About this period several commotions happening in the Dehlí Government, owing to the rebellion of Sultán Salím, the death of Akbar, and revolt of Sultán Khusro, successively, Ambar had leisure to regulate his country, levy great armies, and even dared to seize several of the imperial districts. When the authority of the emperor Jahángír was established, he sent frequent armies to the Dakhin, but Ambar was not to be subdued. He at length gave up the places taken from the Mughals to the prince Sháh Jahán, to whose interest he became attached, and continued loyal till his death which took place in the year 1626 A. D., 1035 A. H., in the 80th year of his age, He was buried in Daulatábád, under a splendid dome which he had erected. After his death Fatha Khán his son succeeded him.

**Malik Aziz,** ملك عزیز, *vide* Malik ul-Azíz 'Usmán, or 'Abú'l Fatha 'Usmán.

**Malik Dinar,** ملك دینار, a Turk of the tribe of Ghuz. He in 1187 A. D., 583 A. H., dispossessed Bahrám Sháh the last prince of Kirmán of the family of Kádard Saljúkí, and put an end to that dynasty.

**Malik Fakhr-uddin,** ملك فخرالدین, king of Bengal commonly called Púrbí. The first Muhammadan chief who invaded Bengal was Malik Muhammad Bakhtyár, in the reign of Kutb-uddín Eybak, king of Dehlí, 1191 A. D., 587 A. H. After him the several governors of that country were appointed from that capital. Malik Fakhr-uddín was originally a soldier in the service of Kadar Khán, governor of Bengal, whom he put to death in the reign of Tughlak Sháh about the year 1338 A. D., 739 A. H., proclaimed himself king, and declared his independence of the throne of Dehlí. He reigned two years and five months, when he was defeated, taken prisoner in a pitched battle in 1340 A. D., and put to death by Malik 'Alí Mubárik, who had also proclaimed himself king under the title of Alá-uddín.

**Malik ibn-Anas, Imam,** امام مالک ابن آنس, one of the four learned doctors of the Sunnís, who are the founders of their faith. He was born at Madína in 714 A. D., 95 A. H., and died there in the reign of the khalíf Hárún al-Rashíd, on Sunday the 28th June, 795 A. D., 7th Rabí' II, 179 A. H., and was buried in the cemetery called Al-Bakía. He is the founder of the second Sunní sect, and is sometimes called "Imám Dár ul-Hijrat," from the circumstance of his birth and death occurring at the city of Madína. In his youth, he had the advantage of the society of Sihl bin-Sa'd, almost the sole surviving companion of the Prophet; and it is supposed that from him he derived his extreme veneration for the traditions. He is the author of the Arabic work called "Muwatta" being a collection of Traditions, and is always looked upon as next in point of authority to the six Sahibs.

**Malik ibn-Nawera,** مالك ابن نویرة, the chief of those who refused to pay the Zakát (or that part of a man's substance which is consecrated to God, as tithes, alms, and the like, and the payment of which is strictly enjoined by the Muhammadan law). He was a person of considerable figure, being the chief of an eminent family among the Arabs, and celebrated for his skill in poetry, as well as his manly qualities and horsemanship. He was murdered by order of Khálid ibn-Walíd in the year 633 A. D., 12 A. H.

**Malik 'Imad,** ملک عماد, a poet who was a cotemporary of Imám Muhammad Ghazzálí.

**Malik, Imam,** امام مالك يعني ابن انس *vide* Imám Malik or Malik Ibn-Anas.

**Malik Jahir,** ملك جاحر, also called Náth Bhanjan. In the well-known town of Mhow in Azimgarh, there is a place which obtains the distinguished title of "Náth Bhanjan" from the great exploits of a saint called Malik Jáhir who ejected the evil genius Deo Náth, together with the original Hindús, and colonized the place with Muhammadans. The story is thus related: During the reign of Jahángír, king of Dehlí, about 1609 A. D., one Abhimán Singh, a Rájpút of the Jatran tribe, having separated from his brethren, owing to the inadequacy of the share allotted to him in his hereditary possessions, took service under that monarch, and on his having embraced the religion of Muhammad, Jahángír granted to him the whole Zamindárí of Azimgarh, under the title of Rájá Abhimán Singh 'Alí Muhammad Nazir-uddaula Khán. From that period up to the time the Nawáb of Audh resumed the grant, the Muhammadans had the supremacy over the Hindús, but in 1801 A. D., when the district was ceded to the British, the Hindús taking courage came and resided there; since then there have always been feuds between the parties.

**Malik Kummi, Mulla,** ملا ملك قمي, a native of Kumm in Persia. He was an excellent poet, and came to the Dakhin in the year 1579 A. D., 987 A. H. He was at first employed by Murtazá Nizám Sháh, and then by Burhán Nizám Sháh, kings of Ahmadnagar. Subsequently he went to Bíjápúr where he was much respected, and the highest honours conferred on him by the king of that place Ibráhím 'Adil Sháh II. He gave his daughter in marriage to Mulla Zahúrí a celebrated poet of that court. Mulla Malik died in 1616 A. D., 1025 A. H., and Zahúrí one year after him. He was called Malik ul-Kalám or the king of poetry. He is the author of a Díwán and several Masnawís.

**Malik Mansur Muhammad-bin-'Usman,** ملك منصور محمد بن عثمان, third Sultán of Egypt of the race of Ayyúb, succeeded his father in November, 1198 A. D., and died in 1200 A. D., when Malik 'Adil Saif-uddín the son of Ayyúb succeeded him and reigned 18 years.

**Malik Mansur,** ملك منصور, *vide* Núr-uddín 'Alí.

**Malik Moizz-uddin, Eaibak,** ایبک ملک معز الدین, a Turkomán slave of the Ayyúbite dynasty who married the Queen Malika Shajrat ul-Dar, the last of the Ayyúbite family and reigned in Egypt. He began his reign in 1250 A. D., 655 A. H., and was murdered in 1257 A. D., 655 A. H. His descendants ruled the country for nearly a hundred years.

*List of the Sultáns or Mamlúks who reigned in Egypt and Hamath in Syria, after the Sultáns of the Ayyúbite family.*

| | A. D. | A. H. |
|---|---|---|
| Malik Moizz Azz-uddín Eaibak Turkmaní Sáhahí began to reign, ........ | 1250 | 648 |
| „ Mansúr Núr-uddín 'Alí bin-Moizz (imprisoned by Muzaffar, ........ | | 655 |
| „ Muzaffar Kut uz-Moizzí (11 months), | | 657 |
| „ Táhir Rukn-uddín, .............. | | 658 |
| „ Sa'íd Muhammad Násir-uddín, .... | | 676 |
| „ 'Adil Badr-uddín (4 months), ...... | | 678 |
| „ Mansúr Abúl Ma'álí Kaládun Sálahí, | | 678 |
| Malik Ashraf Saláh-uddín Khalíl, ........ | | 689 |
| „ Násir Muhammad bin-Kaládún (reigned 44 years), ............ | | 693 |
| „ 'Adil Kutbagha Mansúrí, .......... | | |
| „ Mansúr Hisám-uddín, reigned 2 years died 698 A. D., ................ | | |
| „ Muzaffar Rukn-uddín, reigned 10th died 709 A. D., ................ | | |
| „ Mansúr Abú Bakr (2 months), .... | | |
| „ Ashraf Kuchak (8 months, ........ | | |
| „ Násir Ahmad, died 745 A. D., ...... | | |
| „ Sáláh Ismaíl 'Abú'l Fida, the author of an abridgement of Universal History down to his time. He succeeded his brother Násir Ahmad in 1344 A. D., 745 A. H., .... | | |

In process of time, the old Mamlooks grew proud, insolent and lazy: and the Borgites, a new Militia and slaves of the old Mamlooks, taking advantage of this, rose upon their masters, deprived them of the government and transferred it to themselves about the year 1382 A. D, The Borgites also assumed the name of Mamlooks; and were famous for their valour and ferocity. Their dominion lasted till the year 1517, when they were invaded by Salím I the Turkish Sultán, who defeated them, took possession of their country, and beheaded Tuman Bey the last of the Borgites with 30,000 prisoners.

**Malik Muhammad Jaesi,** ملك محمد جايسي, a poet who was a native of Jáes and the author of the story of Padmáwat in Hindí verse. He lived in the time of the emperor Jahángír.

**Malik Nasir Khan Faruki,** ملك نصيرخان فاروقي, son of Malik Rájá, after whose death in April, 1399 A. D., 801 A. H., he also like his father assumed the ensigns of royalty at Khándesh, and built Burhánpúr. Learned men were invited from all parts, and literature was much promoted. He seized the fort of Asír from 'Asá Ahír, reigned 40 lunar years, and died on the 21st September, 1437 A. D., 20th Rabí' I, 841 A. H. He was buried in the family vault at Tálner by the side of his father, and was succeeded by his son Mírán 'Adil Farúkí.

**Malik Raja Faruki,** ملك راجة فاروقي. The first person who assumed independence in the province of Khándesh was Malik Rájá, the son of Khán Jahán Farúkí, whose ancestors were among the most respectable nobles at the Dehlí court, in the reigns of Alá-uddín Khiljí and Muhammad Tughlak. At the death of his father he was very young, and inherited only a small patrimony. About the year 1370 A. D., 772 A. H., he was appointed governor of Khándesh by Fíróz Sháh Tughlak, and the jágír of Talner conferred on him. After the death of that prince when Diláwar Khán Ghorí assumed independence in Málwá, an intimate connection took place between the latter and Malik Rájá, so much so, that Diláwar Khán gave his daughter in marriage to Malik Nasír the son of Malik Rájá. He reigned 29 lunar years and died on the 28th April, 1399 A. D., 22nd Shabán, 801 A. H. He was buried at the town of Tálner, and was succeeded by his son Malik Nasír Khán.

*The following are the names of the kings of Khándesh.*

1. Malik Rájá.
2. Malik Nasír Khán.
3. Mírán 'Adil Khán.
4. Mírán Mubárik.
5. 'Adil Khán I or 'Alí Sháh.
6. Dáúd Khán.
7. 'Adil Khán II ('Azim Humayún 'Alam Khán).
8. Mírán Muhammad Sháh.
9. Mírán Mubárik II.
10. Mírán Muhammad.
11. Rájá 'Alí Khán.
12. Bahádur Sháh.

**Malik Sarwar,** ملك سرور, *vide* Khwája Jahán.

**Malik Shah,** ملکشاه جلال الدین, surnamed Jalál-uddín was the third Sultán of the first dynasty of the Saljúkís or Saljúkides. He succeeded his father Alp Arsalán in December, 1072 A. D., 465 A. H., and reigned twenty years. His right to the crown was disputed by his brother Kádir Beg, also called Kádard (which see) prince of Kirmán; but that chief was defeated and taken prisoner, and afterwards poisoned or put to death. Malik Sháh subdued almost the whole of Syria and Egypt: and being more fortunate than his father, not only conquered Bukhára, Samarkand and Khwárizm, but received homage from the tribes beyond Jaxartes. After the death of his wazír Nizám ul-Mulk, he moved from Isfahán to Baghdád, with the design of transplanting the khalíf Al-Muktadí, and fixing his own residence in the capital of the Moslem world. The feeble successor of Muhammad obtained a respite of ten days; and before the expiration of the term, the Sultán was summoned by the angel of death. He died in the 38th year of his age in the month of November, 1092 A. D., Shawwál, 485 A. H., a few days after Nizám ul-Mulk his wazír, who was assassinated by a follower of Hasan Sabbáh. The greatness and unity of the Saljúkian empire expired in the person of Malik Sháh. He invented an era called Táríkh Maliksháhí or Jalálí (Jalalian Era). This Era, according to Dr. Hyde commences 15th March, 1079 A. D., corresponding with the 11th Ramazán 471 A. H. Malik Sháh left four sons Barkayárak, Muhammad, Sanjar and Mahmúd, all of whom attained power in their turns. Mahmúd the youngest, was only four years of age when his father died: but the ambition of his mother, the Sultána Khátún Turkán, placed the crown upon his infant head. However, she was soon compelled to resign, and after some time they both died, and Sultán Barkayárak succeeded him.

**Malik Sharki, Mirza,** مرزا ملك شرقي, an author.

**Malik ul-Afzal,** ملك الافضل نورالدين علي, surnamed Núr-uddín 'Alí, the eldest of the seventeen sons of Sálah-uddín Yúsaf ibn-Ayyúb. On the death of his father at Damascus in 1193 A. D., 589 A. H., he took possession of that kingdom, whilst his brother Malik ul-'Azíz 'Usmán obtained that of Egypt, and their brother Malik uz-Záhir continued to hold Aleppo. Damascus was afterwards besieged and taken by his uncle Malik ul-'Adil Saif-uddín Abú Bakr (the Saphadin of Christian writers). Núr-uddín 'Alí in a poetical address to the khalíf Násir, lamented the similarity of his own fate to that of the khalíf 'Alí ibn-Abú Tálib (his namesake) in being thus excluded from his rights by Abú Bakr and 'Usmán; the khalíf in his reply consoled him by the assurance that in him he should find the Násir (protector) whom 'Alí had sought in vain; but the intercession of the khalíf was unavailing to procure the restitution of any part of his territories. In 1198 A. D., however, on the death of his brother, the Sultán of Egypt, Núr-uddín became Atábak, or guardian, to his infant nephew Malik ul-Mansúr, and attempted by the aid of his brother, the Sultán of Aleppo, to recover Damascus from his uncle; but the expedition failed, and Saif-uddín retaliated by invading Egypt, and expelled the young Sultán and his guardian, 1199 A. D. The unfortunate Núr-uddín now retired to Samosata, where he died apparently without issue. He was born in June, 1171 A. D., whilst his father was acting as wazír to the Egyptians. He died suddenly in February, 1225 A. D., Safar 622 A. H., and was buried in Aleppo. *Vide* Núr-uddín 'Alí (Malik ul-Afzal).

**Malik ul-'Aziz 'Usman,** ملک العزیز عثمان, *vide* 'Abú'l Fatha 'Usmán.

**Malli** or **Mallhi Rao Holkar,** مالی یا ملہاری راؤ ھلکر, Rájá of Indor was the son of Khánde Ráo, and grandson of Malhár Ráo I whom he succeeded in 1766 A. D., and died after a reign of nine months. After his death the original family being extinct, Ahlia Bái, the widow of Khánde Ráo, elected Takojí to the ráj.

**Mallu 'Adil Shah,** ملو عادل شاه, of Bíjápúr, succeeded his father Ismá'íl 'Adil Sháh in August, 1534 A. D., Safar, 941 A. H., and was on account of his shameful vices, blinded and deposed after an inglorious reign of only six months by order of his grandmother, and his younger brother Ibráhím was raised to the throne of Bíjápúr in the beginning of the year 1535 A. D., 941 A. H.

**Mallu Khan,** ملو خان, entitled Kádir Sháh, was the ruler of Málwá when Sher Sháh took it about the year 1542 A. D., 949 A. H., and made it over to one of his own officers named Shujá'at Khán or Shujá'a Khán Súr, which see, as also Kádir Sháh.

**Maluk Shah,** ملوك شاه, the father of the historian Shaikh 'Abdul Kádir of Badáon. He died in 1561 A. D., 969 A. H. He is the author of the work called "Jiláe ul-Khawátir."

**Malul,** ملول, the poetical name of Sháh Sharaf-uddín, a dervish of Murádábád. He wrote two Persian Díwáns in which he used the takhallus of Ilhám. He is also the author of a poem called "Haft Mykhána," which he composed in 1777 A. D., 1191 A. H.

**Malwa,** مالوه, kings of, *vide* Diláwar Khán.

**Mamluk,** مملوک, this word signifies in Arabic, a slave in general; but in particular, it means the Turkish and Circassian slaves, whom the kings of the posterity of Sálah-uddín (Saladin) had instructed in military exercises, and who at last made themselves masters of Egypt, and are sufficiently known to us by the name of Mamlukes. These Mamlukes reigned in Egypt 275 lunar years, that is to say, from 1250 to 1517 A. D., 648 to 923 A. H., when Salím I, emperor of the Turks, entirely subdued and exterminated them. The first king of this dynasty was Malik Maizz 'Azz-uddín Eybak, which see.

**Mamnun,** ممنون, poetical title of Mír Nizám-uddín, a son of Kamar-uddín Khán Minnat. He flourished in the time of Akbar Sháh II, king of Dehlí, and is the author of two Persian and Urdú Díwáns. His ancestors were of Sonpat, but he was a native of Dehlí. He was employed by the English Government as a Sadar-us-Sadúr at Ajmer. He died in the year 1844 A. D., 1260 A. H.

**Mamun,** مامون, the son of Hárún al-Rashíd, *vide* Al-Mámún.

**Manbhaoti Begam,** من بهاوتي بيگم, one of the concubines of the emperor Akbar. She built at Agrah on a spot of 40 bighas a garden of which no sign remains now.

**Mangu Kaan** or **Khan,** منگو قاآن یا منگو خان, emperor of Tartary, was the eldest son of Túlí Khán, the son of Changez Khán. He succeeded his cousin Kayúk Khán, the son of Oktái Khán, over the kingdoms of Tartary and Persia about the year 1243 A. D., 640 A. H. He died after a reign of sixteen years in 1258 A. D., 654 A. H., and was succeeded in the kingdom of Tartary by his son Kabláí Khán; his brother Halákú Khán became the sole master of Persia.

**Mani,** ماني, whom we call Manes, was the founder of the sect of the Manichís or Manicheans. In the reign of Sháhpúr, the son of Ardisher, king of Persia, about the year 277 A. D., a painter, named Máni, having learned from the conversation of some Christians, *that the Redeemer had promised to send a Comforter, after him,* formed the wild design of passing for the Paraclete; and, as no opinions are so absurd, as not to be embraced, he soon drew together a multitude of proselytes. Sháhpúr was enraged at this imposture, and wished to punish the author of it; but Máni found means to escape, and fled as far as the borders of China, having first told his followers, that he was going to heaven, and promised to meet them in a certain grot, at the end of the year. In this retreat he amused himself with painting a number of strange figures and views, which at the year's end, he shewed to his disciples, as a work given to him by angels. He was a very ingenious artist, and had a lively fancy, so that his pictures, which were finely coloured, easily persuaded the credulous multitude, in the infancy of the art in Asia, that they were really divine; they were bound together in a book called Artang. which is often alluded to by the Persian poets. Mingling the pure doctrines of Christianity with paganism, he taught that there were two principles of all things, coeternal and coeval, that is, God and the Devil, that from the former all good, and from the latter all evil proceeded. The good being, he called, the author of the new testament, the bad of the old. God, he added, created the soul, the devil, the body. He pretended also to work miracles, and was therefore sent for by Sháhpúr to cure his son, but his pretended power failed him, the child died in his arms, and the disappointed father ordered the prophet to be flayed alive, and his skin stuffed with chaff to be hung up at the gates of the capital, where Epiphanius who refuted his doctrines, saw it. Some say this impostor was put to death in the reign of Bahrám, grandson of Sháhpúr.

**Mani,** ماني, a poet, who although called Kásagar Mázandaráni, *i. e.*, a porcelain manufacturer of Mázandarán; yet his talents introduced him to Muhammad Muhsin Mirzá, a son of Sulṭán Husain Mirzá, in whose service he was killed by the Uzbaks in 1507 A. D., 913 A. H. He is the author of a Díwán.

**Ma'ni,** معني, the poetical name of Ráe Bijai Mal, a brother of Imtiyáz, was living in 1760 A. D., 1174 A. H., and did military service under Nawáb Shujá'-uddaula.

**Manija Begam,** مانيجه بيگم, sister of Núr Jahán Begam, *vide* Kasim Khán Jawení.

**Manik Pal,** مانک پال, rájá of Karoulí. He died in 1805 A. D., and was succeeded by a boy then 13 years of age. In December, 1817 A. D., the Karaulí chief signed a treaty, and put himself under the protection of the British Government.

**Manka al-Hindi** منكه الهندي. Ibn-Abu Usaibia in his work, entitled Ayún al-Anba, on the physicians of India. says, that Manka of India was one of the most distinguished philosophers in the sciences of India, and was well acquainted both with the language of India and Persia. It was he who translated the book of Shánák the Indian, treating on poisons, from the Indian to the Persian language. He lived in the days of Hárún al-Rashíd, and came during his reign, from India to Irák, and attached himself to him.

**Manni Ram Seith,** مني رام, the great banker of Mathura, died in July, 1836 A. D.

**Mannu Lal,** منولال, a Hindú, who is the author of the work called "Guldastáe Nashát."

**Manohar Das,** منوهرداس, *vide* Tousaní.

**Mansa Ram,** منسه رام, father of Rájá Chyte Singh of Banaras. He possessed originally but half the village of Gangapúr, by additions to which, in the usual modes of Hindústán, he laid the foundation of the great zamíndarí of Banaras. He died in 1740 A. D., and was succeeded by his son Balwant Singh.

**Man Singh,** مان سنگه, a rájá of Gwáliar who lived in the time of Sulṭán Sikandar Lodí and his son Sulṭán Ibráhím Lodí, and died about the year 1518 A. D., 924 A. H. He was a prince of great valour and capacity. His son Bikarmájít succeeded him in the rájáship and was living at the time the emperor Babar conquered India.

**Man Singh,** مان سنگه, son or nephew of Rájá Bhagwán Dás Kachhwáhá, ruler of Amer in Ajmer now called Jaipúr and Jainagar. He was appointed governor of Kábul by the emperor Akbar in 1587 A. D., 995 A. H., and in the next year of Behár, Hájípúr and Patna, and after the death of his father in 1589 A. D., 998 A. H., he was honoured with the title of rájá and rank of 7000, and made governor of Bengal. He had 1500 concubines, and every one of them had children; but they all died before him. Mán Singh died in the ninth year of the emperor Jahángír 1614 A. D., 1023 A. H., in the Dakhin, and sixty of his concubines burnt themselves with his corpse. His second son Rájá Bháo Singh succeeded him and died of drinking. The eldest son of Mán Singh was Rájá Partap Singh who died before his father and left a son named Mahá Singh who served under the emperor Jahángír, and after the death of his grandfather and uncle was honoured with the title of Rájá. Mán Singh had built a house on the banks of the river Jamna of which at present towards the river only two broken Burj are to be seen. The Muhalla Mánpánah close to the Jamna Masjid at Ágrah is still very well-known. He died at Berár in 1617 A. D., 1026 A. H. His son Mirzá Rájá Jai Singh served under Sháh Jahán and 'Alamgír. He was poisoned by his son Kírat Singh about the year 1625 A. D. After him his son Rám Singh was reduced to a mansab of 4000; Bishun Singh, reduced to a mansab of 3000, and after him come Jai Singh Sawai, son of Bishun Singh, which see.

**Man Singh,** مان سنگه, rájá of Jodhpúr or Márwár, was a descendant of rájá Jaswant Singh Ráṭhorí, the earliest rájá of this country on record. He succeeded rájá Bhím Singh in 1803 or 1804 A. D. Disasters or disappointments either soured the temper or affected the reason of Mán Singh, who became one of the most sanguinary monsters that ever disgraced the gaddí. His death was announced on the 20th of September, 1843 A. D. The Márwár succession question was settled in favour of Ahmadnagar on the 7th November, 1843, the choice falling not on the young heir of that house, but on his father Takht Singh, who was unanimously elected, and whose son accompanied him as prince royal. Takht Singh is a descendant of the Herori Jaswant. Several of the Zanana ladies and three or four slave girls became Suttí.

**Man Singh, Raja,** مان سنگه راجا, of Audh. His title was Mahárájá Sir Mán Singh Bahádur Kayam Jung, K. C. S. I. He died at Ajuddhia on the 11th October, 1870 A. D. He was Vice-President of the British Indian Association, a post which he held with great success.

**Mansur,** منصور, a khalíf of Baghdád, *vide* Al-Mansúr.

**Mansur,** منصور, the son of Báiḳara Mirzá, and father of Sulṭán Husain Mirzá of Hirát.

**Mansur,** منصور, a poet, who is the author of a Díwán in which are some Kasídas in praise of Sháh Abbas II, who died in 1666 A. D., 1077 A. H., and of Abbas Ḳulí Beg.

**Mansur I, Samani, Amir,** امير منصور ساماني, a prince of the race of the Samanides, was the son of Amír Núh I, and brother to Amír 'Abdul Malik whom he succeeded 961 A. D., 350 A. H. He compelled the Dílamí ruler of Fars and 'Iráḳ to pay him an annual tribute of 150,000 dínars of gold: and the peace, by which this tribute was fixed was cemented by his marriage with the daughter of Rukn-uddaula, the reigning prince of that family. Amír Mansúr died after a reign of 15 lunar years on the 15th of March, 976 A. D., 11th Rajab, 365 A. H., and was succeeded by his son Amír Núh II. His wazír Abú 'Alí bin-Muhammad translated into Persian the Táríkh Tabarí.

**Mansur II Samani, Amir,** امير منصور ثاني, succeeded his father Amír Núh II, in 997 A. D., 387 A. H., on the throne of Khurásán. He occupied it for a short period (little more than a year) which was marked with disgrace and misfortune. He was obliged to fly before his rebellious nobles, who afterwards deprived him of his sight and elevated his younger brother, 'Abdul Malik II, to the throne 998 A. D., 388 A. H.

**Mansur 'Ali Khan,** منصور علي خان, Nawáb of Audh, *vide* Safdar Jang.

**Mansur 'Ali Khan, Sayyad,** منصور علي خان سيد, the present Nawáb of Murshidábád. He was living in 1868.

**Mansur Hallaj,** منصور حلاج, the surname of Shaikh Husain Halláj, a celebrated ascetic, who was a native of Baiza, and originally a cotton-thrasher. The Musalmáns differed in their opinions about the character of this person. Some took him to be a saint, and gave out that he performed miracles; others believed him to be a sorcerer or a juggler, and that he only deceived people with his tricks. He was, however, condemned and sentenced by the khalíf of Baghdád, Maḳtadir, and was put to death, because he used to proclaim "An-ul-haḳ," *i. e.*, "I am the truth," or in other words, "I am God." When they had taken him to the place of execution, they first cut off both his hands, and then his legs; they plucked out his eyes, cut out his tongue, and separated his head from his body. They then burned his mangled corpse to ashes, and threw it into the Tigris. This circumstance took place in the year 919 A. D., 306 A. H., but according to Ibn-Khallikán, on the 24th Zi-Ḳa'da, 309 A. H., corresponding with 26th March, 922 A. D. Shaikh Husain is commonly called Mansúr Halláj though it is the name of his father. He is considered by the Súfís to be one of their most eminent spiritual leaders, who, they believe, had attained the fourth or last stage of Súfiism. An inspired Súfí is said to have demanded of the Almighty why he permitted Mansúr to suffer? The reply was, "This is the punishment for the revealer of secrets."

**Mansur ibn-Alkaem ibn-Almahdi,** منصور ابن القايم ابن المهدي, a prince of Africa who died on Friday the 19th of March, 953 A. D., Friday 29th Shawwál, 341 A. H.

**Mansur, Shah,** منصور شا, *vide* Sháh Mansúr.

**Mansur, Khwaja,** منصور خواجه, *vide* Khwája Mansúr.

**Manu,** من, the son of Brahmá, the first male according to the Hindús. Kapíl was Manu's grandson, and the author of the Sankh Shastar in which he mentions the Gíta, which relates of transactions, which took place at the end of the Dwápar, and the beginning of the Kaljug. Manu is the author of the Institutes that goes by his name; it is said that it existed in the Satjug according to this shlók, "When 1010 years of the Satjug were expired, I Manu, at the full moon of the month Bhadr, by the command of Brahmá finished this Shastar."

**Manuchehr,** منوچهر, one of the ancient kings of Persia of the first or Pishdádián dynasty, who succeeded Faredún. He was a good and pious monarch: but the great prosperity which attended his reign was chiefly owing to the wisdom and courage of his prime-minister, Sám, the son of Narímán, whose descendants Zál and Rustam, even during this reign obtained a celebrity which has led Persian historians and poets to speak only of those events that are connected with their biography. Manúchehr died after a reign of 120 years, and was succeeded by his son Nauzar, in the latter part of whose reign died Sám, the son of Narímán. After the death of Sám, Pashang the king of Túrán invaded Persia with a force of 30,000 men, commanded by his son, Afrásiáb. Two engagements and two single combats took place, Nauzar himself was discomfited by Afrásiáb, who soon afterwards took him prisoner and slew him. This happened in the seventh year of the reign of that unfortunate monarch.

**Manuchehr,** منوچهر, *vide* Ḳábús.

**Manuchehr, Malik or Khakan,** ملک منوچهر يا خاقان, ruler of Shírwán whose panegyrist was Khákání the poet. He was a descendant of Bahrám Chobín, and his title was Khákán, hence the takhallus of Khákání. Manúchehr reigned about the year 1180 A. D., 576 A. H., of the Christian era.

**Manuchehr,** منوچهر, (prince) he was the son of Shaikh Ibráhím, ruler of Shírwán who died in 1417 A. D., 820 A. H. His panegyrist was Kátibí who wrote a chronogram on his death which happened in the year 1412 A. D., 815 A. H., five years before his father.

**Manuchehr,** منوچهر, *vide* Tousaní.

**Manuchehri,** منوچهری, who had the sobriquet of Shast Galla. His name was Hakím Najm-uddín Aḥmad bin-Ya'ḳúb bin-Manúchehrí. He lived at the court of Sulṭán Mahmúd of Ghazní and of his two sons Masa'úd and Muhammad. He acquired much wealth, and hence his sobriquet of Shast Galla, *i. e.*, sixty flocks of sheep. He died in 1090 A. D., 483 A. H., and left a Díwán in Persian.

**Manwi, Maulwi,** مولوی معنوی, an author.

**Manzari,** منظری سمرقندی, of Samarḳand, a poet who was in the service of Bairam Khán at Ágrah, and wrote a poem called "Sháhnámí Khayál," which contains an account of the war of Sikandar Sháh Súr, &c.

**Marghinani,** مرغينانی, his proper name was Burhán-uddín 'Alí bin-Muhammad, but he derived this title from his native country Marghínán a city in Máwarun-nahr. He is the author of the "Hidáya," and several other works. His death happened in 1197 A. D., 593 A. H. *Vide* Burhán-uddín 'Alí.

**Maria,** ماریه, one of the wives of Muhammad by whom he had a son named Ibráhím who died when an infant. She was called Kabtí or Egyptian, because she was sent as a present to Muhammad by Makoukas, king of Alexandria. She died in 637 A. D., 16 A. H.

**Mariam,** مریم. This word in Arabic signifies Mary, and is only applied to the Virgin Mary. The Kurán, in the chapter called Al-Amrán, or the family of Amrán, and in Súra Mariam, confounds Mary the mother of Jesus with Mariam the daughter of Amram and sister of Moses and Aaran. In the book called Al-Sahíh, there is a tradition, that the Apostle of God said, among men there have been many perfect; but among women only four: 'Asia, the wife of Pharaoh; Mary, the daughter of Amrán, Khudyja, the daughter of Khawylid and Fátima, daughter of Muhammad.

**Mariam Makani,** مریم مکانی, a title of Hamída Báno Begam, the mother of the emperor Akbar, which she received after her death. See Hamída Báno.

**Mariam Zamani,** مریم زمانی. She was the daughter of Rájá Beharí Mál Kachwaha, was married to the emperor Akbar Sháh. Her proper name is not known. She was the mother of the emperor Jahángír; she died at A'grah in the time of her son Jahángír in 1623 A. D., 1032 A. H., and the mausoleum at A'grah in Sikandra which was erected by her son over her grave, is called by the people of A'grah, Rauza Mariam.

**Ma'ruf,** معروف, poetical name of Iláhí Bakhsh Khán, younger brother of Fakhr-uddaula Nawáb Ahmad Bakhsh Khán, son of Mirzá 'Arif Khán. He died in the year 1242 A. H., and left two Díwáns in Urdú.

**Ma'ruf Karkhi,** معروف کرخی, he was by birth a Christian, but being convinced that there are not three Gods as the Christians say, but one, he became a convert to Muhammadanism, and his parents followed his example. He afterwards became a very pious Musalmán; was cotemporary with Dáúd Táí and Ibráhím Adham, and became master of Sarí Sakatí. He died in the reign of Mámún, the son of Hárún al-Rashíd on the 31st of August, 815 A. D., 20th Muharram, 200 A. H., and lies buried in a place called Karkh in Baghdád. The heart of Ma'rúf (that is to say the letter R, which is the numeral for 200) is the chronogram for the Hijrí year of his demise.

**Marwan ibn-Hafsa,** مروان ابن حفصه, an eminent Arabian poet, on whom the khalíf Mahdí, on one occasion, bestowed the sum of 70,000 dirhams (£1600) as a reward for merit.

**Marwan I,** مروان ابن الحکم, son of Hakam, was the fourth khalíf of the race of Umayya. He was proclaimed khalíf at Damascus after the death of Mu'áwia II, in 684 A. D., 64 A. H. He was also called, "Ibn-Taríd," the son of the expelled, because Muhammad had banished his father Hakam for divulging a secret. He died after a reign of 298 days on the 12th April, 685 A. D., 2nd Ramazán 65 A. H. He is said by some authors to have been poisoned by his wife, Zainab, the widow of Mu'áwia II. Her, he had married, with a promise that her son Khálid should succeed him, but afterwards altering the succession in favour of his own son 'Abdul Malik, young Khálid reproached him with his breach of promise: upon this Marwán calling him bastard, the child complained to his mother, who to be revenged for this affront, is said to have poisoned him or smothered him with a pillow.

**Marwan II,** مروان الحمار, surnamed Himár or the ass, was the son of Muhammad the son of Hakam, and the fourteenth and last khalíf of the house of Umayya. He was nephew to Marwán I. After deposing Ibráhím the son of Walíd II, he ascended the throne of Damascus in 745 A. D., 26th Zil-hijja, 132 A. H., and was defeated and slain on the 5th August, 750 A. D. in a battle fought against Abú'l Abbás al-Saffáh who was previously proclaimed khalíf by the inhabitants of Kúfa on Friday the 29th of November, 749 A. D., 13th Rabí' II, 132 A. H. Marwán before his accession to the throne, had been governor of Mesopotamia, and had received, by his Georgian warfare, the honorable epithet of the ass of Mesopotamia or Al-Himár, a warlike breed of asses, that never fly from an enemy.

**Masa'ud I, Sultan,** سلطان مسعود اول, son of Sultán Mahmúd of Ghazní. He after cruelly depriving his brother Muhammad of sight, mounted the throne of Ghazní 1030 A. D., 421 A. H. He made several incursions into India to maintain the tranquillity of those possessions which his father had subdued. But he had no time to attack others: all his means were required to defend himself from a formidable tribe of Tartars, called Saljúkí, who had, for a considerable time past, made predatory incursions into Khurásán, and other parts of his dominions. He carried on a petty war against different branches of this powerful tribe for some time, and with various success, till he was completely defeated in a great action fought in Khurásán with Tughral Beg Saljúkí on Friday the 16th of June, 1038 A. D., 9th Ramazán, 429 A. H., and was obliged to fly towards Láhor, which he resolved to make the future capital of his government. On his march, he was deposed by his mutinous army, and his brother Muhammad Makahúl the blind, was again placed on the throne. Masa'úd remained in confinement for several years, and was afterwards assassinated by Ahmad the son of Muhammad Makahúl 1041 A. D., 433 A. H.

**Masa'ud II, Sultan,** سلطان مسعود ثاني, son of Sultán Maudúd, a child of four years old, was raised to the throne of Ghazní after the death of his father in December, 1049 A. D. but was soon deposed after a nominal reign of six days, and Abú'l Hasan 'Alí, the son of Sultán Masa'úd I, was proclaimed emperor.

**Masa'ud III, Sultan,** سلطان مسعود ثالث, the sonof Sultán Ibráhím ascended the throne of Ghazní after the death of his father in 1098 A. D., 492 A. H. He reigned over Ghazní and Láhor 16 years; had for his wife the sister of Sultán Sanjar, the Saljúkide who had made peace with his father. Sultán Masa'úd died in 1114 A. D., 508 A. H., and was succeeded by his son Sherzád or Shernazád.

**Masa'ud IV, Sultan,** سلطان مسعود رابع, the son of Sultán Muhammad Saljúkí, and brother of Tughral II, whom he succeeded to the throne of Hamdan. He began to reign about the year 1134 A. D., 529 A. H., and died 1152 A. D., 1st Rajab, 547 A. H., Atábak Eldiguz was his minister.

**Masa'udi,** مسعودی, the famous historian who visited India, Ceylon and the coast of China in the year 915 A. D. He is the author of the work entitled "Ma'dan ul-Jawáhir" Mines of Gems, of which the first part has been well translated by Dr. A. Sprenger. The first of his compositions is "Akhbár uz-Zaman," an enormous work of at least twenty volumes; the second is the "Kitáb ul-Ausath," being the complement to the Akhbár; and the third "Mines of Gems" or as some call it the "Meadows of Gold," forming at the same time the extract and the supplement of the two others. He died 956 A. D., 345 A. H. In describing the early discoveries of his countrymen inside the Great Pyramid in Egypt, he says, that some of them found in the lowest part of the Pyramid a vase containing a quantity of fluid of an unknown quality. They also discovered in a large hall a quantity of golden coins put up in columns, every piece of which was of the weight of 1000 dinars. In another place they found the image of an old man, made of green stone sitting upon a sofa, and wrapped up in a garment. Before him were statues of little boys. Having proceeded further they met with the image of a cock made of precious stones and placed upon a green column. Continuing their researches they came to a female idol of white stone and lions of stone on each side. This, he says, occurred in the time of Yarid bin-'Abdullah, supposed, says Colonel Howard Vyse, to have been a king of Egypt.

**Masa'ud Ghazi, Salar,** سالار مسعود غازی, a celebrated Muhammadan martyr commonly called Ghazí Miyain, whose tomb is at Bahráich in Audh. He was the son of Sálár Sáhú, and related to Sulṭán Mahmúd of Ghazní; his mother being that monarch's sister. He had forcibly taken possession of a Hindú temple in Bahráich, upon which the Hindús surrounded him from all sides, a battle ensued in which Masa'úd Ghází was slain, and several of his adherents cut to pieces. This circumstance took place on the 15th of June, 1033 A. D., 14th Rajab, 424 A. H., at which time he was only 19 years old. To commemorate his martyrdom a festival takes place every year at Bahráich on the first Sunday in the month of Jeiṭh, which falls exactly on the 29th day after our Easter Sunday, and very seldom on any other day. The festival terminates with the flying of kites.

**Masa'ud Hisari, Maulana,** مولانا مسعود حصاری, a poet who was living in the commencement of Akbar's reign, and wrote the chronogram of the emperor Humáyún's death which took place in 1556 A. D., 963 A. H.

**Masa'ud, Khwaja,** خواجه مسعود of Bak, a place near Bukhára. It is said that he was for some time a king in Máwarun-nahr, but a dervish at heart. He is the author of several works on Súfyism, one of which is the "Umm al-Nasáeh." He has also composed a Díwán which he called "Núr ul-Áin," the light of the eye, containing more than 3,000 verses.

**Masa'ud, Khwaja,** خواجه مسعود, *vide* Khwája Masa'úd.

**Masa'ud Sa'd Salman,** مسعود ساد سلمان, a poet and native of Jurján. He flourished in the time of Manúchehr, ruler of that country, about the year 1060 A. D., 452 A. H. He is the author of a Díwán in Arabic and Persian.

**Mas-hafi,** مصحفی, an Urdú poet of Lakhnau, whose proper name is Ghulám Hamdání. His native country was Amroha in the district of Murádábád. He died about the year 1824 A. D., 1240 A. H. He is the author of several Díwáns and biographies in Persian and Urdú.

**Masha-ullah,** ما شا الله, the surname of an author who is also styled "Al-Misrí," or the Egyptian. It is also the name of a Jew, who was a great astronomer, and lived in the time of the khalífs Al-Mansúr and Al-Mámún.

**Ma'shuk 'Ali, Maulana Muhammad** معشوق علي مولانا محمد of Jaunpúr, a learned Musalmán and author of several works in prose and poetry. He died in the year 1852 A. D., 1268 A. H.

**Masih,** مسيح, the poetical name of Hakím Rukná Káshí, which see.

**Masih,** مسيح, whose proper name was Hátim, is the author of the poem called "Ḳissae Manúchehr," containing the story of Manúchehr, which he composed in 1660 A. D., 1070 A. H., and dedicated it to Sháh Jahán the emperor of Dehlí.

**Masiha,** مسيحا, poetical title of Hakím Muhammad 'Alí Khán, who is the author of an Urdú Díwán.

**Masihai, Akhund,** اخوند مسيحاى of Káshán, whose poetical name is Sáhib, a man who possessed every ornament of learning and accomplishments, had been a pupil and son-in-law of 'Aḳá Husain of Khwánsár, and gained the admiration of all mankind by his good qualities and agreeable society. He composed much in verse, and has left elegant compositions in prose. He died at Isfahán in the beginning of the 18th century.

**Masihi,** مسيحى, a Turkish poet of great repute at Constantinople, who flourished in the reign of the emperor Sulaimán II, styled the Lawgiver. His works are preserved in the archives of the Royal Society. Masíhí died in 1512 A. D., 918 A. H.

**Masihi, Mulla,** ملا مسيحى, also called Masíhái, was the poetical name of Sa'd-ulláh, an adopted son of Muḳarrab Khán. He was a native of Pánípat, and flourished in the time of the emperor Jahángír. He translated the "Ramáyan," which contains the battle of Rám Chand with Ráwan the ten-headed monster, from Hindí into Persian verse.

**Masihi,** مسيحي, *vide* Rukn-uddín Masa'úd Masíhí.

**Masir,** مسير, poetical name of prince Mirzá Hamáyún Kadr, the son of Mirzá Khurshaid Kadr, *vide* Taskhír.

**Masjidi,** مسجدي, poetical title of a poet of Persia.

**Masjid Moth,** مسجد موٹ, built by Mián Bhúya at Dehlí. *Vide* Bhúya.

**Maslah-uddin,** مصلح الدين, proper name of the celebrated Shaikh Sa'dí of Shíráz, *vide* Sa'dí.

**Maslah-uddin al-Lari,** مصلح الدين لارى, a native of Lár in Persia, and author of the work called "Mirat ul-Adwár," the Mirror of the World.

**Masruf,** مصروف, poetical title of Nawáb Khán Bahádur Khán, the son of Jalál-uddín or Zulfiḳár Khán, the son of Háfiz Rahmat Khán of Bareli He is the author of a Díwán. He rebelled against the British in 1857, and consequently was obliged to leave his native country and go to Mecca.

**Masrur,** مسرور, the poetical title of Walí Muhammad Khán who was governor of Lár under Sháh Tahmásp II of Persia.

**Mast,** مست, the poetical appellation of Zulfiḳar 'Alí, which see.

**Ma'sum 'Ali Shah, Mir,** معصوم علي شاه مير a celebrated Súfi teacher, who was a disciple of Sayyad 'Alí Razá, a native of the Dakhin. During the reign of Karím Khán, he went from India to Shíráz, where his followers soon amounted to more than thirty thousand. The orthodox priests took alarm, and prevailed on the mild Karím Khán to banish the saint from his capital, but his reputation was increased by the act of power which proclaimed him dangerous. After Karím Khán's death, Mír Ma'súm, who resided in a small village near Isfahán, deputed his first disciple, Fayáz 'Alí, to teach in that city. That holy person soon died, and was succeeded in his office by his son Núr 'Alí Sháh: who, though young in years, was, (to use the phrase of his historian), "old in piety." The number and rank of Mír Ma'súm's followers excited alarm in the priests of Isfahán, who transmitted so exaggerated an account of the vile heresies of the Súfís to 'Alí Murád Khán, the king, and recommended him so strongly to support the faith, by punishing those whose opinions were alike hostile to true religion and good government, that the monarch, the moment he received their representation, sent orders to cut off the noses and ears of some among the most zealous of the obnoxious sect; and as a further disgrace, to shave the beards of all who had adopted their opinions. The ignorant soldiers intrusted with the execution of this mandate, were not very capable of discriminating between true believers and infidels: and we are assured by a contemporary writer, that many orthodox Muhammadans had their noses and ears cut off, and their beards shaved on this memorable occasion.

Mír Ma'súm 'Alí and Núr 'Alí Sháh, after wandering from one place to another, re-visited Kirmán, where Mushták 'Alí, the most pious of his disciples, was put to death. At Kirmánsháh Núr 'Alí Sháh was placed in confinement: and Mír Ma'súm was murdered when at prayers in the midst of his followers. This sect, however, notwithstanding the efforts of their enemies, continued to increase in numbers; and Núr 'Alí Sháh, with all who adhered to him, were banished the kingdom. His avowed disciples were at this period about sixty thousand; but many more were supposed to be secretly devoted to him. He is said to have been poisoned at Mausal. It is related that two inhabitants of Kirmánsháh, who were distinguished by an extraordinary appearance of zeal, dressed his dinner on the day that he was suddenly attacked by violent spasms, which in a few hours terminated his existence. Their flight led all to suspect them of having poisoned him. Núr 'Alí died at 9 o'clock on the morning of the 3rd June, 1800 A. D., 10th Mu-harram, 1215 A. H. He expired close to the grave of the prophet Jonas, within a league of Mausal.

**Matin,** متین, the poetical name of Shaikh 'Abdul Raza bin-'Abdulláh Matín. He was a native of Isfahán, but of Arabic origin. He came to India in the reign of the emperor Muhammad Sháh, and subsequently went to Lakhnau, where he assumed the garb of a dervish and received a pension from Burhán ul-Mulk Sa'ádat Khán. Having lost his pension owing to the change of rulers, he proceeded to Bengal where he died in 1761 A. D., 1175 A. H., and left a Díwán of 5000 verses.

**Ma'tmid Khan,** معتمد خان, *vide* Ma'tmid Khán.

**Matrazi,** مطرزي, surname of Muwayyad, the grandfather of Shaikh Nizámí of Gauja. He was a poet and an author.

**Maudud Chishti, Khwaja,** خواجه مودود چشتي, son of Khwája Yúsaf the son of Sama'án. His father who died in 1067 A. D., aged 84 lunar years, lies buried at Chisht. Khwája Maudúd is the founder of a religious sect called Chishtí, of which Khwája Mo'ín-uddín Chishtí, whose tomb is at Ajmir, was a follower. Maudúd died on the 8th May, 1153 A. D., 1st Rajab, 527 A. H.

**Maudud, Sultan,** سلطان مودود, the son of Sultán Masa'úd I of Ghazní. He was at Balkh when his father was murdered by Ahmad the son of the reigning Sultán, Muhammad Makahúl; he immediately proclaimed himself king and marched to revenge his father, and having defeated the Sultán's army on the banks of the Indus, made Muhammad and his sons prisoners, and put them all to death 1041 A. D., 433 A. H. The dynasty of Ghazní lost, during the reign of Maudúd, all their possessions in Persia. Maudúd died at Láhor on the 23rd of December, 1049 A. D., 24th Rajab, 441 A. H., having reigned upwards of nine years.

**Mauji,** موجي بدخشاني, of Badakhshán, whose proper name was Muhammad Kasim Khán, is the author of a "Yúsaf Zalekha," containing 6000 verses. He died at Ágrah in 1571 A. D., 979 A. H.

**Maulana 'Ali,** مولانا علي, the son of Mahmúd Kirmání, commonly called Shaháb. He is the author of a History entitled "Maásir Mahmúdí" which he dedicated to Sultán Mahmúd Sháh I, Khiljí, king of Málwá, who reigned from 1436 to 1469 A. D.

**Maulana Hasan,** مولانا حسن, a learned Musalmán who died in the time of Sultán Salím Sháh of Dehlí in the year 1549 A. D. His tomb, which has a Persian inscription in verse, is still to be seen in the Roman Catholic Burial-ground at Ágrah.

**Maulana Husain,** مولانا حسين, was a disciple of Khwája Abú'l Wafá who died in 1432 A. D., 836 A. H. Mauláná Husain is the author of the work called "Maksad Aksa," and of the "Sharah Kasída Burda."

**Maulana Maghrabi,** مولانا مغربي, *vide* Maghrabí.

**Maulana Majd,** مولانا مجد, *vide* Majd (Mauláná).

**Maulana Nasir,** مولانا ناصر, *vide* Násir Bukhárí (Mauláná).

**Maulanae Rum,** مولاناء روم, *vide* Jalál-uddín Rúmí.

**Maulud Muhammad,** مولود محمد, author of a Persian work on Physic, called "Bahr ul-Munáfa," the Sea of Profit, dedicated to Típú Sultán.

**Maulwi Rumi,** مولوی رومي, *vide* Jalál-uddín Rúmí.

**Mauzun,** موزون, poetical appellation of Rájá Rám Naráin of Patna, which see.

**Mawasi,** مواسی, a celebrated poet of Persia, who flourished at the court of Malik Sháh Saljúkí about the end of the eleventh century of the Christian era, and received the designation of Malik ush-Shu'ará, king of poets, and the dignity of an Amír. The poet Khákání made him his model in versification; and so renowned were his odes, that more than a hundred poets endeavoured to imitate his style.

**Mazani,** مازنی, whose proper name is Abú 'Usmán, was an excellent Arabic Grammarian. He died in 863 A. D., 249 A. H.

**Mazani,** مزنی, or Al-Mazaní, *vide* Abú Ibráhím Ismá'íl.

**Mazdak,** مزدک, name of a famous impostor, a native of Persia, surnamed Zandík, that is to say, the impious. He lived in the reign of Kubád the father of Nausherwán the Just. He was imprisoned and afterwards put to death by order of the latter.

**Mazhar,** مظہر, author of a poem containing the story of "Chandar Badan," which he dedicated to Aurangzíb emperor of Dehlí.

**Mazhar,** مظہر, the poetical designation of (Mirzá) Ján Jánán, which see.

**Mazhari, Maulana,** مولانا مظہری کشمیری, a poet of Kashmír who flourished in the time of Akbar.

**Mazhar ul-Hakk,** مظہرالحق, poetical name of Abú 'Abdullah Muhammad Fázil, author of the "Mukhbir ul-Wásilín," a poem containing the chronograms of the most celebrated persons among the Muhammadans. He flourished in the time of the emperor 'Alamgír and died in 1696 A. D., 1106 A. H., *vide* Abú 'Abdullah Muhammad Fázil.

**Mazmun,** مضمون, the poetical appellation of Shaikh Sharaf-uddín a descendant of Shaikh Faríd-uddín Shakarganj. When he was past forty, he took up his abode in the mosque at Sháhjahánábád called Zínat ul-Masájid, and led the life of an ascetic. He was a pupil of Mazhar and 'Arzú, the latter called him "Shái'r-i-Bedána," because he had lost all his teeth. He died about the year 1745 A. D., 1158 A. H.

**Mehr,** مہر, poetical title of Mirzá Hatim 'Alí Beg of Ágrah, formerly a Munsif of Chunár. He is the author of a Díwán and a book called "Panjae Mehr." He was still living at Ágrah in 1873 A. D.

**Mehr,** مہر, poetical name of Nawáb Amín-uddaula Sayyad 'Aghá 'Alí Khán, a son of Mo'tmid-uddaula 'Aghá Mír, the ex-Nawáb of Lakhnau. He was living at Kahnpúr in 1856, and is the author of an Urdú Díwán.

**Mehri,** مہری, poetical name of an author.

**Mehr Nasir,** مہرنصیر, *vide* Mirzá Mehr Nasír.

**Mehrun-nisa Begam,** مہرالنساء بیگم, 5th daughter of 'Alamgír. Her mother's name was Aurangabadí Mahal, She was born in August, 1661 A. D., 3rd Safar 1072 A. H., and married to Prince Ezid Bakhsh, the son of Sulṭán Murád Bakhsh, and died in 1704 A. D., 1116 A. H.

**Mehrun-nisa,** مہرالنساء, daughter of Núr Jahán by Sher Afgan Khán. She was married to Shahriar, the youngest son of Jahángír.

**Mian Mir,** میاں میر, *vide* Shaikh Mír of Láhor and Sháh Mír.

**Minhaj us-Saraj Jurjani,** منہاج السراج جورجاني, a native of Jurjan or Georgia, was an elegant poet and author of the "Tabkát Násirí," which he wrote in 1252 A. D., and dedicated to Násir-uddín Mahmúd king of Dehlí who reigned from 1246 to 1266 A. D. He is also called Ḳazí Sadr Jahán Minháj-uddín Jurjání. *Vide* Abú 'Umar Minháj.

**Minnat,** منت, poetical name of Mír Ḳamar-uddín Minnat, a native of Dehlí. Warren Hastings conferred on him the title of "Malik-ush-Shu'ará," or the king of poets at the recommendation of the Nawáb of Murshidábád. He visited the Dakhan and received 5,000 rupees for a Ḳasída or panegyric which he wrote in praise of the Nizam of Haidarábád. He died at Calcutta in 1793 A. D., 1208 A. H., and left 150,000 verses in Persian and Urdú. Among his compositions is a "Chamanistán" and a "Shakaristán."

**Mir,** میر, this word is an abbreviation of Amír, which in Arabic signifies, a chief, prince and commander. The Sayyads of India are also called Mír.

**Mir,** میر, the poetical designation of Mír Muhammad Taḳí, a Hindústaní poet who flourished in the time of the emperor Sháh 'Alam, and whose poetry is mostly Rekhta. He was a native of Akbarábád and nephew to Siráj-uddín 'Alí Khán 'Arzú. He is the author of six Díwáns and a Tazkira or biography of poets. He died at Lakhnau in the year 1810 A. D., 1225 A. H., *vide* Faiz, and Taḳi (Mír).

**Mir Akhund,** میر اخوند, *vide* Kháwand Sháh.

**Mir 'Alam,** میرعالم, title of Mír Abú'l Ḳasim, the prime-minister of the Nizám of Haidarábád. This nobleman for upwards of thirty years had taken a lead in the administration of affairs in the Dakhin. He died in the month of November, 1808 A. D., and was succeeded by Munír ul-Mulk.

**Mir 'Ali,** میرعلي, surnamed Dámád, or the bridegroom (because he was married to a favourite sister of the great Sháh 'Abbás), was the teacher of a system of philosophy much more pure and sublime than had hitherto been known. His immortal scholar Sadrau has, by his numerous works, proved himself superior to Aristotle in abstract science, though that great philosopher had been hitherto the master of his preceptor and all his predecessors in those branches of learning.

**Mir Amman,** میرامن, a Hindústání lyric poet, whose poetical name was Lutf, which see.

**Miran,** میرن, surname of Mír Sádiḳ, the son of Nawáb Ja'far 'Alí Khán of Bengal, *vide* Mír Sádiḳ.

**Miran 'Adil Khan Faruki,** میران عادل خان فاروقي, third king of Khándesh, succeeded his father Malik Nasír Khán in September, 1437 A. D. He reigned more than three years, expelled the Dakhanís from Khándesh in 1440 A. D., and was murdered in the city of Burhánpúr on Friday the 28th of April, 1441 A. D., 8th Ẕil-ḥijja, 844 A. H. He was buried at Tálner by the side of his father, and succeeded by his son Mírán Mubárik Khán I.

**Miran Ghani,** میران غني, commonly called 'Adil Khán Fárúḳí I, succeeded his father Mírán Mubárik Khán in May, 1457 A. D., Rajab, 861 A. H. to the government of Khándesh, which province under his rule attained a degree of prosperity which it had never known under any of its former rulers. This prince added considerably to the fortifications of Asír, and constructed the strong outwork called Malaigaṛh; he also built the citadel of Burhánpúr, and raised many magnificent palaces in that town. He died after a reign of 48 lunar years on Friday the 8th September, 1503 A. D., 14th Rabí' I, 909 A. H., and was buried at his particular request near the palace of the Daulat Maidán in Burhánpúr. He was succeeded by his brother Dáúd Khán Fárúḳí.

**Miran Husain Nizam Shah,** میران حسین نظام شاہ, ascended the throne of Ahmadnagar in the Dakhin after the murder of his father Murtaza Niẓám Sháh in June 1588 A. D., Rajab, 996 A. H. He being of an impetuous and cruel disposition, began his reign by tyranny and oppression, and was deposed and murdered after a reign of ten months and three days on the 18th of March, 1589 A. D., 11th Jumáda I, 997 A. H., and his cousin Ismá'íl Niẓám Sháh, the son of his uncle prince Burhán Sháh (who was then at the court of the emperor Akbar at Dehli), was raised to the throne.

**Miran Mubarik Khan Faruki I,** ميران مبارک خان فاروقی, succeeded his father Mírán 'Adil Khán Fárúḳí in the government of Khándesh in April, 1441 A. D. He reigned, without undertaking any foreign conquest, or drawing upon himself the hostility of his neighbours, for a period of nearly 17 lunar years. He died on the 17th May, 1457 A. D., 12th Rajab, 861 A. H., was buried at Tálner, and succeeded by his son Mírán Ghaní, commonly called 'Adil Khán Fárúḳí I.

**Miran Mubarik Khan Faruki II,** ميران مبارک‌خان فاروقی, succeeded his brother Mírán Muhammad Khán in the government of Khándesh in 1536 A. D., 943 A. H. He reigned 32 lunar years and died on the night of Wednesday the 24th of December, 1566 A. D., 6th Jumáda II, 974 A. H., and was succeeded by Mírán Muhammad Khán Fárúḳí II.

**Miran Muhammad Khan Faruki I,** ميران محمد خان فاروقی, succeeded to the government of Khándesh after the death of his father 'Adil Khán II, in 1520 A. D., 926 A. H., and after the demise of Bahádur Sháh king of Gujrát and Málwá, who was murdered by the Portuguese at Diu in February, 1537 A. D., he (Muhammad Khán) being the son of Bahádur Sháh's sister, was proclaimed by his mother, in concert with the nobles, king of Gujrát and Málwá, and was formally crowned at Máṇdo with the title of Mírán Muhammad Sháh; but his reign in those provinces was of short duration, for he died suddenly on the 24th of April, 1537 A. D., 13th Ẓi-Ḳa'da, 943 A. H. His body was conveyed to Burhánpúr, and interred in the vault of his father, 'Adil Khán II. His brother Mírán Mubárik Khán II succeeded him in the government of Khándesh, and Mahmúd Sháh (son of Latíf Khán the brother of Bahádur Sháh) to the throne of Gujrát.

**Miran Muhammad Khan Faruki II,** ميران محمد خان فاروقی ثاني, succeeded Mírán Mubárik Khán II in the government of Khándesh in December, 1566 A. D., and died after a reign of ten years in 1576 A. D., 984 A. H. He was succeeded by his brother Rájá 'Alí Khán.

**Miran Shah, Mirza,** مرزا ميران‌شاه, the eldest surviving son of Amír Taimúr (Tamerlane) was born in the year 1367 A. D., 769 A. H. He had the government of 'Iráḳ, 'Azurbeján, Dayárbikr and Syria during the lifetime of his father, and after his death he reigned 3 years 3 months and 7 days over those countries, when he was slain in a battle against Ḳara Yúsaf the Turkmán on the 20th of April, 1408 A. D., 24th Ẓi-Ḳa'da, 810 A. H., aged 41 lunar years 7 months and 10 days. He had several sons, *viz.*, Abú Bakr Mirzá, 'Alí Mirzá, Umar Mirzá who succeeded him, Mirzá Khalíl, Sulṭán Muhammad Mirzá, Mirzá Ayjal and Mirzá Sayúrghamish.

**Mir Bakir Damad,** ميرباقر داماد, he was called Dámád because he was the son-in-law of Sháh 'Abbás I, king of Persia. He is the author of the work entitled "Ufk ul-Mubín," and the marginal notes on the "Sharah Mukhtasar Usúl". He died in the year 1630 A. D., 1040 A. H., *vide* Muhammad Bakir Dámád.

**Mir Buzurg,** ميربزرگ, author of a work on Súfyism called "Durr ul-Ma'rfat."

**Mir Dard,** ميردرد, *vide* Dard (Mír).

**Mir Haidar,** مير حيدر, *vide* Haidar (Mír).

**Mir Haidar Rafiki Mua'mmai,** مير حيدر رفيقي معمائي, the punster and poet, flourished in the time of Sháh Ismá'il Safwí II of Persia, and was living about the year 1577 A. D., 985 A. H., *vide* Haidar Mua'mmái, and Rafí-uddín Haidar Ráfa'í.

**Mir Haji,** ميرحاجي. The convict Mír Hájí, the murderer of Captain Douglas and others during the mutiny at Dehlí, was executed on Tuesday morning the 29th of December, 1868 A. D., in front of the Láhor Gate of the city of Dehlí, facing the apartments which were the scene of the murders for which he suffered death.

He was brought from jail to the place of execution under a strong Police Guard; he mounted the scaffold with a firm step; while the rope was being adjusted he muttered in a low voice "Brethren, remember your Kalma," and then repeated in the same low tone two or three times "La illah" &c., &c., soon after which the trap fell, and all was over, almost without a struggle. After hanging the usual time, the body was made over to the friends of the convict.

**Mir Husaini,** ميرحسيني, author of the Zád ul-Musáfirín *Vide* Husain bin-Hasan al-Husainí.

**Mir Ja'far,** مير جعفر, nawáb of Bengal, *vide* Ja'far 'Alí Khán.

**Mir Jumla,** مير جمله, title of Mír Muhammad Amín of Sháhristán in Persia, came to India in the time of Jahángír 1618 A. D., 1027 A. H., and served under him for several years. In the reign of Sháh Jahán, he was raised to the rank of 5000 with the title of Mír Jumla. He died on the 22nd of August, 1637 O. S., 10th Rabí' II, 1047 A. H.

**Mir Jumla,** ميرجمله, title of Mír Muhammad Saíd the prime-minister of 'Abdullah Ḳuṭb Sháh of Golkanḍa. He had formerly been a diamond merchant and had been known and respected throughout the Dakhin for his wealth and abilities long before he attained high station. His son, Muhammad Amín, a dissolute and violent young man, had drawn on himself the resentment of 'Abdullah Ḳuṭb Sháh, and had involved his father in a dispute with the court at Dehlí. Mír Jumla in the year 1656 A. D., 1066 A. H., threw himself on the protection of the emperor Sháh Jahán, in whose service he remained; became the chosen counsellor of the prince Aurangzíb, and afterwards one of the most useful instruments of his ambitious designs. On the accession of Aurangzíb 'Alamgír, he was sent in pursuit of Sulṭán Shujáa' and appointed governor of Bengal. The title conferred on him by 'Alamgír, was Mu'azzam Khán, KhánKhánán Sipah Sálár. He held the rank of 7000. In the fourth year of the emperor 1662 A. D., he went on an expedition against the kingdom of Asám. He marched from Dacca in Bengal about the month of February, and entered Asám by Ghorágháṭ; from thence he proceeded with very little opposition to the capital Ghargáon, which he took and plundered; but the rainy season setting in soon after, which inundated great part of the country, his supplies were cut off by the Asámians, and his troops becoming sickly, it was with great difficulty the army effected its retreat. The unfortunate general fell a victim to the climate a few days after his re-entering Bengal. He died at Khizarpúr in Kúch Behár on the 31st March, 1663 A. D., 2nd Ramaẓán, 1073 A. H. The history of this expedition was written by Shaháb-uddín Aḥmad Tálásh in 1663 A. D., 1073 A. H.

**Mir Jumla,** ميرجمله, title of 'Abdullah a nobleman and private favourite of the emperor Farrukh-siyar, was promoted for some time to tho Súbadárí of Bihár. In the first year of the emperor Muhammad Sháh, he was appointed to the rank of Ṣadr us-Ṣudúr, and died in the 13th year of his reign, about the year 1731 A. D., 1144 A. H.

**Mir Khund,** ميرخواند, *vide* Kháwand Sháh.

**Mir Mannu,** ميرمنو, *vide* Mo'ín ul-Mulk.

**Mir Masum,** ميرمعصوم بهكرى, of Bihkar, was an officer of the rank of 1000 in the time of Akbar and Jahángír, but an excellent poet. He is the author of a Díwán, and a Masnawí called "Ma'dan ul-Afkár," written in imitation of the "Makhzan ul-Asrár," and of a history of Sindh, called "Táríkh Sindh." He died at Bihkar in 1606 A. D., 1015 A. H.

**Mir Muhammad Khan Talpur,** مير محمد خان تلپور, one of the Ex-Amírs of Sind. He was lately one of the members of the Bombay Legislative Council. He died at Haidarabád (Sind) on the 17th of December, 1870 A. D. Much respected, his remains were followed to the family mausoleum by the Commissioner, the Judge, and the Collector, of the district. He lies in the place originally intended for his late father, Mír Murád 'Alí, who preferred lying out in the open air, where the sun and moon could shed their light on his grave. He died in his 60th year. There now remain only three of the once numerous Talpúr family at Haidarabád, all aged men at whose death in the course of time the once troublesome family will be extinct. The conquest of their territory and the overthrow of their power, furnish one of the most remarkable and interesting episodes in British Indian history.

**Mir Muhammad, Munshi,** منشي مير محمد, author of a collection of Letters.

**Mir Muhammad, Sayyad,** سيد مير محمد, the great Mahdawí of Jaunpúr.

**Mir Mu'izzi,** مير معزى, *vide* Amír Moizzí.

**Mir Murtaza,** ميرمرتضي المدعوبعلم الهدى, surnamed Al-Mad'ú bi-ilm il-Huda. He died on the 25th September, 1044 A. D., 30th Safar, 436 A. H.

**Mir Razi,** مير رضى, a poet who received a lakh of Rupees from a prince of Dehlí for a Ghazal he composed.

**Mir Sadik,** ميرصادق, commonly called Mírán, was the son of Mír Ja'far 'Alí Khán, nawáb of Bengal. He was killed by lightning when asleep in his tent on the night of the 2nd July 1760 A. D., 18th Ẓi-Ḳa'da, 1173 A. H. He had killed several women of his harem with his own hand. Being reproached by the British Resident with the murder of one of the women, he answered, "What, shall not I kill an old woman, who goes about in her litter to stir up people against my father?"

**Mir Sharaef 'Allama,** مير شرف علامه, *vide* Sharíf Jurjaní.

**Mir Sayyad Jama Baf,** ميرسيد جامه باف, the weaver, was an excellent poet of Persia who came to India in 1562 A. D., 969 A. H. in the time of the emperor Akbar, and died in the year 1565 A. D., 973 A. H. His compositions mostly were Rubáis, consequently he is sometimes called Mír Rubá'í.

**Mir Taki,** ميرتاكي, *vide* Mír.

**Mirza,** ميرزا, is an abbreviation of Amírzáda, which in Persian signifies, the son of a prince or nobleman. It is also written Mirzá, which has been adopted in this work. The descendants of Amír Taimúr were all called Mirzás till Bábar Sháh, who assumed the honorable title of Bádsháh, and the princes were called Sulṭáns and Salátíns.

**Mirza,** مرزا, *vide* Mírzá.

**Mirza 'Ali Beg,** مرزا علي بيگ, *vide* 'Alí Beg (Mirzá).

**Mirza 'Ali, Nawab,** نواب مرزا علي. He was executed at Dehlí on Tuesday the 9th July 1844 A. D., for the murder of two dancing-girls in that city. The Fatwá was given by Mauláná Ṣadr-uddín Khán Bahádur, Ṣadr us-Ṣudúr.

**Mirza Haidar,** مرزا حيدر, *vide* Haidar (Mirzá) also called Haidar Doghlát.

**Mirza Hasan,** مرزا حسن, *vide* Hasan (Mirzá).

**Mirza 'Isa,** مرزا عيسى, and Mirzá Inayat-ullah, governors of Tatta in the time of the emperor Sháh Jahán, where they died. Their tombs are magnificent edifices built of yellow marble, beautifully carved, with flowers in bas-relief, and surpassing all the buildings of the place. The inscription gives the year of 1648 A. D., 1058 A. H.

**Mirza Jan,** مرزا جان, whose poetical name was Jání, was the father of Mirzá Ján Jánán.

**Mirza Jangli,** مرزا جنگلي, Nawáb Sa'ádat 'Alí's second brother.

**Mirza Jana,** مرزا جانا, and Mirzá Ghází, two Wazírs who lived in the reign of the emperor 'Alamgír. Their tombs are in Tatta, and the inscription shows the date to be 1683 A. D., 1095 A. H.

**Mirza Khan,** مرزا خان, author of the "Tuhfat ul-Hind," a work on Hindú music &c., composed under the patronage of 'Azim Sháh. It contains a minute account of Hindú literature in all, or most of its branches: he professes to have extracted his elaborate chapter on music, with the assistance of Pandits, from the Rágarnava, or Sea of Passions, the Rágdarpana or Mirror of Modes, &c.

**Mirza Mehr Nasir,** مرزا مهرنصير, a physician in the service of Karím Khán, king of Persia, and author of a Masnawí. Amongst the many poems which have celebrated the charms and delights of the Spring, his Masnawí holds the highest place. He flourished about the year 1770 A. D., 1184 A. H.

**Mirza Muhammad,** مرزا محمد, surnamed Bulbul, a celebrated lutanist of Persia. It is related by Sir William Jones, that an intelligent Persian repeated to him again and again, that he had more than once been present when Mirzá Muhammad was playing to a large company in a grove near Shíráz, where he distinctly saw the nightingales trying to vie with the musician, sometimes warbling on the trees, sometimes fluttering from branch to branch, as if they wished to approach the instrument whence the melody proceeded, and at length dropping on the ground in a kind of ecstacy, from which they were soon raised by a change of the mode.

**Mirza Muhsin,** مرزا محسن, brother of Nawáb Safdar Jang. His title was Nawáb Izzat-uddaula, which see.

**Mirza Nasir,** مرزا نصير, the father of the maternal grandsire of Nawáb Shujá-uddaula. He came into Hindústán in the beginning of the reign of the emperor Bahádur Sháh the son of 'Alamgír, by whom he was appointed to an office of trust at Patna about the year 1708

A. D., 1120 A. H., where he died and where his tomb yet remains. He had two sons, the second of whom, Muhammad Amín, on being apprised of the death of his father, left Persia, and about the year 1718 A. D. visited the court of the emperor Farrukh-siyar. He was appointed by this prince, governor of the fort of Ágrah; and soon rising to greater honours, he ultimately became the viceroy of Audh, by the title of Burhán ul-Mulk Sa'ádat Khán.

**Mirza Nasir,** مرزا نصير, a poet who came to India from Mazindarán in the reign of the emperor Sháh 'Alam the blind. His son Malik Muhammad Khán received the title of Nawáb Samsám-uddaula Malik Muhammad Khán Diler Jang, from Nawáb Zulfikár-uddaula Najaf Khán and after some time died in Jaipúr in 1804 A. D., 1219 A. H.

**Mirza Rustam,** مرزا رستم, a prince of Ḳandahár, being driven to difficulties by his own brothers and the Uzbaks, came to the court of Akbar in 1593 A. D., 1001 A. H., and presented the king with the fort of Ḳandahár, for which the government of Multán was conferred on him, and he was ranked among the Amírs of the empire. He was the son of Mirzá Sulṭán Husain the grandson of Sháh Ismá'íl king of Persia.

**Misa'ab,** مصعب, brother of 'Abdulláh ibn-Zuber on whose part he was governor of Basra in the time of the Khalífs Marwán I, and his son 'Abdul Malik. He was killed in a battle fought against the troops of the latter, about the year 690 A. D., 71 A. H., and while 'Abdul Malik was at Kúfa during an entertainment, Misa'ab's head was presented to him; upon which one of the company took occasion to say, "I saw Husain's head in this same castle presented to 'Ubaid-ullah; 'Ubaid-ullah's to Almukhtár; Almukhtár's to Misa'ab; and now at last Misa'ab's to yourself." This observation so affected the Khalíf, that either to avert the ill omen, or from some other motive, he ordered the castle to be immediately demolished. Misa'ab had been 'Abdul Malik's intimate friend before he was Khalíf, but marrying afterwards Sakína the daughter of Husain, and 'Ayesha the daughter of Talha, by these marriages he was engaged in the interest of two families who were at mortal enmity with the house of Umayya.

**Miskin,** مسكين, the poetical name of several poets of

**Miskin Shah,** مسكين شاه, a spiritual teacher of the chiefs of Karnál, in the Balághaṭ districts, Southern Hindústán, whose mausoleum stands a mile distant from the town of Karnál. He is the author of a Díwán.

**Mitti,** متي, a person of the tribe of Indians called Kalál, whose profession was to keep watch at the gate of the kings and noblemen of India, and to run before them in their retinue. Some of them were raised even to the rank of 1500. This man was employed by Núr Jahán Begam, was well-educated and became a poet in the time of Jahángír. He is the author of a Díwán.

**Mohan Lal, Munshi,** منشى موهن لال, the son of Pandit Budh Singh, the son of rájá Maní Rám, of Kashmír descent. His father was a resident of Dehlí. He was a student of the Dehlí College and accompanied Lieutenant Burnes and Dr. J. G. Gerard in the capacity of a Persian Munshí to Persia in January, 1832, and wrote a Journal of his travels entitled "Journal of a Tour through the Panjáb, Afghánistán, Turkistán, Khurásán and part of Persia," published at Calcutta in 1834.

**Mohan Lal,** موهن لال, a Hindú who adopted "Anís" for his poetical name. He is the author of a Tazkira called "Anís ul-Ahbab," compiled in 1783 A. D., 1197 A. H. He informs us that when 'Asaf-uddaula the nawáb of Audh saw the Tazkira of the contemporary poets of Hazín, he ordered him to compile a similar work on Indian poets.

**Mohan Singh,** موهن سنگه, son of Ráo Ḳaran, murdered by one Muhammad Sháh about the year 1671 A. D., his women burned themselves alive with his corpse.

**Moi'zzi,** معزي, *vide* Amír Moi'zzí.

**Moi'zz-li-din allah Abi Tamim Ma'd,** معزلدين الله ابي تميم معاد, the son of Ismá'íl surnamed Al-Mansúr. He was the 4th Khalíf of Barbary, and the first king of Egypt of the Fatimite dynasty who began to reign in the former country in 952 A. D., 30th Shawwál 341 A. H. The greatest achievement performed by this Khalíf was his conquest of Egypt, and the removal of the Khiláfat from Ḳairwán to that country in 970 A. D., 361 A. H. He subdued all Africa and built the city Al-Ḳáhira in Egypt, commonly called Grand Cairo, and died after a reign of 24 years in 976 A. D., 19th Rabi' II, 365 A. H. *Vide* Muhammad Al-Mahdi.

*List of the kings of the Fatimite dynasty who reigned from 341 to 567 A. H. in Egypt.*

| | A. D. | A. H. |
|---|---|---|
| Moi'zz-li-dín allah Abí Tamím Ma'd, reigned 24 years, | 952 | 341 |
| Al-'Azíz Billáh Abú Nasr Tarár, reigned 21 years, | 976 | 365 |
| Hákim-bi-amr allah Abú Mansúr, reigned 25 years, | 996 | 386 |
| Táhir-li-ázáz-dín allah Abú'l Hasan bin-Hakim, | 1020 | 411 |
| Mustanasir Billáh Abú Tamím bin-Táhir, | 1036 | 427 |
| Mustaa'lí Billáh Abú'l Ḳásim Aḥmad bin-Mustanasir, | 1094 | 487 |
| Amar be ahkám allah Abú 'Alí Mansúr bin-Mustaa'lí, | 1100 | 495 |
| Háfiz-li-dín allah 'Abdul Majíd bin-Muhammad bin-Mustazehr | 1130 | 524 |
| Al-Záfir-bi-'Abdullah Ismá'íl bin-Háfiz, | 1147 | 542 |
| Fáez-bi-nasr allah Ísa bin-Záfir, | 1152 | 547 |
| 'Azid-li-dín allah bin-Yúsaf bin-Háfiz in whose time Egypt was taken by Sálah-uddín (Azid died in 1173 A. D.), | 1158 | 553 |

**Moi'zz-uddin,** معز الدين, title of the emperor Jahándár Sháh.

**Moi'zz-uddin,** معز الدين, surname of Ḳaiḳubád the grandson of Sulṭán Ghayás-uddín Balban.

**Moi'zz-uddin Husain Kart, Malik,** معز الدين ملك حسين كرت, the seventh king of the dynasty of Kart or Kard. He succeeded his brother Malik Háfiz in 1322 A. D., reigned over Hirát, Ghazní &c., about 38 years (some say only 12), and completely subdued the Sarbadáls. He died about the year 1370 A. D., 771 A. H., and was succeeded by his grandson Ghayás-uddín the son of 'Alí.

**Moi'zz-uddin Muhammad Ghori,** معز الدين محمد غوري, *vide* Shaháb-uddín Muhammad Ghorí.

**Moi'zz-uddin Muhammad, Mir,** مير معز الدين محمد, he was so exquisite a caligrapher that a thousand verses written by him sold for 10,000 dínárs. He was living about the year 1585 A. D., 993 A. H.

**Moi'zz-uddaula,** معز الدوله, the brother of 'Imád-uddaula 'Alí Bóya. He was nominated Wazír to the Khalíf Al-Rází Billáh in 936 A. D., and held that office during the reigns of Al-Muttakí and Al-Mustakfí, the latter of whom he afterwards dethroned, and continued through life to exercise absolute authority over Al-Mutía, the son of the Khalíf Al-Muktadir, whom he elevated to the throne. He was the youngest of the three brothers. He governed 'Irak 21 years and 11 months and died at Baghdád on Monday the 1st of April, 967 A. D., 17th Rabí' II, 356 A. H. He was succeeded by his son 'Izz-uddaula Bakhtaiár, who was killed in battle in 968 A. D., 356 A. H., by Azd-uddaula, the son of Rukn-uddaula who succeeded him in the office of wazír to the Khalíf of Baghdád.

**Momin, Mir,** مير مومن استرابادي, of Astarábád, an author.

**Momin,** مومن, Hakím Muhammad Mómin Khán, a physician and the best poet of his time in Dehlí. He wrote Persian and Rekhta poetry, and has left a Díwán in Persian and several Masnawís. He fell from the roof of his house and broke his arm in 1852 A. D., 1268 A. H., and died after a few days.

**Momin 'Ali, Shaikh,** شيخ مومن علي, a poet whose poetical name was Maftún.

**Mubid,** موبد, the takhallus of Zinda Rám of Kashmír. He was a pupil of Mirzá 'Abdul Ghaní Beg Kabúl, and is the author of a Díwán. He died in 1759 A. D., 1172 A. H.

**Mubid Shah,** موبد شاه, a Guebre who turned Musalmán and wrote a history of the religions in the time of the emperor Akbar, entitled "Dabistán." The intention of the author appears to have been to furnish to Akbar, a pretended historical basis of the religion which this emperor had invented, and which he was desirous to introduce. For this reason, the author commences with a very long chapter on the religion of the Mahábádians, which is a mere web of incoherent fables. Sir William Jones first mentioned this work. Gladwin published in the "New Asiatic Miscellany," its first chapter, together with an English translation. Leyden in the 9th volume of the Asiatic Researches, translated the chapter on the Illuminati, and the text of the whole work was published at Calcutta in 1809. The Oriental Translation Society also published the whole in English.

**Mu'in-uddin,** معين الدين, author of the "Ganj Sa'ádat," dedicated to the emperor 'Alamgír.

**Mu'in-uddin Chishti, Khwaja,** خواجه معين الدين چشتي, a celebrated Muhammadan saint whose tomb is at Ajmír. He was born at Sístán in 1142 A. D., 537 A. H., came to India and was residing at Ajmír when Pithaura, rájá of that place, was taken prisoner and put to death by Shahab-uddín Ghorí surnamed Moi'zz-uddín Muhammad Sám in 1192 A. D., 633 A. H. Mo'ín-uddín died in 1236 A. D., aged 97 lunar years. The inside of the mausoleum is both magnificent and solemn, the floor is paved with pure marble, the walls nicely latticed, the ceiling beautifully white and smooth. In the centre stands the tomb, covered with very valuable brocade. At the head of the tomb is placed a large silver censer, from which the smoke of the burning incense diffuses its fragrance all over the place night and day.

**Mu'in-uddin Isfarari, Maulana,** مولانا معين الدين اسفراري, author of the "Táríkh Mubárik Sháhí."

**Mu'in-uddin Jawini, Maulana,** مولانا معين الدين جويني, a native of Jawín, and author of the "Nigáristán," (the gallery of pictures). A miscellaneous work upon moral subjects, in prose and verse, which he wrote in imitation of the Gulistán of Sa'dí. There is a beautiful copy of this book, says Sir Wm. Jones, in the Bodleian library at Oxford. He was a contemporary of Shaikh Sa'ad-uddín Hamwia who died in the year 1252 A. D. 650 A. H.

**Mu'in-uddin Muhammad,** معين الدين محمد هروي of Hirát, an author of several works, among which are "Táríkh Músawí," a history of the Jews; describing their origin, sufferings in Egypt &c. The "Rauzat ul-Jannat," containing a minute description of the city of Hirát, dedicated to Sultán Husain Abú'l Ghází Bahádur in 1493 A. D., 900 A. H. The "Mia'ráj ul-Nabúat," or the ascent of the prophet, detailing some of the grossest falsehoods that human invention ever suggested. Among many shocking circumstances of his journey to heaven, it is related that he saw the souls of his father and mother swimming in the liquid fire of hell; and being about to interpose for them, he was told that if he then interceded for unbelievers, his intercession for the faithful on the Day of Judgment would not be admitted: he therefore left them to their fate. This work was written in 1486 A. D., 891 A. H. He is also the author of the "Rauzat ul-Waezín."

**Mu'in-uddin,** معين الدين, commonly called Bhanbú, the son of Zábita Khán, which see.

**Mu'in ul-Mulk Rustam Hind,** معين الملك رستم هند, commonly called Mír Mannú, was the son of Ya'tmád-uddaula Kamar-uddín Khán, Wazír. He was appointed governor of Láhor by the emperor Ahmad Sháh of Dehlí after the battle of Sarhind against Ahmad Sháh Abdálí in which his father was killed in 1748 A. D., 1161 A. H. He died suddenly in the year 1754 A. D., 1167 A. H.

**Mujid,** موجد, the takhallus of a poet who is the author of a Díwán.

**Munis, Haji,** حاجي مونس, author of a Díwán which he completed in 1723 A. D., 1135 A. H.

**Musa, Sayyad,** سيد موسي. He fell in love with Moháni a jeweller's daughter in the time of the emperor Akbar; an account of whom may be seen in the Tárikh Badáoní.

**Musi bin-'Ukba,** موسي بن عقبة, author of the work called "Kitáb Maghází." He died in 758 A. D., 141 A. H.

**Musi Kazim, Imam,** امام موسي كاظم, was the seventh Imám of the race of 'Alí, and succeeded his father Imám Jáfar Sádik who was the sixth. He was born 745 A. D., 128 A. H., and died in the reign of the Khalíf Hárún al-Rashíd on the 1st September, 799 A. D., 25th Rajab, 183 A. H. He is buried at Baghdád on the west bank of the Tigris, opposite to the mausoleum of Abú Haníta, which is on the east bank, and as one of his grandchildren, named Imám Muhammad Takí was buried afterwards in the same vault, they are called Kázimín. His mother's name was Hamída. It is said that he was imprisoned by Harún al-Rashíd for ten years, and then poisoned.

**Musi Raza,** موسي رضا, *vide* 'Alí Músí Razá (Imám).

**Muswi Khan,** موسوی خان, an amír of high rank in the time of the emperor 'Alamgír. His proper name was Mirzá Moi'zz or Moi'zz-uddín Muhammad, a descendant of Imám Músí Razá. He was a good poet, and had at first assumed *Fitrat* for his poetical name, but afterwards changed it to Múswí, to which the title of Khán was added by the emperor. He died in the Dakhin in 1690 A. D., 1101 A. H., aged 51 years. *Vide* Fitrat. His jagír at Ágrah extended from the Kacheri ghát to the Dargah of Sayyad near the Rájghát. The ground contained nearly 300 bighas.

**Mo'takid Khan,** معتقد خان, son of Iftikhár Khán, an officer of the rank of 4000 in the time of the emperor Sháh Jahán. He died on the 17th of October, 1651 O. S., 12th Ẕi-Ka'da, 1061 A. H., at Jaunpúr, of which place he was then governor.

**Mo'takid-uddaula,** معتقد الدولہ, the title of Mán Khán, the brother of Údham Bái, the mother of the emperor Aḥmad Sháh of Dehlí on whose accession to the throne in 1748 A. D., 1161 A. H., he was raised to the rank of 6,000 with the above title.

**Mo'tamid Billah,** معتمد باللہ, *vide* Al-Mo'tamid Billáh.

**Mo'tamid Khan,** معتمد خان, a nobleman of the reign of the emperor Jahángír, who wrote the second part (the first part was written by Jahángír himself) of the "Ikbál-náma Jahángírí," a Memoir of that monarch from his accession to the throne in 1605 A. D., 1014 A. H. After the death of Mír Jumla 1637 A. D., 1047 A. H., he was appointed Mír Bakhshí by Sháh Jahán. He died 1639 A. D., 1049 A. H., *vide* Muhammad Hadí. There is an old Masjid still standing in the city of Ágrah supposed to be erected by him.

**Mo'tamid Khan,** معتمد خان, a nobleman, who lived in the time of the emperor 'Alamgír and built the Masjid of Gwaliar in the year 1661 A. D., 1072 A. H., which is at the present time in perfect good order.

**Mo'tamid-uddaula Bahadur Sardar Jang,** معتمد الدولہ بہادر سردار جنگ. He was Díwán to Salábat Jang of Haidarábád, and died in 1774 A. D., 1188 A. H.

**Mo'tarazzi,** معترزی, surname of Nasr bin-'Abdus Sa'íd, also named Burhán-uddín bin-'Abdul Mukárim. He was one of the most illustrious Arabian grammarians. He died 1213 A. D., 610 A. H.

**Mo'tasim Billah,** معتصم باللہ, khalíf of Baghdád, *vide* Al-Mo'tasim Billáh.

**Mo'tazid Billah,** معتضد باللہ, khalíf of Baghdád, *vide* Al-Mo'tazid Billáh.

**Moti Begam,** موتي بيگم, one of the wives of the emperor Sháh Jahán; who built a garden called Mótí Bágh on the banks of the Jamna near the Rájghát at Ágrah; no traces of it are to be seen now, but the ground on which it was built is still called Mótí Bágh, and some of its land is under cultivation.

**Mu'ajiz,** معاجز, poetical title of Muhammad Nizám Khán, an Afghán who was an author and died at Dehlí in 1749 A. D., 1162 A. H.

**Mu'awia I,** معاويہ, the son of Abú Sufián, the son of Harb, and general of the khalífs 'Umar and 'Usmán. After avenging his master's (Osman's) death, he seized his kingdom 644 A. D., and became the first khalíf of the race of Umayya or Ommiades. He took Rhodes and after destroying the Colossus, he attacked Sicily, and carried devastation to the gates of Constantinople. After beseiging in vain the capital for seven years, he purchased peace by an annual tribute. During this seige, the Greek fire is said to have been invented. He died on the 7th of April, 680 A. D., New Moon of Rajab, 60 A. H., after having reigned from Hasan's resignation, 19 lunar years 3 months and 27 days, and was buried at Damascus his capital, which was made the residence of the khalífs as long as the house of Umayya continued on the throne. Mu'áwia had embraced the Muhammadan religion at the same time with his father, which was in the year of the victory. Muhammad made him his secretary, and 'Umar gave him the lieutenancy of Syria, which he held during four years of that khalíf's life. 'Usmán continued him in that post during the whole space of his reign, which was about 12 years. Four years more he kept Syria in his own hands by force, whilst he held out against 'Alí. Taking altogether, therefore, he had held possession of Syria, either as governor or khalíf, for nearly 40 years. There are different reports about his age; some say 70 years and others 75. He was succeeded by his son Yezíd I.

*Khalífs of the house of Umayya who reigned at Damascus.*

1. Mu'áwia I.
2. Yezíd I.
3. Mu'áwia II.
4. Marwán I.
5. 'Abdul Malik.
6. Walíd I.
7. Sulaiman.
8. 'Umar, son of 'Abdul Azíz.
9. Yezíd II.
10. Hashám.
11. Walíd, son of Yezíd II.
12. Yezíd III.
13. Ibrahím, son of Walíd.
14. Marwán II, the last of the Ommaides.

**Mu'awia II,** معاويہ, son of Yezíd I, and the third khalíf of the race of Umayya. He succeeded his father in September, 683 A. D., 64 A. H., at Damascus, but being of a weakly constitution, and unable to bear the fatigues of government, resigned the crown six weeks after his inauguration, and died soon after without naming a successor. Therefore, as soon as he had made his abdication, the officers of the court proceeded to the election of a khalíf and their choice fell upon Marwán, the son of Hakam. In the meantime 'Abdullah the son of Zuber had been declared khalíf in Arabia, 'Irák, Khurásán, Egypt, and a great part of Syria. *Vide* 'Umar al-Maksús.

**Mua'zzi, Amir,** امير مغري, a nobleman at the court of Sulṭán Malikshah Saljúḳí. He is the author of a Díwán in Persian. He was living at the time of the Sulṭán's death which happened in 1092 A. D., *vide* Amír Moizzí.

**Mu'azzam Khan,** معظم خان خانخانان, Khán Khánán entitled Mír Jumla, which see.

**Mu'azzam, Khwaja,** خواجہ معظم, *vide* Khwaja Mu'azzam.

**Mu'azzam, Muhammad,** محمد معظم, *vide* Bahádur Sháh I.

**Mubarik 'Ali Khan,** نواب مبارک علي خان, Nawáb of Bengal, Behár and Urisa, placed on the masnad on the 23rd of December, 1824 A. D.

**Mubarik Shah Khilji,** مبارک شاہ خلجي, surnamed Ḳuṭb-uddín, ascended the throne of Dehlí (according to Firishta) on the 22nd of March, 1317 A. D., 7th Muḥarram, 717 A. H. after the death of his father Sulṭán 'Alá-uddín Khiljí, and the murder of Káfúr a slave of the latter who had aspired to the throne and had raised Shaháb-uddín 'Umar Khán a boy of seven years of age, the youngest son of the late Sulṭán to the throne. Amír Khusro, the celebrated Persian poet who had served three kings before, wrote a book in his name, for which he was remunerated by the king with an elephant load of silver-pieces. Mubárik Sháh reigned four years, and was murdered on the 4th April, 1321 A. D., 5th Rabí' I, 721 A. H., by his wazír, Malik Khusro, a favourite slave to whom he had confided all the powers of the State. This man ascended the throne with the title of Khusro Sháh, but was assassinated five months after by Ghází Khán Tughlaḳ, governor of the Panjáb, who took the title of Ghayás-uddín Tughlaḳ Sháh. The house of Khiljí terminated with Mubárik Sháh.

**Mubarik Shah,** مبارک شاه, the son of Khizir Khán ascended the throne of Dehlí after the death of his father on the 22nd May, 1421 A. D., 19th Jumáda I, 824 A. H. He reigned 13 lunar years 3 months and 16 days, and was murdered on the 18th of April, 1434 A. D., 5th Ramazán, 837 A. H. in a masjid where he had gone to say his prayers, by Ḳází 'Abdus Samad, Sadháran Khattrí and others, who raised Muhammad Sháh, his nephew, to the throne.

**Mubarik Shah Sharki,** مبارك شاه شرقي, whose former name was Malik Wásil or Karanfal, was the adopted son of Khwája Jahán Sharḳí whom he succeeded 1401 A. D., 803 A. H. to the government of Jaunpúr, and perceiving that the kingdom of Dehlí was thrown into disorder and anarchy, he, with the consent of the officers of his government, assúmed the royal canopy, and caused coin to be struck in his name under the above title. He died after a short reign of 18 months in the year 1402 A. D., 804 A. H., and was succeeded by his younger brother Ibráhím Sháh Sharḳí.

**Mubarik, Shaikh,** *vide* Shaikh Mubárik.

**Mubarik-uddaula,** مبارك الدوله, the youngest of the three sons of Mír Ja'far 'Alí Khán, Nawáb of Bengal. He succeeded his brother Saif-uddaula in March, 1770 A. D., on the same terms as his brother, *viz.*, to receive a pension of sixteen lacs of rupees, and the business of Názim to be managed by deputy. He died at Murshidábád in September, 1793 A. D., and was succeeded by his son Názir ul-Mulk, Wazír-uddaula. Mubárik-uddaula is mentioned in Forster's Travels as the grandson of Mír Ja'far and son of Míran. Hamilton says Mubárik-uddaula died in 1796 A. D.

**Mubarik-ullah, Mirza,** مرزا مبارک الله, a Persian poet.

**Mubariz Khan,** مبارز خان, a nobleman who, in the commencement of the reign of Muhammad Sháh of Dehlí, was governor of Haidarábád, and was killed in a battle which he fought at the instigation of the emperor against Nizám ul-Mulk on the 1st of October, 1724 O. S., 23rd Muḥarram, 1137 A. H., and his head sent to court with part of his spoils.

**Mubariz ul-Mulk,** مبارز الملك, a title of Nawáb Sarbaland Khán.

**Mubtila,** مبتلا, takhallus of Shaikh Ghulám Muhí-uddín Ḳureshí of Mírath. He is the author of several works. He was living in 1807 A. D., 1222 A. H.

**Mudki Rao,** مدكي راؤ, *vide* Jhanko Ráo Sendhía.

**Mu'in Jawini,** معين جويني, *vide* Mo'ín-uddín Jawíní.

**Mufid, Mulla,** ملامفيد, *vide* Mullá Mufíd.

**Mufid, Shaikh,** شيخ مفيد, *vide* Abú 'Abdullah Muhammad bin-Muhammad al-Na'mání.

**Mufrid,** مفرد, poetical name of Muhammad 'Alí Beg.

**Mughal Beg,** مغل بيگ, a nobleman of the reign of the emperor Akbar. He is the author of the work entitled "Samrát ul-Kuds," commonly called "Tazkira Mashá-ekh."

**Mughira,** مغيره, *vide* Al-Mughíra.

**Mughis-uddin, Ḳazi,** قاضي مغيث الدين. He flourished in the reign of Sulṭán 'Alá-uddín Khiljí.

**Muhakkik Tusi,** محقق طوسي, of Tús, author of the Muiyar ul-Ashár, a book on the art of poetry. He died in the year 1273 A. D., 672 A. H., *vide* Nasír-uddín Túsí.

**Muhabbat Khan, Nawab,** نواب محبت خان, whose takhallus is Muhabbat, was also called Muhabbat-ulláh Khán, one of the sons of Háfiz Rahmat Khán. In composing Rekhta, he was a pupil of Mirzá Ja'far 'Alí Hasrat, and in Persian, a pupil of Makín. He resided at Lakhnau and received a handsome allowance from the British Government as well as from the nawáb 'Asaf-uddaula. He has written a Masnawí called "Asrár Muhabbat," containing the loves of "Sísí and Pánú," at the request of Mr. Johnson who had the title of Mumtáz-uddaula, and is also the author of a Díwán. According to a chronogram of Jurat, he died in 1807 A. D., 1222 A. H.

**Muhammad,** محمد, (or Mahomed) the Arabian prophet, author of the "Ḳurán," was born on Monday the 20th of April, 571 A. D., 10th Rabí' I, A. H. at Mecca in Arabia, and was of the tribe of Ḳuresh, the noblest of the country. Arab writers make him to be descended in a right line from Ishmael the son of Abraham; but do not pretend to any certainty in the remote part of his genealogy. He lost his father, 'Abdullah, before he was two years old, and his mother, 'Amina, before he was six; but their attention was supplied by the care of his grandfather 'Abdul Muttalib, who at his death, which happened two years after, left him under the guardianship of his son Abú Tálib with whom he continued till he was twenty-five, when he was placed in the service of a woman, named Khudyja, the widow of a rich merchant at Mecca, who sent merchandize into Syria. This woman fell in love with Muhammad, the driver of her camels, and married him. In his frequent journeys through Arabia, he had observed the various sects which divided the opinions of the eastern Christians, and he considered that nothing could so firmly secure to him the respect of the world as laying the foundation of a new religion. He, in his 40th year assumed the title of the Apostle of God, and gradually increased his fame and his followers by the aid of pretended visions. When he found himself exposed to danger at Mecca, he left the city, and retired to Madína, where his doctrines found a more friendly reception. This event which happened in the year 622 A. D., forms the celebrated era of the Muhammadans, called the hijra or hijrí, which signifies Separation. At Madína the prophet erected his standard, and as for thirteen years before he had endeavoured to spread his doctrines by persuasion, he now propagated them by the sword. In the eleventh year of the Hijra the prophet fell sick, and after a confinement of thirteen days, he died on Monday the 8th of June, 632 A. D., 12th Rabí' I, 11 A. H., aged 63 lunar years. He was buried in the same place where he died, in the chamber of the most beloved of his wives 'Ayesha, the daughter of Abú Bakr, at Madína, where his remains are still preserved. It is very remarkable that though Muhammad himself so often declared in the Ḳurán that he wrought no miracles, yet his followers have ascribed a great many to him. For instance, they affirm, that he caused water to flow from his fingers; that he split the moon in two; that the stones, trees, and beasts acknowledged him to be the true prophet sent from God, and saluted him as such; that he went one night from Mecca to Jerusalem, from whence he ascended up to heaven, where he saw and conversed with God, and came back again to Mecca before the next morning; with many more miracles equally incredible. Muhammad permitted by his law, four wives to each of his followers; but did not limit himself to that number; for he observed that a prophet, being peculiarly gifted and privileged, was not bound to restrict himself to the same laws as ordinary mortals. The authors who give him the smallest number of wives, own that he had fifteen, four of whom, however, never shared connubial rites. Their names and the year when they died, are as follow:

| | | A. D. | A. H. |
|---|---|---|---|
| 1. | Khudyja, the daughter of Khawylid died 3 years before the Hijrí era, aged 65, ...................... | 619 | .. |
| 2. | Súda, daughter of Zama'a, died, .... | 674 | 54 |
| 3. | 'Ayesha, daughter of Abú Bakr, died aged 66, ...................... | 677 | 57 |
| 4. | Hafsa, daughter of 'Umar Khattáb, died, ...................... | 665 | 45 |
| 5. | Umm Salma, daughter of Abú Umayya, outlived all Muhammad's wives, and died, ...................... | 679 | 59 |
| 6. | Umm Habíba, daughter of Abú Sufyán, died, ...................... | 664 | 44 |
| 7. | Zainab, daughter of Jahash, widow of Zaid, Muhammad's slave, died, .... | 641 | 20 |
| 8. | Zainab, daughter of Khuzyma, died 2 months after the above, .......... | 641 | 20 |
| 9. | Maimúna, daughter of Harith, died, | 671 | 51 |
| 10. | Jawyria, daughter of Harith, ...... | 670/5 | 50/56 |
| 11. | Safyá, daughter of Hai bin-Akhtab, died, ...................... | 670 | 50 |
| 12. | Maria Copti, or the Egyptian, of whom was born Ibráhím, .............. | 637 | 16 |

By Khudyja his first wife, he had six children, two sons and four daughters, *viz.*, Ḳasim and 'Abdullah who is also called Táhir; and Zainab, Rukia, Umm Kulsúm and Fátima; all of whom died before their father, excepting Fátima who was married to 'Alí, and survived her father six months.

**Muhammad I,** محمد اول, (or Mahomet I) Sultán of the Turks, was the son of Báyezíd I (Bajazet) whom he succeeded in 1413 A. D., 816 A. H., after an interregnum of eleven years, during which time his brother Sulaimán had taken possession of Brusa. He was a brave and politic monarch, conquered Cappadocia, Servia, Wallachia, and other provinces, and was at peace with Manuel Palœologos, emperor of Constantinople, to whom he restored some of his provinces, and died at Andrianople of a bloody-flux 1422 A. D., 825 A. H., aged 47 years. He was succeeded by his son Murád II (Amurath).

**Muhammad II,** محمد ثاني, (Mahomet II) emperor of the Turks, surnamed the Great, succeeded his father Murád II (Amurath) in February, 1451 A. D., Muḥarram, 855 A. H. His reign was begun with preparations for war; he besieged Constantinople, and conveyed over the land some of his gallies into the harbour, which the Greeks had shut up against the invaders. Constantinople was taken by him on Tuesday the 29th of May, 1453 A. D., 20th Jumáḍa I, 857 A. H., and in her fall poured forth her fugitive philosophers and learned men to revive literature in the Western world. Muhammad by his victories, deserved the name of Great; and the appellation of Grand Seignor, which he assumed, has descended to his successors. After subduing two empires, twelve tributary kingdoms and two hundred towns, he was preparing for the subjugation of Italy, when a colic proved fatal to him, and he died on Thursday the 3rd May, 1481 A. D., 3rd Rabí' I, 886 A. H., after a reign of 31 lunar years. His death was the cause of universal rejoicings over the Christian world, whose religion he had sworn to exterminate, for the tenets of Muhammad. He was of an exceeding courage and strength, of a sharp wit, and very fortunate; but withal, he was faithless and cruel: and in his time occasioned the death of 80,000 Christians of both sexes. His son Báyezíd II succeeded him.

**Muhammad III,** محمد ثالث, emperor of the Turks, succeeded his father Murád III in January, 1595 A. D., Jumáḍa I, 1003 A. H. to the throne of Constantinople. He began his reign by ordering nineteen of his brothers to be strangled, and ten of his father's wives to be drowned, whom he supposed to be with child. He made war against Rodulphus II, emperor of Germany, and invaded Hungary with an army of 200,000 men, but his progress was checked by Maximillian the emperor's brother, who would have obtained a decisive victory, had not his troops abandoned themselves to pillage. Muhammad, obliged to retire from Hungary, buried himself in the indolence of his seraglio. He died of the plague, after a reign of 9 years in January, 1604 A. D., Shábán, 1012 A. H., aged 59 years, and was succeeded by his son Ahmad I.

**Muhammad IV,** محمد رابع, emperor of the Turks, was the son of Ibráhím, whom he succeeded on the throne of Constantinople in 1649 A. D., 1059 A. H. He pursued the war with the Venetians, and after reducing Candia, with the loss of 200,000 men, he invaded Poland. His arms proved victorious, but the disgrace was wiped off by the valour of Sobeski, king of Poland, who the next year routed his enemies at the battle of Choezim. He was deposed in 1687 A. D., 1098 A. H., and sent to prison where he died in 1691 A. D., 1102 A. H. He was succeeded by his brother Sulaimán II.

**Muhammad Abd,** محمد عبد, author of a Persian work on Jurisprudence called "Asás ul-Islám," the Foundation of Muhammadanism, and of one called "Fiḳha Sunnatf wa-Jamáa't."

**Muhammad 'Adil Shah,** محمد عادل شاه, king of Bíjápúr, succeeded his father Ibráhím 'Adil Sháh II, in the year 1626 A. D., 1036 A. H. As the armies of the emperor of Dehlí were daily extending their conquests in the Dakhin, and he knew that should the country of Aḥmadnagar be reduced, his own would become the object of attack, he assisted Nizám Sháh against the imperial arms; and more than once suffered for his conduct, being obliged to purchase peace by large contributions. In the year 1634 A. D., 1044 A. H. the armies of the emperor Sháh Jahán invaded the Dakhin on three quarters and laid waste the country of Bíjápúr without mercy. After the reduction of Daulatábád and other forts, with most part of the kingdom of Nizám Sháh, Muhammad 'Adil Sháh agreed to pay a considerable tribute to the emperor. He was the last king of Bíjápúr who struck coins in his own name. In the latter part of his reign, his vassal Sewájí, the son of Sáhú Bhósla, by stratagem and treachery obtained great power, and the foundation of the Bíjápúr monarchy became weakened. He died in November, 1656 A. D., Muḥarram, 1067 A. H. and was succeeded by his son 'Alí 'Adil Sháh II. His tomb at Bíjápúr called "Gol Gumbaz," has a dome which measures 130 feet in diameter which can be seen from 30 miles distance. A beautiful view is seen from the roof; the tomb being at the very end of the city, all the remarkable places present themselves to us, and the eye loses itself in the vast number of cupolas, domes, and minarets crowded together. Conspicuous among these are seen the fair proportions of the Rauza or tomb of Ibráhím 'Adil Sháh.

**Muhammad Afzal,** محمد افضل, author of the work named "Madínat ul-Aubia." It gives an account of the creation of the world, and a history of all the prophets prior to the birth of Muhammad.

**Muhammad Afzal, Shaikh,** شيخ محمد افضل, son of Shaikh 'Abdur Rahím, a pírzada and native of Gházípúr, who by the command of his murshid or spiritual guide, Mír Syyid Muhammad of Kálpí, fixed his residence at Allahábád where he held a school and passed the remainder of his life in teaching Arabic and Persian, and making proselytes. He is the author of several works; was born on the 28th October, 1628 O. S., 10th Rabí' I, 1038 A. H., and died aged 87 lunar years on Friday the 2nd of January, 1713 O. S., 15th Ẕil-ḥijja, 1124 A. H. His descendants are still at Allahábád. He used "Afzal" for his poetical name.

**Muhammad Akbar,** محمد اكبر, the emperor Akbar is sometimes so called.

**Muhammad Akbar,** محمد اكبر, the youngest son of the Emperor Aurangzib 'Álamgír. He rebelled against his father, went to Persia and died there in 1115 A. H.

**Muhammad Akbar,** محمد اكبر, son of Muhammad Gesú Daráz of Kulbarga. He is the author of a Persian work on Theology entitled "'Akáed Akbarí," containing the principles of the Muhammadan faith.

**Muhammad 'Ala-uddin bin Shaikh 'Ali al-Hiskafi,** محمد علاء الدين بن شيخ علی الحسكفي, author of the work on Jurisprudence called the Fatáwá Durr al-Mukhtár," which is a commentary on the Tanwír ul-Absár, containing a multitude of decisions.

**Muhammad 'Ali Hazin,** محمد علی حزين, *vide* Hazín.

**Muhammad 'Ali,** محمد علي, author of an Inshá or collection of Letters.

**Muhammad 'Ali Khan,** محمد علی خان, eldest son of Faiz-ullah Khán the Rohela chief of Rámpúr. He succeeded his father in 1794 A. D.

**Muhammad 'Ali Khan,** محمد علي خان, Nawáb of the Carnatic, was the son of Anwar-uddín Khán. After his father's death he was confirmed to the government of the Carnatic by Nawáb Násir Jang in 1750 A. D., and placed on the masnad by the assistance of the English. He died aged 78 years, on the 13th October, 1795 A. D.; and his son 'Umdat ul-Umrá succeeded him.

**Muhammad 'Ali Khan, Rohela,** محمد علی خان, he succeeded his father Faiz-ullah Khán in September, 1794 A. D. to his jágír of Rámpúr. *Vide* Faiz-ullah Khán.

**Muhammad 'Ali Mahir,** محمد علی ماهر, *vide* Máhir.

**Muhammad 'Ali Khan,** محمد علي خان, Nawáb of Tonk, son of the Pindari chief Amír Khán, succeeded his father to the gaddí of Tonk in 1834, and was deposed in 1867 on account of the Lawa massacre. His state came under the immediate control of the Political Department in the end of 1870 when his son Ibráhím 'Alí Khán was installed as Nawáb of Tonk.

**Muhammad 'Ali, Mir,** مير محمد علي, of Burhánpúr, author of the Mirat-us-Safá."—(See *All the Year Round,* Vol. XVIII, p. 157.)

**Muhammad 'Ali,** محمد علي, Viceroy of Egypt. Upwards of twelve centuries have passed since Egypt fell under the arms of the successful General of the Khalíf Omar; for a little over five centuries it remained in the possession of the successors of the conqueror; their power was put to an end by the Turkmans in 1171 A. D., and about eighty years afterwards the latter were in their turn expelled by the Mamlooks. The Mamlooks raised one of their own number to the throne, with the title of Sulṭán, and the dynasty lasted till 1517, when the last of the Mamlook Sulṭáns was put to death by the Turkish Sulṭán Salam, who appointed a Pasha to the government assisted by a council of twenty-four Mamlook beys or chiefs. This state of things lasted till 1798, when the French under Bonaparte landed in Egypt, and after destroying the Mamlooks, were themselves attacked and defeated by the British in 1801. After the departure of the British, the country fell into anarchy till it was restored by Muhammad 'Alí, who by the massacre of the remaining Mamlooks made himself master of the situation. The treaty of London in 1841 made the government of Egypt hereditary in the family of Muhammad 'Alí, and Ismá'íl Pasha is his grandson. Egypt has now ceased to be a province of Turkey. Its ruler has had all the powers of an independent sovereign conceded to him by the Farmán which dates from the 8th of June, 1873 A. D. Muhammad was born in 1769, entered the Turkish army, and in 1799 was sent to Egypt at the head of a contingent to co-operate with the British against the French invaders. Here his fine military qualities rapidly developed themselves, and he at length became the Commander of the Albanian Corps d'armee in Egypt. He was soon after involved in disputes with the Mamlooks who had long practically ruled Egypt. They were at length entirely exterminated in 1820. He declared himself independent of the Porte in 1838, and died on the 2nd August, 1849 A. D. He was succeeded by his son or grandson Ismá'íl Pasha.

**Muhammad 'Ali Shah,** محمد علي شاه, whose former title was Nawáb Nasír-uddaula, was the son of Sa'ádat 'Alí Khán, Nawáb of Audh. He was placed on the throne of Lakhnau by the British, after the death of his nephew, Sulaimán Jáh Nasír-uddín Haidar, on the 8th of July, 1837 A. D., 4th Rabí' II, 1253 A. H. at the age of 70 years, and took the title of Abú'l Fatha Moín-uddín Sulṭán Zamán Muhammad 'Alí Sháh. He reigned exactly five lunar years, and died at Lakhnau on Tuesday the 17th May, 1842 A. D., 5th Rabí' II, 1258 A. H., when his son Suryya Jáh Amjad 'Alí Sháh succeeded him.

**Muhammad al-Mahdi,** محمد المهدي, the first khalíf or king of Barbary of the race of the Fatimites. He began to reign in 908 A. D., 296 A. H., and was supposed to be a descendant of Husain the son of 'Alí and Fátima, whence the race is called Fátimite. His descendants conquered Egypt. He died in 933 A. D., 321 A. H., and was succeeded by his son Káem Biamr-ullah, who died in 945 A. D., 334 A. H., and was succeeded by his son Mansúr Billáh in 952 A. D., 341 A. H. *Vide* Maizli-ud-din-Allah.

**Muhammad Amin,** محمد امين, son of Daulat Muhammad al-Husainí al-Balkhí, is the author of the work called "Anfa' ul-Akhbár," or Useful Chronicle; was in the service of Nawáb Sipahdar Khán, who receives a long and laudatory notice at the close of the work. He concluded it in 1626 A. D., 1036 A. H., and styled it Anfa' ul-Akhbár, because the Hijrí year 1036 A. H. in which it was completed, is represented by the letters composing those words. He resided chiefly at Aḥmadnagar.

**Muhammad Amin,** محمد امين, author of the work entitled "'Asrár ul-Ma'ání," a collection of poems on the the conquests of the emperor 'Alamgír, and a panegyric on several cities of the Dakhin, which previous to its being subdued by his arms, was esteemed the garden of India. He also wrote another work on Theology entitled "Haḳíḳat Ilm Iláhí."

**Muhammad Amin Khan,** محمد امين خان, son of Muhammad Sa'íd Mír Jumla. He served under the emperors Sháh Jahán and 'Alamgír, and was raised to the rank of 5000. He died on the 6th May, 1682 O. S., 8th Jumáḍa I, 1093 A. H. at Aḥmadábád Gujrát.

**Muhammad Amin Khan,** محمد امين خان, entitled Ya'tmád-uddaula, was the son of Mír Bahá-uddín, the brother of Nizám ul-Mulk 'Asaf Jáh, and came to India in the reign of 'Alamgír under whom he served for several years. He was the chief counsellor of the emperor Muhammad Sháh, and was appointed Wazír with the above title after the death of Sayyad Husain 'Alí Khán and the imprisonment of his brother Sayyad 'Abdullah Khán in 1720 A. D., 1133 A. H., but he had scarcely entered on his office, when he was taken ill and died suddenly on the 17th of January, 1721 O. S., 29th Rabí' I, 1133 A. H. After his death the office of prime-minister was only filled by a temporary substitute, being ultimately designed for Nizám ul-Mulk 'Asaf Jáh, who was then in the Dakhin.

**Muhammad Amin Razi,** محمد امين رازي, *vide* Amín Aḥmad, author of the Haft Aḳlím.

**Muhammad Amir Khan,** محمد اميرخان, of Ágrah, author of the "Maulúd Nádirí" containing the history and miracles of 'Abdul Kadir Gíláni in Urdú, written in 1847 A. D., 1263 A. H., *vide* Muhammad Ḳásim.

**Muhammad Ansar,** محمد انصار, author of the work called "Malfúzát Shaikh Aḥmad Maghrabi" or the Memoirs of Shaikh Aḥmad Khaṭṭú, a very celebrated Súfí of Gujrát, whose tomb is at Ahmadábád, and still held in veneration. It was written in 1445 A. D., 849 A. H.

**Muhammad 'Arif, Mirza,** ميرزا محمد عارف, a poet who was contemporary with Násir 'Alí.

**Muhammad Aslam, Kazi,** قاضي محمد اسلم, who lived in the time of Shalydan.

**Muhammad, Atabak,** اتابك محمد, *vide* Atábak Muhammad.

**Muhammad 'Azim,** محمد اعظم, an historian who wrote a history of Kashmír in continuation of one written by Haidar Malik. It is amusing to observe, says Mr. H. M. Elliot, the extravagant praises which this orthodox historian confers upon 'Alamgír, whom he infinitely prefers to the noble and enlightened Akbar of whom he complains that he "treated all his subjects alike!" not favouring the Muhammadans above the Hindús. Was ever a nobler tribute paid to a ruler?

**Muhammad Bakhtyar Khilji,** محمد بختيار خلجي, was appointed governor of Bengal by Sulṭán Ḳuṭb-uddín Eybak about the year 1203 A. D., 600 A. H. He made Lakhnauṭí the seat of his government.

| | A.D. | A.H. |
|---|---|---|
| Muhammad Bakhtyár Khiljí, ........ began | 1203 | 600 |
| Muhammad Sherán Azz-uddín, slain in battle with the infidels, ..................... | 1205 | 602 |
| 'Alí Murdán 'Alá-uddín Khiljí slain, ...... | 1208 | 605 |
| Husám-uddín Ghausí slain, ............ | 1212 | 609 |
| Násir-uddín bin-Shams-uddín, ......... | 1227 | 624 |
| Mahmúd bin-Shams-uddín, became Sulṭán of Hindústán,.......................... | 1229 | 627 |
| Tughán Khán, governor under Sulṭána Rizia, | 1237 | 634 |
| Tijí or Tají, .......................... | 1243 | 641 |
| Taimúr Khán Ḳirán, ................... | 1244 | 642 |
| Saif-uddín, ........................... | 1246 | 644 |
| Ikhtiár-uddín Malik Uzbak, ............. | 1253 | 651 |
| Jalál-uddín Khání, .................... | 1257 | 656 |
| Táj-uddín Arsalán, ..................... | 1258 | 657 |
| Muhammad Tátár Khán, ................ | 1260 | 659 |
| Moi'zz-uddín Tughral, ................ | 1277 | 676 |
| Násir-uddín Baghrá Khán, son of Ghayas-uddín Balban, considered-1st sovereign of Bengal, ........................... | 1282 | 681 |
| Ḳadar Khán, viceroy of Muhammad Sháh I, Tughlaḳ, ........................... | 1325 | 725 |
| Fakhr-uddín Sikandar, assumes independence, | 1340 | 741 |
| 'Alá-uddín Mubárik, .................. | 1342 | 743 |
| Shams-uddín Muhammad Sháh Iliás Bhangara, ............................... | 1343 | 744 |
| Sikandar Sháh bin-Shams-uddín, ......... | 1359 | 760 |
| Ghayás-uddín 'Azim Sháh bin-Sikandar Sháh, | 1308 | 769 |
| Saif-uddín Sulṭán us-Salátín bin-Ghayás-uddín,............................. | 1374 | 775 |
| Shams-uddín bin-Sulṭán us-Salátín,........ | 1384 | 785 |
| Kansa, a Hindú, ....................... | 1386 | 787 |
| Jalál-uddín Muhammad Sháh (Chitmal bin-Kansa),............................ | 1392 | 794 |
| Aḥmad Sháh bin-Jalál-uddín, ........... | 1409 | 812 |
| Násir Sháh (descendant of Shams-uddín Iliás), | 1427 | 830 |
| Bárbak Sháh bin-Násir Sháh began, ...... | 1457 | 862 |
| Yúsaf Sháh bin-Bárbak Sháh, ........... | 1474 | 879 |
| Sikandar Sháh,......................... | 1482 | 887 |
| Fatha Sháh, .......................... | 1482 | 887 |
| Sháhzáda Sulṭán, an eunuch, .............. | 1491 | 896 |
| Fíróz Sháh Habshí, ..................... | 1492 | 897 |
| Mahmúd Sháh bin-Fíróz Sháh, ........... | 1494 | 899 |
| Muzaffar Sháh Habshí, ................. | 1495 | 900 |
| 'Alá-uddín Husain Sháh bin-Sayyad Ashraf, | 1498 | 903 |
| Nasrat Sháh bin-'Alá-uddín Husain, ...... | 1521 | 927 |
| Mahmúd Sháh bin-'Alá-uddín Husain, defeated by, ............................ | 1534 | 940 |
| Faríd-uddín Sher Sháh, ................ | 1537 | 944 |
| Humayún held court at Gaur also called Jannatábád, .......................... | 1538 | 945 |
| Sher Sháh, again, ..................... | 1539 | 946 |
| Muhammad Khán, ...................... | 1545 | 952 |
| Khizir Khán Bahádur Sháh bin-Muhammad Khán,.............................. | 1555 | 962 |
| Jalál-uddín bin-Muhammad Khán, ....... | 1561 | 968 |
| Sulaimán Kiráni,........................ | 1564 | 971 |
| Báyezíd bin-Sulaimán, .................. | 1573 | 981 |
| Dáúd Khán bin-Sulaimán, defeated by Akbar's forces under Munaim Khán,........ | 1573 | 981 |

**Muhammad Azim Khan,** محمد اعظم خان, ex-amír of Kabúl, *vide* Azim Khán.

**Muhammad Baki, Khwaja,** خواجه محمد باقي, a Muhammadan saint who died on the 20th October, 1603

A. D., 25th Jumáda II, 1012 A. H., and is buried at Dehlí close to the Kadam Rasúl. Nizám-uddín Ahmad has mentioned him in his work called Karámát ul-Aulia.

**Muhammad Bakhsh,** محمد بخش, whose poetical name is Mahjúr, is the author of a work in Urdú called Nauratan or the nine jewels containing numerous stories which he completed in the first year of Nawáb Ghazí-uddín Haidar of Lakhnau or 1230 A. H. He is also the author of two other works of the same description one called "Gulshan Naubahár" and the other "Chár Chaman."

**Muhammad Bakir,** محمد باقر مجلسي, surnamed Majlisí (or the Ornament of Assemblies) the son of Muhammad Takí, was Shaikh ul-Islám or high priest of the city of Isfahán, and one of the most celebrated Shia lawyers and learned scholar that Persia ever produced in general literature, law and theology. Such was the esteem in which he was held, that Sháh Sulaimán pressed upon him the hand of his daughter, which, strange to say, he declined. One alone of this celebrated man's works, called "Hakk ul-Yekín" which he dedicated to Sháh Husain, extends to fourteen folio volumes. It contains a body of the theology of the Shias, and quotes and refutes the arguments opposed to the opinions advanced, illustrating the whole with evidences of the truth of the Shia doctrines and with numerous traditions. Besides this, he wrote on many other subjects. One of his works treating exclusively of Hadís, is called "Bahr ul-Anwár." He died 1698 A. D., 1110 A. H., aged 72 years.

**Muhammad Bakir Damad, Mir,** مير محمد باقر داماد. His father Sayyad Mahmúd was styled Dámád, because he was the son-in-law of Shaikh 'Alí 'Amilí. He was a native of Astrábád in Persia. Muhammad Bákir his son was also styled Dámád, because he married the daughter of Sháh 'Abbás I, king of Persia. He resided for many years in Isfahán, and is the author of several compilations, one of which is called Utkil Mubun. He died 1630 A. D., 1040 A. H., *vide* Mír Bákir Dámád.

**Muhammad Bakir, Imam,** امام محمد باقر, the son of Imám Zain-ul 'Abidín, was the fifth Imám of the race of 'Alí. He was born on the 17th of December, 676 A. D., 3rd Safar, 57 A. H., and died in the month of May or June, 731 A. D., Rabí' I, 113 A. H. His corpse was carried to Madína and interred at the Bakía cemetery, in the vault wherein was deposited the bodies of his father and his father's uncle; it is placed under the same dome which covers the tomb of 'Abbás. Some authors have given the day of his death to be 28th January, 733 A. D., which corresponds with the 7th Zil-hijja, 114 A. H.

**Muhammad Beg Khan,** محمد بيگ خان, *vide* Hájí Muhammad Beg Khán.

**Muhammad bin-'Abdul 'Aziz,** محمد بن عبد العزيز, surnamed Wajúdí, author of the work in Turkí called "Sháhid wa-Ma'ní." He died in the year 1612 A. D., 1021 A. H.

**Muhammad bin-'Abdur Rahman,** محمد بن عبد الرحمان, surnamed bin-'Alí Laila, was a very celebrated Musalmán doctor, and Kází of the city of Kúfa, where he was born in 693 A. D., 74 A. H., and died in the year 765 A. D., 148 A. H.

**Muhammad bin-Abu Bakr,** محمد بن ابوبكر, *i. e.*, the son of 'Abú Bakr the first khalíf after Muhammad. He was made governor of Egypt by the khalíf 'Ali, but was taken prisoner soon after in a battle fought against Amrú ibn-ul-'As the deputy of Muáwia I, who killed him, and, inclosing his dead body in the skin of an ass, burned it to ashes in 657 A. D., 38 A. H.

**Muhammad bin-Ahmad,** محمد بن احمد هروي, of Hírát, author of the "Tarjuma Fatúh 'Arabí," containing the conquests of the Arabian Tribes and the domestic quarrels of the Muhammadans, commencing from the Khiláfat of 'Abú Bakr 632 A. D., 11 A. H., and continued till the murder of Husain at the battle of Karbala in 680 A. D., 61 A. H. This work is translated from the Arabic, and was written in 1199 A. D., 595 A. H.

**Muhammad bin-'Ali,** محمد بن علي, author of the Arabic work entitled "Abnái ul-Janán," containing the Life of Muhammad and Memoirs of his companions.

**Muhammad bin-'Amru at-Tamimi,** محمد بن عمرو التميمي, author of a biographical work on the lives of eminent Shias.

**Muhammad bin-Isa Tirmizi,** محمد بن عيسي ترمذي, author of the work called "Jáma' Tirmizí." It is also called "Sunan Tirmizí" and likewise "Al-'Ilal." He was a pupil of al-Bukhárí, and died in 892 A. D., 279 A. H.

**Muhammad bin-Is,** محمد بن عيس, author of the "Risála Almua'jjam fee Asha'ár al-'Ajam."

**Muhammad bin-Husain,** محمد بن حسين, author of an Arabic work on Jurisprudence called "Badáya-ul-Hidáya," and of another in Arabic and Persian entitled "Hayát ul-Fawád." He died 1686 A. D., 1098 A. H.

**Muhammad bin-Ibrahim Sadr Shirazi Kazi ul-Kuzat,** محمد بن ابراهيم صدر شيرازي قاضي القضات, who is also called Mullá Sadr, is the author of the marginal notes on the "Ulhyyát."

**Muhammad bin-Idris, Imam,** امام محمد بن ادريس, the founder of the third orthodox sect, who is said to have been the first that reduced the Science of Jurisprudence into a regular system, and made a discriminating collection of Traditions. He died 819 A. D., 204 A. H.

**Muhammad bin-Is-hak-un-Nadim,** محمد بن اسحاق النديم, commonly called Abú Ya'kúb al Warrak, author of the "Kitáb ul-Fehrist," the most ancient record of Arabian literature, written 987 A. D., 377 A. H. This work, though mentioned by Hájí Khalfa, had hitherto escaped the industry of European explorers, but a portion of it (four books) has been found in the Royal Library of Paris, and the remainder in Herr von Hammer-Purgstall's collection. By a passage in the Fehrist, that learned gentleman has found that the *Thousand and One Nights* (Arabian Nights) had a Persian origin. In the eighth book, the author says that the first who composed tales and apologues were the kings of the first dynasty of the Persians; then those of the Arsacides the third of the four ancient dynasties of Persia: these tales were augmented and amplified by the Sasanides. The Arabs, he then proceeds to say, translated them into their tongue, composing others like them. The first book of this kind was the *Hazár Afsána*, or Thousand Tales, the subject of which the writer explains, mentioning Shahrzáda and Dínárzáda as the two females who practice the *ruse* upon the king. "It is said," continues the author, "that this book was composed by Humáe, the daughter of Bahman." The truth is, that the first who had these tales told him at night, was Alexander the Great, in order that he might keep awake, and be upon his guard. The kings who came after him made use, for the same purpose, of the Thousand Tales, which fill up a thousand nights, and two hundred conversations beside, in the light of the moon, which were related in a number of nights. Asiatic Journal, Vol. XXXI, p. 237.

**Muhammad bin-Ismail,** محمد بن اسمعيل, *vide* Muhammad Ismá'íl and Al-Bakharí.

**Muhammad bin-Jarir Tabari,** محمد بن جرير طبری, author of several works. He died in 941 A. D., 330 A. H.

**Muhammad bin-Yakub al-Kulini,** محمد بن يعقوب القوليني, author of the Arabic work called Káfí which is of high authority among the sect of the Shia.

**Muhammad bin-Ḳasim,** محمد بن قاسم, was a cousin of the khalíf Walíd I, and son-in-law of Hajjáj bin-Yúsaf Saḳafí. He by the command of the khalíf in the year 711 A. D., 92 A. H., marched with a large army to Sindh and having defeated and killed the rájá of that country took possession of it on Thursday the 23rd June, 712 A. D., 10th Ramaẓán, 93 A. H. From amongst the prisoners captured in the fort of Alor, two daughters of the rájá were sent to Damascus, and the khalíf sent them to his harem, consigning them to the care of his people until their grief should be assuaged. After two months, they were brought to the presence of the khalíf; when they raised the veils from their faces, the khalíf was smitten with their beauty, and asked their names; one was called Girpáldeo, the other Súrajdeo. The khalíf ordered one to his own bed; she said, "O my Lord, I am not fit for the king's service, we have both for three days been with Bin-Ḳásim, who after dishonouring us, sent us here." The king was highly incensed, and directed that his servants should seize Bin-Ḳásim, sew him up in a cow-hide, and send him to Syria. When Bin-Ḳásim received this order, he directed the messengers to do as they were directed. They obeyed the order, covered Bin-Ḳásim with a raw cow-hide: after enduring the torture for three days he died. They then put his body into a box, and conveyed it to the khalíf who opening it in the presence of the two women, said, "Behold how absolute is my power, and how I treat such servants as Bin-Ḳásim." The women replied, "Oh king, just men ought not to be precipitate in great affairs, or be too hasty to act, either upon the representation of friends or foes." The khalíf asked their meaning, they said, "We made this accusation against Bin-Ḳásim because of the hatred we bore him, seeing that he slew our father, and through him we lost all our property and possessions, and became exiles from our own country; but Bin-Ḳásim was like a father and brother to us, he looked not on us for any bad purpose, but when our object was revenge for the blood of our father, we accused him of this treachery: this end attained, do with us as you will." The khalíf on hearing this, suffered great remorse: he ordered the two women to be tied to horses, and dragged to death, and they buried Bin-Ḳásim in the burial place at Damascus. See Journal Asiatic Society, Vol. VII, Part I, pp. 305-307.

**Muhammad bin-Ḳawam-uddin,** محمد بن قوام الدين, author of a Persian Dictionary called "Bahr-ul-Fazáel," the sea of excellence.

**Muhammad bin-Khawand,** محمد بن خاوند, *vide* Kháwand Sháh.

**Muhammad bin-Mahmud,** محمد بن محمود الاسترشی, commonly called Al-Isturúshí, author of the "Fusúl al-Isturúshí," a work principally restricted to decision, respecting mercantile transactions. He died in 1227 A. D., 625 A. H.

**Muhammad bin-Musa,** محمد بن موسي, of Khwárízm, author of a work on Algebra called "Aljabr wal-Muḳabila." This work was translated into English by Frederic Rosen.

**Muhammad bin-Murtaza,** محمد بن مرتضی محسن, surnamed Muhsan, author of a Shia law-book called the "Mufatih" on which a commentary was written by his nephew, who was of the same name, but surnamed Hádí.

**Muhammad bin-Tahir, II,** محمد بن طاهر ثاني, succeeded his father in the government of Khurásán and was the last of the race of Táhirians. He was taken prisoner in a battle by Ya'ḳúb bin-Lais about the year 874 A. D., 260 A. H., who took possession of Khurásán. Thus ended the race of the Táhirians in Khurásán who governed that province for upwards of 54 lunar years.

**Muhammad bin-Tunish al-Bukhari,** محمد بن تنيش البخاری, author of the work called "'Abdullah-náma," containing the history of the Uzbak Tartars originally from Dasht Ḳapchák, on the northern shores of the Caspian Sea. In 1494 A. D., they invaded Transoxania under Sháh Beg Khán; and having driven out the descendants of Taimúr, retained possession of that country. The prince whose memoirs are the chief subject of this work, was 'Abdullah Khán; he was a contemporary of the renowned Akbar emperor of Hindústán, with whom he kept up constant correspondence and interchange of ambassadors, and died 1595 A. D., 1005 A. H. This book was dedicated to Nizám-uddín Kókaltash.

**Muhammad bin-Ya'kub,** محمد بن يعقوب, author of the work called Ḳámús, *vide* Fírozabádí.

**Muhammad bin-Ya'kub al-Kálini ar-Razi,** محمد بن يعقوب الكلينی, who is called the Raís ul-Muhaddisín, or chief of the traditionists, is the author of the "Jáma' ul-Káfí," which is reckoned one of the books of the Ḳutub Arba'. It is of vast extent, comprising no less than thirty books; and its author is said to have been employed twenty years in its composition. He also wrote several other works of less note and died at Baghdád in 939 A. D., 328 A. H.

**Muhammad bin-Yusaf,** حكيم محمد بن يوسف هروی, a physician of Hirát and author of an Arabic Dictionary, called "Bahr-ul-Jawáhir," or the Sea of Jewels, said to be an Encyclopædia or Dictionary of Arts and Sciences.

**Muhammad bin-Yusaf,** محمد يوسف هروی, of Hirát, author of the "Táríkh Hind." This work no doubt (says Mr. H. M. Elliot) is the same as "Risálae Ajáeb wa-Gharáeb-i-Hindústán," since the author of that treatise also bears the name of Muhammad Yúsaf Hirwí. This author appears to have been contemporary with, and to have conversed with Khwája Hasan of Dehlí who was a disciple of Nizám-uddín Aulia who died in 1325 A. D.

**Muhammad Bukhari, Sayyad,** محمد بخاری سيّد, father of Sayyad Aḥmad Jalal Bukharí. He had many disciples in the time of Sháh Jahán. Close by the western gate of the Rauza of Tajganj is his shrine. He died in the year 1045 A. H.

**Muhammad Damishki,** محمد دمشقي, name of an illustrious Persian poet, who lived in the time of Fázil the son of Ahia the Barmakí or Barmecide.

**Muhammad Ghayas-uddin,** محمد غياث الدين, the son of Jalál-uddín, the son of Sharaf-uddín, author of the Persian Dictionary, entitled "Ghayás ul-Lughát," which he completed after fourteen years' labour in the year 1826 A. D., 1242 A. H., also of the "Miftáh ul-Kunúz," "Sharah Sikandar-náma," "Nuskha Bágh o-Bahár," and several poems and Kasídas &c. He was an inhabitant of Mustafábád, commonly called Rámpúr in the Pergunnah of Sháhábád, Lakhnau.

**Muhammad Gesu Daraz, Sayyad,** سيد محمد گيسودراز, of Kulbarga in Daulatábád, a famous Muhammadan saint, who was a disciple of Shaikh Nasír-uddín Chirágh, Dehlí. He was born at Dehlí on the 30th of July, 1321 A. D., 4th Rajab, 721 A. H. His proper name is Sudar-uddín Muhammad Husainí, but he was commonly called Muhammad Geisú Daráz, on account of his having long ringlets. He lived at Kulbarga in the reign of the Bahmaní Sultáns, and had the address to engage Prince Ahmad Sháh, to become his disciple, and build him a fine house and a superb convent. When this prince ascended the throne, in 1422 A. D., 825 A. H., the credit of the saint became so great, that from the lord to the artificer, all made it their glory to follow his instructions; so that his tomb became a place of pilgrimage to all sects. He died in the Dakhin in the beginning of the reign of Ahmad Sháh in 1422 A. D., and is buried at Hasanábád, commonly called Kulbarga. His tomb is a magnificent edifice covered with a dome, in the middle of an extensive court. During the reigns of the Dakhin Sultáns, great sums of money were occasionally offered to his descendants who reposed near the saint, in vows and presents, and many villages were assigned by the kings to defray the expenses of the tomb. He is said to be the author of several works, among which are the "Adáb ul-Muríd," the "Wajúd ul-'Ashikín;" containing the whole duty of a Súfí disciple, &c., and also of a book of Fables in Persian entitled "Asmár ul-Asrár." His son named Muhammad Akbar, is the author of the "Akáed Akbarí," containing the principles of the Muhammadan faith.

**Muhammad Ghazzali,** محمد غزالي, *vide* Ghazzálí.

**Muhammad Ghori,** محمد غوري, *vide* Shaháb-uddín Ghorí.

**Muhammad Ghaus Jilani, Hazrat Shaikh,** جيلاني حضرت شيخ محمد غوث, a celebrated Muhammadan saint whose tomb is at Uchcha of the Gílánís in Multán, and round whose shrine this town was built and after whom it was named. He was a descendant of Shaikh 'Abdul Kádir Jílání Baghdádí, and came to Uchcha about the year 1394 A. D. The Dáúdputtras have continued to be his muríd or disciples, and the muríd of his successors from the time of their first leaving Shikárpúr.

**Muhammad Ghaus, Shaikh,** شيخ محمد غوث گواليري, of Gwáliar, his proper name is Hají Hamíd-uddín, styled Ghaus-ul-'Alam, one of the greatest saints of India, who is said to have resided for twelve years in the practice of asceticism in the jangal which lies at the foot of the Chunár hills, consuming the leaves and fruits of the forest as his sole food; and so celebrated was he for the fulfilment of his blessings and predictions, that even powerful kings used to come and visit him and pay their respects. He afterwards went to Gwáliar, where he engaged himself in the pursuits of his holy calling and in making proselytes; and managed to content himself with the proceeds of a jágír, which yielded a crore of tangas. He was the murshid or master of Shaikh Wajíh-uddín 'Alw of Gujrát, and died on the 14th September, 1562 O. S., 14th Muharram, 970 A. H. The chronogram of the year of his death is "Shaikh Auliabúd," *i. e.*, Shaikh was a saint. He is the author of several works, among which are the "Jawáhir ul-Khamsa," and another entitled "Gulzár Abrár" containing the memoirs of all the Súfí Shaikhs of India with their places of burial and many other particulars. His brother Shaikh Phúl who served under the emperor Humáyún, was killed at Agrah 1537 A. D., 945 A. H., by the adherents of Mirzá Handál who had rebelled against his brother. His tomb is on a hill near the fort of Bayána. They were the descendants of Khwája Faríd-uddín Muhammad 'Attár in the seventh generation. Their grandfather's name was Mo'ín-uddín Kattál, whose tomb is in Jaunpúr, and father's name Kiyam-uddín. He lies buried in Zahúrábád commonly called Kunbra, in Ghazípúr. A small work entitled "Munákib Ghausia" containing the adventures of Muhammad Ghaus, was written by Sayyad Fazl-ullah in the year 941 Hijrí, 24 years before the death of the saint.

**Muhammad Ghaus Khan,** محمد غوث خان, *vide* Siráj-uddaula Muhammad Ghaus Khán.

**Muhammad Ghaus Zarrin,** محمد غوث زرّين, of Bijnaur. He lived in the time of Nawáb 'Asafuddaula of Lakhnau and is the author of a Chahár Darwesh in Persian.

**Muhammad Hadi,** محمد هادي, a nobleman of the Court of the emperor Jahángír, who wrote the last part of the "Túzak Jahángírí," during the last four years of that emperor's reign; Jahángír wrote the first part up to the 17th year of his reign, and the second part was written by Matmid Khán.

**Muhammad Hakim, Mirza,** ميرزا محمد حكيم, son of the emperor Humáyún and half-brother of Akbar, was born at Kábul on the 18th of April, 1554 A. D., 15th Jumáda I, 961 A. H. In the reign of his brother, the emperor Akbar, he had the government of Kábul, of which he remained during his life in undisturbed possession. He had twice invaded the Panjáb; once in 1566 A. D., 974 A. H., and the second time in February, 1581 A. D., Muharram, 989 A. H., when the emperor found it necessary to proceed himself with an army, and Mirza Muhammad Hakím was obliged to retreat before him. He died at Kábul in the 30th year of the emperor Akbar, on the 26th of July, 1585 O. S., 16th Amardád Ilahí corresponding with 16th Sha'bán, 993 A. H., aged 32 lunar years. After his death Rájá Bhagwán Dás and his son Mán Singh were sent to Kábul by the emperor to take charge of that province. His mother's name was Máh Chúchak Begam.

**Muhammad Hanif,** محمد حنيف, also called Muhammad bin-'Alí, was the third son of 'Alí, and because he was not descended from his wife Fatima as Hasan and Husain were, is not reckoned amongst the Imáms, notwithstanding there were many who after Husain's death secretly acknowledged him to be the lawful khalíf or Imám. He died in the year 700 A. D., 81 A. H.

**Muhammad Hasan Burhan,** محمد حسن برهان, author of the Persian Dictionary called "Burhán Káta'," dedicated to 'Abdullah Kutb Sháh of Haidarabád and Golkanda, 1651 A. D., 1061 A. H.

**Muhammad Hasan,** محمد حسن هلوي, of Dehlí who flourished about the year 1604 A. D., 1013 A. H., is the author of a Masnawí or poem containing the praises of the prophet, of his chaste wives and of great saints.

**Muhammad Hashim,** محمد هاشم, *vide* Kháfí Khán.

**Muhammad Husain,** محمد حسين, author of a Persian work on Theology called "Aḳáed Husain."

**Muhammad Husain Khan,** محمد حسين خان, the present nawáb of Kalpí, his title is 'Azím ul-Mulk.

**Muhammad Husain Mirza,** محمد حسن مرزا, *vide* Ibrahím Husain Mirzá.

**Muhammad Husain, Shaikh,** شيخ محمد حسين شهرت, whose poetical name is Shuhrat, was an excellent poet and a physician. He was a native of Arabia, but completed his studies at Shíráz and came to India where he was employed by the prince 'Azim Sháh as a physician. In the reign of Farrukh-siyar the title of Hakím-ul-Mumálik was conferred on him. He went on a pilgrimage to Mecca in the time of the emperor Muhammad Sháh, and after his return to India, he died in the month of April, 1737 A. D., Ẕil-ḥijja, 1149 A. H., at Dehlí. He is the author of a Díwán consisting of 5000 verses.

**Muhammad Ibn-Alahmar,** محمد ابن الأحمر, or more properly Ibn al-Ahmar, one of the Moorish kings of Granada in Spain and founder of the Alhambra, a celebrated fortress or palace which was regarded by the Moors of Granada as a miracle of art, and had a tradition that the king who founded it dealt in magic, or at least was deeply versed in alchemy, by means of which, he procured the immense sums of gold expended in its erection. The name of this monarch, as inscribed on the walls of some of the apartments of the Alhambra, was Abú 'Abdullah, but is commonly known in Moorish history as Muḥammad Ibn-Alahmar. He was born in Arjona, in 1195 A. D., 591 A. H. of the noble family of the Baní Nasar; when he arrived at manly years, he was appointed Alcayde or governor of Arjona and Jaen, and gained great popularity by his benignity and justice. Some years afterwards, on the death of Ibn-Húd, when the Moorish power of Spain was broken into factions, many places declared for Muḥammad Ibn-Alahmar; he seized upon the occasion, made a circuit through the country, and was everywhere received with acclamation. It was in the year 1238 A. D., that he entered Granada amidst the enthusiastic shouts of the multitude. He was proclaimed king with every demonstration of joy, and soon became the head of the Moslems in Spain, being the first of the illustrious line of Baní Nasar that had sat upon the throne. He caused the mines of gold and silver, and other metals found in the mountainous regions of his dominions, to be diligently worked, and was the first king of Granada who struck money of gold and silver with his name, taking great care that it should be skilfully executed. It was about this time, towards the middle of the 13th century, that he commenced the splendid palace of the Alhambra. He retained his faculties and vigour to an advanced age. In his 79th year, he took the field on horseback, accompanied by the flower of his chivalry, to resist an invasion of his territories, but was suddenly struck with illness, and in a few hours he died vomiting blood, and in violent convulsions. *Vide* Yúsaf Abú'l Hájí.

**Muhammad ibn-Husam,** محمد ابن حسن, *vide* Ibn-Husám.

**Muhammad ibn-Jurir ut-Tabari,** محمد ابن جرير الطبرى, the son of Jurír, an Arabian author, who died about the year 942 A. D., 330 A. H.

**Muhammad ibn-Zikaria al-Razi,** محمد ابن زكريا الرازي. See Rázi.

**Muhammad ibn-Is-hak,** محمد ابن اسحاق, the earliest biographer of Muḥammad the Arabian prophet. He died about the year 151 A. H., fifteen years after the overthrow of the Ummiada dynasty.

**Muhammad 'Imad,** محمد عماد who flourished about the year 1371 A. D., 773 A. H., is the author of the following admired poems: "Misbáh ul-Hidáet," "Múnis ul-Abrár," "Masnawí Kattiat," and "Muhabbat-náma," *vide* 'Imád Faḳíh.

**Muhammad, 'Imam,** محمد امام, *vide* 'Imám Muhammad.

**Muhammad Is-hak,** محمد اسحاق, author of the work called "Siar ul-Nabí wa-'Asár Sahába."

**Muhammad Isma'il Bukhari,** محمد اسماعيل بخارى, who is also called Abí 'Abdullah bin-Ismá'íl al-Bukhárí, is the author of the "Sahíh ul-Bukhárí," a book held in the highest estimation, and considered, both in spiritual and temporal matters, as next in authority to the Ḳurán. It contains 9,880 traditions, selected from 167,000; recording not only all the revelations, inspirations, actions, and sayings, of Muhammad, but also explaining many of the difficult passages of the Ḳurán. It relates besides many miracles and anecdotes of the ancient prophets, and other inspired persons. He was born in the year 810 A. D., 194 A. H., and died in the month of June, 870 A. D., Rajab, 256 A. H. He is commonly called Al-Bukharí, which see.

**Muhammad Isma'il, Moulwi,** مولوى محمد اسماعيل, author of the "Sirát ul-Mustaḳím" or "The True Path," containing an account of the peculiar tenets held by the followers of Sayyid Aḥmad the modern Muhammadan zealot and reformer, with whose name we have recently become familiar. This work is one of the most important of several treatises which have been composed by that sect. The main object of the author in composing it, was, in the first instance probably to shew his own learning; in the next, to justify the claims of Sayyid Aḥmad, (of whom he was a constant and confidential adherent,) as a devotee, gifted with a surpassing degree of religious capacity and illumination. It makes reference especially, in its explanations and allusions, to the peculiar divisions which prevail in India, among those who aspire to the honors of religious initiation. These are generally numbered as the followers of one or other, of three venerated Pírs, each of whom has given a name to a distinct school or sect; the first, the "Taríḳa-i-Ḳádiria," which traces its origin to 'Abdul Ḳádir Jílání. Another, the "Taríḳa-i-Chishtia," so called from its founder Khwája Mo'ín-uddín Chishtí, whose tomb is at Ajmer; the third, the "Taríḳa-i-Naḳshbandia," derived from a Khwája Bahá-uddín Naḳshband, a native of Bukhára. It was one of the peculiar pretensions of Sayyid Aḥmad, that he held himself privileged to be the founder of a school of his own, to which he gave the name of the "Taríḳa-i-Muhammadia." His book was written some time about the year 1822 A. D., and it is to be remarked, as a new feature in the history of efforts for the propagation of Muhammadanism, or for the reform of its corruptions, how extensively the emissaries of this sect have availed themselves of the press to disseminate their tenets. The "Sirát ul-Mustaḳím," the "Taḳwíat ul-Ímán," the "Hidáet ul-Mominín," and a little tract attached to it, named the "Múzih ul-Kabír wa'l Bidaa't," and two other tracts, entitled the "Nasíhat ul-Muslimín," and "Tambíh ul-Gháfilín," have all been printed at private presses in Calcutta or at Huglí. See Sayyid Aḥmad.

**Muhammad Jani,** محمد جاني, author of the work

called "'Asar Aḥmadí," a minute history of Muhammad and the twelve 'Imáms, with various anecdotes respecting them.

**Muhammad Jogi, Mirza,** محمد جوگي, son of Sháh-rukh Mirzá, the son of Amír Taimúr. He died 1444 A. D., 848 A. H., two years before his father, aged 43 lunar years.

**Muhammad Karim,** محمد کريم, the son of prince Azím-ush-Shán, the son of the emperor Bahádur Sháh. He was murdered by order of the emperor Jahándár Sháh his uncle, in April 1712 A. D., 1124 A. H.

**Muhammad Ḳasim,** محمد قاسم, the original name of the celebrated historian, Firishta.

**Muhammad Ḳasim,** محمد قاسم, *vide* Násir-uddín Ḳabbácha.

**Muhammad Ḳasim,** محمد قاسم, son of Hájí Muhammad Surúrí Káshání, and author of the "Farhang Surúrí," a dictionary of the Persian language, dedicated to Sháh 'Abbás Bahádur Khán, king of Persia, 1599 A. D., 1008 A. H. *Vide* Surúrí.

**Muhammad Ḳasim Khan Badakhshani,** محمد قاسم خان موجي, whose poetical name was Maují, was an officer in the service of the emperors Humáyún and Akbar. He died in 1571 A. D., 979 A. H., at A'grah, and is the author of an "Yúsaf Zalekha," containing the loves of Joseph and Potiphar's wife. *Vide* Maují.

**Muhammad Ḳasim, Mir,** مير محمد قاسم, author of the "'Ibrat-náma," which he wrote after the invasion of Nádir Sháh, about the year 1739 A. D., 1152 A. H.

**Muhammad Ḳasim, Sayyad,** سيد محمد قاسم, of Danapúr, author of the work entitled "Aijáz Ghausia" in Urdú, which he composed in the year 1855 A. D., 1271 A. H., containing the history and miracles of the celebrated saint of Baghdád, 'Abdul Ḳádir Gílání.

**Muhammad Kazim, Mirza,** مرزا محمد کاظم, the son and successor of Mirzá Muhammad Amín, private Munshí or Secretary to 'A'lamgír, and author of the history called "'A'lamgír-náma." It is a history of the first ten years of the reign of the emperor 'A'lamgír to whom it was dedicated in the 32nd year of his reign, 1689 A. D., 1100 A. H. When it was presented to him, he forbade its being continued; and prohibited all other historians or authors from relating the events of his life, preferring (says his panegyrist) the cultivation of inward piety to the ostentatious display of his actions. This monarch, whose reign is admired by the Muhammadans, and detested by the Hindús, after having imprisoned his father, mounted the throne of Dehlí in 1658 A. D., 1068 A. H. At this period the glory of the house of Bábar may be said to have arrived at its zenith. The empire extended from the north-west mountains of Ḳábul to the southern limits of Chittagong; and the kings of Golkonḍa and Bíjápúr paid tribute. He is also the author of a "Sháhnáma," a "Roz-náma," or Journal, and another work entitled "Akhbár Hasania."

**Muhammad Khalil-ullah Khan,** محمد خليل اللهخان, surnamed Ashk, is the author of a history of Amír Hamzá, uncle of Muhammad, which he professes to have drawn from a compilation made by order of Sulṭán Mahmúd, the Ghaznavide; and observes, "What renders this present history at all times interesting is this, that it informs us of the customs of various nations, and that it instructs us in the art of doing battle, and of taking towns and kingdoms. Accordingly Maḥmúd, to avoid the necessity of counsel from any one, had portions of it read to him as a daily observance."

**Muhammad Khan Bangash, Nawab,** محمد خان بنگش, styled Ghazanfar Jang, a Rohela chief of the tribe of Bangash. He founded the city of Farrukhábád in the name of his patron the emperor Farrukh-siyar. In the reign of Muhammad Sháh 1730 A. D., 1143 A. H. he was appointed governor of Málwa, but unable to cope with the Marhaṭṭas on account of their repeated incursions, he was removed in 1732 A. D., 1145 A. H., and appointed governor of Allahábád. Muhammad Khán having planned the reduction of the Bundelas of whom rájá Chatursál was chief, entered that country in 1733 A. D., 1146 A. H. with an army, and took several places; but as he was but little acquainted with the roads, Chatursál, with the assistance of Peshwá Bájí Ráo, surrounded him suddenly with an army. The nawáb, unable to combat a superior force, took refuge in the fortress of Jaitgaṛh, where he was closely blockaded by the enemy for some time, when his son Ḳáem Jang having collected an army of the Afgháns, marched to Jaitgaṛh and escorted his father in safety to Allahábád. The imperial ministers, making a pretence of Muhammad Khán's ill-success, removed him from the Súbadárí. He died in the month of June, 1743 A. D., Jumáda I, 1156 A. H., and was succeeded in his jágír by his son Ḳáem Jang, commonly called Ḳáem Khán.

*The following is a list of the Nawábs of Farrukhábád.*

Muhammad Khán, Bangash.
Ḳáem Jang, son of ditto.
Aḥmad Khán, brother of Ḳáem Jang.
Muzaffar Jang, son of Aḥmad Khán.
Tafazzul Husain Khán.

**Muhammad Khan, Mir,** مير محمد خان, commonly called Khán Kalán, was the eldest brother of Shams-uddín Muhammad Anka Khán. He served under the emperors Humáyún and Akbar, and was made governor of the Panjáb by the latter, which office he held for several years, and died 1575 A. D., 983 A. H. He was an excellent poet, and has left a Díwán in Persian, and another in the Turkish language. He was a native of Ghazní, and therefore chose for his poetical name "Ghaznawí." There is a work on Súfíism entitled "Burhán ul-I'mán," either written by him or some other Muhammad Khán.

**Muhammad Khan Shaibani,** محمد خان شيباني, *vide* Sháhí Beg Khán Uzbak.

**Muhammad Khan, Sultan,** سلطان محمد خان, also called Muhammad Ḳáán and Khán Shahíd, was the eldest son of Sulṭán Ghayás-uddín Balban, king of Dehlí, who had appointed him viceroy of all the frontier provinces, *viz.*, Multán, Láhor, Debalpúr and other districts. This prince was blest with a bright and comprehensive genius, taking great delight in learning and the company of learned men. He, with his own hand, made a choice collection of the beauties of poetry, selected from the most famous in that art. The work consisted of 20,000 couplets, and was esteemed the criterion of taste. Among the learned men in the prince's court, Amír Khusro and Khwája Hasan bore the first rank in genius and in his esteem. The throne of Persia was at this time filled by Arghún Khán, the son of Abḳa Khán, and grandson of Halákú Khán. Timar Khán Changezí who was then an Amír of mighty renown in the empire of the race of

Changez Khán, and governed Hirát, Ḳandahár and other districts; invaded Hindústán with 20,000 chosen horse. Having ravaged all the villages about Debalpúr and Láhor, he turned towards Multán. The prince Muhammad Sulṭán hearing of his designs, hastened to the banks of the river of Láhor, where both armies drew up in order of battle, and engaged with great fury. The prince, unfortunately, received a fatal arrow in his breast, by which he fell to the ground, and in a few minutes expired. Very few of the unfortunate Muhammad's party escaped from this conflict. Among the fortunate few, was Amír Khusro, the poet, who relates this event at large, in his book called "Khizir Khání." This event took place on Friday, the 9th of March, 1285 A. D., 30th Ẕil-ḥijja, 683 A. H.

**Muhammad Khan Talpur,** محمد خان تالپور, *vide* Mír Muhammad Khán Tálpúr.

**Muhammad Khuda Banda, Sultan,** محمد خدا بندہ, surnamed Sulṭán Sikandar Sháh, was the eldest son of Sháh Tahmásp I; was born in the year 1531 A. D., 938 A. H., and succeeded to the throne of Persia on the death of his brother Sháh Ismá'íl II, in November, 1577 A. D., 985 A. H. The fortunes of this monarch, who from a natural weakness in his eyes, was incapable of rule, had been for many years upheld by the character of his eldest son, Hamza Mirzá, and his power terminated at the death of that prince, who fell under the blow of an assassin in his own private apartments on the 24th November, 1586 A. D., 22nd Ẕil-ḥijja, 994 A. H. The chiefs of Khurásán immediately proclaimed 'Abbás, the king's second son, as king of Persia, and in the year 1588 A. D., 996 A. H., marched with him to Ḳazwín, the capital of the empire, which they took possession of without opposition, and the unfortunate Muhammad was deserted by every inhabitant of Ḳazwín and by his own army.

**Muhammad Khuda Banda, Sultan,** محمد خدا بندہ, surnamed Aljáilú, a descendant of Changez Khán, succeeded his brother Sulṭán Gházán Khán, the son of Arghún Khán to the throne of Persia in May, 1304 A. D., Shawwál, 703 A. H. He is said to have been a just prince, and was the first monarch of Persia who proclaimed himself of the sect of 'Alí. He gave a public proof of his attachment to this sect, by causing the names of the twelve Imáms to be engraven on all the money which he coined. He built the celebrated city of Sultánia in 'Azurbeján or Media, which he made the capital of his dominions, and where he afterwards was buried. The dome over his tomb is fifty-one feet in diameter, and is covered with glazed tiles. He died on the 17th December, 1316 A. D., 1st Shawwál, 716 A. H., after a reign of 13 lunar years, and was succeeded by his son Sulṭán Abú Sa'íd Bahádur Khán.

**Muhammad Khusro Khan,** محمد خسرو خان, author of a Medical work called "Makhzan ul-Adwia."

**Muhammad Ḳuli Khan,** محمد قلي خان, governor of Allahábád, was the son of Mirzá Muhsin, the brother of Nawáb Safdar Jang of Audh. In the year 1759 A. D., 1172 A. H., he, under the royal standard of the prince 'Alí Gohar (afterwards Sháh 'Álam) who had procured from his father, 'Álamgír II, grants of Bengal, Behár and Urysa, marched towards Patna, where, on his arrival, the place was besieged and the siege was carried on for some days with briskness; but he was obliged to raise the siege and retreat on receiving intelligençe that Shujáa'-uddaula (who was his first cousin and the son of Safdar Jang), had treacherously seized Allahábád and possessed himself of that province. On his arrival at Allahábád in 1761 A. D., 1174 A. H., he was seized and imprisoned, and ultimately put to death in the fort of Jalálábád by order of Shujáa'-uddaula, he being jealous of his ambitious views in assisting the prince in the invasion of Bengal, and regarding Allahábád as his right, it having been given only in deputation by his father, Safdar Jang, to Muhammad Ḳulí Khán, who had refused to surrender it to the son.

**Muhammad Ḳuli Ḳutb Shah,** محمد قلي قطب شاہ, *vide* Ḳulí Ḳutb Sháh II.

**Muhammad Ḳuli Salim,** محمد قلي سليم, *vide* Salím.

**Muhammad Kuresh, Mirza,** محمد قريش ميرزا, the second son of Bahádur Sháh. His title of succession to the throne of Dehlí, was acknowledged by the British Government, in 1856 with this condition that on the king's death he would receive the title of Sháhzada.

**Muhammad Ḳutb Shah,** محمد قطب شاہ, the fifth Sulṭán of the Ḳutbsháhí dynasty of Golkanḍa, and nephew or brother of Muhammad Ḳulí Ḳutb Sháh, whom he succeeded in January, 1612 A. D., Ẕi-Ḳa'da, 1020 A. H. He was living in 1620 A. D., 1029 A. H. After his death, 'Abdullah Ḳutb Sháh was raised to the throne of Golkanḍa.

**Muhammad Lad,** محمد لاد, author of the Dictionary called "Muwyyad ul-Fuzlá."

**Muhammad Lari, Mulla,** محمد لاری, author of a work which goes after his name, *viz.*, "Tálíf Mullá Muhammad Lárí."

**Muhammad Maghrabi, Maulana,** مولانا محمد مغربي, *vide* Maghrabí.

**Muhammad Makahul,** محمد مكحول, *vide* Muhammad (Sulṭán).

**Muhammad Ma'sum,** محمد معصوم, the son of Shaikh Aḥmad Sarhindí, was born in the year 1598 A. D., 1007 A. H., and died in 1668 A. D., 1079 A. H. aged 72 lunar years.

**Muhammad Ma'sum Nami, Amir,** امير محمد معصوم نامی of Bakkar, was one of the nobles of the court of Akbar. He wrote five Masnawís or Poems, containing 10,000 verses; one is in the metre of "Haft Paikar," one in the measure of the "Sikandar-náma," one called "Parí Súrat," is in the measure of "Lailí and Majnún," one called "Husn wa-Náz," is in the metre of "Yúsaf Zalekhá," and one in the measure of the "Makhzan ul-Asrár." He also wrote two Díwáns of Ghazals and two Sákí-námas. He once paid a visit to Sháh 'Abbás, king of Persia, accompanied with no less than one thousand followers.

**Muhammad Mir, Sayyad,** مير محمد. His proper name is Kamál-uddín Haidar. He was a native af Lakhnau, and translated the History of Rasselas from English into Urdú for the Ágrah School Book Society, in the year 1839 A. D.

**Muhammad Mirza,** محمد مرزا, son of Míránsháh and grandson of Amír Taimúr, was a pious prince, and not being ambitious, he remained with his brother Mirzá Khalíl-ulláh, ruler of Samarḳand; and when that country was taken by Mirzá Sháhrukh his uncle, and made over to his own son Mirzá Ulagh Beg in 1408 A. D., 811 A. H., he passed the remainder of his life with the latter and died about the year 1441 A. D., 845 A. H., recommending his son Mirzá Abú Sa'íd to him.

**Muhammad Muhsin of Kashan, Mulla,** ملا محمد محسن كاشاني, author of the "Tafsír Sáfi."

**Muhammad Muhsin,** محمد محسن, the rebel Tahsíldár of Pailání who joined the mutineers in the year 1857 A. D., and was, together with 'Imdád 'Alí the rebel Deputy Collector, hanged at Banda on the 24th April, 1858 A. D.

**Muhammad Mukim,** محمد مقيم, *vide* Nizám-uddín Ahmad Khwája.

**Muhammad Muzaffar,** محمد مظفر, surnamed Mubáriz-uddín, was the founder of the dynasty of Muzaffarians in Fars. He held a high station at the court of Sultán Abú Sa'íd Khán, king of Persia; but after his death, which happened in 1335 A. D., when trouble and confusion began to reign on all sides, he retired to Yazd and took possession of that country. In the year 1353 A. D., 754 A. H., he took Shíráz from Sháh Shaikh Abú Is-hák, and having seized him after some time, put him to death, and became master of Fars. His son Sháh Shujáa' rebelled against him in 1359 A. D., 760 A. H., deprived him of his sight and ascended the throne at Shíráz. Muhammad Muzaffar died in the year 1364 A. D., 765 A. H. This dynasty governed Fars 77 years, during which, seven princes enjoyed power, *viz.*:

1. Mubáriz-uddín Muhammad Muzaffar or Muzaffaruddín.
2. Sháh Shujáa', son of ditto.
3. Sháh Mahmúd, his brother.
4. Sultán Ahmad.
5. Sháh Mansúr, son of Muzaffar, in whose time Shíráz was taken by Amír Taimúr.
6. Sháh Ahia.
7. Sháh Zain-ul 'Abidín, the son of Sháh Shujáa'.

The last two reigned only a few months. *Vide* Muzaffar.

**Muhammad Nasir,** محمد نظير, *vide* Khwája Násir.

**Muhammad Nasir Ahmad,** محمد نظير احمد, Deputy Collector of Settlements in Jalain, author of the work named "Mirat at Urús" or the "Bride's Mirror," an admirable tale of domestic life among the Muhammadans of India, for which a reward of 1000 Rupees was conferred on him by the Lieutenant-Governor in 1870 A. D.

**Muhammad Ufi,** محمد عوفي, who flourished in the 16th century of the Christian era, is the author of a biography, called "Tazkira Muhammad Ufi."

**Muhammad Ufi,** محمد عوفي, author of a Tazkira or biography called "Labáb ul-Albáb," and of another work entitled "Jáma' ul-Hikáyát." The latter he compiled in 1228 A. D., 625 A. H. He was a native of Marv which, under the Saljúk princes, was the capital of Persia. *Vide* Núr-uddín Muhammad Ufi.

**Muhammad Parizada,** محمد پريزاده, an author whose work is continually studied throughout the Othmánli empire, not only by all the ministers and statesmen of the Porte but likewise by the Greek princes and dragomans.

**Muhammad Rafi-uddin Muhaddis,** محمد رفع الدين محدث, *vide* Rafí-uddín.

**Muhammad Rafia Waez,** محمد رفيع واعظ, a celebrated preacher at Isfahán, was a contemporary of Mirzá Sáeb and Táhir Wahíd. He is the author of a Díwán in Persian, as also of a poem containing the battle of Sháh 'Abbás with Elam Khán, ruler of Túrán, and one called "Abwáb ul-Janán," a religious book.

**Muhammad Raza Khan,** محمد رضا خان, he was selected for the office of chief minister by the English, after the death of Jafar 'Ali Khán, Nawáb of Bengal, to the young Nawáb Najm-uddaula, the son of the late Nawáb in 1765 A. D.

**Muhammad Raza,** محمد رضا, author of the Arabic work on Theology, called, "Ashrakát Alwia" Heavenly Illuminations, and of another on Jurisprudence entitled "Intikháb ul-Ahkám."

**Muhammad Saki,** محمد ساقي, *vide* Mustai'd Khán.

**Muhammad Sadr-uddin,** محمد صدر الدين, surnamed Abú'l Ma'álí, which see.

**Muhammad Salah Kambu,** محمد صالح كمبو, author of the "'Amal Sálah."

**Muhammad Salah, Shaikh,** شيخ محمد صالح, Kamboh, brother to Shaikh Ináyet-ullah, is the author of the book called "Behar Chaman."

**Muhammad Salah, Mir,** مير محمد صالح, lived in the time of the emperors Jahángír and Sháh Jahán about the year 1628 A. D., 1037 A. H. His poetical name was Kashfí, which see.

**Muhammad Salah, Mirza,** مرزا محمد صالح, *vide* Sipahdár Khán.

**Muhammad Salah, Mirza,** مرزا محمد صالح, author of the "Latáef Khayáb," or the Beauties of Imagination. It contains extracts from all the poets of any celebrity, with memoirs of the authors; and ought to have been named the Beauties of Poetry; being of the nature of the English compilation of Select Extracts. It was commenced by the author in 1731 A. D., 1144—1155 A. H., and finished by Ja'far Nasír in 1742 A. D.

**Muhammad Salah, Shaikh,** شيخ محمد صالح, author of the "Bahár Sakhun" and the "Táríkh Sháhjahání", also of a poem called "Arám Jan" which he completed in 1646 A. D., 1056 A. H.

**Muhammad Sarbadal,** محمد سربدال, was the chief of a kind of vagabonds called Sarbadáls, who had made themselves master of the city of Sabzwár and of some others in Khurásán. This personage was also called Sayyid Muhammad, and although he was head of a gang of highwaymen or robbers, yet he was much esteemed for his probity.

**Muhammad Shafia',** محمد شفيع دهلوي, of Dehlí, author of the work called "Mirát ul-Wáridát," or Mirror of Occurrences, a compendious history of the Mughal empire, from the death of Akbar to the invasion of Nádir Sháh. He undertook this work at the request of a nobleman in the reign of Muhammad Sháh.

**Muhammad Shah,** محمد شاه, the son of prince Faríd-uddín, the son of Khizir Khán, king of Dehlí. He was placed on the throne after the assassination of his uncle Mubárik Sháh in April, 1434 A. D., Ramaẓán 837 A. H. He reigned 12 lunar years and died on the 20th of January, 1446 A. D., 22nd Shawwál 849 A. H. He was succeeded by his son Sulṭán 'Alá-uddín.

**Muhammad Shah,** محمد شاه, the son of Aḥmad Sháh, succeeded his father to the throne of Gujrát in July, 1443 A. D., Rabí' I, 847 A. H. He reigned eight lunar years, 9 months and 4 days, and was poisoned by his wife on the 12th February, 1451 A. D., 10th Muḥarram, 855 A. H. He was succeeded by his son Ḳutb Sháh also called Ḳutb-uddín.

**Muhammad Shah,** محمد شاه, the son of Hoshang Sháh, ascended the throne of Málwá after the death of his father on the 17th July, 1434 A. D., 9th Ẓil-ḥijja, 837 A. H. He reigned about nine months and was poisoned by Muhammad Khán (the son of Malik Mughís his prime minister) who ascended the throne under the title of Mahmúd Sháh Khiljí in May, 1435 A. D.

**Muhammad Shah,** محمد شاه, emperor of Dehlí, surnamed Roshan Akhtar or the Brilliant Star, was the son of the prince Jahán Sháh one of the three brothers who perished in disputing the crown with their eldest brother Jahándár Sháh, the son of Bahádur Sháh. He was born on Friday the 7th of August, 1702 O. S., 24th Rabí' I, 1114 A. H., and crowned by the two Sayyads after the death of Rafí-uddaula, on the 29th September, 1719 A. D., 25th Ẓi-Ḳada, 1131 A. H. On his accession it was determined that the names of his two predecessors, *viz.*, Rafí-uddarját and Rafí-uddaula who reigned about three months each, should be struck out of the list of kings, and that his reign should commence from the death of the emperor Farrukh-siyar. Muhammad Sháh reigned 30 lunar years, 6 months and 10 days, and died one month after the battle of Sarhind which his son fought against Aḥmad Sháh Abdálí. His death took place on Thursday the 16th of April, 1748 A. D., 27th Rabí' II, 1161 A. H. at the age of 47 lunar years, 1 month and 3 days. He was buried in the court before the mausoleum of Nizám-uddín Aulia at Dehlí, and was succeeded by his son Aḥmad Sháh. This emperor may be termed the last of the race of Amír Taimúr who reigned in Dehlí and enjoyed any power. The few princes of that sovereign's family who were raised to the throne after Muhammad Sháh were mere pageants, whom the nobles of the court elevated or cast down as it suited the purposes of their ambitions.

**Muhammad Shah 'Adil** or **'Adli,** محمد شاه عادل, an Afghán of the tribe of Súr, whose original name was Mubáriz Khán, was the son of Nizám Khán Súr, the brother of Sher Sháh, and brother-in-law of Salím Sháh after whose death in 1554 A. D., 961 A. H., having murdered his son Fíroz, a boy of twelve years of age who had been raised to the throne, he assumed royal dignity with the title of Muhammad Sháh 'Adil. He was illiterate, hated men of learning and kept company with illiterate persons like himself, whom he raised to the highest dignities in the State; among whom, one Hímú, a Bania or Indian shopkeeper, whom his predecessor Salím Sháh had made superintendent of the markets, was intrusted with the whole administration of affairs. This naturally created him enemies among the Afghán chiefs, who having conspired against his life, revolted from his authority. Ibráhím Khán Súr, who had the king's sister for his wife, soon after raised a considerable army, and, getting possession of the city of Dehlí, ascended the throne in 1555 A. D., 962 A. H., and assumed the ensigns of royalty. Muhammad Sháh, finding himself betrayed, fled to Chunár, and contented himself with the government of the eastern provinces. He was slain in a battle fought at Munger with Bahádur Sháh, king of Bengal, 1556 A. D., 963 A. H. The period of his reign at Dehlí was only eleven months.

**Muhammad Shah Bahmani I,** محمد شاه بهمني اول, the second king of the Bahmaní dynasty, was the son of Sulṭán 'Alá-uddín Hasan Kángoh Bahmaní, whom he succeeded to the throne of the Dakhin in February, 1358 A. D., 19th Ẓi-Ḳada, 776 A. H. He reigned 17 lunar years and died on the 21st of March, 1375 A. D. His son Mujáhid Sháh succeeded him.

**Muhammad Shah Bahmani II,** محمد شاه بهمني ثاني, the thirteenth Sulṭán of the Bahmaní dynasty, was the son of Humáyún Sháh the Cruel. He succeeded his brother Nizám Sháh to the throne of the Dakhin in July, 1463 A. D. in his ninth year; and the affairs of government were conducted, as in the reign of his late brother, by Khwája Jahán and Khwaja Mahmúd Gáwán, under the direction of the queen mother. The former was murdered after some time, and the title of Khwája Jahán was conferred on Mahmúd Gáwán, adding the duties of Wakíl-us-Saltanat to his other functions. Muhammad Sháh reigned nearly 20 lunar years, and died a year after he had caused his minister Mahmúd Gáwán to be put to death, *i. e.*, on the 24th March, 1482 A. D., 1st Ṣafar, 887 A. H. His son Mahmúd Sháh II succeeded him. The year of Muhammad Sháh's death is comprised in a Persian verse, the translation of which runs thus:

Sulṭán Muhammad Sháh, ruler of kings,
When suddenly summoned to yield up his breath,
Abandoned the Dakhin, and all worldly things,
And "*the ruin of the Dakhin,*" recorded his death.

**Muhammad Shah Sharki,** محمد شاه شرقي, succeeded to the throne of Jaunpúr after the death of his father Mahmúd Sháh Sharḳí, in 1452 A. D., 856 A. H., and was killed after five months in a battle which he fought against his brother Husain Sháh Sharḳí, who succeeded him.

**Muhammad Shahid,** محمد شهيد, whose garden is still to be seen on the left bank of the Jamna at Ágrah where the swimmers of Ágrah assemble after bathing in the Jamna in the rainy season.

**Muhammad Shah, Sayyad,** سيد محمد شاه, son of Sayyad Walí of Pandúa, author of a collection of documents containing Forms of Letters, Parwanas, instruments or Contracts of Law, &c., &c., entitled "Jáma' ul-Dastúr," written about the year 1800 A. D.

**Muhammad Shah Tughlak I,** محمد شاه تغلق, whose former name was Malik Fakhr-uddín Júnán, succeeded his father Ghayás-uddín Tughlaḳ Sháh on the throne of Dehlí in February, 1325 A. D., 725 A. H. He took the fort of Nagarkót in 1337 A. D. and built several royal buildings and places in Dehlí. It was in his reign that 'Alá-uddín Hasan Kangóh raised the standard of royalty in the Dakhin, 1347 A. D., 748 A. H., where his descendants reigned for several generations. Muhammad Sháh died at Ṭhaṭṭa on the banks of the river Sindh on the 20th of March, 1351 A. D., 21st Muḥarram, 752 A. H., after a reign of nearly 27 lunar years. He was succeeded by his cousin Sulṭán Fíróz Sháh Bárbak, the son of Sipah Salár Rajab.

**Muhammad Shah Tughlak II,** محمد شاه تغلق ثاني, surnamed Násir-uddín, was the son of Fíróz Sháh Tughlaḳ. He was born on the 3rd June, 1353 A. D., 3rd Jumáda I, 754 A. H. He ascended the throne of Dehlí in the lifetime of his father in the year 1387 A. D., but was soon after deposed and expelled by the chiefs. He remained at Nagarkót till the reign of Abú Bakr Sháh, when he proceeded towards Dehlí with a large army, and after some repulses proving victorious, ascended the throne in August, 1390 A. D., 792 A. H. He is the founder of a fortress in Jalesar which he called Muhammadábád. He reigned 3 years and 7 months, and died on the 19th February, 1394 A. D., 17th Rabí' II, 796 A. H., and his body was deposited at Dehlí in the same vault with that of his father. He was succeeded by his son Humáyún, who, on ascending the throne, assumed the name of 'Alá-uddín Sikandar Sháh, but died suddenly after a short reign of 45 days, and his brother Sulṭán Mahmúd succeeded him.

**Muhammad Shah,** محمد شاه, king of Persia, was the son of 'Abbás Mirzá, and grandson of Fatha Abú Sháh, whom he succeeded to the throne of Persia in 1834 A. D., and died in 1847 A. D.

**Muhammad Sharif Hakkani,** محمد شريف حقاني, author of a poem called "Aynak-e-Dil," which he completed in 1685 A. D., 1096 A. H.

**Muhammad Shah,** محمد شاه, present ruler of Badakhshán. He was placed in his present position by Amír Sher 'Alí of Ḳábul to whom he is bound to pay tribute, the amount of which in 1870 A. D., was £8100, and 500 horses. His predecessor was the intimate friend of 'Abdul Rahmán Khán, the pretender to the Afghán throne, who was opposed by Sher 'Alí in 1868 A. D.

**Muhammad Sharif, Khwaja,** خواجه محمد شريف, a nephew of Mauláná Umaidí. He was wazír to Sháh Tahmasp Safwí I, and governor of Yezd, Abarkóh and afterwards of Isfahán for several years, and died in 1538 A. D., 945 A. H.

**Muhammad, Sharif, Mir,** مير محمد شريف, author of a Masnawí or poem containing felicitations on the accession to the throne of Lakhnau, of Ghází-uddín Haidar, completed in 1814 A. D., 1229 A. H.

**Muhammad Shirin Maulana,** مولانا محمد شيرين, commonly called Mauláná Maghrabí, which see.

**Muhammad Shaikh,** شيخ محمد, author of the works called "Jámi Jahán-námá," and the "Nafs Rahmání," containing meditation on the unity of God, and rules for solitary devotion, *vide* Shaikh Muhammad.

**Muhammad Sufi, Maulana,** مولانا محمد صوفي, author of the work called "Maikhána wa-Butkhána," or the wine shop and idol house. He was a native of Mázindarán, and was residing in 1725 A. D., 1038 A. H. at Ahmadábád in Gujrát, and afterwards for some time in Ḳashmír.

**Muhammad, Sultan,** سلطان محمد, the last king of the ancient race of the sovereigns of Badakhshán, taken prisoner in battle by Sulṭán Abú Sa'íd, a descendant of Amír Taimúr, and slain together with all his children and relations in 1466 A. D., 871 A. H.

**Muhammad, Sultan,** سلطان محمد, who was afterwards surnamed Makahúl or the Blind, was the second son of Sulṭán Mahmúd of Ghazní. He succeeded his father in 1030 A. D. in the absence of his elder brother Masa'úd, who after five months deprived him of his sight and placed him in close confinement, where he remained till he was again reinstated by the army in 1038 A. D., and his brother Masa'úd deposed. He reigned at Láhor for two years, after which he was defeated and put to death by Sulṭán Maudúd the son of Masa'úd 1044 A. D.

**Muhammad, Sultan,** سلطان محمد, was the second son of Sulṭán Malikshâh Saljúkí, after whose death he ruled over Azurbejan, but when his eldest brother Barkayárak died in 1104 A. D., 498 A. H., he seized Baghdád also and assumed the title of Sulṭán. This prince died at Isfahán 1118 A. D., Ẕil-ḥijja, 511 A. H., and was succeeded by his son Mahmúd, who, however, was soon reduced by his uncle, Sulṭán Sanjar, to the condition of a dependent. Mahmúd died 1131 A. D., 15th Shawwál, 525 A. H., aged 27 years at Hamdan after a reign of 14 years.

**Muhammad, Sultan,** سلطان محمد, surnamed Ḳuṭb-uddín, succeeded his father 'Alá-uddín Takash as Sulṭán of Khwárizm in 1200 A. D., 596 A. H. He was defeated by the celebrated conqueror Changez Khán, his country pillaged, and almost all his family made prisoners in 1218 A. D., 615 A. H. He died of a broken heart in March, 1221 A. D., Ẕil-ḥijja, 617 A. H. His son Jalál-uddín for a long time bore up against the torrent that had overwhelmed his father, but was at last subdued. He was slain in 1230 A. D., 627 A. H. *Vide* Takash.

**Muhammad, Sultan,** سلطان محمد, son of Báisanghar Mirzá. *Vide* Bábar (Sulṭán) and Sulṭán Muhammad.

**Muhammad, Sultan Mirza,** محمد سلطان مرزا, or Sulṭán Mirzá, the son of Awais Mirzá, the son of Báikara, the son of Mansúr, a prince of the house of Amír Taimúr. He accompanied the emperor Bábar Sháh to India, and after his death rebelled against his son the emperor Humáyún, and though subdued and pardoned, his five sons, *viz.*, Muhammad Husain Mirzá, Ibráhím Husain Mirzá, Masa'úd Husain Mirzá, Ulagh Mirzá, and Sháh Mirzá, and three of his nephews took advantage of the general disturbance which took place in 1566 A. D., 974 A. H., and revolted at Sambhal, the government of which had been assigned to their father. At first they were overpowered without an effort and were confined in the fort of Sambhal by order of the emperor Akbar, but when that monarch marched in the year 1567 A. D., 975 A. H. for the purpose of subduing Málwá; they made their escape to Gujrát and sought an asylum with Changez Khán, governor of Baroach, where they sowed the seeds of future troubles, which only ended with the subjugation of the kingdoms by Akbar in 1572 A. D., 980 A. H., *vide* Ibráhím Husain Mirzá. Muhammad Sulṭán Mirzá was, on account of his sons' rebellion, confined in the fort of Bayána about the year 1567 A. D. where he died some years after.

**Muhammad Sultan,** محمد سلطان, the eldest son of Jahángír Mirzá. After his father's death, he was named by his grandfather, heir of all his dominions, but died before him in 1404 A. D., 805 A. H.

**Muhammad Tahir Nasirabadi,** محمد طاهر نصيرابادي, author of a biography called "Tazkira Muhammad Táhir." He lived in the reign of 'Abbás Sháh I of Persia.

**Muhammad Tahir,** محمد طاهر, *vide* Ináyet Khán.

**Muhammad Taki, Imam,** امام محمد تقي, also called Muhammad al Jawád, was the ninth Imám of the race of 'Alí, and the son of Imám 'Alí Músí Razá who was the eighth. He was born in the year 811 A. D., 195 A. H., and is said to have been poisoned in 835 A. D., 220 A. H. He is buried at Baghdád near the tomb of his grandfather Imám Músí Kázim, the son of Ja'far Sádiḳ. His wife's name was Umm ul-Fazl, the daughter of the khalíf Mámún.

**Muhammad Taki, Mir,** ميرمحمد تقي, *vide* Taḳí (Mír).

**Muhammad Tughlak Shah,** محمد تغلق شاه, *vide* Muhammad Sháh Tughlaḳ.

**Muhammad Wala,** محمد والا, author of the work called "Najm ul-Hidáet," containing much good advice, written according to the Súfí faith.

**Muhammad Walah, Sayyad,** سيد محمد واله, author of the "Risála Dastúr ul-Nazm," or the art of writing poetry, with specimens of the various measures.

**Muhammad Yar Khan,** محمد يارخان, the son of Aitmad Khán, nobleman of the time of the emperor 'Alamgír.

**Muhammad Yusaf,** محمد يوسف, a native of Ḳábul, who came to India and was employed in the service of the emperor Akbar. He was a good poet and died in the year 1562 A. D., 970 A. H.

**Muhammad Yusaf 'Ali Khan Bahadur,** محمد يوسف علي خان, the present loyal nawáb of Rámpúr (1859—1872) who succeeded Muhammad Saíd Khán in 1855.

**Muhammad Zahid, Mir,** مير محمد زاهد, son of Muhammad Aslam, an author who flourished in the reign of Sháh Jahán and 'Alamgír, and died in the year 1690 A. D., 1101 A. H.

**Muhammad Zaman,** محمد زمان, a celebrated punster and poet of Persia, who came to India in the reign of Akbar, but after a few years returned to his native country where he died some years before or after 1600 A. D.

**Muhammad Zaman,** محمد زمان, *vide* Ḳásim Khán, Súbadár of Ḳábul.

**Muhip Narayan,** مهيپ نارايں, rájá of Banares, he was living in 1789 A. D., nephew of Rájá Cheyt Singh and grandson of Rájá Balwunt Singh. The Rájá's daughter was wife of Bábú Dirgbijai Singh, from whom the present Mahárájá is descended.

**Muhi,** محي, takhallus of a poet who flourished about the year 1592 A. D., 1001 A. H., and is the author of a Díwán.

**Muhit,** محيط, *vide* Rámjas Munshí.

**Muhi-uddin,** محي الدين, author of a heroic poem called "Taríkh Najíb-náma," in praise of Najíb Khán, styled Najíb-uddaula, an Afghán chief who distinguished himself during the reign of the unfortunate 'Alamgír II, emperor of Dehlí.

**Muhi-uddin bin-Arabi, Shaikh,** شيخ محي الدين بن عربي, a celebrated learned Muhammadan of Persia, who was born in 1166 A. D., 561 A. H., died in 1239 A. D., 637 A. H., and is buried at Damascus. He is the author of a work in Arabic called "Fatúhát Makkia," *vide* Ibn-Arabí.

**Muhi-uddin Abdul Ḳadir bin-Abi ul-Wafa** محي الدين عبدال قادر بن ابي الوافه, *vide* 'Abdul Ḳádir bin 'Abí ul-Wafá Misrí.

**Muhi-uddin Tusi, Shaikh,** محي الدين طوسي, a native of Tús, and author of the work called "Kanz ul-'Ashiḳín," a treatise on divine love; abridged from the "Kímiá-e-Sa'ádat." He was a co-temporary of 'Umar Mirzá, and was living in 1408 A. D., 811 A. H.

**Muhi-uddin,** محي الدين, author of the work called "Irshád Yáfa'í."

**Muhib,** محب, poetical name of Sayyad Ghulám Nabí of Bilgrám who was slain in a battle which took place between Nawáb Safdar Jang and Aḥmad Khán, Nawáb of Furrukhábád on the 5th February, 1752 A. D., 29th Ṣafar, 1165 A. H.

**Muhib,** محب, poetical name of Shaikh Walí-ullah of Dehlí, who was a pupil of Sauda, and is the author of a Díwán.

**Muhib-uddin Said Hasan al-Yaghawi,** سيد محب الدين حسين, surnamed Guz, an author who died in 1132 A. D., 526 A. H.

**Muhib-ullah, Ḳazi,** قاضي محب الله, who, in the reign of 'Alamgír, was appointed Ḳází of Lakhnau and afterwards of Haidarábád in the Dakhin. On the accession of Bahádur Sháh to the throne of Dehlí, 1707 A. D., 1119 A. H., he was honoured with the Sadárat of all India. He is the author of several works, among which are the "Kitáb Sallam," and "Muslim."

**Muhindar Singh, Maharaja,** مهيندر سنگه مهاراجه, Rájá of Bhadawar (1870).

**Muhib-ullah, Shaikh,** شيخ محب الله, a pírzáda of Allahábád who died there in the year 1648 A. D., 1058 A. H. He is the author of a work called "'Ibádat ul Khawás" on Ethics.

**Muhsin 'Ali Khan, Sayyad,** محسن علي خان شايد, the son of Sayyad Sháh Husain, the son of Sayyad Arab Sháh, was an excellent poet, and is the author of a Díwán and a biography of Urdú poets called "Sarápá Sakhun."

**Muhsin Fani,** محسن فاني, an excellent poet and author, whose proper name was Shaikh Muhammad Muhsin and poetical title Fání. He held the appointment of Sadárat of the province of Allahábád for several years in the time of the emperor Sháh Jahán; and when that monarch conquered Balkh in 1646 A. D., 1056 A. H., amongst the spoil which fell into the hands of the emperor belonging to Nazar Muhammad Khán, the ruler of that province, was a Díwán composed by Muhsin Fáni which he had sent as a present to that ruler with verses in his praise; this annoyed the emperor, and Muhsin was forthwith dismissed from his office. He received, however, a small pension and passed the remainder of his life at Kashmír where he died in 1670 A. D., 1081 A. H. His Díwán contains about 7,000 verses.

**Muhtadi Billah,** مهتدي بالله, *vide* Al-Muhtadí.

**Muhtashim 'Ali Khan,** محتشم علي خان, *vide* Hashmat.

**Muhtashim, Maulana,** مولانا محتشم, a poet of Kashan and master of Fakhrí bin-Mauláná Sulṭán Muhammad Amírí of Hirát. He wrote three Díwáns, *viz.*, "Sabáya," "Jalália," and "Shabábia," besides a Díwán of Ḳasídas in praise of the Imáms and princes consisting of about 8,000 verses, and a Risála of Mua'mmas or enigmas and chronograms. There is a Kasída quoted on the accession of Sháh Isma'íl Safwí to the throne of Persia, of 66 misras, each of which contains a chronogram for the year 1576 A. D., 984 A. H.

**Mui'zzi,** معزي, *vide* Moi'zzí.

**Mui'zz-li-din-allah,** معزالدين الله, *vide* Moi'zz-li-dín-allah.

**Mui'zz-uddin,** معز الدين, *vide* Moi'zz-uddín.

**Mui'zz-uddaula,** معزالدوله, *vide* Moi'zz-uddaula.

**Mujaddid Alif Sani,** مجدد الف ثاني, *vide* Aḥmad Sarhindí (Shaikh).

**Mujahid Shah Bahmani,** مجاهد شاه بهمني, succeeded his father Muhammad Sháh I Bahmaní on the throne of the Dakhin in March, 1375 A. D., Shawwál, 776 A. H. He was murdered after a reign of three years on the night of the 14th of April, 1378 A. D., 17th Ẕil-ḥijja, 779 A. H., by his uncle Dáúd Khán who ascended the throne by the title of Dáúd Sháh.

**Mujib,** شاه مجيب, or Sháh Mujíb, author of a history of the loves of Joseph and Potiphar's wife called "Yúsaf wa-Zalekha," in Urdú verse composed in 1824 A. D., 1240 A. H.

**Mujir,** مجير بيلقاني, poetical name of 'Abdul Mukárim Mujír-uddín of Bílḳán, a town in Azurbeján. He was a pupil of Khákání, and is the author of a Díwán. He died in 1198 A. D., 594 A. H. He flourished in the time of Ḳizal Arsalán, and was a co-temporary of Zahír-uddín Fáryábí.

**Mujir-uddin Bilkani,** مجيرالدين بيلقاني, *vide* Mujír.

**Mujrim,** مجرم, poetical name of Rahmat-ullah, who is the author of an Urdú Díwán.

**Mujrim,** مجرم, poetical title of Ghulám Husain of Patna, the father of Ishḳí, whose proper name was Shaikh Muhammad Wajíh.

**Mukalil bin-Sulaiman,** مكالل بن سليمان, author of a Commentary on the Ḳurán. He died in the year 723 A. D., 105 A. H.

**Mukanna,** مقنع, *vide* Al-Makna or Mukanna.

**Mukarrab Khan,** مقرب خان, *vide* Masíhí (Mulla).

**Mukarram Khan, Nawab,** نواب مكرم خان, governor of Multán in the time of 'Alamgír.

**Mukim Khan,** مقيم خان, held the rank of 700 in the time of the emperor Akbar, and was raised to a high rank in the time of Jahángír. He had a home at Agrah on the banks of the Jamna at a place still called Mukím Khán ka Ghát.

**Mukhlis,** مخلص, the poetical name of Ráe 'Anand Ráe, a Khattrí, who was the father-in-law of Tansukh Ráe, and a pupil of Mirzá Bedil. He died in the fourth year of Aḥmad Sháh's reign 1751 A. D., 1164 A. H. His works contain 50,000 verses. He is also called Mukhlis Hindí, to distinguish him from Mukhlis Káshí.

**Mukhlis,** مخلص, the poetical appellation of Mukhlis 'Alí Khán, commonly called Mír Báḳir. He was Nawáb Nawázish Khán, Shahámat Jang's sister's son, and is the author of a Díwán in Urdú.

**Mukhlis Kashi,** مخلص كاشي, a poet of Persia.

**Mukhtar bin-Mahmud bin-Muhammad az-Zahidi Abu ar-Rija al-Ghazmini,** مختار بن محمود, surnamed Najm-uddín, is the author of "Ḳuniat al-Muniat," a collection of decisions of considerable authority. He died 1259 A. D., 658 A. H.

**Mukhtari,** مختاري, a Persian poet.

**Mukhtar-uddaula,** مختار الدوله, *vide* Murtazá Khán.

**Muktadi Billah,** مقتدي بالله, *vide* Al-Muktadí.

**Muktadir Billah,** مقتدر بالله, *vide* Al-Muktadir.

**Muktafi Billah,** مكتفي, *vide* Al-Muktafí.

**Mulhim,** ملهم, a poet who flourished about the year 1706 A. D., 1118 A. H., and is the author of a Díwán.

**Mulla Ahmad,** ملا احمد, *vide* Aḥmad (Mulla).

**Mulla 'Ali al-Hafiz al-Kastamumi,** ملا علي الحافظ القستمومي, author of the Commentary on the Hadís ul-Arbaín of Shaikh Ismá'íl Haḳḳí.

**Mulla 'Ali Ḳusanji,** ملا علي قوسنجي, who also wrote a Háshia or marginal notes on the Kashshaf, besides the one written by Tuftázání. He died about the year 1405 A. D. 808 A. H.

**Mulla Husain Waez,** ملا حسين وايز, *vide* Husain Waez (Mauláná).

**Mulla Furati,** ملا فراتي, author of the work entitled the "Ḳarak Sawál" containing forty questions with the answers of Muhammad, according to tradition.

**Mulla 'Imad,** ملا عماد, author of a work on Súfiism in Persian, called "Hashia Mullá 'Imád."

**Mulla Firoz,** ملا فيروز, a Pársí priest. The Pársís of Bombay entertain the most liberal feelings in favour of science and literature: they possess great wealth, and commercial relation with every part of Asia. The mission sent by them some years ago to Persia at their own expence of Kans, the father of Mullá Fíroz, the Editor of the *Dasatir*, for the purpose of making inquiries relative to the remnant of the Pársís in that country; the discovery by Kans while on that mission of a copy of the *Dasatir* in the Pahlawí language, and the English translation of that curious work, published by Mulla Fíroz at Bombay in 1818 shew the spirit and perseverance with which the Pársís of Bombay have instituted inquiries connected with the history of their country, *vide Transactions, Royal Asiatic Society*, Vol. III, Appendix, p. iv.

**Mulla Jami Lahouri Namdar Khani,** ملا جامي لاهوری نامدارخاني, whose poetical name is Bekhud, was very will skilled in composing chronograms, and has left a thick Díwán of Ghazals, &c. He died in 1675 A. D., 1086 A. H.

**Mulla Jiwan,** ملا جیون امیٹھوی, of Amaiṭhí, whose proper name was Shaikh Aḥmad, was the tutor of the emperor 'A'lamgír. He is the author of the Commentary on the Ḳurán called "Tafsír Aḥmadí." He is also called Mullá Jián Jaunpúrí, and is said to have died 1718 A. D., 1130 A. H.

**Mulla Ḳasim,** ملا قاسم مشهدی, of Mashhad, author of an Insha, or Collection of Letters.

**Mulla Khusro,** ملا خسرو, author of a law treatise, entitled "Ghurar ul-Ahkám," and a Commentary on the same work called the "Durar al Hukkám." Mulla Khusro, who is one of the most renowned of the Turkish jurisconsults, completed his work in 1478 A. D., 883 A. H. and died in 1480 A. D., 885 A. H.

**Mulla Malik Ḳummi,** ملا ملک قمی, *vide* Malik Ḳummí.

**Mulla Mir,** ملا میر, he lived in the time of the emperor Akbar. In 1566 A. D., 974 A. H., he constructed a well at A'grah, and Ashraf Khán Mír Munshí wrote the chronogram of the year of its construction. It is a subtractive one.

**Mulla Mufid Balkhi,** ملا مفید بلخی, a native of Balkh, was an excellent poet. He came to India and died at Multán in the time of the emperor 'A'lamgír, 1674 A. D., 1085 A. H. He is the author of a Díwán. A subtractive chronogram on his death written by Sarkhush.

**Mulla Muhsin,** ملا محسن, *vide* Faiz.

**Mulla Mukimai,** ملا مقیمای, an author who lived in the time of Sháh Jahán.

**Mulla Shah,** ملا شاه, a native of Badakhshán, was a learned and pious Musalmán. He was a disciple of Mián Sháh Mír of Láhor and Murshid or spiritual guide of the unfortunate prince Dárá Shikóh, the eldest son of the emperor Sháh Jahán, who highly respected him and visited him on his tour to Ḳashmír, where he (Mulla Sháh) had built a place for his residence. He died at Ḳashmír in the commencement of the reign of the emperor 'A'lamgír, about the year 1660 A. D., 1070 A. H.

**Mulla Sharif,** ملا شریف, author of a Díwán, on the loves of "Shírín and Khusro," dedicated to Sulṭán Ḳulí Ḳuṭb Sháh of Golkoṇḍa in 1515 A. D., 921 A. H.

**Mulla Sheri,** ملا شیری, *vide* Sherí (Mulla).

**Mulla Shikebi,** ملا شکیبی, an excellent poet who served under 'Abdul Rahím Khán, KhánKhánán, and was living in 1592 A. D., 1000 A. H.

**Mullazada,** ملا زاده, of Patna, author of an Urdú translation of the novel called "Bahár Dánish," which he named "Izhár Dánish."

**Mullazada,** ملازاده, author of the marginal notes on the "Mukhtasir Ma'ání wa-Bayán."

**Multan,** بادشاهان ملتان, kings of, *vide* Yúsaf (Shaikh).

**Mumtaz,** ممتاز, the poetical name of two poets. One of whom is named Maulwí Ihsán-ulláh.

**Mumtaz Mahal,** ممتاز محل, the favorite wife of the emperor Sháh Jahán, for whom he built the celebrated edifice at A'grah called the Táj, *vide* Arjumand Báno Begam.

**Mumtaz Shikoh,** ممتاز شکوه, second son of the emperor Sháh Jahán.

**Mumtaz-uddaula, Nawab,** ممتاز الدوله نواب, the grandson of Muhammad 'Alí Sháh, king of Audh. He was living in 1868 A. D. The nawáb, during the disorders consequent on the Mutiny at Lakhnau, declared his opinions by entering into a contract to give his daughter in marriage to the nominee of the rebels, Birjís Kadr. For this conduct he was adjudged to suffer the loss of his pension, Rs. 700 per mensem.

**Munai'm,** منعم, poetical name of Núr ul-Haḳ, Ḳází of Barẹlí, who was an excellent Persian poet, and has written upwards of 300,000 verses; among his compositions is a commentary on the Ḳurán in verse, and Arabic and Persian Ḳasídas, several Masnawís, and three Persian Díwáns. He was living at Dehlí in 1786 A. D., 1200 A. H.

**Munai'm Khan, KhanKhanan,** منعم خان خانخانان, a nobleman who was raised to the high dignity of prime minister by the emperor Akbar, after the dismissal of Bairám Khán, KhánKhánán in 1560 A. D., 967 A. H.; was appointed governor of Jaunpúr after the death of Khán Zamán, where he built that famous bridge on the river Gúmtí in the year 1567 A. D., 975 A. H. He was latterly appointed governor of Bengal after the defeat of Dáúd Sháh, king of that country in 1575 A. D., 983 A. H. From the period of Muhammad Bakhtyar Khiljí to that of Sher Sháh the city of Gaur, which is also called Lakhnauṭí, had been the capital of Bengal, after which, owing to its insalubrity, it had been abandoned for Khawáspúr Ṭanḍa. Munai'm Khán, however, admiring the spot, gave orders for its repairs, and made it his residence; but he soon fell a victim to its unhealthy climate, and died there on the 12th October the same year, 9th Rajab, 983 A. H.

**Munai'm Khan,** منعم خان, the son of Sulṭán Beg Barlás, a nobleman who had been the emperor Bahádur Sháh's principal officer at Ḳábul, was, on the accession of that emperor to the throne of Dehlí, appointed his wazír with the title of KhánKhánán. He died some time before that monarch's death about the year 1711 A. D., 1123 A. H. He is the author of the work called "Ilhámát Munai'mí."

**Munai'm, Shaikh,** شیخ منعم, a poet who served under prince Sulṭán Shujáạ, governor of Bengal, and was present in the battle fought by that prince against his brother the emperor 'A'lamgír in December, 1658 A. D., after which he was never heard of. For his poetical name, he used his own in his compositions.

**Munir Lahouri, Mulla,** ملا منیرلاهوری, a poet of Láhor, was the son of Mulla 'Abdul Majíd of Multán. He formerly took the words "Sakhun Sanj" for his poetical title, but afterwards used "Munír" in his compositions. His proper name was Abú'l Barkát. He died at A'grah on Saturday the 31st August, 1644 A. D., 7th Rajab, 1054 A. H., and left about 30,000 verses and an Inshá which goes after his name, *viz.*, "Insháe Munír."

**Munna Jan,** منا جان, *vide* Nasír-uddín Haidar.

**Munni Begam,** مني بيگم, a concubine of Mír Ja'far, Nawáb of Bengal. After his death and the death of his two sons Najm-uddaula and Saif-uddaula, she was appointed guardian to Mubárik-uddaula, the infant son of the late Nawáb, by Warren Hastings, in preference to others whose claims were more forcible. The guardianship was taken away from the Begam in 1776 A. D. She was the mother of Najm-uddaula, died 1779 A. D., 1st Sha'bán 1103 A. H.

**Munshi,** منشي, takhallus of Jaswant Ráe Munshí. He is the author of a Díwán, and was living in 1712 A. D., 1124 A. H.

**Munshi,** منشي, poetical title of Munshí Múlchánd, a Káyeth and native of Dehlí. He was a pupil of the poet Nasír, and is the author of some fragments of the Sháhnáma in Urdú. He died about the year 1822 A. D.

**Munsif,** منصف, poetical title of Fázil Khán, who is the author of a Díwán, and was living in 1704 A. D., 1116 A. H.

**Murad I, Sultan,** اول سلطان مراد, whom our English authors call Amurath I, and who is also called Murád Khán Ghází and Khwáwandgár Rúm, was the third Sultán of the race of Usmán or Othmán. He succeeded his father Arkhan (Orchan) on the Turkish throne in 1359 A. D., 760 A. H., and was known for his cruelties towards his son, and those who espoused his cause. He advanced into Europe, and made Adrianople his capital in 1360 A. D. He was a great warrior and obtained 37 victories, in the last of which he perished 1389 A. D., 791 A. H., aged 71, by the hand of a soldier. He (or as some say his father) was the first who established the formidable force of the Jánisarís. His son Báyezíd I, succeeded him.

**Murad II, Sultan,** ثاني سلطان مراد, succeeded his father Muhammad I as Ottoman emperor, in 1422 A. D., 825 A. H., and was the first Turk who used cannon in the field of battle. In 1443 A. D., 847 A. H., he resigned the crown in favour of his son Muhammad II, but finding him incapable to hold the reins of government, he abandoned his retirement and defeated the famous Sikandar Beg (Scanderbeg,) and routed the Hungarians. According to Gibbon, he died on the 2nd February, 1451 A. D., Ẕil-hijja, 854 A. H., and was succeeded by his son Muhammad II, who afterwards took Constantinople.

**Murad III, Sultan,** ثالث سلطان مراد, succeeded his father Salím II to the throne of Constantinople in December, 1574 A. D., Shabán, 982 A. H., and to rid himself of all competitors, he, at his first coming to the crown, caused his five brothers to be strangled in his presence. This act of cruelty so affected his mother that she destroyed herself. He took from the disagreeing Persians, Armenia, Media, and the city of Tauris, and the fort Gaino from the Hungarians. He died on the 18th January, 1595 A. D., Jumáda I, 1003 A. H., aged 50 lunar years. At the time of his death such a sudden and terrible tempest arose, that many thought the world would then be dissolved. He was succeeded by his son Muhammad III. Sulṭán Murád is the author of the work called "Fatúhát-us-Siyám."

**Murad IV, Sultan,** رابع سلطان مراد, son of Aḥmad I, emperor of Constantinople, succeeded his uncle Mustafa I, who was deposed the second time in 1623 A. D., 1032 A. H. He took Baghdád in 1637 A. D., 30,000 of whose inhabitants he put to the sword, though he had promised them protection. He died on the 8th February, 1640 A. D., 1049 A. H., aged 18, of excessive intoxication, and was succeeded by his brother Ibráhím.

**Murad Baksh, Sultan,** سلطان مراد بخش, youngest son of the emperor Sháh Jahán, by whom he was appointed governor of Gujrát, Ṭhaṭṭa and Bihkar. He was seized and imprisoned in the fort of Gwáliar, by the orders of his brother the emperor 'Álamgír, after the first battle he fought against his brother Dárá Shikóh, and was subsequently murdered, 1662 A. D., 1072 A. H., at Gwáliar and buried within the fort.

**Murad Mirza,** مرزا مراد, also called Sulṭán Murád and Sháh Murád, was the second son of the emperor Akbar. His mother's name was Salíma Sulṭána Begam. He was born on Thursday the 8th June, 1570 A. D., 978 A. H. in the house of the venerable Shaikh Salím Chishtí at Síkrí. The Hindús, on account of his being born in the mountainous country of Síkrí, used to call him Paháṛí. After this prince's birth, the emperor, considering the village of Síkrí a propitious spot, two of his sons having been born there, ordered the foundation of a city to be laid, which, after the conquest of Gujrát, he called Fathapúr. This prince was sent by his father to conquer the Dakhin in 1595 A. D., 1004 A. H., where he fell sick and died on the 1st of May, 1599 A. D., 15th Shawwál, 1007 A. H. He was at first buried at Sháhpúr, but afterwards his corpse was removed to Dehlí and laid by the side of Humáyún the prince's grandfather.

**Murassa' Rakam,** مرصع رقم, title of the author of the "Nautarz Muṛassạ." *Vide* Tahsín.

**Murauwat,** مروت, poetical name of Saghír 'Alí, a poet, who is the author of a story in Urdú called "Tilismát Ishḳ," composed in 1792 A. D., 1207 A. H.

**Murshid Khan,** مرشد خان, a poet, who flourished in the time of Jahángír, and is the author of a Díwán.

**Murshid Ḳuli Khan,** مرشد قلي خان, a nobleman of the time of the emperor Sháh Jahán, who was Faujdár of Muthurá, and was killed there in 1638 A. D., 1048 A. H.

**Murshid Ḳuli Khan,** مرشد قلي خان, nawáb of Bengal, *vide* Ja'far Khán.

**Murshid Ḳuli Khan,** مرشد قلي خان, Rustam Jang, son-in-law of Shujá-uddaula, governor of Bengal, by whom he was appointed governor of Katak. Being defeated by Mahábat Jang, Nawáb of Bengal, he fled to the Dakhin in the year 1739 A. D. where he died. He was a good poet, and his poetical name was Sarshár.

**Murtaza Khan,** سيد مرتضى خان, a Sayyad, who on the accession of Nawáb 'Asaf-uddaula to the masnad of Lakhnau, was appointed by him his náib or deputy, with the title of Mukhtár-uddaula, but Basant 'Alí Khán, an old khwája sará (eunuch) of the nawáb's father, being offended at the influence he had over the nawáb, resolved to remove him; and for this purpose having invited him to an entertainment, murdered him, and was himself slain the same day by order of the nawáb. This circumstance took place in the month of March, 1776 A. D., Ṣafar, 1190 A. H.

**Murtaza Khan,** مرتضى خان, a relative of Dost 'Alí, the Nawáb of Arkat, under whom the atrocious seizure of Trichinopoly was perpetrated by Chanda Ṣaḥib. The nawáb was succeeded by his son Safdar 'Alí, who after overcoming the effects of poison prepared for him by Murtaza Khán, fell by the poignard of a Paṭhán assassin hired for the work by the same person. A storm was raised which he had not the courage to encounter, and disguising himself in female attire, he escaped from Arkat to his own fort of Vellore. Two years afterwards, the youthful son and successor of Safdar 'Alí met the fate of his father, and common report attributed to Murtaza Khán a principal share in the contrivance of this murder also. Such was the man to whom the patronage of Dupleix, who was at that time grievously at a loss for money, was extended, for Murtaza Khán had the reputation of being extremely rich, and was selected by Dupleix for a new Nawáb of Arkat. He was solemnly installed in his new dignity, but finding that his presence was indispensable at Vellore, he returned thither after some time in 1752 A. D.

**Murtaza Khan Anju,** مرتضی خان انجو, a nobleman of the reign of the emperor Sháh Jahán. At the time of his death which took place 1629 A. D., 1038 A. H., he was governor of Ṭhaṭṭa.

**Murtaza Khan,** مرتضی خان, *vide* Shaikh Faríd, and Faríd Bukhárí.

**Murtaza, Mir,** میر مرتضی, surnamed "Al-Madau bi-ilm ul-Huda." He died in September, 1046 A. D., Ṣafar, 436 A. H.

**Murtaza Nizam Shah I,** مرتضی نظام شاه, ascended the throne of Aḥmadnagar in the Dakhin after the death of his father Husain Nizám Sháh I, in 1565 A. D., 972 A. H., and as he was then in his minority, his mother Khunza Sulṭána became for six years chief manager of affairs, after which the Sulṭán took the affairs under his own management. He reigned about 24 lunar years, and becoming mad, his son Mírán Husain Nizám Sháh shut him up in a warm bathing-room, and shutting fast the doors and windows to exclude all air, lighted a great fire under the bath, so that the Sulṭán was speedily suffocated by the steam and heat. This circumstance took place about the 15th January, 1589 A. D., 8th Rabí' I, 997 A. H. But according to the work of Jámạ ul-Hind, he was poisoned by his son on the 5th June, 1588 A. D., corresponding with 18th Rajab, 996 A. H.

**Murtaza Nizam Shah II,** مرتضی نظام شاه, a nominal prince and a descendant of the Nizám Sháhí kings of Aḥmadnagar, who was raised to the throne by Malik Ambar, the Abyssinian and others after the capture of Bahádur Nizám Sháh in 1600 A. D., 1009 A. H. He was put to death about the year 1628 A. D., 1038 A. H., by Fatha Khán, the son of Malik Ambar, who placed his son Husain, an infant of ten years on the throne. Husain was afterwards confined for life by the emperor Sháh Jahán in the fortress of Gwáliar. *Vide* Fatha Khán.

**Musahib, Mirza,** مرزا مصاحب, a poet who flourished after the poet Sáeb whom he imitates, and was probably living in 1745 A. D., 1158 A. H.

**Musannifak,** مصنفك, surname of Mulla 'Alá-uddín 'Alí bin-Muhammad, an Arabian author, who died 1470 A. D., 875 A. H.

**Musibat,** مصیبت, poetical name of Sháh Ghulám Ḳuṭb-uddín, eldest brother of Sháh Muhammad Afzal of Allahábád. He went on a pilgrimage to Mecca and died there in 1773 A. D., 1187 A. H.

**Mushfaki,** مشفقي, a poet who was born at Bukhárá in the year 1538 A. D., 945 A. H., and composed a Díwán which he completed in 1575 A. D., 983 A. H.

**Mushtak,** مشتاق, the poetical name of Mír Said 'Alí of Isfahán who was alive in the year 1760 A. D., 1174 A. H.

**Mushtak,** مشتاق, poetical title of Mushták Husain of Agrah. He is the author of a Díwán, and since he was a pupil of Bahádur Sháh the ex-king of Dehlí, in every one of his Ghazals he has mentioned in the last verse the poetical name of the king, *viz.*, Zafar.

**Mushtak,** مشتاق, poetical appellation of Muhammad Ḳulí Khán of Patna, a son of Háshim Ḳulí Khán. He was a pupil of Muhammad Roshan Joshish, and Darogha of the household of Nawáb Zain-uddín Aḥmad Khán Haibat Jang. He died in 1801 A. D., 1216 A. H.

**Mushtaki,** سید مشتاقي, *vide* Rizk-ulláh (Shaikh).

**Muslim bin-Amr,** مسلم بن عمر, the father of Ḳutaiba. He was slain in battle along with Misaa'b ibn-Zuber, about the year 690 A. D., 71 A. H.

**Muslim bin-Hajjaj Naishapuri,** مسلم بن حجاج نیشاپوري, or Ḳashmirí, author of the "Saḥíh Muslim," a succinct collection of Traditions, and of the "Masnad Kabír." He died in the year 875 A. D., 261 A. H. The Saḥíh Muslim is considered as almost of equal authority with the Saḥíh ul-Bukhárí, and indeed by some, especially by the African doctors, is preferred to that work. The two collections are constantly quoted together under the name of the Saḥíhain or two Saḥíhs. Muslim is said to have composed his work from 300,000 traditions. *Vide* 'Abdullah Abú Muslim.

**Muslim ibn-'Ukba,** مسلم بن عقبة, was made governor of Medína by Yezíd, the son of Mu'áwia I, 682 A. D., 63 A. H., to chastise the insolence of the inhabitants of that place, who had rebelled against him, which done, he marched directly with his army towards Mecca, but died by the way in September, 683 A. D., Muḥarram, 64 A. H.

**Muslim ibn-Okail,** مسلم ابن عقیل, nephew of 'Alí and cousin of Imám Husain whom he wished to assist against Yezíd, the son of Mu'áwia, but was beheaded along with Háris on the 8th September, 680 A. D., 8th Ẕil-ḥijja, 60 A. H., and their heads sent as a present to Yezíd by 'Obaid-ulláh ibn-Zayád. This event took place a few days before the death of Imám Husain.

**Mustaa'sam Billah,** مستعصم بالله, the 37th or last khalíf of the house of 'Abbás, *vide* Al-Mustaa'sam.

**Musta'in Billah,** مستعین بالله, *vide* Al-Musta'ín Billáh.

**Mustafa,** مصطفی, a title of Muhammad.

**Mustafa I, Sultan,** سلطان مصطفی, succeeded his brother Aḥmad I (Achmet) as emperor of Turkey or Constantinople in 1617 A. D., Ẕi-Ḳa'da, 1025 A. H., which was a novelty never before heard of in this kingdom, it being the Grand Seignor's policy to strangle all the younger brothers; however, this Mustafa was preserved, either because Aḥmad, being once a younger brother, took pity on him, or because he had no issue of his own body, and so was not permitted to kill him. It is said that Aḥmad once intended to have shot him, but at the instant he was seized with such a pain in his arm and shoulder, that he cried out "Muhammad will not let him die." He carried himself but insolently and cruelly, and was deposed and sent to prison in 1618 A. D., 1027 A. H., when 'Usmán, his nephew, was raised to the throne. 'Usmán was murdered in 1621 A. D., 1030 A. H., and Mustafa again restored, and ultimately strangled by his Janisarís in 1623 A. D., 1032 A. H. He was succeeded by Murád IV.

**Mustafa II, Sultan,** سلطان مصطفى, son of Muhammad IV succeeded Aḥmad II in 1695 A. D., 1106 A. H. as emperor of Constantinople. He was an able warrior, and after defeating the Imperialists at Temswar, he attacked the Venetians, Poles and Russians. He retired to Adrianople, where he forgot himself in lascivious pleasures, till a revolt of his subjects compelled him to descend from his throne in 1703 A. D., 1115 A. H. He died of melancholy six months after. He was succeeded by his brother Aḥmad III.

**Mustafa III, Sultan,** سلطان مصطفى, son of Aḥmad III, succeeded his nephew 'Usmán III as emperor of Constantinople in 1757 A. D., 1171 A. H. He spent his time in his seraglio, and left the government to his favorites. He died on the 21st January, 1774 A. D., 1187 A. H., and was succeeded by his brother Aḥmad IV, also called 'Abdul Hamíd.

**Mustafa IV, Sultan,** سلطان مصطفى, son of Aḥmad IV, succeeded Salím III on the 29th of May, 1807 A. D., 1222 A. H., as emperor of Constantinople. He reigned one year, and was deposed and slain in 1808 A. D., 1223 A. H., when Mahmúd II was raised to the throne.

**Mustafa bin-Muhammad Sa'id,** مصطفى, author of the Persian Commentary on the Ḳurán, entitled "Aḳsám 'Ayát Ḳurán."

**Mustai'd Khan,** مستعد خان, surnamed Muhammad Sáḳí, was employed as Munshí or secretary to 'Ináyet-ullah Khán, wazír of Bahádur Sháh, and is the author of the "Másir-i-'Álamgírí," the history of the emperor 'Álamgír. He had been a constant follower of the court for forty years, and an eye-witness of many of the transactions he records. He undertook the work by desire of his patron, and finished it in 1710 A. D., 1122 A. H. being only three years after the decease of 'Álamgír.

**Mustajab Khan,** مستجاب خان, one of the sons of Háfiz Rahmat Khán, and author of the work called "Gulistán-i-Rahmat" being a history of his father. He died in February, 1833 A. D., 2nd Shawwál, 1248 A. H., aged 74 lunar years.

**Mustakfi Billah,** مستكفي بالله, *vide* Al-Mustakfí Billáh.

**Mustanjad Billah,** مستنجد بالله, *vide* Al-Mustanjid.

**Mustanasar Billah,** مستنصر بالله, *vide* Al-Mustanasar.

**Mustarashid Billah,** مسترشد بالله, *vide* Al-Mustarshid.

**Mustazi Billah,** مستضي بالله, *vide* Al-Mustazí.

**Mustazahar Billah,** مستظهر بالله, *vide* Al-Mustazhir.

**Musailima,** مسيلمه, commonly called Kazzáb or the Liar, was an impostor who arose in the time of Muhammad in one of the provinces of Arabia, named Hajar. As success in any project seldom fails to draw in imitators, Muhammad having raised himself to such a degree of power and reputation, by acting the prophet, induced others to imagine they might arrive at the same height by the same means. His most considerable competitors in the prophetic office was Musailima and Al-Aswad. Musailima pretended to be joined in commission with Muhammad, and published revelations in imitation of the Ḳurán. He sent Muhammad a letter, offering to go halves with him, in these words: "From Musailima, the apostle of God, to Muhammad, the apostle of God. Now, let the earth be half mine and half thine." But Muhammad believing himself too well established to need a partner, wrote him this answer: "From Muhammad the apostle of God, to Musailima the liar. The earth is God's; he giveth the same for inheritance unto such of his servants as he pleaseth; and the happy issue shall attend those who fear him." During the few months which Muhammad lived after the setting up of this new imposture, Musailima grew very formidable; Abú Bakr, Muhammad's successor, in the second year of his reign and the 12th of Hijrí, (633 A. D., 12 A. H.,) sent an army against him under the command of Khália, the son of Walíd, who defeated and slew him in battle. Al-Aswad set up for himself the very year that Muhammad died; but a party, sent by Muhammad, broke into his house by night, and cut off his head. They received the appellation of "The two Liars."

**Mutia' Billah,** مطيع بالله, khalífa of Baghdád, *vide* Al-Mutía' Billáh.

**Mutjali,** متجلي, poetical name of Sayyad Ḳutb-uddín.

**Mutnabbi** متنبي, or Al-Mutnabbi, surname of Abú Tyyeb Aḥmad bin-Husain, one of the most celebrated of the Arabian poets, born at Kúfa in 915 A. D., 303 A. H. He had acquired an extensive knowledge of pure Arabic, drawn from the best sources, and this he has handed down in his poetical compositions. He flourished about the year 950 A. D., 339 A. H.; his father was a water-carrier in Kúfa. His principal patron was Saif-uddaula, prince of Damascus, of the family of Hamdan. The surname of "Al-Mutnabbí," (the pretended prophet) was given him because he had set up for a prophet in the flat country near Sawáma, where he was followed by a great multitude of the Banú Kalab and other tribes; but Lúlú, governor of Emessa, having marched against him took him prisoner and dispersed his partizans. He kept Mutnabbí in confinement for a long period, and having at length brought him back to the Muslim faith, he set him at liberty. He was attacked by a chief of the tribe of Ásad, at the head of a troop of partizans: a combat took place in which he was killed with his son Al-Muhassad and his slave Muflik. This event happened in the month of September, 965 A. D., 354 A. H.

**Muttaki Billah,** متقي بالله, a khalíf of Baghdád, *vide* Al-Muttaḳí.

**Mutalibi,** مطلبي, surname of Muhammad bin-Idrís al-Sháfa'í, who was one of the four Imáms, or chief of the four orthodox sects amongst the Musalmáns.

**Mutwakhil Ali Allah,** متوكل على الله, a khalíf of Baghdád, *vide* Al-Mutwakkil.

**Muwyyad al-Hulla, (Shaikh),** شيخ مويد الحلي, *vide* Abú'l Ḳásim of Hulla.

**Muwyyad-uddaula,** مويد الدولة, son of Rukn-uddaula, the son of Alí Bóya the Bóyaite. He succeeded to a part of his father's dominions in Persia in September 976 A. D., Muḥarram 366 A. H. He was taken captive and imprisoned by Hisám-uddaula at Jurjan in January 984 A. D., Sha'bán, 373 A. H., and his brother Fakhr-uddaula Abú'l Hasan Alí got possession of the empire.

**Muwyyad-uddaula,** مويدالدولة, the son of Nizám ul-Mulk, the celebrated wazír of Sultán Alp Arsalán and his son Malikshâh. He served as minister to Barkayárak, the son of the latter for some time, and when dismissed by that monarch, he joined his brother Muhammad in an attack upon Barkayárak; but was taken, and put to death by that prince.

**Muzaffar or Muzaffarian,** مظفر و مظفريان, a dynasty

of petty rulers of Fars or Persia. From the period at which the fortunes of the family of Halákú began to decline, *i. e.*, after the death of Sulṭán Abú Sa'íd in 1335 A. D. till the conquest of Persia by Ámír Taimúr, the province of Fars was governed by a dynasty of petty rulers, who took the name of Muzaffar from their founder, Mubáriz-uddín Muhammad whose title was Al-Muzaffar, or the Victorious, which title he received on his victory over Abú Isháḳ, the governor of Shíráz in 1353 A. D., 754 A. H. The capital of this family was Shíráz, which is said to have attained its great prosperity under their rule. *Vide* Muhammad Muzaffar.

**Muzaffar,** مظفر, the poetical name of a person who flourished about the year 1690 A. D., 1102 A. H. The name of his Murshid or spiritual guide was Alí Amjad, in whose praise he has written some Ghazals.

**Muzaffar Husain Mirza,** مظفر حسین مرزا, was the son of Sulṭán Husain Mirzá, ruler of Khurásán, after whose death in May 1506 A. D., Ẕil-hijja 911 A. H. he conjointly with his brother Badí-úzzamán Mirzá, ascended the throne of Hirát; but they did not enjoy it long, for Sháhí Beg Khán, the Uzbak, defeated them in May 1507 A. D., Muḥarram 913 A. H. and took possession of the country. Muzaffar Husain Mirzá, who had gone to Astarábád, died there the same year.

**Muzaffar Husain Mirza,** مظفر حسیر مرزا, of the royal Safwí race of Persia, was the son of Sulṭán Husain Mirzá, the son of Bahrám Mirzá, the son of Sháh Ismá'íl Safwí. He left his jágír of Ḳandahár, and proceeded to India; and on his arrival at the court of the emperor Akbar in August 1595 A. D. was appointed an amír of 5000. The Sarkár of Sambhal was assigned to him in jágír, and Ḳandahár (which was made over to the emperor,) to Sháh Beg Kábulí. About the year 1609 A. D. Mirzá Khurram (afterwards Sháh Jahán) was married to a daughter of Muzaffar Husain who received the title of Ḳandahárí Begam.

**Muzaffar Husain Mirza,** مظفر حسین مرزا, was the son of Ibráhím Husain Mirzá and Gulrukh Begam. He was married to Khánam Sulṭán, the daughter of the emperor Akbar in 1593 A. D., and was living in 1600 A. D.

**Muzaffar Jang,** مظفر جنگ, also called Muzaffar Husain Khán, Nawáb of Farrukhábád, whose original name was Diler Himmat Khán. He succeeded his father Aḥmad Khán Bangash in the month of November, 1771 A. D., Sha'bán, 1185 A. H., and received the above title from the emperor Sháh 'Alam, who was then proceeding to Dehlí from Allahábád. He ceded his territory to the English on receipt of a pension of 108,000 rupees on the 4th June, 1802 A. D. After his death, his grandson Tafazzul Husain Khán succeeded him.

**Muzaffar Jang,** مظفر جنگ, whose original name was Hidáet Muhín-uddín, was the favourite grandson of the celebrated Nizám ul-Mulk, the Súbadár of Haidarábád. He was the son of that nobleman's daughter, and on his death, he collected an army and gave out that his grandsire had in his will not only appointed him to inherit the greatest part of his treasures, but had likewise nominated him to succeed to the government of the southern provinces. Násir Jang, his uncle, who had taken possession of his father's wealth, was enabled to keep his father's army in pay; and this was so numerous, that the forces which Muzaffar Jang had collected were not sufficient to oppose him with any probability of success. Muzaffar Jang subsequently went to Arkát (Arcot) where he defeated and killed Anwar-uddín Khán, the nawáb of that place, by the assistance of the French in a battle fought on the 23rd of July, 1749 A. D., and was acknowledged the lawful Súbadár of the Dakhin. He was, however, after some months obliged to surrender himself to Násir Jang, who kept him in close confinement; but after the murder of Násir Jang in December, 1750 A. D., 17th Muḥarram, 1164 A. H., he was again raised to the masnad by the assistance of the French. His reign was, however, of short duration, for he was not long after assassinated by the same persons who had raised him to power. His death took place on the 3rd of February, 1751 A. D., 17th Rabí' I, 1164 A. H., when Salabat Jang, the third son of the old Nizám, was placed on the masnad by the French.

**Muzaffar Ḳawami, Maulana,** مولانا مظفر قوامي, *vide* Ḳawámí.

**Muzaffar Khan, Nawab,** نواب مظفر خان, was the younger brother of Amír ul-Umrá Khán Daurán Abdus Samad Khán, by whose interest he was appointed governor of Ajmeir in the reign of Farrukh-siyar, and was ordered to march with a numerous army against the Marhaṭṭa chief Malhár Ráo Holkar, who had invaded the territories of the Maharájá Jaising Sawáí of Amber (now called Jaipúr). Muzaffar Khán was slain along with his brother in the battle which took place between the emperor Muhammad Sháh and Nádir Sháh in the month of February, 1739 A. D., Ẕi-Ḳa'da, 1151 A. H.

**Muzaffar Khan,** مظفر خان, a nobleman who was appointed governor of Ágrah by the emperor Jahángír in the year 1621 A. D., 1030 A. H. He built the mosque in the city of Ágrah, called "Kálín or Kalí Masjid," in the year 1631 A. D., 1041 A. H. which is still standing but in a ruinous state.

**Muzaffar Khan Tirbati,** مظفر خان تربتي, a nobleman who was appointed governor of Bengal by the emperor Akbar in 1579 A. D., 987 A. H. In his time Bábá Khán Ḳákshál rebelled against the emperor, took Gaur, slew Muzaffar Khán at Ṭánḍa in April, 1580 A. D., Rabí' I, 988 A. H., and became independent for some time.

**Muzaffar, Maulana,** مولانا مظفر, a celebrated poet of Hirát in Khurásán, who lived in the time of Sulṭán Ghayás-uddín Kart, and Sháh Shujáa' of Shíráz.

**Muzaffar Shah I,** مظفر شاه, whose original name was Muzaffar Khán, was the first king of Gujrát. He was born at Dehlí on the 30th June, 1342 A. D., 25th Muḥarram, 743 A. H. His family had been elevated from menial stations in the household of the kings of Dehlí. He was, however, appointed governor of Gujrát in 1391 A. D., 794 A. H. by Sulṭán Muhammad Tughlaḳ II, king of Dehlí, in the room of Farhat ul-Mulk who had rebelled against the king; a battle took place in which the latter lost his life. In the year 1396 A. D., 799 A. H. Muzaffar Khán caused himself to be proclaimed king under the title of Muzaffar Sháh, and directed coin to be struck in his name. He died after a reign of nearly 20 years, on the 27th July, 1411 A. D., 6th Rabí' II, 814 A. H., in the 71st year of his age, and was succeeded by his grandson Aḥmad Sháh the son of Tátár Khán.

*Ḳings of Gujrát.*

1. Muzaffar Sháh I.
2. Aḥmad Sháh I, his grandson, the son of Tátár Khán.
3. Muhammad Sháh, surnamed Karím, the merciful.
4. Ḳuṭb Sháh.
5. Dáúd Sháh, his uncle, deposed in favour of
6. Mahmúd Sháh I, surnamed Baiḳara, who made two expeditions to the Dakhin.
7. Muzaffar Sháh II.

8. Sikandar Sháh, assassinated.
9. Mahmúd Sháh II, displaced by Bahádur and confined.
10. Bahádur Sháh who was murdered by the Portuguese.
11. Mírán Muhammad Sháh Farúķí of Málwá.
12. Mahmúd II, released from prison.
13. Aḥmad Sháh II, a spurious heir, set up by the minister.
14. Muzaffar Sháh III, a supposititious son of Mahmúd, and the last king in whose time Gujrát was taken by Akbar.

**Muzaffar Shah II,** مظفر شاه, was born on Thursday the 10th April, 1470 A. D., 20th Sha'bán, 875 A. H., and succeeded his father Sulṭán Mahmúd Sháh I, Baiķara on the throne of Gujrát, in the 41st year of his age, in November, 1511 A. D., Sha'bán, 917 A. H. He reigned nearly 15 years, and died on Saturday the 17th of February, 1526 A. D., 3rd Jumáḍa I, 932 A. H., aged 56 lunar years. He was buried at Sarkích. His son Sikandar Sháh succeeded him.

**Muzaffar Shah III,** مظفر شاه, a supposititious son of Mahmúd Sháh III, named Nathú, was raised to the throne of Gujrát by Ya'tmád Khán, the prime minister, after the death of Aḥmad Sháh II in 1561 A. D., 968 A. H. In the year 1572 A. D., 980 A. H., the emperor Akbar was invited by Ya'tmád Khán to occupy Gujrát as in former times; upon which Akbar advanced on the capital of that kingdom which he took possession of on the 20th of November of the same year 14th Rajab, 980 A. H., and re-united it to Dehlí as a province of Hindústán. Muzaffar Sháh, who had abdicated his throne in favour of Akbar, was sent to Ágrah in the first instance, but was subsequently remanded into close confinement, from which he not only made his escape but flying into Gujrát, collected a respectable force, attacked the viceroy Ķuṭb-uddín Khán, and slew him in action; and after an imprisonment of nearly nine years, re-ascended the throne of Gujrát. His reign was, however, of short duration; for in the year 1583 A. D., 991 A. H., Akbar having deputed Mirzá Khán KhánKhánán, the son of Bairám Khán to re-take Gujrát, Muzaffar Khán was defeated in a pitched battle and fled to Júnagaṛh; and as he was pursued by Khán 'Azim, he cut his throat with a razor. His head was then cut off and sent to court. His downfall terminated the dynasty of the Muhammadan kings of Gujrát; ever since which period that kingdom has been considered as a province of Dehlí.

**Muzaffar Shah Purbi,** مظفر شاه پوربي, whose former name was Siddí Badar, was an Abyssinian slave; he murdered his sovereign Mahmúd Sháh, and ascended the throne of Bengal in 1495 A. D., 900 A. H. He reigned three years, and was killed in a battle fought with his minister Sayyad Sharíf, who succeeded him with the title of 'Ala-uddín II, in 1498 A. D., 904 A. H.

**Muzaffar-uddin,** مظفرالدين, *vide* Sunķar.

**Muzaffar-uddin,** مظفرالدين, *vide* Muhammad Muzaffar.

**Muzaffar-uddin Zangi,** مظفرالدين زنگي, *vide* Sunķar.

---

# N.

**Nabi-Effendi,** نبي افندي, a Turkish poet, well acquainted with the classic writers of Greece and Rome. He flourished in the 17th century. *Lempriere's Universal Biography.*

**Nadim Gilani,** نادم گيلاني, an author who came to India, and was a cotemporary of Nazírí of Naishápúr.

**Nadir,** نادر, poetical title of Mirzá Kalb Husain, Deputy Collector of Etáwah. *Vide* Kalb Husain.

**Nadira Begam,** نادره بيگم, daughter of Sulṭán Parwez, the son of the emperor Jahángír. She was married to prince Dárá Shikóh, the eldest son of the emperor Sháh Jahán, on the 23rd January, 1634 A. D., by whom she had two sons, *viz.*, Sulaimán Shikóh and Sipehr Shikóh. She died through fatigue in May, 1659 A. D., Ramaẓán, 1069 A. H. at Dáwar, the country of Malik Jíwan, where her husband had fled along with her after his defeat at Ajmeir. She was buried in the Khanqa of Mian Mír at Lahor.

**Nadir Shah,** نادر شاه, also called Nádir Ķulí Khán, and Tahmasp Ķulí Khán, the greatest warrior Persia has ever produced. He was the son of a shepherd, born in the province of Khurásán, 1687 A. D., but by selling some of his father's sheep, he collected a number of desperate followers who shared his dangers and the booty gained in plundering caravans. By degrees he saw himself at the head of 6,000 brave adherents, and his assistance was solicited by Sháh Tahmasp II, king of Persia, whose throne was usurped by Ashraf, the chief of the Afghâns. With impetuous valour, Nádir attacked and routed the enemy, and then seated his master on the throne of his ancestors at Isfahán 1730 A. D. He then pursued the flying Afghâns to Ķandahár, and on his return, taking advantage of the odium created by an unfavourable treaty made by Sháh Tahmasp with the Turks during his absence, he deposed the king; and his son, an infant of six months he proclaimed Sháh, by the name of 'Abbás III. This event took place on the 16th August, 1732 A. D., 1145 A. H. In his name, Nádir assumed to himself the sovereign power, and after having recovered all that had been taken from Persia, he concluded a peace with the Ottoman Porte in 1736 A. D. On the death of the young Sháh 'Abbás the same year, he signified his intention of resigning his honours; but the nobles, excited by his private intrigues, invested him with the sovereign power. The historian of Nádir is careful in informing us, that the crown of Persia was placed upon the head of the conqueror exactly at 20 minutes past 8 in the morning of the 26th February, 1736 A. D., Shawwál, 1148 A. H. Nádir, now elevated to the height of his ambition, wisely saw that war was the only support of his greatness, and therefore with a numerous army he marched against India in 1739. The Mughal empire was rapidly conquered, 200,000 men were put to the sword, and a booty of one hundred and forty-five millions, in which was the imperial throne set with diamonds of an immense value, called the Peacock Throne, was brought away by him from Dehlí. He latterly became capricious, proud and tyrannical, and was guilty of such cruelty, that the nobles conspired against him and assassinated him on the night of Sunday the 10th May, 1747 A. D., 10th Jumáḍa I, 1160 A. H., after he had reigned 20 years over one of the most extensive and powerful empires of the world. He was buried at Mashhad nine days after his death. His nephew and murderer 'Alí Ķulí Khán who took the title of 'Alí Sháh or 'Adil Sháh, succeeded him. On his accession, he put to death thirteen of the sons and grandsons of Nádir; the only descendant of the conqueror that was spared, was his grandson, Sháhrukh, the son of Raza Ķulí, who was 14 years of age. 'Adil Sháh was soon after deprived of sight and imprisoned. After him Ibráhím his brother reigned for some time in 1748 A. D., Sháhrukh in 1749 A. D., Sulaiman in 1750 A. D., Ismá'íl bin-Sayyad Mustafa from 1750 to 1759 A. D., and after him Karím Khán Zand and 'Aķá Muhammad Khán Ķájár, which see.

**Nafis bin-'Iwaz,** نفيس بن عوض, author of the Arabic work, called "Hall-i-Mújiz ul-Ḳánún." He was a contemporary of Mirzá Ulagh Beg.

**Naftuya,** نفطويه, or Niftúya, was called so, because an offensive smell like naphtha issued from his body. He was an author, and died in 912 A. D., 300 A. H. His proper name is Abú 'Abdullah Ibráhím.

**Naila,** نيلا, the mother of Fíróz Sháh and the daughter of Rájá Mal Bhaṭṭí.

**Naishapuri,** نيشاپوري, or Naisábúrí, an Arabian author, who took his poetical name from Naishápúr his birthplace; he is called by European writers Nisaburiensis. He has collected in a little book the grave and witty sayings of Muhammad and his successors, and some of the kings of Persia.

**Naiyar and Rakhshan,** رکشن یا نیار, are the poetical titles of Nawáb Ziyá-uddín Aḥmad Khán, the son of Nawáb Aḥmad Bakhsh Khán of Fírozpúr and Láhor.

**Najabat Khan KhanKhanan, Nawab,** نواب نجابت خان خانخانان, a nobleman of the reign of the emperor 'A͡lamgír, by whom he was much respected. His proper name was Mirzá Shujáa, he was the son of Mirzá Sháhrukh, and the grandson of Mirzá Sulaimán of Badakhshán. He was born on the 25th November, 1603 A. D., and died on the 13th December, 1664 A. D., 4th Jumáda I, 1075 A. H. at Ujjain. He held the rank of 5000 at the time of his death.

**Najabat, Mir,** میر نجابت, author of a poem called "Gulkushtí," on the art of wrestling, a Sharah of which has been written by Siráj-uddín 'Alí Khán 'Arzú; and another by Munshí Ratan Singh of Lakhnau. *Vide* Naját (Mír).

**Najaf Khan,** نجف خان, styled Amír ul-Umrá Zulfiḳar-uddaula, was born in Persia of a family said to be related to the Safwí sovereigns of that empire, and in his infancy was, with many of his relations, a prisoner to the usurper Nádir Sháh, who kept all the personages, any way allied to the throne, in confinement for his own security. At the request of Mirzá Muhsin Khán, the brother of Nawáb Safdar Jang, who was sent on an embassy to Nádir Sháh by Muhammad Sháh the emperor, after his invasion of Hindústán, Najaf Khán and a sister much older than himself were released. This lady married her deliverer, and Najaf Khán accompanied her and her husband to Dehlí. He was treated with parental affection by Mirzá Muhsin, and at his death attached himself to Muhammad Ḳulí Khán his son, the governor of Allahábád, who was shortly after seized and put to death by his first cousin Nawáb Shujá-uddaula the son of Safdar Jang. Najaf Khán upon this event, retired with a few followers into Bengal, and offered his services to the Nawáb Mír Ḳásim 'Alí Khán, then at war with the English, who gave him great encouragement. When Ḳásim 'Alí took refuge with Shujá-uddaula, Najaf Khán not choosing to trust himself in the power of the latter, repaired to Bundelkhand, and served Gumáu Singh, one of the chiefs of that country. Upon the flight of Shujá-uddaula, after the battle of Buxar, he offered his services to the English, representing himself as the rightful lord of the province of Allahábád, was received with respectful welcome, and even put in possession of a part of it; but when peace was concluded with the Nawáb Wazír, the English discovering the falsehood of his claim, set it aside, and rewarded his attachment with a pension of two lakhs of rupees and strong recommendations to the emperor Sháh 'Alam. The recompense was greater than his services to the English, as he had kept up a correspondence with Shujá-uddaula, whom he would have joined, had he been successful in the battle of Kóṛá. From Allahábád he accompanied the emperor Sháh 'Alam to Dehlí in 1771 A. D., and having reduced the city of A͡grah from the Jáṭs, he was appointed Amír-ul-'Umrá with the title of Zulfikár-uddaula. The Rájás of Jaipúr and several other Hindú princes were his tributaries. He died on the 22nd of April, 1782 A. D., 1169 A. H., in the 49th year of his age.

**Najashi,** نجاشي, *vide* 'Abú'l Husain Aḥmad.

**Najat, Mir,** میر نجات اصفهاني, of Isfahán, whose proper name was Mír 'Abdul A͡l, is the author of a Díwán. He was a cotemporary of Táhír Wahíd who wrote a Preface to that work. He is also, it seems, the author of another poem on the art of wrestling called "Gulkushtí." Some of the authors call him Mír Najábat. *Vide* Najábat (Mír).

**Naji,** ناجي, poetical name of Muhammad Shákir, who lived in the reign of the emperor Muhammad Sháh, and was cotemporary with the poets Walí, Hátim, Mazmún, and 'Abrú.

**Najib Khan,** نجيب خان, *vide* Najíb-uddaula.

**Najib-uddin Farsi,** نجيب‌الدين فارسي, a poet of Persia who died about the year 1231 A. D., 628 A. H., and left a Díwán.

**Najib-uddaula,** نجيب‌الدوله, the title of Najíb Khán, a Rohela chief, and nephew of Basharát Khán. He came into Rohelkhand during the administration of 'Alí Muhammad Khán. He was at first appointed to the charge of a very small party, not consisting of more than twelve horse and foot. But his courage and activity soon brought him to the notice of his patron, who entrusted him with a respectable military command, and procured for him in marriage the daughter of Dúndé Khán the Rohela chief. He subsequently espoused the imperial cause, and was honourably received at Dehlí by the wazír Ghází-uddín Khán, and being soon after promoted to the command of the army, he attacked Safdar Jang, who had avowedly announced his hostile disposition to the court, and compelled him to cross the Ganges 1753 A. D., 1167 A. H. On the successful conclusion of this campaign, in which he was wounded, he received from the emperor Aḥmad Sháh the title of Najíb-uddaula. He was created Amír-ul-'Umrá to the emperor 'A͡lamgír II, by Aḥmad Sháh Abdálí on the return to Ḳandahár in 1757 A. D., 1170 A. H., but was soon after that conqueror's departure, deprived of his office by the wazír Ghází-uddín Khán, who conferred it on Aḥmad Sháh Bangash the Nawáb of Farrukhábád as a return for his services. Najíb-uddaula was present in the famous battle fought by Aḥmad Sháh Abdálí with the Marhaṭṭas in January, 1761 A. D., and on his departure to Ḳandahár, was again restored to his former situation of Amír-ul-'Umrá, and was entrusted with the care of the city of Dehlí and protection of the royal family. He governed Dehlí and the few districts yet in possession of the royal family with moderation and justice till his death which took place in October, 1770 A. D., Rajab, 1184 A. H., when he was succeeded in his dominions by his son Zábita Khán who continued to protect the royal family; the emperor Sháh 'Alam residing at Allahábád with the English. Najíb-uddaula was buried at Najíbábád a city founded by him.

**Najib-un-Nisa Begam,** نجیب النسا بیگم, the sister of the emperor Akbar, and the wife of Khwája Hasan Nakshbandí.

**Najm Sani,** نجم ثاني, a famous wazír of Sháh Ismá'íl Safwí I, whose proper name was Mirzá Yár Ahmad. He was taken prisoner in a battle fought against the Uzbaks, and put to death on the 12th of November, 1512 A. D., 3rd Ramazán, 918 A. H., by order of 'Abdullah Khán Uzbak, king of Túrán.

**Najm-uddin 'Abu Hafs 'Umar bin-Muhammad,** نجم الدين ابو حفص عمر بن محمد, *vide* Nasafí.

**Najm-uddin 'Abu'l Hasan 'Ali bin-Daud,** نجم الدين ابوالحسن علي بن داود, commonly called Kahkarí, from Kahkar, a place in Chaldea, situated near Basra, where he was born in 1172 A. D., 568 A. H. He was a descendant of Zuber bin-Awám, and a famous jurisconsult, and a good grammarian. He led a very retired and austere life, and was one of the most celebrated professors of the Hanífian sect, in the college named Ruknia, in the city of Damascus, where he died in 1274 A. D., 645 A. H., aged 77 lunar years.

**Najm-uddin 'Abru, Shah,** شاه نجم الدين آبرو, a poet of Dehlí, who flourished in the reign of the emperor Sháh 'Alam.

**Najm-uddin Fahdani,** حافظ نجم الدين فهداني, or Kahdaní (Háfiz) author of an Arabic work entitled "Itaháf ul-Wará bi-Akhbár ul-Kurá."

**Najm-uddin Kubra, Shaikh,** شيخ نجم الدين كبرى, a celebrated pious Musalmán, who was slain at Khwárizm at the time when the troops of Changez Khán, the Tartar, invaded that kingdom in 1221 A. D., 618 A. H.

**Najm-uddin Muhammad 'Umar-al-Samarkandi,** نجم الدين محمد عمر السمرقندي, author of a Medical work in Arabic called "Asbáb wa 'Alámat."

**Najm-uddin Razi,** نجم الدين رازى معروف به يدالله, commonly called "I'dullah" or the hand of God.

**Najm-uddaula,** نجم الدولة, whose proper name is Mír Phúlwárí, was the eldest son of Mír Ja'far 'Alí Khán, Nawáb of Bengal, Behár, and Urissa. He succeeded his father in February, 1765 A. D., Sha'bán, 1178 A. H., and the same year the East India Company received from the emperor Sháh 'Alam the appointment of Díwán of the three provinces of Bengal. Najm-uddaula died of the small-pox, after a reign of one year and four months, on the 3rd May, 1766 A. D., 22nd Zi-Ka'da, 1179 A. H., and was succeeded by his brother Saif-uddaula.

**Naki, Imam,** نقي امام, *vide* 'Alí Nakí (Imám).

**Naki Kamara,** نقي كمره, a poet who died in 1622 A. D., 1031 A. H., and left a Díwán.

**Nakib Khan,** نقيب خان, the grandson of Yahia bin-'Abdul-Latíf, which see.

**Nakhshabi,** نقشابي, poetical name of a person, who is the author of the "Tútí-náma" or Tales of a Parrot. When he flourished or when he died is not known.

**Na'man, Mir,** مير نعمان, a poet who died at Agrah on the 4th of March, 1648 A. D., 18th Safar, 1058 A. H., and was buried there.

**Na'mat 'Ali Khan,** نعمت علي خان, author of a work called "Sháh-náma," containing an account of the Muhammadan kings of India.

**Na'mat Khan,** نعمت خان عالي, whose poetical name is 'Alí, and who afterwards received the title of Dánishmand Khán, was Comptroller of the Kitchen to the emperor 'Alamgír, and a constant attendant on his person. He is the author of a number of excellent poems; one of which is called "Husn wa-Ishk," but that held in the greatest estimation is a satire on the conquest of Golkonda by 'Alamgír, 1687 A. D., in which the author lashes not only the generals, but even the emperor himself, whose conduct in destroying the Muhammadan kings of Bíjápúr and Golkonda, while the Marhattas and other Hindú chiefs had exalted the standard of defiance, was much disapproved of by many of the zealous Musalmáns. The officers and soldiers were also much disgusted by incessant wars in the Dakhin, and the very great hardships they suffered during his campaigns in that country. This book goes by the name of the author, "Na'mat Khán 'Alí," and has no other name. It is sometimes called "Wakáya Na'mat Khán 'Alí." He also compiled a very excellent book on Oriental Cookery. The whole of his work is called "Khwán Na'mat," or the Table of Delicacies. He died in the reign of the emperor Bahádur Sháh, 1708 A. D., 1120 A. H. *Vide* Dánishmand Khán.

**Na'mat-ullah,** سيد نعمت الله نارنوني, a Sayyad of Nárnaul and a pious Musalmán who is said to have performed miracles. He had reared a hawk by whose aid he procured his subsistence for several years. He afterwards proceeded to Akbarnagar commonly called Rájmahál in Bengal, where the prince Sultán Shujáa', the son of the emperor Sháh Jahán then governor of that province, with several of his 'Umrá, became his disciples. He died in the year 1666 A. D., 1077 A. H., at a place called Fírozpúr, east of Rájmahál where he had received a jágír from the prince. He was a saint and a poet.

**Na'mat-ullah, Khwaja,** خواجه نعمت الله, author of the history of the Afgháns or early Abdálís, an account of which is given in the Journal of the Asiatic Society of Bengal, Vol. XIV, p. 445. It is called "Táríkh Afghání," translated by Bernhard Dorn, Ph. D. &c.

**Na'mat-ullah Wali, Sayyad Shah Nur-uddin,** سيد شاه نورالله نعمت الله ولي, a descendant of Imám Músí Kázim. He was a learned and pious Musalmán, and an excellent poet. He is said to have performed miracles; was the disciple of Shaikh 'Abdullah Yáfa'í, but followed the tenets of Imám Sháfa'í. He is the author of nearly 500 books and pamphlets. He died in the time of Sháhrukh Mirzá the son of Amír Taimúr, 1424 or 1431 A. D., 827 A. H., aged 75 years, and is buried at Máhán, a village of Kirmán in Persia. Sayyad was his poetical title.

**Nami,** نامي, a poet who died in 1533 A. D., 940 A. H.

**Nami,** نامي, *vide* Muhammad Ma'súm Námí.

**Nami ul-Nami,** نامي النامي, surname of 'Abú'l 'Abbás ibn-Muhammad al-Dazamí al-*Massifi*, who was an excellent Arabic poet. He died 1008 A. D., 399 A. H., aged 90 years.

**Namkin,** قاسم خان نمکین, poetical title of Ḳásim Khán, who lived in the time of the emperor Jahángír.

**Namud,** نمود, *vide* Taskhír.

**Nana,** نانا, a corruption of Nánhá, or Nannhá, is the appellation by which Bálájí Ráo Peshwá was commonly known in Hindústán, and is by most supposed to be a title of State; but as we are informed, it arose from the nickname given him when a child by his father; Nannhá signifying a little man.

**Nana,** نانہاپہرنویس, or Nánhá Farnawís or Pharnawís, was the Kárkun of Mádhó Ráo Peshwá.

**Nana,** ننہا صاحب, or Nánhá Sáhib, the nickname of Dhondhúpant of Biṭhúr near Kahnpúr. This miscreant was an adopted son of Bájí Ráo II, the ex-Peshwá of Púná who died in December, 1852 A. D. According to Mr. Shephard's narrative of the Kahnpúr Mutiny, Bájí Ráo died on the 28th January, 1851 A. D. Of all the butcheries in the disturbances of 1857, that enacted by this vile wretch, stands pre-eminent. Out of seven hundred and fifty living souls (all Christians) in the strength and vigour of life, few escaped to tell the horrible tale. Lieutenants Delafosse and Thomson of the 53rd N. I., Ensign Brown, 56th N. I., and two other, soldiers, were the only survivors of the massacre. Three men and four women are reported to have also escaped and reached Allahábád. They escaped the massacre in the river and were hid in Kahnpúr, until the arrival of General Havelock's forces. The pension of the ex-Peshwá amounting to 8 laks of rupees per annum, was not continued to the Nánhá, and this appears to have been his principal, if not sole grievance, though he invariably maintained friendly relations with the European residents, and indeed on many occasions treated them with apparently cordial hospitality. His residence was at Biṭhúr, situated ten miles from Kahnpúr, where he owned an estate left him by his patron the ex-Peshwá, and he was allowed a retinue of 500 infantry and cavalry, with three guns of small callibre, and these troops were of course entirely independent of European authority. A proclamation was issued by the Governor-General in March, 1858 A. D., wherein a reward was offered of one lakh of rupees to any person, who should deliver Nánhá Dhondhúpant of Biṭhúr to the district officer commanding in any military camp or at any military post; and, in addition to the pecuniary reward, a free pardon was guaranteed to any mutineer, deserter or rebel (excepting the Nawábs of Farrukhábád, Bareli, Banda and Rájá of Mainpúrí) who should so deliver up the Nánhá Sáhib.

**Nanak,** نانك شاہ, or Nánhak Sháh, the founder of the sect called Sikhs, was born in the year 1469 A. D. He was the son of a Hindú grain-merchant, and disciple of Sayyad Husain, or as some say of Kabír, and consequently a sort of Hindú deist, but his peculiar tenet was universal toleration. He maintained that devotion was due to God, that forms were immaterial, and that Hindú and Muhammadan worship were the same in the sight of the Deity. During his travels, Nánhak was introduced to the emperor Bábar, before whom he is said to have defended his doctrine with great firmness and eloquence. Nánhak died in the month of August, 1539 A. D., aged 70 years. After his sect had silently increased for more than a century, it excited the jealousy of the Musalmán government, and its spiritual chief, the Gurú Arjun, was put to death in 1606 A. D., within a year after the decease of the emperor Akbar. This tyranny changed the Sikhs from inoffensive quietists into fanatical warriors. They took up arms under Hargóbind, the son of their martyred pontiff, who inspired them with his own spirit of revenge and of hatred to their oppressors.

*The following are the names of the Sikh Gurús from Nánhak.*

| | | | |
|---|---|---|---|
| Gurú Nánhak Sháh, the founder of the sect, | died | 1539 | A. D. |
| „ Angad, who wrote some of the sacred books, | „ | 1552 | |
| „ Amardás, | „ | 1574 | |
| „ Rámdás who beautified Amritsir, | „ | 1581 | |
| „ Arjunmal, he compiled the 'Adi Granth, | „ | 1606 | |
| „ Hargóbind, who was the first warlike leader, | „ | 1644 | |
| „ Har Ráe, grandson of Hargóbind, | „ | 1661 | |
| „ Har Krishan, son of Har Ráe, | „ | 1664 | |
| „ Teigh Bahádur, uncle of Har Krishan, | „ | 1675 | put to death. |
| „ Gobind, son of Teigh Bahádur. He remodelled the Sikh government. He was assassinated by a Paṭhán soldier in, | „ | 1708 | Assassinated. |
| „ Banda, put to death by the Musalmáns, | „ | 1715 | put to [death. |
| 12 Misals of the Sikhs captured Láhor and occupied the Panjab. | | | |
| Charat Singh of Sukelpaka misal, | „ | 1774 | |
| Maha Singh his son, extended his rule, and his wife became regent, and Lakhpat Singh her minister, | „ | 1792 | |
| Ranjít Singh established Láhor independency in 1805, *vide* Ranjít Singh, | „ | 1839 | 27th [June. |

**Nandkumar,** نندکمار, a rich Máhájan of Calcutta and Faujdár of Huglí. All the power of the State had been committed to him without control, in the time of the Nawáb Ja'far 'Alí Khán. He was a treacherous enemy to the English. He was convicted of a forgery, condemned to suffer death, and was hanged at the appointed place of execution in Calcutta on the 5th August, 1775 A. D., 7th Jumádạ II, 1189 A. H. His treasure and effects were given up to his son Rájá Gúrdás. It is said there were fifty-two lakhs of rupees in money, and about the same amount in jewels and rich goods. In his house were found the seals of several eminent persons which he had forged. The Bráhmans of Calcutta were struck with such horror when that execution took place, that they rushed into the sacred waters of the river to purge themselves of the pollution of such a sight, and looking upon Calcutta as a second Aceldama or field of blood, they crossed the river and settled at Bali, six miles from the scene of execution. They gradually extended their habitation beyond Bali and formed the village U'tarpara.

**Narayan Rao Peshwa,** نارایں راو پیشوا, the third son of Balájí Ráo Peshwá, succeeded his brother Madhó Ráo in November, 1770 A. D. He was assassinated by his paternal uncle Raghunáth Ráo, better known by the name Rághoba, in August 1772 A. D., and was succeeded by his infant son Sewájí Madhó Ráo, Raghunáth Ráo failing in his views joined the English at Surat.

**Nargisi,** نرگسي, an author who died at Ḳandahár in 1530 A. D., 937 A. H., and has left a Díwán.

**Nassi,** نرسي, the Narses of the Greeks, a king of the Sásánian dynasty, succeeded his brother Bahrám III 393 A. D., on the throne of Persia, and after a reign of nine years abdicated it in favor of his son, Hurmuz II; and survived that act but a short period.

**Narsingh Deo Bundeila, Raja,** راجه نرسنگهدیو بندیله, son of Rájá Madhukar Sáh Bundeila, who died in the reign of the emperor Akbar 1592 A. D., 1000 A. H. He served prince Mirzá Salim (afterwards Jahángír) for several years and by his orders slew Abú'l Fazl the prime minister of his father Akbar in 1602 A. D., 1011 A. H. In the first year of Jahángír, he was raised to the rank of 3000, and subsequently to that of 4000. The Hindú temple at Muthura (Muttra) which 'Alamgír afterwards converted into a mosque, was built by him at a cost of three lakhs of rupees. He died in the year 1626 A. D., 1036 A. H.

**Nasai,** نسائي, *vide* Abú 'Abdul Rahmán Nasáí. He was a native of Nasá, a town in Khurásán.

**Nasafi,** نسفي, or Al Nasafí whose proper name is Abú'l Barakát 'Abdullah bin-Aḥmad, commonly called Háfiz-uddín Al Nasafí, is the author of a law-book entitled "Wáfí," and its commentary called the "Káfí." He is also the author of the "Kanz ul-Daḳáeḳ," a book of great reputation, principally derived from the Wáfí, and containing questions and decisions according to the doctrines of Abú Hanifa, Abú Yúsaf, the Imám Muhammad, Zafar, Al Sháfa'í, Málik, and others. Many Commentaries have been written on this work: the most famous is the "Bahr ar-Ráeḳ" by Zain-ul-'Abidín bin-Nujaim al-Misrí. Nasafí died 1310 A. D., 710 A. H., *vide* Háfiz-uddín Nasafí.

**Nasafi,** نسفي, surname of Najm-uddín Abú Hafs 'Umar bin-Muhammad, a celebrated doctor, and author of the "'Aḳáed al-Nasafí," a book in Arabic containing the fundamental and principal articles of the Muhammadan religion. This work is greatly esteemed by the Musalmáns, who prefer it to many others of the same title. A commentary on the above work was written by Taftazání. Nasafí died in 1142 A. D., 537 A. H.

**Nasibi, Baba,** بابا نصيبي of Gílán, was a court poet of Sulṭán Ya'ḳúb. He died at Tabrez, in 1537 A. D., 944 A. H., and left a Díwán containing about 5,000 verses.

**Nasibi, Mirza Muhammad Khan,** نصيبي مرزا محمد خان, came from Persia to Lakhnau in the reign of Nasír-uddín Haidar; and died under Amjad Alí Sháh before or after the year 1845 A. D., 1261 A. H. He is the author of several poems.

**Nasim,** نصيم, poetical title of Lachhmí Naráyan, Rájá of Benares.

**Nasim,** نصيم, poetical appellation of Paṇḍit Dayá Shankar, who is the author of a story called "Gulzár Nasím," in Urdú verse, composed in 1838 A. D., 1254 A. H.

**Nasim,** نصيم, poetical title of Asghar 'Alí Khán of Dehlí.

**Nasir,** نصير, poetical name of Mír Nasír 'Alí of Lakhnau.

**Nasir,** نصير, takhallus of Nasír-uddín Hamdání, who flourished about the year 1606 A. D., 1015 A. H., in which year he visited Shíráz. He is the author of a Díwán.

**Nasir,** نصير, poetical name of Sháh Nasír-uddín, an Urdú poet, commonly called Mían Kallú. He was a native of Dehlí and the son of Sháh Gharíb. In the latter part of his life, he proceeded to Haidarábád and was employed by Mahárájá Chandú Lál in whose service he died about the year 1840 A. D. He has left an Urdú Díwán, containing more than 100,000 verses which were collected together after his death by one of his pupils named Mahárháj Singh.

**Nasir Khan,** نصيرخان, ruler of Haidarábád in Sindh, succeeded his brother Mír Núr Muhammad Khán in 1842 A. D. He was imprisoned and sent down to Calcutta by the English in 1843 A. D., 6th Rabí' II, 1261 A. H., where he died on the 16th of April 1845 A. D.

**Nasir Khan Faruki,** نصيرخان فيروقي, *vide* Malik Nasír Khán.

**Nasir-uddin,** نصيرالدين, title of Aḥmad Sháh, the present king of Persia. *Vide* Aḥmad Sháh.

**Nasir-uddin,** نصيرالدين, author of the Arabic work on Jurisprudence called "Fatáwí Ibráhímí."

**Nasir-uddin,** نصيرالدين, king of Persia, *vide* Nasír-uddín.

**Nasir-uddin Haidar,** نصيرالدين حيدر, king of Audh, was the son of Ghází-uddín Haidar whom he succeeded on the throne of Lakhnau on the 30th October 1827 A. D., 28th Rabí' I, 1243 A. H. with the title of Sulaimán Jáh Nasír-uddín Haidar. He reigned ten years, and died on the 7th of July 1837 A. D., 3rd Rabí' II, 1253 A. H., in which year died also William IV, king of England, and Akbar II, king of Dehlí. Nasír-uddín Haidar was succeeded by his uncle Nasír-uddaula, who took the title of Abú Muzaffar Mói-uddín Muhammad 'Alí Sháh, and Munná Ján the illegitimate son of Nasír-uddín Haidar was sent to the fort of Chunár where he died on the 15th January 1846 A. D., 16th Muḥarram 1262 A. H.

**Nasir-uddin Mahmud,** نصيرالدين محمود چراغ دهلي, also called by Firishta Nasír-uddín Mahmúd Awadhí, surnamed Chirágh Dehlí or the Candle of Dehlí, a celebrated Muhammadan saint, who was a disciple of Shaikh Nizám-uddín Auliá, whom he succeeded on the masnad of Irshád or Spiritual Guide, and died on Friday the 16th of September, 1356 A. D., 18th Ramazán, 757 A. H. He is buried at Dehlí in a mausoleum which was built before his death by Sulṭán Fíróz Sháh Bárbak, one of his disciples, and close to his tomb Sulṭán Bahlól Lódí was afterwards buried. He is the author of a work called Khair-ul-Majális.

**Nasir-uddin Tusi, Khwaja,** خواجه نصيرالدين طوسي, the famous philosopher and astronomer who was employed by Halákú Khán, the grandson of Changez Khán to form the I'lkhání Tables &c. He was the son of Imám Fakhr-uddín Muhammad Rází, was born at Tús in Khurásán on Saturday the 3rd of March 1201 A. D., 11th Jumáda I, 597 A. H., and though a somewhat over-zealous Shía, was one of the best, and certainly the most universal scholar that Persia ever produced. He wrote on all subjects, and some of his works are to this day standard books in Persian Universities. He was a fair Greek scholar, and made a new translation of Euclid into Arabic, wherein he proves most of the propositions, sometimes in two, three, and four ways, wholly different from the demonstrations of the Greek author. He likewise translated the Almajisti, and wrote a volume of learned explanatory notes upon it. He also wrote several works on geometry, astronomy, philosophy, theology, and dissertations on miscellaneous subjects. During the Mughal persecutions he wandered among the mountains of Khurásán, and was taken captive by Alauddín Muhammad, a descendant of Hasan Sabbah who forced him to remain with him for several years and employed him as his wazír. It was during his captivity, that he wrote the most celebrated of all his treatises, a well-known and excellent little work on moral philosophy, which he styled "Akhláḳ Násirí," or the morals of Nasír in complement to Nasir-uddín 'Abdul Rahím, governor of the fortress of Dez; but this flattery did not procure him his liberty, he remained in that mountainous region till he was released by Halákú Khán in November 1256 A. D., 654 A. H. It was Nasír-uddín that persuaded Halákú to march against Baghdád, which was taken in 1258 A. D. The "Akhláḳ Násirí" is a translation in Persian of the "Kitáb-ut-Tahárat fil Hikmat Amalí," an Arabic work by Abú Alí Muhammad of Mecca. There are two other works on Súfiism which he wrote, one called "Aosáf-ul-Ashráf," the Praises of the Virtuous, and the other "Bahar-ul-Maání," the Sea of Truth. He is also the author of a work entitled "Khilláfat-náma Iláhí," and of another work on Prosody called "Másr-ush-shohra." Nasír-uddín died in the reign of Abákáán the son of Halákú on the 24th June, 1274 A. D., 18th Ẓil-ḥijja 672 A. H., and was buried at Baghdád near the tomb of Imám Músí Ḳázim. His brutal severity towards Ibn Hájib, a helpless captive, is an everlasting stain on the otherwise illustrious character of this distinguished man. *Vide* Al-Mustaạsim Billáh.

**Nasir-uddaula,** نصيرالدوله, Nizám of the Haidarábád State, succeeded his father Sakandar Jáh on the 23rd May 1829 A. D. and died in May 1857 A. D. His son ascended the masnad with the title of Nawáb Afzal-uddaula.

**Nashat,** نشاط, the poetical name of Ráe Phukní Mal, a Hindú, who was Díwán or Treasurer of 'Álamgír's wazír.

**Nashati,** نشاطي, a poet who died 1508 A. D., 914 A. H.

**Nashwan bin-Said Himiri al-Yemani,** نشوان بن سعيد حميرى اليمني, author of the work called "Shams-ul-'Ulúm," or the Sun of Science. He died 1177 A. D., 573 A. H.

**Nasikh,** ناسخ, poetical title of Shaikh Imám Bakhsh, a celebrated poet of Lakhnau where he died in 1838 A. D., 1254 A. H. He is the author of an Urdú Díwán.

**Nasir,** محمد نصيرخان ناصر, the takhallus of Muhammad Nasír Khán, who is the author of a Díwán, and was living in 1807 A. D., 1222 A. H.

**Nasir,** ناصر, poetical name of Nawáb Násir Jang, son of Muzaffar Jang Bangash. He died in 1813 A. D., 1228 A. H., on a day when an eclipse of the sun had taken place.

**Nasir,** ناصر, poetical title of Sạádat Khán, the son of Risalat Khán. He is the author of five Díwáns and a biography.

**Nasir 'Ali, Mulla,** ملا ناصرعلي, a poet of Sháhjahánábád, whose poetical name was 'Alí. He was born at Sarhind, and died at Dehlí in March, 1697 A. D., Ramaẓán, 1108 A. H., and is buried near the mausoleum of Nizám-uddín Auliá. He was a fertile poet and has left a Díwán and a Masnawí.

**Nasir Bukhari, Maulana,** مولانا ناصر بخاري, a learned Musalmán who lived like a Dervish and wrote poetry on different subjects. He was a contemporary of Salmán Sáwají, who died in 1377 A. D., 779 A. H.

**Nasir Billah,** ناصر بالله, a Khalíf of Baghdád, *vide* Al-Násir Billáh.

**Nasir Jang, Nawab Nizam-uddaula,** ناصرجنگ نواب نظام الدوله, was the second son of Nizám-ul-Mulk 'Asaf Jáh, whom he succeeded in the government of the Dakhin in May, 1748 A. D., Jumáda II, 1161 A. H. He reigned two years and a half, and was slain on the 5th December, 1750 A. D., 17th Muḥarram, 1164 A. H. by a conspiracy of his own servants, assisted by the French who surprised his camp while he was engaged in quelling a rebellion raised by his nephew, Muzaffar Jang, who had been imprisoned by him. On his death Muzaffar Jang was placed on the masnad of the Dakhin by the conspirators; but this young prince did not long enjoy his dignity, for he was assassinated almost immediately after his accession by the same persons who had raised him to power. This event took place on the 2nd February, 1751 A. D., 17th Rabí' I, 1164 A. H. Násir Jang was buried at Burhánpúr near the tomb of his father.

**Nasir, Khwaja,** خواجه ناصر, a poet who was contemporary with Salmán Sáwají. *Vide* Násir Bukhárí.

**Nasir bin-Khusro, Hakim,** حكيم ناصربن خسرو, the author of the work, called "Zadíl Musafarín" from which book the compiler of the Hajat Darakoke Núruddín Shírází, has so largely borrowed. He was a genuine Kuresh, and must have written under the short reign of al-Wasiq Billáh, the ninth Khalíf of the house of Abbás, who reigned between the year 840 and 841 A. D., *vide* Transactions Royal Asiatic Society, Vol. III, p. 32. 'Alí Raza the 8th Imám, and great-grandfather of Násir bin-Khusro died in the year 818 A. D., 204 A. H.

**Nasir Khusro,** ناصرخسرو, a celebrated physician and poet of Isfahán, whose poetical name was Hujjat. He is the author of several works, among which are the two following, *viz.*, "Róstái-náma" in verse, and "Kanz-ul-Haḳaeḳ" in prose. He has also left us a Díwán consisting of 30,000 verses. He was a contemporary of Khwája 'Abú'l Hasan Jurjání and the celebrated physician Avicenna. Some say that he was a Deist, and others considered him to be an Atheist, on which account he was persecuted by the Muhammadans, and fled from one city to another, till at last he was obliged to conceal himself among the hills of Badakhshán. Daulat Sháh has given a very interesting account of Násir Khusro in his Tazkira. In 1872 there was discovered among the Elliot papers an Arabic work by Násir Khusro, on the buildings and water-works of Jerusalem. He is most precise in his information. It is said, that if this work had been found a little earlier, it might have saved the Palestine exploration Committee some diggings and considerable outlay. There is also a work of the same kind in Persian called "the Travels of Násir Khusro," which he wrote in 1052 A. D., corresponding with 444 A. H.

**Nasir Shah Purbi,** ناصرشاه پوربي, a lineal descendant of Shams-uddín Bhangára, was placed on the throne of Bengal in 1427 A. D., 831 A. H., after the murder of Násir-uddín Ghulám, who had usurped the throne for several days after the death of his master Aḥmad Sháh. General Briggs, in his translation, says that he reigned only two years, whereas it appears from Major Stewart's Bengal History, which seems to be correct, that he reigned 32 years, consequently his death must have happened in the year 1458 A. D., 863 A. H. He was succeeded by his son Bárbak. He is also called Násir Husain Sháh as appears from an Arabic Inscription on a mosque lately discovered in the district of Hughli in Bengal by H. Blochmann, Esq., M. A., Professor, Calcutta Madrasa.

**Nasir, Shaikh,** شيخ ناصر اكبرابادي, of Akbarábád, a Musalmán saint who is said to have performed a number of miracles, and was highly respected by the emperor Sháh Jahán. He died on the 7th June, 1647 A. D., 13th Jumáda I, 1057 A. H., and was buried at Agrah.

**Nasir-uddin Ḳabbacha** or **Fattah,** ناصر الدين قباچه يا فتاح, ruler of Sindh. It is related in several Histories such as the "Khulásat ul-Hikáet," the "Haj-náma," and the History of Hájí Muhammad Ḳandahárí, that the first establishment of the Muhammadan faith in the country of Sindh took place in the time of Hajjáj bin-Yúsaf, governor of Basra, at the time when Walíd the son of the Khalíf 'Abdulmalik was ruler of the provinces of both 'Iráḳs. Hajjáj deputed Mahmúd Husain in the year 706 A. D., 87 A. H. with a select army into Mikráu, and he subdued that country; and made converts of many of the inhabitants called Ballochís. He afterwards deputed Budmín to conquer Díbál (modern Ṭhaṭṭa on the Indus). Budmín failed in his expedition, and lost his life in the first action. Hajjáj, not deterred by this defeat, resolved to follow up the enterprise by another. In consequence, in the year 712 A. D., 93 A. H., he deputed his cousin Imád-uddín Muhammad bin-Ḳásim the son of Aḳíl or Ukail Thaḳafí or Saḳafí with six thousand soldiers to attack Díbál, and he in a short time conquered the place, and Rájá Dáhir, the ruler of Díbál was slain in battle. After the death of Muhammad bin-Ḳásim, a tribe who trace their origin from the Ansárís, established a government in Sindh; after which the zamíndárs, of the tribe of Súmara, usurped the power, and held independent rule over the kingdom of Sindh for the space of 500 years. In the course of years, the dynasty of Súmara was subverted, and the country subdued by another dynasty called Súmana, whose chief assumed the title of Jám. During the reigns of these dynasties in Sindh, the Muhammadan kings of India Proper, such as those of Ghazní, Ghór and Dehlí, invaded Sindh, and seizing many towns, appointed Muhammadan governors over them. Among these rulers, Násir-uddín Ḳabbácha asserted his independence, and caused the public prayers to be read in his name as king of Sindh. Násir-uddín was one of the Turkish slaves of Shaháb-uddín Muhammad Ghórí, who made him governor of Uchcha in Multán about the year 1203 A. D., 600 A. H. He espoused the daughter of Sulṭán Ḳuṭb-uddín Eaibak viceroy, and afterwards king of Dehlí, after whose death in 1210 A. D., 607 A. H., having seized many of the towns subjected to the Sindh government, he reduced the territory of the Súmanas to the small tract of country around Ṭhaṭṭa, and relinquishing the allegiance to the throne of Dehlí, became independent. Besides Sindh, his kingdom embraced the provinces of Multán, Kohrám and Sursatí. He was twice attacked by Táj-uddín Elduz of Ghazní, but he successfully repelled both these invasions. In 1225 A. D. Shams-uddín Altimsh, king of Dehlí, made several attempts to remove him from his government, and even marched for that purpose as far as Uchcha, when Násir-uddín having no hopes of eventually repelling the arms of the Dehlí monarch, placed his family and personal attendants with his treasure, in boats, and endeavoured to occupy a contiguous island; when a storm coming on, the boat foundered, and every one perished. This monarch reigned in Sindh and Multán for a period of 22 years. In the latter end of the reign of Muhammad Tughlaḳ of Dehlí, Sindh owned allegiance to that monarch; nevertheless, occasionally taking advantage of local circumstances, the Sindhís contrived, for a considerable period, to shake off their allegiance. The first of the family of which we have any account was Jám Afrá.

*The following is a list of the Jám dynasty of Súmana, originally Rájpúts.*

| A. H. | No. | | | A. D. |
|---|---|---|---|---|
| 737 to 740 A. H. | 1. | Jám Afrá, reigned 3 years and 6 months from 1336 A. D., and .......... | died | 1339 |
| 754 „ | 2. | „ Chobán, his brother, reigned 14 years and .. | „ | 1353 |
| 769 „ | 3. | „ Baní, son of Jám Afrá, reigned 15 years and .. | „ | 1367 |
| 782 „ | 4. | „ Timmají, son of Jám Afrá, reigned 13 years, | „ | 1380 |
| 793 „ | 5. | „ Saláh-uddín, converted to Muhammadanisn, .. | „ | 1391 |
| 796 „ | 6. | „ Nizám-uddín, his son, .. | „ | 1393 |
| 812 „ | 7. | „ 'Alísher, his son, ...... | „ | 1409 |
| „ „ | 8. | „ Giran, son of Timmáji, died on the 2nd day after his accession. | | |
| 827 „ | 9. | „ Fatha Khán, son of Iskandar Kháh, ........ | „ | 1423 |
| 854 „ | 10. | „ Tughlak, his brother invaded Gujrát, reigned 27 years, and was succeeded by his kinsman Jám Mubárak, who was deposed after a reign of 3 days, .............. | „ | 1450 |
| 856 „ | 11. | „ Sikandar, son of Fatha Khán, reigned 18 months and ................ | „ | 1452 |
| „ „ | 12. | „ Sanjar, a descendant of the former kings of Sindh was elected in 1452, reigned 8 years and ................ | „ | 1460 |
| 894 „ | 13. | „ Nizám-uddín, commonly called Jám Nanda, was contemporary with Hasan Langa, king of Multán, reigned 30 years, and .......... | died | 1489 |
| 927 „ | 14. | „ Fíróz his son, reigned about 33 years, when Sháh Beg Arghún, governor of Kándahár in 1520 A. D. marched to conquer Sindh, and occupied the whole country, even to the possession of Ṭhaṭṭa, .. | „ | 1520 |
| 930 „ | | Sháh Beg Arghún, reigned 3 years, ...... | „ | 1523 |
| 966 „ | | Sháh Husain Arghún, .. | „ | 1554 |
| 982 „ | | Mahmúd of Bakkar, reigned till 1572 A. D. when the emperor Akbar annexed Sindh to the empire. | | |

**Nasir-uddin Ḳazi Baizawi,** ناصر الدين قاضي بيضاوي, the son of Imám Badr-uddín Umar bin-Fakhr-uddín 'Alí Baizáwí. *Vide* Baizáwí.

**Nasir-uddin Khilji, Sultan,** سلطان ناصرالدين خلجي, was the son of Sulṭán Ghayás-uddín Khiljí, king of Málwá. He ascended the throne of that kingdom a few days before the death of his father which happened on the 25th October, 1500 A. D., 27th Rabí' II, 906 A. H. He reigned eleven years and four months; and having previously declared his third son Mahmúd, his successor, died about the year 1511 A. D., 917 A. H.

**Nasir-uddin Mahmud, Sultan,** نصرالدين محمود سلطان, son of Sulṭán Shams-uddín Altimsh, succeeded his nephew Sulṭán 'Aláuddín Masa'úd Sháh in June, 1246 A. D. to the throne of Dehlí. He reigned 20 years, was imprisoned, and died on the 18th February, 1266 A. D., when Ghayás-uddín Balban succeeded him.

**Nasir-uddin Mahmud,** ناصرالدین محمود بغرا خان, surnamed Baghrá Khán, governor of Bengal, was the son of Sulṭán Ghayás-uddín Balban, and the father of Móizz-uddín Kaiḳubád who was, during the absence of his father in Bengal, made king of Dehlí. When Sulṭán Ghayás-uddín Tughlaḳ in 1324 A. D. marched in person towards Bengal, he was then living, and came from Lakhnauṭí to pay his respects bringing with him many valuable presents. He was confirmed in his government of Bengal, and permitted to assume the ensigns of royalty. He died in the time of Muhammad Tughlaḳ Sháh. *Vide* Baghrá Khán.

**Nasir-uddin Muhtashim,** ناصرالدین محتشم, is the person in whose name Khwája Násir-uddín Túsi wrote the work entitled "Akhláḳ Násirí."

**Nasir-uddin Murtaza,** ناصرالدین مرتضی, author of several works, one of which is called "Risála Misbáh ilm Nahv." He died in 1213 A. D., 610 A. H.

**Nasr,** نصر, commonly called Nasr Badakhshí, is the poetical name of Mirzá 'Abú Nasr of Badakhshán who was an author, and died in 1668 A. D., 1078 A. H.

**Nasr Ahmad,** نصراحمد, a grandson of Sámán. He was appointed governor of Bukhárá by the Khalíf Mo'tamid Billáh in 875 A. D., *vide* Ismá'íl Sámání.

**Nasrabadi,** نصرابادی, the full name of this author was Muhammad Táhir; he was born at Nasrábád (which is in the district of Isfahán) about the year 1616 A. D., 1025 A. H., and is the author of the biography called "Tazkíra Nasrábádí," which he wrote in the year 1672 A. D., 1083 A. H., and added about nine biographies ten years after.

**Nasr 'Asim,** نصرعاصم, was the first who introduced the diacritical marks in the Ḳurán by order of the Khalíf 'Usmán.

**Nasrat,** نصرت, the poetical title of Diláwar Khán who is the author of a Díwán. He died in 1726 A. D., 1139 A. H.

**Nasrati,** نصرتي, a celebrated poet of the Dakhin, who is the author of a heroic poem in Hindí and the Dakhiní dialect, called "'Alí-náma," which contains the conquests or wars of Sulṭán 'Alí 'Adil Sháh of Bíjápúr. This prince, to whom the work was dedicated, was assassinated in 1580 A. D., 938 A. H. Nasratí is also the author of two other poems called "Gulshan Ishḳ," and "Guldastae 'Ishḳ," the former is the tale of Rájá Manohar and the princess Chintáwatí, and the latter contains a variety of odes and amatory poems, also dedicated to his patron the Sulṭán, between the year 1560 and 1570 A. D.

**Nasrat Jang,** نصرت جنگ, *vide* Khán Dourán Nasrat Jang.

**Nasrat Khan,** نصرت خان, *vide* Khán Dourán Nasrat Jang.

**Nasrat Shah,** نصرت شاه, the son of Fatha Khán, the son of Fíróz Sháh Tughlaḳ. The throne of Dehlí which was vacated by Sulṭán Mahmúd Sháh on the invasion of Amír Taimúr in 1399 A. D., was taken possession of by Nasrat Sháh on that conqueror's return to Persia. He reigned eleven months and was defeated in a battle by his cousin Eḳbál Khán the son of Zafar Khán who succeeded him in 1400 A. D. The Súbahs had rendered themselves independent in their own governments, during the misfortunes and confusions of the empire. Gujrát was seized upon by Khán 'Azim Zafar Khán; Málwá by Diláwar Khán; Ḳanauj, Audh, Kaṛa and Jaunpúr by Sulṭán-ush-Sharaḳ Khwája Jahán; Láhor, Díbálpúr, and Multán by Khizir Khán; Samána by Khalíl Khán; Bayána by Shams Khán; Mahóba by Muhammad Khán bin-Malikzada Fíróz, and so on.

**Nasrat Shah,** نصرت شاه, who is called by General Briggs, Nasíb Sháh, succeeded his father 'Aláuddín in the government of Bengal in 1524 A. D., 930 A. H. When the emperor Bábar slew Ibráhím the son of Sikandar Lodí, and ascended the throne of Dehlí in 1526 A. D., 932 A. H., many of the adherents of the Lodí dynasty sought protection at the court of Bengal, and among others the prince Mahmúd (brother to Ibráhím Lodí) also took refuge there, and his sister became the wife of the king. Nasrat Sháh died in 1538 A. D., 945 A. H., and Mahmúd who was then one of his ministers succeeded in usurping his throne. About this period Sher Khán, who afterwards ascended the throne of Dehlí, attacked and defeated Mahmúd in action, and eventually expelled him from Bengal, whence he fled to the court of Dehlí, where representing his grievances, the emperor Humáyún marched with an army and took the kingdom of Bengal from Sher Khán whom he defeated in a general action. Sher Khán rallying his defeated troops in the year 1542 A. D., 949 A. H., succeeded in re-conquering Bengal. On his death, and after the accession of his son Salím Sháh to the throne of Dehlí, the province of Bengal was made over to Muhammad Khán Afghán, one of the officers of his court, on whose death his son declared his independence, and proclaimed himself king under the title of Bahádur Sháh.

**Nasr bin-Ahmad Samani,** نصرت بن احمد ساماني, *vide* Nasr Sámání.

**Nasr Samani, Amir,** امیر نصر ساماني, the third Sulṭán or Amír of the race of Sámán or Samanides, was eight years old when he succeeded his father Amír Aḥmad on the throne of Bukhárá and Khurásán 914 A. D., 301 A. H. He enjoyed a long and prosperous reign and died at Bukhárá 943 A. D., Rajab, 331 A. H., leaving all his territories in peace. He was succeeded by his son Amír Núh I. Ródakí the poet lived in his time.

**Nasr-ullah,** نصر الله بن عبدالحمید بن ابي المعالي, the son of 'Abdul Hamíd bin-Abí ul-Ma'álí, a poet who flourished in the reign of Bahrám Sháh of Ghazní, in whose name he wrote the book called "Kallela Damna," or Pilpay's Fables, which he translated from the Arabic into Persian. *Vide* 'Abú'l Ma'álí the son of 'Abdul Majíd.

**Nasr-ullah,** نصرالله, king of Bukhára, who died in the year 1860 A. D. He was a great tyrant, a greater probably never ruled a people. When on his death-bed, and so weak as to be scarcely able to make himself understood, he directed one of his wives to be brought into his room. The poor lady's brother had recently been in rebellion, and the news of his defeat and capture reached the tyrant when on his deathbed. Unable to glut his eyes with the sight of their execution, he wreaked his vengeance on his own wife, because she was sister to the rebel chief. She was beheaded before his eyes now about to close in death. Laden with every crime that could burden the conscience of a responsible king, Nasr-ullah died, leaving the throne to his son and successor Muzaffar-uddín who was living in 1873 A. D.

**Nasr-ullah bin-'Abdullah al-Akhmi Alazhari,** نصرالله بن عبدالله, a celebrated poet who died in the year 1173 A. D., 569 A. H. He is also called Kalakas, and Alaaz al-Iskandarí.

**Nasir-uddin Shah,** ناصرالدین شاہ, king of Persia, was born in 1831 A. D., was the eldest son of Muhammad Sháh, the eldest son of 'Abbás Mirzá, so well-known for his partiality to the English, and the great-grandson of Fatha 'Alí Sháh. Násir-uddín ascended the throne after the death of his father, on the 4th September, 1848 A. D., in his 19th year. He visited Russia, London, France, Germany &c. in 1873 A. D.

**Natik,** ناطق نیشاپوري, a poet of Naishápúr, who came to India, and was the master of Jawáhir Singh the poet.

**Natik,** ناطق, the poetical name of Gul Muhammad Khán of Dehlí. One of his works is called Jawhar ul-Muazzim. He died in 1848 A. D., 1264 A. H.

**Nawai,** نوائي, the poetical name of Amír Alísher.

**Nawai, Mulla,** ملا نواى خراساني of Khurásán. He came to India and found a patron in prince Daniál the son of Akbar, and died at Burhánpúr in 1610 A. D., 1019 A. H. He is the author of a Díwán.

**Nawal Rae, Raja,** راجه نول راى, a Káyeth of the Saksena tribe in the service of Nawáb Safdar Jang; was by degrees raised to higher rank with the title of Rájá, and was appointed his deputy to settle the affairs of the province of Farrukhábád which was seized by the Nawáb after the death of its ruler Nawáb Káem Jang. Nawal Ráe was slain in a battle fought against Ahmad Khán the brother of the late Nawáb, on the 3rd August, 1750 A. D., 10th Ramazán 1163 A. H.

**Nawal Singh,** راجه نول سنگه, the Ját Rájá of Bhartpúr who succeeded his brother Ráe Ratan Singh after the death of Kehrí Singh his nephew, about the year 1769 A. D., 1183 A. H., and died in the year 1776 A. D. at the time when the fort of Díg was besieged by Nawáb Najaf Khán. After his death his nephew Ranjít Singh, the son of Kehrí Singh, the son of Súrajmal Ját, succeeded him.

**Nawawi,** نوي بن شرف, the son of Sharaf whose proper name was Abú Zikariá Yehia; is the author of several works on different subjects. One of his works is called "Tahzíb-ul-Asmáe" a biographical dictionary of Illustrious Men, another the "Fatáwá-an-Nawáwí" a collection of decisions of some note. He also composed a smaller work of the same nature, entitled "'Uaiún-al-Masáel al-Muhimmat" arranged in the manner of question and answer. He died 1278 A. D., 676 A. H.

**Nawazish Khan,** نوازش خان, author of the "Gulzár Dánish."

**Nawedi,** نویدي, a poet who is the author of a Díwán. He was living in 1645 A. D., 1055 A. H. This person appears to be another Nawedí besides the one whose proper name was Khwája Zain-ul-'Abidín, which see.

**Naweri,** نویری, an historian who wrote the Life of Sultán Bibars, the sovereign of Egypt. He died in 1331 A. D., 732 A. H.

**Nazari, Hakim,** حکیم نزاری, *vide* Nizárí (Hakím).

**Nazar Muhammad Khan,** نذر محمد خان, ruler of Balkh. He was defeated by the emperor Sháh Jahán and his country taken possession of by that monarch in 1646 A. D., 1056 A. H.

**Nazar Muhammad Khan,** نذر محمد خان, Nawáb of Bhopál succeeded his father Wazír Muhammad in March, 1816 A. D.

**Nazar,** نضربن شمیل, son of Shumíl, whose proper name is Abú'l Hasan Nazar, was an author of several works He died at Marv 820 A. D., 204 A. H.

**Nazir,** نظیر, the poetical title of a poet of Ágrah, whose proper name was Shaikh Walí Muhammad. He is the author of a poem or Díwán containing Persian, Urdú and Hindí verses on different subjects. He has besides composed a "Tarjíhband" in Urdú on the Pand-náma of Sa'dí. He supported himself by teaching, and his poetry is much esteemed by the bazar people of Ágrah. He died at Ágrah on Monday the 16th August, 1830 A. D., 26th Safar, 1246 A. H., and is buried at Tájganj.

**Naziri,** نظیری نیشاپوری, poetical title of Muhammad Husain of Naishápúr. He came to India where he found a patron in 'Abdul Rahím Khán KhánKhánán. In 1603 A. D., 1012 A. H. he made the pilgrimage to Mecca, and after his return he paid a visit to his patron and then settled in Ahmadabád, Gujrát, where he died in 1613 A. D., 1022 A. H. He is the author of a Persian Díwán.

**Nazim Hirwi,** ناظم هروی, a poet of Hirat, who is the author of a Díwán and a "Yúsaf Zalekha," which he completed in the year 1648 A. D., 1058 A. H.

**Nazir Bakhtyar Khan,** ناظر بختیار خان, a man of letters, who led a private life near Farídábád, within a few miles of Ágrah, and is the author of the work called "Mirat 'Alam," or the Mirror of the World. This work contains the history of the first ten years of the emperor 'Álamgír. He is also called Bakhtáwar Khán, which see.

**Nazim-ul-Mulk, Nazir-ul-Mulk,** ناظرالملك ناظم الملك, Wazír-uddaula, the son of Mubárik-uddaula, the Nawáb of Bengal whom he succeeded 28th September, 1793 A. D., and died in April, 1810 A. D. He was succeeded by his son Zain-uddín 'Alí Khán.

**Nekodar,** نیکودار, surname of Ahmad Khán, king of Persia, which see.

**Neko Siar, Sultan,** سلطان نیکو سیر, son of Muhammad Akbar, the youngest son of 'Álamgír Aurangzeb.

**Nigahi,** نگاهي of Arán near Káshán, is the author of a poem or Masnawí called "Mukhtár-náma," of about 30,000 verses in the metre of the Sháh-náma, and one called "Mehr-wa-Mushtarí," in imitation of Assár's Masnawí.

**Nihal Singh,** نیهال سنگه, Rájá of Kapúrthala. He died in the year 1852 A. D., having made his last will and testament, in which he left the throne with nearly the whole of his kingdom to his eldest son, Randhír Singh, and to his two younger sons, Bikarma Singh and Suchait Singh, he assigned a jagír of one lakh each, in case they disagreed with their brother. The Government of India was made the executor of the will. After the Rájá's death, his eldest son Randhír Singh, ascended the gaddí. His younger brother Suchait Singh fell out with him, and asked the British Government to execute his father's will in regard to him. Lord Dalhousie at once ordered the separation of a jágír of one lakh from the Kapúrthala Ráj according to the provisions of the will. The other brother, Bikarana Singh, is a worthy man, and much attached to the British rule. Like his royal brother, he performed important services to the English Government in 1857, and was rewarded for them with a jágír in Audh, and titles besides. He received his jágír of one lakh in Kapúrthala in 1868.

**Nirpat Rae,** نرپت راي, a Hindú who was in the service of Sarhindí Begam the wife of Sháhjahán. He also built a garden at Ágrah on a spot of 28 bígas.

**Nirpat Singh,** نرپت سنگه, present Rájá of Panna.

**Nisar,** نثار دهلوي, of Dehlí, a poet who is the author of a Persian Díwán.

**Nisari,** نثاري, poetical name of a person who is the author of the work called "Chahár Gulzár."

**Nisbati,** نسبتي تهانيسري, of Thánesar, a poet who has left a Díwán in Persian.

**Nizam,** نظام, the poetical name of 'Imád-ul-Mulk Ghází-uddín Khán III.

**Nizam of Astrabad,** نظام استرابادي, an extremely pious man, who died in 1515 A. D., 921 A. H., and left besides a Díwán, a Masnawí which bears the title of "Bilkais and Sulímán," and contains the story of Solomon and the Queen of Sheba.

**Nizam Ahmad,** نظام احمد, author of the work called "Ráhat-ul-Kulúb," Delight of Hearts, containing the sayings of Shaikh Faríd-uddín Shakarganj, a Muhammadan saint who is buried at Ajodhan, a place commonly called Patan in Multán.

**Nizam 'Ali Khan,** نواب نظام علي خان, Nawáb or Názim of Haidarábád in the Dakhin, was the son of the famous Nizám-ul-Mulk 'Asaf Jáh. He deposed and imprisoned his brother Salábat Jang on the 27th of June, 1762 A. D., 4th Zil-hijja, 1175 A. H. and assumed the government of the Dakhin; but his power was much curtailed by the Marhattas, who obliged him to resign a great part of his territories and pay a tribute for the remainder. He made Haidarábád the seat of his government, reigned 42 lunar years, and died on the 17th of August, 1802 A. D., 16th Rabí' II, 1217 A. H. He was succeeded by his son Nawáb Sikandar Jáh.

**Nizam Bai,** نظام باي, the mother of the emperor Jahándar Sháh, and wife of Bahádur Sháh.

**Nizam Dast Ghaib,** نظام دست غيب, a poet.

**Nizami,** نظامي, the surname of 'Abú Majd bin-Yúsaf Al-Mutrazí, was one of the most illustrious poets of Persia.

**Nizami Ganjawi, Shaikh,** شيخ نظامي گنجوي, also called Nizám-uddín Ganjawí, a very celebrated poet who was a native of Ganja. He is the author of the poem called "Sikandar-náma," the history of Alexander the Great, which is one of the most celebrated Romances of the East, and is written in admirable poetry. The number of works attributed to Nizámí amount to nine or ten, among which are the five following poems called the Khamsa, or the five books, *viz.* :—

1. "Makhzan-ul-Asrár" the Magazine of Mysteries, which he dedicated to Bahrám Sháh.
2. "Lailí-wa-Majnún" dedicated to Khákán Manúchehr, ruler of Shírwán.
3. "Khusro-wa-Shírín," } dedicated to Kizal Arsalán for
4. "Haft Paikar," } which he received from that chief fourteen villages free of rent.
5. Sikandar-náma, which was his last work and which he finished on the 15th of October, 1200 A. D., 4th Muharram 597 A. H., and died the same year, aged 84. This book, it seems he had dedicated to Tughral III, Saljúkí, some years before his death, for Tughral died in 1194 A. D. Some authors say that Nizámí died in 1209 A. D., 606 A. H.

To Nizámí is accorded the palm for the best poem on the loves of Khusro and Shírín, to Jámí, for those of Yúsaf and Zalekha, and to Hátifí, for the *most* musical, *most* melancholy version of the sad tale of Lailí and Majnún. His Díwán contains nearly 20,000 verses on all subjects.

**Nizami 'Uruzi,** نظامي عروضي سمرقندي, of Samarkand, was a pupil of Amír Mu'izzí who lived in the time of Maliksháh. He is the author of a poem entitled "Waisa-wa-Rámín" and of another work in verse called "Chahár Makála."

**Nizam Haji Yemani,** نظام حاجي يمني, author of the "Lataéf Ashrafí" which explains the origin of the Súfís, their tenets, customs, dress, mystical phrases, moral obligations, and every other particular of their sect. Dedicated to Sayyad Ashraf Jahángír Sámání, 1446 A. D., 850 A. H.

**Nizam ibn al-Husain al-Sawai,** نظام ابن الحسين الساوئ, author of the three last portions of the "Jáma Abbásí" *vide* Bahá-uddín Muhammad (Shaikh).

**Nizam Khan Ma'jiz,** نظام خان معجز, a poet who is the author of a Díwán in Persian.

**Nizam, Mirza,** مرزا نظام, a poet who died in 1629 A. D., 1039 A. H., and is the author of a Persian Díwán.

**Nizam Sakka,** نظام سقه, is the name of a person who was a water-bearer, and saved the emperor Humáyún from being drowned in the river Chounsá after his first defeat by Sher Sháh, near Patna. It is said that the emperor after his return to Ágrah, rewarded this man by allowing him to sit on the throne for half a day and then honoured him with the dignity of an Amír.

**Nizam Shah Bahmani,** نظام شاه بهمني, son of Humáyún Sháh the cruel, whom he succeeded on the throne of the Dakhin in September, 1461 A. D., 865 A. H. when only 8 years of age, the queen-mother acting as regent. Mahmúd Gáwán, who now held the government of Berar, was appointed wazír, and Khwája Jahán assumed the office of Wakíl-us-Saltanat and was made governor of Tilangána. By the happy co-operation and unanimity of these two personages and the queen-mother, a woman of great abilities, the injuries occasioned by the tyranny of the late king, were soon repaired. Nizám Sháh died suddenly on the night of his marriage, being the 29th of July, 1463 A. D., 13th Ẕi-Ḳa'da, 867 A. H., after a reign of two years and one month, and was succeeded by his brother Muhammad Sháh II.

**Nizam, Shaikh,** شیخ نظام, one of the authors of the "Fatáwá 'Álamgírí," a work on jurisprudence. Of the collections of decisions now known in India, none is so constantly referred to, or so highly esteemed, as this work. It was compiled by Shaikh Nizám and other learned men, and commenced in the year 1656 A. D., 1067 A. H., by order of the emperor 'Álamgír, by whose name the collection is now designated. It was translated into Persian by order of 'Álamgír's daughter, Zeib-un-Nisa.

**Nizam, Shaikh,** شیخ نظام, his poetical name was Zamírí, which see.

**Nizam-uddin, Mir,** نظام الدین میر, *vide* Mamnún.

**Nizam-uddin Ahmad, Khwaja,** خواجه نظام الدین احمد, author of the "Tabḳát Akbarí" which is also known as "Táríkh Nizámí" a general history of India, dedicated to the emperor Akbar about the year 1593 A. D., 1002 A. H. He was the son of Khwája Muhammad Muḳím of Hirat, who was one of the dependants of the emperor Bábar Sháh, and who, at the latter part of that king's reign, was raised to the office of Díwán of the household. After the death of Bábar when Gujrát was conquered by Humáyún, and the provinces of Aḥmadábád was entrusted to Mirzá 'Askarí, Khwája Muḳím was appointed wazír to the Mirzá. He accompanied Humáyún to Ágrah after that monarch's defeat by Sher Sháh at Chounsá. The Khwája subsequently served under Akbar. His son Nizám-uddín, in the 29th year of Akbar's reign, was appointed Bakhshí of Gujrát, to which office he continued for a long time. He died on the 28th October, 1594 A. D., 23rd Ṣafar, 1003 A. H. on the banks of the Ráwí, and was buried in his own garden at Láhor. The following chronogram by 'Abdul Ḳádir Badáoní, translated by Mr. H. M. Elliot, records the date of his death. "Mirzá Nizám-uddín has departed in haste; but with honour has he gone to his final doom. His sublime soul has fled to the celestial regions, and Kádirí has found the date of his death in these words 'A jewel without price has left this world.'"

**Nizam-uddin Ahmad,** نظام الدین احمد بن محمد صانع, son of Muhammad Sálah, author of a work called "Majmúa'-us-Sanáyạ," or Collection of Arts, containing some beautiful poetical inventions, compiled in the year 1650 A. D., 1060 A. H. and published in the Lithographic Press at Lakhnau in 1845 A. D., 1260 A. H. He is also the author of the work called "Karamat-ul-Aulia," containing a minute detail of the (pretended) miracles performed by the twelve Imáms and other saints of the Muhammadan faith, written in 1657 A. D., 1067 A. H.

**Nizam-uddin Ganjawi,** نظام الدین گنجوی, *vide* Nizámí Ganjawí.

**Nizam-uddin Aulia, Shaikh,** شیخ نظام الدین اولیا, styled Sulṭán-ul-Musháekh. He was one of the noblest disciples of Shaikh Faríd-uddín Shakarganj, and a most celebrated saint among the Musalmáns. He was born at Badáon, in October, 1236 A. D., Ṣafar, 634 A. H., and died at Dehlí on Wednesday the 3rd of April, 1325 A. D., 18th Rabí' I, 725 A. H., where he lies buried, and his tomb, which is in Ghayáspúr, is visited by the Muhammadans to this day. Amír Khusro, the poet, was one of his disciples. Sayyid Aḥmad, the father of Nizám-uddín, is buried at Badáon.

**Nizam-uddin Sihali, Maulana,** مولانا نظام الدین سهالی, son of Ḳuṭb-uddín, is the author of the "Sharah" or marginal notes on the "Sadra," and "Shams Bázighá," &c. &c. He died in 1748 A. D., 1161 A. H.

**Nizam-uddin Sikham, Amir,** امیر نظام الدین سخم, a poet who was a contemporary of Amír Alísher, and a panegyrist of Mirzá Sulṭán Aḥmad of Samarḳand.

**Nizam-uddaula,** نظام الدوله, Nawáb of Haidarábád, *vide* Násir Jang.

**Nizam-uddaula, Nawab,** نظام الدوله, whose original name was Mar Phulwárí, was the eldest son of Mír Ja'far 'Alí Khán, Nawáb of Bengal, whom he succeeded in February, 1765 A. D. and assumed the above title. His mother's name was Manní Begam. He died about the month of May, 1766 A. D., Ẕil-ḥijja, 1179 A. H., and was succeeded by his brother Saif-uddaula.

**Nizam-ul-Mulk Muhammad,** نظام الملک محمد, (the son of 'Alí Sayyad Junaidí, to whom the Jámạ-ul-Hikayat is dedicated), was the general of Shams-uddín Altamsh, king of Dehlí. He was living in 622 A. H.

**Nizam-ul-Mulk,** نظام الملک, a justly celebrated minister of Sulṭán Alp Arsalán, second king of the Saljúkides, and afterwards of his son Malikshâh; to his virtue and ability is attributed the success and prosperity of their reign. After an administration of 30 years, the fame of the wazír, his wealth and even his services, were transformed into crimes. This venerable statesman, at the age of 39 years, was dismissed by his master, accused by his enemies, and was stabbed by an assassin, who was a follower of Hasan Sabbáh, the Old Man of the mountain, on Friday night the 15th of October, 1092 A. D., Ramaẓán, 485 A. H. at a place called Naháwand. His body was carried to Isfahán where he was interred with great pomp. It is said that the assassin was suborned against him by Malikshâh, who was fatigued to see him live so long. The Sulṭán survived him 35 days only. Nizám-ul-Mulk appears to be the author of the work, entitled "Siar-ul-Malúk."

**Nizam-ul-Mulk,** نظام الملک آصف جاه, entitled 'Asaf Jáh, whose original name was Chín Kulich Khán, was the son of Ghází-uddín Khán Fíroz Jang a favourite officer of the emperor 'Álamgír, under which monarch he also distinguished himself. In the reign of the emperor Farrukh-siyar, he held the government of Morádábád and was afterwards appointed governor of Málwá, which province he restored to a flourishing condition, but the reputation he acquired rendered him an object of jealousy to the two brothers, Sayyad 'Abdullah Khán and Husain 'Alí Khán, who wished to remove him to another quarter less favourable to his interest than the frontier of the Dakhin; but Nizám-ul-Mulk not willing to quit his post, excused himself, and resolved to seek an independent power in the Dakhin. The disturbed state of that country gave him a pretence for raising troops, and turned his attention to the conquest of the Dakhin. By intrigue and money he obtained possession of the fort of Asírgaṛh about the year 1717 A. D., and procured the junction of several officers of the province. He was pursued from Hindústán by the force under Diláwar Khán and another under 'Álam 'Alí Khán, both of whom he defeated and slew in battle in April, 1720 A. D., and at last remained without a rival in the Dakhin. In the reign of Muhammad Sháh, after the death of the two Sayyads, he was invited to court by that emperor; and on his arrival at Dehlí, the high office of wizárat was conferred on him, but Nizám-ul-Mulk being soon disgusted with the state of things at court, sent in his resignation, and marched off for the Dakhin, and though he continued to send honorary presents, on fixed occasions to the emperor, he thenceforth conducted himself, in other respects, as an independent prince, and governed the provinces of the Dakhin for 30 years with great ability and success. He was present in the battle which took place between Muhammad Sháh and Nádir Sháh, and is the progenitor of the present Nizáms of Haidarábád. He died on the 22nd May, 1748 A. D., 4th Jumáda II, 1161 A. H., thirty-seven days after the death of the emperor Muhammad Sháh, aged 104 lunar years, and was buried at Burhánpúr near the tomb of Sháh Burhán-uddín Gharíb. He left behind him six sons, *viz.*, Ghází-uddín, Násir Jang, Salábat Jang, Nizám 'Alí, Basálat Jang and Mughal 'Alí, and was succeeded in the government of the Dakhin, by the second, Mír Ahmad surnamed Násir Jang, who was present at Burhánpúr when his father died; the eldest Ghází-uddín Khán then residing at Dehlí in the office of Amír-ul-'Umra. Násir Jang was assassinated in December, 1750 A. D., and Muzaffar Jang a grandson of Nizám-ul-Mulk was placed on the throne, and soon after assassinated in February, 1751 A. D.; Salábat Jang, by the influence of the French, was then proclaimed and reigned until 1761 A. D., when he was imprisoned, and in 1763 A. D. put to death by his brother Nizám 'Alí, who ascended the throne and reigned until the 6th August, 1803 A. D. when he died, and was succeeded by his eldest son Mirzá Sikandar Jáh. Sikandar Jáh died on the 23rd May, 1829 A. D., and was succeeded by his son Mír Farkhunda 'Alí Khán the present Nizám (1858). Nizám-ul-Mulk appears to be the author of a Díwán which was found in the Library of Típú Sultán called "Díwán 'Asaf Nizám-ul-Mulk."

**Nizam-ul-Mulk Bahri,** نظام الملک بحری, the father of Ahmad Nizám Sháh Bahrí who was the first king of the Nizám Sháhí dynasty. Nizám-ul-Mulk was originally a Bráhman of Bíjánagar, but being taken prisoner in his infancy by the army of Sultán Ahmad Sháh Bahmaní, was made a Musalmán, and was educated as one of the royal slaves. He finished his education under the same tutor with the king's eldest son Sultán Muhammad, and became eminently learned in Persian and Arabic literature. On the accession of Sultán Muhammad II to the throne of the Dakhin in 1463 A. D., he was raised to the rank of a thousand and the charge of the royal falconry was entrusted to him, on which account he was called Bahrí, *i. e.*, a falconer. By degrees he rose to the highest honours and was appointed governor of Tilangána. On the death of Muhammad Sháh in 1482 A. D., he by his will became first minister to his son Sultán Mahmúd II, who added Bír and other districts to his jágír. This he committed to his son Malik Ahmad, who took up his residence at Khaibar and employed himself diligently in the affairs of his government, and after his father's death set up a separate dynasty in the Dakhin called Nizám Sháhí, the capital of which was Ahmadnagar. Nizám-ul-Mulk who had the sole power of the administration in his hands, latterly paid little or no regard for the king's authority, was murdered by the orders of the Sultán about the year 1486 A. D., 891 A. H., or some time afterwards.

**Nizam-ul-Mulk Mahmud,** نظام الملک محمود, the son of Abí Sa'íd Junaidí, a general and wazír of Shams-uddín Altamsh, king of Dehlí. He died in the reign of Sultána Razia, on the mountains of Sirmor where he had taken refuge from his enemies about the year 1238 A. D.

**Nizari, Hakim,** حکیم نزاري قهستاني, of Kohistán, a man of talents, but given to gaieties and pleasure, particularly to wine. He travelled much, and in his travels he met Sa'dí and other distinguished men. Towards the end of his life he retired from the world and lived by agriculture. He died in 1320 A. D., 720 A. H., and left besides a Díwán, two Masnawís.

**Nuh I, Samani, Amir,** امیر نوح ساماني, the fourth king of the Samánian dynasty, succeeded his father Amír Nasr to the throne of Khurásán and Bukhárá in 942 A. D., 331 A. H., and died in 954 A. D., 343 A. H. His son 'Abdulmalik succeeded him.

**Nuh II, Samani, Amir,** امیر نوح ساماني دویم, seventh king of the Samánian dynasty, surnamed 'Abú'l Kásim, succeeded his father Amír Mansúr I in March, 976 A. D., Rajab, 365 A. H. His reign was marked by extraordinary vicissitudes of fortune. He was contemporary with Subaktagín, a chief of high reputation, who had established a principality at Ghazní. He died in 997 A. D., Rajab, 387 A. H., and was succeeded by his son Mansúr II.

**Nur 'Ali Shah,** نور علي شاه, a leader of the Súfí sect and disciple of Ma'súm 'Alí Sháh, is supposed to have been poisoned, and died on the 3rd June, 1800 A. D., 10th Muharram, 1215 A. H. close to the grave of the prophet Jonas, within a league of Mousal, *vide* Masúm 'Alí Sháh.

**Nuri,** قاضي نور الدين اصفهاني تخلص به نوری, poetical appellation of Kází Núr-uddín of Isfahán who died in 1592 A. D., 1000 A. H., and left a Díwán.

**Nuri,** نوری, a poet who is the author of the "Maulúd Núria," in verse, which he dedicated to Sultán 'Abú'l Muzaffar Ya'kúb Bahádur Khán, commonly called Ya'kúb Beg. He died in the year 1482 A. D., 887 A. H.

**Nuri,** نوری, *vide* Núr-uddín Safaidúní.

**Nur Jahan Begam,** نورجهان بیگم, the favourite Sultána of the emperor Jahángír, was the daughter of the wazír Ya'tmad-uddaula whose tomb is at Agrah. She had attracted the notice of the prince Sultán Salím (afterwards Jahángír); but was, at the suggestion of his father the emperor Akbar, in order to withdraw the lady from the attentions of the prince, married to Sher Afghán Khán, a young Persian lately come into the service, and to whom Akbar gave a jágír in Bengal. After the death of his father, Jahángír appointed Kutb-uddín Khán his foster-brother the son of Shaikh Salím Chishtí, as governor of Bengal with the intention that he might procure for him the object of his passion. Kutb-uddín Khán on his arrival at Burdwán was slain by Sher Afghán Khán, who was himself despatched by Kutb-uddín's attendants. Núr Jahán was seized and sent as a prisoner to Dehlí, and was at first placed by the emperor among the attendants of his mother, but he subsequently married her in the sixth year of his reign 1610 A. D., 1019 A. H., changed her name, which was Mehr-un-Nisá, into Núr Jahán (the light of the world), and raised her to honours such as had never before been enjoyed by the consort of any king in India. From this period her ascendancy knew no bounds; the emperor took no step without consulting her; and on every affair in which she took an interest, her will was law. A circumstance so uncommon in an Asiatic government is thus recorded on the coins of that period. "By order of the emperor Jahángír, gold acquired a hundred times additional value by the name of the empress Núr Jahán." Her father Mirzá Ghayás or Ayas was made prime minister with the title of Ya'tmád-uddaula; and her two brothers were raised to the first rank of 'Umra, by the titles of Ya'tkád Khán, and 'Asaf Khán. One of the accomplishments by which she captivated Jahángír, is said to have been her facility in composing extemporary verses. After the death of her husband, she was treated with much respect and allowed a stipend of £250,000 a year. She survived Jahángír eighteen years, and died aged 72 in 1645 A. D., 1055 A. H., at Láhor, where she was buried in the mausoleum of her husband close to his tomb; some say, near the tomb of her brother 'Asaf Khán on the banks of the Ráwí, at Láhor. Hugh Murray in his History of British India, p. 230, by his erroneously asserting, that she was buried in the mausoleum at Ágrah called the Táj Mahal, has misguided many others. Even so late as the year 1858 A. D., the author of the "History of the Indian Revolt," page 109, says "that this was the mausoleum of Sháh Jahán and his favourite wife Núr Jahán."

**Nur Muhammad,** سید نور محمد بداونی, a Sayyad of Badáon, was a learned and pious Musalmán of the sect of Nakshband. He died on the 3rd August, 1723 A. D., 11th Zi-Ka'da, 1135 A. H.

**Nur Manzil,** نور منزل, name of a garden in Ágrah, built by the emperor Jahángír, which is now called Bágh Dahra. There is a large well in the garden, so large that it is more like a tank.

**Nur-uddin Ahmad, Shaikh,** شیخ نورالدین احمد, surnamed Kutb 'Alam, which see.

**Nur-uddin Arsalan Shah, Atabak,** نورالدین ارسلان شاہ اتابک, a prince of Mousal and Mesopotamia, of the family of Zangí, and grand-nephew of the famous Núr-uddín, Sultán of Aleppo and Damascus. He succeeded his father, Azz-uddín Masa'úd, 1193 A. D., 589 A. H., (the year of the death of Sálah-uddín). During a reign of 18 years, he established in some measure the declining power of his house, and compelled the minor princes of his family, to acknowledge his supremacy as lord paramount. He died 1210 A. D., 607 A. H., regretted by his subjects as a mild and beneficent ruler. His son Azz-uddín, after a reign of between seven and eight years, was succeeded by an infant son bearing the title of Núr-uddín Arsalán II who survived him only a few months.

**Nur-uddin 'Ali, Malik Mansur,** نورالدین علي ملک منصور, the second Sultán of the dynasty of Tartar or Baharite Mumlúks in Egypt, was placed on the throne by the Amírs after the assassination of his father Malik Moi'zz 'Azz-uddín Eibak, 1257 A. D., 655 A. H., at the age of fifteen. His short reign of two years was troubled by continual feuds among the Mamlúk chieftains, and attempts on the part of the Ayyúbite princes of Syria to recover the lost sway of their family in Egypt; and the apprehension of an irruption of the Mughals under Halákú, who had taken Baghdád and destroyed the Khiláfat, shewed the necessity of substituting a ruler of matured years and experience. The Amír Kutuz accordingly assumed the reigns of government, 1259 A. D., 657 A. H., and no more is heard of Núr-uddín. *Vide* Malik Moi'zz 'Azz-uddín.

**Nur-uddin bin-Lutf-ullah,** نورالدین بن لطف الله, better known as Háfiz 'Abrú, which see.

**Nur-uddin 'Ali, Malik-ul-Afzal,** نورالدین علي ملک الافضل, the eldest of the seventeen sons of Sálah-uddín; born 1170 A. D., 565 A. H. In the partition of his father's extensive dominions, which followed his death in 1193 A. D., Damascus and Southern Syria with Palestine fell to the lot of Núr-uddín; but in the dissensions which soon followed, he was stripped of his kingdom by his uncle Saif-uddín 'Abú Bakr (the Saphadin of Christian writers), and his brother 'Usmán, made Sultán of Egypt, 1196 A. D. *Vide* Malik-ul-Afzal.

**Nur-uddin Mahmud, Malik-ul-'Adil,** نورالدین محمود ملک العادل one of the most celebrated and powerful of the Muhammadan rulers of Syria in the age of the Crusades, born 1117 A. D, 511 A. H., was a younger son of 'Imád-uddín Zangí, the second of the dynasty of the Atábaks of 'Irak and Syria. At the death of his father, who was murdered by his own Mamlúks at the siege of Jabbár, 1146 A. D., 541 A. H., Núr-uddín hastening to Aleppo with the signet of the deceased prince, secured the possession of that city and of his father's Syrian dominions; while Mesopotamia, with Mousal for a capital, fell to the lot of the elder brother Saif-uddín; and the feeble attempts of Alp Arsalán, a prince of the house of Saljúk, to assert his ancestral claims to the dominion of these provinces, were easily frustrated by the combined power of the two brothers. The earliest exploits of the reign of Núr-uddín were in continuance of the Holy War which his father had assiduously waged against the Latin Christians of Palestine: Josceline de Courtenay, whose capital of Edessa had been taken by Zangí a few years previous, was signally repulsed in an attempt to recover it, and the Christian inhabitants, who had aided the enterprise, were put to the sword without mercy by command of Núr-uddín, who even levelled the fortifications of the town to prevent its ever again becoming a bulwark to the kingdom of Jerusalem. The recovery of this important fortress was the avowed object of the second Crusade, undertaken 1148 A. D., 543 A. H., under Louis VII of France and the emperor Conrad: but of the mighty hosts which they led from Europe, only a miserable and dispirited remnant escaped the arrows of the Suljúkí Turks in their march through Anatolia to Palestine, the project of retaking Edessa was abandoned as hopeless, the siege of Damascus, which was attacked by the crusading monarchs in conjunction with Baldwin III of Jerusalem, was foiled when on the eve of success by the address with which the minister of the Muslim prince Mujír-uddín fomented the mutual jealousies of the Christian leaders; and this vast armament, which if properly directed might have overwhelmed the rising power of Núr-uddín, only served by its failure to extend and confirm it. Resuming the offensive immediately after the departure of the crusaders, he invaded the territory of Antioch, and in a pitched battle (27th June, 1149 A. D.,) routed and slew the prince Raymond, whose head was sent as a trophy to the Khalíf at Baghdád; and though he sustained a severe defeat in the following year from his ancient opponent Josceline de Courtenay, who surprised his camp, this disgrace was amply compensated by the captivity of that active leader, who was soon after seized while hunting by a marauding party of Turkmans, and died in confinement, while the remaining dependencies of Edessa, the fortress of Aintab, Tellbasher, Ravendan, &c., fell almost without resistance into the power of Núr-uddín, whose dominions now included the whole of Northern Syria. Mujír-uddín was still the nominal ruler of Damascus and the southern portion, but the government was entirely in the hands of his wazír Mo'ín-uddín Anár, whose daughter Núr-uddín had married; and after the death of this able minister, the inhabitants, alarmed at the capture of Ascalon by Baldwin III in 1153 A. D., and dreading an attack from the Christians, voluntarily offered their allegiance to Núr-uddín (1154) as the price of his protection. The weak Mujír-uddín resigned his power, and sought an asylum at the court of the Khalíf of Baghdád, which then seems to have been the usual retreat of deposed princes; while Núr-uddín, the circuit of whose realms now encompassed on all sides by land the Latin territories in Palestine, and extended to the frontiers of the Fatimite possessions in Egypt, fixed his capital at Damascus, which he raised from the ruinous state in which it had been left by an earthquake, and adorned with mosques, fountains, colleges, and hospitals. The death of Baldwin III in 1162 A. D., released Núr-uddín from the ablest of his antagonists, his brother and successor, Almaric, or Amoury, being far inferior to Baldwin, both in prowess and abilities. Mesopotamia, ruled by the Sultán's nephews, acknowledged his supremacy as head of the family; he was now, by his officers, absolute master of Egypt; his name was recited with that of the Khalíf Mustazí of Baghdád in all the mosques throughout his dominions, and even in the holy cities of Mecca and Medina, which Túrán Sháh, brother of Sálah-uddín, had made dependencies of Egypt. But the power and glory of Núr-uddín had now attained their highest pitch, the three remaining years of his life were unmarked by any memorable achievement, and disquieted by the forebodings of the future downfall of his house by the ambition of Sálah-uddín, who, though still ostensively acting as his lieutenant, and making public professions of loyalty and obedience, had in fact become independent master of Egypt, and eluded or disregarded all the orders of his nominal sovereign. Núr-uddín was preparing to march into Egypt to reduce or expel his refractory vassal, when an attack of quinsy terminated his life at Damascus after a prosperous reign of 27 years on the 26th of May, 1173 A. D., 21st Shawwál, 569 A. H. His son Malik-us-Sálah Ismá'íl, a youth, 11 years old, succeeded to the titular sovereignty of his extensive dominions, but was speedily stripped, by Sálah-uddín, of Damascus and the greater part of Syria, and died 8 years afterwards, reduced to the sovereignty of Aleppo and its dependencies.

**Nur-uddin Muhammad, Mirza,** مرزا نور الدين محمد, son of 'Alá-uddín Muhammad, the son of Khwája Husain. He was married to the daughter of the emperor Bábar, named Gulrukh Begam, by whom he had Salíma Sultána Begam who was married to Bairám Khán.

**Nur-uddin Muhammad Ufi,** نور الدين محمد عوفي, the author of the "Jáma'-ul-Hikáyát," a collection of historical anecdotes. This work he wrote and dedicated to Nizám-ul-Mulk Mahmúd, a general of Shams-uddín Altimsh, king of Dehlí, about 1230 A. D., *vide* Muhammad U'fí, and Sadr-uddín U'fí.

**Nur-uddin Safaiduni, Mulla,** ملا نور الدين سفيدوني, entitled Nawáb Tarkhán, was a native of Jám in Hirat and brought up at Mashhad. He was a favourite companion of the emperor Humáyún; and as the Pargana of Safaidún had been conferred on him as jágír, he was consequently called Safaidúní. He cut a canal from the river Jamna to Karnál in the year 1569 A. D., 977 A. H., and named it "Sheikhú Nahr," in honour of the prince Sultán Salím, who was born in that year and was nicknamed by his father the emperor Akbar, Sheikhú Bábá. He was an excellent poet and has left a Díwán or book of Odes. His poetical title was Núrí.

**Nur-uddin Shirazi,** نور الدين شيراجي, *vide* Hakím Núr-uddín Shírází.

**Nur-uddin, Shaikh,** شيخ نور الدين, an historian who wrote the history of Kashmír in Persian called "Táríkh Kashmír," which in after times was continued by Haidar Malik and Muhammad 'Azim.

**Nur-ul-Hak, Shah or Shaikh,** شاه نورالحق, surnamed Al-Mashrakí, Al-Dehlawí and Al-Bukhárí, was the son of Shaikh 'Abdul Hak bin-Saif-uddín of Dehlí. He is the author of the "Zubdat-ut-Tawaríkh," which is an enlarged edition of his father's history, and was composed in order that by improving the style and supplying the omissions, he might render it worthy the acceptance of his patron, Shaikh Faríd-uddín Bukhárí, with whom he was connected by marriage, and who under the title of Murtaza' Khán managed for some time the affairs of the empire in the reign of the emperor Jahángír. He has also written a Sharah on the "Sahíh Bukhárí" and "Muslim." He died in the reign of the emperor 'Alamgír, 1662 A. D., 1073 A. H.

**Nur-ul-Hak,** قاضي نور الحق بريلي, Kází of Barelí, *vide* Munai'm.

**Nur-ullah Shustari, Mir,** مير نورالله شوستري, who is sometimes called Núr-ullah bin-Sharíf-ul-Husainí-ush-Shústarí, was a nobleman at the court of the emperor Akbar. He is the author of the work called "Majális-ul-Mominín." This great biographical work, is a mine of valuable information respecting the most notable persons who professed the Shia faith. The author has given an entire book or section (the fifth Majális) to the lives of the traditionists and lawyers, and has specified the principal works by each learned doctor at the end of their respective histories. Núr-ullah was a zealous Shia and suffered in the year 1610 A. D., 1019 A. H. for his religious opinions in the reign of Jahángír, *vide* Súfí.

**Nur-un-Nisa Begam,** نور النسا بيگم, the daughter of Ibráhím Husain Mirzá by Gulrukh Begam. She was married to prince Mirzá Salím afterwards Jahángír.

**Noubat Khan, Nawab,** نواب نوبت خان, an officer of the reign of the emperor Akbar, whose mausoleum is in old Dehlí close to the seraglio of Sháh-Jahán. It was built in the year 1565 A. D., 973 A. H. and is called "Nílí Chhatrí" on account of its having a blue canopy at the top. It is now in a ruinous state.

**Noudar** or **Nouzar,** نودر, an ancient king of Persia of the Pishdadian dynasty, *vide* Manúchehr.

**Nounihal Singh,** نونهال سنگه, *vide* Kharag Singh, ruler of the Panjáb.

**Nouras Bano Begam,** نورس بانو بيگم, the wife of Shahnawáz Khán, wazír. She was living in September, 1659 A. D., Muharram, 1070 A. H.

**Nousherwan,** نوشيروان عادل, surnamed 'Adil or the Just (Chosroes of the Greeks), was the son of Kubád, king of Persia, at whose death 531 A. D., he ascended the throne of that kingdom. The accounts given by Eastern and Western authors, of the successes of this king in his invasions of the Roman empire, differ but very little. Some of the former have falsely asserted that he took an emperor of the Romans prisoner; and they have all, with a partiality that, in national historians writing of this monarch, seems almost excusable, passed over the few reverses which his arms sustained. But the disgraceful peace which the emperor Justinian purchased at the commencement of the reign of Nousherwán, the subsequent war, the reduction of all Syria, the capture of Antioch, the unopposed progress of the Persian monarch to the shores of the Mediterranean, his conquest of Iberia, Calchos, and the temporary establishment of his power on the banks of the Phasis, and on the shores of the Euxine, are facts not questioned by his enemies. They, however, assert, that his genius, as a military leader, even when his fortune was at the highest, was checked by Belisarius, who was twice sent to oppose his progress; and whose success, considering his want of means, and the character of the court he served, was certainly wonderful. In all the negotiations which took place between the emperor Justinian and Nousherwán, the latter assumed the tone of a superior. His lowest servants were treated, at the imperial court, in a manner calculated to inflame the pride, and raise the insolence of a vain and arrogant nation: and the impressions which this conduct must have made, were confirmed by the agreement of the Roman emperor to pay 30,000 pieces of gold; a sum which could have been of no importance to Nousherwán, but as it showed the monarch of the Western world in the rank of one of his tributaries. In a second war with the Roman emperors Justin and Tiberius, Nousherwán, who though 80 years of age, still led his armies, experienced some reverses of fortune: but the perseverance and valour of the aged sovereign were ultimately rewarded by the conquest of Dara and the plunder of Syria, 572 A. D. He died after a prosperous reign of 48 years about the year 579 A. D., and was succeeded by his son Hurmuz IV.

Muhammad, who was born during the reign of Nousherwán, 571 A. D., used to boast of his fortune, in being born when so just a king reigned. This is great praise, and from a source that cannot be suspected of flattery.

**Nousherwan Kirmani,** نوشيروان كرماني, an author who translated the "Ardai Viráf-náma" originally written in the Zend, into the modern Persian. Another translation was made by Zaratash Bairám in Persian prose and one in verse. This work was translated into English by Mr. J. A. Pope and published at London in 1816. See Ardai Viráf.

**Nouzar,** نوذر, an ancient king of Persia, *vide* Manúchehr.

**Nuzhat,** نزهت, poetical name of Muhammad 'Azím of Dámghán, a poet who is the author of a Díwán. He died in 1724 A. D., 1137 A. H.

---

# O.

**Oktai Ḳaan or Khan,** اقتاء قاآن, the eldest surviving son of Changez Khán whom he succeeded to the dominions of Tartary and Northern China, being crowned as Kháḳán or emperor 1227 A. D., 624 A. H. He died by excess of wine seven months after his brother Chughtái, about the month of January, 1242 A. D., 639 A. H. He was of a mild and generous disposition and governed his conquered subjects with impartiality and justice. As a warrior, he was brave, but prudent, and as a sovereign, equitable and benevolent. He was succeeded by his son Kayúk Khán.

*List of the Kháḳáns of Tartary.*

| | A. D. |
|---|---|
| Oḳtái Ḳáán, eldest son of Changez Khán, began .. | 1227 |
| Kayúk Khán, son of Oḳtái Ḳáán .............. | 1242 |
| Mangú Ḳáán, eldest son of Túlí Khán .......... | 1243 |
| Ḳablái Khán, son of Mangú Káán, succeeded to the kingdom of Tartary in 1259 A. D. and died in 1294 A. D. His brother Halákú Khán, after the death of his father, succeeded to the kingdom of Persia, *vide* Halákú Khán ............... | 1259 |

**Oodham Bai,** اودهم بائي, the mother of the emperor Aḥmad Sháh, the son of Muhammad Sháh of Dehlí. On the accession of her son to the throne, she received the titles of Nawáb Bái, Nawáb Ḳudsia, and Sáhiba Zamání, and her brother Mán Khán was raised to the rank of 6000 with the title of Mo'taḳid-uddaula.

**Orkhan,** اورخان, the son of Othmán or Osmán, the son of Amír Tughral. After his father's death he made himself Sulṭán of the Turks at Brusa in 1327 A. D., 727 A. H. by the destruction of his elder brothers. He added largely to the territories of his father, and formed a body of infantry, afterwards formidable to Europe—the Yenícherí or Jannisárís. He died about the year 1359 A. D., 760 A. H. and was succeeded by his son Murád I (Amarath).

---

# P.

**Padmawati,** پدماوتي, daughter of the Rájá of Ceylon, who was carried off forcibly by Ratan Sain, Rájá of Chittour, and taken away from him by Sulṭán 'Alá-uddín when he conquered Chittour about the year 1303 A. D., 703 A. H. Her story called "Ḳissae Padmáwat," has been written in Persian poetry by Husain of Ghazní, and there is also a version in the Bhákha language in verse, by Malik Muhammad Jáesí. There is another in Persian prose by Ráe Gobind Munshí who wrote it, in 1652 A. D., 1062 A. H., and called it "Tukfat-ul-Kulúb," which is also a chronogram for that year. In the year 1796 A. D., 1211 A. H., another translation into Urdú verse was written by two poets, the first part by Mír Ziyá-uddín 'Ibrat, and the last by Ghulám 'Alí 'Ishrat.

**Palas or Palash,** پالاس, (the Valens of Roman History) succeeded his father Fíroz I on the throne of Persia 484 A. D. He reigned four years, and was succeeded by his brother Ḳubád.

**Panahi,** پناهي, a celebrated poet and artist, who, says 'Ashik, "broke the pencil of the Frank painters, and by painting a single rose-leaf could metamorphose Winter into Spring."

**Parhez Bano Begam,** پرهيز بانو بيگم, daughter of Sháh Jahán by Kandharí Begam. She died in the year 1675 A. D., 1086 A. H.

**Parsaji,** پرساجي, also called Parsárám Bhosla, the son of Rághojí Bhosla, succeeded his father in the government of Berár or Nágpúr in March, 1816 A. D., but being an idiot, he was soon after strangled by Múdhají surnamed 'Apá Sáhib, who was acknowledged by the English.

**Parsaram Bhao or Bhosla,** پرسرام بهاو, *vide* Parsájí.

**Partap Singh,** پرتاپ سنگه, Rájá orRáná of Udaipúr, was the son of Udai Singh, the son of Ráná Sanga. Partáp Singh, who is still idolized by his countrymen for the heroism with which he repelled the attacks of the Mughals, and preserved the germ of national independence in his wild fastnesses, reigned in 1614 A. D., and recovered the greater portion of his dominions before Akbar died. He founded the capital of Udaipúr, and died in 1594 A. H.

**Partab or Partap Pal,** پرتاپ پال, present Rájá of Karoulí.

**Partap Singh,** پرتاپ سنگه, eldest son of Rájá Mán Singh, the son or nephew of Rájá Bhagwán Dás Kachhwáhá of Amber. He died before his father, and left a son named Maha Singh, the father of Mirzá Rájá Jai Singh.

**Partap Singh,** پرتاپ سنگه, Rájá of Jaipúr. He succeeded his father Mádho Singh in 1778 A. D., and died in 1803 A. D., when he was succeeded by his son Rájá Jagat Singh. Don Pedro de Silva was employed by Partáp Singh as a physician, at the time when Colonel Polier visited Jaipúr in search of the Vedas of the Hindús, about the year 1788 A. D. His son or grandson Augustine de Silva who received pension from the Rájá of Bhartpúr died in the year 1856 A. D.; his son Joseph de Silva is now at A'grah, and the pension is still (1857) continued to him. After the death of Jagat Singh who died without issue, Rájá Jai Singh III, posthumous, believed supposititious, succeeded him 1818 A. D.

**Partap Singh Narayan,** پرتاپ سنگھ ناراین, Rájá of Sitára, the son of Rájá Sáhú, commonly called Abba Sáhib and grandson of Rághojí Bhosla. He was closely confined by the Peshwa Bájí Ráo. After the dethronement of Apá Sáhib, he was released from confinement and formally enthroned by the English on the 11th April, 1818 A. D., and a part of the Púna territories assigned for his support. On the 25th September, 1819 A. D., a treaty was concluded between the British Government and the Rájá, ceding to him the districts he subsequently possessed. He violated his treaty, was deposed in 1839, and died at Benares in 1847 A. D. He left only one daughter, but was reported to have adopted Balwant Singh Bhosla, as her son. His next brother having died without issue in 1821; the third brother Sháhjí *alias* Appa Sáhib succeeded in 1839 A. D. and died 5th April, 1848 A. D., leaving no issue.

**Parwana,** پروانه, poetical name of Kúnwar Jaswant Singh, a son of Rájá Bení Bahádur. He died in 1832 A. D., 1248 A. H.

**Parwiz, Sultan,** سلطان پرویز, second son of the emperor Jahángír. His mother's name was Sáhib Jamál, daughter of Khwája Hasan, uncle of Zain Khán Koka. He was born at Kábul about the year 1590 A. D., 998 A. H. and died at Burhánpúr in his 38th year on the 28th of October, 1625 A. D., 6th Safar, 1035 A. H. At a place called Sultánpúr near A'grah on a spot of 450 bíghas, he had built many splendid buildings now in ruins.

**Pashang,** پشنگ, an ancient king of Túrán, and father of Afrásiáb.

**Payam,** پیام, the poetical name of Mír Sharaf-uddín who died at A'grah in the year 1753 A. D., 1166 A. H.

**Payami,** پیامي, the poetical name of 'Abdul-Salám. He lived during the reign of Akbar; *vide* A'in Translation I, 601; [and Sprenger, p. 119].

**Pir Ali Hajwiri, Shaikh,** شیخ پیرعلي هجوري, a native of Hajwír, a village in Ghazní, and author of the work called "Kashf-ul-Mahjúb." He died about the year 1064 A. D., 456 A. H., and is buried at Láhor.

**Pir Badar,** پیر بدر, a celebrated Musalmán saint whose tomb is at Chitagún in Bengal and is evidently of great antiquity. There is a stone scraped into furrows, on which, it is said, Pír Badar used to sit; there is also another bearing an inscription, which from exposure to the weather, and having on it numerous coats of whitewash, is illegible. There is a mosque near the tomb, with a slab of granite, bearing an illegible inscription, apparently from the Kurán. At a short distance is the Masjid of Muhammad Yásín with an inscription conveying the year of the Hijrí 1136. (1724 A. D.)

**Pelaji** or **Belaji,** پیلاجي, the second Gaikowár and Rájá of Baroda. In 1721 A. D. he laid the foundation of the future greatness of Baroda on the firm foundation of a most sagacious policy. He was murdered by the Rájá of Jaudpúr while engaged in the congenial occupation of lifting some of the Rájá's property. He was succeeded by his son Damají who was an unworthy representative of his illustrious sire. He had the audacity to declare open war against the Peshwa while the Peshwa was unencumbered with any other quarrels, and as the result of this unequal contest, he lost half of his possessions, and was forced to hold the other half himself as a fief from the Peshwa. Syají, the son of Daurojí, was a fool, and Anand Ráo was a fool, that is, not fools in the conventional and uncomplimentary sense of the word, but literally fools—persons of weak intellect. But they were the heirs to the throne, and it was sought to make them the victims of an usurpation. The British Government was horrified at this iniquity and they stepped in to prevent it. Afterwards when the British were engaged in their fresh struggle with the Peshwa, Baroda sided with us. The Marhatta confederacy was broken up, and in the final settlement, the Gaikowár received a large accession of territory. Anand Ráo died in 1819 A. D., and was succeeded by Saiají Ráo. Since then we have maintained what was called by the term of the treaty our *alliance* with Baroda.

**Pir Muhammad,** پیر محمد جهانگیر, was the eldest son of Jahángír Mirzá and grandson of Amír Taimúr. He was sent to India some time before his grandfather, *viz.*, in the year 1397 A. D., 799 A. H., and had already taken possession of Multán when his grandfather invaded it. He was a brave prince and his grandfather had bequeathed his crown to him; but he was at Kandahár when his grandfather died; and Khalíl Sultán, another grandson, who was present with the army, obtained the support of several powerful chiefs, and the possession of Samarkand, the capital of the empire. A contest took place between these princes, which terminated unfavourably for Pír Muhammad, who was put to death by the treachery of his own minister six months after the death of his grandfather, 1405 A. D., 808 A. H.

**Pir Muhammad, Mulla, of Shirwan,** ملا پیر محمد شرواني an officer who held the rank of 5000 in the time of the emperor Akbar. He was drowned in the river Narbada in pursuit of Báz Bahádur, king of Málwá, 1561 A. D., 969 A. H.

**Pir Muhammad, Shah,** شاہ پیر محمد, a Pírzáda or Mutwallí of the Dargáh at Saloun, who died in 1688 A. D., 1099 A. H.

**Pir Muhammad,** پیر محمد, *vide* Aghar Khán.

**Peshwa,** پیشوا, *vide* Bálájí Ráo Bishwanáth Peshwa.

**Peroses,** پیروسیس of the Greeks, *vide* Fíroz.

**Perron, General,** پیرن جنریل, a French soldier who came to India and was employed by Nizám 'Alí Khán of Haidarábád as a Colonel. When on the 1st of September, 1798 A. D. a treaty was concluded between the English and the Nawáb, Perron with his French troops were discharged from his service and employed by Daulat Ráo Scindhia the Gwáliar Chief. When M. Duboigne who had the command of the districts of Koel, Alígurh &c., went home, Mon. Perron was appointed General and succeeded him, and continued in command till Lord Lake on the 29th of August, 1803 A. D. took these places, and General Perron being defeated, went over to Lakhnau. He subsequently went home to France.

**Persia,** پارسیاه. For ancient kings of Persia of the 1st or Pishdádian dynasty, *vide* Kaimurs.

For ancient kings of the 2nd or Kayánian dynasty, *vide* Kaiḳubád.

The ancient kings of the Greek dynasties founded after the death of Alexander the Great by his generals who were called by the Persians Ashkánians and Ashghánians or Arsacidœ of the Greeks, are not given in this work.

For the ancient kings of Persia of the Sásánian race called by the Persians Malúk-ut-Tawáef or Petty Kings, *vide* Ardisher Bábagán.

**Phul, Shaikh,** شیخ پهول, a brother of the saint Muhammad Ghaus of Gwáliar, which see. He is also called Phúl Shahíd. His tomb is on a hill near the fort of Bayana.

**Piari Bano,** پیاري بانو, the second wife of prince Shujáa', son of the emperor Sháh Jahán. She bore him three daughters and two sons. She was so famed for her wit and beauty, that songs were made and sung in her praise in Bengal; and the gracefulness of her person had even become proverbial. After her husband's melancholy death in Arracan, she dashed her head against a stone and died, and two of her daughters poisoned themselves, while the third was married to the Rájá of that place.

**Pindar Razi,** پندار رازی, a poet of Rei whose proper name is Kamál-uddín, and who lived at the court of Sultán Majd-uddaula, son of Fakhr-uddaula, about the year 1009 A. D., 400 A. H., and wrote poetry in Arabic, Persian and the Dílamí language.

**Pirthi Raj,** پرتهي راج, the Chauhán Rájá of Ajmere and Dehlí who, in his last battle with Shaháb-uddín Ghorí in 1192 A. D. was taken prisoner and conveyed to Ghazní where he stabbed himself, or was put to death. He is also called Pithoura.

**Pirthi Raj Rathor,** پرتهي راج راتهور, a Hindú chief who held a high rank in the service of the emperor Sháh Jahán, and died in the Dakhin 1656 A. D., 1066 A. H. After his death his brother Rám Singh and his son Keisrí Singh were raised to suitable ranks.

**Pirthi Singh,** پرتهي سنگه, *vide* Mádho Singh Kachhwáha.

**Pithoura,** پتهورا, *vide* Pirthí Ráj the Chauhán Rájá.

**Purbahae Jami,** پوربهاء جامي, a poet, who was a native of Jám a village in Hirát. He flourished in the reign of Arghún Khán and was cotemporary with Humám Tabrezí.

**Pur Hasan Asfaraeni,** پور حسن اسفرايني, a very pious Musalmán who was a native of Asfaráen. He was a disciple of Shaikh Jamál-uddín Zákir, a cotemporary of Shaikh Razí-uddín Alí Lálá, and a good poet, and has left a Díwán consisting of Persian and Turkish Ghazals. In his Persian poems, he uses for his poetical appellation, his own name, *viz.*, "Púr Hasan," and in his Turkish compositions, "Hasan Ughlí."

**Pran Sukh,** پران سک, a learned Hindú, of the Ḳáyeth caste, who is the author of an Inshá or specimens of letter writing, entitled "Insháe Ráhat Ján," written in the reign of the emperor Muhammad Sháh and completed in the year 1750 A. D., 1163 A. H.

**Prithi Raj,** پرتهي راج, *vide* Pirthí Ráj.

**Prithi Singh,** پرتهي سنگه, Mahárájá of Kishangaṛh, situated to the south of Jaipúr intervening between the territory of the British province of Ajmere. The ruler of this small but prosperous state, Mahárájá Prithí Singh, is described as a man of high character. He was living in 1872.

**Puranmal,** پورنمل راجه, Rájá of Amber now called Jaipúr. He gave his daughter in marriage to Akbar Sháh in the year 969 A. H. He is also called Bihárí Mal, which see.

**Purdil,** پردل, a poet who flourished in the time of 'Álamgír, and is mentioned in the "Mirat-ul-Khayál."

---

# R.

**Raba'a Basri,** رابعهٔ بصري, a very celebrated pious lady of Basra, who had a good knowledge of all the traditions. She is said to have constructed a canal from Baghdád to Medina, was a contemporary of Sarí Saḳtí, and died in 801 A. D., 185 A. H.

**Rabit,** رابط, poetical name of Moulwí Abdul Ahad.

**Raek,** رایق, author of the biography called "Tazkira Ráeḳ," an abstract of which was made by Siráj-uddaula Muhammad Ghaus Khán Nawáb of the Karnatik in 1842 A. D.

**Rae Gobind Munshi,** راي گبیند, a Kayeth who is the author of the story of Padmáwat in Persian, entitled, "Tuhfat-ul-Kulúb" which he wrote in the year 1652 A. D., 1062 A. H.

**Rae Lonkaran,** راي لونکرن, Rájá of the Pargana of Sambhar, lived in the time of the emperor Akbar, and died in the 11th year of Jahángír, 1615 A. D., 1024 A. H. He was a good Persian scholar, and used to compose verses; his poetical name was Tousaní. He was succeeded in his territories by his son Manóhar Dás, whose poetical title, some authors say, was Tousaní and not his father's. *Vide* Tousání.

**Rae Indarman,** رای اندرمن, a Hindú, by caste a Bais of Hisár, and author of a work called "Dastúr-ul-Hisáb." He was living in 1768 A. D., 1182 A. H.

**Rae Phukni Mal,** رای پهکني مل, *vide* Nashát.

**Rae Maldeo,** رای ملديو, *vide* Maldeo Ráe.

**Rae Rae Singh,** رای رای سنگه, son of Ráe Kalián Mal Raṭhor, a descendant of Ráe Máldeo and zamíndar of Bikaner in the time of the emperor Akbar. Ráe Kalián Mal with his son served under that monarch for several years, and received his niece in marriage. Ráe Singh subsequently gave his daughter in marriage to Sulṭán Salím, who, on his accession to the throne, conferred on him the rank of 5,000. Ráe Singh died in the year 1612 A. D., 1021 A. H.

**Rae Rayan Raja Bikarmajit,** رای رایان راجه بکرماجیت, was the title of a Bráhman named Sundardás who at first served under the prince Sháh Jahán in the capacity of a Munshí. He afterwards rose by degrees to higher dignities and received the above title from the emperor Jahángír. When Sháh Jahán rebelled against his father, Bikarmájít, who was then with the prince, fell in the battle which took place between the troops of the prince and his father about the year 1621 A. D., 1030 A. H.

**Rae Sarjan Hara,** رای سرجن هاڑا, Rájá of Ranthanbúr in the province of Ágrah, lived in the time of the emperor Akbar. After his death Ráo Bhoj Hárá succeeded him.

**Rae Shew Das,** رای سیو داس, a Khattrí who was appointed deputy to Rájá Jai Singh Súbádar of Ágrah in the time of Muhammad Sháh. He built a fine garden at Ágrah on the banks of the Jamna which goes still after his name, Bágh Shew Dás.

**Rae Tansukh Rae,** رای تنسکه رای, a Hindú whose poetical name was Shauk, was the son of Ráe Majlis Ráe, who was Náeb of the Díwán Khálsa of Ágrah. He is the author of a Tazkíra of Persian poets called "Safínat-ush-Shauk," and also of a small Díwán of 1000 verses. He was living at Ágrah in 1756 A. D., 1170 A. H.

**Rafai, Sayyad,** رافعي سايد. Was an inhabitant of Dehlí and lived on for a long time in an old mosque which he repaired. He died about the year 1867 A. D., 1233 A. H.

**Rafa'i,** رافعي, whose proper name was Imám-uddín, is the author of the "Tadwín," and several works in Persian.

**Rafa'i,** شيخ محي الدين حسين رافعي, surnamed Shaikh Muhí-uddín Husain. He died about the year 1422 or 1427 A. D., 825 or 830 A. H.

**Rafi or Rafia',** مرزا حسن بيگ رفيع, the poetical name of Mirzá Hasan Beg who was employed as secretary to Nazar Muhammad Khán the ruler of Túrán. He came to India about the year 1646 A. D., 1056 A. H. in the reign of the emperor Sháh Jahán, who conferred on him the mansab of 500. He died in the time of 'Álamgír.

**Rafi Khan Bazil, Mirza,** مرزا رفيع خان باذل, author of the work called "Hamlae Haidarí," containing the wars of Muhammad, and the first four Khalífas, *viz.*, Abú Bakr, 'Umar, 'Usmán and 'Alí, in heroic verse consisting of 40,000 verses. He was a native of Dehlí and a descendant of Ja'far *Sarond* Mashhadí. For some years he had the command of the fort of Gwáliar in the time of 'Álamgír, after whose death he lived in retirement at Dehlí, where he died in 1711 A. D., 1123 A. H. He is also the author of a Díwán of Ghazals. His poetical name is Bázil.

**Rafizi Mua'mmai,** رفيعي معمائی, *vide* Mír Haidar Rafíkí.

**Rafi-u'ddarjat,** رفيع الدرجات, the son of Rafí-ush-Shán and grandson of Bahádur Sháh. He was raised to the throne of Dehlí by the two Sayyads, *viz.*, 'Abdullah Khán and his brother Husain 'Alí Khán, after the dethronement of the emperor Farrukh-siyar on the 18th February, 1719 A. D., 8th Rabí II, 1131 A. H., but died in little more than three months of a consumption at Ágrah on the 28th May the same year, 19th Rajab, 1131 A. H., when another youth of the same description, younger brother to the deceased was set up by the Sayyads under the name of Rafí-uddaula Sháh Jahán Sání, who came to the same end in a still shorter period. Both were buried in the mausoleum of Khwája Kutb-uddín Kákí at Dehlí. After their death the Sayyads pitched on a healthier young man as their successor, who ascended the throne by the title of Muhammad Sháh.

**Rafi-u'ddin,** رفيع الدين, a poet who is the author of a very curious and entertaining Díwán or collection of poems. He was a native of Hindústán, and probably of that province which is called the Dakhin. He served in a military capacity, and attached himself to the person of the illustrious emperor Akbar whom he first met at Kashmír in the year 1592 A. D. and received from that monarch the reward of his poetical labours. His Díwán which he commenced writing in the kingdom of the Dakhin, was brought to a conclusion in 1601 A. D., 1010 A. H. It contains about 15,000 distichs.

**Rafi-u'ddin Haidar Rafa'i Mua'mmai, Amir,** امير رفيع الدين حيدر رفعي معمائی, is said to have composed more than 12,000 verses of chronograms, &c., but did not collect them. He was living in 1585 A. D., 993 A. H. This person appears to be the same with Mír Haidar Rafíyí Mua'mmáí.

**Rafi-uddin Lubnani,** رفيع الدين لبناني, native of Lubnán, a village in Isfahán. He was cotemporary with the poets Asír-uddín Admání, Sharaf-uddín Shafrowa, and Kamál-uddín Ismá'íl. He is the author of a Díwán.

**Rafi-uddin, Shaikh Muhammad,** شيخ رفيع الدين محمد, surnamed Muhaddis or traditionist who died in 1547 A. D., 954 A. H., and was buried in the Hawelí of Asaf Jáh at Ágrah.

**Rafi-uddaula,** رفيع الدوله, younger brother of the emperor Rafí-uddarjat, which see.

**Rafi-u'sh-Shan,** رفيع الشان, (prince) son of the emperor Bahádur Sháh, killed in battle against Jahándár Sháh his brother. *Vide* Jāhándár Sháh.

**Rafi-u's-Sauda, Mirza,** مرزا رفيع السودا, *vide* Saudá.

**Rafi Waez,** رفيع واعظ, a poet who is the author of a Díwán. *Vide* Muhammad Rafí Wáez.

**Raghib,** راغب, poetical title of a poet of Shíráz whose proper name is Kalb Husain Beg.

**Raghoba,** رگهوبا, *vide* Raghunáth Ráo.

**Raghoji Bhosla I,** رگهوجي بهوسله. Was nominated "Seiná Sahib Sabha," or general of the Marhatta confederacy, in 1734 A. D., received a sanad from the Peshwa and became the first Rájá of Berár or Nágpúr in 1740 A. D. in which year a great revolution took place in the Marhatta government. The Rájá of Sitára, Rámrájá, a weak prince, being upon the throne, it was concerted between the two principal officers of the state, Bájí Ráo the Peshwá, and Rághójí Bhosla, the Bakhshí or Commander-in-Chief, to divide the dominions of their master. In consequence of this arrangement, the former assumed the government of the western provinces, continuing at the ancient capital of Púna; the latter took the eastern, and fixed his residence at Nágpúr, a principal city in the province of Berár; whilst Rámrájá was confined to the fortress of Sitára, the Peshwa administering the government in his name. Hence the distinction between the Marhattas of Púna and Berár. Rághojí was the son of Vimbojí who was killed in Audh during the lifetime of his father Parsojí, who was Bakhshí under his brother Sáhojí the son of Sambhojí the son of Sewájí the founder of the Marhatta empire. Rághójí Bhosla died in 1749 or

1753 A. D., and transmitted his government to his son Jánojí, who dying in 1772 A. D., left his inheritance to his nephew and adopted son Rághójí Bhosla II the son of his younger brother Madhújí. This occasioned a contention between Jánojí's brother Samojí and Madhújí. The former claimed the government in the right of priority of birth, and the latter as father and guardian of the adopted child. They were accordingly engaged in hostility until the death of Sámojí or Sabhoji, who was killed in an engagement with his brother on the 27th of January, 1775 A. D. From that period the government of Beṛár was held by Madhojí or Madhújí Bhosla.

*Bhosla Rájás of Nágpúr or Beṛár.*

| | | A. D. |
|---|---|---|
| Raghojí Bhosla I | died | 1753 |
| Jánojí or Ránojí | „ | 1772 |
| Madhojí | „ | 1788 |
| Raghojí Bhosla II | „ | 1816 |
| Parsojí (strangled by Apa Sahib) | „ | 1816 |
| Múdojí (Apâ Sahib) was acknowledged by the English in 1816 and | deposed | 1818 |
| Partáp Singh Náráyan grandson of Raghojí Bhosla put on the throne | | 1818 |
| Rághójí Bhosla III, | | 1853 |

**Raghoji Bhosla II,** رگهوجي بهوسله, succeeded his father Madhojí Bhosla in the government of Beṛár or Nágpúr in May, 1788 A. D. and died on the 22nd of March, 1816 A. D., when his son Parsojí succeeded him.

**Raghunath Shah,** رگهوناتهه شاه, of the Mandla district, who was a direct descendant of the eldest branch of the Gond dynasty, was executed in 1857 A. D. for rebellion, and his estates confiscated. Fifteen years later the Government gave his widow Mare Kúṇwar a compassionate allowance of Rs. 120 per annum.

**Raghoji Bhosla III,** رگهوجي بهوسله, Rájá of Beṛár. He died in 1853 A. D., not only without heirs but without any male relations who could support a legitimate claim to the Ráj; thereupon the Governor General quietly annexed that large country to the Company's dominions.

**Raghunath Rao,** رگهوناتهه راؤ, commonly called Raghóba, a Marhaṭṭa chief who was at one time much connected with the English. He was the son of Bájí Ráo Peshwá I, and father of the last Peshwá Bájí Ráo II, and paternal uncle of Mádhó Ráo Peshwá II. He usurped the Peshwáship after the death of Náráyan Ráo, youngest son of Bálájí Ráo Peshwá. On the death of Bálájí Ráo, who left two sons Mádhó Ráo and Náráyan Ráo, both minors, the power of the state was for some years wielded by his brother Raghunáth as regent. Mádhó Ráo was enabled to take the reins of government into his own hands after some time, but died in 1772 A. D., and was succeeded by his brother Nárâyan Ráo. He was soon after murdered in consequence of a plot which Raghobá had formed against him. Raghobá was acknowledged Peshwá after his death; but it appeared soon after that the widow of Náráyan Ráo was with child. The ministers proclaimed the event during Raghobá's absence. He was defeated and fled to Surat.

**Rahim Beg, Mirza,** رحيم بيگ مرزا of Sardhána, author of a small work on Persian and Arabic poetry, entitled "Makhzan Shuárá" which he composed in the year 1852 A. D., 1268 A. H. It is also called "Wasílat-ush-Shuárá."

**Rahia,** راحيه, one of the earliest professors of Muhammadanism, although he was not present at the battle of Badar. Muhammad used to say of him, that of all men he had ever seen Rahia did most resemble the angel Gabriel. He died in the year 670 A. D., 50 A. H.

**Rahim-uddin Bakht, Mirza,** رحيم الدين بخت مرزا and Mirzá Muhsin Bakht (princes of Dehli and grandsons of Sháh Alam) who came to Ágrah from Benares when the Duke of Edinburgh came to Ágrah in 1870 A. D.

**Rahmat-ullah,** رحمت الله, author of the history of the martyr Malik 'Umar, who is buried at Bahráich. He composed this poem 750 years after the death of the saint.

**Raiha,** رايحه, poetical name of Mír Muhammad 'Alí of Sayálkót who died in 1737 A. D., 1150 A. H.

**Raja,** راجه, poetical title of Rájá Balwán Singh, son of Rájá Cheyt Singh of Benares. He is a pensioner of the British Government, and is living at Ágrah, and is the author of a Díwán in Urdú.

**Raja Ali Khan, Faruki,** راجه علي خان فاروقي, succeeded his brother Mírán Muhammad Khán II, in the Government of Khándesh in 1576 A. D. At this period the princes of Hindústán, from Bengal to Sindh including Málwá and Gujrát, had been subdued by the victorious arms of the emperor Akbar; and Rájá 'Alí Khán, in order to avoid so unequal a contest, dropped the title of king, which his brother had assumed, and wrote a letter to Akbar, begging that he might be considered as his vassal and tributary. In order to convince him of his sincerity, he sent him many rich and valuable presents. After the death of Burhán Nizám Sháh II, king of Aḥmadnagar in the year 1596 A. D., 1004 A. H., the prince Mirzá Murád and Mirzá Khán KhánKhánán the son of Bairám Khán, marched for the purpose of subduing the Dakhin. Rájá 'Alí Khán accompanied them, and was killed with many officers of distinction, by the explosion of a powder tumbril, in the famous battle fought between KhánKhánán and Suheil Khán, general of the Aḥmadnagar forces. His death happened on the 26th January 1597 A. D., 18th Jumáda II, 1005 A. H. after he had reigned 21 years. His body was carried to Burhánpúr, where he was buried with due honours. He was succeeded by his son Bahádur Khán Farúḳí.

**Rajab Salar,** رجب سالار, brother of Tughlaḳ Sháh, and father of Sulṭán Fíróz Sháh, king of Dehlí. His tomb is in Bahraich.

**Raja Kans Purbi,** راجه کنس پوربي, a Hindú zamíndár who succeeded in placing himself on the throne of Bengal after the death of Shams-uddín II Púrbí in 1386 A. D., and became the founder of a new dynasty. He reigned seven years and died in 1392 A. D., 795 A. H., and was succeeded by his son Jítmal who became a Musalmán, and assumed the name of Jalál-uddín.

**Raja Ram,** راجه رام, the brother of Sambhájí the Marhaṭṭa chief by another mother. He succeeded his brother in July 1689 A. D. On his accession Sambhájí in April 1680, was seized and sent to reside in one of the forts of the Karnatic, with a decent appanage, but without any power in the government, and there he continued to reside till the death of his brother (July 1689) when he was acknowledged his successor. In his time the fortress of Sitára was taken by 'Álamgír on the 21st April, 1700 A. D., 13th Ẕil-Ḳá'da 1111 A. H., but before it fell, Rájá Rám died of the small-pox the same year at Jhinjí. He was succeeded by his son Karan, who survived him but a few days, when another son of his, named Seiwa an infant only two years old was put on the masnad under the guardianship of Rám Chánd Paṇdit and regency of his mother, Tárá Báí. But when, after the death of 'A'lamgír, Rájá Sáhú or Sáhjí II, was released from confinement, he was put aside, and Sáhjí was crowned at Sitára in March 1708 A. D.

*List of Rájás.*

Rájás of Berar or Nágpúr, *vide* Raghojí Bhosla I.
„ of Chittour and Nágpúr, *vide* Ráná Sanka or Máldeo Ráo.
„ of Gwáliar, *vide* Ránojí Scindhia.
„ of Jaipúr or Jainagar, *vide* Bihárí Mal or Sandhal dewa.
„ of Málwá or Indor of the Holkar family, *vide* Malhár Ráo I.
„ of Márwár or Jodhpúr, *vide* Jodhá Ráo and Máldeo Ráo.
„ of Bhartpúr, *vide* Chúraman Jáṭ.
„ of Sitára, *vide* Sáhjí.
„ of Indor *vide* Malhár Ráo Holkar I.

**Raj Indar Goshain,** راج اندر گوسائین, chief of a sect of Hindú ascetics who used to go about stark naked. He had under his command an army of those people, and was employed by Nawáb Safdar Jang. He was killed in the battle fought by his employer against the emperor Aḥmad Sháh who had dismissed him from his office of wizárat. His death took place on the 20th June, 1753 A. D., 17th Shábán, 1166 A. H.

**Raj Singh Kuchhwaha, Raja,** راج سنگه کچهواها, son of Rájá Askaran, brother of Rájá Bihárí Mal. Served under the emperors Akbar and Jahángír, and died in the year 1615 A. D., 1024 A. H.

**Raj Singh, Rana,** رانا راج سنگه, of Chittour and Udaipúr, succeeded his father Ráná Jagat Singh 1652 A. D., 1062 A. H., and was honoured by the emperor Sháh Jahán with the rank of 5000. In his time the fort of Chittour was demolished by order of the emperor 'A'lamgír. He died in the 24th year of that monarch, 1680 A. D., 1091 A. H., and was succeeded by his son Ráná Jai Singh.

**Raju Ḳattal,** راجو قتال, surnamed Sayyad Sado-uddín a Musalmán saint and brother of Makhdúm Jahánián Jahán Gasht Shaikh Jalál. He is the author of the "Tuhfat-un-Nasayeh," which contains much good advice though written according to the Súfí School. His tomb is at Uchcha in Multán where he died in the year 1403 A. D., 806 A. H.

**Rajwara,** راجواره, name of a place at A'grah built by several Rájás, such as Rájá Jaswant Singh, Rájá Jai Singh, Rájá Mán Singh, Rájá Bharath, Rájá Bohar Singh, Rájá Beattal Dás son of Rájá Gopál Dás, Rájá Dwárka Dás and others, they built their house at A'grah at a place which is now called (Mauza Rájwára).

**Ramai** or **Rami,** رامی, *vide* Sharaf-uddín Rámí.

**Ram Charan Mahant,** رام چرن مهنت, the founder of the Rámsanehí sect, was a Rámáwant Bairágí, born 1719 A. D. in a village in the principality of Jaipúr. Neither the precise period, nor the causes which led him to abjure the religion of his fathers now appear: but he steadily denounced idol-worship, and suffered on this account great persecution from the Bráhmans. On quitting the place of his nativity in 1750 A. D., he wandered over the country, and eventually repaired to Bhílwáṛa, in the Udaipúr territory, where, after a residence of two years, Bhím Singh, Ráná or prince of that state, was urged by the priests to harass him to a degree which compelled him to abandon the town. The chief of Sháhpúra offered the wanderer an asylum at his court, where he arrived in the year 1767 A. D., but he does not seem to have settled there permanently until two years later, from which time, it may be proper to date the institution of the sect. Rám Charan expired in April, 1798 A. D., in the 79th year of his age, and his corpse was reduced to ashes in the great temple at Sháhpúra. Rám Charan composed 36,250 Sabds or hymns, each containing from five to eleven verses. He was succeeded in the spiritual directorship by Rámjan, one of his twelve disciples. This person died at Sháhpúra in 1809 A. D. after a reign of 12 years 2 months and 6 days. He composed 18,000 Sabds. The third hierach Dulhá Rám succeeded him and died in 1824 A. D. He wrote 10,000 Sabds, and about 4000 Sakí, or epic poems, in praise of men eminent for virtue not only of his own faith, but among Hindús, Muhammadans and others. After him Chatra Dás ascended the gaddí, and died in 1831 A. D. He is said to have composed 1000 Sabds, but would not permit their being committed to paper. Náráyan Dás the fourth in descent from Rám Charan, succeeded him and was living in 1835 A. D. See *Journal Asiatic Society of Bengal*, Vol. 4, page 65.

**Ramdeo,** رامديو, a Rájá of Deogír (now Daulatábád) became a tributary to Sulṭán 'Alá-uddín Sikandar Sání, and died in the year 1310 A. D., 710 A. H.

**Ramin,** رامین, a lover, the name of whose mistress was Waisa. Their story, entitled "Rámín and Waisa" has been written in Persian poetry by Nizámí 'Urúzí.

**Ramjas Munshi,** منشي رام جس, whose poetical name was Muḥíṭ, was a Khattrí by caste, and his father Lálá Gangá Bishun whose poetical title was 'A'jiz, resided at Láhor, but Muḥíṭ was born in Dehlí. He obtained an appointment in the Customs Department at Benares which gave him 1,200 rupees a year. He is the author of several Masnawís, such as "Muḥíṭ-i-'Ishḳ," "Muḥíṭ-i-Dard," "Muḥíṭ-i-Gha'm," &c. He also translated some books on mysticism from the Sanskrit, as "Muḥíṭ-ul-Ḥaḳáiḳ," "Muḥíṭ-ul-Asrár," "Gulshán-i-Ma'rifat," "Muḥíṭ Ma'rifat," &c.

**Ramji,** رامجي, son of Rájá Bhagwán Dás the uncle of the celebrated Rájá Mán Singh. He, together with his two brothers, Bijai Rám and Sayám Rám, was crushed to death under the feet of an elephant by order of the emperor Jahángír in the early part of his reign.

**Ram Mohan Rae,** رام موهن راى, afterwards Rájá Rám Mohan Ráe, a Bráhman of a respectable family in Bengal, whose birth and mission are briefly stated in Maunder's Biographical Treasury, was early celebrated for his precocious genius, high linguistic attainments, and other natural gifts which in his after-life procured for him the reputation of a reformer. Among several other reforms, the degenerate state of Hindúism demanded his earliest attention, and he with his wonted zeal and assiduity, took upon himself to introduce a reform which at the risk of his purse and reputation, he succeeded in a great measure in affecting among his former co-religionists. His object was to reconstruct and varnish the old Hindúism, and not to abandon it altogether as some of the modern pseudo-reformers propose. He picked up morals and precepts from the Vedas, Dussanas and Upanishads, which he thought most appropriate and instructive; but never accepted them as revelations. He likewise borrowed rules and precepts from other religions, but more particularly from Christianity. His originality of mind, his natural logical powers, his mastery of mental and moral philosophy, and above all his ardent desire to establish the true knowledge of God among his countrymen, made him discard all the prevailing religions of the world as revelations. When in England, the Rájá always attended the Unitarian church and much approved of its doctrines. He embarked for England and arrived at Liverpool on the 8th April, 1831 A. D. and died at Stapylton Grove near Bristol, while on a visit to that country, for the purpose of giving information and of promoting the interests of his countrymen, by advocating a more liberal intercourse with India. After his death his followers in Bengal strictly adhered to the faith, and multiplied in number by thousands. The works of Sir W. Hamilton and Bishop Berkeley have also become their guides in points of philosophy. In a word the Brahmists are not idolaters, as considered by some, nor infidels as supposed by many. They are rather the religious and enlightened people of the age as they consider themselves. Rájá Rám Mohan translated the Upanishads of the Yajur Veda according to the Comment of Sankar A'chárya, into English, establishing the unity and incomprehensibility of the Supreme Being, whose worship alone can tend to eternal beatitude. A translation of the Vedant (an abridgment of all the sacred writings) in Hindústání and Bengalí, was made by this Hindú philosopher and philanthropist. The Rájá also published an abstract of it in English. His tomb is in Arno's Vale cemetery in Bristol.

**Ramraj,** رام‌راج, a Rájá of Bíjánagar or Bijaiánagar, who was slain in battle against the four Muhammadan princes of the Dakhin. This celebrated action took place on the banks of the Krishna river on Friday the 25th of January 1565 A. D., 20th Jumáda II, 972 A. H. It cost Rámráj his life, and ended in the defeat of the Hindú army with the loss of nearly one hundred thousand men. Rámráj being defeated, was taken prisoner and brought before Husain Nizám Sháh who ordered his head to be struck off, and caused it to be placed on the point of a long spear to be announced to the army; and afterwards kept at Bíjápúr as a trophy.

**Ram Narayan, Raja,** رام نا راین. He was deputy governor of Patna in the time of Mír Ja'far 'Alí Khán the Nawáb of Bengal. Mír Kásim 'Alí, on his accession to the masnad in 1760 A. D., 1174 A. H. having detected embezzlements of large sums from the revenues, the jágírs, and pay of the troops, confiscated his effects. About seven lacs of rupees in money and goods were found in his house, and nearly the same sum was recovered from persons to whom it had been entrusted by himself and his women. He was then kept in confinement with several others on suspicion. In August 1763 A. D., Muharram, 1177 A. H., a few days before Mír Kásim 'Alí's defeat by the English on the banks of the Udwa nala, he commanded these persons to be put to death, and Rájá Rám Náráyan was drowned in the Ganges with a bag of sand tied round his neck. Rám Náráyan was a Persian scholar and wrote poetry in Persian and Urdú, having adopted the word "Mauzún" for his poetical name.

**Ramraja,** رام‌راجه, succeeded Sáhjí II as Rájá of Sitára in December, 1749 A. D. He was the adopted son of Sáhjí and grandson of Tárá Báí. He died on the 12th December, 1777 A. D., having a short time before his death adopted Abba Sáhib the son of Trimbakjí Bhosla. This adopted son was formally enthroned under the title of Sáhú, but was always kept a close prisoner by the Peshwá.

**Ram Singh,** رام سنگه, present Rájá of Kótá and Búndí (1858 A. D.).

**Ram Singh Hara,** رام سنگه هاڑا, and Dalpat Ráo Bundela, two Hindú chiefs who served under the emperor 'Álamgír in the military capacity, and were both killed at the same instant by a cannon shot in the battle which ensued between 'Azim Sháh and his eldest brother Bahádur Sháh, on the 8th of June, 1707 A. D., 18th Rabí' I, 1119 A. H.

**Ram Singh, Munshi,** رام سنگه منشي, author of a collection of letters entitled "Gulshan Ajáeb," written in 1716 A. D., 1128 A. H.

**Ram Singh Rathor,** رام سنگه راتهور, son of Abhai Singh, Rájá of Jodhpúr. He poisoned Bakhat Singh his uncle, and usurped the throne. At his death 1773 A. D., disorganization prevailed in Márwár, promoted by the Marhattas, who then got footing in Rájpútána, and by the evils generated by its feudal institutions. At Tonga, however, the Rathors defeated De Boigne, the celebrated general of Scindhia; but they were crushed at the subsequent battles of Pátan and Mairta by the reigning prince Bijai Singh.

**Ram Singh I,** رام سنگه راجه, Rájá of Jaipúr, he was honoured after the death of his father Rájá Jai Singh I, by the emperor 'Álamgír in 1666 A. D. with the title of Rájá, and put in possession of his father's territories. His son Bishun Singh succeeded him after his death about the year 1675 A. D.

**Ram Singh Sawai II,** رام سنگه سوائی, present Rájá of Jaipúr, son of Jai Singh III, was born a few months before the death of his father whom he succeeded in January, 1834 A. D. He became a member of the Governor General's Council in 1869 A. D.

**Ranas of Chittour and Udaipur,** رانا. *Vide* Ráná Sanká.

**Rana Amar Singh,** رانا امر سنگه, the son of Ráná Partáp Singh of Chittour. He rebelled against the emperor Jahángír for some time, but was at last compelled by force of arms to acknowledge fealty to the throne of Dehlí. The emperor ordered to be cut in marble, the images of Amar Singh and his son Karan, which, when finished and brought to him, he took to Ágrah and placed in the garden-seat, called *Jharokha Darshan,* where the people assembled every morning to pay their respects to the emperor. Amar Singh died in 1619 A. D., 1029 A. H., but the images were cut while he was living.

**Rana Karan,** رانا کرن, son of Amar Singh, the son of Ráná Partáp Singh, the son of Ráná Udai Singh the son of Ráná Sanká. He succeeded his father Amar Singh in the ráj of Udaipúr 1619 A. D., and died in the first year of the reign of Sháh Jahán, 1628 A. D., when his son Ráná Jagat Singh succeeded him, and was honoured by the emperor with the title of Ráná and rank of 5000. Jagat Singh died 1652 A. D. and was succeeded by his son Ráj Kúnwar, who received the title of Ráná Ráj Singh.

**Rana Mal,** رانا مل, a Rájá of Bhatner who lived in the reign of Sultán Ghayás-uddín Tughlak. His daughter named Naila, was married to Sálár Rájab the brother of the Sultán and father of Sultán Fíroz Sháh Tughlak.

**Rana Raj Singh of Chittour,** رانا راج سنگه, *vide* Ráj Singh (Ráná).

**Rana Sanga** or **Sanka,** رانا سانکا, Rájá of Chittour. His son Udai Singh is the founder of the capital Udaipúr. The Udaipúr chief is, in the estimation of all the Hindú dynasties of India, *par excellence* the head, without a rival and free from stain. It is true that the independence of the "great Ránás of Chittour" was assailed by the Moguls, and that they succumbed to circumstances; but they never acknowledged a superior in birth or descent. The family dates back upwards of a thousand years. It was in 1614 A. D., in the reign of the emperor Jahángír, that the house was first compelled by force of arms to surrender that complete independence it had then maintained for eight hundred years, and to acknowledge fealty to the throne of Dehlí. In 1512 we first hear of the renowned Ráná Sangá of Chittour. His army consisted of 80,000 horse, supported by 500 war elephants. Seven Rájás of the highest rank, and a hundred and thirteen of inferior note attended his stirrup in the field. The Rájás of Jaipúr and Márwár served under his banner, and he was the acknowledged head of all the Rájpút tribes. In 1527 A. D. he espoused the cause of the dethroned dynasty of Dehlí. All the princes of Rájpútána ranged themselves under his banner, and he advanced with 100,000 men to drive Babar across the Indus. The first conflict took place at Biana where the advanced guard of the Moguls was totally routed by the Rájpúts. In 1568 A. D. Udai Singh, the son of Ráná Sangá, came under the displeasure of Akbar. He fled and left the defence of his capital Chittour to Rájá Jaimal who was killed by Akbar himself. His death deprived the garrison of all confidence, and they determined to sell their lives as dear as possible. The women threw themselves on the funeral pile of the Rájá, and the men rushed frantically on the weapons of the Moguls and perished to the number of 8000. In 1614 Partáp Singh reigned and recovered the greater portion of his dominion before Akbar died. In 1678 A. D., Aurangzíb marched against Udaipúr and succeeded in subjugating it, but the alienation of the Rájpúts from the Moguls was now complete, and never changed. The great boast of the chiefs of Udaipúr is, that their house never gave a daughter to the Mogul zanana. Jaipúr and Jodhpúr did, and gloried in these imperial alliances as conferring additional dignity on their families.

*List of the Ránás of Udaipúr.*

| | | A. D. |
|---|---|---|
| Ráná Sánká .......................... | died | 1528 |
| „ Udai Singh, son of Ráná Sánká .... | „ | |
| „ Partáp Singh, son of Udai Singh .... | „ | 1594 |
| „ Amar Singh, son of Partáp Singh .... | „ | 1619 |
| „ Karan, son of Amar Singh, embellished Udaipúr .................. | | |
| „ Jagat Singh, son of Ráná Karan, tributary to Sháh Jahán, .......... | „ | 1652 |
| „ Ráj Singh, son of Jagat Singh ...... | „ | 1680 |
| „ Jai Singh, son of Ráj Singh. | | |
| „ Amar Singh II. | | |
| „ Sangram Singh. | | |
| „ Jagat II pays chouth to the Marhattas. | | |

**Ranbir Singh, Maharaja,** مہاراجہ رنبیر سنگہ, the present independent ruler of Kashmír, is the son of Mahárájá Guláb Singh whom he succeeded about the month of July or August, 1857 A. D.

**Ranchhor Das,** رنچہور داس, a learned Káyeth of Jaunpúr, and author of a work on the art of writing prose and poetry, entitled "Dakáek-ul-Inshá," which he wrote in the year 1732 A. D., 1145 A. H.

**Randhir Singh,** رندہیر سنگہ, the Ját Rájá of Bhartpúr, was the eldest son of Ranjít Singh whom he succeeded. After his death, his brother Baldeo Singh ascended the Masnad of Bhartpúr.

**Randhir Singh, Raja,** رندہیر سنگہ, of Kapúrthalla, is the son of the Alúwala chieftain near Jalandhar, in the Panjáb who claimed equal rank with Mahárájá Ranjít Singh, but whose fortune diminished as that of his rival increased. During the disturbances of 1857 A. D., he rendered excellent service to the State in and around Jalandhar, for which he has been rewarded, though with no very liberal hand.

**Rana of Jhansi,** رانا جهنشي, *vide* Gangá Báí.

**Rangin,** رنگین, takhallus of Sa'ádat Yár Khán, who is the author of a poem called "Mehr-wa-Máh," a story of the Sayyad's son, and the jeweller's daughter who lived at Dehlí in the reign of Jahángír. He is also the author of several Díwáns and also a curious Díwán in Urdu rather indecent, in which he has brought in all the phrases of the women of the seraglio of Dehlí and Lakhnau. He died in October, 1835 A. D., Jumáda II, 1251 A. H., aged 80 years.

**Ranjit Singh,** رنجیت سنگہ, the Ját Rájá of Bhartpúr, was the son of Kehrí Singh, the brother of Ratan Singh and Jawáhir Singh, the sons of Súrajmal Ját, the founder of the principality. He succeeded his uncle Rájá Nawáb Singh in 1776 A. D., 1190 A. H. He was despatched by Scindhia to raise the siege of Ágrah, near which a bloody battle was fought on the 16th of June, 1788 A. D., 12th Ramazán, 1202 A. H., in which Ismá'íl Beg was completely defeated, with the loss of all his cannon, baggage, and stores. He was succeeded by his son Randhír Singh.

**Ranjit Singh, Maharaja,** مہاراجہ رنجیت سنگہ, the Sikh ruler of the Panjáb and faithful and highly-valued ally of the British Government, was the son of Mahá Singh, born 1780 A. D., 1255 A. H., and established Láhor independency in 1805 A. D. At his death which happened on the 27th June, 1839, minute-guns to the number of 60 corresponding with the years of the deceased were fired from the ramparts of the forts of Dehlí, Ágrah, Allahábád and all the principal stations of the army. Four of his Ránís and seven slave girls burnt themselves with his corpse. He was succeeded in the Ráj by his eldest son Kharag Singh.

*The following are the names of his successors.*

| | A. D. |
|---|---|
| Kharag Singh, son of Ranjít Singh, died 5th November .................................. | 1840 |
| Nounihál Singh, son of Kharag Singh, died 17th November .................................. | 1840 |
| Ráni Chanda Kúnwar, widow of Kharag Singh. | |
| Sher Singh, brother of Kharag Singh, .. murdered | 1843 |
| Dalíp Singh, a son of Ranjít Singh in whose time the Panjáb was annexed to the British Government 1846 A. D. He was baptized 8th March, 1853 A. D., and in now living in England. | |

**Ranoji Scindhia,** رانوجي سیندهیه, the founder of the Scindhia family of Gwáliar was born at Patílí near Púna, and served first under a chief, who commanded the body-guard of Bájí Ráo the first Peshwá. From this inferior station he gradually rose, and afterwards accompanied the Peishwá in the expedition which was undertaken at the close of the reign of Rájá Sahújí against the province of Málwá. This province was afterwards divided into three parts, of which the first was allotted to Bájí Ráo the Peshwá; the second to the Rájá of Sitára, the third to the family of Holkar. As a reward for the services which Ránójí rendered in the expedition against Málwá, the Peshwá granted a considerable portion of the shares belonging to himself and to the Rájá of Sitára to Ránójí; which grant was afterwards confirmed in jágír to his descendants, now the Rájás of Gwáliar. He died in 1750 A. D., and left five sons, *viz.*, Jiápá, Jotíba, Dattájí,

Madhójí and Jokají. Jíápá succeeded his father and was assassinated in his tent in 1759 A. D.; his brother Mádhójí succeeded him, and although illegitimate, was confirmed in the jágír by Mádhó Ráo Peshwá. He was the most powerful of the native princes of that day. He died at Púná in 1794 A. D. and was succeeded by his grandnephew and adopted son Daulat Ráo Scindhia then only 13 years of age. He married Bájí Bái and died on the 21st of March, 1827 A. D.

*List of the Scindhia family, now Rájás of Gwáliar.*

| | Began | died |
|---|---|---|
| Ránójí Scindhia the first of the race ...... | 1724 | 1750 |
| Jíápá, son of Ránójí .................. | 1750 | 1759 |
| Mádhojí or Mahájí Scindhia, brother of Jíápá, | 1759 | 1794 |
| Daulat Ráo Scindhia, son of Anand Ráo and adopted son of Mádhojí (who fixed his camp at Gwáliar in 1817) .......... | 1794 | 1827 |
| Bájí Bái, his widow who adopted Jhankójí and acted as regent .................. | 1827 | |
| Jhankójí, assumed the reins of government | 1833 | 1843 |
| Jíájí Scindhia, adopted son of Jhankójí .... | 1843 | |

**Ranoji Bhosla,** رانوجي بهوسله, *vide* Jánójí Bhóslá.

**Rao Bahadur Singh,** راو بهادر سنگه, a petty rájá of the Doáb of the Gújar tribe of Rájpúts and ruler of Ghás-hera and Koel, nominally dependant on Dehlí. The Nawáb Safdar Jang in one of his contests had been deserted by Ráo Bahádur Singh, whose punishment was entrusted by the emperor, to Súraj Mal Ját, with the grant of all the lands and castles he might wrest from his opponent. He performed the duty triumphantly. Bahádur Singh was killed in the siege of Ghás-hera, and that and Koel acknowledged the sovereignty of the Ját prince. These events occurred in 1753 A. D., and form an episode in the "Suján Cherittra," a heroic poem.

**Rao Dalip** or **Dalpat Rao Bundela,** راو دليپ, *vide* Rám Singh Háṛá.

**Rao Amar Singh,** راو عمار سنگه, whose daughter was married to Sulaiman Shikoh.

**Rao Raj Singh Rathor** راو راج سنگه راٹهور. He commanded the advanced body of the army of the emperor 'Álamgír in the Dakhin. He died about the year 1675 A. D., 1086 A. H.

**Rao Jodha (Rathor),** راو جدهو, of Jodhpúr. He had 23 brothers who had separate fiefs. He founded Jodhpúr, and removed from Mandor, about the year 1458 A. D.

**Rao Maldeo,** راو مالديو, *vide* Máldeo Ráo.

**Rao Ratan Singh,** راو رتن سنگه, a rájá of Bhartpúr, *vide* Ratan Singh.

**Rao Ratan Singh Hara,** راو رتن سنگه هارا, son of Ráo Bhój Háṛá, the son of Ráo Sarjan Háṛá, Rájá of Búndí. He succeeded his father in the ráj about the year 1607 A. D., 1016 A. H. The rank of 5,000 was conferred on him by Jahángír with the title of Sarbaland Háṛá, and subsequently with that of Rámráj. He died 1630 A. D., 1040 A. H.

**Rasa,** رسا, poetical name of Mirzá Eizid Bakhsh, which see.

**Rashid,** رشيد, or Ibn Raschid or Averroes, *vide* Ibn-Rashíd.

**Rashid Pasha,** رشيد پشاه, a celebrated Turkish Statesman, was born at Constantinople about 1800 A. D. Though a Turk, he was one of the most enlightened men of his time, and was well-versed in foreign languages, general literature and science. He died 7th January, 1858 A. D.

**Rashidi of Samarkand,** رشيدي سمرقندي, or of Balkh, surnamed Watwát, a poet celebrated for his ready wit and smallness of stature. He was a descendant of 'Umar Khattáb and a native of Balkh, but brought up at Samarḳand. He flourished in the time of Sultán Atsiz son of Khwárizm Sháh one of the Sulṭáns of Khwárizm. He was a contemporary of Anwarí, and was in the fort of Hazár Asp, while besieged by Sultán Sanjar, in whose service Anwarí was. During the seige the two poets wrote very severe satires against the parties of each other, which they exchanged by means of arrows; but the fort being at length taken, Watwát was made prisoner. He was, however, released at the intercession of Anwarí, and they both became intimate friends. He was called Watwát, which is the name of a small animal, on account of his being of a small stature and thin in body. He died in the year 1182 A. D., 578 A. H., in the time of Sultán Sháh the son of Arsalán, the son of Atsiz, aged 97 years, at Jurjánia in Khwárizm. He is the author of the "Misbáh Sharíf," an extensive collection of poems on various subjects, and different metres, also of several other works, one of which is called "Hadáeḳ-us-Sehr." He is also called Rashíd-uddín Abdul Jalíl Watwát 'Umarí. His Díwán contains 15,000 verses.

**Rashid Mehrban,** رشيد مهربان, a man who was the leading Zoroastrian inhabitant of Yezd in Tehran and enjoyed the confidence of the Sháh of Persia. He was assassinated by the Musalmáns at Yezd on the 28th of November, 1874.

**Rashid-uddin Watwat,** رشيدالدين وطواط, *vide* Rashídí Samarḳandí and Watwát.

**Rashid-uddin Amir,** امير رشيدالدين, whose full name is Fazl-ulláh Rashíd-uddín-ibn-'Imád-uddaula Abú'l Khair-ibn-Mawaffiḳ-uddaula. He is the author of the "Jáma'-ut-Tawáríkh," or Collection of Histories, which he completed in 1310 A. D., 710 A. H., and deposited in the mosque constructed by him at Tabrez. He was born in the city of Hamdán in 1247 A. D., 645 A. D., was by profession a physician, and it was probably from his skill in the science of medicine that he procured office under the Tartar Sulṭáns of Persia. He passed part of his life in the service of Abá Khán, king of Persia. At a subsequent period, Gházán Khán, who was a friend to literature, appointed him to the post of Wazír in 1298 A. D., 697 A. H. in conjunction with Sa'd-uddín who became his enemy. Rashíd-uddín was maintained in his office by Aljaitú, surnamed Khudá Banda, the brother and successor of Gházán Khán, and was treated by him with great consideration and rewarded with the utmost liberality. Rashíd-uddín in his first rupture with Sa'd-uddín, was compelled in self-defence to denounce him, and to cause him to be put to death. Amír 'Alí Sháh Júbán a person of low origin, was appointed Sa'd-uddín's successor at Rashíd-uddín's request, but they soon fell out, and shortly after the death of Aljáitú who was succeeded by his son Sultán Abú Sa'íd, Amír 'Alí Sháh so far succeeded in prejudicing the Sulṭán against the old minister, that he was removed from the wizárat in 1317 A. D., 717 A. H. A short time afterwards he was recalled, but it was not long before he again lost favour at court, and was accused of causing the death of his patron Aljáitú Khán. It was charged against him that he had recommended a purgative medicine to be administered to the late king, in opposition to the advice of another physician, and that under its effects the king had expired. He was condemned to death, and his son Ibráhím, the chief butler, who was only 16 years old, and by whose hands the potion was said to have been given to the king, was put to death before the eyes of his parent, who was immediately afterwards cloven in twain by the executioner. His head was borne through the streets of Tabreiz, and proclaimed by the public crier as the head of a Jew. Rashíd-uddín was 73 years old when he died, and his death occurred on the 19th July, 1318 A. D., 17th Jumáda I, 718 A. H. His eldest son Ghayás-uddín was subsequently raised to the same dignities as his father, and met with an equally tragical death. Amír 'Alí Sháh continued by his address to maintain his high honours and the favour of his master for the space of six years when he died; being the only Wazír, since the establishment of the Mongol monarchy, who had not met with a violent death. Besides the "Jáma'-ut-Táwáríkh," Rashíd-uddín composed several other works, such as the "Kitáb-ut-Tauzíhát," "Miftáh-ut-Tafásír," and the "Risálat-us-Sultániat," *vide* Fazl-ulláh. The body of Rashíd-uddín was buried near the mosque which he had constructed in Tabrez, but by a strange fatality, it was not destined to repose quietly in this, its last asylum. Nearly a century after his death, the government of Tabreiz together with Azurbeján, was given by Taimúr to his son Míránsháh. This young prince, naturally of mild disposition, had become partially deranged in consequence of an injury of the head occasioned by a fall from his horse, and one day, during a temporary access of madness, caused the bones of Rashíd-uddín to be exhumed, and they were finally deposited in the cemetery of the Jews.

**Rashid Billah,** راشد بالله, a Khalífa of Baghdád, *vide* Al-Rashíd Billáh.

**Rashk,** رشك, poetical name of 'Alí Aosat, who is the author of a dictionary and three Urdú Díwáns, the last of which he composed in 1845 A. D., 1261 A. H.

**Rasikh,** راسخ, the poetical appellation of Mír Muhammad Zamán of Sarhind. He was a Sayyad, and a respectable officer in the service of prince 'Azim Sháh, the son of the emperor 'Alamgír. He was an excellent poet, and died in the year 1695 A. D., 1107 A. H. at Sarhind.

**Rasikh,** راسخ, the poetical title of Ghulám 'Alí of Patna, a Dervish, who died in 1824 A. D., 1240 A. H., and has left an Urdú Díwán.

**Rathor,** رتهور, a tribe of Rájpúts or Rájás, who reigned in Jodhpúr Márwár. *Vide* Máldeo.

**Ratan Singh,** رتن سنگه, also called Ráo Ratan Singh, was the second son of Súrajmal Ját. He succeeded his brother Jawáhir Singh in the ráj of Bhartpúr in 1768 A. D., 1182 A. H., and was not long after murdered by a low assassin named Rúpa Nand, who pretended to be a transmuter of metals, and whom the Rájá had threatened with death. Ratan Singh reigned ten months and thirteen days, and left an infant son named Kehrí Singh, during whose minority, internal commotions, occasioned by contests for the regency, principally contributed to the success of Najaf Khán with whom the Játs were then at war. Kehrí Singh dying was succeeded by his uncle Nawal Singh, the brother of Ratan Singh.

**Raughani,** روغني, a jester in the service of the emperor Akbar. He is the author of a Díwán consisting of 3,000 verses. He appears to have died in Kábul in the country of the Káfirs in 1573 A. D., 981 A. H. The following chronogram on his death expresses the estimation in which he was held by his contemporaries: "He has given his life in Káfiristán like a dog."

**Rayah** رايح, poetical name of Mír Muhammad 'Alí, a Persian poet.

**Rayazi of Hirat,** رياضي هروى, an author and poet who flourished in the time of Sháh Ismá'íl I Safwí. He left a Masnawí of 8,000 verses containing an account of the reign of Sultán Husain Mirzá of Hirát, and had begun a poem on the exploits of Sháh Ismá'íl, but did not finish it. He died in 1515 A. D., 921 A. H.

**Rayazi of Samarkand,** رياضي سمرقندى, an author who died in 1479 A. D., 884 A. H.

**Raymond, General,** رايمند, a French chief in the service of the Nizám of Haidarábád. He died in the middle of the year 1798 A. D., and was succeeded by General Perron.

**Raza, Imam,** امام رضا, *vide* 'Alí Músí Razá.

**Raza Kuli Mirza,** رضا قلي مرزا, the eldest son of Nádir Sháh. He was blinded by his father in 1741 A. D., 1154 A. H.

**Razi, Maulana,** رضي نيشاپورى, of Naishápúr, a poet, whose proper name is Razí-uddín Muhammad, and who instead of writing his takhallus in his Díwán, usually writes "Banda." He died in 1202 A. D., 598 A. H., and is the author of a work on Jurisprudence, entitled "Muhít."

**Razi, Shaikh,** شيخ رضي, *vide* Shaikh Razí.

**Razi,** راضي, poetical title of Fasáhat Khán who flourished about the year 1700 A. D., 1112 A. H., and is the author of a Díwán and a Masnawí.

**Razi,** رازى, takhallus of Muhammad-bin-Zikaria, who assumed the poetical name of Rází, because he was a native of the city of Rái. He was one of the first physicians of the Khalífa Muktadir Billáh, and a great philosopher and astronomer. He died in the year 922 A. D., 311 A. H., and is the author of several works: one of which is called "Al-Háwí" or "Al-Háwí fi'l Tibb" which he wrote from the Sanskrit.

**Razi,** رازى, poetical name of Mír 'Askarí, entitled 'Akil Khán, the Wazír of the emperor 'Alamgír, *vide* 'Akil Khán (Nawáb).

**Razi Billah,** راضي بالله, *vide* Al-Rází Billáh.

**Razi-uddin 'Ali Lala,** رضي الدين, *vide* 'Alí Lálá.

**Razi-uddin Muhammad-bin-'Ali Shatibi,** رضي الدين محمد بن علي شاطبي, an Arabian author, who died 1285 A. D., 684 A. H.

**Razi-uddin Naishapuri,** رضي الدين, *vide* Rázi (Maulana) Rází-uddín Muhammad.

**Razia Sultana,** رضية سلطانة, a queen of Dehlí, *vide* Sultána Rázía.

**Rihai,** رهائي, poetical name of a poet, who is the author of a Díwán. He died in the year 1572 A. D., 980 A. H.

**Rihi,** رهي, poetical name of Majd-uddín Hamkar Fársí, which see.

**Rihi,** رهي, author of a collection of poems on religious subjects entitled "Durr-i-Aḳáed."

**Rijai,** رجائي, poetical name of Hasan 'Alí, a native of Hirat, who died in the year 1558 A. D., 965 A. H.

**Rind,** رند, poetical name of Sayyad Muhammad Khán, son of Mirzá Ghayás-uddín Muhammad Khán, Bahádur Nasrat Jang, who died in the year 1813 A. D., 1228 A. H., at Lakhnau. Rind is the author of a Díwán in Urdú. He was living in 1850 A. D., 1267 A. H.

**Rind,** رند پوتيكا, poetical name of Jání Mánkí Lál a Kayeth of Dehlí. He is the author of a small Díwán in Persian which he published in the year 1851 A. D.

**Rizk-ullah, Shaikh,** شيخ رزق الله, whose poetical name is Mushtákí, was the uncle of Shaikh 'Abdul Haḳ bin-Saif-uddín of Dehlí, and brother of Shaikh Núr-ul-Haḳ's grandfather, Shaikh Núr-ul-Haḳ being the son of 'Abdul Haḳ. Rizḳ-ulláh is the author of a history called "Wáka'át Mushtáḳí," written by him in the reign of Sultán Sikandar. He was a Persian as well as a Hindí poet. In Persian compositions he used "Mushtáḳí" for his poetical title, and in Hindí, "Rájan;" and he is also the author of a work in Hindí which he called "Jót Niranjan." He was born in the year 1495 A. D., 901 A. H., and died in 1561 A. D., 969 A. H. He had eight brothers, all of whom were men of learning.

**Roshan 'Ara Begam,** روشن ارا بيگم, the youngest daughter of Sháhjahán. She died about the year 1669 A. D., 1080 A. H., and is buried at Sháhjahánábád in her own garden called the Garden of Roshan 'Ará.

**Roshan-uddaula Rustam Jang,** روشن الدولة رستم جنگ, whose proper name was Zafar Khán, was a nobleman of the reign of Muhammad Sháh. He is the founder of the Sonahrí Masjid (golden mosque) at Dehlí, situated near the Kótwálí Chabútra, and built in the year 1722 A. D., 1134 A. H. Another mosque or college called the Masjid of Róshan-uddaula, situated in the vicinity of Káziwara at Dehlí which he had inlaid all over with gold, was built by him in 1725 A. D., 1137 A. H. This is that college, on the roof of which Nádir Sháh took post, and from whence he gave orders to slaughter the inhabitants of that city. Róshan-uddaula died in the 14th year of Muhammad Sháh 1732 A. D., 1145 A. H.

**Roshan-uddaula, Nawab,** روشن الدولة, brother to the late Nizám of Haidarábád, died of apoplexy on the 27th July, 1870 A. D.

**Rounak,** رونق, poetical name of Rám Saháe, a Hindú, who was an excellent Persian poet.

**Rounaki,** رونقي, a poet of Hamdán who died in 1622 A. D., 1031 A. H.

**Roz Afzun, Nazir,** ناظر روز افزون خواجه سرا, a celebrated Khwája Sará or eunuch of the emperor Muhammad Sháh. The garden called Bágh Názir at Sháhjahánábád, Dehlí, was built by him in the year 1748 A. D., 1161 A. H.

**Roz Bihan, Shaikh,** شيخ روزبهان, surname of Abú Muhammad ibn-Abí Nasr-al-Baḳilí, a learned and pious Musalmán who is the author of the commentary on the Ḳurán called "Tafsír Aráesh," "Safwat-al-Masháríb," and several other works. He died in July, 1209 A. D., Muharram 606 A. H., *vide* Abú Muhammad Róz Bihán.

**Rudaki,** رودكي, a celebrated Persian poet and musician who flourished in the reign of Amír Nasr the son of Ahmad Sámání; and though born blind, soon attained, from the superiority of his genius, the highest rank at the court of that liberal ruler. History, indeed, gives no instance of a poet so honoured. His establishment was raised by Nasr to a level with that of the proudest nobles: and we may conjecture the style in which Rudakí lived, when assured that he was served by two hundred slaves, and that his equipment was conveyed, when he attended his patron in the field, by four hundred camels. He turned the Arabic translation of Pilpay's Fables into modern Persian verse in 925 A. D., 313 A. H., and received from his royal master a reward of 40,000 dirhams. He is the first who wrote a Díwán or book of Odes in Persian. His original name is Faríd-uddín 'Abú 'Abdulláh, but he assumed the title of Rudakí from Rudak the place of his birth in Samarkand or Bukhárá. His death happened in the year 954 A. D., 343 A. H.

**Ruhani, Amir,** امير روحاني, a most learned poet and philosopher. He was a native of Samarḳand and a pupil of Rashídí. He fled from Bukhárá, after that city was taken by Changez Khán about the year 1226 A. D., 623 A. H., and sought protection at Dehlí in the reign of Sultán Altimsh, where he wrote many excellent poems.

**Ruhi Baghdadi,** روحي بغدادي, a Turkish poet of celebrity. His satires are very forcible and striking, and his manner not unlike that of Juvenal.

**Ruhi,** روحي, poetical name of Sayyad Ja'far of Zánbírpúr. He died in the year 1741 A. D., 1154 A. H., *vide* Sayyad Ja'far.

**Ruhul Amin Khan, Shaikh,** شيخ روح الامين خان, son of Ḳází Muhammad Sa'íd of Bilgram. He was related to Shaikh Aláh Yár Khán the martyr, whose sister he married. He was an excellent poet and wrote a poem containing 7,000 verses. He held the rank of 6,000 with a jágír and 2,000 sawárs. He acted as deputy to Nawáb Sipahdár Khán, and after his death to Nawáb Mubáriz-ul-Mulk Sarbaland Khán, Súbadár of Allahábád. He was subsequently made governor of 22 maháls in the Panjáb in the time of Muhammad Sháh, and was killed in battle against Nádir Sháh at Karnál on Tuesday the 13th of February, 1739 A. D., 15th Zi-Ḳa'da, 1151 A. H.

**Ruh-ullah Khan,** روح الله خان, an Amír who held the high office of Mír Bakhshí or Pay Master General, in the reign of the emperor 'Alamgír. He died in the Dakhin in the 36th year of the emperor, on the 8th of August, 1692 A. D., 5th Zil-hijja, 1103 A. H. After his death his son Khánazád Khán, who was grand-steward of the emperor's household and treasurer of the privy purse, was also honoured with the title of Rúh-ulláh Khán II, and died about the year 1703 A. D., 1115 A. H.

**Rukayya,** رقية, a daughter of Muhammad. She was at first married to 'Utba, the son of Abú Lahab, Muhammad's uncle, and after being divorced by him, was married to 'Usmán the son of Affán. She died about the month of March, 624 A. D., 2 A. H., a few days after the battle of Badar.

**Rukia,** سلطان رقيه, *vide* Sulṭána Rukia.

**Rukia,** رقيه, *vide* Rukayya.

**Rukia Sultana Begam,** رقيه, *vide* Sulṭána Rukia.

**Rukn Kashi, Hakim,** حكيم ركن كاشي, a physician and poet who adopted "Masíh" for his poetical name. He was a respectable attendant of the court of Sháh Abbás the Great, king of Persia, but having taken offence on some cause or other, he came to India and passed some years in the service of the emperor Akbar and his successors Jahángír and Sháh Jahán, during whose reign he went on a pilgrimage to Mecca and returning from thence to Persia, he died there some years after, in 1646 A. D., 1056 A. H., or, as some authors say, about the year 1656 A. D., 1066 A. H., and left near 100,000 verses. His nephew Rahmat Khán also called Hakím Ziyá-uddín son of Hakím Ḳutba, served under Sháh Jahán and 'Álamgír, and died about the year 1664 A. D., 1075 A. H.

**Rukn-uddin Dabir,** ركن الدين دبير, author of the "Shamáel Atkia," a record of the excellencies of the saints, and of the wonders and miracles performed by the Almighty; with an eulogium on Muhammad, dedicated to Burhán-uddín Súfí.

**Rukn-uddin Firoz, Sultan,** سلطان ركن الدين فيروز, the son of Sultán Shams-uddín Altimsh, king of Dehlí, on whose death he ascended the throne on the 1st of May, 1236 A. D., Shabán, 633 A. H., but was after six months deposed by the nobles, and his sister Sulṭána Razia was placed on the throne on the 19th of November the same year. Rukn-uddín died in confinement some time after.

**Rukn-uddin Ḳabai,** ركن الدين قبائي, a poet who was a pupil of Asír-uddín Asmání. He was a native of Ḳabai in Turkey, and cotemporary with the poet Ma'jizí.

**Rukn-uddin Masa'ud Masihi, Maulana,** مولانا ركن الدين مسعود مسيحي, author of the Arabic work on the practice of Medicine called "Zábitat-ul-Iláj." He was also a good poet and was living about the year 1585 A. D., 993 A. H.

**Rukn-uddin, Shaikh,** شيخ ركن الدين, surnamed Abú'l Fatha, a Muhammadan saint, was the son of Shaikh Sadr-uddín 'Arif and grandson of Shaikh Bahá-uddín Zikaria of Multán. He lived in the time of Sultán 'Alá-uddín Sikandar Sání about the year 1310 A. D., 710 A. H., and was a contemporary of Nizám-uddín Aulia. Shaikh Jalál, who is commonly called Makhdúm Jahánián, as well as Shaikh 'Usmán Syyáh, were his disciples.

**Rukn-uddaula,** ركن الدوله, was the brother of 'Imád-uddaula 'Alí Bóya, the founder of the race of the Bóyaites, whom he succeeded on the throne of Fars and 'Irák 949 A. D., 338 A. H. He was lord of Isfahán, Rei, Hamdán and all Persian 'Iráḳ, and father of the three princes, 'Azd-uddaula, Muwayyad-uddaula and Fakhr-uddaula, between whom he shared his possessions, which they governed with the greatest ability. He continued to reside in 'Iráḳ after the death of his brother, and gave over the charge of the affairs of Fars to his eldest son 'Azd-uddaula. Besides 'Imád-uddaula he had another brother Moiz-uddaula younger than himself, who was wazír to the Khalíf Al-Rázi Billáh and his three successors. Rukn-uddaula died at Rei on Friday night the 15th of September, 976 A. D., 18th Muḥarram, 366 A. H., and was buried in the mausoleum which bears his name at Shíráz. He is said to have reigned 44 lunar years 1 month and 9 days, *viz.*, he governed Persia during the life of his brother more than 16 years, and after his death he reigned nearly 28 years. He was succeeded by his son Muwayyad-uddaula. *Vide* 'Alí Bóya.

**Rukn-uddaula,** ركن الدوله, a minister of the Nizám of Haidarábád, who was put to death by his master about the year 1794 A. D. His subserviency to the views of the Marhaṭṭas has generally been considered one of the chief causes which induced the Nizám to put him to death.

**Rukn-uddaula Ya'tkad Khan,** ركن الدوله اعتقاد خان, whose original name was Muhammad Murád, was by birth a Kashmírian, and native of the same place as Sáhiba Niswán, mother of Farrukh-siyar. He was introduced by her to the emperor, whom he persuaded that he could easily effect the destruction of the two brother Sayyads without coming to open war, or causing confusion in the State. Farrukh-siyar, gratified by his flatteries, suddenly promoted him to the rank of 7000 with suitable jágírs and the title of Rukn-uddaula. The district of Murádábád was taken from Nizạm-ul-Mulk, and being with additional lands created into a Súbadárí, was conferred on him, but after the dethronement of Farrukh-siyar in 1719 A. D., 1131 A. H., by the Sayyads, he was disgraced, put under strict confinement, his fortune confiscated and severe tortures were also inflicted upon his person, to compel a disclosure of his wealth. He died during the reign of Muhammad Sháh.

**Rukta,** رقته, name of a place built by the emperor Akbar about ten kós from Jammagar where all his Begams and relations had built their houses as far as Gaughat. This was a park or pleasure-ground.

**Rumani,** رماني, a learned Musalmán, whose proper name was Abú'l Hasan 'Alí-bin-Ísá. He died 994 A. D., 384 A. H.

**Rup Singh, Raja,** راجه روپ سنگه, gave his daughter in marriage to Muhammad Muazzim, the son of 'Álamgír in the year 1661 A. D., 1072 A. H.

**Rustam,** رستم, a celebrated hero of Persia, whom some Persian historians call Rustam Dástán, and Rustam Zábulí because he was a native and governor of Zábulistán. This personage, who was the greatest and most famous of all Persian heroes, was the son of Zál or Zálzar, and grandson of Sám the son of Narímán. He was killed in a battle he fought against Bahman the sixth king of the dynasty of the Kayániáns.

**Rustam 'Ali, Maulana,** مولانا رستم علي, son of 'Alí 'Asghar of Ḳanauj. He is the author of the Commentary on the Ḳurán called "Tafsír Saghír." He died in 1764 A. D., 1178 A. H.

**Rustam Bastami, Khwaja Nizam-uddin,** خواجه رستم بسطامي, an author who died in 1431 A. D., 834 A. H., and appears to be the same with the following item.

**Rustam Kadd Khoziani, Khwaja,** خواجه رستم قد خوزياني, a poet who was a native of Khózián a village in Bastám, and flourished about the year 1408 A. D., 811 A. H. He was a panegyrist of Sulṭán 'Umar, son of Míránsháh, ruler of Khurásán, and a contemporary of Sháhrukh Mirzá. In the "Mirat-ul-Khayál" he is also said to be contemporary with Ibn-ul-Arabí, but this cannot be correct, for Ibn-ul-Arabí died in 1240 A. D., 638 A. H., and Sultán 'Umar and Sháhrukh lived in the early part of the ninth century of the Hijra.

**Rustam Zaman Khan,** رستم زمان خان. *Vide* Alah Yár Khán.

**Ryazi,** رياضي, *vide* Rayází.

---

# S.

**Sa'adat,** سعادت, poetical name of Mír Sa'ádat 'Alí, a resident of Amroha and pupil of Sháh Wiláyet-ulláh. He is the author of a poem called "Seilí Sakheon" containing the story of two Lovers who lived in the time of Nawáb Kamar-uddín Khán, wazír.

**Sa'adat 'Ali Khan, Nawab,** نواب سعادت علي خان, surnamed Yeman-uddaula, was raised to the masnad of Audh at Lakhnau by Sir John Shore, Governor-General, after the death of his brother Nawáb 'Asaf-uddaula and the dethronement of that Nawab's adopted son Wazír 'Alí Khán, on the 21st of January, 1798 A. D., 4th Shabán, 1212 A. H. He died after a reign of nearly 17 years on the 11th July, 1814 A. D., 22nd Rajab, 1229 A. H., and was succeeded by his son Ghází-uddín Haidar who was afterwards crowned king of Audh. In the treaty with Sa'ádat 'Alí Khán, the annual subsidy was fixed at 76 lacs of rupees and the English force in Audh at 10,000 men. The fort of Allahábád was also surrendered to the English. Twelve lacs of rupees were to be paid to the English as compensation for the expense of placing him on the masnad, and he was restrained from holding communication with any foreign state, employing any Europeans or permitting any to settle in his dominions without the consent of his British ally.

**Sa'adat Khan,** سعادت خان برهان الملك, styled Burhán-ul-Mulk, whose former name was Muhammad Amín, was originally a merchant of Khurásán. He is the progenitor of the nawábs and kings of Audh. His father Nasír Khán came to India during the reign of Bahádur Sháh, and after his death his son Muhammad Amín came also. In the commencement of the emperor, Muhammad Sháh's reign he held the faujdárí of Bayána, and was in the year 1724 A. D., 1136 A. H., appointed governor of Audh with the title of Sa'ádat Khán in the room of Rájá Girdhar who was appointed governor of Málwá. He afterwards received the title of Barhán-ul-Mulk and was present in the battle with Nádir Sháh, and died on the night previous to the massacre of Dehlí by that monarch, *i. e.*, on the 9th of March, 1739 A. D., 9th Zil-hijja, 1152 A. H., and was buried at Dehlí in the mausoleum of his brother Sayádat Khán. His only child was a daughter, who was married to his nephew Abú'l Mansúr Khán Safdar Jang the son of Sayádat Khán who succeeded him in the government of Audh.

*List of the Nawábs and kings of Lakhnau.*

Burhán-ul-Mulk Sa'ádat Khán.
Abú'l Mansúr Khán Safdar Jang.
Shujá-uddaula, son of Safdar Jang.
'Asaf-uddaula, son of Shujá-uddaula.
Wazír 'Alí Khán.
Sa'ádat 'Alí Khán.
Ghází-uddín Haidar, son of Sa'ádat 'Alí Khán, who was made king of Audh by Lord Hastings.
Nasír-uddín Haidar, son of ditto.
Muhammad 'Alí Sháh, brother of Ghazí-uddín Haidar.
Amjad 'Alí Sháh, son of M. A.
Wájid 'Alí Sháh, the son of Amjád 'Alí Sháh, the last king of Audh in whose time that country was annexed to the British Government.

**Sa'adat-ullah Khan,** سعادت الله خان, a regular and acknowledged Nawáb of the Karnatic, who having no issue, adopted two sons of his brother, appointing the elder, Dost 'Alí, to succeed him in the Nawábship, and conferring on the younger, Bákir 'Alí, the government of Velore; he likewise directed that Ghulám Husain, the nephew of his favourite wife, should be Díwán or prime-minister to his successor. Having reigned from the year 1710 to 1722 A. D., 1122 to 1135 A. H., he died much regretted by his subjects. According to the "Másir-ul-Umra," he held the Nawábship of the Karnatic from the time of 'Alamgír to the year 1732 A. D., 1145 A. H., Dost 'Alí and his son Hasan 'Alí were killed in battle against the Marhattas on the 20th of May, 1740 A. D. His son Safdar 'Alí succeeded him, but was poisoned by his brother-in-law Murtaza 'Alí and died on the 2nd October, 1742 A. D. After his death Murtaza 'Alí was acknowledged Nawáb of the Karnatic. But in March, 1744 A. D., Nizám-ul-Mulk the súbadár of the Dakhin, having appointed one of his officers, named Anwar-uddín, Nawáb of Arkot, he (Murtaza 'Alí) was deposed.

**Sa'adat Yar Khan,** سعادت يار خان, son of Muhammad Yár Khán, the son of Háfiz Rahmat Khán the Rohela chief, is the author of a work called "Gruli Rahmat" being a History of his grandfather Háfiz Rahmat, written in 1833. This work is an abridgment of the Gulistán Rahmat written by Mustaza Khán, his uncle.

**Sa'adat Yar Khan,** سعادت يار خان, son of Muhkan-uddaula Tahmásp Beg Khán Ya'tkád Jang Bahádur. *Vide* Rangín.

**Sabahi,** صباحي, the poetical name of Akhund Masíhá.

**Sabat,** ثبات, poetical name of Mír Muhammad 'Azím the son of Mír Muhammad Afzal Sábit, born at Allahábád in 1710 A. D., 1122 A. H. He died in 1748 A. D., 1161 A. H., and left a Díwán of about 4,000 verses.

**Sabir,** صابر, poetical name of Mír Said 'Alí, a famous musician who wrote a work in Persian containing instructions on music.

**Sabir,** صابر, poetical title of Sháhzáda Mirzá Kádir Bakhsh of Dehlí. He is the author of a Díwán in Urdú.

**Sabir,** صابر, *vide* Shahádín Adíb Sábir.

**Sabit,** ثابت, the poetical title of Mír Muhammad Afzal of Dehlí who died in 1738 A. D., 1151 A. H., and left a Díwán in Persian of 5,000 verses.

**Sabit,** ثابت, poetical title of Khwája Hasan, an Urdú poet who is the author of a Díwán. He died in 1821 A. D., 1236 A. H.

**Sabit-bin-Kirra,** ثابت بن قرة, who translated Euclid and several other works into Arabic from the Greek, and died in the year 901 A. D., 288 A. H.

**Sabik,** سابق, poetical appellation of Mirzá Yúsaf Beg, a poet whose brothers were mansabdárs in the service of the emperor 'Alamgír, though he was a dervish and died in 1687 A. D., 1098 A. H.

**Sabuhi,** صبوحي, a poet in the service of the emperor Akbar. He died in the year 1564 A. D., 972 A. H.

**Sabr,** صبر, poetical title of Mír Husain 'Alí of Lakhnau, a pupil of Asghar 'Alí Khán Nasím of Dehlí.

**Sabri,** صبري, also called Roz Bihán, a Persian poet of Isfahán.

**Sabzwari,** سبزواري, a native of Sabzwár and author of the "Sawána Sabzwárí," which contains a description of the city of Daulatábád in the Dakhin, with a particular account of all the Súfis and holy men that are buried in its vicinity, written in 1318 A. D., 718 A. H.

**Sadafi,** صدفي, a poet who flourished in the time of Muhammad Sháh. He is the author of a Díwán which is usually called "Díwán Sadafí," but the true title given by the author is "Ráz-ul-'Arifí.

**Sadashiu Bhau,** شداشيو بهاؤ, a Marhaṭta chief, son of Chimnájí and nephew of the Peshwá Bálájí or Bájí Ráo. He was slain in battle against Aḥmad Sháh Abdálí on the 14th of January, 1761 A. D., 6th Jumáda II, 1174 A. H. After his death several pretenders started up, calling themselves the Bháú. In 1779 one appeared in Benares and began to levy troops and raise disturbances in the city, upon which he was seized and confined in the English garrison at Chunar, from whence he was released by Mr. Hastings in 1782.

**Sada Sukh,** شدا سوك, son of Bishun Parshád the son of Guláb Ráe, a Káyeth of Allahábád and author of a work on the art of writing prose and poetry entitled "Murassa Khurshaid" which he wrote in 1802 A. D., 1217 A. H. He also wrote a book of Anecdotes in Urdú.

**Sa'd-bin-Sharif Jaunpuri,** سعد بن شريف جونپوري, author of a Persian work called "Dastúr-ul-Musallín."

**Sa'd-bin-'Abdullah-al-Asha'ri,** سعد بن عبدالله الاشعري, or Ibn-ul-Faráez, author of a treatise on the law of Inheritance, entitled, "Ihtijáj-ush-Shia." He died 913 A. D., 301 A. H.

**Sa'd-bin-Zangi, Atabak,** اتابك سعد بن زنگي, *vide* Sunḳar, or Sanḳar.

**Sa'd-ibn-Ahmad,** سعد ابن احمد, Ḳází of Toleda. He died 1069 A. D., 462 A. H.

**Sa'di, Shaikh,** شيخ سعدي شيرازي, of Shíráz, a celebrated Persian poet, commonly called Shaikh Maslah-uddín Sa'dí-al-Shírází. He was born at Shíráz about the year 1175 A. D., 571 A. H., and died in 1292 A D., 691 A. H., aged 120 lunar years. During his youth he served as a soldier both against the Hindús and Christians: by the latter he was taken prisoner, and obliged to work at the fortifications of Tripoli, whence he was liberated by a person who gave him his daughter in marriage: but the lady was of so bad a temper that the poet complained he had exchanged his slavery for a worse bondage. He was a great traveller; and made the pilgrimage of Mecca fourteen times. He was a disciple of the venerated Súfí, 'Abdul Ḳádir Gílání, or at least, adopted his opinion. His tomb is still to be seen in the neighbourhood of Shíráz. Besides the Gulistán and Bostán, he is the author of a large collection of Odes and Sonnets. There is likewise a short collection of poetical pieces attributed to him called "Al-Khabísát" or the book of Impurities. The author, however, seems to have repented of having written these indecent verses, yet endeavours to excuse himself on account of their giving a relish to other poems, "as salt is used in the seasoning of meat." His works, all of which are held in great estimation, are the following:—

| | |
|---|---|
| A Preface. | Rubá'yát. |
| Majális Khán. | Fardiát. |
| Resala Sáhib Díwán. | Ghazaliát. |
| Gulistán. | Mukaltiát. |
| Bostán. | Murakkabát. |
| Pandnáma. | Al-Khabísát. |
| Ḳasáed Arabí. | Tarjiát. |
| Ḳasáed Fársí. | Kitáb-al-Badáya. |
| Marásí. | Kitáb Tyyobát. |
| Mulamma'át. | Al-Khawátím. |
| Muzahhabát. | |

A very good edition of Sa'dí's works was published in Calcutta by Mr. Harrington: with an English Preface containing the memoirs of the author, and many other interesting anecdotes; and Mr. Gladwin of Bengal has favoured the public with a very good translation of the Gulistán. Jamí calls Sa'dí, "the Nightingale of the Groves of Shíráz."

**Sa'di,** سعدي دكهني of the Dakhin, who is the author of some verses which are erroneously ascribed to Sa'dí of Shíráz.

**Sa'did Usi,** صديد اوسي, an excellent poet, author of the "Jáma-ul-Makiát."

**Sa'did-uddin Gazaruni,** صديد الدين گازروني, author of an Arabic work on Medicine called "Almughní."

**Sadik,** صادق, his proper name is Sádiḳ 'Alí, and he is the author of the "Chahár Bágh Haidarí," dedicated to Nawáb Ghází-uddín Haidar of Lakhnau, who died in 1827 A. D., 1243 A. H. It contains rather selections from ancient authors than original poetry.

**Sa'dik Muhammad Khan,** صادق محمد خان ازادها زهي ازادوار, a mansabdár of 4000: died 1597 A. D., 1005 A. H., buried at Dholpúr. He was a Persian, cousin to Núr Jahán, one of whose sisters he married. He was esteemed one of Akbar's best officers.

**Sadik,** صادق, the poetical name of Mír Ja'far Khán, grandson of Said Muhammad Ḳádirí. He is the author of a work called "Baháristán Ja'farí." He was a native of Dehlí where he died some years before 1782 A. D., 1196 A. H., and was buried in the same vault wherein his grandfather was interred, and which is over the nala of Bairám Dai in Dehlí.

**Sadiki,** صادقي, poetical name of Sádik Beg of the tribe of Afshár. He is the author of a Díwán and a Tazkira or Biography of poets in Turkí.

**Sadik Khan,** صادق خان, the son of 'Aḳá Tákir whose poetical name was Waslí, and grandson of Muhammad Sharaf Hajrí, and nephew and son-in-law of Ya'tmád-uddaula Tehrání. He held a high rank in the time of Akbar and Jahángír, and died on the 7th of October, 1630 A. D., 9th Rabí' I, 1040 A. H., in the reign of the emperor Sháh Jahán.

**Sadik Khan,** صادق خان. was a spiritual guide of the emperor Akbar the Great. He died in 1597 A. D., 1006 A. H. To the left of the road, about half way between Sikandra and Agrah, are some tombs in the fields; one with an adjacent hall of 64 pillars, is believed to be the resting-place of this saint. *Vide* Keene's Ágrah Guide, p. 44.

**Sadik Khan,** صادق خان, brother of Karím Khán, king of Persia. He took possession of Shíráz after the death of Zakí Khán; reigned nearly two years, and was murdered on the 14th March, 1781 A. D., *vide* Karím Khán.

**Sadr-uddin Ardibeli,** صدرالدين اردبيلي, *vide* Sadr uddín Músa.

**Sadr Jahan,** صدر جهان, a learned Muhammadan who lived in the time of Sulṭán Ḳulí Ḳuṭb Sháh, king of Golkanḍa who reigned from 1512 to 1543 A. D., 918 to 949 A. H. He is the author of a Persian work called "Marghúb-ul-Kulúb," a history of that king.

**Sadr Jahan, Kazi,** قاضي صدر جهان, *vide* Minháj-us-Siráj.

**Sadr Jahan, Mir,** مير صدر جهان, a well educated and learned Musalmán, a native of a village near Lakhnau. He was an officer of 4000 in the service of the emperor Akbar, in the 31st year of whose reign, 1585 A. D., 993 A. H., he was sent on an embassy together with Hakím Humám to 'Abdullah Khán Uzbak, ruler of Túrán, whose father Iskandar Khán had died at that time. He lived 120 years, and at the time of his death, which took place in 1611 A. D., 1020 A. H., he was so much emaciated by old age, that there was nothing left in him but bones.

**Sadr-uddin bin-Ya'kub, Mulla,** ملا صدر الدين بن يعقوب, author of a collection of decisions in Persian entitled "Fatáwá Ḳará Kháni," which was arranged some years after his death by Ḳará Khán, in the reign of Sulṭán 'Aláuddín.

**Sadr-uddin Musa, Shaikh,** شيخ صدرالدين موسى, the son of Shaikh Safí-uddín the celebrated founder of the Safwí kings of Persia. *Vide* Shaikh Safí and Ismá'íl Sháh I Safwí.

**Sadr-uddin Muhammad,** صدرالدين محمد, son of Zabardast Khán, and author of the work called "Irshád-ul-Wazrá," written in the reign of the emperor Muhammad Sháh.

**Sadr-uddin Muhammad bin-Is-hak Ḳunawi,** صدرالدين محمد بن اسحاق قونوي, a native of Iconium and an author, who died in 1273 A. D., 672 A. H.

**Sadr-uddin Muhammad, Mir,** مير صدرالدين محمد, author of the "Jawáhir-náma," a book on Arts and Sciences.

**Sadr-uddin Muhammad,** صدرالدين محمد, surnamed Abú'l Ma'álí, which see.

**Sadr-uddin, Ufi Maulana,** مولانا صدرالدين عوفي, author of the Jáma'-ul-Hikáyát." He is also called Núr-uddín Muhammad Úfí, which see.

**Sadr-uddin, Shaikh,** شيخ صدرالدين, the son of Shaikh Bahá-uddín of Multán. He died in 1309 A. D., 709 A. H., at Multán and is buried there.

**Sadr-uddin Sayyad 'Ali Khan,** صدرالدين سيد علي خان, son of Sayyad Nizám-uddín Aḥmad Husainí. He was the best Arabic poet of his time, and is the author of the following works "Ḳitáb Badíạ'," "Salafat," and "Sharah Sahífa Kámila."

**Sa'd-uddin of Dehli,** سعدالدين دهلوى, author of the works called Sharḥ "Kanz-ul-Daḳáiḳ," and "Sharah Manár." He died in 1486 A. D., 891 A. H.

**Sa'd-uddin of Kashghar,** سعدالدين كاشغر, the spiritual guide of Jámí. He died 1456 A. D., 860 A. H.

**Sa'd-uddin Hamwia,** سعدالدين حمويه, entitled Shaikh-ul-Masháeḳ, is the author of several works, one of which is called "Sajanjal-ul-Arwáh," The Mirror of the Soul, and another entitled "Ḳitáb Mahbúb," the Beloved book. He died in the year 1252 A. D., 650 A. H.

**Sa'd-uddin,** سعدالدين, a Turkish historian, was born in 1536 and died at Constantinople in 1599. His history, entitled, the "Táj-ul-Tawáríkh" (the Crown of Histories) a work held in high estimation by scholars, gives a general account of the Ottoman empire from its commencement in 1299 till 1520. He also wrote the "Salím-náma" or History of Salím I, which is chiefly a collection of anecdotes regarding that prince.

**Sa'd-uddin Tuftazani, Mulla,** ملا سعدالدين تفتازاني, *vide* Tuftázaní.

**Sa'd-ullah Khan,** سعد الله خان, the son of the Rohela chief 'Alí Muhammad Khán, whom he succeeded to the Rohela territories in 1749 A. D., 1162 A. H., but retired with a pension of eight lacs of rupees annually from Háfiz Rahmat Khán, and died in the year 1761 A. D., 1175 A. H., at Aoṉla. His brother 'Abdullah Khán was killed in the battle which took place between Háfiz Rahmat Khán and Nawáb Shujá-uddaula, 1774 A. D., 1188 A. H. After his death his brother Faiz-ulláh Khán succeeded him in the Rohela territories of Rámpúr.

**Sa'd-ullah Khan,** سعدالله خان, whose title was Khán 'Alam, was sent as ambassador to the king of Persia by the emperor Sháh Jahán. He died in the year 1631 A. D., 1044 A. H.

**Sa'd-ullah Khan Wazir,** سعد الله خان وزير, surnamed 'Allámí Fahhámí, and entitled Jumlat-ul-Mulk, was the most able and upright minister that ever appeared in India. He makes a conspicuous figure in all the transactions of the emperor Sháh Jahán, and is constantly referred to as a model in the correspondence of the emperor 'Álamgír during the long reign of that monarch. He died on the 9th of April, 1656 A. D., 22nd Jumáḍa II, 1066 A. H., aged 48 lunar years. After his death the mansab of 700 and 100 Sawars was conferred on his son Lutf-ulláh Khán, a boy of 11 years of age.

**Sa'd-ullah Khan,** سعد الله خان, the brother-in-law of Mahmúd Khán, Nawáb of Bijnour, and Munsif of Amroha. He, together with Jalál-uddín Khán, the Nawáb's brother, was tried and convicted by Court Martial, and shot by order of General Jones on the 23rd April, 1858, at Kote Khádir within eight miles of Najíbábád on account of their rebellion.

**Sa'd-ullah Kirmani,** سعد الله كرماني, author of the work called "Fatúhát Míránsháhí," containing an account of the conquests made by Míránsháh the son of Amír Taimúr.

**Sa'd-ullah, Shaikh,** شيخ سعدالله دهلوى, of Dehlí, a descendant of Islám Khán who was wazír to one of the kings of Gujrát; and as he was a disciple of Sháh Gul whose poetical name was Wahdat a descendant of Shaikh Aḥmad Mujaddid, consequently he lived like a dervish, and assumed the title of Gulshán for his poetical name. He died at Dehlí on the 13th December, 1728 A. D., 21st Jumádạ I, 1141 A. H.

**Saeb, Mirza,** مرزا صايب, the poetical name of Mirzá Muhammad 'Alí of Tabrez, a celebrated poet of Persia, who in the latter part of the reign of the emperor Jahángír came to India as a merchant. He became intimate with Zafar Khán, a nobleman of the court, who being appointed governor of Kashmír in those days by Sháh Jahán, took him along with him to that country. From Kashmír he returned to Isfahán where he was honoured with the title of "Malik-ush-Shu'árá" or the king of poets, by Sháh Abbás king of Persia. He wrote Ghazals in an entirely new style, and may therefore be considered as the founder of the new school. He died in 1669 A. D., 1080 A. H., and was buried at Isfahán. His Díwán in Persian contains 80,000 verses.

**Saeb, Mirza,** مرزا صايب, a Hindústání poet and author of the "Mirat-ul-Jamál," or the Mirror of Beauty, a very eccentric work, containing a distinct poem in praise of each of his mistresses' features, limbs, and perfections.

**Saidai Gilani,** سيدائي گيلانی, came to India in the time of Jahángír, and as he was very clever and of great abilities, he was made a Darogah of the Zargár Khána or goldsmith's shop. and received the title of Bedil. He is the author of a Díwán, Nukat Bedil Rukaat Bedil and Chahar Ansur. He died about the year 1116 A. D.

**Sa'id-bin-Mansur,** سعيد بن منصور, author of the works called "Sunan and Zuhd." He died in 842 A. D., 227 A. H.

**Sa'id-bin-Masa'ud of Shiraz,** بن مسعود شيرازي سعيد, author of the Tarjuma Maulúd," a complete history of Muhammad, translated from the Arabic about the year 1358 A. D., 759 A. H.

**Sa'id-bin-Muhammad,** سعيد بن محمد, author of the works called "Minháj-ul-'Abidín" and "Sa'íd-náma," containing moral and philosophical treatises on the virtues, vices, passions, rewards, punishments, &c.

**Sa'id-bin-Musayyab,** سعيد بن مسيب, son-in-law of Abú Hureira. He was one of the seven Fiḳhas of Madína; made forty pilgrimages to Mecca, and died in 713 A. D., 94 A. H.

**Sa'id-bin-Zand,** سعيد بن زند, was the last of those ten companions who had a positive promise of paradise from Muhammad. He died in the year 671 A. D., 51 A. H.

**Sa'id Hirwi,** سعيد هروي, a poet who was a native of Hirat and contemporary with Ḳází Shams-uddín Tibsí.

**Sa'id Khan Ḳureshi,** سعيد خان قريشي, whose proper name was Shaikh Muhammad, was a native of Multán. He was a good poet and a wit, and was employed by the prince Sultán Murád Bakhsh son of Sháh Jahán at the time when he was governor of Gujrát; and afterwards by prince Dárá Shikóh, after whose death he was employed by the emperor 'Alamgír, and died in November, 1676 A. D., Ramazan, 1087 A. H., at Multán where he was buried in a monument which he had built whilst living. He is the author of a Díwán.

**Sa'id Khan, Hakim,** حكيم سعيد خان, a physician of Kaem who lived in the time of Sháh 'Abbás II of Persia, and is the author of a Díwán.

**Sa'id Khan, Muhammad,** محمد سعيد خان, present Nawáb of Rámpúr (1858).

**Sa'id Muhammad Kirmani,** سعيد محمد كرماني, author of the "Siar-ul-Aulia," containing the memoirs of all the principal Súfí Shaikhs and saints. Written in 1594 A. D., 1003 A. H.

**Safdar 'Ali Khan,** صفدر علي خان, nawáb of Arkaṭ son of Dost 'Alí murdered by his brother-in-law Murtazá 'Alí Khán of Vellore on the 2nd October, 1742 A. D.

**Safdar Jang,** صفدر جنگ, Nawáb of Audh, whose proper name was Mirzá Muḳím and surname Mansúr 'Alí Khán, was the son of Sayádat Khán. and nephew and son-in-law of Burhán-ul-Mulk Sa'ádat Khán whom he succeeded in the government of Audh after paying two crores of rupees to Nádir Sháh in the beginning of the year 1152 A. D., 1152 A. H., or April. 1739 A. D.. 1161 A. H. He was appointed wazír in 1748 A. D. on the accession of the emperor Aḥmad Sháh (in the room of Nizám-ul-Mulk who had died that year), and assumed the whole administration of the imperial authority for several years. He was, however, dismissed from the wizárat in 1752 A. D., 1166 A. H., and died on his way to Audh at Pápargháṭ on the 17th of October, 1753 A. D., 17th Ẕil-ḥijja. 1167 A. H. He was buried for some time at Guláb Báṛí in Faizábád his seat of government, but afterwards his remains were conveyed to Dehlí and interred in the vicinity of the Dargáh of Sháh Mardán where a splendid mausoleum was built over his tomb. He was succeeded in the government of Audh by his son Nawáb Shujá-uddaula.

**Safi Khan,** صفي خان, son of Islám Khán Mashhadí, a nobleman who served under the emperors Sháh Jahán and 'Alamgír.

**Safi Mirza,** صفي ميرزا, the son of Sháh 'Abbás I. He was murdered by the instigation of his father who hated him, about the year 1611 A. D., 1020 A. H.

**Safi, Shah,** شاه صفی, king of Persia, *vide* Sháh Safí.

**Safi, Shaikh,** شيخ صفی, *vide* Shaikh Safí.

**Safir of Faryab,** سفير, poetical name of a poet of Fáryáb.

**Safi-uddin Muhammad,** صفي الدين محمد, son of Husain Wáez. He is the author of a book called "Rishhát," which is a chronogram for 909 A. H., in which year it was completed. (1503 A. D., 909 A. H.) It contains the sayings of his Murshid or spiritual guide Obeidulláh Ahrár who resided at Samarḳand. *Vide* 'Alí Wáez.

**Safi-uddin, Shaikh,** شيخ صفی الدين, *vide* Ismá'íl Sháh Safwí and Shaikh Safí.

**Saffah,** سفّاح, *vide* Al-Saffáh.

**Safia,** صفيه, daughter of a Jew of Khaibar, whom Muhammad married after the battle of Khaibar. She was one of the most beloved wives of the prophet, whom she survived for forty years of widowhood. She died about the year 670 A. D., 50 A. H.

**Safshikan Khan,** صف شكن خان, title of Muhammad Táhir, a nobleman of the rank of 3000, who served under the emperor 'Alamgír and died 1676 A. D., 1085 A. H.

**Safwi Kha'n,** صفوي خان, a descendant of the royal house of Persia of the Safwí family. He held a high rank in the service of the emperor 'Alamgír, and was killed in the battle which took place between the two brothers 'Azim Sháh and Bahádur Sháh on the 8th June, 1707 A. D., 18th Rabí I, 1119 A. H.

**Saguna Ba'i Sa'heb,** سيگونه بائي صاحب, Ráni of Sitára and widow of the late Mahárájá of Sitára Chatrapatí Appa Saheb who died about the year 1874 A. D.

**Saha'bi,** سحابي, poetical name of a poet who wrote poetry in Persian, and is the author of a Díwán.

**Sahar,** سحر, poetical title of Sayyad Násir 'Alí who died in 1833 A. D., 1249 A. H.

**Sahara'wi,** صحراوي, *vide* Abú'l Kásim Al-Saharáwí.

**Sahba',** صهبا, whose original name was 'Abdul Báḳí, was a poet who flourished about the year 1653 A. D., 1063 A. H. in the time of the emperor 'Alamgír.

**Sahba'i,** صهبائی, poetical name of Maulwí Imám Bakhsh. He translated the Arabic work called "Hadáeḳ-ul-Balághat," into Persian, and is the author of several Persian and Urdú works. He was living in 1854 A. D., 1271 A. H.

**Sahba'n,** سحبان, the son of Wáil Kheyáí, who lived in the time of Harún-al-Rashíd. Shaikh Sádí in his Gulistán says, that Sahbán Wáil has been considered as unrivalled in eloquence, insomuch that if he spoke before an assembly for the space of a year, he did not repeat a word twice, and if the same meaning occurred he repeated it in a different form.

**Sa'hib,** صاحب, the poetical appellation of Hakím Kázim, commonly called "Masíh-ul-Bayán." He was a physician and also a poet, and held the rank of 500 in the reign of 'Alamgír. He died two or three years before Mirzá Sáeb the poet about the year 1667 A. D., 1077 A. H., and left two or three Díwáns. He imitated Jalál-uddín Rúmí and wrote several Masnawís or poems, *viz.*, "Aína Khána", "Parí Khána", "Maláhat Aḥmadí", "Sabáhat Yúsafí", "Gul Muhammadí", and "Aufás Masíhí".

**Sa'hib,** صاحب, *vide* Masíhái (Akhúnd).

**Sa'hib Balkhi,** صاجب بلخي, a poet of Balkh who wrote panegyrics in praise of some of the kings of Badakhshán. He flourished in the 9th century of the Hijra.

**Sa'hib,** صاحب, (Aloysius Reinhardt) a son of Shamrú or Sombre, who had the title of Mazaffar-uddaula Mumtáz-ul-Mulk Nawáb Zafaryáb Khán Bahádur Nasrat Jang. He held (says an author) sometimes assemblies of poets in his house, and is said to have been a pleasant man, but a great scoundrel. He was a pupil of Khairátí Khán Dilsóz. He died in the prime of life, and was buired at Agra in the small Catholic Church built by his father. He was grandfather of the late Dyce Sombre.

**Sa'hib Jama'l,** صاحب جمال, wife of the emperor Jahángír and a relative of Zain Khán Koka. She was the mother of Sulṭán Parweiz.

**Sa'hib Ḳira'n,** صاحب قران, this is the title the Orientals as well as Arabs, Persians and Turks have given to Amír Taimúr (Tamerlane), because he was born in a particular planetary aspect (*vide* next article but one).

**Sa'hib Kira'n,** صاحب قران, the poetical title of Sayyad Imám 'Alí of Bilgram who became distracted in 1813 A. D., 1228 A. H., and wrote indecent and satirical poetry. He came to Lakhnau in the time of Nawáb 'Asaf-uddaula.

**Sa'hib Ḳira'n Sa'ni,** صحب قران ثاني, or Sáhib Ḳirán the Second, a title of the emperor Sháh Jahán. The first being Taimúr or Tamerlane the founder of the family. The word means "nearness" and is used in Astrology to express a planetary conjunction. Taimúr and his descendant, the builder of the Táj, were both born when Jupiter and Venus were "in the same house." *Vide* Sháh Jahán.

**Sa'hiba Zama'ni,** صاحبة زماني, daughter of the emperor Muhammad Sháh. She was sought in marriage by 'Alamgír II, but she refused him. Her mother, Malika Jahán, claimed the protection of Aḥmad Sháh Abdálí against 'Alamgír's designs upon her daughter, and he carried them both to Kábul in 1757 A. D., and some time after espoused Sáhiba Zamání himself.

**Sa'hji** or **Sa'huji Bhosla I,** ساهجي يا ساهوجي, a Mahraṭṭa chief who rose to considerable rank in the time of Malik Ambar an Abyssinian chief of Aḥmadnagar. He afterwards entered the service of the king of Bíjápúr and was continued in his jágír, which had fallen to that state in the partition of the Aḥmadnagar territory. He was subsequently employed on conquests to the southward, and obtained a much more considerable jágír in the Mysore country including the towns of Sira and Bangalore. When at a great age, he was killed by a fall in hunting, about the year 1664 A. D. He was the father of the celebrated Sewájí, who though the son of a powerful chief, begun life as a daring and artful captain of banditti, ripened into a skilful general and an able statesman, and left a character which has never since been equalled or approached by any of his countrymen. Sáhjí, in consequence of some dispute with his first wife, separated from her, and married Toka Bái, by whom he had, Ekójí, who afterwards became king of Tanjore.

*List of the family of Sewájí or Rájás of Sitára.*

| | A. D. |
|---|---|
| Sáhjí, Ṣúbadár of the Karnatik under 'Alamgír, bestows jágírs on his sons—Tanjore on Ekójí—and dies | 1664 |
| Sewájí, his son commences predatory expeditions | 1647 |
| —— plunders Surat, and assumes the title of rájá | 1664 |
| —— establishes a military government 1669 and dies | 1680 |
| Rájá Rám, set up by minister, imprisoned at Ráegarh | 1680 |
| Sambhájí assumed the sovereignty 1680—executed at Talápúr | 1689 |
| Santa, usurped power—murdered | 1698 |
| Rájá Rám again proclaimed 1698 A. D., at Sitára and died | 1700 |
| Tárá Bái, his wife, assumed regency | 1700 |
| Sewájí II, son of Sambhá, nicknamed Sáhújí, released on 'Alamgír's death, and crowned at Sitára in March, 1708, and died in | 1749 |
| Rám Rájá, nominal successor,—power resting with minister or Peishwa, died 12th December | 1777 |
| Sabú surnamed Abba Saheb, the adopted son of Rám Rájá succeeded | 1777 |
| Partáp Singh the son of Sabú, reinstated at Sitára by the British, 11th April | 1818 |

**Sa'hji, Sa'huji** or **Sa'u Bhosla II,** ساهجي, ساهوجي, يا ساو, the son of Sambhájí the Marhaṭṭa chief, after whose death in 1689 A. D., 15th Muḥarram, 1101 A. H he (though then an infant) was acknowledged as Rájá, and his uncle Rájá Rám nominated to be regent during his minority; but when subsequently the infant Rájá fell into the hands of 'Alamgír, and was confined, Rájá Rám proclaimed himself Rájá on the ground of the captivity of his nephew. In his time the fort of Sitára was taken by 'Alamgír on the 21st April, 1700 A. D., 13th Zi-Ka'da, 1111 A. H., but before it fell, Rájá Rám had died of the small-pox at Jhinjí, and had been succeeded by his son Sewá, a child of two years, under the regency of his mother Tárá Báí, the widow of the deceased. After the death of 'Alamgír, Sáhjí was released from confinement by 'Azim Sháh, and was acknowledged by the Marhattas as their principal chief, and crowned at Sitára in March, 1708 A. D. During his reign, the Marhattas having overrun and plundered almost every part of Hindústán, excepting Bengal, extended their territories from the Western Sea to Urisa, and from Agrah to the Karnátik, forming a tract of near one thousand miles long by seven hundred wide. His minister, the Peishwá Bátojí Bishwanáth, gained such an ascendancy over the mind of his master, as to persuade Sáhjí to delegate to him the exercise of all authority and power in the state. During the latter part of his reign, Sáhjí shut himself up in Sitára, and his person and government were almost forgotten. Sáhjí died (some time after the death of Nizám-ul-Mulk) about the month of December, 1749 A. D. after a reign of 50 years. He was succeeded by his adopted son Rám Rájá the grandson of Tárá Báí, power resting with the minister or Peishwá. Before his death he intrusted the Peishwá with the sole management of the Marhatta empire, and directed that Kolhápúr, then governed by Sambhájí the son of Rájá Rám, should be always considered as an independent kingdom.

**Sa'hu**, ساهو, also called Abba Sáheb, was the son of Trimbakjí Bhosla, and adopted son of Rám Rájá, whom he succeeded on the masnad of Sitára on the 12th December, 1777 A. D. He was always kept a close prisoner. After his death, his son Partáp Singh succeeded him.

**Saja'wandi**, سجاوندي, *vide* Siráj-uddín Muhammad bin-'Abdur Rashíd-al-Sajáwandí.

**Sajja'd, Mir**, مير سجاد, an Urdú poet of Agrah who was a pupil of Sháh Najm-uddín 'Abrú.

**Sakafi**, ثقفي, or Thakafí, whose original name is Abú Isá, was an excellent Arabic grammarian and author. He died in 766 A. D., 149 A. H.

**Sakina Ba'no Begam**, سكينه بانو بيگم, sister of Mirzá Muhammad Hakím half-brother to the emperor Akbar. She was married to Sháh Ghazí Khán the nephew of Nokíb Khán.

**Sakina**, سكينه, daughter of Imám Husain. After her father's death she was married to Misaab the brother of 'Abdulláh the son of Zubeir.

**Sakha'**, سخا, poetical name of Záhid 'Alí Khán an author.

**Sakha'wi**, سخاوي, author of the history of the Kázís of Egypt.

**Sakhun**, سخن, a poet of Agrah, named Mír Abdus Samad who died in 1727 A. D., 1140 A. H.

**Sakka**, سقّه بخاري, or Dervish Sakká of Bukhára. He died in 1555 A. D., 962 A. H., and is the author of a Díwán.

**Sakka Bardwa'ni**, سقّه بردواني, author of a Díwán found in the Library of Típú Sultán.

**Sakka'ki**, سكاكي. This word which in Arabic signifies a cutler, was the surname of Abú Ya'kúb Yúsaf bin-Abú Bakr, who was also called Siráj-uddín-al-Khwárizmí. He was a great author and master of Záhidí. One of his works is called "Misbáh-ul-Ulúm." He was born in 1160 A. D., 555 A. H., and died in the year 1229 A. D., 626 A. H.

**Sakhi Sarwa'r**, سخي سرور, a Muhammadan saint. See Sultán Sakhí Sarwar.

**Sala'bat Jang**, صلابت جنگ, the third son of Nizám-ul-Mulk 'Asif Jáh, was placed by the French on the masnad of the Dakhin after the assassination of Muzaffar Jang his nephew which took place on the 3rd February, 1751 A. D., 17th Rabí I, 1164 A. H. Monsieur Bussy the French General was created by him a nobleman of the empire, and the Northern Sircars granted in jágír to his nation. Monsieur Bussy continued to conduct the affairs of the Dakhin, till, by the intrigues of Nizám 'Alí, brother to Salábat Jang his counsellor Haidar Jang being assassinated on the 12th May, 1758 A. D., 3rd Ramazán, 1171 A. H., and the English who had patronized Muhammad 'Alí Khán in the province of Arkát growing powerful, he was obliged to return to the French territories to the assistance of his countrymen. Nizám 'Alí being without a rival, deposed and imprisoned Salábat Jang on the 26th June, 1762 A. D., 4th Zil-hijja, 1175 A. H., and assumed the government. Salábat Jang remained in confinement till his death which happened on the 29th September, 1763 A. D., 20th Rabí' I, 1177 A. H.

**Sala'bat Kha'n**, صلابت خان, a nobleman who held the office of Mír Bakhshí or pay-master general in the time of the emperor Sháh Jahán. He was stabbed in the presence of the emperor by a Rájpút chief named Amar Singh Ráthor the son of Gaj Singh, on the evening of Thursday the 25th of July, 1644 A. D., 30th Jumáda I, 1054 A. H., in the fort of Agrah. His tomb is still to be seen in the vicinity of Agrah. Amar Singh was pursued and cut down near one of the gates of the fort, which goes after his name, Amar Singh Gate.

**Sala'bat Kha'n**, صلابت خان, a nobleman who on the accession of the emperor Ahmad Sháh to the throne of Dehlí in 1748 A. D., 1161 A. H. was raised to the rank of Mír Bakhshí or pay-master general with the title of Zulfikár Jáng.

**Saladin**, *vide* Sálah-uddín Yúsaf the son of Ayyúb.

**Sala'h**, صالح, author of the Masnawí or poem called "Náz wa Nayáz," which he composed about the year 1523 A. D., 930 A. H.

**Sala'h bin-Muba'rik-al-Bukhari**, صالح بن مبارك, author of the "Mukámát Khwája Bahá-uddín," containing the memoirs of the celebrated Shaikh Bahá-uddín, founder of the Nakshbandí Order.

**Sa'lah, Mi'r**, مير صالح كشفي, styled Kashfí, was the son of 'Abdulláh Miskín. He died in the year 1650 A. D. 1060 A. H. at Agrah and lies buried there. *Vide* Kashfí.

**Sala'h-uddin Yusaf**, صالح الدين يوسف, the son of Ayyúb (the same who is called by Christian writers Saladin), a celebrated Sultán of Syria and the first king of Egypt of the Ayyúbite family, equally renowned as a warrior and legislator. It is said that he supported himself by his valour, and the influence of his amiable character, against the united efforts of the chief Christian potentates of Europe, who carried on the most unjust wars against him, under the false appellation of Holy Wars. He reigned in Egypt and Syria from 1173 to 1193 A. D., 568 to 588 A. H., and in the year following he died at Damascus, leaving seventeen sons, who divided his extensive dominions. He was succeeded by his son Malik-ul-'Azíz 'Usmán in the government of Egypt, but as none of his successors possessed the enterprising genius of Sálah-uddín, the history of Egypt from that time to the year 1250 A. D. affords nothing remarkable. At this time the reigning Sulṭán Malik-al-Sálah was dethroned and slain by the Mamlúks, a kind of mercenary soldiers who served under him. In consequence of this revolution, the Mamlúks became masters of Egypt, and chose a Sulṭán from among themselves. *Vide* Mamlúk.

*Sulṭáns of Egypt of the Ayyúbite family.*

| | | A. D. |
|---|---|---|
| Sálah-uddín Yúsaf bin-Ayyúb, began 1168 .. | died | 1193 |
| Malik-ul-'Azíz 'Usmán, son of Sálah-uddín,.. | „ | 1197 |
| Malik Mansúr Muhammad bin-'Usman, .... | „ | 1200 |
| Malik 'Adil Saif-uddín Abú Bakr bin-Ayyúb, | „ | 1218 |
| Malik Kámil Muhammad, son of Saif-uddín, | „ | 1237 |
| Malik 'Adil Abú Bakr bin-Kámil, ......... | „ | 1239 |
| Malik Sálah Ayyúb Najm-uddín bin-Kámil, he was slain in battle with the Franks,.... | | 1249 |
| Malik Muazzim Túrán Sháh bin-Sálah, .... | „ | 1250 |
| Malika Shajrat-uddurr, a slave girl of Malik Sálah, she reigned three years and died in | | 1255 |
| Malik Ashraf Músa bin-Yúsaf, reigned 5 years. | | |

Malik Moizz 'Azz-uddín Eaibak, a Turkoman slave or Mamlúk of the Ayyúbite dynasty, married the queen Malika Shajrat-uddurr, and ascended the throne of Egypt. His descendants ruled for nearly one hundred years, and were called the Mamlúkites.

**Salamat 'Ali,** سلامت علي, the city Munsif of Allahábád who became a rebel and was hung in June, 1857 A. D. at that station.

**Salamat 'Ali Khan, Hakim,** حكيم سلامت علي خان of Benares, author of a Treatise on Music, who lived about the commencement of the present or nineteenth century.

**Salami** or **Salmi,** سلمي, this word which signifies a native of Baghdád, was also the surname of Abú'l Hasan Muhammad bin-Obeid-ullah, who was one of the most illustrious Arabian poet of his time. He lived at the court of 'Azd-uddaula, a Sulṭán of the dynasty of the Bóyaides, who reigned at Fars and 'Iráḳ from 976 to 983 A. D.

**Salar Masa'ud Ghazi,** سالار مسعود غازي, *vide* Masa'úd Ghází (Salár).

**Salhahan** or **Salivahana,** سالباهن, is said to have been the son of a potter and to have lived at Patar on the Godavarí. His era is still in use in the Dakhin, its date is 78 A. D.

**Salim,** سليم, the poetical title of Muhammad Ḳulí, who came to India from Persia during the reign of Sháh Jahán and was employed by Islám Khán, wazír. He is the author of a Díwán and also of a Masnawí which he wrote in Persia, and in which he describes Lahiján. But when he came to India, he altered the heading and called it a description of Kashmír. He died in the year 1647 A. D., 1057 A. H.

**Salim,** مير محمد سليم, Mír Muhammad Salím of Paṭna a merchant who died at Murshidábád in 1781 A. D., 1195 A. H., and left a Masnawí in Urdú.

**Samdik Phra Paramidr,** سامدّيك فري پرميدّر, king of Siam who came to Hindústán in the beginning of 1872, and was received in Calcutta, Lakhnau, Bombay, &c., &c. with all the honours due to high rank.

**Salim I, Sultan,** سلطان سليم, emperor of the Turks or Constantinople, and the greatest monster of that monstrous race, was the second son of Báyezíd II whom he defeated in a battle, and after poisoning him and murdering eight of his brothers or nephews, ascended the throne of Turkey on the 6th April, 1512 A. D., 18th Ṣafar, 918 A. H. He subverted the Mamlúks of Egypt, bringing it with Palestine, Syria, and Arabia under the yoke of the Turks. He invaded the kingdom of Persia; subdued and slew Aladeules, the mountain king of Armenia and reduced his kingdom to the form of a Turkish province. He repressed the forces of the Hungarians by a double invasion. But when intending to turn all his forces upon the Christians, he was suddenly seized with a cancer on his back whereby he died on Friday the 21st of September, 1520 A. D., 6th Shawwal, 926 A. H. on the very spot where he had formerly unnaturally assaulted his aged father. He was succeeded by his son Sulaimán I, surnamed The Magnificent.

**Salim II, Sultan,** سلطان سليم succeeded his father Sulaimán I, surnamed The Magnificent, as emperor of the Turks in September, 1566 A. D., Ṣafar, 974 A. H. He was an idle and effeminate emperor; but his deputies took from the Venetians the isle of Cyprus, and from the Moors the kingdom of Tunis and Algiers. Over this emperor the Christians were victorious in that famous sea-fight called the battle of Lepanto, when he lost above 35,000 men besides his fleet. Devoting his time to the several pleasures of his seraglio, he died, little respected, on the 9th December, 1574 A. D., Shaban, 982 A. H., aged 52, and was succeeded by his son Sulṭán Murád III.

**Salim III, Sultan,** سلطان سليم, son of Mustafá III, was born in 1761 A. D., Rajab, 1203 A. H., and succeeded to the throne of Turkey on the death of his uncle Aḥmad IV, in April, 1789 A. D. He began his reign with a war with Catharine II of Russia, in which peace was purchased by great sacrifices of territory. At a later period Egypt was invaded by the French; but they were defeated, and compelled to quit the country, by the English, in 1801. A revolt of the Jannisarís deposed Salím on the 28th of July, 1807 A. D., Jumáda I, 1222 A. H., and raised Mustafá IV to the throne; but he was deposed after a reign of one year, and Mahmúd II made emperor 1808 A. D.

**Salim Chishti, Shaikh,** شيخ سليم چشتي of Fathapúr Síkrí, surnamed Shaikh-ul-Islám, a Muhammadan saint who, during his life was greatly revered by the emperor Akbar. It is said that by his prayers the king was blessed with several children. His father Bahá-uddín was a descendant of Shaikh Faríd Shakarganj. He was born at Dehlí in 1478 A. D., 883 A. H., was a disciple of Khwája Ibráhím Chishtí, and resided on a hill close to the village of Síkrí in the province of Ágrah. By the liberality of the emperor, he built a splendid Masjid or mosque on the hill, called the Masjid of Fathapúr Síkrí. which was completed in 1571 A. D., 979 A. H., at a cost of 5 lacs of rupees. He died a few months after its completion on the 13th February, 1572 A. D., 27th Ramaẓán, 979 A. H., aged 96 lunar years, and was buried on the top of the hill where his tomb is to be seen to this day. He was one of the chief saints of Hindústán, and his sayings are worthy of commemoration. After his death his son Badr-uddín succeeded him to the guddí. His pedigree runs thus: "Shaikh Salím Chishtí, the son of Bahá-uddín, the son of Shaikh Sulaimán, the son of Shaikh 'Adam, the son of Shaikh Músá, the son of Shaikh Maudúd, the son of Shaikh Badr-uddín, the son of Shaikh Faríd-uddín of Ajúdhun, commonly called Shakarganj." Twenty-four times Salím Chishtí is said to have gone on a pilgrimage to Mecca and returned again. His bread was made of singháras that were produced in the reservoir of Síkrí. His son Ḳutb-uddín was killed in Bengal by Sher Afkan, first husband of Nur Jahán. His grandson Islám Khán, the son of Badr-uddín was raised by the emperor Jahángír to the rank of an Amír and was appointed governor of Bengal in 1608 A. D., 1017 A. H. *Vide* Islám Khán.

**Salim Shah Sur,** سليم شاه سور, also called Islám Sháh and Jalál Khán, was the younger son of the emperor Sher Sháh. His elder brother 'Adil Khán being absent at his father's death, Jalál Khán ascended the throne in the fortress of Kalinjar on the 29th of May, 1545 A. D., 17th Rabí' I, 952 A. H., and assumed the title of Islám Sháh, which by false pronunciation was turned to that of Salím Sháh. He reigned nine years and became afflicted with a fistula, of which he died at Gwáliar 1554 A. D., 961 A. H., in which year also died Mahmúd Sháh king of Gujrát, and Burhán Nizám Sháh king of Aḥmadnagar. In commemoration of the remarkable circumstance of these monarchs dying almost at the same time, Mauláná 'Alí the father of the celebrated historian Firishta, wrote a short epitaph, in which the words "the ruin of kings," exhibit the Hijrí year 961 A. D. The remains of Salím Sháh were conveyed to Sahsarám and buried close to his father's tomb, Salím Sháh was succeeded by his son the prince Fíroz, then 12 years of age, who was placed on the throne by the chiefs of the tribe of Súr, at Gwáliar. He had not reigned three days (some say three months) when Mubáriz Khán the son of Nizám Khán Súr, at once the nephew of the late Sher Sháh, and brother-in-law of Salím Sháh, assassinated the young prince, and ascending the throne, assumed the title of Muhammad Sháh 'Adil.

**Salima Sultana Begam,** سليمه سلطانه بيگم. The mother of this lady was Gulrukh Begam the daughter of the emperor Bábar Sháh who gave her in marriage to Mirzá Núr-uddín Muhammad by whom she had Salíma. Salíma was married to Bairám Khán KhánKhánán in 1558 A. D., the marriage took place at Jalandhar with the consent of the emperor Akbar who was present at the nuptials. After the death of Bairám Khán in 1561, she became the wife of the emperor, by whom she had a daughter named Sháhzáda Khánam, and a son named Sultán Murád. She was well-versed in Persian and had a good genius for poetry. She dide in the reign of the emperor Jahángír 1612 A. D., 1021 A. H.

**Salima Bano Begam,** سليمه بانو بيگم, the daughter of Sulaiman Shikoh, the son of Dára Shaikh, was married to Prince Muhammad Akbar, Aurangzeb's fourth son. Their offspring was Níkasiar who was proclaimed emperor at Ágrah and imprisoned by Rukn-uddaula.

**Salimi** or **Hasan Salimi, Maulana,** حسن سليمي مولانا, a poet who died and was buried at Sabzwar, in the year 1450 A. D., 854 A. H. He has left a Díwán.

**Salghur,** سلغر, from whom the Atábaks of Fárs were descended, was a Turkish general in the service of the Saljúḳí kings, and was entrusted with the charge of one of the princes of that race and appointed to the government of Fárs and some adjoining provinces. Salghur managed not only to keep his government during his life, but to transmit it to his descendants, seven of whom held Fárs as governors, *viz.* :—

1. Maudúd, the son of Salghur.
2. Fazlán-Shubán-Karra, who received the government from Alp Arsalán, rebelled, but was subdued by Nizám-ul-Mulk the prime-minister of the Sultán.
3. Rukn-uddaula.
4. Atábak Jalál-uddín Jawálí.
5. Atábak Kuraja, who built a college at Shíráz, and a palace called Takht Kuraja.
6. Atábak Mankús.
7. Búzába, who is said to have been a just and wise governor. After the death of Búzába who was the last of these governors, Atábak Sunḳar the great grandson of Salghur, succeeded in 1148 A. D., and became a powerful ruler. *Vide* Sunḳar and Muzaffar.

**Salibi** or **Thalibi, Imam,** ثالبي, author of the Taríkh Ghadr-us-Siar," and "Táríkh Aráes."

**Saliha Bano,** صالحه بانو, the daughter of Kásim Khán and wife of the emperor Jahángír who gave her the title of Bádsháh Mahal.

**Salik Ḳazwini,** and **Salik Yezdi,** سالك قزويني سالك يزدي. These two poets, one from Kazwín and the other from Yezd, flourished in the time of the emperor Sháh Jahán, and both died in the reign of 'Álamgír. Sálik Ḳazwíní died ln 1699 A. D., 1080 A. H., and the other, one year after him.

**Salik,** سالك, poetical title of Sháh Ibrahím.

**Salim,** حاجي محمد اسلم, author of a Díwán which he completed in 1701 A. D., 1082 A. H. His proper name is Hájí Muhammad Aslam.

**Saljuk,** سلجوق, *vide* Saljúḳí.

**Saljuki,** سلجوقي, a dynasty of Tartar kings who derive their name from Saljúk, a chief of great reputation, who had been compelled to quit the court of Bíghú Khán the sovereign of the Turks of Ḳapchák. Saljúḳ, who had proceeded with his tribe to the plains of Bukhárá, embraced the religion of Muhammad and acquired the crown of martyrdom in the war against the infidels. His age of an hundred and seven years, surpassed the life of his son Mikáíl; and Saljúḳ adopted the care of his two grandsons Tughral and Ja'far; the eldest of whom, at the age of 45 years was invested with the title of Sultán in the royal city of Naishápúr. It is said that Mikáíl became known to Sultán Mahmúd of Ghazní, and was greatly honoured by that monarch. They relate, that on Mahmúd asking the ambassador of their chief, what force they could bring to his aid; "Send this arrow," said the envoy, presenting one of two which he held in his hand, "and 50,000 horse will appear!"—"Is that all?" exclaimed Mahmúd. "Send this," said he presenting the other, "and an equal number will follow." "But suppose I was in extreme distress," observed the monarch, "and wanted your utmost exertions?"—"Then," replied the ambassador, "send my bow, and 200,000 horse will obey the summons!" The proud conqueror heard with secret alarm, this terrifying account of their numbers: and we are told that he anticipated the future overthrow of his empire. Tughral Beg and his brother served for several years under Sultán Mahmúd. In 1036 A. D., 429 A. H., the former resisted Sultán Masa'úd the son of Mahmúd, and received investiture as Sultán of Khurásán from the Khalífa of Baghdád. *Vide* Tughral Beg who was the first king of the Saljúk dynasty of Persia. Kadard was the first of Saljúk dynasty who reigned in Kirmán; Sulaimán or Kutlamish, the first Sultán of Saljúk dynasty who reigned in Rúm or Anatolia.

**Salman,** سلمان, a poet who died in 1530 A. D., 937 A. H.

**Salman, 'Aka,** آقا سلمان, also called Mirzá Hisábí, is the author of a commentary on the Preface of the Gulistán of about 3000 lines. He devoted himself to Súfyism and wrote a treatise thereon. He also compiled an Arabic Commentary on Kúsanjí's Persian treatise on astronomy; another work of his is called "Aosáf-ul-Bilád." He was living in 1585 A. D., 993 A. H.

**Salman Farsi,** سلمان فارسي, or the Persian. Is said to have been a native of a small place near Isfahán, and that on passing one day by a Christian Church, he was so much struck by the devotion of the people, and the solemnity of the worship, that he became disgusted with the idolatrous faith in which he had been brought up. He afterwards wandered about the East, from city to city, and convent to convent, in quest of a religion, until an ancient monk, full of years and infirmities, told him of a prophet who had arisen in Arabia to restore the pure faith of Abraham. He then journeyed to Mecca, and became a convert to Muhammadanism. This Salmán rose to power in after years, and was reputed by the unbelievers of Mecca to have assisted Muhammad in compiling his doctrines. He died at Madáen in Persia in 653 A. D., 33 A. H.

**Salman Sawaji,** سلمان ساوجي, a celebrated Persian poet, native of Sáwa, surnamed Jalál-uddín Muhammad, who flourished in the time of Amír Shaikh Hasan Jaláyer also called Hasan Buzurg, and his son Sultán Aweis, rulers of Baghdád. In the latter period of his life he became blind, and having retired from the world, died in the year 1377 A. D., 779 A. H. He is the author of a poem entitled "Jamsheid-wa-Khursheid," and of the "Firák-náma," and several other works, and also of a Díwán.

**Sam,** سام, the son of Narímán, and grandfather of Rustam the celebrated hero of Persia. *Vide* Zál and Manúchehr.

**Samanini,** ثمانيني, commonly called so, but his proper name is Abú'l Kásim 'Umar, and his father's name Sábit He was an excellent Arabic grammarian and died in 1050 A. D., 442 A. H.

**Sam Mirza,** سام مرزا, the son of Sháh Ismá'íl I. He is the author of the work called "Tuhfa Sámí," being a biography of the contemporaneous poets of Persia, compiled in 1550 A. D., 957 A. H. His poetical name is Sámí.

**Samrat Jagannatha,** شمرات جگناتهه, a Bráhman, who made a version of Euclid's Elements by order of Sewái Jai Singh, Rájá of Jaipúr, in Sanskrit and called it "Rekhi Ganita."

**Sam Sultan Bahadur,** سام سلطان بهادر, a native of Gujrát, and author of the "Táríkh Bahádur Sháhí."

**Saman,** سامان, the great-grandfather of Ismá'íl Sámán, the first king of the Samánides. His grandson Nasr Ahmad was appointed governor of Bukhárá by Mo'tamid the Khalífa of Baghdád, in 874 A. D., 261 A. H., *vide* Ismá'íl Samání.

**Samani,** ساماني, a dynasty of Muhammadan kings who reigned over Transoxania, holding its court at Bukhárá. Its power extended over Khwárizm, Máwar-un-Nahr, Jurján; Síwastán and Ghazní. This dynasty continued to reign in Bukhárá for a period of 128 years, when it became extinct by the death of its last prince 'Abdul-malik II, in 999 A. D., 389 A. H. The first king of this race was Ismá'íl Sámání, great-grandson of Sámán, a robber-chief from whom this dynasty took its name.

**Samani** or **Samnani,** ساماني, an Arabian author who in the 6th century of the Hijrí wrote a dictionary of the names of all the Arabian authors, entitled "Fi'l Ansáb," which in the succeeding century was abbreviated by Ibn-al-Asír, and this extract again shortened by Sayútí. *Vide* Jalál-uddín Sayútí.

**Sama-ullah, Shaikh,** شيخ سماء الله, or Samá-uddín, one of the great Masháekhs of India, and brother of Shaikh Isháḳ. He lived in the time of Sultán Bahlól Lodí, and died according to 'Abdul Haḳ in 1496 A. D., 901 A. H., and lies buried on the banks of the Hauz Shamsí at Dehlí.

**Sammugarh,** ساموگر, a place in Ágrah built by the emperor Akbar.

**Sambhaji,** سنبهاجي, the son of Sewájí Bhosla the Marhaṭṭa chief and second rájá of Sitára. He was at Parnála when his father died and a faction endeavoured to secure the succession to Rájá Rám, a son of Sewájí by another wife. But Sambhájí supported by the greater part of the troops, who had been the companions of his contests with the forces of the emperor 'Álamgír, established his sovereignty. He behaved with great cruelty to his opponents, imprisoned Rájá Rám and reigned nine years. He succeeded his father in April, 1680 A. D., generally spent his time in female pleasure and excessive drinking, and possessed no talents for government. He listened to the advice of no one, having a conceited opinion of his own abilities, and chose for his favourite Kab Kalás or Kálúsáh, a Bráhman with whom he acted such scenes as made him hateful to the world. He was taken prisoner together with his wife and children by the officers of the emperor 'Álamgír, who ordered him to be executed. His eyes were first destroyed with a hot iron, his tongue cut out, and he was at last beheaded along with his favourite. This event took place in July or August, 1689 A. D., 1100 A. H. His son Sáhjí also called Sáo or Sáhú, an infant, was acknowledged rájá by the Marhaṭṭas, but he was soon after taken prisoner by 'Álamgír and confined till the death of that monarch when he was released. *Vide* Sáhjí II.

**Sambhu Singh,** سنبهو سنگه, Maharana of Udaipúr and Meiwar, who was invested a G. C. S. I. on the 6th of December, 1871 A. D., died on the 7th October, 1874 A. D., at the early age of 27. He succeeded to the guddí of Mewar by adoption in 1862. His elevation was great and sudden, as his father, a brother of the late Rána Sarúp Singh had fallen under suspicion of conspiring to gain his way to the throne by poisoning the invalid Sarúp; and, while the father died under the hands of assassins in a prison within the walls of the palace, the son, along with other members of the family suffered for several years the most cruel persecution.

**Samnani,** سمناني, one of the chief followers of the Súfí sect who died in 1335 A. D., 736 A. H., six years before Khwája Kirmání. *Vide* Ata-uddaula Samnání.

**Samru** or **Sombre,** سامرو, *vide* Shamrú.

**Samsam-uddaula,** صمصام الدوله, title of Sháhnawáz Khán, which see.

**Samsam-uddaula** or **Samsam Jang,** صمصام الدولہ, صمصام جنگ, the son of Samsám-uddaula Sháhnawáz Khán, who received the same title after his father's death. Both of them held distinguished positions in the court of the Nizám of Haidarábád. *Vide* Sháhnawáz Khán.

**Samsam-uddaula,** صمصام الدولہ, the son of Mirzá Nasír who came to India from Mázindaran in the reign of the emperor Sháh Alam. Samsám-uddaula whose original name was Malik Muhammad Khán, received the title of Nawáb Samsám-uddaula Malik Muhammad Khán Dilair Jang from Nawáb Najaf Khán. He died in Jaipúr in 1804 A. D., 1219 A. H.

**Samsam-uddaula,** صمصام الدولہ, entitled Khán Daurán, held the high rank of Amír-ul-'Umrá in the reign of the emperor Muhammad Sháh. *Vide* Khán Daurán.

**Sana',** صانع, poetical name of Shaikh Nizám-uddín Aḥmad commonly called Basí Mián. He flourished about the year 1738 A. D., 1151 A. H.

**Sanai, Husain,** حسین ثنائی, *vide* Khwája Husain Sanaí.

**Sanai, Shaikh,** شیخ ثنائی, commonly called Hakím Sanáí, a celebrated poet and native of Ghazní, who flourished in the reign of Bahrám Sháh, son of Masa'úd Sháh of Ghazní. He is the author of several poems. His last work which he dedicated to Bahrám Sháh, is called the "Hadíḳa," or "Hadíḳat-ul-Haḳáeḳ," the Garden of Truth, a very beautiful poem on the unity of God and other religious subjects, said to contain 30,000 verses. This book he finished 1131 A. D., 525 A. H., in which year he is supposed to have died, aged 62 years. He is also the author of a small work containing about 280 verses, entitled "Ramúz-ul-Anbia wa Kanúz-ul-Aulia," and of a Díwán.

**Sanai, Maulana,** مولانا ثنائی, author of a poem, entitled Bágh Iram.

**Sana-ullah, Maulana,** مولانا ثنا اللہ, Ḳází of Panípat, flourished about the year 1539 A. D., 946 A. H., and is the author of the commentary called "Mazharí" and other works; one of which is called Saif-ul-Maslúf.

**Sandhal Deo,** ٹندھال دیو, one of the Rájás of Ameir, now called Jaipúr, After him reigned Gokul or Kantal, and after him reigned Pújandeva or Pajúrjí about the year 1185 A. D. He married the daughter of Prithi Rájá. After him Malesi, after him the following rájás reigned in succession, Bíjaljí, Rajdeo, who was defeated by Mahmúd II, 1251 A. D. Kílan, Kantal, who built the city of Ameir, Júnsi, Udaikaran, Nar Singh, Banbeír, Udheirao, Chandarsein, Prithiraj, murdered by his son Bhím, Ayskaran; after him reigned Bharamal also called Púranmal and Biharímal, which see.

**Sangham Lal,** سنگہم لال, a Hindú whose poetical name was Izzat. He was a pupil of Mirzá Ján Jánán Mazhar, and was living at Ágrah 1760 A. D., 1174 A. H.

**Sanjar, Mir,** میر سنجر also called Sháh Sanjar Bíjápúrí, was the son of Mír Haidar Káshí the punster. He was an excellent poet and flourished in the time of Sulṭán Ibráhím 'Adil of Bíjápúr. He died in 1612 A. D., 1021 A. H., and left a Díwán.

**Sangram Shah,** سنگرام شاہ, Rájá of Kharakpúr in South Bihár, defied the Mughal armies in the time of Akbar, lost his life in a struggle, and his son and successor were forced to become converts to Islám.

**Sanjar Shah,** سنجر شاہ, the son of Tughan Sháh II. He was cotemporary with Takash Khán who married his mother and adopted him; but when he rebelled against him, Takash blinded him.

**Sanjar, Sultan,** سلطان سنجر, the third son of Sulṭán Malikshàh Saljúḳí. He held at his father's death, 1092 A. D., the government of Khurásán, and took little concern in the troubles that ensued on that event: but after the death of his brother, Sulṭán Muhammad, he may be deemed the actual sovereign of Persia. He forced Bahrám Sháh, a monarch of the race of Ghazní, whose capital was Láhor, to pay him tribute; and Aláuddín, prince of Ghór, who had defeated Bahrám Sháh and taken Ghazní, yielded in his turn to the superior fortune of Sanjar, by whom he was defeated, made prisoner and tributary to the house of Saljúḳ. But Sanjar, after a long reign marked by singular glory and success, was destined to experience the most cruel reverses of fortune. In the year 1140 A. D., 535 A. H., he advanced far into Tartary to attack Gour Khán, the monarch of Ḳara Khatá, and suffered a signal defeat in which almost his whole army was cut to pieces, his family taken prisoner, and all his baggage plundered. He next marched, 1153 A. D., 547 A. H., against the Turkman tribe of Ghuz who had withheld their usual tribute of 40,000 sheep: an action ensued, in which he was defeated and taken prisoner. During his long confinement of four years, his dominions were ruled by his favourite Sulṭána Khátún Turkán: at whose death in 1156 A. D., 551 A. H., Sanjar made an effort to escape and was successful; but he lived only a short time after he regained his liberty, for he died on Friday the 24th May, 1157 A. D., 11th Rabí' II, 552 A. H., in the 73rd year of his age, and was buried in Marv. The Saljúḳ dynasty in Khurásán ceased with his existence, and most part of his kingdom fell into the possession of Khwárizm Sháh Atsiz ibn-Muhammad ibn-Anushtakím the grandfather of Takash Khwárizm Sháh. The poets of his court were Adíb Sábir, Rashíd Wátwát, Abdul Wáṣa, Jabalí, Faríd Kátib, Anwarí, Malik 'Imád Zauzaní, and Sayyad Husain of Ghazní.

**Sanka,** سنقا, *vide*Ráná Sánká.

**Sankar,** سنقر, *vide* Sunḳar.

**Saraj-uddin,** سراج الدین, *vide* Siráj-uddín.

**Sarbaland Khan,** سربلند خان, an Amír of the time of the emperor 'Alamgír, who held the rank of 4000 and died in the year 1679 A. D., 1090 A. H.

**Sarakhsi** or **Al-Sarakhsi,** سرخسي, *vide* Abú Bakr Muhammad-al-Sarakhsí.

**Sarbadal,** سربدال, a tribe of Afgháns of Sabzwár. *Vide* 'Abdul Razzáḳ.

**Sarbaland Khan,** سربلند خان, entitled Nawáb Mubáriz-ul-Mulk, was governor of Patna in the time of Farrukh-siyar, and was recalled to court about the year 1718 A. D., 1130 A. H. In the reign of the emperor Muhammad Sháh he was appointed governor of Gujrát 1724 A. D., 1137 A. H., but in 1730 A. D., 1143 A. H. was removed from his government on account of his consenting to pay the Marhaṭṭas the Chouth or part of the revenue of that province, and Rájá Abhay Singh the son of Ajít Singh Raṭhor was appointed to succeed him. Sarbaland Khán made some opposition to his successor, but was defeated and prevented from coming to court by the emperor. He was, however, after some time appointed governor of Allahábád, 1732 A. D., 1145 A. H., when he deputed his son Khánazád Khán to command, himself residing at court. He died in 1745 A. D., 1158 A. H.

**Sardar Singh,** سردار سنگه, present Rájá of Bikaneir, (1857).

**Sari Sakti,** سري سقطي, a celebrated Musalmán saint, was called Saḳtí because he formerly dealt in metals, but afterwards became a disciple of Marúf Karkhí. He was the uncle of Shaikh Junaid as well as his master. The following anecdote is related on good authority: Sarí Saḳtí said that for thirty years he never ceased imploring divine pardon for having once exclaimed, "*Praise be to God!*" and on being asked the reason, he said: "A fire broke out in Baghdád, and a person came up to me and told me that my shop had escaped, on which I uttered those words, and even to this moment I repent having said so, because it showed that I wished better to myself than to others." He died on Wednesday the 9th of August, 870 A. D., 6th Ramazán, 256 A. H., and is buried at Baghdád. Some authors say that he died three years before that period.

**Sarfaraz Khan, Nawab,** نواب سرفراز خان, entitled 'Alá-uddaula, was the son of Nawáb Shuja-uddaula or Shuja-uddín, governor of Bengal, whom he succeeded on the 13th March, 1739 A. D., 13th Ẕil-ḥijja 1151 A. H. He reigned one year and two months, and was slain in an attack made by Alahwardí Khán Mahábat Jang on the 29th April, 1740 A. D., 13th Ṣafar, 1153 A. H. The cause of this murder is thus recorded: "'Alá-uddaula having accidentally met the niece of his wazír Mahábat Jang, a young lady who bore the repute of being the most beautiful woman of the age, first commanded, and then entreated, her to withdraw her veil, that he might enjoy one look at her face. The modest damsel, overwhelmed with confusion and terror, entreated the prince's pardon, and, pleading eloquently for her honour, declined to gratify his curiosity; but he, being charmed with her exquisite grace and the delicious tones of her voice, was fired with a hasty determination, and himself withdrew the veil. He gazed in ardent admiration on her lovely countenance for a few seconds; then dropping the drapery, he asked forgiveness for his rudeness, and paying the beauty some princely compliment, passed on. The unhappy girl fled in tears to her father, 'Atáulláh, and to her uncle the wazír, and with mixed indignation and shame, declared the sad tale of her disgrace, and immediately afterwards destroyed herself with poison. Suffice it to say, that the prince became their victim within a few hours."

**Sarfi Sawaji,** صرفي سناوجي, a poet named Shaikh Yaḳúb who flourished in the time of the emperor Akbar, and wrote a chronogram on the death of Amír Fath-ulláh Shírází and Hakím Abú'l Fatha Gíláni, both of whom died in 1589 A. D., 997 A. H. He was a native of Sáwa in Persia and came to India where he died in 1595 A. D., 1003 A. H., and left a Díwán.

**Sarfoji,** سرفوجي, Rájá of Tanjore, a descendant of Ekkojí, the brother of the celebrated Síwájí the Marhaṭṭa chief. By the treaty of 25th October, 1799 A. D., the English Government decided between two rival claimants, to place Sarfojí upon the masnad, on condition that he transferred the management of his territory to the British, consenting to receive in lieu of its revenue, an annual payment of £118,350. The absolute sovereignty of the fortress and city of Tanjore itself, were at the same time guaranteed to the prince. Sarfojí died in 1832 A. D., and was succeeded by his only son Síwájí, who reigned 23 years and died on the 29th October, 1855 A. D., leaving no legitimate son to succeed him. The surviving family consisted of the following persons: *viz.*, The Queen Dowager, 16 wives, 2 daughters, 2 sisters, 6 natural sons, 11 natural daughters, and 54 collaterals.

**Sarhindi Begam,** سرهندي بيگم, one of the wives of Sháhjahán, who built a garden at Ágrah, no traces of which are left now.

**Sarkhush,** سرخوش, the poetical name of Muhammad Afzal who was born in 1640 A. D., 1050 A. H., flourished in the time of the emperor 'Álamgír. He wrote a biography of the poets of his own time, entitled "Kalmát-ush-Shu'ará," the letters of which, if taken according to their respective numbers, will give the year in which it was written, *viz.*, 1682 A. D., 1093 A. H. He was a good poet, had the good fortune to become acquainted with almost all men of talents of his day. He died at the advanced age of 76 years about the year 1714 A. D., 1126 A. H., and left besides the above-mentioned work, four Masnawís or poems, *viz.*, "Husn-o-Ishḳ," "Núr-i-'Alí," "Sáḳí-náma," and "Sháh-náma Muhammad 'Azim."

**Sarmad** or **Muhammad Sarmad,** سرمد, Ḳazí of Seringapatam in the time of Típú Sulṭán, by whose request he translated into Persian a work in the Dakhaní dialect, and called it "Khulása Sulṭání."

**Sarmad,** سرمد, the poetical name of an Armenian merchant who came to India in the reign of the emperor Sháh Jahán. In one of his journeys towards Ṭhaṭṭa, he fell so passionately in love with a Hindú girl, that he became distracted and would go about the streets stark naked. He was well-versed in the Persian language and was a good poet. In the beginning of the reign of 'Álamgír, he was sentenced to death on account of his disobeying the orders of that emperor who had commanded him not to go about naked. This event took place about the year 1661 A. D., 1072 A. H. Some say that the real cause of his execution was a Rubáí which he had composed, the translation of which is "The Mullas say that Muhammad entered the heavens; but Sarmad says that the heavens entered Muhammad." His tomb is close to the Jamạ Masjid at Dehlí.

**Sarmadi,** سرمدي, Takhallus of Muhammad Sharíf of Isfahán. He died 1606 A. D., 1015 A. H.

**Sarup Chand,** سروپ چند, a Hindú, who is the author of a history called "Sahíh-ul-Akhbar."

**Sarsabz,** سارشابز, poetical name of Mirzá Zain-ul-Abidín Khán, son of Nawáb Salar Jang. He is the author of a Díwán.

**Sarup Singh, Rana,** رانا سروپ سنگه, present Rájá of Udaipúr, (1857) died 1862 A. D.

**Sarshar,** سرشار, the poetical name of Murshid Ḳulí Khán Rustum Jang, son-in-law of Nawáb Shujá-uddín of Bengal. He was living in the time of Nawáb Mahábat Jang.

**Sarwar,** سرور, poetical name of 'Azim-uddaula Nawáb Mír

Muhammad Khán Bahádur, a son of 'Azim-uddaula Abú'l Kásim Muzaffar Jang. He died in 1834 A. D., Shawwál, 1250 A. H., and left besides the Tazkira called "Umda-e-Muntakhiba," a thick Díwán.

**Sarwat,** سروت, *vide* Jugal Kishór.

**Sata,** ساطع, takhallus of a poet.

**Satesh Chandar Rae Bahadur,** چندرای بهادر سیتش, Mahárájá of Nadea, the great-grandson of Rájá Kishan Chandar Rae who aided the English in despoiling Siráj-uddaula, died November, 1870 A. D.

**Sayadat Khan,** سیادت خان, brother of Islám Khán, a nobleman of the reign of Sháh Jahán; he died in the month of July, 1659 A. D. His son's name was Fazl-ulláh Khán.

**Sayyad Ahmad Kabir,** سید احمد کبیر, grandfather of Sayyad Jalál Bukhárí, and a Musalmán saint, whose tomb is in Bijaimandil near the tomb of Sháh Muhammad Khayálí at Dehlí.

**Sayyad Ahmad,** سید احمد منصف دهلي, Munsif of Dehlí in the British Government service, was the son of Sayyad Muhammad Muttakí Khán Bahádur, and author of the work called "Asár Sanádíd," containing a description of old Dehlí and Sháhjahánábád, and also of another work, entitled "Silsilat-ul-Malúk." The native place of his ancestors, is Arabia. They removed afterwards to Hirat, and during the reign of Akbar the Great, they came into India. Ever since that period, they have enjoyed royal titles and dignity. He was living in 1857 A. D., 1273 A. H.

**Sayyad Ahmad,** سید احمد, brother of the celebrated Sayyad Jalál Bukhárí. He was left in charge of Gujrát by Dárá Shikóh in 1659 A. D. His elder brother's name was Sayyad Jafar Khán. His tomb is near Tájganj at Agrah.

**Sayyad Ahmad Khan,** سید احمد خان, *vide* Ahmad Khán (Sayyad).

**Sayyad Ahmad,** سید احمد بریلوي, of Bareilí, who raised a religious war with the Sikhs in the Panjáb and was killed at Balákot. He began life in an indifferent school for the character of reformer and saint, which he ultimately assumed, as a sawár serving with Amír Khán's free-booting horse in Málwá. Quitting that service, he repaired to Dehlí, and became a disciple of Sháh 'Abdul 'Azíz, a very celebrated devotee of the city; the fame of whose knowledge and piety has been widely extended throughout this side of India. It is frequently said by natives, that it was from Sháh 'Abdul 'Azíz, that Sayyad Ahmad derived the peculiar opinions which he subsequently promulgated, and the design which he adopted of preaching up a religious war. It is at least certain, that the chief of his first disciples, and the most constant associates of all his fortunes, were two near relatives of 'Abdul 'Azíz, one his nephew, Maulwí Muhammad Ismá'íl, author of the Sirát-ul-Mustakím, the other his son-in-law, and also partially a contributor to the book, named Maulwí 'Abdul Hai. By these persons, Muhammad Ismá'íl is generally esteemed to have been a man of much talent and learning. The extreme honour which he and his brother Maulwí paid to Sayyad Ahmad, who was himself nearly illiterate, had a powerful effect in attracting towards him the respect of the vulgar. They rendered him almost menial offices, running, it is said, with their shoes off, by the side of his palankeen, when, he moved out with his servants. From his first leaving Dehlí, he assumed the name of a religious teacher, and commenced spreading his religious doctrines. The general spirit by which these were animated (identical nearly with that of the tenets of the Arabian Wahábís, of whom the sect of Sayyad Ahmad may perhaps be accurately termed an Indian imitation) was the ardent profession of Muhammadanism in its primitive simplicity and fervour, and the utter rejection of all idolatrous or superstitious innovations, whencesoever derived. The manner in which they were at first actually received was, however, highly favourable. When Sayyad Ahmad at last came down to Bengal, he had got together many followers, and had established an extensive reputation. He arrived in Calcutta with a considerable retinue towards the end of 1821 A. D., and immediately a great majority of the Muhammadans of the place, of all ranks and stations, flocked to become, or to profess themselves, his disciples. In the early part of 1822, he proceeded with his friends, the two Moulwís, to Mecca, from whence he returned in October of the next year, having touched for a few days at Bombay, where, with reference to the shortness of his stay, his success, in gaining numerous followers, was nearly as remarkable as in Calcutta. In December, 1823 A. D., he again started for Upper India. The next important event of his career, his commencing a religious war in the Láhor territories, did not occur till after a considerable interval, though the enterprise was one in which he had long openly announced his intention to engage. Its date is given in the "Targhíb-ul-Jihád," or "Incitement of Religious War," a little treatise written in Hindústání during the continuance of the struggle, by a Maulwí of Kanauj, with the view, as its name purports, of rousing the Faithful to rally round the standard which had been raised in the Panjáb. "The tribe of Sikhs," says the indignant Maulwí, "have long held sway in Láhor and other places. Their oppressions have exceeded all limits. Thousands of Muhammadans they have unjustly killed, and on thousands have they heaped disgrace. The 'Azán, or summons for prayer, and the killing of cows, they have entirely prohibited. When at length their insulting tyranny could no longer be borne, Sayyad Ahmad, going to the direction of Kábul and Kandahár, roused the Muhammadans of those countries, and nerving their courage for action in the service of God, some thousands of believers became ready at his call to tread the path of God's service; and on the 21st December, 1826 A. D., 20th Jumáda I, 1242 A. H., the Jihád against the Káfir Sikhs began." The events of this war were watched with a natural interest by the Muhammadan population of India generally, whether followers of Sayyad Ahmad or not. Many of the inhabitants of our Western Provinces went in bodies to range themselves under his standard; and his emissaries gathered large contributions of money and jewels, even from our own distant Presidencies, and from the principal Muhammadan towns of the Dakhin. The prominent occurrences of the war, the perseverance with which it was kept up, the temporary and occasional successes which Sayyad Ahmad met with, and his ultimate death in battle, are well known. With his death, the struggle appears to have entirely ceased.—*Journal Asiatic Society of Bengal,* Vol. I, p. 480.

**Sayyad 'Ali** or **Sayyad 'Ali Hamdani,** علي همداني سید, a famous Sayyad who fled to Kashmír from his native city of Hamdán where he had incurred the wrath of Amír Taimúr. Seven hundred Sayyads are said to have accompanied his flight to Kashmír in the reign of Sultán Kutb-uddín. He arrived in that province in 1380 A. D., 782 A. H. He remained at Kashmír six years and named it the "Garden of Solomon" (Bágh Sulaimán). He died at Paklí whilst on his return to Persia. His son Mír Muhammad Hamdání, also a fugitive, brought in his train three hundred Sayyads to Kashmír, where he remained twelve years. These two immigrations of fugitive Sayyads fixed the religion of the country, and were doubtless the chief cause of the religious persecutions which ensued in the following reign.

**Sayyad 'Ali Shirazi,** سيد علي شيرازي, the saint of the Jokhia Sindhi tribe. His tomb is in Tatta. The inscription bears the date 1776 A. D., 1190 A. H.

**Sayyad 'Ali bin-Shahab-uddin Hamdani,** سيدعلي بن شهاب الدين همداني, author of the "Tazkirat-ul-Malúk," treating upon religion, articles of faith, duty of kings to their subjects, &c., &c.

**Sayyad Husain Shahid, Amir,** اميرسيد حسين شهيد, a Muhammadan saint or martyr, who was slain on the 9th of May, 1538 A. D., 9th Ẓil-ḥijja, 944 A. H. in the time of the emperor Humáyún, and is buried at a place called Náikí Mandí at A'grah, where his tomb is to be seen to this day bearing a Persian inscription in verse.

**Sayyad Kabir, Sayyad,** سيد سيد كبير. His tomb is still to be seen at A'grah near a place called Sulṭánganj, and from the inscription on the tombstone, we learn that he died in 1609 A. D., 1018 A. H.

**Sayyad Muhammad or Said Muhammad,** سيد محمد, author of an Arabic work on Theology called "Asrár 'Ulúm."

**Sayyad Muhammad,** سيد محمد, a poet whose poetical name is Rind, *vide* Rind.

**Saydi, Mir,** ميرصيدي, a poet of Persia who in 1654 A. D., 1064 A. H. came to India in the reign of Sháh Jahán. It is said that in one instance he received a present of 5000 rupees from Jahán 'Ará Begam the daughter of the emperor, and in another one lac for his poems. He died in 1672 A. D., 1083 A. H. and is the author of a Díwán containing, 4,000 verses.

**Saifi of Bukhara, Mulla,** ملا سيفي بخاري. He is the author of two Díwáns, one of Ghazals, and the other for the use of trades-people. *Vide* the following article.

**Saifi of Naishapur,** سيفي نيشاپوري, a poet who flourished in the reign of Aláuddín Takask of Khwarizm. There are several other poets of this name, such as Saifí of Bukhára, Amír Hájí Saif-uddín Saifí, a nobleman at the court of Amír Taimúr, &c. One of them is the author of a small work on the art of writing poetry, called "Urúz Saifí" which he wrote in the year 1491 A. D., or 896 A. H. This work was translated into English in 1872 A. D. by H. Blochmann, M. A.

**Saif Khan,** سيف خان, a nobleman of the reign of the emperor 'A'lamgír, who was appointed governor of the Súba of A'grah in September, 1659 A. D., 1070 A. H.

**Saif Khan,** سيف خان, the brother of Zain Khán Koka.

**Saif Khan,** سيف خان بن ابراهيم خان, son of Ibráhím Khán, Fatha Jang governor of Bengal by a sister of the empress Núr Jahán, named Malika Báno Begam. His aunt the empress, having no sons by Jahángír, adopted Saif Khán as her own, and he was from his tender years brought up at court by the empress. He was subsequently governor of Bardwán where after some years as he was riding on an elephant through the street, a child was accidently trodden to death. The parents loudly demanded an exemplary punishment on the driver. Saif Khán refused their request and ordered them to be driven away. They made their complaint to the emperor, who ordered Saif Khán to make them ample amends for their loss; but Saif Khán threw them into prison which coming to the ears of the emperor, he sent for Saif Khán at Láhor, and for his disobedience had him trodden to death in the presence of the child's parents.

**Saif Khan Koka,** سيف خن كوكه, eldest brother of Zain Khán Kóka, who was raised by the emperor Akbar to the rank of 4000. He was killed in battle against Muhammad Husain Mirzá at Aḥmadábád Gujrát in the year 1572 A. D., 980 A. H.

**Saif-uddin Lachin, Amir,** اميرسيف الدين لاچين, a Turk of the tribe of Láchín, came to India about the year 1253 A. D., 651 A. H., and served under several emperors of Dehlí. He is the father of 'Azz-uddín 'Alí Sháh, Hisám-uddín Aḥmad and of Abú'l Hasan who is commonly called Amír Khusro, the celebrated poet of Hindústán.

**Saif-uddin Asfarikati,** سيف الدين اسفراكاتي, a poet who was a native of Asfaríkat a town in Máwar-unnahr. He flourished in the time of one of the Sulṭáns of Khwárizm, named Alp or Apal Arsalán who reigned after Atsiz and died in 1166 A. D., 561 A. H. Saif-uddín has left a Díwán containing 12,000 verses.

**Saif-uddaula,** سيف الدوله, a prince of Hamdán who reigned about the year 967 A. D., 356 A. H.

**Saif-uddaula or Saif-uddin,** سيف الدوله, son of 'Alá-uddín Hasan Ghórí, whom he succeeded in the kingdom of Ghór and Ghazní 1156 A. D., 551 A. H., and made over the latter province to his cousin Ghayás-uddín Muhammad the son of Sám. He was slain in a battle he fought against the Ghizán Turkmans 1163 A. D., 558 A. H., after a reign of seven years, and was succeeded by his cousin Ghayás-uddín.

**Saif-uddaula,** سيف الدوله whose proper name is Mír Najábat 'Alí Khán, was the second son of Mír Ja'far 'Alí Khán, governor of Bengal, Behar and Urysa. He succeeded his brother Najm-uddaula who died of small-pox, in May, 1766 A. D., Ẓil-ḥijja, 1179 A. H., and assumed the title of Saif-uddaula. A pension was granted to him by the English, and the business of Náẓim managed by deputy. He lived after this three years and ten months, and died on the 10th March 1770 A. D., 8th Ẓi-Ḳa'da, 1183 A. H. He was succeeded by his younger brother Mubárik-uddaula, a minor.

**Saif-uddaula,** سيف الدوله. This man, who was a faithful follower of Mirzá Najaf Khán, was a Hindú Rájpút called Raṭhor, a native of Bikaneir. Having been in service at Allahábád under the brother of the late Wazír, father of Muhammad Ḳulí; he became a Muhammadan about the year 1866, and was appointed to the charge of districts returning 20 lacs a year, with the title of Saif-uddaula.—*Mr. H. G. Keene's Moghul Empire*, page 110.

**Saif-uz-zafar Naubahari,** سيف الظفر بنجرنوبهار, author of a work called "Durr-ul-Majális," containing anecdotes of various persons from the earliest ages to the time of Abú Sa'íd Abú'l Khair who died in 1048 A. D., 440 A. H., together with a description of heaven and hell. He is also called Sayúf Zafar Naubahárí.

**Sayyad,** سيد, the Sayyads who are also called Mírs, are the descendants of 'Alí, the son-in-law of the prophet.

**Sayyad Abdullah,** سيد عبد الله, son of Sayyad 'Abdul

Kádir Gílání, the great saint of Baghdád. His tomb is in the city of Tatta in Sindh.

**Sayyad,** سيد, the poetical title assumed by Sayyad Namat-ullah Walí.

**Sayyad Ahmad Jalal Bukhari,** احمد جلال بخاري سيد. *Vide* Abú Jalál Bukhárí.

**Sayyad 'Ali,** سيد علي, *vide* Sayyad 'Alí.

**Sayyad Husain** or **Mir Husain,** سيد حسين, a celebrated Muhammadan of Ghazní who died at Hirát in December, 1317 A. D., Shawwál, 717 A. H., aged 117 lunar years. He is the author of works called Nazhat-ul-Arwáh and Kanz-ul-Ramúz.

**Sayyad Husain, Makhdum,** مخدوم سيد حسين, a contemporary of Shaikh Nizám-uddín Aulia, and author of the work called "Siar-ul-Aulia. See Wajíh-uddín Mubárik Kirmání.

**Sayyad Husain,** سيد حسين خنگ سوار, commonly called Khink Sawár. It is mentioned in the Akbar-náma, that Sayyad Husain came to India with Shaháb-uddín Ghórí, who after his conquest of India in 1192 A. D., 588 A. H. left him behind as governor of Ajmeir where he died some years after, and was buried on the hill where the fort of Ajmeir then stood. He is now venerated by the Muhammadans as a saint.

**Sayyad Ismail Shah,** سيد اسمعيل شاه, commonly called "Pír Chattar," a Muhammadan saint, whose tomb is situated about two thousand paces out of the western gates of the city of Broach on the northern bank of the Narbada. The tomb is said to be upwards of three hundred years old. It is built of the ordinary form in a small enclosure. It is shaded by a Khizni tree which grows by the side of the eastern wall out of the enclosure. In the middle of the tomb is a reservoir about 5 feet 4 inches by 1 foot 8 inches, and in depth about 1 foot 2 inches. In the midst of the water there rises about one inch above it, a small island, or the inner tomb, of 4 feet by 1. This miraculous reservoir is always full to the brim of very cold water. Hundreds of visitors go to the shrine every Thursday, and drink a tumbler full of the water, but it never diminishes nor increases.

**Sayyad Ja'far,** سيد جعفر زنبيرپوري of Zamírpúr or Zambírpúr, was a descendant of Sayyad Namat-ullah Walí. His poetical name was Rúhí. He died on the 30th of October, 1741 A. D., 1st Ramazán, 1154 A. H., and is buried at Zambírpúr, a place situated thirty miles from Lakhnau.

**Sayyad Ja'far Khan,** سيد جعفر خان, the eldest son of Sayyad Jalál Bukhárí, and brother of Sayyad Ahmad. After his father's death he sat on the masnad of Irshád as a spiritual guide. He lived in the time of the emperor 'Alamgír.

**Sayyad Jalal Bukhari,** سيد جلال بخاري, *vide* Shaikh Jalál.

**Sayyad Jalal Bukhari,** سيد جلال بخاري, son of Sayyad Muhammad Bukhárí and a descendant of Sayyad Ahmad Kabír. A very proud and learned Musalmán who held the rank of 6000 in the reign of the emperor Sháh Jahán. He was born on the 11th February, 1595 A. D., 11th Jumáda, II, 1003 A. H. and died in 1647 A. D., 1057 A. H. and is buried near the gate of the city of Dehlí. Some say his tomb is near Tájganj at Agrah.

**Sayyad Sharif Jurjani,** سيد شريف جرجاني, *vide* Sharíf Jurjání.

**Sayyad Said,** سيد سعيد, Sultán of Oman, and Imám of Muskat, who at the age of 16, ascended the throne in 1803 A. D. and reigned till his death in 1856. His dominions, after his death, were divided among two of his sons, one of whom is established at Zanzibár, the other resides at Muskat, and has the sovereignty of the Asiatic Provinces.

**Sayyad Tehrani,** سيد طهراني, author of a Díwán found in Típú Sultán's Library.

**Sayyad Said,** سيد سعيد, Imám of Muskat. The connection of the British with Muskat commenced in the beginning of the present century, when in conjunction with the then Imám, Sayyad Saíd, the English were engaged in suppressing the Wahabí pirates who infested the Persian Gulf and the Indian Ocean. Sayyad Saíd lived to a great age and filled the throne of Muskat for about fifty years. He died in 1856 A. D., and was succeeded by his son Thowayní who has recently been murdered by his son Salím. The old Imám left several sons, one of whom received as his share the kingdom of Zanzibár and the other Sayyad Turkí another chiefship.

In the year 1868 A. D., one Azan bin-Ghais, aided by the other potentates, having attacked and driven the Sultán from the throne, occupied it himself. Sultán Salím fled to Bandar Abbás, where he is now. The new ruler Azan bin-Ghais is no doubt connected with the Wahabís and supported by them.

**Sayadat, Mir Jalal-uddin,** سيادت, a son of Mír Jamál-uddín Muhaddis. He flourished about the year 1670 A. D., 1081 A. H., and is the author of a Díwán.

**Sayuf Zafar, Naubahari,** سيوف ظفر نوبهارى, this is his correct name, however see under Saif-uz-zafar Naubahárí.

**Sayuti,** سيوطي, *vide* Jalál-uddín Sayútí.

**Sidi** or **Sayyad Maula,** سيدى مولا, a venerable sage, in a mendicant dress, who travelled from Jurján towards the east and arriving at Dehlí, set up a great academy and house of entertainment for travellers and the poor of all denominations. Though he was very religious, and brought up in the Muhammadan faith, yet he followed some particular tenets of his own, so that he never attended public worship. He kept no women nor slaves for himself, and lived upon rice only; yet his expenses in charity were so great, that, as he never accepted any presents, men were astonished whence his finances were supplied, and actually believed, that he possessed the art of transmuting other metals into gold. He made nothing of bestowing two or three thousand pieces of gold to relieve the wants of any noble family in distress. In short, he displayed more magnificence in his feasts than the princes themselves. He expended daily upon the poor 1000 maunds of flour, 500 maunds of meat, 80 maunds of sugar, besides rice, oil, butter and other necessaries in proportion. He latterly began to bestow titles and offices upon his disciples, and to assume a tone and manner sufficiently indicative of his design on the throne. One of his followers dissatisfied with the part assigned to him, went privately to the king (Jalál-uddín Fíroz Khiljí) and disclosed the plot. The king caused him to be apprehended and trodden to death by an elephant. This event happened in the year 1291 A. D., 690 A. H., and is accounted one of the most remarkable events that took place in the reign of that monarch, for many believed him entirely innocent of the charge.

**Sidi 'Ali Kapudan,** سيدي علي كپدان, or Captain of the fleet of Sulṭán Sulaiman I, emperor of Constantinople. He is the author of the work called "Mirat-ul-Mumálik," or Mirror of Countries, containing a description of his journey overland from the Indian shores to Constantinople; and of the "Muhít," that is the Ocean, a Turkish work on Navigation in the Indian Seas. This work the author finished at Aḥmadábád the capital of Gujrát in December, 1554 A. D., Muḥarram, 962 A. H. It was translated by the Baron Joseph von Hammer, Professor, Oriental Languages, at Vienna, and communicated through the Journal of the Asiatic Society of Bengal in 1837.

**Simi Naishapuri,** سيمي نيشاپوري, a very learned Musalmán of Naishápúr. It is said that in one night and day, he composed 3,000 verses. He flourished in the time of Prince 'Aláuddaula (the son of Báisanghar Mirzá) who reigned at Hirát 1447 A. D.

**Sina, Abu Sina** or **Avicenna,** سينا, *vide* Abú Sína.

**Sirati,** سيرتي, a poet who wrote Kasídas, of which some are panegyrics on Sadiḳ Khán and his son Jafar Khán Rází, kings of Persia, the latter of whom was murdered in 1785 A. D., 1199 A. H.

**Seibuya,** سيبويه, an author who received this name on account of his keeping an apple (seib) in his hand, and smelling it often, but his proper name was Abú Bashar 'Umar. He died in 796 A. D., 180 A. H., aged 32 years. See Ḳutrib.

**Seindhia,** سيند هيه, for Rájás of the Seindhia family, *vide* Ránójí Seindhia.

**Seiwaji** or **Siwaji,** سيواجي, a celebrated chief of the Bhosla family and founder of the Marhaṭṭa States in the Dakhin, of whose origin we have the following account. Bhím Sen, ráná of Udaipúr, the first in rank among the Hindú princes, had a son named Bhág Singh by a concubine of a tribe very inferior to his own. On the death of his father, Bhág Singh finding himself despised and neglected by his relations, the Sisodhia rájpúts, who from the low caste of his mother, regarded him only as a bastard, and not of their tribe, became weary of the indignities shewn him; and moved from Udaipúr to Khándesh where he embraced the service of a Zamíndár, named Rájá 'Alí Móhan. He afterwards retired into the Dakhin, where he purchased a tract of land near the present Marhaṭṭa capital of Púna, and settled upon it as Zamíndár, in which situation he died. Bhág Singh had four sons, two of whom, Mallújí and Bambújí, being of an enterprising spirit, entered into the service of Jádho Ráe, a Marhaṭṭa chief of distinguished rank at the court of Bahádur Nizám Sháh. Mallújí had a son named Sáhjí or Sáújí who married the daughter of Jádho Ráe, and thus the Bhósla family became incorporated with the Marhaṭṭas, and are commonly esteemed as such in Hindústán. Sáhjí, after the death of his father, left Aḥmadnagar with his followers and entered into the service of Ibrahím 'Adil Sháh, king of Bíjápúr, who gave him a jágír in the Karnatic, with a command of ten thousand horse. Soon after this in May, 1627 A. D. his son Sewájí, afterwards so celebrated in the Dakhin, was born, from the daughter of Jádho Ráe Marhaṭṭa. Sáhjí having disagreed with his wife, sent her, with the infant Sewájí, to reside at Púna, of which, and the vicinity, he had obtained a grant. Sewájí though neglected by his father was properly educated, and at the age of seventeen excelled in every accomplishment. Military fame was his first passion; and the government of Bíjápúr being now weakened by intestine divisions and the encroachments of the Mughals, he had soon an opportunity of signalizing himself among other rebels. He raised a banditti, and plundered the neighbouring districts, and having now taken possession of the jágír, raised more troops, successfully levied contributions on several Zamíndárs, and much extended the limits of his territories. At this crisis the prince Aurangzeib, governor of the imperial territories in the Dakhin, was meditating the overthrow of his brother Dárá Shikóh, the favourite son of the emperor Sháh Jahán, who was now in a dangerous state of health. For this purpose he was preparing an army to march to Ágrah; and, observing the enterprizing genius of Sewájí, sent him an invitation to his service. Sewájí pretending to be struck with horror at the rebellion of a son against a father, received the prince's messenger with indignity, drove him from his presence, and ordered the letter he had brought, to be tied to the tail of a dog. Aurangzeib for the present stifled his resentment, but never would forgive Sewájí's insolence, and hence may be dated his tedious war in the Dakhin, and finally the ruin of the Mughal empire by the Marhaṭṭas. Aurangzeib having left the Dakhin in 1658 A. D., 1068 A. H., Siwají resolved to turn the inactivity of the imperial troops, and the weakness of the Gólkanḍa and Bíjápúr princes, to the utmost advantage. He took the strong fortress of Rájgaṛh, which he fixed upon as the seat of his government. The Bíjápúr government having in vain desired his father Sáhjí, (who disclaimed all connection with him) to repress the excesses of his son, at length sent against him a considerable force under a general named Afzul Khán. Sewájí with artful policy invited him to come and receive his submission. Afzul Khán advanced without opposition to his tent, when he was stabbed by the treacherous Zamíndár in embracing him. Upon a signal given, the Marhaṭṭás rushed from an ambuscade, attacked the unsuspecting army of Bíjápúr, which, deprived of their chief, was quickly defeated. Sewájí plundered their rich camp, and by this victory became master of all Kókan, the Zamíndárs of which flocked to acknowledge his authority, to save their possessions. The strong fortress of Sitára and other places also opened their gates to receive him. In the course of only three years, Sewájí became a powerful prince, his authority being acknowledged over almost the whole coast of Máṛwár. He built palaces and erected fortifications in every part of his country; gave much trouble to the emperor 'Álamgír; reigned more than twenty years, and left a character which has never since been equalled or approached by any of his countrymen. He died on the 14th April, 1680 A. D., 24th Rabí' I, 1091 A. H., but according to Elphinstone's History of India, on the 5th April the same year, aged 53 years. His funeral pile was administered with the same sacrifices as had been devoted the year before to the obsequies of the Mahárájá Jaswant Singh of Jodhpúr; attendants, animals, and wives, were burnt with his corpse. He was succeeded by his son Sambha or Sambhájí.

**Seoji** or **Shioji,** سيوجي, a grandson of the renowned Jaichánd, the last Ráṭhor monarch of Ḳanauj. He with a few retainers migrated in the year 1212 A. D., and planted the Ráṭhor standard in Máṛwár. His successors in process of time, by valour, and by taking advantage of the times, enlarged the state, and in 1432 A. D., Jódhá Ráo of Máṛwár, founded the modern capital of Jódhpúr, to which he transferred the seat of government from Mandór. The name of Máṛwár is a corruption of Márúwár, also called Márú-deis, or "the region of death." Anciently, and properly, it included the entire western desert, from the Satlaj to the ocean.

**Shabib,** شبيب بن يزيد بن نعيم, the son of Yezíd, the son of Naḍím, was a Khárajite. It is related that his father Yezíd was sent by 'Usmán the Khalíf to assist the Syrian Muhammadans against the Greeks in the twenty-fifth year of the Hijra. The Musalmáns obtaining the victory, the Christians were exposed for sale. Among the captives Yezíd espied a beautiful maid, whom he bought, and married. She proved with child of Shabíb, who was born on the 10th of the month of Zil-hijja, being the day on which the pilgrims kill the sacrifices at Mecca. He opposed Hajjáj the governor of Mecca for a long time, and was at last drowned in a river. His body being drawn out, his head was cut off and sent to Hajjáj. This happened in 696 A. D., 77 A. H.

**Shadan,** شاداں, poetical title of Ráe Chandra Lál, an Amír in the service of the Nizám of Haidarabád.

**Shaddad,** شداد, the Adite, was the son of 'Adand the first king of the 'Adites, a race of ancient Arabs; the smallest of their tribe is said to have been 60 cubits high, and the largest 100 cubits. 'Ad had two sons, Shadíd and Shaddád; on the death of their father they reigned conjointly over the whole earth. At length Shadíd died, and his brother Shaddád ruled after him. Shaddád was fond of reading the ancient books, and when he met with descriptions of Paradise and of the world to come, his heart enticed him to build its like upon the earth. A pleasant and elevated spot being fixed upon, Shaddád despatched one hundred chiefs to collect skilful artists and workmen from all countries. He also commanded the kings of Syria and Onnus to send him all their jewels and precious stones. Forty camel-loads of gold, silver, and jewels were daily used in the building, which contained a thousand spacious quadrangles of many thousand rooms. In the areas were artificial trees of gold and silver, whose leaves were emeralds, and fruit clusters of pearls and jewels. The ground was strewed with ambergris, musk and saffron. Between every two of the artificial trees was planted one of delicious fruit. This romantic abode took up 500 years in the completion. To this paradise he gave the name of Irám. When finished, Shaddád marched to view it, and when arrived near, divided two hundred thousand youthful slaves, whom he had brought with him from Damascus, into four detachments, which were stationed in cantonments prepared for their reception on each side of the garden, towards which he proceeded with his favourite courtiers. Suddenly was heard in the air a voice like thunder, and Shaddád, looking up, beheld a personage of majestic figure and stern aspect, who said, "I am the Angel of Death, commissioned to seize thy impure soul." Shaddád exclaimed, "Give me leisure to enter the garden," and was descending from his horse, when the seizer of life snatched away his impure spirit, and he fell dead upon the ground. At the same time lightnings flashed, and destroyed the whole army of the infidel; and the rose-garden of Irám became concealed from the sight of man.

It was during the reign of Muáwia, the first Khalíf of Damascus, that some of the principal incidents connected with the Paradise of Shaddád, are said to have taken place. This Paradise, though invisible, is still supposed to be standing in the deserts of Aden, and sometimes, though very rarely God permits it to be seen.

Crighton, in his "History of Arabia," says that "The whole fable seems a confused tradition of Belus and the ancient Babylon; or rather, as the name would import, of Benhadad, mentioned in Scripture as one of the most famous of the Syrian kings, and who, we are told, was worshipped by his subjects."

**Shadid, Kazi,** قاضي شديد, an eminent Musalmán doctor and author who died in the year 1447 A. D., 851 A. H.

**Shadid,** شديد, an author, whose proper name is Muhammad bin-Farámurz.

**Shadman, Sultan,** سلطان شادمان, a poet who had assumed the title of Sultán on account of his being a descendant of the royal race of Gihkars, whose territory was between the countries of the Panjáb and Hasan Abdal. He flourished in the reign of the emperor Sháh Jahán, and is the author of a Díwán. He wrote some beautiful verses in praise of the peacock throne on its completion in the year 1635 A. D, 1044 A. H. for which he was very handsomely rewarded by the emperor. He died in the reign of 'Álamgír 1668 A. D., 1079 A. H.

**Shad-ul-Mulk,** شاد الملک یاسعد الملک, a celebrated courtezan whom Sultán Khalíl the grandson of Amír Taimúr had secretly married, and at last lost his kingdom on her account. *Vide* Khalíl (Sultán).

**Sha'ib,** شعيب, the name of Jethro, the father-in-law of Moses.

**Sha'ib,** شعيب, the title of a poet of Isfahán, who wrote the poem called "Wámik and Uzra."

**Shaek,** شايق, the poetical name of Yúsaf Beg, a poet of Dehlí, who passed a retired life although his other brothers were mansabdárs in the service of the emperor 'Álamgír. He died 1687 A. D., 1098 A. H.

**Shaek,** شايق, poetical name of Mír Ghulám 'Alí bin-Sayyad Fatha 'Alí Razawí Jálisí. He flourished under Ghází-uddín Haidar king of Audh who reigned at Lakhnau from 1814 to 1827 A. D., 1229 to 1243 A. H. He is the author of a Díwán.

**Shaek,** نذيرالدين حسن شايق, poetical name of Nazír-uddín Hasan, son of Sháh Ghulám Muhí-uddín Aweisí. He is the author of a work called "Masdar Fayúz" a grammar to learn the Persian language, which he wrote at Bareili in the year 1815 A. D., 1230 A. H., when in the service of Nawáb Ahmad Yár Khán.

**Shafa'i, Imam,** امام شافعي, surname of Abú Abdullah Muhammad bin-Idrís, who was thus surnamed from Shafia one of his forefathers who was a descendant of 'Abdul Mutallib, grandfather of Muhammad. It is from that origin that the Sunnís give to this doctor the title of Imám-ul-Mutallibí, as well as that of 'Arif Billáh, or learned in God. He was born at Ghaza a city of Palestine on the very day that Abú Hanífa died 767 A. D., 150 A. H., and eventually became the founder of the third of the chief Sunní sects. He died in Egypt on Friday the 20th January, 820 A. D., 30th Rajab. 204 A. H., aged 54 lunar years He is the author of several works, and is said by all Sunní writers to have been a learned and virtuous man, who laboured to arrange the traditions so as to render them useful as a code of laws. In his youth he was a pupil of Málik ibn-'Aus. His followers were at one time very numerous in Khurásán; but at present his opinions are rarely quoted, either in Persia or India. He is reputed to have composed two collections of traditions, namely, the "Masnad" and the "Sunan." Besides the works on the traditions, he is said to have composed a most excellent treatise on jurisprudence, called "Al-Fikh-ul-Akbar;" but it has been questioned whether he was the author.

**Shafa'i,** شافعى, poetical appellation of a poet. See Haníf (Imám).

**Shafa'i, Hakim,** حكيم شفائي, poetical title of Sharaf-uddín Hasan, a physician and poet who is the author of several Masnawís, one of which is called "Namakdán Hakíkat" the Salt-cellar of Truth. He died in 1628 A. D., 1037 A. H., *vide* Sharaf-uddín Hasan Shafáí.

**Shafari,** شفاری, one of the three authors who composed the poems entitled "Lamaát-ul-Arab."

**Shah Abbas I,** شاہ عباس, *vide* Abbás (Sháh I.)

**Shah Abbas II,** شاہ عباس, *vide* Abbás (Sháh II.)

**Shahab-uddin,** شہاب الدین, author of a Medical work in Persian, called "Asrár Atibba."

**Shahab-uddin Abu'l Fazl Ahmad-al-'Uskalani,** شہاب الدین ابوالفضل احمد العسقلانی, author of a work on Traditions, entitled "Bulúgh-al-Marám." an abridgement of which called "Muntakhib Bulúgh-al-Maráni" was printed at Calcutta with an interlinear Urdú translation. 'Uskaláni died in 1448 A. D., 852 A. H., *vide* Ibn-Hajar.

**Shahab-uddin Adib Sabir,** شہاب الدین ادیب صابر, a celebrated poet at the court of Sultán Sanjar Saljúkí. He was a contemporary of Anwarí and Rashídí, and was drowned in the river Jaihún by order of Sultán Atsiz of Khwárizm who was an enemy of Sultán Sanjar. When Atsiz raised in Khwárizm the standard of revolt against Sanjar, the latter sent Adíb as a spy to the court of Atsiz that he might continually keep him informed of the intentions of his enemy. It so happened that Atsiz despatched an assassin who was to murder Sanjar on Friday. Adíb sent the intelligence of the plot and portrait of the assassin in advance to Sanjar. The plot was thus frustrated, but Adíb paid with his life for his fidelity to his former patron. Atsiz ordered that his hands and feet be tied, and that he be thrown into the Oxus. This happened in 1152 A. D., 546 A. H. He has left a Díwán of Kasídas, called "Kasáed Adíb Sábir."

**Shahab-uddin Ahmad bin-Mahmud-al-Siwasi,** شہاب الدین احمد بن محمود الشواسی, author of a most celebrated Commentary on the Sirájia of Sajáwandí. He died 1400 A. D., 803 A. H.

**Shahab-uddin Ahmad Talash,** شہاب الدین احمد تالاش, author of the "Tárikh Mulk Asham," which contains the account of an expedition undertaken against the kingdom of Asám in the 4th year of the reign of 'Alamgír 1661 A. D., by Muazzim Khán KhánKhánán, written in 1663. *Vide* Mír Jumla.

**Shahab-uddin Ahmad,** شہاب الدین احمد, son of Muhammad Makdisí of Jerusalem, author of the "Sharah Lámia Shatibia." He died 1328 A. D., 728 A. H. There appears to be another Shaháb-uddín the son of Yúsaf Chilpí, who is said to be the author of the above work. He died in the year 1355 A. D., 756 A. H.

**Shahab-uddin Ahmad,** شہاب الدین احمد, author of the "Fatáwá Ibráhím Sháhí" which was composed by order of Ibráhím Sháh of Jáunpúr in the ninth century of the Hijra.

**Shahab-uddin Burhanpuri,** شہاب الدین برھانپوری, author of the Fountain of Truth, called "Ayn-ul-Maání," an Essay on the knowledge of God, &c., written in the year 1588, *vide* Majd-uddín Ahmad.

**Shahab-uddin Ahmad bin-Yahia,** شہاب الدین احمد بن یحیی, an Arabian author who died in 1317 A. D.

**Shahab-uddin Burulusi,** شہاب الدین برُلُسي, author of a work on Súfyism called "Durr-ul-Ghauwás."

**Shahab-uddin, Kazi,** قاضي شهاب اليدين دولتا بادي, of Daulatábád, author of the Commentary on the Kurán, called "Bahr Mauwáj," in Persian. He received the title of Malik-ul-'Ulmá, king of the learned from Sultán Ibráhím Sharkí of Jaunpúr, and died in the year 1437 A. D., 842 A. H. He is also the author of the work entitled "Munákib-us-Saádat."

**Shahab-uddin, Maulana,** مولانا شہاب الدین, author of the marginal notes on the Kurán, called "Hashia Shaháb Hifáchí."

**Shahab-uddin, Mua'mmai,** شہاب الدین معمائی, or the Punster. He accompanied the emperor Bábar Sháh to India; was a good poet and wrote a book of Enigmas, on account of which he received the title of Muammái or the Punster. He died in the reign of the emperor Humáyún 1535 A. D., 942 A. H., and Khúndamír, the historian, found the year of his death in the words "Shaháb-ul-Sákib" or Shaháb the Sublime.

**Shahab-uddin Muhammad Ghori,** شہاب الدین محمد غوری, surnamed Moizz-uddín Muhammad Sám. He was appointed governor of Ghazní in 1174 A. D., 570 A. H. by his elder brother Ghayás-uddín Muhammad, Sultán of Ghór and Ghazní. He defeated and took prisoner Khusro Malik, the last prince of the race of the Ghaznavides 1186 A. D., 582 A. H., and subdued Khurásán and great part of India. He fought two battles with Pithoura the Rájá of Ajmeir, who was made prisoner and put to death along with Khánde Ráe, king of Dehlí in 1192 A. D., 588 A. H. His brother Ghayás-uddín died in 1203 A. D., 599 A. H., when he succeeded to the throne and reigned over Ghór, Ghazní and India three years. He was murdered by the Gihkars on his way to Ghazní on the 14th March, 1206 A. D., 2nd Shabán, 602 A. H. after he had reigned 32 years from the commencement of his government over Ghazní, and 3 from his accession to the throne. His remains were taken to Ghazní and buried there in a new vault which had been built for his daughter. He was succeeded by his nephew Ghayás-uddín Mahmúd the son of Ghayás-uddín Muhammad.

**Shahab-uddin 'Umar,** شہاب الدین عمر, son of Sultán 'Alá-uddín Sikandar Sání, king of Dehlí, *vide* Káfúr and 'Alá-uddín.

**Shahab-uddin Suharwardi,** شیخ شہاب الدین سہروردي, generally called Shaikh Maktúl, and Katíl-ulláh, because he was put to death by the famous general Sálah-uddín (Saladin) of Aleppo, for having more philosophy than religion. According to the work called Haft Aklím, he was starved or put to death at Aleppo in 1189 A. D., 585 A. H., aged 36 or 38 years. He is the author of the Commentaries called "Sharah Hayákal," and "Sharah Ayzáh." In the 4th Vol. of Hájí Khalfá, p. 236, he is said to be the author of another work called "Akl Surkh."

**Shahab-uddin Suharwardi, Shaikh,** شیخ شہاب الدین سہروردي, the son of Abú Najíb; was born at Suharward in January, 1145 A. D., Rajab, 539 A. H. He was a pious Shaikh, most assiduous in his spiritual exercises and the practise of devotion. He is the author of several works, among which is one called "Awárif-ul-Maárif" also called "Awárif-ul-Hakáek." He died on the 26th September, 1234 A. D., 1st Muharram, 632

A. H., in his 93rd year, at Baghdád, where he was buried. There is another work in Arabic found in the Library of Típú Sulṭán, entitled "Hikmat-ul-Ashrák," of which he is said to be the author.

**Shahab-uddin, Sultan,** سلطان شهاب الدين, the son of Sulṭán 'Alá-uddín whom he succeeded on the throne of Kashmír, 1356 A. D., 757 A. H. He turned his attention to foreign conquest, and during the succeeding ten years subdued Thibet, Káshghar, Badakhshán and Kábul. He then, according to the historian Haidar Malik, invaded Hindústán with an immense army, and is said to have worsted Fíróz Sháh king of Dehlí in a pitched battle on the banks of the Satlaj; the result of which was to cause that potentate to acknowledge his supremacy. Shaháb-uddín then returned to Kashmír, where his religious zeal led him to destroy the idol temples at Bijbihárí and elsewhere. He died after a reign of 19 years, 1376 A. D., and was succeeded by his brother Kutb-uddín, during whose reign, the famous Sayyad 'Alí Hamdání arrived at Kashmír.

**Shahadat,** شهادت, poetical name of Mirzá Sálah of Balkh, who died in 1742 A. D., 1155 A. H.

**Shah 'Alam,** شاه عالم, king of Dehlí, whose original name was 'Alí Góhar, was the son of the emperor 'Alamgír II, by Zínat Mahal surnamed Bilál Kúnwar; was born on the 15th of June, 1728 A. D., 17th Zi-Ka'da, 1140 A. H. In the year 1758 A. D., 1172 A. H., fearing he might be made a prisoner by 'Imád-ul-Mulk Ghází-uddín Khán the minister of his father, he left Dehlí to try his fortune in Bengal, the Nawáb of which province, Siráj-uddaula had been deposed by the assistance of the English, and Mír Jafar set up in his room. He was in Behár, when he received the intelligence of the murder of his father, and having assumed the imperial authority, he ascended the throne on the 25th of December, 1759 A. D., 4th Jumáda I, 1173 A. H. with the title of Sháh 'Alam. After the defeat of Shujá-uddaula his prime-minister, at Buxar on the 23rd October, 1764 A. D., 26th Rabí' II, 1178 A. H., and his flight to the upper province, the king followed the English to Allahábád where he granted the East India Company the Sanad of the Díwání of Bengal dated 12th August, 1765 A. D., 24th Safar, 1179 A. H., on the Company agreeing to pay the emperor 24 lacs of rupees annually from the revenues of the three provinces, *viz.*, Bengal, Behár, and Urysa. This important business being settled by Lord Clive, he returned to Calcutta, leaving General Smith to attend the emperor, but in fact to rule him; for the General resided in the fortress, and his majesty in the town; and the sound of the imperial naubat in the fort being disagreeable to General Smith, he forbad the band to play, nor did the servants of the emperor refuse. Sháh 'Alam continued to reside at Allahábád under the protection of the English till the year 1778 A. D., 1185 A. H. when growing weary of his retirement, he proceeded to Dehlí where he arrived on the 25th of December the same year, but not long after fell into the power of Ghulám Kádir Khán a Roheila chief, who put out his eyes on the 10th of August, 1788 A. D., Ramazán, 1185 A. H. Sháh 'Alam after this event re-assumed the throne and died on the 19th November, 1806 A. D., 7th Ramazán, 1221 A. H., aged 81 lunar years. Sháh 'Alam's poetical name was 'Aftáb. He was a good poet, and has left a Díwán called Díwán 'Aftáb, in Persian and Urdú verses. His remains were deposited close to the tomb of Bahádur Sháh adjoining the Motí Masjíd near the Dargáh of Kutb Sháh.

**Shah 'Alam,** شاه علم, a celebrated Muhammadan saint, was the son of Kutb 'Alam, which see.

**Shah 'Ali, Hazrat,** حضرت شاه علي, a pious Sayyad who is the author of several works on religion, in Persian, Arabic, and Gujrátí. He died at Ahmadábád Gujrát in 1565 A. D., 973 A. H., and was buried there.

**Shah 'Ali Muhammad,** شاه علي محمد, author of the "Tajjalliát Rahmání," an explanation of the Súfí tenets and mystical phrases, &c.

**Shah Begam,** شاه بيگم, the mother of Sulṭán Khusro the son of the emperor Jahángír. *Vide* Khusro (Sulṭán).

**Shahbaz Banda Nawaz,** شاهباز بنده نواز, author of two books called "Ishk-náma, and Sárdat-náma," containing Essays on divine love, the soul, future state, &c.

**Shahbaz Khan Kambu,** شاهباز خان كمبو, a descendant, in the sixth generation, of Hájí Jamál who was a disciple of Shaikh Bahá-uddín of Multán. He passed the first part of his life as a Dervish or mendicant, but was afterwards employed by the emperor Akbar, and raised to the dignity of an Amír. He was appointed governor of Bengal in 1584 A. D., 992 A. H., and died in the 44th year of the reign of that monarch, 1599 A. D., 1008 A. H., aged 70 years. He was buried at Ajmeir near the mausoleum of Khwája Mo'ín-uddín Chishtí. His liberality and the money he expended was so great, that it made the people think that he had in his possession the Philosopher's Stone.

**Shah Beg Arghun** or **Urghun,** شاه بيگ ارغون, king of Sindh and founder of the Arghún family, was the son of Mirzá Zunnún Beg Arghún, the commander-in-chief and head of the nobles at the court of Sulṭán Husain Mirzá king of Khurásán, and governor of Kandahár and the provinces of Shál, Sitúnak and Arghún. Mirzá Zunnún met his death in attempting to resist an invasion under Muhammad Khán Shaibání Uzbak. After his death the government of Kandáhar devolved on his son Sháh Beg Arghún. When the emperor Bábar Sháh invaded the province of Kandahár, Sháh Beg unable to resist him retreated towards Sindh, and having overcome Jám Fíróz the last king of the Samána dynasty, 1521 A. D., 927 A. H., he settled himself as king in that country. His reign was, however, but of short duration, for he died two years and some months after the conquest, in the year 1524 A. D., 930 A. H., and his eldest son Sháh Husain Arghún succeeded him.

**Shah Begam,** شاه بيگم, this was the title conferred by Jahángír on his first wife who was the daughter of Bhagwán Dás the son of Rájá Behárí Mal. She was married to prince Salím (afterwards Jahángír) in 1584 A. D., 993 A. H., and became the mother of Sulṭán Khusro who was born in 1587 A. D., 995 A. H. When Jahángír rebelled against his father Akbar, and was living independently at Allahábád he gave himself up more than ever to debauchery. He had always entertained a peculiar dislike for his eldest son Sulṭán Khusro whose own levity and violence seem to have given him reasons for his displeasure. Some circumstance in their disputes so affected Khusro's mother, that she swallowed poison (opium) in 1603 A. D., 1012 A. H., and died at Allahábád where she was buried in a place called Sulṭán Khusro's garden, where her son Sulṭán Khusro also was afterwards buried.

**Shah Begam,** شاه بيگم, a daughter of Muhammad Mukím, brother of Sháh Beg Arghún, governor of Kandahár and afterwards king of Sindh. She was married to Kásim Kóka, who was killed in the wars of the Uzbaks. On the conquest of Kandahár by Bábar Sháh, she was taken away to Kábul.

**Shah Begam,** شاه بیگم, mother of Khán Mirzá of Badakhshán, traced her genealogy to Alexander the Great.

**Shah Dai-ullah, Shirazi,** شاه داعی الله شیرازی, a pupil of Sháh Namat-ulláh Walí. He was a mystical poet, and a great saint. His tomb which is at Shíráz is a place of pilgrimage.

**Shahi,** شاهي, poetical title of Prince Mirzá Núr-uddín the son of Mirzá Khán Bakht, the son of Mirzá Sulaimán Shikoh.

**Shahi Beg Khan Uzbak,** شاهي بیگ خان اذبگ, also called Shaibání Khán, who after he had conquered Transoxiana, invaded Khurásán, took Hirát in 1507 A. D., 913 A. H., and extinguished the principal branch of the house of Taimúr. He was, however, defeated and slain in a battle against Sháh 'Ismaíl I, Safwí, in 1510 A. D., 916 A. H., when his scull was overlaid with gold, and made into a drinking cup by that monarch. After his death Taimúr Sultán succeeded him and Jání Beg Sultán and 'Abdulláh Khán divided Bukhárá between themselves. The Uzbaks were Tartars who came from the borders of Russia, where they had been governed by a race of princes descended from Shaibání, the grandson of Changez Khán; but they derived their name from Uzbak, the seventh of their race, who introduced the Muhammadan religion among them. The last prince of this tribe was Burgú Khán, who was slain by Sháh Bakht, upon which the Uzbaks quitted their ancient habitation, and conquered Khurasán, Khwarizm, &c.

**Shahi, Mir** or **Amir,** میر شاهي, poetical name of 'Aká Malik son of Jamál-uddín Fírozkohí. His mother was the sister of Khwája Muwyyad, a chief of the race of Sarbadáls of Sabzwár. He was himself a native of Sabzwár and a very learned man. He wrote a beautiful hand, was a good musician and painter. He flourished in the time of Baisanghar Mirzá and Sultán Bábar, and died at Astrabád in 1450 A. D., 854 A. H., aged more than 70 years. He was buried at his own request at Sabzwár. He is the author of a biography of poets called "Majmúa-ush-Shuará" and of a Díwán entitled "Díwán Sháhí."

**Shahid,** شاه, *vide* Ghulám Imám Shahíd.

**Shah Ghulam Azim,** شاه غلام عظیم, son of Sháh Abul Maálí, the son of Sháh Ajmal of Allahábád. He is the author of two Díwáns and a Masnawí. *Vide* Afzal.

**Shah Girami** or **Mirza Girami,** شاه گرامي, a poet who lived in the dress of a Kalandar and Dehlí and died in the year 1743 A. D., 1156 A. H.

**Shah Gul,** شاه گل, *vide* Wahdat.

**Shah Hatim,** شاه حاتم, surname of Shaikh Zahír-uddín a Hindústání poet. *Vide* Hátim.

**Shah Husain Arghun,** شاه حسین ارغون, king of Sindh, succeeded his father Sháh Beg Arghún in 1524 A. D., 930 A. H. He reigned 32 years and died in 1555 A. D., 962 A. H. After his death the government of Sindh was divided between two rivals, Mahmúd the governor of Bakkar and Mirzá Ísa Turkhán governor of Thatta, who both assumed the title of king, and between whom frequent dissensions arose, and battles were fought. The emperor Akbar on coming to Láhor reduced the whole of the province of Bakkar exclusive of the fort, till at last Mahmúd was willing to give it up, and Akbar deputed Geisú Khán to receive it, but Mahmúd died before his arrival, 1574 A. D., 982 A. H., after a reign of 20 lunar years, and Akbar thus became possessed of Upper Sindh, and put an end to the hopes of the race of Mahmúd. Ísa Turkhán who took possession of Thatta after the death of Sháh Husain, died after a reign of 13 years in 1567 A. D., 976 A. H.

**Shah Husain Safwi,** شاه حسین صفوي, succeeded his father Sháh Sulaimán, king of Persia in 1694 A. D., 1134 A. H. In the year 1722, Mahmúd, an Afghán chief of Kandahár beseiged Isfahán, and compelled Sultán Husain to surrender and resign his crown to him. This circumstance occurred on the 23rd of October the same year 1135 A. H., and the unfortunate Sultán was confined in a small palace, where he remained seven years; when a reverse of fortune which threatened their downfall led his enemies, whose chief was Ashraf the successor of Mahmúd, to put an end to his existence. This melancholy event took place in November, 1729 A. D., 1142 A. H. The Safwian family may be said to have actually terminated with Sultán Husain. His son Tahmasp, assumed the title of king, and struggled for a few years with his fate, but a weak effeminate, and debauched youth, was unsuited for such times: and he only merits a place in history, as his name furnished a pretext for the celebrated Nádir Sháh to lay the foundation of his great power.

**Shah Husain Sayyad,** سید شاه حسین, *vide* Hakíkat.

**Shahidi,** شاهدي, poetical name of Mír 'Abdul Wáhid of Bilgrám, which see.

**Shaista Khan, Nawab,** شایسته خان نواب, the son of Asaf Khán the prime minister.

**Shahidi Kummi,** شاهدي قمي, an author who was a native of Kumm, and died in 1529 A. D., 935 A. H.

**Shah Jalal,** شاه جلال, a Muhammadan saint of great sanctity, whose tomb is in Sylhet. This shrine has a large number of attendants to minister at it, and the pigeons and other birds which flock there, are held as sacred as the birds within the temple of Mecca.

**Shah Jahan,** شاه جهان, emperor of Dehlí, surnamed Shaháb-uddín Muhammad Sáhib Kirán Sání, was the third son of the emperor Jahángír. He was born at Láhor on the 5th January, 1593 A. D., 29th Rabí' I, 1000 A. H., and named Mirzá Khurram. His mother Balmatí was the daughter of Rájá Udai Singh, son of Rájá Maldeo of Jodhpúr, and sister to Rájá Súraj Singh. At the time of his father's death he was absent in the Dakhin, but the throne was secured for him by his father-in-law, 'Asaf Khán the wazír, the brother of Núr Jahán Begam. He marched towards Láhor on hearing of the throne being at his disposal; and began his reign 4th February, 1628 A. D., 8th Jumáda II, 1037 A. H. He was the most magnificent prince that ever appeared in India. The most striking instance of his pomp and prodigality was his construction of the famous Peacock throne. It took its name from two peacocks fashioned splendidly in sapphires, emeralds, rubies and other appropriate jewels which formed the chief ornament of a mass of bullion and precious stones that dazzled every beholder. Tavernier, a jeweller by profession, reports, that it cost nearly six millions and a half sterling. His greatest splendour was shown in his buildings. He founded a new city at Dehlí called after him Sháhjahánábád, but of all the structures erected by him, there is none that bears any comparison with the Táj Mahal at Ágrah, a mausoleum of white marble decorated with mosaics, which for the richness of the material, the chasteness of the design, and the effect at once brilliant and solemn, is not surpassed by any edifice, either in Europe or Asia. Táj Mahal is a corruption of Mumtáz Mahal, the name of Sháh Jahán's favourite wife, whose sepulchre it forms. Sháh Jahán reigned thirty years and was deposed and confined in the fort of Ágrah by his son 'Álamgír Aurangzeib on th 9th of June, 1658 A. D., 17th Ramaẓán, 1068 A. H., and died at Ágrah after an imprisonment of 7 years and 10 months, on Monday night the 23rd of January, 1666 A. D., 26th Rajab, 1076 A. H., aged 76 lunar years 3 months and 17 days, and was buried in the Táj close to his wife's tomb. There were living at the time of his imprisonment, four of his sons and four daughters. Of the sons, the eldest was Dárá Shikóh, the second Sulṭán Shujáạ, the third 'Álamgír and the fourth Murád Bakhsh; but 'Álamgír, who succeeded his father, murdered two of his brothers, *viz.*, Dárá and Murád, and the third Sulṭán Shujáạ died in Arracan, or was murdered by the Rájá of that country. His daughters were Arjuman 'Ará, Geití 'Ará, Jahán 'Ará and Dahr 'Ará, (or Roshan 'Ará).

Inscription on a gold coin of Sháh Jahán of enormous size and value struck in 1064 A. H.

سکه بر مهر دو صد مهری زد از لطف اله
ثانیٔ صاحب قرین شاه جهان دین پناه
روی زر باد از نقش سکه اش عالم فروز
تاشود از پرتو خورشید روشن روي ماه

Reverse.

از صدق ابوبکـــر شد ایمـــان انـــور
اســلام قوي دست شد از عدل عمـــر
ذین تازه شد از شرم و حیـــا عثمـــان
از علـــم علي یافت ولایت زیـــور

**Shah Karak,** شاه کرك, a celebrated Muhammadan saint who is buried at Kaṛa, a city in the province of Allahábád, and whose tomb is still held sacred by the Musalmáns. It is mentioned by Firishta, that the day before the assassination of Sulṭán Jalál-uddín Fíroz in 1296 A. D., Sulṭán 'Alá-uddín visited this holy man, who rising from his pillows repeated the following extempore verses. "He who cometh against thee, shall lose his head in the boat, and his body shall be thrown into the Ganges;" which, they say, was explained a few hours after by the death of the unfortunate king, whose head fell into the boat upon this occasion. Sháh Kaṛak died between the years 1296 and 1316 A. D.

**Shah Jahan Begam of Bhopal,** شاه جاهان بیگم, succeeded to the principality of Bhopal on the death of her mother Sikandar Begam, on the 30th of October, 1868. Her Highness in 1871 married her own minister Muhammad Sádik Hasan Khán, by the advice or consent of the Supreme Government. This is her second husband. She commanded that in future he should be addressed thus: Motamid-ul-Muhárn Muhammad Sádik Hasan Khán Sahib Bahádur, second minister of the State of Bhopál.

**Shah Ḳasim,** شاه قاسم, a pious and learned Musalmán who died in the year 1584 A. D., 992 A. H., and Khwája 'Abdul Razá wrote the chronogram of the year of his death.

**Shah Ḳudrat-ullah,** شاه قدر الله, *vide* Ḳudrat.

**Shah Ḳuli Khan Mahram,** شاه قلی خان محرم, a nobleman of the court of the emperor Akbar. He held the rank of 5,000, and was sent with prince Sulṭán Salím to Ajmeir accompanied by Rájá Mán Singh, to chastise the Amírs under the Rájá of Udaipúr in 1598 A. D., 1007 A. H. The emperor Jahángír says in his Memoirs, that in the first year of his reign 1605 A. D., he gave the daughter of Mirzá Handál, named Sulṭán Begam, in marriage to Sháh Ḳulí Khán Mahram, but his death is mentioned in another work, *viz.*, "Másir-ul-Umra," to have taken place in the month of December, 1600 A. D., 18th Azar, 1009 A. H., at Ágrah.

**Shah Madar,** شاه مدار, a celebrated Muhammadan saint, whose proper name was Badí-uddín. He was a disciple of Shaikh Muhammad Taifúrí Bastámí, and is the founder of the sect called Madária in India. Many curious anecdotes are related of him. He died on the 20th December, 1434 A. D., 838 A. H., aged 124 years, and is buried at Makanpúr in Ḳanauj, where a great assembly is held every year at his tomb. He was a cotemporary of Ḳází Shaháb-uddín Daulatábádí who lived in the time of Sulṭán Ibráhím Sharḳí of Jaunpúr.

**Shah Mahmud of Isfahan,** شاه محمود اسفهاني, *vide* Sháh Shujáạ.

**Shah Mansur,** شاه منصور, last Sulṭán of the dynasty of the Muzaffarians, was the son of Sháh Muhammad Muzaffar. He reigned in 'Iráḳ and Fars after Sháh Zain-ul-'Abidín whom he deprived of sight and took possession of Shíráz. He was defeated by Amír Taimúr, who put him to death on Thursday the 22nd of May, 1393 A. D., 10th Rajab, 795 A. H.

**Shah Mansur,** شاه منصور, *vide* Khwája Mansúr.

**Shah Mir,** شاه میر, also called Míán Mír whose proper name was Shaikh Muhammad, was a descendant of the Khalíf 'Umar, and a very pious Musalmán. He is reckoned amongst the Muhammadan saints. He was born at Shístan 1550 A. D., 957 A. H., came to Láhor where he resided 60 years, and died there on Tuesday the 11th August, 1635 A. D., 7th Rabí' I, 1045 A. H., aged 88 lunar years. He is buried at a place called Háshimpúr near Láhor. He had numerous disciples, one of whom was Mullá Sháh, the spiritual guide of the prince Dárá Shikóh, the eldest son of the emperor Sháh Jahán. He is the author of the work called "Ziyá-ul-Ayún," or the Light of the Eyes, containing the rules for propriety of conduct through life.

**Shah Mir,** شاه میر, first Muhammadan king of Kashmír, The original inhabitants of Kashmír appear to have been the followers of Brahmá. The period of the first establishment of the Muhammadan faith in that country took place during the reign of Rájá Seina Déva, about the year 1315 A. D., 715 A. H., when a person called Sháh Mír, coming to Kashmír in the habit of a Dervish, was admitted into the service of that prince. Upon the death of the rájá, he was appointed prime minister to his son and successor Rájá Ranjan. When this rájá died, Anand Dev, who succeeded him, also made Sháh Mír his minister. The whole of this family not only gained great ascendancy over the rájá, but also over the minds of the people, till the rájá, becoming jealous of their power, forbade them the court. This exclusion drove Sháh Mír into rebellion, when having occupied the valley of Kashmír with his troops, most of the officers of the rájá's government also joined him. This insurrection soon brought the rájá to the grave, who died of a broken heart in the year 1327 A. D., 727 A. H., leaving his widow regent. Sháh Mír after some years married

Kaula Deví, the wife of the rájá, who embraced the Muhammadan faith; an event which secured to him the country which he had before nearly usurped. It is related by another author, that when preparations for the marriage were commenced, the devoted princess despairing and indignant, surrounded by her train of maidens, advanced into the presence of the usurper, and upbraiding him for his ingratitude and treachery, stabbed herself before him. Thus perished by her own hand the last Hindú sovereign of Kashmír, and Sháh Mír, who is considered the first Muhammadan king of that country, ascended the throne under the title of Sulṭán Shams-uddín, in the year 1341 A. D., 742 A. H. He died in 1344 or 1349 A. D., 745 or 750 A. H., and was succeeded by his son Jamsheid.

*List of the Muhammadan Kings of Kashmír.*

1. Sulṭán Shams-uddín Sháh Mír.
2. Jamsheid, son of Sháh Mír, reigned 14 months, and was expelled by his younger brother 'Alá-uddín 'Alísheir, and slain.
3. 'Alá-uddín 'Alísheir, son of Sháh Mír, reigned 13 years.
4. Shaháb-uddín, son of 'Alá-uddín reigned 19 years and died 1376 A. D.
5. Ḳuṭb-uddín, brother of Shaháb-uddín, during whose reign the famous Sayyad 'Alí Hamdání arrived in Kashmír. He reigned 15 years.
6. Sikandar, surnamed Butshikan, who destroyed all images and subverted the Hindú religion, was the son of Ḳuṭb-uddín, and a contemporary of Amír Taimúr. He reigned about 25 years.
7. 'Alí Sháh, the son of Sikandar, reigned nearly 7 years.
8. Zain-ul-'Abidín, brother of 'Alí Sháh, reigned 52 years, and died about the year 1474 A. D.
9. Haidar Sháh, son of Zain-ul-'Abidín, reigned little more than a year, and was killed by a fall from his palace.
10. Sulṭán Hasan, son of Haidar Sháh, reigned 12 years in excess and drunkenness.
11. Muhammad Sháh, a child of seven years of age, son of Hasan Sháh. He had several battles with Fatha Khán, and after a reign of 11 years was imprisoned by his uncle.
12. Fatha Khán, who took the title of Fatha Sháh, reigned 10 years.

Muhammad Sháh re-ascended the throne in 1506 and reigned two months, and then Fatha Sháh one year, after which Muhammad Ṣháh ascended the throne the third time, and was deposed after a reign of 19 years. He was once more raised to the throne and died in 1533 after an interrupted reign of 50 years.

Ibráhím, the son of Muhammad, reigned 5 years.

Mubárik Sháh also called Nazuk and Barbak, son of Ibráhím, ascended the throne and after a reign of 3 months was expelled by the army of the emperor Humáyún, who being defeated by Sheir Sháh in 1541, had fled his country, and had retreated to Láhor, whence he sent an army under the command of Mirzá Haidar Doghlát, who invading Kashmír, conquered that province, and reigned there 10 years.

Mirzá Haidar Doghlat, after a reign of nearly 10 years, was killed in a night-attack in 1551 A. D., 958 A. H. After his death, the leading men divided the country into three principalities among themselves, though for form's sake, Názuk, the son of Ibráhím, was again seated on the throne, and was again deposed the second time, by his brother.

Ibráhím II was placed on the throne by Daulat Chak, and after a short time was deposed and blinded, and his brother

Ismá'íl was raised to the throne in 1556. He reigned nearly two years, and was succeeded by his son

Habíb who ascended the throne and reigned 3 years, after which he was imprisoned by Ghází Chak.

Ghází Chak declared himself king and assumed the title of Ghází Sháh, and reigned 4 years, when being attacked with a leprosy, abdicated the throne in 1563 A. D.

Husain Sháh, his brother mounted the throne, reigned 6 years and was compelled to abdicate in favour of his brother 'Alí Khán in 1569 A. D.

'Alí Sháh ascended the throne in 1569, and in the year 1572, Mullá Ishḳí and Ḳází Sadr-uddín came as ambassadors from the court of Dehlí, the result of which was that Akbar was proclaimed emperor of Kashmír in the public prayers; and 'Alí Sháh at the request of Akbar, sent his niece the daughter of his brother Husain Sháh to be married to the prince Salím. In the year 1578, 'Alí Sháh was killed by a fall from his horse after a reign of 9 years and was succeeded by his son.

Yúsaf Chak who proceeded to the court of Akbar in 1586 and his son.

Yaḳúb Chak succeeded to the throne in consequence of his father's detention at the court of Dehlí. In the year 1587 A. D., 995 A. H. Akbar appointed Muhammad Ḳásim Khán, Amír-ul-Bahr (Admiral) to march and subdue Kashmír. Yaḳúb was defeated and at last seized and sent to Dehlí in 1588, where Akbar enrolled Yúsaf Sháh and his son Yaḳúb among the nobles of his government. Each of them received estates in the province of Behár, and from that period the kingdom of Kashmír has been a province of Dehlí.

**Shah Muhammad, Khalifa,** خلیفه شاه محمد, author of the book called "Insháe Jámạ-ul-Ḳawánín," commonly called "Insháe Khalífa," containing forms of letters.

**Shah Murad,** شاه مورد, *vide* Murad Mirzá.

**Shahnawaz Khan,** شاه نواز خان, son of 'Abdul Rahím Khán KhánKhánán. His daughter was married to prince Sháh Jahán. He died in the year 1028 A. H.

**Shahnawaz Khan,** شاهنواز خان, a nobleman of the reign of the emperor Sháh Jahán, was the son of 'Asaf Khán wazír, and father-in-law of the emperor 'Alamgír, and of his brother prince Murád Bakhsh. But the author of the Másir-ul-Umrá says that he was the son of Mirzá Rustam Ḳandahárí. He was appointed governor of Gujrát in the room of the prince Murád Bakhsh who was imprisoned by order of his brother 'Alamgír in July, 1658 A. D. When Dárá Shikóh through various adventures, after his flight from Multán, came to Aḥmadabád Gujrát, Sháhnawáz Khán his maternal uncle was then in that city, and his daughter the wife of Murád Bakhsh was in his palace. Her bitter supplications against 'Alamgír, the impending murderer of her husband, prevailed on him to join the cause of Dárá, for whom he levied an army, and marched with him towards Ajmeir where on their arrival, a bloody battle ensued between the armies of Dárá and 'Alamgír, on Sunday the 13th of March, 1659 A. D., Jumádạ II, 1069 A. H. which ended in the defeat and flight of Dárá and death of Sháhnawáz Khán who fell by the lance of Dileir Khán. He was buried by the orders of 'Alamgír in the mausoleum of Khwája Moí'n-uddín Chishtí at Ajmeir.

**Shahnawaz Khan,** شاهنواز خان, a nobleman of Sháh 'Alam's court, author of the book called Miraat-e-Aftáb-numai a work on the history of Modern Dehlí.

**Shahnawaz Khan,** شمس الدوله شاهنواز خان, entitled Samsám-uddaula. The original name of this nobleman was 'Abdul Razzák; he was descended from the family of Sadát of Khawáf in Khurásán, but his great-grandfather Amír Kamál-uddín left Khawáf, and came to Hindústán in the reign of the emperor Akbar, when he was admitted amongst the nobles of the court of Dehlí. Mírak Husain, the son of Kamál-uddín held a situation in the service of the state, in the reign of Jahángír. The son of Mírak Husain, Mírak Moi'n-uddín, commonly called Amánat Khán, was in great favour with Sháh Jahán, and rose to the first rank. He retained also the patronage of 'Álamgír, was appointed by him to various important governments as those of Láhor, Multán, Kábul and Kashmír. Amánat Khán was the ablest man in the court, and a great favourite of 'Álamgír. When the emperor resided in Upper India, he bestowed the Súbadárí of the Dakhin on Khán Jahán Bahádur Kokaltásh about the year 1670 A. D., 1081 A. H., and Amánat Khán was appointed Díwán of the Dakhin or Paymaster General, and Historiographer. He had four sons of eminent character; the first 'Abdul Ḳádir Dayánat Khán, was the keeper of the Privy Purse. The second Mír Husain Amánat Khán, was the public treasurer and governor of Súrat: after his death the latter post was assigned to his elder brother. The third son was Mír 'Abdul Rahmán Wizárat Khán who was promoted to the Díwání of Málwá and Bíjápúr. He was an excellent poet and composed a Díwán under the poetical title of Bikrámí. The fourth son Ḳásim Khán was Díwán of Multán. Mír Hasan 'Alí the son of Ḳásim Khán was the father of Nawáb Samsám-uddaula Sháhnawáz Khán. He was born on the 10th of March, 1700 A. D., 29th Ramaẓán, 1111 A. H. at Láhor, but repaired to 'Aurangábád at an early age, and took up his abode with his relations and kinsmen who resided there before him. He was engaged first by Nizám-ul-Mulk 'Asaf Jáh under whom and his son Násir Jang he served as Díwán of Beṛáṛ for several years. In the time of Salábat Jang, he was raised to the rank of 7000 with the title of Samsám-uddaula. On the 12th of May, 1758 A. D., 3rd Ramaẓán, 1171 A. H., the day on which 'Abdul Rahmán Haidar Jang, the counsellor of Monsieur Bussy the French General, was assassinated by the instigation of Nizám 'Alí the brother of Salábat Jang, he also was murdered in the confusion together with his youngest son Mír 'Abdul Nabí Khán, but his two other sons, Mír 'Abdur Salám and Mír 'Abdul Hai escaped. The remains of the father and son were interred in the tomb of their ancestors in the southern part of the city of 'Aurangábád. The chronogram of this event gives the following: "We have been murdered by 'Abdul Rahmán." Sháhnawáz Khán is the author of the work called "Másir-ul-Umráe Taimúria" containing the Memoirs of the nobility who served in Hindústán and the Dakhin under the house of Taimúr. It was commenced by him, but he left it unfinished, and in the turbulent scenes which attended his death, the manuscript was scattered in various directions, and was considered as lost: some short time afterwards Mír Ghulám 'Alí Azád, a friend of his collected the greater portion of the missing leaves, and restored the work to its entire form with a few additions, amongst which was the life of the author: at a subsequent period again, his son Mír 'Abdul Hai Khán who had received the title of Samsám-uddaula Samsám Jang after his father's death, completed the work in the form in which it now occurs, in the year 1779 A. D., and died on the 28th April, 1782 A. D., 15th Jumádạ I, 1196 A. H.

**Shah Nur Ashhari,** شاه نورا شهري, a famous poet who was a pupil of Zahír-uddín Fáryábí and flourished in the reign of Sulṭán Muhammad Khwárizm Sháh son of Takash. He died at Tabrez in 1204 A. D., 600 A. H.

**Shah Nur,** شاه نور, a celebrated Dervish and saint who died on the 2nd February, 1693 A. D., and was buried in the vicinity of 'Aurangábád where his tomb is still visited by the Muhammadans.

**Shahpur,** شاه پور, *vide* Sháhpúr.

**Shahristani,** شهرستاني, *vide* 'Abú'l Fatha Muhammad-ash-Shahristaní.

**Shahrukh, Mirza,** شاهرخ مرزا, the son of Razá Ḳulí and grandson of Nádir Sháh. His father Razá Ḳulí's mother Fátima Sulṭán Begam was the daughter of Sháh Sulṭán Husain Safwí. Sháhrukh was raised to the throne some time after the death of his grandfather, but was soon after seized and deprived of sight. He retired to Mashhad, which province he was allowed to hold in his possession till the time of his death which happened at Dámghán in 1796 A. D. His death was the consequence of the tortures that had been inflicted upon him by 'Aḳá Muhammad, king of Persia, who by this act extorted from him many precious stones of great value which had once belonged to Nádir Sháh.

**Shahrukh, Mirza,** مرزا شاهرخ, was the fourth son of Amír Taimúr and held the government of Khurásán at his father's death which took place in February, 1405 A. D. After the imprisonment of Sulṭán Khalíl his nephew, ruler of Samarḳand 1408 A. D., 811 A. H., he marched from Khurásán to take possession of his dominions. His authority was immediately acknowledged, not only in Samarḳand, but over all Transoxania. He was brave and generous, but not an ambitious prince: and during a reign of 42 years, we hear of no wars in which he was engaged, except with the Turkmán tribes of Asia Minor whose power Taimúr had overcome, but not destroyed. Mirzá Sháhrukh was born at Samarḳand on the 21st July, 1377 A. D., 14th Rabí' I, 779 A. H., and died at Fisháward in the province of Rei, on the Persian new year's day, *viz.* Sunday, the 12th March, 1447 A. D., 25th Ẓil-ḥijja, 850 A. H., aged 71 lunar years. He reigned 42 years during which the conquests of his father in India seem to have remained in subjection to his authority. At his death he left 5 sons, *viz.*, Mirzá Ulagh Beg, Ibráhím Mirzá, Mirzá Báisanghar, Sayúrghamish and Muhammad Júgí. He was succeeded by his son Mirzá Ulagh Beg.

**Shahrukh Mirza,** شاهرخ مرزا, a descendant of Amír Taimúr, was the son of Ibráhím Mirzá, the son of Mirzá Sulaimán ruler of Badakhshán. His mother's name was Muhtarim Khánam. About the year 1575 A. D., 983 A. H., he forcibly took possession of Badakhshán from his grandfather and reigned there about 10 years, after which in 1585 A. D., 993 A. H. that province was conquered by 'Abdulláh Khán Uzbak, and Sháhrukh compelled to fly to India, where he was kindly received by the emperor Akbar, who gave him his daughter Shakar-un-Nisá Begam in marriage in the year 1593 A. D., 1001 A. H. and raised him to the rank of an Amír of 5,000. In the time of Jahángír the rank of 7,000 was conferred on him. He died at Ujjain 1607 A. D., 1016 A. H., and was buried there.

**Shahruk Mirza** or **Mirza Shahruk,** شارک مرزا مرزا شارک, who had a Jagír in Gujrát, was murdered by his younger brothers in the year 1032 A. H.

**Shahryar,** شهريار, a king of Persia of the Sasánian race, who reigned in Persia a few months in 629 A. D., *vide* Sheiróya.

**Shahryar, Sultan,** سلطان شهريار, the youngest son of the emperor Jahángír, was married to a daughter of Núr Jahán Begam by her former husband Sher Afghán Khán. On the death of Jahángír in 1627 A. D., 1037 A. H. this prince who was then at Láhor, seized the royal treasure, bought over the troops, and forming a coalition with the two sons of his uncle the late prince Daniál, marched out to oppose 'Asaf Khán the wazír, who had released prince Dáwar Bakhsh surnamed Buláḳí the son of Sulṭán Khusro from prison and proclaimed him king. The battle ended in Sháhryár's defeat, he fled but being given up by his adherents, was imprisoned and blinded. He was after three months put to death together with Dáwar Bakhsh and the two sons of Daniál, named Tahmur and Hoshang by order of Sháh Jahán who ascended the throne on the 4th February, 1628 A. D., 8th Jumáda II, 1037 A. H.

**Shah Sadr,** شاه صدر, a Muhammadan saint whose tomb is situated at the foot of a large mountain of Siwistán, at the distance of about 300 yards from the village of Lakki in Sindh which belongs to the Sayyads of that place. This famous saint, says Lutf-ullah in his Autography, originally came from Arabia, and brought thousands of infidels to the light of Islám from the darkness of idolatry in Sindh. The year of his death is not known, but his tomb was built here by order of Nádir Sháh, king of Persia, in 1155 A. H. Tradition states, that Nádir in a dream was invited by this saint to come to Amarkote where he was to find a very large treasure. Nádir having acted upon the visionary command, discovered the treasure promised to him, and received a very large amount, as a tribute from the Amírs of Sindh. Nádir then bestowed a large sum of money upon the Sayyads of the village, directed them to have the edifice built over the remains of the saints. This they carried into execution, and the following inscription at the door of the shrine gives the date of its completion :—

"I inquired of intellect the year of its date.
"Inspiration informed me, It is the Paradise of the members of the sacred house." 1742 A. D., 1155 A. H.

All Sayyads of Sindh that are called Lakki Sayyads, are, I am informed (says Lutf-ullah) the descendants of this saint, whose parentage ascends up to the Imám 'Alí Naki. I am therefore inclined to think that the word Lakki is a corruption of Naki, which is the name of the tenth Imám.

**Shah Safi,** شاه صفي, grandson of Sháh Abbás the Great, king of Persia. His father's name was Safí Mirzá and his original name Bahrám Mirzá. He succeeded his grandfather in January, 1629 A. D., Jumáda I, 1038 A. H. and took the title of Sháh Safí. He was a capricious tyrant; and every year of his rule presented the same horrid and disgusting scene of barbarous cruelty. All the princes of the blood royal, and almost every minister, or general of family or character, were either put to death, or deprived of their eyes, by command of this monarch. He reigned nearly 14 years, died in May, 1642 A. D., Ṣafar, 1052 A. H., and was succeeded by his son, Abbás II.

**Shah Sharaf-uddin,** شاه شرف الدين, a Muhammadan saint who died in the year 1379 A. D., 781 A. H., and is buried in Behár, where his monument is still standing and is visited by the Muhammadans. There is an inscription in the Kúfí character over the entrance to the dargáh, which however time has rendered illegible with the exception of the date of the death of the saint, and of the erection of the tomb in 1569 A. D., 977 A. H. The dargah is held in great veneration by the Muhammadans who at the 'Urs or anniversary of the death of the saint, assemble from all parts of the country, it is said to the number of 50,000. He is also called Makhdúm-ul-Mulk Sháh Sharíf-uddín and Shaikh Sharíf. The emperor Sikandar Sháh the son of Bahlól Lodí went to visit his tomb about the year 1495 A. D., 900 A. H., *vide* Sharaf-uddín Aḥmad 'Ahia Manerí.



**Shah Sharif** or **Sharif-uddin,** شاه شريف, *vide* Sháh Sharaf-uddín.

**Shah Shujaa'** or **Shuja'-ul-Mulk,** ياشجاع الملک شاه شجاع, king of Kábul, was the youngest son of Taimúr Sháh the son of Aḥmad Sháh Abdálí. He was sent to Kashmír by his brother Muhammad Sháh and imprisoned in the fort of the Kóh-i-Márán in 1812 A. D. from which place he was released in 1814 by Ranjít Singh and detained at Láhor as a prisoner till his escape to the British territories. He was placed by the British Government on the throne of Kábul on the 8th May, 1839 A. D., and was murdered by his nephew, a son of Zamán Sháh on the 2nd May, 1842 A. D. He is the author of a biographical sketch of his own life written at Lúdhiana in 1826-27. This work was translated by Lieut. Bennet, of the Artillery, and published in the Asiatic Journal, Vol. XXX, p. 6, under Asiatic Intelligence.

**Shah Shujaa',** شاه شجاع, Sulṭán of the Muzaffarians whose capital was Shíráz. It is said that this prince was in such a manner plagued by a malady called Júu'l Baḳar, or canine hunger, that he could not satisfy his hunger, neither on his journey, nor when he was at rest. He deprived his father Muhammad Muzaffar of his sight in 1359 A. D., and held the reins of government in his own hands. His brother Sháh Mahmúd of Isfahán beseiged Shíráz in 1364, took possession of that country and died before his brother in 1375 A. D., 9th Shawwal, 776 A. H. after a reign of 16 years. Sháh Shujaa' died on Sunday the 9th of October, 1384 A. D., 21st Shabán, 786 A. H. He was succeeded by his son Zain-ul-'Abidín, who on the approach of Amír Taimúr to Shíráz retired to Tishtar, where his uncle Sháh Mansúr seized him and deprived him of his sight. Shíráz was bestowed by Amír Taimúr on Sháh Ahia the son of Muzaffar, but it was soon after taken by Sháh Mansúr, in whose possession it remained till it was retaken by that conqueror in 1393 A. D., 795 A. H. There is a garden near Shíráz called Haft-tan, which contains the remains of Sháh Shujáa, and has, on one side of it, a small building, ornamented with a variety of pictures.

**Shah Sufi,** شاه صوفي, a Muhammadan saint whose shrine is at a village called Súfípúr in the Pargana of Fírozábád in Agrah. It is related by the Khádims of the dargáh that in the reign of the emperor Akbar, Sháh Súfí a faḳír of some celebrity wandered from Isfahán to India, and took up his hermitage among the Jamna ravines near the city of Chandwár, then the county town of the Pargana of the same name, and which from the remains which still cover the surrounding country for miles—ruined mosques, dilapidated octagon mausolea, fallen entrance gates and such like works of costly strength, must have been an important post in a fiscal and military point of view. All the time from which the fable of Sháh Súfí's miracles commence, Rájá Chandarsen was the lord of the fort of Chandwár, and a troublesome tributary of the Dehlí court. Non-compliance with the royal demands for payment of revenue, brought upon the rájá the investment of his fort by the army of Akbar, who is said to have commanded his forces in person, and to have prosecuted his attack with no approach to success for a period, which the credulous or imposing Khádims of the establishment have exalted into a term of ten years. In the language of Oriental metaphor, the emperor is said to have planted a mangoe tree on the commencement of the seige, and to have eaten the fruit of it, ere his success was secured. This success he owed to the anchorite of the ravines Sháh Súfí. During a severe land storm, the lamps of the entire camp were put out, and the light of the Sháh's hut alone glimmered in the surrounding darkness. This extraordinary fact led to the Sháh's being visited by some of the courtiers. The miraculous character of the event being much commented on by the visitors, the Sháh acknowledged himself to be under the special favour of Heaven—and in the end the conversation turned upon the difficulties of the seige, and the grateful sense of the hermit's interference which the sovereign would entertain in the event of its being brought to a close by his holy means. The Sháh promised the required aid, and declared that the fort should be captured by a fixed day. Thus much for the emperor. In respect to the rájá, the Sháh acted very effectually upon his superstitious fears—told him that the fort was destined to fall, and proffered his own miraculous powers to secure for the rájá, a safe and honourable retreat for himself, family and valuables. The whole were accordingly passed invisible through the beseiging camp, and the rájá quitted Hindústán for the eastward. In return for this valuable service, the emperor bestowed half of an hamlet of Chandwár on the Sháh. The place assumed the name of Safípúr, and has since been inhabited by the descendants of the Sháh. The decease of Sháh Safí took place soon after the grant was made, and he was buried on the brow of a deep ravine, a handsome tomb being erected over his remains. The mausoleum is still in good order and forms a picturesque object in the midst of the desolation of the Jamna ravines in the vicinity of Chandwár and Fírozábád. Its pretty dome and minarets commanding as they do, the heights of the Jamna ravines, often lead the voyagers on the river to visit the shrine of the saint, and landwards the building is an object of interest and beauty, which (says Mr. Mansel, Collector of Ágrah in a letter to the Commissioner of Revenue at Ágrah 29th May, 1839 No. 125) all would regret to see lost to the country. There are several dáláns, a handsome gate, and a small mosque comprised within the building, and the whole is kept in occasional good repair by the outlay of part of the funds of the grant. The fable of the whole is palpable. Indeed the rájá who, under the name of Chandersen, was ousted from Chandwár, lived it is supposed by those best acquainted with the annals of Fírozábád, in the reign of 'Alá-uddín, and his descendants were the party who fell under the displeasure of Akbar.

**Shah Sub-han,** شاه شوبان, a Muhammadan saint who died in 1200 A. D., 596 A. H.

**Shah Sulaiman Safwi,** شاه سليمان صفوي, the son of Sháh Abbás II, king of Persia, whom he succeeded on the 26th August, 1666 A. D., 5th Rabí' I, 1077 A. H. He reigned over Persia 29 years, and died in 1694 A. D., 1106 A. H. He was succeeded by his son Sháh Husain Safwí.

**Shah Tahir Junaidi,** شاه طاهر جنيدي, also called Dakhaní, was the youngest brother of Sháh Jafar. He came to India in the time of the emperor Humáyún, and went afterwards to the Dakhin and was appointed minister to Burhán Nizám Sháh I of Aḥmadnagar. He was of the Shia sect, and succeeded in converting his sovereign to the Shia persuasion in the year 1537 A. D., 944 A. H., and induced him to exchange the white canopy and scarlet pavilion for the green standard assumed by the followers of 'Alí. Sháh Táhir died in the Dakhin 1545 A. D., 952 A. H. He was an excellent poet and is the author of several works.

**Shah Taki or Shaikh Taki,** شاه ياشيخ تقي, a Muhammadan saint who died between the years 1413 and 1421 A. D., and is buried at a place called Jhúsí in the province of Allahábád where a great crowd of Musalmáns assemble every year and make offerings on his tomb.

**Shah Turkman,** شاه تركمان, a Musalmán saint who died in February, 1241 A. D., 24th Rajab, 638 A. H., and lies buried in Sháhjahánábád (Dehlí) at a place called Dargáh Sháh Turkman.

**Shah Wali Muhammad,** شاه والي محمد, a saint whose dargáh is in Ágrah.

**Shah Wali Ullah,** شاه ولي الله, *vide* Ishtiyák.

**Shahzada Khanam,** شاهزاده خانم, a daughter of the emperor Akbar by Salíma Begam. She was living in the commencement of the reign of her brother Jahángír.

**Shahzada Sultan,** شاه زاده سلطان, *vide* Sultán Sháhzáda.

**Shah Zaman,** شاه زمن, *vide* Zamán Sháh.

**Shaista Khan, Amir-ul-Umra,** اميرالامرا شايسته خان. His original name is Abú Tálib, or Mirzá Murád. He was the son of 'Asaf Khán wazír, and grandson of Yaṭmád-uddaula. After the death of his father 1641 A. D., he was appointed wazír by the emperor Sháh Jahán. The large Jamạ Masjid which stood (till 1857) on the banks of the Jamna river to the west of the fortress of Allahábád, was built by him in the time of Sháh Jahán and completed in the year 1646 A. D., 1056 A. H. His son Khudábanda Khán also held a high rank in the time of 'Álamgír, and was appointed Faujdár of the Karnatic Bíjápúr, and subsequently, after the death of Ruh-ullah Khán, he held the post of grand steward of the household. Shaista Khán was appointed governor of Beṛaṛ by Sháh Jahán in 1638: and in 1652 to the more important command of Gujrát. In 1656 he was employed by 'Álamgír (Aurangzeib) at that time viceroy of the Dakhin, to serve as lieutenant to his eldest son Sulṭán Muhammad in the war of Golkanḍa. In the contentions of Sháh Jahán's sons for the throne in 1658, he served with Dárá Shikóh, whom he betrayed by giving intelligence and guides of Aurangzeib. He was appointed in July, 1659 A. D., governor of the Dakhin in the room of Muhammad Muạzzim the son of the emperor 'Álamgír who was recalled to the presence, and in 1666 as governor of Bengal. He kept his court at Dacca and by his injustice provoked a war with Job Charnock, Governor of the factory of the East India Company at Golágháṭ near Huglí. He died in the reign of 'Álamgír on the 31st May, 1694 A. D., 16th Shawwál, 1105 A. H., aged 93 lunar years. Some traces of his Rauza and garden are still to be seen at Ágráh on the banks of the Jamna.

**Shakar-un-Nisa Begam,** شكر النسا بيگم, the daughter of the emperor Akbar, who gave her in marriage to Mirzá Sháhrukh, son of Ibráhím Mirzá. She is buried in the mausoleum of Akbar at Sikandra in Ágrah. Her mother's name was Bíbí Daulat Sháh.

**Shakik Balkhi,** شقيق بلخي, a celebrated pious Musalmán. He died on the 20th January, 791 A. D., 9th Ramaẓán, 174 A. H. in the reign of the Khalíf Hárún-al-Rashíd, and was buried at Khatlán.

**Shakir,** شاكر, the poetical name of Nizám-ul-Mulk 'Asaf Jáh.

**Shakir,** شاكر, the poetical name of 'Abdur Rahmán, author of the poetical work called "Gulistán Musarrat," which he also named "Hadáek-ul-Mạání. He wrote this book at Lakhnau during the reign of Amjád 'Alí Sháh in 1845 A. D., 1261 A. H., and finished it in the time of Wájid 'Alí Sháh.

**Shali,** شالي**,** author of a Díwán, which goes after his name, Díwán Sháhlí.

**Shama'-ul-Mulk,** شمع الملک**,** title of the ruler of Jurján named Ḳábús.

**Shamgar,** شگر**,** *vide* Ḳábús. He is called Shamgír by Daulat Sháh.

**Shamru, Samru** or **Sombre,** شمرو**.** His real name was Walter Reinhard, a person of obscure parentage in the Electorate of Treves. He entered early as a common soldier the service of the French, taking for his *Nom-de-Guerre*, Summer, which his comrades, from his saturnine complexion, turned into Sombre, and the Indians, by corruption, Samrú and Shamrú. At length he repaired to Bengal, and enlisted in one of the Swiss Companies then employed at Calcutta; but at the end of eighteen days deserted to the French at Chandarnagar, where he became a Serjeant. Deserting this post, he fled into the Upper Provinces and was for some time a private trooper in the cavalry of Safdar Jang, father to Shujá-uddaula. This service he quitted, and led a vagabond life in different provinces; but in 1760 was with the rebel Faujdár of Purnia Khádim Husain Khán. Upon his being expelled from Bengal, Shamrú left him and entered into the service of Gregory, an Armenian, then in high favour with Nawáb Ḳásim 'Alí Khán and distinguished with the title of Gúrgín Khán. From him he had the command of a battalion of sepoys, and afterwards obtained from the nawáb the addition of another. In this station he massacred the English captives at Patna in 1763. Some time previous to the battle of Buxar, he treacherously deserted Ḳásim 'Alí with his corps, and embraced the service of the Nawáb Shujá-uddaula, who had gained him over by bribes. Upon the nawáb's defeat at Buxar, he was entrusted with the protection of the Begams, and remained with the nawáb till he had made peace with the English; when, fearful of being delivered up to them, he retired to Ágrah, and entered into the pay of the Jáṭ rájá Jawáhir Singh; but quitted him for the service of the rájá of Jaipúr, who soon dismissed him on a remonstrance from the English General. He then again served the Jáṭs; quitted them once more, and came to Dehlí, from whence he followed the fortunes of Nawáb Najaf Khán, in whose service he died. Such are the outlines of the fortune of this man, who had some merit as a soldier, but wholly obscured by a treacherous and blood-thirsty disposition. His corps was continued after his death, in the name of his son and a favourite concubine, who received for their maintenance the sum of 65,000 rupees per month. He died or was murdered in the year 1778 A. D., 1192 A. H., at Ágrah, where his tomb is to be seen in the Roman Catholic Burial-ground with a Persian inscription in verse, mentioning the year of his death and his name. *Vide* next article.

**Shamru Begam,** شمرو بیگم**,** the celebrated princess of Sardhana, whose original name is Zeib-un-Nisa, was the wife, or rather concubine of Shamrú or Sombre. She held an extensive jagír at Sardhana, and died on the 27th of January, 1836 A. D., 8th Shawwál, 1251 A. H., aged 88 lunar years. She was buried in the church of Sardhána of which she was the founder. She was one of the oldest and most sincere allies of the English. At her death she left upwards of six lakhs of rupees to various charitable and pious purposes, and gave instructions for founding a college for young men, to serve on the apostolic mission of Thibet and Hindústán. Captain Mundy in his "Journal of a Tour in India," says that the history of her life, if properly known, would form a series of scenes, such as perhaps, no other female could have gone through. Colonel Skinner had often, during his service with the Mahraṭṭas, seen her, then a beautiful young woman, leading on her troops to the attack in person, and displaying in the midst of carnage, the greatest intrepidity and presence of mind. The Begam contracted a lawful marriage in 1793. Her first lord, Reinhardt, who bought her when a young and handsome dancing girl; married, and converted her to the Roman Catholic religion. Her second husband was a French adventurer, a soldier of fortune named Levassoult who commanded her small army. It is of this man that the following anecdote is related, which is wondrous strange, if it be true. Skinner used to say that her husband had become possessed of wealth, power, and a numerous army; of these his ambitious wife coveted the undivided possession, and she then accomplished her purpose. A mutinous disposition, on the subject of pay, having manifested itself among his body-guard, the Begam, then about twenty-five, exaggerated the danger to her husband, and got intelligence conveyed to him that the rebels had formed a plan to seize and confine him, and to dishonour his wife. They, consequently, arranged to escape together from the fury of the soldiery: and at night, started secretly from their palace, in palankeens. Towards morning the attendants, in great alarm, announced that they were pursued; and our heroine, in well-feigned despair, vowed that, if their escort was overcome, she would stab herself to the heart. The devoted husband, as she expected, swore he would not survive her. Soon after, the pretended rebels came up, and after a short skirmish drove back the attendants, and forced the bearers to put down the palankeens. At this instant he (Sombre) heard a scream and his wife's female slave rushed up to him, and exclaimed that her mistress had stabbed herself to death. The husband, true to his vow, instantly seized a pistol, and blew out his own brains. His tomb is at Sardhana.

**Shamsheir Bahadur I,** شمشیر بهادر**,** an illegitimate offspring of the Peshwá Bájí Ráo Marhaṭṭa by a Musalmán concubine named Mastání, who brought him up in the Muhammadan religion. He was severely wounded in that famous battle which took place between the Marhaṭṭas and Aḥmad Sháh Abdálí in January, 1761 A. D., got to Ḍíg where Súrajmal Ját had his wounds treated with the greatest care, but he died soon after, and was buried at Ḍíg.

**Shamsheir Bahadur II,** شمشیر بهادر**,** Nawáb of Banda, was the eldest son of 'Alí Bahádur, the son of Shamsheir Bahádur I, the son of Bájí Ráo Peishwá. He succeeded to the territories of his father in Bundelkhand about the year 1802 A. D., but subsequently a pension or stipend of four lacs of rupees annually was granted him in perpetuity by the British Government. He died on the 30th August, 1823 A. D., 24th Ẕil-Ḳa'da, 1238 A. H., and was succeeded by his brother Zulfiḳár 'Alí Khán.

**Shams Fakhri,** شمس فخري**,** a poet.

**Shamsheir Khan,** شمشیر خان**,** a nobleman at whose request a prose abridgement of the Sháhnáma of Firdausí was made by Tawakkul Munshí in 1652 A. D., 1063 A. H.

**Shams Shahab Afif,** شمس شهاب عفیف**,** the son of Malik Sad-ul-Mulk who was Amaldár of Abúhar and Dibálpúr in the reign of Sulṭán Ghayás-uddín Tughlak. He was born the very day that Sulṭán Fíroz Sháh came into the world, *i. e.*, in the year 1309 A. D., 709 A. H., and was the grandfather of Shams Siráj Afíf, the author of the Taríkh Fíroz Sháhí.

**Shams Siraj Afif,** شمس سراج عفیف**,** the grandson of

Shams Shaháb Afíf, was an historian who flourished in the reign of Sulṭán Fíroz Sháh Bárbak, king of Dehlí who reigned from 1351 to 1388 A. D. He is the author of the entire history of that monarch, called "Táríkh Fíroz Shahí," in which he relates that when that emperor built the city of Fírozábád adjoining to that of (old) Dehlí in the year 1354 A. D., 755 A. H., he (the author) was then twelve years of age, and that the red stone pillar in the Koshak of Fírozábád near the mosque or Jamą Masjid, was brought by that emperor in the same year with great expense and labour from a place called Naweira in the vicinity of Sitaura near Khizirábád, a city situated on the foot of a mountain, ninety cós distant from (old) Dehlí, where it then stood. The whole length of this pillar, says the author, was 32 gaz; 8 of which the king ordered to be buried in the earth or sunk in the building and the remaining 24 to be above the surface. This pillar was called by the emperor, "Mínar Zarrín," *i. e.*, the Golden Minar. The second pillar which the emperor set up within his hunting place, called Shikárgáh Fíroz Sháh, was brought from Mírath, and was somewhat smaller than the one just mentioned. This pillar is now called the Láth of Fíroz Sháh. These two pillars were even at that period, as they are now, believed by the Hindús to have been the hand sticks of a famous hero of antiquity named Bhím Sen. The character engraved round these two pillars, the most intelligent and learned men of all religions were not able to decipher. He also observes that the high Minar in the Jamą Masjid called "Kúwat-ul-Islám" in (old) Dehlí was built by Sulṭán Shams-uddín Altimsh. The author was living at the time of Tamerlane's invasion to India in 1398 A. D., 801 A. H., whom he has mentioned in his work.

**Shams Tabreizi,** شمس تبريز, *vide* Shams-uddín Muhammad Tabreizí.

**Shams Tibsi,** شمس تبريز, *vide* Shams-uddín Tibsí (Kází).

**Shams-uddin Ahmad,** شمس الدين احمد, author of the "Khulásat-ul-Munákib," containing the Lives of ten celebrated Súfí Shaikhs.

**Shams-uddin Ahmad Khan,** شمس الدين احمد خان, a descendant of the Sayyads of Naishápúr. He held the rank of 5000 in the reign of the emperor Akbar, and died in 1591 A. D. 999 A. H.

**Shams-uddin 'Ali Khan,** شمس الدين علي خان, author of the "Muntakhib-ul-Hasnát" which contains the history of the eighth Imám, *viz.*, 'Alí Razá bin-Músa also called 'Alí Músí Razá, who died 818 A. D., and whose tomb is at Mashhad (formerly called Tús) in Khurásán, and is still an object of pilgrimage to the Persians; also memoirs of his descendants. This work was translated from the Arabic of Abú Jạfar.

**Shams-uddin-al-Shafa'i,** شمس الدين الشافعي, author of the Arabic work called "Ayún-ul-Asar;" containing the wars and conquests of Muhammad, his successors and companions, interspersed with various anecdotes of his generals.

**Shams-uddin Altimsh, Sultan,** شمس الدين التمش سلطان, a king of Dehlí, whose original name was Altimsh. In his childhood he was bought from a merchant by Sulṭán Ḳuṭb-uddín Eybak, king of Dehlí, who afterwards gave him his daughter in marriage. He expelled 'Arám Sháh, the son of Ḳuṭb-uddín from the throne of Dehlí, 1210 A. D., 607 A. H., and declared himself king with the title of Shams-uddín. He defeated and imprisoned Táj-uddín Eldúz, king of Ghazní who came to Láhor with a large army in 1215 A. D. He beseiged for a whole year the fortress of Gwáliar and took it in 1233, and after a reign of 26 years, died on the 30th April, 1236 A. D., 633 A. H. His son Sulṭán Rukn-uddín Fíroz succeeded him. It is supposed that the Ḳuṭb Mínár in old Dehlí, which is now commonly called the Láṭh of Ḳuṭb Sáhib because it stands close to the dargáh of the celebrated saint Khwája Ḳuṭb-uddín Bakhtyár Kákí, was built and completed by Sulṭán Shams-uddín Altimsh some time before the year 1236 A. D. A part of it was injured by lightning and was repaired and completed on the 26th October, 1501 A. D., 13th Rabí' II, 907 A. H. by Fatha Khán Masnad 'Alí in the reign of Sulṭán Sikandar Sháh Lodí.

**Shams-uddin Bahmani, Sultan,** شمس الدين بهمني سلطان, the son of Sulṭán Mahmúd Bahmaní. He was placed on the throne of the Dakhin on the 14th of June, 1397 A D., 17th Ramaẓán, 799 A. H., after the dethronement of his brother Ghayás-uddín, by Lálchín, who was now honoured with the title of Malik Náeb or regent. Shams-uddín had reigned only five months and seven days, when Fíroz Khán, the son of Sulṭán Dáúd Sháh, having deposed him, sent him together with Lálchín to confinement, and ascended the throne with the title of Fíroz Sháh Rózafzún on Thursday the 15th of November, 1397 A. D., 23rd Ṣafar, 800 A. H.

**Shams-uddin bin-Mubarik,** شمس الدين بن مبارك, author of the "Sharah Hikmat-ul-Ain."

**Shams-uddin Fakir, Mir,** مير شمس الدين فقير, a native of Dehlí, and author of the work, called "Hadáeḳ-ul-Balághat," or Garden of Eloquence, a treatise on the rhetoric, poetry and rhyme of the Persians.

**Shams-uddin Kart I, Malik,** ملک شمس الدين کرت, also called Malik Shams-uddín Muhammad Kart, the son of Abá Bakar Kart, was the founder of the dynasty of Kart or Kard, a tribe of Turks. He commenced his reign in the year 1268 A. D., 666 A. H., over Hirát, Ghor, Ghazní and Kábul. His mother was the daughter of Malik Rukn-uddín Ghórí, who before his death in 1245 A. D., 643 A. H., had named him to be his successor, and which was subsequently confirmed by Mangú Khán and Halákú Khán, kings of Persia. His descendants continued to reign over those countries for 119 lunar years and two months, till they were extinguished by Amír Taimúr (Tamerlane) in 1381 A. D. He was a cotemporary of Abaḳá Khán, king of Persia, and died at Tabreiz in January, 1278 A. D., Shaban, 676 A. H. after a reign of ten years and was succeeded by his son Malik Shams-uddín II.

*Kings of the dynasty of Kart or Kard.*

1. Malik Shams-uddín Muhammad Kart I.
2. ,, Shams-uddín II, his son, also called Rukn-uddín.
3. ,, Fakhr-uddín Bahman, his son.
4. ,, Ghayás-uddín Kart, his brother.
5. ,, Shams-uddín Kart III, his son.
6. ,, Háfiz, his brother.
7. ,, Moi'zz-uddín Husain, his brother.
8. ,, Ghayás-uddín, the son of 'Alí and grandson of Moi'zz-uddín, the last king of this race.

**Shams-uddin Kart II, Malik,** شمس الدين کرت ملک, second king of the dynasty of Kart, was the son of Shams-uddín Kart I, whom he succeeded in January, 1278 A D., 676 A. H. He was a cotemporary of Abáḳá Khán the Tartar king of Persia, and reigned about 28 years over Hirat, Ghazní, Balkh, &c. He died on Thursday the 2nd of September, 1305 A. D., 12th Safar, 705 A. H., and was succeeded by his son Malik Fakhr-uddín Bahman.

**Shams-uddin Kart III, Malik,** شمس الدين كرت ملك, the fifth Sultán of the dynasty of Kart who reigned over Hirat, Balkh, Ghazní and Kábul. He succeeded his father Ghayás-uddín Kart in 1329 A. D., 729 A. H. reigned ten months and died in 1330 A. D., 730 A. H., He was succeeded by his brother Malik Háfiz, who was slain in 1332. After him Moi'zz-uddín Husain his brother ascended the throne.

**Shams-uddin Khan,** نواب شمس الدين خان, the nawáb of Fírozpúr, was the son of Nawáb Ahmad Bakhsh Khán, a jagírdár of Pargana Fírozpúr and Lohárí. It was at his instigation that Karím Khán one of his confidants murdered Mr. W. Fraser the British Commissioner of Dehlí, on the evening of the 22nd March, 1835 A. D., for which act Karím Khán was hanged on the 26th August following, and subsequently the nawáb, who after a full investigation of the case, being found guilty, was executed on the 8th of October of the same year at Dehlí. Nawáb Shams-uddín was the Jagírdár of Fírozpúr, the town of a large district of the same name, situated at a distance of sixty miles to the south-west of Dehlí. He enjoyed a revenue variously estimated at from three to ten lacs of rupees a year. The actual cause of his animosity towards Mr. Fraser, and the reason which induced him to instigate his murder, will perhaps ever remain a mystery. The supposition is, that Mr. Fraser had, in the faithful discharge of his duty, apportioned to Amín-uddín and Ziya-uddín, the younger brothers of the nawáb, a part or whole of Lohárí, an extensive estate, to which the latter considered himself the best entitled.

**Shams-uddin Khawafi, Khwaja,** شمس الدين خوافي خواجه, the son of an Amír of Khawáf in Khurásán by name Khwája 'Alá-uddín. Shams-uddín held a high rank in the service of the emperor Akbar, and was appointed Díwán of the Panjáb in 1599 A. D., 1008 A. H., but died after a few months at Láhor.

**Shams-uddin Muhammad,** شمس الدين محمد, author of the works called "Bakhtyár-náma," and "Sindbád-náma."

**Shams-uddin Muhammad Anka Khan,** شمس الدين محمد عنكا خان, *vide* 'Azim Khán.

**Shams-uddin Muhammad Assar,** شمس الدين محمد عصار, *vide* Assár.

**Shams-uddin Muhammad-bin-Abdullah-al-Ghuzzi, Shaikh,** شمس الدين محمد بن عبدالله الغزى, author of the "Tanwír-ul-Absár," which he composed in 1586 A. D., 995 A. H., and enriched with a variety of questions and decisions. It is considered to be one of the most useful books according to the Hanafí doctrines, and has been frequently commented upon. The most noted of these commentaries is one written by the author himself, entitled "Manh-al-Ghasffar."

**Shams-uddin Muhammad ibn-Nasar,** شمس الدين محمد ابن نصر, author of the work called "Mujma-ul-Bahryn." He lived in the time of Táj-uddín Eldúz.

**Shams-uddin Muhammad bin-Killai,** شمس الدين محمد, author of the "Faráez-ul-Fárikía," a treatise on the Law of Inheritance according to Sháfaí's doctrine. He died in 1375 A. D., 777 A. H.

**Shams-uddin Muhammad bin-Hamza,** شمس الدين محمد بن حمزة, surnamed Fanárí. He was an author and died in the year 1431 A. D., 834 A. H. He wrote a commentary which is considered one of the best glosses on the Sirájia of Sajáwandí.

**Shams-uddin Muhammad Kuswi, Khwaja,** خواجه شمس الدين محمد كوسوي, a descendant of Shaikh Ahmad Jám. He died on Saturday the 31st of March, 1459 A. D., 26th Jumáda I, 863 A. H., and is buried near the Jama Masjid at Hirát, close to the tomb of Fakíh Abú Yezíd Marghazí.

**Shams-uddin Muhammad Sahib Diwan,** شمس الدين محمد صاحب ديوان, held the office of Díwán and prime minister in the reign of Halákú Khán and his son Abáká Khán the Tartar kings of Persia. In the first year of the reign of Arghún Khán, the son of Abáká Khán, he was accused by his enemies of causing the death of the king's father by poison, and was executed at Kara Bágh of Tabrez on Monday the 16th of October, 1284 A. D., 4th Shabán, 683 A. H. He was a good poet and is the author of the work called "Risála Shamsia dar ilm Mantak," a work on the science of Logic. His brother Alá-uddín, surnamed Atá Malik, is the author of a History entitled Jahán Kushá.

**Shams-uddin Muhammad Tabrezi, Maulana,** مولانا شمس الدين محمد تبريزى, commonly called Shams Tabrezí, a celebrated Muhammadan of Tabrez. He was the master of Jalál-uddín Maulwí Rúmí who wrote a book of odes in his name entitled the Díwán of Shams Tabrezí. He was murdered by 'Alá-uddín Mahmúd, the son of the Maulwí and thrown into a well 1247 A. D., 645 A. H. He is considered by the Súfís to be one of the most celebrated martyrs of their sect. He was, they say, sentenced to be flayed alive, on account of his having raised a dead person to life. We are told that, after the law had been put in force, he wandered about, carrying his own skin, and solicited some food to appease his hunger, but he had been excommunicated as well as flayed, and no one would give him the slightest help. After four days he found a dead ox: but he could not obtain fire to dress it. Wearied out with the unkindness of men, he desired the sun to broil his meat. It descended to perform the office; and the world was on the point of being consumed, when the holy Shaikh commanded the flaming orb to resume its station in the heavens.

**Shams-uddin Purbi I,** شمس الدين پوربي, surnamed Bhangeira. His proper name was Khwája Iliás. He ascended the throne of Bengal after the assassination of 'Alá-uddín Púrbí about the year 1343 A. D., 744 A. H. For thirteen years he resisted with success the forces of the king of Dehlí, who could never succeed during the whole of that period in making any impression upon him. He died after a reign of 16 years 1358 A. D., 760 A. H, and was succeeded by his son Sikandar Sháh Púrbí.

**Shams-uddin Purbi II,** شمس الدين پوربي, ascended the throne of Bengal after the death of his father Sultán-us-Salátín 1383 A. D., and died after an inglorious reign of three years 1386 A. D., 788 A. H. He was succeeded by Rája Kans Púrbí.

**Shams-uddin Tabreizi,** شمس الدين تبريزي, *vide* Shams-uddin Muhammad Tabreizi.

**Shams-uddin Tibsi, Kazi,** قاضي شمس الدين طبسي, one of the learned men of Khurásán, and an excellent poet, who attended the court of Nizám-ul-Mulk Wazír to Sultán Jalál-uddín Malikshah. He died about the year 473 A. H.

**Shams-ul-'Umra, Amir Kabir Nawab,** شمس الامرا امير كبير نواب, a nobleman or Amír-ul-'Umra of the court of the Nizám of Haidarábád. He was born in 1780 A. D., and survived three successive Nizáms. The first was Nizám 'Alí Khán by whom the nawáb was originally appointed "Commander of the household troops," during the troubled periods of Típú Sultán's reign. On Nizám 'Alí's death in 1803 A. D., the Nawáb lived to see Mír Akbar 'Alí *alias* Sikandar Jáh, raised to the masnad, and subsequently on the decease of this prince in 1830, saw him succeeded by Násir-uddaula, the late Nizám, from whom he received the title of "Amír Kabír" in acknowledgment of his services to the state. As a geometrician he stood unrivalled, and the compilation styled after himself "Shams-ul-Handisa" besides other works published by him on the Arts and Sciences, distinguish him as an author. He died on the 10th April, 1863 A. D., when he had just completed the 83rd year of his age, and was the oldest nobleman then living in Haidarabád. He left two sons, both are good men. The elder of the two has inherited his father's vast estates and his official titles. The younger received most of his father's immense wealth during his lifetime, and many jagírs since his death.

**Shams-un-Nisa Begam,** شمس النسا بيگم, the daughter of Hakím Kamar-uddín Khán of Benares, but her place of residence is at Lakhnau. She is the author of a small Díwán and was living in the year 1272 A. H.

**Shani,** شاني, a poet who flourished in the reign of Sháh Abbás I, king of Persia, and died in the year 1614 A. D., 1023 A. H. He is sometimes called Maulana Shání Taklú.

**Shapur,** شاپور, a poet of Teherán who died 1638 A. D., 1048 A. H. His tomb is at a place called Surkháb in Tabreiz. He had the title of Malik-ush-Shoárá or king of poets.

**Shapur** or **Shahpur I,** شاپور, (the Sapores of the Greeks) the second king of Persia of the Sasanian dynasty, was the son of Ardisheir Bábigán. He began to reign about the year 240 A. D., and carried his arms into the Roman territories, gained many important victories over that nation, whose emperor, Valerian, he made prisoner and flayed him alive. According to Persian historians, Shápúr reigned 31 years, and died about the year 271 A. D. He was succeeded by his son Hurmuz I, the Hormisdes of the Greeks.

**Shapur II,** شاپور, surnamed Zú'l Aktáf, was the son of Hurmuz II, king of Persia, and was born 310 A. D. a few months after the death of his father, on which account the Persian historians say, that his reign was a few months longer than his life. He died 381 A. D., aged 71 years. During his long reign, he raised his country to a state of the greatest prosperity; having defeated all his enemies, and extended the limits of his empire in every direction. He was succeeded by his son Ardisheir II.

**Shapur III,** شاپور, the son of Shápúr II, and the uterine brother of Ardisheir II, whom he deposed, and mounted the throne of Persia 385 A. D. This prince who is described as virtuous and beneficent, reigned over Persia only five years. He was killed by the fall of his tent, the pole of which struck the monarch as he slept.

**Sharaf-ibn-Shams-uddin,** شرف ابن شمس الدين, author of the "Sharaf-náma" a Persian History of the Dynasties which have governed in Kurdistán. It was translated into English by Professor Charmoy.

**Sharaf Jahan, Mirza,** مرزا شرف جهان, an author whose father Kází Jahán held a high appointment at the court of Sháh Tahmasp Safwí, but being suspected of being a Sunní, he was deprived of it. Sharaf Jahán died in 1561 A. D., 968 A. H.

**Sharaf Kazwini,** شرف قزويني, a poet who was a native of Kazwín, and is the author of a Persian Díwán. He came to the Dakhin in the reign of Kutb Sháh in whose service he died.

**Sharaf-uddin Ahmad Ahia Maneiri, Shaikh,** شيخ شرف الدين احمد احيا منيري, a celebrated saint of Behár. He and his eldest brother Shaikh Jalál-uddín were the disciples of Shaikh Najm-uddín Firdausí. Sharaf-uddín was a contemporary of Shaikh Nizám-uddín Aulia. He resided at Behár, and is the author of the works called "Mádan-ul-Máání," and "Mukátibát Ahia Maneirí," the latter contains the whole duty of a Súfí in a series of 250 letters addressed to his disciples and friends. He died in the year 1379 A. D., 781 A. H., and his tomb (an exact delineation of which has been given by Mr. Daniel) stands near the junction of the river Són with the Ganges, and is still the resort of devout Muhammadans. He is called Maneirí because he resided in a town called Maneir near Patna. The tomb of his fathor Shaikh Ahia or Yehia is in the town of Maneir. (Journal Asiatic Society of Bengal, Vol. XIV, part I, pp. 138-140.) See also Sháh Sharaf-uddín.

**Sharaf-uddin 'Ali Yezdi, Maulana,** مولانا شرف الدين علي يزدي, a learned man and author of several works. He lived at the court of Sultán Ibráhím, the son of Sháhrukh Mirzá, at whose request he wrote in a beautiful style, the "Zafar-náma," also called Táríkh Sáhib Kiráni," a history of the celebrated conqueror Amír Taimúr (Tamerlane), whose dominions extended from the borders of China to the shores of the Mediterranean. This work was finished in four years and dedicated to Sháhrukh Mirzá, 1425 A. D., 828 A. H. It has been translated by P. De la Croix, and the heads of it may be found in Gibbon's sixth volume of the Decline of the Roman Empire. Sharaf-uddín may be considered as the Panegyrist of Taimúr, while the work of Ahmad-ibn-Arabsháh is a coarse satire on that conqueror. He is also the author of the "Sharb Burda." Sharaf-uddín who used Sharaf for his poetical name, died about the year 1446 A. D., 850 A. H.

**Sharaf-uddin Ashrafi Samarkandi,** شرف الدين اشرفي سمرقندي, a poet of Samarkand who died in the year 1199 A. D., 595 A. H.

**Sharaf-uddin Hasan Shafai of Isfahan,** شرف الدين حسن شفائي اصفهاني. He is the author of the following Masnawís or poems, *viz.*, Namakdán Hakíkat," "Mehr-o-Muhabbat," and "Dída Beidar." He died in the year 1628 A. D., 1038 A. H.

**Sharaf-uddin Husain, Mirza,** مرزا شرف الدين حسين, the son of Khwája Móín who was of the race of Khwája

Shákir Násir-uddín 'Abdulláh one of the greatest saints of Turkistán. Sharaf-uddín Husain was the son-in-law of the emperor Humáyún and was governor of Ajmeir. He with another chief named Abú'l Maálí, had revolted at Nágor, before the Uzbak rebellion took place in Málwá, about the year 1561 A. D., 969 A. H., had defeated the emperor Akbar's troops, and advanced towards Dehlí. They were afterwards driven back in their turn, and forced to seek for safety, the latter beyond the Indus, and the former to Aḥmadábád in Gujrát where he joined the Mirzás at Barouch, in the year 1568 A. D., 976 A. H.

**Sharaf-uddin Panipati,** شرف الدين پاني پتي, *vide* Abú 'Alí Kalandar.

**Sharaf-uddin Rami, Maulana,** شرف الدين رامي مولانا, author of a Díwán and the "Hadáek-ul-Hakáek," which treats on metric and poetic compositions, and has been written in imitation of, or competition with, Rashíd-uddín Watwát's Hadáek-us-Sehr. He flourished in the reign of Sháh Mansúr and died 1393 A. D., 795 A. H.

**Sharaf-uddin Shafrawa,** شرف الدين شفروده, a poet of Isfahán, who flourished in the reign of Tughral III, and was cotemporary with the poet Mujír. He is the author of the work called "Itbak-uz-Zahab" which he wrote in imitation of Itwak-uz-Zahab of Zamakhsharí.

**Sharaf-uddin, Shah,** شاه شرف الدين, *vide* Sháh Sharaf-uddín.

**Sharaf-uddaula,** شرف الدوله, a nobleman of the reign of the emperor Muhammad Sháh. He is the founder of the Masjid situated in the Daríba Bázár at Dehlí which he built in the year 1723 A. D., 1135 A. H.

**Sharaf-uddaula, Nawab,** نواب شرف الدوله, ex prime-minister of Audh, was a native of Kashmír. His ancestors were "Rafúgurs" or shawl-darners. At an early age he travelled to the Dakhin, where he obtained employment under the Nizám. He did not, however, remain long at Haidarábád; the reputed splendour of the court of Lakhnau brought him to Audh where he found he had an uncle, the celebrated Maulwí Ahia, the residency Wakíl during the reign of Násir-uddín Haidar. On the accession of Muhammad 'Alí Sháh to the throne in 1839 A. D., Maulwí Ahia was advanced to the post of prime-minister, *vice* Hakím Mahdí, deceased, and Sharaf-uddaula was appointed residency Wakíl *vice* his uncle promoted. Maulwí Ahia dying soon after, Sharaf-uddaula succeeded him as prime-minister. He held the office up to the time of Muhammad 'Alí Sháh's death which took place in May, 1842 A. D., when Amjád 'Alí Sháh succeeding to the throne, he nominated his favourite, Amín-uddaula to the premiership, obliging Sharaf-uddaula to retire. By the Resident personally the nawáb was so much esteemed that, after he lost office, he, the Resident, deemed him the fittest man in Lakhnau to manage the very responsible and important concerns of the Husainabád Imámbárah, of which he induced the king to make him "Wasíkadár," or stipendiary. Sharaf-uddaula was known by every one to be the most sincerely attached friend the British had in Audh. He was, therefore, looked upon with much jealousy and rancour by all the courtiers, but especially by Nawáb 'Alí Nakí Khán, the father-in-law and prime-minister of Wájid 'Alí Sháh the last king. Viewing him always as his rival, 'Alí Nakí often contemplated his ruin, and at one time in league with Nawáb Wasí 'Alí Khán, one of the famous abominables of the court of Lakhnau, he would have compassed his end, as he had succeeded in getting the king to issue an order of banishment against Sharaf-ud daula, with his whole family, but for the timely interference of the Resident who had the order revoked. During the early part of the rebellion (in 1857) the insurgents surrounded his house, insisting that he should become prime-minister of the rebel government. He refused and tried to excuse himself in every way, but they forcibly installed him in the office, which he knew he only nominally held, since Mammú Khán was the ruling spirit with the Begam. On the arrival of General Havelock's force for the relief of the Lakhnau garrison, he was in the Keisar Bágh and received a bullet in the shoulder. When the final grand attack was made on the city by the Commander-in-Chief, which caused the Begam and her party to remove to the Músa Bágh, Sharaf-uddaula took advantage of the confusion and skulked behind, and endeavoured to steal out of the city, when he was recognised by some sepoys, who bound him with cords, took him to Maulwí Aḥmad-ulláh Sháh, who after starving him for four days had him put to death.

**Sharif Jurjani, Mir or Sayyad,** مير شريف جرجاني, whose full name is Sayyad Sharíf 'Alí bin-Muhammad, is the author of the "Háshia Kashsháf" and "Hashia Tafsír Anwár-ut-Tauzíl," also of an Arabic work on philosophy called "'Adáb-ul-Sharíf," and the marginal notes on the "Sharah Matla-ul-Anwár" and on the "Mawákif Azdia" a work on Jurisprudence in Arabic. He also wrote a Commentary on the Sirájia of Sajáwandí, which he named "Sharífia." He was born in 1339 A. D., 740 A. H., and died in July, 1413 A. D., 6th Rabí' II, 816 A. H.

**Sharif Khan Amir-ul-'Umra,** شريف خان امير الامرا, son of Khwája Abdus Samad, a nobleman of the reign of the emperor Jahángír, who in the first year of his reign conferred on him the rank of 5,000 and appointed him governor of Haidarábád in the Dakhin where he died after some years. He was an excellent poet and has left a Díwán. His poetical name was Farsí.

**Sharif Muhammad,** شريف محمد, author of the Persian work on Jurisprudence called "Fatáwa Faeróz Sháhí," dedicated to Fíróz Sháh, king of Dehlí.

**Sharifi Maulana,** مولانا شريفي, a native of Balkh who was a physician, poet and a good musician. He has written several panegyrics in praise of the king of Badakhshán.

**Sharif-uddin Muhammad Abdullah-al-Mousali-al-Basri,** شريف الدين محمد عبدالله الموصلي, author of a Díwán which he called "Díwán Murtazá Alí."

**Sharm,** شرم, *vide* Shams-un-Nisa Begam.

**Shatibi,** شاطبي, *vide* Abú Muhammad Shátibí.

**Shayek,** شايق, *vide* Sháek.

**Shayurghamish, Mirza,** شيورغمش مرزا, a son of Sháhrukh Mirzá.

**Shirazi,** شيرازي, an author who wrote a Commentary on the Tahrír-ul-Majastí of Is-hák bin-Husain, and named it "Hall Mushkilát Majastí."

**Shirin,** شيدي. This word or name which signifies in Persian, sweet, charming or agreeable, is the name of a lady well-known throughout the East. Some call her Mary and others Irene. The Greeks only describe her as a Roman by birth, a Christian by religion; but she is represented as the daughter of the emperor Maurice in the Persian and Turkish romances, which celebrated the love of Khusro for Shírín, of Shírín for Farhád the most beautiful youth of the East. This celebrated beauty has been accused of giving those affections, which a monarch so anxiously sought, to the lowly Farhád, in whose breast her beauties kindled a flame, which deprived him of reason and life. We are told that the son of Khusro, after putting his father to death, sought the favours of his father's mistress; who appeared to consent, but desired to take one look at the remains of his father. The murdered body of her former lover was shown to her, and she immediately put an end to her existence by stabbing herself. *Vide* Farhád.

**Shidi,** شیدي, an African.

**Shidi Foulad Khan,** شیدي فولاد خان, *vide* Fouládi Khán Shídí.

**Shefta,** شیفته, his proper title and name is Nawáb Mustafá Khán of Dehlí, the son of Nawáb Murtazá Khán. He was a good poet and had adopted two poetical names, *viz.*, Shefta and Hasratí. In the art of poetry he was a pupil of Momin who died 1852 A. D., 1250 A. H. He is the author of a Díwán and a biography of Urdu poets which he wrote in 1834 called Gulshán Beikhár.

**Shaikh 'Alai,** شیخ علائی, a philosopher of Bayana, who made a great noise in the world in the reign of Sultán Salím Sháh by introducing a new system of religion. He called himself Imám Mahdí who is believed to be the last of the prophets. This impostor raised great disturbances in the empire, converted some thousands by force and persuasion. After being twice banished by the king, he returned, and kindled fresh troubles, for which he was scourged to death at Ágrah, by order of the king 1548 A. D., 955 A. H. He remained firm to his doctrine in the agonies of death; but his religion was not long maintained by his disciples. *Vide* Áín Translation, (Abú'l-Fazl's Biography).

**Shaikh 'Alam,** شیخ عالم, who wrote a book on the Music of India, and called it Mádhoánal or Mádhó Náek, after the name of the musician who first wrote it in Hindí.

**Shaikh 'Ali,** شیخ علی, author of the "Jawáhir-ul-Samania."

**Shaikhi 1st,** شیخي, a poet, on whom Murád I had conferred a wazírship. The following amusing anecdote of this poet is recorded by an author. In the early part of his career Shaikhí suffered much from a complaint in the eyes, and, being very poor, he was so inconsequent as to open a shop for the sale of eye-water. The price was an asper a bottle. One day, however, a stranger, passing by and observing the bloodshot eyes of the poet, stopped to purchase a bottle, and in paying for it laid down two aspers. "I charge but one asper," said Shaikhí, "do you not know that?" "Certainly I know it," said the stranger, and therefore you see I give you a second." "Give me a second!" replied Shaikhí angrily. "for what?" "To enable you to buy one of your own bottles, my friend," replied the other coolly, "and cure yourself!" The poet shrugged his shoulders and shut up his shop. He flourished about the year 1395.

**Shaikhi 2nd,** a Turkish poet, who was contemporary with Ahmadí.

**Shaikh Buhlul,** شیخ بهلول, the brother of the saint Muhammad Ghaus of Gwáliar. He was put to death in Ágrah by Mirzá Handal, the brother of the emperor Humayún about the year 1539 A. D., 945 A. H. His tomb is on a hill near the fort of Byana.

**Shaikh Farid Bhakari,** شیخ فرید بهکري, a native of Bhakar, and author of the work called "Zakhírat-ul-Kawánín," which he composed in the time of the emperor Sháh Jahán 1650 A. D., 1060 A. H.

**Shaikh Farid Bukhari,** شیخ فرید, a nobleman, who in the first year of Jahángír, was raised to the rank of 5,000, with the title of Murtazá Khán, and appointed Paymaster General of the army. He died in the year 1616 A. D., 1025 A. H.

**Shaikh Ibrahim,** شیخ ابراهیم, an uncle of the poet Hazín. He is the author of the "Ráfa'-ul-Khiláf," which contains glosses on various works, and of the "Káshif-ul-Ghawáshí" being glosses on the Kashsháf as far as the 49th Súra, and of a commentary on Euclid. He died at Láhiján in 1707 A. D., 1119 A. H.

**Shaikh Jalal,** شیخ جلال, surnamed Makhdúm Jahánian Jahángasht; a celebrated saint of Multán, the son of Sayyad Ahmad Kabír the son of Sayyad Jalá'l Bukhárí. He was the disciple of Shaikh Rukn-uddín Abú'l Fatha, grandson of Shaikh Bahá-uddín Zikaria. He is said to have travelled all over the world, and is on that account called Jahángasht. He made seven pilgrimages to Mecca and brought from there a stone bearing the foot mark of the prophet, which he made over to Sultán Fíróz Sháh Tughlak who became one of his disciples. Shaikh Jalál was born on the 8th February, 1308 A. D., 14th Shabán, 707 A. H., and died on Wednesday, the 3rd February, 1384 A. D., 10th Zil-hijja 785 A. H., aged 78 lunar years; he was buried at Uchcha in Multán. The Persian inscription is engraved on the gate of his mausoleum, which is annually visited by the pilgrims of distant countries. It is a popular belief that a fool can get restored to perfect sense by eating the earth of his tomb. He is the founder of the sect of Malang and Jalália Fakírs in India, and is the brother of Sayyad Ráju Kattál. His memoirs were written by one of his disciples and is called "Kitáb Kutbí." *Vide* Thomas, Chronicles of the Pathán kings, p. 94 *n.*

**Shaikh Jalal of Thanesar,** شیخ جلال بخاري, a celebrated pious Musalmán who lived in the time of the emperor Akbar, and died on the 10th of January, 1582 A. D., 14th Zil-hijja 989 A. H., and lies buried at Thánesar.

**Shaikh Jamali, Maulana,** مولانا شیخ جمالي, was a native of Dehlí and an excellent Persian poet. He at first took for his poetical title "*Jalálí*", but subsequently at the request of his *murshid* Shaikh Samá-uddín, changed into, "*Jamálí.* From Dehlí he proceeded on a pilgrimage to Mecca, and on his return he came to Hirat in the time of Sultán Husain Mirzá, where he resided for several years and became acquainted with the celebrated Maulwí Jámí. He is the author of the work entitled "Siar-ul-'Arifín" or Lives of the Pious, as also of a Díwán. He died in the time of the emperor Humáyún 1535 A. D., 942 A. H., and lies buried at old Dehlí where his tomb is still to be seen. His son Shaikh Gadáí Kambóh served under Bairám Khán for several years, rose to a suitable rank and died in 1568 A. D., 976 A. H.

**Shaikh Jun** or **Jiwan bin-Abi Sa'id-al-Makki,** شیخ جون, author of the "Núr-ul-Anwár fí Sharh-al-Manár, a law treatise.

**Shekh Mir,** شيخ مير, a nobleman and one of the best generals of 'Alamgír, whose cause he espoused and was killed in the last battle which took place between that emperor and his eldest brother Dárá Shikóh at Ajmeir on Sunday the 13th of March, 1659 A. D., 29th Jumáda II, 1069 A. H. He was buried by the orders of 'Alamgír close to the tomb of Khwája Mo'ín-uddín Chishtí at Ajmeir.

**Shekh Mir of Lahor,** شيخ مير. He is also called Sháh Mír, and is said to have been a pious Musalmán and spiritual guide of Mullá Sháh. He died in August, 1635 A. D., 1045 A. H., and is buried at Láhor. *Vide* Sháh Mír.

**Shekh Mubarak of Nagor,** شيخ مبارک ناگوري, father of Shekh Faizí and Abú'l Fazl the celebrated wazír of the emperor Akbar. He is the author of the Commentary on the Kurán called "Munba-ul-Ayún," and of another work entitled "Jawáma-ul-Kalám." He was born in the year 1505 A. D., and died at Láhor on the 5th August, 1593 A. D., 17th Zil-Ka'da, 1001 A. H., and was buried at Agrah where in the same compound it is supposed Faizí, Abú'l Fazl and Ladlí their sister were buried. His father's name was Shekh Músá, who was a Turk by birth.

**Shekh Mufid,** شيخ مفيد, *vide* Abú 'Abdulláh Muhammad bin-Muhammad-al-Namání.

**Shekh Muhammad,** شيخ محمد, author of a work on Súfiism in Persian called "Chehal Risála," or forty Chapters, *vide* Muhammad (Shekh).

**Shekh Muwyyad,** شيخ مويد, *vide* Abú'l Kasim of Hulla.

**Shekh Nizam,** شيخ نظام, *vide* Nizám (Shekh).

**Shekh Razi,** شيخ رضي, son of Hasan, author of the Sharah on the Káfia and Sháfia of Ibn-Hájib. He died in 1287 A. D., 686 A. H.

**Shekh Safi** or **Safi-uddin,** شيخ صفي, the celebrated founder of the sect of Súfís in Persia, from whom were descended the royal Safwí family. He dwelt in Ardibeil in Media and died there. His son Shekh Sadr-uddín Músa was held in such high estimation, that he was honoured by a visit from the great conqueror Amír Taimúr. That monarch was so much pleased by the Shekh's conversation, that at his request he released all the prisoners taken in Asia Minor and Turkey. Many of the captives were persons of wealth and family, who afterwards enriched their benefactor by costly presents and acknowledged him as their tutelar saint. Their respect and that of their descendants was continued to him and his posterity. Shekh Safí died at Ardibeil on the 7th of August, 1335 A. D., 17th Zil-hijja, 735 A. H.

**Shekh Razi,** شيخ رضي, son of Hasan, author of the "Sharah on the Káfia and Sháfia of Ibn-Hajib." He died in 1287 A. D., 686 A. H.

**Shekh Saduk,** شيخ صدوق, also called Abú Jafar Muhammad bin-'Alí Babawia. *Vide* Babawia.

**Shekh Sharif,** شيخ شريف, *vide* Sháh Sharaf-uddín.

**Shekh Taki,** شيخ تقي, *vide* Sháh Takí.

**Shekh Yusaf,** شيخ يوسف, *vide* Yúsaf (Shekh).

**Sher Afgan Khan,** شير افگن خان, a Turkman nobleman of high lineage and great renown, was the first husband of the celebrated Núr Jahán Begam. He served in the wars of Akbar with extraordinary reputation, and had a jágír at Bardwán where he was slain 1607 A. D., 1019 A. H., in an encounter with the Governor, Kutb-uddín. His original name was Asta Fillo, and 'Alí Zula Beg, but having killed a lion, he was dignified with the title of Sher Afgan Khán or the destroyer of Lions. The Emperor Jahángír married the widow some years after which gave rise to a legend of the Emperor's having caused his death.

**Sher 'Ali Khan, Amir of Kabul,** شير علي خان, the youngest son of Dost Muhammad Khán.

**Sher 'Ali Afsos, Mir,** مير شير علي افسوس, *vide* Afsós.

**Sheri Maulana,** مولانا شيري, a poet who flourished in the reign of the emperor Akbar. When the fortress of Chittor was taken by that monarch in December, 1567 A. D., Jumáda II, 975 A. H., and the fort of Rinthanpúr on the 22nd March, 1569 A. D., 3rd Shawwál, 976 A. H., in which year the fort of Agrah was also completed, Sherí was then living, and wrote the chronogram of all three. He was slain together with rájá Bírbal and other officers of note in a battle fought against the Yúsafzaí Afgháns of Sawád and Bijúr in February, 1586 A. D., Rabí' I, 994 A. H. The author of the "Másir-ul-'Umrá" says, that he was the nephew of Khwája Jahán Hirwí a nobleman of the court of Akbar, who died in November, 1574 A. D., Shaban, 982 A. H., and that Sherí died in 1581 A. D., 989 A. H. He is the author of a Díwán.

**Sher Khan Lodi,** شير خان لودي, the son of 'Alí Amjád Khán Lodí who died on the 13th of November, 1673 A. D., 14th Shaban, 1084 A. H. Sher Khán is the author of a Tazkira or biography of poets called "Mirat-ul-Khayáb," or the Mirror of Imagination, which he wrote in the year 1691 A. D., 1102 A. H., in the reign of the emperor 'Alamgír. It contains an account of the most celebrated poets, and besides it treats on almost every science cultivated by the Musalmáns: music, medicine, cosmography, oneiroscopy, talismans, &c.

**Sheroya,** شيرويه, the Siroes of the Greeks, was the son of Khusro Parwez, or Chosroes, king of Persia, whom he threw into a dungeon and subsequently murdered 628 A. D., 7 A. H. He reigned only eight months and died 629 A. D., 8 A. H. At the death of Sheroya, an ambitious noble raised Ardisher the infant son of that prince to the throne: but another noble of the name of Shahryár, disapproving this measure, marched from the province which he governed, seized Madáin, put Ardisher to death after he had reigned five months, and usurped the crown, which however he held only a few days, having been slain by the adherents of the royal family. These not being able to discover any heir male of the house of Sasán, elevated Túrándukht the daughter of Khusro Parwez to the throne.

**Sher Shah,** شير شاه, a native of Hissar. His original name was Faríd. His father Hasan was an Afghán of the tribe of Súr, and a native of Roh at Pesháwar who had received from Jamál Khán the governor of Jaunpúr, the districts of Sahsarám and Tánda in jágír for the maintenance of 500 horse. Faríd was for some time in the service of Muhammad Lohání king of Behár, and on his killing a tiger, received from him the title of Sher Khán. He defeated the emperor Humáyún once at Behár on the 26th June, 1539 A. D., 9th Safar, 946 A. H., and the second time on the 17th of May, 1540 A. D., 10th Muharram, 947 A. H., at Kanauj, when he pursued him through Ágrah and Láhor to Khúsháb; from whence Humáyún eventually retreated towards the Indus. Sher Khán by this victory became the sovereign of Dehlí, assumed the title of Sher Sháh, and ascended the throne on the 25th January, 1542 A. D., 7th Shawwál, 948 A. H. In the 5th year of his reign he moved towards Kalingar one of the strongest forts in Hindústán. The batteries were advanced close to the walls, a breach was made, and a general assault was ordered, when a shell, which was thrown against the fort, burst in the battery in which the king stood. The explosion communicating to a powder magazine, several gunners were blown up, and the king so much scorched, that his recovery was hopeless. In this condition he encouraged the prosecution of the attack, and continued to give his orders, till in the evening news was brought him of the reduction of the place. He then cried out, "Thanks to the Almighty God!" and expired. His death happened on the 24th May, 1545 A. D., 12th Rabí' I, 952 A. H. His corpse was conveyed to Sahsarám the family estate, where it was buried in a magnificent sepulchre, which is still to be seen standing in the centre of a reservoir of water, built during his own life. Tradition adds, that during his reign, such was the public security. that travellers rested and slept with their goods by the highways without apprehension of robbery. He was succeeded by his son Salím Sháh.

**Sher Singh,** شیر سنگه, ruler of the Panjáb, was the second son of Kharag Singh the son of Ranjít Singh. After the death of his eldest brother Nau Nihál Singh, which took place on the 17th November, 1840 A. D., his mother Ráni Chánd Kúnwar managed the affairs of his country for two months, when Sher Singh her second son deprived her of that power and became the sole manager. On the 13th September, 1843 A. D., the royal palace was taken by a powerful body of troops and Sher Singh and his son Partáp Singh was murdered by Sardár Ajít Singh —every child and all of Sher Singh's and Partáp Singh's wives were brought out and murdered; amongst the rest, one of Sher Singh's sons, only born the previous evening. After Sher Singh's death, Rájá Dalíp Singh the youngest son of Mahárájá Ranjít Singh was placed on the Masnad. *Vide* Kharag Singh.

**Sherzad, Sultan,** سلطان شیرزاد, son of Sultán Masaúd III, of Ghazní, whom he succeeded 1114 A. D., 508 A. H., and was murdered after one year by his brother Arsalán Sháh, who ascended the throne 1115 A. D., 509 A. H.

**Shia** or **Shia',** شیعه. Those Muhammadans who assert the rights of 'Alí, are called Shias or Shiites or Sectaries, whilst those who consider the first three Khalífas preceding 'Alí as the rightful successors of Muhammad, are called Sunnís or Sannites or Traditionists. The animosity which exists between the Shias and Sunnís, fully equals that of the Protestants and Papists of former times. It was owing to their dissensions that Baghdád was taken, and the Khiláfat overturned. The Turks and Arabs are Sunnís; the Persians and most of the Muhammadans of India are Shias A complete history of the Shias will be found in a work called "Majális-ul-Mominín." The Shia doctrines were adopted by the Persians at the foundation of the Safwí dynasty in 1500 A. D., 905 A. H., and from that period until the present time, have prevailed as the national religion and law of Persia, notwithstanding the violent efforts to substitute the Sunní creed made by the Afghán usurper Ashraf, and the great Nádir Sháh.

**Shibli,** شبلي, *vide* Abú Bakr Shiblí.

**Shikeibi, Maulana,** مولانا شکیبي, a poet of Persia whose proper name is Muhammad Razá. He came to India in the reign of the emperor Akbar, and died in the time of Jahángír 1614 A. D., 1023 A. H.

**Shimbhu,** شمبهو, a Bráhman, who is the author of a "Zafar-náma" or book of victory, containing a poetical account of the military career of General Lake.

**Shinasi,** شناسي, title of a poet who died in the year 1627 A. D., 1037 A. H., and is the author of a work called "Fazl-náma."

**Shio Ramdas,** شیو رامداس, a poet whose poetical title was Hayá, which see.

**Shitab Rae, Raja,** راجه شتاب راي, was by caste a Káyeth, and a native of Dehlí; in his youth he served 'Aká Sulaimán, the favourite dependant of Samsám-uddaula, son of Khán Daurán Amír-ul-'Umra to the emperor Muhammad Sháh. Upon the death of Samsám-uddaula, he obtained the office of imperial Díwán at Patna. Attaching himself to the English in the several revolutions, he became their chief adviser in their connections with the country powers. He was an able statesman, and understood completely the direction of finance. He died about the year 1777 A. D., 1187 A. H.

**Shahrat** or **Shuhrat,** شهرت, the poetical title of Nawáb Hakím-ul-Mumalik, *vide* Muhammad Husain (Shekh).

**Shorish,** شورش, a poet, whose proper name is Gholám Husain and who is the author of a biography of Urdú poets. He died in 1781 A. D., 1195 A. H.

**Shouk,** شوق, the poetical name of Mír Muhammad Bákir father of Mír Muhammad 'Atá Husain Khán Tahsín.

**Shouk,** شوق, poetical name of Maulwí Kudrat-ulláh, who has left a Díwán and a Biography of poets called Tabkat-ush-Shoara.

**Shouk,** شوق, poetical name of Ráe Tansukh Ráe, which see.

**Shoukat of Bukhara,** شوکت بخاري, a poet who died at Isfahán in 1695 A. D., 1107 A. H., and left a Díwán in Persian. His proper name is Muhammad Is-hák.

**Shouki,** شوقي, a poet of Tabreiz, but he is usually called Hirwí, *i. e.*, of Hirát. He left the service of Sám Mirzá, son of Sháh Tahmasp Safwí and went with the emperor Humáyún to Kabul where he died in 1546 A. D., 953 A. H.

**Shouki, Amir,** امیر شوقي, a nobleman and poet who lived in the time of the emperor Sháh Jahán. His proper name was Mír Muhammad Husain. He died in 1634 A. D., 1044 A. H.

**Shujaa' Khan** or **Shujaa't Khan,** شجاع خان, a relative of Sher Sháh, king of Dehlí, who conferred the government of Málwá on him after the expulsion of Mallú Khán entitled Ḳádir Sháh in 1542 A. D., 949 A. H He governed Málwá for a period of 12 years and died in 1554 A. D., 962 A. H. After his death his eldest son Malik Báyezíd assuming the title of Báz Bahádur, took the reins of government in his own hands.

**Shujaa', Sultan,** سلطان شجاع, *vide* Sulṭán Shujáạ.

**Shujaa't Khan, Nawab,** نواب شجاعت خان, a nobleman in the service of the emperor 'Álamgír, *vide* Fakhr-un-Nisa Begam. He was a mansabdár of 4000 in the time of Sháh Jahán. He had a house at Ágrah of which no traces now remain.

**Shuja-uddin,** نواب شجاع الدين, nawáb of Bengal, also called by some Shujá-uddaula, was a native of Burhánpúr, and a descendant of a Turkish tribe of Afgháns in Khurásán. During 'Álamgír's campaigns in the Dakhin, he married Zeib-un-Nisá the daughter of Murshid Ḳulí Jạfar Khán Súbadár of Bengal, and accompanied him to that province. Jạfar Khán, who died in the year 1726 A. D., 1138 A. H., left at his death the succession to his government to his grandson 'Alá-uddaula Sarfaráz Khán; but Shujá-uddín his father having more interest at the court of Dehlí than his son, procured the Súbadárí for himself, and in the year 1735 A. D., 1148 A. H., the province of Behár also was conferred on him by the emperor Muhammad Sháh. Shujá-uddín was celebrated for his clemency, justice and good qualities. He died after 12 years' government of Bengal on the 13th of March, 1739 A. D., 13th Ẕil-ḥijja, 1151 A. H., just at the time when Nádir Sháh was at Dehlí. As there were only a few days remaining for the commencement of the Hijrí year 1152 A. D., at his death. He was succeeded by his son 'Alá-uddaula Sarfaráz Khán, a young prince, whose character as a moral and religious man stands high on the pages of native history.

**Shuja-uddaula, Nawab,** نواب شجاع الدولة, who played a conspicuous part in the early history of British India, was the son of Mansúr 'Alí Khán Safdar Jang, governor of Audh. His original name is Jalál uddín Haidar; he was born in the year 1731 A. D., 1144 A. H., and after the death of his father succeeded to the government in October, 1753 A. D, Ẕil-ḥijja, 1167 A. H. He was present in the famous battle which took place between Aḥmad Sháh Abdálí and the Marhaṭṭas in January, 1761; was appointed wazír to the emperor Sháh 'Alam; was defeated at Buxar by the English on the 23rd October, 1764 A. D., 26th Rabí' II, 1178 A. H., and died at Faizabád, the seat of his government, in the midst of his victories and highest prosperity, on the 29th of January, 1775 A. D., 24th Ẕi-Ḳa'da, 1188 A. H. By his own subjects he was sincerely beloved, and the sons of Háfiz Rahmat Khán, whose country he had seized, wept at his death. He was buried at a place called Guláb Bárí in Faizábád, and was succeeded by his eldest son 'Asaf-uddaula. For a legendary account of his death see Keene's *Fall of the Mughal Empire*, p. 117.

**Shuja-ul-Mulk, Shah,** شاه شجاع الملك, *vide* Sháh Shujáạ.

**Shukr-ullah,** شكر الله, author of the history called "Bahjat-ut-Tawaríkh."

**Shukr-ullah Khan I, Nawab,** شكرالله خان نواب, a nobleman in the service of the emperor Aurangzeib who died about the year 1698 A. D., 1110 A. H.

**Shukr-ullah Khan II, Nawab,** شكرالله خان نواب, son of Shukr-ulláh Khán I, was an Amír in the service of the emperor Aurangzeib 'Álamgír. He was appointed governor of Mewát in 1702 A. D., 1114 A. H.

**Shaibani,** شيباني, an author whose proper name was Abú Amrú Is-hák. He died at Baghdád in the year 828 A. D., 213 A. H.

**Shaibani Khan,** شيباني خان, *vide* Sháhí Beg Uzbak.

**Shaida, Mulla,** ملا شيدا, title of a poet who flourished in the latter part of the reign of Jahángír and commencement of the emperor Sháh Jahán. He was one of the Sheikhzádas of Fathapúr Síkrí, and a contemporary of the poets Tálib Kálím, Ḳudsí, Hakím Házik and Nawáb Islám Khán wazír. His works contain more than 50,000 verses. He has left a Masnawí of 12,000 verses in the style of the "Makhzan-ul-Asrár" of Nizámí. He died in 1652 A. D., 1062 A. H., in Kashmír and was buried there. He also had a house at Ágrah.

**Shaida,** شيدا, poetical appellation of Mír Fatha 'Alí of Lakhnau, author of the story of the Owl and the Grocer entitled "Búm-o-Baḳḳál." He was contemporary with Fidwí, author of an Yúsaf and Zaleikha in Urdú.

**Siamak,** سيامک, the son of Ḳayomurs and the father of Hoshang, the second king of the Pishdadian dynasty of Persia.

**Siawakhsh,** سياوخش, son of Kaikáús, king of Persia of the Kayánian dynasty. He was murdered by Afrásiáb king of Túrán.

**Sihl** or **Sehl bin-Sa'd,** سهل بن سعد, ene of the companions of Muhammad.

**Sijaj,** سجاج, a false prophetess cotemporary with Musylima another impostor. She was a Christian of extraordinary talents and eloquence, and being prompted by an aspiring ambition, she announced herself a prophetess, and uttering her string of rhapsodies in rhyme, declared that they came inspired from above. Struck by her success, Musylima thought it advisable to temporize with her, and accordingly having sent agents, invited her to a private conference, Sijáj consented and came to an interview; she was deceived and having forfeited all pretensions to that purity, which is the highest attribute of her sex, she fell from her proud pre-eminence, and became a mere debased, and contaminated woman. She subsequently enrolled herself among the proselytes of the Ḳurán.

**Sikandar, Alexander the Great,** سكندر ذوالقرنين, called by Muhammad in the Ḳurán, "Zú'lkarnyn" the Two Horned Man; probably by reason of his head being figured as Ammon, with the Ram's Horns, on coins and medals. Eastern commentators have been at a loss to decide who is intended, but generally agree that he was a being favoured of, and who believed in the true God; that guided by the prophet Khizir, he reached the Land of Darkness, near the Fountain of Life, but he could not obtain permission to take a draught of the Eternal Spring. He died in 327 A. D., at the age of 33 years. He conquered Darius king of Persia in 331 B. C. and in 327 he proceeded to invade India. He crossed the Indus without opposition. He was afterwards opposed by a rájá who is called by the Greek Porus whose army was utterly routed.

**Sikandar,** سکندر, poetical name of Khalífa Sikandar who used to write beautiful Marsias in the Púrbí, Márwárí and Panjábí language, and is the author of a poem containing the story of the Fish, the Ferryman and king Dilkhwár.

**Sikandar 'Adil Shah,** سکندر عادل شاه, the last of the kings of Bíjápúr. He succeeded his father 'Alí 'Adil Sháh II when an infant about the year 1672 A. D., 1083 A. H., but never acquired any real power, being the tool of his nobility. In the year 1686 A. D., 4th Ẕi-Ḳa'da, 1097 A. H , on Monday the 13th of September Bíjápúr was taken; the young prince made prisoner, and the kingdom with its remaining dependencies was reduced to the Mughal yoke by the emperor 'Álamgír. He died after three years' imprisonment.

**Sikandar (Prince),** سکندر شاهزاده, the son of 'Umar Shaikh Mirzá the son of Amír Taimúr, after whose death he had several battles with his two brothers, Pír Muhammad and Mirzá Rustam, and took possession of Fars and Isfahán which they had received as inheritance from their grandfather; on which account, his uncle Sháhrukh Mirzá, having defeated him in a battle, put out both his eyes. This circumstance took place in 1414 A. D., 817 A. H.

**Sikandar Begam,** سکندر بیگم, the ruler of Bhopál. She was born in 1816 A. D. Her father was one of the Paṭhán or Afghán soldiers of fortune, who after the death of the emperor Aurangzeib, declared himself independent in Bhopal. On his death his wife was declared Regent by his troops, and his daughter Sikandar Begam heir. She married her cousin Jahángír in spite of her mother upon condition that her husband swore to leave her the direct and visible control of all affairs. Her husband Jahángír died in 1845 A. D. She was publicly presented with the Grand Cross of the Star of India at the Durbar at Ágrah. She died on the 30th October, 1868 A. D. Her Highness had conducted the administration of her principality since the year 1847 when she was first appointed Regent, with ability and success until the day of her decease. Her eldest daughter Sháhjahán Begam succeeded her.

**Sikandar Jah,** نواب سکندر جاه, nawáb or Nizám of Haidarabád, succeeded his father Nawáb Nizám 'Alí Khán to the masnad of the Dakhin on the 16th August, 1802 A. D , 16th Rabí' II, 1217 A. H., and died on the 23rd of May, 1829 A. D., 19th Ẕi-Ḳa'da, 1244 A. H., after a reign of 28 lunar years and some months. He was succeeded by his son Mír Farkhunda 'Alí Khán, who took the title of Nasír-uddaula.

**Sikandar Kadr, Mirza,** سکندر قدر, the son of Prince Khurshaid Kadr, *vide* Taskhír.

**Sikandar Khan Uzbak,** سکندر خان اذبك, a descendant of the royal house of that tribe also called Sikandar Khán of Káshghar. He accompanied the emperor Humáyún to India, was created a nobleman by that monarch. He accompanied Mirzá Haidar who took possession of Kashmír in 1543, and died at Lakhnau in the reign of the emperor Akbar on the 18th September, 1572 A. D., 10th Jumáḍa I, 980 A. H.

**Sikandar Munshi,** سکندر منشي, Secretary to Sháh Abbás I, king of Persia. He is the author of the "Táríkh 'Alam Aráe Abbásí," a history of that monarch, in three books, which he dedicated to him in 1616 A. D., 1025 A. H., *vide* Iskandar Munshí.

**Sikandar Shah,** سکندر شاه, king of Gujrát, succeeded his father Muzaffar Sháh II, in February, 1526 A. D., 19th Shabán, 932 A. H., and after a reign of only three months and seventeen days was assassinated on the 30th May the same year. After his death his younger brother Nasír Khán was raised to the throne under the title of Muhammad Sháh II.

**Sikandar Shah Lodi, Sultan,** سکندر شاه لودي, whose original name was Nizám Khán, was the son of Sulṭán Bahlól Lódí whom he succeeded in July, 1489 A. D , Shabán, 895 A. H. He was the first Musalmán king who made Ágrah his capital. In his time a violent earthquake took place, when many houses were thrown down and several thousands of inhabitants lost their lives. This happened on Sunday the 6th July, 1505 A. D., 3rd Ṣafar, 911 A. H. It was in his reign that the Hindús first commenced reading Persian. He reigned 21 lunar years and some months, and died at Ágrah on Sunday the 17th of February, 1510 A. D., 7th Ẕi-Ḳa'da, 915 A. H., Colonel Dow and General Briggs in their translation of Firishta say, that Sikandar Sháh died in the year of the Hijrí 923 corresponding with 1517 A. D , and that he reigned 28 years and some months; this is evidently a mistake, for the words "Tárí Shud" shew the year of his death to be 915 A. H., consequently the period of his reign only 21 years. He was succeeded by his son Ibrahím Husain Lódí. Sikandar Lódí in his time had built a small fort at Ágrah on the right bank of the river Jamna and called it Badalgarh. The emperor Akbar in the 10th year of his reign, *viz.*, in 972 A. H., having demolished this part laid the foundations of another part of redstone which was completed in the course of 8 years superintended by Ḳasim Khán Mír Bahar this fort had three gotis and two windows and cost 36 lacs of rupees. This fort was accidently burnt down in the time of Sháh Alam and Madho Rao Sendhia.

**Sikandar Shah Purbi,** سکندر شاه پوربي. He was raised to the throne of Bengal after the death of his father Shams-uddín Bhangeiṛa, about the year 1358 A. D., 760 A. H. He had not long entered on his rule before his country was invaded by Fíroz Sháh Tughlaḳ king of Dehlí, who was, however, induced to retreat on Sikandar Sháh promising to pay an annual tribute. He reigned in peace for a period of nine years and died in 1367 A. D., 769 A. H., when he was succeeded by his son Ghayás-uddín Púrbí.

**Sikandar Shah Sur,** سکندر شاه سور. His original name was Aḥmad Khán Súr, a nephew of Sher Sháh. He ascended the throne of Dehlí after defeating Sulṭán Ibráhím Súr in a battle fought in May, 1555 A. D., Jumáḍa II, 962 A. H. He had not long enjoyed his good fortune however, when he was obliged to repair to the Panjáb to oppose the emperor Humáyún, who having returned from a long exile, was now advancing to recover his dominions. He engaged Bairám Khán the general of the army near Sarhind, was defeated on the 22nd June, 1555 A. D., 3rd Shabán, 962 A. H., and fled to the Sewálik mountains from whence he was afterwards expelled by the emperor Akbar 1557 A. D., 27th Ramaẓán, 964 A. H., and sought refuge in Bengal, where he died after two years.

**Sikandar Shikoh Mirza,** سکندر شکوه, a cousin of Bahádur Sháh II, king of Dehlí. He was executed for the murder of his wife in July, 1838 A. D.

**Sikandar, Sultan,** سلطان سکندر, king of Kashmír, surnamed "But Shikan," or Destroyer of Idols, was the grandson of Sháh Mír Darweish who introduced the Muhammadan religion into Kashmír. Sikandar by the assistance of his mother, succeeded his father Sultán Ḳuṭb-uddín 1393 A. D., 796 A. H., his authority being acknowledged by all the nobles and other officers, and became one of the most powerful kings that ever reigned in Kashmír. Various magnificent temples and images of the Hindús did this Sulṭán lay in ruins; which conduct obtained him the glorious title of "But Shikan," or Iconoclast. He reigned 22 years and 9 months and died in 1416 A. D., 819 A. H. In his time Tamerlane invaded India and presents passed between him and Sikandar. He was succeeded by his son Sulṭán 'Alí Sháh.

**Sikandar Turkman,** سکندر ترکمان, *vide* Ḳará Muhammad.

**Silhaddi,** سلهدي, a rájá of Raisín, who was made prisoner by Bahádur Sháh of Gujrát and was forced to become a Muhammadan in the year 1531 A. D., 938 A. H., and afterwards when the fort of Raisín was surrendered by his brother Lachhman to the king, Rání Durgáwatí, the daughter of Rana Sanka, Rana of Chittor and wife of Rájá Silhaddí, with a heroic fortitude invoking curses on the heads of those who should not revenge her cause, set fire to a pile with which she had caused the female apartments to be surrounded, containing seven hundred beautiful women; she plunged into the flames, and they were all consumed. Silhaddí and Lachhman his brother with one hundred of their blood-relations, now putting on their armour, rushed impetuously on the Gujrát troops, and bravely met their fate the same year.

**Sindbad Hakim,** سندباد حكيم, author of a Díwán or book of Odes which he completed in the year 1374 A. D., 776 A. H., and dedicated to Sháh Mahmúd Bahmaní.

**Sindh,** سنده, history of, *vide* Násir-uddín Ḳabbácha.

**Sipahdar Khan,** سپه دار خان, whose proper name is Mirzá Muhammad Sálah, was a native of Tabrez, and his ancestors were reckoned among the nobles of that country. In the year 1592 A. D., 1000 A. H., he left Persia for Hindústán in company with Khwája Beg Mirzá son of Maṣúm Beg Safwí. On his arrival in India, he obtained the honour of an interview with the emperor Akbar. Mansabs suitable to his dignity as well as the government of Gujrát were conferred on him, time after time. When, after the death of prince Murád in 1599 A. D., 1007 A. H., prince Daniál went to the Dakhin and captured the fort of Aḥmadnagar the capital of Nizám Sháh, the government of that country was conferred upon Khwája Beg Mirzá and Sipahdár Khán.

**Sipahdar Khan,** سپه دار خان, was the second son of Khán Jahán Bahádur, the foster-brother of the emperor 'Álamgír. He was raised to the rank of 3000 by that monarch 1691 A. D., 1103 A. H. with the government of the province of Allahábád which he held for several years. His brother Himmat Khán was killed by an arrow in an action with the Marhaṭṭas about the year 1698 A. D., 1110 A. H., and soon after, their father Khán Jahán Bahádur died in the imperial camp.

**Sipehr Shikoh,** سپه سيكو, third son of Dara Shikoh *vide* Sulaiman Shikoh. He was confined in the fort of Gwáliár by 'Álamgír who in his 16th year, 1085 A. H., sent for him from Gwáliár, got him married with his daughter Badr-un-Nisa of whom was born prince 'Alí Tabar.

**Siraj,** سراج, takhallus of Siráj-uddín Husain of Aurangábád who is the author of the "Díwán Muntakhib," containing extracts from no less than 680 poets, and which he completed in 1756 A. D., 1109 A. H.

**Siraj Kummi,** سراج قمي, a poet who was a native of Kumm in Persia and contemporary with Salmán Sáwají.

**Siraj-uddin,** سراج الدين, son of Núr-uddín, author of the "Sharah Bukhárí," and "Sharah 'Umda." He died in 1401 A. D., 804 A. H., see Bilkainí.

**Siraj-uddin 'Ali Khan,** سراج الدين علي خان آرزو, whose poetical title is 'Arzú, was a native of Akbarábád (Ágrah), and a descendant of Shaikh Muhammad Ghaus of Gwáliár. He was an excellent poet and an officer of rank in the time of the emperor Farrukh-siyar. He is the author of several works, among which is a Díwán and a biography entitled "Majmúa-ul-Nafáes," which is also called "Tazkira Arzú," containing the memoirs of the Indian poets who have written Persian, Hindústání and Dakhaní poems. Arzú in 1734 A. D., 1147 A. H. met at Dehlí the poet Hazín who had just come from Persia. The jealousy between the two poets induced 'Arzú to write a treatise entitled "Tambíh-ul-Gháfilín," in which he points out the errors in Hazín's poems. He died at Lakhnau on the 27th of January, 1756 A. D., 23rd Rabí' II, 1169 A. H., and was buried there for some time, but afterwards his remains were removed to Dehlí by his nephew Muhammad Husain Khán. Beside the abovementioned works, he is the author of the following:

- Móhibat Uzma.
- 'Atia Kubrá.
- Siráj-ul-Lughát.
- Chirágh Hidáet.
- Gharáeb-ul-Lughát.
- Khayábán.
- Mustiláhát-ush-Shuará.
- Jawáb Yatarázát Munír.
- Sharah Kasáed 'Urfí.
- Sharah Sikandar-náma.
- Sharah Mukhtasir-ul-Maání.
- Sharah Gulkushtí Mír Naját.
- Nawádir-ul-Alfarz, a Hindustání Dictionary.

**Siraj-uddin Husain,** سراج الدين حسين, *vide* Siráj.

**Siraj-uddin Muhammad bin-'Abdur Rashid-al-Sajawandi,** محمد بن عبد الرشيد آل شيزاوندي سراج الدين, author of the "Sirájia," which is sometimes called "Faráez as-Sajáwandí." This book is of the highest authority on the law of inheritance amongst the Sunnís of India. It has been commented upon by a vast number of writers, upwards of forty being enumerated in the "Kashf-uz-Zunún. The most celebrated of these Commentaries, and the one most generally employed to explain the text, is the "Sharífia" by Sayyad Sharíf 'Alí bin-Muhammad-al-Jurjání. The original text of the "Sirájia," together with that of the "Sharífia," was published in Calcutta in 1829. A Persian translation of the Sirájia and Sharífia was made by Maulwí Muhammad Ráshid by order of Warren Hastings, and published in Calcutta in 1812 A. D. The most celebrated Commentaries on the Sirájia next after the Sharífia, are, that by Shaháb-uddín Aḥmad bin-Mahmúd-as-Siwásí; one by Burhán-uddín Haidar bin-Muhammad-al-Hirwí; another by Shams-uddín bin-Hamza-al-Fanárí; and lastly, a Persian Commentary entitled "Al-Faróez-at-Tájífí Sharh Faráez-as-Sirájí by 'Abdul Karím bin-Muhammad-al-Hamdání.

**Siraj-uddin Muhammad bin-'Umar Halabi,** سراج الدين محمد, an author who died 1446 A. D., 850 A. H.

**Siraj-uddin Sawai, Maulana,** سراج الدين ساوئي مولانا, one of the celebrated poets of Sámána a city in the province of Dehlí. He is the author of the work called "Khiljí-náma." When Sulṭán Jalál-uddín Fíroz Khiljí, before his accession to the throne, was governor of Sámána, the poet was ill-treated by some of his people, and as the Sulṭán took no notice of it then, he wrote the abovementioned book, in which he satirized the governor and the Khiljís. However the Sulṭán after his accession to the throne of Dehlí in 1289 A. D. sent for the poet, and he having tied a rope round his own neck presented himself like a criminal before the king, who embraced him and made him one of his principal confidants. The poet afterwards wrote several panegyrics in praise of the Sulṭán.

**Siraj-uddin, Shaikh,** شیخ سراج الدین, a celebrated Muhammadan saint, whose relics are deposited in an island in the river Krishna near the town of Kursí, in the district of Ráebágh Bíjápúr, in southern Hindústán.

**Siraj-uddin 'Umar,** سراج الدین عمر, who after the death of his brother Zain-ul-'Abidín Nujaim completed the work called "Bahr-ar-Ráeḳ" about the year 1562 A. D., 970 A. H., and wrote another but inferior commentary on the Kanz-ul-Daḳáeḳ entitled the "Nahr-ul-Fáeḳ."

**Siraj-uddaula Muhammad Ghaus Khan,** سراج الدولہ محمد غوث خان, nawáb of the Karnatic whose poetical name was 'Azim, is the author of the work called "Tazkira Subh Watan," being a biography of the poets of Karnatic, compiled in 1842 A. D., 1258 A. H. It is an abstract of the Tazkira of Ráeḳ also called "Guldasta Karnatik."

**Siraj-uddaula,** نواب سراج الدولہ, nawáb of Bengal, formerly named Mirzá Mahmúd, was the eldest son of Zain-uddín Aḥmad, styled Haibat Jang, the nephew and son-in-law of Alahwardí Khán Mahábat Jang governor of Bengal. On the death of his grandfather Mahábat Jang, which happened on the 10th of April, 1756 A. D., 9th Rajab, 1169 A. H., he succeeded him in the government of that province, and immediately taking offence at the English, for their protection to a native officer, said to have escaped from Dacca with treasure, he attacked Calcutta, carried it on the 20th June the same year, and allowed his officers to shut up 146 European prisoners in a small military prison room called the "Black Hole," in which 123 of the number, perished during the night. Mr. Drake the governor of Calcutta escaped on board a ship with a few Englishmen and retired to Madras. At that time Colonel Clive commanded the Company's forces in the province of Arkoṭ. It was agreed by the government of Madras that he should repair with a force to Bengal and endeavour to regain the factory of Calcutta. Colonel Clive and Admiral Watson left Madras with 900 Europeans and 1500 sepoys. He reached Falta on the 20th December and re-took Calcutta on the 2nd January, 1757 A. D., 1170 A. H., and forced Siráj-uddaula into a treaty, offensive and defensive, on the 9th of February following. Clive, subsequently made a secret treaty with Mír Jaʿfar, an officer of the Nawáb, and advanced in June towards Murshidábád, the nawáb's capital. On the 23rd of June, 1757 A. D., Clive fought the battle of Plassey against 18,000 horse and 50,000 Infantry, and aided by the treachery of Mír Jaʿfar, routed the Nawáb's troops. Siráj-uddaula fled, but in a few days was seized and cruelly assassinated on the 4th July, 15th Shawwál, 1170 A. H., by order of Míran the son of Mír Jaʿfar. Thus perished Siráj-uddaula in the 20th year of his age and the 15th month of his reign. On the 29th June Mír Jaʿfar was raised to the masnad, and from that date, the influence of the British may be said to have become paramount in Bengal. His tomb is not far from that of Mahábat Jang.

**Suda,** سودہ, daughter of Zamaa, the second wife of Muhammad, He married her after the death of his first wife Khudyja and before his marriage with Ayesha the daughter of Abú Bakr. She died in 674 A. D., 54 A. H., forty-three years after the death of Muhammad.

**Sudi,** سودی, a Turkish poet, who wrote a commentary on the Díwán-i-Háfiz in the Turkish language. The names of Shorí, Sayyad 'Alí, Lamaí, Surúrí and Shamaí occur also as commentators on Háfiz; but Súdí excels all as an enlightened and accurate critic, not only on account of his eminent success in correcting the exuberances of this fanciful and extravagant mode of interpretation, but of the singular happiness with which he has illustrated the ambiguous and more obsolete allusions of the Poet.

**Sufi,** صوفی, a sect among the Muhammadans. Kází Núrullah of Shustar, a Persian author of very high reputation for his piety and judgment, has given an excellent account of the Súfís and their doctrine in the Majális-ul-Mominín, a treatise on the Shia faith. "The Súfís" (he there says) "are of two classes: those who desire human knowledge, and pursue it in the accustomed way, observing the common ordinances of religion, are called Mutakallam (advocates or observers): those who practise austerities and strive to purify their souls, are called Súfís." This word literally means, *pure, clean.* The celebrated Moulwí Rúmí has the following play upon it in one of his lines. Súfí na Shawad Sáfí tá dar narasad jamí. The Súfí will not be pure till he takes one cup. This is said to have a mystical meaning.

**Sufi, Mulla Muhammad Sufi of Amol,** ملا محمد صوفی, author of a "Sáḳí-náma," which he composed in the year 1592 A. D., 1000 A. H.

**Songsters,** سنگسطرس, celebrated Indian, *vide* Tánsein.

**Surajmal Jat,** سورجمل جاٹ, rájá of Bhartpúr, was the son of Badan Singh Jáṭ whom he succeeded to the ráj a few years before 1750 A. D., 1163 A. H. His younger brother Partáp Singh, built the fort of Kumbhír or Kumeir. After the departure of Aḥmad Sháh Abdálí from India to Ḳandahár, Súrajmal taking advantage of the weakness of the empire made himself master of all the countries that were dependant on Ágrah and ultimately of the town itself, and many other important places, but fell in battle with the Roheila chief Najíb-uddaula in December, 1763 A. D., 1177 A. H. His son Jawáhir Singh succeeded him.

**Suraj Singh, Raja,** راجہ سورج سنگھ, son of Udai Singh Raṭhor, the son of Ráe Maldeo. After the death of his father, 1594 A. D., 1002 A. H., he was raised by Akbar to a suitable rank, and served under that emperor and his son Jahángír, for several years. The mansab of 5,000 was conferred on him by the latter. He died in the Dakhin 1619 A. D., 1028 A. H., and Rájá Gaj Singh his son succeeded him; and as his father was uncle to the emperor Sháh Jahán on the mother's side, he was in a short time raised to the rank of 5,000. Gaj Singh died on the 6th May, 1638 A. D., 2nd Muḥarram, 1048 A. H. His son Amar Singh killed Salábat Khán Mír Bakhshí in 1624 A. D., 1054 A. H., and was himself cut to pieces at one of the gates of the Fort of Ágrah, now called Amar Singh Gate.

**Surdas,** سورداس, son of Bábá Rámdás, a Hindú poet and an excellent musician, who flourished about the 16th or 17th century. He is the author of the work called Súr Ságar," in Hindí, &c.

**Souda,** سودا, his real name is Mirzá Muhammad Rafia, to which he subsequently added his poetical title "Soudá," and is now commonly known by the appellation of Mirzá Rafiús Soudá. He was a native of Dehlí but resided at Lakhnau, and his Díwán and Kasáed contain a variety of poems on various subjects; also Idyls. Elegies and other miscellaneous pieces in Hindústání verse. These volumes are held in the highest estimation all over India. They include a number of encomiastic poems on the late Nawáb 'Asaf-uddaula of Lakhnau, and many other persons of high rank and power, both at Lakhnau and Dehlí; not the least remarkable of which is an eulogy on the late Mr. Richard Johnson. The satires of this poet are also numerous and admirable; but having created him many enemies, to avoid the consequences of their anger, he feigned himself insane, and took the poetical name of Soudá or madman, but he is frequently known by the appellation of "Malik-ush-Shuará," or king of poets. He died at Lakhnau in the year 1781 A. D., 1195 A. H., aged 70 years. 'Asaf-uddaula of Lakhnau gave him a stipend of 6,000 rupees a year. He was a pupil of Siráj-uddín 'Alí Khán 'Arzú.

**Soudai, Baba of Abiward,** بابا سودائي ابيوردي, a poet who had formerly assumed for his poetical title "Kháwarí" but as he used to go about the streets without a turban or shoes, people gave him the title of "Soudáí," *i. e.*, distracted, which he subsequently used in all his compositions. He lived in the time of Sháhrukh Mirzá. He died 1448 A. D., aged 80 years.

**Soz,** سوز, the poetical name of Sayyad Muhammad, who flourished in the reign of the emperor Sháh 'Alam, and is the author of a small Díwán in Urdú. He died in 1797 A. D., 1212 A. H. Another Soz is mentioned in the "Mirat-ul-Khayál" who lived in the time of 'Alamgír. He was a native of Bukhárá and brought up in India.

**Sozan,** سوزان, poetical appellation of Nawáb Ahmad 'Alí Khán Shoukat Jang son of Nawáb Iftikhár-uddaula Mirzá 'Alí Khán, and nephew of Nawáb Sálár Jang. He lived in the time of Nawáb 'Asaf-uddaula of Lakhnau, and is said to have been a good Urdú poet.

**Sozani, Hakim,** حكيم سوزني, surnamed Shams-uddín Muhammad of Samarkand, a Persian poet who derived his origin from Salmán Fársí one of the first companions of Muhammad. Some authors say he was a native of the city of Nakhshab, and others pretend of Samarkand. It is said that when he was a student at Bukhárá, he conceived so great a friendship for the apprentice of a needle-maker, that he himself learned that profession, and he therefore assumed the takhallus of Sózaní. (Sozan means a needle.) He is considered the best humoristic poet of his time, and is the author of a poem called "Kasáed Sózaní," or elegies, written in a very devout style, containing nearly 8,000 verses. During his youth he was a great debauchee; but when advanced in years, he became very devout, made the pilgrimage of Mecca and died in 1173 A. D., 569 A. H., at Samarkand, aged 80 years. One of his friends declared that he had appeared to him after his death (in a dream) and said that God had forgiven all his sins for the sake of one of his verses, in which expressing his humility and contrition, he says, "O Lord, I offer unto thee an oblation, not to be found in thy treasury. Accept thou my sins, my poverty, my repentance and my nothingness."

**Subaktagin,** ناصر الدين سبكتگين, surnamed Násir-uddín, a man of Turkish descent, who, according to some historians, was purchased as a slave by Alaptagín Sultán of Ghazní, who perceiving in him the promise of future greatness, raised him by degrees to posts of confidence and distinction; and his character obtained him the support of all the adherents and officers of that prince. He was raised to the throne of Ghazní after the death of Abú Is-hák the son of Alaptagín 977 A. D., 367 A. H. He enlarged its dominions, and became the first of a family, called Ghaznawí, and by us Ghaznavides, which outshone, at one period, the glory of the proudest dynasties of Asiatic monarchs. He conquered a part of India, which, when connected with his former possessions of Ghazní and Kábul, gave him a kingdom that extended from Khurásán to the Panjáb. Subaktagín reigned 20 lunar years, and died in August, 997 A. D., Shaban, 387 A. H., aged 56, near Balkh, from which place his remains were conveyed to Ghazní for interment. He was succeeded by his son the celebrated Sultán Mahmúd. Including Subaktagín sixteen kings of his race reigned at Ghazní and Láhor. Their names are as follow:—

*List of the Ghaznavide dynasty of Persia and India, including Khurásán, Mawar-un-nahr, Bukhárá, &c., Capital Ghazni.*

1. Násir-uddín Subaktagín.
   Ismaíl appointed successor, but displaced by his brother.
2. Sultán (Yemin-uddaula Abú'l Kásim) Mahmúd.
3. Muhammad, his son, deposed instantly and blinded.
   Muhammad, restored and again deposed.
4. Masaúd I, another son, deposed and killed.
5. Maudúd, son of Masaúd.
6. Masaúd II, reigned only six days.
7. Abú'l Hasan 'Alí son of Masaúd I.
8. Abdur Rashíd son of Mahmúd.
9. Farrukhzad son of Masaúd.
10. Ibráhím his brother.
11. Masaúd III son of Ibráhím.
12. Sheizád.
13. Arsalán Sháh.
14. Bahrám Sháh fled to Láhor.
15. Khusro Sháh ruled at Láhor.
16. Khusro Malik ruled at Láhor.

*Kings of the family of Ghór.*

Alá-uddín Hasan Ghorí.
Malik Saif-uddín.
Ghayás-uddín Muhammad Ghorí.
Shaháb-uddín Muhammad Ghorí.
Táj-uddín Eldúz.

**Subhan Bakhsh, Maulwi,** مولوی سبحان بخش, author of a modern history of jurisprudence, or rather of jurists in Urdú, compiled from the works of Ibn-Khallikán and Sayútí, entitled "Farjuma Táríkh-al-Hukmáe wa Tazkirat-al-Mufassirín." It was published at Dehlí in 1848 A. D.

**Sub-hani, Maulana,** مولانا سبحاني, a poet whose native country was Najaf Ashraf, commonly called Kúfa, from which place he never stirred all the time of his life. He lived at the same period in which Shaikh Faizí and Zahúrí flourished, and wrote nothing but Rubáis in the Persian language on different subjects of which 12,000 were collected after his death.

**Sub-hi,** صبحي, a poet who served under Sultán Shujáa the son of Sháh Jahán.

**Suchet Singh,** سچت سنگه, a Sikh chief, who joined the rebels after the murder of Mahárájá Sheir Singh, was attacked by Híra Singh, near Láhor, his force dispersed and himself killed about the 6th April, 1844. On hearing of the death of this chief, no less than 95 females of his family sacrificed themselves at Lamba.

**Sufian Souri,** صفيان ثوري, whose proper name was Abú 'Abdullah, was born at Kúfa in 713 A. D., 95 A. H. He was a master of the highest authority in the Traditions and other Sciences. He died in the time of the Khalífa Al-Mahdí, about the year 777 A. D., 160 A. H., and is buried at Basra, where he had concealed himself in order to avoid accepting the office of Ḳází.

**Suhyli Khurasani,** سهيلي خراساني, whose full name is Amír Shaikh Aḥmad Suhylí, also called Nizám-uddín Aḥmad Shykham, was seal-bearer to Sulṭán Husain Mirzá of Hirát. The work called "Anwár Suhylí," was dedicated to him by Husain Wáez. He is the author of a Díwán. His death took place in 1501 A. D., 907 A. H.

**Sukman bin-Ortak,** سقمان بن ارتك, first king of the princes of the Turkmán Ortakites who reigned at Amid and Khaifa. The following is a list of this race :—

| | A. D. | A. H. |
|---|---|---|
| Sukmán bin-Ortak, .................... | 1097 | 490 |
| Ibráhím bin-Sukmán, .................... | 1104 | 498 |
| Rukn-uddín Dáúd, .................... | 1128 | 522 |
| Fakhr-uddín Ḳará Arsalán bin-Dáúd, .... | 1149 | 544 |
| Núr-uddín Muhammad bin-Ḳará Arsalán, | 1166 | 562 |
| Ḳuṭb-uddín Sukmán bin-Muhammad. .... | 1185 | 581 |
| Malik-us-Sálah Násir-uddín Mahmúd, .... | 1200 | 597 |
| Malik-ul-Masaúd bin-Mahmúd,.......... | 1221 | 618 |
| Malik-ul-Kámil nephew of the celebrated Sálah-uddín (Saladin), he took Amid, | 1231 | 629 |

**Sultan Ahmad Jalayer,** سلطان احمد جليار, *vide* Hasan Buzurg.

**Sultan 'Ali Khurasani,** سلطان علي خراساني, author of the Persian work on Medicine called "Dastúr-ul-Iláj," which he wrote in 1334 A. D., 734 A. H., and dedicated to Sulṭán Abú Saíd Bahádur Khán.

**Sultan 'Ali Mashhadi,** سلطان علي مشهدى, a native of Mashhad. He was not so much distinguished as a poet as he was as a caligrapher. He was in caligraphy, a pupil of Mauláná Azhar, who was a pupil of Jafar, and Jafar was a pupil of Mauláná Mír 'Alí the inventor of the Naskhtalíḳ. Mauláná Sulṭán 'Alí lived at the court of Mirzá Báiḳara and found a patron in Amír 'Alísheir. He was upwards of 63 years of age in 1550 A. D., 957 A. H.

**Sultana Begam,** سلطانه بيگم, a daughter of the emperor Bábar Sháh.

**Sultana Begam,** سلطانه بيگم, a daughter of Mirzá Handál the brother of the emperor Humáyún. She was married to Sháh Ḳulí Mahram. Her sister named Ruqia Sulṭána was married to the emperor Akbar.

**Sultana Razia,** سلطانه رضيه, daughter of Shams-uddín Altimsh king of Dehlí. She was raised to the throne after the deposition of her brother Rukn-uddín Fíróz in November, 1236 A. D. She was deposed in November, 1239 A. D., and confined in the fort of Bitahnda, from which place she made her escape and contrived to raise an army with which she marched towards Dehlí; but was defeated and put to death by her brother Bahrám Sháh, who ascended the throne. The reign of Sulṭána Razia lasted 3 lunar years 6 months and 6 days. Her tomb is still to be seen in old Dehlí.

**Sultana Rukia** or **Ruqia,** سلطانه رقيه, the daughter of Mirzá Handal the son of the emperor Babar, was the first or chief wife of the emperor Akbar, by whom he had no children. Consequently when Sháh Jahán was born to Jahángír, his grandfather Akbar made him over to her to be brought up by her. She was also the patroness of Núr Jahán; and died at Ágrah in January, 1626 A. D., Jumáda I, 1035 A. H., aged 84 lunar years.

**Sultan Ahmad bin-Masa'ud,** سلطان احمد, author of the Arabic work called "Asmái-ul-Rijál."

**Sultan Ahmad Mirza,** سلطان احمد مرزا. Aḥmad Mirzá (Sulṭán).

**Sultan Husain Mirza,** سلطان حسين مرزا, surnamed Abú'l Ghází Bahádur, was the son of Mirzá Mansúr, the son of Mirzá Báiḳara, the son of Mirzá 'Umar Shaikh, the son of Amír Taimúr. After the death of Sulṭán Abú Saíd Mirzá, he contrived to make himself master of Khurásán, and ascended the throne at Hirát on the 24th of March, 1469 A. D., 10th Ramazan, 873 A. H. The great victories which this prince gained over the numerous competitors for the throne, as well as over the Uzbaks, obtained him the title of Ghází, or victorious. The court of this prince boasted of many eminent men. The celebrated historian Khandamír was his subject, and Amír 'Alísher his wazír. He reigned in Khurásán 38 lunar years and 4 months, and died according to the "Tabkát Akbarí," on the 10th of May, 1506 A. D., corresponding with the 16th Ẓil-ḥijja, 911 A. H. aged 70 years, and was buried at Hirát. He was succeeded by his two sons Badíu'zzamán Mirzá and Muzaffar Husain Mirzá, who reigned conjointly for some time over Khurásán. The former in the year 1507 A. D., 913 A. H., was driven from his dominions by Sháhí Beg Khán Uzbak; and his brother, who usurped the throne and reigned a short time at Hirát, afterwards shared the same fate. Sulṭán Husain Mirzá is the author of the work called "Majális-ul-Ishḳ," a very entertaining novel, containing a variety of stories, principally on the subject of love. He had a turn for poetry, and composed a Díwán in Turkí. His poetical name was Husainí.

**Sultan Husain Safwi,** سلطان حسين صفوى, *vide* Sháh Husain Safwí.

**Sultan Ibrahim,** سلطان ابراهيم, *vide* Ibráhím (Sulṭán).

**Sultan Khusro,** سلطان خسرو, *vide* Khusro (Sulṭán).

**Sultan Mahmud,** سلطان محمود, *vide* Mahmúd (Sulṭán) of Ghazní.

**Sultan Mahmud Mirza,** سلطان محمود مرزا, the son of Sulṭán Abú Saíd Mirzá who was sovereign of the greater part of Mawar-un-nahr and Badakhshán. His takhallus or poetical name was "Zillí."

**Sultan Mirza,** سلطان مرزا, *vide* Muhammad Sulṭán Mirzá.

**Sultan Muhammad Saljuki,** سلطان محمد بن جلال الدين ملكشاه, the son of Sulṭán Jalál-uddín Malikshah. He succeeded his brother Barkayáraḳ in December, 1104 A. D., 498 A. H., and after a reign of about 13 years died in 1118 A. D., 511 A. H., *vide* Muhammad (Sulṭán).

**Sultan Muhammad,** سلطان محمد بن مرزا بايسنغر, the son of Mirzá Báisanghar the son of Mirzá Sháhrukh, the son of Amír Taimúr. He was defeated in a battle against his brother Bábar Sulṭán, taken prisoner and put to death in January, 1452 A. D., Ẓil-ḥijja, 855 A. H.

**Sultan Murad,** سلطان مراد, *vide* Murad Mirzá.

**Sultan Muhammad,** سلطان محمد بن عالمگیر, the eldest son of the emperor 'Álamgír. He died 30 years before his father, on the 5th December, 1676 A. D., 8th Shawwál, 1087 A. H., in the fort of Gwáliar where he was confined by his father, and was buried near the mausoleum of Ḳutb-uddín called Ḳutb Sháh, at Dehlí.

**Sultan Sakhi Sarwar,** سلطان ساقي سرور, a Muhammadan saint. His shrine is situated at the mouth of the Sierí Pass leading in the direction of Kándahar, and is built at the "Dámanpahár." Though not much reverenced in the Darájat, it is said that from 180,000 to 200,000 pilgrims both Musalmáns and Hindús from the Panjab and Sindh, visit it annually. In February, March and April disciples assemble in large numbers, and the fair is over in April.

**Sultan Shah,** سلطان شاه, son of Alp Arsalán, Sulṭán of Khwárizm. Some time after his father's death, which took place in 1162 A. D., 557 A. H., he was defeated in several battles by his elder brother Alá-uddín Takash, and obliged to fly to the forests where he died from hunger and distress, about the year 1193 A. D., Ramaẓán, 589 A. H.

**Sultan Shahzada,** سلطان شهزاده, an eunuch of Fatha Sháh king of Bengal whom he murdered, and ascended the throne 1491 A. D., 896 A. H. He reigned only a few months and was assassinated the same year by Malik Andíl who succeeded him and took the title of Fíróz Sháh Púrbí.

**Sultan Parwez,** سلطان پرویز, *vide* Parwez Sulṭán.

**Sultan Shujaa',** سلطان شجاع بن شاهجهان, second son of the emperor Sháh Jahán, was born at Ajmeir on Sunday the 12th of May, 1616 A. D., 4th Jumáda I, 1025 A. H., and married to the daughter of Mirzá Rustam Safwí brother of Muzaffar Husain Mirzá of the royal house of Persia. He was appointed governor of Bengal by his father, which country he governed with justice and clemency till the accession of his brother the emperor 'Álamgír and the defeat of Dárá Shikóh in 1658, when he marched with a powerful army towards Dehlí. He was defeated by 'Álamgír on the 5th January, 1659 A. D., 19th Rabí' II, 1069 A. H. at a place called Khajúa, about thirty miles west of Allahábád, and pursued by Mír Jumla and Sulṭán Muhammad the eldest son of 'Álamgír to Bengal, from which place he was obliged to seek refuge in Arakan where, after two years, 1660 A. D., 1071 A. H., he was put in a boat with all his family and sunk in the river by order of the rájá of that country.

**Sultan-ul-Nisa Begam,** سلطان النسا, eldest daughter of the emperor Jahángír and sister of Sulṭán Khusro. Her mother was the daughter of Rájá Bhagwán Dás, and she was born in the year 1586 A. D., 994 A. H., After the death of her brother Sulṭán Khusrau, she erected a tomb for herself close to her brother Sulṭán Khusrau's grave at Allahábád, but died at Ágrah and lies buried there in the mausoleum of the emperor Akbar.

**Sultan-us-Salatin Purbi,** سلطان السلاطين, was elevated to the throne of Bengal on the death of his father Ghayás-uddín Púrbí 1373 A. D., 775 A. H. This prince was benevolent, merciful and brave. He died after a reign of ten years 1383 A. D., 785 A. H., and was succeeded by his son Shams-uddín II Púrbí.

**Sultan Walad,** سلطان ولد, son of the celebrated Maulwí Rúmí. He is the author of a beautiful poem on the Súfí doctrines, &c., written in imitation of the Masnawí of his father 1291 A. D., 690 A. H., and also of a Díwán, and another work called "Walad-náma" containing an account of his father and grandfather.

**Sulaiman,** سليمان, a Khalíf of the house of Umayya, and son of 'Abdulmalik. He succeeded his brother Walíd I in Syria 714 A. D., 96 A. H., and died after a reign of three years 717 A. D., 99 A. H.

**Sulaiman,** سليمان, the son of Báyezíd I, (Bajazet) was proclaimed emperor of the Turks in 1402 A. D., 805 A. H., at the time when his father was taken captive by Amír Taimúr. He displayed great valour, but his glory was tarnished by his excessive love of pleasure. He was dethroned and murdered in 1410 A. D. by his brother Músa, who in his turn was defeated and assassinated by another brother Muhammad I who ascended the throne in 1413 A. D. This Sulaimán is not reckoned among the Turkish Sulṭáns.

**Sulaiman I, Sultan,** سلطان سليمان, surnamed the Magnificent, was the son of Salím I, whom he succeeded as emperor of the Turks in September, 1520 A. D., Shawwál, 926 A. H. His reign was splendid. He defeated the Mamlúks in Egypt, and made peace with Sháh Ismá'íl I Safwí king of Persia, after which he carried his arms against Europe and took Belgrade. In 1522 he attacked Rhodes and took it, and then invaded Hungary and defeated the Hungarians at Mohatz in 1526. The conquest of Buda was followed by the siege of Vienna, but after twenty unsuccessful assaults, he retreated with the loss of 80,000 men. In 1534 he made war against Sháh Tahmásp Safwí, and invaded Tauris and Persia, but suffered a defeat, and was disappointed in his attack on Malta. He died on the 4th September, 1566 A. D., Safar, 974 A. H., having lived 76 solar years and reigned 46. He was a prince more just and true to his word than any other of his predecessors, but a great terror to all Christians. His son Sulṭán Salím II succeeded him.

**Sulaiman II, Sultan,** سلطان سليمان, emperor of Turkey who succeeded his brother Muhammad IV in 1687 A. D., 1098 A. H., was a very indolent prince. He died in the year 1691 A. D., 1102 A. H., and was succeeded by his brother Aḥmad II.

**Sulaiman bin-Ahmad Tahrani,** سليمان بن احمد طهراني, author of the "Muajjam Kabír, "Muajjam Ausat," "Muajjam Saghír," "Daláel-ul-Nabúat," and many other works. He died in 971 A. D., 360 A. H.

**Sulaiman bin-Ahmad,** سليمان بن احمد, author of the book called "Umdat," a Turkish work on Navigation in the Indian Seas written in the year 1511 A. D., 917 A. H., and five others of the same description, called the "Fawáed," the "Hawia," the "Tuhfat-ul-Fahúl," the "Minháj," and the "Ḳiládat-ul-Shamús."

**Sulaiman bin-Kutlamish,** سليمان بن قتلمش by the aid of Malikshâh Saljúḳí who took his father prisoner, became the first king of the Saljúḳ dynasty of Rúm or Anatolia whose capital was Iconium. He began his reign in 1077 A. D., 470 A. H., reigned eight years, and destroyed himself through fear of Takash or Turtash the son of Alp Arsalán. After him there was an interregnum of seven years from 1085 to 1092 A. D., when his son Daúd ascended the throne.

*Kings of the Saljúḳ dynasty who reigned in Iconium.*

1. Sulaimán bin-Kutlamish.
2. Daúd son of Sulaimán, having gained a victory over his enemies ascended the throne in 1092 A. D., and died in 1107.
3. Kulich Arsalán his brother, who in a battle with Atábak Jáwalí fell into a canal with his horse and was drowned in 1116 A. D.
4. Masaúd son of Ḳulich Arsalán died in 1156 A. D.
5. 'Azz-uddín Ḳulich Arsalán son of Masaúd. He destroyed the first Crusade army and died in 1188 A. D.
6. Ḳuṭb-uddín Malikshâh son of 'Azz-uddín, deposed in 1192 A. D.
7. Ghayás-uddín Kaikhusro son of 'Azz-uddín deposed in 1200 A. D.
   Ghayás-uddín Kaikhusro restored 1203 A. D.
8. Rukn-uddín Sulaimán son of 'Azz-uddín Ḳulich Arsalán deposed in 1203 A. D.
9. Ḳizal or Ḳulich Arsalán son of Rukn-uddín deposed by Ghayás-uddín Kaikhusro in 1203 A. D.
10. 'Azz-uddín Kaikáús bin-Kaikhusro began to reign in 1210 and deposed in 1219 A. D.
11. 'Alá-uddín Kaiḳubád bin-Kaikhusro, poisoned in 1236 or 1239 A. D.
12. Kaikhusro son of Kaiḳubád. He was invaded by the Mughal princes, descendants of Changez Khán.
    'Azz-uddín Kaikáús restored and reigned in nominal conjunction with his brothers Rukn-uddín and 'Alá-uddín sons of Kaikhusro 1245 A. D.
13. Rukn-uddín Ḳulich Arsalán son of Kaikhusro began in 1257 A. D.
14. Ghayás-uddín Kaikhusro son of Rukn-uddín began 1267 A. D.
15. Masaúd bin-'Azz-uddín Kaikáús died in 1308 A. D., 708 A. H. He was the last of this race.

**Sulaiman Badakhshi, Mirza,** مرزا سليمان بدخشي, ruler of Badakhshán, was the son of Khán Mirzá, the son of Mahmúd Mirzá, the son of Sultán Abú Saíd Mirzá, a descendant of Amír Taimúr. When his father Khán Mirzá died in the year 1521 A. D., 927 A. H., he was then only seven years old, consequently that province fell into the hands of the emperor Bábar who was then in Kábul; he appointed his son Humáyún to take charge of that country; but when Bábar conquered Dehlí in 1526 A. D., 932 A. H., he after four years restored that kingdom to Mirzá Sulaimán, in whose possession it remained till the year 1575 A. D., 983 A. H., when it was usurped by his grandson Sháhrukh Mirzá the son of Ibráhím Mirzá, who intended to assassinate him. Mirzá Sulaimán was obliged to fly to India, where on his arrival, he was received by the emperor Akbar with the greatest affection and kindness. He subsequently made a pilgrimage to Mecca and returned to India in 1587 A. D., 995 A. H., where after two years he died at Láhor on Saturday the 12th of July, 1589 A. D., 8th Ramazán, 997 A. H., aged 77 lunar years.

**Sulaiman Kadr, Mirza,** سليمان قدر, a prince, the son of Mirzá Khurshaid Kadr, the son of Mirzá Asmán Kadr. Their poetical titles were Taskhír, Kaisar and Namúd, *vide* Kaisar.

**Sulaiman Baiza,** سليمان بيضا, an author.

**Sulaiman Ḳirani,** سليمان قراني, was made governor of Bengal after the deposition of Bahádur Sháh Afghán in 1549 A. D., 956 A. H., but threw off his allegiance from the throne of Dehlí after the death of Salím Sháh king of Dehlí 1554 A. D., 961 A. H. During his rule he subdued the province of Orissa; and notwithstanding he was virtually independent, he used frequently to send valuable presents to the emperor Akbar. He reigned for a period of 25 lunar years, and died in 1572 A. D., 981 A. H. His eldest son Báyezíd Khán succeeded him, but was murdered after one month, and Dáúd Khán his younger brother ascended the throne with the title of Dáúd Sháh.

**Sulaiman Shah,** سليمان شاه, the son of Muhammad Malikshâh, the Saljúkide. He was much addicted to pleasure and wine, and resigned his crown to Arsalán Sháh the son of Tughral II. He was killed in 1159 A. D.

**Sulaiman Shikoh,** سليمان شكوه, the eldest son of the prince Dárá Shikóh the son of the emperor Sháh Jahán. He was born on the 5th April, 1635 A. D., 26th Ramazán, 1044 A. H. After the defeat and assassination of his father in 1659 A. D., 1069 A. H., he was seized and brought to Dehlí by the officers of 'Alamgír from Sirínagar where he had taken refuge, and imprisoned by that emperor, along with his brother Sipehr Shikóh in the fort of Gwáliar where they both died in a short time, and was buried in the fort of Gwáliar. Sulaimán had also his house built at Agrah close to his father's house.

**Sulaiman Shah,** سليمان شاه, king of Persia, *vide* Sháh Sulaimán.

**Sulaiman Shikoh, Mirza,** مرزا سليمان شكوه, the son of the emperor Sháh 'Alam and brother of Akbar Sháh II king of Dehlí. He died on the 24th February, 1838 A. D., 29th Zil-Ḳa'da, 1253 A. H. at Agrah, and was buried in the mausoleum of the emperor Akbar the Great at Sikandara in Agrah. His tomb is of white marble and has a Persian inscription, mentioning his name and the year of his death. He has left a Díwán in Urdú.

**Sunna,** سنا, this word is used generally to signify all the traditions, both of the sayings and doings of the Prophet, and the term Hadís is employed in the same comprehensive sense. The distinction between the Hadís (sayings) and the Sunan (doings), is not attended to by doctors of the Muslim law; both are generally authoritative.

**Sunni,** سني. Those Musalmáns, who assume to themselves the appellation of orthodox, and uphold the succession of the Khalífas Abú Bakr, Umar, and Usmán, and deny the right of supremacy, either spiritual and temporal to the posterity of 'Alí, are called Sunnís. They are divided into an infinity of sects, but of these there are only four principal ones, which are called after their founders. *Vide* Imáma, and Shia.

**Sunkar or Sankar,** سنقر, son of Maudúd, one of the Atábaks of Fars, who is better known by his title of Atábak Muzaffar-uddín, was the great-grandson of Salghar, the founder of this dynasty. He succeeded Búzába the last governor of Fars of this family, and threw off all dependence upon the Saljúḳí Sultáns about the year 1148 A. D., 543 A. H. He made his residence the city of Shíráz, which afterwards became the capital of his family. He died 1161 A. D., 556 A. H., and was succeeded by his brother.

Muzaffar-uddín Zangí, who after a peaceful reign of 14 years, left the government to his son Takla in 1175 A. D., 571 A. H.

Takla, who acquired fame by employing, as his wazír, the victorious Khwája Amín-uddín of Gázarún, reigned 20 years, and at his death, which happened 1195 A. D., 591 A. H., the government of Fars fell to his brother.

Atábak Sad bin-Zangí, who made a successful attack upon Isfahán. The memory of Atábak Sad is to this day held in great respect at Shíráz. He surrounded that city by a wall, and built the Jáma Masjid or chief mosque, which still remains a monument of his piety and munificence. He reigned more than 30 lunar years, and died about the year 1226 A. D., 623 A. H. He was succeeded by his son.

Atábak Abú Bakr also called Abú Nasr, a son every way worthy of his father. He gave an extraordinary proof of his foresight in his early conciliation of Changeiz Khán, to whom he sent a mission, and some valuable presents. The conqueror received the advance with favour, conferred the Turkish title of Kutlak Khán upon him; and the province of Fars through the wisdom of its prince, was exempted from that destruction which fell on all those in its vicinity. In his time lived the celebrated Sadí of Shíráz who wrote the Gulistán in his name. Abú Bakr died at Shíráz in 1260 A. D., 5th Jumáda II, 658 A. H., after a long and prosperous reign of 34 years, and left his government to his son. Daulat Sháh says he died in 667 A. H.

Atábak Sad II, who, at the time of his father's death, was with the army of Halákú Khán the grandson of Changeiz Khán, hastened to take possession of his inheritance, but was seized by an illness, which terminated his existence before he could reach his capital. His infant son

Atábak Muhammad was placed upon the masnad; and the rule devolved upon the child's mother Khátún Turkán: but her authority received a great shock in the death of her son, who two years and a half after his advancement, fell from the terrace of his palace, and was killed on the spot, 1262 A. D., 660 A. H. After his death

Muhammad Sháh, a chief of the family of Salghar was elevated to the dignity of Atábak, but Khátún Turkán, after eight months being displeased with his conduct, seized him and sent him prisoner to Halákú Khán: while she elevated his brother Saljúk Sháh to the government.

Saljúk Sháh, with a view of confirming his power, married Khátún Turkán; but afterwards in a fit of intoxication, ordered one of his slaves to strike off her head. Some officers of the emperor Halákú Khán, who were present, expressed their feelings at this horried act and were instantly put to death. When Halákú heard of these proceedings, he immediately ordered the execution of his brother Muhammad; and Saljúk, dreading the vengeance of the emperor, fled to Kázarún: but was seized and put to death, 1263 A. D., 661 A. H.

Ísh, the daughter of Atábak Sad who reigned one year, got married to Mangú Taimúr the son of Halákú, which put an end to this family, which lasted 120 lunar years.

**Supkaran** or **Subhkaran Bundeila**, صبهکرن بندیله, a Rájpút, who was an Amír of 2500 in the service of the emperor 'Alamgír. He died at Bahádurgarh in the Dakhin about the year 1678 A. D., 1089 A. H., and was much lamented by all who knew him. Many of his women buried themselves upon the funeral pile with his corpse. He was a soldier unequalled, had in repeated battles won the prize of valour, and was in general successful. After his death his son Dalpat Ráo was exalted to the rank of 500 by the emperor.

**Surur**, سرور, poetical name of Mirzá Rajab 'Alí Beg of Lakhnau. He is the author of a Díwán and several other works and of a beautiful story in Urdú called "Fisána Ajáeb" which he completed in the first year of the reign of Nasír-uddín Haidar, 1828 A. D., 1244 A. H.

**Surur**, سرور, poetical name of Lachhmí Rám.

**Sururi**, سروري, poetical title of Hájí Muhammad, a poet who died in 1561 A. D., 969 A. H. He was the son of a shoemaker, and had so excellent a memory, that he knew more than 30,000 verses by heart. He composed a dictionary called "Mujma-ul-Furs," and a book in which he explains the difficult words of Nizámí and other poets. *Vide* Muhammad Kásim son of Surúrí. He also wrote a Commentary in the Turkish language on the Díwán of Hafiz.

**Sururi**, سروري, poetical appellation of Razí-uddín a brother of Maftún. He is the author of several Persian poems, besides which he has composed from 10 to 12 thousand Urdú verses. He was alive in 1796 A. D. 1211 A. H.

**Suryya Jah**, ثریاجاه, *vide* Amjad 'Alí Sháh, king of Audh.

**Swami Bhopat Rae Begam**, سواحي بهوپت رای بیغم, a Khattrí who resided at Patan near Jammú in the Panjáb. He translated, from the Sanskrit into Persian the Prabodh Chand (Chandrodaya) Nátak a very curious work on Theosophy, and dedicated it as well as several other treatises on Súfyism to Naráyan Chand.

# T.

**Taban**, تابان, the poetical name of Mír 'Abdul Hai of Dehlí, a youth whose extraordinary beauty was the theme of contemporary poets, and of whose personal charms, it is related that they were the envy of the other sex, and the admiration of all who beheld him. He was slain at an early age in consequence of having himself formed a very unbecoming attachment. His odes are in high estimation for delicacy and elegance of sentiment, and even the poet Souda was among the number of his admirers. *Gilchrist's Hindústání Grammar.* He lived in the time of the emperor Muhammad Sháh.

**Tabari**, طبري, a celebrated historian of Tabaristán, and author of the "Táríkh Tabarí." He was a famous Imám of Baghdád, and the Livy of the Arabians. He finished his General History in 914 A. D., 302 A. H. At the request of his friends, he reduced his work of 30,000 sheets to a more reasonable size. He died 922 A. D., 310 A. H. *Vide* Abú Jafar-at-Tabarí, and Abú Alí the wazír of Mansúr.

**Taba Taba**, طبا طبا, a poet whose proper name was Mír Rafí-uddín Husain, a Sayyad, who being of the Tabátabá tribe, used it as his poetical name. He was living in 1601 A. D., 1010 A. H.

**Tabiat**, طبیعت, poetical name of Shaikh Saif-uddín Muhammad, a poet who lived in 1742 A. D., 1155 A. H.

**Tadbir**, تدبیر, poetical title of Prince Sikandar Kadr.

**Tadrawi** or **Tazrawi Ab-hari**, تدروي, a nephew of Nargisí. He came from Rome to India, died there 1567 A. D., 975 A. H., and was buried at Ágrah. He is the author of a memoir or Masnawí called "Risála Hasan-o-Yúsaf Muhammad Khán."

**Tafta**, تفته, poetical name of Munshí Hargopál of Sikandarábád, by caste a Káyeth. He is the author of a Persian Díwán which he completed and published in the Lithographic Press at Ágrah in 1851 A. D., 1267 A. H.

and of a Parody on the verses of the Gulistán in verse, entitled "Tazmín Gulistán," published in 1858 A. D., 1274 A. H.

**Tafazzul Husain Khan,** تفضل حسين خان, the rebel Nawáb of Farrukhábad. He was the grandson and successor of Muzaffar Jang, also called Muzaffar Husain Khán. This man, a British protegé, murdered sixty-two Englishmen, women, and children, during the insurrection of 1857, under circumstances of the most cold-blooded atrocity. After months of unavailing pursuit, Major Barrow, Commissioner of the district of Audh, to which he had fled, offered him his life provided he had himself committed no murders. The Nawáb surrendered, was tried, found guilty, and sentenced to death. The Governor-General, however, while fully coinciding in the verdict, held that the word of a British officer must be maintained, declared the criminal exempt from the punishment of death, on the condition that he should immediately quit the British territory for ever. If, ran the order, he accept this condition, he will be conveyed to the frontier as a convict under a Military guard and there set at liberty. If he refuse the condition, or if having accepted it, he shall break it, or attempt to break it, now, or at any future time, the capital sentence pronounced upon him will be carried out. The Nawáb elected to be sent to Mecca. Accordingly on the 23rd of May, 1859 A. D., he was taken to the Magistrate's office under a European Guard, and there fettered. He was allowed to see his children but not his wife. Two hundred men of the Fathagarh Levy were ordered to guard him to Bombay on his way to Mecca.

**Taftazani** or **Tuftazani,** تفتازاني, which is sometimes erroneously written Tughtázání, is the surname of an author who was called so from his birth-place, a city in Khurásán. His proper name is Mulla Sad-uddín Masaúd bin-'Umar. He is the author of the Commentaries on the "Maázid", "'Akáed" and "Kashsháf"; and also of the "Sharah Sharaf Zanjáni", "Mutouwal", which he dedicated to Malik Husain Kart and "Mukhtasir Talkhís," dedicated to Jání Beg. There is another work entitled "Sharah Halláj," which is also attributed to him. In the latter part of his life he served under Tamerlane and died at Samarkand. According to the Muntakhib-ut-Tawáríkh, he was born in 1322 A. D., 722 A. H., and died on the 10th January, 1390 A. D., 22nd Muharram, 792 A. H., but according to Hájí Khalfa in 791 A. H.

**Taghallub,** تغلب, a learned and pious Musalmán whose proper name was Abú'l Abbás Ahmad. He was the Imám of the inhabitants of Kúfa, and died at Baghdád in the year 903 A. D., 290 A. H.

**Tahawi** or **Al-Tahawi,** طحاوي, *vide* Abú Jafar bin-Muhammad Tabáwí.

**Tahir** and **Ghani,** غني طاهر, poetical names of Mirzá Muhammad Táhir commonly called Ghaní Kashmírí, which see.

**Tahir,** طاهر, the grandson of Amrú bin-Lais, which see.

**Tahir I** or **Tahir ibn-Husain-al-Khuzai',** طاهر ابن حسين الخذاعی, surnamed Yeminain (Ambidexter). He was one of Al-Mamún's ablest supporters and one of the greatest generals of his age. He defeated and slew 'Alí Ibn-Ísá in battle 811 A. D., 195 A. H., and sent his head as a present to the Khalíf Al-Mámún his employer, who amply rewarded Táhir for his services. And when that prince was residing at Marv the capital of Khurásán, he revolted against his brother Al-Amín the Khalíf of Baghdád, and despatched Táhir with an army to attack him at Baghdád which place he took in 813 A. D., Safar, 198 A. H., and having slain Al-Amín, sent his head to Khurásán that it might he presented to Al-Mámún his brother, who conferred the government of Khurásán upon Táhir and his descendants with almost absolute and unlimited power. Táhir died on Saturday the 15th of November, 822 A. D., 24th Jumáda II, 207 A. H , at Marv, and his son Talha was appointed wazír in his room. The following is a list of his descendants.

Táhir I, died 207 A. H.
Talha his son.
'Abdullah son of Táhir died 230 A. H.
Táhir II son of 'Abdullah.
Muhammad son of Táhir II and last prince of this race.

**Tahir II,** طاهرابن عبد الله, great-grandson of Táhir I, and son of Abdulláh whom he succeeded in the government of Khurásán in the reign of Al-Mustaín Billáh and died a natural death. He was succeeded by his son Muhammad the last prince of this race.

**Tahir bin-Ahmad-al-Bukhari, Imam Iftikhar-uddin,** طاهربن احمد البخاری, author of a work on Ilm-ul-Fatáwa or science of decisions, entitled the "Khulásat-ul-Fatáwá," a select collection of decisions of great authority. He was also the author of the "Khazínat-ul-Wakiát," and the "Kitáb-an-Nisáb" on which books the Khulásat was grounded, and to which many subsequent collections are indebted for numerous valuable cases. He died 1147 A. D., 542 A. H.

**Tahir Billah,** طاهربالله, *vide* Al-Táhir Bi-amrullah a Khalíf of Baghdád.

**Tahir Bukhari,** طاهر بخاری, a very pious Musalmán of Bukhárá and an excellent poet, who flourished in the reign of Sultán Bábar of Hirát.

**Tahir Abiwardi,** طاهرابیوردی, a poet who flourished in the time of Sultán Báisanghar.

**Tahir Muhammad bin-Imad-uddin Hasan bin-Sultan 'Ali bin-Haji Muhammad Husain Sabzwari,** طاهر محمد بن عماد الدين حسن. He is the author of the history called "Rauzat-ut-Táhirín," the Garden of the Immaculate. It is a general history and was commenced in 1602 A. D., 1011 A. H., three years before the death of Akbar and concluded in 1606 A. D., 1015 A. H. Sir H. M. Elliot in his "Historians of India," calls it the "Rauzat-us-Safá," this is evidently a mistake, for that book was written by Mír Kháwand Sháh who died in 1498 A. D.

**Tahir Wahid, Mirza,** مرزا طاهروحيد, son of Husain Khán Kazwíní, commonly called Wákaa Nawís, the news-writer, was one of the greatest poets of the age. He was historigrapher of Sháh Abbás II, and afterwards wazír to Sháh Sulaimán, kings of Persia. Mirzá Sáeb, who died in 1669 A. D., was one of his cotemporaries. Táhir Wahíd is the author of a Díwán containing 60,000 verses, and of a history of the Safwí kings of Persia. One of his works which he wrote, in 1656 A., D., 1066 A. H., is called "Mirat-ul-Ai'jaz" and one, which contains letters written by him for the king of Persia, goes after his name, and is called "Táhír Wahíd." He died in 1696 A. D., 1108 A. H.

**Tahir-al-Azaz din Allah,** طاهر الاعز دين الله, son of Hákim Abú Mansúr, succeeded his father 1020 A. D. on the throne of Egypt. He reigned 15 years, and left his crown to a son under seven years of age, named Al-Mustanasar Billáh. Táhir died in 1036 A. D., 427 A. H.

**Tahmasp I, Shah Safwi,** شاه طهماسپ صفوي, king of Persia, was born on Wednesday the 22nd of February, 1514 A. D., 26th Ẕilḥijja, 919 A. H., and succeeded his father Sháh Ismạil I to the throne of Persia, on the 24th May, 1524 A. D., 19th Rajab, 930 A. H., when he was ten years of age. The reign of this prince owes much of its celebrity to the truly royal and hospital reception he gave to the emperor Humáyún 1543 A. D., when that monarch was forced to fly from India, and to take shelter in his dominions. All the means of the kingdom were called forth to do honour to the royal guest: and they were as liberally furnished to replace him upon his throne. Sháh Tahmasp died at the age of 64 after a reign of more than 53 lunar years, on Tuesday the 15th of May, 1576 A. D., 15th Ṣafar, 984 A. H. His fourth son Ismạíl Mirzá succeeded him. According to his own request he was buried at Mashhad.

**Tahmasp II, Shah, Safwi,** شاه طهماسپ صفوی, king of Persia was the son of Sulṭán Husain. He assumed the title of king of Persia after the confinement of his father by Mahmúd the Afghán chief, and struggled a few years with his fate; but a weak, effeminate, and debauched youth was unsuited for such times: and he only merits a place in history, as his name furnished a pretext for the celebrated Nádir Ḳulí Khán to lay the foundations of his great power. He was confined at Sabzwár in Khurásán, and put to death by Razá Ḳulí Khán, the son of Nádir Sháh who was then absent in his expedition to India in 1739 A. D., 1151 A. H.

**Tahmasp Ḳuli, Mirza,** مرزا طهماسپ قلی, a Turk, and an excellent poet, who flourished in the time of the emperor Sháh Jahán, and wrote a beautiful chronogram consisting of nineteen verses in Persian on the marriage of the emperor's eldest son Dárá Shikóh, each hemistich of which gives the year 1633 A. D., of the Hijra, 1043 A. H.

**Tahmurs,** طهمورث, commonly called Deoband or the Magician binder, a title which he derived from the success with which he warred against the enemies of his family. He succeeded his father Hoshang, and was the third king of Persia of the first or Pishdadian dynasty. He governed Persia 30 years, and was succeeded by his nephew, the famous Jamshed.

**Tahsin,** تحسين, poetical name of Mír Muhammad 'Atá Husain Khán of Lakhnau who lived in the court of Nawáb Mansúr 'Alí Khán, Safdar Jang, and had the title of Murassạ Raḳam. His father Mír Muhammad Bákir whose poetical name was Shauḳ, was also a learned man and a poet. Tahsín is the author of the works called "Zawábit Angreizí" "Tawáríkh Ḳásimí," "Insháe Tahsín," and of the "Nautarz Murrassạ," an Urdú version of the Four Darweishes, which he wrote in the commencement of the reign of Nawáb 'Asaf-uddaula about the year 1775 A. D. *Vide* Atá Husain Khán.

**Tahsin 'Ali Khan,** تحسين علي خان خواجة سرا, an eunuch of Nawáb 'Asaf-uddaula of Lakhnau. He died in the time of Nawáb Sạádat 'Alí Khán in August, 1813 A. D., Shabán, 1228 A. H.

**Taimur,** تيمور, *vide* Amír Taimúr.



**Taimur Shah,** تيمور شاه, the eldest son of Aḥmad Sháh Abdálí, succeeded his father to the throne of Ḳábul and Ḳandahár in 1772 A. D., 1186 A. H., after murdering Sháh Walí Khán his father's wazír, who intended to crown his son-in-law prince Sulaimán a younger brother of Taimúr. He reigned 20 years over Ḳábul, Ḳandáhár and Khurasán and died 17th May, 1793 A. D., 7th Shawwál, 1207 A. H., aged 47 years. He left several sons, *viz.*, Humayún Sháh, Zamán Sháh, Mahmúd Sháh, Sháh Shujáạ, Fíroz Sháh, Abbás and Ayyúb. On Taimúr's death, a powerful faction headed by his favourite wife, and supported by Páinda Khán entitled Sarfaráz Khán, the head of the Barakzaí family, placed Sháh Zamán upon the throne, at Ḳábul; Humayún the elder brother, proclaimed himself king of Ḳandahár, and Mahmúd became the ruler of Hirát.

**Taimur Sultan,** تيمور سلطان, the successor of Shaibání Khán the chief of the Uzbaks, after whose death in 1510 A. D., 916 A. H., he took possession of Samarḳand, and Jání Beg Khán and 'Abdullah Khán divided Bukhárá between themselves.

**Tajalli,** تجلي, poetical title of 'Alí Razá, an encomiast of 'Aḳá Husain Khwánsárí. He is the author of a poem called "Mạráj-ul-Khayál. He died in 1677 A. D., 1088 A. H.

**Tajara Begam,** تاجارا بيگم, the mother of Wájid 'Alí the ex-king of Lakhnau, who proceeded to England after the annexation of Audh to the British possessions and died in France in 1857 A. D. *Vide* Jawad 'Alí.

**Taji,** تاجي, poetical appellation of Mír Muhammad Husain, the native country of whose forefathers was Andján in Persia. He flourished in the time of 'Álamgír, and is the author of a Díwán.

**Tajrid,** تجريد, a poet who is the author of a Díwán.

**Taj-uddin 'Abdul Wahhab bin-as-Sabki,** تاج الدين عبدالوهاب بن اشبكي, author of the "Tabaḳát-ash-Sháfi'at." There are numerous biographical collections treating of the lives of the principal followers of Sháfạí besides the one just mentioned which have similar titles, but the most noted is by Táj-uddín. He died in 1369 A. D., 771 A. H.

**Taj-uddin Abu Ja'far bin-Sukman,** تاج الدين ابو جعفر بن سقمان, an author who died 1118 A. D., 512 A. H.

**Taj-uddin Abu'l Fazl,** تاج الدين ابو الفضل بن طاهر, son of Táhir, ruler of Sístán also called Nímróz which country he received from Sulṭán Sanjar Saljúḳí sometime about the year 1150 A. D., 545 A. H. The following is a list of his descendants who reigned in Sístán till the invasion of Changeiz Khán.

1. Táj-uddín 'Abú Jạfar.
2. Shams-uddín Muhammad son of Táj-uddín, who along with his sister was slain by his own subjects.
3. Táj-uddín Harb son of 'Izzul Mulk who is said to have reigned 60 years.
4. Bahrám Sháh son of Táj-uddín in whose time lived Abú Nasr Faráhí the author of the "Nisáb-us-Subián."
5. Nasrat-uddín son of Bahrám, who was killed in battle against his brother Rukn-uddín.
6. Rukn-uddín son of Bahrám, who was slain at the time of the invasion of Changeiz Khán.

7. Shaháb-uddín Muhammad son of Táj-uddín slain in battle.
8. Táj-uddín who defended himself for two years in the fort of Sístán which was at last taken and every soul put to the sword by the troops of Changeiz Khán.

**Taj-uddin Elduz,** تاج‌الدین یلدوز, king of Ghazní. It is related that Shaháb-uddín Muhammad Ghórí who had no children excepting a daughter, took pleasure in educating Turkish slaves, whom he afterwards adopted. Four of these slaves, besides Ḳuṭb-uddín Eaibak, became great princes, of whom Táj-uddín Eldúz was one. On the death of Shaháb-uddín, in 1206 A. D., 602 A. H., the Turkí officers espoused the cause of his nephew prince Mahmúd, the son of Ghayás-uddín Ghórí; but Mahmúd being unambitious, and naturally indolent, remained satisfied with the throne of his ancestors at Ghór, and proclaimed Eldúz king of Ghazní, content to receive homage from that chief. Eldúz had several battles with Ḳuṭb-uddín Eaibak kirg of Dehlí, and some time after his death, he recruited his army and marched to India with a view to conquer that country, but was defeated near Dehlí by Shams-uddín Altimsh in 1215 A. D., 611 A. H., and being taken prisoner, was imprisoned in Badáon, where, according to some accounts, he died a natural death, but according to others, he was poisoned. The whole length of his reign was nine years. A list of the Sulṭáns of the Slave Dynasty of Ghór, who reigned in India, is given under Ḳuṭb-uddín Eaibak.

**Taj-uddin Gazruni,** تاج‌الدین گازرونی, author of the "Bahr-i-Sạádat" the Sea of Felicity, a Persian work containing Essays on the goodness of God, the Creation of the world, on Virtue and the necessity of observing the moral duties, proved by various quotations from the Ḳurán.

**Taj-uddin Sangreiza,** تاج‌الدین سنگریزه, a Persian poet who lived in the time of Ghayás-uddín Balban king of Dehlí, about the year 1274 A. D., 670 A. H.

**Taj-uddin 'Umar bin-'Ali,** عمربن علي فقهي تاج‌الدین, surnamed Fiḳahí, an Arabian author who died in the year 1331 A. D., 731 A. H.

**Taj-ul-Mulk,** تاج الملك, whose original name was Malik Tájú, was appointed wazír by Khizir Khán king of Dehlí in the first year of his reign 1414 A. D., 817 A. H., with the above title. He died on the 13th January, 1421 A. D., 8th Muḥarram, 824 A. H., and his eldest son Sikandar succeeded him in the office of wizárat under the title of Malik-ush-Sharḳ."

**Takash** or **Turtash,** تكش, which see.

**Takash** or **Taksh,** تكش, surnamed 'Alá-uddín Sulṭán of Khwárizm, the son of Alp Arsalan the son of Atsiz a descendant of the prince of that country, who had been cupbearer to the celebrated Sulṭán Sanjar king of Persia. He defeated and slew Tughral III Saljúḳí in a battle 1194 A. D., 590 A. H. At his death which happened 4th July, 1200 A. D., 19th Ramaẓán, 596 A. H., he left his kingdom to his son Sulṭán Muhammad surnamed Ḳuṭb-uddín, whose reign was at its commencement, splendid and successful: but his fortune fell before that great destroyer of the human race, Changeiz Khán: by whom he was defeated, his countries pillaged and almost all his family made prisoners. He died of a broken heart 1220 A. D., 617 A. H. His son Jalál-uddín, who was the last of this dynasty of kings, long bore up against the torrent that had overwhelmed his father: but was at last subdued. He was slain 1230 A. D.

**Takhat** or **Takht Singh,** تخت سینگه, Rájá of Jodhpúr Márwár, who was raised to the gaddí after the death of his father Rája Mán Singh in November, 1843 A. D. He died on the 12th February, 1873 A. D., and was succeeded by his eldest son Jaswant Singh to whom he had resigned the reins of government some months before his death.

**Takla,** تكله, a king of Fárs, *vide* Sunḳar.

**Takoji Holkar,** تكوجی هولکر, the nephew of Malhár Ráo Hólkar I, was elected and placed on the masnad of Indour by Ahlia Bái the widow of Khande Ráo son of Malhár Ráo in 1767 A. D. on the death of her son Mallí Ráo. He reigned 30 years and died on the 15th August, 1797 A. D., leaving two legitimate sons Kashí Ráo and Malhár Ráo; and two illegitimate sons Ithojí and Jaswant Ráo. After the death of Takójí, his eldest son Káshí Ráo succeeded him; but the country was usurped by Daulat Ráo Scindhia for some time and afterwards made over to Jaswant Ráo.

**Takoji Holkar,** تكوجی هولکر, rájá of Indour, was raised to the gaddí in 1844 A. D., and was living in 1857.

**Tala',** طالع, the poetical name of Mirzá Nizám-uddín brother to Mirzá Ḳuṭb-uddín Máel. He was an excellent poet and flourished in the time of the emperor 'Alamgír, and was living about the year 1696 A. D., 1108 A. H.

**Talaiha ibn-Khawailid,** طليحه ابن خويلد, one of the false prophets who pretended to prophecy like Muhammad, and lied against God, saying, that inspiration came down to him from heaven. He was received into favour by the Saracens 638 A. D., 17 A. H., by saving the life of Sarjabíl ibn-Hasaní in a battle against the Greeks, and was subsequently employed by the Khalíf 'Umar in his wars against the Persians.

**Talash,** تلاش, the poetical name of Shaháb-uddín Aḥmad, which see.

**Taleiha ibn-Khaweilid,** طليحه, a false prophet. About the 12th year of the Hijra, several persons, perceiving the success and prosperity of Muhammad and his followers, set up also for prophets in hope of meeting the like good fortune, and making themselves eminent in the world. Such were Osad-al-Abbasí and Taleiha, with several others whose attempts however quickly came to nothing. *Vide* Talaiha.

**Talha,** طلحه بن طاهر, the son of Táhir the general of the Khalíf al-Mámún. He succeeded his father in the government of Khurásán in 822 A. D., 213 A. H., and after a reign of 6 years died a natural death in 828 A. D. His son 'Alí was killed the same year in a battle against the rebels at Naishapúr.

**Talha ibn-'Obeidullah,** طلحه بن عبيدالله. He, together with Zubeir and 'Ayesha the widow of Muhammad, were 'Alí's irreconcilable and implacable enemies. The Kúfians, Egyptians and the greatest part of the Arabians were for 'Alí. A part of the Basorians favoured Talha but the rest supported Zubeir. He was killed with Zubeir in a battle against 'Alí at Basra with an arrow by Marwán the then Secretary of 'Alí 656 A. D., 36 A. H.

**Talib 'Amuli,** طالب آملي, a celebrated poet of 'Amul in Persia, who came to India in the reign of the emperor Akbar, and lived till the time of the emperor Jahángír, and was honoured by that monarch with the title of "Malik-ush-Shu'árá" or the king of poets 1619 A. D., 1028 A. H. He died in the year 1625 A. D., 1035 A. H., aged nearly 100 years, in Kashmír, and left a Díwán of 14,000 verses.

**Talib Jajurmi,** طالب جاجرمی, author of a poem called "Manázira Góli-o-Chougán," Dispute between the Bat and the Ball, which he dedicated to Sulṭán 'Abdulláh, the son of Sulṭán Ibráhím, the son of Sháhrukh. He died in 1450 A. D., 854 A. H., and is buried close to the tomb of Khwája Háfiz at Shíráz.

**Talib Kalim,** طالب کلیم, *vide* Abú Tálib Kalím.

**Talmasani,** تلمساني, a poet.

**Tamanna,** تمنا, author of a small Díwán in Urdú.

**Tamas,** تامس, *vide* George Thomas.

**Tamerlane** or **Timarlang,** تمرلنگ, *vide* Amír Taimúr.

**Tana Shah,** تاناشاہ, *vide* Abú'l Hasan Ḳuṭbsháh.

**Tanha,** تنہا, poetical title of 'Abdul Latíf Khán, who is the author of a Díwán.

**Tanha,** تنہا, poetical name of Muhammad 'Alí.

**Tanuki,** طانوقي, surname of Abú'l 'Alá, one of the most celebrated Arabian poets of the tribe of Tánúḳ which has produced many clever men.

**Tansen,** تانسین, a celebrated Hindí musician or singer who flourished in the time of Akbar, and was employed by him. He was originally in the service of a Rája named Rám Chand, and was sent to court at the special request of the emperor. He died in the 34th year of that monarch's reign 1588 A. D., 996 A. H.

The musicians both vocal and instrumental in India ever since the Musalmán conquests, who have been highly esteemed, and whose names are handed down to posterity with much respect by different authors, are as follow: Gopál, Amír Khusro the poet, Baijú, Bháno, Panḍwá, Bakhshú, Lohang, Sulṭán Husain Sharḳí of Jaunpúr, Rája Mán of Gwáliar founder of the Dhurpad, in whose time also lived the four following, *viz.*, Chárjú, Bhagwán, Ḍhondhí, and Ḍálú. Tánsein, Subhán Khán, Súrgayán Khán of Fathapúr, Chánd Khán and his brother Súraj Khán, Tántarang Khán the son of Tánsein, Madan Ráe, Rámdás and his son Súrdás a blind moral poet and musician, Báz Bahádur, Munḍia, Mían Panḍ, Mían Dáúd Mullá Is-háḳ, Shaikh Khizir, Sheikh Beichú, Hasan Khán Ṭeiní, Súrat Sein and his brother Lálá Deibí, Mirzá 'Aḳil, Mián Shórí, Ghulámí, Lál Khán, Nílam Prakásh, and the *Bin* players Fíróz Khán and Naubat Khán.

**Tantia Topi,** تانتیا توپي, a famous rebel chief of 1857. He was captured in the jungles of Perone on the 7th, and hanged on the 18th of April, 1859. It is said that before his death he solemnly affirmed that he was the instigator of the Cawnpúr massacre, and that the Náná who had sworn to protect the Europeans was angry with him for his conduct and never saw him afterwards. If true, this confession was made evidently with the view of saving the Náná, when it would no longer injure himself. At his confession Tántiá described himself as a Bráhman of high caste, a native of Púna, which place he had left about 30 years before for Central India, where he became an Artillery soldier (Tópí). He next obtained employment in the Náná's establishment at Biṭhúr in connection with the Treasury, and was so employed in 1857 when the mutiny broke out. He also said, that he commanded the rebel army of 8,000 men which attacked Colonel Greathead's column on the parade ground at Ágrah on the 10th October, 1857. He declared he was aware of the arrival of the column from Dehlí before he opened fire on the encampment that morning, and did not suppose he had only the Ágrah brigade to deal with, as we imagined. He was deceived, however, after the action had commenced, by seeing a re-enforcement of European redcoats coming up (Greathead's men being dressed in Khákhi) for whose appearance and apparent numbers (for they were reported to be 2,500 men) he could not account, but supposing them to be new arrivals from down-country, he immediately retreated; otherwise he would have held his ground, and not have allowed Col. Greathead to win so easy a victory. Tántia also mentioned that the largest force he ever commanded was at the battle of Betwa, when he had under him 22,000 fighting men, and 130 pieces of ordnance of various calibres.

**Tapish,** تاپش, the poetical name of Munshí Ghulám Muhammad Khán editor of the Newspaper called "Audh Akhbar." He was living in 1871 A. D.

**Taqi Aohadi,** تقي اوحدی, a Persian poet who came to India and was living at Ágrah in 1614 A. D., 1023 A. H. He is the author of a Díwán.

**Taqi, Imam,** امام تقي, *vide* Muhammad Taḳí.

**Taqi Kashani,** تقي کاشاني, *vide* Taḳí-uddín Muhammad Káshání.

**Taqi, Mir,** میرتقي, a Persian and Urdú poet who is the author of six Díwáns and several other works. He was a native of Ágrah and died at Lakhnau in 1810 A. D., 1225 A. H. His father's name was Muhammad Muttaḳí. His poetical name is Mír, which see.

**Taqi-uddin Muhammad bin-Ahmad bin-'Ali Hasani Fasi,** تقی‌الدین محمد بن احمد بن علي, author of the work called "Shafa-ul-Gharám." He died 1428 A. D., 832 A. H.

**Taqi-uddin Muhammad Kashani,** تقی‌الدین محمد کاشاني, son of Sharaf-uddín 'Alí Husainí Zikrí. He was born at Káshán about the year 1539 A. D., 946 A. H., and is the author of a biography called "Khulásat-ul-Ashạár, wa Zubdut-ul-Afkár" compiled in the year 1585 A. D., 993 A. H.

**Taqi-uddin Sabaki,** تقی‌الدین سبقي, son of Abdul Káfí. He is the author of more than 150 works on different subjects. He died in 1349 A. D., 750 A. H.

**Taqi-uddin Tamimi,** تقی‌الدین تمیمي, author of a biographical treatise giving an account of the Hanafí lawyers, arranged in alphabetical order, entitled "Tabaḳát us-Saniat fí Tarájim-ul-Hanafiat." He died in 1596 A. D., 1005 A. H.

**Tara Bai,** تارا بای, the wife of Rájá Rám, the brother of Sambhají the son of Seiwájí Bhosla the Marhaṭṭa chief of Sitára. After the death of her husband in March, 1700 A. D., she ruled as regent in the name of her son, Seiwá, a child of two years, over the territories acquired by Seiwájí. But on 'Álamgír's death in 1707 A. D., when Sáhú, the son of Sambhají was released by 'Azim Sháh, he (Sáhú) quickly made himself master of Sitára and imprisoned Tárá Bai.

**Tara Begam,** تارا بیگم, one of the wives of the emperor Akbar. She had a garden in Ágrah consisting of 40 bígas of ground, now in ruins.

**Tarbiat Khan,** تربیت خان, a nobleman of 4000 who served under the emperor 'Álamgír as Mír 'Atash or Commander of Artillery. After the death of that monarch, he espoused the cause of his son 'Azim Sháh and was killed in the battle against Bahádur Sháh, 1707 A. D., 1119 A. H. He had, on a spot of land of 13 bígas, built a house at Ágrah on a piece of ground called Tajára or Majára outside the fort opposite to Amar Singh Darwáza.

**Tarbiat Khan Barlas,** تربیت خان برلاس, title of Shafí-ulláh Khán, a native of Persia, who came to India and served under the emperors Sháh Jahán and 'Álamgír. At the time of his death he held the rank of 4,000, and was governor of Jaunpúr where he died 1685 A. D., 1096 A. H.

**Tari,** تاري, poetical title of Mullá 'Alí Muhaddis.

**Tarkhan** or **Nawab Tarkhan,** نواب ترخان, *vide* Núr-uddín Safaiduni, (Mulla).

**Tarki,** ترکي, the first Sultán or emperor of, and his descendants; *vide* Usmán or Uthmán.

**Tarmadi, Tarmizi** or **Tirmizi,** ترمدي, *vide* Tirmizí which is the correct name.

**Tasalli,** تسلي, the poetical name of Ibráhím of Shíráz who came to India and was living in 1623 A. D., 1032 A. H. He is the author of a Díwán.

**Taskhir,** تسخیر, poetical title of Prince Mirzá Sulaimán Ḳadr, the son of Mirzá Khurshaid Ḳadr. *Vide* Ḳaisar.

**Tashbihi,** تسبیهي, *vide* Akbar 'Alí Tashbíhí.

**Tashkparizada,** تاشکپري زاده, surname of Mulla Aḥmad bin-Mustáfa, a celebrated Arabian who died 1560 A. D., 968 A. H.

**Tasir,** تاثیر, the poetical title of Mirzá Muhsin who is the author of a Díwán. He flourished about the year 1718 A. D., 1130 A. H.

**Taslim,** تسلیم, title of Muhammad Háshim of Shíráz. He came under 'Álamgír to India, and is ths author of a Díwán. He was living in 1697 A. D., 1109 A. H.

**Tatar Khan,** تاتار خان, adopted son of Tughlaḳ Sháh and prime minister of Sulṭán Muhammad Sháh Tughlaḳ. He is the author of a Commentary on the Ḳurán, entitled "Tafsír Tátár Khání," and of another work on Muhammadan Law, called "Fatáwí Tátár Khání." He died in the reign of Sulṭán Fíroz Sháh Bárbak.

**Tatar Khan,** تاتار خان, of Khorasan; a *Mansabdar* of one thousand under Akbar. He was Governor of Dehlí, and died there, 1588 A. D., 986 A. H.

**Tatar Khan,** تاتار خان, son of Muzaffar Sháh I, King of Gujrát, and father of Aḥmad Sháh I.

**Taufal Khan,** توفل خان, prime minister, *vide* Burhán 'Imád Sháh.

**Tauli Khan,** تولي خان, the fourth son of Changeiz Khán. On the death of his father, 1227 A. D., he succeeded to the kingdoms of Persia, Khurasán and Ḳábul and died three years after. He left several sons, among whom the two eldest, *viz.*, Mangú Khán and Halákú Khán were the most famous.

**Taurandukht,** توران دخت, the daughter of Khusro Parweiz. She was elevated on the throne of Persia some time after the death of her brother Sheiroya 631 A. D. We are told by Persian historians that this queen restored the sacred cross, which had been borne away from Jerusalem by Khusro Parweiz: and by that act, acquired great power with the Roman emperor. But this is evidently erroneous: for there is no doubt that the emperor Heraclius, when he returned from Persia, carried that precious relic to Constantinople, which was deemed a more splendid trophy of victory, than all his spoils and conquests. Túrándukht ruled Persia only one year and four months. She was succeeded by her cousin and lover Sháh Shananda. He had reigned only one month when he was deposed, and 'Azarm or Arzamídukht, another daughter of Khusro Parweiz was raised to the throne 632 A. D. This princess, who was alike distinguished by her sense and beauty, resolved to take the whole management of the affairs of the kingdom into her hands. She would not even appoint a wazír. But the fatal passion of a Persian noble defeated all her designs. Farrukh Hurmuz the governor of Khurásán, fell violently in love with her, or perhaps, with her dominions. He proceeded to court and made his love known to his royal mistress; she refused her hand, and he was soon after murdered through her instigation. As soon as his melancholy fate was known to his son Rustam, he collected a large army, and marched from Khurásán to Madain. The queen was unable to oppose him; and the young chief revenged his father by putting her to a cruel death. After her demise, Farrukhzád the son of Khusro Parweiz by a female singer of Isfahán was raised to the throne, but before he had reigned a month, his days were terminated by poison. Such were the events which immediately preceded the reign of Yezdijard III, and the fall of the Persian monarchy.

**Tauran Shah,** توران شاه, surnamed Mulik-ul-Muạzzim, was the brother of the famous Salah-uddín who had appointed him as his lieutenant in Damascus. He died at Alexandria on the 1st of July, 1180 A. D., 5th Ṣafar, 576 A. H.

**Tauran Shah, Khwaja,** خواجه توران شاه, surnamed Jalál-uddín, was wazír of Sháh Shujáạ ruler of Shíráz, and died on the 3rd of April, 1385 A. D.

**Tausi Maulana,** مولانا طوسي, apoet of Khurásán who flourished in the reign of Bábar Sulṭán, after whose death, he went over to Azurbeijan in the time of Jahán Sháh, and died there 1487 A. D., 892 A. H.

**Tauti Begam,** توتي بیگم, one of the wives of the emperor Akbar. She had built a garden in Ágrah called Tota Bágh; there is also a tank in Ágrah which is called Tota ka Tál.

**Tauti, Maulana,** مولانا طوطي ترشیزي of Tarshish, a learned Musalmán and a good poet. He flourished in the time of Bábar Sulṭán and died at Hirát in the year 1462 A. D., 866 A. H. As Tutí means in Persian a parrot, consequently Amír 'Alísheir found the year of his death to be contained in the word "Khurús," which means a cock.

**Taufik, Mulla,** ملا توفيق كشميري of Kashmír, a Persian poet.

**Tausani,** توسني, the poetical name of Manóhar Dás, who, though a Hindú, was also called Muhammad Manóhar and Mirzá Manóhar. He flourished in the reign of the emperor Akbar. The name of his father was Lónkaran (Salt Manufacturer). He was rája of Sambhar. *Vide* Ráe Lónkaran.

**Tawakkul bin-Isma'il bin-Haji Ardibeili,** توكل بن اسمعيل, author of the work entitled "Safwat-us-Safá," containing the history of the celebrated Shaikh Safí, the founder of the sect of Súfís in Persia, and from whom were descended the royal Safwí family, written in 1397 A. D., 800 A. H.

**Tawakkul Munshi,** توكل منشي, author of the work called "Sháhnáma" "Shamsher Khání," a prose abridgment of the celebrated Sháhnáma of Firdausí, written in 1652 A. D., 1062 A. H. A translation of this was again made in Urdú verse by a poet in the reign of the emperor Sháh Akbar II, 1810 A. D., 1225 A. H.

**Taya'** or **Tai Billah,** طايع بالله, a khalíf of Baghdád. *Vide* Al-Táya̤ Billáh.

**Tayyabi,** طيبي, author of the "Háshia Kashsháf," and "Sharah Mashkút-ul-Masábíh." He died in 1342 A. D., 743 A. H.

**Tazrawi,** تذروی, *vide* Tadrawí.

**Tegh Bahadur,** تيغ بهادر, a gúrú or chief of the Sikhs, who having collected his followers, levied contributions from the inhabitants of his neighbourhood, in conjunction with Háfiz 'Adam, a Musalmán devotee and his votaries, He was put to death as a dangerous heretic in the 17th year of the emperor 'A̕lamgír's reign, 1673 A. D., 1084 A. H. His body was divided into four parts and hung in the city.

**Tek Chand,** ٹیک چند, whose takhallus is Chánd, was the son of Balrám a Hindú of Sarhind. He is the author of the "Guldastae Ishḳ," Nosegay of Love, a Masnawí or poem containing the story of Kámrúp in Persian verse. He flourished in the time of 'A̕lamgír.

**Tek Chand, Munshi,** ٹیک چند, whose poetical title is Bahár, was a Hindú, by caste a Khattrí and author of a work entitled "Bahár Ajam," a voluminous dictionary of Persian idioms, and another called "Nawádir-ul-Masádir." The former work he completed in the year 1739 A. D., 1152 A. H. He also wrote another work called "Abtál Zarúrat."

**Thatta, rulers of,** ٹهٹ ٹهه. *Vide* Násir-uddín Ḳabbácha.

**Tippu Sahib,** ٹیپو صاحب, *vide* Ṭípú Sulṭán.

**Tipu Shah** or **Tippu,** ٹیپو شاه, a celebrated Muhammadan devotee of Arkaṭ, from whom the famous Ṭípú Sulṭán the sovereign of Mysore was named. His mausoleum still continues, a favourite resort of the pious, and Haidar 'Alí Khán the father of Ṭípú Sulṭán had a particular veneration for him. Típú or Tippú in the Canarese language signifies a tiger.

**Tipu** or **Tippu Sultan,** ٹیپو سلطان, the son of Haidar 'Alí Khán of Mysore. He was born in the year 1749, and succeeded his father in December, 1782 as ruler of Mysore. During the American war he joined the French against the English; but after the breaking out of the French revolution, he was alone exposed to the fortunes of the war. In 1790 he was defeated in Travancore, and yielding to the British arms, he consented, in 1792, to make peace with Lord Cornwallis by delivering up his two sons as hostages, and paying, besides part of his dominion, above three millions sterling. His intrigues with the French, and his machinations to destroy the English power, renewed the war in 1799. He was attacked by the British in his very capital, and was killed whilst bravely defending himself on the ramparts on the 4th of May, 1799 A. D., 28th Ẕil-Ḳa'da, 1213 A. H., aged 52 years He was buried in the mausoleum of his father in the garden named Lál Bágh. Ṭípú, though oppressive and capricious, patronized the arts, and his fondness for literature was displayed in the collection of books found in his palace, consisting of various works in the Sanskrit language of the 10th century, translations of the Ḳurán, MSS. of the history of the Mughal victories and historical memoirs of Hindústán, all which were deposited in the Library of Calcutta, and a catalogue of them was written by Captain Stewart and published. Ṭípú Sulṭán is the author of two books or collections of letters, one entitled "Farmán-ba-nám 'Alí Rájá," and the other "Fath-ul-Majáhidín," a part of the latter has been translated and published by Mr. B. Crisp of Bengal.

**Tirandaz Khan,** تيرانداز خان, a slave of the emperor Akbar Sháh the Great, was raised to high rank and received the title of Khán. He built his house on a spot of ground consisting of six bígas in A̕grah towards the south of the house of Islám Khán Rúmí. He was raised to the rank of 2000 and appointed governor of Aḥmadabád by the emperor Sháh Jahán.

**Tirmizi,** ترميزي, also called Hakím-al-Tirmizí. This was the title or surname of Abú 'Abdul áh Muhammad bin-'Alí, an author and philosopher of Tirmiz in Persia, who died in the year 869 A. D., 255 A. H.

**Todar Mal** or **Torar Mal,** ٹوڈر مل, the celebrated minister of Finance or Díwán of the emperor Akbar Sháh, was a Hindú of the tribe of Khattrí of Láhor. He was appointed Súbadár of Bengal in 1580 A. D., 988 A. H., and died at Láhor in the 36th year of the reign of that monarch, on Monday the 10th of November, 1589 A. D., 11th Muḥarram, 998 A. H. Abú'l Fazl describes him as entirely devoid of avarice and quite sincere, but of a malicious and vindictive temper, and so observant of the fasts and other superstitions of the Hindús, as to draw down on him reproof even from Akbar.

**Tufail,** طفيل, the name of 'Alí's nephew.

**Tughan Khan,** طغان خان, the Muhammadan governor of Bengal in 1243 A. D. He invaded the principality of Jaházpúr in Urysa, and was defeated by its rája, who pursued him into Gour, his metropolis; but reinforcements from Audh compelled the rája subsequently to retreat.

**Tughan Taimur Khan,** طغان تيمور خان, a descendant of the Mughal kings of Persia and ruler of Jurján. After the death of Sulṭán Abú Saíd and Arpa Khán, he conquered several provinces of Khurásán and subdued the Sarbadáls of that place. He was at last slain by Khwája Ahia Kiratí chief of the Sarbadáls on Saturday the 14th of December, 1353 A. D., 16th Zi Ka'da, 754 A. H.

**Tughan Shah I,** طغان شاه, a prince of the Saljúkian family whose seat of government was Naishápúr. This prince is said to have been defeated in his younger days, in a battle fought against Ibráhím bin-Nayál, who took him prisoner and blinded him. After some time his uncle Tughral Beg seized Ibráhím in 952 A. D., 451 A. H., murdered him, and restored the kingdom to his cousin Tughán Sháh. The poet Arzaḳí lived in his time and wrote several panegyrics in his praise.

**Tughan Shah II,** توگان شاه, a prince of the Saljúk dynasty, who ascended the throne of Persia after the death of Sulṭán Sanjar and after several battles was defeated and slain by Takash the Sulṭán of Khwarizm and died in 1185 A. D., 581 A. H.

**Tughlak,** تغلق, a slave of Sulṭán Ghayás-uddín Balban. His son, after murdering Khusro Sháh, ascended the throne of Dehlí and assumed the title of Ghayás-uddín Tughlaḳ in 1321 A. D.

**Tughlak Shah,** تغلق شاه, *vide* Ghayás-uddín Tughlaḳ Sháh and Muhammad Tughlaḳ Sháh.

**Tughrai, Mulla,** طغرئ ملا, an author who lived in the middle of the 11th century of the Hijrí.

**Tughrai,** طغرائي, surname of Hasan Abí Isma'íl of Isfahán, a celebrated wazír of the king of Mousal, Sulṭán Masaúd Saljúkí. He was called Tughráí on account of his excellence in the species of writing styled Tughrá, and also had the title of "Honors of Writers," but better known in Europe by his admired Arabic poem, entitled "Carmen Tughrai." Being taken prisoner in a battle where his sovereign was defeated by his brother Mahmúd 1120 A. D., 514 A. H., he was put to death by that prince's wazír who hated him for his great abilities. A collection of the poems of Tughráí has been made, the most celebrated of which is that called "Láma-ul-'Ajam."

**Tughrai,** طغرائي, title of Amír Yemín-uddín of Alashhad, a poet and author of the Kulliát Tughráe Mashhadí, a collection of poems, odes, elegies, &c. which also contains the following prose works, all of which are entertaining novels; *viz.:* "Mirat-ul-Maftúh," "Kanz-ul-Maání," "Majmúa-ul-Gharíb," "Chashmae Faiz," and "Anwár-ul-Mubárak." He died at a place called Fareomud in 1324 A. D., 724 A. H. There is an Insha supposed to have been written by him entitled "'Inshae Tughráí." He was cotemporary with the Tartar king of Persia Muhammad Khuda Banda and his son Abú Saíd.

**Tughral Beg,** طغرل بيک, (the Tangrolipix of the Greeks) was the son of Mikáíl the son of Saljúḳ, and the first Sulṭán of the race of the Saljúkides. Tughral Beg and his brother Jafar Beg Dáúd, were in the service of Sulṭán Mahmúd of Ghazní. After defeating Sulṭán Masaúd I son of Sulṭán Mahmúd in a battle fought in 1038 A. D., 429 A. H., he assumed the title and state of a sovereign at Naishápúr. He subdued 'Iráḳ, took Baghdád, and by its reduction, became master of the person of the Khalífa Al-Ḳáem Billáh, who invested him as Sulṭán of Khurásán, appointed him viceregent or vicar of the holy prophet, and the lord of all Muhammadans. He gave his sister in marriage to the khalíf, and his nephew Alp Arsalan afterwards married the daughter of the khalíf Al-Muktadí The Saljúḳ family divided into three branches and settled in Hamdan, Kirmán and Rúm or Anatolia. Tughral Beg died after a reign of 25 lunar years 1063 A. D., 455 A. H., aged 70 lunar years, and as he had no issue, he was succeeded by his nephew Sulṭán Alp Arsalán the son of Abú Jafar Dáúd. The following are the names of the Sulṭáns of the Saljúḳ dynasty of Irán or Persia:—

1. Tughral Beg the son of Mikáíl the son of Saljúḳ.
2. Alp Arsalán, nephew of Tughral Beg.
3. Malikshah the son of Alp Arsalán.
4. Barkayárak the son of Malikshah. In his reign the empire was divided, he retaining Persia; Muhammad his brother, Syria and Azarbaiján, and Sulṭán Sanjar, Khurásán and Máwarun-nahr.

**Tughral II,** طغرل, also called Tughral king (Sulṭán) of the race of Saljúḳ, was the son of Sulṭán Muhammad the son of Alp Arsalán. He was raised to the dignity of Sulṭán by his uncle Sulṭán Sanjar 1132 A. D., 525 A. H., after the death of his brother Sulṭán Mahmúd, and after a reign of three years died in October, 1134 A. D., Muharram, 529 A. H., aged 25 years. His brother Masaúd succeeded him.

**Tughral III,** طغرل, a Sulṭán of the Saljúkian family, was the son of Arsalán Sháh the son of Sulṭán Muhammad the brother of Sulṭán Sanjar. After the death of Sulṭán Sanjar, 1157 A. D., 552 A. H., Persia continued, for a period of forty years, to be distracted with the wars of different branches of the Saljúkian dynasty. The last who exercised power was Tughral III who succeeded his father Arsalán Sháh in January, 1176 A. D., Jumáda II, 571 A. H., and after a reign of ten years was seized and imprisoned by his uncle and wazír Ḳizal Arsalán, who resolved to usurp the throne, but fell by the hand of an assassin in 1191 A. D., 587 A. H., and the kingdom restored to Tughral. He was, however, after some years defeated in a battle, taken prisoner and executed by Takash ruler of Khwárizm, 1194 A. D., 590 A. H., and his head sent to Násir the khalífa of Baghdád. With this prince terminated the Saljúkiar monarchs of Persia, who had governed that country, from the commencement of his reign of Tughral I to the death of Tughral III, 158 years.

**Tughtazani,** تغتازاني, *vide* Tuftazání.

**Tokaji Holkar,** توکاجي حلکر, *vide* Takójí.

**Tuktamish Khan,** تقتمش خان, ruler of Dasht Kapchák whom Amír Taimúr defeated in 1395 A. D.

**Tulshi Bai,** تلشي بائ, the widow of Jaswant Rao Holkar, *vide* Jaswant Rao Holkar.

**Tulshi Das,** تلشي داش, a Bráhman and a celebrated poet among the Hindús. He is the author of the "Ramáyan" in the Bhákha dialect. He flourished in the reign of the emperors Akbar and Jahángír, was originally an inhabitant of Rájápúr near Chitarkót and Tarhuwán; but went about as an ascetic from one place to another, and died at Benares on the 24th of October, 1623 A. D. In the Bhákhá or pure Hindí, there are still extant many elegant poems, songs, &c., the productions of Hindui poets, *viz.*, Kab Gang, Tulshí, Bihárí, Girdhar, Lálach, Súrdás, Kabír, Náuhak, and to these we may add the names of Malik Muhammad Jáyesí, Ahmad Wahab, Muhammad Afzal, Amír Khán, &c., as they composed in both dialects. Girdhar Dás is the author of another Ramáyan. *Vide* Girdhar Dás.

**Turkan Khatun,** ترکان خاتون, a daughter of Sulṭán Jalál-uddín of Khwárizm. She was given in marriage by Halákú Khán, to Malik Sháh son of Badr-uddín Lúlú, prince of Mausal.

**Turkan Khatun,** ترکان خاتون, wife of Sulṭán Jalál-uddín Malikshâh.

**Turkman,** ترکمان, the poetical name of a person whose father was a native of Shíráz, but he was born in India, and was living about the year 1690 A. D., 1102 A. H.

**Turtush,** ترتش, a brother of Malikshâh the Saljúkian, against whom he rebelled and was compelled to save himself by leaving the kingdom. This appears to be the same person called by Ibn-Khallikán, Tutush the son of Alp Arsalán, who took prisoner Atsiz a Sulṭán of Khwarizm and put him to death on the 21st October, 1078 A. D., 11th Rabí' II, 471 A. H. Turtush was slain in a battle fought against his nephew Barkayarak̤ on Sunday the 25th February, 1095 A. D., 17th Ṣafar, 488 A. H., aged 30 years.

**Tutash,** تتش, *vide* Turtush.

# U

**'Ubeid or 'Ubeid,** عبید, a poet who lived in the time of Sulṭán Ghayás-uddín Tughlak̤ Sháh, and was buried alive on account of his having raised a false report that the king was dead, and that a great revolution had taken place at Dehlí. This event took place in the second year of the king's reign, 1322 A. D., 722 A. H.

**'Ubeid Khan,** عبید خان, ruler of the Uzbaks, was contemporary with Sháh Tahmásp I Safwí king of Persia, who in a battle defeated his troops and gave them a signal overthrow in 1527 A. D., 935 A. H.

**'Ubeid-ullah,** عبید الهٰ, sovereign of the Uzbaks. This monarch was the nephew of the celebrated Sháhí Beg Khán, the conqueror. He commenced his reign about the year 1542 A. D., 949 A. H.

**'Ubeid-ullah Ahrar Nakshband,** عبید الهٰ احرار نقشبند, a celebrated learned Musalmán and saint of Khurásán, among the number of whose disciples Maulwí Jámí was one. He died in the month of February, 1491 A. D., Rabí' II, 896 A. H., and is buried at Samark̤and. Amír Alísher, the celebrated wazír of Sulṭán Husain Mirzá, who much respected him, found the chronogram of the year of his death in the words "Khuld Barín."

**'Ubeid-ullah bin-Masa'ud,** عبید الهٰ بن مسعود, author of a Commentary on the Wik̤áya a work on juris prudence, entitled "Sharh Wik̤áya." He is also the author of the "Nikáya" which is sometimes called "Mukhtasir-al-Wik̤áya," being in fact, an abridgment of that work. 'Ubeid-ullah died 1349 A. D., 750 A. H. See Mahmúd surnamed Burhán-ash-Shariát.

**'Ubeid-ullah ibn-Ḳais (or Qais),** عبید الله ابن قیس, a distinguished Arabian poet, who commemorated the death of Misaa'b the son of Zubeir, who was on terms of friendship with him, and had fought in his cause in the year 690 A. D., 71 A. H.

**'Ubeid-ullah ibn-Zayad,** عبید الهٰ ابن زیاد, was appointed governor of Kúfa by the khalíf Yezíd in the room of Al-Naṃán 679 A. D., 60 A. H. He beheaded Muslim, Husain's cousin, and his troops surrounded Husain at Karbala, who having desperately engaged his troops, was after long resistance cut to pieces with all his men in October, 680 A. D., Muḥarram, 61 A. H. In the reign of 'Abdulmalik, 'Ubeid-ullah was sent to Kúfa with leave to plunder it for three days; but before he reached that city, Al-Mukhtár, then ruler of that place, sent his forces against him under the command of Ibráhím the son of Alashtar, when after a sharp engagement, 'Ubeid-ulláh's forces were beaten and himself killed in the camp. Ibráhím having cut off his head, sent it to Al-Makhtár, and burnt his body. This circumstance took place in August 686 A. D., Muḥarram, 67 A. H.

**'Ubeid-ullah-al-Mahdi,** عبید الله المهدي, a chief of Barbary in Africa, who in 910 A. D., 298 A. H., rebelled against the king of that country of the race of Aghlab, and assumed the title of Khalíf of Ḳairwán (the ancient Cyrene, and residence of the Aghlabite princes). To give the greater weight to his pretensions, he also took the surname of Al-Mahdí, the director. According to some, also, he pretended to be descended in a right line from 'Alí the son of Abú Tálib, and Fátima the daughter of Muhammad; for which reason, the Arabs called him and his descendants Fatimites. He likewise encouraged himself and his followers by a traditional prophecy of Muhammad, that at the end of 300 years the sun should rise out of the West. Having at length driven the Aghlabites into Egypt, where they became known by the name of Maghrabians, he extended his dominions in Africa and Sicily, making Kairwán the place of his residence. He sent several of his generals at different times to conquer Egypt, but they were always defeated and obliged to fly to Ḳairwán. Al-Mahdí reigned in Barbary 24 years, and was succeeded by his son Abul Ḳásim, who then took the surname of Al-Ḳáyem Mahdí.

**'Ubeid Zakani,** عبید زاکاني, a celebrated jester and poet, was contemporary with the poet Salmán Sáwají. He composed several ludicrous verses on Jahán Khátún the wife of Khwája Amín-uddín, wazír of Sháh Abú Is-hák̤ ruler of Shíráz. He is the author of the work called "Risála dar ilm Bayán," which he dedicated to the king, and also of a Díwán. He died in 1370 A. D., 772 A. H.

**Udaipuri Begam,** اودیپوري بیگم, the favourite wife of the emperor 'Álamgír, and the mother of the prince Kámbakhsh whom his father cherished with the utmost tenderness, as the son of his old age. She was living in 1686 A. D. She is believed to have been a Sisodia from Jodhpur.

**Udai Singh,** رانا اودي سنگه, Ráná of Chittor was the son of Ráná Sanka the emperor Babar's competitor, but a man of feeble character. In his time the fort of Chittor was taken by the emperor Akbar in March, 1568 A. D., Shaban, 975 A. H. His son Ráná Partáp founded the new capital called Udaipúr, which is still occupied by his descendants. Ráná Partáp Singh died 1595 A. D., 1004 A. H., and Amar Singh his son succeeded him and died in the 14th year of Jahángír, 1620 A. D., 1029 A. H.

**Udai Singh Rathouri,** اودي سنگه راتهوري, commonly called Moṭa Rája. was the son of Ráe Máldeo of Jódhpúr Máṛwár. He served under the emperor Akbar, and in the year 1586 A. D., 994 A. H., gave his daughter named Bálmatí in marriage to Sulṭán Salím (afterwards Jahángír) by whom he had Sháh Jahán. He was raised to high rank, and Jódhpúr his native country given him in jágír. He died 1594 A. D., 1002 A. H., and four of his wives burned themselves with his corpse. After his death his son Súraj Singh succeeded him.

**Ugarsen,** اوگرسین راجه, a rája who is said to have reigned at Ágrah several centuries before the time of

Sulṭán Sikandar Lodí. After him Ágrah became a village of Bayana, the name of the rája of which place was Bín.

**Ulfati,** الفتي, poetical name of Ḳulich Khán of Andján, which see.

**Ulagh Beg Mirza** or **Ulugh Beg,** الغ بيغ مرزا, a prince celebrated for his knowledge in Astronomy, was the son of Mirzá Sháhrukh the son of Amír Taimúr. He reigned at Samarḳand for 40 years during the lifetime of his father whom he succeeded in March, 1447 A. D., 851 A. H. He was a prince who made peaceful studies the chief object of his life, and had entirely neglected the art of war. He assembled all the astronomers of his kingdom, and the celebrated Tables which are known by his name, *viz.*, "Zíj Ulagh Beg" were the result of his labours. He is said to have had very large instruments for making his observations; particularly a quadrant as high as the church of Santa Sophia at Constantinople, which is 180 Roman feet. His fate was cruel, he was defeated, taken prisoner, and put to death by his son Mirzá 'Abdul Latíf on the 27th of October, 1449 A. D., Ramaẓán, 853 A. H. It is a consolation to know that this unnatural prince enjoyed the power he had attained, by so monstrous a crime, only for the short space of six months: he was slain by his own soldiers. Ulagh Beg's Catalogue of fixed stars rectified for 1434 A. D., was published by Hyde at Oxford in 1665 in 4to. with learned notes.

**'Umar-al-Maksus,** عمر المكوس, the favourite master of the khalíf Mu'áwia II, who after his father's death consulted him whether he ought, or not, to accept the khiláfat. His master told him, that if he thought himself able to administer justice duly to the Musalmáns, he ought to accept it; but otherwise he ought not to charge himself with it. This khalíf had scarcely reigned six weeks, when he found himself two weak to sustain the weight of the government, and resolved to lay it down. This he did, and had no sooner renounced the khiláfat, but he shut himself up in a chamber from whence he never stirred till he died, not long after his abdication, of the plague, according to some, and according to others of poison. The family of Umayya was so greatly irritated at his proceedings, that they vented their resentment upon the person of 'Umar-al-Maksús, whom they buried alive, because they supposed that it was by his advice that Mu'áwia deposed himself. This circumstance took place in the year 683 A. D., 64 A. H.

**'Umar bin-'Abdul Aziz,** عمر بن عبد العزيز, grandson of Marwán I, was the ninth khalíf of the house of Umayya. He succeeded Sulaimán at Damascus in September or October, 717 A. D., 99 A. H., and died after a reign of two years and some months in February, 720 A. D., 101 A. H., at Dyr Samán. He was succeeded by Yezíd II. This khalíf ('Umar 'Abdul Azíz) was eminent above all others for temperance and self-denial, insomuch, that according to the Muhammadan faith, he was raised to Muhammad's bosom, as a reward for his abstinence in an age of corruption.

**'Umar bin-'Abdul Aziz,** عمر بن عبد العزيز, was an eminent Musalmán who died in the year 742 A. D., 124 A. H.

**'Umar bin-'Abdul Aziz bin-Maja,** عمر بن عبدالعزيز بن ماجه, commonly called Husám-ush-Shahíd, author of a most esteemed Commentary. He was killed 1141 A. D., 536 A. H. *Vide* Abú Bakr Aḥmad bin-'Umar-al-Khassáf.

**'Umar bin-'Abdullah,** عمر بن عبدالله, a famous Arabian poet who flourished in the time of the khalíf 'Abdulmalik. *Vide* Jamíl.

**'Umar bin-Khattab,** عمر بن خطاب, one of the favourite companions and father-in-law of Muhammad. He succeeded Abú Bakr Sadíḳ as second khalífa after Muhammad in August, 634 A. D., Jumáda II, 13 A. H. He spread his conquests over Syria and Phœnicia, and took Jerusalem after an obstinate siege in 637 A. D., 16 A. H. His generals extended his conquests over Persia and Egypt and increased the worshippers of Muhammad. The fall of Alexandria under his power was marked by the destruction of its celebrated library, but he restored the canal between the Nile and the Red Sea. During his reign the Muhammadans conquered 36,000 towns, destroyed, 4,000 Christian temples, and built 1,400 mosques. He was the first who was called "Amír-ul-Momínín" or the Lord of the Believers, and this title was ever afterwards used by all succeeding khalífs. He was married seven times, and one of his wives was Umm Kulsúm the daughter of 'Alí. He was stabbed on Wednesday the 3rd of November, 644 A. D., 25th Ẕilḥijja, 23 A. H., by a Persian slave named Fíróz whilst saying his morning prayers in a mosque, and died three days after, aged 63 lunar years. He reigned 10 years 6 months and 8 days, and was succeeded in the khiláfat by 'Usmán the son of 'Affán. Waring in his "*Tour to Shíráz*," mentions that while he was at Shíráz (1802 A. D.,) the Persians (who are Shias) celebrated the death of the khalíf 'Umar. "They erected a large platform, on which they fixed an image, disfigured and deformed as much as possible. Addressing themselves to the image, they began to revile it for having supplanted 'Alí the lawful successor of Muhammad; at length having exhausted all their expressions of abuse, they suddenly attacked the image with stones and sticks, until they had shattered it into pieces. The inside was hollow, and full of sweetmeats, which were greedily devoured by the mob who attended the ceremony."

**'Umar Khan Khilji,** عمر خان خلجي, the youngest son of Sulṭán 'Alá-uddín Khiljí a boy of seven years of age, was raised to the throne of Dehlí after the death of his father, by Malik Káfúr the eunuch, in December, 1316 A. D., Shawwál, 716 A. H. Malik Káfúr was assassinated after 35 days and soon after 'Umar Khán was deposed by his brother Mubarak Khán who ascended the throne in January, 1317 A. D., 716 A. H.

**'Umar Khayam,** عمر خيام. He was originally a tent-maker and hence his *takhallus* of Khayám. He is held to be one of the most remarkable of Persian poets, unprecedented in regard to the freedom of his religious opinion. The Voltaire of Persia, his works gave great offence to the priests, but are, nevertheless, highly esteemed by general readers, apparently with justice, as the animation and brilliancy of his style are unquestionable. His hatred of hypocrisy and the tricks of false devotees, appears his crime in the eyes of the supposed pious; his tolerance of other creeds was looked upon with equal suspicion and dislike. He was born at Naishapúr, and devoted much of his time to the study of astronomy, of which science he was a distinguished professor; but it is said that, instead of his studies leading him to the acknowledgment of the Supreme Being, it prompted his disbelief. The result of his reflections on this important subject is given in a poem of his, much celebrated under the title of "Rubáyát 'Umar Khayám." He was the friend of Hasan Sabbáh, the founder of the sect of the Assassins, and, it has been conjectured, assisted him in the establishment of his diabolical doctrine and fellowship. Some allowance must, however, be made for the prejudices of his historians, who would, of course, neglect nothing calculated to cast odium on one so inimical to their superstitions. 'Umar Khayám seems particularly to direct his satire against the mysticism of Mawásí, the most exalted poet of his time, though inferior in this extraordinary and incomprehensible style to the later followers of the same school, Attár and the great Mulla. However reprehensible his mockery would be if really directed against religion in general, it scarcely deserves the severity it met with, when we consider that it was the abuses he attacked and the absurdities he ridiculed; and as for the incongruities introduced into his poems, and his professed love of pleasure, he is only following or rather pointing out as absurd, the contradictions of the mystic poets, which are difficult enough to reconcile to the understanding, whether allegorical or not. The following will give an idea of the style of 'Umar Khayám :

"Ah! ye who long that, in time's coming night
Your names should shine in characters of light,
Let not this duty ever be forgot;—
Love well your neighbour; do him no despite."

"Ah! strive your best no human heart to wring,
Let no one feel your anger burn or sting;
Would you be wrapped in everlasting joy,
Learn how to suffer, and cause no suffering."

Some English versions of the Quatrains by Mr. Edward Fitzgerald have been published by Quaritch of London. 'Umar Khayám was contemporaneous with Hasan Sabbah, Nizám-ul-Mulk wazír of Malikshâh, and Mawásí the poet. Khushgo in his Tazkira has recorded the year of 'Umar Khayám's death 1123 A. D., 517 A. H., and this appears to be correct. Wajid 'Alí in his Matla-ul-Ulúm says that he died in 1121 A. D., 515 A. H.

**'Umar Mahrami,** عمرمهرامي, author of a work called "Hujjat-ul-Hind," written in 1645 A. D.

**'Umar Mirza,** عمرمرزا, one of the sons of Míránshâh the son of Amír Taimúr. He was defeated and wounded in a battle fought against Sháhrukh Mirzá and died after a few days in May, 1407 A. D., 809 A. H.

**'Umar Sahlan (Kazi Mir) Sawaji,** سهلان ساوجي قاضي عمر, author of a work on the science of Logic and Philosophy called "Masábir Nasírí," which he dedicated to Nasír-uddín Mahmúd the wazír of Sultán Sanjar.

**'Umar Shaikh Mirza,** عمرشيخ مرزا, second son of Amír Taimúr. He was governor of Persia during the lifetime of his father, and was killed in battle in 1394 A. D., 799 A. H, aged 40 years. Báikara Mirzá who succeeded him was one of his sons.

**'Umar Shaikh Mirza,** عمرشيخ مرزا, one of the eleven sons of Sultán Abú Saíd Mirzá, the son of Sultán Muhammad, the son of Míránsháh, the son of Amír Taimúr. He was the father of Bábar Sháh king of Dehlí; born at Samarkand in the year 1456 A. D., 860 A. H., and held the government of Andiján during the lifetime of his father which, with the united principality of Farghána, he continued to govern after his death which took place in 1469 A. D., 873 A. H. He died after a reign of 26 lunar years and 2 months on Monday the 9th of June, 1494 A. D., 4th Ramazán, 899 A. H. by the fall of a scaffold upon which he stood to see his pigeons flying; aged 39 lunar years. His son Bábar, then in his eleventh year, was advanced to the throne by his nobles and assumed the title of Zahír-uddín.

**'Umdat-ul-Mulk,** عمدت الملک, a title of Nawáb Amír Khán.

**'Umdat-ul-Umra,** عمدة الامرا, the eldest son of Muhammad 'Alí Khán the Nawáb of the Karnátik. He succeeded his father in October, 1795 A. D., and died on the 15th July, 1801 A. D., on his death the English resolved to take the functions of government into their own hands. 'Alí Husain, the next heir, refused to comply. The English in consequence, raised 'Azim-uddaula, the nephew of the deceased Nawáb, to the nominal throne, on condition of his renouncing the powers of government in their favour.

**Umm Habiba,** ام حبيبه, one of the wives of Muhammad. She was the daughter of Abú Sufián the father of Mu'áwia I, and died in 664 A. D., 44 A. H.

**Umm Habiba,** ام حبيبه, daughter of Rabia and fourth wife of 'Alí, by whom she had one son named 'Umar.

**Umm Hanna,** ام حنى, a daughter of Abú Tálib and sister of 'Alí the son-in-law of Muhammad.

**Umm Jamil,** ام جميل, daughter of Harb, sister of Abú Sufián and wife of Abú Lahab. Because she fomented the hatred which her husband bore to Muhammad, the passage in the Kurán, Ch. CXI was revealed against them.

**Umm Makri,** ام مقري, one of the principal Muhammadan saints. born at Ghazní; who acquired such great reputation by his sanctity, that Sultán Mahmúd often went to consult him, and refused to sit down in his presence, out of respect to his virtues. He lived about the year 1000 A. D.

**Umm Salma,** ام سلمه, daughter of Abú Umayya and wife of Muhammad. She outlived all the wives of that prophet and died in 679 A. D., 59 A. H.

**Umyd,** اميد, the poetical name of Mirzá Muhammad Raza, whose title was Kizalbásh Khán, which see.

**Umydi, Maulana,** مولانا اميدي, one of the best poets of his time, born at Tehrán a province of Rei. Najm Sání, Mír 'Abdul Bákí and Khwája Habíb-ulláh who were nobles in the service of Sháh Ismaíl Safwí, were his intimate friends; but Sháh Kawám-uddín Núr Bakhshí who was also one of the courtiers, and was his enemy, murdered him one night in the year 1519 A. D., 925 A. H.

**Ung** or **Ang,** انک, which see.

**Uns,** أنس, poetical name of Munshí Lálchánd, *vide* Lálchánd.

**'Unsari,** عنصري, commonly called Abú'l Kásim 'Unsarí, a native of Balkh and one of the learned men who lived at the court of Sultán Mahmúd of Ghazní. He was a pupil of Abú'l Farah Sanjarí and master of the poets Asjadí and Farrukhí. He is esteemed to hold the first rank, as to genius, in that age; for besides being one of the best poets, he was a great philosopher, versed in all the known sciences, and all the learned languages of those times. Four hundred poets and learned men, besides all the students of the university of Ghazní acknowledged him for their master. Among the works of 'Unsarí there is an heroic poem upon the actions of Sultán Mahmúd. The king one night in a debauch having cut off the long tresses of his favourite slave, Ayaz, was much concerned in the morning for what he had done. 'Unsarí accosted him with some extempore lines on the occasion, which so pleased the king that he ordered his mouth to be thrice filled with jewels. He wrote a Díwán consisting of 30,000 couplets, and died according to Daulat Sháh, in the reign of Sulṭán Masaúd I the son of Sulṭán Mahmúd 1040 A. D., 431 A. H. Dr. Sprenger in his Catalogue of Persian Books, says, p. 15, "that 'Unsarí died in 1049 A. D., 441 A. H."

**Unsi,** انسي, a poet, whose proper name was Muhammad Sháh. He died in 1565 A. D., 973 A. H.

**'Uqail,** عقيل, the brother of 'Alí the son of 'Abú Tálib, who not being entertained by his brother according to his quality joined Mu'áwia 660 A. D., 40 A. H., who received him with open arms, and assigned him large revenues. His son Muslim, who espoused the cause of his uncle Husain, was beheaded by 'Ubeid-ullah ibn-Zayád in the reign of Yezíd.

**'Urfi, Maulana,** مولانا عرفي, a native of Shíráz and an excellent poet. His proper name is Jamál-uddín, but he is better known by his poetical title 'Urfí. He first came to the Dakhin, and thence to Agrah where he passed a few years in the service of Hakím Abú'l Fatha Gílání, after whose death in 1589 A. D., 997 A. H., 'Abdul Rahím Khán, KhánKhánán introduced him to the emperor Akbar who finding him to be a well learned man, and a good poet, employed him among his own officers. Not long after he died in the year 1591 A D., 999 A. H., aged 36 years at Láhor where he was buried; but as he had expressed his wish in one of his odes that his remains should be transported to Najaf Ashraf where 'Alí is buried, his bones were accordingly after some years sent to that place by Mír Sábir Isfahání and re-interred there. He is the author of several works, of which his Díwán and Kasáed are most-esteemed, and were, even during his lifetime, very popular and sold in every street.

**'Urian,** عريان, poetical name of Mirzá Asad.

**'Uskalani,** عسقلاني, an author, *vide* Shaháb-uddín Abú'l Fazl Aḥmad.

**'Usman, Osman** or **Othman,** عثمان, the first Sulṭán of the Turks, was the son of Amír Tughral who died in 1288 A. D., 687 A. H. His grandfather Sulaimán was a native of Balkh which country he left on the invasion of Changez Khán in 1214 A. D., 611 A. H., and went to Rome where he was drowned. 'Usmán served under Sulṭán 'Alá-uddín Kaikubad one of the Saljúkian Sulṭáns of Iconium in Karamania; had received a grant of land in the direction of ancient Phrygia, where he took Brusa from the Greek emperor, and laid the foundation of that power called after him Ottoman or 'Usmania and on the destruction of the Sulṭánate of Iconium in 1299 by the Mongols, succeeded in obtaining possession of a portion of Bithynia. According to the work "Haft Aklím," the first year of his reign is fixed 1289 A. D., 688 A. H., and that he reigned 38 lunar years and died in 1327 A. D., 727 A. H., and was buried at Brusa. His son Orkhán succeeded him.

*List of the Emperors of Turkey of the 'Usmán or Ottoman family.*

'Usmán or Osmán.
Orkhán son of 'Usmán.
Murád I son of Orkhán.
Báyezíd I son of Murád.
Sulaimán son of Báyezíd.
Muhammad I son of Báyezíd.
Murád II son of Muhammad.
Muhammad II son of Murád.
Báyezíd II son of Muhammad II.
Salím I son of Báyezíd.
Sulaimán I surnamed the Magnificent, son of Salím.
Salím II son of Sulaimán.
Murád III son of Salím II.
Muhammad III son of Murád III.
Aḥmad I son of Murád III.
Mustapha I son of Murád III.
'Usmán I son of Aḥmad I.
Murád IV son of Aḥmad I.
Ibráhím son of Aḥmad I.
Muhammad IV son of Ibráhím.
Sulaimán II son of Ibráhím.
Aḥmad II son of Ibráhím.
Mustafa II son of Muhammad IV.
Aḥmad III son of Muhammad.
Mahmúd I son of Mustafá II.
'Usmán II son of Mustafá II.
Mustafá III son of Aḥmad III.
Aḥmad IV son of Aḥmad III.
Salím III son of Mustafá III.
Mustafá IV son of Aḥmad IV.
Mahmúd II son of Aḥmad IV.
Abdul Majíd son of Mahmúd II.
Abdul Aziz son of Mahmud II

**Usman, Osman** or **Othman I,** عثمان, son of Aḥmad I, (Achmet) succeeded his uncle, Mustafá I (who was deposed in 1618) on the Turkish throne, and being unsuccessful in his wars against Poland in 1621, was by the Jannisárís slain in an uproar 1622 A. D., and Mustafá again restored; but this he enjoyed not long, for the same hand that raised him to the throne, again plucked him down in 1623, and raised Murád IV to be their king.

**'Usman II,** عثمان, brother of Mahmúd I (or as some call him Muhammad V) whom he succeeded to the throne as emperor of Constantinople in 1754 A. D., 1168 A. H. He renewed, under severe penalties, the Muhammadan law, that his subjects should drink no wine. He died after a short reign in 1757 A. D., 1171 A H., aged 59 years, and was succeeded by Mustafá III his nephew.

**'Usman,** عثمان بن عفان, the son of 'Affán, the son of 'Abú'l 'As the son of Umayya, was one of the favourite companions of Muhammad. He succeeded 'Umar as third Khalíf after Muhammad, in November 644 A. D., Muḥarram, 24 A H., and was murdered after a reign of nearly twelve years in his own house at Medina by Muhammad the son of Abú Bakr, Ammar ibn-Yasar and several others on the 30th June, 655 A. D., 18th Zil-ḥijja, 35 A. H., aged 82 years. His corpse lay unburied for three days; at last it was removed bloody at it was, and buried in the same clothes he was killed in, without so much as being washed, and without the least funeral solemnity. The dissensions which arose on the death of the Prophet, with regard to the succession to the Khiláfat, were revived with renewed fury when, on the murder of 'Usmán, the noble and unfortunate 'Alí succeeded to the dignity of Amír-ul-Mominín; and they eventually caused the division of Islám into two great parties or sects, called respectively the Sunnís, and the Shias who differ materially in the interpretation of the Ḳurán, and in admitting or rejecting various portions of the oral law. The hatred entertained between these rival sects has been the cause of constant religious wars and persecutions scarcely to be surpassed in the history of any nation or creed, and still separate the followers of Muhammad into two classes, by a barrier more insurmountable than that which divides the Roman Catholic from the Protestant.

**'Usman bin-Isa bin-Ibrahim Sadik,** عثمان بن عيسى, author of a collection of traditions in Arabic called "Gháet-ut-Touzíh."

**'Usman Mukhtari,** عثمان مختاري, a poet who flourished in the reign of Sultán Ibráhím of Ghazní and was a cotemporary of Sheikh Sanáí the poet.

**'Utba,** عتبة, the son of Abú Lahab. He was married to Rukyya third daughter of Muhammad, but repudiated her afterwards. It is said that he was torn to pieces by a lion in the presence of a whole caravan when on a journey to Syria.

**'Uzaeri Razi,** عضايري رازي, one of the learned men and poet of the court of Sultán Mahmúd of Ghazní, whose poetical performance as a panegyrist are esteemed very good, for one of which he received a present of 4000 dirhams from the Sultán. He is called Assaberi Rázi, in the Dictionary of the Religious Ceremonies of the Eastern nations. He was a native of Rei, consequently the word Rází is fixed to his name.

**Uzbak,** اذبك, atribe of Turks.

**Uzlat,** عذلت, the poetical name of Sayyad 'Abdul Walí, the son of a very learned and pious man named Sadulláh in whom Aurangzeib had very great confidence. After the death of his father, he went down to Murshidábád and was supported by Alahwardí Khán. After the demise of his patron in 1756, he went to the Dakhin where he died and left a Díwán.

**Uzzan Hasan,** أذن حسن, (or Hasan the Long) who is also called Hasan Beg, was the founder of the tribe of Turkmans called 'Akkoinlos, or the White Sheep. After he had extirpated his rival Jahán Sháh the son of Kará Yúsaf in 1467 A. D. and put all his relations to death, he engaged in a war with Sultán Abú Saíd Mirzá king of Persia who fell into his hands and was slain 1449 A. D., Uzzan Hasan from this event, became sovereign of a great part of the dominions of the house of Taimúr. After he had made himself master of Persia, he turned his arms in the direction of Turkey: but his career of greatness was arrested by the superior genius of the Turkish emperor, Muhammad II, from whom he suffered a signal defeat, which terminated his schemes of ambition. He died after a reign of eleven years at the age of seventy on the 7th of December, 1477 A. D., 882 A. H. Catherine Commenus, who is called by the Persians Carum Commoniah, was married to him. She had a daughter named Martha, married to Shaikh Haidar, father of Sháh Ismaíl Safwí, first monarch of the Safwian dynasty of Persia. Uzzan Hasan was succeeded by his son Yakúb Beg.

# V.

**Victoria Gaurama, Princess,** وكٹعديا گاوراما.

The Princess Victoria Gouráma is daughter of his Highness Prince Bír Rájindar Wadér, ex-rájá of Kurg (Coorg) a small principality of Hindustán, situated near the Mysore country; its greatest length is about seventy miles, and the mean breadth about twenty-two miles. Haidar 'Alí contrived in the middle of the last century, to get possession of Kurg by treachery; but in 1787 the young rájá, Bír Rájindar, his prisoner, escaped from confinement through the aid of several of his subjects and succeeded in establishing himself in his dominions. At his death, in 1808, he left the succession to an infant daughter, to the exclusion of his brother, to whom of right it belonged according to ancient usages; but the young princess soon after abdicated in favor of her uncle, with the sanction of the British Government.

The Princess Victoria Gauráma was born in February 1841. The melancholy circumstance of the death of the mother, two days after the birth of the child, seems to have led to increased affection for his offspring on the part of the father, who from his own previous convictions in favor of Christianity, determined that his favorite daughter should be brought up in the principles of the Christian faith. From this period the ex-rájá entertained an anxious desire to visit Europe, in order that, when she had arrived at a suitable age, she might be introduced into European society; and thereby receive such impressions as would promote a feeling favourable to Christianity. Accordingly in the early part of 1852, the prince quitted India for England, leaving at the city of Benares the rest of his family, consisting of eleven children, with their mothers. On his arrival in England the object of his visit was made known to the Queen, who at once most kindly and graciously consented to become sponser to the young princess. The baptismal ceremony was performed by the Archbishop of Canterbury in the private chapel of Buckingham Palace on 30th June, 1852, in the presence of Her Majesty, the Prince Consort, and numerous other members of the royal family: the princess received the prefix of "Victoria" to her Indian name of "Gauráma," by which she had been called after one of the pagan divinities of her country.

The princess is said to have become a good scholar under the care of these charged with her education. Her personal appearance was exceedingly interesting and intelligent, and the complexion of her skin but little darker than that what Europeans call a deep brunette. Her portrait, which Winterhalter painted by command of Her Majesty, is at Buckingham Palace.—*The Art Journal*, Vol. III, p. 293.

**Vikramaditya,** بيكرا ماديتيا, commonly called Bikramájít, which see.

# W.

**Wa'il Khuzai',** واعل خزاعي, an Arabian poet who lived in the time of Harún-al-Rashíd and his son Mamúh. He was cotemporary with Imám 'Alí Músí Raza, and is the author of a Díwán in Arabic wherein he praises the charms of his beloved Salmí.

**Waez,** واعظ, *vide* Husain Wáez, and Muhammad Rafí Wáez.

**Wafa,** وفا, *vide* Ayn-ul-Mulk Hakím.

**Wafa,** وفا, poetical name of Mirzá Sharaf-uddín 'Alí Husainí of Kumm. He came to India in 1749 A. D., 1162 A. H., and is the author of a short Díwán.

**Wafa,** وفا, poetical name of Dayánáth a Kashmírí of Barelí. He is the author of a poem called "Gul wa Bulbul" the Nightingale and the Rose, which he composed in 1847 A. D., 1263 A. H.

**Wafai,** وفاى, title of a poet.

**Wahab or Wahhab,** وهاب, the son of 'Abdul Manáf, was the father of 'Amina the mother of Muhammad.

**Wahdat,** وحدت, poetical name of Shaikh Jamál-uddín the great-grandfather of Shaikh Muhammad Hazín. He is the author of several works, *viz.*, "Elucidation of the miracle of the Moráj, or Ascent of the prophet;" "An Explanation or Commentary in Persian on the Kulliát of the Ḳánún," which he wrote at the desire of Khán Aḥmad Khán, king of Gílán. "An Epistle or Treatise on the confirmation of a Necessary Being;" "A Treatise on the Solution of Obscurities in the Section of Surds or Solids;" an extensive "Commentary on the Fisús or Gems of Faryábí," and a Díwán containing 2,000 couplets.

**Wahdat,** وحدت, poetical name of 'Abdul Ahad, who was familiarly called Sháh Gul, a son of Shaikh Muhammad Saíd and grandson of Shaikh Aḥmad Sarhindí. He resided mostly in the Kóṭila near Dehlí and is the author of a Díwán. He died in 1714 A. D., 1126 A. H.

**Wahid,** واحد, *vide* Tahir Wahíd.

**Wahidi,** وحيدي, poetical title of Wahíd-uddín, which see.

**Wahid-uddin Tabreizi,** وحيدالدين تبريزي, a poet of Persia whose poetical title is Wahídí. He is the author of a treatise written professedly upon versification.

**Wahidi,** واحدي, poetical name of 'Alí son of Aḥmad, which see.

**Wahmi,** وهمي, poetical appellation of Hájí Tahmásp Ḳulí, a poet who flourished in India between the years 1637 and 1647 A. D., 1047 and 1057 A. H.

**Wahshat,** وحشت, poetical title of Shaikh 'Abdul Wáhid who was a descendant of Imám Muhammad Ghazzálí. He was an excellent poet born and brought up in Ḳasba Thánesar. He flourished in the reign of 'Alamgír, and is the author of a Díwán.

**Wahshi Yezdi, Maulana of Yezd,** وحشي يزدي مولانا, author of the Masnawí or poem called "Názir wa Manzúr" which he completed in the year 1559 A. D., 966 A. H., and of another poem called Farhad and Shírín in the metre of Nizamei's Khusro and Shírín and several other works. He died in 1584 A. D., 992 A. H.

**Wajih-uddin Ahmad Maghrabi,** وجيه الدين احمد مغربي, commonly called Shaikh Aḥmad Khaṭṭú, which see.

**Wajih-uddin Mubarak Kirmani,** وجيه الدين مبارک كرماني, a Sayyad and a disciple of Nizám-uddín Aulia. He was commonly called Sayyad Khúrd or the little Sayyad. He is the author of the work called Siar-ul-Aulia." See Sayyad Husain (Makhdúm).

**Wajih-uddin, Shaikh,** شيخ وجيه الدين, of Gujrát, a disciple of Shaikh Muhammad Ghaus of Gwáliar. He was a learned man, is the author of several works, and his poetical name was Alwí. He died on the 30th of November, 1589 A. D., 1st Ṣafar, 998 A. H., and was buried in Aḥmadabád Gujrát.

**Wajid 'Ali,** واجد علي, author of an Urdú Grammar entitled "Guldastae Anjuman" which he wrote and published at Agrah in the year 1849 A. D., and another work called "Matlạ-ul-Ulúm."

**Wajid 'Ali Shah,** واجد علي شاه, the last king of Audh was the son of 'Amjad 'Alí Sháh, after whose death he ascended the throne at Lakhnau, in 1847 A. D., 1263 A. H. In his time Audh was annexed to the British Government on the 7th of February, 1856. His poetical title is Akhtar, and is the author of three Díwáns and three Masnawís in Urdú. This ex-king is now living in Calcutta, pensioned by Government.

Inscription on his coin.

سکه زد بر سيم و زر از فضل و تاميد اله
ظل حق واجد علي سلطان عالم بادشاه

**Wakidi,** واقدي, surname of Muhammad bin-'Umar, an author who wrote in Arabic the work called "Tabaḳát Wáḳidí," containing the history of the conquests of Syria by the generals of 'Umar, during the years 638-9 A. D. He died in the year 824 or 834 A. D., 209 or 219 A. H. Ibn-Jauzí relates that Wáḳidí who dwelt at Baghdád, when removing to the Eastern bank of the Tigris, required 120 camels to convey his books. *Vide* Abú Abdulláh Muhammad ibn-'Umar-ul-Wáḳidí.

**Wakif,** واقف, the poetical name of a poet whose proper name is Núr-ul-Ayn. He was a native of Paṭiála of which place his father was a Ḳází. He was contemporary with the poet 'Arzú, and died about the year 1776 A. D., 1190 A. H. He is commonly called Wákif Lahorí and his Díwán contains about 800 Persian Ghazals.

**Wala,** والا, poetical name of Islám Khán, which see.

**Walad,** ولد, *vide* Sultán Walad, who is also called Mauláná Walad.

**Walah,** واله, poetical name of Said Muhammad, author of a poem called "Dastúr-ul-Nazm."

**Walah,** اله, poetical title of 'Alí Ḳulí Khán of Dághistán He is the author of a Tazkira entitled "Rayáz-ush-Shu'árá." It is an universal biographical dictionary of Persian poets, and contains about 2,500 articles. He came to India in 1734 A. D., 1147 A. H., where he composed the above work in 1748 A. D., 1161 A. H., and died after nine years in 1757 A. D., 1170 A. H. He is the father of Gunna Begum, which see.

**Walajah, Prince,** شهزاده واليدجاه, son of 'Azim Sháh. He along with his brother Beidár Bakht, was killed in the battle fought by his father against the emperor Bahádur Sháh his eldest brother in 1707 A. D.

**Walajah,** والاجاه, a title of Muhammad 'Alí Khán, nawâb of the Karnatik, who died in 1795 A. D., aged 87 years.

**Wali,** والي, poetical name of Najaf 'Alí Beg, an author.

**Wali,** والي, poetical name of Sháh Walí-ulláh a native of Gujrát, but passed the greatest part of his life in the Dakhin. He was living in the time of the emperor 'Alamgír and is the first poet who wrote a Díwán in Urdú. A copy of this book was brought to Dehlí in 1720 A. D., 1132 A. H. which induced many poets of that city to apply themselves to Urdú poetry. *Vide* Hátim.

**Wali, of Dasht Bayaz,** ولي دشت بياضي, a place in Khurásán. He was a contemporary with Mirzá Muhammad Ḳulí Mailí who came to India in 1571 A. D., 982 A. H. Walí is the author of a Persian Díwán. *Vide* Walí (Mauláná).

**Walidad Khan and Ahmad 'Ali Khan,** ولیداد خان, rebel leaders in Bulandshahr (N. W. P.) during the troubles of 1857.

**Wali Kalandar,** والي قلندر, a poet who lived in the time of Báisanghar Mirzá.

**Wali Muhammad Khan Uzbak,** ولي محمد خان اذبک, king of Túrán, was the son of Jání Beg Khán by 'Abdulláh Khán Uzbak's daughter. He was raised to the throne of Túrán after the death of his brother Bákí Beg Khán, and visited Sháh Abbás king of Persia in 1611 A. D., 1020 A. H. He reigned 6 years and was killed in battle about the year 1612 A. D.

**Wali Muhammad, Hazrat,** حضرت ولي محمد نارنولي, of Narnoul a Musalmán saint who died on the 13th of November, 1647 A. D., 25th Shawwál, 1057 A. H.

**Wali, Maulana,** مولانا ولي دشت بياضي, a famous poet of Dasht Bayáz in Khurásán, who was a contemporary of Mauláná Zamírí, and was put to death by order of Taimúr Sulṭán Uzbak, who had taken possession of Khurásán in the reign of Sulṭán Muhammad Khudá Banda, king of Persia who reigned from 1577 to 1588 A. D., 985 to 995 A. H. He is the author of a Persian Díwán. *Vide* Walí of Dasht Bayáz.

**Wali Ram,** ولي رام, a Hindú, who was usually called Banwálí Dás, is the author of a Masnawí.

**Wali-ullah, Maulwi Shah,** مولوی شاه ولي اله دهلوي, of Dehlí, author of the commentary on the Ḳurán in Persian, entitled "Fath-ul-Rahmán."

**Wali-ullah Husaini, Maulwi Muhammad,** مولوی محمد ولي اله حسيني, author of a commentary on the Ḳurán, called "Nazm-ul-Jawáhir," which he wrote in 1821 A. D., 1236 A. H.

**Walid,** وليد بن عتبه, the son of 'Utba, was made governor of Medina by Mu'áwia I, but was removed from the government of that city by Yezíd I in favour of Amrú the son of Saíd who was then governor of Mecca.

**Walid I,** وليد بن عبدالملک, seventh Khalíf of the house of Umayya. He succeeded his father 'Abdulmalik in Syria 705 A. D., 96 A. H., and died after a reign of 9 years and some months about the year 714 A. D. Spain was conquered in his time by his generals. He was succeeded by his brother Sulaimán.

**Walid II,** وليد بن يزيد, son of Yezíd II, succeeded his uncle Háshim in Syria as eleventh Khalíf of the race of Umayya in 743 A. D., 126 A. H. He reigned little more than a year and was slain in 744, when his son Yezíd III, succeeded him.

**Wali-uddin 'Abu 'Abd-ullah Muhammad bin-'Abdullah-al-Katib, Shaikh,** شيخ ولي الدين ابو عبداله, author of the "Mishkát-ul-Masábíh" a new and augmented edition of the Masábíh of Al-Baghwí, which he completed in 1336 A. D., 737 A. H. It is a concise collection of traditions, principally taken from the Six Books or Sahíhs and arranged in chapters according to subjects. This collection was translated by Captain Matthews in 1809.

**Wamik,** وامق, the celebrated lover of Azrá. The poet Farkhárí has written a poem on their love adventures.

**Waraka,** ورقه, a lover, the name of whose mistress was Gulsháh.

**Waraka bin-Naufat,** ورقه بن نوفل, a cousin of Khudyja the wife of Muhammad. In the days of ignorance he learned the Christian religion, translated the gospel into Arabic, gave himself up to devotion, and opposed the worship of idols. He became a convert to Muhammadanism about the year 611 A. D., lived to a great age, and towards the end of his life became blind.

**Warusta,** وارسته لاهوري, a poet of Láhor, who is the author of a work called "Jang Rangárang," being a collection of verses of all the poets who have written on different matters. He was living in 1766 A. D., 1180 A. H.

**Wasfi,** وصفي, *vide* Abdulláh Tirmizí.

**Wasik** or **Wathik Billah,** واثق باله, a Khalífa of Baghdád. *Vide* Al-Wásiḳ Billáh.

**Wasik, Mulla,** ملا واثق, name of a poet.

**Wasili,** ملاواثق, *vide* 'Alá-ud-dín (Sayyad).

**Wasil Khan of Kashmir,** واصل خان كشميري, author of the "Mahárájnáma," in the Preface of which he praises Nawáb 'Asaf-uddaula, Mahárája Nirmal Dás and Lála Hulás Ráe.

**Wasili,** واصلي, poetical appellation of Mír Imám Wardí Beg, who is the author of a Díwán, and was living at Lakhnau in 1780 A. D., 1194 A. H.

**Wasli,** وصلي, the poetical title of 'Aḳa Táhir the father of Sádiḳ Khán.

**Wasti,** واسطي, poetical name of Mír 'Abdul Jalíl Bilgramí, which see.

**Watwat,** وطواط, the nickname of the poet Rashídí, which see. It is also the surname of Muhammad bin-Ibrahím, the son of Ahia the son of 'Alí-al-Kátibí, an Arabian author.

**Wazah,** واضح, the poetical title of Mirzá Mubárik styled Irádat Khán the grandson of Nawáb `Azim Khán of the time of Jahángír. He took instructions in the art of poetry from Mír Muhammad Rásikh and became an excellent poet; but in the latter part of his life, he led a retired life, became a Ḳalandar and died in 1716 A. D., 1128 A. H. *Vide* Irádat Khán.

**Wazah,** واضح, poetical name of 'Aḳá 'Alí Asghar who was originally a manufacturer of gold thread. He was living in 1720 A. D., 1132 A. H., and is the author of a Díwán.

**Wazir,** وزير, the poetical title of Khwája Wazír son of Khwája Faḳír of Lakhnau. He died in 1854 A. D., 1270 A. H., and is the author of a Díwán in Urdú.

**Wazir,** وازي, poetical name of Shaikh Wazír, author of two Díwáns, Persian and Urdú.

**Wazir 'Ali Khan,** وزير علي خان, for a short time Nawáb of Lakhnau, was the adopted son of Nawáb 'Asaf-uddaula on whose death in September, 1797 A. D., he was raised to the masnad of Audh at Lakhnau, but after a short interval grounds for disputing the authenticity of his pretensions having been established, he was deposed on the 21st of January, 1798 A. D. by Sir John Shore, and Saádat 'Alí Khán the brother of the late Nawáb was placed on the masnad. Wazír 'Alí was sent to Benares where he murdered Mr. Cherry the Political Agent on Monday the 14th of January, 1799 A. D., 8th Shában, 1213 A. H. He at first fled to Butwal and afterwards took refuge with the rája of Jaipúr, a powerful independent chief who refused to give him up unless under a stipulation of his life being spared. To this it was thought prudent to accede, and being accordingly given up to the British in December following, he was brought down to Calcutta and confined at Fort William in a bomb-proof, divided by iron gratings in three parts. The longest, in the centre, was occupied by Wazír 'Alí, and the other two by Sentries, one English and one native. After many years captivity, he was transported to a more suitable prison in the palace built for Típú Sultán's family in the fort of Vellore, where the females of his family subsequently joined him, and there he died. Lord Teignmouth, in the Life of his father, states that Wazír 'Alí died in rigorous confinement in Fort William and this is said to be a mistake. His death took place in the month of May, 1817 A. D., Rajab, 1232 A. H., after 17 years 3 months and 4 days' confinement, and was buried at Kásí Bághán close to a tomb of one of the sons of Típú Sultán. He was then in his 36th year. His mother was the wife of a Farrash. The expenses of his marriage in 1795 amounted to 30 lakhs of rupees, while 70 rupees were sufficient to defray all the cost of his funeral in 1817, a strange reverse of fortune.

**Wazir Khan,** وزیرخان, surname of Muhammad Táhir an officer of the rank of 5000 who served under the emperor 'Alamgír. In the latter years of his life he was appointed governor of Málwa where he died 1672 A. D. His nephew Rafí Khán is the author of the "Hamlae Haidarí."

**Wazir Muhammad, Nawab of Bhopal,** وزیرمحمد, an ally of the British Government, died in March, 1816 A. D., and his son Nazar Muhammad Khan succeeded him.

**Wazir Khan,** وزیرخان, an Amír of the Court of the emperor Sháhjahán by whom he was raised to the rank of 5000 into the title of Wazír Khán and the Súbadarship of the Panjáb. He built a splendid masjíd at Láhor in 1044 A. H., which is still in good preservation. His proper name was Hakím Alím-uddín.

**Wazir-uddaula,** وزیرالدوله, title of Wazír Muhammad Khán, the Nawáb of Tonk, the son of Nawáb Amír Khán the Pindara Chief, died in June, 1864 A. D.

**Wazir-uddaula,** وزیرالدوله, *vide* Názir-ul-Mulk Wazír-uddaula.

**Wikar-ul-Umra,** وکرال عمرا, the son of Shams-ul-Umrah Nawáb of Haidarabád Dakhin.

**Wisal,** وصال, the poetical name of Mirzá Kóchak of Shíráz, author of a "Farháa wa Shírín."

**Wisali,** وصالي, poetical name of Sayyad 'Alá-uddin a modern poet of Khurásán who was settled in Audh. He is the author of an Elegy on the Imáms, *vide* 'Alá-uddín (Sayyad).

**Wizarat Khan,** وزارت خان, whose proper name is Mír Abdur Rahmán, was the second son of Amánat Khán Mírak, an excellent poet. His poetical name was Bikramí. He flourished in the time of the emperor 'Alamgír and has left a Díwán. *Vide* Bikramí.

**Wys Karani,** بیش کراني, *vide* Aweis Karaní.

# X.

**Xavier, Hieronymo,** a Catholic Missionary who came from Goa to Dehlí in the reign of the emperor Jahángír. He is the author of a religious work in Persian entitled the "Mirror of Truth" which he dedicated to the emperor in the year 1609 A. D., and which has been preserved in the Library of Queen's College, Cambridge. A reply to this book was written a few years after its appearance by Ahmad ibn-Zain-ul-'Abidín Alalwí, to which he gave the title of "The divine rays in refutation of Christian error." A copy of which is also preserved in the same College. This work was written by the author in the month of November, 1621 A. D., Muharram, 1031 A. H.

# Y.

**Yadgar Muhammad, Mirza,** مرزا یادگار محمد, the son of Mirzá Muhammad, the son of Mirzá Báisánghar, the son of Mirzá Sháhrukh, the son of Amír Taimúr. After the death of Mirzá Báisanghar, his grandfather, he succeeded him as governor of Khurásán in 1434 A. D., and held that situation till the death of Sultán 'Abú Saíd Mirzá, who being taken prisoner by Uzzan Hasan, was made over to Yádgár Muhammad in 1469 A. D., 873 A. H. who slew him. After his death Sultán Husain Báikara took possession of Hirát, with whom Yádgár Muhammad had several battles; but was at last slain in a night attack on the 25th of August, 1470 A. D., 27th Safar, 875 A. H. He was the last of the descendants of Sháhrukh Mirzá, and is said to have written excellent poetry.

**Yadgar Nasir, Mirza,** مرزا یادگار ناصر, brother of the emperor Bábar Sháh. When the emperor Humáyún after his return from Persia marched in person in the year 1546 A. D., 953 A. H. to reduce Badakhshán, Yádgár Násir having attempted to stir up a sedition in the royal army, was upon conviction, sentenced to death, though he was uncle to the king.

**Yafa'i, Imam,** امام يافعي, a Muhammadan doctor whose proper name was 'Abdullah bin-Asad. He was a native of Yáfa in Syria from which he was called Yáfaí. He is also called Kutb Mecca, and Yáfaí Nazal-ul-Haramyn. Sháh Namat-ullah was one of his disciples. He is the author of several works in Arabic, among which are "Durr-ul-Nazm fí Munáfa-ul-Kurán," "Rauzat-ul-Rayázín fí Hikáet-ul-Sálahín," "Khulásat-ul-Mufákhir fí Munákib-ush-Shaikh 'Abdul Kádir," and the "Mirat-ul-Janán fí Hawádis-uz-Zamán" the latter containing Memoirs of all the Muhammadan Generals and other illustrious Characters, from the commencement of the Hijrí era 622 A. D. to the year 1300 A. D., a very interesting work. Yáfaí, according to some, died in 1354 A. D., and according to others in 1366 A. D., 755 or 767 A. H., but the latter date appears to be correct. He is sometimes called 'Abdullah bin-'Abdul Yáfaí.

**Ya'jaz,** اعجاز, the poetical name of Shaikh Muhammas Saíd a native of Agrah and an excellent poet. He wda living about the year 1691 A. D., 1102 A. H. in the reign of the emperor 'Alamgír, and was employed in the service of Nawáb Mukarram Khán, Názim of Multán. He was a contemporary of the poet Sarkhush, who has mentioned him in his biography called "Kalmat-ush-Shu'ára.

**Ya'kub Beg** or **Sultan Ya'kub,** يعقوب بيگ, the son of Uzzan Hasan, whom he succeeded in 1477 A. D., 882 A. H. and became the king of the Turkmán tribes called Akkoinlú or the White Sheep. After his death he was succeeded by his son Alwand Beg who was defeated about the year 1500 A. D., 996 A. H., by Sháh Ismá'íl I, Safwí.

**Ya'kub bin-Idris,** يعقوب بن ادريس, *vide* Kirmání.

**Ya'kub bin-Lais Saffar, Amir,** بن ليث صفاري اميريعقوب. He is also called Yakút and is the first who rebelled against the Abbasides and is the founder of the dynasty of the Safárí or Safarides which signifies a pewterer. He raised himself from a humble station of a coppersmith, to the rank of a sovereign in Sístán, and having obtained the possession of Khurásán and Tabaristán in 874 A. D., 260 A. H. from Muhammad the son of Tahir II whom he took prisoner, he was declared rebel by the Khalíf Mo'tamid, in consequence of which he marched with a powerful army towards Baghdád in the year 878 A. D., 265 A. H., but died on the road after a reign of eleven years. He was succeeded by his brother Amrú bin-Lais. *Vide* Lais.

**Ya'kub, Sultan,** سلطان يعقوب, *vide* Ya'kúb Beg.

**Yakut,** ياقوت, *vide* Ya'kúb bin-Lais.

**Ya'mali of Hirat,** اعمالي هراتي, a poet who is th author of a Persian Díwán.

**Yari, Maulana,** مولانا ياري, an author.

**Yehia bin-'Abdur Rahman,** يحيى بن عبدالرحمان, author of the Arabic work on Theology called "Ayn-ul-Ilm," the fountain of science, and one entitled "Afzal-us-Salát, a collection of Traditions.

**Yehia bin-'Abul Mansur,** يحيى بن ابوالمنصور, one of the greatest astronomers that lived in the time of the Khalíf Al-Mánsúr.

**Yehia bin-Ahmad-al-Hilli** or **Hulli,** احمد الحلي يحيى بن, who was celebrated for his knowledge of traditions, is well known amongst the Imámia sect for his works on jurisprudence, is the author of the "Jama-ush-Sharáya" and the "Madkhal dar Usúl Fikh which are in the greatest repute. He died 1280 A. D., 679 A. H.

**Yehia bin-Aktam,** يحيى بن اكثم, was Chief Justice during the Khiláfat of Al-Mamún. He died in the reign of the Khalíf Al-Mutwakkil 856 A. D., 242 A. H.

**Yehia bin-Khalid,** يحيى بن خالد, Grand wazír of Harún-al-Rashíd, whose son Jafar-al-Barmakí, was put to death by order of that khalíf 803 A. D., 187 A. H.

**Yehia bin-Ma'az Razi,** يحيى بن معاذ رازي, a very learned Muhammadan who died on the 9th August, 871 A. D., 18th Ramazán, 257 A. H., and was buried at Naisbápúr.

**Yehia Kashi, Mir,** ميريحيى كاشي, one of the celebrated poets of the reign of the emperor Sháhjahán. On the completion of the palace and city of Sháhjahánábád in the year 1648 A. D., 1058 A. H., he wrote a chronogram for which he was rewarded by that monarch with 5000 rupees. He died in the year 1654 A. D., 1064 A. H.

**Yehia Maneiri,** يحيى منيري, a celebrated saint who is buried at Maneir, *vide* Sharaf-uddin Ahmad Ahia Maneirí.

**Yehia, Mulla of Naishapur,** ملايحيى نيشاپوري. His poetical name is Fattáhí. He is the author of a Díwán and of the Persian work called "Shabistán Khayál," "the Chamber of Imagination." He flourished in the reign of Sháhrukh Mirzá, and died 1448 A. D., 852 A. H.

**Yekin,** يقين, the poetical name of Inaám-ulláh Khán, an Urdú poet who has left in a Díwán or collection of Hindí poems, principally on love subjects. He was the son of Azhar-uddín Khán Bahádur Mubárak Jang, a grandson of the Mujaddid Alif Sání, or Reformer of the second thousandth year, and a pupil of Mirzá Jánjánán Mazhar, who was so fond of him that he wrote most of his poetry in his name; he was killed at the age of 25 years in the time of Ahmad Sháh about the year 1750 A. D., 1163 A. H. by his own father, because he brought disgrace on his family. His Díwán is very celebrated.

**Yelduz,** يلدوز, *vide* Táj-uddín Eldúz.

**Yemin-uddin, Am r,** اميريمين الدين, entitled Malik-ul-Fuzla or prince of the learned, was the father of Amír Mahmúd commonly called ibn-Yemín, *vide* Amír Yemín-uddin, also Tughrái.

**Yemin-uddin, Amir,** امير يمين الدين نزلاباري, a poet who was a native of Nazlábád in the province of Baihak in Persia. He was cotemporary with the poets Kátibí and 'Alí Shaháb. He is the author of several Masnawís, *viz.*, "Misbáh-ul-Kulúb containing Dialogues between the Candle and the Moth; "Mishkát-ul-Tálibín" dialogues between Wisdom and Love; and the story of "Fatha and Fathúh."

**Yemin-uddin Tughrai of Mashhad,** يمين الدين طغرائي, *vide* Tughrái Mashhadí.

**Yezdi,** يزدي, author of a treatise concerning divine love, called "Risálat fí bayán Muhabbat."

**Yezdijard I,** يزدجرد, surnamed Al-'Athim or Al-'Asim, the sinner (the Isdigertes of the Greeks) whom some authors term the brother, and others the son of his predecessor Bahram IV, whom he succeeded to the throne of Persia 404 A. D. This monarch is represented by Persian historians, to have been a cruel prince, and we are told, the nation rejoiced when he was killed by the kick of a horse. He died after a reign of .6 years, and was succeeded by his son Bahram V.

**Yezdijard II,** يزد جرد, (the Isdigertes II of the Romans), succeeded his father Bahram V to the throne of Persia 438 A. D. He was a wise and brave prince and reigned 18 years.

**Yezdijard III,** يزدجرد, the son of Shahryár and grandson of Khusro Parwez, was raised to the throne of Persia after the dethronement of the queen Arzamí Dakht, 632

A. D. He is the Isdigertes III of the Greeks, and a cotemporary of 'Umar the Khalíf of Arabia. This prince who appears to have been as weak as he was unfortunate, sat upon the throne only nine years; that being the period from his elevation to the battle of Nahawand which decided the fate of Persia, and which from its date 641 A. D., fell under the dominion of the Arabian Khalífs. For a period of ten years afterwards this monarch was a fugitive, possessed no power whatever. He first fled to Sístán, then to Khurásán, and lastly, to Marv where he was murdered 651 A. D., 31 A. H. He was the last sovereign of the house of Sásán, a dynasty which ruled Persia for 415 years. It is from the commencement of his reign that the Persian Era, which is in use to this day in Persia, is called after him the Era of Yezdijard. It began on Tuesday the 16th of June, 632 A. D., 20th Rabí' I, 11 A. H. being only eight days after Muhammad's death.

**Yezid,** يزيد بن ابو سفيان, the son of Abú Sufián. He died by the plague that raged in Syria in the year 639 A. D. The mortality both among men and beasts was so terrible, that the Arabs call that year "'Am-ul-ramada," or the year of destruction. By this pestilence the Saracens lost 25,000 men, among whom were Abú 'Obeida, general of the Saracen army at Syria, Sarjabíl, ibn-Hasana formerly Muhammad's secretary, and Yezíd ibn-Sufián.

**Yezid I,** يزيد بن معاويه, the son of Mu'áwia and the second Khalíf of the house of Umayya. His inauguration was performed at Damascus on the same day that his father died, *viz.*, on the new moon of the month of Rajab, corresponding with the 7th of April, 680 A. D. 1st Rajab, 60 A. H. He was a man of considerable taste and refinement, an eloquent orator, and an admired poet. Some specimens of his composition, which are still extant, display no ordinary powers of mind. The first and the last lines of the ode with which the bard of Persia, the celebrated Háfiz, opens his magnificent Díwán, are borrowed from Yezíd. It was once sarcastically asked of Háfiz, "How could a distinguished poet like yourself stoop to borrow from Yezíd, who was not only a usurper, but also the murderer of Imám Husain?" He answered, "Which of you, seeing a dog running away with a diamond, would not stop the brute, and rescue the jewel from its unclean mouth?" By Persian authors, Yezíd is never mentioned without abomination, and ordinarily this imprecation is added to his name, "Lanat-ulláh," that is, the curse of God be upon him;" in reference not to his vices, but to the death of Husain, the son of 'Alí, whom he first of all attempted to destroy by poison, and afterwards caused to be killed, with all his family, on the plains of Karbala. Under his khiláfat the Musalmáns conquered all Khurásán and Khwárizm, and put the territories of the princes of Samarkand under contribution. The motto of his seal was, "God is our Lord." Yezíd died on the 31st of October, 683 A. D., 4th Rabí' I, 64 A. H. in the 39th year of his age, after he had reigned three years and eight months, and was succeeded by his son Muáwia II. His mother's name was Maisana a Bedouin of the tribe of Kalabí.

Yezíd was a debauchee and is represented by Moslem writers as an Atheist.

**Yezid II,** يزيد بن عبدالملك, the ninth Khalíf of the race of Umayya, was the son of the Khalíf 'Abdulmalik. He succeeded 'Umar the son of 'Abdul Azíz in 720 A. D., 101 A. H. in Syria, and died after a reign of four years, 724 A. D., 105 A. H. His brother Hashám succeeded him.

**Yezid III,** يزيد بن وليد, the twelfth Khalíf of the house of Umayya, succeeded his father Walíd II in Syria 744 A. D., 126 A. H., and died the same year after he had reigned six months. He was succeeded by his brother Ibráhím.

**Yunas bin-Abdur Rahman-al-Yuktaini,** يونس بن عبد الرحمان, a celebrated Shia traditionist. Amongst other works, he wrote the "'Ilal-al-Hadís," the "Ikhtiláf-al-Hadís," and the "Jáma-al-Kabír." He is said to have made forty-five pilgrimages to Mecca, and fifty-four 'Umrats when he merely visited the sacred city, and to have written the surprising number of 1,000 volumes, controverting the opponents of the Shia doctrines. He died at Madína in 823 A. D., 208 A. H.

**Yusaf of Ahmadabad,** يوسف احمد ابادي, author of an Arabic work on Theology called, "Akáed Yúsaf."

**Yusaf,** يوسف, author of a collection of letters called "Badáyu'l Insha" or wonders of letter writing. It is also called "Insháe Yúsafí.

**Yusaf Abu'l Haji,** يوسف ابوالحاجي, one of the Moorish kings of Granada, and the Finisher of the celebrated palace of the Alhambra. He ascended the throne of Granada in the year 1333, and his personal appearance and mental qualities were such as to win all hearts. He established schools in all the villages, with simple and uniform systems of education; he obliged every hamlet of more than twelve houses to have a mosque, and prohibited various abuses and indecorums, that had been introduced into the ceremonies of religion and the festivals and public amusements of the people. His attention was also directed towards finishing the great architectural works commenced by his predecessors, and erecting others on his own plans. The Alhambra, which had been founded by the good Muhammad ibn-Alahmar, was now completed. He constructed the beautiful gate of Justice, forming the grand entrance to the fortress, which he finished in 1348. He likewise adorned many of the courts and halls of the palace, as may be seen by the inscriptions on the walls, in which his name repeatedly occurs. In the year 1354, as he was one day praying in the royal mosque of the Alhambra, a maniac rushed suddenly from behind, and plunged a dagger in his side. He was borne to the royal apartments, but expired almost immediately. The murderer was cut to pieces, and his limbs burnt in public, to gratify the fury of the populace.

**Yusaf Adil Shah,** يوسف عادل شاه, whose original name was Yúsaf 'Adil Khán, was the founder of the 'Adil Sháhí dynasty of Bíjápúr. He was a nobleman in the service of Muhammad Sháh II Bahmaní, king of the Dakhin. When the Sultán left this world, and dissentions began to prevail in the kingdom, most of the foreign officers and soldiers attached themselves to Yúsaf 'Adil Khán; who, seeing the ministers of Sultán Mahmúd II, the successor of the late king bent on his destruction, withdrew himself from Ahmadábád, with his family and followers, to his government of Bíjápúr, and resolving to become the founder of a kingdom, he began to add to his territories by conquest. In the year 1489 A. D., 895 A. H., he, with the assent of Malik Ahmad Bahrí, assumed the title of Sháh, and read the khutba of Bíjápúr in his own name. Yúsaf 'Adil Sháh died at Bíjápúr in 1510 A. D., 916 A. H. of a dropsical disorder after he had reigned with great prosperity 21 years, in the 75th year of his age, and was succeeded by his son Ismá'íl 'Adil Sháh.

*List of the kings of the 'Adil Sháhí dynasty.*

| | A. D. |
|---|---|
| Yúsaf 'Adil Sháh, supposed to be the son of Murád II of Anatolia; purchased for the bodyguard at Aḥmadábád from a merchant. He began to reign | 1489 |
| Ismá'íl 'Adil Sháh, son of Yúsaf | 1510 |
| Mallú 'Adil Sháh, son of Ismá'íl, reigned six months | 1534 |
| Ibráhím 'Adil Sháh I, son of Ismá'íl | 1535 |
| 'Alí 'Adil Sháh I, son of Ibráhím | 1557 |
| Ibráhím 'Adil Sháh II, son of Tahmásp the son of 'Alí A. Sháh | 1579 |
| Muhammad 'Adil Sháh, son of Ibráhím II | 1626 |
| 'Alí 'Adil Sháh II, son of Muhammad | 1660 |
| Sikandar 'Adil Sháh the last king of Bíjápúr | 1672 |

**Yusaf 'Ali Khan,** يوسف علي خان, Nawáb of Rámpúr. His Highness was one of the few princes who were faithful to the British Government in the troublous times of 1857, when the whole of the N. W. Provinces were in a state of revolt and insurrection. Lord Canning rewarded him with liberal grants of land worth a lac per annum, whilst Her Majesty was pleased to confer on him the Star of India. He died at his capital in Rohilkhand on the 21st of April, 1865 A. D., 24th Ẓi-Ḳa'da, 1282 A. H.

**Yusaf Amiri, Maulana,** مولانا يوسف امري, a Persian poet who flourished in the time of Sháhrukh Mirzá and wrote panegyrics in praise of his son Baisanghar Mirzá.

**Yusaf bin-Muhammad,** يوسف بن محمد, author of a medical work called "Fáedat-ul-Akhbár."

**Yusaf bin-Junaid,** يوسف بن جنيد, generally known by the name of Akhí Chalabí. *Vide* Ḳází Khán.

**Yusaf bin-Hasan-al-Mukaddasi,** يوسف بن حسن المقدسي, author of a portion of the "Tabaḳát-al-Hanbaliat." He died in 1466 A D., 871 A. H. *vide* Abú'l Husain bin-Abú Yalí.

**Yusaf Hamadani,** يوسف همداني, a celebrated learned Musalmán of Hamadán who died in the year 1141 A. D., 536 A. H.

**Yusaf Khan, Mirza,** يوسف خان. A Mansabdar of 2,500 in the 30th year of Akbar, and subsequently governor of Kashmir. Later still served with distinction under Abú'l Fazl in the Dakhin; died Jam. II. 1010 A. H. Was a native of Mashad, of the Sáyyid tribe.

**Yusaf, Mir,** مير يوسف استرابادي, of Astrabád who was living in 1580 A. D., 988 A. H. and wrote a chronogram on the death of the poet Kásim Káhí, who died that year.

**Yusaf Muhammad Khan,** يوسف محمد خان, Commander of Five Thousand under Akbar, whose foster-brother he was. Died of drink, 973 A. H.

**Yusaf Muhammad Khan,** يوسف محمد خان, author of a history of the reign of Muhammad Sháh emperor of Dehlí, called "Taríkh Muhammad Sháhí."

**Yusaf Shah Purbi,** يوسف شاه پوربي, the son of Bárbak Sháh whom he succeeded to the throne of Bengal in 1174 A. D., 887 A. H. He reigned 8 years and died in 1482 A. D. His son Fatha Sháh succeeded him.

**Yusaf, Maulana, of Naishapur,** مولانا يوسف نيشاپور, is the first person who wrote a book on the art of writing poetry in Persian; he flourished about two hundred years after Khulíl bin-Aḥmad of Baṣra who had also written on the same subject in Arabic.

**Yusaf, Shaikh,** شيخ يوسف, first king of Multán. The introduction of the Muhammadan faith into Multán, says Firishta, first took place in the latter part of the first century of the Hijra, about the year 700 A. D. by the conquest of that country by Muhammad Kásim, after whom, until the reign of Sulṭán Mahmúd of Ghazní, no account is to be traced of its history. Mahmúd conquered Multán from the infidels; but on the decline of the Ghazní power, the inhabitants succeeded in expelling the Muhammadans, and establishing a separate government. From the period of its subjugation by Muhammad Ghórí, it remained tributary to Dehlí until the year 1443 A. D., 847 A. H. when the governor of that province like most others of the kingdom at the same period, declared independence. After which time several princes reigned in succession. The first of these was one Shaikh Yúsaf a man of learning, wisdom and high character, of the tribe of Ḳureish, whom the inhabitants of Multán selected to be ruler over the people of Multán and Uchcha, when the public prayers were read and money coined in his name. Shaikh Yúsaf had reigned but two years, when his father-in-law, Ráe Sehra of the tribe of Langa having seized him, sent him under a guard to Dehlí, and mounted the throne under the title of Ḳuṭb-uddín Mahmúd Langa. Abú'l Fazl in the 'Ayín-i-Akbarí, assigns seventeen years for the reign of Shaikh Yúsaf.

*Muhammadan kings of Multán.*

| | A. D. |
|---|---|
| Shaikh Yúsaf who established an independent monarchy, began | 1443 |
| Ráe Sehra or Ḳuṭb-uddín Mahmúd Langa | 1445 |
| Husain Langa I | |
| Mahmúd Khán Langa | 1502 |
| Husain Langa II, who began 1524 A. D., was overcome by Sháh Husain Arghún, and subsequently Multán became a province of the empire under the emperor Humáyún. | |

**Yusaf, Shaikh of Gujrat,** شيخ يوسف گجراتي, author of the "Tazkirat-ul-Atḳiyá."

**Yusaf Khan,** يوسف خان, governor of Sindh, who live in the time of the emperor Sháh Jahán. In his time (says Múnshí Lutf-ullah) he built an Ídgah, in Tatta a splendid mosque, where all true believers gather together twice a year, and perform the divine service. Its inscription is in beautiful large Nastalik characters, as follows :—

"Yúsaf Khán, the powerful lord, erected this place of worship as high as his fortune. The year of its finishing is found by cherubion—the temple of Makka for the virtuous." 1633 A. D., 1043 A. H.

There are upwards of 400 mosques in the city of Tatta, (says Lutf-ullah) but almost all of them going to decay. There is also a Grand Mosque (Juma Masjid) begun by Sháh Jahán, in 1647 A. D., 1057 A. H. and finished by Aurangzeib in 1072 A. H. The edifice is a magnificent one about 200 yards long by 30 broad, built of baked bricks and mortar. The whole site is roofed with 100 domes, every one of them painted in a different style from another. The inscriptions carved round the great arch of stone, and those upon the two Lata stones, are excellently done in large letters. In short, the whole scene presents a picture of beauty and solemnity to the spectator.

# Z.

**Zabita Khan,** ضابطه خان, a Roheila chief, and son of Najíb-uddaula Amír-ul-Umrá. After the death of his father in October, 1770 A. D., Rajab, 1184 A. H. he continued to protect the royal family at Dehlí till the return of the emperor Sháh 'Alam from Allahábád in December, 1771 A. D., Ramazán, 1185 A. H., when he was convicted of having been deficient in respect to the royal authority while the emperor resided at Allahábád, and having abused his trust by corrupting the ladies of the harem especially the princess Khairunnisa the king's sister. His territories were seized, and he was compelled to make his escape to Shujá-uddaula the nawáb of Audh. But not long after, the Marhaṭṭas obliged the emperor to confer on Zábita Khán, the rank of Amír-ul-Umrá, and to restore him the grant of almost all the districts of which he had only a few months before been deprived by their assistance. Zábita Khán was the father of that traitor, Ghulám Ḳádir Khán, who subsequently blinded the emperor Sháh 'Alam. His second son, by name Mu'ín-uddín Khán commonly called Bhanbú Khán, received a pension of 5,000 rupees from the British Government, and after his death a pension of one thousand rupees monthly was granted to his two sons Mahmúd Khán and Jalál-uddín Khán. The elder rebelled in 1857 and being subsequently arrested died in Meerut jail.

**Zaer** or **Zayer,** زاير, poetical name of Shaikh Muhammad Fákhir of Allahábád who died in 1751 A. D., 1164 A. H.

**Za'ifa Khatun,** ضعيفه خاتون, sister to Sultán Sanjar, married to Malik Táj-uddín Abú'l Fazl, a descendant of the royal family of Amrú bin-Lais.

**Zafar,** ظفر, the poetical name of Abú Zafar Siráj-uddín Bahádur Sháh the ex-king of Dehlí. *Vide* Bahádur Sháh.

**Zafar,** ظفر, poetical title of Ṭíká Rám, a Hindú.

**Zafar Khan,** ظفرخان, the original name of (Nawáb) Roshan-uddaula, which see.

**Zafar Khan,** ظفرخان, son of Sultán Fíróz Sháh Bárbak, was murdered by Khán Jahán the prime minister in 1385 A. D., 787 A. H.

**Zafar Khan,** ظفرخان, the title of Khwája Ihsán-ulláh, a nobleman of the reign of the emperor Sháh Jahán, and father of Ináyet Khán who was the author of the work called "Sháh Jahán-náma." Zafar Khán held the rank of 3000, and died at Láhor 1662 A. D., 1073 A. H. His poetical name was Ihsán, which see.

**Zagatai, Jagatai,** ظفرتي, *vide* Chagatái (Khán) which is more consonant to the Turkish pronunciation.

**Zahid, Shaikh,** شيخ زاهد كيلاني, of Gílán, a pious Musalmán who resided in Ardibail, a city in Azurbaiján, about 25 miles to the east of Taurus or Tabrez, and was the father-in-law of the celebrated Shaikh Safí or Safí-uddín Ardibeilí. He died 1335 A. D., 735 A. H.

**Zahid,** زاهد, whose proper name is Mirzá Záhid-uddín, the son of Mirzá Kam Bakhsh, the son of Mirzá Sulaimán Shikoh, the son of Sháh Alam king of Dehlí. He is the author of a Díwán.

**Zahidi,** زاهدي, a learned Muhammadan who wrote excellent Commentaries on the Ḳurán in Arabic as well as in Persian, called "Tafsír Záhidí." He died in 1260 A. D., 658 A. H.

**Zahik,** ضاحك, the poetical name of Mír Ghulám Husain the father of Mír Hasan of Lakhnau. He is the author of an Urdú Díwán and every Ghazal of his are full of jokes.

**Zahir Faryabi,** ظهير فاريابي, *vide* Zahír-uddín Fáryábí.

**Zahir Kirmani,** ظهير كرماني, author of a poem called "Majma-ul-Bahryn," containing the story of Manóhar, composed in the year 1749 A. D., 1162 A. H.

**Zahir-uddin Abu Bakr Muhammad bin-Ahmad-al-Bukhari,** ظهير الدين ابو بكر محمد بن آحمد البخاري, who died in 1222 A. D., 619 A. H., is the author of the "Fatáwa-az-Zahíria," a collection of decisions.

**Zahir-uddin 'Isa, Shaikh,** ظهيرالدين عيسى, a son of Shaikh Aḥmad Jám and author of a work called "Ramúz-ul-Hakáeḳ."

**Zahir-uddin Faryabi,** ظهيرالدين فاريابي, a native of Fáryáb, was an excellent poet and the pupil of Rashídí. He flourished in the reign of Tughral III Saljúḳí and Atábak Kizal Arsalán. He died at Tabriz 1201 A. D., 598 A. H., and is buried close to the tomb of Kháḳání at Surkháb in Tabriz. He is the author of a Díwán. Some authors say that the style of his poetry is far better than Anwarí's. Another poet has written, that "Should you come across with the Díwán of Zahír Faryábí, steal it, though you find it in the Ḳaba."

**Zahir-uddin Marghashi,** ظهيرالدين مرغشي, author of the "Taríkh Tabaristán."

**Zahir-uddin Makhdum,** ظهيرالدين مخدوم, an Arab, Egyptian, or subject of the Turkish empire, who is thought to have been despatched to assist the Muhammadan princes of Malabar against the Portuguese, and to have during his stay in India, composed an historical account of Malabar in the Arabic language, which terminates with the Hijrí year 987 A. H., corresponding with the year of our Lord 1580 A. D.

**Zahir-uddin, Mir,** ظهير الدين, son of Mir Khalib-ulla of Yazd, came from Persia to Lahore temp. Jahángir, and rose to high employ.

**Zahir-uddaula Bahadur,** ظهيرملك, (Prince) of Arkot, son of Azím Jáh Bahádur. He succeeded to the Masnad after the death of his father in January, 1874 A. D.

**Zahuri, Mulla,** ملا ظهوري ترشيزي, a native of Tarshish a city of Sabzwár in Persia. His proper name is Núr-uddín. After completing his studies he came to the Dakhin in the reign of Ibráhím 'Adil Sháh II of Bíjápúr, and passed the remainder of his days in his service. He dedicated his Sáḳí-náma, a celebrated poem, containing 4,000 verses to Burhán Nizám Sháh II of Aḥmadnagar who made him a present of seven elephants loaded with valuables. He is also the author of several other works, among which are the "Mína Bazár," "Ruḳaat Zahúrí," "Seh Nasr," a Díwán "Risála Nauras," "Khwán Khalíl," and "Gulzar Ibráhím," the last three he dedicated to his patron Ibráhím 'Adil Sháh. Zahúrí died one year after his father-in-law Mulla Malik Ḳummí, *i. e.*, in 1617 A. D., 1026 A. H., aged more than 90.

**Zahur-uddin, Isa,** ظهورالدين عيسى, son of Shaikh-ul-Islám Aḥmad Jám, and author of the work called Ramúz-ul-Haḳáeḳ. *Vide* Záhír-uddín Ísa.

**Zain Khan,** زين خان, son of Khwája Maksud, of Herát. A connection of Akbar and Jahángír, and Mansabdár of 4,500, afterwards promoted to 5000: an accomplished soldier and literary man, died of drink in 1010 A. H.

**Zakaria,** زكريا, *vide* Bahá-uddín Zikaria.

**Zakaria bin-Muhammad bin-Mahmud-al-Kamuli-al-Kazwini,** زكريا بن محمد بن محمود الكمولي القزويني, a native of Ḳazwín, and author of the "'Ajáeb-ul-Makhlúḳát," or the Wonders of the Creation, which he completed in the year 1363 A. D., 764 A. H. There are several copies of this work to be found in the public Libraries of London, and in private collections, some of them containing beautiful and correct drawings of all the beasts, fishes, birds, trees, and even monsters, described in the book: and the account of metals and gems, a subject that has attracted great public attention of late, contains in particular much curious information.

**Zakaria bin-Muhammad Ansari of Egypt,** زكريا بن محمد انصاري مصري, an author who died 1520 A. D.

**Zakaria Khan,** زكريا خان, thes on of Abdus Samad Khán, styled Saif-uddaula Bahádur Jang. He held the government of Láhor at the period of Nádir Sháh's invasion to India 1739 A. D., 1151 A. H., and died in the year 1745 A. D., 12th Jumáda II, 1158 A. H. His eldest son succeeded him in the government with the title of Sháh nawáz Khán.

**Zaki,** ذكي همداني, a poet of Hamdan, who lived in the time of Sháh Tahmásp Safwí, and died about the year 1621 A. D., 1030 A. H. He is the author of a Díwán.

**Zaki,** ذكي, poetical name of Jafar 'Alí Khán of Dehlí who lived in the time of the emperor Sháh 'Alam.

**Zaki** or **Safi-uddin Zaki Maraghai,** ذكي, but he was simply called Zakí. He was a poet and died in 1210 A. D., 607 A. H.

**Zaki Khan,** ذكي خان, who usurped the throne of Persia after the death of Karím Khán in March, 1779 A. D., but was assassinated after two months. *Vide* Karím Khán.

**Zakhmi, Hazrat,** حضرت ذكي, author of a Persian Díwán.

**Zakhmi,** زخمي, takhallus of Fakhr-uddaula Dabír-ul-Mulk Rája Ratan Singh Bahádur. He was a native of Lakhnau where he was minister of Finance. He died in 1850 A. D., 1266 A. H. and left a considerable Library at Bareli. A few years before his death, *viz.*, in 1846 A. D. he had embraced the Muhammadan faith.

**Zal,** زال, also called Zálzar, the son of Sám and grandson of Narímán. He was the father of Rustam, and these three personages, *viz.*, Sám, Zál and Rustam pass for the most famous heroes of Persia; they belong to the reigns of Manúchehr, Bahman and Afrásiáb. It was Zál who drove Afrásiáb king of the Turks out of Persia and put the crown on the head of Zú or Zab, son of Tahmásp, a descendant of one of the kings of the Pishdádian dynasty. This same Zál was put in prison by Bahman son of Isfandiár; but he made his escape, and married Rúdába, daughter of Mehráb governor of Kábulistán, who became the mother of Rustam; unfortunately, however, he fell into the hands of Bahman again, who put him to death.

**Zalali Hirwi,** زلالي هروي, a poet who was a native of Hirat and died in the year 1525 A. D., 931 A. H.

**Zalali Khwansari, Mulla,** ملازلالي خوانسا خمي, who is sometimes called Hakím Zalálí, was a native of Khwánsár. He was a pupil of Mirzá Jalál Asír, and is the author of the following seven Masnawís or poems, *viz.*, "Sulaimán-náma," "Shíala Dídár," "Maikhána," "Husn Gulútoz," "Azur wa Samundar," "Zarra wa Khursheid" and "Mahmúd Ayáz," which was his last composition and which he commenced in 1592 A. D., 1001 A. H., and completed in 23 years in 1615 A. D., 1024 A. H., but died before he could arrange it. This was done in India, and Mulla Tughráí wrote a Preface to it.

**Zalali Shirazi,** زلالي شيرازي, an author who died in 1541 A. D., 948 A. H.

**Zalim Singh,** ظالم سنگه, the present rája of Koṭa.

**Zamakhshari,** زمخشري, *vide* Jár-ulláh.

**Zaman Shah,** زمان شاه, king of Kábul and Ḳandahár, was the son of Taimúr Sháh and grandson of the celebrated Aḥmad Sháh Abdálí. He ascended the throne of Kábul after the death of his father in 1793 A. D., 1207 A. H. He advanced to Láhor in 1796 A. D., 1210 A. H. and threatened to visit Dehlí, but soon retreated to his own dominions, tranquillity of which had been disturbed by the rebellion of one of his brothers. He was blinded by his younger brother Mahmúd Sháh of Hirát about the year 1800 A. D., and confined in the Bálá Hisár. When in the year 1839, the British Government placed Sháh Shujáạ on the throne of Kábul, Zamán Sháh was proclaimed king by the Afgháns in January, 1842 A. D.

**Zamani, Yezdi,** زماني يزدى, a Persian poet who died in 1612 A. D., 1021 A. H.

**Zamir,** ضمير, the poetical name of Sayyad Hidáet 'Alí Khán styled Naṣír-uddaula Bakhshí-ul-Mulk Asad Jang Bahádur, a relative of Alah Wardí Khán Mahábat Jang, Nawáb of Bengal. He held for some time the Súbadárí of Patna where he died in the beginning of the reign of Sháh 'Alam, and is buried at Husainábád.

**Zamir,** ضمير, poetical name of Sayyad Aḥmad the brother of Sayyad Imtiyáz Khán Humá.

**Zamir,** ضمير, poetical name of Naráyan Dás, a Hindú.

**Zamiri, Maulana,** مولانا ضميرى, a celebrated poet of Persia who flourished about the year 1538 A. D., 945 A. H. in the time of Sháh Tahmásp Safwí. He is the author of the following six poems, *viz.*, "Naz wa Nayáz," "Wámiḳ wa Azra," "Bahár wa Khizán," "Lailí wa Majnún," "Sikandar-náma," and "Jannat-ul-Akhiyár." He also wrote two Díwáns of Kasídas called "Saháef Yamál" and "Isdáf Láal." He died in 1565 A. D., 973 A. H.

**Zamiri, Maulana,** مولانا ضميرى, the poetical name of Shaikh Nizám, who was the son of Shaikh Sulaimán's sister. They were both inhabitants of Bilgrám, and both were employed in the service of the emperor Humáyún after his conquest of India the second time. Shaikh Sulaimán died in the reign of the emperor Akbar, on the 1st September, 1589 A. D., 1st Ẕi-Ḳa'da, 997 A. H., and Mauláná Zamírí, who was an excellent poet, died at Safaidún 1595 A. D., 1003 A. H., and nawáb Mubarak Khán of Dehlí found the chronogram of his death to consist of the words "Ah! Ah! Nizám."

**Zamzam,** زمزم, a famous well at Mecca which the Muhammadans pretend was made from the spring of water, which God shewed to Hagar and Ishmael whom Abraham had driven from his house, and obliged to retire to Arabia.

**Zangi Shahid,** زنکي شهيد, a Muhammadan saint whose Dargáh is in Ágrah towards the gate of the Hatheapul.

**Zardasht,** زردست, the celebrated Persian Magian Zoroaster. The religion of the first Persians appears to have been the worship of the planets; but in the reign of Darius Hystaspes or Gashtasp, the adoration of fire and the elements was introduced by Zardasht, and continued to be the religion of the State until its conquest by the Muhammadans. The fugitives known as Gabrs and Parsís, still follow this faith. The doctrines and practices of this system are collected in a work called Avesta, or Zand Avesta, being written in the Zand language. The Zand Avesta was translated into French, by Anquetil Du Perron and subsequently much studied and elucidated by Rask, Barnouf and other Continental scholars.

**Zarra,** ذره, the poetical name of Mirzá Bhuchchú of Dehlí or Lakhnau, who has left a Persian Díwán which he completed in 1774 A. D., 1188 A. H.

**Zarra,** ذره, the poetical title of Mirzá Rája Rám Náth who served under the emperor Sháh 'Alam the blind. He chose the takhallus of "Zarra" *i. e.*, atom or dust, in reference to "'Aftáb," the poetical appellation of his patron the king.

**Zeib-un-Nisa Begam,** زيب النسا بيگم, a daughter of the emperor 'Álamgír, born on the 5th of February, 1639 A. D., 10th Shawwál, 1048 A. H.; was well versed in Persian and Arabic, had the whole Ḳurán by heart, wrote a beautiful hand, and is the author of a commentary on the Ḳurán entitled "Zeib-ul-Tafásír." She was also a good poetess, and has left a Díwán in Persian. Her poetical name was "Makhfí." She died, unmarried, in the year 1702 A. D., 1113 A. H. Her tomb was close to the Kabulí gate at Dehlí, but was demolished when the Rájpútana Railway was constructed.

**Zila'i,** زيلعي, the son of Yúsaf, a learned Musalmán and author, who died 1361 A. D., 762 A. H.

**Zilli,** ظلي, poetical name of Sulṭán Muhammad Mirzá, which see.

**Zinat Mahal,** زينت محل, the wife of Bahádur Sháh, king of Dehlí, who was still living in 1873 in British Burma as a State prisoner.

**Zinat-un-Nisa Begam,** زينت النسا بيگم, a daughter of the emperor 'Álamgír. She died in 1710 A. D., 1122 A. H. and is buried in the yard of the mosque called "Zínat-ul-Masájid," in Dehlí. This mosque which is built of red stone, was erected by her, and is situated on the banks of the Jamna at a place called Dariáganj in Sháhjahánábád.

**Zingis Khan,** ظنقي خان, *vide* Changez Khán.

**Zinut Mahal,** زينت محل, the title of Bilál Kúṇwar the mother of Sháh 'Alam king of Dehlí.

**Ziyad,** زياد, supposed to be an illegitimate son of Abú Sufián by a woman named Abia. He was Mu'áwia's brother by the father's side, and was publicly acknowledged by him to be his brother. He was reckoned one of the companions of Muhammad although he was born in the first year of the Hijrat, 622 A. D., and was but eleven years old when Muhammad died. In Alí's reign he was made lieutenant of Persia; this office he discharged much to his own credit, and to the advantage of the people. He was a man of incomparable parts, and singular greatness of spirit. Besides the lieutenancy of Baṣra, Mu'áwia gave Ziyád those of Khurásán, Sajistán, India, Bahrein and Ammán. He died of the plague on his fingers, on the 22nd of August, 673 A. D., 3rd Ramaẕán, 53 A. H. in the 53rd (lunar) year of his age, and was buried near Kúfa. A little before his death, he gathered the people together, and filled both mosque and street, and castle with them, in order to impose upon them by oath the renunciation of the line of 'Alí; but the plague had just seized him, and the accident was afterwards looked upon by all as a providential deliverance.

**Ziyae Barani,** ضياء برني, *vide* Ziyá-uddín Baraní.

**Ziyae Burhanpuri,** ضياء برهانپوري, author of a Persian Díwán.

**Ziya-uddin Ahmad Khan, Nawab,** ضياءالدين خان, the son of Nawáb Aḥmad Baksh Khán of Fírozpúr and Loharí. His poetical name is Nyyar and Rakhshán. He succeeded to his father's estate on the 1st January, 1870.

**Ziya-uddin Barani,** ضياالدين برني, also called Ziyáe Baraní, flourished in the reign of Sulṭán Muhammad Sháh Tughlaḳ and Fíróz Sháh Tughlaḳ, kings of Dehlí, and is the author of the history called "Taríkh Fíróz Sháhí," which gives an account of eight kings from the first year of Sulṭán Ghayás-uddín Balban 1266 A. D., to the sixth year of Sulṭán Fíróz Sháh Tughlaḳ 1356 A. D., 757 A. H., at which period our author was 74 (lunar) years of age. His uncle Malik 'Alá-ul-Mulk was Kotwál of the city of Dehlí in the reign of Sulṭán Alá-uddín Khiljí, and his father who held the title of Muwayyad-ul-Mulk, was appointed in the first year of that monarch 1296 A. D. to the Nayábat of Baran or Baran Shahr, now called Bulandshahr, which city appears to have been the birthplace of our author, on which account he calls himself in the above-mentioned history Ziyáe Baraní. Baran is also the name of a Pergunnah in Bulandshahr.

**Ziya-uddin Ghazanfar, Maulana,** ضياالدين غضفر مولانا, was born at Kumm but educated at Káshán. Besides many Kasídas and Ghazals &c., he left a Masnawí called "Pír wa Jawán" of about 3,000 verses. He was living about the year 1585 A. D., 993 A. H.

**Ziya-uddin Khujandi,** ضياالدين خجندی, a poet who died in 1225 A. D., 622 A. H.

**Ziya-uddin Nakhshabi,** ضياالدين نخشبي, author of the "Túti-náma," or Tales of a Parrot in Persian, and also of a story called "Gulreiz," containing the story of Prince Maṣúm Sháh and the princess Naushába. He is also the author of a treatise entitled "Lazzat-un-Nisá," (*vide* Hasan 'Alí the poet laureate).

**Ziya-ullah, Sayyad,** سيد ضياالله, an author who died in 1691 A. D., 1103 A. H.

**Zohak,** ضحاک, *vide* Zuhák.

**Zouk,** ذوق, poetical title of Shaikh Muhammad Ibráhím of Dehlí, an Urdú poet who passed the greatest part of his life in the service of Akbar II, king of Dehlí, and was living about the year 1837 A. D.

**Zouki Ardastani,** ذوقي اردستاني, a poet who died in 1635 A. D., 1045 A. H.

**Zouzani,** زوزني, whose full name and title is Al-Ḳází-al-Imám Sayyad Abú 'Abdullah-al-Zouzaní, was the author of the "Sharah Ḳasáed-ul-Saba-al-Muallaḳát," an esteemed Commentary in Arabic on the seven celebrated poems which were written in letters of gold, and suspended to the door of the temple of Mecca previous to the mission of Muhammad. Their authors were Amri-al-Kais, Tarafa, Zaheir, Labíd, Antar, Amrú, and Harath. These poems have been so elegantly translated by Sir William Jones, that had he never published any thing else, they would have stampt his fame, as a man of taste, a good poet, and an excellent Oriental scholar.

**Zu** or **Zab,** زو يا زب, a descendant of the ancient kings of Persia, whom Zál, the father of Rustam, raised to the throne of Persia, and drove Afrásiáb king of the Turks who had conquered it, out of that kingdom. Zú died after he had conquered Fars, and was succeeded by his son Karshásp. This prince, who was soon set aside as incompetent by Zál, is considered by Persian authors as the last of the first or Pishdádian dynasty: who according to their own computation, governed Persia 2,450 years. The names of twelve kings only of their race have been preserved. After Karshásp, Kaiḳubád who is the first king of the second or Kayánian dynasty, was proclaimed king of Persia.

**Zubari,** زبري, the son of Muslim, an Arabian author who died in 742 A. D., 124 A. H.

**Zubdatun-nisa,** زبدة النساء, the fourth daughter of the emperor 'Alamgír. Her mother's name was Nawáb Baí. She was born on the 26th Ramazán 1061 A. H., was married to one of Dara Shikoh's sons. She died a few days before her father in the same month and year, 1118 A. H.

**Zubeida Khatun,** زبيده خاتون, the wife of Hárún-al-Rashíd. She was the daughter of Abú Jafar the son of the Khalíf Al-Mansúr, and mother of the Khalíf Al-Amín. Her chastity was ample, her conduct virtuous. She died at Baghdád in June, 831 A. D., Jumáda I, 216 A. H. She is said to have built the city of Tabrez in 806 A. D., 190 A. H.

**Zuber,** زبير بن بكار, the son of Bakkár, a Kazí of Mecca and author of the "Kitáb Sunan and Kitáb Akhbár Madína. He died in the year 870 A. D., 256 A. H.

**Zuber ibn-al-Awam,** زبير ابن الاوام, was the father of 'Abdullah ibn-Zubeir, and an enemy of 'Alí. He was slain by Amrú ibn-Jarmuz 656 A. D., and his head carried to 'Alí, who not approving this act of his, Amrú drew has sword and ran himself through.

**Zuha'k** or **Zohak,** ضحاک, or Azdahák, a tyrant of Persian mythology who overcame Jamshid king of Persia in a battle, and became the king of that country. There are various accounts of the descent of Zuhák. Some say he was an Arabian, but descended from Ḳyomurs: others trace his descent to Shaddád, and term him a Syrian; and it has even been conjectured that he was the Astyages of the Greeks. All agree in one fact, that he was of a cruel and sanguinary temper. He is described as having had two dreadful cancers on his shoulders, which the Persian fabulists have changed into snakes, whose hunger nothing could appease but the brains of human beings: two of his subjects were slain daily to furnish the horrid meal: till the manly indignation of Káwa or Gáwa a blacksmith of Isfahán, whose two sons were on the point of being sacrificed, relieved the empire from this tyrant, and raised Fareidún, a prince of the Pishdadian dynasty to the throne. The fable perhaps indicates an ancient subjugation of Persia by a Median or Tartar tribe who used the serpent, a dragon, for their standard. There is a ruin near Bámián called by the people "The Castle of Zohák.

**Zujja'j,** زجّاج, whose proper name was Abú Is-háḳ Ibráhím bin-Muhammad, was the author of several works. He died at Baghdád in the year 923 A. D., 311 A. H., when he was upwards of 80 years old.

**Zuka,** ذكا, poetical name of Mír Aulád Muhammad of Bilgram, a nephew of Mír Ghulám Alí 'Azád. He was living in 1761 A. D., 1175 A. H.

**Zuka'h,** ذوكاه, poetical name of Khubchand Kayeth of Dehlí, author of a biography of poets in Urdú.

**Zulfika'r 'Ali,** ذوالفقار علي, whose poetical name is Mast, was the author of a Tazkira entitled "Rayáz-ul-Wifák," containing the biography of the poets of Calcutta and Benares who wrote Persian verses; it was completed in 1814 A. D., 1229 A. H. at Benares. He is also the author of several other works.

**Zulfika'r 'Ali Khan,** ذوالفقار علي خان, Nawáb of Banda, was the son of 'Alí Bahádur, ruler of Bundeilkhand. He succeeded his brother Shamsheir Bahádur on the 30th of August, 1823 A. D., 22nd Zil-hijja, 1238 A. H. He was succeeded by 'Alí Bahádur Khán.

**Zulfika'r Jang,** ذوالفقار جنگ, a title of Salábat Khán.

**Zulfika'r Khan,** ذوالفقار خان, a nobleman of the reign of the emperor Sháh Jahán. He is the father of Asad Khán whose son also held this title. He died in 1659 A. D., Muharram, 1070 A. H.

**Zulfika'r Khan Turkman,** ذوالفقار خان ترکمان, an officer who served under Sháh Jahán and died in 1647 A. D., 1057 A. H.

**Zulfika'r Khan, Amir-ul-Umra,** ذوالفقار خان نصرت جنگ امير الامرا, styled Nasrat Jang, whose former title was Yatkád Khán, was the son of Asad Khán, a nobleman of the reign of 'Alamgír: he was born 1657 A. D., 1067 A. H. and held several appointments under that emperor. On the accession of Bahádur Sháh in the year 1707 A. D., 1119 A. H. the title of Amír-ul-Umrá was conferred on him with the government of the Dakhin. It was by his aid and intrigues that Jahándár Sháh, after the death of his father Bahádur Sháh, overcame all his brothers and ascended the throne of Dehlí, when he was appointed to be chief Vazír; but after the defeat of that emperor in the battle against Farrukh-siyar, he was taken up and strangled by order of the latter as a punishment for his conduct. His head with that of the late emperor Jahándár Sháh who had also been put to death in prison, were carried on poles, and their bodies hanging feet upwards across an elephant, were exposed in the new emperor's train, when he made his triumphant entry to the palace at Dehlí. This event took place in January, 1713 A. D., Zil-hijja, 1124 A. H. The aged minister Asad Khán Z's father was compelled to attend the procession, accompanied by the ladies of his family as spectators of their own disgrace. Asad Khán, who in hopes of making peace with the new emperor had persuaded his son to visit him, and had thus put him in his power, with tears in his eyes, wrote the following chronogram on his death: ابراهيم الميل را قربان نمود (Abraham sacrificed Ishmael.) Mehr-un-Nisa Begam, the daughter of Yemín-uddaula 'Asaf Khán was his mother, and Shaista Khán the son of 'Asaf Khán was his father-in-law.

**Zulfikar of Sabzwari,** ذوالفقار سبزواری, a Sayyad and a great poet, who flourished in the reign of Sulṭán Muhammad of Khwarizm about 1200 A. D.

**Zulkadar-uddaula,** ذوالفقار الدوله, a title of Najaf Khán.

**Zulkadar,** ذوالقدر, *vide* Zulḳadar.

**Zulkadar,** ذوالقدر, the poetical name of Mirzá Muhammad Míhsia, a Turk of the tribe of Zulḳadar, the meaning of which in the Turkish language is an archer that never misses his aim. This title he assumed for his takhallus. He flourished about the year 1688 A. D., 1100 A. H., and is the author of a Díwán.

**Zulkarnyn,** ذوالقرنين, master of two horns, a title of Alexander the Great, probably based on coins representing him in the character of Ammon.

**Zunnun** or **Zu'l Nur Misri,** ذوالنون مصری, surnamed Abú'l Fazl Túbán, son of Ibráhím, a celebrated Muhammadan saint of Egypt whose merits were great in number, and who is said to have performed many miracles, and to have been the founder of the sect of Súfí in Egypt, where he was held in the greatest estimation. It is related in the "Nafahát," that at his death when they were carrying him for burial, a large flock of birds, of the kind that was never seen before, overshadowed his coffin to the grave. He died in February, 860 A. D., Ẓi-Ḳa'da, 245 A. H., and a chapel was built over his tomb in Egypt, where a number of other holy men are buried. The work called "Latáef-ul-Akhbár," contains the Memoirs of this famous saint.

**Zyd (or Zaid) bin-Sabit, Abu Sa'd,** زيد بن ثابت, one of Muhammad's secretaries, to whom he dictated the Ḳurán. He wrote that copy which was used by the Khalífs or Imáms at the command of 'Usmán the son of Affán the third Khalíf after Muhammad. He died about the year 665 A. D., 45 A. H., some say that he died in 673 A. D., 54 A. H. He is the earliest authority on the Ilm-al-Faráez and may be called the father of the law of inheritance. Muhammad is reported to have said to his followers—"The most learned among you in the laws of heritage is Zyd;" and the Khalífas 'Umar and 'Usman considered him without an equal as a judge, a jurisconsult, a calculator in the division of inheritances, and a reader of the Ḳurán.

**Zyd bin-Haria,** زيد بن حارث, of the tribe of Kalb, was the emancipated slave of Muhammad who married his divorced wife Zynab. See the following article. Zyd was killed in the eighth year of the Hijrat in an attak on the Greeks at Muta in Syria, 629 A. D., 8 A. H.

**Zynab,** زينب بنت جحش, the daughter of Jahash and the wife of Muhammad. She was formerly married to Zy the emancipated slave of the prophet. Towards the end of the fifth year of the Hijrat 626 A. D., Muhammad going into the house of Zyd, did not find him at home, but happening to espy his wife, he could not conceal the impression made upon him, but cried out, "Praise be to God, who turneth men's hearts as he pleaseth!" Zynab heard him, and told it to her husband when he came home. Zyd, who had been greatly obliged to Muhammad, was very desirous to gratify him, and offered to divorce his wife. Muhammad pretended to dissuade him from it, but Zyd easily perceiving how little he was in earnest, actually divorced her. Muhammad thereupon took her to wife, and celebrated the nuptials with extraordinary magnificence, keeping open house upon the occasion. She died nine years after the death of Muhammad in the year 641 A. D., 20 A. H.

**Zynab,** زينب بنت خزيمه, the daughter of Khuzyma, was also one of the wives of Muhammad, and died two months after the preceding one in the year 641 A. D., 20 A. H.

**Zynab,** زينب, a daughter of Muhammad married to Abú'l 'As. This man, who was an unbeliever, was taken prisoner to the battle of Badar, and the prophet would fain have drawn his son-in-law to him, and enrolled him among his disciples, but Abú'l 'As remained stubborn in unbelief. Muhammad then offered to set him at liberty on condition of his returning to him his daughter. To this he agreed, and Zyd, the faithful freedman of the prophet was sent with several companions to Mecca to bring Zynab to Medina, where after her arrival, Abú'l 'As was released.

**Zyn Khan Koka,** زين خان كوكه, the foster-brother of the emperor Akbar. He was the son of Khwája Maḳsúd Hirwí; his mother, whose name was Píchah Ján, was employed as an Anaga or nurse on Akbar in his childhood, consequently Zyn Khán was called Kóka or foster-brother to Akbar who raised him in course of time to the rank of 4,500. Subsequently his uncle Khwája Hasan's daughter was married to Sulṭán Salím, and became mother of Sulṭán Parwez. In the year 1586 A. D., 994 A. H., Zyn Khán was despatched with a considerable detachment against the Afgháns of Sawád and Bijour, but he was defeated, and Khwája Arab Bakhshí, Rája Bírbal, Mulla Sherí and many other persons of distinction, with 8,000 men, were killed in the action. In 1588 he was appointed to the government of Kábul. He died at Ágrah on the 6th of Mehr 1009 A. H., corresponding with the 19th of September, 1600 A. D. He is said to have been the best musician of the time of Akbar, but a bad poet. He played chiefly Hindí tunes. (The same as Zain Khán, q. v.)

**Zyn-uddin Ahmad 'Ali Khan,** زين الدين علي خان, succeeded Názir-ul-Mulk Nawáb Názim of Bengál at Murshidábád in April, 1810 A. D.

**Zyn-uddin bin-Ahmad,** زين الدين بن احمد, commonly called Ibn-Rajab, is the author of the "Sharah Tirmizí", "Sharah Bukhárí", and "Tabaḳát Hanábila." He died in 1393 A. D., 795 A. H. He is sometimes called Zyn-uddín Abdul Rahmán bin-Aḥmad, *vide* Abú'l Husain.

**Zyn-uddin 'Ali-al-Sai'li,** زين الدين علي السيلي, commonly called the second Shahíd, author of a valuable and voluminous commentary upon the Sharáyạ-al-Islám, entitled the "Masálik-ul-Afhám."

**Zyn-uddin Muhammad Hafi, Shaikh,** زين الدين حافي, an excellent poet and author who flourished in the reign of the emperor Humáyún. He was called Háfí on account of his walking barefoot.

**Zyn-ul-'Abidin,** زين العابدين, metropolitan of Seringapatam and author of the work called "Muwayyad-ul-

Jáhidín," a poem consisting of 52 odes or hymns, one of which was ordered to be chaunted in the mosques, throughout the kingdom of Mysore, every Friday. They are in sixteen different kinds of metre, and were compiled by order of Ṭípú Sulṭán, to rouse the zeal of his Muhammadan subjects, against the Hindús and the Christians.

**Zyn-ul-'Abidin Ibrahim bin-Nujim-al-Misri,** زين العابدين بن نجيم, author of the Commentary on the Kanz-ul-Daḳáiḳ entitled "Bahr ar-Ráiḳ" which he left incomplete at his death, but it was finished by his brother, Siráj-uddín 'Umr, who also wrote another and inferior Commentary on the same work, entitled "Nahr-ul-Fáiḳ." Zyn-ul-Abidín died in 1562 A. D., 970 A. H. The "Ashbáh wán Nazáir" is also an elementary work of great reputation by Zyn-ul-'Abidín, also the "Fatáwa az-Zynia," which contains decisions, and were collected by his son Aḥmad about 1562 A. D.

**Zyn-ul-'Abidin 'Ali Abdi,** زين العابدين علي ابدي, *vide* Khwája Zyn-ul-Abidín 'Alí Abdí.

**Zyn-ul-'Abidin, Imam,** زين العابدين امام, surnamed Alí Asghar, was the son of Imám Husain, and the fourth Imám of the race of Alí. His mother's name was Salafa or Shahr Báno, said to be the daughter of Yezdijard III king of Persia. She was one of the captives when Persia was conquered, and sold to 'Alí, who gave her to his son Husain. It is said that the Khalíf Walíd I. suspecting him of a design upon the Khiláfat, said to him, alluding to his mother's having been exposed for sale as a slave, "You are unworthy to reign, as being the son of a slave." The Imám answered, "Hagar the mother of Ishmael the son of Abraham, was a slave, yet Muhammad was descended from her." The Khalif blushed and was silent. He was born in 657 A. D., 37 A. H., and died in the reign of the Khalíf Walíd I in the month of October, 713 A. D., Muḥarram, 95 A. H. He was buried in the cemetry called Baḳír in Medina close to his uncle Imám Hasan's tomb.

**Zyn-ul-Abidin Khan, Nawab,** زين العابدين خان نواب, the son of Nawáb Ghulám Husain Khán and grandson of Nawáb Fyz-ullah Beg Khán. His poetical name is 'Arif. He died in 1855 or 1856 A. D., 1272 A. H.

**Zyn-ul-'Abidin, Sultan,** زين العابدين سلطان, son of Sulṭán Sikandar, ascended the throne of Kashmír, after taking prisoner his brother 'Alí Sháh in a battle in 1423. This prince improved the country more than any of his predecessors. He built bridges, towns and forts, and erected at Naushahra a noble palace, twelve stories high, each story of fifty rooms. He also enlarged and beautified the city of Srínagar his capital. He died in 1474 A. D. after a reign of 52 lunar years, and was succeeded by his son Hydar Sháh who after reigning little more than a year, was killed by a fall from his terrace 1475 A. D., and was succeeded by his son Sulṭán Hasan.